2017–2018
OREGON BLUE BOOK

Compiled and
published by

Dennis Richardson
Secretary of State

Julie Yamaka, Managing Editor
Phil Wiebe, Copy Editor
Gary Halvorson, Photo and Web Editor

Archives Division
Office of the Secretary of State
Salem, Oregon 97310

i

Acknowledgements and special thanks to the following people:

Office of the Secretary of State:
  Archives Division, Mary Beth Herkert, State Archivist
    Fact gathering and verification: Nicholas Adelman, Matt Brown, Chris Fuller,
      Amandeep Gulaini, Katherine Hill, Theresa Rea, Austin Schulz and Todd Shaffer
    Graem Sawyer, section formatting for online publishing
    Proofreader: Kay Kinsley
    Publications Unit: Steve Mabry and Colleen Needham
    Section review: Stephanie Clark and Layne Sawyer, Managers
  Business Services Division: Jeff Morgan, Director; Godfre Kouka
  Elections Division: Brenda Bayes, Manager

Department of Administrative Services, Chief Financial Office and Geospatial Enterprise Office, maps

Employment Department, Research Division: Nick Beleiciks, State Employment Economist, Economy Section, Dave Yamaka, graphics

Office of the State Court Administrator: Kim Blanding, Judicial Section

Oregon Chief Education Office: Melissa Navas and Higher Education Coordinating Commission: Endi Hartigan, Education Section

www.bluebook.state.or.us

Orders:
Office of the Secretary of State
Oregon Blue Book
255 Capitol St. NE, Suite 180
Salem, OR 97310
503-378-5199

TABLE OF CONTENTS

Preface and Dedication by Dennis Richardson, Secretary of State
Foreword by Kate Brown, Governor

Color illustrations and photographs following page 224

Dennis Richardson
SECRETARY OF STATE

STATE OF OREGON
SECRETARY OF STATE
136 STATE CAPITOL
SALEM, OREGON 97310-0722

January 2017

Dear Oregonians,

Our entire team is proud to present the 2017–2018 edition of the *Oregon Blue Book*, the state's directory, almanac and fact book. For more than a century, this publication has provided the official record of Oregon's rich history, diverse economy and accessible governance — each edition preserved forever. The Oregon State Archives Division spends countless hours gathering the data and photos, then compiling the elements in this book to make Oregon history come alive.

This edition of the *Blue Book* is particularly exciting because its unique theme shines a spotlight on an element of Oregon life that truly unifies our shared experience: Oregon's breathtaking outdoor recreational adventures. The awe and wonder of our state's natural beauty blesses Oregonians of all ages, for all ages. In the informative and colorful pages that follow, you will learn about the pathways of public access and the many ways to enjoy Oregon's environmental beauty and recreational opportunities.

In addition, the youngest Oregonians have a special opportunity to present their perspectives on our state's outdoor activities with the *Blue Book* student essay contest. Access to nature and outdoor adventures are crucial for developing minds and bodies, and Oregon children have countless opportunities to play, explore and experience our state's geology, hydrology and biology. While reading these student essays, I hope you'll be transported back in time to a childhood memory of a school bus field trip, a state park hike or favorite family camping experience—memories from your own formative years.

As a people, our lives are as intertwined as the hiking trails that crisscross the state. The backbone of this system is the Pacific Crest Trail, and no dedication to the Oregon outdoors would be complete without its inclusion. The trail's golden anniversary is nearly upon us as we prepare to commemorate the 50th anniversary of the National Trails System Act signed into law by President Lyndon Johnson in 1968 — the genesis for the creation of the massive 2,659-mile trail connecting California, Oregon and Washington. We hope you agree that Oregon's 430 miles of the trail are the most spectacular of all! We are pleased to present a color insert of the Pacific Crest Trail in this edition of the *Blue Book*. The Oregon section of the trail traverses Crater Lake National Park and ancient, dormant volcanoes such as Diamond Peak, Mount Washington, Three Fingered Jack, The Three Sisters, Mount Jefferson and Mount Hood. Explore the insert and, then, explore the trail for yourself.

Oregonians have so much for which to be thankful, and this publication helps us remember and record the many significant elements that make Oregon great. A special thanks is due to the Oregon State Archivist Mary Beth Herkert and her team for all their diligent and dedicated work on this publication. We also have created a corresponding Web site if you prefer the digital version, which is fully search-able. Just visit http://bluebook.state.or.us in your Web browser and dive in to all its great content. I look forward to the years ahead and the future chapters that will fill the *Oregon Blue Book*.

Sincerely,

Dennis Richardson
Secretary of State

Dedication
Victor Atiyeh

The 2017–2018 edition of the Oregon Blue Book is dedicated to the memory of Governor Vic Atiyeh.

Victor "Vic" Atiyeh was a first-generation American who grew up in an ethnically diverse neighborhood in Northeast Portland. His father had immigrated to the United States in the early 1900s from what is now Syria.

As a youth, Atiyeh began his lifelong involvement with the Boy Scouts of America and played football at Portland's Washington High School. While at Washington, he was nominated by his fellow students to serve as senior class president. It was his first experience with public service and would not be his last.

As a successful businessman, Atiyeh was running his family's rug and carpet business when he was recruited to campaign for a seat in the Oregon House of Representatives. He was elected in 1958 and represented a portion of Washington County in the House until being elected to the state Senate in 1964.

In 1979, Atiyeh became the nation's first Arab-American governor. His election came when the lingering effects of a national recession had devastated the housing market, which, in turn, hurt Oregon's timber industry.

Out of economic necessity, Governor Atiyeh worked to diversify the state's economy. Many of Oregon's largest industries can be traced back to the leadership of Governor Atiyeh, including viticulture, tourism and technology. Today's trade with Asian countries, which has become a key component of Oregon's economy, was initiated in part by his many trips abroad to promote Oregon and the many products manufactured and grown here.

Throughout his political career, Vic Atiyeh emphasized inclusion and recognized the importance of diversity through his work with the state's many minority populations and groups. His ability to reach across the aisle and find common ground with others was a true testament to his character and effectiveness as a legislator and governor.

After leaving the governor's office in 1987, aspiring political candidates often sought Governor Atiyeh's sage wisdom and counsel. He was always generous with his time and happy to share his experience with others.

Those who knew Governor Vic Atiyeh speak of him with respect and reverence. His calm and reasoned approach helped Oregonians through challenging times. He was Oregon's senior statesman until his death on July 20, 2014 at age 91. This year's Oregon Blue Book is dedicated to honoring Vic Atiyeh and his lifetime of dedicated service to family, to community and to his beloved State of Oregon.

Kate Brown
GOVERNOR

STATE OF OREGON
GOVERNOR
254 STATE CAPITOL
SALEM, OREGON 97301-4047
(503) 378-3111
www.oregon.gov

January 2017

To My Fellow Oregonians,

The core of our responsibility in state government is to serve Oregon's people by ensuring we have healthy families and safe communities. We must be careful stewards of our precious natural resources to preserve the beauty and bounty of Oregon for generations to come. We must build a seamless system of education from cradle to career and foster a robust economy. We must work toward inclusivity so that all people who call Oregon home feel welcome and safe here.

In the pages of this *Oregon Blue Book,* you will learn more about what makes Oregon special — its symbols, geography, history, and governance. You'll also get a glimpse of the people in elected office, at state agencies, and on boards and commissions who work to address our state's most important issues, including education, human services, health, the economy, and the environment.

Public engagement is a critical component of our democracy. Your voice matters to us, and I encourage you to become involved in making your community more inclusive and livable, so we can work alongside one another to build a future where each of us thrives.

Sincerely,

Kate Brown
Governor

New in this Edition . . .

Cascade Mountains Recreation

The featured exhibit in this edition of the *Oregon Blue Book* uses photos, artwork and memorabilia to highlight the colorful history of recreation in the Cascade Mountains over the years.

Skiing, fishing, hiking, and camping were favorite pursuits in the early 1900s. They still remain popular, but have been joined by newer sports such as snowboarding, snowmobiling and mountain biking. Get a taste of the wide variety of possibilities.

You can find this exhibit in the color insert located after page 224. The insert also offers images of state symbols and an Oregon physical features map. The photo tour of the State Capitol found in previous editions is still available online at: bluebook.state.or.us

Outdoor Recreation History

Check out the history of outdoor recreation on page 374! This new feature takes a look at how all, including the earliest Oregonians, enjoy the natural wonders that the geography of Oregon presents.

The history traces the development of outdoor recreation into the industry it is today and touches upon the efforts made to balance the recreational, industrial and environmental resources of our state.

Student Essays About Oregon Recreation

Secretary of State Jeanne P. Atkins asked Oregon elementary students to write essays describing their favorite things to do in the state's great outdoors. She asked middle school students where they would take first-time visitors for Oregon outdoor activities.

The essays show a strong appreciation for nature and recreation. From hiking to surfing to snowshoeing to fishing, the young writers prove that outdoor recreation will continue to hold a special place in the hearts of Oregonians for years to come.

Seven of the essays are displayed in this edition of the *Oregon Blue Book*. Two of them include student illustrations See the essays, which are shown as submitted, on pages viii, 126, 154, 162, 188, 276, and 386-387.

Ever-changing Oregon Information

We called, emailed and faxed hundreds of government offices, television and radio stations, newspapers, cultural institutions and others in an effort to gather the most up-to-date information for this edition of the *Oregon Blue Book*.

Several sections, such as Executive, Economy, Government Finance, and Education, have been rewritten to reflect changes.

Of course, in addition to this print edition, don't forget the online *Oregon Blue Book*. We continue to add new information as we receive it throughout the year so you can stay abreast of ongoing changes to Oregon's governmental and cultural institutions. See it at: www.bluebook.state.or.us

MIDDLE SCHOOL STUDENT ESSAY
Wahclella Falls

Soren Nilsen-Goodin, Essay Contest Winner
Lisa Colombo's Sixth Grade Class
Southwest Charter School, Portland

Located near the Columbia River, it's an amazing place to hike, to swim and to have fun. As soon as you walk into the forest everything stops. The bustling of the city stops. The sound of cars speeding down the road stops. Everything stops. Except for Nature. The sounds of nature start. The pleasant sound of birds chirping. Trees swaying and especially the waterfall. The closer you get to the waterfall it sounds like thunder. Thunder and rain. And then you look at the creek. You see fish jumping in the rapids. You think about what a pleasant day there having. Just like you. And this is why I would take a friend to Wahclella Falls.

Wahclella Falls in the Columbia River Gorge. *(Photo courtesy Kelvin Kay via Wikimedia)*

A boy spends a lazy afternoon fishing on the shore of Anthony Lake in the Elkhorn Mountains.
Oregon State Archives Scenic Photograph 20130718-3299

Facts, like maps, help us envision a complete picture of Oregon. This section includes an almanac with interesting statistics and general information about Oregon, a list of Oregon Olympic Games medal winners, "Oregon, My Oregon"—our state song, and a map of Oregon showing counties and major roads.

ALMANAC

For entries with an asterisk (*), see related photo in the color insert pages.

Abbreviation, Oregon: OR (postal)

Airports/Heliports: 97 public, 377 private

Alternative Energy Projects, Largest

Geothermal Projects

Neal Hot Springs, Malheur County, 2012: 22 megawatts peak capacity

Klamath Falls Geothermal District Heating System, City of Klamath Falls, OIT campus, providing heat to downtown buildings, 2010: 2.1 megawatts peak capacity

Solar Projects

Outback Solar, Lake County, 2012: 4,950 megawatts peak capacity

Oregon solar projects, various locations, 2011: 4,574 megawatts

ProLogis (seven warehouse rooftop projects) Multnomah and Clackamas Counties, 2010: 2,400 megawatts peak capacity

Black Cap Solar, Lake County, 2012: 2,000 megawatts peak capacity

Wind Projects

Shepherds Flat wind energy facilities, Gilliam and Morrow Counties, 2012: 338 turbines generating 898 megawatts peak capacity, comprising one of the largest land-based wind farms in the world

Biglow Canyon Wind Farm, Sherman County, 2010: 217 turbines generating 450 megawatts peak capacity

Klondike III Wind Project, Sherman County, 2007: 176 turbines generating 300 megawatts peak capacity

Stateline Wind Project, Umatilla County, 2001: 229 turbines generating 222 megawatts peak capacity

Altitudes

Highest: Mt. Hood (11,239')

Lowest: Pacific Ocean (sea level)

Amusement Park, Oldest

Oaks Amusement Park, Portland: Opening on May 30, 1905, it is one of the oldest continuously operated amusement parks in the United States.

Animal, State*

The 1969 Legislature named the American Beaver *(Castor canadensis)* the Oregon state animal. Prized for its fur, the beaver was over-trapped by early settlers and eliminated from much of its original range. Through management and protection, the beaver has been reestablished in waterways throughout the state. The beaver has been referred to as "nature's engineer," and its dam-building activities are important to natural water flow and erosion control. Oregon is known as the "Beaver State." The beaver is Oregon State University's mascot.

Apportionment, U.S. House of Representatives
(number of U.S. Representatives from Oregon)

1860–1880.......... 1
1890–1900.......... 2
1910–1930.......... 3
1940–1970.......... 4
1980–Present....... 5

Awards (Nobel, Pulitzer)

1934: Medford *Mail Tribune,* Pulitzer, Journalism

1939: Ronald Callvert, *The Oregonian,* Pulitzer, Editorial Writing

1954: Linus Pauling, Nobel, Chemistry

1956: Walter H. Brattain, Nobel, Physics

1957: Wallace Turner and William Lambert, *The Oregonian,* Pulitzer, Local Reporting

1962: Linus Pauling, Nobel, Peace

1999: Richard Read, *The Oregonian,* Pulitzer, Explanatory Writing

2001: Carl Weiman, Nobel, Physics

2001: *The Oregonian,* Pulitzer, Public Service

2001: Tom Hallman, Jr., *The Oregonian,* Pulitzer, Feature Writing

2005: Nigel Jaquiss, *Willamette Week,* Pulitzer, Investigative Reporting

2006: Rick Attig and Doug Bates, *The Oregonian,* Pulitzer, Editorial Writing

2007: *The Oregonian,* Pulitzer, Breaking News Reporting

2010: Dale T. Mortensen, Nobel, Economics

2014: *The Oregonian,* Pulitzer, Editorial Writing

Beverage, State

Milk was designated Oregon's state beverage in 1997. The Legislature recognized that milk production and the manufacture of dairy products are major contributors to the economic well-being of Oregon agriculture.

Bird, State*

The Western Meadowlark *(Sturnella neglecta)* was chosen the Oregon state bird in 1927 by an Oregon Audubon Society's poll of Oregon's school children. Native throughout western North America, the bird has brown plumage with buff and black markings. Its underside is bright yellow with a black V-shape on the breast. The outer tail feathers are mainly white and are easily visible when it flies. The Western Meadowlark is known for its distinctive, flute-like song.

Births: 46,102 (2015)

Borders and Boundaries

Washington on the north;
California on the south;
Idaho on the east;
Pacific Ocean on the west;
Nevada on the southeast.

Bridges

Highest: Thomas Creek Bridge, north of Brookings, 345'

Longest: Astoria-Megler Bridge, Astoria, 21,474'
Covered bridges: 51
33 covered bridges are located in the Willamette Valley, 19 in Lane County

Buildings, Tallest (Portland)
1. Wells Fargo Tower (1972), 546', 41 floors
2. U.S. Bancorp Tower (1983), 536', 42 floors
3. KOIN Tower (1984), 509', 35 floors

Cities, Total Incorporated: 241
Largest Populations (2015)
1. Portland (613,335)
2. Eugene (163,400)
3. Salem (160,690)
4. Gresham (107,065)
5. Hillsboro (97,480)
6. Beaverton (94,215)

Counties, Total: 36
Largest Area, Square Miles
1. Harney (10,228)
2. Malheur (9,928)
3. Lake (8,359)
4. Klamath (6,135)
5. Douglas (5,071)

Smallest Area, Square Miles
1. Multnomah (465)
2. Hood River (533)
3. Benton (679)
4. Columbia (687)
5. Yamhill (718)

Largest Populations (2015)
1. Multnomah (777,490)
2. Washington (570,510)
3. Clackamas (397,385)
4. Lane (362,150)
5. Marion (329,770)

Crustacean, State
The 2009 Legislature designated the Dungeness Crab *(Metacarcinus magister)* as the official state crustacean. The action followed petitioning by the 4th grade class of Sunset Primary School in West Linn. Common to the Pacific coastline from the Alaskan Aleutian Islands to Santa Cruz, California, Dungeness Crab is considered the most commercially important crab in the Pacific Northwest.

Dance, State
In 1977, the Legislature declared the Square Dance to be the Oregon state dance. The dance is a combination of various steps and figures danced with four couples grouped in a square. The pioneer origins of the dance and the characteristic dress are deemed to reflect Oregon's heritage. The lively spirit of the dance exemplifies the friendly, free nature and enthusiasm that are a part of the Oregon character.

Deaths: 35,709 (2015)
Divorces: 13,831 (2015)
Electoral Votes for U.S. President: 7

Fair, Oregon State: Early History
1858: The State Fair was unofficially started by a group of farmers known as the Oregon Fruit-growers Association.

1861: The first official Oregon State Fair was held along the Clackamas River in the Gladstone/Oregon City area.

1862: The second State Fair took place in Salem, at the same location where it is held today.

1871: Women's suffrage activists Susan B. Anthony and Abigail S. Duniway camped at the State Fairgrounds during an extended visit to Oregon.

Father of Oregon*
The 1957 Legislature bestowed upon Dr. John McLoughlin the honorary title of "Father of Oregon" in recognition of his great contributions to the early development of the Oregon Country. Dr. McLoughlin came to the Northwest region in 1824 as a representative of the Hudson's Bay Company.

Fish, State*
The Chinook Salmon *(Oncorhynchus tsha-wytscha)*, also known as the spring, king or tyee salmon, is the largest of the Pacific salmons and the most highly prized for the fresh fish trade. Declared the Oregon state fish by the 1961 Legislature, the Chinook Salmon is found from southern California to the Canadian Arctic. Record-sized catches of 53 inches and 126 pounds have been reported.

Flag, State*
The Oregon state flag, adopted in 1925, is navy blue with gold lettering and symbols. Blue and gold are the state colors. On the flag's face the legend "STATE OF OREGON" is written above a shield, which is surrounded by 33 stars. Below the shield, which is part of the state seal, is written "1859," the year of Oregon's admission to The Union as the 33rd state. The flag's reverse side depicts a beaver. Oregon has the distinction of being the only state in The Union whose flag has a different pattern on the reverse side. The dress or parade flag has a gold fringe, and the utility flag has a plain border.

Flower, State*
The Legislature designated the Oregon Grape *(Mahonia aquifolium)* as the Oregon state flower by resolution in 1899. A low-growing plant, the Oregon Grape is native to much of the Pacific Coast and is found sparsely east of the Cascades. Its year-round foliage of pinnated, waxy green leaves resembles holly. The plant bears clusters of small yellow flowers in early summer and a dark blue berry that ripens late in the fall. The fruit can be used in cooking.

Fossil, State*

The Legislature designated the Metasequoia, or Dawn Redwood *(Metasequoia glyptostroboides)*, as the Oregon state fossil by resolution in 2005. The Metasequoia flourished in the Miocene Epoch of 25 to 5 million years ago and left its record embedded in rocks across the Oregon landscape. While long extinct in Oregon, paleontologists discovered living 100-foot Metasequoia trees in a remote area of China in the 1940s and brought specimens back to the United States for propagation, thus ensuring that live Metasequoia trees can be found today. It can grow to 200 feet in height.

Fruit, State*

The Legislature designated the pear *(Pyrus communis)* as the Oregon state fruit by resolution in 2005. Oregon produces a variety of pears, including Comice, Anjou, Bosc and Bartlett. The pear ranks as the top-selling tree fruit crop in the state and grows particularly well in the Rogue River Valley and along the Columbia River near Mt. Hood.

Gemstone, State*

The 1987 Legislature designated the Oregon Sunstone as the Oregon state gemstone. Uncommon in its composition, clarity and colors, it is a large, brightly colored transparent gem in the feldspar family. The Oregon Sunstone attracts collectors and miners and has been identified as a boon to tourism and economic development in southeastern Oregon counties.

Geographic Center

The geographic center of Oregon lies in Crook County, 25 miles south-southeast of Prineville.

Gorge, Deepest

Hells Canyon, Wallowa County: Up to 7,913' in depth along the Snake River, it is the deepest gorge in North America.

Highways, Special Designation

Historic Columbia River Highway: The 74-mile stretch of the Columbia River Highway from Troutdale to The Dalles was built from 1913 to 1922. For many years, it was designated U.S. 30. Beginning in the 1950s, Interstate 84 replaced the historic highway as the main route through the Columbia Gorge. The historic highway became a National Scenic Byway All-American Road in 1999. In 2000, the U.S. Secretary of the Interior designated it a National Historic Landmark, which recognized the highway as a significant national heritage resource. The route became the first highway in the country to be given either of these national designations.

Oregon 99: Originally known as the Pacific Highway, Oregon 99 runs from the Oregon/California border north to Junction City, where it splits into Oregon 99E and Oregon 99W. The Pacific Highway, once designated as U.S. 99, U.S. 99E and U.S. 99W, was the main north–south highway in Oregon from the 1920s until Interstate 5 replaced it in 1964.

U.S. 101: Completed in the 1930s, the Oregon Coast Highway (U.S. 101) runs the length of Oregon's Pacific Coast from Astoria on the Columbia River to the Oregon/California border. The highway was designated an Oregon Scenic Byway in 1991 and a National Scenic Byway All-American Road in 2002.

Veterans Memorial Highways: Beginning with WWI in 1917, 479,600 Oregon veterans have served our nation during five major wars—WWI, WWII, Korea, Vietnam, Persian Gulf/Afghanistan/Iraq. Over 6,000 lost their lives and 15,000 were wounded during those wars. Five border-to-border highways were designated by the Legislature and three governors to honor these veterans:

WWI Veterans Memorial Highway: U.S. 395,

WWII Veterans Historic Highway: U.S. 97,

Korean War Veterans Memorial Highway: Interstate 5,

Vietnam Veterans Memorial Highway: Interstate 84, and

Persian Gulf, Afghanistan and Iraq Veterans Memorial Highway: U.S. 101.

Interstate 5 was also designated a Purple Heart Trail.

In a project managed by the Bend Heroes Foundation, 67 veterans memorial highway signs were installed along the five highways at no expense to taxpayers.

Hot Springs

Notable hot springs: Alvord, Austin, Bagby, Belknap, Bigelow, Blue Mountain, Breitenbush, Couger (Terwilliger), Crane, East Lake, Echo Rock, Hart Mountain (Antelope), Hot Lake, Hunter's, Juntura, Kah-Nee-Ta, Kropp, Lehman, Luce, McCredie, Olene Gap, Paulina Lake, Snively, Summer Lake, Umpqua, Wall Creek, Weberg, Whitehorse

Hydroelectric Projects and Dams, Largest

John Day Dam: Columbia River, 1971, 2,160 megawatts

The Dalles Dam: Columbia River, 1957, 2,100 megawatts

Bonneville Dam: Columbia River, 1938 (produced first power in 1937, first commercial power in 1938), 1,218 megawatts

McNary Dam: Columbia River, 1954, 980 megawatts

Insect, State*

In 1979, the Legislature designated the Oregon Swallowtail Butterfly *(Papilio oregonius)* as the Oregon state insect. A true native of the Northwest, the Oregon Swallowtail is at home in the lower sagebrush canyons of the Columbia River and its tributaries, including the Snake River watershed.

This strikingly beautiful butterfly has a wingspan of 2-1/2 to 3 inches and is bright yellow and black with a reddish-orange hindspot.

Jails and Prisons

31 jails operated by county sheriffs

14 institutions operated by the Department of Corrections, including the Oregon State Penitentiary, which is Oregon's only maximum security prison

One federal correctional institution

Judicial Districts: 27

Lakes

Deepest: Crater Lake, 1,946' (deepest in the United States)

Largest:

Upper Klamath Lake, 61,543 surface acres

Malheur Lake, 49,700 surface acres

Note: Size may vary depending on seasons and precipitation. At times, Malheur Lake may have a larger surface area than Upper Klamath Lake.

Number: Approximately 6,150 lakes/reservoirs

Legal Holidays and
Days of Special Observance

New Year's Day (observed)
1/2/17, 1/1/18, 1/1/19

Martin Luther King, Jr.'s Birthday (observed)
1/16/17, 1/15/18, 1/21/19

Presidents' Day
2/20/17, 2/19/18, 2/18/19

Memorial Day
5/29/17, 5/28/18, 5/27/19

Independence Day
7/4/17, 7/4/18, 7/4/19

Labor Day
9/4/17, 9/3/18, 9/2/19

Veterans Day (observed)
11/10/17, 11/12/18, 11/11/19

Thanksgiving Day
11/23/17, 11/22/18, 11/28/19

Christmas Day
12/25/17, 12/25/18, 12/25/19

Additionally, other days may be legal holidays in Oregon, such as those appointed by the governor as a holiday or those appointed by the president of the United States as a day of mourning, rejoicing or other special observance, when the governor also appoints that day as a holiday.

Whenever a holiday falls on a Sunday, the following Monday shall be observed as the holiday. Whenever a holiday falls on a Saturday, the preceding Friday shall be observed as the holiday.

The governor may also proclaim days or weeks in special recognition to individuals or groups or to promote issues and causes.

Lighthouses

Cape Arago Lighthouse, Coos Bay: lighted 1934; deactivated 2006

Cape Blanco Lighthouse, Port Orford: lighted 1870

Cape Meares Lighthouse, Tillamook: lighted 1890; deactivated 1963

Cleft of the Rock Lighthouse, Yachats (privately owned, not open to the public): lighted 1976

Coquille River Lighthouse, Bandon: lighted 1896; deactivated 1939

Heceta Head Lighthouse, Florence: lighted 1894

Port of Brookings Lighthouse, Brookings (privately owned, not open to the public): lighted 1997

Tillamook Rock Lighthouse, Cannon Beach: lighted 1881; deactivated 1957

Umpqua River Lighthouse, Reedsport: lighted 1894

Yaquina Bay Lighthouse, Newport: lighted 1871–74; reactivated 1996

Yaquina Head Lighthouse, Newport: lighted 1873

Marriages: 27,794 (2015)

Microbe, State

In 2013, the Oregon Legislature designated *Saccharomyces cerevisiae* as the state microbe. The yeast converts sugar into carbon dioxide and ethanol, an essential process for leavening bread and brewing alcoholic beverages, making Oregon an internationally recognized hub of craft brewing.

Mileage Distances (in Oregon), Highways and Interstates

Interstate 5: 308 miles

Interstate 84: 375 miles

U.S. 20: 451 miles

U.S. 26: 471 miles

U.S. 97: 289 miles

U.S. 101: 363 miles

U.S. 395: 384 miles

Mileage Distances, Road (from Portland)

Albuquerque, New Mexico	1,360
Atlanta, Georgia	2,595
Boise, Idaho	430
Chicago, Illinois	2,120
Denver, Colorado	1,240
Fargo, North Dakota	1,500
Houston, Texas	2,270
Los Angeles, California	965
Miami, Florida	3,255
New York, New York	2,895
Omaha, Nebraska	1,655
Phoenix, Arizona	1,335
St. Louis, Missouri	2,045
Salt Lake City, Utah	765
San Francisco, California	635
Seattle, Washington	175

Mother of Oregon*

Honored by the 1987 Legislature as the "Mother of Oregon," Tabitha Moffatt Brown "represents the distinctive pioneer heritage and the charitable and compassionate nature of Oregon's people." At 66 years of age, she financed her own wagon for the trip from Missouri to Oregon. The boarding school for orphans that she established later became known as Tualatin Academy and eventually, was chartered as Pacific University.

Motto, State

"She Flies With Her Own Wings" was adopted by the 1987 Legislature as the Oregon state motto. The phrase originated with Judge Jessie Quinn Thornton and was pictured on the territorial seal in Latin: *Alis Volat Propriis*. The new motto replaces "The Union," which was adopted in 1957.

Mountains, Major

Blue Mountains: This northeastern Oregon mountain chain is part of the Columbia Plateau, which also extends into southeastern Washington. Lava flows cover much of the surface, and the upper, wooded slopes have been used for lumbering. Recreation and livestock grazing are the mountains principal economic uses. The highest elevation is Rock Creek Butte (9,105'), located on the Elkhorn Ridge a few miles west of Baker City.

Cascade Range: This lofty mountain range extends the entire north–south length of Oregon east of the Willamette Valley. It lies about 100 to 150 miles inland from the coastline and forms an important climatic divide, with the western slopes receiving abundant precipitation but the eastern slopes very little. The western slopes are heavily wooded, with the eastern section mainly covered by grass and scrub plants. Many lakes and several large rivers are in the mountains, the latter harnessed for hydroelectric power. The range is used frequently for outdoor recreation, including camping, hiking and skiing. The highest elevations are Mt. Hood (11,239'), located in Clackamas and Hood River Counties, and Mt. Jefferson (10,495'), located in Jefferson, Linn and Marion Counties.

Coast Range: The Coast Range runs the length of the state along the western coastline, from the Columbia River in the north to the Rogue River in the south. These mountains contain dense softwood forests which, historically, made lumbering an important economic activity. Their eastern slopes mark the western edge of the Willamette Valley. The highest elevation north of Coquille is Mary's Peak (4,097'), located in Benton County. The highest elevation south of Coquille is Mt. Bolivar (4,319') in Coos and Curry Counties.

Klamath Mountains: The Klamath Mountains in southwestern Oregon are sometimes included as part of the Coast Range. These mountains include numerous national forest and wildlife preserves and contain scenic portions of the Klamath River. The highest elevation is Mt. Ashland (7,532'), located in Jackson County.

Steens Mountain: This is a massive, 30-mile-long mountain in the Alvord Valley featuring valleys and U-shaped gorges that were cut by glaciers one million years ago. It is located in Harney County in southeastern Oregon and is 9,773' in elevation.

Mushroom, State*

The 1999 Legislature recognized the Pacific Golden Chanterelle *(Cantharellus formosus)* as the Oregon state mushroom. This mushroom is a wild, edible fungus of high culinary value that is unique to the Pacific Northwest. More than 500,000 pounds of Pacific Golden Chanterelles are harvested annually in Oregon, representing a large portion of the commercial mushroom business.

Name of Oregon

The first written record of the name "Oregon" comes from a 1765 proposal for a journey written by Major Robert Rogers, an English army officer. It reads, "The rout . . . is from the Great Lakes towards the Head of the Mississippi, and from thence to the River called by the Indians Ouragon." His proposal rejected, Rogers reapplied in 1772, using the spelling "Ourigan." The first printed use of the current spelling appeared in Captain Jonathan Carver's 1778 book, *Travels Through the Interior Parts of North America 1766, 1767 and 1768*. He listed the four great rivers of the continent, including "the River Oregon, or the River of the West, that falls into the Pacific Ocean at the Straits of Annian."

While no definitive pronunciation of "Oregon" is given in *Oregon Geographic Names,* the most common pronunciation by long-time Oregonians is "OR-ee-gun."

National Cemeteries
Willamette, Portland
Eagle Point, Eagle Point
Roseburg, Roseburg

National Fish Hatcheries
Eagle Creek, Estacada
Warm Springs, Warm Springs

National Forests
Deschutes, Fremont-Winema, Malheur, Mt. Hood, Ochoco, Rogue River-Siskiyou, Siuslaw, Umatilla, Umpqua, Wallowa-Whitman, Willamette

National Grassland
Crooked River, near Madras

National Historic Sites
Crater Lake's Superintendent's Residence; Fort Astoria; Fort Vancouver (Oregon, Washington); Jacksonville's Historic District; Portland's Pioneer Courthouse, Old Town Historic District and Aubrey Watzek House; Timberline Lodge; University of Oregon's Deady and Villard Halls; Lower Klamath National Wildlife Refuge; Oregon Caves Chateau; John Day's Kam Wah Chung Company Building; Joseph's Wallowa Lake Site; Lake County's Fort Rock Cave

National Monuments
Cascade-Siskiyou, near Ashland
John Day Fossil Beds, located in three units near Kimberly, Mitchell and Fossil

Newberry National Volcanic Monument, near Bend

Oregon Caves, near Cave Junction

National Parks

Crater Lake

Lewis and Clark National Historical Park (Oregon, Washington)

Nez Perce National Historical Park (Oregon, Idaho, Montana, Washington)

National Recreation Areas

Hells Canyon National Recreation Area (Oregon, Idaho)

Oregon Dunes National Recreation Area

National Scenic Area

Columbia River Gorge

National Trails

California National Historic Trail

Lewis and Clark National Historic Trail

Oregon National Historic Trail: 2,170 miles from Independence, Missouri, to the Willamette Valley of Oregon, passing through Missouri, Kansas, Nebraska, Wyoming, Idaho and Oregon.

National Wildlife Refuges

Ankeny, near Jefferson

Bandon Marsh, near Bandon

Baskett Slough, near Dallas

Bear Valley, near Klamath Falls

Cape Meares, near Tillamook

Cold Springs, near Hermiston

Hart Mountain National Antelope Refuge, near Lakeview

Klamath Marsh, near Klamath Falls

Malheur, near Burns

McKay Creek, near Pendleton

Nestucca Bay, near Pacific City

Oregon Islands, off southern Oregon coast

Siletz Bay, near Lincoln City

Three Arch Rocks, off coast near Oceanside

Tualatin River, near Sherwood

Upper Klamath, near Klamath Falls

Wapato Lake, near Sherwood

William L. Finley, near Corvallis

Nut, State*

The hazelnut, or filbert, *(Corylus avellana)* was named the state nut by the 1989 Legislature. Oregon grows 99 percent of the entire U.S. commercial crop. The Oregon hazelnut, unlike wild varieties, grows on single-trunked trees up to 30 or 40 feet tall. Adding a unique texture and flavor to recipes and products, hazelnuts are preferred by chefs, bakers, confectioners, food manufacturers and homemakers worldwide.

Parks, State

257 parks totaling over 109,000 acres; day use attendance of 47.63 million (July 1, 2014–June 30, 2015) ranking 3rd in nation; more than 1,000 miles of managed trails; boat docks/ramps in approximately 50 parks; 53 campgrounds

Physical Dimensions

United States Rank in Total Area: 9

Land Area: 95,988 square miles

Water Area: 2,390 square miles

Total: 98,378 square miles

Coastline: 363 miles

Poet Laureate*

In 2016, Governor Kate Brown named Elizabeth Woody Oregon's poet laureate, noting that "Woody's words bring to life the landscapes, creatures and people who make Oregon special." Woody succeeds Peter Sears, poet laureate from 2014 to 2016. She is Oregon's eighth poet laureate since 1921.

Born on the Navajo Nation reservation in Ganado, Arizona, Woody has lived in Warm Springs and Portland much of her life and is an enrolled member of the Confederated Tribes of Warm Springs.

Woody received the 1995 William Stafford Memorial Award for Poetry from the Pacific Northwest Bookseller's Association and was a poetry finalist for the 1994 Oregon Book Awards. She has published poetry, short fiction and essays. Her first book of poetry *Hand into Stone* won a 1990 American Book Award. Other published works include *Luminaries of the Humble* and *Seven Hands, Seven Hearts*.

Population

Oregon is ranked 39th in population density with 42 inhabitants per square mile.

1850	12,093	1940	1,089,684
1860	52,465	1950	1,521,341
1870	90,923	1960	1,768,687
1880	174,768	1970	2,091,533
1890	317,704	1980	2,633,321
1900	413,536	1990	2,842,321
1910	672,765	2000	3,421,399
1920	783,389	2010	3,831,074
1930	953,786	2015	4,013,845

Precipitation

Record 24-hour maximum rainfall: 14.3" on November 6, 2006, at Lees Camp in the Tillamook County Coast Range

Average yearly precipitation at Salem: 39.7"

Record 24-hour snowfall: 39" on January 9, 1980, at Bonneville Dam

Record annual snowfall: 903" in 1950 at Crater Lake

Reservoir, Longest: Lake Owyhee, 52 miles

Rivers, Longest

Partially in the State of Oregon:

Columbia River: 1,243 miles

Snake River: 1,078 miles

Entirely in the State of Oregon:

John Day River: 284 miles

Deschutes River: 252 miles

Willamette River: 187 miles

Rock, State*

The thunder egg (geode) was named the Oregon state rock by the 1965 Legislature after rockhounds throughout Oregon voted it as their favorite rock. Thunder eggs range in diameter from less than one inch to over four feet. Nondescript on the outside, they reveal exquisite designs in a wide range of colors when cut and polished. They are found chiefly in Crook, Jefferson, Malheur, Wasco and Wheeler Counties.

Schools, Public

Education Service Districts 19
Schools 1,239
School Districts 197
Student population (2015–2016) 567,407

Seal, State*

The state seal consists of an escutcheon, or shield, supported by 33 stars and divided by an ordinary, or ribbon, with the inscription "The Union." Above the ordinary are the mountains and forests of Oregon, an elk with branching antlers, a covered wagon and ox team, the Pacific Ocean with setting sun, a departing British man-of-war ship signifying the departure of British influence in the region, and an arriving American merchant ship signifying the rise of American power. Below the ordinary is a quartering with a sheaf of wheat, plow and pickax, representing Oregon's mining and agricultural resources. The crest is the American Eagle. Around the perimeter of the seal is the legend "State of Oregon 1859." On September 17, 1857, the Constitutional Convention adopted a resolution that authorized the U.S. president to appoint a committee of three—Benjamin F. Burch, L. F. Grover and James K. Kelly—to report on a proper seal for the State of Oregon. Harvey Gordon created a draft, to which the committee recommended additions to be included in the state seal.

Seashell, State*

In 1848, conchologist (shell expert) John Howard Redfield named the *Fusitriton oregonensis* after the Oregon Territory. Commonly called the Oregon hairy triton, the shell is one of the largest found in the state, reaching lengths up to five inches. The shells are found from Alaska to California and wash up on the Oregon coast at high tide. The Legislature designated the state shell in 1991.

Shoes, Oldest

Sandals that are 9,300 years old, made of sagebrush and bark, were found at Fort Rock Cave in Central Oregon in 1938 by archaeologist Luther Cressman.

Skiing

Downhill: Anthony Lakes, near Union; Mt. Ashland, near Ashland; Mt. Bachelor, near Bend; Mt. Bailey snowcat skiing, near Diamond Lake; Cooper Spur, at Mt. Hood; Ferguson Ridge, near Joseph; Hoodoo, near Sisters; Mt. Hood Meadows, at Mt. Hood; Skibowl, at Mt. Hood; Spout Springs, near Elgin; Summit, at Government Camp; Timberline, at Mt. Hood; Warner Canyon, near Lakeview; Willamette Pass, near Oakridge; Wing Ridge in the Wallowas

Cross Country: National Forests: Deschutes, Fremont-Winema, Malheur, Mt. Hood, Ochoco, Rogue River-Siskiyou, Umatilla, Umpqua, Wallowa-Whitman, Willamette. Also, Crater Lake National Park and Hell's Canyon National Recreation Area.

Soil, State

The Legislature designated Jory soil as Oregon's state soil by concurrent resolution in 2011. The Jory soil is distinguished by its brick-red, clayish nature as it has developed on old volcanic rocks through thousands of years of weathering. It is estimated to exist on more than 300,000 acres of western Oregon hillsides and is named after Jory Hill in Marion County.

Jory soil supports forest vegetation such as Douglas fir and Oregon white oak. Many areas with the soil have been cleared and are now used for agriculture. Jory soil, coupled with the Willamette Valley climate, provides an ideal setting for various crops, including wine grapes, wheat, Christmas trees, berries, hazelnuts and grass seed.

Song, State

J. A. Buchanan of Astoria and Henry B. Murtagh of Portland wrote "Oregon, My Oregon," in 1920. With this song, Buchanan and Murtagh won a statewide competition sponsored by the Society of Oregon Composers, gaining statewide recognition. The song became the Oregon state song in 1927. (See music score on page 11.)

Standard of Time

The standard time zones were established by Congress in 1918. Oregon lies within the Pacific Standard Time zone with the exception of most of Malheur County along the Idaho border, which is on Mountain Standard Time. Daylight Saving Time is in effect from March through November.

Clocks "spring forward" one hour at 2:00 a.m. on the second Sunday of March: 3/12/17, 3/11/18, 3/10/19.

Clocks "fall back" one hour at 2:00 a.m. on the first Sunday of November: 11/5/17, 11/4/18, 11/3/19.

Temperatures, Records and Averages

Highest: 119°F on July 29, 1898, in Pendleton and on August 10, 1898, in Prineville

Lowest: -54°F on February 9, 1933, in Ukiah (50 miles south of Pendleton) and on February 10, 1933, in Seneca (105 miles southwest of Baker City)

Average January/July Temperatures:
Burns .... January 24.8°F/July 66.6°F
Grants Pass .... January 40.9°F/July 71.8°F

Newport............ January 45.7°F/July 57.9°F
Redmond .... January 32.7°F/July 65.9°F
Salem................ January 41.2°F/July 67.6°F

Tree, State*

The Douglas Fir *(Pseudotsuga menziesii),* named for David Douglas, a 19th century Scottish botanist, was designated the Oregon state tree in 1939. Great strength, stiffness and moderate weight make it an invaluable timber product said to be stronger than concrete. Averaging up to 200' in height and six feet in diameter, heights of 325' and diameters of 15' can also be found.

Trees, Largest

American Chestnut *(Castanea dentata):* 106' tall, 219" circumference, Multnomah County

Baker Cypress *(Cupressus bakeri):* 98' tall, 107" circumference, Josephine County, Rogue River National Forest

Bigleaf Maple *(Acer macrophyllum):* 119' tall, 463" circumference, Lane County

Bitter Cherry *(Prunus emarginata):* 83' tall, 35" circumference, Marion County

Black Cottonwood *(Populus balsamifera):* 154' tall, 348" circumference, Marion County

Black Walnut *(Juglans nigra):* 112' tall, 312" circumference, Multnomah County

California Laurel *(Umbellularia californica):* 101' tall, 601" circumference, Curry County

Douglas Fir *(Pseudotsuga menziesii):* 327' tall, 444" circumference, Coos County

English Oak *(Quercus robur):* 69' tall, 156" circumference, Polk County

Giant Chinkapin *(Chrysolepis chrysophylla):* 106' tall, 182" circumference, Douglas County

Incense Cedar *(Calocedrus decurrens):* 138' tall, 484" circumference, Josephine County

Knobcone Pine *(Pinus attenuate):* 117' tall, 118" circumference, Josephine County

Monterey Pine *(Pinus radiata):* 94' tall, 234" circumference, Coos County

Noble Fir *(Abies procera):* 216' tall, 252" circumference, Linn County

Oregon Ash *(Fraxinus latifolia):* 81' tall, 285" circumference, Multnomah County

Oregon White Oak *(Quercus garryana):* 97' tall, 288" circumference, Multnomah County

Pacific Dogwood *(Cornus nuttallii):* 61' tall, 150" circumference, Multnomah County

Pacific Willow *(Salix lucida):* 70' tall, 102" circumference, Washington County

Ponderosa Pine *(Pinus Ponderosa):* 167' tall, 348" circumference, Deschutes County

Port Orford Cedar *(Chamaecyparis lawsoniana):* 242' tall, 522" circumference, Coos County, Siskiyou National Forest

Sugar Pine *(Pinus lambertiana):* 255' tall, 290" circumference, Douglas County

Tanoak *(Lithocarpus densiflorus):* 135' tall, 303" circumference, Curry County

White Alder *(Alnus rhombifolia):* 91' tall, 151" circumference, Polk County

Source: www.americanforests.org

Tribes, Federally-Recognized

Nine federally-recognized tribes with reservation lands in Oregon:

Burns Paiute Tribe (349 members)

Confederated Tribes of Coos, Lower Umpqua and Siuslaw (1,144 members)

Confederated Tribes of the Grand Ronde Community (5,306 members)

Confederated Tribes of Siletz (5,080 members)

Confederated Tribes of the Umatilla Indian Reservation (3,016 members)

Confederated Tribes of Warm Springs Reservation (5,214 members)

Coquille Indian Tribe (1,041 members)

Cow Creek Band of Umpqua Tribe (1,722 members)

Klamath Tribes (3,700 members)

One federally-recognized tribal community: Celilo Village, located east of The Dalles

One federally-recognized tribal government in Oregon and Nevada: Fort McDermitt Paiute-Shoshone Tribe

Waterfall, Highest

Multnomah Falls, 620'

(sidebar) **Almanac**

Olympic Games Medalists from Oregon (1906–2016)

1906

Kerrigan, H.W. (Bert)	High Jump	Bronze

1908

Gilbert, Alfred C.	Pole Vault	Gold
Kelly, Dan	Broad Jump	Silver
Smithson, Forrest	Hurdles	Gold

1912

Hawkins, Martin	Hurdles	Bronze

1920

Balbach, Louis J.	Diving	Bronze
Kuehn, Louis (Hap)	Diving	Gold
Ross, Norman	Swimming	Gold (3)
Sanborn-Payne,Thelma	Diving	Bronze
Sears, Robert	Fencing	Bronze

1924

Newton, Chester	Wrestling	Silver
Reed, Robin	Wrestling	Gold

1928		
Hamm, Edward B.	Broad Jump	Gold

1932		
Graham, Norris	Rowing	Gold
Hill, Ralph	5000m	Silver
LaBorde, Henri J.	Discus	Silver

1936		
Robinson, Mack	200m	Silver

1948		
Beck, Lewis W. Jr.	Basketball	Gold
Brown, David P.	Rowing	Gold
Gordien, Fortune	Discus	Bronze
Helser (de Morelos), Brenda	Swimming	Gold
Zimmerman-Edwards, Suzanne	Swimming	Silver

1952		
Proctor, Hank	Rowing	Gold
Smith, William T.	Wrestling	Gold

1956		
Fifer, James	Rowing	Gold
Gordien, Fortune	Discus	Silver

1960		
Davis, Otis	400m	Gold (2)
Dischinger, Terry G.	Basketball	Gold
Imhoff, Darrall	Basketball	Gold
Wood, Carolyn	Swimming	Gold

1964		
Carr, Ken	Basketball	Gold
Counts, Mel G.	Basketball	Gold
Dellinger, William S.	Track and Field	Bronze
Freeman, Kevin	Equestrian	Silver
Saubert, Jean M.	Skiing	Silver/Bronze
Schollander, Don	Swimming	Gold (4)

1968		
Fosbury, Richard D.	High Jump	Gold
Freeman, Kevin	Equestrian	Silver
Garrigus, Thomas I.	Trapshooting	Silver
Johnson Bailes, Margaret	4x100m Relay	Gold
Sanders, Richard J.	Wrestling	Silver
Schollander, Don	Swimming	Gold/Silver

1972		
Freeman, Kevin	Equestrian	Silver
Peyton McDonald, Kim	Swimming	Gold
Sanders, Richard J.	Wrestling	Silver

1976		
Peyton McDonald, Kim	Swimming	Gold
Wilkins, Mac M.	Discus	Gold

1984		
Burke, Douglas L.	Water Polo	Silver
Herland, Douglas J.	Rowing	Bronze
Huntley (Ruete), Joni	High Jump	Bronze
Johnson, William D.	Skiing	Gold
King (Brown), Judith	400m Hurdles	Silver

	Menken-Schaudt, Carol	Basketball	Gold
	Schultz, Mark P.	Wrestling	Gold
	Wilkins, Mac M.	Discus	Silver

1988		
Brown, Cynthia L.	Basketball	Gold
Lang, Brent	Swimming	Gold

1992		
Johnson, Dave	Decathlon	Bronze
Jorgenson, Dan	Swimming	Bronze

1994		
Street, Picabo	Skiing	Silver

1996		
Deal, Lance	Hammer	Silver
MacMillan, Shannon	Soccer	Gold
Milbrett, Tiffany	Soccer	Gold
O'Brien, Dan	Decathlon	Gold
Schneider, Marcus	Rowing	Bronze
Steding, Katy	Basketball	Gold

1998		
Street, Picabo	Skiing	Gold

2000		
French, Michelle	Soccer	Silver
Kinkade, Mike	Baseball	Gold
Lindland, Matt	Wrestling	Silver
MacMillan, Shannon	Soccer	Silver
Milbrett, Tiffany	Soccer	Silver
Thompson, Chris	Swimming	Bronze

2002		
Steele, Dan	Bobsled	Bronze
Klug, Chris	Snow Board	Bronze

2004		
Hansen, Joey	Rowing	Gold
Johnson, Kate	Rowing	Silver
Zagunis, Mariel	Fencing	Gold

2008		
Cox, Stephanie Lopez	Soccer	Gold
Inman, Josh	Rowing	Bronze
Ward, Rebecca	Fencing	Bronze (2)
Windes, Elsie	Water Polo	Silver
Zagunis, Mariel	Fencing	Gold/Bronze

2012		
Bailey, Ryan	4x100m Relay	Silver
Eaton, Ashton	Decathlon	Gold
Rupp, Galen	10,000m	Silver
Windes, Elsie	Water Polo	Gold

2016		
Crouser, Ryan	Shot Put	Gold
Eaton, Ashton	Decathlon	Gold
Hill, Kim	Volleyball	Bronze
Rupp, Galen	10,000m	Bronze
Zagunis, Mariel	Fencing	Bronze

Olympic Games medal information courtesy of Jack Elder, Olympian, Luge 1972

State Song

Words
J.A. Buchanan

Music
Henry B. Murtagh

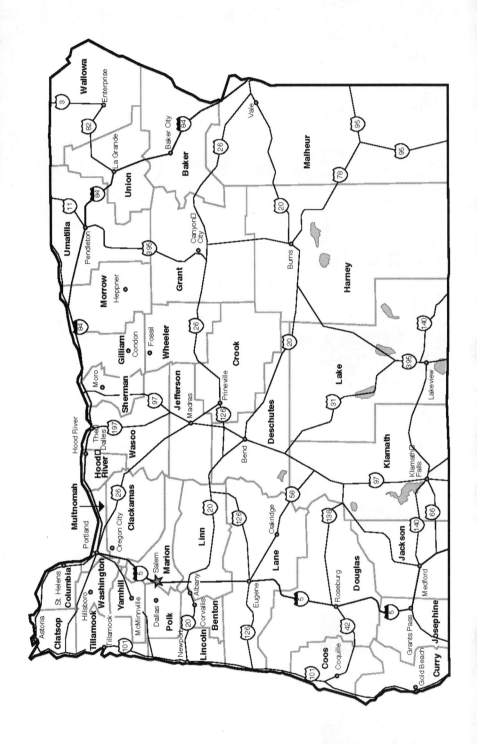

Two women ride horses on the beach at Nehalem Bay State Park in Tillamook County.
Oregon State Archives Scenic Photograph DSC0151-7

Oregonians elect five officials for statewide office to manage our executive branch of government: governor, secretary of state, treasurer, attorney general, and commissioner of the bureau of labor and industries. This section introduces these officials, describes their responsibilities and lists the administrative agencies and the services they provide.

KATE BROWN was born in Torrejón de Ardoz, Spain, on June 21, 1960. After spending most of her childhood in Minnesota, Brown earned a Bachelor of Arts degree in Environmental Conservation, with a Certificate in Women's Studies, from the University of Colorado at Boulder. She earned her law degree and Certificate in Environmental Law from the Northwestern School of Law at Lewis & Clark College in Portland.

Brown has taught at Portland State University and practiced family and juvenile law. She was appointed to the Oregon House of Representatives in 1991. In 1996, after serving two more House terms, she won election to the Oregon Senate. Two years later, she was elected Senate Democratic Leader and, in 2004, became the first woman to serve as Oregon's Senate Majority Leader.

In her legislative career, Brown made Oregon's government more accessible by holding legislative committee hearings around the state. She also ensured funding for a comprehensive review of Oregon's ethics laws, spearheaded legislation creating ORESTAR (Oregon Elections System for Tracking and Reporting), a searchable online database of campaign contributions and expenditures, and reformed Oregon's initiative process to reduce fraud and protect the citizen's right to petition.

In 2008, Brown was elected Oregon's 24th secretary of state and, in 2012, she was reelected. As secretary of state, she created Business Xpress, an online portal to provide resources for starting, expanding, operating or relocating businesses in Oregon. Brown also worked to modernize and streamline the state's voting and voter registration processes.

On February 18, 2015, in accordance with the Oregon Constitution, Secretary of State Brown was sworn in as Oregon's 38th governor after Governor John Kitzhaber resigned. She was then elected governor on November 8, 2016.

Governor Kate Brown

State Capitol Building, 900 Court St. NE, Suite 254, Salem 97301; 503-378-3111

Kate Brown, Portland; Democrat; appointed 2015; elected 2016; term expires January 2019.

The governor is elected to a four-year term and is limited to two consecutive terms in office during any 12-year period. The governor must be a U.S. citizen, at least 30 years old and an Oregon resident for three years before taking office.

The governor provides leadership, planning and coordination for the executive branch of state government. She appoints many department and agency heads within the executive branch and appoints members to nearly 300 policymaking, regulatory and advisory boards and commissions.

The governor proposes a two-year budget to the Legislature, recommends a legislative program to each regular session and may also call special sessions. She reviews all bills passed by the Legislature and may veto measures she believes are not in the public interest.

The governor chairs both the State Land Board, which manages state-owned lands, and the Oregon Progress Board, which sets strategic goals for Oregon. The governor acts as the superintendent of public instruction, directs state government's coordination with local and federal governments and is commander-in-chief of the state's military forces.

The governor appoints judges to fill vacancies in judicial office, has extradition authority and may grant reprieves, commutations and pardons of criminal sentences.

If the office of governor becomes vacant, the office passes, in order, to the secretary of state, state treasurer, president of the Senate and speaker of the House of Representatives. There is no lieutenant governor in Oregon.

For additional information, see page 19.

DENNIS MICHAEL RICHARDSON is Oregon's 26th secretary of state. Born July 30, 1949, Dennis grew up with the core belief that we all have an obligation to serve those in need and speak for those who cannot speak for themselves.

As a young man, Dennis deployed to Vietnam as a combat helicopter pilot in the U.S. Army. His service engrained in him the values of courage, commitment and leadership for a lifetime. After his military service, Dennis married his wife Cathy and attained his baccalaureate and law degrees from Brigham Young University before settling in Central Point, Oregon.

Married 43 years, Dennis and Cathy are parents of one son and eight daughters. In addition to his other responsibilities, Dennis volunteers his time mentoring job seekers and serving on the board of ACCESS (Aging Community Coordinated Enterprises and Supportive Services), the Community Action Agency of Jackson County.

Secretary Richardson practiced law for more than three decades and, while doing so, he served on the Central Point City Council and six terms in the Oregon House of Representatives, where he was unanimously elected speaker pro tempore. He also served as co-chair of the Joint Ways and Means Committee and successfully led the state out of a $3.5 billion budget deficit without raising taxes.

Secretary Richardson will apply his experience, knowledge and leadership to help restore accountability, transparency and the people's trust in state government. His commitment is to be a watchdog over public spending, while increasing access to public records, confidence in public elections, and a business-friendly, job-creating climate in Oregon.

Secretary of State Dennis Richardson

136 State Capitol Building, 900 Court St. NE, Salem 97310-0722; 503-986-1523

Dennis Richardson, Central Point; Republican; elected 2016; term expires January 2021.

The secretary of state is one of three constitutional officers of the executive branch elected statewide. The secretary serves a four-year term and can hold office for a second consecutive term.

The responsibilities of the secretary of state include leadership roles in the following areas:

Chief elections officer: The secretary interprets and applies state election laws, compiles and publishes the *Voters' Pamphlet* and supervises all elections, local and statewide.

Auditor of public accounts: He examines and audits accounts of all publicly funded boards, commissions and agencies.

Corporation Division: The secretary keeps public records of businesses authorized to transact business in Oregon, nonprofit corporations, and trade and service marks. Other public business records include notices of security interests in movable and personal property, statutory liens and warrants.

Chief records officer of the state: The secretary houses and provides access to the permanently valuable records of state government through the Archives Division and provides storage for inactive state agency records through the State Records Center.

State Land Board member: The secretary shares responsibility with the governor and treasurer for supervising and managing state-owned lands.

Oregon Sustainability Board: The secretary serves as chair. This board promotes practices that strive to optimize an organization's financial, environmental and social performance.

The secretary is custodian of the Seal of the State of Oregon, and he regulates Oregon notaries public. He also publishes the *Oregon Blue Book*.

If the office of governor becomes vacant, the office passes to the secretary of state. There is no lieutenant governor in Oregon.

For additional information, see page 21.

TOBIAS READ is Oregon's 29th state treasurer. Born in Montana and raised in Idaho, he moved to Salem, Oregon to attend Willamette University before getting his Master of Business Administration degree at the University of Washington. He brings a wide range of public-sector and private-sector experience to the office—he worked for two U.S. Treasury secretaries, at the Nike Corporation, and has most recently served as a state representative in Oregon for a decade.

As a state representative, Tobias was known for focusing on the issues that contribute to a growing economy—a high-quality education, innovation, and funding for our roads and bridges. He strove to fund full-day kindergarten and give every district the opportunity to offer it. During the 2015 legislative session, he led the effort to pass the Oregon Retirement Savings Plan, making it easier for more than a million Oregonians who don't get retirement plans from their employers to save for their retirements.

As state treasurer, Tobias' first priority is to focus on managing Oregon's money responsibly and with transparency. He is also working hard to help Oregonians save for college and retirement so that everyone in Oregon has a chance to succeed.

Tobias lives in Beaverton with his wife Heidi and their two children.

State Treasurer Tobias Read

159 State Capitol Building, 900 Court St. NE, Salem 97301-4043; 503-378-4329

Tobias Read, Beaverton; Democrat; elected 2016; term expires January 2021.

The state treasurer is a constitutional officer and a statewide elected official. The treasurer serves a four-year term and, if reelected, can hold office for two terms.

The treasurer serves as the chief financial officer for the state and is responsible for the prudent financial management of billions of taxpayer dollars. The treasurer also serves as the state's chief investment officer and has the duty of investing the monies of numerous funds such as the Public Employees Retirement Fund, the State Accident Insurance Fund and the Common School Fund.

The treasurer serves on a variety of state financial boards and on the State Land Board, which has a fiduciary duty to manage state trust lands for the benefit of the Common School Fund.

The Office of the State Treasurer is a highly sophisticated organization with a wide range of financial responsibilities, including managing the investment of state funds, issuing state bonds, serving as the central bank for state agencies and administering the Oregon 529 College Savings Network.

The treasurer manages a portfolio of about $88 billion, with investments diversified across a spectrum of asset classes from stocks to real estate.

For additional information, see page 23.

ELLEN F. ROSENBLUM, a former federal prosecutor and state trial and appellate judge, was first elected to a four-year term as Oregon's 17th attorney general in November 2012 and was reelected to a second term November 8, 2016. She is the first woman to serve as Oregon attorney general. Her priorities include consumer protection and civil rights—advocating for and protecting Oregon's children, seniors, immigrants and crime victims and those saddled with education-related debt. She is committed to assisting district attorneys and local law enforcement in prosecuting elder abuse and complex crimes and has made crimes against children as well as consumer Internet privacy high priorities.

Attorney General Rosenblum has been active in local and national organizations of lawyers, judges and attorneys general. She has served on the Executive Committee of the National Association of Attorneys General and is the immediate past chair of the Conference of Western Attorneys General. She has served as secretary of the American Bar Association and is the chair of the ABA Section of State and Local Government Law. She co-founded the section's Attorneys General and Department of Justice Issues Committee.

Attorney General Ellen F. Rosenblum

Justice Building, 1162 Court St. NE, Salem 97301; 503-378-4400

Ellen F. Rosenblum, Portland; Democrat; appointed June 2012; elected November 2012; reelected 2016; term expires January 2021.

The attorney general is the chief legal officer of the State of Oregon and heads the Department of Justice and its nine divisions.

The attorney general controls and supervises all court actions and legal proceedings in which the state of Oregon is a party or has an interest. The attorney general also has full charge and control of all legal business of all state departments, boards and commissions that require the services of legal counsel. She prepares ballot titles for measures to be voted upon by the people of Oregon and appoints the assistant attorneys general to act as counsel for the various state departments, boards and commissions.

The attorney general gives written opinions upon any question of law in which the state or any public subdivision may have an interest when requested by the governor, by any state agency official or by any member of the Legislature. The attorney general and her assistants are prohibited by law from rendering opinions or giving legal advice to any other persons or agencies.

Services and responsibilities of the attorney general and the Department of Justice are representation of the state's interests in all civil and criminal cases before the state and federal courts, serving as legal counsel to state agencies and offices, consumer protection and information services, supervision of charitable trusts and solicitations, enforcement of state and federal antitrust laws in Oregon, assistance to the state's district attorneys, administration of the state's crime victims' compensation program, investigations of organized crime and public corruption, and the establishment and enforcement of child support obligations for families who receive public assistance.

The term of office for attorney general is four years.

For additional information, see page 25.

BRAD AVAKIAN serves as the commissioner of the Bureau of Labor and Industries (BOLI) where he works for strong and fair enforcement of Oregon's civil rights laws and wage and hour protections. With emphasis on apprenticeships and the return of career and technical education, Avakian has led efforts to ensure that employers have access to a skilled, competitive workforce.

Avakian was born February 4, 1961. A proud product of Beaverton's public schools, Avakian earned a Bachelor of Science degree in psychology from Oregon State University in 1984 and a Juris Doctor degree from Lewis & Clark Law School in 1990.

After law school, Avakian opened a civil rights law practice to fight housing and employment discrimination. In response to music program cuts in local schools, Avakian worked with parents and educators to create the Southwest Music School.

Avakian served in the Oregon House of Representatives and, later, in the Oregon Senate representing Washington County and Northwest Portland. As a legislator, Avakian was a strong advocate for public education, Oregon's environment and working families. Avakian was honored as "Consensus Builder of the Year" in 2007 for his work passing the Oregon Renewable Energy Act and an expanded Bottle Bill. He also worked to strengthen the state's civil rights laws, including cosponsoring the landmark Oregon Equality Act of 2007.

At BOLI, Avakian championed the return of 21st century shop classes to 340 Oregon middle schools and high schools serving more than 160,000 students. He worked with legislators to pass the country's first civil rights bill for unpaid interns and oversaw wage and civil rights enforcement that directed more than $25 million back to unfairly treated Oregonians.

Avakian lives in northeastern Washington County with his wife and high school sweetheart Debbie and their two children, Nathan and Claire.

Commissioner of the Bureau of Labor and Industries Brad Avakian

State Office Building, 800 NE Oregon St., Suite 1045, Portland 97232; 971-673-0761

Brad Avakian, Beaverton; nonpartisan; appointed April 2008; elected November 2008; reelected 2012 and 2014; term expires January 2019.

The commissioner is chief executive of the Bureau of Labor and Industries. The commissioner also chairs the State Apprenticeship and Training Council. The term of the commissioner is four years.

The commissioner enforces state laws prohibiting discrimination in employment, housing, public accommodation and vocational, professional and trade schools. The position also has the authority to initiate a "commissioner's complaint" on behalf of victims of discrimination.

Through the Wage and Hour Division, the commissioner administers state laws relating to wages, hours of employment, basic working conditions, child labor and prevailing wage rates, and licenses certain industries to ensure quality professional services. The division oversees the Wage Security Fund that covers workers for unpaid wages in certain business closures and enforces group health insurance termination notification provisions.

The commissioner also directs the state's registered apprenticeship training system that gives workers the opportunity to learn a job skill while earning a living. The program benefits employers by providing a pool of skilled workers to meet business and industry demands.

The agency has expanded its support for employers so that they can more easily comply with frequently complex state and federal employment law. The Administrative Prosecution Unit prosecutes the agency's contested wage and hour and civil rights complaints. The commissioner issues final orders in all contested cases, except commissioner's complaints.

For additional information, see page 27.

OFFICE OF THE GOVERNOR

Kate Brown, Governor
Address: State Capitol Bldg., 900 Court St. NE, Suite 254, Salem 97301
Phone: 503-378-3111
Fax: 503-378-8970
Web: www.oregon.gov/gov/pages/index.aspx
Statutory Authority: ORS Chapter 176
Duties and Responsibilities: The governor is the chief executive of Oregon. The Oregon Constitution charges the governor with faithfully executing the laws, making recommendations to the Legislature and transacting all necessary business of government. The governor may veto bills of the Legislature and shall fill vacancies by appointment.

Arrest and Return (Extradition)

Address: State Capitol Bldg., 900 Court St. NE, Suite 160, Salem 97301
Phone: 503-378-3111
Fax: 503-378-3514
Contact: Fran Lushenko, Extradition Officer
Statutory Authority: ORS 133.743–133.857
Duties and Responsibilities: Arrest and Return provides administrative services for Oregon's extradition program.

Constituent Services Office

Address: State Capitol Bldg., 900 Court St. NE, Suite 160, Salem 97301
Phone: 503-378-4582
Fax: 503-378-6827
Duties and Responsibilities: The Constituent Services Office aids Oregonians in navigating state services and listens when citizens have ideas or suggestions about state government. The Constituent Services staff reports regularly to the governor, noting issues in state government that need attention. The office seeks to treat all inquiries fairly, to examine each situation objectively and to respond in a clear and helpful way.

Diversity, Equity and Inclusion, Office of

Address: Public Service Bldg., 255 Capitol St. NE, Suite 126, Salem 97310
Phone: 503-378-6833
Fax: 503-378-3225
Contact: Serena Stoudamire, Director of the Office of Diversity, Equity and Inclusion/ Affirmative Action;
Nakeia Daniels, Affirmative Action Manager;
Eloisa Miller, Economic and Business Equity Manager
Duties and Responsibilities: The Office of Diversity, Equity and Inclusion is responsible for the development and execution of a broad-based program that advances the public engagement mission and equity goals of the Office of the Governor in conjunction with major social, economic and political institutions and programs. The office is responsible for ensuring compliance with the Title VII Affirmative Action directives of the 1964 Civil Rights Act and Oregon Revised Statutes 659A by sharing and interpreting their objectives. The office responds to issues and concerns of Oregonians raised at the Constituent Services Office; identifies opportunities to increase equity and inclusion throughout out all policy areas; and works with the executive appointments staff to broaden diversity in the recruitment, confirmation, and ongoing participation of volunteer members of statewide boards and commissions. Additionally, the office works in collaboration with all state agencies to implement solutions to effectively promote, create and sustain equity and inclusion in contracting for Oregon's disadvantaged, minority-owned, woman-owned, emerging small businesses and service-disabled veteran-owned businesses, and sets state agency compliance standards for statewide contracting practices.

Education

Address: 775 Court St. NE, Salem 97301
Phone: 503-373-1283
Fax: 503-378-6827
Email: lindsey.d.capps@oregon.gov
Contact: Lindsey Capps, Education Policy Advisor
Duties and Responsibilities: For the state's children to succeed and thrive, Oregon is building a seamless system of education from cradle to career to ensure that every student is ready to learn and prepare for a future in which they can compete in the global workforce and be economically secure. The education policy advisor represents the governor on education issues, guiding policy and priority setting for early learning through higher education. Under the governor, the chief education officer serves as education policy advisor, coordinating with multiple state agencies and convening key stakeholders to advance strategies to ensure equitable access, opportunity and outcomes for students across the unified public education system.

Education Office, Chief

Address: 775 Court St. NE, Salem 97301
Phone: 503-373-1283
Email: education.investment@state.or.us
Web: http://education.oregon.gov
Contact: Lindsey Capps, Chief Education Officer
Statutory Authority: 2011 Oregon Laws, Chapter 519, Section 1

Duties and Responsibilities: The Chief Education Office oversees the building of a seamless system of public education that meets the diverse learning needs of every Oregon student from cradle to career. The purpose of the office is to elevate policies and practices to improve student learning outcomes and achieve statewide educational goals; ensure educational equity, opportunity and access to multiple pathways of learning from early childhood through postsecondary education; eliminate systemic barriers for students and growing the capacity of the unified public education system to serve student success; provide for a well-supported, culturally responsive education workforce; build collaborative partnerships with education stakeholders to further the design and effective implementation of state agency initiatives; and implement a statewide data system to evaluate and inform education policy and programs.

As the successor to the Oregon Education Investment Board, the office fulfills these duties by convening key stakeholders across education sectors and providing strategic leadership and coordination to multi-agency research, planning and policymaking. For these purposes, the chief education officer provides direction and oversight to state education agencies including the Early Learning Division, Youth Development Division, Oregon Department of Education, Higher Education Coordinating Commission and the Teachers Standards and Practices Commission.

Energy

Address: Public Service Bldg., 255 Capitol St. NE, Suite 126, Salem 97310
Phone: 503-986-6545
Fax: 503-378-3225
Email: ruchi.sadhir@oregon.gov
Contact: Ruchi Sadhir, Energy Policy Advisor
Duties and Responsibilities: The energy policy advisor works on a range of matters related to energy and climate change. Greenhouse gas emissions from the energy sector, including power plants and transportation fuels, is the largest cause of climate change. The energy policy advisor is focused on meaningfully reducing greenhouse gas emissions to combat climate change while keeping energy reliable and costs affordable to benefit Oregonians and the state economy. The policy advisor works on strategies for the public and private utility sector, energy transmission and distribution, transportation fuels, and energy infrastructure improvements.

Jobs and Economy

Address: State Capitol Bldg., 900 Court St. NE, Suite 160, Salem 97301
Phone: 503-378-5884
Fax: 503-378-6827

Duties and Responsibilities: Building Oregon's economy is a top priority for the governor. State government can and must play a key role in creating a favorable environment for the private sector to build a vibrant and innovative economy. The jobs and economy advisor is focused on identifying ways to ensure that Oregon companies become more competitive and sustainable and on ensuring that economic recovery touches every part of Oregon, urban and rural. It is also important to maintain connections at the regional, national and international levels. The multi-state initiatives director is focused on positioning Oregon at the forefront of a clean economy, health care transformation, and innovation in building and maintaining public infrastructure.

Labor and Workforce

Address: State Capitol Bldg., 900 Court St. NE, Suite 160, Salem 97301
Phone: 503-373-1558
Fax: 503-378-5540
Email: elana.pirtle-guiney@oregon.gov
Contact: Elana Pirtle-Guiney, Labor and Workforce Policy Advisor
Duties and Responsibilities: The Labor and Workforce policy advisor represents the governor on labor and collective bargaining issues. In addition, the advisor guides development of state-level policy related to education and workforce issues by providing leadership for, and serving as a liaison between, state and local efforts in education, training and workforce development and by ensuring alignment of statewide, local and regional strategic plans through collaboration with local workforce investment boards. The advisor seeks input from business and industry organizations, labor organizations, state agencies, local education providers, local government, community-based organizations, and public and private postsecondary colleges and schools.

Natural Resources Office

Address: Public Service Bldg., 255 Capitol St. NE, Suite 126, Salem 97310
Phone: 503-986-6535
Fax: 503-378-3225
Contact: Jason Miner, Natural Resources Policy Manager
Statutory Authority: ORS 173.610
Duties and Responsibilities: The governor's natural resources team convenes regular meetings of state natural resource agencies to ensure that state policies are consistently applied across agencies. The office facilitates resolution of policy differences between state agencies, federal agencies and between agencies and stakeholders, and provides direction and coordination for agencies on regulatory, planning and environmental issues that span multiple agencies. Examples include

coordination of species recovery efforts, water quality monitoring and enhancement, multipurpose water development and ocean conservation.

Public Safety and Oregon Military Department

Address: State Capitol Bldg., 900 Court St. NE, Suite 160, Salem 97301
Phone: 503-986-6550
Fax: 503-378-6872
Email: heidi.moawad@oregon.gov
Contact: Heidi Moawad, Public Safety and Oregon Military Department Policy Advisor
Duties and Responsibilities: The Public Safety and Oregon Military Department policy advisor works with the leadership of the Department of Corrections, Oregon State Police, Oregon Youth Authority, Oregon Criminal Justice Commission, Oregon Board of Parole and Post-Prison Supervision, Department of Public Safety Standards and Training, Oregon National Guard and the Office of Emergency Management. The advisor works closely with stakeholders in the public safety community around the state and with state and local groups to achieve the governor's public safety goals.

Regional Solutions

Address: State Capitol Bldg., 900 Court St. NE, Suite 160, Salem 97301
Phone: 541-610-7215
Fax: 503-378-6827
Email: annette.liebe@oregon.gov
Contact: Annette Liebe, Director
Duties and Responsibilities: Regional Solutions is an innovative, collaborative approach to community and economic development in Oregon. The state, in partnership with Oregon colleges and universities, established Regional Solutions Centers throughout Oregon. Each center works with community leaders at the local level to identify priorities, solve problems and seize opportunities to complete projects. These centers integrate state agency work and funding with other government, private and civic sector partners to ensure that projects are completed as efficiently as possible.

Transportation

Address: Public Service Bldg., 255 Capitol St. NE, Suite 126, Salem 97310
Phone: 503-986-6545
Fax: 503-378-3225
Contact: Karmen Fore, Senior Director for Federal/Regional Affairs and Transportation Policy Advisor
Duties and Responsibilities: The transportation policy advisor is focused on leading the governor's efforts to develop sustainable, multimodal transportation systems that move Oregon's people and cargo more efficiently.

Veterans

Address: 700 Summer St. NE, Salem 97301
Phone: 503-373-2388
Fax: 503-373-2362
Contact: Cameron Smith, Veterans Policy Advisor
Duties and Responsibilities: The veterans policy advisor works closely with the Oregon Department of Veterans' Affairs to ensure that the more than 320,000 veterans in Oregon access the benefits they have earned through their service. The position is also a link to ensure that veterans' interests are represented on the governor's staff and incorporated into broader policy areas to improve veterans' health, education and economic opportunity.

Washington, D.C., Office

Address: Hall of the States, Suite 134, Washington, D.C. 20001
Phone: 202-508-3847
Email: drew.johnston@oregon.gov
Contact: Drew Johnston, Washington, D.C., Director;
Karmen Fore, Senior Director for Federal/Regional Affairs (Oregon)
Duties and Responsibilities: The governor's Washington, D.C., office serves as liaison between state government, including the the Office of the Governor and state agencies, and federal government, including the U.S. Congress and the Oregon congressional delegation, the presidential administration and federal agencies. Federal decisions have an outsized impact on state affairs, and the office monitors and advocates on behalf of the state of Oregon. The office also serves as the state's principal connection to many outside organizations, including the National Governors Association and the Western Governors' Association.

OFFICE OF THE SECRETARY OF STATE

Dennis Richardson, Secretary of State
Leslie Cummings, Deputy Secretary of State
Address: 136 State Capitol Bldg., Salem 97310-0722
Phone: 503-986-1523
Fax: 503-986-1616
Email: oregon.sos@state.or.us
Web: http://sos.oregon.gov/Pages/default.aspx
Legal Authority: Oregon Constitution, Article VI, Section 2; ORS Chapters 177, 240
Duties and Responsibilities: The Office of the Secretary of State is one of three constitutional offices established at statehood. The secretary of state is the auditor of public accounts, chief elections officer, chief records officer and custodian of the Seal of the State of Oregon.

Archives Division

Address: 800 Summer St. NE, Salem 97310
Phone: 503-373-0701
Fax: 503-378-4118
Email: archives.info@state.or.us
Web: http://sos.oregon.gov/archives/Pages/
default.aspx
Contact: Mary Beth Herkert, State Archivist
Statutory Authority: ORS 177.120, Chapter
183, 192.001–192.170, 357.805–357.885
Duties and Responsibilities: The State Archives
was created by the Oregon Legislature in 1945 and
received its initial funding in 1947. The primary
function of the State Archives was to manage
public records at all levels of government in
Oregon by authorizing their retention and disposition and to identify, preserve and provide access to
the permanently valuable public records of the
state. Today, the State Archives acts as the state's
information manager (Records Management Unit)
by managing public records from creation until
final disposition and as the state's information
broker (Reference Unit) by identifying, preserving
and providing access, through its website and in
person, to the permanently valuable public records
of the state. In addition, the division is responsible
for filing, codifying and publishing Oregon's
Administrative Rules; compiling and publishing the
Oregon Blue Book; filing Official Documents;
providing advice and assistance on a variety of public records issues; and managing the State Records
Center for non-permanent, paper records storage
and the Security Copy Depository for microfilm.

The State Archives is home to the original
Oregon Constitution.

State Historical Records Advisory Board

Address: 800 Summer St. NE, Salem 97310
Phone: 503-378-5196
Fax: 503-378-4118
Web: http://sos.oregon.gov/archives/Pages/
shrab-main.aspx
Contact: Mary Beth Herkert, State Coordinator

Audits Division

Address: Public Service Bldg., 255 Capitol St.
NE, Suite 500, Salem 97310
Phone: 503-986-2255; Hotline: 1-800-336-8218
Fax: 503-378-6767
Email: SOS.audits@state.or.us
Web: http://sos.oregon.gov/audits/Pages/
default.aspx
Contact: Mary Wenger, Interim Director
Statutory Authority: ORS 177.170–177.180,
Chapter 297
Duties and Responsibilities: Created in 1929, the
Audits Division conducts audits to protect the pub-
lic interest and improve Oregon government. The

division ensures that public funds are properly
accounted for, spent in accordance with legal
requirements and used to the best advantage. These
efforts evoke Oregon's first auditor whose duties
were defined in the Territorial Statutes "to lessen
the public expenses, use public money to best
advantage, promote frugality in public office, and
generally, for better management." The division
conducts its work according to the professional
standards published by the U.S. Government
Accountability Office, and all its audits are
available to the public on the secretary of state's
website.

Corporation Division

Address: Public Service Bldg., 255 Capitol St.
NE, Suite 151, Salem 97310
Phone: 503-986-2200
Fax: 503-986-6355
Web: http://sos.oregon.gov/business/Pages/
default.aspx
Contact: Peter Threlkel, Director
Statutory Authority: ORS Chapters 56, 58, 60,
62, 63, 65, 67, 68, 79, 80, 87, 128, 194, 554,
647, 648
Duties and Responsibilities: The origins and functions of the Corporation Division date back to 1862.
The division provides timely document processing
services and convenient access to information
about businesses, notaries, secured transactions and
government resources for a prosperous Oregon.
The division assists the public in registering
business entities and filing public notice of records
of debt, commissions notaries public, and provides
certification of records and notarized documents.
The division provides access to public record information in the form of copies, certificates, lien
searches, computer reports, and on-line database
access to allow the public and businesses to know
with whom they are doing business.

The Office of Small Business Assistance assists
businesses who experience difficulty in their interactions with a state agency and connects businesses
with state and non-state resources. The office acts
as an ombudsman to help resolve problems
between businesses and state agencies.

The division helps entrepreneurs start a business
in Oregon by ensuring government registration
processes are as fast and easy as possible. These
efforts help accomplish the secretary of state's
vision to deliver better results to Oregonians
through more efficient and effective service delivery, greater transparency and accountability, and
using innovation to connect Oregonians to their
government.

Elections Division

Address: Public Service Bldg., 255 Capitol St. NE, Suite 501, Salem 97310-0722
Phone: 503-986-1518
Fax: 503-373-7414
Email: elections.sos@state.or.us
Web: http://sos.oregon.gov/voting-elections/Pages/default.aspx
Contact: Steve Trout, Director
Statutory Authority: ORS Chapters 246–260
Duties and Responsibilities: The Elections Division ensures the uniform interpretation and application of Oregon's election laws and enforces federal election laws. It monitors and supervises election administration of the country's first vote-by-mail system in all 36 counties and provides the public, elected officials, candidates, media and interested parties advice and assistance in all matters related to elections. Though some of its duties were performed prior to statehood in 1859, the Elections Division was officially created in 1957 when the secretary of state was named the chief elections officer for the state.

The division manages the statewide voter registration database and the electronic system for tracking and reporting campaign finance transactions. The division accepts filings for state offices, receives and verifies initiative and referendum petitions, and monitors campaign contributions and expenditure reports. The division publishes and distributes the *Voters' Pamphlet* for all state elections and investigates alleged election law violations.

Internal Support:

Business Services Division

Address: Public Service Bldg., 255 Capitol St. NE, Suite 180, Salem 97310
Phone: 503-986-2204
Fax: 503-378-4991
Contact: Jeff Morgan, Director

Human Resources Division

Address: Public Service Bldg., 255 Capitol St. NE, Suite 105, Salem 97310
Phone: 503-986-2168
Fax: 503-986-2175
Contact: Jackie Steffens, Director

Information Systems Division

Address: Public Service Bldg., 255 Capitol St. NE, Suite 103, Salem 97310
Phone: 503-986-1519
Contact: Chris Molin, Director

OFFICE OF THE STATE TREASURER

Tobias Read, State Treasurer
  Darren Q. Bond, Deputy State Treasurer
Address: 159 State Capitol Bldg., 900 Court St. NE, Salem 97301
Phone: 503-378-4329
Fax: 503-373-7051
Email: oregon.treasurer@state.or.us
Web: www.oregon.gov/treasury/Pages/index.aspx
Statutory Authority: ORS Chapter 178
Duties and Responsibilities: The state treasurer is a constitutional officer and a statewide elected official. The treasurer serves as the chief financial officer for the state and is responsible for the prudent management of billions of taxpayer dollars. The treasurer serves a four-year term and may serve only two consecutive terms. The Office of the State Treasurer is the state's financial services hub and oversees a range of financial responsibilities, including managing the investment of state funds, issuing state bonds, serving as the central bank for state agencies and administering the Oregon 529 Savings Network and Oregon Retirement Savings Plan.

In addition, the office coordinates policy development, legislative and public initiatives, financial literacy outreach and public engagement. The state treasurer, by constitutional authority, serves on the State Land Board and, by statute, on a number of public financial boards, including the Oregon Investment Council and State Debt Policy Advisory Commission.

Executive Division

Address: 159 State Capitol Bldg., 900 Court St. NE, Salem 97301
Phone: 503-378-4329
Contact: Darren Q. Bond, Deputy State Treasurer
Duties and Responsibilities: The Executive Division coordinates agencywide business services including strategic planning, internal auditing and accounting, human resource functions, project management, procurement and communications.

Debt Management Division

Address: 350 Winter St. NE, Suite 100, Salem 97301-3896
Phone: 503-378-4930
Fax: 503-378-2870
Contact: Laura Lockwood-McCall, Director
Duties and Responsibilities: The Debt Management Division oversees the sale, issuance and ongoing management of all state bonds, serves as a resource for debt-issuing local governments and maintains a statewide bond calendar, and

serves as the state's liaison to rating agencies and investors with regard to the state's financial condition.

Facilities Authority, Oregon

Address: 1600 Pioneer Tower, 888 SW Fifth Ave., Portland 97204
Phone: 503-802-2102
Contact: Gwendolyn Griffith, Executive Director
Statutory Authority: ORS 289.100
Duties and Responsibilities: The Oregon Facilities Authority was created in 1989 and is empowered to issue low-cost bonds to assist non-profit organizations with the financing of property and facilities for health, housing, educational and cultural uses. The authority reviews proposed projects and makes recommendations to the state treasurer about the issuance of bonds.

Municipal Debt Advisory Commission

Address: 350 Winter St. NE, Suite 100, Salem 97301-3896
Phone: 503-378-4930
Fax: 503-378-2870
Contact: Laura Lockwood-McCall, Debt Management Division Director
Statutory Authority: ORS 287.030
Duties and Responsibilities: The Municipal Debt Advisory Commission collects and reports information related to Oregon local government debt and provides policy input to the Legislature on debt matters of local governments.

Private Activity Bond Committee

Address: 350 Winter St. NE, Suite 100, Salem 97301-3896
Phone: 503-378-4930
Fax: 503-378-2870
Contact: Laura Lockwood-McCall, Debt Management Division Director
Duties and Responsibilities: The Private Activity Bond Committee allocates tax-exempt private activity bond allotments provided to the state under federal tax law.

State Debt Policy Advisory Commission

Address: 350 Winter St. NE, Suite 100, Salem 97301-3896
Phone: 503-378-4930
Fax: 503-378-2870
Contact: Laura Lockwood-McCall, Debt Management Division Director
Statutory Authority: ORS 286.550–286.555
Duties and Responsibilities: The State Debt Policy Advisory Commission, chaired by the state treasurer, prepares annual reports regarding outstanding tax-supported and non-tax-supported debt

and makes recommendations to the governor and Legislature regarding affordable levels of state indebtedness.

Finance Division

Address: 350 Winter St. NE, Suite 100, Salem 97301-3896
Phone: 503-378-4633
Fax: 503-373-1179
Contact: Cora Parker, Director
Duties and Responsibilities: The Finance Division provides cash management services to all Oregon state agencies and hundreds of Oregon local government entities, including cities, counties, schools and special districts. The division also helps protect public funds deposited at private banks and credit unions through collateralization requirements governed by ORS chapter 295. As the central bank for state agencies, the division manages millions of financial transactions annually, including cash deposits, electronic fund transfers, and check issuance. The division also administers the Local Government Investment Pool, which provides a short-term investment vehicle for local governments for the period between when revenue is received and when it is needed to pay public bills.

Short Term Fund Board

Address: 350 Winter St. NE, Suite 100, Salem 97301-3896
Phone: 503-378-4552
Fax: 503-378-2870
Contact: Heidi Rawe
Statutory Authority: ORS 294.885
Duties and Responsibilities: The purpose of the board is to advise the state treasurer and the Oregon Investment Council in the management and investments of the Oregon Short Term Fund and the Local Government Investment Pool. The treasurer serves as an ex officio member and appoints three members to the board. The governor appoints the remaining three members.

Investment Division

Address: 16290 SW Upper Boones Ferry Rd., Tigard 97224
Phone: 503-431-7900
Contact: John Skjervem, Chief Investment Officer
Duties and Responsibilities: The Investment Division manages the financial and real asset portfolios comprised by the Public Employees Retirement Fund, State Accident Insurance Fund, Oregon Short Term Fund, Common School Fund and numerous other state and agency accounts. On June 30, 2016, the combined market value of these funds totaled $89 billion, which included a $70 billion balance for the Public Employees Retirement Fund, the largest trust fund under

division management. Each managed fund has a unique risk and return profile and is broadly diversified across asset class, geography and investment strategy. The division also manages the investment program for the state's deferred compensation plan, serves as staff for the Oregon Investment Council and strives to save taxpayers and beneficiaries money by meeting each fund's specific investment objective at the lowest possible net cost.

Investment Council, Oregon

Address: 350 Winter St. NE, Suite 100, Salem 97301-3896
Phone: 503-378-4000
Contact: John Skjervem, Chief Investment Officer
Statutory Authority: ORS 293.706
Duties and Responsibilities: The Oregon Investment Council sets policy for all state investment trust funds and discharges its responsibilities consistent with state law and governing fiduciary standards. The state treasurer and director of the Public Employees Retirement System are ex officio council members, and the governor appoints four members whose service is subject to Senate confirmation. The council approves guidelines for all state investment activities and delegates day-to-day management authority to the Office of the State Treasurer's Investment Division.

Other Groups:

Oregon 529 Savings Network

Address: 350 Winter St. NE, Suite 100, Salem 97301-3896
Phone: 503-373-1903
Web: www.oregon529network.com
Contact: Michael Parker, Executive Director
Statutory Authority: ORS 348.841
Duties and Responsibilities: The Oregon 529 Savings Network gives Oregonians a tax-advantaged option to save for future education expenses and expenses incurred by Oregonians with disabilities. The Oregon plans are administered by the Oregon 529 Savings Board. The plans are qualified under Section 529 of the federal Internal Revenue Code. Investors qualify for state tax deducations for deposits, and all gains are state and federal tax free if used for qualified expenses.

Oregon offers two education-related 529 plans: the Oregon College Savings Plan, which is sold directly to investors, and the MFS 529 Savings Plan, sold exclusively through financial advisors. Both plans operate independently of each other but are governed by the same state and federal laws.

The Oregon ABLE (Achieving a Better Life Experience) Savings Plan was launched in 2016 and gives disabled Oregonians the ability to save and receive the same tax benefits. In addition, under federal law, as much as $100,000 in assets may be saved in ABLE accounts and not jeopardize eligibility for vital public assistance programs.

Oregon Retirement Savings Plan

Address: 159 State Capitol Bldg., 900 Court St. NE, Salem 97301
Phone: 503-378-4329
Web: www.oregon.gov/Retire/Pages/index.aspx
Contact: Lisa Massena, Executive Director
Statutory Authority: ORS 178.200
Duties and Responsibilities: Enacted by the 2015 Legislature to address a crisis of inadequate savings, the Oregon Retirement Savings Plan serves Oregonians who do not have access to a retirement savings option, such as a 401(k) plan. More than half of the Oregon workforce does not have access to a plan at work.

The plan will launch in phases starting in 2017 and is overseen by the Oregon Retirement Savings Board, which is chaired by the state treasurer. Two legislators sit as ex officio members and the governor appoints four members whose service is subject to Senate confirmation.

Information Services Division

Address: 350 Winter St. NE, Suite 100, Salem 97301-3896
Phone: 503-378-3436
Contact: Nancy O'Halloran, Chief Information Officer
Duties and Responsibilities: The Information Services Division provides enterprise-level information technology across the Office of the State Treasurer divisions, programs and business units in support of the state treasurer's mission.

DEPARTMENT OF JUSTICE

Ellen F. Rosenblum, Attorney General
   Frederick M. Boss, Deputy Attorney General
Address: 1162 Court St. NE, Salem 97301
Phone: 503-378-6002
Fax: 503-378-4017
Web: www.doj.state.or.us/Pages/index.aspx
Statutory Authority: ORS Chapter 180
Duties and Responsibilities: The Office of Attorney General was created by the Legislature in 1891. The Department of Justice was later established by the Legislature in 1947 and is the equivalent of the state's law firm. With nine divisions and approximately 1,300 employees, the agency is headquartered in Salem and has nine legal and 12 child support offices throughout the state. The department, which is led by the attorney general, is dedicated to the ethical and independent legal representation of state government, including all elected and appointed officials, agencies, boards and commissions. The department also advocates for and protects all Oregonians, especially the most

vulnerable, such as children and seniors. In all, the department and the attorney general have responsibility and authority under more than 350 state statutes.

The mission of the department is to serve state government and support safe and healthy communities throughout Oregon by providing essential justice services. The attorney general and the nine divisions are dedicated to providing ethical, independent and high quality legal services to state government; safeguarding consumers from fraud and unfair business practices; fighting crime and helping crime victims; advocating for vulnerable children; supporting families through the collection of child support; enforcing environmental protections; defending the civil rights of all Oregonians; and pursuing justice and upholding the rule of law.

Appellate Division

Address: 1162 Court St. NE, Salem 97301
Phone: 503-378-4402
Web: www.doj.state.or.us/Pages/index.aspx
Contact: Benjamin Gutman, Solicitor General
Duties and Responsibilities: The Appellate Division is responsible for representing the state's interests in all civil, criminal and administrative cases before state and federal appellate courts. Under supervision of the solicitor general, division attorneys articulate and defend the state's laws and legal policies in written briefs and oral arguments before the Oregon Court of Appeals, Oregon Supreme Court, United States Court of Appeals and Supreme Court of the United States. The division supports district attorneys by providing advice and training on legal issues. The division also creates and maintains a set of legal publications on various subjects of criminal law.

Child Support, Division of

Address: 1215 State St., Salem 97301;
    Mail: 1162 Court St. NE, Salem 97301
Phone: 503-947-4388
Web: http://oregonchildsupport.gov/Pages/
    index.aspx
Contact: Kate Cooper Richardson,
    Administrator
Duties and Responsibilities: The Division of Child Support administers the child support program for the state, providing child support services to Oregonians. Services include locating absent parents, establishing paternity, establishing child and medical support orders, modifying and enforcing support orders, and receiving and distributing child and medical support payments. Child support services are provided to all parents regardless of income. The division maintains local branches around the state and works in partnership

with county district attorneys' offices to deliver child support services through the Child Support Program. The program collects and distributes more than $360 million in child support annually, a vital component to ensuring the well-being of Oregon families.

Civil Enforcement Division

Address: 1162 Court St. NE, Salem 97301
Phone: 503-934-4400
Web: www.doj.state.or.us/Pages/index.aspx
Contact: Lisa M. Udland, Administrator
Duties and Responsibilities: The Civil Enforcement Division is responsible for civil law enforcement statewide. The Charitable Activities Section enforces laws regarding charitable trusts and solicitations and regulates bingo and raffle operations. The Civil Recovery Section is responsible for obtaining judgments and collecting debts owed to state agencies. It also provides legal services to the Division of Child Support. The Financial Fraud/Consumer Protection Section protects Oregon consumers from predatory marketplace practices. Its responsibilities include enforcement of laws pertaining to unlawful business practices, antitrust, securities, civil racketeering and charitable solicitations. The Medicaid Fraud Unit is part of a federally subsidized program for deterring fraud committed by Medicaid health care service providers. It detects and prosecutes cases of criminal abuse or neglect in health care facilities receiving Medicaid funds. The Child Advocacy Section provides legal advice, juvenile court and administrative hearing representation to the Department of Human Services, Child Welfare Programs. It handles cases involving allegations of child abuse and neglect.

Crime Victims' Services Division

Address: 1162 Court St. NE, Salem 97301
Phone: 503-378-5348; Toll-free 1-800-503-7983
Fax: 503-378-5738
Email: cvsd.email@doj.state.or.us
Web: www.doj.state.or.us/victims/pages/
    index.aspx
Contact: Shannon Sivell, Director
Duties and Responsibilities: The mission of the Crime Victims' Services Division is to reduce the impact of crime on victims' lives by supporting statewide victim services programs, promoting victims' rights, compensating victims for their economic damages and providing victims access to information and resources in a compassionate, responsive and dedicated manner.

Criminal Justice Division

Address: 1162 Court St. NE, Salem 97301
Phone: 503-378-6347
Fax: 503-373-1936
Web: www.doj.state.or.us/Pages/index.aspx
Contact: Michael Slauson, Chief Counsel
Duties and Responsibilities: The Criminal Justice Division is the Department of Justice's primary crime fighting unit. The division is divided into three sections: Special Investigations and Prosecutions, Organized Crime, and Criminal Intelligence. The division provides investigative, trial and training support to Oregon's district attorneys and law enforcement agencies. In addition, the division investigates and prosecutes organized crime, Internet crimes against children, public corruption and human trafficking cases. The division leads or participates in several important criminal and anti-terrorism information sharing and analysis programs through its Oregon TITAN Fusion Center and High Intensity Drug Trafficking Area Investigation Service Center.

District Attorneys

The Oregon Constitution describes the dual functions of the district attorney as the prosecuting attorney and law officer of the state and counties. Elected to a four-year term, the district attorney serves as the public prosecutor, represents the state in criminal proceedings and initiates proceedings for punishable offenses. The district attorney enforces child support orders, represents the state in juvenile matters and undertakes inquests into the cause and manner of certain deaths. Though elected by county voters, the district attorney is a state officer whose salary is paid by the state and who, in most cases, is prohibited from privately practicing law.

District attorneys by county: Baker, Matt Shirtcliff; Benton, John Haroldson; Clackamas, John S. Foote; Clatsop, Joshua Marquis; Columbia, R. Steven Atchison; Coos, R. Paul Frasier; Crook, Daina A. Vitolins; Curry, Everett Dial; Deschutes, John Hummel; Douglas, Rick Wesenberg; Gilliam, Marion Weatherford; Grant, Jim Carpenter; Harney, Joseph W. Lucas; Hood River, John T. Sewell; Jackson, Beth Heckert; Jefferson, Steven F. Lariche; Josephine, Ryan Mulkins; Klamath, Robert W. Patridge; Lake, Sharon Forster; Lane, Patricia W. Perlow; Lincoln, Michelle Branam; Linn, Doug Marteeny; Malheur, David M. Goldthorpe; Marion, Walter Beglau; Morrow, Justin Nelson; Multnomah, Rod Underhill; Polk, Aaron Felton; Sherman, Wade McLeod; Tillamook, William Porter; Umatilla, Daniel R. Primus; Union, Kelsie McDaniel; Wallowa, Mona K. Williams; Wasco, Eric J. Nisley; Washington, Robert Hermann; Wheeler, Gretchen M. Ladd; Yamhill, Brad Berry

General Counsel Division

Address: 1162 Court St. NE, Salem 97301
Phone: 503-947-4540
Web: www.doj.state.or.us/Pages/index.aspx
Contact: Steven A. Wolf, Chief Counsel
Duties and Responsibilities: The General Counsel Division provides a broad range of legal services to state agencies, boards and commissions, including day-to-day legal advice necessary for the state's operation. The division is composed of the following sections headed by attorneys-in-charge: Business Activities, Business Transactions, Government Services, Health and Human Services, Labor and Employment, Natural Resources, and Tax and Finance.

Trial Division

Address: 158 12th St. NE, Salem 97301;
   Mail: 1162 Court St. NE, Salem 97301
Phone: 503-947-4700
Web: www.doj.state.or.us/Pages/index.aspx
Contact: Steve Lippold, Chief Trial Counsel
Duties and Responsibilities: The Trial Division defends the state, its agencies, employees and elected and appointed officials in civil litigation brought in state and federal courts. The division also defends district attorneys in civil suits brought against them. The division includes four sections, each with a particular area of focus. The Civil Litigation Section handles a wide variety of cases that may be tried to a jury in state and federal courts. These cases fall into five general categories: torts, employment, commercial disputes, prisoner civil rights lawsuits and real estate condemnation. The Criminal and Collateral Remedies Litigation Section defends convictions secured by county district attorneys against collateral attacks brought by the convicted person. The Defense of Agency Orders Litigation Section defends state agency decisions when they are challenged in circuit court. The Special Litigation Unit handles complex class-action lawsuits, elections litigation and other high-profile or sensitive matters in which the state or its agencies may be plaintiffs or defendants.

BUREAU OF LABOR AND INDUSTRIES

Brad Avakian, Commissioner of the Bureau of Labor and Industries
Address: 800 NE Oregon St., Suite 1045,
   Portland 97232
Phone: 971-673-0761; Oregon Relay System
   TTY: 711
Fax: 971-673-0762
Email: mailb@boli.state.or.us
Web: www.oregon.gov/BOLI/Pages/index.aspx
Statutory Authority: ORS Chapter 651

Duties and Responsibilities: The mission of the Bureau of Labor and Industries (BOLI) is to protect employment rights, advance employment opportunities and protect access to housing and public accommodations that are free from unlawful discrimination. The Oregon Legislature founded the agency in 1903.

The principal duties of BOLI are to protect the rights of workers and citizens to have equal, non-discriminatory treatment through the enforcement of anti-discrimination laws that apply to workplaces, housing and public accommodations; to encourage and enforce compliance with state laws relating to wages, hours, and terms and conditions of employment; to educate and train employers to understand and comply with both wage and hour, and civil rights law; and to promote the development of a highly skilled, competitive workforce in Oregon through the apprenticeship program and through partnerships with government, labor, business, and educational institutions.

BOLI employs nearly 100 professionals and is headquartered in Portland. Regional offices can be found in Eugene and Salem.

BOLI Regional Offices:

Eugene
Address: 1400 Executive Pkwy., Suite 200, Eugene 97401
Phone: 541-686-7623
Fax: 541-686-7980

Salem
Address: 3865 Wolverine St. NE, Bldg. E-1, Salem 97305
Phone: 503-378-3292
Fax: 503-378-7636

Commissioner's Office and Program Services Division

Address: 800 NE Oregon St., Suite 1045, Portland 97232
Phone: 971-673-0781; Oregon Relay System TTY: 711
Fax: 971-673-0762
Web: www.oregon.gov/BOLI/Pages/index.aspx
Contact: Christine Hammond, Deputy Labor Commissioner
Statutory Authority: ORS Chapter 651
Duties and Responsibilities: The Commissioner's Office develops legislative initiatives, oversees communications for the agency and manages constituent correspondence and public engagement. The office also oversees legislatively directed reporting and serves as staff for legislative workgroups and the Oregon Council on Civil Rights. Other duties include intergovernmental relations, strategic planning and budget management. The Administrative Prosecution Unit convenes administrative law hearings in contested cases for both wage and hour and civil rights determinations.

Apprenticeship and Training Division

Address: 800 NE Oregon St., Suite 1045, Portland 97232
Phone: 971-673-0760; Oregon Relay System TTY: 711
Fax: 971-673-0768
Web: www.oregon.gov/BOLI/Pages/index.aspx
Contact: Stephen Simms
Statutory Authority: ORS 334.745–334.750, Chapter 660
Duties and Responsibilities: The Apprenticeship and Training Division promotes apprenticeship in a variety of trades by working with business, labor, government, and educational organizations to increase training and employment opportunities throughout the state. Apprenticeship is occupational training that includes on-the-job experience with classroom learning. The division registers occupational skills standards and agreements between apprentices and employers and works with local apprenticeship committees to ensure quality training and equal opportunity, especially for women and people of color, in technical craft jobs.

Apprenticeship and Training Division Regional Offices:

Bend
Address: 1645 NE Forbes Rd., Suite 106, Bend 97701-4990
Phone: 541-322-2435
Fax: 541-389-8265

Medford
Address: 119 N Oakdale Ave., Medford 97501
Phone: 541-776-6270
Fax: 541-776-6284

State Apprenticeship and Training Council

Address: 800 NE Oregon St., Suite 1045, Portland 97232
Phone: 971-673-0760; Oregon Relay System TTY: 711
Contact: Stephen Simms, Secretary; Brad Avakian, Chair
Statutory Authority: ORS 660.110
Duties and Responsibilities: The State Apprenticeship and Training Council oversees apprenticeship committees, programs and policies and approves apprenticeship committee members. The commissioner of the Bureau of Labor and Industries serves as the chairperson, and the director of the Apprenticeship and Training Division serves as its secretary.

Civil Rights Division

Address: 800 NE Oregon St., Suite 1045, Portland 97232
Phone: 971-673-0764; Oregon Relay System TTY: 711
Fax: 971-673-0765
Web: www.oregon.gov/BOLI/Pages/index.aspx
Contact: Amy Klare
Statutory Authority: ORS 30.670, 30.685, 345.240, 654.062, Chapter 659A
Duties and Responsibilities: The Civil Rights Division is tasked with defending the rights of all Oregonians to have equal opportunity in employment, housing, public accommodations and career schools. The investigators, managers and support staff that make up the division are a crucial part of BOLI's mission to protect employment rights, advance employment opportunities and protect access to housing and public accommodations that are free from discrimination.

Wage and Hour Division

Address: 800 NE Oregon St., Suite 1045, Portland 97232
Phone: 971-673-0844; Oregon Relay System TTY: 711
Fax: 971-673-0769
Web: www.oregon.gov/BOLI/Pages/index.aspx
Contact: Gerhard Taeubel, Administrator
Statutory Authority: ORS Chapters 279, 652, 653, 658, ORS 654.251
Duties and Responsibilities: The Wage and Hour Division enforces laws covering state minimum wage and overtime requirements, working conditions, child labor, farm and forest labor contracting, and wage collection. The division enforces the payment of prevailing wage rates required to be paid to construction workers on public works projects. BOLI determines and publishes prevailing wage rates based on an annual construction industry survey.

Prevailing Wage Advisory Committee

Address: 800 NE Oregon St., Suite 1045, Portland 97232
Phone: 971-673-0844
Contact: Gerhard Taeubel, Administrator
Statutory Authority: ORS 279C.820
Duties and Responsibilities: The Prevailing Wage Advisory Committee was legislatively established in 2003. The committee assists the BOLI commissioner in the administration of the Prevailing Wage Rate Law.

Technical Assistance for Employers Program

Address: 800 NE Oregon St., Suite 1045, Portland 97232

Phone: 971-673-0824; Oregon Relay System TTY: 711
Web: www.oregon.gov/BOLI/Pages/index.aspx
Contact: Jennifer Germundson, Manager
Duties and Responsibilities: The Technical Assistance for Employers Program offers guidance to Oregon businesses and organizations so they can understand Oregon employment law and avoid potential violations. The program holds employment law seminars throughout the state and publishes employer handbooks on wage and hour, civil rights, family leave laws and other important topics. The staff fields daily calls from Oregon employers seeking guidance on employment-related matters.

OTHER STATE AGENCIES, BOARDS AND COMMISSIONS

Beyond the previous five main executive offices, there are other agencies, boards, commissions and programs that carry out executive branch duties. The following section contains information about these entities. Each description includes basic contact information and when available, a summary of the entity's duties and responsibilities.

In general, the agencies are listed alphabetically by substantive name. For example, the Department of Human Services appears as "Human Services, Department of." Programs under the main agency are listed under that agency's heading. Thus, Self Sufficiency Programs would appear within the larger entry for Department of Human Services. These subdivisions are also listed alphabetically by substantive name with a few exceptions, such as when a board or commission is connected directly to the main agency office.

The *Oregon Blue Book* Index is helpful for locating individual agencies, boards, commissions or programs.

ACCOUNTANCY, OREGON BOARD OF

Address: 3218 Pringle Rd. SE, Suite 110, Salem 97302-6307
Phone: 503-378-4181
Fax: 503-378-3575
Web: www.oregon.gov/BOA/Pages/index.aspx
Contact: Martin Pittioni, Executive Director; Scott Wright, CPA, Chair
Statutory Authority: ORS Chapter 673
Duties and Responsibilities: The Oregon Board of Accountancy was created in 1913 by the Oregon Legislature. The board, with a staff of nine, protects the public through licensure of approximately 8,000 Certified Public Accountants (CPAs) and Public Accountants (PAs) and through registration of approximately 1,000 public accounting firms.

Applicants for licensure must meet minimum standards in terms of education, work experience and successful completion of the national CPA exam. Thereafter, licensees must demonstrate professional accounting competency at licensure renewal by meeting continuing education standards of 80 hours of education every two years for active licensees. The board also protects the public through its investigation function. Complaints are accepted in any written format from members of the public and other sources and may be self-initiated by the board. If an investigation finds a violation of board statutes or rules, licensees are held accountable for their conduct through disciplinary action.

The CPA profession is fundamentally about trust in the quality of audits, the accuracy of financial statements and the competency of any other professional service performed by CPAs, including tax services. The board holds licensees accountable for adhering to all professional and ethical standards that apply to their practice. The public can verify the status and disciplinary history of an Oregon licensee or public accounting firm on the board's website. The public can also verify CPA credentials nationally through the National Association of State Boards of Accountancy website at www.cpaverify.org.

ADMINISTRATIVE SERVICES, DEPARTMENT OF

Address: 155 Cottage St. NE, Salem 97301-3972
Phone: 503-378-3104
Fax: 503-373-7643
Email: oregon.info@oregon.gov
Web: www.oregon.gov/DAS/Pages/index.aspx
Contact: Katy Coba, Chief Operating Officer and Director
Statutory Authority: ORS 184.305
Duties and Responsibilities: The Department of Administrative Services (DAS) is the central administrative agency of Oregon state government and home to Oregon's Chief Operating Officer. DAS supports state agencies by providing a strong and stable management infrastructure for statewide personnel, finance, information systems and services, asset management, procurement, publishing and distribution and risk management. DAS employs about 850 people, with offices primarily in the Salem area.

DAS exists to effectively implement the policy and financial decisions made by the governor and the Oregon Legislature, to manage and coordinate projects involving multiple state agencies and to serve as a catalyst for innovation and improvement across all of state government. DAS supports Oregonians by supporting the state agencies, boards and commissions they rely on each day.

Chief Operating Officer, Office of the

Address: 155 Cottage St. NE, Salem 97301-3965
Phone: 503-378-3104
Fax: 503-373-7643
Email: oregon.info@oregon.gov
Web: www.oregon.gov/DAS/Pages/index.aspx
Contact: Katy Coba, Chief Operating Officer and Director
Statutory Authority: ORS 184.315
Duties and Responsibilities: The Office of the Chief Operating Officer (COO) provides leadership and policy direction to the department and all other state executive branch agencies. It oversees DAS's public affairs, economic analysis, legislative, information technology (internal to DAS) and project management work. The office is headed by the Chief Operating Officer, who is appointed by the governor. COO staff also provides support to state government's Enterprise Leadership Team, which is comprised of state agency leaders and serves as an advisory board to the governor and COO on long-term strategic policies and statewide initiatives.

Chief Financial Office

Address: 155 Cottage St. NE, U10, Salem 97301-3965
Phone: 503-378-3106
Fax: 503-373-7643
Email: CFO.info@oregon.gov
Web: www.oregon.gov/das/Financial/Pages/Index.aspx
Contact: George Naughton, Chief Financial Officer
Statutory Authority: ORS 184.335
Duties and Responsibilities: The Chief Financial Office prepares the Governor's Recommended Budget and monitors the development and execution of state agency budgets. The office provides management review services, issues certificates of participation to finance capital construction and infrastructure, helps agencies manage about three million acres of public lands and coordinates the state's bonded debt process. The office manages the financial system infrastructure for state government, which includes accounting, payroll and financial reporting. It also oversees DAS's internal audits and business services.

Chief Human Resources Office

Address: 155 Cottage St. NE, U30, Salem 97301-3967
Phone: 503-378-3622
Fax: 503-373-7684
Email: chro.hr@oregon.gov
Web: www.oregon.gov/das/HR/Pages/Index.aspx

Contact: Madilyn Zike, Chief Human Resources Officer
Statutory Authority: ORS 240.055
Duties and Responsibilities: The Chief Human Resources Office is responsible for statewide human resource systems, policies and initiatives. This encompasses human resource management and consultation and includes establishing and maintaining classification and compensation plans, training and development, administering and maintaining the central state employee database, overseeing personnel recruitment and labor relations and performing Public Employees Retirement System reconciliation for all state agencies. The office also provides direction and services to promote a stable and qualified workforce in state government. In addition, it offers DAS and client agencies a variety of human resource-related services, including human resource consultation, recruitment and position management.

DAS Business Services

Address: 155 Cottage St. NE, U90, Salem 97301-3972
Phone: 503-373-7607
Email: janet.e.savarro@oregon.gov
Web: www.oregon.gov/das/Financial/Pages/dbs.aspx
Contact: Janet Savorro, Administrator
Duties and Responsibilities: DAS Business Services (DBS) provides a comprehensive group of essential services to support the business of DAS and other public agencies. It is comprised of three sections: Administration and Business Support Services, Budget and Rate Development Services and Performance Management and Survey Analysis. DBS also provides support to the following four DAS Customer Utility Boards: Enterprise Technology Services Board, Enterprise Asset Management Board, Enterprise Goods and Services Board and Enterprise Human Resource Services Board.

Enterprise Asset Management

Address: 1225 Ferry St. SE, U100, Salem 97301-4281
Phone: 503-428-3362
Fax: 503-373-7210
Email: fac.info@oregon.gov
Web: www.oregon.gov/das/Pages/EAM.aspx
Contact: Shannon Ryan, Administrator
Statutory Authority: ORS Chapters 270, 276, 279A, 279C, 283
Duties and Responsibilities: Enterprise Asset Management (EAM) provides centralized services to state government, including motor pool and surplus property. In addition, the division acquires and maintains space for state agencies, provides property management, real property transaction services (buy, sell and lease), project management,

space planning, state building operations and maintenance and landscape maintenance. EAM also manages parking and commuter programs for state employees in Salem and Portland.

Enterprise Goods and Services

Address: 1225 Ferry St. SE, Salem 97301
Phone: 503-378-4642
Fax: 503-373-1626
Email: bret.west@oregon.gov
Web: www.oregon.gov/das/Pages/EGS.aspx
Contact: Bret West, Administrator
Statutory Authority: ORS 184.305, ORS Chapters 278, 279, 282, 283
Duties and Responsibilities: Enterprise Goods and Services provides centralized services to state government, including accounting and payroll, mail distribution and printing, procurement, self-insurance and risk control and financial system management.

State Chief Information Officer, Office of the

Address: 155 Cottage St. NE, 4th Floor, Salem 97301
Phone: 503-378-3175
Fax: 503-378-3795
Email: OSCIO.Info@oregon.gov
Web: www.oregon.gov/das/OSCIO/Pages/Index.aspx
Contact: Alex Pettit, State Chief Information Officer
Statutory Authority: ORS 182.122, 184.475, 184.477, 291.038, 291.039
Duties and Responsibilities: The Office of the State Chief Information Officer is an independent official directly responsible to the governor. The state chief information officer operates as the governor's primary advisor for statewide enterprise technology and telecommunication projects and programs, implementation of the Information Technology (IT) Governance framework, and establishment of Oregon's long-term IT strategy using the Enterprise Information Resource Management Strategy. It is comprised of four sections: Enterprise Security Office, IT Governance, Enterprise Shared Services and Enterprise Technology Services.

Other Groups:

Economic Analysis, Office of

Address: 155 Cottage St. NE, U20, Salem 97301-3966
Phone: 503-378-3405
Fax: 503-373-7643
Email: OEA.info@oregon.gov
Web: www.oregon.gov/DAS/OEA/Pages/index.aspx

Contact: Mark McMullen, State Economist
Duties and Responsibilities: The Office of Economic Analysis prepares state economic and revenue forecasts and the long-term population and employment forecasts. The office assesses long-term economic and demographic trends, evaluates their implications and conducts special economic and demographic studies. The office also prepares state criminal and juvenile population forecasts and manages the Highway Cost Allocation Study.

Governor's Council of Economic Advisors

Address: 155 Cottage St. NE, U20, Salem 97301-3966
Phone: 503-378-3405
Fax: 503-373-7643
Contact: Joseph Cortright, Chair
Duties and Responsibilities: The Governor's Council of Economic Advisors is a group of 12 economists from academia, finance, utilities and industry. This group works in conjunction with the Office of Economic Analysis.

Public Lands Advisory Committee

Address: 155 Cottage St. NE, U10, Salem 97301-3965
Phone: 503-378-3106
Fax: 503-373-7643
Email: CFO.info@oregon.gov
Web: www.oregon.gov/das/Financial/CapFin/Pages/plac.aspx
Contact: Tom Byler, Chair
Statutory Authority: ORS 270.120, 270.100(1)(d)
Duties and Responsibilities: The Public Lands Advisory Committee's primary role is to advise DAS on all real property acquisitions, exchanges or terminal dispositions valued at $100,000 or more, for which the department must give its consent.

Public Officials Compensation Commission

Address: 155 Cottage St. NE, U30, Salem 97301-3967
Phone: 503-378-2065
Fax: 503-373-7684
Email: Oregon.pocc@state.or.us
Web: https://www.oregon.gov/das/HR/Pages/pocc.aspx
Statutory Authority: ORS 292.907
Duties and Responsibilities: The Public Officials Compensation Commission's primary role is to review and make recommendations to the Legislature on the amount of annual salary to be paid for the following elected officials: governor, secretary of state, treasurer, attorney general, commissioner of the Bureau of Labor and Industries, members of the Legislature, chief justice and judges of the Supreme Court, and judges of the Court of Appeals, Circuit Courts and Tax Courts.

ADVOCACY COMMISSIONS OFFICE, OREGON

Address: 421 SW Oak St., Suite 770, Portland 97204; Mail: 1819 SW 5th Ave., #313, Portland 97201
Phone: 503-302-9725
Fax: 503-473-8519
Email: OACO.mail@oregon.gov
Web: www.oregon.gov/OAC/Pages/index.aspx
Contact: Lucy Baker, Administrator
Statutory Authority: ORS 185.005–185.025
Duties and Responsibilities: The Oregon Advocacy Commissions Office (OACO) was created in 2005 to support Oregon's Commission on Asian and Pacific Islander Affairs, Commission on Black Affairs, Commission on Hispanic Affairs and the Commission for Women.

In that role, OACO supports each commission's work advising the governor, Legislature and departmental leadership on policies affecting communities of color and women; growing leadership from their communities within government; and building success for Asian, Pacific Islander, Black and Hispanic Oregonians, and for women in Oregon.

Asian and Pacific Islander Affairs, Commission on

Address: 421 SW Oak St., Suite 770, Portland 97204; Mail: 1819 SW 5th Ave., #313, Portland 97201
Phone: 503-302-9725
Fax: 503-473-8519
Email: OACO.mail@oregon.gov
Web: www.oregon.gov/OCAPIA/Pages/index.aspx
Contact: Mari Watanabe, Chair
Statutory Authority: ORS 185.610–185.625
Duties and Responsibilities: The Oregon Commission on Asian and Pacific Islander Affairs (OCAPIA) was established in 1995 and originally had a trade and economic development focus. The 1999 Legislature amended the commission's functions to place a greater emphasis on advocacy, policy research and leadership development.

The goal of OCAPIA is to facilitate communication and dissemination of information between state government and Asian and Pacific Islander communities. This not only benefits Oregon's Asian and Pacific Islander Americans, but also provides the state with information on how to best provide services to all its citizens. Volunteers who are already leaders in their communities aid the commission with their knowledge and relationships.

The commission is composed of 11 members, nine of whom are appointed by the governor and confirmed by the Senate to serve three-year terms. The president of the Senate and the speaker of the House each appoint a member to serve a two-year term. The commission strives for ethnic as well as geographic diversity in its appointments.

Black Affairs, Commission on

Address: 421 SW Oak St., Suite 770, Portland 97204; Mail: 1819 SW 5th Ave., #313, Portland 97201
Phone: 503-302-9725
Fax: 503-473-8519
Web: www.oregon.gov/OCBA/Pages/index.aspx
Email: OACO.mail@oregon.gov
Contact: James Morris, Chair
Statutory Authority: ORS 185.410–185.430
Duties and Responsibilities: The Commission on Black Affairs works for the implementation of economic, social, legal and political equality for Oregon's African American and Black populations.

The commission is authorized by law to monitor existing programs and legislation designed to meet the needs of the African American and Black community; identify and research concerns and issues affecting the community in order to recommend actions and programs to the governor and the Legislature; act as a liaison between the community and Oregon's government; encourage African American and Black representation on state boards and commissions; and establish special committees as needed.

The commission is composed of 11 members, nine of whom are appointed by the governor and confirmed by the Senate to serve three-year terms. The president of the Senate and the speaker of the House each appoint a member to serve a two-year term. The commission strives for ethnic as well as geographic diversity in its appointments.

Hispanic Affairs, Commission on

Address: 421 SW Oak St., Suite 770, Portland 97204; Mail: 1819 SW 5th Ave., #313, Portland 97201
Phone: 503-302-9725
Fax: 503-473-8519
Email: OACO.mail@oregon.gov
Web: www.oregon.gov/Hispanic/Pages/index.aspx
Contact: Alberto Moreno, Chair
Statutory Authority: ORS 185.310–185.330
Duties and Responsibilities: The Oregon Commission on Hispanic Affairs (OCHA) was created by the 1983 Legislature to work for economic, social, legal and political equality for Hispanics in Oregon. The commission monitors existing programs and legislation to ensure that the needs of Hispanics are met. The commission researches problems and issues and recommends appropriate action, maintains a liaison between the Hispanic community and government entities and encourages Hispanic representation on state boards and commissions.

In addition, the commission focuses on and responds to the wider statewide context of equity and social well-being, identifies and seeks solutions to disparities in services and programs for the ethnically diverse Hispanic/Latino/Indigenous community, and encourages good public policy development. In networking with numerous Hispanic community, civic, cultural/ethnic and professional organizations, OCHA also promotes civic engagement, economic development and ongoing mentoring for the next generation of leaders.

The commission is composed of 11 members, nine of whom are appointed by the governor and confirmed by the Senate to serve three-year terms. The president of the Senate and the speaker of the House each appoint a member to serve a two-year term. The commission strives for ethnic as well as geographic diversity in its appointments.

Women, Commission for

Address: 421 SW Oak St., Suite 770, Portland 97204; Mail: 1819 SW 5th Ave., #313, Portland 97201
Phone: 503-302-9725
Fax: 503-473-8519
Email: OACO.mail@oregon.gov
Web: www.oregon.gov/Women/Pages/index.aspx
Contact: Dr. Barbara Spencer, Chair
Statutory Authority: ORS 185.510–185.560
Duties and Responsibilities: In 1964, Governor Mark Hatfield established the Governor's Commission on the Status of Women to advise him of the needs and concerns of Oregon women. In 1983, the commission gained independent status as the Oregon Commission for Women, with a directive to strive for women's equality through the implementation of beneficial programs and policies. The commission continues this work by advocating for women in the community, providing information on women's issues to the governor and Legislature, serving as a link for women to state agencies and providing services to individual women in Oregon.

The commission is composed of 11 members, nine of whom are appointed by the governor and confirmed by the Senate to serve three-year terms. The president of the Senate and the speaker of the House each appoint a member to serve a two-year term. The commission strives for ethnic as well as geographic diversity in its appointments. It also presents awards annually to honor Oregon's outstanding women.

AGRICULTURE, DEPARTMENT OF

Address: 635 Capitol St. NE, Salem 97301-2532
Phone: 503-986-4550
Fax: 503-986-4750
Email: info@oda.state.or.us
Web: www.oregon.gov/ODA/Pages/index.aspx
Contact: Alexis Taylor, Director
Statutory Authority: ORS Chapter 576
Duties and Responsibilities: The Oregon Department of Agriculture (ODA) has a three-fold mission: ensure food safety and provide consumer protection; protect the natural resource base for present and future generations of farmers and ranchers; and promote economic development and expand market opportunities for Oregon agricultural products. The three broad policy areas of the mission statement are interdependent. Without a strong and healthy natural resource base—particularly land and water—there is little or no agricultural production to promote and market. Without assurance that the food produced in Oregon is safe, there is little chance that many agricultural products will be of interest to potential customers.

The agency was formed in 1931 when the Oregon Legislature consolidated 13 separate boards, bureaus and commissions. ODA relies on close partnerships with other state and federal agencies, Oregon State University's College of Agricultural Sciences and numerous non-government organizations to help carry out the agency's mission. The 10-member State Board of Agriculture advises ODA on policy issues, develops recommendations on key agricultural issues and provides advocacy of the state's agriculture industry in general. New responsibilities for the agency include an industrial hemp program and the addition of a cannabis policy coordinator to incorporate the state's cannabis production into existing ODA programs and requirements.

ODA employs about 480 people and is headquartered in Salem, with its marketing and laboratory programs located in Portland at the Food Innovation Center. In addition, several inspectors and other staff members' responsibilities are spread geographically to provide services across the state.

Food and Animal Health Programs

Phone:
  Animal Health Program (State Veterinarian): 503-986-4680
  Food Safety Program: 503-986-4720
  Livestock Identification Program (Brands): 503-986-4681

Email: spage@oda.state.or.us
Contact: Stephanie Page, Director
Duties and Responsibilities: This program area provides inspections for all facets of Oregon's food distribution system (except restaurants) to ensure food is safe for consumption, to protect and maintain animal health and to ensure animal feeds meet nutritional and labeling standards.

Internal Services and Consumer Protection Programs

Phone:
  Laboratory Services: 503-872-6644
  Weights and Measures Program: 503-986-4670
Email: jbarber@oda.state.or.us
Contact: Jason Barber, Director
Duties and Responsibilities: These programs provide consumer protection and fair competition among businesses while facilitating interstate commerce and international trade by ensuring the accuracy and uniformity of Oregon's Commercial Weighing System and the quality of motor fuels sold in Oregon. The program area provides laboratory analysis and technical support to the Oregon Department of Agriculture's enforcement programs, and it also administers programs dealing with wolf depredation compensation and egg-laying hen cage space.

Market Access and Certification Programs

Agricultural Marketing and Development Program
  Address: 1207 NW Naito Pkwy., Suite 104, Portland 97209-2832
  Phone: 503-872-6600
Commodity Inspection Program
  Phone: 503-986-4620
Email: leng@oda.state.or.us
Contact: Lindsay Eng, Director
Duties and Responsibilities: These programs help Oregon's agricultural producers successfully add value, sell and ship products to local, national and international markets by promoting and creating demand for products through marketing activities, inspection and certification.

Natural Resources Programs

Phone:
  Natural Resources Programs: 503-986-4700
  Pesticides Program: 503-986-4635
Email: rjaindl@oda.state.or.us
Contact: Ray Jaindl, Director
Duties and Responsibilities: These programs address water quality, water quantity and natural resource conservation on agricultural lands. They

also address the proper use of pesticides, labeling and sale of fertilizer, as well as field burning in the Willamette Valley. Program goals are accomplished through outreach efforts, compliance, monitoring and coordination with other natural resource agencies.

Plant Protection and Conservation Programs

Phone: 503-986-4636
Email: hrogg@oda.state.or.us
Contact: Helmuth Rogg, Director
Duties and Responsibilities: These programs protect Oregon's agricultural industries and natural environment from harmful plant pests, diseases and noxious weeds; enhance the value and market-ability of exported nursery stock, Christmas trees, seeds and other agricultural products; and further the conservation of threatened and endangered plants.

State Board of Agriculture

Address: 635 Capitol St. NE, Salem 97301-2532
Phone: 503-986-4558
Fax: 503-986-4750
Contact: Kathryn Walker, Assistant to the Board
Statutory Authority: ORS Chapter 561
Duties and Responsibilities: The 10-member State Board of Agriculture advises ODA on policy issues, develops recommendations on key agricultural issues and provides advocacy of the state's agriculture industry in general.

Agricultural Commodity Commissions

Most commodity commissions conduct promotional, educational, production and market research projects. The commissions are authorized by ORS chapters 576, 577 and 578. They are funded by assessments on the producers of the commodities. The director of the Oregon Department of Agriculture appoints the members of all 23 commissions.

Albacore Commission

Address: PO Box 983, Lincoln City 97367-0983
Phone/Fax: 541-994-2647
Web: www.oregonalbacore.org
Contact: Nancy Fitzpatrick, Executive Director

Alfalfa Seed Commission

Address: PO Box 688, Ontario 97914-0688
Phone: 541-881-1335
Email: duanekressly@hotmail.com
Contact: Edith Kressly, Administrator

Beef Council

Address: 1827 NE 44th Ave., Suite 315, Portland 97213
Phone: 503-274-2333
Web: www.orbeef.org
Contact: Will Wise, Executive Director

Blueberry Commission

Address: PO Box 3366, Salem 97302-0366
Phone: 503-364-2944
Web: www.oregonblueberry.com
Contact: Bryan Ostlund, Administrator

Clover Commission

Address: PO Box 3366, Salem 97302-0366
Phone: 503-364-2944
Web: www.oregonclover.org
Contact: Bryan Ostlund, Administrator

Dairy Products Commission

Address: 10505 SW Barbur Blvd., Portland 97219-6853
Phone: 503-229-5033
Web: https://odncouncil.org
Contact: Pete Kent, Executive Director

Dungeness Crab Commission

Address: PO Box 1160, Coos Bay 97420-0301
Phone: 541-267-5810
Web: www.oregondungeness.org
Contact: Hugh Link, Executive Director

Fine Fescue Commission

Address: PO Box 3366, Salem 97302-0366
Phone: 503-364-2944
Web: www.oregonfinefescue.org
Contact: Bryan Ostlund, Administrator

Hazelnut Commission

Address: 21595-A Dolores Way NE, Aurora 97002-9738
Phone: 503-678-6823
Web: www.oregonhazelnuts.org
Contact: Meredith Nagely, Administrator

Hop Commission

Address: PO Box 298, Hubbard 97032
Phone: 503-982-7600
Web: www.oregonhops.org
Contact: Michelle Palacios, Administrator

Mint Commission

Address: PO Box 3366, Salem 97302-0366
Phone: 503-364-2944
Web: www.oregonmint.org
Contact: Bryan Ostlund, Administrator

Orchardgrass Seed Producers Commission

Address: 6745 SW Hampton St., #101, Portland 97223
Phone: 503-924-1181
Web: www.oregonorchardgrass.org
Contact: Misty Slagle, Administrator

Potato Commission

Address: 9320 SW Barbur Blvd., Suite 130, Portland 97219-5405
Phone: 503-239-4763
Web: www.oregonspuds.com
Contact: Bill Brewer, Executive Director

Processed Vegetable Commission

Address: 6745 SW Hampton St., #101, Portland 97223
Phone: 503-924-1181
Web: http://horticulture.oregonstate.edu/content/oregon-processed-vegetable-commission-0
Contact: Misty Slagle, Administrator

Raspberry and Blackberry Commission

Address: 4845 B SW Dresden Ave., Corvallis 97333-3915
Phone: 541-758-4043
Web: www.oregon-berries.com
Contact: Philip Gütt, Administrator

Ryegrass Growers Seed Commission

Address: PO Box 3366, Salem 97302-0366
Phone: 503-364-2944
Web: www.ryegrass.com
Contact: Bryan Ostlund, Administrator

Salmon Commission

Address: PO Box 983, Lincoln City 97367-0983
Phone/Fax: 541-994-2647
Web: http://oregonsalmon.org
Contact: Nancy Fitzpatrick, Executive Director

Sheep Commission

Address: 1270 Chemeketa St. NE, Salem 97301
Phone: 503-364-5462
Web: http://oregonsheepcommission.com
Contact: Richard Kosesan, Administrator

Strawberry Commission

Address: 4845 B SW Dresden Ave., Corvallis 97333-3915
Phone: 541-758-4043
Web: www.oregon-strawberries.org
Contact: Philip Gütt, Administrator

Sweet Cherry Commission

Address: 2667 Reed Rd., Hood River 97031-9609
Phone: 541-386-5761
Web: www.osweetcherry.org
Contact: Dana Branson, Administrator

Tall Fescue Commission

Address: PO Box 3366, Salem 97302-0366
Phone: 503-364-2944
Web: www.oregontallfescue.org
Contact: Bryan Ostlund, Administrator

Trawl Commission

Address: 16289 Hwy. 101 S, Suite C, Brookings 97415
Phone: 541-469-7830
Web: www.ortrawl.org
Contact: Brad Pettinger, Director

Wheat Commission

Address: 1200 NW Naito Pkwy., Suite 370, Portland 97209-2800
Phone: 503-467-2161
Web: www.owgl.org/about-us/oregon-wheat-commission
Contact: Blake Rowe, Executive Director

APPRAISER CERTIFICATION AND LICENSURE BOARD

Address: 3000 Market St. NE, Suite 541, Salem 97301
Phone: 503-485-2555
Fax: 503-485-2559
Email: Kalley.J.Morris@oregon.gov
Web: www.oregonaclb.org
Contact: Gae Lynne Cooper, Administrator
Statutory Authority: ORS Chapter 674
Duties and Responsibilities: The Appraiser Certification and Licensure Board (ACLB) was created in 1991 with the responsibility to protect the public and Oregon financial institutions through regulation and supervision of licensed and certified real estate appraisers and appraisal management companies in the state. In addition, the ACLB ensures that real estate appraisals are issued in writing and conducted in compliance with federal guidelines (Title XI of the Financial Institutions Reform, Recovery, and Enforcement Act of 1989), Oregon statutes and rules and the Uniform Standards of Professional Appraisal Practice. The ACLB is a semi-independent agency with six full time staff members who serve the public and eight board members appointed by the governor.

Architect Examiners, State Board of

Address: 205 Liberty St. NE, Suite A, Salem 97301
Phone: 503-763-0662
Fax: 503-364-0510
Email: architectboard@orbae.com
Web: www.orbae.com
Contact: Maria Brown, Administrator
Statutory Authority: ORS 671.010–671.220
Duties and Responsibilities: The State Board of Architect Examiners was created by the Legislature in 1919 to regulate the practice of architecture. The agency serves Oregonians by assuring that persons practicing architecture in Oregon are properly qualified and licensed. The agency determines the standards for architect and architectural firm licensure, which consist of a combination of education, examination and experience. The agency enforces the laws governing the practice of architecture in Oregon by investigating alleged violations and disciplining those who violate the law. The agency consists of seven board members and five staff and is headquartered in Salem.

Aviation, Oregon Department of

Address: 3040 25th St. SE, Salem 97302-1125
Phone: 503-378-4880
Fax: 503-373-1688
Email: aviation.mail@state.or.us
Web: www.oregon.gov/Aviation/Pages/index.aspx
Contact: Mitch Swecker, Director
Statutory Authority: ORS 835.100
Duties and Responsibilities: The mission of the Oregon Department of Aviation is to advocate for the safe operation of aviation in Oregon and the growth and economic development of airports and their communities. It is governed by a seven-member board of directors appointed by the governor and the staff size is 14 full-time eqivalent employees. The Aviation Board was formed in 1921, and it developed the system of airports in Oregon. It performed many of the functions that the Federal Aviation Administration (FAA) does today. The board provides policy oversight for the agency and is the modal committee for the *Connect*Oregon program.

The department manages 28 state airports with approximately 300 lease or access agreements with tenants. It also registers airports, pilots and aircraft and is responsible for a Statewide Capital Improvement Program in coordination with the FAA and federally funded public use airports around the state. The state operates a Pavement Management Program for runways and taxiways that preserves the life of airport pavement and reduces mainte-nance and repair costs at 66 airports around the state.

The department is funded by Other Funds revenue. In 2015, the Legislature increased taxes on jet fuel and aviation gas which enables a grant assistance program for public use airports and pro-vides funding for an FAA grant match, economic development, disaster resiliency and assistance for rural commercial air service.

Blind, Commission for the

Address: 535 SE 12th Ave., Portland 97214
Phone: 971-673-1588; Toll-free: 1-888-202-5463
Fax: 503-234-7468
Email: ocb.mail@state.or.us
Web: www.oregon.gov/blind
Contact: Dacia Johnson, Executive Director
Statutory Authority: ORS 346.110–346.570
Duties and Responsibilities: The mission of the Commission for the Blind (OCB) is to empower Oregonians who are blind to fully engage in life. The commission was established in 1937 and has evolved to be a consumer driven organization with a citizen governing body, appointed by the governor, that represents consumer organizations, education, ophthalmology/optometry, businesses and individual citizens who are blind. The agency operates under its enabling statutes and through the Workforce Innovation and Opportunity Act of 2014. The commission has 57 full-time equivalent staff who provide services throughout the state.

OCB's major program objectives include helping Oregonians who are blind get and keep jobs that allow them to support themselves and their families; training Oregonians in alternative skills related to blindness such as adaptive technology, white cane travel, Braille and activities of daily living; helping seniors and individuals with vision loss who are unable to work live with high levels of independence and self-sufficiency so they can remain in their homes and stay active in their com-munities; and licensing and supporting business owners who operate food service and vending oper-ations in public buildings and facilities throughout the state.

Business Development Department, Oregon (Business Oregon)

Address: 755 Summer St. NE, Suite 200, Salem 97301-1280
Phone: 503-986-0123; TTY: 1-800-735-2900
Fax: 503-581-5115
Web: www.oregon4biz.com
Contact: Chris Harder, Director
Statutory Authority: ORS 285A.070

Duties and Responsibilities: The Oregon Business Development Department, operating as Business Oregon, has offices in Salem and Portland with field offices around the state that house business development and finance officers as well as infrastructure regional coordinators. The agency works to create, retain, expand and attract businesses that provide sustainable, living-wage jobs for Oregonians through public-private partnerships, leveraged funding and support of economic opportunities for Oregon companies and entrepreneurs. The agency's programs, resources and assistance help Oregon's communities and businesses with expansion projects, export opportunities, access to capital, certifications and to build infrastructure capacity that addresses public health safety and compliance issues.

CHIROPRACTIC EXAMINERS, BOARD OF

Address: 3218 Pringle Rd. SE, Suite 150, Salem 97302-6311
Phone: 503-378-5816
Fax: 503-362-1260
Email: oregon.obce@oregon.gov
Web: www.oregon.gov/OBCE/Pages/index.aspx
Contact: Cassandra C. Skinner, J.D., Executive Director
Statutory Authority: ORS Chapter 684
Duties and Responsibilities: The Oregon Board of Chiropractic Examiners (OBCE) was created in 1915 and is responsible for administering the Chiropractic Practice Act, as well as establishing the rules and regulations governing chiropractic in Oregon. The seven-member board is comprised of five licensed chiropractors and two public members who are appointed by the governor for three-year terms.

The OBCE's mission is to serve the public, regulate the practice of chiropractic, and promote quality, competent and ethical health care. The board's programs include application, examination, continuing education, public information and investigation of complaints. If violations are found, the board issues disciplinary actions and/or rehabilitation plans to meet competency standards.

COLUMBIA RIVER GORGE COMMISSION

Address: PO Box 730, White Salmon, WA 98672
Phone: 509-493-3323
Fax: 509-493-2229
Email: info@gorgecommission.com
Web: www.gorgecommission.org
Contact: Nancy Andring, Administrative Assistant
Statutory Authority: ORS 196.150

Duties and Responsibilities: The Columbia River Gorge Commission was established by a compact between Oregon and Washington in 1987 in response to 1986 federal legislation establishing the 300,000-acre Columbia River Gorge National Scenic Area. The commission works in partnership with the U.S. Forest Service, six counties and four tribes to implement a regional management plan to protect and provide for the enhancement of the scenic, natural, cultural and recreational resources of the Columbia River Gorge and to protect and support the area's economy.

CONSTRUCTION CONTRACTORS BOARD

Address: 201 High St. SE, Suite 600, PO Box 14140, Salem 97309-5052
Phone: 503-378-4621
Fax: 503-373-2007
Email: ccbemails@ccb.state.or.us
Web: www.oregon.gov/CCB/Pages/index.aspx
Contact: James Denno, Administrator
Statutory Authority: ORS 701.205
Duties and Responsibilities: The Construction Contractors Board (CCB) protects Oregonians by preventing and resolving construction contracting problems. The agency licenses contractors, investigates complaints against licensees and penalizes unlawful contractors. The CCB educates the public about how to avoid problems on construction projects and helps mediate disputes between homeowners and licensed contractors.

Formed in 1971 as the Builders Board to license residential contractors, the agency was subsequently renamed and authority expanded to regulate commercial contractors as well. To become licensed, contractors must meet minimum education and experience requirements and pass a test. Licensed contractors are subject to continuing education requirements.

The CCB employs approximately 60 people. Enforcement officers and dispute mediators are deployed across the state. The board is made up of nine members appointed by the governor and confirmed by the Oregon Senate. Members represent different segments of the construction industry, the public and local government.

CONSUMER AND BUSINESS SERVICES, DEPARTMENT OF

Address: 350 Winter St. NE, Salem 97301-3878; PO Box 14480, Salem 97309-0405
Phone: 503-378-4100
Fax: 503-378-6444
Email: dcbs.info@oregon.gov
Web: www.oregon.gov/DCBS/Pages/index.aspx

Contact: Patrick Allen, Director
Statutory Authority: ORS Chapter 705
Duties and Responsibilities: The Department of Consumer and Business Services (DCBS) is Oregon's largest business regulatory and consumer protection agency. The department administers state laws and rules to protect consumers and workers in the areas of workers' compensation, occupational safety and health, financial services, insurance, and building codes. The department was formed in 1993 to serve as an integrated umbrella agency over most state functions affecting businesses in order to improve efficiency and effectiveness.

DCBS employs about 900 people and is headquartered in Salem. Several of its divisions have offices around the state. Oregon OSHA has field offices in Portland, Bend, Eugene, Salem, Medford and Pendleton. The Workers' Compensation Division has a Medford office that provides return-to-work services. The Building Codes Division has field offices in Coos Bay and Pendleton. The Workers' Compensation Board conducts hearings around the state with staffed offices in Eugene, Medford, Portland and Salem.

Building Codes Division

Address: 1535 Edgewater St. NW,
PO Box 14470, Salem 97309-0404
Phone: 503-378-4133
Fax: 503-378-2322
Web: www.oregon.gov/bcd/Pages/index.aspx
Contact: Mark Long, Administrator
Statutory Authority: ORS Chapters 446, 447, 455, 460, 479, 480, 693
Duties and Responsibilities: The Legislature, in 1973, established a statewide uniform building code and created the Building Codes Division to administer it. A statewide building code helps ensure a minimum level of safety in all areas of the state and a uniform regulatory environment for businesses, the general public and contractors. The division adopts building codes with the advice of seven statutory boards. The division certifies inspectors, licenses trade professionals and establishes training and education requirements; provides code and rule interpretation and dispute resolution; enforces license, code and permit requirements to prevent unsafe conditions; and conducts inspections where local entities do not. The division also streamlines building permit processes through ePermitting and other programs.

Building Codes Advisory Boards

Address: PO Box 14470, Salem 97309-0404
Phone: 503-373-7613
Web: www.oregon.gov/BCD/boards/Pages/index.aspx
Contact: Brett Salmon, Policy and Technical Services Section Manager

Boiler Rules, Board of

Statutory Authority: ORS 480.535, 705.250
Duties and Responsibilities: Started in 1961, the Board of Boiler Rules formulates and adopts rules for the safe construction, installation, inspection, operation, maintenance and repair of boilers and pressure vessels and reviews staff enforcement actions. The governor appoints the board's 11 members to four-year terms, subject to Senate confirmation.

Building Codes Structures Board

Statutory Authority: ORS 455.132, 455.144, 705.250
Duties and Responsibilities: Dating back to 1973, the Building Codes Structures Board helps the DCBS director administer the Structural Program, Prefabricated Structures Program, Accessibility to People with Physical Disabilities Program and certain energy programs. The governor appoints the board's nine members to four-year terms, subject to Senate confirmation.

Construction Industry Energy Board

Statutory Authority: ORS 455.492, 705.250
Duties and Responsibilities: The Construction Industry Energy Board, started in 2009, evaluates proposed state building code standards and proposed administrative rules relating to the energy use and energy efficiency aspects of the electrical, structural, prefabricated structure and low-rise residential specialties. The proposed standards evaluated by the board may include energy conserving technology, construction methods, products and materials. The board has 11 members.

Electrical and Elevator Board

Statutory Authority: ORS 455.138, 455.144, 479.680, 705.250
Duties and Responsibilities: The Electrical and Elevator Board, started in 1949, helps the DCBS director administer the electrical and elevator programs. The board also oversees the licensing and enforcement of these programs to ensure that the people involved are appropriately licensed and the work meets minimum safety standards. The governor appoints the board's 15 members to four-year terms, subject to Senate confirmation.

Mechanical Board

Statutory Authority: ORS 455.140, 705.250
Duties and Responsibilities: The Mechanical Board, formed in 2004, helps the DCBS director administer the code and associated administrative rules adopted for mechanical devices and equipment. The governor appoints the 10-member board, subject to Senate confirmation.

Plumbing Board, State

Statutory Authority: ORS 693.115, 705.250
Duties and Responsibilities: Created in 1935 under the State Board of Health, the State Plumbing Board licenses individuals to engage in the business, trade or calling of a journeyman plumber. The board establishes license, business and supervising plumber registrations, examinations and continuing education fees. The governor appoints the board's seven members, subject to Senate confirmation.

Residential and Manufactured Structures Board

Statutory Authority: ORS 455.135, 705.250
Duties and Responsibilities: The Residential and Manufactured Structures Board, created in 2004, helps the DCBS director administer the low-rise residential dwelling program. The governor appoints the board's 11 members, subject to Senate confirmation.

Financial Regulation, Division of

Address: 350 Winter St. NE, Salem 97301-3881; PO Box 14480, Salem 97309-0405
Phone: 503-378-4140
Fax: 503-378-7862
Email: dcbs.dfcsmail@oregon.gov
Web: http://dfr.oregon.gov/Pages/index.aspx
Contact: Laura Cali, Administrator
Statutory Authority: ORS Chapters 59, 86A, 97, 446, 465, 646A, 697, 705–717, 723, 725, 725A, 726, 731–735, 737, 742, 743, 743A, 744, 746, 748, 750, 752
Duties and Responsibilities: Insurance regulation in Oregon began in 1887, when the secretary of state was given ex officio powers as insurance commissioner. The Department of Insurance, which later became the Insurance Division, was created in 1909. Regulation of financial institutions dates to 1907, when banks became subject to the State Banking Board. Securities-related regulation began a few years later in 1913, when the Corporation Department was created to license security brokers and regulate savings and loan associations.

On January 1, 2016, the Division of Finance and Corporate Securities and the Insurance Division were merged into one division: the Division of Financial Regulation.

The division regulates banks and credit unions, check cashing, debt management services, financial and investment advisors, insurance industry, mortgage industry, money transmitters, pawnshops, payday and title lenders and securities. The division investigates consumer complaints, analyzes and monitors financial and insurance institution finances, reviews all insurance policies before they are sold in Oregon, licenses companies and professionals and registers securities and other investments.

Health Insurance Marketplace, Oregon

Address: 350 Winter St. NE, Salem 97301-3883; PO Box 14480, Salem 97309-0405
Phone: Toll-free: 855-268-3767
Email: info.marketplace@oregon.gov
Web: http://healthcare.oregon.gov
Contact: Berri Leslie, Administrator
Statutory Authority: ORS Chapter 741
Duties and Responsibilities: The Oregon Health Insurance Marketplace replaced Cover Oregon on July 1, 2015. DCBS administers the marketplace, which seeks to improve the lives of Oregonians by providing individuals and small businesses with access to affordable, high-quality health insurance. The marketplace oversees health insurance products sold to Oregonians through HealthCare.gov and provides local support, education and assistance to help Oregonians find the plan that best meets their health and financial needs.

Occupational Safety and Health Division, Oregon

Address: 350 Winter St. NE, Salem 97301-3882; PO Box 14480, Salem 97309-0405
Phone: 503-378-3272 (Voice/TTY); Toll-free in Oregon only: 1-800-922-2689 (Voice/TTY)
Fax: 503-947-7461
Email: admin.web@oregon.gov
Web: www.osha.oregon.gov
Contact: Michael Wood, Administrator
Statutory Authority: ORS Chapter 654
Duties and Responsibilities: The Oregon Occupational Safety and Health Division (Oregon OSHA) was created in 1973 to administer the Oregon Safe Employment Act. Oregon OSHA is responsible for working with employers and employees to reduce and prevent occupational injuries, illnesses and fatalities and for enforcing Oregon occupational safety and health standards. The division inspects workplaces for occupational safety and health hazards, investigates complaints about safety and health issues on the job and investigates fatal accidents to determine if the Oregon Safe Employment Act has been violated. The division also provides technical, educational and consultative services to help employers and employees implement and improve injury and illness prevention plans.

Workers' Compensation Division

Address: 350 Winter St. NE, Salem 97301-3879; PO Box 14480, Salem 97309-0405
Phone: 503-947-7810
Fax: 503-947-7581
Email: workcomp.questions@oregon.gov
Web: http://wcd.oregon.gov
Contact: Lou Savage, Administrator
Statutory Authority: ORS Chapters 654, 656, 659A
Duties and Responsibilities: Oregon's workers' compensation system was created in 1913, with major reforms enacted in 1990 and 1995. The Workers' Compensation Division administers and regulates statutes and rules to ensure that employers provide coverage for their workers, provide treatment and benefits to help injured workers return to work as quickly as possible, and resolve disputes as quickly, fairly and with as little litigation as possible. The division facilitates injured workers' early return-to-work through incentive programs funded through the Workers' Benefit Fund; helps resolve medical, vocational, disability and other disputes; and provides consultation, training and technical services to people and businesses within the system.

Injured Workers, Ombudsman for

Address: 350 Winter St. NE, Salem 97301-3878; PO Box 14480, Salem 97309-0405
Phone: 503-378-3351; Toll-free: 1-800-927-1271
Fax: 503-373-7639
Email: oiw.questions@oregon.gov
Web: www.oregon.gov/DCBS/OIW/Pages/index.aspx
Contact: Jennifer Flood, Ombudsman
Statutory Authority: ORS 656.709
Duties and Responsibilities: The Legislature created the office of the Ombudsman for Injured Workers in 1987 to serve as an independent advocate for injured workers. The office was expanded as part of the major reforms to the workers' compensation system in 1990. The office investigates and attempts to resolve workers' compensation related complaints. Also, the office provides information to injured workers to enable them to protect their rights and makes recommendations for improving ombudsman services and the workers' compensation system.

Small Business Ombudsman for Workers' Compensation

Address: 350 Winter St. NE, Salem 97301-3878; PO Box 14480, Salem 97309-0405
Phone: 503-378-4209
Fax: 503-373-7639
Email: david.waki@oregon.gov
Web: www.oregon.gov/DCBS/SBO/Pages/sbo.aspx
Contact: David Waki, Ombudsman
Statutory Authority: ORS 656.709
Duties and Responsibilities: The Small Business Ombudsman for Workers' Compensation was created as part of the 1990 workers' compensation reforms to educate and advocate for small businesses. The ombudsman serves as a workers' compensation resource center, assisting small businesses in the areas of insurance and claims processing. This includes the intervention, investigation and resolution of any workers' compensation related issue. Also, the office provides education and information to employers, trade groups, agents and insurers on relevant workers' compensation issues.

Workers' Compensation Management-Labor Advisory Committee

Address: 350 Winter St. NE, Salem 97301-3878; PO Box 14480, Salem 97309-0405
Phone: 503-947-7866
Fax: 503-378-6444
Email: mlac@oregon.gov
Web: www.oregon.gov/DCBS/mlac/Pages/mlac.aspx
Contact: Theresa Van Winkle, Administrator
Statutory Authority: ORS 656.790
Duties and Responsibilities: The Legislature created the Workers' Compensation Management-Labor Advisory Committee (MLAC) as part of the reform of the workers' compensation system in 1990. Workers' compensation issues are often adversarial, creating uncertainty for both workers and employers. MLAC provides an effective forum for business and labor to meet, explore and resolve issues involving the workers' compensation system. MLAC is charged with reviewing and making recommendations on workers' compensation issues to the DCBS director and the Legislature. Members of the committee are appointed by the governor and subject to Senate confirmation. The committee consists of five management and five labor representatives and the DCBS director, who serves as an ex officio member.

Other Groups:

Senior Health Insurance Benefits Assistance

Address: 350 Winter St. NE, Salem 97301; PO Box 14480, Salem 97309-0405
Phone: 503-947-7979; Toll-free: 1-800-722-4134; TTY: 1-800-735-2900

Fax: 503-947-7092
Email: shiba.oregon@oregon.gov
Web: www.oregon.gov/dcbs/insurance/shiba/
Pages/shiba.aspx
Contact: Lisa Emerson
Duties and Responsibilities: Oregon has been providing information to Medicare beneficiaries and their families since the late 1980s. The Senior Health Insurance Benefits Assistance (SHIBA) program officially began in 1992 under a grant from the federal government. Since March 1, 2016, SHIBA has been part of the Oregon Health Insurance Marketplace. SHIBA uses trained staff and volunteers to help people with Medicare benefits make health insurance decisions. Volunteers are available in most counties throughout Oregon to help beneficiaries and their family members understand Medicare benefits, choose a supplemental insurance policy and enroll in a prescription drug benefits. SHIBA counseling services are free of charge.

Workers' Compensation Board

Address: 2601 25th St. SE, Suite 150, Salem 97302-1280
Phone: 503-378-3308
Fax: 503-373-1684
Web: www.oregon.gov/wcb/pages/index.aspx
Contact: Holly Somers, Chair
Statutory Authority: ORS Chapter 656
Duties and Responsibilities: Oregon's workers' compensation system was created in 1913, and the duties of the board were established to resolve workers' compensation disputes. The Workers' Compensation Board became its own agency in 1965 and provides timely and impartial resolution of disputes arising under the Workers' Compensation Law and the Oregon Safe Employment Act. The board is a five-member body appointed by the governor for four-year terms, subject to Senate confirmation. The board conducts contested case hearings and provides mediation for workers' compensation matters, as well as for Oregon OSHA citations and orders. The board is the appellate body that reviews administrative law judge workers' compensation orders on appeal, exercises own motion jurisdiction, and reviews Claim Disposition Agreements (Compromise and Release of workers' benefits). Also, the board hears appeals from Oregon Department of Justice decisions regarding applications for compensation under the Crime Victim Assistance Program and resolves disputes between workers and workers' compensation carriers arising from workers' civil actions against third parties.

CORRECTIONS, DEPARTMENT OF

Address: 2575 Center St. NE, Salem 97301-4667
Phone: 503-945-0927
Fax: 503-373-1173
Web: www.oregon.gov/doc/Pages/index.aspx
Contact: Colette S. Peters, Director
Statutory Authority: ORS Chapter 423
Duties and Responsibilities: The Department of Corrections was created by the Legislature in June 1987 and works to promote public safety by holding offenders accountable for their actions and reducing the risk of future criminal behavior. The department has custody of adults sentenced to prison for more than 12 months, housing approximately 14,500 adults in 14 state prisons throughout the state. It also oversees community parole and post-prison supervision of 32,000 individuals in Linn and Douglas Counties. The department is recognized nationally among correctional agencies for providing adults in custody with the cognitive, education and job skills needed to become productive citizens when they transition back to their communities. Due to these efforts, Oregon's recidivism rate is about 28 percent.

Administrative Services Division

Address: 3691 State St., Salem 97301
Phone: 503-428-5500
Fax: 503-363-4170
Contact: Daryl Borello, Assistant Director
Duties and Responsibilities: The Administrative Services Division supports the daily business of the Department of Corrections. General Services covers Facilities Services; Central Distribution, including canteen food purchasing, radio and warehouse operations; and Information Services. The Human Resources Division manages the personnel-related services of recruitment, affirmative action, employee development and training, employee safety and risk management and organization and leadership development. It also provides assistance in administering the department's classification, compensation, human resources policies and labor contracts.

Chief Financial Officer, Office of the

Address: 2575 Center St. NE, Salem 97301-4667
Phone: 503-945-9007
Fax: 503-945-7150
Contact: Steve Robbins, Chief Financial Officer
Duties and Responsibilities: The Office of the Chief Financial Officer is responsible for determining the resources necessary to support the existing and growing offender populations. The office develops and executes the department's Long-Range Construction Plan to ensure appropriate institutions are in place to house offenders entering

the system. Fiscal Services include contracts, purchasing, accounting and Central Trust.

Communications, Office of

Address: 2575 Center St. NE, Salem 97301-4667
Phone: 503-945-9999
Fax: 503-373-1173
Web: www.oregon.gov/DOC/OC/Pages/index.aspx
Contact: Elizabeth Craig, Administrator
Duties and Responsibilities: The Office of Communications is responsible for furthering the department's mission and goals through close collaboration with external and internal stakeholders, both inside and beyond the realm of public safety. Serving as a trusted source of accurate information, this office ensures the department is a transparent governmental organization that members of the public can access at any time. The office includes internal and external communications, media relations, legislative and government relations, public record/information coordination and rules coordination.

Community Corrections

Address: 3691 State St., Salem 97301
Phone: 503-428-5500
Fax: 503-363-4170
Web: www.oregon.gov/DOC/CC/pages/index.aspx
Contact: Jeramiah Stromberg, Assistant Director
Duties and Responsibilities: Community Corrections works in partnership with local, county-operated community corrections agencies. The Department of Corrections operates Community Corrections in Linn and Douglas Counties. Activities include supervision, community-based sanctions, and services directed at offenders who have committed felony crimes and have been placed under supervision by the courts (probation), the Board of Parole and Post-Prison Supervision or the local supervisory authority (parole/post-prison supervision).

Inspector General, Office of the

Address: 2575 Center St. NE, Salem 97301-4667
Phone: 503-945-9043
Fax: 503-373-7092
Web: www.oregon.gov/DOC/INSPEC/Pages/index.aspx
Contact: Craig Prins, Inspector General
Duties and Responsibilities: The Office of the Inspector General provides an oversight function on behalf of the director and deputy director of the Department of Corrections. The office was created in 1990 as recommended by an investigative report to the governor. The inspector general has broad responsibility for oversight of suspected, alleged or actual misconduct within the department, reporting to the director or deputy and to other officials as required by law and the department Code of Conduct.

Offender Management and Rehabilitation Division

Address: 2575 Center St. NE, Salem 97301-4667
Phone: 503-945-9055
Fax: 503-373-1173
Web: www.oregon.gov/DOC/OMR/Pages/index.aspx
Contact: Heidi Steward, Assistant Director
Duties and Responsibilities: The Offender Management and Rehabilitation Division is responsible for carrying out the Department of Corrections' mission to reduce the risk of future criminal conduct by offenders incarcerated in prison. This division includes the operation of intake; correctional case management; population management; inmate work programs; inmate services, including visiting, inmate mail and legal libraries; religious services; sentence computation; offender records; victim services; and institution programs such as workforce development, education, cognitive programs and addictions treatment programs.

Operations Division

Address: 2575 Center St. NE, Salem 97301-0470
Phone: 503-945-0950
Fax: 503-373-1173
Web: www.oregon.gov/DOC/OPS/Pages/index.aspx
Contact: Mike Gower, Assistant Director
Duties and Responsibilities: Oregon's adult prisons are centrally administered by the assistant director of operations to ensure that Oregon's 14 prisons are safe, civil and productive so that inmates can pursue the goals specified in their corrections plans. Experienced staff help shape positive behavior. To hold inmates accountable for their actions, the Operations Division's responsibilities encompass prison management, health services, mental health services, inmate transportation, security threat group (gang) management, emergency preparedness and most inmate work crew activities.

Oregon Corrections Enterprises

Address: 3691 State St., Salem 97301
Phone: 503-428-5500
Fax: 503-363-4170
Web: www.oce.oregon.gov
Contact: Ken Jeske, Administrator
Duties and Responsibilities: Oregon Corrections Enterprises (OCE) is semi-independent from the Department of Corrections. By working with the department, state agencies, non-profit agencies and the public, OCE builds partnerships that sustain work opportunities for adults in custody. OCE

explores new business opportunities and partnerships while working to reduce recidivism and save money for Oregon's taxpayers.

State Prisons:

Coffee Creek Correctional Facility

Address: 24499 SW Grahams Ferry Rd., Wilsonville 97070
Phone: 503-570-6400
Fax: 503-570-6417
Web: www.oregon.gov/DOC/OPS/PRISON/pages/cccf.aspx
Contact: Rob Persson, Superintendent
Operational Since: 2001
Capacity: 1,685
Number of Staff: 412
Minimum-security and medium-security facility accommodating all of Oregon's female inmates and providing intake services to all male inmates

Columbia River Correctional Institution

Address: 9111 NE Sunderland Ave., Portland 97211-1799
Phone: 503-280-6646, ext. 241
Fax: 503-280-6012
Web: www.oregon.gov/DOC/OPS/PRISON/pages/crci.aspx
Contact: Rick Angelozzi, Superintendent
Operational Since: 1990
Capacity: 553
Number of Staff: 131
Minimum-security prison

Deer Ridge Correctional Institution

Address: 3920 East Ashwood Rd., Madras 97741
Phone: 541-325-5999
Web: www.oregon.gov/DOC/OPS/PRISON/pages/drci.aspx
Contact: Tim Causey, Superintendent
Operational Since: 2007
Capacity: Minimum-security, 774; Medium-security, 1,228
Number of Staff: 176

Eastern Oregon Correctional Institution

Address: 2500 Westgate, Pendleton 97801-9699
Phone: 541-276-0700
Fax: 541-276-1841
Web: www.oregon.gov/DOC/OPS/PRISON/pages/eoci.aspx
Contact: Jeri Taylor, Superintendent
Operational Since: 1985
Capacity: 1,659
Number of Staff: 438
Medium-security prison

Mill Creek Correctional Facility

Address: 5465 Turner Rd. SE, Salem 97317
Phone: 503-378-2600
Fax: 503-373-7424
Web: www.oregon.gov/DOC/OPS/PRISON/pages/mccf.aspx
Contact: Jeff Premo, Superintendent
Operational Since: 1992
Capacity: 240
Number of Staff: 49
Minimum-security work camp

Oregon State Correctional Institution

Address: 3405 Deer Park Dr. SE, Salem 97310-9385
Phone: 503-373-0125
Fax: 503-378-8919
Web: www.oregon.gov/DOC/OPS/PRISON/pages/osci.aspx
Contact: Christine Popoff, Superintendent
Operational Since: 1959
Capacity: 890
Number of Staff: 253
Medium-security facility

Oregon State Penitentiary

Address: 2605 State St., Salem 97310-0505
Phone: 503-378-2453
Fax: 503-378-3897
Web: www.oregon.gov/DOC/OPS/PRISON/pages/osp.aspx
Contact: Jeff Premo, Superintendent
Operational Since: 1866
Capacity: 2,194
Number of Staff: 590
Maximum-security penitentiary, including death row inmates, and minimum-security facility

Powder River Correctional Facility

Address: 3600 13th St., Baker City 97814-1346
Phone: 541-523-6680
Fax: 541-523-6678
Web: www.oregon.gov/DOC/OPS/PRISON/pages/prcf.aspx
Contact: Brad Cain, Superintendent
Operational Since: 1989
Capacity: 286
Number of Staff: 92
Minimum-security prison. Alcohol and drug treatment facility for inmates preparing to transition from prison back into their communities.

Santiam Correctional Institution

Address: 4005 Aumsville Hwy. SE, Salem 97317
Phone: 503-378-2144
Fax: 503-378-8235
Web: www.oregon.gov/DOC/OPS/PRISON/pages/sci.aspx
Contact: Brandon Kelly, Superintendent

Operational Since: 1992
Capacity: 440
Number of Staff: 113
Minimum-security prison

Shutter Creek Correctional Institution

Address: 95200 Shutters Landing Ln., North Bend 97459-0303
Phone: 541-756-6666
Fax: 541-756-6888
Web: www.oregon.gov/DOC/OPS/PRISON/pages/scci.aspx
Contact: Kimberly Hendricks, Superintendent
Operational Since: 1990
Capacity: 302
Number of Staff: 88
Minimum-security prison

Snake River Correctional Institution

Address: 777 Stanton Blvd., Ontario 97914-8335
Phone: 541-881-5000
Fax: 541-881-5009
Web: www.oregon.gov/DOC/OPS/PRISON/pages/srci.aspx
Contact: Mark Nooth, Superintendent
Operational Since: 1991
Capacity: 3,062
Number of Staff: 893
Multi-security prison, Oregon's largest correctional institution

South Fork Forest Camp

Address: 48300 Wilson River Hwy., Tillamook 97141-9799
Phone: 503-842-2811
Fax: 503-842-7943
Web: www.oregon.gov/DOC/OPS/PRISON/pages/sffc.aspx
Contact: Rick Angelozzi, Superintendent
Operational Since: 1951
Capacity: 204
Number of Staff: 56
Minimum-security work camp

Two Rivers Correctional Institution

Address: 82911 Beach Access Rd., Umatilla 97882
Phone: 541-922-2001
Fax: 541-922-2046
Web: www.oregon.gov/DOC/OPS/PRISON/pages/trci.aspx
Contact: John Myrick, Superintendent
Operational Since: 2000
Capacity: 1,878
Number of Staff: 482
Medium and minimum-security facility

Warner Creek Correctional Facility

Address: 20654 Rabbit Hill Rd., Lakeview 97630-5000
Phone: 541-947-8200
Fax: 541-947-8231
Web: www.oregon.gov/DOC/OPS/PRISON/pages/wccf.aspx
Contact: Steve Brown, Superintendent
Operational Since: 2005
Capacity: 406
Number of Staff: 102
Minimum-security facility

COUNSELORS AND THERAPISTS, OREGON BOARD OF LICENSED PROFESSIONAL

Address: 3218 Pringle Rd. SE, Suite 250, Salem 97302-6312
Phone: 503-378-5499
Email: lpct.board@state.or.us
Web: www.oregon.gov/OBLPCT/Pages/index.aspx
Contact: Charles Hill, Executive Director
Statutory Authority: ORS 675.705–675.835
Duties and Responsibilities: The Board of Licensed Professional Counselors and Therapists was created in 1989 to protect Oregon consumers seeking mental health counseling and marriage and family therapy services. The board determines if individuals meet the initial and continuing education, training and examination standards for licensure and issues new and renewal licenses to those who are qualified. The board develops policies and standards for professional practice and enforces disciplinary action against counselors, therapists and interns who engage in misconduct or are incompetent. It also issues civil penalties to individuals practicing in Oregon without a license or engaging in misrepresentation. The eight members of the board are appointed by the governor and confirmed by the Senate for three-year terms.

CRIMINAL JUSTICE COMMISSION, OREGON

Address: 885 Summer St. NE, Salem 97301
Phone: 503-378-4830
Fax: 503-378-4861
Email: julie.vaughn@oregon.gov
Web: www.oregon.gov/CJC/Pages/index.aspx
Contact: Michael Schmidt, Executive Director
Statutory Authority: ORS 137.651–137.680
Duties and Responsibilities: The Oregon Criminal Justice Commission, created in 1995, serves as the policy development forum for state

and local criminal justice systems. Eleven staff persons provide data analysis, planning and grant administration expertise to public safety officials. They work collaboratively with stakeholders to improve Oregon's criminal justice systems. Nine commissioners direct the staff's work. The agency directly impacts criminal justice systems by administering statewide grant programs for specialty courts and justice reinvestment programs. The agency administers Oregon's sentencing guidelines, serves as the State Administering Agency for the Byrne Justice Assistant Grant program and houses the Statistical Analysis Center.

DENTISTRY, OREGON BOARD OF

Address: 1500 SW 1st Ave., Suite 770, Portland 97201
Phone: 971-673-3200
Fax: 971-673-3202
Email: information@oregondentistry.org
Web: www.oregon.gov/dentistry/Pages/index.aspx
Contact: Stephen Prisby, Executive Director
Statutory Authority: ORS Chapter 679, ORS 680.010–680.205, 680.990
Duties and Responsibilities: The Board of Dentistry is the second oldest licensing board in Oregon, created by an act of the Legislature on February 23, 1887. The mission of the board is to protect the public by assuring that the citizens of Oregon receive the highest quality oral health care possible.

The goals of the board are to protect the public from unsafe, incompetent or fraudulent practitioners and to encourage licensees to practice safely and competently in the best interests of their patients. The board does this by testing the competency of applicants through written and clinical examinations; requiring continuing education of all licensees; investigating complaints and enforcing the provisions of the Dental Practice Act and rules of the board; communicating board policies and other pertinent information to all licensees on a regular basis; acting as a resource to consumers in determining the adequacy of their dental treatment; and working with other health care boards and associations to develop partnerships for forging a viable health care delivery system.

The activities of the board are funded from license application, renewal, examination and permit fees paid by dentists and dental hygienists. No state General Funds (tax revenues) are allocated for its operations.

EDUCATION, DEPARTMENT OF

Address: 255 Capitol St. NE, Salem 97310-0203
Phone: 503-947-5600
Fax: 503-378-5156
Email: ode.frontdesk@ode.state.or.us
Web: www.ode.state.or.us
Contact: Dr. Salam Noor, Deputy Superintendent of Public Instruction
Statutory Authority: ORS 326.111
Duties and Responsibilities: The Oregon Department of Education (ODE) oversees the education of over 560,000 students in Oregon's public kindergarten through grade 12 education system. Oregon has over 1,200 public K–12 schools organized into 197 school districts and 19 education service districts. Over 100 of these schools are public charter schools. These schools and districts employ over 63,000 teachers, administrators and other school and district staff. ODE encompasses early learning, public preschool programs, the state School for the Deaf, regional programs for children with disabilities and education programs in Oregon youth corrections facilities.

While ODE is not in the classroom directly providing services, the agency (along with the State Board of Education) focuses on helping districts achieve both local and statewide goals and priorities through strategies such as developing policies and standards, providing accurate and timely data to inform instruction, training teachers on how to use data effectively, administering numerous state and federal grants, and sharing and helping districts implement best practices

State Board of Education

Address: 255 Capitol St. NE, Salem 97310-0203
Phone: 503-947-5991
Fax: 503-378-5991
Email: jessica.nguyen-ventura@ode.state.or.us
Web: www.ode.state.or.us/search/results/?id=144
Contact: Jessica Nguyen-Ventura, State Board Coordinator
Statutory Authority: ORS 326.011–326.075
Duties and Responsibilities: The State Board of Education works to ensure that every Oregon public school student has equal access to high quality educational services that promote lifelong learning and that prepare students for their next steps following high school graduation, including college, work and citizenship.

The Legislature created the board in 1951 to oversee the state's schools. The board sets educational policies and standards for Oregon's 197 public school districts and 19 educational service districts. All of these agencies have separate governing bodies responsible for transacting business within their jurisdictions. The state board is the body responsible for administrative rules that the Department of Education implements.

The board is comprised of seven members appointed by the governor and confirmed by the Senate. Five members represent Oregon's five congressional districts, and two members represent the state at large. Members serve four-year terms and are limited to two consecutive terms. Board members elect their chair each year. The state board meets at least six times per year, and the public is welcome to attend board meetings.

Fair Dismissal Appeals Board

Address: 255 Capitol St. NE, Salem 97310-0203
Phone: 503-947-5651
Fax: 503-378-5156
Web: www.ode.state.or.us/search/page/?id=3676
Contact: Cindy Hunt, Government and Legal Affairs Manager
Statutory Authority: ORS 342.930
Duties and Responsibilities: The Fair Dismissal Appeals Board (FDAB) consists of 24 members appointed by the governor from specific categories: six public school administrators, six contract teachers, six school board members and six who must have no occupational affiliation with a school district. Each category must be further distributed by size of school district.

FDAB was created to hear appeals of teacher and administrator dismissals by school districts. FDAB is staffed by the superintendent of public instruction through the FDAB executive secretary. Once an appeal is filed with FDAB, a three-member panel is selected by the board's executive secretary to hear the appeal and render a decision.

Quality Education Commission

Address: 255 Capitol St. NE, Salem 97310-0203
Phone: 503-947-5670
Fax: 503-378-5156
Web: www.ode.state.or.us/search/results/?id=166
Contact: Brian Reeder, Assistant Superintendent
Statutory Authority: ORS 327.497–327.506
Duties and Responsibilities: The Quality Education Commission was created by statute in 2001. The commission's charge is to identify educational best practices and to estimate the level of funding required to ensure that the state system of kindergarten through grade 12 public education meets the goals established in statute. To fulfill that charge, the commission researches educational best practices and estimates the costs of implementing them. The model used to estimate educational costs, known as the Quality Education Model, is maintained by the commission with assistance from the Department of Education. The model has been enhanced and improved since it was first developed in 1999 and represents the most comprehensive tool to estimate the costs of educational improvements in Oregon.

Early Learning Division

Address: 775 Summer Street NE, Suite 300, Salem 97301
Phone: 503-947-5929
Email: EarlyLearning.OEIB@state.or.us
Web: http://oregonearlylearning.com
Contact: David Mandell, Director
Statutory Authority: ORS 326.425, 417.710, 417.727
Duties and Responsibilities: The mission of the Early Learning Division is to support all of Oregon's young children and families so they will have opportunities to learn and thrive. The division values equity, integrity and collective wisdom for creating positive impacts for children and families. As part of the 40/40/20 education goal (40 percent of Oregonians earning a baccalaureate degree or higher, 40 percent an associate's degree or certificate in a skilled occupation and 20 percent a high school diploma or its equivalent) and with a vision for a seamless education system from birth through college, the division was created in 2013 to focus on the future of children.

The division's work includes supporting safe early learning environments, improving the health and development of young children, ensuring children are entering school ready to learn, helping parents gain access to affordable, quality child care and helping to develop a professional early learning workforce.

Youth Development Council and Division

Address: 255 Capitol St. NE, Salem 97310-0203
Phone: 503-378-6250
Fax: 503-378-5156
Web: www.ode.state.or.us/search/results/?id=387
Contact: Iris Bell, Executive Director and Administrator
Statutory Authority: ORS 417.847, 417.850, 417.852–417.854, 417.855
Duties and Responsibilities: The Youth Development Council was created by House Bill 4165 in 2012 and further developed in House Bill 3231 in 2013, with an understanding that, despite existing initiatives to align systems and policies in support of students, there are youths who encounter various forms of adversity throughout their lives. This can be so significant it creates real and detrimental barriers to education and workforce success. To help youths get back on the path to high school graduation, college and/or a career, the Legislature created the council.

The council is tasked with supporting the education system by developing state policy and administering funding to support community and school-based youth development programs, services and initiatives for youths ages six to 24. The council advocates for youths through changes in state law, policy and funding for programs and services that support youth education, career/workforce development and juvenile crime prevention.

Efforts funded through the council are effective evidence, research and practice-based prevention and intervention approaches. These approaches are required to be culturally appropriate, specific to sexual orientation and gender-identity, and must address various barriers to educational and workforce success.

EMPLOYMENT DEPARTMENT

Address: 875 Union St. NE, Salem 97311
Phone: 503-947-1470; Toll-free: 1-800-237-3710
Fax: 503-947-1472
Email: Oed_info@oregon.gov
Web: www.Employment.Oregon.gov
Contact: Kay Erickson, Director;
Statutory Authority: ORS 657.601
Duties and Responsibilities: The mission of the Employment Department is to support business and promote employment by providing unemployment insurance benefits to those who are out of work through no fault of their own, by matching qualified job seekers to businesses who need their skills and by providing timely and accurate economic and labor market information.

With the passage of the Social Security Act in 1935, the federal government laid the groundwork for the unemployment insurance program. The State Unemployment Compensation Commission was formed in 1935 and, in January of 1938, the first unemployment check, for $15, was issued to James H. Allen in Ontario.

In 1957, a division was formed to research and collect unemployment and economic data. That Research Division was combined with the State Employment Service and the State Unemployment Compensation Commission to form the Department of Employment in 1959.

In 1971, the Legislature established the Department of Human Resources (DHR), with Employment as one of its divisions. The Employment Division operated within DHR until 1993, when Governor Barbara Roberts signed legislation to form the Employment Department.

Today, the department employs approximately 1,200 staff providing vital services to Oregonians, including managing the state's unemployment insurance program, offering job search assistance to individuals, helping businesses find quality workers, providing up-to-date labor market information and providing fair and impartial administrative hearings.

Unemployment Insurance Division

Address: 875 Union St. NE, Salem 97311
Phone: 503-947-1330
Fax: 503-947-1668
Web: www.oregon.gov/EMPLOY/
Unemployment/Pages/default.aspx
Contact: David Gerstenfeld, Director
Statutory Authority: ORS 657.601
Duties and Responsibilities: Unemployment insurance benefits replace part of the income lost when workers become unemployed through no fault of their own. This softens the impact job losses have on workers and their communities. The division is responsible for paying benefits to eligible claimants in an accurate and timely manner, deciding eligibility issues, discouraging fraud and collecting taxes to fund the program.

The money used to pay Oregon unemployment insurance benefits comes from Oregon employers' state payroll taxes. The taxes collected are deposited in a trust fund used to pay unemployment insurance benefits to unemployed Oregon workers.

Workforce and Economic Research Division

Address: 875 Union St. NE, Salem 97311
Phone: 503-947-1229
Fax: 503-947-1210
Web: www.QualityInfo.org
Contact: David Yamaka, Interim Director
Statutory Authority: ORS 657.601
Duties and Responsibilities: The division's team of economists, workforce analysts and researchers collect and analyze statewide and regional labor market information. They help organizations and businesses apply that information in their day-to-day operations. Analysts provide concise, up-to-date information about the local and state economies and their effects on the workforce. Research staff studies the labor force and related topics, supplies data and analysis to new and expanding firms and analyzes occupational supply and demand, which is gathered through surveys sent to employers.

In addition to offering general information, staff produces special reports upon request. Businesses, in turn, use this labor market information to identify challenges and opportunities. Economic development planners, educators and training providers, job applicants, legislators and the news media also regularly rely on this information to learn about workforce issues that affect Oregonians.

Workforce Operations Division

Address: 875 Union St. NE, Salem 97311
Phone: 503-947-1277

Fax: 503-947-1658
Contact: Jim Pfarrer, Director
Statutory Authority: ORS 657.601
Duties and Responsibilities: The Workforce Operations Division of the Employment Department serves employers by recruiting workers with skills matching employers' needs. The department helps job seekers find jobs that match their skills, provides them with information about trends in occupations and refers job seekers to appropriate training programs.

The division partners with the Office of Community Colleges and Workforce Development of the Higher Education Coordinating Commission, local Workforce Development Boards, local training providers and the Department of Human Services Self-Sufficiency and Vocational Rehabilitation programs to form the state's workforce system, WorkSource Oregon.

The division also oversees programs aimed at assisting certain groups, such as military veterans, migrant seasonal farmworkers and workers adversely affected by foreign trade.

Other Groups:

Administrative Hearings, Office of
Address: 4600 25th Ave. NE, Suite 140, Salem 97301; Mail: PO Box 14020, Salem 97309-4020
Phone: 503-947-1918
Fax: 503-947-1920
Email: rema.a.bergin@oregon.gov
Web: www.oregon.gov/OAH/Pages/index.aspx
Contact: Gary Tyler, Chief Administrative Law Judge
Statutory Authority: ORS 183.605
Duties and Responsibilities: The Office of Administrative Hearings was created by the Legislature in 1999 to provide an independent and impartial forum for citizens and businesses to dispute state agency actions against them. Sixty-five professional administrative law judges hold more than 30,000 hearings a year for approximately 70 state agencies. By statute, all administrative law judges are required to be "impartial in the performance of [their] duties and shall remain fair in all hearings." Oregon is the 22nd state with an independent central panel of administrative law judges.

Employment Appeals Board
Address: 875 Union St. NE, Salem 97311
Phone: 503-947-2098
Fax: 503-378-2129
Contact: Susan Rossiter, Chair
Statutory Authority: ORS 657.685–657.690

Duties and Responsibilities: The three-member Employment Appeals Board is appointed by the governor to review hearing decisions issued in contested unemployment insurance claims cases. The board performs new revisions of 2,500 to 3,000 cases per year, with authority to affirm, modify, reverse or remand for additional evidence the decisions of administrative law judges at the Office of Administrative Hearings. Final written decisions of the board are subject to review by the Oregon Court of Appeals.

Employment Department Advisory Council
Address: 875 Union St. NE, Salem 97311
Phone: 503-947-1361
Fax: 503-947-1472
Contact: Melissa Leoni, Council Staff
Statutory Authority: ORS 657.695
Duties and Responsibilities: The Employment Department Advisory Council includes volunteer representatives of the public, management and labor. Council members are appointed by the governor. The council assists the director of the Employment Department in the effective development of policies and programs with respect to unemployment insurance, employment services and labor market information.

EMPLOYMENT RELATIONS BOARD
Address: 528 Cottage St. NE, Suite 400, Salem 97301-3807
Phone: 503-378-3807
Fax: 503-373-0021
Email: Emprel.Board@oregon.gov
Web: www.oregon.gov/ERB
Contact: Adam Rhynard, Board Chair
Statutory Authority: ORS Chapters 240, 663, ORS 243.650–243.795, 662.010–662.455
Duties and Responsibilities: The Employment Relations Board resolves disputes concerning labor relations for an estimated 3,000 different employers and 250,000 employees in the public and private sectors under its jurisdiction. The board administers the collective bargaining law that covers public employees of the state of Oregon and its cities, counties, school districts and other local governments; hears and decides appeals from state employees concerning personnel actions; and administers the collective bargaining law that regulates private employers who are not covered by the National Labor Relations Act.

ENERGY, STATE DEPARTMENT OF

Address: 550 Capitol St. NE, Salem 97301
Phone: 503-378-4040; 1-800-221-8035 (Toll-free in Oregon)
Fax: 503-373-7806
Email: askenergy@oregon.gov
Web: www.oregon.gov/ENERGY/Pages/index.aspx
Contact: Michael Kaplan, Director
Statutory Authority: ORS Chapters 469, 470
Duties and Responsibilities: The State Department of Energy's mission is "Leading Oregon to a safe, clean, and sustainable energy future." The department works with many stakeholders to help implement the state's energy goals and policies. The work is diverse—from helping Oregonians improve the energy efficiency of their homes, businesses and schools, to overseeing the state's interests in the cleanup project at the Hanford nuclear site in Washington. The department provides policy expertise to prepare for Oregon's future energy needs and offers technical and financial resources to encourage adoption of and investment in energy efficiency and renewable energy resources. The department also staffs the Energy Facility Siting Council, which has jurisdiction over large energy generating and transmission facilities within the state. This effort brings together project developers, local and regional governments, citizens and others to make sure proposed projects are approved, built, operated and decommissioned consistent with all applicable laws and regulations. The department was created in 1975 and has about 90 employees.

Energy Facility Siting Council

Address: 550 Capitol St. NE, Salem 97301
Phone: 503-378-4040; 1-800-221-8035 (Toll-free in Oregon)
Contact: Barry Beyeler, Chair

Hanford Cleanup Board, Oregon

Address: 550 Capitol St. NE, Salem 97301
Phone: 503-378-4040; 1-800-221-8035 (Toll-free in Oregon)
Contact: Kristen McNall, Chair

ENGINEERING AND LAND SURVEYING, STATE BOARD OF EXAMINERS FOR

Address: 670 Hawthorne Ave. SE, Suite 220, Salem 97301
Phone: 503-362-2666
Fax: 503-362-5454
Email: osbeels@osbeels.org

Web: www.oregon.gov/OSBEELS/Pages/index.aspx
Contact: Mari Lopez, Administrator
Statutory Authority: ORS 672.240
Duties and Responsibilities: Since 1919, the Oregon State Board of Examiners for Engineering and Land Surveying (OSBEELS) has regulated the practice of engineering. In 1945, regulation of the land surveying profession was added. In 1987, OSBEELS absorbed administrative oversight for Certified Water Right Examiners. In 2005, legislation was passed to include authority to regulate the practice of photogrammetric mapping.

The 11-member board, along with 15 staff, assures that professional engineers, land surveyors, photogrammetrists and certified water right examiners registered to practice in Oregon are qualified in fields in which technical and professional knowledge and skills are required. This is accomplished by setting standards of qualification for licensure; ensuring only individuals fully qualified by education, experience and examination are granted the privilege by license to practice engineering, land surveying, photogrammetric mapping and water right examination in Oregon; requiring that all licensed practitioners maintain competency; reviewing relevant laws and rules and revising them expeditiously; vigorously and impartially pursuing enforcement of regulatory laws and rules by carefully investigating any complaints or information relating to violations; and effectively disseminating information regarding board goals and activities to licensees and the public.

OSBEELS transitioned to semi-independent status in 1999. There are no tax dollars used for the board's operation. Activities are supported entirely by fees received from applicants and licensees. OSBEELS currently regulates more than 25,000 licensed professionals.

ENVIRONMENTAL QUALITY, DEPARTMENT OF

Address: 700 NE Multnomah St., Suite 600, Portland 97232
Phone: 503-229-5696; Toll-free (Oregon only): 1-800-452-4011
Fax: 503-229-6124
Web: www.oregon.gov/DEQ/Pages/index.aspx
Contact: Richard Whitman, Interim Director
Statutory Authority: ORS Chapters 454, 459, 466, 467, 468
Duties and Responsibilities: The Department of Environmental Quality (DEQ) is responsible for protecting and enhancing Oregon's water and air quality, managing the proper disposal of solid and hazardous wastes, providing assistance in cleaning up contaminated properties and enforcing Oregon's environmental laws. The agency was formed in 1969 to replace the State Sanitary Authority, which had been created in 1938 when

citizens overwhelmingly supported an initiative to clean up the Willamette River.

As environmental problems have become more complex, DEQ's role has expanded to fight climate change with policies to reduce greenhouse gas emissions, prevent toxic chemical releases and reduce risks from toxins already in the environment. DEQ is helping Oregonians solve environmental problems by encouraging personal responsibility and providing communities with technical assistance.

DEQ employs approximately 650 scientists, engineers, geologists, toxicologists, inspectors, legal and policy staff, technicians, managers and professional support staff across the state.

DEQ's headquarters are located in Portland along with its Northwest Region office. Other regional offices include the Eastern Region in Bend, the Western Region in Eugene and field offices in Coos Bay, Klamath Falls, La Grande, Medford, Pendleton, Salem, The Dalles and Tillamook. The Laboratory and Environmental Assessment Office is in Hillsboro, and seven Vehicle Inspection Stations are located in the Portland and Medford areas. The agency director has the authority to issue civil penalties for violations of pollution laws and standards. DEQ relies on several citizen advisory committees and government officials to guide its decisions.

Environmental Quality Commission

Address: 700 NE Multnomah St., Suite 600, Portland 97232
Phone: 503-229-5695
Fax: 503-229-6124
Contact: Greg Aldrich
Duties and Responsibilities: The Environmental Quality Commission, DEQ's policy and rulemaking board, adopts administrative rules, issues orders, reviews appeals of fines or other DEQ actions and hires the DEQ director. The governor appoints commission members to four-year terms.

Environmental Solutions Division

Address: 700 NE Multnomah St., Suite 600, Portland 97232
Phone: 503-229-5696; Toll-free (Oregon only): 1-800-452-4011
Fax: 503-229-6124
Web: www.oregon.gov/DEQ/Pages/index.aspx
Contact: Wendy Wiles, Administrator
Duties and Responsibilities: The Environmental Solutions Division is responsible for collecting and analyzing environmental information and developing sound and effective environmental strategies. The division ensures that technical and scientific expertise is available to inform and carry out these responsibilities. In partnership with others, the division takes a comprehensive and holistic view of environmental impacts and seeks to create solutions that reduce negative impacts.

Operations Division

Address: 700 NE Multnomah St., Suite 600, Portland 97232
Phone: 503-229-5696; Toll-free (Oregon only): 1-800-452-4011
Fax: 503-229-6124
Web: www.oregon.gov/DEQ/Pages/index.aspx
Contact: Lydia Emer, Administrator
Duties and Responsibilities: The Operations Division has lead responsibility to ensure that DEQ's work is delivered in a consistent and effective manner across media and regions. The division collaborates with the other divisions to ensure that implementation planning is central to policy development. The division works to optimize the delivery of programs and services to Oregonians, and implements and supports specific programs in DEQ's regional divisions.

FILM AND VIDEO OFFICE, OREGON

Address: 123 NE 3rd Ave., Suite 210, Portland 97232
Phone: 971-254-4020
Email: shoot@oregonfilm.com
Web: www.oregonfilm.org
Contact: Tim Williams, Executive Director
Statutory Authority: ORS 284.305
Duties and Responsibilities: The Oregon Film and Video Office has been helping production companies find, secure and utilize Oregon's magnificent locations since 1968. The office's mission is to promote the development of the film, television and multimedia industry in Oregon and to enhance the industry's revenues, profile and reputation within Oregon and among the industry internationally. The office administers the state's Oregon Production Investment Fund and Greenlight Oregon Labor Rebate programs that incentivize film, television and multimedia production in Oregon.

FISH AND WILDLIFE, OREGON DEPARTMENT OF

Address: 4034 Fairview Industrial Drive SE, Salem 97302
Phone: 503-947-6000; Toll-free: 1-800-720-6339 (ODFW); Licensing and Controlled Hunts Information: 503-947-6102
Email: odfw.info@state.or.us
Web: www.odfw.com
Contact: Curt Melcher, Director
Statutory Authority: ORS 496.080–496.166
Duties and Responsibilities: The statutory obligation and mission of the Oregon Department of Fish and Wildlife (ODFW) is to "protect and

enhance Oregon's fish and wildlife and their habitats for use and enjoyment by present and future generations." ODFW accomplishes this mission through its fish and wildlife divisions and regional offices. Staff in these divisions and in the regional and field offices are supported by administrative divisions which include information and education, human resources, information systems and administrative services. The Oregon State Police play a key role in the mission through enforcement of fish and wildlife regulations. The seven-member Fish and Wildlife Commission, appointed by the governor, hires the agency director, sets policy and adopts administrative rules. The director oversees agency administration and the day-to-day operations of the agency.

Fish and Wildlife Commission, Oregon

Address: 4034 Fairview Industrial Dr. SE, Salem 97302-1142
Phone: 503-947-6033
Web: www.dfw.state.or.us/agency/commission
Contact: Director's Office
Statutory Authority: ORS 496.090
Duties and Responsibilities: The Oregon Fish and Wildlife Commission consists of seven members appointed by the governor for staggered, four-year terms. One commissioner must be from each congressional district, one from east of the Cascades and one from west of the Cascades.

The commission was formed July 1, 1975, when the formerly separate fish and wildlife commissions were merged. ODFW consists of the commission, a commission-appointed director and a statewide staff of approximately 1,000 permanent employees. Commissioners formulate general state programs and policies concerning management and conservation of fish and wildlife resources and establish seasons, methods and bag limits for recreational and commercial take.

Fish Division

Address: 4034 Fairview Industrial Dr. SE, Salem 97302-1142
Phone: 503-947-6201
Fax: 503-947-6202
Web: www.dfw.state.or.us/fish
Contact: Ed Bowles, Administrator
Statutory Authority: ORS 496.124, 506.142
Duties and Responsibilities: As part of ODFW's mission to protect and enhance Oregon's fish and wildlife and their habitats, the department is charged by statute to protect and propagate fish in the state. This includes direct responsibility for regulating harvest of fish, protection of fish, enhancement of fish populations through habitat improvement, and the rearing and release of fish into public

waters. ODFW maintains hatcheries throughout the state to provide fish for program needs.

Restoration and Enhancement Board

Address: 4034 Fairview Industrial Dr. SE, Salem 97302-1142
Phone: 503-947-6259
Web: www.dfw.state.or.us/fish/RE
Contact: Kevin Herkamp, Coordinator
Statutory Authority: ORS 496.286–496.291
Duties and Responsibilities: On June 29, 1989, the Oregon Fisheries Restoration and Enhancement Act of 1989 was signed into law. The Act allows the Department of Fish and Wildlife to undertake a comprehensive program to restore state-owned fish hatcheries, enhance natural fish production, expand hatchery production and provide additional public access to fishing waters. The department's program provides increased recreational fishing opportunities and supports and improves the commercial salmon fishery.

Information and Education Division

Address: 4034 Fairview Industrial Dr. SE, Salem 97302-1142
Phone: 503-947-6011
Fax: 503-947-6009
Contact: Rick Hargrave, Administrator
Duties and Responsibilities: This division directs and/or provides all communications and education services for the department. These services include strategic outreach programs, informational campaigns, media and public relation communications, public involvement activities, special events, hunter education programs, aquatic and angler education programs, additional education activities, creation of publications and videos and website management.

Wildlife Division

Address: 4034 Fairview Industrial Dr. SE, Salem 97302-1142
Phone: 503-947-6300
Fax: 503-947-6330
Web: www.dfw.state.or.us/wildlife
Contact: Ron Anglin, Administrator
Statutory Authority: ORS 496.124
Duties and Responsibilities: The Wildlife Division has direct responsibility for monitoring the numbers and health of wildlife species, setting population conservation and management objectives, overseeing wildlife habitat restoration and maintenance and regulating harvest of game animals. The Oregon Conservation Strategy is a key part of the division.

Access and Habitat Program

Address: 4034 Fairview Industrial Dr. SE,
Salem 97302-1142
Phone: 503-947-6087
Web: www.dfw.state.or.us/lands/AH
Contact: Isaac Sanders, Coordinator
Statutory Authority: ORS 496.228
Duties and Responsibilities: In 1993, the Oregon Legislature created the Access and Habitat Program. The new law created an incentive-based program to improve public hunting access and wildlife habitat on private lands in Oregon. The program's motto, "Landowners and Hunters Together for Wildlife," conveys the program's basic mission to foster partnerships between landowners and hunters for the benefit of the wildlife they value. The program also seeks to recognize and encourage the important contributions made by landowners to the state's wildlife resource.

The funding for the program comes from three sources: a $4 surcharge on all hunting licenses, the annual auction and raffle of 10 deer and 10 elk tags, and funding from the Green Forage and Deer Enhancement and Restoration Program.

FOREST RESOURCES INSTITUTE, OREGON

Address: 317 SW 6th Ave., Suite 400, Portland
97204-1705
Phone: 971-673-2944
Fax: 971-673-2946
Web: OregonForests.org; KnowYourForest.org;
LearnForests.org; OregonForestLaws.org;
WhyBuildWithWood.org
Contact: Paul F. Barnum, Executive Director
Statutory Authority: ORS 526.600–526.675
Duties and Responsibilities: The Legislature created the Oregon Forest Resources Institute (OFRI) in 1991 to advance public understanding of forests, forest management and forest products and to encourage sound forestry through landowner education. OFRI is governed by a 13-member board of directors and is funded by a portion of the forest products harvest tax. OFRI's nine-member staff develops programs, publications and information-rich websites for the general public, family forest landowners and kindergarten through grade 12 teachers and students. OFRI helps the public understand the social, environmental and economic importance of Oregon's forests, and the environmental benefits of forest products. The institute does this through its educational advertising and websites as well as through producing topical publications, videos and speaker presentations. OFRI is headquartered in Portland and has a satellite office and 15-acre demonstration forest at The Oregon Garden in Silverton.

FORESTRY DEPARTMENT, STATE

Address: 2600 State St., Salem 97310
Phone: 503-945-7200
Fax: 503-945-7212
Email: information@oregon.gov
Web: www.oregon.gov/ODF/Pages/index.aspx
Contact: Peter Daugherty, State Forester
Statutory Authority: ORS Chapters 321, 477,
526, 527, 530, 532
Duties and Responsibilities: For over 100 years, Oregon's State Department of Forestry (ODF) has operated with a singular vision: ensuring the sustainability of Oregon's forests. That vision is manifested through the triple priorities of protecting forestland from wildfire, enforcing Oregon's Forest Practices Act and managing Oregon's state-owned forests. These priorities are managed through ODF's three primary operational divisions.

Forest Protection Division: Since 1911, ODF has served as the state's largest fire department, today protecting just over half of Oregon's forests from wildfire. This includes all of Oregon's privately owned forests, as well as state and local government-owned forests, and, by contract, more than two million acres of U.S. Bureau of Land Management's forests in western Oregon. These lands represent a value of more than $60 billion.

Private Forests Division: This division oversees Oregon's Forest Practices Act. Enacted in 1971 and modified many times since, the Act regulates stream and water quality protection, timber harvesting, tree planting, road construction and maintenance, air quality from prescribed burning, chemical use and other practices on private forest lands.

State Forests Division: The department's third principal business is managing the 3 percent of the forest landbase that is owned by the state, about 821,000 acres. State-owned forests are located primarily in northwest Oregon in the Tillamook, Clatsop and Santiam State Forests. The recently dedicated Gilchrist State Forest is in northern Klamath County and the Sun Pass State Forest is just south of Crater Lake. The 93,000-acre Elliott State Forest, Oregon's first state forest, is on the south coast near Coos Bay.

ODF manages most of these lands to achieve what Oregon statutes and administrative rules call the "greatest permanent value," which means a balance of social, economic and environmental values. The agency does this while generating more than $80 million each year, two-thirds of which is distributed according to state law to the counties and local taxing districts where the forests reside. The agency's State Forests Division manages this portfolio.

ODF is overseen by the State Board of Forestry. The department is served by more than 600 permanent employees and over 600 seasonal employees, operating out of its Salem-based headquarters and 32 field offices throughout Oregon.

Board of Forestry, State

Phone: 503-945-7210
Contact: Tom Imeson, Chair
Statutory Authority: ORS Chapter 526
Duties and Responsibilities: The State Board of Forestry is a seven-member citizen board appointed by the governor and confirmed by the Senate. The mission of the board is to lead Oregon in implementing policies and programs that promote sustainable management of Oregon's public and private forests. Its primary responsibilities are to supervise all matters of forest policy within Oregon, appoint the state forester, adopt rules regulating forest practices and provide general supervision of the state forester's duties in managing ODF.

No more than three members may receive any significant portion of their income from the forest products industry. There must be at least one member from each of the state's three major forest regions: northern, southern and eastern. The term of office is four years, and no member may serve more than two consecutive full terms. The state forester serves as secretary to the board.

Emergency Fire Cost Committee

Address: 2600 State St., Salem 97310
Phone: 503-945-7449
Contact: Tim Keith, Fund Administrator
Statutory Authority: ORS 477.750–477.775
Duties and Responsibilities: The Oregon Forest Land Protection Fund was established by the Legislature as an insurance fund with the purpose of equalizing emergency fire suppression costs among the various State Department of Forestry protection districts. The emergency funding system is designed to operate as an "insurance policy" whereby all districts contribute (pay premiums) into the fund so that money will be available to any individual district to pay fire suppression costs for emergency fires.

Family Forestlands, Committee for

Address: 2600 State St., Salem 97310
Phone: 503-945-7482
Contact: Lena Tucker, Private Forests Division Chief
Statutory Authority: ORS 526.016
Duties and Responsibilities: The Committee for Family Forestlands researches policies impacting family forestland viability, resource protection and forestry benefits. Based on its findings, the com-

mittee recommends actions to the State Board of Forestry and state forester.

The 13-member committee includes seven voting and six non-voting members. Voting members include four family forest owners and one representative each from the environmental community, forest products industry and general public. Non-voting ex officio members may include representatives from ODF, Oregon State University, Oregon small forestland groups, forestry-related industry associations and the Oregon Forest Resources Institute.

Forest Stewardship Coordinating Committee

Address: 2600 State St., Salem 97310
Phone: 503-945-7482
Contact: Lena Tucker, Private Forests Division Chief
Statutory Authority: U.S. Cooperative Forestry Assistance Act, 16 U.S.C. 2101 et seq.
Duties and Responsibilities: The Stewardship Coordinating Committee (SCC) advises the state forester on policies and procedures for U.S. Forest Service, state and private forestry programs, such as Forest Legacy and Forest Stewardship. The committee consists of representatives from state and federal natural resource agencies, private forest landowners, consulting foresters and forest industry and conservation organizations.

The SCC also serves as the forestry subcommittee to the Oregon Technical Advisory Committee, which advises both the U.S. Department of Agriculture (USDA) Farm Services Agency and USDA Natural Resource Conservation Service on federal farm and forestry assistance programs.

Forest Trust Land Advisory Committee

Address: 2600 State St., Salem 97310
Phone: 503-945-7351
Contact: Liz Dent, State Forests Division Chief
Statutory Authority: ORS 526.156
Duties and Responsibilities: The Forest Trust Land Advisory Committee is a group of elected county commissioners that advises the State Board of Forestry and state forester on matters related to state forestlands managed by ODF. The council represents the 15 counties with state forestlands on policy matters related to the management of the forestlands and distributions of revenues produced from those lands. The counties who receive revenues from these forestlands are Benton, Clackamas, Clatsop, Columbia, Coos, Douglas, Josephine, Klamath, Lane, Lincoln, Linn, Marion, Polk, Tillamook and Washington.

The committee's roster is established in November when the Council for Forest Trust Land Counties elects their board of directors at the annual meeting of the Association of Oregon Counties.

Regional Forest Practice Committees

Address: 2600 State St., Salem 97310
Phone: 503-945-7482
Contact: Lena Tucker, Private Forests Division Chief
Statutory Authority: ORS 527.650
Duties and Responsibilities: Regional Forest Practice Committees are panels of citizens that advise the State Board of Forestry on current forestry issues and forest management approaches. Three Regional Forest Practice Committees, serving the northwest, southwest and eastern regions of the state, were created by the 1971 Oregon Forest Practices Act. Under Oregon law, a majority of committee members must be private forest landowners and persons involved with logging or forest operations.

Smoke Management Advisory Committee

Address: 2600 State St., Salem 97310
Phone: 503-945-7200
Duties and Responsibilities: In 1989, the Legislature directed the state forester to establish a Smoke Management Advisory Committee to provide advice and assistance to the State Department of Forestry Smoke Management program. The state forester appoints three members: an industrial forestland owner representative, a non-industrial forestland owner representative and a public representative. A U.S. Forest Service representative and a U.S. Bureau of Land Management representative are also invited to serve as members. Each member serves a two-year term that is renewable after the two-year period.

Committee members gather for public meetings in Salem twice a year to discuss and provide advice to the Smoke Management program regarding current prescribed burning and smoke intrusion trends, program fund balance, implementation plan items and other current issues and projects of the program.

State Forests Advisory Committee

Address: 2600 State St., Salem OR 97310
Phone: 503-945-7200
Duties and Responsibilities: The State Forests Advisory Committee (SFAC) is comprised of citizens and representatives of timber, environmental and recreation groups. The SFAC provides a forum to discuss issues, opportunities and concerns and offer advice and guidance to ODF on the implementation of the Northwest Oregon State Forests Management Plan. The plan provides guidance for managing 616,000 acres within the Tillamook, Clatsop and Santiam State Forests and several scattered state-owned forest tracts in Benton, Polk, Lincoln and Lane Counties through a balanced approach to generate revenue, while prioritizing environmental and social benefits.

GEOLOGIST EXAMINERS, STATE BOARD OF

Address: 707 13th St. SE, Suite 114, Salem 97301
Phone: 503-566-2837
Fax: 503-485-2947
Email: osbge.info@state.or.us
Web: www.oregon.gov/OSBGE/Pages/index.aspx
Contact: Christine Valentine, Administrator
Statutory Authority: ORS 672.615
Duties and Responsibilities: The mission of the State Board of Geologist Examiners, established in 1977, is to safeguard the health, welfare and property of Oregonians with respect to geologic practice in Oregon. The board accomplishes this primarily through registration of geologists. The board also reviews complaints about geologist conduct and practice or unlicensed geologic practice and has authority to impose civil penalties, suspend, revoke or not renew registrations or seek other resolutions as appropriate. In addition, the board works to inform the public, government agencies and others about the practice of geology.

The board sets examination, education and experience standards for geologist registration and for a specialty certification in engineering geology, evaluates applications for examination and registration based on these standards and administers national exams and an engineering geology specialty examination. Geologists licensed in other states or jurisdictions can apply for registration in Oregon but must meet all of the board's standards.

More than 1,100 geologists are registered to practice in Oregon with over 250 also holding certification in engineering geology. The board is composed of four Oregon registered geologists, the state geologist and a public member, and is served by two staff, an executive director and registration specialist.

GEOLOGY AND MINERAL INDUSTRIES, STATE DEPARTMENT OF

Address: 800 NE Oregon St., Suite 965, Portland 97232
Phone: 971-673-1555
Fax: 971-673-1562
Web: www.oregon.gov/DOGAMI/Pages/index.aspx
Contact: Brad Avy, State Geologist
Statutory Authority: ORS Chapters 516, 517, 520, 522

Duties and Responsibilities: The Department of Geology and Mineral Industries (DOGAMI) increases understanding of Oregon's geologic resources and hazards through science and stewardship.

DOGAMI was established in 1937 as an independent state agency. Its early focus on mining and rural economic development has expanded to include helping Oregonians understand and prepare for the natural hazards that accompany the state's spectacular geology.

Today, DOGAMI's mission is to provide earth science information and regulation to make Oregon safe and prosperous. The Geologic Survey and Services program develops maps, reports and data to help Oregon manage natural resources and prepare for natural hazards such as earthquakes, tsunamis, landslides, floods, volcanic eruptions and coastal erosion. The Mineral Lands Regulation and Reclamation program oversees the state's mineral production and works to minimize impacts of natural resource extraction and to maximize the opportunities for land reclamation.

DOGAMI has a staff of approximately 45 people.

Department of Geology and Mineral Industries Governing Board

Contact: Lisa Phipps, Chair
Duties and Responsibilities: A five-member governing board of citizens, appointed by the governor and confirmed by the Senate, oversees the Department of Geology and Mineral Industries. The board sets policy, oversees general operations and adopts a strategic plan every six years to guide DOGAMI's mission and objectives.

Field Offices:

Albany (Mineral Land Regulation and Reclamation program)
Address: 229 Broadalbin St. NW, Albany 97321
Phone: 541-967-2039
Fax: 541-967-2075

Baker City
Address: 1995 3rd St., Suite 130, Baker City 97814
Phone: 541-523-3133

Newport Coastal Field Office
Address: 313 SW 2nd St., Suite D, Newport 97365
Phone: 541-574-6658

GOVERNMENT ETHICS COMMISSION, OREGON

Address: 3218 Pringle Rd. SE, Rm. 220, Salem 97302-1544
Phone: 503-378-5105
Fax: 503-373-1456
Email: ogec.mail@oregon.gov

Web: www.oregon.gov/OGEC/Pages/index.aspx
Contact: Ronald A. Bersin, Executive Director
Statutory Authority: ORS 171.725–171.785, 192.660, 192.685, ORS Chapter 244
Duties and Responsibilities: The Oregon Government Ethics Commission (OGEC), established by vote of the people in 1974, is responsible for enforcement of government ethics laws. Oregon government ethics laws prohibit public officials from using their office for financial gain and require public disclosure of economic conflict of interest. The OGEC also enforces state laws that require lobbyists, and the entities they represent, to register and periodically report their lobbying expenditures. The third area of OGEC jurisdiction is the executive session provisions of the public meetings law.

The OGEC is a nine-member citizen commission served by nine staff members who focus on regulation and prevention through education.

HEALTH AUTHORITY, OREGON

Address: 500 Summer St. NE, E20, Salem 97301-1097
Phone: 503-947-2340; 877-398-9238
Fax: 503-947-2341
Email: OHA.DirectorsOffice@state.or.us; OHPB.Info@state.or.us
Web: www.oregon.gov/OHA/Pages/index.aspx
Contact: Lynne Saxton, Director
Statutory Authority: ORS 413.032
Duties and Responsibilities: The Oregon Health Authority (OHA) is responsible for improving the lifelong health of Oregonians, improving quality and increasing access to health services, and containing and lowering health care costs. It was created by the 2009 Legislature to ensure that every Oregonian has access to affordable, sustainable, high-quality health care and to ensure health equity for all Oregonians. One of the ways it does that is through an innovative system of coordinated care organizations (CCOs). These CCOs serve most of the more than 1 million members of the Oregon Health Plan, Oregon's Medicaid program. The 16 CCOs work with partners in all 36 Oregon counties to provide better care at lower cost and ensure that their members' physical, behavioral and dental health needs are met.

OHA is overseen by the nine-member citizen Oregon Health Policy Board and carries out its work through several program areas.

Health Policy and Analytics collects and analyzes data about health care and health reform in Oregon so that legislators, policymakers, providers and individuals can make informed health-related decisions. The Health Systems Division is comprised of the Medical Assistance Program, which operates the Oregon Health Plan, and Addictions and Mental Health, which helps Oregonians achieve physical, mental and social well-being by integrating physical and behavioral care. These two former divisions were combined in the 2015–2017 biennium.

The Oregon State Hospital operates in-patient psychiatric facilities in Salem and Junction City, as well as Pendleton Cottages for patients in Eastern Oregon who are nearing the point when they can return to their communities. The Office of Equity and Inclusion works to eliminate health gaps and and make health care more accessible. The Public Health Division works to improve health for Oregonians through prevention activities and environmental health regulation.

Health Policy Board, Oregon
Address: 500 Summer St. NE, Salem 97301
Phone: 503-947-2340; 877-398-9238
Fax: 503-947-2341
Email: OHPB.Info@state.or.us
Web: www.oregon.gov/OHA/OHPB/Pages/
index.aspx
Statutory Authority: ORS 413.032
Duties and Responsibilities: The nine-member Oregon Health Policy Board (OHPB) serves as the policy-making and oversight body for the Oregon Health Authority. The board is committed to providing access to high-quality, affordable health care for all Oregonians and to improving population health.

OHPB was established by the Legislature in 2009 through House Bill 2009, which made the Oregon Health Authority responsible for most state health care services and for reforming the state's health care system. The board is responsible for improving access to health care, the quality of that care and containing the growth in its cost.

Educators Benefit Board, Oregon
Address: 500 Summer St. NE, Salem 97301
Phone: 503-378-6610; Toll-free: 1-888-469-6322
Fax: 503-378-5832
Email: oebb.benefits@state.or.us
Web: www.oregon.gov/OHA/OEBB/Pages/
index.aspx
Contact: Kathy Loretz, Executive Director
Statutory Authority: ORS 243.864
Duties and Responsibilities: The Oregon Educators Benefit Board provides a choice of benefit plans for most of Oregon's kindergarten through grade 12 school districts, education service districts and community colleges, as well as a number of charter schools and local governments.

Equity and Inclusion, Office of
Address: 421 SW Oak St., Suite 750, Portland 97204

Phone: 971-673-1240; 971-673-1285 (Director);
TTY: 711
Fax: 971-673-1128
Web: www.oregon.gov/OHA/oei/pages/
index.aspx
Contact: Leann Johnson, Director
Email: Leann.R.Johnson@state.or.us
Statutory Authority: ORS 431.137
Duties and Responsibilities: The Office of Equity and Inclusion works with diverse communities throughout Oregon to eliminate health gaps and disparities by making health care more accessible and ensuring the delivery of care consistent with state and federal civil rights guidelines. It operates a Traditional Health Worker program to help ensure that culturally competent care is delivered by a diverse workforce. Its Health Care Interpreter program trains and certifies bilingual persons to provide high-quality health care interpretation to Oregon's growing diverse populations.

Health Licensing Office (HLO)
Address: 700 Summer St. NE, Suite 320, Salem 97301-1287
Phone: 503-378-8667; TTY: 503-373-2114
Fax: 503-370-9004
Email: hlo.info@state.or.us
Web: www.oregon.gov/oha/hlo/Pages/index.aspx
Contact: Holly Mercer, Director
Statutory Authority: ORS 676.600–676.992
Duties and Responsibilities: The Health Licensing Office works with multiple boards, councils and programs to oversee a variety of health and health-related professions. It protects Oregonians' health and safety by ensuring that these professionals are trained and qualified to practice. The office tests people who apply for professional licenses, inspects facilities, responds to consumer complaints and disciplines practitioners who violate state requirements.

HLO, Advanced Estheticians, Board of Certified
Web: www.oregon.gov/OHA/hlo/Pages/Board-
Certified-Advanced-Estheticians.aspx
Duties and Responsibilities: In July 2015, House Bill 2642 created the Board of Certified Advanced Estheticians to oversee the safe practice of advanced nonablative esthetics in Oregon. The board has nine members appointed by the governor. Licensing in advanced esthetics began on July 1, 2016.

HLO, Athletic Trainers, Board of
Web: www.oregon.gov/oha/hlo/Pages/Board-
Athletic-Trainer.aspx
Statutory Authority: ORS 688.701–688.734
Duties and Responsibilities: The Board of Athletic Trainers oversees the practice of athletic

trainers in Oregon. It has five members appointed by the governor.

HLO, Behavior Analysis Regulatory Board

Web: www.oregon.gov/oha/hlo/Pages/Board-Behavior-Analysis-Regulatory.aspx
Statutory Authority: ORS 676.800–676.805
Duties and Responsibilities: The Behavior Analysis Regulatory Board oversees the licensing of behavior analysts and assistant behavior analysts and the registration of behavior analysis interventionists, all of whom treat individuals with autism spectrum disorder. The board has nine members appointed by the governor and subject to confirmation by the Senate.

HLO, Cosmetology, Board of

Web: www.oregon.gov/oha/hlo/Pages/Board-Cosmetology.aspx
Statutory Authority: ORS 690.005–690.992
Duties and Responsibilities: The Board of Cosmetology oversees the practice of cosmetologists in Oregon. It has seven members appointed by the governor and subject to confirmation by the Senate.

HLO, Board of Denture Technology

Web: www.oregon.gov/OHA/hlo/Pages/Board-Denture-Technology.aspx
Statutory Authority: ORS 680.500–680.990
Duties and Responsibilities: The Board of Denture Technology oversees the practice of denturists in Oregon. It has seven members appointed by the governor and subject to confirmation by the Senate.

HLO, Dietitians, Board of Licensed

Web: www.oregon.gov/OHA/hlo/Pages/Board-Licensed-Dietitians.aspx
Statutory Authority: ORS 691.405
Duties and Responsibilities: The Board of Licensed Dietitians oversees the practice of dietitians in Oregon. It has seven members appointed by the governor.

HLO, Electrologists and Body Art Practitioners, Board of

Web: www.oregon.gov/oha/hlo/Pages/Board-Body-Art-Practitioners.aspx
Statutory Authority: ORS 690.350–690.992
Duties and Responsibilities: The Board of Electrologists and Body Art Practitioners oversees the practices of tattoo artists, electrologists and body piercers, including specialty piercers and earlobe-only piercers. It has seven members appointed by the governor and subject to confirmation by the Senate.

HLO, Environmental Health Registration Board

Web: www.oregon.gov/OHA/hlo/Pages/Board-Environmental-Health-Registration.aspx
Statutory Authority: ORS 700.005–700.995
Duties and Responsibilities: The Environmental Health Registration Board oversees the practices of environmental health specialists and waste water specialists in Oregon. It has seven members appointed by the governor.

HLO, Hearing Aids, Advisory Council on

Web: www.oregon.gov/OHA/hlo/Pages/Board-Advisory-Council-Hearing-Aids.aspx
Statutory Authority: ORS 694.015–694.991
Duties and Responsibilities: The Advisory Council on Hearing Aids oversees the practice of hearing aid specialists in Oregon. It has seven members appointed by the governor and subject to confirmation by the Senate.

HLO, Midwifery, Board of Direct Entry

Web: www.oregon.gov/oha/hlo/Pages/Board-Direct-Entry-Midwifery.aspx
Statutory Authority: ORS 687.405–687.991
Duties and Responsibilities: The Board of Direct Entry Midwifery oversees the practice of licensed direct entry midwives in Oregon. It has seven members appointed by the governor and subject to confirmation by the Senate.

HLO, Nursing Home Administrators Board

Web: www.oregon.gov/OHA/hlo/Pages/Board-Nursing-Home-Administrators.aspx
Statutory Authority: ORS 678.800
Duties and Responsibilities: The Nursing Home Administrators Board oversees the practice of nursing home administrators in Oregon. It has nine members appointed by the governor and confirmed by the Senate.

HLO, Respiratory Therapist and Polysomnographic Technologist Licensing Board

Web: www.oregon.gov/OHA/hlo/Pages/Board-Respiratory-Therapist-Polysomnographic-Technologist-Licensing.aspx
Statutory Authority: ORS 688.800–688.995
Duties and Responsibilities: The Respiratory Therapist and Polysomnographic Technologist Licensing Board oversees the practices of respiratory therapists and polysomnographic technologists in Oregon. It has seven members appointed by the governor and subject to confirmation by the Senate.

HLO, Sex Offender Treatment Board

Web: www.oregon.gov/OHA/hlo/Pages/Board-Sex-Offender-Treatment.aspx
Statutory Authority: ORS 675.360–675.410
Duties and Responsibilities: The Sex Offender Treatment Board oversees the practices of clinical and associate sex offender therapists in Oregon. It has seven members appointed by the governor.

Health Policy and Analytics Division

Address: 421 SW Oak St., Suite 850, Portland, 97204
Phone: 503-947-2340; 877-398-9238
Fax: 503-947-2341
Web: www.oregon.gov/oha/analytics/Pages/index.aspx
Contact: Leslie Clement, Director
Duties and Responsibilities: The Health Policy and Analytics Division collects and analyzes health data from throughout the state and makes reports and recommendations to OHA leaders, the governor and the Legislature based on that data. The division also provides support to the Health Policy Board, the Medicaid Advisory Committee, the Health Care Workforce Committee and others. The chief medical officer supports the work of many programs and committees that are part of the health transformation effort, including the Patient Centered Primary Care Home program, Transformation Center, and Health Evidence Review Commission.

Health Systems Division

Address: 500 Summer St. NE, E44, Salem 97301-1118
Phone: 503-945-5772
Contact: Varsha Chauhan, MD, Director
Duties and Responsibilities: The Health Systems Division manages the Oregon Health Plan, Oregon's Medicaid program, which covers more than 1.1 million Oregonians. It also manages the statewide behavioral health system, whose mission is to integrate addiction services and mental health care with the state's physical health system. The division also oversees the Children's Wraparound Program, which works with the state's coordinated care organizations to ensure that children with special needs receive integrated care.

Public Employees' Benefit Board

Address: 500 Summer St. NE, E89, Salem 97301
Phone: 503-373-1102
Fax: 503-373-1654
Email: inquiries.pebb@state.or.us
Web: www.oregon.gov/DAS/PEBB/Pages/index.aspx
Contact: Kathy Loretz, Executive Director
Statutory Authority: ORS 243.125

Duties and Responsibilities: The Public Employees' Benefit Board (PEBB) designs, contracts and administers benefits for state employees, including medical and dental coverage; life, accident, disability and long-term care insurance; and flexible spending accounts. PEBB also offers health care insurance options for retirees not yet eligible for Medicare.

Public Health Division

Address: 800 NE Oregon St., Suite 930, Portland 97232
Phone: 971-673-1222
Fax: 971-673-1299
Email: health.webmaster@state.or.us
Web: http://public.health.oregon.gov
Contact: Lillian Shirley, Public Health Director
Statutory Authority: ORS Chapters 97, 431–475, 624
Duties and Responsibilities: The Public Health Division improves lifelong health for all Oregonians by promoting health and preventing the leading causes of death, disease and injury in the state. The division assesses the public's health through data collection and uses that information to develop policies and programs that support improved health outcomes for all Oregonians. The division oversees health promotion and prevention activities, health care facility licensing, environmental health regulation, public health emergency preparedness, epidemiological outbreak investigations and the Oregon State Public Health Laboratory.

The division works with local health departments, tribes, community organizations, health care providers, coordinated care organizations and other partners. The Public Health Advisory Board and other advisory committees provide guidance to the division.

State Hospital, Oregon

Address: 2600 Center St. NE, Salem 97301
Phone: 503-945-2800; TTY: 800-735-2900
Fax: 503-947-2900
Web: www.oregon.gov/oha/osh/pages/index.aspx
Contact: Greg Roberts, Superintendent
Statutory Authority: ORS 179.321
Duties and Responsibilities: The Oregon State Hospital provides in-patient psychiatric care for adults from throughout the state. With two campuses, one in Salem and one in Junction City, the hospital's primary goal is to help people recover from their illnesses and return to the community.

HIGHER EDUCATION COORDINATING COMMISSION

Address: 255 Capitol St. NE, Salem 97310-0203
Phone: 503-378-5690
Fax: 503-378-8395
Email: info.HECC@state.or.us
Web: http://www.oregon.gov/HigherEd/Pages/index.aspx
Contact: Ben Cannon, Executive Director
Statutory Authority: ORS 351.735
Duties and Responsibilities: : The Higher Education Coordinating Commission (HECC) is dedicated to fostering and sustaining pathways to opportunity and success for all Oregonians through an accessible, affordable and coordinated network for educational achievement beyond secondary education. Established in 2011, the HECC is responsible for advising the Legislature, governor and the chief education office on higher education policy. Its statutory authorities include the development of biennial budget recommendations for postsecondary education in Oregon, making funding allocations to community colleges and public universities, approving new academic programs in the public system, allocating Oregon Opportunity Grants (state need-based student aid), authorizing degrees proposed by private and out-of-state providers, licensing private career and trade schools and overseeing veterans education programs.

The HECC is a 14-member volunteer board supported by the executive director, who oversees the agency, including the Offices of the Executive Director, Policy and Communications, Student Access and Completion, Community College and Workforce Development, Public University Coordination, Private Postsecondary Education, Operations, and Research and Data.

Community Colleges and Workforce Development, Office of

Address: 255 Capitol St. NE, Salem 97310
Phone: 503-378-8648
Fax: 503-378-8434
Email: ccwd.info@state.or.us
Web: www.oregon.gov/CCWD/Pages/index.aspx
Contact: Patrick Crane, Director
Statutory Authority: ORS 326.051
Duties and Responsibilities: The HECC Office of Community Colleges and Workforce Development (CCWD) provides coordination, leadership and resources to Oregon's network of 17 locally governed community colleges, 18 adult basic skills providers, nine local workforce boards, and other partners. Established in 1999, it has responsibility for coordinating community college programs and

services, developing biennial budget recommendations for the Community College Support Fund, allocation of state funding, coordination of the academic approval process for community colleges and reporting to the Legislative Assembly. CCWD also coordinates and provides statewide administration of the federally funded Workforce Investment and Opportunity Act (WIOA); Title IB Adult, Youth, Dislocated Worker programs; WIOA Title II Adult Education and Family Literacy programs; Carl Perkins Career and Technical Education Act programs; the non-federally funded Oregon Youth Conservation Corps; and the General Educational Development (GED) programs. In 2013, the Legislature established the HECC as the state rulemaking authority for community colleges, transferring authorities previously held by the State Board of Education.

Private Postsecondary Education, Office of

Address: 255 Capitol St. NE, Salem 97310
Phone: 503-378-5690
Fax: 503-378-8395
Web: http://www.oregon.gov/highered/Pages/index.aspx
Contact: Juan Báez-Arévalo, Director
Statutory Authority: ORS Chapter 345, 348.594–348.615; 10 USC 1606, 1607; 38 USC
Duties and Responsibilities: The HECC Office of Private Postsecondary Education oversees the quality, integrity and diversity of private postsecondary programs in Oregon for the benefit of students and consumers. The office includes the Office of Degree Authorization (ODA), Private Career Schools Licensing Unit and the State Authorizing Agency (SAA) for Veterans Education. ODA works to ensure the quality of degrees and certificates offered by private degree-granting colleges in Oregon and out-of-state public and private degree-granting colleges; evaluates requests to start new degree programs in Oregon or offer academic programs for college credit to Oregon citizens from outside the state; protects existing degree programs offered by private colleges from detrimental duplication by publicly-funded institutions; and protects Oregonians from fraudulent use of substandard academic credentials and fraudulent degrees.

The Private Career Schools Licensing Unit licenses private career schools and provides educational leadership, technical assistance, training and support to private career schools in Oregon. In the interest of Oregon students, the unit works closely with schools on licensing requirements such as business and fiscal standards, as well as instructional and curricular requirements.

The SAA for Veterans Education is responsible for granting the necessary approval needed for the

Department of Veterans Affairs to pay veterans and other eligible persons their G.I. Bill education benefits. The SAA approves programs at high schools, public universities, private and independent universities and colleges, community colleges, flight schools and private career and trade schools located in Oregon.

Student Access and Completion, Office of

Address: 1500 Valley River Dr., Suite 100, Eugene 97401
Phone: 541-687-7400; Toll-free: 1-800-452-8807
Fax: 541-687-7414
Email: public_information@osac.state.or.us
Web: www.OregonStudentAid.gov
Contact: Bob Brew, Director
Statutory Authority: ORS Chapter 348
Duties and Responsibilities: The HECC Office of Student Access and Completion (OSAC) administers a variety of state, federal and privately funded student financial aid programs for the benefit of Oregonians attending institutions of postsecondary education. OSAC administers Oregon's largest state-funded, need-based grant program, the Oregon Opportunity Grant, which assists students with financial aid to attain a postsecondary education at an Oregon community college, public university or four-year private nonprofit institution; the Oregon Promise grant program for recent high school and GED graduates planning to attend an Oregon community college; and a number of publicly funded programs serving targeted groups of students, including former foster youth, students with childcare expenses and children of deceased and disabled public safety officers.

OSAC's Scholarship Program works in partnership with the state's largest foundations, private individuals, financial institutions, employers and membership organizations to administer scholarships for the benefit of Oregon students. OSAC also offers outreach and mentoring programs that help create a college-going culture in Oregon, including Oregon ASPIRE, the state's mentoring program to help middle school, high school and college students access education and training beyond high school with the help of trained volunteers.

University Coordination, Office of

Address: 255 Capitol St. NE, Salem 97301
Phone: 503-378-5690
Fax: 503-378-8395
Email: info.HECC@state.or.us
Web: www.oregon.gov/highered/Pages/index.aspx
Contact: Veronica Dujon, Director of Academic Planning and Policy; Andrew Rogers, Director of University Finance
Statutory Authority: ORS Chapter 350

Duties and Responsibilities: The HECC Office of University Coordination provides academic and fiscal coordination related to Oregon's seven public universities (Eastern Oregon University, Oregon Institute of Technology, Oregon State University, Portland State University, Southern Oregon University, University of Oregon and Western Oregon University), including coordination of the academic program approval process, statewide initiatives and legislative directives to enhance postsecondary pathways and student success. The office also develops biennial budget recommendations for the Public University Support Fund, Public University State Programs, capital investments, fiscal reporting and analysis, and the allocation of state funding through the Student Success and Completion funding model.

HOUSING AND COMMUNITY SERVICES DEPARTMENT

Address: 725 Summer St. NE, Suite B, Salem 97301-1266
Phone: 503-986-2000
Email: housinginfo@oregon.gov
Web: www.oregon.gov/OHCS/Pages/index.aspx
Contact: Margaret Salazar, Director
Statutory Authority: ORS 456.555
Duties and Responsibilities: Oregon Housing and Community Services (OHCS) is Oregon's housing finance agency providing financial and program support to create and preserve opportunities for quality, affordable housing for Oregonians of lower and moderate income.

OHCS administers programs that provide housing stabilization—from preventing and ending homelessness and assisting with utilities to keep someone stable, to financing multifamily affordable housing and encouraging home ownership. It delivers these programs primarily through grants, contracts and loan agreements with local partners and community-based providers and has limited direct contact with low-income beneficiaries. OHCS's sources of funds are varied and include federal and state resources with complex regulatory compliance requirements. Stewardship, compliance monitoring and asset management are all critical roles for OHCS.

Housing Stability Council, Oregon

Address: 725 Summer St. NE, Suite B, Salem 97301-1266
Phone: 503-986-2005
Fax: 503-986-2132
Email: housinginfo@oregon.gov
Web: www.oregon.gov/ohcs/OSHC/Pages/index.aspx
Contact: Kris Klemm, Executive Assistant to the Director

Statutory Authority: ORS 456.567
Duties and Responsibilities: The Oregon Housing Stability Council consists of nine members and is the governing body for the Housing and Community Services Department. The council approves affordable housing projects, sets direction on statewide housing policy and serves as an advisory body to the agency. The council also serves as a public body for engagement with stakeholders, housing advocates and the public on affordable housing issues and policy decisions.

Chief Financial Office

Address: 725 Summer St. NE, Suite B, Salem 97301-1266
Phone: 503-986-2000
Fax: 503-986-2020
Email: housinginfo@oregon.gov
Web: www.oregon.gov/OHCS/Pages/index.aspx
Contact: Caleb Yant, Chief Financial Officer
Statutory Authority: ORS 456.555
Duties and Responsibilities: OHCS's Chief Financial Office includes the Finance Section, the Budget Section and the Information Services Section. The office provides essential services to support OHCS's leadership and workforce to achieve the department's mission.

The Finance Section includes grants and monitoring, procurement and contracts and general accounting functions for all aspects of the department. Key program areas of the department rely on community partners serving people with low incomes, and grants and contracts are critical for success in reaching low-income Oregonians. This section ensures accountability and stewardship of resources.

The Budget Section manages and reports on all aspects of the agency's budget. The section works closely with partners at the Legislative Fiscal Office and the Department of Administrative Services to provided needed reports and budget documents throughout the biennium. The section provides critical operational support for the agency.

The Information Services Section is responsible for maintaining information technology systems and infrastructure for the agency. It provides operational support for all other areas of the agency. In addition, it provides data and research support to ensure programs are effective and efficient and the agency is engaged with best practices.

Housing Finance Division

Address: 725 Summer St. NE, Suite B, Salem 97301-1266
Phone: 503-986-2000
Fax: 503-986-2020
Email: housinginfo@oregon.gov
Web: www.oregon.gov/OHCS/Pages/index.aspx

Contact: Julie Cody, Assistant Director
Statutory Authority: ORS 446.525–446.543, 456.515–456.723, 458.210–458.310, 458.600–458.650, 458.655–458.665
Duties and Responsibilities: The Housing Finance Division administers federal and state funded multifamily rental housing resources to facilitate the increased availability of safe, decent, affordable housing for Oregonians with low incomes. This includes the development of new multifamily units and the acquisition and rehabilitation of existing multifamily units, the support of homeownership for low- and moderate-income Oregonians through single family programs, the long term maintenance of affordable multifamily housing through asset management and compliance, debt management, and foreclosure assistance under the Oregon Homeownership Stabilization Initiative.

Housing Stabilization Division

Address: 725 Summer St. NE, Suite B, Salem 97301-1266
Phone: 503-986-2000
Fax: 503-986-2020
Email: housinginfo@oregon.gov
Web: www.oregon.gov/OHCS/Pages/index.aspx
Contact: Claire Seguin, Assistant Director
Statutory Authority: ORS 456.587, 458.505–458.530, 458.600–458.650
Duties and Responsibilities: The Housing Stabilization Division administers services for Oregonians with low and extremely low incomes to help stabilize their housing as well as achieve greater economic stability. Services include work to prevent and end homelessness, emergency rental assistance, energy bill payment assistance and weatherization assistance as well as other anti-poverty programs such as the Individual Development Accounts.

The division ensures that affordable housing projects across Oregon maintain compliance with state and federal regulations and are safe and healthy properties for the residents. The division's responsibilities also include contract administration on behalf of the U.S. Department of Housing and Urban Development, and human resources and facilities functions.

Public Affairs Division

Address: 725 Summer St. NE, Suite B, Salem 97301-1266
Phone: 503-986-0951; 503-986-0990, Assistant Director
Fax: 503-986-2020
Email: housinginfo@oregon.gov
Web: www.oregon.gov/OHCS/Pages/index.aspx
Contact: Rem Nivens, Assistant Director
Statutory Authority: ORS 456.555

Duties and Responsibilities: OHCS's Public Affairs Division includes Federal Planning, Housing Integrators (formerly known as Regional Advisors to the Department) and Government Relations and Communications. Public Affairs is the primary division that engages with the public, stakeholders, elected officials and the media.

HUMAN SERVICES, DEPARTMENT OF

Address: 500 Summer St. NE, Salem 97301
Phone: 503-945-5944
Fax: 503-581-6198
Email: communications.dhs@state.or.us
Web: www.oregon.gov/DHS/Pages/index.aspx
Contact: Clyde Saiki, Director
Statutory Authority: ORS 409.010
Duties and Responsibilities: The Department of Human Services (DHS) Director's Office is responsible for overall leadership, policy development and administrative oversight for all programs, staff and offices in DHS. These functions are coordinated by the chief of staff with the Office of the Governor, the Legislature, other state and federal agencies, partners and stakeholders, communities of color, local governments, advocacy and client groups and the private sector.

Key functions include Federal Financial Policy, Governor's Advocacy, Legislative Relations, Media and Communications, Legal Affairs, Rules Coordination, Tribal Relations, Community Engagement, Equity and Multicultural Services, Information Technology, the Office of the Chief Financial Officer, Finance and Human Services. The Director's Office includes the deputy director, who is responsible for Shared Services, Internal Audits, Business Intelligence, Licensing and Regulatory Oversight, Continuous Improvement, Business Supports, Adult Abuse Prevention and Investigations and Program Integrity.

The mission of DHS is to help Oregonians in their own communities achieve safety, well-being and independence through opportunities that protect, empower, respect choice and preserve dignity. DHS believes that every Oregon child and youth in its care deserves to grow up safely—with support for success in school; every Oregon adult deserves to live in safety—free from abuse, neglect and financial exploitation; every Oregonian has the right to live as independently as possible—with dignity, choice and self-determination; and every Oregonian can work to the best of their abilities to contribute to their family and their community.

Governor's Advocacy Office

Address: 500 Summer St. NE, E02, Salem 97301
Phone: 503-945-5665
Fax: 503-945-6904
Contact: Zachary Gehringer, Administrator
Duties and Responsibilities: The Governor's Advocacy Office handles client complaints related to DHS services. This office operates independently in the investigations performed and reports directly to the governor by providing a quarterly report on the status of the complaints. The team in this office works closely with field and central office staff, program staff, the Office of the Governor, key stakeholders and the DHS Director's Office to successfully, equitably and respectfully reach a conclusion.

Aging and People with Disabilities Programs

Address: 500 Summer St. NE, E02, Salem 97301
Phone: 503-947-1100
Fax: 503-373-7823
Contact: Ashley Carson-Cottingham, Director
Duties and Responsibilities: The DHS Aging and People with Disabilities (APD) programs assist a diverse population of older adults and people with disabilities to achieve well-being through opportunities for community living, employment, family support and long-term services that promote independence, choice and dignity. The program's goals are to ensure the safety and protection of the population whom APD serves, with a focus on prevention; facilitate awareness of and easy access to services; serve people in an equitable and culturally sensitive manner; promote high quality services by APD, its local partners and providers; and increase advocacy efforts to improve outcomes for APD consumers.

During the 2017–2019 biennium, APD expects to serve over 5,000 people age 60 and older through Oregon Project Independence; over 36,000 older adults and people with physical disabilities per month with long-term care services paid through Medicaid; over 450,000 older individuals with Older Americans Act services; and over 150,000 Oregonians with direct financial support services.

Oregonians needing information about these programs may contact the Aging and Disability Resource Connection (ADRC) of Oregon. The ADRC is a collaborative public-private partnership that streamlines consumer access to the aging and disability service delivery system. The ADRC is free to Oregonians and provides information and assistance that empowers people to make informed decisions. Through trained options counselors, Oregonians can develop action plans to address long-term service and support needs that align with their preferences, financial situations, values and needs. During the last biennium, the ADRC received over 18,000 calls and 164,000 website inquiries. Employees from both APD local offices and Area Agencies on Aging throughout Oregon are responsible for providing direct client services and for determining eligibility of the aging and people with disabilities for medical programs provided through the Oregon Health Authority.

APD is impacted by demographic growth in the older adult population and is serving an increasingly diverse population. APD strives to identify disparities in outcomes for diverse populations and identify strategies to serve individuals in a culturally and linguistically appropriate manner.

Deaf and Hard of Hearing Services Program

Address: 500 Summer St. NE, E16, Salem 97301
Phone: 503-947-1189; Toll-free: 1-800-521-9615
Fax: 503-947-5184
Contact: Jeff Puterbaugh
Statutory Authority: ORS 185.230

Medicaid Long-Term Care Quality and Reimbursement Advisory Council

Address: 500 Summer St. NE, E02, Salem 97301
Phone: 503-930-7293
Fax: 503-373-7823
Contact: Ann McQueen
Statutory Authority: ORS 410.500

Governor's Commission on Senior Services

Address: 500 Summer St. NE, E02, Salem 97301
Phone: 503-945-6993
Fax: 503-373-7823
Contact: Max Brown
Statutory Authority: ORS 410.320

Child Welfare Programs

Address: 500 Summer St. NE, E48, Salem 97301
Phone: 503-945-5600
Fax: 503-581-6198
Web: www.oregon.gov/DHS/Pages/index.aspx
Contact: Lena Alhusseini, Director
Duties and Responsibilities: DHS Child Welfare Programs help improve family capacity to provide safe and permanent living environments for foster children of all ages. The programs' goals are to achieve safe and equitable reductions in the number of children experiencing foster care. This is accomplished by protecting children from abuse and neglect and safely maintaining them in their homes whenever possible and appropriate; finding safe, permanent, stable homes for children when needed; ensuring children in foster care are well cared for, remain connected to family, siblings and support networks and receive appropriate services; providing culturally appropriate and equitable treatment for all children served; and practicing quality assurance and improvement for defining, measuring and improving outcomes for children and families.

Child Welfare Programs serve children and families when children are subject to abuse and neglect. Child protection workers respond to all reports of child abuse and neglect. If a child cannot be safe at home, a foster care placement is made. Child Welfare has a renewed focus and energy around keeping children safe and reducing its foster care population by implementing a system that prevents out-of-home placements and increases a timely and safe return to families.

The program areas within Child Welfare are Child Safety, Well-Being, Permanency, Program Design and Delivery and Federal Program Performance and Reporting

In federal fiscal year 2015, 11,238 children spent at least one day in foster care, 69,972 reports of abuse and neglect were received, 32,682 reports were referred for investigation and 6,708 reports found abuse or neglect involving 10,402 victims. Of these, 46.6 percent of the victims were younger than six years old.

Child Welfare Advisory Committee

Address: 500 Summer St. NE, E62, Salem 97301
Phone: 503-945-6653
Fax: 503-945-6969
Contact: Gina Scott
Statutory Authority: ORS 418.005

Family Services Review Commission

Address: 500 Summer St. NE, E48, Salem 97301
Phone: 503-947-6071
Fax: 503-373-7032
Contact: Kim Fredlund, Self-Sufficiency Programs Director
Statutory Authority: ORS 411.075

Independent Living Council

Address: 500 Summer St. NE, E87, Salem 97301
Phone: 503-945-6204
Fax: 503-945-8991
Contact: Shelly Emery
Statutory Authority: Exec. Order No. 94-12

Refugee Child Welfare Advisory

Address: 500 Summer St. NE, E48, Salem 97301
Phone: 503-945-6739
Fax: 503-373-7032

Contact: Oscar Herrera
Statutory Authority: ORS 418.941

State of Oregon Rehabilitation Council

Address: 500 Summer St. NE, E87, Salem 97301
Phone: 503-945-6256; Toll-free: 1-877-277-0513
Fax: 503-945-8991
Contact: Rhonda Hunter
Statutory Authority: ORS 344.735

Developmental Disabilities Programs

Address: 500 Summer St. NE, E02, Salem 97301
Phone: 503-945-6918; Toll-free:1-800-282-8096
Fax: 503-373-7823
Contact: Lilia Teninty, Director
Duties and Responsibilities: The DHS Intellectual and Developmental Disabilities (I/DD) Services program provides support across the lifespan to Oregonians. Its mission is to help individuals be fully engaged in life and, at the same time, address critical health and safety needs. The I/DD program strives to support individuals with intellectual and developmental disabilities and their families by promoting and providing services that are person-centered, self-directed, flexible, community inclusive, culturally appropriate, and supportive of the discovery and development of each individual's unique gifts, talents and abilities. This gives people with disabilities the opportunity to have fulfilling and meaningful lives and contribute to and enjoy their communities.

As a result of the state's adoption of the Community First Choice Option, an increased number of children and adults with I/DD are able to access Medicaid-funded, community-based services to meet their needs, instead of having to meet crisis eligibility in order to access the appropriate level of support.

DHS I/DD programs are committed to providing an array of options that are properly distributed to ensure access through equitable and culturally competent services; being responsive to emerging consumer demands for individualized, self-directed services; ensuring the health and safety of individuals served; promoting maximum independence and engagement in homes and communities; and leveraging the use of available federal funding options.

Individuals eligible for services must have an intellectual or developmental disability that significantly impedes their ability to function independently. Intellectual and developmental disabilities include cerebral palsy, Down syndrome, autism and other neurological conditions originating in the brain that occur during childhood. These disabilities are expected to be lifelong in their effect and have a signficant impact on the person's ability to function independently. Some people with I/DD may also have significant medical or mental health needs. Most individuals with I/DD meet Medicaid financial eligibility requirements. The majority of I/DD program services are now administered under the Medicaid State Plan Community First Choice Option. Case management and employment services are available through traditional, home and community-based service waivers.

Oregon Disabilities Commission

Address: 500 Summer St. NE, Salem 97301
Phone: 503-945-6993
Fax: 503-373-7823
Contact: Max Brown, Administrative Support
Statutory Authority: ORS 185.130
Duties and Responsibilities: Initially formed in 1983 and re-formed in 2005 after a brief hiatus, the Oregon Disabilities Commission (ODC) is a governor-appointed commission within DHS. The commission is composed of 15 members broadly representative of major public and private agencies who are experienced in, or have demonstrated particular interest in, the needs of individuals with disabilities. A majority of the members are individuals with disabilities. The ODC acts as a coordinating link between and among public and private organizations serving individuals with disabilities.

The mission of ODC is to secure economic, social, legal and political justice for individuals with disabilities through systems change. To carry this out, the commission identifies and hears the concerns of individuals with disabilities and uses the information to prioritize public policy issues which should be addressed; publicizes the needs and concerns of individuals with disabilities as they relate to the full achievement of economic, social, legal and political equity; and educates and advises the DHS, governor, Legislature and appropriate state agency administrators on how public policy can be improved to meet the needs of individuals with disabilities.

Self-Sufficiency Programs

Address: 500 Summer St. NE, E48, Salem 97301
Phone: 503-945-5600
Fax: 503-373-7032
Contact: Kim Fredlund, Director
Duties and Responsibilities: The mission of Self-Sufficiency Programs (SSP) is to meet the emotional and material needs of program participants and ensure that every family has an educational or career pathway to economic security. SSP is designed to provide low-income Oregonians with

services to create stability and prepare participants for employment so they are equipped to work their way out of poverty. The programs emphasize the safety and healthy development of children and often serve to prevent abuse or neglect that may lead to out-of-home placement in the more expensive foster care program. Oregonians access SSP services when they are in need and have no other alternatives. Participants access services through a network of local offices in every county.

SSP works to achieve its mission by focusing on four foundational operating principles: family engagement, economic stability, collective impact, and integrity and stewardship. The services offered through SSP are Employment Related Day Care, Supplemental Nutritional Assistance Program, Temporary Assistance for Needy Families (TANF), TANF-related programs such as the Job Opportunity and Basic Skills program and Family Support and Connections, Temporary Assistance for Domestic Violence Survivors, Refugee Program, Youth Services Program and Program Design and Delivery.

Challenges from the Great Recession linger, and SSP caseloads continue to be significantly higher than they were prior to the recession. Many SSP participants are working but have lower wages or fewer hours than they did prior to the recession and don't earn enough to make ends meet on their own. There continues to be an uneven distribution of poverty based on factors such as geography, race, ethnicity and age. In Oregon, poverty rates in rural counties tend to be higher than urban areas.

Vocational Rehabilitation Services, Office of

Address: 500 Summer St. NE, E87, Salem 97301
Phone: 503-945-5880
Fax: 503-947-5025
Contact: Trina Lee, Director
Statutory Authority: ORS 344.510–344.630
Duties and Responsibilities: The mission of the Office of Vocational Rehabilitation Services (VR) is to assist Oregonians with disabilities to achieve and maintain employment and independence. VR provides a variety of services, such as helping youth with disabilities transition to jobs as they become adults, helping employers realize the benefit of employing people with disabilities and partnering with other state and local organizations that coordinate employment and workforce programs. A total of 316,222 working-age Oregonians experience a disability, but only 36 percent are employed. Employment helps people with disabilities progress towards self-sufficiency, become involved in their communities and live more engaged and satisfying lives.

All working-age Oregonians who experience a disability and are legally entitled to work are potentially eligible for VR services. Individuals who experience a medical, cognitive or psychiatric diagnosis that results in a functional impediment to employment are typically eligible for services. Approximately 95 percent of all eligible clients currently served by VR are people with significant disabilities. These individuals experience multiple functional impediments requiring several services provided over an extended period of time. VR has counselors with expertise in the areas of intellectual and developmental disabilities (I/DD), deafness and hearing impairments, mental health, motivational intervention, spinal injury and traumatic brain injury.

VR services are provided by rehabilitation counselors and support staff who deliver direct client services through 34 field offices and multiple, single-employee, stations in WorkSource Oregon Centers and other human services agencies across the state. As the demographics in Oregon are changing, VR is adapting in order to provide culturally-specific services to Oregonians and help diversify the state's workforce.

In federal fiscal year 2015, VR helped 15,378 individuals and obtained 2,723 employment outcomes, including 454 individuals with (I/DD) and 262 with psychiatric disabilities who obtained jobs. Of those 454 individuals with I/DD, 239 are maintaining their jobs through supported employment services. In addition, VR contracts with 39 school districts and consortia on behalf of 115 schools to provide services for approximately 1,300 students each year.

Other Group:

Oregon Council on Developmental Disabilities

Address: 540 24th St. NE, Salem 97301
Phone: 503-881-9529
Fax: 503-945-9947
Contact: Jaime Daignault, Executive Director
Statutory Authority: 42 USC 15001
Duties and Responsibilities: The Oregon Council on Developmental Disabilities is made up of self-advocates, family members, representatives of advocacy organizations and community organizations that provide services and supports to people with developmental disabilities. Counsel members also include representatives of state agencies that receive federal funding on behalf of people with developmental disabilities, and are appointed by the governor to serve up to two consecutive four-year terms.

Council members work together to determine goals and objectives in the five-year state plan, allocate funds to state plan activities and review the council's progress annually. The council is supported by seven full-time staff who are charged with implementing the state plan.

The council's mission is to advance social and policy change so people with developmental disabilities, their families and communities may live, work, play and learn together. The council's vision is that all communities welcome and value people with disabilities and their families.

LAND CONSERVATION AND DEVELOPMENT, DEPARTMENT OF

Address: 635 Capitol St. NE, Suite 150, Salem 97301-2540
Phone: 503-373-0050
Fax: 503-378-5518
Web: www.oregon.gov/LCD/Pages/index.aspx
Contact: Jim Rue, Director
Statutory Authority: ORS Chapters 92, 195, 196, 197, 215, 222, 227, 268, 308
Duties and Responsibilities: The Department of Land Conservation and Development (DLCD) is a small state agency with a broad mission. With about 55 permanent staff, the department is responsible for making Oregon's statewide land use program work for communities in all parts of the state. DLCD does this through partnerships with cities and counties, state development agencies (Transportation and Business Oregon) and natural resource agencies (Agriculture, Forestry, Water Resources, State Lands, Environmental Quality and Fish and Wildlife) as well as citizens. The department is guided in policy development by the Land Conservation and Development Commission (LCDC) whose members are appointed by the governor. In addition, the Director's Office provides overall management and policy direction.

Community Services Division

Address: 635 Capitol St. NE, Suite 150, Salem 97301-2540 (Regional Offices in Bend, Eugene, La Grande, Medford and Portland)
Phone: 503-934-0018
Fax: 503-378-5518
Web: www.oregon.gov/LCD/Pages/commserv. aspx
Contact: Rob Hallyburton, Manager
Duties and Responsibilities: The Community Services Division, formed in 2003, administers grant programs for local governments and provides technical land use planning assistance from several regional offices and Salem to local government planners and officials, the general public and interest groups. The division reviews local comprehensive plan amendments and provides expertise on a wide range of subjects related to city and county comprehensive plans. Staff in this division includes regional representatives around

the state as well as urban, rural and economic development specialists.

Grants Advisory Committee

Address: 635 Capitol St. NE, Suite 150, Salem 97301-2540
Phone: 503-934-0018
Contact: Rob Hallyburton
Statutory Authority: ORS 197.639
Duties and Responsibilities: The Grants Advisory Committee is appointed by the Land Conservation and Development Commission. It advises the commission and the department on the allocation of grants and technical assistance funding from General Fund sources and other issues assigned by the commission.

Ocean and Coastal Services Division

Address: 635 Capitol St. NE, Suite 150, Salem 97301-2540 (Offices in Newport, Tillamook and Portland)
Phone: 503-373-0050
Fax: 503-378-6033
Web: www.oregon.gov/LCD/OCMP/Pages/ index.aspx
Contact: Patty Snow, Manager
Duties and Responsibilities: The Ocean and Coastal Services Division, created in 1976, oversees Oregon's federally designated coastal program providing grants and technical assistance to coastal communities. The division provides assistance related to four statewide coastal planning goals and to coastal hazards. The division also oversees development of Oregon's Territorial Sea Plan in cooperation with other agencies and conducts federal consistency reviews for federal projects and permits proposed in the Oregon coastal zone.

Planning Services Division

Address: 635 Capitol St. NE, Suite 150, Salem 97301-2540
Phone: 503-373-0050
Fax: 503-378-5518
Web: www.oregon.gov/LCD/Pages/planserv. aspx
Contact: Matt Crall, Manager
Duties and Responsibilities: The Planning Services Division contains specialized planning programs, including the Transportation and Growth Management Program, Floodplain Management and Natural Hazards Planning, Measure 49 Services and the Oregon Sustainable Transportation Initiative.

Other Groups:

Citizen Involvement Advisory Committee

Address: 635 Capitol St. NE, Suite 150, Salem 97301-2540
Phone: 503-373-0050
Contact: Sadie Carney
Statutory Authority: ORS 197.160
Duties and Responsibilities: ORS 197 established the state's Citizen Involvement Advisory Committee (CIAC) to advise LCDC and local governments on matters pertaining to citizen involvement. CIAC is an advisory body with no explicit or implied authority over any local government or state agency. The CIAC has eight volunteer members, including one from each of Oregon's five congressional districts and three chosen at-large. Committee members are appointed to four-year terms by LCDC.

Local Officials Advisory Committee

Address: 635 Capitol St. NE, Suite 150, Salem 97301-2540
Phone: 503-373-0050
Contact: Amie Abbott
Statutory Authority: ORS 197.165
Duties and Responsibilities: LCDC appoints the Local Officials Advisory Committee (LOAC) for the purpose of promoting mutual understanding and cooperation between LCDC, DLCD and local governments in implementing and improving the statewide land use planning system. LOAC is comprised of persons serving as city or county elected officials and its membership reflects the city, county and geographic diversity of the state.

LAND USE BOARD OF APPEALS

Address: 775 Summer St. NE, Suite 330, Salem 97301-1283
Phone: 503-373-1265
Web: www.oregon.gov/LUBA/Pages/index.aspx
Contact: Michael A. Holstun, Board Chair
Statutory Authority: ORS 197.810
Duties and Responsibilities: In 1979, the Oregon Legislature created the Land Use Board of Appeals (LUBA) as an agency with exclusive jurisdiction to review appeals of land use decisions made by cities, counties, districts and state agencies. Prior to LUBA's creation, appeals of land use decisions were heard in 36 different county circuit courts, and sometimes before the Land Conservation and Development Commission. In creating LUBA, the Legislature intended to provide a simpler and faster process for resolving land use disputes and also to promote a consistent interpretation of state and local land use laws. LUBA's decisions are reviewable by appeal to the Court of Appeals. LUBA's secondary mission is to publish its orders and opinions which citizens, decision-makers and participants in land use processes can use to guide future land use decision-making.

LUBA is the first tribunal of its kind in the United States. The governor appoints the three-member board to serve four-year terms, subject to confirmation by the Oregon Senate. Each board member must be a member of the Oregon State Bar. The board is assisted by two administrative staff and a staff attorney.

LANDSCAPE ARCHITECT BOARD, STATE

Address: 707 13th St. SE, Suite 114, Salem 97301
Phone: 503-589-0093
Fax: 503-485-2947
Email: oslab.info@state.or.us
Web: www.oregon.gov/LANDARCH/Pages/index.aspx
Contact: Christine Valentine, Administrator
Statutory Authority: ORS 671.459
Duties and Responsibilities: Since 1981, the State Landscape Architect Board has been charged with safeguarding Oregonians through the regulation of landscape architecture practice in the state. The board reviews complaints related to registrant practice and unlicensed practice and sets examination, education and experience standards for landscape architect licensure. Landscape architects licensed in other states or jurisdictions can apply for registration in Oregon but must meet all of the board's standards. More than 490 landscape architects are registered to practice in Oregon. Firms that provide landscape architectural services must also be registered.

The board is composed of four Oregon registered landscape architects and three public members and is served by two staff filling the roles of executive director and registration specialist.

Landscape architects design, manage and protect the natural and built environment through the application of science and design expertise. They address various project components such as plantings, irrigation systems, site lighting, grading, drainage and erosion control, and settings for structures, roadways, walkways and similar features. Landscape architects work on a wide array of private and public projects with goals to keep the public safe from hazards, protect and maximize natural resources and prevent damage to property due to changes in the built environment.

LANDSCAPE CONTRACTORS BOARD, STATE

Address: 2111 Front St. NE, Suite 2-101, Salem 97301
Phone: 503-967-6291
Fax: 503-967-6298
Email: lcbinfo@lcb.state.or.us
Web: www.oregon.gov/lcb
Contact: Elizabeth Boxall, Administrator
Statutory Authority: ORS 671.510–671.760
Duties and Responsibilities: The State Landscape Contractors Board (LCB) was created in 1972, became semi-independent in 2002 and is responsible for regulating landscape construction work in Oregon. The agency is overseen by a board of seven individuals, appointed by the governor, who serve a maximum of six years. Five of the seven members are from the landscaping industry and two represent the general public.

The LCB promotes consumer protection and contractor competency in the Oregon landscape contracting industry through five major program areas: Examinations, Licensing, Enforcement, Claims/Dispute Resolution and Education. As of June 30, 2015, there were 4.5 full-time employees overseeing the five programs of the agency and administering over 2,500 licensees, including both business and individual licenses.

LIBRARY, STATE

Address: 250 Winter St. NE, Salem 97301-3950
Phone: 503-378-4243
Fax: 503-585-8059
Web: www.oregon.gov/OSL/Pages/index.aspx
Contact: MaryKay Dahlgreen, State Librarian
Statutory Authority: ORS Chapter 357
Duties and Responsibilities: The Oregon State Library (OSL) is responsible for providing quality information services to state government, quality library services to blind and print-disabled Oregonians, and leadership, grants and other assistance to improve library service for all Oregonians. It was established as the Oregon Library Commission in 1905, becoming the Oregon State Library in 1913. Since its founding, the library has been governed by an independent board of trustees. The present board consists of nine members from throughout the state who are appointed by the governor.

OSL has occupied the State Library building on the Capitol Mall since 1939. The library staff of about 40 is organized into an operations division and three program divisions.

The Government Information and Library Services Division provides research and reference assistance to state government and to persons on official state business. Specialized collections include federal and state government publications and a comprehensive collection of materials about Oregon. The library also provides public access to Oregon state government documents.

The Library Support and Development Services Division includes planning for statewide library development, providing equal access to information resources for K–12 students through the Oregon School Library Information System, collecting and reporting library statistics and administering state and federal library grant programs. Current priorities are improving early literacy services to children in public libraries and facilitating access to library services for all Oregonians.

The Oregon Talking Book and Braille Library is the Oregon Regional Library for the Library of Congress' National Library Service for the blind and physically handicapped. Oregonians who are unable to read standard print because of a visual or physical disability are eligible for free library services. Books and magazines are available in audio format and in Braille.

LIQUOR CONTROL COMMISSION, OREGON

Address: 9079 SE McLoughlin Blvd., Portland 97222-7355
Phone: 503-872-5000; Toll-free: 1-800-452-6522
Fax: 503-872-5266
Web: www.oregon.gov/OLCC/Pages/index.aspx
Contact: Steve Marks, Executive Director
Statutory Authority: ORS Chapters 471, 472, 473, 475B
Duties and Responsibilities: The Oregon Liquor Control Commission (OLCC) supports businesses, public safety and community livability through education and the enforcement of liquor and marijuana laws. OLCC places emphasis on addressing alcohol and marijuana sales to minors and visibly intoxicated people.

OLCC was created in 1933 by a special legislative session after national prohibition ended. The agency advocates responsible alcohol consumption by managing and distributing distilled spirits, licensing and regulating businesses that sell and serve alcohol and training and issuing permits for alcohol servers. In 2014, the agency took on added responsibilities of licensing, regulating and tracking Oregon's new recreational marijuana industry, as well as issuing marijuana worker permits. The OLCC is also responsible for administering Oregon's Bottle Bill.

Five citizen commissioners set policy for the OLCC. The agency also relies on advisory committees, government officials and citizens to guide its decision-making. The agency employs 263 people and is headquartered in Portland. There are regional OLCC offices in Bend, Eugene, Medford and Salem, as well as numerous satellite offices throughout the state.

LONG-TERM CARE OMBUDSMAN, OFFICE OF THE

Address: 3855 Wolverine St. NE, Suite 6, Salem 97305-1251
Phone: 503-378-6533; Toll-free: 1-800-522-2602; TTY: 711
Fax: 503-373-0852
Email: ltco.contact@ltco.state.or.us
Web: www.oregon.gov/ltco/pages/index.aspx
Contact: Fred Steele, Ombudsman
Statutory Authority: ORS 441.402–441.419
Duties and Responsibilities: The Office of the Long Term Care Ombudsman has operated for 30 years with the mission to enhance the quality of life, improve the level of care, protect individual rights and promote the dignity of each Oregon citizen who is residing in a long-term care facility such as a nursing home, residential care facility, assisted living facility or adult foster home. In the last several years, this mission has expanded to include programs for individuals with intellectual/developmental disabilities and mental health concerns living in licensed care settings such as residential treatment facilities, 24-hour group homes and foster care homes.

The agency identifies, investigates and resolves complaints on behalf of residents using a network of trained and certified volunteer ombudsmen. In addition, it monitors the complex long-term and residential care systems which, in addition to facilities, include a number of state and local agencies. The ombudsman makes recommendations to the Legislature and the governor on long-term and residential care issues. The agency establishes productive relationships with senior organizations, disability and mental health organizations, advocacy groups and cooperative associations that impact the lives of long-term and residential care residents.

The agency's recent expansion also includes the addition of the Oregon Public Guardian (OPG) program, which serves as a court appointed, surrogate decision maker for adults incapable of making some or most decisions about themselves and their affairs and who have no one else to serve as a guardian or conservator. Those in need of OPG's services include persons with age-related neurocognitive issues, persons with serious and persistent mental health issues and persons with intellectual/developmental disabilities.

LOTTERY, OREGON STATE

Address: PO Box 12649, Salem 97309
Phone: 503-540-1000; TTY: 503-540-1068
Fax: 503-540-1168
Email: lottery.webcenter@state.or.us
Web: www.oregonlottery.org
Contact: Barry Pack, Director
Statutory Authority: ORS Chapter 461
Duties and Responsibilities: As a result of two voter initiatives, Oregonians created the Oregon State Lottery in 1984. The lottery's mission, "Operate a lottery with the highest standards of security and integrity to earn maximum profits for the people of Oregon commensurate with the public good," directs the efforts of the over 400 statewide lottery employees. Oregon's lottery is both a public trust and a market-driven business. Lottery revenues—over $1 billion a year since 2006—result in transfers to the state to help fund public endeavors.

ORS 461.500 provides that at least 84 percent of total annual revenues be returned to the public, with at least 50 percent being returned as prizes and the remainder used for designated public purposes. The remaining 16 percent of annual revenues are available for the payment of administrative expenses. Lottery administrative expenses are currently at just under 4 percent of revenue, which makes the agency entirely self-funded, with no tax money contributed to its operation, programming or development.

Since it began selling tickets in 1985, the Oregon State Lottery has grown to become the second largest revenue producer for the state, following income tax revenues, and continues to do good things for Oregon. Since 1985, the lottery has transferred nearly $10 billion to help support public education, economic development, state parks and watershed enhancement. It has also paid players over $30 billion in prizes and provided over $80 million for problem gambling treatment and awareness.

MARINE BOARD, STATE

Address: PO Box 14145, Salem 97309-5065
Phone: 503-378-8587
Fax: 503-378-4597
Email: marine.board@state.or.us
Web: www.oregon.gov/OSMB/Pages/index.aspx
Contact: Scott Brewen, Director
Statutory Authority: ORS Chapter 830
Duties and Responsibilities: The State Marine Board was established in 1959 by the Legislature in response to the federal Boating Safety Act of 1958. The agency's mission is to serve Oregon's recreational boating public through education, enforcement, access and environmental stewardship for a safe and enjoyable experience. The agency is governed by a volunteer, five-member board, who serve at the pleasure of the governor.

The board adopts boating regulations to promote safety, reduce conflict, preserve traditional boat uses and protect the environment. The agency has 40 staff and four primary program areas: Boating

Safety, Policy and Environmental, Registration and Boating Facilities.

The agency is responsible for titling and registering motorboats, registering guides/outfitters and licensing charter boats. The agency contracts with county sheriff's offices and the Oregon State Police to enforce boating laws on state waters. The agency also provides grants and engineering services to governments (cities, counties, park districts, port districts, state and federal) to develop and maintain boat ramps, parking, restrooms and temporary moorage facilities.

The agency encourages safe and sustainable boating through its Boating Safety Education, Aquatic Invasive Species Prevention, Clean Marina and Clean Boater programs. Additionally, the agency collaborates on statewide issues with boaters who serve on Boat Oregon Advisory Teams. The teams meet regularly to evaluate boating issues and discuss ways the agency can improve its operations to better serve Oregon's recreational boaters.

MASSAGE THERAPISTS, STATE BOARD OF

Address: 728 Hawthorne Ave. NE, Salem 97301
Phone: 503-365-8657
Fax: 503-385-4465
Email: OBMT.info@state.or.us
Web: www.oregon.gov/OBMT/Pages/index.aspx
Contact: Kate Coffey, Executive Director
Statutory Authority: ORS 687.011–687.991
Duties and Responsibilities: The functions of the State Board of Massage Therapists date back to 1951 when the Legislature adopted a comprehensive bill for the Oregon State Board of Examiners, which was empowered to regulate conduct for massage establishments, issue licenses, refuse, revoke or suspend licenses and establish requirements for massage schools. The laws for massage therapy have been modified over the years. In 1975, Senate Bill 390 passed and the administration for licensing massage therapists changed to the State Board of Massage Therapists. The mission of the board is to protect the public by regulating and monitoring the practice of massage therapy in Oregon.

MEDICAL BOARD, OREGON

Address: 1500 SW 1st Ave., #620, Portland 97201-5847
Phone: 971-673-2700
Fax: 971-673-2670
Email: omb.info@state.or.us
Web: www.oregon.gov/OMB/Pages/index.aspx
Contact: Kathleen Haley, Executive Director
Statutory Authority: ORS Chapter 677

Duties and Responsibilities: The Oregon Medical Board has been protecting Oregon citizens through the regulation of the practice of medicine since 1889. The agency now licenses and regulates Medical Doctors (MD), Doctors of Osteopathic Medicine (DO), Doctors of Podiatric Medicine (DPM), Physician Assistants (PA) and Acupuncturists (LAc).

The 13-member board is composed of physicians, a physician assistant and two members of the public. The board sets qualifications for licensure and grants licenses to applicants who meet those requirements. It investigates complaints and disciplines licensees who violate state law (the Medical Practice Act). The board also supports rehabilitation and education for licensees in an effort to promote access to quality care for all Oregonians.

The board oversees more than 21,000 licensees. It is located in Portland and is staffed with nearly 40 employees.

MEDICAL IMAGING, BOARD OF

Address: 800 NE Oregon St., Suite 1160A, Portland 97232
Phone: 971-673-0215
Fax: 971-673-0218
Email: OBMI.Info@state.or.us
Web: www.oregon.gov/OBMI/Pages/index.aspx
Contact: Ed Conlow, Executive Director
Statutory Authority: ORS 688.405–688.605, 688.915

Duties and Responsibilities: The Board of Medical Imaging (OBMI), created by legislation in 1977, currently licenses and oversees over 5,000 medical imaging technologists who are qualified to practice radiography, radiation therapy, sonography, nuclear medicine and magnetic resonance imaging (MRI). In addition, the OBMI oversees the educational requirements and issues permits for 600 limited x-ray machine operators. Licensure assures that imaging technologists are properly educated and trained. In turn, Oregon consumers of health care services can be confident that diagnostic and therapeutic imaging procedures are conducted as accurately and safely as possible. Accurate imaging procedures improve patient safety and help contain health costs by aiding in the prevention of health problems through effective diagnosis and treatment. Members of the board are appointed by the governor and confirmed by the Senate for three-year terms. There are twelve board members, including four physicians, three public members and five medical imaging licensees who represent each of the five medical imaging modalities. The board has three employees and is located at the Portland State Office Building.

Military Department, Oregon

Address: 1776 Militia Way SE, PO Box 14350, Salem 97309-5047
Phone: 503-584-3980; Toll-Free: 1-800-452-7500
Web: www.oregon.gov/OMD/Pages/index.aspx
Contact: Major General Michael E. Stencel, Adjutant General
Statutory Authority: ORS 396.305
Duties and Responsibilities: The Oregon Military Department was the first state agency created in Oregon. It administers, equips and trains the Oregon Army and Air National Guard. During peacetime and for natural disasters, the department responds to the governor in support of the citizens of Oregon. During wartime, the Oregon Army and Air National Guard can be federalized in support of national missions as directed by the U.S. president. The department administers 39 readiness centers/armories, seven maintenance centers, four training sites, two Army Aviation Support Facilities and two Air National Guard bases. Each community with sufficient population to support Guard activities has a National Guard unit assigned to it. In addition, the department oversees the Oregon Office of Emergency Management.

The National Guard is found in both the United States and Oregon Constitutions. Its tradition and history are grounded in its mission statement: "A ready force equipped and trained to respond to any contingency. When we are needed, we are there."

Command Group

Address: PO Box 14350, Salem 97309-5047
Phone: 503-584-3991
Fax: 503-584-3987
Email: tagor@mil.state.or.us
Contact: Major General Michael E. Stencel, Adjutant General
Duties and Responsibilities: The Command Group consists of the adjutant general; Joint Force Headquarters, including the assistant adjutants general for support and operations; Land Component commander; Air Component commander; and the interagency director. The group administers all components of the Oregon National Guard in cooperation with the governor and state Legislature.

Installations Division

Address: PO Box 14350, Salem 97309-5047
Phone: 503-584-3914
Fax: 503-584-3584
Email: agi-s@mil.state.or.us
Contact: Roy Swafford, Director
Duties and Responsibilities: The Installations Division provides and maintains quality installa-

tions to support the missions of the Oregon Army National Guard.

The division supports the Oregon National Guard and the citizens of Oregon by providing facilities for localized and statewide emergencies and for training and housing soldiers and equipment, and by providing environmental support for tactical training and the execution of federal and state missions.

The division's rental program allows community groups and private parties to use armories on an as-available basis.

Public Affairs Office

Address: AGPA, PO Box 14350, Salem 97309-5047
Phone: 503-584-3917
Fax: 503-584-3912
Email: agpa@mil.state.or.us
Contact: Stephen Bomar, Director of Public Affairs
Duties and Responsibilities: The Public Affairs Office supports the adjutant general's communication plan. This includes community outreach, social media, print, video and graphic design efforts. Oregon's Military Department and National Guard bring more than $350 million in annual economic impact to the state.

In addition, strategic communications for internal audiences across the Army and Air National Guard and state personnel are as critical to the success of the organization as maintaining and building external stakeholder relationships.

Other Groups:
Emergency Management, Office of

Address: 3225 State St., Salem 97301;
PO Box 14370, Salem 97309-5062
Phone: 503-378-2911; TTY: 503-373-7857
Fax: 503-373-7833
Web: www.oregon.gov/OMD/OEM/Pages/index.aspx
Contact: Andrew Phelps, Director
Statutory Authority: ORS Chapter 401
Duties and Responsibilities: The Office of Emergency Management executes the governor's responsibilities to maintain an emergency services system to deal with emergencies or disasters that may present threats to the lives and property of Oregon's citizens. The agency coordinates and facilitates emergency planning, preparedness, response and recovery activities with state and local emergency service agencies and organizations.

Youth Challenge Program
Address: 23861 Dodds Rd., Bend 97701
Phone: 541-317-9623

Fax: 541-382-6785
Web: www.oycp.com
Contact: Dan Radabaugh, Director
Duties and Responsibilities: The Oregon National Guard Youth Challenge Program is a statewide accredited, public, alternative high school that serves 16 to 18-year-old high school dropouts. The program is guided by military principles, structure and discipline, and consists of two phases. During the residential phase, cadets (students) live on-site for five months and attend school, where they earn credits to return to high school and earn their GED or high school diploma. The post-residential phase is a mandatory 12-month mentoring period during which cadets work with mentors from their home towns.

MORTUARY AND CEMETERY BOARD, STATE

Address: 800 NE Oregon St., Suite 430, Portland 97232-2195
Phone: 971-673-1500
Fax: 971-673-1501
Email: mortuary.board@state.or.us
Web: www.oregon.gov/MortCem/Pages/index.aspx
Contact: Michelle Sigmund-Gaines, Executive Director
Statutory Authority: ORS 97.170, 97.931, 692.300, 692.415
Duties and Responsibilities: The State Mortuary and Cemetery Board was created June 6, 1921. The board's programs affect those who have suffered a loss, those who make final arrangements and those who provide death care goods and services. In order to protect the public, it is the board's responsibility to ensure that all of Oregon's death care facilities are properly licensed and to regulate the practice of individuals and facilities engaged in the care, preparation, processing, transportation and final disposition of human remains. Engaging in certain death care activities without a license is the only crime within the board's jurisdiction. Approximately 63,000 deaths will occur in Oregon during the 2015–2017 biennium. Death care services are provided by approximately 2,400 practitioners and facilities throughout the state. The board is self-supporting and derives its financing from licensing, examination and a portion of the death certificate filing fee (not the fees derived from the purchase of a certified copy of a death certificate). The board currently has six employees and one office located in Portland.

NATUROPATHIC MEDICINE, OREGON BOARD OF

Address: 800 NE Oregon St., Suite 407, Portland 97232
Phone: 971-673-0193
Fax: 971-673-0226
Email: obnm.info@state.or.us
Web: www.oregon.gov/obnm/Pages/index.aspx
Contact: Anne Walsh, Executive Director
Statutory Authority: ORS Chapter 685
Duties and Responsibilities: The Oregon Board of Naturopathic Medicine was established by the 1927 Legislature to protect consumers of naturopathic medicine by enforcing practice standards. The profession has grown from 200 in 1998 to over 1,100 in 2016. The board is staffed with 2.5 full-time equivalent positions to support the seven-member board that includes two public members and five licensed naturopathic physicians. The board carries out the provisions of its authority by conducting background checks, examining, issuing and renewing licenses, approving educational opportunities for licensees, investigating complaints and taking action when discipline is appropriate. The board is an Other Funds agency and derives its financing from licensing fees.

NORTHWEST POWER AND CONSERVATION COUNCIL

Address: 851 SW 6th Ave., Portland 97204-1347
Phone: 503-229-5171
Fax: 503-229-5173
Email: info@nwcouncil.org
Contact: Bill Bradbury, Henry Lorenzen, Oregon Council Members
Statutory Authority: ORS 469.805
Duties and Responsibilities: The Pacific Northwest Power and Conservation Council came into being with the passage of the Northwest Power Act of 1980. The Power Act established an interstate compact consisting of Oregon, Washington, Montana and Idaho, each state having two governor-appointed representatives. The council has two major planning functions under the Act: developing a fish and wildlife program to protect, mitigate and enhance fish and wildlife populations affected by the development of the federal Columbia River hydropower system, and the development of a 20-year regional power plan. The council updates these plans on a roughly five-year rotation. The council describes its mission as ensuring, through public participation, an affordable and reliable energy system while enhancing fish and wildlife in the Columbia River Basin. In addition to the eight council members, there is a

staff of approximately 50, mostly in Portland but also located in offices spread throughout the four states.

NURSING, OREGON STATE BOARD OF

Address: 17938 SW Upper Boones Ferry Rd., Portland 97224-7012
Phone: 971-673-0685
Fax: 971-673-0684
Email: oregon.bn.info@state.or.us
Web: www.oregon.gov/OSBN/Pages/index.aspx
Contact: Ruby R. Jason, MSN, RN, NEA-BC, Executive Director
Statutory Authority: ORS 678.010–678.445
Duties and Responsibilities: Since 1911, the Oregon State Board of Nursing (OSBN) has regulated nursing practice and education in protection of the public's health, safety and well-being. It oversees the licensure, certification, education and compliance of the approximately 80,000 registered nurses, licensed practical nurses, nursing assistants and advanced practice nurses in Oregon.

The nine OSBN board members are appointed by the governor and include a mix of public members and nursing professionals. They represent a variety of nursing practice settings and geographic locations. Board members serve three-year terms. The OSBN meets regularly throughout the year and may hold special meetings if necessary. The OSBN employs a staff of about 50 who provide customer service and assist the board in carrying out its mission.

OCCUPATIONAL THERAPY LICENSING BOARD

Address: 800 NE Oregon St., Suite 407, Portland 97232
Phone: 971-673-0198
Fax: 971-673-0226
Email: nancy.schuberg@state.or.us
Web: www.oregon.gov/otlb/Pages/index.aspx
Contact: Nancy Schuberg, Executive Director
Statutory Authority: ORS 675.210–675.340
Duties and Responsibilities: The Occupational Therapy Board was created in 1977 to regulate the practice of occupational therapy. The role of the board is to investigate complaints and take appropriate action, make and enforce laws and rules regarding occupational therapy practice, establish continuing education requirements, process applications and issue license and renewals, and collect fees and authorize disbursements of funds. The mission of the board is to protect the public by supervising occupational therapy practice. The board is comprised of five volunteer members: two

occupational therapists, one occupational therapy assistant and two public members. Each member is appointed by the governor and may serve up to two four-year terms. The board is self-supporting and activities are financed solely from licensure and related fees.

OPTOMETRY, OREGON BOARD OF

Address: 1500 Liberty St. SE, Suite 210, Salem 97302
Phone: 503-399-0662
Fax: 503-399-0705
Email: shelley.g.sneed@oregon.gov
Web: www.oregon.gov/obo/Pages/index.aspx
Contact: Shelley Sneed, Executive Director
Statutory Authority: ORS Chapter 683
Duties and Responsibilities: The Oregon Board of Optometry was enacted in 1905 to protect Oregonians from the dangers of unqualified and improper practice of optometry. The board is comprised of five governor-appointed members; four are licensed optometrists and one is a public member. Members serve three-year terms and oversee the agency and its functions. The board is staffed by two full-time staff who assist board members in enforcing the agency's laws and rules. There are currently about 1,250 active and inactive licensed optometrists in Oregon. Oregonians can submit complaints to the board for review if they believe an optometrist has breached Oregon law or given an improper standard of care.

PARKS AND RECREATION DEPARTMENT, STATE

Address: 725 Summer St. NE, Suite C, Salem 97301
Phone: 503-986-0707;
Campground Reservations: 1-800-452-5687;
Parks Information: 1-800-551-6949
Fax: 503-986-0794
Email: Lisa.sumption@oregon.gov
Web: www.oregon.gov/OPRD/Pages/index.aspx
Contact: Lisa Sumption, Director
Statutory Authority: ORS Chapters 97, 358, 390
Duties and Responsibilities: The State Parks and Recreation Department (OPRD) exists to protect and provide outstanding natural, scenic, recreational, cultural and historic places for the enjoyment and education of present and future generations. The state park tradition in Oregon began in 1922 with the first state park: a land donation on the Luckiamute River in the Willamette Valley became what is now Sarah Helmick State Recreation Site. Originally a division of the Highway

Commission and later, its successor the Oregon Department of Transportation, the State Parks and Recreation Department was created as an independent agency in 1989. Today, OPRD focuses on protecting Oregon's special outdoor and historic places, providing opportunities for great experiences and sustaining Oregon's quality outdoor recreation and heritage resources for the future. To accomplish this, OPRD provides one of the most popular state park systems in the nation—more than 250 properties serving over 45 million visitors a year—and manages other key recreation and heritage programs: Oregon's stunning public ocean shore, scenic waterways and first-of-their-kind scenic bikeways, the State Historic Preservation Office, archaeology services, historic cemeteries and all-terrain vehicle safety certifications. OPRD programs serve Oregon communities directly with grants and advice related to outdoor recreation, museums and historic "Main Street" revitalization.

OPRD has about 840 positions totaling about 575 full-time equivalent employees, with a large number of employees being seasonal. The governor-appointed State Parks and Recreation Commission sets OPRD's policy direction. The department is funded by state park visitor fees, a share of state recreational vehicle license revenues, some federal funds and a share of Oregon Lottery profits constitutionally dedicated to parks by Oregon voters in 1998 and 2010.

Historic Preservation Office, State

Address: 725 Summer St. NE, Suite C, Salem 97301
Phone: 503-986-0684
Fax: 503-986-0793
Email: chrissy.curran@oregon.gov
Web: www.oregonheritage.org
Contact: Christine Curran, Heritage Division Manager and Deputy State Historic Preservation Officer
Statutory Authority: ORS 358.612
Duties and Responsibilities: The State Historic Preservation Office (SHPO) was established in 1967, a year after the U.S. Congress passed the National Historic Preservation Act. Under federal and state mandates, the SHPO manages programs that create opportunities for individuals, organizations and local governments to become directly involved in the protection of significant historic and cultural resources.

The SHPO creates these opportunities through archaeological services, grant programs, planning assistance, tax incentive programs and federal programs such as the National Register of Historic Places. In addition, the Certified Local Government Program and the Oregon Main Street Network collaborate with communities to develop compre-

hensive revitalization strategies based on a community's unique assets, character and heritage.

The OPRD director is Oregon's designated State Historic Preservation Officer.

Historic Preservation, State Advisory Committee on

Address: 725 Summer St. NE, Suite C, Salem 97301
Phone: 503-986-0684
Fax: 503-986-0793
Email: chrissy.curran@oregon.gov
Web: www.oregonheritage.org
Contact: Christine Curran, Heritage Division Manager
Statutory Authority: ORS 358.622
Duties and Responsibilities: The State Advisory Committee on Historic Preservation is a nine-member group that reviews nominations to the National Register of Historic Places. The members are professionally recognized in the fields of history, architecture, archaeology and other related disciplines. The committee holds public meetings in February, June and October each year at different locations within the state.

Heritage Commission, Oregon

Address: 725 Summer St. NE, Suite C, Salem 97301
Phone: 503-986-0696
Fax: 503-986-0793
Email: Todd.Mayberry@oregon.gov
Web: www.oregonheritage.org
Contact: Todd Mayberry, Coordinator
Statutory Authority: ORS 358.570
Duties and Responsibilities: The Oregon Heritage Commission, established to secure, sustain, enhance and promote Oregon's heritage, is a nine-member governor-appointed commission that has broad responsibilities as a connector and catalyst for hundreds of organizations and thousands of Oregonians devoted to preserving and interpreting Oregon's heritage resources. Its programs include the Heritage and Museum Grant Programs, technical assistance for heritage organizations and an annual conference. It also gives annual Heritage Excellence Awards and designates Oregon Heritage Traditions, All-Star Communities, and Statewide Celebrations.

Historic Cemeteries, Oregon Commission on

Address: 725 Summer St. NE, Suite C, Salem 97301
Phone: 503-986-0685
Fax: 503-986-0793
Email: Kuri.gill@oregon.gov
Web: www.oregonheritage.org
Contact: Kuri Gill, Coordinator

Executive

Statutory Authority: ORS 97.772–97.784
Duties and Responsibilities: Established in 1999, the Oregon Commission on Historic Cemeteries maintains a list of historic cemeteries and gravesites in Oregon. It works to promote public education on the significance of historic cemeteries and to provide financial and technical assistance for restoring, improving and maintaining their appearance.

Historic Trails Advisory Council

Address: 725 Summer St. NE, Suite C, Salem 97301
Phone: 503-986-0684
Fax: 503-986-0793
Email: chrissy.curran@oregon.gov
Web: www.oregonheritage.org
Contact: Christine Curran, Heritage Division Manager
Statutory Authority: Executive Order 98-16
Duties and Responsibilities: In 1998, the governor established the Oregon Historic Trails Advisory Council (OHTAC) to oversee and provide advice on Oregon's 16 historic trails. Nine volunteer citizens comprise OHTAC to advise the state on locating, preserving and encouraging use of historic trails by Oregonians and visitors. The group meets three times a year. Guided by experts and/or local residents, OHTAC evaluates and records trail conditions, and discusses opportunities for marking and interpreting the trails.

The council collects and shares information on trails, encourages local communities and agencies to develop directional and interpretive signs, brochures and maps, and helps them find resources to protect and share these irreplaceable corridors of history.

PAROLE AND POST-PRISON SUPERVISION, STATE BOARD OF

Address: 2575 Center St. NE, Suite 100, Salem 97301-4621
Phone: 503-945-9009
Fax: 503-373-7558
Web: www.oregon.gov/bopps/Pages/index.aspx
Contact: Brenda Carney, Executive Director; Michael Wu, Board Chair
Statutory Authority: ORS Chapter 144
Duties and Responsibilities: The Board of Parole and Post-Prison Supervision works in partnership with the Department of Corrections and local supervisory authorities to protect the public and reduce the risk of repeat criminal behavior. The board imposes prison terms and makes release decisions on offenders whose criminal conduct occurred prior to November 1, 1989. The board sets conditions of supervision for all offenders being released from prison, imposes sanctions for violations of supervision and determines whether discharge from parole supervision is compatible with public safety. Discharge from supervision for offenders sentenced under sentencing guidelines occurs automatically upon expiration of the statutory period of post-prison supervision. The board's decisions are based on applicable laws, victims' interests, public safety and the recognized principles of offender behavioral change.

The full-time board was authorized in 1969. In 1975, the board was enlarged to five members, with the stipulation that at least one member must be a woman. The membership was reduced to three in 1992; however, legislation increased the board back to five in 2015. The governor appoints members for four-year terms and also determines the chair and vice-chair. Members can serve a maximum of two terms. Board staff consists of an executive director, a supervising executive assistant and 22 support staff. The board works closely with the Department of Corrections and local community corrections agencies.

In 2013, new legislation was passed for a sex offender notification level system, which was amended in 2015. This system will improve community education and notification of high-risk registered sex offenders in Oregon and will introduce opportunities for low risk offenders to be reclassified to a lower notification level and/or receive relief from registration if they meet statutory requirements. In the 2015–17 and 2017–19 biennia, the board will conduct assessments for over 4,000 registered sex offenders. In January 2019, the board will begin conducting hearings to determine eligibility for reclassification and/or relief from registration for those registrants who meet statutory requirements.

PATIENT SAFETY COMMISSION, OREGON

Address: PO Box 285, Portland 97204-0285
Phone: 503-928-6158
Fax: 503-224-9150
Email: info@oregonpatientsafety.org
Web: http://oregonpatientsafety.org
Contact: Melissa Parkerton, Interim Executive Director
Statutory Authority: ORS 442.820–442.835, Chapter 686
Duties and Responsibilities: The Oregon Patient Safety Commission (OPSC) was created by the Legislature in 2003 to reduce the risk of serious adverse events occurring in Oregon's health care system and to encourage a culture of safety. OPSC is located in Portland and has 13 staff members that support three key programs.

The Patient Safety Reporting Program (PSRP) is a voluntary program for health care organizations to contribute information about adverse events, why they occur and strategies to make care safer. OPSC analyzes and shares aggregate patient safety information to enhance quality and safety statewide. All PSRP contributions are protected under state law, creating a safe environment where patient safety innovation can thrive.

Early Discussion and Resolution (EDR) provides a constructive way forward when a patient is seriously injured during health care. Open conversations between health care providers and patients about what happened can bring resolution and closure to those involved. In Oregon, when such conversations are initiated through EDR, they are protected under state law.

Quality Improvement Initiatives are mission-driven, grant-funded patient safety initiatives that support implementation of best practices in Oregon's health care system. Current work includes a grant to enhance infection prevention readiness and infrastructure in a variety of health care settings across the continuum of care.

PHARMACY, STATE BOARD OF

Address: 800 NE Oregon St., Suite 150, Portland 97232-2162
Phone: 971-673-0001
Fax: 971-673-0002
Email: pharmacy.board@state.or.us
Web: www.oregon.gov/Pharmacy/Pages/index.aspx
Contact: Marcus Watt, Executive Director
Statutory Authority: ORS Chapters 475, 689
Duties and Responsibilities: The State Board of Pharmacy was created in 1891. Its purpose is to enforce high quality standards of pharmacy practice and regulate drugs to uphold the safety, health and welfare of the public. Today, the board is appointed by the governor and consists of nine members: five licensed pharmacists, two public members and two pharmacy technicians. There are also 20 staff members, led by the executive director, who are located at the Portland headquarters. They implement the board's policies, statutes and rules through licensure and compliance. Currently, there are 27,182 licensees, which include pharmacists, preceptors, pharmacy technicians, interns, and drug outlets, including pharmacies, manufacturers, wholesalers and charitable pharmacies. Licensing fees solely finance the activities of the board. In the last year, Oregon became the first state to implement contraceptive prescribing authority for pharmacists.

PHYSICAL THERAPIST LICENSING BOARD

Address: 800 NE Oregon St., Suite 407, Portland 97232-2187
Phone: 971-673-0200
Fax: 971-673-0226
Web: www.oregon.gov/PTBrd/Pages/index.aspx
Contact: James Heider, Executive Director
Statutory Authority: ORS 688.160
Duties and Responsibilities: The Physical Therapist Licensing Board was created in 1971 to regulate the practice of physical therapy in Oregon. The board's primary purpose is the protection of the public. The board achieves this by establishing and regulating professional standards of practice, which ensure that physical therapists and physical therapist assistants are properly educated, hold valid/current licenses, practice within their scope of practice and continue to receive ongoing training throughout their careers. Physical therapy practice is governed by state statutes and rules that define the scope of practice. The board issues licenses, promulgates rules, monitors continuing competency, investigates complaints, issues civil penalties for violations and may revoke, suspend or impose probation on a licensee or place limits on a licensee's practice.

The board regulates over 5,000 active licensees and employs two full-time and one part-time staff. The board is comprised of eight volunteer members: five physical therapists, one physical therapist assistant and two public members. Each member is appointed by the governor and confirmed by the Senate to serve a four-year term. A board member may be reappointed to one subsequent term. The board is self-supporting, and activities are financed solely from licensure and related fees.

POLICE, DEPARTMENT OF STATE

Address: 3565 Trelstad Ave. SE, Salem 97317
Phone: 503-378-3720
Fax: 503-378-8282
Email: ask.osp@state.or.us
Web: www.oregon.gov/OSP/Pages/index.aspx
Contact: Travis Hampton, Superintendent
Statutory Authority: ORS 181A.015
Duties and Responsibilities: The Department of State Police was created in 1931 to serve as a rural patrol and to assist local city police and sheriffs' departments. Some of the agency's specialized programs and services include transportation safety; major crime investigations; forensic services, including DNA identification, automated fingerprint identification and computerized criminal history files; drug investigation; fish and wildlife

enforcement; gambling enforcement and regulation; state emergency response coordination; state Fire Marshal Service and Conflagration Act coordination; coordination of federal grants for public safety issues; coordination of Criminal Justice Information Standards; medical examiner services; Special Weapons and Tactics (SWAT); and serving as the point of contact to the National Office of Homeland Security.

The Oregon State Police employs more than 1,300 sworn and professional staff in the areas of patrol, criminal investigation, forensic services, medical examiner, state fire marshal, gaming regulation, fish and wildlife regulation, public safety communications, and information management, with a biennial budget of approximately $327 million in total funds.

Criminal Investigations Division

Address: 3565 Trelstad Ave. SE, Salem 97317
Phone: 503-378-3720
Fax: 503-378-8282
Email: ask.osp@state.or.us
Web: www.oregon.gov/OSP/CID/Pages/
index.aspx
Contact: Captain Jon Harrington
Statutory Authority: ORS 181A.145
Duties and Responsibilities: The Criminal Investigations Division (CID) is the investigative resource of the Department of State Police and delivers statewide services in support of the agency's vision to provide "Premier Public Safety Services for Oregon."

The CID's Major Crimes Section, Drug Enforcement Section, and Sex Offender Registration Unit work in conjunction with other state police divisions to enhance livability and safety by protecting the people, property and natural resources of Oregon.

Detectives are strategically located across the state to support local law enforcement with major criminal investigations and to serve on interagency teams. They also provide primary criminal investigative services on state property and at state institutions.

Criminal Justice Information Systems and Law Enforcement Data System

Address: 3565 Trelstad Ave. SE, Salem 97317
Phone: 503-378-5565
Fax: 503-378-2121
Email: Helpdesk.leds@state.or.us
Web: www.oregon.gov/osp/CJIS/Pages/
index.aspx
Statutory Authority: ORS 181A.280

Duties and Responsibilities: The Criminal Justice Information Systems and Law Enforcement Data System provide information-sharing services for security background checks and for assisting law enforcement and criminal justice agencies in their investigations. The unit also includes the Oregon State Athletic Commission that works to protect the public and participants involved in ring sports.

Fish and Wildlife Division

Address: 3565 Trelstad Ave. SE, Salem 97317
Phone: 503-378-3720
Fax: 503-378-8282
Email: osp.fwd@state.or.us
Web: www.oregon.gov/OSP/FW/Pages/
index.aspx
Contact: Captain Jeff Samuels
Statutory Authority: ORS 181A.015
Duties and Responsibilities: The purpose of the Fish and Wildlife Division is to ensure compliance with the laws and regulations that protect and enhance the long-term health and equitable utilization of Oregon's fish and wildlife resources and the habitats upon which they depend. Other important services include public safety and enforcement of criminal and traffic laws.

Forensic Services Division

Address: 3565 Trelstad Ave. SE, Salem 97317
Phone: 503-378-3720
Fax: 503-363-5475
Email: osp.forensics@state.or.us
Web: www.oregon.gov/OSP/FORENSICS/
Pages/OSP%20FORENSICS.aspx
Contact: Captain Alex Gardner
Statutory Authority: ORS 181A.150
Duties and Responsibilities: The Forensic Services Division is a nationally accredited forensic laboratory system serving all state and local law enforcement agencies, medical examiners and prosecuting attorneys in Oregon. The division also performs forensic analysis on criminal cases for the defense upon a court order.

The division provides Oregon's only full service forensic laboratory system. Analysts provide technical assistance and training, evaluate and analyze evidence, interpret results, and provide expert testimony related to the full spectrum of physical evidence recovered from crime scenes.

Gaming Division

Address: 3400 State St., G-750, Salem 97301
Phone: 503-378-6999
Fax: 503-378-6878
Email: ask.osp@state.or.us
Web: www.oregon.gov/OSP/GAMING/Pages/
index.aspx
Contact: Major Joel Lujan
Statutory Authority: ORS 181A.090

Duties and Responsibilities: The Gaming Division consists of the Lottery Gaming Section and Tribal Gaming Section, both working to ensure that all gaming activities are conducted with fairness, integrity, honesty and security.

Medical Examiner Division

Address: 13309 SE 84th Ave., Suite 100, Clackamas 97015
Phone: 971-673-8200
Email: eugene.gray@state.or.us
Web: www.oregon.gov/OSP/SME/Pages/index.aspx
Contact: Dr. Karen Gunson, Medical Examiner
Statutory Authority: ORS Chapter 146
Duties and Responsibilities: The purpose of the Medical Examiner Division is to provide direction and support to the state death investigation program. The medical examiner manages all aspects of the state medical examiner program and has responsibility for technical supervision of county offices in each of Oregon's 36 counties.

Patrol Services Division

Address: 3565 Trelstad Ave. SE, Salem 97317
Phone: 503-378-3720
Fax: 503-378-8282
Email: Ask.osp.@state.or.us
Web: www.oregon.gov/OSP/PATROL/Pages/index.aspx
Contact: Captain Teresa Bloom
Statutory Authority: ORS Chapter 181A
Duties and Responsibilities: The purpose of the Patrol Services Division is to provide a uniform presence and law enforcement services throughout the state, with a primary responsibility for crash reduction, crime reduction and other transportation safety issues, as well as to respond to emergency calls-for-service on Oregon's state and interstate highways.

State Fire Marshal, Office of

Address: 3565 Trelstad Ave. SE, Salem 97317
Phone: 503-378-3473
Fax: 503-373-1825
Email: oregon.sfm@state.or.us
Web: www.oregon.gov/osp/sfm/Pages/index.aspx
Contact: Jim Walker, State Fire Marshal
Statutory Authority: ORS 476.020
Duties and Responsibilities: The Office of State Fire Marshal works to protect citizens, their property and the environment from fire and hazardous materials.

PSYCHIATRIC SECURITY REVIEW BOARD

Address: 610 SW Alder St., Suite 420, Portland 97204
Phone: 503-229-5596
Fax: 503-224-0215
Email: psrb@psrb.org
Contact: Juliet Britton, J.D., Executive Director
Statutory Authority: ORS 161.327, 426.701, 426.702, Chapter 419C
Duties and Responsibilities: The Psychiatric Security Review Board was originally established in 1977 to supervise individuals who successfully asserted the insanity defense (Guilty Except for Insanity or GEI) to a criminal charge. Recognizing the rehabilitative needs of individuals diagnosed with a persistent mental illness, Oregon has invested in a mental health system designed for this population. With public safety as its focus, the board has successfully reintegrated clients into the community with a five-year average 0.51 percent adult recidivism rate. In recent years, the board's responsibilities have expanded to supervise youth and certain civil commitments. Additionally, it has been designated by the Legislature as the "relief" authority for two different populations: GEI sex offenders who request relief from sex offender registration and those who are barred from possessing a firearm due to a mental health determination (primarily civil commitment) who request restoration of firearm rights.

The board is comprised of an adult panel and a juvenile panel. Each consists of five members, appointed by the governor for four-year terms and confirmed by the Senate. The adult panel is comprised of a psychiatrist and a psychologist experienced in the criminal justice system, an experienced parole and probation officer, an attorney experienced in criminal trial practice and a member of the general public. The juvenile panel has a child psychiatrist, child psychologist, parole and probation officer experienced in juvenile criminal justice, an attorney experienced in juvenile criminal trial practice and a member of the general public.

The agency employs 11 staff and has a biennial budget of approximately $2.5 million.

PSYCHOLOGIST EXAMINERS, STATE BOARD OF

Address: 3218 Pringle Rd. SE, Suite 130, Salem 97302-6309
Phone: 503-378-4154
Fax: 503-374-1904
Web: www.oregon.gov/OBPE/Pages/index.aspx
Contact: Charles J. Hill, Executive Director
Statutory Authority: ORS 675.010–675.150

Duties and Responsibilities: The Board of Psychologist Examiners was created in 1963 to protect Oregon consumers of psychological services. The board determines if individuals meet the initial and continuing education, training and examination standards for licensure and issues new and renewal licenses to those who are qualified. The board develops policies and standards for professional practice and enforces disciplinary action against psychologists, psychologist associates and residents who engage in misconduct or are incompetent. It also issues civil penalties to individuals practicing in Oregon without a license or engaging in misrepresentation. The nine members of the board are appointed by the governor and confirmed by the Senate for three-year terms.

PUBLIC EMPLOYEES RETIREMENT SYSTEM

Address: 11410 SW 68th Pkwy., Tigard 97223; PO Box 23700, Tigard 97281-3700
Phone: 888-320-7377; TTY: 503-603-7766
Fax: 503-598-1218
Web: www.oregon.gov/PERS/Pages/index.aspx
Contact: Steve Rodeman, Executive Director
Statutory Authority: ORS 237.350–237.980, 238.005–238.750, 238A.005–238A.475, 243.401–243.507
Duties and Responsibilities: The Public Employees Retirement System (PERS) has administered retirement benefits for Oregon's public sector workers (state, local government and school district employees) since 1945. PERS serves approximately 210,000 active/inactive members, 135,000 benefit recipients and 925 employers. The system pays approximately $3.7 billion in benefits annually; about $3.3 billion is paid to Oregon residents. Those in-state payments support an estimated 35,999 jobs in Oregon. Investment income provided 73.8 percent of total PERS revenue from 1970–2014, with member contributions providing 5.6 percent and employer contributions providing 20.6 percent. Nearly 35 percent of PERS members are currently eligible to retire.

Public Employees Retirement Board

Address: PO Box 23700, Tigard 97281-3700
Phone: 503-598-7377
Contact: John Thomas, Chair
Statutory Authority: ORS 238.630

Oregon Savings Growth Plan Advisory Committee

Address: 800 Summer St. NE, Salem 97301
Phone: 503-378-3730
Web: www.oregon.gov/PERS/OSGP/Pages/index.aspx
Contact: Mark Carlton, Chair

PUBLIC SAFETY STANDARDS AND TRAINING, DEPARTMENT OF

Address: 4190 Aumsville Hwy. SE, Salem 97317
Phone: 503-378-2100
Fax: 503-378-4600
Web: www.oregon.gov/DPSST/Pages/index.aspx
Contact: Eriks Gabliks, Director
Statutory Authority: ORS 181A.355–181A.995, 206.010–206.015, 243.950–243.974, 703.010–703.325
Duties and Responsibilities: The mission of the Department of Public Safety Standards and Training (DPSST) is to promote excellence in public safety by delivering quality training and developing and upholding professional standards for police, fire, corrections, parole and probation and telecommunications personnel, in addition to licensing private security providers and private investigators in Oregon.

DPSST also trains and certifies Oregon Liquor Control Commission regulatory specialists, regulates and licenses polygraph examiners, determines sheriff candidates' eligibility to run for office and administers the Public Safety Memorial Fund. DPSST strives to provide resources and certification programs that public safety officers and organizations need to maintain the highest professional skill standards for service to Oregon's communities and citizens. These services are based at DPSST's 236-acre academy and extend across the state through a network of regional training coordinators.

DPSST is governed by a 24-member board and five discipline-specific policy committees. DPSST serves more than 42,000 public safety constituents across the state and employs 160 full-time staff and approximately 400 part-time employees and agency loaned instructors.

The functions of DPSST date back to 1961 with the establishment of the Board on Police Standards and Training. Since its inception, the addition of the corrections, parole and probation, telecommunications and emergency medical dispatch, fire, private security, private investigator and regulatory specialist disciplines expanded the board's oversight and the name transitioned to the Board on Public Safety Standards and Training. The growth in scope of the board required the establishment of DPSST in 1997 as the agency to facilitate the standards and training requirements set forth by the board. DPSST also provides staffing for the board and police committees and works with various board advisory committees and workgroups

DPSST's campus is home to the Fallen Law Enforcement Officers Memorial and the Fallen Firefighters Memorial. Memorial ceremonies for each are hosted annually to honor the officers and firefighters who have been killed in the line of duty.

Public Safety Standards and Training, Board on

Address: 4190 Aumsville Hwy. SE, Salem 97317
Phone: 503-378-2100
Web: www.oregon.gov/DPSST/BD/Pages/index.aspx
Contact: Jason Myers, Chair; Patricia Patrick-Joling, Vice Chair
Statutory Authority: ORS 181A.360
Duties and Responsibilities: In addition to statutes set by the Oregon Legislature, DPSST's overall mission is guided by the 24-member Board on Public Safety Standards and Training and five discipline-specific public safety policy committees. Membership of the board is outlined in ORS and provides a comprehensive representation of the constituent base.

The board and committees are integrally involved in setting standards for employment, training and certification or licensure of public safety professionals, fire service professionals, private security professionals, private investigators and polygraph examiners. Board and committee meetings are held quarterly to review standards and curriculum, administrative rule changes, requests for waivers of the standards and cases addressing the denial or revocation of certification or licensure. In addition, the board and committees assist DPSST in setting the agency's goals for the future through guidance and input regarding policy direction and strategic planning.

PUBLIC UTILITY COMMISSION

Address: PO Box 1088, 201 High St. SE, #100, Salem 97308-1088
Phone: 503-373-7394
Fax: 503-378-6163
Email: puc.commission@state.or.us
Web: www.puc.state.or.us/Pages/Index.aspx
Contact: Michael Dougherty, Chief Operating Officer
Statutory Authority: ORS Chapters 756, 757, 758, 759, 772
Duties and Responsibilities: The Public Utility Commission (PUC) is responsible for regulating rates and services offered by private Oregon electric and natural gas utilities, telecommunications companies and water companies. The commission's actions are governed by state and federal laws and judicial decisions. The PUC consists of the following programs:

The Utility Program serves as the technical and analytical arm of the agency. Its professional staff analyzes all utility filings, helps build a factual record in contested case proceedings, investigates and recommends policy options, inspects utility facilities and undertakes many other activities needed for the commission to carry out its mission and serve ratepayers. The program is funded through a Utility Gross Operating Revenue Fee of up to 0.3 percent of gross operating revenues. The Utility Program also receives federal funds through the Pipeline Hazardous Material Safety Administration.

The Residential Service Protection Fund consists of four programs that provide adequate and affordable telephone service to Oregonians. These programs provide assistance to low-income Oregonians with a discount on monthly telephone service; Oregonians with disabilities that need adaptive telecommunications equipment to communicate effectively on the telephone; Oregonians with medical hardships who must have telephone access at all times; and Oregonians with hearing or speech disabilities who are provided the ability to place or receive calls through specially trained relay operators. The program is funded through a surcharge, currently $.07, which is assessed against each paying retail subscriber who has telephone or cellular service with access to the Oregon Telecommunications Relay Service.

The Policy and Administration Program consists of the three commissioners, the chief operating officer, Business Services, Commission Services, Consumer Services Section, Human Resources and Information Systems.

The Administrative Hearings Division conducts rulemaking and contested case hearings on issues concerning utility services. Hearings involve mergers and acquisitions, rate proposals and consumer complaints. The section also oversees records management, public records requests and agency compliance with the Administrative Procedures Act.

Maritime Pilots, Oregon Board of

Address: 800 NE Oregon St., Portland 97232
Phone: 971-673-1530
Fax: 971-673-1531
Web: www.puc.state.or.us/BMP/Pages/Index.aspx
Contact: Eric Burnette, Executive Director; Susan Johnson, Administrator
Statutory Authority: ORS Chapters 670, 776
Duties and Responsibilities: The Oregon Board of Maritime Pilots (OBMP) is a part of the PUC for budget and administrative purposes. OBMP protects public health, safety and welfare by ensuring that only the best-qualified persons are licensed to pilot vessels. OBMP is an independent occupational licensing and regulatory agency for state maritime pilots.

A maritime (or marine) pilot is a local navigational and ship-handling expert who directs the course and speed of vessels based upon knowledge of wind, weather, tides, currents and local geography. Replacing a vessel lost through negligent navigation, injuries or deaths among the vessel's crew, loss of cargo, environmental damage and cleaning up spills of hazardous materials are costly. Piloting requires education, experience and licensure, and commands salaries commensurate with other professional occupations, such as physicians and attorneys.

OBMP regulates the rates pilots charge for their services. It also monitors pilot performance and investigates pilot performance in any reportable casualty. OBMP encourages safe piloting practices. It has two full time equvalent positions and falls under the governor's A Thriving Oregon Economy and Excellence in State Government focus areas.

OBMP receives no General or Lottery funds. Revenues are received from annual pilot license fees, board operations fee (assessed on vessels entering or leaving the Columbia River, Coos Bay, and Yaquina Bay), reimbursements from rate hearings and miscellaneous receipts.

RACING COMMISSION, OREGON

Address: 800 NE Oregon St., Suite 310, Portland 97232
Phone: 971-673-0207
Fax: 971-673-0213
Email: jack.mcgrail@state.or.us
Web: www.oregon.gov/RACING/pages/index.aspx
Contact: Jack McGrail, Executive Director
Statutory Authority: ORS 462.210
Duties and Responsibilities: The Oregon Racing Commission (ORC) was established in 1933. The agency regulates all aspects of live horse racing in Oregon. The ORC is the nation's leader in licensing multi-jurisdictional, simulcast, advance deposit wagering companies. The agency promotes the safety of the sport for all participants, equine and human, and ensures the integrity of the contests for the wagering public. There is one commercial race meet held in Portland and five summer fair race meets around the state, which include locations at Union, Grants Pass, Prineville, Tillamook and Harney County. The mission of the agency is to regulate and facilitate all aspects of the pari-mutuel (wagering) industry in Oregon for the benefit of the citizenry, the licensees, the participants and the economy of the state. The agency employs 12.27 full-time equivalent employees and licenses 3,700 horse racing participants, nine advance deposit wagering companies and four tote companies.

REAL ESTATE AGENCY

Address: 530 Center St. NE, Suite 100, Salem 97301
Phone: 503-378-4170
Fax: 503-378-2491
Email: orea.info@state.or.us
Web: www.oregon.gov/REA/pages/index.aspx
Contact: Gene Bentley, Commissioner
Statutory Authority: ORS 696.375
Duties and Responsibilities: The Real Estate Agency is responsible for licensing, registering and regulating real estate brokers, principal real estate brokers, property managers, escrow agents, real estate marketing organizations and membership campgrounds. It also regulates aspects of condominium filings, timeshare filings and manufactured dwelling subdivisions.

In 1919, the Oregon Legislature passed the first effective real estate license law in the United States. The Insurance Department issued the first real estate licenses. Over the years, different state offices have been responsible for real estate licensing. The current Real Estate Agency was created in 1987.

The agency is managed by a real estate commissioner appointed by the governor. The commissioner is advised by the nine-person Real Estate Board. About 28 agency employees serve over 20,000 licensees and registrants.

Real Estate Board

Address: 530 Center St. NE, Suite 100, Salem 97301
Phone: 503-378-3720
Fax: 503-378-8282
Email: orea.board@state.or.us
Web: www.oregon.gov/rea/about_us/Pages/Real_Estate_Board.aspx
Contact: Gene Bentley, Commissioner
Statutory Authority: ORS 696.405
Duties and Responsibilities: The Real Estate Board consists of seven industry members and two public members appointed by the governor. It meets at least six times a year. The board advises the real estate commissioner and the governor's office on real estate industry matters. It is also responsible for reviewing experience waiver requests and continuing education provider qualification petitions for approval.

REVENUE, DEPARTMENT OF

Address: 955 Center St. NE, Salem 97301-2555
Phone: 503-378-4988; Toll-free 800-356-4222; TTY: 800-886-7204
Fax: 503-945-8738
Email: questions.dor@oregon.gov
Web: www.oregon.gov/dor/Pages/index.aspx
Contact: Nia Ray, Director

Statutory Authority: ORS 305.025

Duties and Responsibilities: The Oregon Department of Revenue started as the Oregon Tax Commission in 1909. The department has nearly 1,000 employees who help achieve its mission of making revenue systems work to fund the public services that preserve and enhance the quality of life for all citizens. The department administers more than 30 tax programs, including personal income tax, corporation taxes, cigarette and tobacco taxes and marijuana tax. Revenue's tax programs provided 96 percent of Oregon's General Fund revenue for the 2013–15 biennium.

While the department does not collect property taxes, it ensures property tax laws are applied fairly and equitably across Oregon's 36 counties. The Property Tax Division administers the property tax deferral program, determines the value of industrial and centrally assessed properties, and supports and trains county appraisers and assessors. Revenue also collects debt on behalf of nearly 300 public agencies, commissions and boards.

The department is headquartered in Salem, with district offices in Portland, Gresham, Bend, Eugene and Medford.

SOCIAL WORKERS, STATE BOARD OF LICENSED

Address: 3218 Pringle Rd. SE, Suite 240, Salem 97302-6310
Phone: 503-378-5735
Fax: 888-252-1046
Email: randy.harnisch@state.or.us
Web: www.oregon.gov/BLSW/Pages/index.aspx
Contact: Randy Harnisch, Executive Director
Statutory Authority: ORS 675.510–675.600
Duties and Responsibilities: Social workers in Oregon are licensed mental health professionals who work in a variety of settings from schools and social service agencies to hospitals and hospice facilities. The State Board of Licensed Social Workers was created to ensure that individuals serving the public as social workers have the education and skills to do the job safely, effectively and efficiently. Currently, there are about 5,500 licensed social workers in Oregon, and that number is growing as social workers' skills are used to provide services in communities across the state.

The board has seven members, four who are social workers and three who are not social workers and who represent the public. The board has its office in Salem and has six staff members: three working to issue and renew licenses, two working to monitor and investigate complaints and an executive director to oversee the operation of the agency. Board meetings are held monthly in Salem and are open to the public.

The board was created in 1979 to set policy and adopt rules for social workers. Currently, the board offers four license types: Registered Baccalaureate Social Worker (RBSW), Licensed Master's Social Worker (LMSW), Clinical Social Work Associate (CSWA) and Licensed Clinical Social Worker (LCSW). These four licenses allow license holders to call themselves "social workers" and, in the case of the CSWA and LCSW, to work with clients directly as clinical social workers.

SPEECH-LANGUAGE PATHOLOGY AND AUDIOLOGY, STATE BOARD OF EXAMINERS FOR

Address: 800 NE Oregon St., Suite 407, Portland 97232-2162
Phone: 971-673-0220; TDD: 503-731-4031
Fax: 971-673-0226
Email: speechaud.board@state.or.us
Web: www.oregon.gov/BSPA/Pages/index.aspx
Contact: Erin K. Haag, Executive Director
Statutory Authority: ORS 681.205–681.505
Duties and Responsibilities: Audiologists and speech-language pathologists provide vital services to Oregonians in hospitals, home health settings, private practices, early intervention programs, early childhood special education programs and in Oregon's kindergarten through grade 12 school system. The State Board of Examiners for Speech-Language Pathology was established in 1973 to license and regulate the performance of audiologists, speech-language pathologists, and, as of 2013, speech-language pathology assistants, to ensure consumer protection. The office is staffed by three employees (2.5 full-time equivalent) and overseen by the board, which is made up of two audiologists, two speech-language pathologists, one otolaryngologist and two public members.

STATE FAIR COUNCIL

Address: 2330 17th St. NE, Salem 97301
Phone: 971-701-6573
Fax: 503-947-3206
Web: http://oregonstatefaircouncil.org
Contact: Michael Paluszak, Director and CEO
Statutory Authority: ORS 565.456
Duties and Responsibilities: The Legislature passed Senate Bill 7 in 2013 to create the State Fair Council as a public corporation, and management of the fair and exposition center was transferred to this new entity. The council oversees the Oregon State Fair and Exposition Center to showcase Oregon products and people; to educate and communicate to the citizens of Oregon about the needs, issues and context of the key industries of the state,

with emphasis on agriculture, forestry, technology and manufacturing; and to create an event that celebrates all of Oregon and Oregonians in an atmosphere of responsible community involvement and citizenship. The exposition center hosts the annual state fair at the end of August through Labor Day and provides a venue for meetings, concerts, trade shows and other events the rest of the year from its location in the heart of Salem. From 2005–2014, the state stair and exposition center were operated by the State Parks and Recreation Department.

STATE LANDS, DEPARTMENT OF

Address: 775 Summer St. NE, Suite 100, Salem 97301-1279
Phone: 503-986-5200
Fax: 503-378-4844
Email: dsl@dsl.state.or.us
Web: www.oregon.gov/DSL/Pages/index.aspx
Contact: James T. Paul, Director
Statutory Authority: ORS Chapter 273
Duties and Responsibilities: The Department of State Lands (DSL) is the administrative arm of the State Land Board, Oregon's oldest board. Established by the Oregon Constitution, the State Land Board has been composed of the governor (chair), secretary of state and state treasurer throughout its history.

At statehood in 1859, the federal government granted Oregon about 3.4 million acres of land for financing public education. The State Land Board oversees these state-owned "school lands" which now total only about a fifth of the original acreage. Land types include range and agricultural land, commercial land, forest land and mineral and energy resources. Revenues from these lands are dedicated to the Common School Fund, a trust fund for kindergarten through grade 12 public schools. Distributions from the fund's earnings are sent twice a year to the state's 197 school districts. The State Land Board and the department also are charged with protecting public rights to use state-owned waterways for navigation, fishing, commerce and recreation.

Over time, the Oregon Legislature assigned various additional responsibilities to the agency, including administering the state's unclaimed property program (1957); protecting state wetlands and waterways (1967: removal-fill law; 1989: wetland conservation law); and serving as the state partner for the South Slough National Estuarine Research Reserve (1974). The department also administers the estates of people who die without a will and without known heirs.

DSL employs just over 100 people and is headquartered in Salem in a building that is an asset of the Common School Fund. The Eastern Region Office is located in Bend, and the South Slough National Estuarine Research Reserve is headquartered in Charleston on the south coast. In addition to the Director's Office and State Land Board, agency program areas operate under two divisions: Operations (Aquatic Resource Management and Common School Fund Property) and Administration (Business Operations and Support Services, and the South Slough).

South Slough National Estuarine Research Reserve

Address: PO Box 5417, 61907 Seven Devils Rd., Charleston 97420
Phone: 541-888-5558
Fax: 541-888-5559
Web: www.oregon.gov/DSL/SSNERR/Pages/index.aspx
Contact: Gary Cooper, Manager
Statutory Authority: ORS 273.554
Duties and Responsibilities: The South Slough National Estuarine Research Reserve is a 5,900-acre protected area located on the South Slough inlet of the Coos Estuary in Charleston, near Coos Bay. Established in 1974 by the Oregon Legislature, it is a partnership with the National Oceanic and Atmospheric Administration and DSL. The mission of the South Slough Reserve is to improve the understanding and management of estuaries and coastal watersheds in the Pacific Northwest. The South Slough was the first of 28 reserves nationwide and is the only program of its kind in Oregon.

The reserve has two core areas of service: education and science. Education staff provide classes and training for a wide variety of clients, including schoolchildren, science teachers, local decision-makers, and professionals involved in managing estuaries and coastal watersheds. The reserve's interpretive center offers informative displays and a system of hiking trails for tourists and area residents. Scientists provide research data for national and regional organizations.

The reserve is guided by an eight-member, governor-appointed, Management Commission, chaired by the director of DSL. Staff are located at both the reserve's Interpretive Center and at the University of Oregon's Institute of Marine Biology in Charleston. The reserve employs 16 full-time staff, is supported by a large cadre of volunteers and hosts numerous student researchers and interns on an annual basis. The Friends of South Slough, a membership, all-volunteer nonprofit group, assists the reserve with its educational and research activities and obtains grants and other funding to promote and support the reserve's programs.

TAX PRACTITIONERS, STATE BOARD OF

Address: 3218 Pringle Rd. SE, Suite 120, Salem 97302-6308
Phone: 503-378-4034
Fax: 503-585-5797
Email: tax.bd@oregon.gov
Web: www.oregon.gov/OBTP/Pages/index.aspx
Contact: Howard Moyes, Executive Director; Susan Gallagher-Smith, Chair
Statutory Authority: ORS 673.605–673.740
Duties and Responsibilities: The Oregon Legislature created the State Board of Tax Practitioners in 1974 to protect consumers from incompetent and unethical tax return preparers, the first law and organization of its kind in the country. Today, the board licenses and regulates nearly 4,000 individual tax practitioners and more than 1,200 tax preparation businesses. The board is comprised of seven volunteer members who serve staggered three-year terms. Six of the members are licensed tax consultants, and the seventh member represents the general public. Four full-time staff administer day-to-day operations. The board is completely self-funded through licensing and examination fees and civil penalties. Its stringent licensing, examination and continuing education standards exceed those of the Internal Revenue Service.

TEACHER STANDARDS AND PRACTICES COMMISSION

Address: 250 Division St. NE, Salem 97301
Phone: 503-378-3586
Fax: 503-378-3758
Email: contact.tspc@oregon.gov
Web: www.oregon.gov/tspc/Pages/index.aspx
Contact: Monica Beane, Executive Director
Statutory Authority: ORS 342.350
Duties and Responsibilities: The Teacher Standards and Practices Commission was created by the Oregon Legislature in 1965 to advise the State Board of Education on licensure, education and performance of teachers, and other matters on which the board requested assistance. In 1973, the Legislature created a new state agency and transferred the full responsibility for educator licensure, educator licensure preparation programs and maintenance of professional standards of conduct to the commission. In 1979, authority for appointment of commission members was moved from the State Board of Education to the governor. The commission employs about 25 employees and processes approximately 20,000 licensure applications a year. The commission's responsibilities apply to professional conduct for candidates enrolled in educator preparation, licensure and charter school registrations for teachers and administrators, licensure for personnel service specialists (school counselors, school psychologists and school social workers) and certification for school nurses employed by Oregon public schools, preprimary through grade 12. The commission has oversight of approximately 20 public and independent college and university educator preparation licensure programs. The commission works in cooperation with the Chief Education Office to ensure well-rounded policy throughout Oregon's public education services.

TOURISM COMMISSION, OREGON

Address: Headquarters: 250 Church St. SE, Suite 100, Salem 97301; 319 SW Washington St., Suite 700, Portland 97204
Phone: 971-717-6205
Fax: 971-717-6215
Email: info@traveloregon.com
Web: www.traveloregon.com
Contact: Todd Davidson, CEO
Statutory Authority: ORS 284.101–284.146
Duties and Responsibilities: The Oregon Tourism Commission, doing business as Travel Oregon, drives economic growth and job creation by strengthening tourism throughout the state. The commission works to enhance visitors' experiences by providing information, resources and trip planning tools that inspire travel and consistently convey the exceptional qualities of Oregon. The commission aims to improve Oregonians' quality of life by strengthening the economic impact of the state's $10.8 billion tourism industry, which employs more than 105,000 Oregonians.

Created in 1995 and made semi-independent by the Legislature in 2003, Travel Oregon is led by a nine-member governor-appointed board and employs 43 staff members, who market the state with inspirational and innovative advertising campaigns, publications, destination development and community enrichment, and who manage the state's Welcome Centers. Travel Oregon works with local communities, industry associations, government agencies and private businesses in the implementation of its industry and legislatively-approved biennial strategic plan.

The agency ensures broad economic impact across the state by partnering with Oregon's regional tourism associations.

TRANSPORTATION, DEPARTMENT OF

Address: 355 Capitol St. NE, Salem 97301-3871
Phone: 503-986-3200; 1-888-ASK-ODOT (275-6368) for questions and concerns
Fax: 503-986-3432
Web: www.oregon.gov/ODOT/Pages/index.aspx
Contact: Matthew L. Garrett, Director
Statutory Authority: ORS 184.615
Duties and Responsibilities: The Department of Transportation's (ODOT) mission is to provide Oregonians with a safe, efficient transportation system that supports economic opportunity and livable communities. ODOT is actively involved in developing Oregon's multimodal system of highways and bridges, public transit services, rail passenger and freight systems and bicycle and pedestrian paths. ODOT manages driver licensing and vehicle registration programs, motor carrier operations and transportation safety programs.

Office of the Director

Address: MS 11, 355 Capitol St. NE, Salem 97301-3871
Phone: 503-986-4214
Fax: 503-986-3432
Contact: Travis Brouwer, Assistant Director for Public Affairs
Duties and Responsibilities: The Office of the Director is made up of the director; Public Affairs, including the Communications and Government Relations Sections; and the Office of Civil Rights. The director oversees ODOT's biennial budget and manages Oregon's statewide transportation policy and development of surface transportation, driver and vehicle safety and licensing and motor carrier programs. The assistant director for public affairs directs the activities of the ODOT executive team in setting overall policy and strategic direction. The Government Relations Section analyzes local, state and federal laws and rules that affect transportation. The Communications Section helps citizens understand transportation programs and issues through the agency's outreach and information efforts, which include community relations, public information, employee communications and media relations. Public Affairs provides staff support for the Office of the Director, the Oregon Transportation Commission and other advisory committees. The Office of Civil Rights manages and implements ODOT's federal and state regulatory civil rights programs.

Transportation Commission, Oregon

Address: MS 11, 355 Capitol St. NE, Salem 97301-3871
Phone: 503-986-3450
Fax: 503-986-3432

Contact: Jacque Carlisle, Commission Assistant
Statutory Authority: ORS 184.615–184.620
Duties and Responsibilities: The Oregon Transportation Commission is a five-member volunteer citizen board. The governor appoints the members with the consent of the Senate. Members serve a four-year term and may be reappointed. When making appointments, the governor considers the geographic regions of the state and ensures that at least one member is a resident east of the Cascades. In addition, not more than three members may belong to any one political party.

Driver and Motor Vehicle Division

Address: 1905 Lana Ave. NE, Salem 97314-0100
Phone: 503-945-5000; Toll-free (Portland): 503-299-9999
Fax: 503-945-0893
Web: www.oregon.gov/ODOT/DMV/Pages/index.aspx
Contact: Tom McClellan, Administrator
Statutory Authority: ORS 184.615(3)
Duties and Responsibilities: The Driver and Motor Vehicle Division (DMV) promotes transportation safety, protects financial and ownership interests in vehicles, provides driver licenses and identification cards for Oregon residents and collects revenues for Oregon's highway system. DMV generated about $322 million for Oregon's transportation system in fiscal year 2015.

DMV has been part of the Department of Transportation since 1969, but its core functions date back to 1905. The "D" in DMV stood for "department" only for about 12 years—from 1956 to 1969. For more than half a century before that, driver licensing and motor vehicle registration and titling were part of Oregon's Office of the Secretary of State.

DMV contributes to public safety by licensing only qualified persons and vehicles to drive on Oregon roads. DMV issues titles to protect the financial and ownership interests in vehicles. There are currently more than 3.5 million licensed drivers and more than 4.2 million registered vehicles in Oregon. DMV plays a major role in fraud prevention by enforcing strict identification standards in issuing driver licenses and ID cards, and providing driver and vehicle data to law enforcement and courts electronically.

DMV services touch almost every Oregonian by issuing nearly 600,000 driver licenses and ID cards, 850,000 vehicle titles, and 2 million vehicle registrations each year. DMV also regulates and inspects about 3,500 vehicle- and driver-related businesses, such as auto dealers and dismantlers.

Each day, DMV serves more than 12,000 customers in its 60 field offices across Oregon, and each year, DMV serves about 1.7 million customers by telephone. Many transactions can be performed online.

Through the multi-year Service Transformation Program, DMV is focused on updating business processes and tools, enhancing services and providing services in ways that today's customers, business partners and the Legislature expect.

Highway Division

Address: 4040 Fairview Industrial Dr. SE, Salem 97302-1142
Phone: 503-986-6625
Fax: 503-986-3150
Web: www.oregon.gov/odot/hwy/Pages/index.aspx
Contact: Paul Mather, Administrator
Statutory Authority: ORS 184.615(3)
Duties and Responsibilities: The Highway Division is responsible for the design, maintenance, operation and construction of about 8,000 miles of state highways. The division's activities include identifying highway needs; maintaining state highway routes; acquiring rights of way; designing highways, bridges and related structures; awarding highway construction contracts; supervising contractors; obtaining federal highway funds; testing materials; evaluating environmental impacts of proposed projects; and conducting traffic studies and other research projects.

ODOT's five regional offices are responsible for transportation operations in their geographic area. Each region has several district offices responsible for transportation system maintenance.

Motor Carrier Transportation Division

Address: 3930 Fairview Industrial Dr. SE, Salem 97302-6351
Phone: 503-378-5849
Fax: 503-373-1940
Web: www.oregontruckingonline.com
Contact: Gregg Dal Ponte, Administrator
Statutory Authority: ORS Chapters 803, 810, 818, 823, 825, 826
Duties and Responsibilities: The Motor Carrier Transportation Division (MCTD) ensures the safety of commercial trucks and buses and collects fees for their use of the roads. The division collects weight-mile tax and truck registration fees from trucking companies. MCTD also maintains a size and weight enforcement program to ensure that trucks are following size and weight requirements put in place to protect infrastructure and safety, and it issues over-size, overweight and other special variance permits. MCTD enforces commercial vehicle laws, including regulations on driver hours of service. Each year, MCTD and its partner agencies inspect thousands of trucks to ensure that equipment is in good working order and that drivers meet all safety requirements.

MCTD's Trucking Online Internet service brings permit processing, road-use tax reporting and payment, and other truck transactions as close as the nearest computer.

MCTD operates the Green Light preclearance program, which uses weigh-in-motion scales and transponder readers to screen trucks as they travel at highway speed so they don't have to stop at a weigh station if everything is in order. Green Light has pre-cleared more than 21 million trucks, saving the trucking industry 1.7 million hours of travel time and nearly $209 million in operating costs in the 18 years it has operated. Keeping trucks moving also reduces air pollution.

Oregon's truck inspection efforts have paid off in keeping unsafe drivers off the roads. In 2015, of the truck drivers inspected in Oregon, 14.5 percent were placed out-of-service for a critical safety violation. The current national rate of drivers placed out-of-service is 5.51 percent.

Rail and Public Transit Division

Address: 555 13th St. NE, Suite 3, Salem 97301-4179
Phone: 503-986-4077
Fax: 503-986-3183
Web: www.oregon.gov/ODOT/PT/Pages/index.aspx; www.oregon.gov/ODOT/RAIL/Pages/index.aspx
Contact: Hal Gard, Administrator
Statutory Authority: ORS 184.615(3)
Duties and Responsibilities: ODOT combined its rail and public transit programs into a single Rail and Public Transit Division to encourage multi-modal collaboration and gain additional efficiencies. The consolidated division works with transit districts and transportation providers throughout the state, supports intercity passenger bus and rail service and ensures the safety of rail and transit systems. In addition, the division provides grants to local and regional governments and non-profit organizations for transportation services. Programs in this division include Transit, Intercity Passenger Rail and Bus, and Rail and Transit Safety.

Transportation Development Division

Address: 555 13th St. NE, Suite 2, Salem 97301-4178
Phone: 503-986-3421
Fax: 503-986-4173
Web: www.oregon.gov/ODOT/TD/Pages/index.aspx

Contact: Jerri Bohard, Administrator
Statutory Authority: ORS 184.615
Duties and Responsibilities: The Transportation Development Division (TDD) provides guidance on, and support for, policies and planning that enhance Oregon's multimodal transportation system. TDD produces statewide transportation plans and policies, assists local governments and transportation organizations in their planning, collects and analyzes data to support planning and strategic investment decisions, oversees transportation research, and manages grant programs, including the *Connect*Oregon program for non-highway investments. TDD also develops the Statewide Transportation Improvement Program, or STIP, which is the state's four year transportation capital improvement program, and is responsible for managing all federal highway transportation funds that flow to the state. The sections in TDD are Planning, Transportation Data, Active Transportation and Research.

Bicycle and Pedestrian Advisory Committee

Address: 555 13th St. NE, Suite 2, Salem 97301-4178
Phone: 503-986-3555
Web: www.oregon.gov/ODOT/HWY/BIKEPED/Pages/index.aspx
Contact: Sheila Lyons, Program Manager
Statutory Authority: ORS 366.112

Oregon Freight Advisory Committee

Address: 555 13th St. NE, Suite 2, Salem 97301-4178
Phone: 503-986-3525
Web: www.oregon.gov/ODOT/TD/TP/pages/ofac.aspx
Contact: Roseann O'Laughlin, Senior Transportation Planner
Statutory Authority: ORS 366.212

Transportation Safety Division

Address: MS 3, 4040 Fairview Industrial Dr. SE, Salem 97302-1142
Phone: 503-986-4190
Fax: 503-986-3143
Web: www.oregon.gov/ODOT/TS/Pages/index.aspx
Contact: Troy E. Costales, Administrator
Statutory Authority: ORS 184.615(3), 802.300
Duties and Responsibilities: The Transportation Safety Division works with partners to organize, plan and implement statewide transportation safety programs that have helped reduce Oregon's highway fatality rate 60 percent since 1980. The division conducts campaigns focused on behaviors, including safety belts, child safety seats, impaired drivers, speeding, young drivers and motorcycle safety. It partners with law enforcement, safety advocates and others to promote transportation safety through the "Four E's": education, enforcement, engineering and emergency response. The division awards more than 500 grants and contracts to partners and other service providers each year.

Oregon Transportation Safety Committee

Address: MS 3, 4040 Fairview Industrial Dr. SE, Salem 97302-1142
Phone: 503-986-4188
Contact: Mike Laverty, Chair

Governor's Advisory Committee on DUII (Driving under the Influence of Intoxicants)

Address: MS 3, 4040 Fairview Industrial Dr. SE, Salem 97302-1142
Phone: 503-986-4188
Contact: Chuck Hayes, Chair

Governor's Advisory Committee on Motorcycle Safety

Address: MS 3, 4040 Fairview Industrial Dr. SE, Salem 97302-1142
Phone: 503-986-4188
Contact: David Peterson, Chair

TRAVEL INFORMATION COUNCIL

Address: 1500 Liberty St. SE, Salem 97302
Phone: 503-378-4508; Toll-free: 1-800-574-9397
Fax: 503-378-6282
Web: http://ortravelexperience.com
Contact: Nancy DeSouza, Executive Director
Statutory Authority: ORS 377.835
Duties and Responsibilities: The Oregon Travel Information Council—doing business as Oregon Travel Experience (OTE)—is a semi-independent state agency formed by the Legislature in 1972. OTE's programs enhance the public's motoring experience and community economic development by helping travelers navigate to essential services, attractions and points of historic interest. The agency is responsible for the operation of 29 highway safety rest areas at 17 locations around the state under an interagency agreement with the Oregon Department of Transportation. OTE administers the statewide "Blue Logo" Sign Program and information centers that identify gas, food, lodging and attractions on highways throughout Oregon, and leads the Oregon Heritage Tree and Oregon Historical Marker programs.

The nine-member governing council, composed of eight volunteers appointed by the governor and one member of the Oregon Transportation Commission, guide the work of the agency. Members are selected for their knowledge of, experience with or interest in economic development, travel within Oregon, recreational opportunities in Oregon and Oregon's history and natural history.

VETERANS' AFFAIRS, DEPARTMENT OF

Address: 700 Summer St. NE, Salem 97301-1285
Phone: 503-373-2000; Toll-free: 1-800-828-8801; TTY: 503-373-2217
Fax: 503-373-2362
Web: www.oregon.gov/ODVA/Pages/index.aspx
Contact: Cameron Smith, Director
Statutory Authority: ORS 406.020
Duties and Responsibilities: The Oregon Department of Veterans' Affairs (ODVA) was founded in 1945 to, in the words of then-Governor Earl Snell, "provide every possible service and assistance to our returning veterans." Today, the ODVA's mission is to help ensure over 330,000 veterans spanning four generations and five major eras of warfare have access to the best care, resources and opportunities that the nation's veteran benefit system can offer. Through its offices in Salem and Portland, ODVA funds, trains and certifies national, statewide and county Veteran Service Offices that provide free benefits counseling and claims services to veterans, survivors and dependents. In recent years, its Veterans Services Division has been increasingly focused on serving minority groups within the diverse veterans population, including women, tribal, incarcerated and LGBTQ veterans. Other key initiatives include the agency's conservatorship program, the ORVET Home Loan Program and the Oregon Veterans' Homes in Lebanon and The Dalles.

Advisory Committee to the Director of Veterans' Affairs

Address: 700 Summer St. NE, Salem 97301-1285
Phone: 503-373-2383
Contact: Dennis Guthrie, Chair
Statutory Authority: ORS 406.210
Duties and Responsibilities: The committee consists of nine people, all veterans appointed by the governor, who advise the director and staff of the ODVA on a wide variety of matters. The committee members act as advocates for veterans' issues and represent veterans' concerns across Oregon.

Aging Veterans' Services

Address: 700 Summer St. NE, Salem 97301-1285
Phone: 503-373-2028

Fax: 503-373-2391
Contact: Mary Jaeger, Director
Duties and Responsibilities: ODVA's Aging Veterans' Services includes its Conservatorship Program, which helps veterans, survivors and dependents who are legally designated "protected persons" to preserve and manage their estates while providing income and assets for shelter, medical, personal and other needs. This division also operates two Oregon Veterans' Homes located in Lebanon and The Dalles where skilled nursing, rehabilitative and Alzheimer's disease care is provided for veterans, spouses and Gold Star parents (parents whose children died while serving in the U.S. Armed Forces).

Home Loan Program

Address: 700 Summer St. NE, Salem 97301-1285
Phone: 503-373-2051;
Toll-free: 1-800-828-8801, 1-888-673-8387 (within Oregon)
Fax: 503-373-2393
Contact: Cody Cox, Manager
Duties and Responsibilities: Administered by the ODVA since its inception, the ORVET Home Loan Program is designed to provide eligible veterans with home loans at the lowest possible interest rates.

Veterans' Services Division

Address: 700 Summer St. NE, Salem 97301-1285
Phone: 503-373-2249
Contact: Eric Belt, Administrator; Mitch Sparks, Director
Duties and Responsibilities: The Veterans' Services Division includes funding, certification for, and training of, national, statewide and county Veteran Service Offices that provide free benefits counseling and claims services to veterans, survivors and dependents. This division includes support for specific minority groups within Oregon's increasingly diverse veteran population, including women, tribal, incarcerated and LGBTQ veterans.

VETERINARY MEDICAL EXAMINING BOARD

Address: 800 NE Oregon St., Suite 407, Portland 97232
Phone: 971-673-0224
Fax: 971-673-0226
Email: ovmeb.info@state.or.us
Web: www.oregon.gov/OVMEB/Pages/index.aspx
Contact: Lori Makinen, Executive Director
Statutory Authority: ORS 686.210

Duties and Responsibilities: In 1903, the Legislature enacted the Veterinary Practice Act, which authorizes the Veterinary Medical Examining Board to regulate the practice of veterinary medicine in Oregon. The board licenses veterinarians, Certified Veterinary Technicians and Euthanasia Technicians, ensuring that every applicant meets state and national requirements for education, testing and experience. The board protects the public and the public's animals by making and enforcing rules for competency, health and safety standards for veterinarians and facilities. With a staff of three located in Portland, the board processes license applications and renewals, proposes and adopts or repeals rules and investigates complaints alleging violations of the Veterinary Practice Act. The board is comprised of eight volunteer members: five veterinarians, two members of the public and one Certified Veterinary Technician. The board was the first in the country to elect a Certified Veterinary Technician to serve as chair. In 2016, the board began registering veterinary facilities in Oregon and, in 2017, will begin inspections to ensure practices meet all minimum standards.

WATER RESOURCES DEPARTMENT

Address: 725 Summer St. NE, Suite A, Salem 97301
Phone: 503-986-0900
Fax: 503-986-0904
Web: www.oregon.gov/OWRD/Pages/index.aspx
Contact: Tom Byler, Director
Statutory Authority: ORS Chapters 536, 537, 538, 540, 541, 542, 543, 543A
Duties and Responsibilities: The foundation of Oregon's water quantity laws go back to the settlement of the West; however, establishment of a comprehensive set of water laws and an office to oversee the state's water resources did not occur until the office of State Engineer was created in 1905 and the Water Code was passed in 1909. The Water Code required that, with some exceptions, in order to use water in the state an individual had to first obtain a water right. Over time, a variety of offices, boards and commissions managed water resources and the water rights system.

Today, the Water Resources Department is the state agency charged with administration of the laws governing the management and distribution of surface and groundwater resources. The present form of the department was created in 1975, and the Water Resources Commission was established in 1985.

The department's core functions are to protect existing water rights, process water right transactions, facilitate voluntary streamflow restoration, increase understanding of demands on the state's water resources, provide accurate and accessible water resource data and facilitate water supply solutions. The department also protects public health and safety through its dam safety and well construction programs.

The department is currently organized into the following divisions: Director's Office, Administrative Services, Field Services, Technical Services and Water Right Services. Department headquarters and the Northwest Regional office are in Salem. The department also has four other regional offices and 15 small field offices throughout Oregon.

Director's Office

Address: 725 Summer St. NE, Suite A, Salem 97301
Phone: 503-986-0910
Contact: Tom Byler
Duties and Responsibilities: The Director's Office develops and supervises policies and programs to ensure that water management practices follow Oregon Water Law, oversees implementation of the State's Integrated Water Resources Strategy and serves as the principal contact with the Legislature and stakeholder groups. In addition, the Water Resources Development Program provides funding and technical assistance to help individuals and communities meet their water needs.

Water Resources Commission

Address: 725 Summer St. NE, Suite A, Salem 97301
Phone: 503-986-0900
Contact: Cindy Smith, Commission Assistant
Statutory Authority: ORS 536.022
Duties and Responsibilities: The seven-member Water Resources Commission oversees department activities and sets policy consistent with state law.

Field Services Division

Address: 725 Summer St. NE, Suite A, Salem 97301
Phone: 503-986-0847
Contact: Ivan Gall, Administrator
Duties and Responsibilities: The Field Services Division carries out the department's mission by enforcing the state's water laws and implementing the Water Resources Commission's policies in the field. The division has sole responsibility for the regulation of water uses based upon the water rights of record. Staff also inspects wells for protection of the groundwater resource, inspects dams for the protection of the public and collects streamflow and groundwater data for use by staff and the public.

Water Right Services Division

Address: 725 Summer St. NE, Suite A, Salem 97301
Phone: 503-986-0819
Contact: Dwight French, Administrator
Duties and Responsibilities: With some exceptions, in order to use water in Oregon, one must obtain a water right. The Water Right Services Division is responsible for the processing of water right permits to meet a variety of needs, including agriculture, drinking water, fish, wildlife, recreation and industry. In addition, the division processes other water right transactions that allow water right holders to change how their existing rights are used, including changes involving the transfer or lease of water instream. The division also adjudicates water right claims that pre-date the 1909 water code, as well as federal and tribal rights.

Groundwater Advisory Committee

Address: 725 Summer St. NE, Suite A, Salem 97301
Phone: 503-986-0900
Contact: Justin Iverson, Department Liaison; Garry Zollman, Chair
Statutory Authority: ORS 536.090
Duties and Responsibilities: The Groundwater Advisory Committee's nine members, appointed by the Water Resources Commission, represent a range of interests and expertise. The committee, established by the Legislature in 1977, advises the commission and WRD on rules, legislation and groundwater public policy and the licensing of well constructors, and reviews proposed expenditure of revenues generated from start card fees collected by WRD prior to a well construction.

Klamath River Basin Compact

Address: 6600 Washburn Way, Klamath Falls 97603
Phone: 541-973-4431
Contact: Chrysten Lambert, Chair, Klamath Falls, federal government representative; Tom Byler, Oregon representative; Curtis Anderson, California representative
Statutory Authority: 542.610
Duties and Responsibilities: Members of the Klamath River Basin Compact facilitate intergovernmental cooperation in development and proper use of the water resources of the Klamath River Basin.

Western States Water Council

Address: 682 E Vine St., Suite 202, Murray, UT 84107
Phone: 801-685-2555
Web: www.westernstateswater.org

Contact: Tony Willardson, Executive Director; Tom Byler, Oregon Executive Committee Member
Duties and Responsibilities: Created in 1965, the Western States Water Council facilitates cooperation among western states in the conservation, development and management of water resources. The council consists of representatives appointed by the governors of 18 western states: Alaska, Arizona, California, Colorado, Idaho, Kansas, Montana, Nebraska, Nevada, New Mexico, North Dakota, Oklahoma, Oregon, South Dakota, Texas, Utah, Washington and Wyoming.

WATERSHED ENHANCEMENT BOARD, OREGON

Address: 775 Summer St. NE, Suite 360, Salem 97301-1290
Phone: 503-986-0178
Fax: 503-986-0199
Email: darika.barnes@oweb.state.or.us
Web: www.oregon.gov/OWEB/Pages/index.aspx
Contact: Meta Loftsgaarden, Executive Director
Statutory Authority: ORS Chapter 541
Duties and Responsibilities: The Oregon Watershed Enhancement Board (OWEB) provides grants to help Oregonians take care of local streams, rivers, wetlands and natural areas. Community members and landowners use scientific criteria to decide jointly what needs to be done to conserve and improve rivers and natural habitats in the places where they live. OWEB grants are funded from the Oregon Lottery, federal dollars and salmon license plate revenue. The agency, which was created in 1999, is led by a 17-member citizen board drawn from the public at large, tribes, and federal and state natural resource agency boards and commissions. Headquartered in Salem, OWEB has 34 employees, six of whom are regional field representatives located in offices around the state.

WINE BOARD, OREGON

Address: 4640 SW Macadam Ave., Suite 240, Portland 97239
Phone: 503-228-8336
Fax: 503-228-8337
Email: info@oregonwine.org
Web: www.oregonwine.org; industry.oregonwine.org
Contact: Tom Danowski, Executive Director
Statutory Authority: ORS 576.753
Duties and Responsibilities: The Oregon Wine Board was established as a semi-independent state agency in 2003. The board consists of nine volunteer members appointed by the governor for a term of three years. The board and eight staff members

work on behalf of all Oregon wineries and independent growers throughout the state's diverse winegrowing regions managing marketing, research and education initiatives that support and advance the Oregon wine and wine grape industry.

YOUTH AUTHORITY, OREGON

Address: 530 Center St. NE, Suite 500, Salem 97301-3777
Phone: 503-373-7205
Fax: 503-373-7622
Email: oya.info@oya.state.or.us
Web: www.oregon.gov/OYA/Pages/index.aspx
Contact: Fariborz Pakseresht, Director
Statutory Authority: ORS Chapters 419A, 419C, 420, 420A
Duties and Responsibilities: The passage of Senate Bill 1 in 1995 established the Oregon Youth Authority (OYA). OYA protects the public and reduces crime by holding youth accountable for their behavior and providing opportunities for reformation in safe environments.

OYA provides treatment, education and job training services to youths aged 12 to 25. OYA exercises legal and physical custody over youths who commit offenses between the ages of 12 and 18 and have been committed to OYA by county juvenile courts, and physical custody over youths sentenced as adults to the legal custody of the Oregon Department of Corrections, but placed with OYA due to their young age.

OYA employs approximately 1,000 people throughout Oregon with central offices in Salem; provides probation and parole services in all 36 counties in Oregon; operates 11 close-custody facilities; and contracts with a range of residential treatment providers and foster parents to ensure youth receive the most appropriate combination of placement, treatment and other services needed to leave OYA's custody ready to lead productive, crime-free lives.

A boy slides down a snowy slope on an inner tube near Diamond Lake Lodge in 1976.
Oregon State Archives Photograph OHD8792

Oregon's judicial branch of government helps individuals, businesses and government groups resolve disputes, protect their rights and enforce their legal duties. Oregon judges review cases for compliance with federal, state and local laws. This section describes the judicial system and introduces Oregon's judges.

OREGON SUPREME COURT

Address: Supreme Court Bldg., 1163 State St., Salem 97301-2563
Records and Case Information: 503-986-5555; Oregon Relay 711
Fax: 503-986-5560

The Supreme Court of Oregon has seven justices elected by nonpartisan, statewide ballot to serve six-year terms. Justices elected to the Supreme Court must be United States citizens, members of the Oregon State Bar, and residents of Oregon for at least three years. The court has its offices and courtroom in the Supreme Court Building, one block east of the State Capitol in Salem. The members of the court elect one of their number to serve as chief justice for a six-year term.

Powers and Authority

The Supreme Court was created, and its role largely defined, by Article VII of the Oregon Constitution, as amended. It is primarily a court of review in that it reviews the decisions of the Court of Appeals in selected cases. The Supreme Court usually selects cases with significant legal issues calling for interpretation of laws or legal principles affecting many citizens and institutions of society. When the Supreme Court decides not to review a Court of Appeals case, the Court of Appeals' decision becomes final. In addition to its discretionary review function, the Supreme Court hears direct appeals in death penalty, lawyer and judicial discipline, and Oregon Tax Court cases. It may accept original jurisdiction in mandamus, quo warranto and habeas corpus proceedings. It also reviews ballot measure titles, prison siting disputes, reapportionment of legislative districts, and legal questions on Oregon law referred by federal courts.

Administrative Authority

The chief justice is the administrative head of the Judicial Department and exercises administrative authority over and supervises the appellate, circuit and tax courts. The chief justice makes rules and issues orders to carry out necessary duties and requires appropriate reports from judges and other officers and employees of the courts. As head of the Judicial Department, the chief justice appoints the chief judge of the Court of Appeals and the presiding judges of all state trial courts from the judges elected to those courts. The chief justice adopts certain rules and regulations respecting procedures for state courts. The chief justice also supervises a statewide plan for budgeting, accounting and fiscal management of the judicial department.

The chief justice and the Supreme Court have the authority to appoint lawyers, elected judges and retired judges to serve in temporary judicial assignments.

Admission and Discipline of Lawyers and Judges

The Supreme Court admits lawyers to practice law in Oregon and has the power to reprimand, suspend or disbar lawyers whose actions have been investigated and prosecuted by the Oregon State Bar. In admitting lawyers, the Supreme Court acts on the recommendation of the Board of Bar Examiners, which conducts examinations for lawyer applicants each February and July and which screens applicants for character and fitness to practice law. The Supreme Court appoints at least 14 members to the Board of Bar Examiners. The board includes two public members who are not lawyers. The Supreme Court also has the power to censure, suspend or remove judges after investigation and recommendation by the Commission on Judicial Fitness and Disability.

OREGON COURT OF APPEALS

Address: Supreme Court Bldg., 1163 State St., Salem 97301-2563
Records and Case Information: 503-986-5555; Oregon Relay 771
Fax: 503-986-5865

Created in 1969 as a five-judge court, the Court of Appeals was expanded to six judges in 1973, to ten judges in 1977 and to 13 judges in 2012. The judges, otherwise elected on a statewide, nonpartisan basis for six-year terms, must be United States citizens, members of the Oregon State Bar and qualified electors of their county of residence. The chief justice of the Supreme Court appoints a chief judge from among the judges of the Court of Appeals.

Court of Appeals judges have their offices in the Justice Building in Salem and usually hear cases in the courtroom of the Supreme Court Building. The court ordinarily sits in panels of three judges. The Supreme Court has authority to appoint a Supreme Court justice, a circuit court judge or an Oregon Tax Court judge to serve as a judge pro tempore of the Court of Appeals. In 1995, the Court of Appeals established an Appellate Settlement Conference Program for mediation of cases in that court.

Jurisdiction

The Court of Appeals has jurisdiction to review appeals of most civil and criminal cases and most state administrative agency actions. The exceptions are appeals in death penalty, lawyer and judicial disciplinary, and Oregon Tax Court cases, which go directly to the Oregon Supreme Court.

Reviews and Decisions

A party aggrieved by a decision of the Court of Appeals may petition the Supreme Court for review within 35 days after the Court of Appeals issues its decision. The Supreme Court determines whether to review the case. The Supreme Court allows a petition for review whenever at least one fewer than a majority of the Supreme Court judges participating vote to allow it.

OREGON TAX COURT

Address: Robertson Bldg., 1241 State St., 4th Floor, Salem 97301-2563
Phone: 503-986-5645; TTY: 503-986-5651
Fax: 503-986-5507

The Oregon Tax Court has exclusive, statewide jurisdiction in all questions of law or fact arising under state tax laws, including income taxes, corporate excise taxes, property taxes, timber taxes, cigarette taxes, local budget law and property tax limitations.

The Oregon Tax Court consists of the Magistrate Division and the Regular Division. The judge of the Oregon Tax Court appoints a presiding magistrate and one or more other magistrates to serve in the Magistrate Division.

Trials in the Magistrate Division are informal proceedings. Statutory rules of evidence do not apply, and the trials are not reported. The proceedings may be conducted by telephone or in person. A taxpayer may be represented by a lawyer, public accountant, real estate broker or appraiser.

All decisions of the magistrates may be appealed to the Regular Division of the Oregon Tax Court.

Appeals from the Magistrate Division are made directly to the Regular Division of the Oregon Tax Court. The judge of the Oregon Tax Court presides over trials in the Regular Division. The Regular Division is comparable to a circuit court and exercises equivalent powers. All trials are before the judge only, no jury, and are reported. The parties may either represent themselves or be represented by an attorney. Appeals from the judge's decision are made directly to the Oregon Supreme Court.

The judge serves a six-year term and is elected on the statewide, nonpartisan judicial ballot.

CIRCUIT COURTS

Each county has a circuit court, which is a state trial court of general jurisdiction. However, except for cases involving the termination of parental rights, Gilliam, Sherman and Wheeler Counties also have "county courts," which exercise jurisdiction in juvenile cases. In addition, Gilliam, Grant, Harney, Malheur, Sherman and Wheeler Counties' county courts exercise jurisdiction in probate, adoption, guardianship and conservatorship cases.

Circuit court judges are elected on a nonpartisan ballot for a term of six years. They must be citizens of the United States, members of the Oregon State Bar, residents of Oregon for at least three years and residents of their judicial district for at least one year, except Multnomah County judges, who may

reside within ten miles of the county. There are 173 circuit judges serving 36 Oregon counties. The circuit judges are grouped in 27 geographical areas called judicial districts. Multnomah County District has 38 circuit judges; Lane, 15; Marion and Washington, 14; Clackamas, 11; Jackson, 9; Deschutes, 7; Coos-Curry, 6; four districts have five judges, three districts have four judges, six districts have three judges, three districts have two judges and three districts have one judge.

To expedite judicial business, the chief justice of the Supreme Court may assign any circuit judge to sit in any judicial district in the state.

Senior Judges

Under Oregon law, a judge who retires from the circuit court, Oregon Tax Court, Court of Appeals or Supreme Court, except a judge retired under the provisions of ORS 1.310, may be designated a senior judge of the state by the Supreme Court and is eligible for temporary assignment by the Supreme Court to any state court at or below the level in which he or she last served as a full-time judge. The current roster of senior judges follows:

From the Supreme Court: Richard Baldwin, Wallace P. Carson, Jr., Paul J. De Muniz, Robert D. Durham, W. Michael Gillette, Susan M. Leeson, Hans Linde, Virginia L. Linder, Edwin Peterson, R. William Riggs, George Van Hoomissen

From the Court of Appeals or Oregon Tax Court: Carl N. Byers, Mary J. Deits, Walter Edmonds, Rick T. Haselton, William L. Richardson, David Schuman, John Warden, Robert Wollheim

From the circuit courts: Pamela L. Abernethy, Ted Abram, Marshall L. Amiton, G. Philip Arnold, Fred Avera, Raymond Bagley, Glen D. Baisinger, Frank L. Bearden, Mary Ann Bearden, William Beckett, Douglas G. Beckman, Linda Bergman, Jack A. Billings, Alan C. Bonebrake, Sid Brockley, Nancy W. Campbell, Cynthia Carlson, H. Ted Carp, Joseph F. Ceniceros, Ronald E. Cinniger, Rita B. Cobb, Allan H. Coon, Ross Davis, Don A. Dickey, Henry R. Dickinson, Jr., Jim Donnell, Hugh C. Downer, Jr., James R. Ellis, Greg Foote, Kimberly C. Frankel, Jackson L. Frost, Stephen A. Gallagher, Mark Gardner, Robert S. Gardner, Randolph L. Garrison, David Gernant, Michael J. Gillespie, James C. Goode, Dennis Graves, Joe Guimond, David Hantke, Daniel L. Harris, Wayne R. Harris, Barbara Haslinger, Eveleen Henry, Bryan T. Hodges, Janet S. Holcomb, William Horner, Robert J. Huckleberry, Don Hull, Rodger Isaacson, Nely L. Johnson, Donald Kalberer, Mitchell A. Karaman, John V. Kelly, Karla J. Knieps, Frank D. Knight, Dale R. Koch, Thomas W. Kohl, Thomas Kolberg, Paula J. Kurshner, Kristena La Mar, Darryl Larson, William Lasswell, Terry A. Leggert, Kip Leonard, William O. Lewis, Paul J. Lipscomb, John Lowe, Jon B. Lund, Charles E. Luukinen, William S.

continued on page 98

Judicial

Supreme Court

Balmer, Thomas A.
Chief Justice
Position 1
Served since 2001
Term expires 1/2021

Brewer, David
Associate Justice
Position 2
Served since 2013
Term expires 1/2019

Kistler, Rives
Associate Justice
Position 4
Served since 2003
Term expires 1/2023

Landau, Jack L.
Associate Justice
Position 5
Served since 2011
Term expires 1/2023

Nakamoto, Lynn
Associate Justice
Position 6
Served since 2016
Term expires 1/2019

Walters, Martha Lee
Associate Justice
Position 7
Served since 2006
Term expires 1/2021

Position
Vacant

Associate Justice
Position 3 Vacant
pending Governor's
appointment

Court of Appeals

Hadlock, Erika L.
Chief Judge
Position 9
Served since 2011
Term expires 1/2019

Armstrong, Rex
Associate Judge
Position 10
Served since 1995
Term expires 1/2019

DeHoog, Roger J.
Associate Judge
Position 8
Served since 2016
Term expires 1/2019

DeVore, Joel
Associate Judge
Position 11
Served since 2013
Term expires 1/2021

Duncan, Rebecca
Associate Judge
Position 2
Served since 2010
Term expires 1/2023

Egan, James
Associate Judge
Position 6
Served since 2013
Term expires 1/2019

Flynn, Meagan A.
Associate Judge
Position 7
Served since 2014
Term expires 1/2023

Garrett, Christopher
Associate Judge
Position 1
Served since 2014
Term expires 1/2021

Lagesen, Erin
Associate Judge
Position 12
Served since 2013
Term expires 1/2021

Judicial

Ortega, Darleen
Associate Judge
Position 3
Served since 2003
Term expires 1/2023

Sercombe, Timothy
Associate Judge
Position 4
Served since 2007
Term expires 1/2021

Shorr, Scott A.
Associate Judge
Position 5
Served since 2016
Term expires 1/2019

Tookey, Douglas L.
Associate Judge
Position 13
Served since 2013
Term expires 1/2021

Oregon Tax Court

Breithaupt, Henry C.
Tax Judge
Served since 2001
Term expires 1/2021

continued from page 95

Mackay, Jean K. Maurer, Steven Maurer, Robert B. McConville, John A. McCormick, Rick J. McCormick, Keith E. Meisenheimer, L. A. Merryman, Richard Mickelson, Robert Millikan, Douglas Mitchell, Robert J. Morgan, Thomas M. Mosgrove, Thomas Moultrie, Rudy M. Murgo, Gayle A. Nachtigal, George W. Neilson, Philip L. Nelson, Gerald C. Neufeld, Joseph V. Ochoa, Loyd O'Neal, Rebecca Orf, Ronald J. Pahl, Dale W. Penn, Hollie M. Pihl, J. Burdette Pratt, Steven Price, William G. Purdy, Richard Rambo, Robert Redding, Steven B. Reed, Garry L. Reynolds, Jamese Rhoades, Rick W. Roll, Don H. Sanders, Mark S. Schiveley, Joan G. Seitz, Robert Selander, Lane W. Simpson, Berkeley Smith, Bernard L. Smith, William C. Snouffer, Michael C. Sullivan, Patricia A. Sullivan, Ronald D. Thom, Gary S. Thompson, Carroll Tichenor, Stephen

Tiktin, Eric Valentine, Pierre Van Rysselberghe, Lyle Velure, Robert Walberg, Elizabeth Welch, C. Gregory West, Raymond B. White, Janice R. Wilson, John Wilson, Jan Wyers, Frank J. Yraguen

From the district courts:* Richard J. Courson, Robert L. Gilliland, Charles H. Reeves.

*Effective January 15, 1998, all district courts were abolished and the powers, functions and judges of the district courts were transferred to the circuit courts.

JUDICIAL CONFERENCE

The Oregon Judicial Conference, created under ORS 1.810, is composed of all judges of the Supreme Court, Court of Appeals, Tax Court, circuit courts and all senior judges certified under ORS 1.300. The chief justice of the Supreme Court is chair of the conference, and the state court administrator acts as executive secretary. Under ORS 1.820, the conference may make a continuous survey and study of the organization, jurisdiction, procedure, practice and methods of administration and operation of the various courts within the state.

The Judicial Conference meets annually to conduct their business meeting, attend educational seminars, issue committee reports and adopt resolutions, if any.

STATE COURT ADMINISTRATOR, OFFICE OF THE

Source: Kingsley W. Click, Administrator
Address: 510 Justice Bldg. Mail: Supreme Court Bldg., 1163 State St., Salem 97301-2563
Phone: 503-986-5500; Oregon Relay 711
Fax: 503-986-5503
Web: http://courts.oregon.gov/OJD/OSCA

The state court administrator position was statutorily created in 1971 to assist the chief justice in exercising administrative authority and supervision over the state courts. In 1983, with unification and state funding of the trial and appellate courts, the duties of the position expanded to include supervision of the personnel plan for nonjudge staff and human resources; supervision of the accounting system for the state courts; preparation and management of the consolidated budget, revenue, and collections system; management of the legislative program requirements; inventory of state court property and procurement; internal audit; provision of legal contracts and services; collection and compilation of state court statistics; maintenance of a statewide automated information system; continuing education programs for judges and nonjudge staff; development of statewide administrative, personnel, fiscal and records policies and procedures concerning the courts, public information, and long-range planning for the future needs of the courts. (*See ORS 8.110 and 8.125*)

In addition, the state court administrator oversees staff responsible for managing records of all cases filed with the Supreme Court, Court of Appeals and Oregon Tax Court. The administrator publishes the opinions of the Supreme Court, Court of

Appeals and Oregon Tax Court and oversees the State Law Library. The administrator also has responsibility for administrative management of the Office of the State Court Administrator, including the State Court Security program, State Court Interpreter program, Certified Shorthand Reporters program and the State Citizen Review Board program. Under ORS 30.273, the state court administrator also calculates and posts the annual adjustment to the liability limitations under the Oregon Tort Claims Act.

STATE OF OREGON LAW LIBRARY

Source: Cathryn Bowie, State Law Librarian
Address: 1163 State St., Supreme Court Bldg., Salem 97301-2563
Phone: 503-986-5640; TTY: 503-986-5561
Fax: 503-986-5623
Web: www.oregon.gov/SOLL

The State of Oregon Law Library (SOLL) traces its origins to the organization of the territorial government of Oregon. The Territorial Act of 1848 provided for the establishment of a library "to be kept at the seat of government." An 1851 act provided for the appointment of a librarian and defined the librarian's duties. The library served a broad constituency from its beginnings: "Members of the legislature, and its clerks and officers; Judges of the Supreme and District Courts, and their clerks; Attorney-general and marshall of the Territory; attorneys-at-law, secretary of the Territory; and all other persons, shall have access to the library, and the privileges allowed by law." This inclusive policy was continued with statehood in 1859 and after charge and control of the library was transferred to the Supreme Court in 1905.

Today, the mission of the library is to provide the comprehensive legal resources that the executive, legislative and judicial branches of state government require to serve the public effectively

continued on page 123

Cases Filed in Oregon Courts 2010–2015

	2010	2011	2012	2013	2014	2015
Oregon Supreme Court	1,271	1,191	1,219	1,325	977	886
Oregon Court of Appeals	3,093	2,943	2,910	2,652	2,566	2,598
Oregon Tax Court, Regular	53	71	97	43	37	27
Oregon Tax Court, Magistrate	1,374	1,310	885	580	470	575
Circuit Courts	565,397	552,601	*547,598	*541,928	532,136	503,244

* Combination of two reporting systems as the courts transition to updated computer software

Circuit Court

Abar, Donald D.
Marion
District 3, Position 11

Adkisson, Marci W.
Klamath (P)
District 13, Position 3

Adler, A. Michael
Deschutes
District 11, Position 4

Ahern, Daniel J.
Crook, Jefferson (P)
District 22, Position 2

Albrecht, Cheryl
Multnomah
District 4, Position 31

Allen, Beth
Multnomah
District 4, Position 34

Ambrosini, George
Douglas
District 16, Position 5

Armstrong, Sean E
Marion
District 3, Position 7

Ashby, Wells B.
Deschutes
District 11, Position 6

Avera, Sally
Polk
District 12, Position 1

Bachart, Sheryl
Lincoln
District 17, Position 1

Bagley, Beth
Deschutes
District 11, Position 2

Bailey, Charlie
Washington (P)
District 20, Position 6

Baker, Lindi L.
Josephine (P)
District 14, Position 4

Barnack, Tim
Jackson
District 1, Position 6

Barron, Richard L.
Coos, Curry (P)
District 15, Position 2

Baxter, Greg
Baker (P)
District 8, Position 1

Beaman, Cynthia
Coos, Curry
District 15, Position 6

Bechtold, Paula M.
Coos, Curry
District 15, Position 5

Bennett, J. Channing
Marion
District 3, Position 1

Bergstrom, Eric
Multnomah
District 4, Position 8

Bispham, Carol R.
Linn
District 23, Position 1

Bloch, Eric J.
Multnomah
District 4, Position 20

Bloom, Benjamin M.
Jackson
District 1, Position 7

Bottomly, Leslie G.
Multnomah
District 4, Position 6

Brady, Alta J.
Deschutes (P)
District 11, Position 1

Branford, Thomas O.
Lincoln (P)
District 17, Position 3

Brauer, Christopher R.
Morrow, Umatilla
District 6, Position 5

Brownhill, Paula J.
Clatsop (P)
District 18, Position 1

Broyles, Audrey J.
Marion
District 3, Position 9

Bunch, Dan
Klamath
District 13, Position 5

Burge, Frances
Douglas (P)
District 16, Position 4

Burton, Claudia M.
Marion
District 3, Position 4

Bushong, Stephen
Multnomah
District 4, Position 21

Butterfield, Eric
Washington
District 20, Position 4

Callahan, Cathleen B.
Columbia
District 19, Position 1

Campbell, Monte S.
Polk (P)
District 12, Position 2

Carlson, Charles D.
Lane
District 2, Position 2

Chanti, Suzanne
Lane
District 2, Position 9

Collins, John L.
Yamhill
District 25, Position 1

Connell, David B.
Benton (P)
District 21, Position 3

Conover, R. Curtis
Lane
District 2, Position 12

Crain, Patricia
Jackson
District 1, Position 4

Cramer, William D., Jr.
Grant, Harney (P)
District 24, Position 1

Dahlin, Eric L.
Multnomah
District 4, Position 24

Dailey, Kathleen M.
Multnomah
District 4, Position 25

Darling, Deanne L.
Clackamas
District 5, Position 9

Day, Vance D.
Marion
District 3, Position 5

Delsman, David E.
Linn
District 23, Position 2

Donohue, Matthew J.
Benton
District 21, Position 2

Easterday, Cynthia
Yamhill
District 25, Position 3

Erwin, Andrew R.
Washington
District 20, Position 7

Flint, Bethany P.
Deschutes
District 11, Position 3

Forte, Stephen P.
Deschutes
District 11, Position 7

Frantz, Julie
Multnomah
District 4, Position 10

Fun, James Lee, Jr.
Washington
District 20, Position 13

Garcia, Oscar
Washington
District 20, Position 9

Gerking, Timothy
Jackson (P)
District 1, Position 5

Geyer, Courtland
Marion
District 3, Position 12

Grant, Jenefer
Columbia (P)
District 19, Position 3

Greenlick, Michael A.
Multnomah
District 4, Position 19

Greif, Lisa
Jackson
District 1, Position 8

Grensky, Ron
Jackson
District 1, Position 9

Grove, Ted
Columbia
District 19, Position 2

Hampton, Lynn W.
Morrow, Umatilla
District 6, Position 1

Hart, Thomas M.
Marion
District 3, Position 13

Henry, Patrick W.
Multnomah
District 4, Position 35

Herndon, Robert D.
Clackamas (P)
District 5, Position 7

Hill, Daniel J.
Morrow, Umatilla (P)
District 6, Position 3

Hill, Jonathan R.
Tillamook (P)
District 27, Position 1

Hill, Norman R.
Polk
District 12, Position 3

Hillman, Annette
Crook, Jefferson
District 22, Position 1

Hodson, Jerry
Multnomah
District 4, Position 3

Holland, Lauren S.
Lane
District 2, Position 11

Holmes Hehn, Amy
Multnomah
District 4, Position 14

Hoppe, David G.
Jackson
District 1, Position 2

Hull, Thomas M.
Josephine
District 14, Position 1

Hung, Lung S.
Malheur (P)
District 9, Position 2

Immergut, Karin
Multnomah
District 4, Position 26

Jacquot, Megan L.
Coos, Curry
District 15, Position 4

James, Bronson D.
Multnomah
District 4, Position 15

James, Mary
Marion
District 3, Position 6

Janney, Andrea M.
Klamath
District 13, Position 1

Johnson, Kathleen E.
Douglas
District 16, Position 3

Jones, Edward J.
Multnomah
District 4, Position 23

Jones, Jeffrey S.
Clackamas
District 5, Position 1

Kantor, Henry
Multnomah
District 4, Position 30

Karabeika, Heather L.
Clackamas
District 5, Position 8

Kasubhai, Mustafa
Lane
District 2, Position 3

LaBarre, Jerome
Multnomah
District 4, Position 7

Judicial

Landis, Erin Keith
Malheur
District 9, Position 1

Leith, David E.
Marion
District 3, Position 8

Letourneau, Donald R.
Washington
District 20, Position 3

Lieuallen, Jon S.
Morrow, Umatilla
District 6, Position 2

Litzenberger, Marilyn
Multnomah
District 4, Position 38

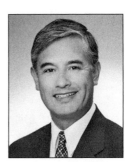

Lopez, Angel
Multnomah
District 4, Position 22

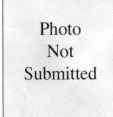

Photo
Not
Submitted

Love, Valeri L.
Lane
District 2, Position 8

Loy, Michael S.
Multnomah
District 4, Position 33

Margolis, Jesse
Coos, Curry
District 15, Position 3

Marshall, Christopher J.
Multnomah
District 4, Position 5

Marshall, William A.
Douglas
District 16, Position 2

Matarazzo, Judith H.
Multnomah
District 4, Position 28

Matyas, Cindee S.
Clatsop
District 18, Position 3

McAlpin, Jay A.
Lane
District 2, Position 7

McHill, Thomas
Linn
District 23, Position 5

McIntosh, Dawn M.
Clatsop
District 18, Position 2

McIntyre, Kerrie K.
Lane
District 2, Position 13

McKnight, Maureen H.
Multnomah
District 4, Position 13

Mejia, Lorenzo A.
Jackson
District 1, Position 1

Menchaca, Ricardo
Washington
District 20, Position 8

Merten, Maurice K.
Lane
District 2, Position 6

Miller, Eve L.
Clackamas
District 5, Position 2

Miller, Walter R., Jr.
Deschutes
District 11, Position 5

Mooney, Josephine H.
Lane
District 2, Position 10

Murphy, Daniel R.
Linn (P)
District 23, Position 3

Nelson, Adrienne C.
Multnomah
District 4, Position 4

Newman, Michael
Josephine
District 14, Position 3

Nichols, Robert F.
Lake (P)
District 26, Position 1

Norby, Susie
Clackamas
District 5, Position 11

Novotny, DeAnn L.
Linn
District 23, Position 4

Olson, John A.
Gilliam, Hood River,
Sherman, Wasco,
Wheeler (P)
District 7, Position 1

Osborne, Roxanne B.
Klamath
District 13, Position 2

Ostrye, Karen
Gilliam, Hood River,
Sherman, Wasco,
Wheeler
District 7, Position 3

Pagán, Ramón A.
Washington
District 20, Position 14

Partridge, Lindsay R.
Marion
District 3, Position 10

Pellegrini, Cheryl
Marion
District 3, Position 3

Judicial

Prall, Tracy A.
Marion (P)
District 3, Position 2

Raines, Keith R.
Washington
District 20, Position 5

Rasmussen, Karsten H.
Lane (P)
District 2, Position 1

Rastetter, Thomas
Clackamas
District 5, Position 10

Ravassipour, Kelly W.
Jackson
District 1, Position 3

Rees, David
Multnomah
District 4, Position 9

Rigmaiden, Clara L.
Lane
District 2, Position 15

Roberts, Beth
Washington
District 20, Position 12

Roberts, Leslie
Multnomah
District 4, Position 37

Rooke-Ley, Ilisa
Lane
District 2, Position 5

Ryan, Thomas
Multnomah
District 4, Position 18

Sanders, Paulette
Lincoln
District 17, Position 2

Silver, Gregory F.
Multnomah
District 4, Position 12

Simmons, Ann Marie G.
Douglas
District 16, Position 1

Sims, Theodore E.
Washington
District 20, Position 1

Skye, Kelly
Multnomah
District 4, Position 17

Stauffer, Janet L.
Gilliam, Hood River,
Sherman, Wasco,
Wheeler
District 7, Position 2

Steele, Kathie F.
Clackamas
District 5, Position 6

Stone, Martin E.
Coos, Curry
District 15, Position 1

Stone, Ronald W.
Yamhill (P)
District 25, Position 2

Stuart, Diana
Multnomah
District 4, Position 27

Svetkey, Susan M.
Multnomah
District 4, Position 16

Temple, Eva J.
Morrow, Umatilla
District 6, Position 4

Tennyson, Katherine
Multnomah
District 4, Position 1

Thompson, Kirsten E.
Washington
District 20, Position 2

Trevino, Mari
Tillamook
District 27, Position 2

Tripp, Susan
Marion
District 3, Position 14

Upton, Suzanne
Washington
District 20, Position 10

Van Dyk, Douglas V.
Clackamas
District 5, Position 4

Villa-Smith, Kathryn L.
Multnomah
District 4, Position 29

Vogt, Debra
Lane
District 2, Position 14

Walker, Kenneth
Multnomah
District 4, Position 11

Waller, Nan G.
Multnomah (P)
District 4, Position 2

Weber, Katherine
Clackamas
District 5, Position 5

West, Russell B.
Union, Wallowa (P)
District 10, Position 2

Wetzel, Michael
Clackamas
District 5, Position 3

Wiles, Ladd
Yamhill
District 25, Position 4

Williams, Gary
Crook, Jefferson
District 22, Position 3

Williams, Locke A.
Benton
District 21, Position 1

Wipper, Janelle F.
Washington
District 20, Position 11

Wittmayer, John
Multnomah
District 4, Position 36

Wogan, Cameron F.
Klamath
District 13, Position 4

Wolf, John A.
Gilliam, Hood River,
Sherman, Wasco, Wheeler
District 7, Position 4

Wolke, Pat
Josephine
District 14, Position 2

Wyatt, Merri Souther
Multnomah
District 4, Position 32

Zennaché, Charles
Lane
District 2, Position 4

CIRCUIT COURT JUDGES BY DISTRICT

District 1—Jackson
Jackson County Justice Bldg., Medford 97501

Barnack, Tim
Pos. 6, Exp. 1-4-21, 541-776-7171 x168

Bloom, Benjamin M.
Pos. 7, Exp. 1-7-19, 541-776-7171 x230

Crain, Patricia
Pos. 4, Exp. 1-2-23, 541-776-7171 x112

Gerking, Timothy G. (presiding judge)
Pos. 5, Exp. 1-7-19, 541-776-7171 x172

Greif, Lisa
Pos. 8, Exp. 1-4-21, 541-776-7171 x108

Grensky, Ron
Pos. 9, Exp. 1-7-19, 541-776-7171 x169

Hoppe, David
Pos. 2, Exp. 1-4-21, 541-776-7171 x173

Mejia, Lorenzo A.
Pos. 1, Exp. 1-4-21, 541-776-7171 x164

Ravassipour, Kelly W.
Pos. 3, Exp. 1-4-21, 541-776-7171 x163

District 2—Lane
Lane County Courthouse, Eugene 97401

Carlson, Charles D.
Pos. 2, Exp. 1-4-21, 541-682-4257

Chanti, Suzanne
Pos. 9, Exp. 1-2-23, 541-682-4254

Conover, R. Curtis
Pos. 12, Exp. 1-7-19, 541-682-4497

Holland, Lauren S.
Pos. 11, Exp. 1-2-23, 541-682-4415

Kasubhai, Mustafa
Pos. 3, Exp. 1-4-21, 541-682-4256

Love, Valeri L.
Pos. 8, Exp. 1-7-19, 541-682-4753

McAlpin, Jay A.
Pos. 7, Exp. 1-7-19, 541-682-4240

McIntyre, Karrie K.
Pos. 13, Exp. 1-2-23, 541-682-4218

Merten, Maurice K.
Pos. 6, Exp. 1-2-23, 541-682-4258

Mooney, Josephine H.
Pos. 10, Exp. 1-7-19, 541-682-3601

Rasmussen, Karsten H. (presiding judge)
Pos. 1, Exp. 1-7-19, 541-682-4253

Rigmaiden, Clara L.
Pos. 15, Exp. 1-4-21, 541-682-4250

Rooke-Ley, Ilisa
Pos. 5, Exp. 1-2-23, 541-682-4300

Vogt, Debra
Pos. 14, Exp. 1-7-19, 541-682-4027

Zennaché, Charles
Pos. 4, Exp. 1-4-21, 541-682-4259

District 3—Marion
Marion County Courthouse, Salem 97309-0869

Abar, Donald D.
Pos. 11, Exp. 1-7-19, 503-585-4939

Armstrong, Sean E.
Pos. 7, Exp. 1-7-19, 503-588-5026

Bennett, J. Channing
Pos. 1, Exp. 1-7-19, 503-588-7950

Broyles, Audrey J.
Pos. 9, Exp. 1-2-23, 503-588-5492

Burton, Claudia M.
Pos. 4, Exp. 1-2-23, 503-584-7713

Day, Vance D.
Pos. 5, Exp. 1-7-19, 503-585-8485

Geyer, Courtland
Pos. 12, Exp. 1-7-19, 503-373-4445

Hart, Thomas M.
Pos. 13, Exp. 1-2-23, 503-584-7749

James, Mary
Pos. 6, Exp. 1-2-23, 503-373-4303

Leith, David E.
Pos. 8, Exp. 1-7-19, 503-588-5160

Partridge, Lindsay R.
Pos. 10, Exp. 1-7-19, 503-588-5028

Pellegrini, Cheryl
Pos. 3, Exp. 1-4-21, 503-588-5020

Prall, Tracy A. (presiding judge)
Pos. 2, Exp. 1-4-21, 503-588-5030

Tripp, Susan
Pos. 14, Exp. 1-4-21, 503-373-4361

District 4—Multnomah

Multnomah County Courthouse, Portland 97204

Albrecht, Cheryl
Pos. 31, Exp. 1-7-19, 503-988-3835

Allen, Beth
Pos. 34, Exp. 1-4-21, 503-988-3250

Bergstrom, Eric
Pos. 8, Exp. 1-7-19, 503-988-5029

Bloch, Eric J.
Pos. 20, Exp. 1-2-23, 503-988-3954

Bottomly, Leslie G.
Pos. 6, Exp. 1-4-21, 503-988-3404

Bushong, Stephen
Pos. 21, Exp. 1-4-21, 503-988-3546

Dahlin, Eric L.
Pos. 24, Exp. 1-4-21, 503-988-3668

Dailey, Kathleen M.
Pos. 25, Exp. 1-2-23, 503-988-3062

Frantz, Julie
Pos. 10, Exp. 1-4-21, 503-988-3045

Greenlick, Michael A.
Pos. 19, Exp. 1-4-21, 503-988-3214

Henry, Patrick W.
Pos. 35, Exp. 1-7-19, 503-988-5010

Hodson, Jerry
Pos. 3, Exp. 1-7-19, 503-988-5101

Holmes Hehn, Amy
Pos. 14, Exp. 1-4-21, 503-988-3052

Immergut, Karin
Pos. 26, Exp. 1-2-23, 503-988-5008

James, Bronson D.
Pos. 15, Exp. 1-2-23, 503-988-5544

Jones, Edward J.
Pos. 23, Exp. 1-7-19, 503-988-3540

Kantor, Henry
Pos. 30, Exp. 1-4-21, 503-988-3972

LaBarre, Jerome
Pos. 7, Exp. 1-7-19, 503-988-3348

Litzenberger, Marilyn
Pos. 38, Exp. 1-4-21, 503-988-3365

Lopez, Angel
Pos. 22, Exp. 1-2-23, 503-988-3068

Loy, Michael S.
Pos. 33, Exp. 1-4-21, 503-988-3813

Marshall, Christopher J.
Pos. 5, Exp. 1-4-21, 503-988-3274

Matarazzo, Judith Hudson
Pos. 28, Exp. 1-7-19, 503-988-3227

McKnight, Maureen H.
Pos. 13, Exp. 1-4-21 503-988-3986

Nelson, Adrienne C.
Pos. 4, Exp. 1-7-19, 503-988-5047

Rees, David
Pos. 9, Exp. 1-2-23, 503-988-3803

Roberts, Leslie
Pos. 37, Exp. 1-7-19, 503-988-6760

Ryan, Thomas
Pos. 18, Exp. 1-4-21, 503-988-3008

Silver, Gregory F.
Pos. 12, Exp. 1-4-21, 503-988-3069

Skye, Kelly
Pos. 17, Exp. 1-2-23, 503-988-3204

Stuart, Diana
Pos. 27, Exp. 1-4-21, 503-988-3201

Svetkey, Susan M.
Pos. 16, Exp. 1-7-19, 503-988-3060

Tennyson, Katherine
Pos. 1, Exp. 1-4-21, 503-988-3078

Villa-Smith, Kathryn L.
Pos. 29, Exp. 1-7-19, 503-988-3985

Walker, Kenneth
Pos. 11, Exp. 1-4-21, 503-988-3041

Waller, Nan G. (presiding judge)
Pos. 2, Exp. 1-4-21, 503-988-3846

Wittmayer, John
Pos. 36, Exp. 1-4-21, 503-988-3165

Wyatt, Merri Souther
Pos. 32, Exp. 1-7-19, 503-988-3029

District 5—Clackamas

Clackamas County Courthouse, Oregon City 97045

Darling, Deanne L.
Pos. 9, Exp. 1-4-21, 503-557-2841

Herndon, Robert D. (presiding judge)
Pos. 7, Exp. 1-2-23, 503-655-8644

Jones, Jeffrey S.
Pos. 1, Exp. 1-7-19, 503-655-8687

Karabeika, Heather L.
Pos. 8, Exp. 1-4-21, 503-655-8643

Miller, Eve L.
Pos. 2, Exp. 1-2-23, 503-655-8686

Norby, Susie
Pos. 11, Exp. 1-7-19, 503-650-8902

Rastetter, Thomas
Pos. 10, Exp. 1-2-23, 503-655-8432

Steele, Kathie F.
Pos. 6, Exp. 1-4-21, 503-655-8678

Van Dyk, Douglas V.
Pos. 4, Exp. 1-2-23, 503-655-8688

Weber, Katherine
Pos. 5, Exp. 1-2-23, 503-655-8233

Wetzel, Michael
Pos. 3, Exp. 1-7-19, 503-655-8685

District 6—Morrow, Umatilla
Umatilla County Courthouse, Pendleton 97801

Brauer, Christopher R.
Pos. 5, Exp. 1-7-19, 541-278-0341 x222

Hampton, Lynn W.
Pos. 1, Exp. 1-7-19, 541-278-0341 x232

Lieuallen, Jon S.
Pos. 2, Exp. 1-2-23, 541-278-0341 x225

Stafford Hansell Gov't Center, Hermiston 97838

Hill, Daniel J. (presiding judge)
Pos. 3, Exp. 1-2-23, 541-667-3034

Temple, Eva J.
Pos. 4, Exp. 1-7-19, 541-667-3031

District 7—Gilliam, Hood River, Sherman, Wasco, Wheeler
Hood River Co. Courthouse, Hood River 97031

Olson, John A. (presiding judge)
Pos. 1, Exp. 1-4-21, 541-387-6913

Ostrye, Karen
Pos. 3, Exp. 1-4-21, 541-387-6906

Wasco County Courthouse, The Dalles 97058

Stauffer, Janet L.
Pos. 2, Exp. 1-2-23, 541-506-2710

Wolf, John A.
Pos. 4, Exp. 1-2-23, 541-506-2717

District 8—Baker
Baker County Courthouse, Baker City 97814

Baxter, Greg (presiding judge)
Pos. 1, Exp. 1-7-19, 541-523-6303

District 9—Malheur
Malheur County Courthouse, Vale 97918

Hung, Lung S. (presiding judge)
Pos. 2, Exp. 1-7-19, 541-473-5568

Landis, Erin Keith
Pos. 1, Exp. 1-2-23, 541-473-5568

District 10—Union, Wallowa
Union County Courthouse, La Grande 97850
Wallowa County Courthouse, Enterprise 97828

West, Russell B. (presiding judge)
Pos. 2, Exp. 1-4-21, 541-962-9500 x2225;
541-426-4991

Vacant
Pos. 1, Exp. 1-7-19, 541-962-9500 x2231;
541-426-4991

District 11—Deschutes
Deschutes County Courthouse, Bend 97701

Adler, A. Michael
Pos. 4, Exp. 1-2-23, 541-388-5300 x2490

Ashby, Wells B.
Pos. 6, Exp. 1-2-23, 541-388-5300 x2520

Bagley, Beth
Pos. 2, Exp. 1-7-19, 541-388-5300 x2410

Brady, Alta J. (presiding judge)
Pos. 1, Exp. 1-7-19, 541-388-5300 x2450

Flint, Bethany P.
Pos. 3, Exp. 1-7-19, 541-388-5300 x2370

Forte, Stephen P.
Pos. 7, Exp. 1-4-21, 541-388-5300 x2580

Miller, Walter R., Jr.
Pos. 5, Exp. 1-4-21, 541-388-5300 x2550

District 12—Polk
Polk County Courthouse, Dallas 97338

Avera, Sally
Pos. 1, Exp. 1-7-19, 503-831-1776

Campbell, Monte S. (presiding judge)
Pos. 2, Exp. 1-2-23, 503-623-9245

Hill, Norman R.
Pos. 3, Exp. 1-7-19, 503-623-5235

District 13—Klamath
Klamath Co. Courthouse, Klamath Falls 97601

Adkisson, Marci Warner (presiding judge)
Pos. 3, Exp. 1-2-23, 541-883-5503 x251

Bunch, Dan
Pos. 5, Exp. 1-2-23, 541-883-5503 x255

Janney, Andrea M.
Pos. 1, Exp. 1-4-21, 541-883-5503 x247

Osborne, Roxanne Burgett
Pos. 2, Exp. 1-2-23, 541-883-5503 x257

Wogan, Cameron F.
Pos. 4, Exp. 1-2-23, 541-883-5503 x244

District 14—Josephine
Josephine County Courthouse, Grants Pass 97526

Baker, Lindi L. (presiding judge)
Pos. 4, Exp. 1-2-23, 541-476-2309 x243

Hull, Thomas M.
Pos. 1, Exp. 1-7-19, 541-476-2309 x232

Newman, Michael
Pos. 3, Exp. 1-2-23, 541-476-2309 x250, 314

Wolke, Pat
Pos. 2, Exp. 1-7-19, 541-476-2309 x218

Judicial

District 15—Coos, Curry
Coos County Courthouse, Coquille 97423

Barron, Richard L. (presiding judge)
Pos. 2, Exp. 1-2-23, 541-396-4095

Beaman, Cynthia
Pos. 6, Exp. 1-4-21, 541-247-2742
29821 Ellensburg Ave., Gold Beach 97444

Bechtold, Paula M.
Pos. 5, Exp. 1-7-19, 541-751-2337
PO Box 865, North Bend 97459

Jacquot, Megan L.
Pos. 4, Exp. 1-2-23, 541-396-4115

Margolis, Jesse
Pos. 3, Exp. 1-7-19, 541-247-2742
29821 Ellensburg Ave., Gold Beach 97444

Stone, Martin E.
Pos. 1, Exp. 1-2-23, 541-396-4117

District 16—Douglas
Douglas County Justice Bldg., Roseburg 97470

Ambrosini, George
Pos. 5, Exp. 1-7-19, 541-957-2422

Burge, Frances (presiding judge)
Pos. 4, Exp. 1-2-23, 541-957-2420

Johnson, Kathleen
Pos. 3, Exp. 1-2-23, 541-957-2433

Marshall, William A.
Pos. 2, Exp. 1-2-23, 541-957-2436

Simmons, Ann Marie G.
Pos. 1, Exp. 1-4-21, 541-957-2430

District 17—Lincoln
Lincoln County Courthouse, Newport 97365

Bachart, Sheryl
Pos. 1, Exp. 1-4-21, 541-265-4236 x252

Branford, Thomas O. (presiding judge)
Pos. 3, Exp. 1-7-19, 541-265-4236 x223

Sanders, Paulette
Pos. 2, Exp. 1-7-19, 541-265-4236 x224

District 18—Clatsop
Clatsop County Courthouse, Astoria 97103

Brownhill, Paula J. (presiding judge)
Pos. 1, Exp. 1-4-21, 503-325-8555 x301

Matyas, Cindee S.
Pos. 3, Exp. 1-7-19, 503-325-8555 x301

McIntosh, Dawn M.
Pos. 2, Exp. 1-2-23, 503-325-8555 x301

District 19—Columbia
Columbia County Courthouse, St. Helens 97051

Callahan, Cathleen B.
Pos. 1, Exp. 1-4-21; 503-397-2327 x322

Grant, Jenefer (presiding judge)
Pos. 3, Exp. 1-4-21, 503-397-2327 x316

Grove, Ted
Pos. 2, Exp. 1-4-21, 503-397-2327 x314

District 20—Washington
Washington County Courthouse, Hillsboro 97124

Bailey, Charlie (presiding judge)
Pos. 6, Exp. 1-7-19, 503-846-4403

Butterfield, Eric
Pos. 4, Exp. 1-2-23, 503-846-8771

Erwin, Andrew R.
Pos. 7, Exp. 1-4-21, 503-846-8009

Fun, James Lee, Jr.
Pos. 13, Exp. 1-7-19, 503-846-3615

Garcia, Oscar
Pos. 9, Exp. 1-7-19, 503-846-4840

Letourneau, Donald R.
Pos. 3, Exp. 1-7-19, 503-846-3418

Menchaca, Ricardo J.
Pos. 8, Exp. 1-4-21, 503-846-6204

Pagán, Ramón A.
Pos. 14, Exp. 1-4-21, 503-846-3708

Raines, Keith R.
Pos. 5, Exp. 1-4-21, 503-846-3457

Roberts, Beth
Pos. 12, Exp. 1-4-21, 503-846-8643

Sims, Theodore E.
Pos. 1, Exp. 1-2-23, 503-846-8311

Thompson, Kirsten E.
Pos. 2, Exp. 1-4-21, 503-846-8872

Upton, Suzanne
Pos. 10, Exp. 1-2-23, 503-846-6344

Wipper, Janelle F.
Pos. 11, Exp. 1-7-19, 503-846-3852

District 21—Benton
Benton County Courthouse, Corvallis 97330

Connell, David B. (presiding judge)
Pos. 3, Exp. 1-2-23, 541-766-6830

Donohue, Matthew J.
Pos. 2, Exp. 1-4-21, 541-766-6843

Williams, Locke A.
Pos. 1, Exp. 1-4-21, 541-766-6827

District 22—Crook, Jefferson
Jefferson Co. Circuit Court, 129 SW E St., Suite 101, Madras 97741
Crook County Courthouse, Prineville 97754

Ahern, Daniel J. (presiding judge)
Pos. 2, Exp. 1-4-21, 541-475-3317;
541-447-6541

Hillman, Annette
Pos. 1, Exp. 1-7-19, 541-475-3317;
541-447-6541

Williams, Gary
Pos. 3, Exp. 1-4-21, 541-475-3317;
541-447-6541

District 23—Linn

Linn County Courthouse, Albany 97321

Bispham, Carol R.
Pos. 1, Exp. 1-2-23, 541-812-8767

Delsman, David E
Pos. 2, Exp. 1-4-21, 541-812-8766

McHill, Thomas
Pos. 5, Exp. 1-2-23, 541-812-8765

Murphy, Daniel R. (presiding judge)
Pos. 3, Exp. 1-7-19, 541-812-8769

Novotny, DeAnn L.
Pos. 4, Exp. 1-7-19, 541-812-8768

District 24—Grant, Harney

Grant County Courthouse, Canyon City 97820
Harney County Courthouse, Burns 97720

Cramer, William D., Jr. (presiding judge)
Pos. 1, Exp. 1-4-21, 541-573-5207;
541-575-1438

District 25—Yamhill

Yamhill County Courthouse, McMinnville 97128

Collins, John L.
Pos. 1, Exp. 1-2-23, 503-434-7497

Easterday, Cynthia
Pos. 3, Exp. 1-2-23, 503-434-7486

Stone, Ronald W. (presiding judge)
Pos. 2, Exp. 1-7-19, 503-434-7485

Wiles, Ladd
Pos. 4, Exp. 1-4-21, 503-434-3054

District 26—Lake

Lake County Courthouse, Lakeview 97630

Nichols, Robert F. (presiding judge)
Pos. 1, Exp. 1-4-21, 541-947-6051

District 27—Tillamook

Tillamook County Courthouse, Tillamook 97141

Hill, Jonathan R. (presiding judge)
Pos. 1, Exp. 1-2-23, 503-842-2598 x112

Trevino, Mari
Pos. 2, Exp. 1-4-21, 503-842-2598 x114

Circuit Judges Association:

President—Hon. Janet Stauffer
President Elect—Hon. Mary M. James
Secretary—Hon. Lauren Holland
Treasurer—Hon. Benjamin M. Bloom
Immediate Past President—Hon. Josephine H. Mooney

continued from page 99

and to afford all Oregonians access to legal information.

The library provides access to the largest collection of legal information resources in state government, including the primary law of all U.S. jurisdictions and secondary material in virtually all areas of law.

The library operates under the administrative authority of the office of the state court administrator.

Related Organizations

BOARD OF BAR EXAMINERS

Source: Charles Schulz, Admissions Director
Address: 16037 SW Upper Boones Ferry Rd.,
PO Box 231935, Tigard 97281-1935
Phone: 503-620-0222
Web: www.osbar.org/admissions

Jeffrey Alan Howes, Chair, 2017; Nicole L. Robbins, Vice Chair, 2017; Michael A. Casper, member, 2019; Stephanie Eames, member, 2019;

Dr. Randall Green, Ph.D., public member, 2017; Dr. Richard Kolbell, Ph. D., public member, 2017; Misha Isaak, member, 2017; Angela Lucero, member, 2018; Joanna T. Perini-Abbott, member, 2019; Hon. Thomas M. Ryan, member, 2019; Cassandra C. Skinner, member, 2017; Hon. Kelly Skye, member, 2017; Stephanie J. Tuttle, member, 2018; Caroline M. Wong, member, 2017

The Board of Bar Examiners, established in 1913, acts for the Supreme Court in evaluating an applicant's qualifications to practice law in Oregon. Board activities in determining an applicant's qualifications for admission to the Bar include preparation, grading and evaluation of a bar examination; and investigation and evaluation of the character and fitness of each applicant.

OREGON STATE BAR

Source: Helen Hierschbiel, Executive Director and CEO
Address: 16037 SW Upper Boones Ferry Rd.,
PO Box 231935, Tigard 97281-1935
Phone: 503-620-0222; Toll-free: 1-800-452-8260
Fax: 503-684-1366
Web: www.osbar.org

Board of Governors: Michael Levelle, President, Portland, 2017; John R. Bachofner, Vancouver,

2019; James C. Chaney, Eugene, 2017; Christine R. Costantino, Portland, 2019; Eric Foster, Medford, 2020; Robert Gratchner, Public Member, 2019; Guy B. Greco, Newport, 2018; Ray Heysell, Immediate Past-President, Medford, 2016; John E. Mansfield, Portland, 2017; Eddie Medina, Hillsboro, 2020; Vanessa A. Nordyke, President-elect, Salem, 2018; Thomas C. Peachey, The Dalles, 2020; Per A. Ramfjord, Portland, 2018; Kathleen J. Rastetter, Oregon City, 2018; Liani JH Reeves, Portland, 2020; Julia C. Rice, Salem, 2019; Traci Rossi, Public Member, 2020; Kerry L. Sharp, Public Member, 2018; Kate von Ter Stegge, Portland, 2019; Elisabeth Zinser, Public Member, 2017

Established in 1935, the Oregon State Bar is a public corporation and instrumentality of the Oregon Judicial Department that serves the public by regulating lawyers and improving access to justice and the delivery of legal services. The state bar oversees the admission and discipline of Oregon's lawyers. It also operates a lawyer referral service and Tel-Law program, conducts continuing legal education programs, publishes legal and public service material, sponsors a legislative program to improve the laws and judicial system of Oregon, provides malpractice coverage for lawyers in private practice, distributes state funds allocated to legal service programs and monitors the programs for adherence to adopted standards.

COUNCIL ON COURT PROCEDURES

Source: Mark A. Peterson, Executive Director
Address: c/o Lewis & Clark Law School, 10015 SW Terwilliger Blvd., Portland 97219
Phone: 503-768-6505
Email: ccp@lclark.edu

Statutory appointing authority for council members can be found at ORS 1.730.

Members with term-expiration dates:

Judicial member appointed by the Oregon Supreme Court: Justice Jack L. Landau, Salem, 2017

Judicial member appointed by the Oregon Court of Appeals: Judge Rex Armstrong, Salem, 2017

Circuit judge members appointed by the Executive Committee of the Circuit Court Judges Association: Hon. Sheryl Bachart, Lincoln County Circuit Court, 2017; Hon. D. Charles Bailey, Washington County Circuit Court, 2019; Hon. R. Curtis Conover, Lane County Circuit Court, 2017; Hon. Timothy Gerking, Jackson County Circuit Court, 2019; Hon. David E. Leith, Marion County Circuit Court, 2019; Hon. Leslie Roberts, Multnomah County Circuit Court, 2019; Hon. John A. Wolf, Gilliam, Hood River, Sherman, Wasco, and Wheeler County Circuit

Courts, 2017; Hon. Charles Zennaché, Lane County Circuit Court, 2017

Practitioners appointed by the Board of Governors of the Oregon State Bar: Michael Brian, Chair, Medford, 2017; John Bachofner, Vice-Chair, Vancouver, WA, 2017; Jay Beattie, Portland, 2019; Troy S. Bundy, Portland, 2019; Kenneth Crowley, Salem, 2019; Travis Eiva, Eugene, 2017; Jennifer Gates, Portland, 2017; Robert Keating, Portland, 2019; Maureen Leonard, Portland, 2017; Shenoa L. Payne, Portland, 2017; Derek Snelling, Eugene, 2019; Deanna L. Wray, Portland, 2017

Public member appointed by the Oregon Supreme Court: Arwen Bird, Treasurer, Beaverton, 2017

Established in 1977 by ORS 1.725 to 1.760, the council promulgates rules governing pleading, practice and procedure in all civil proceedings in the circuit courts of the state. Promulgated amendments to the rules are submitted to the Legislature in January of odd-numbered years and go into effect on January 1 of the following even-numbered year, unless amended, repealed or supplemented by the Legislature.

COMMISSION ON JUDICIAL FITNESS AND DISABILITY

Source: Susan D. Isaacs, Executive Director
Address: PO Box 1130, Beaverton 97075-1130
Phone: 503-626-6776
Fax: 503-626-6787
Web: http://courts.oregon.gov/CJFD/

Chair Hon. James C. Egan, 2018; Hon. Monte S. Campbell, 2021; Judy Edwards, Public Member, 2018; Annabelle Jaramillo, Public Member, 2019; Jenna Morrison, Public Member, 2020; Judy Parker, 2019; Judy Snyder, 2019; Hon. Debra K. Vogt, 2021; Jeffrey Wallace, 2020

Commission members are volunteers serving four-year terms. Three are judges appointed by the Supreme Court, three are lawyers appointed by the Oregon State Bar and three are citizens appointed by the governor and confirmed by the senate.

Pursuant to ORS 1.410 to 1.480, the Oregon Constitution and the Rules of Judicial Conduct, the commission investigates complaints regarding Oregon judges. If the commission believes there is substantial evidence of misconduct, a public hearing is held. The commission makes recommendations regarding disciplinary actions to the Supreme Court. A judge may be censured, suspended or removed from office by the Supreme Court. The commission cannot change the decision of a judge and does not have jurisdiction over arbitrators, mediators or municipal court judges.

COUNTY COURTS

At one time, county courts existed in all 36 Oregon counties. The title "county judge" is retained in some counties as the title of the chair of the board of county commissioners. There is no requirement that county judges be members of the bar.

Where a county judge's judicial function still exists, it is limited to juvenile and probate matters and occupies only a portion of the judge's time, which is primarily devoted to nonjudicial administrative responsibilities as a member of the county board.

Now, only six counties, all east of the Cascades, have county judges who retain any judicial authority. Gilliam, Sherman and Wheeler have juvenile and probate jurisdiction, while Grant, Harney and Malheur have probate jurisdiction.

MUNICIPAL COURT

Oregon Municipal Judges Association

Source: A. Carl Myers, Director
Address: 1815 Commercial St. S., Salem 97302
Phone: 503-399-9219
Email: carl@feiblemancase.com
Web: www.omjaonline.com

The Oregon Municipal Judges Association participates in arranging continuing educational training sessions for municipal judges. It maintains a listserv system for judges to gain access to other municipal court judges and justices of the peace. The two associations trade off on annual conferences in Oregon. It coordinates with the Oregon Department of Transportation, which has its own annual conference for judges.

Many incorporated cities in Oregon have a municipal court as authorized by charter and state law. Municipal courts have concurrent jurisdiction with circuit and justice courts over all violations and misdemeanors committed or triable in the city in which the court is located. They do not have jurisdiction over felonies. Municipal courts primarily hear traffic violations and crimes; violations of municipal codes and ordinances, including animal, high grass and trash nuisances; vehicle impoundments and forfeitures; and parking and pedestrian violations. They also hear certain minor tobacco, liquor and drug violations.

Municipal courts may be a court of record, although most are not. Municipal court procedures are controlled to a large extent by state law.

A municipal judge need not be an attorney, although most are. Municipal judges are usually appointed by, and serve at the pleasure of, the city council. A few Oregon cities have elected judges. Qualifications for office are determined by the city council or charter. A municipal judge may perform weddings anywhere within the state of Oregon.

JUSTICE COURTS

Source: Joe Charter, Justice of the Peace
Address: 4173 Hamrick Rd., Central Point 97502
Phone: 541-774-1286
Web: www.jacksoncounty.org

Justice court is held by a justice of the peace within the district for which he or she is elected. The county commissioners have power to establish justice court district boundaries. The justice of the peace is a remnant of territorial days when each precinct of the state was entitled to a justice court. Thirty-two justice courts currently administer justice in 21 counties.

Justice courts have jurisdiction within their county, concurrent with the circuit court, in all criminal prosecutions, except felony trials. Actions at law in justice courts are conducted using the mode of proceeding and rules of evidence similar to those used in the circuit courts, except where otherwise specifically provided.

Justice courts have jurisdiction over traffic, boating, wildlife and other violations occurring in their county. Justices of the peace also perform weddings at no charge if performed at their offices during regular business hours.

The justice court has small claims civil jurisdiction where the money or damages claimed do not exceed $7,500, except in actions involving title to real property, false imprisonment, libel, slander or malicious prosecution.

A justice of the peace must be a citizen of the United States, a resident of Oregon for three years, and a resident of the justice court district for one year prior to becoming a nonpartisan candidate for election to that office. They are elected to six-year terms. The names of the Oregon justices of the peace are listed by county in the Local Governments section.

OFFICE OF PUBLIC DEFENSE SERVICES

Source: Nancy Cozine, Executive Director; Per Ramfjord, Chair
Address: 1175 Court St. NE, Salem 97301-4030
Phone: 503-378-3349
Fax: 503-378-2163
Web: www.oregon.gov/OPDS

The Public Defense Services Commission (PDSC) is an independent body that governs the Office of Public Defense Services (OPDS). The chief justice of the Oregon Supreme Court appoints the seven commission members to four-year terms. The commission's primary charge is to establish "a public defense system that ensures the provision of public defense services in the most cost efficient manner consistent with the Oregon Constitution, the United States Constitution and Oregon and national standards of justice[.]"

The PDSC appoints the executive director for OPDS. The OPDS has two divisions: Contract and Business Services (CBS) and the Appellate Division (AD), formerly known as the State Public Defender.

CBS is responsible for administering the public defense contracts that provide legal representation for financially eligible persons in criminal, civil commitment and juvenile proceedings and for processing requests and payments for non-contract fees and expenses. Contracts provide trial-level representation and appellate representation on cases not handled by AD.

AD is the appellate arm of OPDS. The division provides constitutionally mandated representation in the appellate courts to financially eligible persons in misdemeanor and felony criminal offenses, including capital offenses, parents in juvenile dependency cases, and inmates appealing administrative decisions from the State Board of Parole and Post-Prison Supervision.

MIDDLE SCHOOL STUDENT ESSAY
The Oregon Surf

Hayes Blackman, Essay Contest Runner-up
Lynette Gottlieb's Seventh Grade Class
Ashbrook Independent School

Oregon has some of the most special surfing on the planet. If I had a friend visit I would take them surfing. He may not be used to the cold water, but I promise my friend will fall in love with surfing. Getting up for your first time on the board, feeling the salt spray on your face, that is what nature is all about. Surfing is for all ages, whether you're eight or eighty. It is the essence of the outdoors.

I love the beaches and I never want to have to let them go. With all the beautiful places to surf in Oregon my family's favorite is Otter's Crest. It's not terribly large, but it's still amazing. The water can be so chilled that your feet turn blue. If you swim out far enough you discover a marvelous kelp forest. When the water is clear you can see the kelp glisten. I want someone else to see this beauty and fall in love. This beach of mine is what I love and will always savor.

The rugged coastline at Otter Crest. *(Oregon State Archives)*

An ornate head decorates a dragon boat at Portland's Riverplace Marina on the Willamette River.
Oregon State Archives Scenic Photograph 20160507-0558

Oregon's Provisional Legislature first met formally in 1845 in Oregon City. They were a unicameral body that operated on an uncertain schedule. The present bicameral system—two houses with senators and representatives—was adopted in 1859 upon statehood. Today's legislators meet annually in Salem and deal with complex matters and busy schedules. This section introduces the members of the Legislature and describes how the Legislature is organized.

Oregon's Legislative Assembly

Source: Legislative Administration
Address: 900 Court St. NE, Rm. 140-A, Salem 97301
Phone: 503-986-1848
Web: www.oregonlegislature.gov

President of the Senate

Peter Courtney, Senate President
Address: 900 Court St. NE, Rm. S-201, Salem 97301
Phone: 503-986-1600

The Senate president is elected by members of the Senate to select committee chairs and membership, preside over its daily sessions and coordinate its administrative operations. Subject to the rules of the Senate, the president refers measures to committees, directs Senate personnel and mediates questions on internal operations.

The Senate president's staff assists in carrying out official duties, helps coordinate Senate operations and provides a variety of public information services. In cooperation with the speaker of the House, the president coordinates and supervises the work product of the legislative branch of Oregon state government and represents that branch in contacts with the executive and judicial branches. The president's office works closely with all political parties to ensure that session goals are met.

Secretary of the Senate

Lori Brocker, Secretary of the Senate
Address: 900 Court St. NE, Rm. 233, Salem 97301
Phone: 503-986-1851

The secretary of the Senate is an elected officer of the state Senate. The secretary is responsible for and supervises Senate employees engaged in keeping measures, papers and records of proceedings and actions of the Senate. The secretary supervises preparation of the daily agenda, all measures, histories, journals and related publications and is in charge of publication of documents related to the Senate. In addition, the secretary has custody of all measures, official papers and records of the Senate, except when released to authorized persons by signed receipt. The secretary also serves as parliamentary consultant to the Senate, advises officers of the Senate on parliamentary procedure and manages the Honorary Page program.

During the interim, the secretary receives messages from the governor announcing executive appointments requiring Senate confirmation, prepares the agenda for the convening of the Senate and supervises publication of the official record of proceedings.

Speaker of the House of Representatives

Tina Kotek, Speaker of the House
Address: 900 Court St. NE, Rm. 269, Salem 97301
Phone: 503-986-1200

The speaker of the House is elected by House members to preside over the deliberations of the House, preserve order and decorum and decide questions of order. The speaker appoints chairs and members to each committee and refers measures to appropriate committees in accordance with provisions of the rules of the House.

The House speaker's staff coordinates operations of the speaker's office, assists the presiding officer in performing official duties, provides research and policy support in issue areas, provides information to the news media and assists legislators in solving constituent problems. In conjunction with the Senate president's office, the speaker's office coordinates and supervises operations of the legislative branch of government, joint statutory committees and joint interim committees and task forces.

Chief Clerk of the House of Representatives

Timothy Sekerak, Chief Clerk
Address: 900 Court St. NE, Rm. H-271, Salem 97301
Phone: 503-986-1870

The chief clerk, elected by members of the House of Representatives, supervises and keeps a correct journal, and is the official custodian of all other records of House proceedings. The chief clerk notifies the Senate of all acts of the House, certifies and transmits all bills, resolutions and papers requiring Senate concurrence immediately upon their passage or adoption, and secures proper authentication of bills that have passed both houses and transmits them to the governor.

The chief clerk prepares the agenda, coordinates details for the opening organization of the House and acts as parliamentarian as directed by House rules. In addition, the chief clerk supervises and authenticates the revision and printing of the *Senate and House Journal* at the end of the legislative session, and prepares all legislative records that are to be permanently filed with the state archivist.

Caucus Offices

Ginny Burdick, Senate Majority Leader
Address: 900 Court St. NE, Rm. S-223, Salem 97301
Phone: 503-986-1700

Ted Ferrioli, Senate Republican Leader
Address: 900 Court St. NE, Rm. S-323, Salem 97301
Phone: 503-986-1950

Jennifer Williamson (D), House Majority Leader
Address: 900 Court St. NE, Rm. H-295, Salem 97301
Phone: 503-986-1900

Mike McLane (R), House Minority Leader
Address: 900 Court St. NE, Rm. H-395, Salem 97301
Phone: 503-986-1400

Caucus offices provide many services to their members during session and interim periods. Each office is directed by a leader chosen by the respective political party. The operations of the four offices are not identical, but typical services include conducting research, writing speeches and press releases, providing public information services, serving as liaison to state and federal agencies to help solve constituent problems, organizing caucus activities and circulating information about legislative business among caucus members during both session and interim periods.

Organization

Oregon's Legislative Assembly is composed of two chambers, the Senate and House of Representatives. The Senate consists of 30 members elected to four-year terms. Half of the Senate seats are up for election every two years. The House consists of 60 representatives elected to two-year terms. Except in cases of persons selected to fill vacancies, legislators are elected in even-numbered years from single-member districts. Election by single-member district means that each Oregonian is represented by one senator and one representative. To qualify for a seat in the Legislature, one must be at least 21 years of age, a U.S. citizen and reside in the legislative district for at least one year prior to election. Each chamber elects presiding officers to oversee daily sessions and operations and perform other duties set by rule, custom and law. These officers are known as the president of the Senate and speaker of the House.

Functions

The primary functions of the Legislature are to enact new laws and revise existing ones, make decisions that keep the state in good economic and environmental condition and provide a forum for discussion of public issues.

The Legislature reviews and revises the governor's proposed budget and passes tax laws to provide needed revenue. The Oregon Constitution requires that the state must not spend money in excess of revenue.

The Legislature also influences executive and judicial branch decisions. Laws enacted by the Legislature, along with adoption of the budget, establish state policy that directs all state agency activity and impacts the courts. The Senate confirms gubernatorial appointments to certain offices. To ensure that legislative intent is followed, the Legislative Counsel Committee reviews administrative rules of state agencies.

Legislative Process

During the 2015 Regular Session, 847 of 2,641 introduced bills became law. During the 2016 Regular Session, 124 of 253 introduced bills became law.

Most of the discussion and revisions of bills and other measures are done in committees. The process begins when a measure is introduced and referred to a committee. The committee may hear testimony on the measure, frequently from members of the public, and may amend the measure and send it to the floor of its respective chamber for debate. The committee can also table the measure and end its consideration. Unlike many state legislatures, Oregon does not amend measures during floor debate.

After a measure has been considered by a committee and passed by the chamber in which it was introduced, it is sent to the other chamber where a similar procedure is followed.

If both chambers pass a bill in identical form, including any amendments approved by the other chamber, it is enrolled (printed in final form) for the signatures of the presiding officers and governor. The governor may sign the bill, veto it or let it become law without signature. The governor may also veto line items of appropriation bills, but may not veto an act referred for a vote of the people or an act initiated by the people.

The Oregon Constitution and state law require that deliberations of the Legislative Assembly and its committees be open to the public. The law also requires public notice of meetings and maintenance of public meeting records. These practices ensure that the legislative process is open to public scrutiny.

Effective Date of Laws

The regular effective date of a measure is January 1 of the year following passage of the measure. Some measures may contain a provision, such as an emergency clause, that specifies an earlier effective date.

The Oregon Constitution prohibits tax measures from having an emergency clause. This ensures that the people have the right to refer a tax measure for a vote by petition before it goes into effect.

Session Schedule

In 2010, voters approved a ballot measure referred by the Legislature requiring the Legislature to meet annually. Beginning in 2011, the Legislature convenes in February at the State Capitol in Salem, but sessions may not exceed 160 days in odd-numbered years and 35 days in even-numbered years. Five-day extensions are allowed by a two-thirds vote in both houses. In addition, the Legislature may hold an organizational session to swear in newly elected officials, elect legislative leaders, adopt rules, organize and appoint committees and begin introducing bills.

Special sessions to deal with emergencies may be called by the governor or by a majority of each chamber. For example, the Legislative Assembly

Legislative

called itself into a special session in 2002, 2006, 2008 and 2010, Governor Ted Kulongoski called for a special session in 2006, and Governor John Kitzhaber called for a special session in 2012 and in 2013.

Contacting a Legislator and Obtaining Legislative Information

During session, the following numbers are available to obtain legislative information:
• Outside Salem: 1-800-332-2313

• Within Salem: 503-986-1388

During the interim, individual legislators may be reached by calling the telephone numbers listed on pages 141–143 and 149–153. Legislative information may be obtained by calling Legislative Administration at 503-986-1848.

Session Interim

After adjournment of regular or special sessions, the work of the Legislature continues. Legislators study issues likely to be important during future

Chronology of Regular Legislative Sessions in Oregon

Leg. Assembly	Year	Dates	Length in Days	Leg. Assembly	Year	Dates	Length in Days
1	1860	Sept. 10–Oct. 19	40	44	1947	Jan. 13–April 5	83
2	1862	Sept. 8–Oct. 17	40	45	1949	Jan. 10–April 16	97
3	1864	Sept. 12–Oct. 22	41	46	1951	Jan. 8–May 3	116
4	1866	Sept. 10–Oct. 20	41	47	1953	Jan. 12–April 21	100
5	1868	Sept. 14–Oct. 28	44	48	1955	Jan. 10–May 4	115
6	1870	Sept. 12–Oct. 20	39	49	1957	Jan. 14–May 21	128
7	1872	Sept. 9–Oct. 23	45	50	1959	Jan. 12–May 6	115
8	1874	Sept. 14–Oct. 21	38	51	1961	Jan. 9–May 10	122
9	1876	Sept. 11–Oct. 20	40	52	1963	Jan. 14–June 3	141
10	1878	Sept. 9–Oct. 18	40	53	1965	Jan. 11–May 14	124
11	1880	Sept. 13–Oct. 23	41	54	1967	Jan. 9–June 14	157
12	1882	Sept. 11–Oct. 19	39	55	1969	Jan. 13–May 23	131
13	1885	Jan. 12–Feb. 21	40	56	1971	Jan. 11–June 10	151
14	1887	Jan. 10–Feb. 18	39	57	1973	Jan. 8–July 6	180
15	1889	Jan. 14–Feb. 22	39	58	1975	Jan. 13–June 14	153
16	1891	Jan. 12–Feb. 20	39	59	1977	Jan. 10–July 5	177
17	1893	Jan. 9–Feb. 17	39	60	1979	Jan. 8–July 4	178
18	1895	Jan. 14–Feb. 23	40	61	1981	Jan. 12–August 2	203
19	1897	Jan. 11–March 2	*	62	1983	Jan. 10–July 16	188
20	1899	Jan. 9–Feb. 18	40	63	1985	Jan. 14–June 21	159
21	1901	Jan. 14–March 4	50	64	1987	Jan. 12–June 28	168
22	1903	Jan. 12–Feb. 20	39	65	1989	Jan. 9–July 4	177
23	1905	Jan. 9–Feb. 17	40	66	1991	Jan. 14–July 1	168
24	1907	Jan. 14–Feb. 23	41	67	1993	Jan. 11–August 5	207
25	1909	Jan. 11–Feb. 20	41	68	1995	Jan. 9–June 10	153
26	1911	Jan. 9–Feb. 18	41	69	1997	Jan. 13–July 5	174
27	1913	Jan. 13–March 5	51	70	1999	Jan. 11–July 24	195
28	1915	Jan. 11–Feb. 20	41	71	2001	Jan. 8–July 7	181
29	1917	Jan. 8–Feb. 19	43	72	2003	Jan. 13–August 27	227
30	1919	Jan. 13–Feb. 27	46	73	2005	Jan. 10–August 5	208
31	1921	Jan. 10–Feb. 23	45	74	2007	Jan. 8–June 28	171
32	1923	Jan. 8–Feb. 22	46	75	2009	Jan. 12–June 29	169
33	1925	Jan. 12–Feb. 26	46	76	2011	Feb. 1–June 30	150
34	1927	Jan. 10–Feb. 25	47	76	2012	Feb. 1–March 5	34
35	1929	Jan. 14–March 5	50	77	2013	Feb. 4–July 8	155
36	1931	Jan. 12–March 6	54	77	2014	Feb. 3–March 7	33
37	1933	Jan. 9–March 9	60	78	2015	Feb. 2–July 6	155
38	1935	Jan. 14–March 13	59	78	2016	Feb. 1–March 3	32
39	1937	Jan. 11–March 8	57	79	2017	Feb. 1–	
40	1939	Jan. 9–March 15	66				
41	1941	Jan. 13–March 15	62				
42	1943	Jan. 11–March 10	59				
43	1945	Jan. 8–March 17	69				

The House of Representatives never formally convened because its members failed to reach agreement on organization.

sessions, become acquainted with new issues, prepare drafts of legislation and exercise legislative oversight.

Convening of the Senate to Act on Executive Appointments

The Legislative Assembly may require that appointments to state public office made by the governor, be subject to Senate confirmation.

During the legislative session, the Senate president refers executive appointments to a standing or special committee to review the background and qualifications of appointees, ensuring that statutory requirements are met. Appointees may be asked to come before the committee for personal interviews. The committee submits its recommendations to the full Senate for confirmation votes.

During the interim, the secretary of the Senate receives the governor's announcements of executive appointments requiring Senate confirmation. Generally, gubernatorial appointments made during a regular or special session of the Legislature are acted upon by the Senate prior to adjourning *sine die* or final adjournment.

History

Oregon's Provisional Legislature met formally for the first time in Oregon City, December 2 to December 19, 1845. An earlier pre-provisional committee met in August of the same year after the formal ratification of Oregon's Organic Articles and Laws of 1843 and the inauguration of George Abernethy as governor. The first Provisional Legislature, a unicameral body with autonomous powers, conducted its sessions in a rather casual manner and frequently suspended its rules to take care of unexpected situations. It met annually or more frequently until February 1849, five months before the first Territorial Legislature met during July 16 to July 24, 1849, also in Oregon City.

The Territorial Legislature was bicameral. It had an upper council of nine members and a lower house of 18 members elected from the eight existing counties that had regular annual meetings. Unlike the Provisional Legislature, its actions were subject to review in Washington, D.C. At the time of statehood and adoption of the constitution in 1859, the present bicameral system was adopted. The Legislature then met in the fall of even-numbered years until 1885 when the sessions were moved to the early winter months of odd-numbered years to accommodate members who farmed.

Statistical Summary of the Seventy-eighth Legislative Assembly
Source: Legislative Counsel

2015 Regular Session

Session Length	155 Calendar Days
Convened	February 2, 2015
Adjourned	July 6, 2015
Bills Introduced	2,641
Other Measures	158
Total	2,799
Senate Total Membership	**30**
Democrats	18
Republicans	12
President: Peter Courtney (D), Salem	
House Total Membership	**60**
Democrats	35
Republicans	25
Speaker: Tina Kotek (D), Portland	

Bills	House	Senate	Total
Introduced	1,617	1,024	2,641
Passed Both Houses	491	356	847
Vetoed	0	0	0
Became Law	491	356	847
Unsigned by Governor	1*	0	1*
Resolutions and Memorials			
Introduced	95	63	158
Adopted	47	27	74

* HB 3085 referred. Election held May 15, 2016.

2016 Regular Session

Session Length	32 Calendar Days
Convened	February 1, 2016
Adjourned	March 3, 2016
Bills Introduced	253
Other Measures	30
Total	283
Senate Total Membership	**30**
Democrats	18
Republicans	12
President: Peter Courtney (D), Salem	

Senate and House District Numbers

Senate	House Dist.	Senate	House Dist.	Senate	House Dist.	Senate	House Dist.
1	1 and 2	9	17 and 18	17	33 and 34	25	49 and 50
2	3 and 4	10	19 and 20	18	35 and 36	26	51 and 52
3	5 and 6	11	21 and 22	19	37 and 38	27	53 and 54
4	7 and 8	12	23 and 24	20	39 and 40	28	55 and 56
5	9 and 10	13	25 and 26	21	41 and 42	29	57 and 58
6	11 and 12	14	27 and 28	22	43 and 44	30	59 and 60
7	13 and 14	15	29 and 30	23	45 and 46		
8	15 and 16	16	31 and 32	24	47 and 48		

Legislative

House Total Membership			60
Democrats			35
Republicans			25
Speaker: Tina Kotek (D), Portland			

Bills	House	Senate	Total
Introduced	150	103	253
Passed Both Houses	81	62	143
Vetoed	0	0	0
Became Law	70	54	124
Unsigned by Governor	0	0	0
Resolutions and Memorials			
Introduced	15	15	30
Adopted	11	8	19

STATUTORY COMMITTEES AND INTERIM OFFICES

Source: Legislative Administration
Address: 900 Court St. NE, Rm. 140-A, Salem 97301
Phone: 503-986-1848
Web: www.oregonlegislature.gov/la

Legislative Administration Committee

Daron Hill, Legislative Administrator

The Legislative Administration Committee provides services to the Legislative Assembly, its support staff and the public. The committee, authorized by ORS 173.710, includes the president of the Senate, the speaker of the House, members of the Senate appointed by the president and members of the House appointed by the speaker. The committee appoints an administrator to serve as its executive officer. The administrator's office coordinates and oversees the operation of the following administrative units:

Employee Services

Address: Room 140-B
Phone: 503-986-1373

Employee Services provides human resource administration to all legislative employees and legislative job seekers.

Facility Services

Address: Room 49
Phone: 503-986-1360

Facility Services manages the infrastructure of the State Capitol Building, including maintenance, capital improvement projects and space planning. The staff also provides centralized purchasing, mail handling and distribution of legislative publications.

Financial Services

Address: Room 140-C
Phone: 503-986-1695

Financial Services provides budgeting, accounting and financial reporting services to the Legislature.

Special Legislative Sessions in Oregon[1]

Year	Date	Length in Days
1860	Oct. 1–Oct. 2	2
1865	Dec. 5–Dec. 18	14
1885	Nov. 11–Nov. 24	14
1898	Sept. 26–Oct. 15	20
1903	Dec. 21–Dec. 23	3
1909	Mar. 15–Mar. 16	2
1920	Jan. 12–Jan. 17	6
1921	Dec. 19–Dec. 24	6
1933	Jan. 3–Jan. 7	5
1933	Nov. 20–Dec. 9	20
1935	Oct. 21–Nov. 9	20
1957	Oct. 28–Nov. 15	19
1963	Nov. 11–Dec. 2	13[2]
1965	May 21–May 25	5
1967	Oct. 30–Nov. 21	23
1971	Nov. 16–Nov. 22	7
1974	Jan. 24–Feb. 24	15
1975	Sept. 16–Sept. 16	1
1978	Sept. 5–Sept. 9	5[3]
1980	Aug. 4–Aug. 8	5
1981	Oct. 24–Oct. 24	1
1982	Jan. 18–Mar. 1	43
1982	June 14–June 14	1
1982	Sept. 3–Sept. 3	1
1983	Sept. 14–Oct. 4	21
1984	July 30–July 30	1
1990	May 7–May 7	1
1992	July 1–July 3	3
1995	July 28–Aug. 4	8
1996	Feb. 1–Feb. 2	2
2002	Feb. 8–Feb. 11	4
2002	Feb. 25–Mar. 2	6
2002	June 12–June 30	19
2002	Aug. 16–Aug. 20	5
2002	Sept. 1–Sept. 18	18
2006	April 20–April 20	1
2008	Feb. 4–Feb. 22	19
2010	Feb. 1–Feb. 25	25
2012	Dec. 14–Dec. 14	1
2013	Sept. 30–Oct. 2	3

[1]Historical records are not consistent on actual dates.
[2]Nine-day recess, Nov. 22 to Dec. 2, due to death of President Kennedy.
[3]Does not include recess from Jan. 24 to Feb. 11.

Information Services

Address: Room 141
Phone: 503-986-1916

Information Services supports the Legislature by providing computer and mainframe programs and services, legislative publications, electronic access to legislative information and maintenance of computer equipment.

Legislative Media

Address: Room 35
Phone: 503-986-1195
Legislative Media, a division of Information Services, provides audio and video coverage of legislative events, production videos and maintains audio and video equipment in the Capitol.

Visitor Services

Address: Capitol Rotunda Area
Phone: 503-986-1388
Web: https://www.oregonlegislature.gov/capitol historygateway/Pages/Visit-the-Capitol.aspx
Visitor Services provides guided tours and information on the legislative process and Capitol history. It also operates the Capitol Gift Shop.

Legislative Policy and Research Committee and Office of Legislative Policy and Research

Christopher Reinhart, Office of Legislative Policy and Research Director
Address: 900 Court St. NE, Rm. 453, Salem 97301
Phone: 503-986-1813
Fax: 503-986-1814
Web: https://www.oregonlegislature.gov/lpro

The Legislative Policy and Research Committee was established by Senate Bill 1569 in 2016 and consists of the president of the Senate, senators appointed by the president, the speaker of the House of Representatives and representatives appointed by the speaker. The director, who is selected by the committee, serves as executive officer to the committee, manages the Office of Legislative Policy and Research and employs professional staff.

The office provides centralized, professional and nonpartisan research, issue analysis and committee management services for the Legislative Assembly. The office's responsibilities include organizing and administering committee meetings, analyzing measures, providing research and policy options to legislators, and producing committee meeting records.

Legislative Counsel Committee and Office of Legislative Counsel

Dexter Johnson, Legislative Counsel
Address: 900 Court St. NE, Rm. S-101, Salem 97301
Phone: 503-986-1243
Fax: 503-373-1043
Web: www.oregonlegislature.gov/lc

The Legislative Counsel Committee was established by ORS 173.111 and consists of the president of the Senate, senators appointed by the president, the speaker of the House of Representatives and representatives appointed by the speaker. The legislative counsel, who is selected by the committee, serves as executive officer to the committee, manages the Office of the Legislative Counsel and employs a legal and editorial professional staff.

The Office of the Legislative Counsel is responsible for drafting legislative measures for legislators, legislative committees, state agencies and statewide elected officials. The office also provides legal opinions and other legal services to legislators, legislative committees and legislative staff. During legislative sessions, the office drafts amendments to measures and prints introduced, engrossed and enrolled measures for the Legislative Assembly.

The Office of the Legislative Counsel prepares indexes and tables for all measures introduced during a legislative session. At the end of each session, the office publishes *Oregon Laws*, the official compilation of that session's laws. The office also compiles and publishes *Oregon Revised Statutes* (ORS), the official codification of Oregon's statute laws, every two years. Each edition of ORS incorporates the new statutory provisions and amendments to statutory provisions passed by the Legislative Assembly or approved by the voters at an election in the preceding two years. As part of the ORS set, subscribers receive a supplement of laws enacted during the short, even-year regular legislative session. The office also incorporates any new sections or amendments into its annual printing of the *Constitution of Oregon*.

Pursuant to ORS 183.710 to 183.725, the Office of the Legislative Counsel conducts a review of all new administrative rules adopted by state agencies. This review allows the Legislative Assembly to monitor whether an agency's rules are consistent with the agency's constitutional and statutory authority.

Oregon Law Commission

Lane P. Shetterly, Chair
Jeffrey Dobbins, Executive Director
Laura Handzel, Deputy Director
Address: Willamette University College of Law, 245 Winter St. SE, Salem 97301
Phone: 503-370-6973
Web: www.willamette.edu/wucl/centers/olc/

The Oregon Law Commission, established in 1997, is the state's official law reform body. The commission and its work groups help to reform, correct, and revise Oregon law based on suggestions for revision and its own review of Oregon's laws.

The commission consists of 15 commissioners: two persons appointed by the president of the Senate (one of whom must be a senator), two persons appointed by the speaker of the House of Representatives (one of whom must be a representative), the deans (or an appointee) from each of Oregon's three law schools, three persons appointed by the Oregon State Bar, the attorney general, the chief justice of the Supreme Court, the chief judge of the Court of Appeals, a circuit court judge and one person appointed by the governor.

The commission submits a biennial report to the Legislative Assembly. Pursuant to ORS 173.335, the Office of the Legislative Counsel assists the commission in carrying out its duties.

Legislative Fiscal Office

Ken Rocco, Legislative Fiscal Officer
Address: 900 Court St. NE, Rm. H-178, Salem 97301
Phone: 503-986-1828

The Legislative Fiscal Office is a permanent, nonpartisan legislative agency created in 1959, pursuant to ORS 173.410 to 173.450, to serve legislators and committees on matters related to the state's fiscal affairs. The office provides research, analysis, evaluation and recommendations concerning state expenditures, budget issues, agency organization, program administration and state information technology projects. It also provides fiscal impact assessments of proposed legislation and provides staff assistance to the Joint Legislative Committee on Information Management and Technology and the Joint Legislative Audit Committee. The office staffs the Joint Committee on Ways and Means during sessions and the Emergency Board during interims between sessions.

Emergency Board

The Emergency Board, authorized by Article III, section 3, of the Oregon Constitution and by ORS 291.324, consists of the president of the Senate, the speaker of the House of Representatives, the co-chairs of the Joint Committee on Ways and Means, and eight Senate and eight House members, totaling 20 members. Between sessions, the Emergency Board may allocate to state agencies, out of emergency funds appropriated to the board, additional monies to carry on activities required by law for which appropriations were not made. The board may authorize an agency to spend over the budgeted amount by tapping funds that are dedicated or continuously appropriated for the agency. The board may also approve a new budget for a new agency task, or it may authorize transfers of funds between an agency's expenditure classifications.

Joint Committee on Ways and Means

The Joint Committee on Ways and Means, created under ORS 171.555, is the legislative appropriations committee that determines state budget policy. Staffed by the Legislative Fiscal Office and made up of both Senate and House members appointed by the president of the Senate and the speaker of the House, the committee works to determine state budget priorities. This joint appropriation process structure, employed in Oregon and several other states, is especially effective in resolving budgetary differences.

Legislative Revenue Office

Paul Warner, Legislative Revenue Officer
Address: 900 Court St. NE, Rm. 354, Salem 97301
Phone: 503-986-1266

Pursuant to ORS 173.810 to 173.850, the Legislative Revenue Office, established by the 1975 Oregon Legislature, provides nonpartisan analysis of tax and school finance issues.

The legislative revenue officer is appointed by, and responsible to, the House and Senate committees that deal with revenue and school finance.

The office staffs the House and Senate Revenue Committees, writes revenue impact statements for proposed legislation, and researches tax and other revenue related issues.

Legislative Commission on Indian Services

Karen Quigley, Executive Officer
Address: 900 Court St. NE, Rm. 167, Salem 97301
Phone: 503-986-1067
Email: karen.m.quigley@state.or.us
Web: www.oregonlegislature.gov/cis

The Legislative Commission on Indian Services, an advisory body created in 1975 by ORS 172.100 to 172.140, operates as a small agency within the legislative branch. It consists of 14 members. Thirteen members are appointed by legislative leadership to two-year terms: one member from each of Oregon's nine federally-recognized tribal governments, two state senators and two state representatives. The commission may appoint one additional non-voting member from an area in which nonreservation Indians reside and who is associated with an Urban Indian Health Program under Title V of the federal Indian Health Care Improvement Act.

The purpose of the commission is to improve services to American Indians in the state and to promote communication and relations between the state of Oregon and the nine federally-recognized Indian tribes in Oregon.

Commission responsibilities include compiling information about services available to Indians, encouraging and supporting public and private agencies to expand and improve their activities affecting Indians, assessing programs of state agencies operating for the benefit of Indians, and making recommendations for improvement. The commission is the primary point of contact for the state of Oregon for questions about Oregon's American Indians and their issues. The commission plays a significant role in monitoring and facilitating Oregon's state-tribal, government-to-government law and policy.

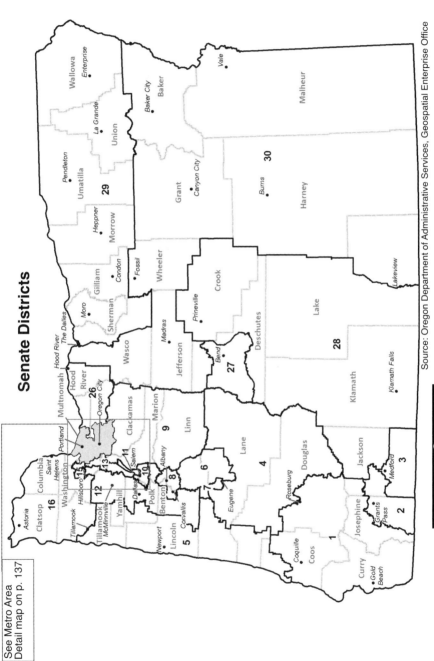

Senate Districts

Legislative

See Metro Area
Detail map on p. 137

House Districts

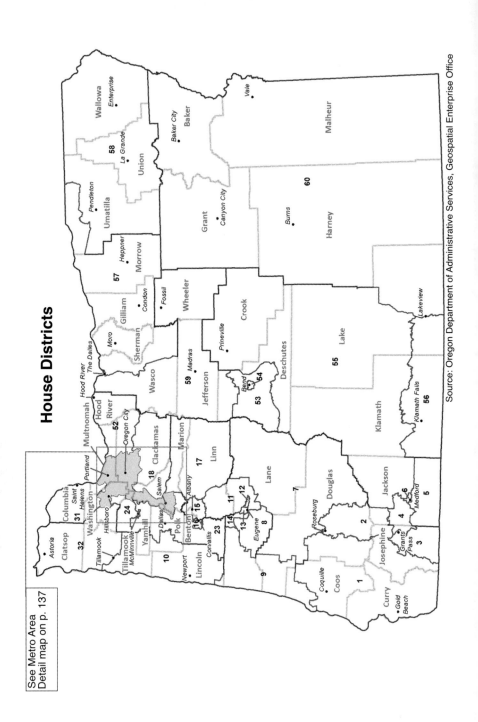

See Metro Area
Detail map on p. 137

Metro Area Detail Maps

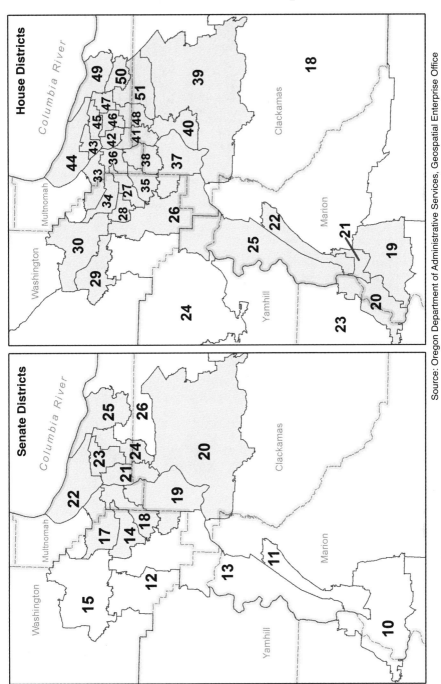

Source: Oregon Department of Administrative Services, Geospatial Enterprise Office

Legislative

President of the Senate

Peter Courtney (Democrat, District 11) was born in Philadelphia, Pennsylvania, on June 18, 1943. He graduated with bachelor and master degrees from the University of Rhode Island and received a law degree from Boston University. Courtney was first elected to the Salem City Council in 1974, where he served until 1981. He began serving in the House of Representatives in 1981 and was first elected to the Senate in 1998. He is serving a record seventh term as president of the Oregon Senate.

Courtney is retired from Western Oregon University, where he was an adjunct professor and served as assistant to University President Mark D. Wiess. He has served on the Salem Mass Transit Board, the United Way Board, and the Board of Directors for the YMCA, and he has coached for the Boys and Girls Club.

Courtney has worked as a political commentator for *The 10 O'Clock News* at KPTV, Channel 12, Portland, and at KSLM Radio, Salem. He married his wife Margie in 1976. They have three sons, Peter, Sean and Adam, two daughters-in-law and one grandson.

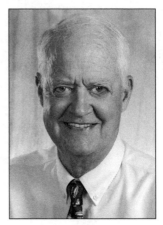

Peter Courtney

Baertschiger, Herman
R—District 2

Beyer, Lee
D—District 6

Boquist, Brian
R—District 12

Burdick, Ginny
D—District 18

Courtney, Peter
D—District 11

DeBoer, Alan
R—District 3

Dembrow, Michael
D—District 23

Devlin, Richard
D—District 19

Ferrioli, Ted
R—District 30

Frederick, Lew
D—District 22

Gelser, Sara
D—District 8

Girod, Fred
R—District 9

Hansell, Bill
R—District 29

Hass, Mark
D—District 14

Johnson, Betsy
D—District 16

Knopp, Tim
R—District 27

Kruse, Jeff
R—District 1

Linthicum, Dennis
R—District 28

Legislative

Manning, Jr., James I.
D—District 7

Monnes Anderson, Laurie
D—District 25

Monroe, Rod
D—District 24

Olsen, Alan R.
R—District 20

Prozanski, Floyd
D—District 4

Riley, Chuck
D—District 15

Roblan, Arnie
D—District 5

Steiner Hayward, Elizabeth
D—District 17

Taylor, Kathleen
D—District 21

Thatcher, Kim
R—District 13

Thomsen, Chuck
R—District 26

Winters, Jackie
R—District 10

State Senators by District

District/Counties	Name/Address/Phone	Occupation/Yr. Elected*	Birthplace/Year
1. Curry and portions of Coos, Douglas, Jackson and Josephine	Jeff Kruse (R) 636 Wild Iris Lane Roseburg 97470 541-673-7201	Co-owner Kruse Farms 2005/2009/2013/2017 (1997–2003)	Oregon 1951
2. Portions of Jackson and Josephine	Herman Baertschiger, Jr. (R) 900 Court St. NE, S-403 Salem 97301 503-986-1702	Forester/Rancher 2013/2017	California 1959
3. Portion of Jackson	Alan DeBoer (R) 900 Court St., NE, S-421 Salem 97301 503-986-1703	Auto Dealer 2017	Oregon 1951
4. Portions of Douglas and Lane	Floyd Prozanski (D) PO Box 11511 Eugene 97440 541-342-2447	Attorney 2005/2009/2015 (1995–2003)	Texas 1954
5. Lincoln and portions of Coos, Douglas, Lane, Polk, Tillamook and Yamhill	Arnie Roblan (D) 900 Court St. NE, S-417 Salem 97301 503-986-1705	Retired School Principal 2013/2017 (2005–2013)	Washington 1948
6. Portions of Lane and Linn	Lee Beyer (D) PO Box 131 Springfield 97477 541-726-2533	Retired Business Advisor 1999/2011/2015 (1991–1997)	Nebraska 1948
7. Portion of Lane	James I. Manning, Jr. (D) 900 Court St. NE, S-205 Salem 97301 503-986-1707	Retired U.S. Army 2017	Missouri 1953
8. Portions of Benton and Linn	Sara Gelser (D) 900 Court St. NE, S-405 Salem 97301 503-986-1708	Educator/Civil Servant 2015 (2007–2015)	Nevada 1973
9. Portions of Clackamas, Linn and Marion	Fred Girod (R) 101 Fern Ridge Rd. SE Stayton 97383 503-769-4321	Dentist 2008/2009/2013/2017 (1993–2007)	Oregon 1951
10. Portions of Marion and Polk	Jackie Winters (R) 900 Court St. NE, S-301 Salem 97301 503-986-1710	Retired Business Owner/ Agency Administrator 2003/2007/2011/2015 (1999/2001)	Kansas 1937
11. Portion of Marion	Peter Courtney (D) 900 Court St. NE, S-201 Salem 97301 503-986-1600	Retired from Western Oregon University 1999/2003/2007/2011/ 2015 (1981–1997)	Pennsylvania 1943
12. Portions of Benton, Marion, Polk, Washington and Yamhill	Brian Boquist (R) 900 Court St. NE, S-311 Salem 97301 503-986-1712	Businessman/Rancher 2009/2013/2017 (2005/2007)	Oregon 1958

Senate terms are four years, and House terms (in parentheses) are two years, unless appointed mid-term.

District/Counties	Name/Address/Phone	Occupation/Yr. Elected*	Birthplace/Year
13. Portions of Clackamas, Marion, Washington and Yamhill	Kim Thatcher (R) 900 Court St. NE, S-307 Salem 97301 503-986-1713	Small Business Owner 2015 (2005/2007/2009/2011/ 2013)	Idaho 1964
14. Portion of Washington	Mark Hass (D) 900 Court St. NE, S-207 Salem 97301 503-986-1714	Brand Manager 2008/2009/2013/2017 (2001–2005)	Rhode Island 1956
15. Portion of Washington	Chuck Riley (D) 900 Court St. NE, S-303 Salem 97301 503-986-1715	Retired Computer Consultant 2015 (2005/2007/2009)	Illinois 1939
16. Clatsop, Columbia and portions of Multnomah, Tillamook and Washington	Betsy Johnson (D) PO Box R Scappoose 97056 503-543-4046	Legislator/Former Commercial Helicopter Pilot 2007/2011/2015 (2001/2003)	Oregon 1951
17. Portions of Multnomah and Washington	Steiner Hayward, Elizabeth (D) 3879 SW Hall Blvd. Beaverton 97005 503-277-2467	OHSU Associate Professor of Family Medicine 2011/2015	New York 1963
18. Portions of Multnomah and Washington	Ginny Burdick (D) 6227 SW 18th Dr. Portland 97239 503-986-1718	Communications Consultant/Legislator 1997/2001/2005/2009/ 2013/2017	Oregon 1947
19. Portions of Clackamas and Multnomah	Richard Devlin (D) 900 Court St. NE, S-213 Salem 97301 503-986-1719	State Senator 2003/2007/2011/2015 (1997–2001)	Oregon 1952
20. Portions of Clackamas and Marion	Alan R. Olsen (R) PO Box 820 Canby 97013 503-936-8605	General Contractor 2011/2015	Illinois 1948
21. Portions of Clackamas and Multnomah	Kathleen Taylor (D) 900 Court St. NE, S-423 Salem 97301 503-986-1721	Management Auditor 2017	Wisconsin 1966
22. Portion of Multnomah	Lew Frederick (D) 900 Court St. NE, S-419 Salem 97301 503-231-2564	Communications Consultant 2017 (2009–2015)	Washington 1951
23. Portion of Multnomah	Michael E. Dembrow (D) 900 Court St. NE, S-407 Salem 97301 503-986-1723	College Teacher 2013/2015 (2009/2011/2013)	Connecticut 1951
24. Portions of Clackamas and Multnomah	Rod Monroe (D) 7802 SE 111th Ave. Portland 97266 503-760-4310	Small Business Owner/ Legislator 1981/1985/2007/2011/ 2015 (1977–1981)	British Columbia, Canada 1942
25. Portion of Multnomah	Laurie Monnes Anderson (D) PO Box 1531 Gresham 97030 503-618-3071	Retired Nurse 2005/2009/2013/2017 (2001/2003)	California 1945

District/Counties	Name/Address/Phone	Occupation/Yr. Elected*	Birthplace/Year
26. Hood River and portions of Clackamas and Multnomah	Chuck Thomsen (R) 900 Court St. NE, S-316 Salem 97301 503-986-1726	Orchardist 2011/2015	Oregon 1957
27. Portion of Deschutes	Tim Knopp (R) 900 Court St. NE, S-309 Salem 97301 503-986-1727	Exec. Vice President Non-Profit Trade Assoc. 2013/2017	Oregon 1965
28. Crook, Klamath and portions of Deschutes, Jackson and Lake	Dennis Linthicum (R) 900 Court St. NE, S-305 Salem 97301 503-986-1728	Software and Applications Developer 2017	California 1956
29. Gilliam, Morrow, Sherman, Umatilla, Union and Wallowa and portion of Wasco	Bill Hansell (R) 900 Court St. NE, S-415 Salem 97301 503-986-1729	Former County Commissioner 2013/2017	Washington 1945
30. Baker, Grant, Harney, Jefferson, Malheur, Wheeler and portions of Clackamas, Deschutes, Lake, Marion and Wasco	Ted Ferrioli (R) 900 Court St. NE, S-323 Salem 97301 503-986-1730	Retired Association Director and Rancher 1997/2001/2005/2009/ 2013/2017	Washington 1951

MEMBERS OF THE OREGON HOUSE OF REPRESENTATIVES

Tina Kotek

Speaker of the House

Beginning with her work to win domestic partnership benefits for faculty and students at the University of Washington in the mid-1990s, Tina Kotek has worked hard to change the world and to empower people to be part of that change.

She began her public service career as a policy advocate for the Oregon Food Bank, working to eliminate hunger for every Oregonian. She went on to serve as the policy director for Children First for Oregon before being elected to the Oregon House of Representatives in 2006.

In her first term in the House, Representative Kotek championed a redesign of the state's welfare program, led the fight to establish statewide nutrition standards for food sold in schools, and helped pass landmark legislation that both ended discrimination based on sexual orientation and created domestic partnerships for same-sex couples.

In 2013, she became the first openly lesbian speaker of any state house in the nation.

In recent legislative sessions, Speaker Kotek was a leader in the movement to give everyone a fair shot at success by championing the successful efforts to expand earned sick leave, strengthen retirement security and ban racial profiling. She worked to strengthen and expand child care options for working parents and fought to pass trailblazing legislation to raise Oregon's minimum wage.

Today, Speaker Kotek and her partner Aimee live in the Kenton neighborhood of North Portland.

Legislative

Alonso Leon, Teresa
D—District 22

Barker, Jeff
D—District 28

Barnhart, Phil
D—District 11

Barreto, Greg
R—District 58

Bentz, Cliff
R—District 60

Boone, Deborah
D—District 32

Buehler, Knute
R—District 54

Bynum, Janelle
D—District 51

Clem, Brian L.
D—District 21

Doherty, Margaret
D—District 35

Esquivel, Sal
R—District 6

Evans, Paul
D—District 20

Fahey, Julie
D—District 14

Gilliam, Vic
R—District 18

Gomberg, David
D—District 10

Gorsek, Chris
D—District 49

Greenlick, Mitch
D—District 33

Hack, Jodi L.
R—District 19

Hayden, Cedric
R—District 7

Heard, Dallas
R—District 2

Helm, Ken
D—District 34

Hernandez, Diego
D—District 47

Holvey, Paul
D—District 8

Huffman, John E.
R—District 59

Legislative

Johnson, Mark
R—District 52

Kennemer, Bill
R—District 39

Keny-Guyer, Alissa
D—District 46

Kotek, Tina
D—District 44

Lininger, Ann
D—District 38

Lively, John
D—District 12

Malstrom, Sheri
D—District 27

Marsh, Pam
D—District 5

McKeown, Caddy
D—District 9

McLain, Susan
D—District 29

McLane, Mike
R—District 55

Meek, Mark
D—District 40

Nathanson, Nancy
D—District 13

Nearman, Mike
R—District 23

Noble, Ron
R—District 24

Nosse, Rob
D—District 42

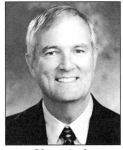

Olson, Andy
R—District 15

Parrish, Julie
R—District 37

Piluso, Carla C.
D—District 50

Post, Bill
R—District 25

Power, Karin
D—District 41

Rayfield, Dan
D—District 16

Reardon, Jeff
D—District 48

Reschke, E. Werner
R—District 56

Sanchez, Tawna
D—District 43

Smith, David Brock
R—District 1

Smith, Greg
R—District 57

Smith Warner, Barbara
D—District 45

Sollman, Janeen
D—District 30

Sprenger, Sherrie
R—District 17

Stark, Duane A.
R—District 4

Vial, A. Richard
R—District 26

Whisnant, Gene
R—District 53

Williamson, Jennifer
D—District 36

Wilson, Carl
R—District 3

Witt, Bradley
D—District 31

State Representatives by District

District/Counties	Name/Address/Phone	Occupation/Yr. Elected*	Birthplace/Year
1. Curry and portions of Coos, Douglas and Josephine	David Brock Smith (R) 900 Court St. NE, H-379 Salem 97301 503-986-1401	Small Business 2017	California 1976
2. Portions of Douglas, Jackson and Josephine	Dallas Heard (R) 900 Court St. NE, H-386 Salem 97301 503-986-1402	Landscape Contractor 2015/2017	Oregon 1985
3. Portion of Josephine	Carl Wilson (R) 900 Court St. NE, H-390 Salem 97301 503-986-1403	Radio Broadcaster 1999/2001/2015/2017	Oklahoma 1952
4. Portions of Jackson and Josephine	Duane A. Stark (R) 900 Court St. NE, H-372 Salem 97301 503-986-1404	Outreach Pastor 2015/2017	Oregon 1978
5. Portion of Jackson	Pam Marsh (D) 900 Court St. NE, H-375 Salem 97301 503-986-1405	Legislator 2017	Missouri 1954
6. Portion of Jackson	Sal Esquivel (R) 900 Court St. NE, H-382 Salem 97301 541-734-4369	Real Estate Broker 2005/2007/2009/2011/ 2013/2015/2017	California 1948
7. Portions of Douglas and Lane	Cedric Hayden (R) PO Box 459 Lowell 97452 503-986-1407	Dental Surgeon, Rancher 2015/2017	Oregon 1968
8. Portion of Lane	Paul Holvey (D) PO Box 51048 Eugene 97405 541-344-5636	Carpenters' Union Representative 2005/2007/2009/2011/ 2013/2015/2017	Oregon 1954
9. Portions of Coos, Douglas, Lane and Lincoln	Caddy McKeown (D) 900 Court St. NE, H-476 Salem 97301 503-986-1409	Port Commissioner 2013/2015/2017	Oregon 1951
10. Portions of Lincoln, Polk, Tillamook and Yamhill	David Gomberg (D) 900 Court St. NE, H-471 Salem 97301 503-986-1410	Small Business Owner 2013/2015/2017	Oregon 1953
11. Portions of Lane and Linn	Phil Barnhart (D) PO Box 71188 Eugene 97401 503-986-1411	State Representative 2001/2003/2005/2007/ 2009/2011/2013/2015/ 2017	New York 1946
12. Portion of Lane	John Lively (D) 900 Court St. NE, H-488 Salem 97301 503-986-1412	Account Manager 2013/2015/2017	Oregon 1946

House terms are two years, and Senate terms (in parentheses) are four years, unless appointed mid-term.

District/Counties	Name/Address/Phone	Occupation/Yr. Elected*	Birthplace/Year
13. Portion of Lane	Nancy Nathanson (D) PO Box 41895 Eugene 97404 541-343-2206	Library Program Staff 2007/2009/2011/2013/ 2015/2017	Texas 1951
14. Portion of Lane	Julie Fahey (D) 900 Court St. NE, H-474 Salem 97301 503-986-1414	Business Consultant 2017	Illinois 1978
15. Portions of Benton and Linn	Andy Olson (R) PO Box 891 Albany 97321 541-967-6576	Retired Law Enforcement 2005/2007/2009/2011/ 2013/2015/2017	Nebraska 1952
16. Portion of Benton	Dan Rayfield (D) 900 Court St. NE, H-286 Salem 97301 503-986-1416	Attorney 2015/2017	California 1979
17. Portions of Linn and Marion	Sherrie Sprenger (R) 900 Court St. NE, H-388 Salem 97301 503-986-1417	Small Business Owner 2008/2009/2011/2013/ 2015/2017	Oregon 1965
18. Portions of Clackamas and Marion	Vic Gilliam (R) PO Box 158 Silverton 97381 971-599-3557	Real Estate and Media 2007/2009/2011/2013/ 2015/2017	Ohio 1953
19. Portion of Marion	Jodi L. Hack (R) 900 Court St. NE, H-385 Salem 97301 503-986-1419	Competitive Grant Writer 2015/2017	Oregon 1969
20. Portions of Marion and Polk	Paul Evans (D) 900 Court St. NE, H-281 Salem 97301 503-986-1420	Educator, Small Business Owner 2015/2017	Oregon 1970
21. Portion of Marion	Brian L. Clem (D) 396 Hoyt St. SE Salem 97302 503-391-9770	Small Business Owner 2007/2009/2011/2013/ 2015/2017	Oregon 1972
22. Portion of Marion	Teresa Alonso Leon (D) 900 Court St. NE, H-283 Salem 97301 503-986-1422	State Representative 2017	Mexico 1975
23. Portions of Benton, Marion, Polk and Yamhill	Mike Nearman (R) 900 Court St. NE, H-378 Salem 97301 503-986-1423	Software Engineer 2015/2017	Wisconsin 1964
24. Portions of Washington and Yamhill	Ron Noble (R) 900 Court St. NE, H-376 Salem 97301 503-986-1424	Retired Law Enforcement 2017	California 1960
25. Portion of Marion	Bill Post (R) 900 Court St. NE, H-387 Salem 97301 503-986-1425	Radio Broadcaster 2015/2017	Arizona 1960

District/Counties	Name/Address/Phone	Occupation/Yr. Elected*	Birthplace/Year
26. Portions of Clackamas, Washington and Yamhill	A. Richard Vial (R) 900 Court St. NE, H-484 Salem 97301 503-986-1426	Farmer/Lawyer 2017	California 1954
27. Portion of Washington	Sheri Malstrom (D) 900 Court St. NE, H-280 Salem 97301 503-986-1427	Registered Nurse 2017	Oregon 1953
28. Portion of Washington	Jeff Barker (D) PO Box 6751 Aloha 97007 503-986-1428	Retired Police Lieutenant 2003/2005/2007/2009/ 2011/2013/2015/2017	Oregon 1943
29. Portion of Washington	Susan McLain (D) 900 Court St. NE, H-477 Salem 97301 503-986-1429	Retired Teacher 2015/2017	Oregon 1949
30. Portion of Washington	Janeen Sollman (D) 900 Court St. NE, H-487 Salem 97301 503-986-1430	Customer Service Specialist 2017	Philippines 1969
31. Columbia and portions of Multnomah and Washington	Bradley Witt (D) 900 Court St. NE, H-374 Salem 97301 503-986-1431	Labor Official 2005/2007/2009/2011/ 2013/2015/2017	Massachusetts 1952
32. Clatsop and portions of Tillamook and Washington	Deborah Boone (D) PO Box 928 Cannon Beach 97110 503-986-1432	Business Owner 2005/2007/2009/2011/ 2013/2015/2017	Oregon 1951
33. Portions of Multnomah and Washington	Mitch Greenlick (D) PO Box 5156 Portland 97208 503-297-2416	Professor Emeritus, OHSU 2003/2005/2007/2009/ 2011/2013/201/2017	Michigan 1935
34. Portion of Washington	Ken Helm (D) 900 Court St. NE, H-490 Salem 97301 503-986-1434	Attorney 2015/2017	California 1965
35. Portions of Multnomah and Washington	Margaret Doherty (D) 16200 SW Pacific Hwy. H-282 Tigard 97224 503-986-1435	Teacher, Small Business Owner 2009/2011/2013/2015/ 2017	California 1950
36. Portion of Multnomah	Jennifer Williamson (D) 900 Court St. NE, H-295 Salem 97301 503-986-1436	Attorney 2013/2015/2017	Oregon 1973
37. Portions of Clackamas and Washington	Julie Parrish (R) 900 Court St. NE, H-371 Salem 97301 503-986-1437	Business Owner 2011/2013/2015/2017	Oregon 1974
38. Portions of Clackamas and Multnomah	Ann Lininger (D) 900 Court St. NE, H-485 Salem 97301 503-986-1438	Attorney 2014/2015/2017	Oregon 1968

District/Counties	Name/Address/Phone	Occupation/Yr. Elected*	Birthplace/Year
39. Portion of Clackamas	Bill Kennemer (R) 900 Court St. NE, H-380 Salem 97301 503-986-1439	Retired Psychologist and County Commissioner 2009/2011/2013/2015/ 2017	California 1946
40. Portion of Clackamas	Mark Meek (D) 900 Court St. NE, H-285 Salem 97301 503-986-1440	Realtor 2017	California 1964
41. Portions of Clackamas and Multnomah	Karin Power (D) 900 Court St. NE, H-274 Salem 97301 503-986-1441	Attorney 2017	New Jersey 1983
42. Portion of Multnomah	Rob Nosse (D) 900 Court St. NE, H-472 Salem 97301 503-986-1442	Labor Representative 2015/2017	Ohio 1967
43. Portion of Multnomah	Tawna Sanchez (D) 900 Court St. NE, H-273 Salem 97301 503-986-1443	Family Services Director 2017	Oregon 1961
44. Portion of Multnomah	Tina Kotek (D) 7930 N Wabash Ave. Portland 97217 503-986-1444	Consultant 2007/2009/2011/2013/ 2015/2017	Pennsylvania 1966
45. Portion of Multnomah	Barbara Smith Warner (D) 900 Court St. NE, H-275 Salem 97301 503-986-1445	Labor Liaison, U.S. Senate 2013/2015/2017	Pennsylvania 1967
46. Portion of Multnomah	Alissa Keny-Guyer (D) 900 Court St. NE, H-272 Salem 97301 503-986-1446	Nonprofit Management 2011/2013/2015/2017	New York 1959
47. Portion of Multnomah	Diego Hernandez (D) 900 Court St. NE, H-373 Salem 97301 503-986-1447	Nonprofit Executive Director 2017	California 1987
48. Portions of Clackamas and Multnomah	Jeff Reardon (D) 900 Court St. NE, H-473 Salem 97301 503-986-1448	Teacher 2013/2015/2017	Washington 1947
49. Portion of Multnomah	Chris Gorsek (D) 900 Court St. NE, H-486 Salem 97301 503-378-1449	Teacher 2013/2015/2017	Oregon 1958
50. Portion of Multnomah	Carla C. Piluso (D) 900 Court St. NE, H-491 Salem 97301 503-986-1450	Retired Police Chief 2015/2017	Oregon 1955
51. Portions of Clackamas and Multnomah	Janelle Bynum (D) 900 Court St. NE, H-284 Salem 97301 503-986-1451	Restaurant Owner 2017	District of Columbia 1975

District/Counties	Name/Address/Phone	Occupation/Yr. Elected*	Birthplace/Year
52. Hood River and portions of Clackamas and Multnomah	Mark Johnson (R) PO Box 1047 Hood River 97031 503-986-1452	Builder/Contractor 2011/2013/2015/2017	California 1957
53. Portion of Deschutes	Gene Whisnant (R) 900 Court St NE, H-383 Salem 97301 503-986-1453	USAF Colonel, Retired 2003/2005/2007/2009/ 2011/2013/2015/2017	North Carolina 1943
54. Portion of Deschutes	Knute C. Buehler (R) 900 Court St. NE, H-389 Salem 97301 503-986-1454	Orthopedic Surgeon 2015/2017	Oregon 1964
55. Crook and portions of Deschutes, Jackson, Klamath and Lake	Mike McLane (R) 900 Court St. NE, H-395 Salem 97301 541-233-4411	Attorney 2011/2013/2015/2017	Alaska 1965
56. Portions of Klamath and Lake	E. Werner Reschke (R) 900 Court St. NE, H-377 Salem 97301 503-986-1456	Online Marketing/Web Development 2017	California 1965
57. Gilliam, Morrow, Sherman and portions of Umatilla and Wasco	Greg Smith (R) PO Box 215 Heppner 97836 541-676-5154	Small Business Owner 2001/2003/2005/2007/ 2009/2011/2013/2015/ 2017	Oregon 1968
58. Union, Wallowa and portion of Umatilla	Greg Barreto (R) 900 Court St. NE, H-384 Salem 97301 503-986-1458	President, Manufacturing Company 2015/2017	California 1955
59. Jefferson, Wheeler and portions of Deschutes and Wasco	John E. Huffman (R) PO Box 104 The Dalles 97058 541-298-5959	Commercial Property Owner, Developer 2007/2009/2011/2013/ 2015/2017	Missouri 1957
60. Baker, Grant, Harney, Malheur and portion of Lake	Cliff Bentz (R) 258 S Oregon St. Ontario 97814 541-889-8866	Attorney 2008/2009/2011/2013/ 2015/2017	Oregon 1952

Legislative

MIDDLE SCHOOL STUDENT ESSAY

Oregon Adventure!

Jake Hale, Essay Contest Runner-up
Scott Buchanan's Eighth Grade Class
Crook County Middle School, Prineville

Oregon's forests are great places to take a friend out who's never been to Oregon. From Spring there's horseback riding, turkey hunting, and even the start of fishing. Then there's Fall, the start of hunting season. My most favorite time of the year.

If I was to have a friend come over to Oregon and stay here, I'd take him out too the Ochoco Mountains. They are a great place for mostly any outdoor activity and have a wide expanse of land. Plus, the Ochocos are my backyard. I've been around them most of my life and I wouldn't trade them for anything.

Since I grew up in a hunting family, I would take my friend out hunting. I'd take him out just for the experience of the beauty of nature and the thrill of being able to provide for you and your family. Whether it be coyotes or sage rats, we'd still have a great time. This is what I do, no one can take it away from me. This is what we find fun in around Central Oregon. I know that that friend who would be coming here would have a blast being in the outdoors of Oregon.

Steins Pillar towers over the forest in the Ochoco Mountains. *(Oregon State Archives)*

A horse and rider jump over an obstacle during a show jumping competition near Parkdale in the Hood river Valley.
Oregon State Archives Scenic Photograph DSC0034–33

Government finance—where government gets its money and how it spends it—affects all Oregonians. The connections between state and local government revenues and state and local government services are important. This section describes revenue sources and distribution.

STATE AND LOCAL GOVERNMENT FINANCE

Source: Department of Administrative Services, Chief Financial Office

State Government

Oregon has a biennial budget. Budgets begin July 1 of odd-numbered years and continue for two years. Oregon law requires all state and local governments to balance their budgets. How does the state government's budget work? The state receives money from a variety of sources which are grouped into funds. These funds are known as the General Fund, Lottery Fund, Other Funds and Federal Funds.

The total Legislatively Approved Budget for the 2015–2017 biennium is $70.9 billion total funds. This is an increase of $4.8 billion, or 7.2 percent, from the 2013–2015 Legislatively Approved Budget of $66.1 billion. The General and Lottery Funds portions of the 2015–2017 budget amounted to $19 billion.

General Fund

The 2015–2017 Legislatively Approved Budget included approximately $18.1 billion in General Fund expenditures—a 25.5 percent share of the total budget. The General Fund is largely made up of personal and corporate income taxes collected by the Oregon Department of Revenue. The personal income tax makes up the largest share of General Fund revenue. It accounts for about 87.2 percent of projected revenue for 2015–2017 as of the June 2016 quarterly revenue forecast. Corporate income taxes are about 6.1 percent of the total revenue amount. Other sources make up the remainder. The largest of these sources are the cigarette tax, estate tax and the liquor apportionment transfer.

General Fund appropriations provide funding to agencies that do not generate revenues, receive federal funds or generate sufficient other funds to support their approved programs. Agencies do not actually receive money from the General Fund. Instead, they expend against an appropriation from the General Fund that is established for general government purposes up to the amount approved in their budget bill. Because General Fund monies can be used for any public purpose and the amount of the General Fund is limited, competition for these monies is keen.

In 1990, voters approved Ballot Measure 5. This reduced local property tax rates, which reduced local revenue and, in turn, shifted much of the responsibility for funding public schools to the state's General Fund. The 2015–2017 Legislatively Approved Budget had $9.8 billion, or 51.5 percent, of the General and Lottery Funds being spent on education.

General Fund revenues for the 2015–2017 biennium are expected to total $18.1 billion. There was a balance carried over from the prior biennium of approximately $528.8 million after a dedicated transfer of $136.7 million was made to the Rainy Day Fund. As of June 2016, the revenue forecast was $24.8 million above the "Close of Session" forecast, bringing total resources to $18.3 billion. The updated projected ending balance for 2015–2017 is $261.8 million.

Lottery Fund

The Lottery Fund derives from the sale of lottery game tickets and from Video Lottery. After prizes and lottery expenses are paid, revenue flows to the Economic Development Fund. A portion of the Lottery Fund is constitutionally dedicated to be spent in specific ways. The remainder is distributed at the discretion of the Legislature for economic development.

The 2015–2017 Legislatively Approved Budget included $958.2 million of expenditures from the Lottery Fund, which is about 1.4 percent of the total

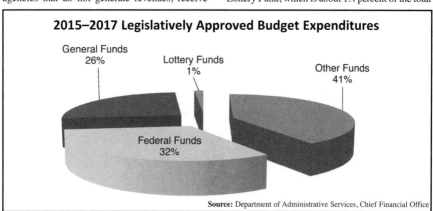

2015–2017 Legislatively Approved Budget Expenditures

General Funds 26%

Lottery Funds 1%

Other Funds 41%

Federal Funds 32%

Source: Department of Administrative Services, Chief Financial Office

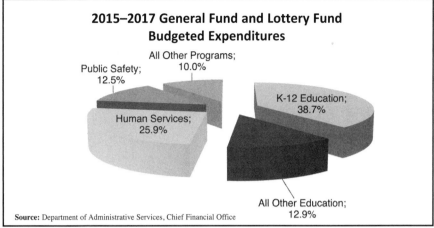

2015–2017 General Fund and Lottery Fund Budgeted Expenditures

- All Other Programs; 10.0%
- Public Safety; 12.5%
- Human Services; 25.9%
- K-12 Education; 38.7%
- All Other Education; 12.9%

Source: Department of Administrative Services, Chief Financial Office

budget. Dedicated spending accounted for about 38 percent of that amount, and debt service accounted for another 24 percent. The remainder was distributed to the State School Fund and a variety of other projects. Overall, about 53 percent of the Lottery Fund is dedicated to education.

Other Funds

The 2015–2017 Legislatively Approved Budget included $29 billion in Other Funds for a 40.9 percent share of the total budget. Other Funds revenue generally refers to monies collected by agencies in return for services. Legislative actions may allow an agency to levy taxes, provide services for a fee, license individuals, or otherwise earn revenues to pay for programs. These Other Funds are often separate and distinct from monies collected for general government purposes (General Fund), and they may be based on statutory language, federal mandate, legal requirements, or for specific business reasons. Some funds are "dedicated"— the income and disbursements are limited by the state's constitution or by another law (for example, the Highway Fund). Other Funds may not be moved from one major program to another. Consequently, competition for these monies is limited.

Federal Funds

The 2015–2017 Legislatively Approved Budget included $22.9 billion in Federal Funds for a 32.3 percent share of the total budget. Federal Funds are monies received from the federal government through entitlement programs, grants and aid awarded to various state agencies.

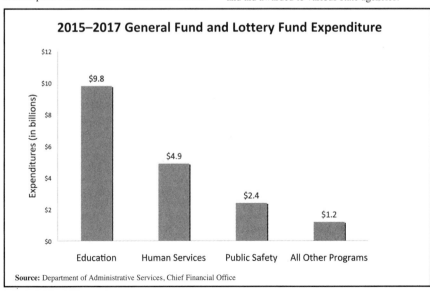

2015–2017 General Fund and Lottery Fund Expenditure

Expenditures (in billions)

- Education: $9.8
- Human Services: $4.9
- Public Safety: $2.4
- All Other Programs: $1.2

Source: Department of Administrative Services, Chief Financial Office

Government Finance

State Budget Process

Oregon state agencies develop biennial budgets according to instructions provided by the Department of Administrative Services, Chief Financial Office. This budget development process begins in even-numbered years, well before the Legislative Assembly convenes in January of the odd-numbered years. Agencies are required to prepare and submit their budget requests to the Chief Financial Office. These budget requests consist of narrative descriptions of agency programs, completed budgetary forms, and reports from the Oregon Budget Information and Tracking System (ORBITS). An agency budget request serves as a conduit to the governor and the Legislature that identifies the agency's needs and priorities.

Agencies begin by building a Current Service Level (CSL) budget, which is the amount of money needed in the upcoming biennium to continue all existing programs, minus one-time monies. An agency may request additions to their CSL budget through policy packages, which describe the purpose and the amount needed. Agencies also must identify program reductions and performance targets. For their 2017–2019 budget requests, agencies begin in March 2016 and submit their completed requests by September 2016. An agency's budget provides an outline of what an agency does, what it costs, and how many people are involved.

After analysis by the Governor's Office and the Chief Financial Office, the governor aligns her priorities with the agencies' requests resulting in the Governor's Recommended Budget. Because the governor has a legal obligation to submit a balanced budget for all of state government, the Governor's Recommended Budget includes the proposed budgets for the Legislative Assembly and the Judicial Department. However, because of separation of power principles, the governor's budget recommendations are advisory only for the other two branches. The governor presents the Governor's Recommended Budget to the Legislative Assembly when it convenes in January of odd-numbered years.

When the Legislative Assembly is in session, a subcommittee of the Joint Ways and Means Committee considers each agency's budget. At the budget hearings, an agency presents its budget request and answers questions asked by members of the committee. Staff members from the Legislative Fiscal Office and the Chief Financial Office are also present at the budget hearings. Members of the public may attend the hearings and request an opportunity to testify. At the end of an agency's budget hearings, the agency's budget goes to the full Ways and Means Committee for a vote and then on to the full House and Senate for a vote. The agency's budget may be amended at any point

in this process, although changes typically occur during the subcommittee hearings. After passage by both chambers, an agency's budget becomes its Legislatively Adopted Budget for the biennium, and it goes into effect July 1 of odd-numbered years. If the Legislature makes changes to the adopted budget in special sessions or through the Emergency Board, it becomes known as the Legislatively Approved Budget.

Kicker Provision

The Oregon Constitution requires the governor to provide an estimate of biennial General Fund revenues.

In 1979, the Legislature placed a condition on those revenue estimates that required excess funds to be "kicked back" to taxpayers if actual revenues exceeded estimated revenues by 2 percent or more of the close-of-session estimate.

For revenues from corporate income and excise taxes, the provision had required that the excess be returned to taxpayers who paid corporate income and excise taxes. However, this provision was amended in November 2012 by the citizen initiative process. Ballot Measure 85 requires that this excess be retained in the General Fund to provide additional funding for public education of kindergarten through twelfth grade. This measure is applicable to biennial estimates on or after July 1, 2013.

For General Fund revenues from all other sources where the actual revenues exceed the estimated revenues by 2 percent or more, the excess is "kicked back" to taxpayers who paid personal income tax. Ballot Measure 85 did not affect this provision. These taxpayers receive the refund by December 1 of the year the biennium ends, which is an odd-numbered year. The refund is an identical proportion of each taxpayer's personal income tax liability for the prior year.

During 2015–2017, $363 million was refunded to personal income tax payers.

Rainy Day Fund and Education Stability Fund

Established in 2007, the Oregon Rainy Day Fund is essentially a savings account for state government. Withdrawals can be made, after a three-fifths vote of approval by the Legislature, if there is a decline in the General Fund for the current or subsequent biennium budgets, there is a prolonged employment decline or the governor declares an emergency. Given the economic conditions in 2009 and 2010, the fund needed to be utilized. The current fund balance is expected to be $387.6 million at the end of the 2015–2017 biennium.

The Education Stability Fund (ESF) was created through a constitutional amendment approved by voters in 2002. The ESF receives 18 percent of net

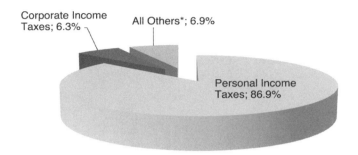

2015–2017 General Fund Revenue Forecast by Source

Corporate Income Taxes; 6.3%

All Others*; 6.9%

Personal Income Taxes; 86.9%

*e.g., cigarette tax, estate tax, liquor apportionment transfer

Source: Department of Administrative Services, Chief Financial Office

lottery proceeds deposited on a quarterly basis. The ESF has similar requirements as the Rainy Day Fund. Like the Rainy Day Fund, the ESF had been drawn down during the last economic downturn to balance budgets in the 2009–2011 and 2011–2013 biennia. Based on the June 2016 revenue forecast, the fund is projected to have a balance of $381.6 million at the end of the 2015–2017 biennium.

State Spending Limit

The state spending limit was first enacted by the 1979 Legislative Assembly. It limited the growth of General Fund appropriations to the growth of personal income in Oregon. The 2001 Legislative Assembly replaced this spending limit with one tying appropriations for a biennium to personal income for that biennium. The appropriations subject to this limit may not exceed 8 percent of projected personal income for the same biennium. The 2003–2005 Legislatively Adopted Budget authorized an expenditure limit of 7.6 percent of projected personal income for the biennium based on the May 2003 revenue forecast. The limit may be exceeded if the governor declares an emergency and three-fifths of the members of both chambers vote to exceed it.

Local Government

Local government in Oregon is predominantly financed by the property tax, although there are other local taxes, such as hotel-motel taxes, transit taxes and, in Multnomah County, a business income tax.

Most local governments must prepare and adopt an annual budget. This includes schools, counties, cities, ports, rural fire protection districts, water districts, urban renewal agencies, and special districts. Oregon's Local Budget Law establishes standard budget procedures and requires citizen participation

in budget preparation and public disclosure of the budget before it is formally adopted. A budget officer must be appointed and a budget committee formed. The budget officer prepares a draft budget and the budget committee reviews and revises it before it is approved. Notices are then published, copies of the budget are made available for public review, and at least two opportunities for public comment are provided.

Local government budgets are usually for a fiscal year beginning July 1 and ending June 30. However, local governments have the option of creating a two-year biennial budget like the state. The governing body must enact a resolution or an ordinance to formally adopt the budget, make appropriations, and levy and categorize any tax. This must be done no later than June 30. Budget revenues are divided into ensuing year property tax and non-property tax revenues.

The Oregon Constitution allows a local government to levy annually the amount that would be raised by its permanent rate limit without further authorization from the voters. When a local government has to increase the permanent rate limit or when the rate limit does not provide enough revenue to meet estimated expenditures, the government may request a local option levy from the voters. Approval requires a "double majority." This means that at least 50 percent of the registered voters must vote, and a majority of those who vote must approve the levy, unless the measure is submitted during an election held in any May or November, which are exempt from the "double majority" approval requirement. Since 1991, the Oregon Constitution has limited the maximum amount of taxes to support the public schools to $5 per $1,000 of real market value. The maximum amount to support

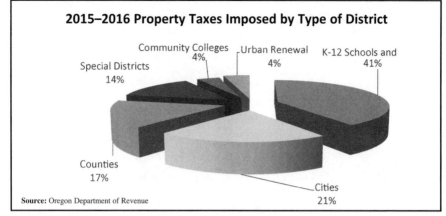

2015–2016 Property Taxes Imposed by Type of District

- Community Colleges 4%
- Special Districts 14%
- Urban Renewal 4%
- K-12 Schools and 41%
- Counties 17%
- Cities 21%

Source: Oregon Department of Revenue

other government operations is $10 per $1,000 of real market value.

Taxes

Personal Income Tax

Oregon residents and nonresidents who earn income in Oregon pay personal income tax.

Oregon's taxable income is the same as federal taxable income with some adjustments. Tax rates range from 5 percent to 11 percent of taxable income. After deductions and credits, the average effective tax rate is about 5.7 percent of adjusted gross income. Since 1993, the income tax brackets have been indexed to changes in the Consumer Price Index. The current standard deduction is $3,895 on a joint return, $1,945 on single and married filing separate returns, and $3,135 for a head of household return.

The personal income tax is the largest source of state tax revenue. In January 2010, Oregon voters approved Ballot Measure 66, which made two changes to personal income tax calculations. First, it established new tax brackets for adjusted gross incomes above $125,000 (single filers) and $250,000 (joint filers) and phased out the federal tax subtraction for those same filers. Second, it allowed a one-year tax exclusion of the first $2,400 of unemployment benefits, as does federal tax law.

Business Taxes

Corporations that do, or are authorized to do, business in Oregon pay an excise tax. Corporations not doing, or that are not authorized to do, business in Oregon, but that have income from an Oregon source, pay income tax. The tax rate is 6.6 percent of Oregon net income. There is a minimum excise tax of $150.

The corporate excise and income tax is the second largest source of state tax revenue. Oregon voters approved Ballot Measure 67 in January

2010. The measure made three changes to Oregon corporate taxation. First, it increased the minimum corporate tax from $10 to $150. Second, it instituted a new corporate income tax rate structure that applies a marginal rate of 7.9 percent to corporate net income above $250,000 in tax years 2009 and 2010. For 2011 and 2012, the rate drops to 7.6 percent. In 2013, the marginal rate is 7.6 percent for net income above $10 million and 6.6 percent for net income below $10 million. Third, it established higher rates for corporate filing fees with the secretary of state.

Property Tax

Property tax rates differ across Oregon. The rate depends on the tax rate approved by local voters and the limits established by the Oregon Constitution. Most properties are taxed by a number of districts, such as a city, county, school district, community college, fire district, or port. The total tax rate on any particular property is calculated by adding all the local taxing district rates in the area. The total tax rate is then multiplied by the assessed value of the property. The county assessor verifies the tax rates and levies submitted by each local taxing district on an annual basis. The county tax collector collects the taxes and distributes the funds to the local districts.

Taxable property includes real property, mobile homes, and some tangible personal property used by business. The state and each county assessor determine the value of property in each county. Measure 5, which was passed by the voters in November 1990, restricted non-school taxes on any property to $10 per $1,000 of real market value. It restricted school taxes on any property to $5 per $1,000 of real market value.

Measure 50 was passed by the voters in May 1997. Measure 50 added another limit to the Measure 5 limits. Now, each property has a real market value and an assessed value. Each taxing district has a fixed, permanent tax rate for operations. Districts may not increase this rate. Voters can approve local option levies for up to five years for operations and up to 10 years or the useful life of capital projects, whichever is less. Local option levies require a "double majority" for approval. Measure 50 established the 1997–1998 maximum assessed value as 90 percent of a property's 1995–1996 real market value. In subsequent tax years, the assessed value is limited to 3 percent annual growth until it reaches real market value. The assessed value can never exceed real market value. New property is assessed at the average county ratio of assessed to real market value of existing property of the same class. For 2008–2009, for all classes of property statewide, total assessed value was about 56 percent of real market value.

Resources

Department of Administrative Services, Chief Financial Office
www.oregon.gov/DAS/financial
The Chief Financial Office publishes the "Budget Process Overview" and *Governor's Recommended Budget.*

Department of Administrative Services, Office of Economic Analysis
www.oregon.gov/DAS/oea/pages/index.aspx
The Office of Economic Analysis publishes periodic Economic and Revenue Forecasts, as well as related demographic data.

Department of Revenue
www.oregon.gov/DOR/index.shtml
The Department of revenue publishes information about taxes in Oregon.

Legislative Fiscal Office
www.oregonlegislature.gov/lfo
The Legislative Fiscal Office publishes detailed analyses of the *Legislatively Adopted Budget* and the *Governor's Recommended Budget.*

Legislative Revenue Office
www.oregonlegislature.gov/lro
The Legislative Revenue Office publishes reports on revenue-related issues including *Oregon Public Finance: Basic Facts,* which serves as an introduction to how Oregon government is financed.

ELEMENTARY SCHOOL STUDENT ESSAY

Mending Lila

Jada Jones, Essay Contest Winner
Illustration by Mizuki Maddock
Ashley Baker's Fourth Grade Class
Yujin Gakuen School, Eugene

Mizuki is my best friend we both heard about this competition. She drew this picture for you and maybe the book.

My most memorable Oregon experience was camping along the Crooked River with family. We fly fished for trout and watched birds hunt in the canyon. This whole area is beautiful.

On the first day of our trip I saw a Monarch butterfly. I got close and noticed a large tear in it's wing. I asked my parents how we could help. They couldn't fix the wing, but said I could find it nectar.

For the next few days I cared for Lila. She held on to me wherever I went. On the fourth day we needed to head back home and I couldn't take her with us. I wished she could fly again and continue her journey. At that moment, Lila said good bye and flew away.

I will always remember this experience. I hope you are able to have an experience in Oregon you will never forget.

Education

A pilot wears a motor on his back while flying a powered paraglider north of Baker City.
Oregon State Archives Scenic Photograph 20160713-4337

As Oregon's population grows and our economy evolves, the strength of our educational institutions is an important public policy issue. This section describes public education in Oregon and also lists independent colleges and universities.

PUBLIC EDUCATION IN OREGON

Source: Oregon Chief Education Office

Public Education in Oregon

Education is critical to ensuring that every Oregonian is prepared for success in a global economy, has economic security, and has the ability to provide for themselves and their families. Education promotes shared values, enriches culture and expands the vitality of individuals and communities. When delivered equitably, education provides opportunity for every Oregonian no matter their race, home language, disability, family income or zip code. Never before has a high-quality education been more important to the lives and well-being of individuals and our communities.

Senate Bill 253 (2011) established the mission of Oregon's education system to achieve key goals for high school and college completion and career readiness. Under these goals, known as "40-40-20," Oregon aspires to achieve the following by 2025:

• 40 percent of adult Oregonians will have earned a bachelor's degree or higher,

• 40 percent will have earned an associate's degree or postsecondary credential as their highest level of education attainment, and

• 20 percent will have earned at least a high school diploma, an extended or modified high school diploma, or the equivalent of a high school diploma as their highest level of education attainment.

These goals reflect a shared commitment by the state and education groups to create the conditions to ensure each young person has access and opportunities throughout their education to thrive and to pursue an education and career path meaningful to them.

To put this commitment into operation, education agencies that serve students from cradle to career have adopted an "Equity Lens" to guide policy making, investment recommendations, program development, and community engagement. The Equity Lens expresses shared values that recognize the unique assets, contributions and capabilities of individual students. It also underscores the importance of working closely with communities to develop strategies and a network of supports for students and their families.

Chief Education Office

Senate Bill 215 (2015) created the Chief Education Office (CEdO) for the purpose of building a seamless system of education from birth to college and career. The CEdO leverages both directing authority and coordinating capacity to lead cross-sector, multi-agency planning and stakeholder convening to eliminate barriers impeding student success, ensuring educational equity and opportunity within all education settings, and achieving statewide goals and student learning outcomes.

The CEdO brings strategic leadership and coordination to key student transition points and other critical areas across the education continuum to improve outcomes for Oregon students, grow the capacity of systems to serve student success, expand pathways of learning, ensure a well-supported, culturally responsive education workforce, and elevate policies and practices to accelerate student learning outcomes through convening, research, and partnerships with educational groups and communities.

The CEdO's focus is to foster stronger connections and alignment from early learning to kindergarten through twelfth grade education, and K–12 education to higher education and the workforce. In doing so, the agency expands student access and opportunity and provides each individual a seamless pathway of learning, with a particular focus on traditionally underserved students and students in poverty.

In 2015, Governor Kate Brown outlined her vision to improve the number of students who complete high school with a plan for their future. Realizing this vision requires a long-term commitment by the state's education system to prioritize equitable access to opportunities and supports that foster success for every student throughout the continuum of their educations.

With a four-year high school graduation rate of 74 percent, Governor Brown has identified improving graduation outcomes as her top education priority. Governor Brown charged the CEdO with engaging with school districts and communities to identify and scale up effective practices and make policy recommendations to ensure more students graduate high school with a plan for their future.

In the 2015–2017 biennium, Governor Brown and legislators prioritized a series of investments designed to improve access and opportunities for the youngest Oregonians and students pursuing a college education or exploring a career. These "wrap-around" investments included resources to establish all-day kindergarten at every school in the state; more than $130 million to expand access to early learning and preschool programs for families who could not have previously afforded them; a near doubling of investments in science, technology, engineering and math (STEM) and Career and Technical Education programs to help engage students in hands-on learning and prepare them for future careers; the creation of the Oregon Promise program that can provide two years of community college tuition at no cost to qualifying high school graduates; and the expansion of the Oregon Opportunity Grant to an additional 16,000 college and university students.

The education system operating in isolation cannot affect the changes necessary to improve student outcomes. Partnerships with communities and groups that span education, health, social service and workforce are critical to successfully expanding student opportunities and putting them on a path towards employment, job training, or post-secondary education.

The CEdO has coordinating oversight of all state education agencies, including:

The **Oregon Early Learning Division** (ELD), established within the Department of Education, is charged with coordinating service delivery systems to improve kindergarten readiness for the 190,294 children who are newborn to six years old across Oregon.

The **Department of Education** (ODE) develops statewide policy and programs, and allocates resources for 576,407 students in Oregon's public K–12 system. ODE is in charge of public preschool programs through its Early Learning Division. It also oversees the Oregon School for the Deaf, regional programs for children with disabilities, and other out-of-school-time educational programs through its Youth Development Division.

The **Youth Development Division** (YDD), established within ODE, is charged with developing state-level policy and administering funding to support community-based youth development programs, services and initiatives that support educational success, focus on crime prevention, reduce high-risk behaviors, and are integrated, measurable and accountable. The division plays an important role in supporting young people ages 16 to 24 who are neither enrolled in school nor participating in the labor force by helping them get back on the path to college and/or career.

The **Higher Education Coordinating Commission** (HECC) was first convened in 2011, and the Legislature established HECC as an agency in 2013 by consolidating existing authorities that were spread across multiple agencies and boards. HECC is the single state entity responsible for ensuring pathways to higher education success statewide and serves as point of coordination for institutions and partners working across the public and private higher education arena. The governance of Oregon's public community colleges and universities is the responsibility of their respective governing boards. In September 2015, about 290,000 students were enrolled in Oregon's 17 public community colleges and seven public universities.

Education Funding

Education-related investments span early learning through higher education and include a range of services, from youth corrections education and Career and Technical Education, to strategic investments designed to support and create opportunities for Oregon's historically underserved students and communities.

Early Learning: The Early Learning Division funds preschools, home visiting, relief nurseries, Early Learning Hubs and other programs for children under the age of five and their families. The Division is also responsible for licensing and monitoring child care programs, as well as providing other supports to child care programs and the early learning workforce. The Early Learning Division's budget for the 2015–2017 biennium is $405.8 million, of which $233.3 million are General Fund dollars. Most of the rest of the funding is federal, a large source of which is the Child Care Development Fund.

Kindergarten through Twelvth Grade: In 1991, the Legislature established a school funding equalization formula to fund K–12 schools. That funding formula, largely based on student enrollment numbers and student demographics, determines how much funding school districts receive from the State School Fund calibrated to the district's local revenue to fill the gap between the district's local revenue.

For the 2015–2016 school year, the State School Fund is providing $5.4 billion to support 576,407 students in 1,239 schools, 197 school districts, and Oregon's 19 education service districts. Of the $5.4 billion in the State School Fund, $3.6 billion is derived from state revenues, comprised of income tax and lottery revenues. The remaining nearly $1.8 billion is considered local revenues and are primarily received from property taxes. Federal and other funds provide a little more than a billion dollars in additional resources for schools.

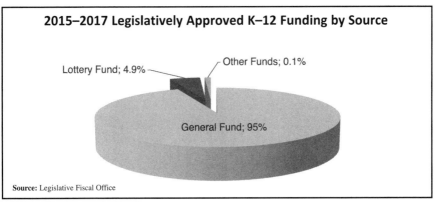

2015–2017 Legislatively Approved K–12 Funding by Source

Lottery Fund; 4.9%
Other Funds; 0.1%
General Fund; 95%

Source: Legislative Fiscal Office

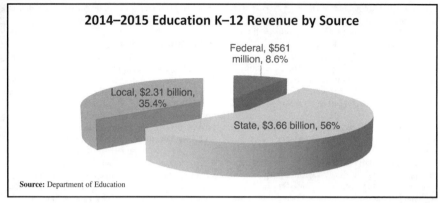

2014–2015 Education K–12 Revenue by Source

Federal, $561 million, 8.6%

Local, $2.31 billion, 35.4%

State, $3.66 billion, 56%

Source: Department of Education

Higher Education: The primary sources of funding for Oregon's public universities and community college are tuition and fees, state funding and other funds, which, for the community colleges includes property tax revenue. Today, tuition and fees account for a higher percentage of total revenue than the other sources. For 2015–2017, the state was able to increase the investment in Oregon's public universities and community colleges after years of underfunding, supporting the state's strategic focus on student success outcomes.

Community College Support Fund (CCSF) is the primary source of state funding supporting educational and operational expenses at Oregon's 17 community colleges. The CCSF is distributed using a formula that aims for equitable distribution of public resources per student, taking into account both CCSF and local property tax dollars. This fund provides investment in a range of educational activities, including associate degrees, transferable postsecondary undergraduate coursework, career and technical education, college credit in high school, adult basic education, literacy and local workforce training. The CCSF for 2015–2017 was $550 million.

The primary sources of state funding for seven public universities' educational, public and research missions are the Public University Support Fund (PUSF), the Sports Action Lottery program, Public University Statewide and State Programs, as well as through financing of capital projects. The PUSF, which totaled $665 million in 2015–2017, is

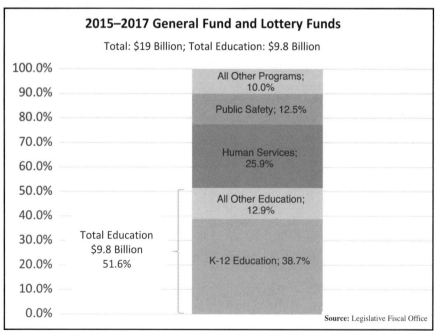

2015–2017 General Fund and Lottery Funds

Total: $19 Billion; Total Education: $9.8 Billion

All Other Programs; 10.0%

Public Safety; 12.5%

Human Services; 25.9%

All Other Education; 12.9%

Total Education $9.8 Billion 51.6%

K-12 Education; 38.7%

Source: Legislative Fiscal Office

distributed by the Student Success and Completion Model, a distribution formula focused on completions and student support, among other state priorities.

Early Learning in Oregon

The 2011 Legislature created the Early Learning Council (ELC), a governor-appointed policy and rulemaking body charged with creating a more coordinated service delivery system that improves kindergarten readiness and ensures that children up to six years old have the holistic supports so critical to educational success. In 2013, the Legislature formed the Early Learning Division to carry out this work overseen by the council. The division also includes the Office of Child Care.

The division's priorities include ensuring quality early learning environments through the implementation of the Quality Rating Improvement System; improving early literacy; increasing alignment between early childhood education and early elementary education; increasing alignment between early childhood education and health care; and providing early learning services to families through home visiting (Healthy Families Oregon and Early Head Start), respite care (Oregon Relief Nurseries) and high quality pre-school (Oregon Pre-Kindergarten Program).

The division is also responsible for implementing Early Learning Hubs — Oregon's community-based service delivery system for young children and their families — across the state.

The ELC, a 17-member, volunteer board, oversees early learning policy for the state and provides strategic direction to the division.

Kindergarten through Twelvth Grade Education in Oregon

In the 2015–2016 school year, there were 576,407 students in Oregon's public K–12 schools. There are more than 29,000 teachers working in close to 1,250 public schools in 197 school districts, led by locally elected school boards.

Students of color represent about 35 percent of Oregon's student population. About 10 percent of students are non-native English speakers. The most common first language for these students is Spanish, followed by Russian, Vietnamese and Chinese. Oregon students and their families speak more than 150 languages.

More than half of Oregon public school students qualify for free and reduced lunch, up 10 percent in the last decade.

Oregon's four-year high school graduation rate is 74 percent.

The governor serves as the superintendent of schools and appoints a deputy to lead the work of the Department of Education. In 2015, Governor Kate Brown appointed Salam Noor to serve as the Deputy Superintendent of Public Instruction for K–12 education. The department works with the State Board of Education to develop policy and strategies to improve outcomes for K–12 students.

The department and the state board work to help school districts achieve both local and statewide goals and priorities through strategies such as developing policies and standards, providing accurate and timely data to inform instruction, training educators to use data effectively, administering numerous state and federal grants, and sharing and helping districts implement best practices.

The goals of the department include graduating students to be college and career ready, closing the achievement and opportunity gaps, improving teacher and administrator effectiveness, increasing performance for all schools and districts and contributing to a strong, seamless education system from early childhood through higher education.

State Board of Education

The Oregon State Board of Education works to ensure that every Oregon public school student has equal access to high quality educational services that promote lifelong learning and prepare them to graduate from high school with a plan for their futures, including college, work and citizenship.

The Oregon Legislature created the Board in 1951 to oversee the state's schools. The board sets educational policies and standards for Oregon's 197 public school districts and 19 educational service districts. All of these agencies have separate, locally-elected governing bodies responsible for transacting business within their jurisdictions. The State Board of Education is the body responsible for promulgating administrative rules that the Department of Education implements.

The board is comprised of seven members appointed by the governor and confirmed by the senate. Five members represent Oregon's five congressional districts, and two members represent the state at large. Members serve four-year terms and are limited to two consecutive terms. Board members elect their chair each year. The board meets at least six times per year and their meetings are open to the public.

Oregon School for the Deaf

Dr. Sharla Jones, Director
Address: 999 Locust St. NE, Salem 97301-5254
Phone: 503-378-3825;
Video phone: 503-400-6180
Fax: 503-378-4701
Web: www.osd.k12.or.us

Established in 1870, the Oregon School for the Deaf (OSD) enrolls students who, because of hearing impairment, require services and supports that are not provided through their regular public school. OSD is funded by legislative appropriation and is operated by the Department of Education. In 2016–2017, 121 students were enrolled at the school at no cost to their families.

HIGHER EDUCATION IN OREGON

Prospective students and families in Oregon can choose from a wide variety of postsecondary education options to earn degrees, certificates and training to build their futures and achieve their career goals. Oregon's higher education system enrolls hundreds of thousands of students in seven public universities, 17 community colleges, the Oregon Health & Science University, over 50 private colleges and universities and hundreds of private career and trade schools.

Higher Education Coordinating Commission

Ben Cannon, Executive Director
Address: 255 Capitol St. NE, Salem 97310-0001
Phone: 503-378-5690
Email: Info.HECC@state.or.us
Web: www.oregon.gov/highered/about/Pages/ commission.aspx

Established in 2011 and vested with its current authority in 2013, the Higher Education Coordinating Commission (HECC) is a 14-member, volunteer commission and agency dedicated to fostering and sustaining the best, most rewarding pathways to opportunity and success for all Oregonians through an accessible, affordable and coordinated network for higher education. For the current list of commissioners, go to: www.oregon.gov/HigherEd/ /about/Pages/commission. The commission is supported by the HECC state agency.

The HECC is the single state entity responsible for ensuring pathways to higher educational success for all Oregonians statewide and serves as a convener of the groups and institutions working across the public and private higher education arena.

The work of the HECC is driven by the state's "40-40-20" educational attainment goal, a clear target against which to measure the state's educational progress. In support of state goals, the commission develops and implements policies and programs to ensure that Oregon's network of colleges, universities, workforce development initiatives and pre-college outreach programs are well coordinated to foster student success. It also advises the Legislature, the governor, and the Chief Education Office on policy and funding to meet state postsecondary goals. The major functions of the HECC include:

• Providing one strategic vision for higher education planning, funding and policy in Oregon,

• Authorizing postsecondary programs and degrees,

• Administering key financial aid, workforce, and other programs, and

• Evaluating and reporting on the success of higher education efforts.

Specific key responsibilities of the HECC include consolidated state budget development for public postsecondary education, including Oregon's seven

universities and 17 community colleges; state funding allocations and approval of academic programs for community colleges and public universities; the distribution model for the state's financial aid programs (Oregon Opportunity Grant, Oregon Promise, and others); approval of missions for public universities; degree authorization for private postsecondary institutions; licensure for private career schools; and approval of institutions to administer students veterans benefits.

The HECC's strategic plan has six key priorities: sharpening and monitoring goal setting, sustaining public college and university funding, simplifying and aligning student pathways, enhancing student success, improving college affordability, and contributing to prosperous workforce, economy, and communities. The plan emphasizes that Oregon has made progress toward the state's 40-40-20 goal, yet not all of the state's populations have experienced equally, the benefits of improving completion rates. The HECC takes a lead role in convening partners to further align programming to close achievement and opportunity gaps for historically underrepresented and low-income student populations, as well as improving connections between Oregon's education and workforce systems.

The HECC agency is organized in the Offices of the Executive Director, Policy, and Communications; Community Colleges and Workforce Development (see Oregon Community Colleges); Student Access and Completion (OSAC); Private Postsecondary Education (see Private and Independent Colleges); University Coordination (see Public Universities); Operations; and Research and Data, and Workforce Investment.

HECC Office of Student Access and Completion

Address: 1500 Valley River Dr., Suite 100, Eugene 97401
Phone: 541-687-7400; Toll-free: 1-800-452-8807
Contact: Bob Brew, OSAC Director and Deputy Executive Director of the HECC
Web: www.oregonstudentaid.gov

The Office of Student Access and Completion (OSAC) administers state, federal and privately funded student financial aid programs for the benefit of Oregonians attending institutions of postsecondary education. OSAC is responsible for the administration of state financial aid and access programs, including budget recommendations, fiscal management, policy and awards of financial aid to Oregon students at private and public institutions statewide. Its financial aid programs include the Oregon Opportunity Grant, Oregon's largest state-funded, need-based grant program for new students planning to go to college and for continuing college students; the Oregon Promise, a tuition grant program for recent high school graduates or GED recipients entering an Oregon community college and other state financial aid programs. OSAC also administers more than 500 scholarship funds in partnership with foundations, private donors and others, and works with partners to improve the college and career readiness of Oregon students through the ASPIRE mentoring program, programs to support students with financial aid applications and more.

Office of Research and Data

Address: 255 Capitol St. NE, Salem 97301
Phone: 503-947-2456
Contact: Amy Cox, Director
Web: www.Oregon.gov/highered

The Office of Research and Data, established in 2013, compiles, analyzes and reports research and data on postsecondary education to inform the HECC, the public, and policymakers on the postsecondary education enterprise. The office conducts research to inform policy decisions and clarify progress toward state goals, especially with regard to student characteristics, enrollment, academic performance and academic pathways. It also reports data on students, courses, programs and institutions to comply with state and federal reporting requirements.

HECC Office of Workforce Investment

Address: 875 Union St. NE, Salem 97301
Phone: 503-947-2442
Contact: Karen Humelbaugh, Director
Web: www.Oregon.gov/highered/Pages/index.aspx

The Office of Workforce Investment, formerly a part of the Office of Community Colleges and Workforce Development, is one of several state entities that contribute oversight, resources, and programming to the workforce development system. The HECC is the administrative entity for federally funded workforce and education programs authorized by the U.S. Workforce Innovation and Opportunity Act (WIOA) serving Oregonians. The office monitors investments to Oregon's workforce system, ensuring programmatic compliance and fiscal accountability; provides policy direction and technical assistance to state and local partners, staff, and other stakeholders; and administers the Oregon Youth Conservation Corps (OYCC).

Community Colleges

Oregon has 17 community colleges governed by locally-elected boards that provide accessible, high quality, lifelong learning opportunities to serve the present and future needs of the state and its citizens.

Oregon's community colleges maintain an open admission policy with equal educational access and opportunity through which hundreds of thousands of students each year advance their education and skills. The colleges train Oregonians for advancement in jobs and careers, award degrees and certificates, support students in preparing to transfer seamlessly to four-year institutions, and partner with high schools to offer access to college curricula, such as dual credit. They provide courses and programs for those who need to develop competencies in literacy and language skills or who are pursuing a general equivalency diploma (GED) or an adult high school diploma. They provide career and technical education programs, which prepare individuals for entry-level employment or occupational advancement, meeting the needs of students and employers. The colleges also provide counseling and career development services, workforce, health and safety curricula, and many other programs and services to serve the needs of Oregon's communities.

HECC Office of Community Colleges and Workforce Development

Address: 255 Capitol St. NE, Salem 97310-0001
Phone: 503-947-2401
Web: www.Oregon.gov/highered/Pages/index.aspx
Contact: Patrick Crane, Director

Established in 1999 and formerly the Department of Community Colleges and Workforce Development, the Office of Community Colleges and Workforce Development (CCWD) provides coordination, convening, research, leadership and resources to Oregon's 17 locally-governed community colleges, 18 adult basic skills providers, community-based organizations and other partners. CCWD is responsible for educational policy and funding coordination to promote student success, including biennial budget recommendations and allocation of state funds to the community colleges, approval of new academic programs, administration of Career and Technical Education (CTE) and Career Pathways, as well as work to improve academic pathways such as accelerated learning and transfer pathways. CCWD administers statewide Adult Basic Skills, federal Title II activities, Oregon's General Educational Development (GED) Program, and works closely with other postsecondary institutions and workforce partners to further the educational and workforce goals for Oregon.

Blue Mountain Community College

Camille Preus, President
Address: 2411 NW Carden Ave., PO Box 100, Pendleton 97801-1000
Phone: 541-276-1260
Web: www.bluecc.edu
Fall 2015 Enrollment: 3,327
2015–2016 Tuition and Fees: $4,757

Central Oregon Community College

Dr. Shirley I. Metcalf, President
Address: 2600 NW College Way, Bend 97703
Phone: 541-383-7700
Web: www.cocc.edu
Fall 2015 Enrollment: 8,575
2015–2016 Tuition and Fees: $4,444

Chemeketa Community College
Julie Huckestein, President
Address: 4000 Lancaster Dr. NE, PO Box 14007, Salem 97309-7070
Phone: 503-399-5000
Web: www.chemeketa.edu
Fall 2015 Enrollment: 14,726
2015–2016 Tuition and Fees: $4,230

Clackamas Community College
Dr. Joanne Truesdell, President
Address: 19600 S Molalla Ave., Oregon City 97045-7998
Phone: 503-594-6000
Web: www.clackamas.edu
Fall 2015 Enrollment: 9,341
2015–2016 Tuition and Fees: $4,268

Clatsop Community College
Chris Breitmeyer, President
Address: 1651 Lexington Ave., Astoria 97103
Phone: 503-325-0910
Web: www.clatsopcc.edu
Fall 2015 Enrollment: 1,694
2015–2016 Tuition and Fees: $4,995

Columbia Gorge Community College
Dr. Frank Toda, President
Address: 400 E Scenic Dr., The Dalles 97058-3434
Phone: 541-506-6000
Web: www.cgcc.edu
Fall 2015 Enrollment: 1,385
2015–2016 Tuition and Fees: $4,770

Klamath Community College
Roberto Gutierrez, President
Address: 7390 S 6th St., Klamath Falls 97603-7121
Phone: 541-882-3521
Web: www.klamathcc.edu
Fall 2015 Enrollment: 2,059
2015–2016 Tuition and Fees: $4,605

Lane Community College
Mary Spilde, President
Address: 4000 E 30th Ave., Eugene 97405-0640
Phone: 541-463-3000
Web: www.lanecc.edu
Fall 2015 Enrollment: 11,292
2015–2016 Tuition and Fees: $4,982

Linn-Benton Community College
Greg Hamann, President
Address: 6500 Pacific Blvd. SW, Albany 97321
Phone: 541-917-4999
Web: www.linnbenton.edu
Fall 2015 Enrollment: 8,778
2015–2016 Tuition and Fees: $4,568

Mount Hood Community College
Debra Derr, President
Address: 26000 SE Stark St., Gresham 97030-3300
Phone: 503-491-6422
Web: www.mhcc.edu
Fall 2015 Enrollment: 9,319
2015–2016 Tuition and Fees: $4,841

Oregon Coast Community College
Dr. Birgitte Ryslinge, President
Address: 400 SE College Way, Newport 97366
Phone: 541-867-8501
Web: www.oregoncoastcc.org
Fall 2015 Enrollment: 1,013
2015–2016 Tuition and Fees: $4,770

Portland Community College
Mark Mitsui, President
Address: PO Box 19000, Portland 97280-0990
Phone: 971-722-6111
Web: www.pcc.edu
Fall 2015 Enrollment: 37,279
2015–2016 Tuition and Fees: $4,703

2014–2015 Components of Revenue for Community Colleges

STATE: General Fund; 36.7%

STUDENTS: Tuition & Fees; 39.6%

LOCAL: Property Taxes; 23.7%

Source: Higher Education Coordinating Commission

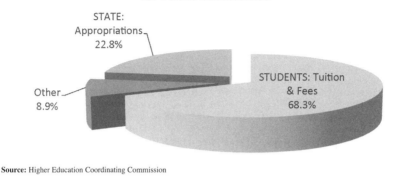

2015–2016 Components of Revenue for Public Universities

STATE: Appropriations 22.8%

Other 8.9%

STUDENTS: Tuition & Fees 68.3%

Source: Higher Education Coordinating Commission

Rogue Community College
Dr. Peter Angstadt, President
Address: 3345 Redwood Hwy., Grants Pass 97527-9291
Phone: 541-956-7500
Web: www.roguecc.edu
Fall 2015 Enrollment: 6,830
2015–2016 Tuition and Fees: $4,905

Southwestern Oregon Community College
Dr. Patty M. Scott, President
Address: 1988 Newmark Ave., Coos Bay 97420
Phone: 541-888-2525
Web: www.socc.edu
Fall 2015 Enrollment: 3,507
2015–2016 Tuition and Fees: $5,481

Tillamook Bay Community College
Connie Green, President
Address: 4301 Third St., Tillamook 97141
Phone: 503-842-8222
Web: www.tillamookbaycc.edu
Fall 2015 Enrollment: 692
2015–2016 Tuition and Fees: $4,725

Treasure Valley Community College
Dana Young, President
Address: 650 College Blvd., Ontario 97914-3498
Phone: 541-881-8822
Web: www.tvcc.cc
Fall 2015 Enrollment: 2,521
2016–2016 Tuition and Fees: $5,310

Umpqua Community College
Debra Thatcher, President
Address: 1140 Umpqua College Rd., Roseburg 97470
Phone: 541-440-4600
Web: www.umpqua.edu
Fall 2015 Enrollment: 4,449
2015–2016 Tuition and Fees: $4,793

Community college tuition and fees figures are based on 15 credit hours, in-district resident status and are annualized. Enrollment numbers are based on fall, fourth-week headcount enrollment.

Public Universities
Oregon's public universities serve as educational, scholarly and research centers that prepare students to succeed in the 21st century workforce and serve the needs of Oregon students and communities. Providing education at the baccalaureate level and beyond, the seven Oregon public universities include Eastern Oregon University (EOU), La Grande; Oregon Institute of Technology (OIT), Klamath Falls and Wilsonville; Oregon State University (OSU), Corvallis and Bend; Portland State University (PSU), Portland; Southern Oregon University (SOU), Ashland; University of Oregon (UO), Eugene; and Western Oregon University (WOU), Monmouth.

In 2014–2015, the public universities collectively awarded 45,151 degrees and certificates across the state. The universities offer bachelor degrees in hundreds of majors and minors, certificate programs, professional programs, graduate programs, as well as research, scholarship, innovation, and public service that directly serve Oregon's communities and industries and the needs of national and international constituents. The universities work closely with Oregon's kindergarten through 12th grade schools and 17 community colleges to provide seamless educational pathways for students to access and complete their college goals.

HECC Office of University Coordination
Address: 255 Capitol St. NE, Salem 97301
Phone: 503-378-5690
Contact: Veronica Dujon, Director, University Academic Planning and Policy;

Andrew Rogers, Director, University Budget and Finance
Web: www.Oregon.gov/highered/Pages/index.aspx

The Office of University Coordination, established in 2013, provides coordination related to Oregon's seven public universities and education sector partners to enhance student success and achieve state educational attainment goals.

The office is responsible for coordination, convening, research, resources, and leadership related to university funding and academic, alignment and transfer policy. The finance unit works with campuses on biennial budget recommendations, fiscal analysis to inform policy maker decisions, and allocation of funding to the universities. The academic unit coordinates processes for academic program review and approval, university mission approval, directives and strategies to improve student pathways between institutions and sectors, and additional policy and legislative initiatives to support student success.

As of July 1, 2015, all of Oregon's public universities, previously under the authority of the State Board of Higher Education (SBHE), are governed by governor-appointed, Senate approved, institutional boards of trustees.

Eastern Oregon University
Tom Insko, President
Address: One University Blvd., La Grande 97850-2899
Phone: 541-962-3512; Toll-free: 1-800-452-8639
Web: www.eou.edu
Board of Trustees: www.eou.edu/governance
Fall 2015 Enrollment: 3,488
2015–2016 Tuition and Fees: $7,757

Oregon Institute of Technology
Dr. Nagi Naganathan, President
Address: 3201 Campus Dr., Klamath Falls 97601-8801
Phone: 541-885-1000
Web: www.oit.edu
Board of Trustees: www.oit.edu/trustees
Fall 2015 Enrollment: 4,786
Klamath Falls 2015–2016 Tuition and Fees: $8,839
Wilsonville 2015-2016 Tuition and Fees: $7,786

Oregon State University
Edward J. Ray, President
Address: 634 Kerr Administration Building, Corvallis 97331-2128
Phone: 541-737-4133
Web: www.oregonstate.edu; www.osucascades.edu
Board of Trustees: http://leadership.oregonstate.edu/trustees
Fall 2015 Headcount Enrollment: 29,576
2015–2016 Tuition and Fees: $10,107
OSU-Cascades Fall 2015 Enrollment: 1,016
OSU-Cascades 2015–2016 Tuition and Fees: $8,790

Portland State University
Wim Wiewel, President
Address: PO Box 751, Portland 97207-0751
Phone: 503-725-4419; Toll-free: 1-800-547-8887
Web: www.pdx.edu
Board of Trustees: www.pdx.edu/board
Fall 2015 Enrollment: 28,076
2015–2016 Tuition and Fees: $8,124

Southern Oregon University
Linda Schott, President
Address: 1250 Siskiyou Blvd., Ashland 97520
Phone: 541-552-7672
Web: www.sou.edu
Board of Trustees: https://governance.sou.edu
Fall 2015 Enrollment: 6,215
2015–2016 Tuition and Fees: $8,145

University of Oregon
Michael H. Schill, President
Address: 110 Johnson Hall, Eugene 97403
Phone: 541-346-3036
Web: www.uoregon.edu
Board of Trustees: trustees.uoregon.edu
Fall 2015 Enrollment: 24,125
2015–2016 Tuition and Fees: $10,289

Western Oregon University
Rex Fuller, President
Address: 345 N Monmouth Ave., Monmouth 97361
Phone: 503-838-8888
Web: www.wou.edu
Board of Trustees: http://www.wou.edu/board/
Fall 2015 Enrollment: 5,445
2015–2016 Tuition and Fees: $8,433

Tuition and fee figures are based on 15 credit hours per term for undergraduate resident students. Certain programs are assessed at different rates than noted. Enrollment numbers are fall, fourth-week enrollment.

OREGON HEALTH & SCIENCE UNIVERSITY

Joseph E. Robertson, MD, MBA, President
Address: 3181 SW Sam Jackson Park Rd., Portland 97239-3098
Web: www.ohsu.edu/xd/
Board of Directors:
http://www.ohsu.edu/xd/about/vision/board.cfm
2015 Enrollment: 2,895

The Oregon Health & Science University (OHSU) includes Oregon's only academic health center and has schools of medicine, dentistry, nursing, public health (in partnership with PSU), and other health care professional programs. OHSU has been organized as a public corporation since 1995 and is governed by a board of directors that is appointed by the governor and confirmed by the Senate. The state continues to support OHSU programs through grants and general funds that totaled $77.3 million in the 2015–2017 biennium.

WESTERN INTERSTATE COMMISSION FOR HIGHER EDUCATION

Address: PO Box 3175, Eugene 97403
Phone: 541-346-5729
Web: www.wiche.edu

The Western Interstate Commission for Higher Education (WICHE) is a regional organization created by the Western Regional Education Compact, adopted in the 1950s by 15 western states. WICHE was created to facilitate resource sharing among the higher education systems of the West. Fifteen states, including Oregon, are members of WICHE, which is governed by three governor-appointed commissioners from each state. Under terms of the compact, each state commits to support WICHE's basic operations through annual dues established by the full commission. Oregon's three commissioners are Ryan Deckert, Portland; Cam Preus, Pendleton; and Hilda Rosselli, Salem.

PRIVATE AND INDEPENDENT COLLEGES

Oregon is home to hundreds of private colleges, universities and career schools providing a wide range of college and career training opportunities to Oregonians.

HECC Office of Private Postsecondary Education

Address: 255 Capitol St. NE, Salem 97301
Phone: 503-947-5716
Contact: Juan Baez-Arevelo, Director
Web: www.oregon.gov/highered/Pages/index.aspx

The Office of Private Postsecondary Education (PPS) oversees the quality, integrity and diversity of private postsecondary programs in Oregon for the benefit of students and consumers.

The office supports the success of private higher education institutions in achieving their missions to educate and train Oregonians for career success, and to provide quality and relevant certificate and degree programs. The office has three parts:
• Office of Degree Authorization (ODA),
• Private Career Schools (PCS) unit, and
• U.S. Department of Veterans Affairs State Approving Agency (SAA).

Serving as the lead regulatory office, the office guides policy and regulatory action that approves programs and institutions serving Oregonians. The PCS unit and ODA serve as the state regulators that approve degree-granting institutions, private career schools, and distance education providers to operate in this state. Without approval or explicit exemption from regulation from the HECC, a school cannot legally operate in our state or offer valid degrees or certificates to Oregonians. A number of private, not-for-profit institutions, including those listed below, are authorized but exempt from ongoing regulation by the HECC because of their longstanding status and having met certain requirements. Other private institutions are regulated and required to renew their authorization on a regular basis.

For current lists of authorized, licensed private programs and institutions, see our Web site at www.oregon.gov/highered/Pages/index.aspx

The SAA approves public and private institutions and programs for postsecondary veteran benefits in Oregon. In order for a veteran, reservist or dependent to use their G.I. Bill Benefits, the educational program must be approved by the SAA.

Oregon Alliance of Independent Colleges and Universities

Web: http://oaicu.org

The mission of the Oregon Alliance of Independent Colleges and Universities is to represent and serve its member institutions, all of which are regionally accredited, not-for-profit, independent colleges and universities in Oregon. This is accomplished through public advocacy, institutional cooperation, and strategic collaboration with the public sector, including business, philanthropy and government. The alliance invests in diverse students, committed educators and relevant learning by partnering with leaders from business and industry, philanthropy and public sector agencies and institutions.

Independent Colleges and Universities

Following is a list of Oregon's independent, non-profit higher education institutions that are regionally accredited and have reached independent/exempt status from ongoing regulatory oversight by the Office of Degree Authorization.

Concordia University, Portland
Dr. Charles Schlimpert, President
Phone: 503-288-9371
Web: www.cu-portland.edu
Fall 2015 enrollment: 7,182

Corban University, Salem
Sheldon Nord, President
Phone: 503-581-8600
Web: www.corban.edu
Fall 2015 enrollment: 1,232

Embry-Riddle Aeronautical University, Portland
Jenifer Stevens, Campus Director
Phone: 503-288-8690
Web: http://worldwide.erau.edu/locations/portland
Fall 2015 enrollment: 175

George Fox University, Newberg
Robin Baker, President
Phone: 503-538-8383
Web: www.georgefox.edu
Fall 2015 enrollment: 3,925

Lewis & Clark College, Portland
Barry Glassner, President
Phone: 503-768-7000
Web: www.lclark.edu
Fall 2015 enrollment: 3,526

Linfield College, McMinnville
Thomas L. Hellie, President
Phone: 503-883-2200
Web: www.linfield.edu
Fall 2015 enrollment: 2,417

Marylhurst University, Portland
Melody Rose, President
Phone: 503-636-8141
Web: www.marylhurst.edu
Fall 2015 enrollment: 982

Mount Angel Seminary, St. Benedict
Rev. Msgr. Joseph Betschart, President-Rector
Phone: 503-845-3951
Web: www.mountangelabbey.org
Fall 2015 enrollment: 170

Multnomah University, Portland
Rev. Craig Williford, President
Phone: 503-255-0332
Web: www.multnomah.edu
Fall 2015 enrollment: 737

National University of Natural Medicine, Portland
David J. Schleich, President
Phone: 503-552-1555
Web: www.ncnm.edu
Fall 2015 enrollment: 631

Northwest Christian University, Eugene
Joseph Womack, President
Phone: 541-343-1641
Web: www.nwcu.edu
Fall 2015 enrollment: 740

Northwest University, Salem
Dr. Carley Kendrick, Dean
Phone: 503-304-0092
Web: https://salem.northwestu.edu
Fall 2015 enrollment: 30

Oregon College of Art and Craft, Portland
Denise Mullen, President
Phone: 503-297-5544
Web: https://ocac.edu
Fall 2015 enrollment: 151

Pacific Northwest College of Art, Portland
Don Tuski, President
Phone: 503-226-4391
Web: www.pnca.edu
Fall 2015 enrollment: 501

Pacific University, Forest Grove
Dr. Lesley Hallick, President
Phone: 877-722-8648
Web: www.pacificu.edu
Fall 2015 enrollment: 3,810

Reed College, Portland
John Kroger, President
Phone: 503-771-1112
Web: www.reed.edu
Fall 2015 enrollment: 1,453

University of Portland, Portland
Rev. Mark L. Poorman, President
Phone: 503-943-8000
Web: www.up.edu
Fall 2015 enrollment: 4,338

University of Western States, Portland
Joseph Brimhall, President
Phone: 503-256-3180
Web: www.uws.edu
Fall 2015 enrollment: 839

Warner Pacific College, Portland
Andrea P. Cook, President
Phone: 503-517-1000
Web: www.warnerpacific.edu
Fall 2015 enrollment: 1,212

Western Seminary, Portland
Rev. Randal Roberts, President
Phone: 503-517-1800
Web: www.westernseminary.edu
Fall 2015 enrollment: 726

Western University of Health Sciences, Lebanon
Dr. Paula M. Crone, Vice President/Dean
Phone: 541-259-0200
Web: http://www.westernu.edu/northwest
Fall 2015 enrollment: 431

Willamette University, Salem
Stephen Thorsett, President
Phone: 503-370-6300
Web: www.willamette.edu
Fall 2015 enrollment: 2,746

A young skier gets airborne while descending Mount Hood near Timberline Lodge on a sunny July day.
Oregon State Archives Scenic Photograph 20140707-9353

Through the organizations described in this section, we are fortunate to have many opportunities to gain greater understanding and appreciation for the arts and culture, history and heritage, Earth sciences and technology of Oregon.

ARTS AND CULTURE IN OREGON

Oregon Arts Commission

Brian Rogers, Executive Director
Address: 775 Summer St. NE, Suite 200, Salem 97301-1280
Phone: 503-986-0082; TDD: 503-986-0123
Fax: 503-986-0260
Web: www.oregonartscommission.org

The Oregon Arts Commission enhances the quality of life for all Oregonians through the arts by stimulating creativity, leadership and economic vitality.

The commission provides leadership, funding and arts programs through its grants, special initiatives and services. The commission works to improve access to the arts all around the state.

The commission continues to function with the primary role of issuing project grants to private non-profit arts organizations. The commission also supports the Oregon Folklife Network.

Oregon Cultural Trust

Brian Rogers, Executive Director
Address: 775 Summer St. NE, Suite 200, Salem 97301-1280
Phone: 503-986-0088; TDD: 503-986-0123
Fax: 503-986-0260
Web: www.culturaltrust.org

Founded in 2001, the Oregon Cultural Trust leads Oregon in cultivating, growing and valuing culture as an integral part of communities. Working with the Oregon Arts Commission, the Oregon Heritage Commission, the Oregon Historical Society, Oregon Humanities and the State Historic Preservation Office, the Cultural Trust inspires Oregonians to invest in a permanent fund that provides grants to cultural organizations. It is governed by a 13-member board of directors. Eleven voting members are appointed by the governor, and the president of the Senate and speaker of the House of Representatives each appoint a member of the Legislature as non-voting, advisory members.

Oregon Humanities

Adam Davis, Executive Director
Address: 921 SW Washington Ave., Portland 97205
Phone: 503-241-0543; Toll-free: 1-800-735-0543
Fax: 503-241-0024
Web: http://oregonhumanities.org

Oregon Humanities is an independent, nonprofit affiliate of the National Endowment for the Humanities. Oregon Humanities, formerly the Oregon Council for the Humanities, was established in 1971 and is one of five statewide partners of the Oregon Cultural Trust. Programs include

Oregon Humanities magazine, the Conversation Project, Humanity in Perspective, Think & Drink and Public Program Grants.

Oregon Humanities' vision is an Oregon that invites diverse perspectives, explores challenging questions and strives for just communities.

Oregon's Major Arts Organizations

Oregon Shakespeare Festival

Bill Rauch, Artistic Director; Cynthia Rider, Executive Director
Address: 15 S Pioneer St., PO Box 158, Ashland 97520
Phone: 1-800-219-8161
Fax: 541-482-8045
Web: www.osfashland.org

The Oregon Shakespeare Festival is one of the largest nonprofit theaters in the country. Established in 1935, it has an annual attendance of almost 400,000. It annually presents more than 760 performances of eleven plays in repertory from mid-February through October on its three stages. The festival also offers backstage tours, classes, lectures, concerts and play readings.

Oregon Symphony Association

Scott Showalter, President and CEO
Address: 921 SW Washington St., Portland 97205
Phone: 503-228-1353; Toll Free: 1-800-228-7343
Fax: 503-416-6302
Web: www.orsymphony.org

Led by Music Director Carlos Kalmar, the Oregon Symphony is one of the largest performing arts organizations in the Pacific Northwest. Its many performances each year include the classical concert series, pops concerts, youth and educational concerts, family concerts and special performances at its home in Portland, as well as in Salem and elsewhere in Oregon.

Portland Art Museum

Brian Ferriso, Executive Director
Address: 1219 SW Park Ave., Portland 97205
Phone: 503-226-2811
Fax: 503-226-4842
Web: www.portlandartmuseum.org

The Portland Art Museum, founded in 1892, is the region's oldest and largest visual and media arts center and one of the state's greatest cultural assets. The museum is a premier venue for education in the visual arts and for the collection and preservation of art for the enrichment of present and future generations.

The internationally renowned museum presents special exhibitions drawn from the world's finest collections. The permanent collection showcases unique American tribal objects and Japanese,

Chinese, and Korean objects up to 3,000 years old. European, modern and contemporary art, Northwest art, photography and graphic arts round out the collection. Located in downtown Portland's cultural district, the museum offers lectures, tours and family activities.

Portland Opera
Christopher Mattaliano, General Director
Address: 211 SE Caruthers St., Portland 97214
Phone: 503-241-1407
Fax: 503-241-4212
Web: www.portlandopera.org
Internationally renowned singers perform with the Portland Opera Orchestra and Chorus in a four-production season at Portland's Keller Auditorium. Although sung in their original languages, the operas are easily understood by an avid and growing audience, thanks to projected English translations. In addition to the Keller Auditorium stage, the Portland Opera Studio Artist program for America's young singers, is featured in its own opera production in the Newmark Theater. The opera's Education and Outreach programs continue year-round, including fully staged traveling opera productions that tour the state, in-school programs, student dress rehearsals, pre- and post-performance lectures, public presentations and radio shows, a costume shop and backstage tours.

The company also presents the Broadway Across America Portland series, delighting regional audiences with nationally touring Broadway productions.

Regional Arts Councils

The Arts Center
Cynthia Spencer, Executive Director
Address: 700 SW Madison Ave., Corvallis 97333
Phone: 541-754-1551
Fax: 541-754-1552
Web: www.theartscenter.net
Serving Benton and Linn Counties

Art Center East
Mika Morton, Executive Director
Address: 1006 Penn Ave., PO Box 541, La Grande 97850
Phone: 541-962-3629
Web: http://artcentereast.org
Serving Baker, Gilliam, Grant, Harney, Malheur, Morrow, Umatilla, Union, Wallowa and Wheeler Counties

Columbia Center for the Arts
Kerry Cobb, Executive Director
Address: 215 Cascade Ave., PO Box 1543, Hood River 97031
Phone/Fax: 541-387-8877
Web: www.columbiaarts.org
Serving Hood River, Sherman and Wasco Counties

Lane Arts Council
Liora Sponko, Executive Director
Address: 1590 Willamette St., Suite 200, Eugene 97401
Phone: 541-485-2278
Web: www.lanearts.org
Serving Lane County

Oregon Coast Council for the Arts
Catherine Rickbone, Executive Director
Address: PO Box 1315, Newport 97365
Phone: 541-265-2787; Toll-free: 1-888-701-7123
Fax: 541-265-9464
Web: www.coastarts.org
Serving Clatsop, Coos, Curry, Lincoln and Tillamook Counties

Regional Arts and Culture Council
Eloise Damrosch, Executive Director
Address: 411 NW Park Ave., Suite 101, Portland 97209-3356
Phone: 503-823-5111
Fax: 503-823-5432
Web: www.racc.org
Serving Clackamas, Multnomah and Washington Counties

Umpqua Valley Arts Association
Andrew Apter, Executive Director
Address: 1624 W Harvard Ave., Roseburg 97471
Phone: 541-672-2532
Fax: 541-672-7696
Web: http://uvarts.com
Serving Douglas County

Local and Regional Arts Agencies in Oregon

Astoria
Astor Street Opry Company
Address: 129 W Bond St., PO Box 743, Astoria 97103
Phone: 503-325-6104
Web: www.shanghaiedinastoria.com

Baker City
Crossroads Carnegie Art Center
Address: 2020 Auburn Ave., Baker City 97814
Phone/Fax: 541-523-5369
Web: www.crossroads-arts.org

Beaverton
Beaverton Arts Commission
Address: 12725 SW Millikan Way, Fifth Floor, PO Box 4755, Beaverton 97005
Phone: 503-526-2299
Fax: 503-526-2479
Web: www.beavertonoregon.gov/arts

Brookings

Manley Art Center
Address: 433 Oak St., PO Box 2568, Brookings 97415
Phone: 541-469-1807

Pelican Bay Arts Association, Manley Art Center
Address: 433 Oak St., PO Box 2568, Brookings 97415
Phone/Fax: 541-469-1807
Email: pbaart@frontier.com

Cannon Beach

Cannon Beach Arts Association and Gallery
Address: 1064 S Hemlock St., PO Box 684, Cannon Beach 97110
Phone: 503-436-0744
Web: www.cannonbeacharts.org

Condon

Greater Condon Arts Association
Address: 403 W Walnut St., PO Box 33, Condon 97823
Phone: 541-384-5114

Coos Bay

Coos Art Museum
Address: 235 Anderson Ave., Coos Bay 97420
Phone: 541-267-3901
Web: www.coosart.org

Coquille

Coquille Valley Art Association
Address: 10144 Hwy. 42, Coquille 97423
Phone: 541-396-3294
Web: coquillevalleyartcenterdotorg.wordpress.com

Elgin

Elgin Opera House Theatre
Address: 104 N 8th St., PO Box 492, Elgin 97827
Phone: 541-663-6324
Web: www.elginoperahouse.com

Forest Grove

Valley Art Association and Gallery
Address: 2022 Main St., PO Box 333, Forest Grove 97116
Phone: 503-357-3703
Web: www.valleyart.org

Grants Pass

Grants Pass Museum of Art
Address: 229 SW G St., PO Box 966, Grants Pass 97528
Phone: 541-479-3290
Web: www.gpmuseum.com

Halfway

Cornucopia Arts Council and Pine Fest
Address: PO Box 921, Halfway 97834
Phone: 541-742-7900
Web: www.pinefest.org

Hermiston

Desert Arts Council
Address: PO Box 554, Hermiston 97838
Phone: 541-379-6992
Web: www.desertartscouncil.com

Hillsboro

Hillsboro Arts & Culture Council
Address: 527 E Main St., Hillsboro 97123
Phone: 503-615-3497
Fax: 503-615-3484
Web: www.hillsboroarts.org

Hood River

Arts in Education of the Gorge
Address: 1009 Eugene St., Hood River 97031
Phone: 541-387-5031
Fax: 541-387-5098
Web: www.gorgeartsined.org

Jacksonville

Art Presence Art Center
Address: 206 N 5th St., Jacksonville 97530
Phone: 541-941-7057
Web: www.art-presence.org

Joseph

Wallowa Valley Arts Council
Address: PO Box 526, Joseph 97846
Phone: 541-432-9105
Web: http://wallowavalleyarts.org

Keizer

Keizer Art Association
Address: 980 Chemawa Rd. NE, Keizer 97303
Phone: 503-390-3010
Web: www.keizerarts.com

Klamath Falls

Klamath Art Association
Address: 120 Riverside Dr., Klamath Falls 97601
Phone: 541-883-1833
Web: http://klamathartgallery.blogspot.com

Klamath Arts Council
Address: PO Box 1706, Klamath Falls 97601
Phone: 541-883-2009

Ross Ragland Theater and Cultural Center
Address: 218 N Seventh St., Klamath Falls 97601
Phone: 541-884-0651
Fax: 541-884-8574
Web: www.rrtheater.org

Lake Oswego

Arts Council of Lake Oswego
Address: 520 First St., PO Box 369, Lake Oswego 97034
Phone: 503-675-3738
Fax: 503-534-5247
Web: www.artscouncillo.org

Lakewood Center for the Arts
Address: 368 S State St., Lake Oswego 97034
Phone: 503-635-3901
Fax: 503-635-2002
Web: www.lakewood-center.org

Lincoln City
Lincoln City Cultural Center
Address: 540 NE Hwy. 101, PO Box 752, Lincoln City 97367
Phone: 541-994-9994
Web: www.lincolncity-culturalcenter.org

Madras
Jefferson County Arts Association and Art Adventure Gallery
Address: 185 SW Fifth St., PO Box 376, Madras 97741
Phone: 541-475-7701
Web: www.artadventuregallery.com

McMinnville
Arts Alliance of Yamhill County
Address: PO Box 898, McMinnville 97128
Web: www.artsallianceyamhillco.org

Medford
Rogue Gallery & Art Center
Address: 40 S Bartlett St., Medford 97501
Phone: 541-772-8118
Fax: 541-772-0294
Web: www.roguegallery.org

Milwaukie
North Clackamas Arts Guild
Address: PO Box 220004, Milwaukie 97269
Phone: 503-454-0447
Web: www.ncartsguild.com

Nehalem
The Art Ranch
Address: 39450 Northfork Rd., Nehalem 97131
Phone: 503-368-7160
Fax: 503-368-7656
Email: lortiz@nehalemtel.net

Newport
Yaquina Art Association and Gallery
Address: 789 NW Beach Dr., Newport 97365
Phone: 541-265-5133
Web: www.yaquinaart.org

Ontario
Four Rivers Cultural Center
Address: 676 SW Fifth Ave., Ontario 97914
Phone: 541-889-8191
Fax: 541-889-7628
Web: www.4rcc.com

Oregon City
Clackamas County Arts Alliance
Address: PO Box 2181, Oregon City 97045

Phone: 503-655-0525
Web: www.clackamasartsalliance.org

Pendleton
Pendleton Center for the Arts
Address: 214 N Main St., Pendleton 97801
Phone: 541-278-9201
Web: www.pendletonarts.org

Salem
Salem Art Association
Address: 600 Mission St. SE, Salem 97302
Phone: 503-581-2228
Fax: 503-371-3342
Web: www.SalemArt.org

Silverton
Silverton Arts Association
Address: 303 Coolidge St., Silverton 97381
Phone/Fax: 503-873-2480
Web: www.silvertonarts.org

Springfield
Emerald Empire Art Association
Address: 500 Main St., Springfield 97477
Phone: 541-726-8595
Fax: 541-726-2954
Web: http://emeraldartcenter.org

Springfield Arts Commission
Address: 225 Fifth St., Springfield 97477
Phone: 541-726-2238
Fax: 541-726-3747
Web: www.springfieldartscommission.org

Tillamook
Tillamook County Arts Network
Web: www.tillamookcountyarts.org

Tualatin
Tualatin Arts Advisory Committee
Address: Tualatin Community Park, 8515 SW Tualatin Rd.; mail: 18880 SW Martinazzi Ave., Tualatin 97062
Phone: 503-691-3060
Fax: 503-691-9786
Web: www.tualatinoregon.gov

Welches
Wy'East Artisans Guild
Address: PO Box 682, Sandy 97055
Email: wyeast@gmx.com
Web: http://wyeastartisansguild.com

Wilsonville
Wilsonville Arts and Culture Council
Address: PO Box 861, Wilsonville 97070
Phone: 503-638-6933
Web: www.wilsonvillearts.org

Woodburn

Woodburn Art Center
Address: 2551 N Boones Ferry Rd., Woodburn 97071
Phone: 503-982-6450
Web: www.woodburnartcenter.com

OREGON HISTORY ORGANIZATIONS

Oregon's Major History and Heritage Organizations

State Archives

Mary Beth Herkert, State Archivist
Address: 800 Summer St. NE, Salem 97310
Phone: 503-373-0701
Fax: 503-378-4118
Email: archives.info@state.or.us
Web: http://sos.oregon.gov/archives/Pages/default.aspx

After being created by the Legislature in 1945, the State Archives received budgetary funding in 1947 with a two-fold mandate: to manage public records at all levels of government in Oregon by authorizing their retention and disposition, and to identify, preserve and provide access to the permanently valuable public records of the state.

The State Archives is a division of the Office of the Secretary of State. The Reference Unit provides access to these records at the State Archives building in Salem and online via the Archives Web site. Holdings include birth, death and marriage records; state agency records, such as those from the Department of Forestry (The Forest Practices Act) and from the Department of Corrections (the original Great Register); records from the courts (probate and circuit court cases) and records from the Legislature.

The oldest records in the Archives holdings include those of the Provisional and Territorial governments; the original Oregon City Plat created by Dr. John McLoughlin, "Father of Oregon;" and the original Oregon Constitution.

National Historic Oregon Trail Interpretive Center

Sarah LeCompte, Center Director
Address: 22267 Hwy. 86, PO Box 987, Baker City 97814
Phone: 541-523-1843
Fax: 541-523-1834
Web: www.blm.gov/or/oregontrail

Operated by the U.S. Department of Interior's Bureau of Land Management (BLM), the National Historic Oregon Trail Interpretive Center is located at Flagstaff Hill on Highway 86, five miles east of Baker City. The 509-acre site features a 23,000 square-foot facility with permanent exhibits offering audio, video, dioramas and artifacts to recreate the experiences of Oregon Trail emigrants. The Interpretive Center also includes exhibits on American tribal culture, mining and the history of the Bureau of Land Management. A 150-seat theater hosts an active schedule of lectures and performances.

From atop Flagstaff Hill, visitors see more than 13 miles of the Oregon Trail route. Visitors may also view close-up trail ruts at the base of Flagstaff Hill. During the summer, living history characters interpret pioneer life at a wagon encampment.

Oregon Commission on Historic Cemeteries

Kuri Gill, Coordinator
Address: 725 Summer St. NE, Suite C, Salem 97301
Phone: 503-986-0685
Fax: 503-986-0793
Email: kuri.gill@oregon.gov
Web: www.oregon.gov/OPRD/HCD/OCHC/

Established in 1999, the Oregon Commission on Historic Cemeteries (OCHC) consists of seven citizens with broad knowledge of the issues relating to the preservation, restoration, upkeep and advocacy for historic burial sites and their importance in Oregon history. An historic cemetery in Oregon is one in which a burial occurred before February 14, 1909, or in which someone who died before that date is buried.

The OCHC coordinates the restoration, renovation and maintenance of historic cemeteries statewide.

They also develop and maintain a listing of historic cemeteries and gravesites in Oregon; award grants to protect and develop historic cemeteries; provide technical assistance on the care of grave markers, structures, railings and curbs, ironwork, fencing and plantings; and develop legislation that would benefit historic cemeteries.

Oregon Geographic Names Board

Philip A. Cogswell, President
Address: 1200 SW Park Ave., Portland 97205
Phone: 503-306-5203
Web: www.ohs.org/about-us/affiliates-and-partners/oregon-geographic-names-board/

Founded in 1908, the board is an advisor to the United States Board on Geographic Names and is associated with the Oregon Historical Society, which maintains the board's correspondence and records. It is composed of 25 appointed board members representing all geographic areas of the state and is served by advisors from government agencies and the private sector.

The board supervises the naming of all geographic features within the state to standardize geographic nomenclature, prevent confusion and duplication in naming geographic features, and correct previous naming errors. The board's recommendations are submitted to the U.S. board in Washington, D.C., for final action.

Oregon Heritage Commission

Todd Mayberry, Coordinator
Address: 725 Summer St. NE, Suite C, Salem 97301
Phone: 503-986-0685
Fax: 503-986-0793
Web: www.oregon.gov/OPRD/hcd/ohc

Oregon's heritage is more than history, and it is more than historic artifacts or documents in a museum. It is brick on an historic downtown building, hand-hewn beams in a homestead barn, smoke rising from a powwow campfire and sounds from a community celebration. Heritage is stories about people and places and traditions handed down by elders.

The mission of the Oregon Heritage Commission is to secure, sustain and enhance Oregon's heritage by coordinating heritage initiatives by public and private organizations; advocating for all levels of support for heritage; educating the public about its extent and value; and promoting and celebrating its diversity. It develops an Oregon Heritage Plan every five years. Its programs include heritage and museum grants, Oregon Heritage Traditions, Oregon Heritage All-Star Communities, the Oregon Heritage Conference, the Oregon Heritage MentorCorps and the Oregon Heritage Excellence Awards.

Established by the 1995 Legislature, the commission is composed of nine gubernatorial appointments, who represent the geographic and cultural diversity of the state, and nine advisory members. The advisory commissioners represent the Oregon Historical Society, the State Library, the State Archives, the State Historic Preservation Office, the State Historic Records Advisory Board, the Department of Education, the Higher Education Coordinating Council, the Department of Land Conservation and Development and the Oregon Tourism Commission.

The commission is housed within the State Parks and Recreation Department and is a statewide partner of the Oregon Cultural Trust.

Oregon Historical Society

Kerry Tymchuk, Executive Director
Address: 1200 SW Park Ave., Portland 97205
Phone: 503-222-1741; TDD: 503-306-5194
Fax: 503-221-2035
Web: www.ohs.org

For more than 100 years, the Oregon Historical Society (OHS) has provided a place for history—a home for Oregon heritage, culture, beginnings and future. The society has expanded far beyond its original mission of collecting, preserving, publishing and sharing Oregon's rich history. Attractions include exhibits covering a wide range of historical topics, lectures and special events, a museum store, its peer-reviewed journal, the *Oregon Historical Quarterly,* and research library with a wealth of books, maps, documents, oral histories, photo-graphs and film footage. OHS also operates educational programs for children and adults, and provides smaller exhibits that travel around the state. Web site content is also available across the state through the OHS digital history projects, including the Oregon History Project, The Oregon Encyclopedia and the Oregon TimeWeb. The museum is open Monday through Saturday, 10:00 a.m. to 5:00 p.m., and Sunday, 12:00 p.m. to 5:00 p.m. Admission covers entrance to both the museum and library (OHS members are free). Multnomah County residents are also admitted free due to a modest levy that was first approved by voters in November 2010 and renewed in May 2016.

Oregon Historic Trails Advisory Council

Christine Curran, Heritage Division Director
Oregon Parks and Recreation Department
Address: 725 Summer St. NE, Suite C, Salem 97301
Phone: 503-986-0684
Fax: 503-986-0793
Web: www.oregon.gov/oprd/HCD/Pages/ohtac.aspx

The Oregon Historic Trails Advisory Council was established by Executive Order 98-16 to recognize all Oregon historic trails as outlined in ORS 358.057. The council is a nine-member committee appointed by the governor and formed to promote public awareness of the significance of Oregon's historic trails, as well as to advise a variety of public and private agencies and organizations on policy matters. The council is Oregon's official liaison to other states, associations and federal agencies in acquiring national, as well as state, recognition of Oregon's historic trails.

The Council represents three National Historic Trails in Oregon—the Lewis and Clark Trail, the Applegate Trail and the Nez Perce Trail—as well as five alternative routes to the Oregon Trail and seven other major Oregon historic trails.

State Historic Preservation Office

Christine Curran, Director and Deputy SHPO
Address: 725 Summer St. NE, Suite C, Salem 97301
Phone: 503-986-0684
Fax: 503-986-0793
Web: www.oregon.gov/oprd/HCD/SHPO/Pages/index.aspx

The State Historic Preservation Office (SHPO) works in partnership with individuals, organizations and government groups to help identify various ways to preserve and use historic sites and places.

The SHPO was established in 1967 to manage and administer programs for the protection of the state's historic and cultural resources. When these resources disappear, Oregonians not only lose the tangible and educational value they contribute to our heritage, we can also lose a real monetary value to our economy and intangible, yet quite meaningful, aspects of Oregon's culture.

SHPO's program coordinators and representatives assist city planners and other officials, property owners and preservation groups in finding forward-thinking solutions to better protect and preserve our past.

By planning for growth and change, while respecting and protecting historic buildings and other important sites, state agencies, local governments and community organizations can play key leadership roles in safeguarding Oregon's cultural heritage resources. By becoming involved in historic preservation efforts at the local level, Oregonians can gain a greater understanding and appreciation of our shared heritage in all its variations.

Tamástslikt Cultural Institute
Roberta Conner, Director
Address: 47106 Wildhorse Blvd., Pendleton 97801
Phone: 541-429-7700
Fax: 541-429-7716
Web: www.tamastslikt.org

Tamástslikt Cultural Institute is dedicated to the accurate depiction and perpetuation of the culture and history of the Cayuse, Umatilla and Walla Walla Tribes. Located on the Umatilla Indian Reservation, Tamástslikt is the only tribally owned and operated interpretive center along the National Historic Oregon Trail. Tamástslikt is a National Park Service certified interpretive site for both the Lewis and Clark and Oregon National Historic Trails. The institute is open Monday through Saturday from 10:00 a.m. to 5:00 p.m.

Visitors to Tamástslikt hear horses rumbling across a grassy plateau, Coyote saving the plants and animals from an ancient monster, generations-old songs in the winter lodge, the bell and translated hymns in the church. They see the brilliant color of dances at a competition powwow, poignant interviews with Tribal warriors and stories from families who have long participated in the Pendleton Round-Up. Ancient tools and art forms, ambient sounds and voices, along with historical photographs and contemporary video footage, combine to create an intriguing experience. One visit yields a new understanding of these peoples and their Eastern Oregon and Southeastern Washington homeland. The Outdoor Living Culture Village is open from Memorial Day through Labor Day.

Local native arts and crafts are available in the spacious museum store. The Kinship Café offers lunch and spectacular views.

Willamette Heritage Center
Bob H. Reinhardt, Executive Director
Address: 1313 Mill St. SE, Suite 200, Salem 97301
Phone: 503-585-7012

Fax: 503-588-9902
Web: www.willametteheritage.org

The Willamette Heritage Center (WHC) connects generations by preserving and interpreting the history of the Mid-Willamette Valley. The 14 historic structures on the WHC's five-acre campus house permanent and changing exhibits, a research library and archive, a textile learning center and event and office spaces.

Early settlement buildings take visitors back to the 1840s, when Euro-American missionaries and immigrants settled in the Mid-Willamette Valley, home of the Kalapuya. The 1841 Jason Lee House and Methodist Parsonage are the oldest standing wooden frame houses in the Pacific Northwest, featured along with the John D. Boon House (1847) and Pleasant Grove Church (1854), built by Oregon Trail immigrants. The 1896 Thomas Kay Woolen Mill, a National Park Service-designated American Treasure, vividly tells the story of industrialization in the Mid-Willamette Valley. Changing exhibits explore and highlight the rich and diverse cultural heritage of the region. The Research Library holds valuable photographs, records, and documents focused on Marion County. The WHC offers a variety of historical courses and tours as well as educational programs and events year-round. These include *Sheep to Shawl* in May, *History Was Here* in July, *Oregon Trail Live* in September, and *Magic at the Mill* in December.

The WHC is a private, 501(c)(3) nonprofit organization formed from the merger of Mission Mill Museum and the Marion County Historical Society. The WHC is open Monday through Saturday, 10:00 a.m. to 5:00 p.m. The Research Library is open Tuesday through Friday, 12:00 p.m. to 4:00 p.m. and by appointment.

Regional Historical Societies and Heritage Organizations

Aurora Colony Historical Society
Old Aurora Colony Museum
Address: 15018 Second Ave., PO Box 202, Aurora 97002
Phone: 503-678-5754
Web: www.auroracolony.org

Baker Heritage Museum
Address: 2480 Grove St., Baker City 97814-2719
Phone: 541-523-9308
Web: www.bakerheritagemuseum.com

Benton County Historical Society & Museum
Address: 1101 Main St., PO Box 35, Philomath 97370
Phone: 541-929-6230
Fax: 541-929-6261
Web: www.bentoncountymuseum.org

Clackamas County Historical Society and Museum of the Oregon Territory
Address: 211 Tumwater Dr., PO Box 2211, Oregon City 97045
Phone: 503-655-5574
Fax: 503-655-0035
Web: www.ClackamasHistory.org

Clatsop County Historical Society
Address: 714 Exchange St., PO Box 88, Astoria 97103
Phone: 503-325-2203
Fax: 503-325-7727
Web: www.cumtux.org; www.oregonfilmmuseum.org

Columbia Gorge Discovery Center & Wasco County Museum
Address: 5000 Discovery Dr., The Dalles 97058
Phone: 541-296-8600
Web: www.gorgediscovery.org

Columbia River Maritime Museum
Address: 1792 Marine Dr., Astoria 97103
Phone: 503-325-2323
Fax: 503-325-2331
Web: www.crmm.org

Coos History Museum & Maritime Collection
Address: 1210 N Front St., Coos Bay 97420
Phone: 541-756-6320
Web: www.cooshistory.org

Crook County Historical Society and Bowman Museum
Address: 246 N Main St., Prineville 97754
Phone: 541-447-3715
Web: www.bowmanmuseum.org

Curry Historical Society and Museum
Address: 29419 S Ellensberg Ave., PO Box 1598, Gold Beach 97444
Phone: 541-247-9396
Web: www.curryhistory.com

Deschutes County Historical Society and Museum
Address: 129 NW Idaho Ave., Bend 97703
Phone: 541-389-1813
Fax: 541-317-9345
Web: www.deschuteshistory.org

Douglas County Museum and Umpqua River Lighthouse Museum
Address: 123 Museum Dr., Roseburg 97471; 1020 Lighthouse Rd., Winchester Bay 97467
Phone: 541-957-7007; 541-271-4631
Web: www.umpquavalleymuseums.org

Four Rivers Cultural Center and Museum
Address: 676 SW Fifth Ave., Ontario 97914
Phone: 541-889-8191
Fax: 541-889-7628
Web: www.4rcc.com

Genealogical Forum of Oregon
Address: 2505 SE 11th Ave., Suite B18, Portland 97202-1061
Phone: 503-963-1932
Web: www.gfo.org

Gilliam County Historical Society
Address: Hwy. 19 at Burns Park, PO Box 377, Condon 97823
Phone: 541-384-4233
Email: gilliamcohistoricalmuseum@gmail.com

Grant County Historical Museum
Address: 101 S Canyon City Blvd., Canyon City 97820
Phone: 541-575-0362
Email: museum@ortelco.net

Harney County Historical Society
Address: 18 W D St., PO Box 388, Burns 97720
Phone: 541-573-5618
Email: harneymuseum@centurytel.net

The History Museum of Hood River County
Address: 300 E Port Marina Dr., PO Box 781, Hood River 97031
Phone/Fax: 541-386-6772
Web: hoodriverhistorymuseum.org

Josephine County Historical Society
Address: 512 SW Fifth St., Grants Pass 97526
Phone: 541-479-7827
Web: www.jocohistorical.org

Lake County Museum
Address: 118 S E St., PO Box 1222 Lakeview 97630
Phone: 541-947-2220
Web: www.lakecountyor.org/links/museum

Lane County Historical Society and Museum
Address: 740 W 13th Ave., Eugene 97402
Phone: 541-682-4242
Fax: 541-682-7361
Web: www.lanecountyhistoricalsociety.org

Lincoln County Historical Society
Address: 545 SW Ninth St., Newport 97365
Phone: 541-265-7509
Fax: 541-265-3992
Web: www.oregoncoasthistory.org

Linn County Historical Museum

Address: 101 Park Ave., PO Box 607 Brownsville 97327
Phone: 541-466-3390
Web: http://www.linnparks.com/museums/linn-county-historical-museum/about/

Malheur Country Historical Society

Address: PO Box 691, Ontario 97914
Email: malheurcountryhist@gmail.com
Web: https://sites.google.com/site/malheur countryhistorical/

The Museum at Warm Springs

Address: 2189 Hwy. 26, PO Box 909, Warm Springs 97761
Phone: 541-553-3331
Fax: 541-553-3338
Web: www.museumatwarmsprings.org

North Lincoln County Historical Museum

Address: 4907 SW Hwy. 101, Lincoln City 97367
Phone: 541-996-6614
Fax: 541-996-1244
Web: www.northlincolncountyhistoricalmuseum. org

Oregon Jewish Museum and Center for Holocaust Education

Address: 1953 NW Kearney St., Portland 97209
Phone: 503-226-3600
Fax: 503-226-1800
Web: www.ojmche.org

Oregon Nikkei Legacy Center and Endowment

Address: 121 NW Second Ave., Portland 97209
Phone: 503-224-1458
Fax: 503-224-1459
Web: www.oregonnikkei.org

Polk County Historical Society

Address: 560 S Pacific Hwy. West, PO Box 67, Rickreall 97371
Phone: 503-623-6251
Web: www.polkcountyhistoricalsociety.org

Sherman County Historical Society and Museum

Address: 200 Dewey St., PO Box 173, Moro 97039
Phone: 541-565-3232
Web: www.shermanmuseum.org

Southern Oregon Historical Society

Address: 106 N Central Ave., Medford 97501
Phone: 541-773-6536
Fax: 541-858-1095
Web: www.sohs.org

Tillamook County Pioneer Museum

Address: 2106 Second St., Tillamook 97141
Phone: 503-842-4553
Fax: 503-842-4553
Web: www.tcpm.org

Troutdale Historical Society

Address: 732 E Historic Columbia River Hwy., Troutdale 97060
Phone: 503-661-2164
Web: www.troutdalehistory.org

Umatilla County Historical Society and Heritage Station Museum

Address: 108 SW Frazer Ave., PO Box 253, Pendleton 97801
Phone: 541-276-0012
Fax: 541-276-7989
Web: www.heritagestationmuseum.org

Washington County Museum

Address: 120 E. Main St., Hillsboro 97123
Phone: 503-645-5353
Web: www.washingtoncountymuseum.org

Yamhill County Historical Society and Museum

Address: 605 Market St., PO Box 484, Lafayette 97127

Yamhill Valley Heritage Center
Address: 11275 SW Durham Ln., McMinnville 97128
Phone: 503-864-2308
Web: www.yamhillcountyhistory.org

EARTH SCIENCES AND TECHNOLOGY

Along with the many state and national parks and forest centers, other organizations have facilities that teach visitors about our natural world and encourage us to explore further.

Oregon's Major Industry, Science and Technology Organizations

Columbia Gorge Discovery Center

Carolyn Purcell, Executive Director
Address: 5000 Discovery Dr., The Dalles 97058
Phone: 541-296-8600
Fax: 541-298-8660
Web: www.gorgediscovery.org
The Columbia Gorge Discovery Center is the official interpretive center for the Columbia River Gorge National Scenic Area. The 26,100 square-foot exhibit wing holds interactive displays which

bring to life the tremendous volcanic upheavals and raging floods that created the Gorge, the theories of why ice ages occur, the mighty river which sculpted patterns for a unique and spectacular diversity of vegetation, wildlife and ancient life ways, the currents that shape our futures in the Gorge and live raptor programs.

Open seven days a week, 9:00 a.m. to 5:00 p.m.

Evergreen Aviation & Space Museum

Larry Wood, Director
Address: 500 NE Captain Michael King Smith Wy., McMinnville 97128
Phone: 503-434-4180
Web: www.evergreenmuseum.org

The Evergreen Aviation & Space Museum is home to the world's largest wooden flying boat, the *Spruce Goose*, the *SR-71 Blackbird*, the *Titan II SLV Missile* and a 3-D digital theater. The museum houses more than 200 historic aircraft, spacecraft and exhibits, artwork and traveling exhibits.

In 2011, the museum opened the 70,000 square-foot Wings & Waves Waterpark, an educational waterpark that includes 10 waterslides, a wave pool and a hands-on water museum.

Across from the McMinnville Airport, three miles southeast of McMinnville on Highway 18, the museum is open 9:00 a.m. to 5:00 p.m. The waterpark is open varied hours depending on the season. Check the Web site for current hours and admission prices.

The High Desert Museum

Dr. Dana Whitelaw, President
Address: 59800 S Hwy. 97, Bend 97702-7963
Phone: 541-382-4754
Fax: 541-382-5256
Web: www.highdesertmuseum.org

The High Desert Museum is nationally acclaimed for its close-up wildlife encounters, living history experiences, Tribal and Western art, cultural exhibits and special programs for all ages. The museum features indoor and outdoor exhibits and natural animal habitats and is renowned for inspiring stewardship of high desert cultural and natural resources. Nature trails meander through the museum's 135 forested acres.

Major permanent exhibits include the *Earle A. Chiles Center on the Spirit of the West*, the *Henry J. Casey Hall of Plateau Indians* and the *Donald M. Kerr Birds of Prey Center*, which is home to many raptors. Outdoor wildlife viewing areas include the "Wind, Earth and Fire" interpretive fire trail. Two North American river otters can be found frolicking in the pond at the *Autzen Otter Exhibit*. Porcupines, badgers, a bobcat and reptiles are among the museum's wildlife collection of more than 100 animals.

The museum's turn of the century working sawmill and replica *High Desert Homestead Ranch* provide authentic settings for its living history performers.

The High Desert Museum is just five minutes south of Bend and is open every day, except Independence Day, Thanksgiving and Christmas. The museum is funded by visitors, members, donors and grants.

Malheur Field Station

Duncan Evered and Lyla Messick, Directors
Address: 34848 Sodhouse Ln., Princeton 97721
Phone: 541-493-2629
Email: mfs@highdesertair.com

Malheur Field Station is an environmental education and research center in the northern Great Basin region in Southeastern Oregon operated by the Great Basin Society, a non-profit organization founded in 1985. The field station provides public lectures, accredited and non-accredited courses, professional development workshops and scout projects. It also hosts individuals, families, birding groups, K–12 school groups and other groups. A member-based consortium of 19 northwest universities, colleges and education organizations guides the academic programs. Friends of Malheur membership benefits include newsletters, bookstore and lodging discounts.

The field station is on the Malheur National Wildlife Refuge, 32 miles south of Burns, a diverse setting of marshlands, desert basins, alkali playas, upland desert scrub steppe, volcanic and glacial landforms, and fault block mountains, providing a rich outdoor classroom for the biologist, geologist, archaeologist, artist, astronomer or environmental science student.

Lodging and food services can be arranged. Basic accommodations range from dormitories and kitchenettes to trailers and recreational vehicle hook-ups.

The field station's Natural History Museum exhibits and bookstore are open to the public.

Oregon Coast Aquarium

Carrie E. Lewis, President and CEO; Brent Denham, Board Chair
Address: 2820 SE Ferry Slip Rd., Newport 97365
Phone: 541-867-3474
Fax: 541-867-6846
Web: http://aquarium.org

The Oregon Coast Aquarium, located in Newport, is a non-profit institution occupying a 32-acre site on Yaquina Bay, adjacent to the Oregon State University Mark O. Hatfield Marine Science Center. Aquarium exhibits are housed in an 80,000 square-foot building and on six acres of elaborately rocked pools, caves, cliffs and bluffs.

Indoor exhibits include four galleries replicating habitats found in coastal wetlands, sandy and rocky shores and off Oregon's coast in deeper waters. Also, indoors are a demonstration lab, Whale Theater, changing exhibit area, full-service cafe and gift shop. Outdoor exhibits include sea otters, harbor seals and sea lions, wave-pummeled tide pools, a coastal cave featuring a giant Pacific octopus, the largest walk-through seabird aviary in North America, a nature trail and a children's play area. The aquarium is open every day, except Christmas, and is handicap accessible.

Oregon Museum of Science and Industry (OMSI)

Nancy Stueber, President; Sue Keil, Board Chair
Address: 1945 SE Water Ave., Portland 97214-3354
Phone: 503-797-4000; 800-955-6674
Web: www.omsi.edu

Established in 1944, the Oregon Museum of Science and Industry is an independent, non-tax-based educational and cultural resource center with an international reputation for excellence in science exhibitry and informal science education. OMSI is dedicated to improving the public's understanding of science and technology through a wide variety of innovative and interactive science programming. More than one million people visit the museum and participate in OMSI's programs every year.

Since 1992, OMSI has occupied a 18.5-acre riverside campus on the east bank of the Willamette River in downtown Portland. The complex includes five exhibit halls; eight interactive science labs; a planetarium; a 300-seat, five-story, Empirical Theater; and the 219-foot U.S.S. *Blueback* submarine moored just outside the building in the river. The museum has river view dining, a science store stocked with hundreds of educational fun toys and an extensive bookstore.

In addition to the exhibits on permanent display, OMSI researches, designs and builds science exhibits for travel to other science centers around the globe. Boasting the largest museum-based, traveling science exhibits program in North America, OMSI has an international reputation for producing popular exhibits.

OMSI also has the largest science outreach education program in the United States, reaching more than 220,000 students across seven western states. OMSI provides education programs to more than 1,900 each year, and OMSI camps serve more than 10,000 children and provide approximately 328,000 hours of science instruction annually. OMSI's education programs include science classes and camp-ins.

OMSI is open Tuesday through Sunday, 9:30 a.m. to 5:30 p.m., from Labor Day through mid-June and is open daily, 9:30 a.m. to 7:00 p.m., from mid-June

through Labor Day. Open all holidays, except Thanksgiving and Christmas.

Oregon State University Hatfield Marine Science Center

Bob Cowen, Director
Address: 2030 SE Marine Science Dr., Newport 97365
Phone: 541-867-0100
Fax: 541-867-0138
Web: http://hmsc.oregonstate.edu

The Hatfield Marine Science Center (HMSC) is Oregon State University's coastal research, teaching and marine extension hub. The center was built on Yaquina Bay in 1965 with the help of the Port of Newport and the federal government, which granted the initial construction funds. Since that time, HMSC facilities have expanded to accommodate over 300 researchers and students from many departments at OSU and from six state and federal agencies. Facilities include a Visitor Center, research and teaching laboratories, including seawater wet lab facilities, and on-site housing for undergraduate and graduate students in residence, and visiting scientists. HMSC is a base for oceanographic research vessels and is adjacent to the site of the National Oceanic and Atmospheric Administration (NOAA) Marine Operations Center – Pacific. As part of OSU's Marine Studies Initiative, HMSC has plans to significantly expand academic programs at HMSC and build a new teaching and research building in Newport. *See* http://marinestudies.oregonstate.edu.

Agencies located at the HMSC include the Oregon Department of Fish and Wildlife Marine Resources Program, the U.S. Environmental Protection Agency Pacific Coastal Ecology Branch, the U.S. Fish and Wildlife Service Oregon Coast National Wildlife Refuge Complex, the U.S. Geological Survey, the USDA's Agricultural Research Service, and NOAA, which includes elements of the Alaska Fisheries Science Center, the Northwest Fisheries Science Center and the Pacific Marine Environmental Laboratory.

HMSC research and education activities aim to increase understanding of coastal and ocean ecosystems and foster sustainable management of marine resources.

The HMSC Visitor Center, managed by Oregon Sea Grant, offers the opportunity to explore over 15,000 square feet of exhibit space featuring interactive, hands-on exhibits and aquaria. The public wing with its beloved touch pool and octopus tank features frequently changing exhibits, including a wave tank exhibit installed in 2012. Computer simulations enable visitors to play the role of scientific explorers while learning about some of the current research underway at the center, and a webcam features the giant Pacific octopus: http://hmsc.oregonstate.edu/visitor/octocam.

Informal education programs and hands-on laboratories can be reserved by school and organized groups, and a dedicated corps of trained volunteers assists visitors with their individual explorations.

Admission to the Visitor Center is by donation. For more information, see http://hmsc.oregonstate.edu/visitor-center.

The HMSC was named in 1983 to honor Mark O. Hatfield, who served Oregon as a state legislator and two-term governor before joining the U.S. Senate in 1966, where he served more than 30 years.

Oregon Zoo

Don Moore, PhD, Director
Address: 4001 SW Canyon Rd., Portland 97221
Phone: 503-220-2540
Fax: 503-226-6836
Web: www.oregonzoo.org

Nestled on 64 acres in the forested hills of Washington Park, the Oregon Zoo is just five minutes west of downtown Portland, easily accessible by public transit and just off Highway 26. Parking charges apply.

The Oregon Zoo is home to more than 2,000 animals from around the world. The Great Northwest area welcomes visitors to the zoo and includes the *Eagle Canyon* exhibit, which surrounds visitors with the splendors of a natural watershed. Visitors have a fish-eye view of salmon, sturgeon and other native fish. Farther up the trail, magnificent bald eagles appear. Visitors discover the importance of rivers and streams and the interconnectedness of animals and the ecosystem. The Great Northwest also features *Condors of the Columbia*—the home of an Oregon native brought back from near-extinction: the California condor. *The Family Farm*—a re-creation of an Oregon Century Farm—is complete with farmhouse and barn, allowing visitors of all ages a chance to interact with sheep, goats and chickens.

The zoo is also the perfect place to learn about animals and explore their habitats around the world. *Red Ape Reserve* showcases orangutans and white-cheeked gibbons. *Predators of the Serengeti* houses lions and cheetahs, while the *Africa Savanna* is home to rhinos, hippos, giraffes and more. The *Africa Rainforest* features fruit bats, monkeys, crocodiles, and many bright and colorful birds, including flamingos. The *Amazon Flooded Forest* gives visitors a peek at some of the many animals living in the most diverse ecosystem in the world. At the Asian elephant habitat, visitors can connect with Portland's elephant family and learn about their care—the Oregon Zoo is recognized worldwide for its Asian elephant program, which has spanned more than 60 years. Other zoo residents include black bears, cougars, polar bears, penguins,

Amur tigers and leopards, all living in lush exhibits recreating their natural habitats.

Visitors can hop aboard the Washington Park and Zoo Railway for a ride through the forested hillsides surrounding the zoo. During the summer, visitors may enjoy the four-mile loop or get off at the International Rose Test Garden and take a stroll, enjoying a view of the city, and catch a later train back to the zoo.

The zoo is a service of Metro and is dedicated to its mission of inspiring the community to create a better future for wildlife. Committed to conservation, the zoo is currently working to save endangered California condors, Oregon silverspot and Taylor's checkerspot butterflies, western pond turtles and Oregon spotted frogs. Other projects focused on saving animals from extinction include studies on Asian elephants, polar bears, orangutans and cheetahs.

University of Oregon Museum of Natural and Cultural History

Jon Erlandson, Director
Address: 1680 E 15th Ave., Eugene 97403-1224
Phone: 541-346-3024
Fax: 541-346-5334
Web: http://natural-history.uoregon.edu

Founded in 1935–1936 by the Oregon Legislature, the Museum of Natural and Cultural History is home to hundreds of thousands of cultural objects, fossils, and biological specimens from Oregon and around the world. The museum is a center of interdisciplinary research and education, serving the global scientific community, Native American tribes, students of all ages, visitors to Oregon and Lane County, and the local community.

The museum offers two permanent exhibits: *Explore Oregon* is devoted to the state's natural history and geology, featuring the sabertooth salmon and other paleontological wonders. *Oregon — Where Past is Present* showcases 15,000 years of cultural history in the state, including 10,000-year-old sandals recovered from Oregon's Fort Rock Cave, as well as tools, coprolites, and other items from the Paisley Caves, Oregon's oldest cultural site.

In addition to these permanent offerings, visitors to the museum enjoy a diverse program of rotating exhibits, spanning the arts, cultural history and scientific research.

Engaging, hands-on displays await visitors of all ages throughout the museum, with touchscreen displays, a curation station and a variety of other interactives. Children especially enjoy digging at a simulated archaeological site and sporting lab coats while interpreting their finds.

Located on the University of Oregon campus near historic Hayward Field, the museum is open

Tuesday through Sunday, 11:00 a.m. to 5:00 p.m. Admission is free on the first Friday of the month. An exhibit talk is offered each day at 2:00 p.m. and is included with the price of admission. Admission Past and Presents, the museum store, is always free.

World Forestry Center
Eric Vines, Executive Director
Address: 4033 SW Canyon Rd., Portland 97221
Phone: 503-228-1367
Fax: 503-228-4608
Web: www.worldforestry.org

Established in 1966, the World Forestry Center, located in Portland's Washington Park, is a private, non-profit forestry education organization. Through classes, tours, the Discovery Museum exhibits and demonstration forests, the center illustrates and interprets benefits of the forest environment and promotes appreciation and understanding of forests and forest resources worldwide.

In 1989, the World Forestry Center established the World Forest Institute (WFI) to meet a growing demand for forestry information and exchange of information on forest trade, regulation, management and forest resources. WFI also manages the International Fellowship Program that provides a unique collaboration between the research community, private industry and the public sector.

The center also operates Magness Memorial Tree Farm in Sherwood, Oregon, an 80-acre demonstration forest that is free and open to the public. The property has a visitors' center and log bunkhouses used for group camping.

ELEMENTARY SCHOOL STUDENT ESSAY
Frog Lake

Colton Anderson, Essay Contest Runner-up
Maggie Harlow's Fifth Grade Class
Memorial Elementary, McMinnville

Frog Lake is nestled in Mt. Hood National Park a mile off the highway. On the Frog Lake Trail about 4 miles up is a beautiful lake about 2 feet at its deepest. During the winter it freezes almost to the bottom. It is surrounded by a dense forest and the wide trail cut right through it. The lake is completely clear all the way to the bottom. My dad and I have snowshoed up there with our skates over our shoulders, sticks, and our puck, and played hockey. He taught me some techniques on skating and puck handling. We camped up there for three days and it was lots of fun. On the third day we hiked back, got in the old S10 and drove home. Once we got home we told stories about how fun it was. I can't wait to go back again!

About the image: Frog Lake is one of many scenic lakes near Mount Hood. Shown to the right is nearby Timothy Lake, another popular destination for recreation in the mountains. To learn more about the subject, see the Cascades recreation photo exhibit in the color section of this book. (*Oregon State Archives*)

Kayaks and other surface water sports equipment stand ready for rent in downtown Brookings on the Oregon Coast.
Oregon State Archives Scenic Photograph 20130911-4204

Historically, Oregon's economy was based on natural resources: timber, fishing and agriculture. Today, the economy is in transition to add manufacturing and service industries with an emphasis on technology. This section describes Oregon's economy.

OREGON'S ECONOMY

Source: Employment Department, Workforce and Economic Research Division

Oregon's economy is robust entering the 2017–2019 biennium following three years of rapid job growth that helped bring the state's unemployment rate to its lowest point in decades. Oregon ranked near the top of all states in terms of improved job growth and decreased unemployment. In early 2016, Oregon's unemployment rate was down to 4.5 percent, lower than the U.S. unemployment rate of 4.7 percent.

During the past three decades, Oregon made the transition from a resource-based economy to a more mixed manufacturing and marketing economy, with an emphasis on high technology. Oregon's hard times of the early 1980s signaled basic changes had occurred in traditional resource sectors — timber, fishing and agriculture — and the state worked to develop new economic sectors to replace older ones. Most important, perhaps, was the state's growing high-tech sector, centered in the three counties around Portland. However, rural Oregon counties were generally left out of the shift to a new economy.

As with the nation, Oregon's expansion from 2004 through 2007 was fueled by growth in construction and services. The recession erased construction's job gains and devastated the economy to the extent that employment in 2010 was at about the same level as in 2000. Job growth was slow during the first three years of recovery, but picked up speed in 2013, as all the major sectors began adding jobs.

Oregon is one of the most trade dependent states in the nation and, to some extent, economic activity in other countries helps drive the state's economy. The value of exports from Oregon to foreign countries was $20.1 billion in 2015. The state's largest trading partners are China, Canada, Malaysia, Japan and South Korea. Of course, Oregon's trade with other U.S. states far exceeds its trade with foreign nations.

The aging population will factor into the future of Oregon's economy. The eldest members of the "Baby Boom" generation, those born between 1946 and 1964, are becoming eligible for Social Security benefits, and many are considering retirement. Nearly one out of four workers in Oregon is already 55 years or older. As the generation ages, employers will need to find new workers with the skills to replace their retiring workforce. At the same time, the growing number of retirees will demand more leisure and health care services.

Employment

Oregon's labor force is more than two million strong. Three out of five of the state's working age

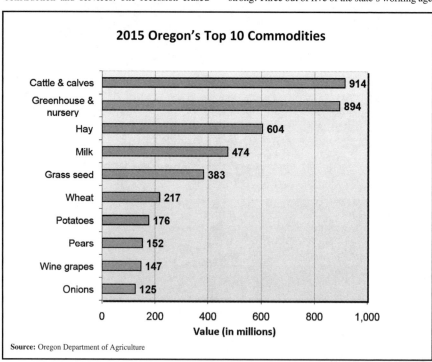

2015 Oregon's Top 10 Commodities

Commodity	Value (in millions)
Cattle & calves	914
Greenhouse & nursery	894
Hay	604
Milk	474
Grass seed	383
Wheat	217
Potatoes	176
Pears	152
Wine grapes	147
Onions	125

Value (in millions)

Source: Oregon Department of Agriculture

population is involved in the labor force. Some are currently looking for a job, many are working for themselves and 1.9 million are employees working at the 143,000 business establishments and government entities across the state. Employment in trade, transportation and utilities accounts for nearly one out of five Oregon jobs, making it the state's largest industry sector. Federal, state and local government jobs are the next largest group, followed by private education and health services, and professional and business services.

Nearly every industry in Oregon was hit hard by the Great Recession. Overall job growth resumed in March 2010, and all the major sectors turned the corner and were adding jobs by early 2014. Total payroll employment reached 1,831,900 in May 2016, nearly 100,000 more jobs than there were when the recession began in December 2007.

Professional and business services added 55,100 jobs during the recovery so far, the most of any sector. Mining and logging, a relatively small sector in terms of number of jobs, added 1,300 jobs.

The trade, transportation and utilities sector has added 39,900 jobs since the recovery began. Private educational services, driven by increasing enrollments, and health care and social assistance, driven by an aging population, never suffered net job losses during the recession. They have added a combined 40,900 jobs during the recovery. Leisure and hospitality, which includes restaurants, hotels and recreational activities, added 36,900 jobs. Other services, which include businesses such as repair and maintenance shops, personal and laundry services and religious and membership organizations, added 6,800 jobs.

The manufacturing sector lost the highest number of jobs during the recession, but has been adding jobs back at a steady pace. So far, 22,900 jobs have been added during the recovery, with 13,700 of those jobs at durable goods manufacturers. In particular, businesses that produce wood products, machinery, and computer and electronic products have been hiring the most workers. The other 8,800 jobs were added by manufacturers of nondurable goods, such as food and beverages.

The construction sector lost a larger share of its jobs than any other sector in Oregon. It was a few years into the recovery before construction firms started hiring, but they were hiring again in 2013. Construction has gained back 21,400 jobs during the recovery.

Oregon's information sector is in flux, with hiring in software publishers being pared by cuts by newspaper, book and directory publishers. Many of the post-recession job gains in this sector have been in Oregon's growing motion picture and video production industry. Overall, the information sector has added 2,500 jobs since early 2010.

Oregon's Top Ten industries by Employment in 2015:

1. Food services and drinking places (144,200)
2. Administrative and support services (93,000)
3. Ambulatory health care services (82,600)
4. Hospitals (55,700)
5. Specialty trade contractors (52,300)
6. Nursing and residential care facilities (48,400)
7. General merchandise stores (42,500)
8. Food and beverage stores (42,500)
9. Computer and electronic product manufacturing (37,800)
10. Social assistance (36,100)

The financial activities sector, which is closely tied to the real estate market, experienced a boom and bust in employment similar to the construction industry, and employment levels continued to fall as the rest of the private sector recovered. Financial activities recently improved and started adding jobs again and now has 2,100 jobs more than in early 2010.

Governments cut jobs over the course of the recovery, driven by reductions in funding local education and spending at the federal level. Local educational employment has stabilized, but federal cuts are expected to continue. Growth in state government jobs is attributed to homecare workers who care for older people and people with disabilities in the person's own home. Government employment is now 9,900 more than it was in early 2010.

Wages

Oregon began a new, three-tier minimum wage rate on July 1, 2016. The tiers vary by geography, with a standard rate of $9.75 per hour in 18 of Oregon's counties and a rate of $9.50 in the remaining nonurban counties. The minimum wage will increase on July 1, 2017, to a standard rate of $10.25, a rate of $11.25 within the Portland Urban Growth Boundary and a rate of $10.00 in nonurban counties. Oregon's minimum wage will increase by $0.50 or $0.75 each year through 2022, depending on the area. Starting in 2023, Oregon's minimum wage will be adjusted annually according to the increase in the U.S. Consumer Price Index.

Although Oregon has a high minimum wage compared with most other states, workers in Oregon tend to work fewer hours per week, and average wage earnings are below the national level. Workers in Oregon earned an average of $929 in weekly earnings in 2015, which is below the national average earnings of $1,018 per week.

Oregon workers earned an annual average of $48,312 in 2015, but the pay workers earn varies widely by industry. The average annual pay in the information industry was $73,565, the most of any broad sector, followed by manufacturing ($65,737) and professional and business services ($64,581). The lowest earnings were at jobs in leisure and hospitality, where pay averaged $19,547 per year.

Of course, the average wage for an industry does not reveal how many low- or high-wage jobs are in an industry. About 12 percent of Oregon jobs have an average wage of less than $10 per hour and another 28 percent are between $10 and $15 per hour. This suggests that more than 60 percent of all jobs pay at least $15 per hour.

Income

Per capita personal income, a broader measure of the income all Oregonians receive from all sources, was $42,974 per person in 2015, which is $3,600 more per person than in 2005 after adjusting for inflation. In addition to wages, personal income includes proprietors' income, income from dividends, interest and rent, and transfer receipts.

The national per capita personal income out performed Oregon over the decade, increasing by $11,765 over the same period and reaching $47,669 in 2015. Oregon's per capita personal income is just 90 percent of the nation's and ranks 32nd among the states and Washington, D.C.

Despite lower average incomes than the nation as a whole, Oregon's poverty rate is less than average. According to the U.S. Census Bureau, 14.3 percent of Oregon residents lived in families with incomes below the poverty threshold during 2011–2013. The U.S. poverty rate was 14.8 percent. Oregon's poverty rate is ranked about 27th in the nation.

Revenue and Taxes

Oregon's state and local governments receive revenue from numerous sources including federal transfer payments; tuition, hospital and other charges; Lottery revenue; and taxes. Of all these sources, half of total state revenue is from taxation. Personal income tax and corporate excise tax are the most significant components of the state General Fund, and property tax is the most significant local tax in Oregon. These three taxes represent 80 percent of all state and local taxes. Oregon does not have a state sales tax.

The personal income tax is the largest source of state tax revenue, expected to account for 87 percent of the state's General Fund for the 2013–15 biennium. Oregon's taxable income is closely connected to federal taxable income. The state

personal income tax rates range from 5 percent to 9.9 percent of taxable income.

The corporate excise and income tax is the second largest source of state tax revenue. The corporate tax rates are 6.6 percent and 7.6 percent of taxable business income. For tax year 2011, less than 3 percent of corporate taxpayers accounted for three-fourths of income and excise tax revenue from C corporations, the most common form of business corporations. The minimum corporate excise tax ranges from $150 to $100,000, depending on the corporation's Oregon sales. Almost 75 percent of all C corporations paid the minimum tax for tax year 2011, but minimum taxpayers accounted for only 14 percent of the total tax paid by C corporations in 2011.

Local governments in Oregon began taxing property before statehood, but the current system is mainly the product of two statewide ballot measures passed in the 1990s, Measures 5 and 50. In Oregon's property tax system, each taxing district is limited to a fixed permanent tax rate, but voters can temporarily increase rates through local options levies or to repay bonds used to fund capital projects. Individual properties have a taxable assessed value equal to, or less than, the real market value that cannot increase by more than 3 percent per year and cannot exceed the real market value. Taxes for an individual property are calculated by applying the tax rates of the local districts to the taxable assessed value of each property and are generally limited to no more than $5 per $1,000 of real market value for education districts and $10 per $1,000 of real market value for all other taxing districts. Levies to repay bonds are outside of this limit.

Additional Information

Department of Agriculture
www.oregon.gov/ODA/Pages/index.aspx

Bureau of Labor and Industries – Minimum Wage
www.oregon.gov/boli/WHD/OMW/Pages/
    Minimum-Wage-Rate-Summary.aspx

Employment Department – Labor Market Information
www.QualityInfo.org

Department of Revenue
http://www.oregon.gov/DOR/Pages/index.aspx

U.S. Department of Labor
www.dol.gov/esa/minwage/america.htm

A couple holds hands as they walk along the beach near Bandon's south jetty.
Oregon State Archives Scenic Photograph DSC0027–22

Oregon's long tradition of open government and citizen involvement depends in part on its citizens receiving accurate and timely information. The media play an important role in providing this information to Oregonians. This section lists Oregon's media resources.

Newspapers Published in Oregon

The following newspapers are published at least once a week. See "Selected Periodicals" following this section for other magazines and journals.

Source: Oregon Newspaper Publishers Association (ONPA)*

Executive Director: Laurie Hieb

Address: 7150 SW Hampton St., Suite 111, Portland 97223

Phone: 503-624-6397

Fax: 503-624-9811

Email: onpa@orenews.com

*For newspapers that are not ONPA members, information was provided independently.

Key: (P) = Publisher, (E) = Editor, (GM) = General Manager

Albany

Albany Democrat-Herald
Mon–Sun a.m.; Jeff Precourt (P); Mike McInally (E); (Mon–Sat), 12,596 (Sun); Estab. 1865
PO Box 130, Albany 97321; 541-926-2211; Fax: 541-926-7209
Web: www.democratherald.com

Ashland

Ashland Daily Tidings
Mon–Sat p.m.; J. Grady Singletary (P); Robert L. Hunter (E); Estab. 1876
PO Box 1108, Medford 97501; 541-776-4411; Fax: 541-776-4376
Web: www.dailytidings.com

Astoria

The Daily Astorian
Mon–Fri p.m.; David Pero (P/E); Estab. 1873
PO Box 210, Astoria 97103; 503-325-3211; Fax: 503-325-6573
Web: www.dailyastorian.com

Baker City

Baker City Herald
Mon, Wed, Fri p.m.; Kari Borgen (P); Jayson Jacoby (E); Estab. 1870
PO Box 807, Baker City 97814; 541-523-3673; Fax: 541-523-6426
Web: www.bakercityherald.com

The Record-Courier
Thur; Gina Perkins (P/E);
Estab. 1901
PO Box 70, Baker City 97814
Web: www.therconline.com

Bandon

Bandon Western World
Wed; Chris Rush (P); Amy Moss-Strong (E); Estab. 1912
PO Box 248, Bandon 97411-0248; 541-347-2423; Fax: 541-347-2424
Web: www.bandonwesternworld.com

Beaverton

Beaverton Valley Times
Thur; Christine Moore (P); Miles Vance (E); Estab. 1921
PO Box 22109, Portland 97269; 503-684-0360; Fax: 503-620-3433
Web: http://portlandtribune.com/beaverton-valley-times-news

Bend

The Bulletin
Mon–Sun a.m.; Gordon Black (P); John Costa (E); Estab. 1903
PO Box 6020, Bend 97708-6020; 541-382-1811; Fax: 541-385-5802
Web: www.bendbulletin.com

Brookings

Curry Coastal Pilot
Wed, Sat; Cindy Vosburg (P); Scott Graves (E); Estab. 1946
PO Box 700, Brookings 97415; 541-469-3123; Fax: 541-469-4679
Web: www.currypilot.com

Brownsville

The Times
Wed; Vance and Holly Parrish (P); Vance Parrish (E); Estab. 1888
PO Box 278, Brownsville 97327; 541-466-5311; Fax: 541-466-5312
Web: www.thebrownsvilletimes.com

Burns

Burns Times-Herald
Wed; Randy Parks (E); Estab. 1887
355 N Broadway Ave., Burns 97720; 541-573-2022; Fax: 541-573-3915
Web: http://btimesherald.com

Canby

Canby Herald
Wed; Georgia Newton (P); John Baker (E); Estab. 1906
PO Box 1108, Canby 97013; 503-266-6831; Fax: 503-266-6836
Web: www.pamplinmedia.com/canby-herald-news

Cave Junction

Illinois Valley News
Wed; Dan Mancuso (P); Laura Mancuso (E); Estab. 1937

PO Box 1370, Cave Junction 97523;
541-592-2541

Web: www.illinois-valley-news.com

Clatskanie

The Clatskanie Chief

Thur; Deborah Steele Hazen (P/E); Estab. 1891

PO Box 8, Clatskanie 97016; Phone/Fax:
503-728-3350

Web: www.thechiefnews.com

Condon

The Times-Journal

Thur; McLaren and Janet Stinchfield (P);
McLaren Stinchfield (E); Circ. 1,306; Estab. 1886

PO Box 746, Condon 97823; 541-384-2421;
Fax: 541-384-2411

Coos Bay

The World

Mon–Thur, Sat; Chris Rush (P); Larry
Campbell (E); Estab. 1878

PO Box 1840, Coos Bay 97420; 541-269-1222;
Fax: 541-269-2725

Web: www.theworldlink.com

Coquille

The Sentinel

Wed; Jean Ivey (P); Kathleen Dimmick (E);
Estab. 1882

61 E First St., Coquille 97423; 541-396-3191;
Fax: 541-396-3624

Corvallis

Corvallis Gazette-Times

Mon–Sun a.m.; Jeff Precourt (P); Mike
McInally (E); Estab. 1862

PO Box 368, Corvallis 97339; 541-753-2641;
Fax: 541-758-9505

Web: www.gazettetimes.com

Cottage Grove

Cottage Grove Sentinel

Wed; John Bartlett (P); Jon Stinnett (E);
Estab. 1889

PO Box 35, Cottage Grove 97424; 541-942-3325;
Fax: 541-942-3328

Web: www.cgsentinel.com

Creswell

The Creswell Chronicle

Thur; Scott J. Olson (P/E); Estab. 1965

PO Box 428, Creswell 97426; 541-895-2197;
Fax: 541-895-2361

Web: www.thecreswellchronicle.com

Dallas

Polk County Itemizer-Observer

Wed; Emily Mentzer (P); Kurt Holland (E);
Estab. 1875

PO Box 108, Dallas 97338; 503-623-2373;
Fax: 503-623-2395

Web: www.polkio.com

Drain

The Drain Enterprise

Thur; Sue Anderson (P/E); Estab. 1950

PO Box 26, Drain 97435; 541-836-2241;
Fax: 541-836-2243

Enterprise

Wallowa County Chieftain

Wed; Marissa Williams (P); Scot Heisel (E);
Estab. 1884

PO Box 338, Enterprise 97828; 541-426-4567;
Fax: 541-426-3921

Web: www.wallowa.com

Estacada

Estacada News

Thur; J. Mark Garber (Pres.); Steve Brown (E);
Estab. 1904

PO Box 549, Estacada 97023; 503-630-3241;
Fax: 503-630-5840

Web: http://portlandtribune.com/estacada-
news-news/

Eugene

Eugene Weekly

Thur; Camilla Mortensen (E); Estab. 1982

1251 Lincoln St., Eugene 97401; 541-484-0519;
Fax: 541-484-4044

Web: www.eugeneweekly.com

The Register-Guard

Mon–Sun a.m.; Logan Molen (P/E);
Estab. 1862

3500 Chad Dr., Eugene 97408; 541-485-1234

Web: www.registerguard.com

Florence

Siuslaw News

Wed, Sat; John Bartlett (P); Ned Hickson (E);
Estab. 1890

PO Box 10, Florence 97439; 541-997-3441;
Fax: 541-997-7979

Web: www.thesiuslawnews.com

Forest Grove

News-Times

Wed; Nikki DeBuse (P); Nancy Townsley (E);
Estab. 1886

2038 Pacific Ave., Forest Grove 97116;
503-357-3181; Fax: 503-296-2828

Web: http://portlandtribune.com/forest-grove-
news-times-news/

Media Directories

Gold Beach

Curry County Reporter
Wed; Matt and Kim Hall (P); Matthew Smith (E); Estab. 1914
PO Box 766, Gold Beach 97444; 541-247-6643; Fax: 541-247-6644
Web: www.currycountyreporter.com

Grants Pass

Grants Pass Daily Courier
Tue–Fri, Sun; Travis Moore (P); Kevin Widdison (E); Estab. 1885
PO Box 1468, Grants Pass 97528-0330; 541-474-3700; Fax: 541-474-3814
Web: www.thedailycourier.com

Gresham

Outlook
Tue, Fri; J. Mark Garber (Pres.); Steve Brown (E); Estab. 1911
PO Box 747, Gresham 97030; 503-665-2181; Fax: 503-665-2187
Web: http://portlandtribune.com/gresham-outlook-news/

Halfway

Hells Canyon Journal
Wed; Steve Backstrom (P/E); Estab. 1984
PO Box 646, Halfway 97834; 541-742-7900; Fax: 541-742-7933

Heppner

Heppner Gazette-Times
Wed; David Sykes (P); Andrea Di Salvo (E); Estab. 1883
PO Box 337, Heppner 97836; 541-676-9228; Fax: 541-676-9211

Hermiston

Hermiston Herald
Wed; Kathryn B. Brown (P); Gary West (E); Estab. 1906
333 E Main St., Hermiston 97838; 541-567-6457; Fax: 541-567-1764
Web: www.hermistonherald.com

Hillsboro

Hillsboro Argus
Wed, Fri; Tom Maurer (E); Estab. 1873
PO Box 588, Hillsboro 97123; 503-648-1131; Fax: 503-648-9191
Web: www.oregonlive.com/argus

Hood River

Hood River News
Wed, Sat; Chelsee Marr (P); Kirby Neumann-Rea (E); Estab. 1905

PO Box 390, Hood River 97031; 541-386-1234; Fax: 541-386-6796
Web: www.hoodrivernews.com

John Day

Blue Mountain Eagle
Wed; Marissa Williams (P); Sean Hart (E); Estab. 1898
195 N Canyon Blvd., John Day 97845; 541-575-0710; Fax: 541-575-1244
Web: www.myeaglenews.com

Keizer

Keizertimes
Fri; Lyndon Zaitz (P); Eric Howald (E); Estab. 1979
142 Chemawa Rd. N, Keizer 97303; 503-390-1051; Fax: 503-390-8023
Web: www.keizertimes.com

Klamath Falls

Herald and News
Tue–Sun a.m.; Mark Dobie (P); Gerry O'Brien (E); Estab. 1906
PO Box 788, Klamath Falls 97601; 541-885-4410; Fax: 541-885-4456
Web: www.heraldandnews.com

La Grande

The Observer
Mon, Wed, Fri; Kari Borgen (P); Andrew Cutler (E); Estab. 1896
1406 Fifth St., La Grande 97850; 541-963-3161; Fax: 541-963-7804
Web: www.lagrandeobserver.com

Lake Oswego

Lake Oswego Review
Thur; J. Brian Monihan (P); Estab. 1920
PO Box 22109, Portland 97269; 503-635-8811; Fax: 503-635-8817
Web: http://portlandtribune.com/lake-oswego-review-news

Lakeview

Lake County Examiner
Wed; Tillie Flynn (Gen. Mgr.); Estab. 1880
739 N 2nd St., Lakeview 97630; 541-947-3378; Fax: 541-947-4359
Web: www.lakecountyexam.com

Lebanon

Lebanon Express
Wed; Jeff Precourt (P); Mike McInally (E); Estab. 1887
90 E Grant St., Lebanon 97355; 541-258-3151; Fax: 541-259-3569
Web: www.lebanon-express.com

Lincoln City

The News Guard
Wed; Mark Smidt (P); Gretchen Ammerman (E); Estab. 1927
PO Box 848, Lincoln City 97367; 541-994-2178; Fax: 541-994-7613
Web: www.thenewsguard.com

Madras

The Madras Pioneer
Wed; Tony Ahern (P); Susan Matheny (E); Estab. 1904
345 SE Fifth St., Madras 97741; 541-475-2275; Fax: 541-475-3710
Web: www.madraspioneer.com

McKenzie Bridge

McKenzie River Reflections
Thur; Ken Engelman (P); Louise Engelman (E); Estab. 1978
59059 Old McKenzie Hwy., McKenzie Bridge 97413; 541-822-3358; Fax: 541-663-4550
Web: http://mckenzieriverreflectionsnewspaper.com

McMinnville

News-Register
Tue, Fri; Jeb Bladine (P); Steve Bagwell (E); Estab. 1866
PO Box 727, McMinnville 97128; 503-472-5114; Fax: 503-472-9151
Web: www.newsregister.com

Medford

Mail Tribune
Mon–Sun a.m.; J. Grady Singletary (P); Cathy Noah (E); Estab. 1906
PO Box 1108, Medford 97501; 541-776-4411; Fax: 541-776-4376
Web: www.mailtribune.com

Milton-Freewater

Valley Herald
Fri; Sherrie Widmer (P/E); Estab. 2001
408 N Main St., Milton-Freewater 97862; 541-938-6688; Fax: 541-938-6689
Web: www.mfvalleyherald.net/home.html

Molalla

Molalla Pioneer
Wed; Georgia Newton (P); Peggy Savage (E); Estab. 1913
PO Box 168, Molalla 97038; 503-829-2301; Fax: 503-829-2317
Web: www.molallapioneer.com

Myrtle Creek

The Douglas County Mail
Thur; Robert L. Chaney, Sr. (P/E); Estab. 1902
PO Box 729, Myrtle Creek 97457; 541-863-5233; Fax: 541-863-5234

Myrtle Point

Myrtle Point Herald
Thur; Matt Hall (P); Matthew Smith (E); Estab. 1889
PO Box 606, Myrtle Point 97458; 541-572-2717; Fax: 541-572-2828

Newberg

The Newberg Graphic
Wed; Allen Herriges (P); Gary Allen (E); Estab. 1888
PO Box 700, Newberg 97132; 503-538-2181; Fax: 503-538-1632
Web: www.newberggraphic.com

Newport

News-Times
Wed, Fri; James Rand (P); Wyatt Haupt (E); Estab. 1882
PO Box 965, Newport 97365; 541-265-8571; Fax: 541-265-3862
Web: www.newportnewstimes.com

Oakridge

Dead Mountain Echo
Thur; Larry and Debra Roberts (P); Larry Roberts (E); Estab. 1973
PO Box 900, Oakridge 97463; 541-782-4241; Fax: 541-782-3323

Ontario

The Argus Observer
Tue–Fri p.m., Sun a.m.; John Dillon (P); Estab. 1896
1160 SW Fourth St., Ontario 97914; 541-889-5387; Fax: 541-889-3347
Web: www.argusobserver.com

Pendleton

East Oregonian
Tue–Sat; Kathryn B. Brown (P); Daniel Wattenburger (E); Estab. 1875
211 SE Byers Ave., Pendleton 97801; 541-276-2211; Fax: 541-276-8314
Web: www.eastoregonian.com

The Pendleton Record
Thur; Marguerite M. Maznaritz (P); Sam Westover (E); Estab. 1911
PO Box 69, Pendleton 97801; 541-276-2853; email: penrecor@uci.net

Port Orford

Port Orford News
Wed; Matt Hall (P/E); Estab. 1958
PO Box 5, Port Orford 97465; 541-260-3638
Web: www.portorfordnews.net

Portland

Daily Journal of Commerce
Mon, Wed, Fri; Brian Hunt (P) Stephanie Basalyga (E); Estab. 1872
921 SW Washington St., Suite 210, Portland 97205; 503-226-1311; Fax: 503-226-1315
Web: www.djcoregon.com

Portland Tribune
Tue, Thur; Mark Garber (E); Estab. 2001
6605 SE Lake Rd., Portland 97222-2161; 503-226-6397; Fax: 503-226-7042
Web: www.portlandtribune.com

The Asian Reporter
Bi-monthly (1st and 3rd Mon); Jaime Lim (P); Estab. 1990
922 N Killingsworth St., Portland 97217; 503-283-4440; Fax: 503-283-4445
Web: www.asianreporter.com

The Oregonian
Mon–Sun a.m. (home delivery Wed, Fri, Sat, Sun a.m.); Chris Anderson (Pres.); Estab. 1850
1550 SW First Ave., Suite 500, Portland 97201; 503-221-8327; Fax: 503-227-5306
Web: www.oregonlive.com/oregonian

The Skanner
Wed; Bernie Foster (P); Bobbie Foster (E); Estab. 1975
415 N Killingsworth St., Portland 97217; 503-285-5555; Fax: 503-285-2900
Web: www.theskanner.com

Willamette Week
Wed; Richard H. Meeker (P) Mark Zusman (E); Estab. 1974
2220 NW Quimby St., Portland 97210; 503-243-2122; Fax: 503-243-1115
Web: www.wweek.com

Prineville

Central Oregonian
Tue, Fri; Tony Ahern (P); Jason Cheney (E); Estab. 1881
558 N Main St., Prineville 97754; 541-447-6205; Fax: 541-447-1754
Web: www.centraloregonian.com

Redmond

The Redmond Spokesman
Wed; Steve Hawes (P); Geoff Folsom (E); Estab. 1910
PO Box 788, Redmond 97756; 541-548-2184; Fax: 541-548-3203
Web: www.redmondspokesmanonline.com

Reedsport

The Umpqua Post
Wed; Chris Rush (P); Larry Campbell (E); Estab. 1996
PO Box 145, Reedsport 97467; 541-269-1222; Fax: 541-271-2821
Web: www.theumpquapost.com

Rogue River

Rogue River Press
Wed; Teresa Pearson (P/E); Estab. 1915
PO Box 1485, Rogue River 97537; 541-582-1707; Fax: 541-582-0201
Web: www.rogueriverpress.com

Roseburg

The News-Review
Tue–Sun a.m.; Tim Smith (GM); Craig Reed (E); Estab. 1867
345 NE Winchester St., Roseburg 97470; 541-672-3321; Fax: 541-957-4265
Web: www.nrtoday.com

Saint Helens

The Chronicle
Wed; Don Patterson (P/E); Estab. 1881
PO Box 1153, Saint Helens 97051; 503-397-0116; Fax: 503-397-4093
Web: www.thechronicleonline.com

Salem

Capital Press
Fri; J. Michael O'Brien (P); Joe Beach (E); Estab. 1928
PO Box 2048, Salem 97303; 800-882-6789; Fax: 503-370-4383
Web: www.capitalpress.com

Statesman Journal
Mon–Sun a.m.; Ryan Kedzierski, President; Estab. 1851
PO Box 13009, Salem 97309; 503-399-6611; Fax: 503-399-6706
Web: www.statesmanjournal.com

Sandy

Sandy Post
Wed; J. Mark Garber (Pres.); Steve Brown (E); Estab. 1937
PO Box 68, Sandy 97055; 503-668-5548; Fax: 503-668-0748
Web: http://portlandtribune.com/sandy-post-news/

Scappoose

South County Spotlight
Wed; Darryl Swan (P/E); Estab. 1961

33548 Edward Ln., Suite 110, Scappoose 97056; 503-543-6387; Fax: 503-543-6380
Web: http://portlandtribune.com/south-county-spotlight-news

Seaside

Seaside Signal
Every other Fri; David Pero (P); Richard Marx (E); Estab. 1905
1555 N Roosevelt Dr., Seaside 97138; 503-738-5561; Fax: 503-738-9285
Web: www.seasidesignal.com

Silverton

Appeal Tribune
Wed; Ryan Kedzierski (P); Estab. 1880
PO Box 35, Silverton 97381; 503-873-8385; Fax: 503-873-8064
Web: www.silvertonappeal.com

Springfield

Springfield Times
Thur; Amber Deyo (P); Henry Houston (E); Estab. 2008
216 Main St., Suite 5, Springfield 97477; 541-741-7368; Fax: 541-203-9413
Web: www.springfieldtimes.net

Stayton

The Stayton Mail
Wed; Steve Silberman (P); Estab. 1894
PO Box 400, Stayton 97383; 503-769-6338; Fax: 503-769-6207
Web: www.staytonmail.com

Sweet Home

The New Era
Wed; Scott Swanson (P/E); Estab. 1929
PO Box 39, Sweet Home 97386; 541-367-2135; Fax: 541-367-2137
Web: www.sweethomenews.com

The Dalles

The Dalles Chronicle
Tue–Fri p.m., Sun a.m., RaeLynn Ricarte (P/E); Estab. 1890
PO Box 1910, The Dalles 97058; 541-296-2141; Fax: 541-298-1365
Web: www.thedalleschronicle.com

Tigard/Tualatin/Sherwood

The Times
Thur; Christine Moore (P); Miles Vance (E); Estab. 1956
PO Box 22109, Portland 97269; 971-204-7735
Web: http://portlandtribune.com/the-times-news

Tillamook

Headlight Herald
Wed; Joe Warren (P); Jordan Wolfe (E) Estab. 1888
PO Box 444, Tillamook 97141; 503-842-7535; Fax: 503-842-8842
Web: www.tillamookheadlightherald.com

Vale

Malheur Enterprise
Wed; Scotta Callister (P); Lyndon Zaitz (GM); Estab. 1909
289 A St. W, Vale 97918; 541-473-3377; Fax: 541-473-3268
Web: www.malheurenterprise.com

Warrenton

The Columbia Press
Fri; Gary Nevan (P/E); Estab. 1922
PO Box 130, Warrenton 97146; 503-861-3331
Web: www.thecolumbiapress.com

West Linn

West Linn Tidings
Thur; J. Brian Monihan (P); Luke Roney (E); Estab. 1981
PO Box 22109, Portland 97269; 503-635-8811; Fax: 503-635-8817
Web: http://portlandtribune.com/west-linn-tidings-news

Wilsonville

Wilsonville Spokesman
Wed; J. Brian Monihan (P); Luke Roney (E); Estab. 1985
PO Box 22109, Portland 97269; 503-682-3935; Fax: 503-266-6836
Web: www.wilsonvillespokesman.com

Woodburn

Woodburn Independent
Wed; Allen Herriges (P); Lindsay Keefer (E); Estab. 1888
PO Box 96, Woodburn 97071; 503-981-3441; Fax: 503-981-1253
Web: www.woodburnindependent.com

SELECTED PERIODICALS PUBLISHED IN OREGON

The State Library has compiled a representative sample of the many periodicals published in Oregon. The first year of each periodical's publication follows its title and publication schedule.

Key: A = Annual; BM = Bi-monthly; BW = Bi-weekly; M = Monthly; Q = Quarterly; SA = Semi-annual; SM = Semi-monthly; W = Weekly

1859: Oregon's Magazine (M) 2009: 1859 Media, LLC, 70 SW Century Dr., Suite 100-218, Bend 97702; 541-728-2764
Web: http://www.1859oregonmagazine.com

Agri-Times Northwest (SM) 1984: Sterling Ag, LLC, PO Box 1626, Pendleton 97801-0189; 541-276-6202; Fax: 541-278-4778
Web: www.agritimesnw.com

Animal Law Review (SA) 1995: Lewis & Clark Law School, 10015 SW Terwilliger Blvd., Portland 97219; 503-768-7000; Fax: 503-768-6783
Web: http://law.lclark.edu/law_reviews/animal_law_review

Backwoods Home Magazine (BM) 1989: PO Box 712, Gold Beach 97444; 541-247-8900; 800-835-2418; Fax: 541-247-8600
Web: www.backwoodshome.com

Book Dealers World (Q) 1980: National Association of Book Entrepreneurs, PO Box 606, Cottage Grove 97424; Phone/Fax: 541-942-7455;
Web: www.bookmarketingprofits.com

Calyx (SA) 1976: PO Box B, Corvallis 97339; 541-753-9384/888-336-2665; Fax: 541-753-0515;
Web: www.calyxpress.org

Cascade Journal (Q) 2014: 147 Shevlin Hixon Dr. #201, Bend 97701; 800-417-3314;
Web: http://cascadejournal.com/

Dialogue (Q) 1961: Blindskills, Inc., PO Box 5181, Salem 97304-0181; 503-581-4224; 800-860-4224; Fax: 503-581-0178
Web: www.blindskills.com

Digger (M) 1988: Oregon Association of Nurseries, 29751 SW Town Center Loop W, Wilsonville 97070; 503-682-5089/888-283-7219; Fax: 503-682-5099; Web: www.oan.org

Environmental Law (Q) 1970: Lewis & Clark Law School, 10015 SW Terwilliger Blvd., Portland 97219; 503-768-6700; Fax: 503-768-6783
Web: http://law.lclark.edu/law_reviews/environmental_law

Eugene Magazine (Q) 2006: Olive Tree, LLC, 1255 Railroad Blvd., Eugene 97401; 541-686-6608; Fax: 541-686-8008
Web: www.eugenemagazine.com

Flyfishing and Tying Journal (Q) 1978: Frank Amato Publications, PO Box 82112, Portland 97282; 503-653-8108; 800-541-9498
Web: www.amatobooks.com

Glimmer Train (Q) 1992: Glimmer Train Press, Inc., PO Box 80430, Portland 97280-1430; 503-221-0836; Fax: 503-221-0837
Web: www.glimmertrain.com/index.html

Heritage Newsletter (M) 1987: Linn County Genealogical Society, PO Box 1222, Albany 97321-0537; 541-791-1618
Web: www.lgsoregon.org

El Hispanic News (M) 1981: PO Box 306, Portland 97207-0306; 503-228-3139; Fax: 503-228-3384
Web: www.elhispanicnews.com

Home Power (BM) 1987: Home Power, PO Box 520, Ashland 97520-0520; 541-512-0201/800-707-6585; Fax: 541-512-0343
Web: https://homepower.com/home

Journal of Environmental Law and Litigation (SA) 1985: 138 Knight Law Center, 1221 University of Oregon, Eugene 97403; 541-346-3844
Web: https://law.uoregon.edu/explore/JELL

El Latino de Hoy: Semanario Latinoamericano de Oregon (W) 1991: 2318 SW 18th Ave., Portland 97201; 503-493-1106/503-493-1126; Fax: 503-493-1107
Web: www.ellatinodehoy.com

Metroscape (SA) 1995: Institute of Portland Metropolitan Studies, Portland State University, PO Box 751, Portland 97207-0751; 503-725-5170; Fax: 503-725-5199
Web: www.pdx.edu/ims/metroscape

Midwifery Today (Q) 1987: PO Box 2672, Eugene 97402; 541-344-7438/800-743-0974; Fax: 541-344-1422
Web: www.midwiferytoday.com

Northwest Labor Press (SM) 1987: PO Box 13150, Portland 97213; 503-288-3311
Web: http://nwlaborpress.org

Noticias Latinas! Latin News! (Q) 1995: Latin Media Northwest, 16239 SE McLoughlin Blvd., Suite 2, Milwaukie 97267; 503-827-5507; Fax: 503-227-7790
Web: www.latinmedianw.com

OLA Quarterly (Q) 1995: Oregon Library Association, PO Box 3067, La Grande 97850; 541-962-5824
Web: http://commons.pacificu.edu/olaq/

Open Spaces: Views from the Northwest (Q) 1998: Open Spaces Publishing, 6327-C SW Capitol Hwy., PMB 134, Portland 97239-1937; 503-313-4361; Web: www.open-spaces.com

Oregon Business Magazine (M) 1981: MIF Publications, Inc., 715 SW Morrison St., Suite 800, Portland 97205; 888-881-5861
Web: www.oregonbusiness.com

Oregon Coast (BM) 1982: Northwest Regional Magazines, 4969 Hwy. 101 #2B, Florence 97439; 541-997-8401/800-348-8401
Web: www.northwestmagazines.com
Oregon Grange Bulletin (BM) 1990: Oregon State Grange, 643 Union St. NE, Salem 97301; 503-316-0106; Fax: 503-316-0109
Web: http://orgrange.org/osg-bulletin/
Oregon Historical Quarterly (Q) 1900: Oregon Historical Society, 1200 SW Park Ave., Portland 97205; 503-306-5220; Fax: 503-221-2035
Web: www.ohs.org/research-and-library/oregon-historical-quarterly/
Oregon Home (Q) 1997: MediAmerica, 715 SW Morrison, Suite 800, Portland 97205; 888-881-5861;
Web: www.oregonhomemagazine.com
Oregon Humanities (Q) 1983: Oregon Humanities, 921 SW Washington St., Suite 150, Portland 97205; 503-241-0543/800-735-0543; Fax: 503-241-0024
Web: http://oregonhumanities.org/
Oregon Hunter (BM) 1983: Oregon Hunters Association, PO Box 1706, Medford 97501; 541-772-7313; Fax: 541-772-0964
Web: http://www.oregonhunters.org/pub.html
Oregon Law Review (Q) 1921: University of Oregon, 1515 Agate St., 1221 University of Oregon, Eugene 97403; 541-346-3844; Fax: 541-346-1596
Web: https://law.uoregon.edu/explore/OLR
Oregon Wheat (BM) 1962: Oregon Wheat Growers League, 115 SE Eighth St., Pendleton 97801-2319; 541-276-7330; Web: www.owgl.org
Oregon's Agricultural Progress (SA) 1953: Oregon State University, Agricultural Experiment Station, 422 Kerr Admin. Bldg., Corvallis 97331-2119; 541-737-3311
Web: http://oregonprogress.oregonstate.edu
Parenting Now! (Q) 1978: 86 Centennial Loop, Eugene 97401; 541-484-5316; Fax: 541-484-1449; Web: https://parentingnow.org/
Peaceworker (M) 2003: 104 Commercial St. NE, Salem 97301; 503-585-2767; Fax: 503-588-0088; Web: http://peaceworker.org
Portland Monthly (M) 2003: SagaCity Media, 921 SW Washington St., Suite 750, Portland 97205; 503-222-5144; Fax: 503-227-8777
Web: www.portlandmonthlymag.com
Random Lengths (W) 1944: PO Box 867, Eugene 97440-0867; 541-686-9925/888-686-9925; Web: www.randomlengths.com
Resource Recycling (M) 1982: PO Box 42270, Portland 97242-0270; 503-233-1305; Fax: 503-233-1356; Web: www.resource-recycling.com
Rubberstampmadness (Q) 1980: RSM Enterprises, Inc., PO Box 610, Corvallis 97339-0610; 541-752-0075/877-782-6762
Web: www.rsmadness.com

Ruralite (M) 1953: Ruralite Services, Inc., 5605 NE Elam Young Pkwy., Hillsboro 97124; 503-357-2105; Web: www.ruralite.org
Skipping Stones (Q) 1988: PO Box 3939, Eugene 97403-0939; 541-342-4956
Web: www.skippingstones.org
Small Farmers Journal (Q) 1976: PO Box 1627, Sisters 97759-1627; 541-549-2064; 800-876-2893; Fax: 541-549-4403
Web: http://smallfarmersjournal.com
Spot Magazine (BM) 2005: PO Box 16667, Portland 97292; 503-261-1162
Web: http://spotmagazine.net/
Take Root (Q) 2011: Duhn & Associates, PO Box 636, Junction City 97448-0636
Web: www.takerootmagazine.com/index.html
Tinnitus Today (3/year) 1975: American Tinnitus Association, PO Box 5, Portland 97207; 503-248-9985/800-634-8978; Fax: 503-248-0024; Web: http://www.ata.org/
True Parent (M) 2014: Index Newspapers, 115 SW Ash St., Suite 600, Portland 97204; 503-294-0840; Web: http://trueparent.com/
Western Places (Irregular) 1992: PO Box 2093, Lake Oswego 97035; 503-635-1379; Web: www.westernplaces.net
Willamette Journal of International Law and Dispute Resolution (A) 1997: Willamette University College of Law, 245 Winter St. SE, Carnegie 105, Salem 97301; 503-370-6632
Web: www.willamette.edu/law/resources/journals/wjildr/
Willamette Law Review (Q) 1978: Willamette University College of Law, 245 Winter St. SE, Salem 97301; 503-370-6186; Fax: 503-375-5463; Web: www.willamette.edu/wucl/resources/journals/review/

OREGON COMMERCIAL RADIO STATIONS

Albany

KHPE-FM (107.9) Contemporary Christian
KWIL-AM (790) Christian Bible Teaching
 PO Box 278, Albany 97321; 541-926-2233; Fax: 541-926-3925; Randy Davison

KRKT-FM (99.9) Country
KTHH-AM (990) Comedy
 2840 Marion St. SE, Albany 97321; 541-926-8628; Fax: 541-928-1261; Larry Rogers

Astoria/Seaside

KAST-AM (1370) News/Talk
KCRX-FM (102.3) Classic Rock
KLMY-FM (99.7) Hot Adult Contemporary
KVAS-AM (1230) Classic Country
KVAS-FM (103.9) Country

285 SW Main Ct., Suite 200, Warrenton 97146;
503-861-6620; Scott Lindahl

KCYS-FM (96.5) Hot Country
PO Box 1258, Astoria 97103; 503-717-9643;
Fax: 503-717-9578; Dave Heick

Baker City

KBKR-AM (1490)

KKBC-FM (95.3)

KCMB-FM (104.7) Country
KVBL-FM (103.1) News/Talk
KWRL-FM (99.9) Adult Contemporary
1009-C Adams Ave., La Grande 97850;
541-963-3405; Fax: 541-963-5090;
Randy McKone

Bandon

KBDN-FM (96.5) Classic Country
PO Box 180, Coos Bay 97420; 541-267-2121;
Fax: 541-267-5229; Philipp Jimenez

Bend/Redmond

KBND-AM/FM (1110/100.1) News/Talk
KLRR-FM (101.7) Adult Contemporary/Adult
Album Alternative
KMTK-FM (99.7) Country
KTWS-FM (98.3) Classic Rock
KWXS-FM (107.7) Contemporary Hit Radio
PO Box 5037, Bend 97708; 541-382-5263;
Fax: 541-388-0456; Jeremy Groh

KBNW-AM (1340/104.5 translator in Bend)
News/Talk/Information
KLTW-FM (95.7/93.7 translator in Prineville)
Adult Contemporary
KQAK-FM (105.7) Classic Hits
KWLZ-FM (96.5) News/Talk/Information
KWPK-FM (104.1) Hot Adult Contemporary
854 NE Fourth St., Bend 97701; 541-383-3825;
Fax: 541-383-3403; Keith Shipman

KICE-AM (940) Sports/Talk
KMGX-FM (100.7) Adult Contemporary
KRXF-FM (92.9) Alternative
KSJJ-FM (102.9) Country
KXIX-FM (94.1) Contemporary Hit Radio
345 SW Cyber Dr., Suites 101–103, Bend
97702; 541-388-3300; Fax: 541-388-3303;
Jim Gross

KNLR-FM (97.5) Contemporary Christian
KNLX-FM (104.9) Contemporary Christian
30 SE Bridgeford Blvd., Bend 97702;
541-389-8873; Fax: 541-389-5291;
Terry Cowan

KRCO-AM (690/96.9 translator in Prineville)
Classic Country

PO Box 690, Prineville 97754; 541-447-6770;
Fax: 541-383-3403; Dave Clemens

Brookings

KDOB-FM (91.5) News/Talk/Christian
2070 Milligan Way, Medford 97504;
541-776-5368; Fax: 541-842-4334;
Perry Atkinson
KURY-AM (910) Adult Standards
KURY-FM (95.3) Classic Hits
PO Box 1029, Brookings 97415;
541-469-2111; Brian Papstein

Burns

KBNH-AM (1230) Country
KORC-FM (92.7) Classic Hits
PO Box 877, Burns 97720; 541-573-2055;
Chris Pruett

Cave Junction

KCNA-FM (102.7)

Coos Bay/North Bend

KBBR-AM (1340) Progressive News/Talk
KOOS-FM (107.3/107.7) Hot Adult
Contemporary
KTEE-FM (94.9/95.7) Adult Album Alternative
PO Box 180, Coos Bay 97420; 541-267-2121;
Fax: 541-267-5129; Philipp Jimenez

KDCB-FM (89.5) News/Talk/Christian
2070 Milligan Way, Medford 97504;
541-776-5368; Fax: 541-842-4334;
Perry Atkinson

KDCQ-FM (92.9) Classic Hits
PO Box 478, Coos Bay 97420; 541-269-0929;
Fax: 541-269-9376; Stephanie Kilmer

KHSN-AM (1230) Sports
PO Box 180, Coos Bay 97420; 541-267-2121;
Fax: 541-267-5129; Lee Taft

KYTT-FM (98.7) Contemporary Christian
580 Kingwood Ave., Coos Bay 97420;
541-269-2022; Fax: 541-267-0114;
Rick Stevens

Coquille

KSHR-FM (97.3) Hot Country
KWRO-AM/FM (630/100.3) Conservative Talk
PO Box 180, Coos Bay 97420; 541-267-2121;
Fax: 541-267-5129; Philipp Jimenez

Corvallis

KEJO-AM (1240) Sports Talk
KLOO-AM (1340) News/Talk
KLOO-FM (106.3) Classic Rock
2840 Marion St. SE, Albany 97321;
541-926-8628; Fax: 541-928-1261;
Larry Rogers

Cottage Grove

KNND-AM (1400)

Dallas
KWIP-AM (880)

Elgin
KRJT-FM (105.9)

Enterprise
KWVR-AM (1340) Talk/Sports/News
KWVR-FM (92.1) Country
   220 W Main St., Enterprise 97828;
   541-426-4577; Fax: 541-426-4578;
   David Frasch

Eugene/Springfield
KDUK-FM (104.7) Top 40 Hits
KFLY-FM (101.5) Mainstream Rock
KOOL-FM (99.1) Classic Hits
KPNW-AM (1120) News/Talk/Sports
   1500 Valley River Dr., Suite 350, Eugene
   97401; 541-284-3600; Fax: 541-484-5769;
   Larry Rogers

KEHK-FM (102.3) Bright Adult Contemporary
KNRQ-FM (103.7) Alternative Rock/Active Rock
KSCR-AM (1320) Business Talk Radio Network
KUGN-AM (590) News/Talk
KUJZ-FM (95.3) Sports/Talk
KZEL-FM (96.1) Quality/Classic Rock
   1200 Executive Pkwy., Suite 440, Eugene
   97401; 541-284-8500; Fax: 541-485-0969;
   B. J. O'Brien

KEQB-FM (97.7) Regional Mexican
KEUG-FM (105.5) Adult Hits
KKNU-FM (93.3) New Country
KMGE-FM (94.5) Adult Contemporary
   925 Country Club Rd., Suite 200, Eugene 97401;
   541-484-9400; Fax: 541-344-9424; John Tilson

KKNX-AM (840) Hits of the '60s through '80s,
   CBS News, OSU Sports
   1142 Willagillespie Rd. #28, Eugene 97401;
   541-342-1012; Fax: 541-342-6201; John Mielke

Florence
KCFM-AM/FM (1250/104.1) Adult Standards/
   Music of Your Life
KCST-FM (106.9) Adult Standards
   PO Box 20000, Florence 97439; 541-997-9136;
   Fax: 541-997-9165; Jon Thompson

Gold Beach
KGBR-FM (92.7) Hot Adult Contemporary
   PO Box 787, Gold Beach 97444-0787;
   541-247-7211; Fax: 541-247-4155;
   Diana St. Marie

Gold Hill
KRWQ-FM (100.3) Country
   (See complete listing in Medford)

Grants Pass
KAJO-AM/FM (1270/99.7) FullService/Talk/
AM Means Actual Music
   888 Rogue River Hwy., Grants Pass 97527;
   541-476-6608; Fax: 541-476-4018; Carl Wilson

KCMD-FM (99.3) Classical Hits
   820 NE Seventh St., Suite 1, Grants Pass
97526
   541-476-2137; Don Monette

KLDR-FM (98.3) Hot Modern Adult
   Contemporary
   888 Rogue River Hwy., Grants Pass 97527;
   541-474-7292; Fax: 541-474-7300; Carl Wilson

KROG-FM (97.1)

KRRM-FM (94.7) Classic Country
   225 Rogue River Hwy., Grants Pass 97527;
   541-479-6497; Fax: 541-479-5726; Herb Bell

Hermiston
KOHU-AM (1360) Country
KQFM-FM (93.7) Adult Contemporary
   PO Box 145, Hermiston 97838-0145;
   541-567-6500; Fax: 541-567-6068; Angela Pursel

Hood River
KCGB-FM (105.5/96.9) Adult Contemporary
KIHR-AM (1340/98.3) Country/Information
   1190 22nd St., Hood River 97031; 541-386-
1511; Fax: 541-386-7155; Gary Grossman

John Day
KJDY-AM/FM (1400/94.5) Country
   PO Box 399, John Day 97845; 541-575-1400;
   Fax: 541-575-2313; Kelly Workman

Klamath Falls
KAGO-AM (1150) News/Talk
KAGO-FM (99.5) Rock
KHIC-FM (98.5) Top 40
KLAD-AM (960) Sports
KLAD-FM (92.5) Country
   404 Main St., Suite 4, Klamath Falls 97601;
   541-882-8833; Fax: 541-882-8836; Rob Siems

KFEG-FM (104.7) Classic Rock
KFLS-AM (1450) News/Talk/Sports
KFLS-FM (96.5) Country
KKKJ-FM (105.5) Contemporary Hit Radio
KKRB-FM (106.9) Adult Contemporary
KRJW-AM (1240) Sports
   1338 Oregon Ave., Klamath Falls 97601;
   541-882-4656; Fax: 541-884-2845;
   Robert Wynne

La Grande
KLBM-AM (1450)
KUBQ-FM (98.7)
KVBL-FM (103.1) News/Talk
   1009-C Adams Ave., La Grande 97850;
   541-963-3406; Fax: 541-963-5091;
   Randy McKone

Media Directories

KWRL-FM (99.9) Adult Contemporary
1009-C Adams Ave., La Grande 97850;
541-963-3405; Fax: 541-963-5090;
Randy McKone

Lakeview

KLCR-FM (95.3) Adult Contemporary
PO Box 1017, Lakeview 97630;
541-947-3325; Woodrow Michael Warren

KORV-FM (93.5) Real Country
629 Center St., Lakeview 97630;
541-417-0149; Marcie Wade

Lebanon

KGAL-AM (1580) News/Talk/Sports
KSHO-AM (920) Adult Standards
PO Box 749, Albany 97321; 541-451-5425;
Fax: 541-451-5429; Charlie Eads

Lincoln City

KBCH-AM (1400) Adult Standards/Talk/Sports
KCRF-FM (96.7) Classic Rock
PO Box 1430, Newport 97365; 541-265-2266;
Fax: 541-265-6397; Dave Miller

McMinnville

KLYC-AM (1260)

Medford/Ashland/Phoenix

KAKT-FM (105.1) Country
KBOY-FM (95.7) Classic Rock
KCMX-AM (880) News/Talk
KCMX-FM (101.9) Adult Contemporary
KTMT-AM (580) ESPN Sports
KTMT-FM (93.7) Hit Adult Contemporary
1438 Rossanley Dr., Medford 97501;
541-779-1550; Fax: 541-776-2360; Joe Mussio

KDOV-FM (91.7) News/Talk/Christian
2070 Milligan Way, Medford 97504;
541-776-5368; Fax: 541-842-4334;
Perry Atkinson

KIFS-FM (107.5) Mainstream Contemporary
Hit Radio
KLDZ-FM (103.5) Classic Hits
KMED-AM (1440) Talk
KRWQ-FM (100.3) Country
3624 Avion Dr., Medford 97504; 541-772-4170;
Fax: 541-857-0326; Mike Wilson

KLVB-AM (730)

KRTA-AM (610)

Monmouth

KSND-FM (95.1) Spanish Language International
Romantica/Oldies
(See complete listing in Woodburn)

Newport

KCUP-AM (1230) News/Talk
KPPT-FM (100.7) Hits of '60s, '70s and Beyond

PO Box 456, Newport 97365; 541-265-5000;
Fax: 541-265-9576; Cheryl Harle

KNCU-FM (92.7) U92 Country
KNPT-AM (1310/98.3 translator) News/Talk/
Sports
KYTE-FM (102.7) Adult Contemporary
PO Box 1430, Newport 97365; 541-265-2266;
Fax: 541-265-6397; Dave Miller

KSHL-FM (97.5) Country
PO Box 1180, Newport 97365; 541-265-3000;
Fax: 541-265-6478; Dick Linn

Ontario

KSRV-AM (1380) Oldies
1725 N Oregon St., Ontario 97914;
541-889-8651; Fax: 541-889-8733;
Jack Armstrong

KSRV-FM (96.1) Adult Hits
5660 Franklin Rd., Suite 200, Nampa, ID 83687
208-465-9966; Fax: 208-465-2922;
Darrell Calton

Pendleton

KTIX-AM (1240) Sports
KUMA-AM (1290) News/Talk
KUMA-FM (92.1) Adult Contemporary
2003 NW 56th Dr., Pendleton 97801;
541-276-1511; Fax: 541-276-1480; David Capps

KWHT-FM (103.5) Country
KWVN-FM (107.7) Variety
13 1/2 E Main St., Suite 202, Walla Walla, WA
99362; 509-522-1383; Fax: 509-522-0211;
David Capps

Port Orford

KDPO-FM (91.9) News/Talk/Christian
2070 Milligan Way, Medford 97504;
541-776-5368; Fax: 541-842-4334;
Perry Atkinson

Portland Area

KBFF-FM (95.5) Adult Contemporary
KINK-FM (101.9) Adult Album Alternative
KUFO-AM (970) Talk
KUPL-FM (98.7) Country
KWLZ-FM (96.3) Hip Hop
KXL-FM (101.1) News/Talk/Sports
KXTG-AM (750) Sports
1211 SW Fifth Ave., Suite 600, Portland 97204;
503-517-6000; Fax: 503-517-6401;
Milt McConnell

KBMS-AM (1480)

KBNP-AM (1410)

KDZR-AM (1640)

KEX-AM (1190) News/Talk
KPOJ-AM (620) Sports Talk
KFBW-FM (105.9) Classic Rock
KKCW-FM (103.3) Adult Contemporary

KKRZ-FM (100.3) Hot Adult Contemporary
KKRZ-HD2 (102.3) Alternative Rock
KLTH-FM (106.7) Classic Hits
KXJM-FM (107.5) Contemporary Hits
    13333 SW 68th Pkwy., Suite 310, Tigard 97223;
    503-323-6400; Fax: 503-323-6664;Robert Dove

KFXX-AM (1080) Sports Talk
KGON-FM (92.3) Classic Rock
KMTT-AM (910) Sports Talk
KNRK-FM (94.7) Alternative Rock
KRSK-FM (105.1) Hot Adult Contemporary
KWJJ-FM (99.5) Country
KYCH-FM (97.1) Variety Hits
    0700 SW Bancroft St., Portland 97239;
    503-223-1441; Fax: 503-223-6909;
    Tim McNamara

KGDD-AM/FM (1150/93.5) Regional Mexican
    5110 SE Stark St., Portland 97215;
    503-233-5284; Fax: 503-234-5583;
    Amador Bustos

KKOV-AM (1550) American Standards
KPAM-AM (860) News/Talk
    6605 SE Lake Rd., Portland 97222-2161;
    503-223-4321; Fax: 503-294-0074;
    Jeanne Winter

KKPZ-AM (1330)

KKSL-AM (1290)

KLVP-AM (1040)

KLVP-FM (88.7)

KOOR-AM (1010) Russian Radio 7
KQRR-AM (1520) Russian Religious
KRYN-AM (1230) Spanish Christian Music
KXET-AM (1130) Russian Religious
KZZR-FM (94.3) Regional Mexican
    5110 SE Stark St., Portland 97215;
    503-234-5550; Fax: 503-234-5583;
    Amador Bustos

KPDQ-AM (800)

KPDQ-FM (93.7)

KUIK-AM (1360) News/Talk/Sports
    PO Box 566, Hillsboro 97123; 503-640-1360;
    Fax: 503-640-6108; Don McCoun

Redmond
KRDM-AM (1240)

Reedsport
KDUN-AM (1030)

KJMX-FM (99.5) Classic Rock
    PO Box 180, Coos Bay 97420; 541-267-2121;
    Fax: 541-267-5129; Philip Jimenez

Roseburg
KKMX-FM (104.3) Adult Contemporary Rock
KQEN-AM (1240) News/Talk
KRSB-FM (103.1) Contemporary Country
KSKR-AM (1490) Sports

KSKR-FM (101.1) Top 40
    1445 W Harvard Blvd., Roseburg 97471;
    541-672-6641; Fax: 541-673-7598; Pat Markham

Saint Helens
KOHI-AM (1600) News/Talk/Sports
    36200 Pittsburg Rd., Suite C, Saint Helens 97051;
    503-397-1600; Fax: 503-397-1601; Marty Rowe

Salem
KBZY-AM (1490)

KYKN-AM (1430) Talk
    PO Box 1430, Salem 97308; 503-390-3014;
    Fax: 503-390-3728; Mike Frith

Scappoose
KFIS-FM (104.1)

Seaside
(see complete listing under Astoria)
KSWB-AM (840) Seaside Sports
    PO Box 682, Seaside 97138; 503-717-5533;
    Fax: 503-717-5550; John Chapman

Stayton
KCKX-AM (1460) ESPN Sports
    PO Box 158, Woodburn 97071; 503-769-1460;
    Fax: 503-981-3561; Donald Coss

Sweet Home
KFIR-AM (720) News/Talk
    PO Box 720, Sweet Home 97386;
    541-367-5115; Fax: 541-367-5233; Michael
Astalis

The Dalles
KACI-AM (1300/103.9) News/Talk
KACI-FM (93.5) Classic Hits
KMSW-FM (92.7) Rock Classics
    PO Box 1517, The Dalles 97058; 541-296-2211;
    Fax: 541-296-2213; Gary Grossman

KLCK-AM (1400) Talk
KRSX-FM (95.9) Adult Contemporary
KYYT-FM (102.3) Contemporary Country
    PO Box 1023, The Dalles 97058; 541-296-9102;
    Shannon Milburn

KODL-AM/FM (1440/99.1) Adult Standards
    PO Box 1488, The Dalles 97058; 541-296-2101;
    Fax: 541-296-3766; Al Wynn

Tillamook
KDEP-FM (105.5) Adult Contemporary
KTIL-AM (1590) Oldies
KTIL-FM (95.9) Mainstream Country
    170 Third St. W, Tillamook 97141;
    503-842-4422; Shaena Peterson

Waldport
KWDP-AM (820) Adult Standards/Sports
    PO Box 1430, Newport 97365; 541-265-2266;
    Fax: 541-265-6397; Dave Miller

Media Directories

Walla Walla, WA

KTEL-AM (1490/100.1) News/Talk
13 1/2 E Main St., Suite 202, Walla Walla, WA
99362; 509-522-1383; 509-522-0211;
David Capps

Woodburn

KSND-FM (95.1) Spanish Language
International Romantica/Oldies

KWBY-AM (940) Spanish Language Music
Regional Mexican/News/Sports
PO Box 158, Woodburn 97071; 503-981-9400;
Fax: 503-981-3561; Donald Coss

Oregon Association of Broadcasters (OAB)

Contact: Bill Johnstone, President/CEO
Address: 9020 SW Washington Square Rd.,
Suite 140, Portland 97223
Phone: 503-443-2299
Fax: 503-443-2488
Web: www.theoab.org

OREGON COMMERCIAL TELEVISION STATIONS

Bend

KBNZ-LD (7) CBS

KOHD-TV (51) ABC
63090 Sherman Rd., Bend 97701;
541-749-5151; Fax: 866-996-3232; Julie Brinks;
Web: http://zolomedia.com

KFXO-LP (39) Fox
62990 O. B. Riley Rd., Bend 97701;
541-382-2121; Fax: 541-382-1616; Bob Singer;
Web: www.ktvz.com/kfxo

KTVZ-TV (21) NBC
62990 O. B. Riley Rd., Bend 97703;
541-383-2121; Fax: 541-382-1616;
Bob Singer; Web: www.ktvz.com

Coos Bay/North Bend

KCBY-TV (11) CBS
3451 Broadway, North Bend 97459; 541-269-
1111; Fax: 541-269-7464; Renard Maiuri;
Web: www.kcby.com

Eugene

KEVU-TV (23) My Network TV
2940 Chad Dr., Eugene 97408; 541-683-3434;
Fax: 541-683-8016; Mark Metzger;
Web: www.kevutv.com

KEZI-TV (9) ABC
PO Box 7009, Eugene 97475; 541-485-5611;
Fax: 541-686-8004; Michael Boring;
Web: www.kezi.com
Sub-channel: KEZI.9+ (9.2) News

KLSR-TV (34) Fox
2940 Chad Dr., Eugene 97408; 541-683-3434;
Fax: 541-683-8016; Mark Metzger;
Web: www.OregonsFOX.com

KMTR-TV (16) NBC
3825 International Ct., Springfield 97477;
541-746-1600; Fax: 541-747-0866;
Greg Raschio; Web: www.kmtr.com
Sub-channel: NMTR (16.2) CW

KVAL-TV (13) CBS
4575 Blanton Rd., Eugene 97405; 541-342-
4961; Fax: 541-342-2635; J.R. Jackson;
Web: www.kval.com
Sub-channel: KVAL 2 (13.2) This TV

Klamath Falls

KDKF-TV (31) ABC
PO Box 4220, Medford 97501; 541-773-1212;
Fax: 541-779-9261; Mark Hatfield;
Web: www.kdrv.com

KOTI-TV (2) NBC
PO Box 2K, Klamath Falls 97601;
541-882-2222; Fax: 541-883-7664; Bob Wise

Medford

KDOV-LP (44) Independent—Faith and Family
2070 Milligan Way, Medford 97504;
541-776-5368; Fax: 541-842-4334;
Perry Atkinson; Web: www.TheDove.us

KDRV-TV (12) ABC
PO Box 4220, Medford 97501; 541-773-1212;
Fax: 541-779-9261; Mark Hatfield;
Web: www.kdrv.com
Sub-channel: KDRV.2 (12.2) Live Well Network

KFBI-TV (48) MyTV48 (See KMVU-DT)

KMCW-TV (14 and KFBI.2) Telemundo
Medford (See KMVU-DT)

KMVU-DT (26) Fox
820 Crater Lake Ave., #105, Medford 97504;
541-772-2600; Dave Olmsted
Sub-channel: KMVU-D2 (26.2) MeTV

KOBI-TV (5) NBC
PO Box 1489, Medford 97501; 541-779-5555;
Fax: 541-779-5564; Bob Wise;
Web: www.kobi5.com

KTVL-TV (10) CBS
1440 Rossanley Dr., Medford 97501;
541-773-7373; Fax: 541-779-0451;
Kingsley Kelley; Web: www.ktvl.com

Portland

KATU-TV (2) ABC
2153 NE Sandy Blvd., Portland 97232;
503-231-4222; Fax: 503-231-4233;
John Tamerlano; Web: www.katu.com

KGW-TV (8) NBC
1501 SW Jefferson St., Portland 97201;
503-226-5000; Fax: 503-226-5158; DJ Wilson;
Web: www.kgw.com
Sub-channels:
MGW (8.2) Live Well Network
NGW (8.3) Estrella TV

KOIN-TV (6) CBS
222 SW Columbia St., Suite 102, Portland
97201-6601; 503-464-0600; Fax: 503-464-0717;
Web: www.koin.com

KPDX-TV (49) My Network TV
14975 NW Greenbrier Pkwy., Beaverton 97006;
503-906-1249; Fax: 503-548-6915;
Patrick McCreery; Web: www.kpdx.com

KPTV-TV (12) Fox
14975 NW Greenbrier Pkwy., Beaverton 97006;
503-906-1249; Fax: 503-548-6915;
Patrick McCreery; Web: www.kptv.com

KRCW-TV (32) CW
10255 SW Arctic Dr., Beaverton 97005;
503-644-3232; Fax: 503-626-3576;
Pam Pearson; Web: www.portlandscw32.com

Roseburg

KPIC-TV (4) CBS
655 W. Umpqua St., Roseburg 97471;
541-672-4481; Fax: 541-672-4482;
Renard Maiuri; Web: www.kpic.com

KTCW-TV (22) NBC
655 W. Umpqua St., Roseburg 97471;
541-746-1600; Fax: 541-747-4482;
Andrew Pitts; Web: www.kmtr.com
Sub-channel: NTCW (46.2) CW

Salem

KPWC-TV (37)

KPXG-TV (22) ION Media Networks
432 NE 74th Ave., Portland 97213;
503-222-2221; Fax: 503-222-4613;
Mary Pierce

KSLM-TV (27)

KWVT-TV (17.1 Eugene to Wilsonville/17.2
Wilsonville to Longview, WA) Independent
17980 Brown Rd., Dallas 97338; 503-930-7228;
Ken Lewetag; Web: http://kwvtsalem.com

The Dalles

KRHP-LD (14) Christian/Family Programming
3350 Columbia View Dr., The Dalles 97058;
541-296-2711; Fax: 541-296-6158; Bob Pettitt
Sub-channels:
KRHP-LD (14.2) National Association of
Religious Broadcasters TV
KRHP-LD (14.3) E/I Children's TV
KRHP-LD (14.4) JCTV (ages 13–35)

Oregon Association of Broadcasters (OAB)

Contact: Bill Johnstone, President/CEO
Address: 9020 SW Washington Square Rd.,
Suite 140, Portland 97223
Phone: 503-443-2299
Fax: 503-443-2488
Web: www.theoab.org

OREGON PUBLIC/ EDUCATIONAL RADIO AND TELEVISION STATIONS

Ashland

KSMF-FM (89.1)
KSOR-FM (90.1)
KSRG-FM (88.3)
Southern Oregon University, 1250 Siskiyou
Blvd., Ashland 97520; 541-552-6301;
Fax: 541-552-8565; Paul Westhelle;
Web: http://ijpr.org

Astoria

KMUN-FM (91.9)
KTCB-FM (89.5 Tillamook)
PO Box 269, Astoria 97103; 503-325-0010;
Joanne Rideout; Web: http://coastradio.org

Bend

KLBR-FM (88.1)
Lane Community College, 4000 E 30th Ave.,
Eugene 97405; 541-463-6000;
Fax: 541-463-6046; John Stark;
Web: http://klcc.org

KOPB-FM (91.5)
KOAB-TV (10.1–10.2)
7140 SW Macadam Ave., Portland 97219;
503-244-9900; Steven M. Bass, OPB President;
Web: www.opb.org

Canyonville

KWRZ-FM (92.3)
University of Oregon, 75 Centennial Loop,
Eugene 97401; 541-345-0800/800-422-4301;
Greg Raschio; Web: www.kwax.com

Coos Bay

KSBA-FM (88.5)
KZBY-FM (90.5)
Southern Oregon University, 1250 Siskiyou
Blvd., Ashland 97520; 541-552-6301;
Fax: 541-552-8565; Paul Westhelle;
Web: http://ijpr.org

Corvallis

KBVR-FM (88.7)
KBVR-TV (26)

Media Directories

Oregon State University Orange Media Network, 2251 SW Jefferson Way, Corvallis 97331; 541-737-6323; Radio: Anthony Heatherly, TV: Luke Van Hoomissen

KOAC-AM (550)
KOAC-FM (103.1)
KOAC-TV (7)
7140 SW Macadam Ave., Portland 97219; 503-244-9900; Steven M. Bass, OPB President; Web: www.opb.org

Enterprise

KETP-FM (88.7)
7140 SW Macadam Ave., Portland 97219; 503-244-9900; Steven M. Bass, OPB President; Web: www.opb.org

Eugene

KEPB-TV (28)
7140 SW Macadam Ave., Portland 97219; 503-244-9900; Steven M. Bass, OPB President; Web: www.opb.org

KLCC-FM (89.7)
Lane Community College, 4000 E 30th Ave., Eugene 97405; 541-463-6000; Fax: 541-463-6046; John Stark; Web: http://klcc.org

KMME-FM (94.9/100.5)
PO Box 5888, Portland 97228; 503-285-5200; Fax: 503-285-3322; Patrick Ryan

KRVM-AM (1280)
Southern Oregon University, 1250 Siskiyou Blvd., Ashland 97520; 541-552-6301; Fax: 541-552-8565; Paul Westhelle; Web: http://ijpr.org

KRVM-FM (91.9)
Eugene Public School District 4J, 1574 Coburg Rd., #237, Eugene 97401; 541-790-6686; Fax: 541-790-6688; Billy Safier; Web: www.krvm.org

KWAX-FM (91.1)
University of Oregon, 75 Centennial Loop, Eugene 97401; 541-345-0800/800-422-4301; Paul Bjornstad; Web: www.kwax.com

Florence

K211BP (90.1)
Eugene Public School District 4J, 1574 Coburg Rd., #237, Eugene 97401; 541-790-6686; Fax: 541-790-6688; Billy Safier; Web: www.krvm.org

KLFO-FM (88.1)
Lane Community College, 4000 E 30th Ave., Eugene 97405; 541-463-6000; Fax: 541-463-6046; John Stark; Web: http://klcc.org/

Gleneden Beach

KOGL-FM (89.3)
7140 SW Macadam Ave., Portland 97219; 503-244-9900; Steven M. Bass, OPB President; Web: www.opb.org

Grants Pass

KAGI-AM (930)
Southern Oregon University, 1250 Siskiyou Blvd., Ashland 97520; 541-552-6301; Paul Westhelle; Web: http://ijpr.org

Gresham

KMHD-FM (89.1)
7140 SW Macadam Ave., Portland 97219; 503-244-9900; Steven M. Bass, OPB President; Web: www.opb.org

Hood River

KHRV-FM (90.1)
7140 SW Macadam Ave., Portland 97219; 503-244-9900; Steven M. Bass, OPB President; Web: www.opb.org

John Day

KOJD-FM (89.7)
7140 SW Macadam Ave., Portland 97219; 503-244-9900; Steven M. Bass, OPB President; Web: www.opb.org

Klamath Falls

KFTS-TV (22)
SOPTV, 34 S Fir St., Suite 200, Medford 97501; 541-779-0808; Fax: 541-779-2178; Mark Stanislawski

KLMF-FM (88.5)
KSKF-FM (90.9)
Southern Oregon University, 1250 Siskiyou Blvd., Ashland 97520; 541-552-6301; Paul Westhelle; Web: http://ijpr.org

KTEC-FM (89.5)
Oregon Institute of Technology, 3201 Campus Dr., Klamath Falls 97601; 541-937-5832; Nick Baer; Web: www.ktec895.com

La Grande

KEOL-FM (91.7)
Eastern Oregon University, One University Blvd., La Grande 97850; 541-962-3698; Nick Creson; Web: www.eou.edu/keol

KTVR-FM (90.3)
KTVR-TV (13)
7140 SW Macadam Ave., Portland 97219; 503-244-9900; Steven M. Bass, OPB President; Web: www.opb.org

Lakeview

KOAP-FM (88.7)
7140 SW Macadam Ave., Portland 97219; 503-244-9900; Steven M. Bass, OPB President; Web: www.opb.org

McMinnville

KSLC-FM (90.3)
Linfield College, #A498, 900 SE Baker St., McMinnville 97128; 503-883-2550; Dr. Michael Huntsberger

Medford

KSYS-TV (8)
SOPTV, 34 S Fir St., Suite 200, Medford 97501; 541-779-0808; Fax: 541-779-2178; Mark Stanislawski

Mendocino, CA

KPMO-AM (1300)
Southern Oregon University, 1250 Siskiyou Blvd., Ashland 97520; 541-552-6301; Paul Westhelle; Web: http://ijpr.org

Mt. Shasta, CA

KLDD-FM (91.9)
KMJC-AM (620)
KNSQ-FM (88.1)
Southern Oregon University, 1250 Siskiyou Blvd., Ashland 97520; 541-552-6301; Paul Westhelle; Web: http://ijpr.org

Myrtle Point

KOOZ-FM (94.1)
Southern Oregon University, 1250 Siskiyou Blvd., Ashland 97520; 541-552-6301; Paul Westhelle; Web: http://ijpr.org

Newport

KLCO-FM (90.5)
Lane Community College, 4000 E 30th Ave., Eugene 97405; 541-463-6000; Fax: 541-463-6046; John Stark; Web: http://klcc.org

Oakridge

KAVE-FM (88.5)
Eugene School District 4J, 1574 Coburg Rd., #237, Eugene 97401; 541-687-3370; Fax: 541-687-3573; Cambra Ward

Pendleton

KRBM-FM (90.9)
7140 SW Macadam Ave., Portland 97219; 503-244-9900; Steven M. Bass, OPB President; Web: www.opb.org

Portland

KBOO-FM (90.7)
20 SE Eighth Ave., Portland 97214; 503-231-8032; Fax: 503-231-7145; Monica Beemer; Web: www.kboo.fm

KBPS-AM (1450)
Benson Polytechnic High School, 515 NE 15th Ave., Portland 97232; 503-916-5828; Kevin Flink

KBVM-FM (88.3)
PO Box 5888, Portland 97228; 503-285-5200; Fax: 503-285-3322; Patrick Ryan

KDUP-AM (1580)
University of Portland Communications Dept., 5000 N Willamette Blvd., Portland 97203; 503-943-7284; Brian Blair

KOPB-FM (91.5);
KOPB-TV (10)
Oregon Public Broadcasting, 7140 SW Macadam Ave., Portland 97219; 503-244-9900; Fax: 503-293-4165; Steven M. Bass, OPB President; Web: www.opb.org

KQAC-FM (89.9)
211 SW Caruthers, Portland 97212; 503-943-5828: Jack Allen; Web: www.allclassical.org

Redding/Burney/Shasta Lake City, CA

KJPR-AM (1330)
KNCA-FM (89.7)
Southern Oregon University, 1250 Siskiyou Blvd., Ashland 97520; 541-552-6301; Fax: 541-552-8565; Paul Westhelle; Web: http://ijpr.org

Reedsport

KLFR-FM (89.1)
Lane Community College, 4000 E 30th Ave., Eugene 97405; 541-463-6000; Fax: 541-463-6046; John Stark; Web: http://klcc.org

KSYD-FM (92.1)
Eugene School District 4J, 1574 Coburg Rd., #237, Eugene 97401; 541-687-3370; Fax: 541-687-3573; Cambra Ward

Rio Dell/Eureka, CA

KNHM-FM (91.5)
KNHT-FM (107.3)
Southern Oregon University, 1250 Siskiyou Blvd., Ashland 97520; 541-552-6301; Fax: 541-552-8565; Paul Westhelle; Web: http://ijpr.org

Roseburg

KMPQ-FM (88.1)
Lane Community College, 4000 E 30th Ave., Eugene 97405; 541-463-6000; Fax: 541-463-6046; John Stark; Web: http://klcc.org

KSRS-FM (91.5)
KTBR-AM (950)
Southern Oregon University, 1250 Siskiyou Blvd., Ashland 97520; 541-552-6301; Paul Westhelle; Web: http://ijpr.org

Media Directories

Talent

KSJK-AM (1230)
 Southern Oregon University, 1250 Siskiyou
 Blvd., Ashland 97520; 541-552-6301;
 Paul Westhelle; Web: http://ijpr.org

The Dalles

KOTD-FM (89.7)
 7140 SW Macadam Ave., Portland 97219;
 503-244-9900; Steven M. Bass, OPB President;
 Web: www.opb.org

Tillamook

KTMK-FM (91.1)
 7140 SW Macadam Ave., Portland 97219;
 503-244-9900; Steven M. Bass, OPB President;
 Web: www.opb.org

Warm Springs

KWSO-FM (91.9)

PO Box 489, Warm Springs 97761;
 541-553-1968; Fax: 541-553-3348;
 Sue Matters

Yreka, CA

KNYR-FM (91.3);
KSYC-AM (1490)
 Southern Oregon University, 1250 Siskiyou
 Blvd., Ashland 97520; 541-552-6301;
 Paul Westhelle; Web: http://ijpr.org

Oregon Association of Broadcasters (OAB)

Contact: Bill Johnstone, President/CEO
Address: 9020 SW Washington Square Rd.,
 Suite 140, Portland 97223
Phone: 503-443-2299
Fax: 503-443-2488
Web: www.theoab.org

The Murray Family rides toward Mount Hood during a 1970 Pacific Crest Trail horse packing adventure.
Photo courtesy Barry G. Murray

The citizens of the United States, through our federal government, own more than half the land in Oregon. Oregon's position on the Pacific Rim has resulted in strong ties between Oregon and other nations. Oregon has nine federally recognized tribes, who have distinct relationships with state government. This section contains information about the federal government, representatives of other nations, and tribes in Oregon.

Jeff Merkley

Democrat. Born in Myrtle Creek, October 24, 1956. Stanford University, B.A., 1979; master's degree in Public Policy from Woodrow Wilson School at Princeton University, 1982. He was Executive Director of Portland Habitat for Humanity before serving as President of the World Affairs Council of Oregon for seven years, where he continues to serve on the Board of Trustees. He and his wife Mary have two children.

Elected to the Oregon House of Representatives, 1999; became speaker of the House in 2007. Elected to the U.S. Senate, 2008; reelected 2014.

Committee member: Appropriations; Budget; Environment and Public Works; Foreign Relations. Term expires 2021.

Washington, D.C., Office: 313 Hart Senate Office Bldg., Washington, D.C. 20510; 202-224-3753; Fax: 202-228-3997; Web and email: www.merkley.senate.gov

District Offices: Bend: 131 NW Hawthorne Ave., Suite 208, Bend 97701; 541-318-1298

Eugene: 405 E Eighth Ave., Suite 2010, Eugene 97401; 541-465-6750

Medford: 10 S Bartlett St., Suite 201, Medford 97501; 541-608-9102

Pendleton: 310 SE Second St., Suite 105, Pendleton 97801; 541-278-1129

Portland: One World Trade Center, 121 SW Salmon St., Suite 1400, Portland 97204; 503-326-3386; Fax: 503-326-2900

Salem: 495 State St., Suite 330, Salem 97301; 503-362-8102

Ron Wyden

Democrat. Born in Wichita, Kansas, May 3, 1949. Stanford University, A.B. in Political Science, 1971; University of Oregon School of Law, J.D., 1974. Co-director, Oregon Gray Panthers, 1974–1980; director, Oregon Legal Services for the Elderly, 1977–1979; public member, Oregon Board of Examiners of Nursing Home Administrators, 1978–1979.

Elected to the U.S. House of Representatives, 1980; reelected 1982, 1984, 1986, 1988, 1990, 1992 and 1994. Elected to the U.S. Senate, 1996; reelected 1998, 2004, 2010 and 2016.

Ranking member of Finance Committee; Committee member: Budget; Energy and Natural Resources; Select Committee on Intelligence; Joint Committee on Taxation. Term expires 2023.

Washington, D.C., Office: 221 Dirksen Senate Office Bldg., Washington, D.C. 20510-3703; 202-224-5244; Fax: 202-228-2717; Web and email: www.wyden.senate.gov

District Offices: Bend: Jamison Bldg., 131 NW Hawthorne Ave., Suite 107, Bend 97701; 541-330-9142; Fax: 541-330-6266

Eugene: Wayne Morse Federal Courthouse, 405 E Eighth Ave., Suite 2020, Eugene 97401; 541-431-0229; Fax: 541-431-0610

La Grande: Sac Annex Bldg., 105 Fir St., Suite 201, La Grande 97850; 541-962-7691; Fax: 541-963-0885

Medford: The Federal Courthouse, 310 W Sixth St., Rm. 118, Medford 97501; 541-858-5122; Fax: 541-858-5126

Portland: 911 NE 11th Ave., Suite 630, Portland 97232; 503-326-7525; Fax: 503-326-7528

Salem: 707 13th St. SE, Suite 285, Salem 97301; 503-589-4555; Fax: 503-589-4749

U.S. Representatives

Suzanne Bonamici—First District

Counties: Clatsop, Columbia, Washington, Yamhill and part of Multnomah

Democrat. Born in Detroit, Michigan, October 14, 1954. University of Oregon, B.A., 1980; University of Oregon School of Law, J.D., 1983. Before going into private practice in Portland, she was a consumer protection attorney for the Federal Trade Commission in Washington, D.C. She and her husband Michael Simon have two children.

Elected to the Oregon House of Representatives, 2006. Appointed to the Oregon State Senate, 2008; elected 2008; reelected 2010. Elected to the U.S. House of Representatives, 2012; reelected 2014 and 2016.

Committee member: Education and the Workforce; and Science, Space and Technology. Term expires 2019.

Washington, D.C., Office: 439 Cannon House Office Bldg., Washington, D.C. 20515; 202-225-0855; Fax: 202-225-9497; Web and email: https://bonamici.house.gov

District Office: 12725 SW Millikan Way, Suite 220, Beaverton 97005; 503-469-6010; Toll-free: 800-422-4003; Fax: 503-326-5066

Greg Walden—Second District

Counties: Baker, Crook, Deschutes, Gilliam, Grant, Harney, Hood River, Jackson, Jefferson, Grants Pass area of Josephine, Klamath, Lake, Malheur, Morrow, Sherman, Umatilla, Union, Wallowa, Wasco and Wheeler

Republican. Born January 10, 1957, in The Dalles, Oregon. University of Oregon, B.S. Owner, Columbia Gorge Broadcasters. Press Secretary and Chief of Staff, Congressman Denny Smith, 1981–1987. He and his wife Mylene have one child.

Elected to Oregon House of Representatives, 1988; served as House Majority Leader, 1991–1993; appointed to Oregon Senate, 1995; served as Assistant Majority Leader.

Elected to the U.S. House of Representatives, 1998; reelected 2000, 2002, 2004, 2006, 2008, 2010, 2012, 2014 and 2016.

Chair of the Energy and Commerce Committee. Term expires 2019.

Washington, D.C., Office: 2182 Rayburn House Office Bldg., Washington, D.C. 20515; 202-225-6730; Fax: 202-225-5774; Web and email: https://walden.house.gov

District Offices: Bend: Jamison Bldg., 1051 NW Bond St., Suite 400, Bend 97701; 541-389-4408; Fax: 541-389-4452

La Grande: 1211 Washington Ave., La Grande 97850; 541-624-2400; Fax: 541-624-2402

Medford: 14 N Central Ave., Suite 112, Medford 97501; 541-776-4646; Fax: 541-779-0204

National/International/Tribal

Earl Blumenauer—Third District

Counties: Most of Multnomah and the northern part of Clackamas

Democrat. Born in Portland, August 16, 1948. Attended Lewis & Clark College and Law School, and Harvard University's Kennedy School of Government. Received B.A. degree, political science, 1970; law degree, 1976.

Elected to Oregon House of Representatives, 1972; reelected 1974 and 1976. Elected to Multnomah County Board of Commissioners, 1978; reelected 1982. Elected to Portland City Council, 1986; reelected 1990 and 1994.

Elected to Congress, 1996; reelected 1998, 2000, 2002, 2004, 2006, 2008, 2010, 2012, 2014 and 2016.

Committee member: Budget; Ways and Means, and its Subcommittees on Health and Trade. Term expires 2019.

Washington, D.C., Office: 1111 Longworth House Office Bldg., Washington, D.C. 20515; 202-225-4811; Fax: 202-225-8941; Web and email: https://blumenauer.house.gov

District Office: 729 NE Oregon, Suite 115, Portland 97232; 503-231-2300; Fax: 503-230-5413

Peter DeFazio—Fourth District

Counties: Coos, Curry, Douglas, Lane, Linn and most of Benton and Josephine

Democrat. Born in Needham, Massachusetts, May 27, 1947. Tufts University, B.A., 1969; University of Oregon, M.A., 1977. Honorable discharge, U.S. Air Force Reserve, 1971. Aide to Congressman Jim Weaver, 1977–1982; elected to Lane County Board of Commissioners, 1982. He and his wife Myrnie L. Daut own a home and live in Springfield.

Elected to the U.S. House of Representatives, 1986; reelected 1988, 1990, 1992, 1994, 1996, 1998, 2000, 2002, 2004, 2006, 2008, 2010, 2012, 2014 and 2016. Ranking member of Transportation and Infrastructure. Term expires 2019.

Washington, D.C., Office: 2134 Rayburn House Office Bldg., Washington, D.C. 20515; 202-225-6416; Fax: 202-225-0032; Web and email: https://defazio.house.gov

District Offices: Coos Bay: 125 Central Ave., Rm. 350, Coos Bay 97420; 541-269-2609; Fax: 541-269-5760

Eugene: 405 E Eighth Ave., Suite 2030, Eugene 97401; 541-465-6732; Toll-free: 800-944-9603; Fax: 541-465-6458

Roseburg: 612 SE Jackson, Rm. 9, Roseburg 97470; 541-440-3523; Fax: 541-440-3525

U.S. REPRESENTATIVES

Kurt Schrader—Fifth District

Counties: Lincoln, Marion, Polk, Tillamook, parts of northern Benton, most of Clackamas and parts of southwestern Multnomah

Democrat. Born in Bridgeport, Connecticut, October 19, 1951. Cornell University, NY, B.A., 1973; University of Illinois, D.V.M., 1977. Owner, Clackamas County Veterinary Clinic. He has five grown children.

Elected to Oregon House of Representatives, 1996; served through 2002; elected to Oregon Senate, 2002; served through 2008.

Elected to the U.S. House of Representatives, 2008; reelected 2010, 2012, 2014 and 2016.

Committee member: Energy and Commerce Subcommittee on Health; Subcommittee on Environment and the Economy. Term expires 2019.

Washington, D.C., Office: 2431 Rayburn House Office Bldg., Washington, D.C. 20515; 202-225-5711; Fax: 202-225-5699;

Web and email: https://schrader.house.gov

District Offices: Oregon City: 621 High St., Oregon City 97045; 503-557-1324; Fax: 503-557-1981

Salem: 544 Ferry St. SE, Suite 2, Salem 97301; 503-588-9100; Toll Free: 877-301-KURT (5878); Fax: 503-588-5517

Congressional Districts

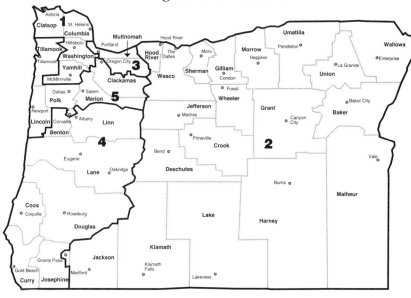

U.S. GOVERNMENT OFFICIALS

President of the United States
Donald J. Trump
Address: The White House, 1600 Pennsylvania Ave., Washington, D.C. 20500
Phone: 202-456-1414
Fax: 202-456-2461
Web: www.whitehouse.gov
Occupational Background: Real estate developer, television personality and beauty pageant owner
Educational Background: University of Pennsylvania Wharton School, bachelor's degree, 1968
Government Experience: None

Vice President of the United States
Michael R. Pence
Occupational Background: Governor, U.S. Representative, radio talk show host, attorney
Educational Background: Hanover College, bachelor's degree, 1981; Indiana University McKinney School of Law, law degree, 1986
Governmen Experience: U.S. House of Representatives 2001–2013; Indiana Governor, 2013–2016

Cabinet

Chief of Staff
Reince Priebus
Address: The White House, 1600 Pennsylvania Ave., Washington, D.C. 20500
Phone: 202-456-1414
Web: www.whitehouse.gov

Department of Agriculture
Thomas Vilsack, Secretary
Address: 1400 Independence Ave. SW, Washington, D.C. 20250
Phone: 202-720-2791
Web: www.usda.gov

Department of Commerce
Wilbur Ross, Secretary*
Address: 1401 Constitution Ave. NW, Washington, D.C. 20230
Phone: 202-482-2000
Web: www.commerce.gov

Department of Defense
James Mattis, Secretary
Address: 1000 Defense Pentagon, Washington, D.C. 20301-1000
Phone: 703-428-0711
Web: www.defense.gov

Department of Education
Betsy DeVos, Secretary*
Address: 400 Maryland Ave. SW, Washington, D.C. 20202
Phone: 202-401-3000
Web: www.ed.gov

Department of Energy
Rick Perry, Secretary*
Address: 1000 Independence Ave. SW, Washington, D.C. 20585
Phone: 800-DIAL-DOE (800-342-5363)
Web: www.energy.gov

Department of Health and Human Services
Tom Price, Secretary*
Address: 200 Independence Ave. SW, Washington, D.C. 20201
Phone: 877-696-6775
Web: www.hhs.gov

Department of Homeland Security
John F. Kelly, Secretary
Address: Washington, D.C. 20528
Phone: 202-282-8000
Web: www.dhs.gov

Department of Housing and Urban Development
Ben Carson, Secretary*
Address: 451 7th St. SW, Washington, D.C. 20410
Phone: 202-708-1112
Web: www.hud.gov

Department of Interior
Ryan Zinke, Secretary*
Address: 1849 C St. NW, Washington, D.C. 20240
Phone: 202-208-3100
Web: www.doi.gov

Department of Justice
Jeff Sessions, Attorney General*
Address: 950 Pennsylvania Ave. NW, Washington, D.C. 20530
Phone: 202-514-2000
Web: www.usdoj.gov

Department of Labor
Andrew Puzder, Secretary*
Address: Frances Perkins Bldg., 200 Constitution Ave. NW, Washington, D.C. 20210
Phone: 1-866-4-USA-DOL (866-487-2365)
Web: www.dol.gov

Department of State
Rex W. Tillerson, Secretary of State*
Address: 2201 C St. NW, Washington, D.C. 20520
Phone: 202-647-4000
Web: www.state.gov

Department of Transportation
Elaine Chao, Secretary*
Address: 1200 New Jersey Ave., Washington, D.C. 20590
Phone: 202-366-4000
Web: www.dot.gov

Department of the Treasury
Steven Mnuchin, Secretary*
Address: 1500 Pennsylvania Ave. NW, Washington, D.C. 20220
Phone: 202-622-2000
Web: www.treasury.gov

Department of Veterans Affairs
David Shulkin, Secretary*
Address: 810 Vermont Ave. NW, Washington, D.C. 20420
Phone: 1-800-827-1000
Web: www.va.gov

Environmental Protection Agency
Scott Pruitt, Administrator*
Address: 1200 Pennsylvania Ave. NW, Washington, D.C. 20460
Phone: 202-564-4700
Web: www.epa.gov

Office of Management and Budget
Mick Mulvaney, Director*
Address: 725 17th St. NW, Washington, D.C. 20503
Phone: 202-395-7254
Web: www.whitehouse.gov/omb

Small Business Administration
Linda McMahon, Administrator*
Address: 409 Third St. SW, Washington D.C. 20416
Phone: 800-827-5722
Web: https://www.sba.gov/

United Nations Ambassador
Nikki Haley, Ambassador
Address: 140 E 45th St., New York, NY 10017
Phone: 212-415-4000
Web: http://usun.state.gov

United States Trade Representative
Robert Lighthizer, Ambassador*
Address: 600 17th St. NW, Washington, D.C. 20508
Phone: 202-395-7360
Web: www.ustr.gov
*Presidential appointee, not yet confirmed by the Senate at press time

U.S. GOVERNMENT IN OREGON
For information about U.S. Government in Oregon, contact the Federal Citizen Information Center at 1-800-FED-INFO (1-800-333-4636), or go to: www.loc.gov/rr/news/fedgov.html.

U.S. DISTRICT COURTS
Main Office:
U.S. Courthouse
Address: 1000 SW Third Ave., Portland 97204

Eugene Divisional Office:
Wayne L. Morse U.S. Courthouse
Address: 405 E Eighth Ave., Suite 2100, Eugene 97401

Medford Divisional Office:
James A. Redden U.S. Courthouse
Address: 310 W Sixth St., Room 201, Medford 97501

Pendleton Divisional Office:
John F. Kilkenny U.S. Courthouse
Address: 104 SW Dorian Ave., Pendleton 97801

MAJOR POLITICAL PARTIES
Democratic National Committee
Address: 430 S Capitol St. SE, Washington, D.C. 20003
Phone: 202-863-8000
Web: www.democrats.org

Democratic State Central Committee of Oregon
Address: 232 NE Ninth Ave., Portland 97232-2915
Phone: 503-224-8200
Web: dpo.org

Independent Party of Oregon
Address: 9220 SW Barbur Blvd., Suite 119, Portland 97219
Phone: 503-687-1206
Web: www.indparty.com

Republican National Committee
Address: 310 First St. SE, Washington, D.C. 20003
Phone: 202-863-8500
Web: https://gop.com

Republican State Central Committee of Oregon
Address: 25375 SW Parkway Ave., #200, Wilsonville 97070
Phone: 503-595-8881
Web: https://oregon.gop

TRIBAL PEOPLES OF OREGON

Source: Legislative Commission on Indian Services
Contact: Karen Quigley, Executive Officer
Address: 900 Court St. NE, Rm. 167, Salem 97301
Phone: 503-986-1067
Fax: 503-986-1071
Web: www.oregonlegislature.gov/cis
Statutory Authority: ORS 172.100–172.140, 182.162–182.168

Oregon's total "American Indian" population, according to the 2010 U.S. Census, included 109,223 people as "American Indian or Alaskan Native". Oregon's "American Indians" live in all 36 counties and are about 3 percent of Oregon's total population. Fewer than 50 percent of Oregon's "American Indian" population are members of the nine federally recognized tribes in Oregon. Other "American Indians" who reside in Oregon are members of tribes in other states, descendants, individuals who "self-identify" as "American Indians" or tribal people from other regions.

Members of Oregon's nine federally recognized tribes speak of being in this area from time immemorial. Village sites and traditional ways are known to date back many thousands of years.

Tribal governments are separate and unique sovereign nations with powers to protect the health, safety and welfare of their enrolled members and to govern their lands. This tribal sovereignty predates the existence of the U.S. government and the state of Oregon. The members residing in Oregon are citizens of their tribes, citizens of Oregon and, since 1924, citizens of the United States of America.

The U.S. Department of the Interior, Bureau of Indian Affairs, oversees tribal interests and administers the federal government's trust obligations. At times, the federal government has been supportive of tribal self-determination and, in other periods, has adopted policies and passed legislation having a negative impact on the ability of tribes to govern as sovereigns. "Termination," one such policy in the 1950s, was an attempt to sever federal trusteeship and support for tribal sovereignty. Of the 109 tribes and bands terminated nationwide, 62 were in Oregon. In 1975, the federal government recognized the failure of its termination policy and passed the Indian Self Determination and Education Assistance Act and, later, the Tribal Self-Governance Act.

Several tribes began the process to restore their status as sovereign nations. In 1977, the Confederated Tribes of Siletz was the second tribe in the nation to achieve restoration. Following Siletz was the Cow Creek Band of the Umpqua Tribe of Indians in 1982, the Confederated Tribes of Grand Ronde in 1983, the Confederated Tribes of Coos, Lower Umpqua and Siuslaw in 1984, the Klamath Tribes in 1986 and the Coquille Indian Tribe in 1989.

Another three federally recognized tribal governments exist in Oregon: the Confederated Tribes of Warm Springs (Treaty of 1855), the Confederated Tribes of Umatilla (Treaty of 1855) and the Burns Paiute Tribe (1972 Executive Order). Fort McDermitt Paiute Shoshone Tribe is a federally-recognized tribe with reservation lands straddling Oregon and Nevada but the tribe's population center is in Nevada. Celilo Village is a federally-recognized tribal entity near The Dalles, jointly administered by the Confederated Tribes of Warm Springs, the Confederated Tribes of Umatilla and the Yakama Indian Nation (Washington).

All Oregon tribal governments have reservation or trust lands created by treaties, statutes or executive branch actions. Tribal governments have regulatory authority over these lands. Tribal governments have been removed by Congress. Nearly 904,000 acres, or at least 1.6 percent of land within Oregon's boundaries, are held in trust by the federal government or are designated reservation lands. Tribal governments have the authority to decide their own membership qualifications and have a right to exclude individuals from their reservations. Just as Oregon does not collect tax on federal lands nor tax federal or local governments or non-profit corporations, Oregon does not tax tribal governments, but all tribal members as individual citizens pay federal taxes and most pay state taxes, with the exception of those who live and work on a reservation or earn money on reservation or trust lands or from trust resources.

Public Law 280 gave the state certain civil and criminal jurisdiction over tribes, with the exception of the Confederated Tribes of Warm Springs, the Confederated Tribes of Umatilla and the Burns Paiute Tribe, which are "non Public Law 280" tribes. Notwithstanding Public Law 280, all Oregon tribes have the authority to elect their own governments and adopt laws and ordinances. Oregon tribal governments have their own departments dealing with governmental services, including law enforcement and tribal court systems. In addition, each tribal government operates programs in the areas of natural resources, cultural resources, education, health and human services, public safety, housing, economic development and other areas to serve their members. Oregon maintains a government-to-government relationship with the tribal governments as directed in ORS 182.162 to 182.168.

Passage of the National Indian Gaming Regulatory Act in 1988 created the opportunity to build gaming centers on reservation and trust lands. Besides providing employment opportunities for tribal members and citizens of surrounding communities, revenues from these tribal enterprises fund health clinics, education, scholarships, housing and other services. All Oregon tribal governments are striving to diversify their revenue streams and are actively pursuing other avenues for generating revenue. These gaming and other enterprises have made these tribal governments some of the largest employers in their counties—generating employment for tax-paying employees, benefiting local communities and the entire state.

Most Oregon tribes are "confederations" of three or more tribes and bands. Each tribe's area of interest may extend far beyond its tribal governmental center or reservation location.

Burns Paiute Tribe

Address: 100 Pasigo St., Burns 97720
Phone: 541-573-2088
Email: dlteeman.burnspaiute@gmail.com
Web: www.burnspaiute-nsn.gov
Restoration: by Executive Order, October 13, 1972
Number of Members: 349
Land Base Acreage: 13,736 acres
Number of people employed by the Tribe: 54

Economy: The Old Camp Casino and RV Park

Points of Interest: Steens Mountain recreational area; Malheur National Wildlife Refuge; Reservation Day Powwow occurs two days each fall about October 13; annual Mother's Day Powwow

History and Culture: The Burns Paiute Reservation is located north of Burns in Harney County. Today's tribal members are primarily the descendants of the "Wadatika" band of Paiutes of central and southern Oregon. The Wadatika, named for the wada seeds collected near Malheur Lake shores, lived on seeds, berries, roots and vegetation they gathered and wild animals they hunted. Their territory included the area from the Cascade Mountains to Boise, Idaho, and the Blue Mountains to Steens Mountain. Paiute legends say that the Paiutes have lived in this area since before the Cascade Mountains were formed, coming from the south as part of a migration through the Great Basin. People of the Burns Paiute Tribe were basket makers who used fibers of willow, sagebrush, tule plant and Indian hemp to weave baskets, sandals, fishing nets and traps. Archeologists have found clothing made from animal and bird hides, and sandals made from sagebrush fibers believed to be close to 10,000 years old. The tribe continues to hunt, gather food and do beadwork and drum-making in traditional ways.

Tribal Court: Tribal Judge Christie Timko; Associate Judge Patricia Davis, 100 Pasigo St., Burns 97720; 541-573-2793

Tribal Council 2016–2017: Chairperson Joe DeLaRosa, Vice-Chair Dean Adams, Secretary Tracy Kennedy, Sergeant at Arms Jarvis Kennedy, Members at Large: Shayla Barney, Cecil Dick and Lucas Samor

Confederated Tribes of Coos, Lower Umpqua and Siuslaw

Address: 1245 Fulton Ave., Coos Bay 97420
Phone: 541-888-9577, 888-280-0726
Email: Bgarcia@ctclusi.org
Web: https://ctclusi.org
Restoration Date: October 17, 1984
Number of Members: 953
Land Base Acreage: about 415 acres
Number of people employed by the Tribes: 542

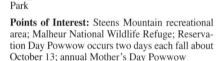

Economy: Three Rivers Casino & Hotel, Ocean Dunes Golf Course, Restoration Forest Plan

Points of Interest: Three Rivers Casino & Hotel; Salmon Ceremony held on the first Sunday in August at the Tribal Hall in Coos Bay; Annual Restoration Day celebrated on or about October 17 each year. The Confederated Tribes of Coos, Lower Umpqua and Siuslaw observe summer and winter solstices and sponsor seasonal events for hunting and gathering.

History and Culture: The tribal people of western Oregon understood the land to be the Spirit expressing itself in the natural world. The people were connected to the land with certainty and gratitude. It sustained, nurtured and made life possible, while supporting all the spirits sharing this world. The tribal economy reflected the relationship of the Creator to the People. Acquiring objects of both aesthetic and utilitarian value was a measure of an individual's wealth and status, yet acquisition was not an end in itself. The annual Potlatch became the setting for individuals to give their possessions to others, further mirroring the Creator's relationship to the People. The spiritual act of gifting your earthly possessions to others remains a powerful personal experience and a statement of faith and trust.

The tribes administered laws with transparency and a focus on the collective rights of the people. Individualism at the expense of community was not tolerated. Victims of an offense participated in the forming of appropriate punishments in a public arena where justice and fairness were, like other decision making processes, a group affair.

By 1854, white settlers began taking Donation Land Claims around Coos Bay. In 1856, the U.S. Army forcibly removed the tribal people to the new 18,000 acre Great Coast Reservation established on a windswept spit on the north side of the mouth of the Umpqua River.

Tribal Court: Tribal Judge J. D. Williams, 1245 Fulton Ave., Coos Bay 97420; 541-888-9577

Tribal Council: Chief Warren A. Brainard (2020), Chairman Mark Ingersoll (2019), Vice-Chair Teresa Spangler (2019), Beverly Bowen (2018), Tara Bowen (2018), Arron McNutt (2018), Doc Slyter (2019)

Coquille Indian Tribe

Address: 3050 Tremont St., North Bend 97459
Phone: 541-756-0904
Email: cit@coquilletribe.org
Web: www.coquilletribe.org
Restoration Date:
June 28, 1989
Number of Members: 1,041
Land Base Acreage:
6,552 acres (in trust)
Free Land: 3,456 acres (three separate parcels)
Number of people employed by the Tribe: 634

Economy: The tribe contributes to the economy of Coos County and its other service area counties, Curry, Douglas, Jackson and Lane, through business ventures, including timber operations; the Mill Casino, Hotel and RV Park; the Laundry Mill; Tribal One Broadband Technologies, LLC; and Sek-wet-Se Nonprofit Corporation. The tribe is the second largest employer in Coos County.

Points of Interest: Dune rides and shipwrecks at Oregon Dunes National Recreation Area; Charleston Harbor; charter fishing for tuna and salmon; crabbing; storm watching; beachcombing; tide pooling; canoeing; and the holiday lights showcase at Shore Acres State Park

History and Culture: The Coquilles' ancestral homelands, more than one million acres of lower Coos Bay and the Coquille River watershed, were ceded by treaties to the U.S. government in 1851 and 1855 in exchange for reservation land that never materialized because the treaties were never ratified by the U.S. Senate. No permanent tribal land existed until 1989, when Congress passed Public Law 101-42 re-establishing the Coquilles as a federally-recognized tribe.

After regaining federal recognition, the Coquille tribal government created programs to provide housing, health care, education, elder care, law enforcement and judicial services to its members. Cultural preservation efforts include learning and teaching oral histories and traditions to members of the tribe.

A congressional act in 1996 restored 5,410 acres of forest land to the tribe. The tribe operates a multi-discipline, natural resources progam to manage its forest lands under certification standards of the Forest Stewardship Council.

Tribal Court: Chief Judge Don Owen Costello, 3050 Tremont St., North Bend 97459; 541-756-0904

Tribal Council: Chief Donald B. Ivy (2019), Chairperson Brenda Meade (2018), Vice-Chair Kippy Robbins (2017), Secretary/Treasurer Joan Metcalf (2018), Representatives: Toni Ann Brend (2018) and Eric Metcalf (2019)

Cow Creek Band of Umpqua Tribe of Indians

Address: 2371 NE Stephens St., Suite 100, Roseburg 97470
Phone: 541-672-9405, 800-929-8229
Web: www.cowcreek.com
Treaty Date: September 19, 1853
Restoration Date: December 29, 1982
Number of Members: 1,722
Land Base Acreage: 1,840 acres (in trust)
Number of people employed by the Tribe: 1,100

Economy: The Cow Creeks were restored without reservation land in 1982. All land held by the tribe has been by purchase. The Seven Feathers Casino Resort in Canyonville, featuring a casino,  hotels, restaurants and entertainment venues, is the tribe's main source of income. Several other businesses, such as the K-BAR cattle ranch in Rogue River, have been acquired in their economic diversification program. Since recognition, the tribe has developed housing, education and social services programs, business corporations, a utility cooperative, a charitable foundation, and a tribal court system. The tribe is one of the largest employers in Douglas County.

Points of Interest: Oregon's Interstate-5 highway passes through Canyonville, the Seven Feathers Resort and the heart of Cow Creek's homeland. The area is one of natural beauty and includes the Umpqua River, the Cascade Mountains, the Pacific Ocean and dunes and a growing wine industry.

History and Culture: The Cow Creeks lived between the Cascade and Coast Ranges in southwestern Oregon, along the South Umpqua River. They hunted deer and elk and fished silver salmon and steelhead as far north as the Columbia River, east to Crater Lake, and south to the Klamath Marsh.

Except for the purpose of the Termination Act in 1954, which called for the immediate termination of federal relations with more than 60 tribes in western Oregon, the Cow Creek's Treaty of 1853 was ignored by the U.S. government for over 128 years until federal recognition in 1982.

Tribal Court: Tribal Judge Ronald Yockim, 2371 NE Stephens St., Suite 100, Roseburg 97470; 541-672-9405

Tribal Council: Chairman Daniel Courtney (2020), Vice-Chair Gary Jackson (2018), Secretary Yvonne Dumont-McCafferty (2018), Treasurer Robert VanNorman (2017), Jessica Bochart (2017), Tom Cox (2019), Rob Estabrook (2018), Roy "Steve" Jackson (2019), Gerald Rainville (2017), George T. Rondeau (2019) and Luann Urban (2020)

Confederated Tribes of The Grand Ronde Community

Address: 9615 Grand Ronde Rd., Grand Ronde 97347
Phone: 503-879-5211, 1-800-422-0232
Email: publicaffairs@grandronde.org
Web: www.grandronde.org
Restoration Date: November 22, 1983
Number of Members: 5,306
Land Base Acreage: about 11,288 acres
Number of people employed by the Tribes: 1,600

Economy: Spirit Mountain Casino, over 10,000 acres of forest lands and wildfire fighting crew

Points of Interest: Spirit Mountain Casino is Oregon's most successful casino, and the tribe dedicates 6 percent of the profits to its Spirit Mountain Community Fund, which supports charitable organizations in an 11-county area of western Oregon. The fund has given more than $55 million to area charities since 1997. The West Valley Veterans Memorial, four granite pillars representing the four branches of the armed services, holds the names of tribal members and area veterans who fought and served their country.

The tribe hosts a Veterans Powwow each July and a Competition Powwow on the third weekend of August. Fort Yamhill Heritage Area nearby tells the story of the relocation, transition and sadness for Grand Ronde's people when they were forced from their ancestral homelands, which extended from the banks of the Columbia River to the Oregon–California border, on to the Grand Ronde Reservation under military guard.

History and Culture: The tribes include Athabaskan-speaking Chasta, Rogue River and Upper Umpqua from southern Oregon. Molalla tribes are from the western Cascade Mountains, Kalapuya Tribes are from the Willamette Valley, and Chinookan-speaking Tumwater, Clackamas, Watlala and Multnomah are from the lower Willamette and Columbia Rivers. Chinuk Wawa became the tribes' common language. Traditional basket making and weaving, skills still practiced today, were important tribal utility and cultural skills.

Tribal Court: Tribal Judge Suzanne Ojibway-Townsend, 9615 Grand Ronde Rd., Grand Ronde 97347; 503-879-2303

Tribal Council: Chair Reyn Leno (2017), Vice-Chair Cheryle J. Kennedy (2019), Secretary Jon George (2018), Kathleen George (2019), Jack Giffen (2019), Tonya Gleason-Shepek (2017), Denise Harvey (2019), Chris Mercier (2017) and Brenda Tuomi (2018)

Klamath Tribes

Address: PO Box 436, 501 Chiloquin Blvd., Chiloquin 97624
Phone: 541-783-2219, 800-524-9787
Email: taylor.tupper@klamathtribes.com
Web: www.klamathtribes.org
Restoration Date: August 27, 1986
Number of Members: 3,700
Land Base Acreage: no reservation land
Number of people employed by the Tribes: Over 300

Economy: Kla-Mo-Ya Casino, a full service travel center and a wellness center

Points of Interest: Kla-Mo-Ya Casino, Crater Lake National Park, Lava Beds National Monument and Tulelake History Museum. Named by *Sunset Magazine* as one of the nation's five best birding hotspots, the Klamath Basin in the Pacific Flyway is a migratory flyway for more than 350 species of birds, including Bald Eagles, Clarke's Grebes and Black Terns.

History and Culture: Traditionally, every March, the c'waam (Lost River Suckerfish) swims up the Sprague River to spawn. A certain snowfall at this time of year heralds the c'waam's return, and the evening sky reveals the fish constellation (three stars in line making "Orion's Belt") on the southwestern horizon. Klamath traditions state that watchmen, or swaso.llalalYampgis, monitored the riverbanks to see exactly when the fish would return. The head "shaman" would then give thanks for their return. Tribal elders continue this ceremony to ensure the survival of a species, tribal traditions, and mankind. The celebration includes traditional dancing, drumming, feasting and releasing of a pair of c'waam into the river. Other annual events include the Restoration Celebration held the fourth weekend in August and the New Year's Eve Sobriety Powwow.

The Klamath Tribes, the Klamath, Modoc and Yahooskin Paiute people, have lived in the Klamath Basin from time beyond memory. Legends and oral history tell about when the world and the animals were created, when the animals and gmok'am'c, the Creator, sat together and discussed the creation of man. According to tribal sayings, if stability defines success, their presence here has been, and always will be, essential to the economic well-being of their homeland.

Tribal Court: Tribal Judge Jeremy Brave-Heart, 118 W. Chocktoot St., PO Box 1260, Chiloquin 97624; 541-783-3020

Tribal Council 2016–2019: Chairman Don Gentry, Vice-Chair Gail Hatcher, Secretary Roberta Frost, Treasurer Brandi Hatcher, Kathleen Hatcher-Mitchell, Jeannie McNair, David Ochoa, Devery Saluskin, Perry Chocktoot and Steve Weiser

Confederated Tribes of Siletz Indians

Address: 201 SE Swan Ave. PO Box 549, Siletz 97380
Phone: 541-444-2532
Web: www.ctsi.nsn.us
Restoration Date: November 18, 1977
Number of Members: 5,080
Land Base Acreage: 15,265 acres
Reservation Land: 4,010 acres
Number of people employed by the Tribes: 1,121

Economy: The Confederated Tribes of Siletz Indians (CTSI) own and operate the Chinook Winds Casino Resort in Lincoln City. The Siletz Tribal Business Corporation manages several businesses, including Hee Hee Illahee RV Resort, Logan Road RV Park and Siletz Tribal Prints & Gifts. The tribe also owns and leases office space in Lincoln City, Eugene, Salem and Portland.

Points of Interest: Chinook Winds Casino and Resort, including ocean-front hotel, restaurants, arcade and childcare; 18-hole golf course in Lincoln City; Nesika Illahee Powwow each August; and the Tribes' Restoration Powwow each November

History and Culture: The Confederated Tribes of Siletz Indians is a diverse confederation of 27 Western Oregon, Northern California and Southern Washington bands. A 1.1 million-acre reservation was established by President Franklin Pierce on November 9, 1855, fulfilling the stipulations of eight treaties. Over time, reservation lands were taken away, and the CTSI were terminated as a tribe in 1954. In 1977, the CTSI was the second tribe in the nation to achieve restoration. In 1980, some reservation lands were re-established. In spite of mistreatment and displacement, the CTSI continues work to recover as much as possible of what was lost.

Since 1980, the tribe has increased its land base to 15,265 acres, which includes 14,666 acres of timberland and 599 acres for cultural preservation, housing, economic purposes, and wildlife habitat enhancement. About 58 percent (9,045 acres) of the land base is in Lincoln County. The tribe provides homes for nearly 192 members and their families and provides over 1,000 jobs.

Tribal Court: Tribal Chief Judge Calvin E. Gantenbein, PO Box 549, Siletz 97380; 541-444-8228

Tribal Council: Chairperson Delores Pigsley (2019), Vice-Chair Alfred "Bud" Lane III (2019), Treasurer Robert Kentta (2017), Secretary Sharon Edenfield (2018), Members: Lillie Butler (2019), Loraine Butler (2017), Reggie Butler, Sr. (2018), Dave Hatch (2018) and Gloria Ingle (2017)

Confederated Tribes of the Umatilla Indian Reservation

Address: 46411 Ti'mine Way, Pendleton 97801
Phone: 541-276-3165
Email: info@ctuir.org
Web: ctuir.org
Treaty Date: June 9, 1855; 12 Stat. 945
Number of Members: 3,016
Land Base Acreage: 172,000 acres
Number of people employed by the Tribes: 1,645

Economy: Prior to the 1855 Treaty, the tribes' economy consisted primarily of intertribal trade, livestock, trade with fur companies, hunting, fishing and gathering. Today, the economy includes agriculture, livestock, tourism, a travel plaza, grain elevator, the Wildhorse Resort (casino, hotel, RV Park, golf course), Tamástslikt Cultural Institute, Cayuse Technologies, and Coyote Business Park, a 520-acre commercial and light industrial business development on the Interstate 84 Highway. The reservation is also home to the Umatilla National Forest Supervisor's Office.

Points of Interest: Tamástslikt Cultural Institute, Wildhorse Resort & Casino, Wildhorse Golf Course, Nix-yá-wii Warriors Memorial, Crow's Shadow Institute of the Arts, Indian Lake Recreation Area, seasonal upland gamebird and turkey hunting

History and Culture: Three tribes make up the CTUIR: Cayuse, Umatilla and Walla Walla. They have lived on the Columbia River Plateau for over 10,000 years, an area of about 6.4 million acres in what is now northeastern Oregon and southeastern Washington. In 1855, the tribes and the United States government negotiated a treaty in which the tribes ceded 6.4 million acres, while reserving a section of land for their exclusive use in the form of a reservation. The CTUIR reserved rights in the treaty, including fishing and hunting rights and the right to gather traditional foods and medicines within the ceded areas.

The traditional religion of the tribes is called "Washat" or "Seven Drums." Native languages are still spoken, and a language preservation program is helping to re-establish the languages.

Tribal Court: Tribal Judge William Johnson, 46411 Ti'mine Way, Pendleton 97801; 541-276-2046

Tribal Council 2015–2017: Chairman Gary Burke, General Council Chair Alan Crawford, Vice-Chair Jeremy Wolf, Treasurer Rosenda Shippentower, Secretary David Close, Members at Large: Armand Minthorn, Justin Quaempts, Aaron Ashley and Woodrow Star

Confederated Tribes of Warm Springs Reservation

Address: PO Box C, Warm Springs 97761
Phone: 541-553-1161
Email: rsuppah@wstribes.org
Web: https://warmsprings-nsn.gov
Treaty Date: June 25, 1855
Number of Members: 4,306
Land Base Acreage: 644,000 acres
Number of people employed by the Tribes: 525

Economy: Under the Corporate Charter, the tribes have established a number of enterprises owned by the tribes, but operated independently of tribal government, that contribute to the economy  of the reservation. These include Warm Springs Power & Water, Warm Springs Forest Products and Kah-Nee-Ta Resort and Casino.

Points of Interest: Kah-Nee-Ta Resort Lodge and Casino, Kah-Nee-Ta Village, RV Park and golf course, Indian Head Casino, and the Museum at Warm Springs

History and Culture: Long before Europeans set foot on the North American continent, the three tribes of the Warm Springs Reservation – the Wasco, the Walla Walla (later called the Warm Springs), and the Paiute – had developed societies beside the Columbia River, Cascade Mountains, and other parts of Oregon. Prior to settling on the reservation, natural food resources were so plentiful that agriculture was unnecessary for the three tribes of the Warm Springs Reservation. Salmon from the nearby Columbia was a staple for the Wasco and Warm Springs bands. The high-plains Paiutes depended more on deer and other large game. All three tribes took advantage of assorted roots, fruits and other plant life. Salmon were hauled out of the Columbia with long-handled dip nets. Roots were pulled from the ground with specialized digging sticks called kapns. Berries were gathered in ornately-woven baskets. Centuries of practice perfected these methods.

Tribal Court: Chief Tribal Judge Anita Jackson, PO Box 850, Warm Springs 97761; 541-553-3454

Tribal Council 2016–2019: Chairman Austin Greene, Jr., Paiute Chief Joe Moses, Warm Springs Chief Delvis Heath, Wasco Chief Alfred Smith, Jr., Representatives: Charles "Jody" Calica, Brigette McConville, Carina Miller, Ron Suppah, Valerie Switzler, Lee Tom, Raymond Tsumpti

OREGON CONSULAR CORPS

A number of foreign nations maintain consulates in Oregon. A consul is an official appointed by a government to live in a foreign city to look after the business and other interests of the home country and to assist and protect its nationals within the consular territory.

A consular representative promotes a country's trade within the assigned area, assists and protects shipping interests, legalizes ships' papers, assists native seamen in distress, adjudicates on some shipping matters, administers oaths, legalizes foreign documents as required by a country's laws, issues passports and visas and explains a country's policies, cultural achievements and its attractions for tourism.

For assistance from a Consul General or an Honorary Consul, please consult the listing of countries below for a representative of the country in which you have an interest.

Austria
Christopher R. Hermann, Honorary Consul
Address: 900 SW Fifth Ave., Suite. 2600, Portland 97204
Phone: 503-552-9733
Email: crhermann@stoel.com

Barbados
H. Desmond Johnson, M.D., Honorary Consul
Address: 4750 SW Trail Rd., Tualatin 97062
Phone: 503-659-0283
Email: bajandoc@hotmail.com

Belgium
John H. Herman, Honorary Consul
Address: 1024 SW Myrtle Dr., Portland 97201
Phone: 503-228-0465
Email: jacherman@aol.com

Canada
Jim Baumgartner, Honorary Consul
Address: 805 SW Broadway, Suite. 1900, Portland 97205
Phone: 503-417-2166
Email: honconcanada@bhlaw.com

Cyprus
Alexander Christy, Honorary Consul
Address: 1130 SW Morrison St., Suite. 510, Portland 97205
Phone: 503-248-0500
Email: alex@alexchristy.com

Czech Republic
Marie R. Amicci, Honorary Consul
Address: 320 A Ave., Suite 5, Lake Oswego 97034
Phone: 503-293-9545
Email: cz_consul_pdx@msn.com

Denmark
Ingolf Noto, Honorary Consul
Address: 1600 Pioneer Tower, 888 SW Fifth Ave., Portland 97204

Phone: 503-802-2131
Email: ingolf.noto@tonkon.com

France
Francoise Aylmer, Honorary Consul
Address: 1600 SW Fourth Ave., Portland 97201
Phone: 503-725-5037
Email: francoise@pdx.edu

Germany
Robert T. Manicke, Honorary Consul
Address: 200 SW Market St., Suite. 1775, Portland 97201
Phone: 503-222-0490
Email: portland-OR@hk-diplo.de

Guatemala
Marta Isabel Guembes Herrera, Consul a.h.
Address: 7304 N Campbell Ave., Portland 97217
Phone: 503-530-0046
Email: guembes@yahoo.com

Iceland
Les Swanson, Honorary Consul
Address: 900 SW 83rd Ave., Portland 97225
Phone: 503-228-1838
Email: lesswanson@comcast.net

Italy
Andrea Bartoloni, Honorary Consul
Address: 1331 NW Lovejoy St., Suite. 900, Portland 97209
Phone: 503-226-8622
Email: ab@aterwynne.com

Japan
Hiroshi Furusawa, Consul General
Address: 1300 SW Fifth Ave., Suite. 2700, Portland 97201
Phone: 503-221-1811
Email: hiroshi.furusawa@mofa.go.jp

Korea, Republic of
Charles Gregory Caldwell, Honorary Consul
Address: 8433 SW 10th Ave., Portland 97219
Phone: 503-768-7457
Email: caldwell@lclark.edu

Latvia, Republic of
Uldis J. Berzins, M.D., Honorary Consul
Address: 655 Medical Center Dr. NE, Salem 97301
Phone: 503-581-5287
Email: ujberzins@aol.com

Liechtenstein, The Principality of
Mary Jean Thompson, Honorary Consul
Address: 2846 NW Fairfax Ter., Portland 97210
Phone: 503-248-4000
Email: mjthompson@tdaportland.com

Lithuania
Randolph L. Miller, Honorary Consul
Address: 333 SE Second Ave., Portland 97214
Phone: 503-234-5000
Email: randy@mooreco.com

Luxembourg
Bill Failing, Honorary Consul
Address: 2649 SW Georgian Pl., Portland 97201
Phone: 503-224-5268
Email: bfailing@europa.com

Malaysia
John L. Blackwell, Honorary Consul
Address: 4708 SW Fairview Blvd., Portland 97221
Phone: 503-740-8404
Email: JohnLBlackwell1@gmail.com

Mexico
Armando Ortiz Rocha, Head Consul
Address: 1305 SW 12th Ave., Portland 97201
Phone: 503-227-1442
Web: http://consulmex.sre.gob.mx/portland

The Netherlands
Hans van Alebeek, Honorary Consul
Address: 1 Bowerman Dr., Beaverton 97005
Phone: 503-716-1500
Email: portland@nlconsulate.com

New Zealand
Charles Swindells, Honorary Consul
Address: 500 NW Hilltop Rd., Portland 97210
Phone: 503-803-7129
Email: cjs@theswindells.org

Norway
Larry K. Bruun, Honorary Consul
Address: 4380 SW Macadam, Suite. 120, Portland 97239
Phone: 503-221-0870
Email: lbruun@wbgatty.com

Philippines, Republic of the
Richard K. Woodling, Consul General, a.h.
Address: 2662 SW Georgian Pl., Portland 97201
Phone: 971-679-6682
Email: Richard.Woodling@comcast.net

Romania
James H. Rudd, Honorary Consul
Address: 888 SW Fifth Ave., Ste. 1200, Portland 97204
Phone: 503-382-5165
Email: rudd@fergwell.com

Thailand
Nicholas J. Stanley, Honorary Consul General
Address: 1136 NW Hoyt St., Suite. 210, Portland 97209
Phone: 503-221-0440
Email: thai@siaminc.com

United Kingdom
Andrew MacRitchie, Honorary Consul
Address: 1 Sansome St., Suite. 850, San Francisco, CA 94104
Phone: 503-227-5669
Email: UKHonConsul@aol.com

Source: Michou Jardini, Oregon Consular Corps, 503-808-0974; www.oregonconsularcorps.com

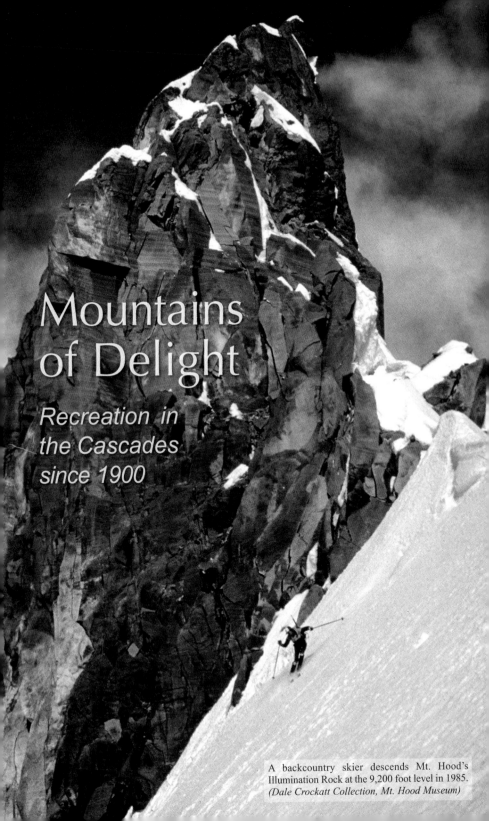

Mountains
of Delight

*Recreation in
the Cascades
since 1900*

A backcountry skier descends Mt. Hood's
Illumination Rock at the 9,200 foot level in 1985.
(Dale Crockatt Collection, Mt. Hood Museum)

Alexander Kingsbery views the Middle Sister (left) and North Sister at sunrise from atop the South Sister in the Three Sisters area of the Cascades. All three peaks rise above 10,000 feet. *(Alexander Kingsbery via Pacific Crest Trail Association)*

Recreation in the Cascades since 1900

Recreation has played a key role in the history of the Cascade Mountains of Oregon since 1900. Residents of the Willamette Valley and other population centers have long escaped the hectic pace of cities and towns to commune with nature and play in the mountains. This exhibit illustrates a wide, but incomplete, range of activities over the decades. The fashions and equipment may have evolved over time, but the interest in Cascades recreation has remained the same.

Camping, fishing, hunting, skiing, hiking and mountain climbing headed the list of favored recreation in the early 1900s. Various camps and retreats catering to youth, fraternal or religious groups thrived and offered many organized recreational pursuits in the Cascades for those willing to brave the often primitive roads. Other visitors preferred the numerous rustic mountain lodges that grew popular throughout the Oregon Cascades. The completion of the Crater Lake Lodge in 1915 and Timberline Lodge in 1938 highlighted this trend. These destinations served as comfortable bases to explore and recreate in the surrounding mountains.

The development of better-paved roads into the mountains beginning in the 1920s, spurred more individual travel. Meanwhile, the federal government built more reservoirs, campgrounds, hiking trails and other infrastructure that drew more visitors to the mountains. While older forms of recreation remain popular, new types, such as snowboarding and mountain biking, have been added. The decades also have seen the growth of motorized recreation such as water skiing, jet skiing and snowmobiling.

Images—Left: Women's 1930s era climbing boots. *(Mazamas Library and Historical Collections Object, Alta M. Loose Collection)*; Right: a vintage mountaineering ice axe. *(Oregon State Archives)*

Two men watch a kitchen worker hand feed scraps to a black bear at Crater Lake National Park in this undated photo. Interactions such as this, once not uncommon, are now known to lead to dangerous and unhealthy outcomes, both for wildlife and for humans. The park has been a recreational destination in the southern Oregon Cascades since its founding in 1902. *(Crater Lake National Park)*

Brightly painted Adirondack chairs on the shore at Lake of the Woods Resort west of Klamath Falls beckon vacationers to sit back, relax and take in the view of the lake. *(Oregon State Archives)*

An original pen and ink drawing captures the relaxed mood of sitting around a fire after a day of skiing on Mt. Hood. The drawing by Douglas Lynch was done circa 1937–1939 for a Timberline Lodge advertising brochure that was never published. *(Friends of Timberline)*

A couple shows off fish caught on Diamond Lake east of Roseburg in 1937. *(Oregon State Archives)*

A student wearing snowshoes employs a much faster travel method by belly sliding down a snowy slope at Crater Lake. *(Stephanie Duwe, NPS, Crater Lake National Park)*

A colorful 1948 Mazamas mountaineering organization poster encourages hikers to join a trail trip into the mountains. *(Mazamas Library and Historical Collections, Marianne and Ty Kearney Collection)*

Skiers take a break at the rim of Crater Lake in 1939. *(Oregon State Archives)*

Two skiers and a park ranger stand next to Ike Davidson's snow machine at Crater Lake National Park circa 1931–1932 in this photo by Charles H. Simson. *(Crater Lake National Park)*

Two women relax at a campground next to Diamond Lake with Mt. Theilsen in the background in 1956. *(Oregon State Archives)*

Tourists at Crater Lake National Park got a thrill in 1927 when Charles Lindbergh flew his "Spirit of St. Louis" airplane over the park as part of an extensive flying tour around the country. Earlier in the year, Lindbergh became the first person in history to fly solo, non-stop from North America to Europe, transforming himself into an instant international celebrity in the process. This photo is by Fred H. Kiser. *(Crater Lake National Park)*

Two people canoe through lake fog on Lake Harriet in the Cascade Mountains of Clackamas County. *(Oregon State Archives)*

The Pacific Crest Trail (PCT), a north-south hiking route that traces the crests of the Sierra Nevada and Cascade mountains from Mexico to Canada, offers some of the purest recreation in the Cascades. Originally proposed in the 1920s, it gained National Scenic Trail status in 1968.

The trail winds through the Oregon Cascades for 460 miles, crossing Crater Lake National Park and several wilderness areas before dropping over 3,000 feet into the Columbia River Gorge at Cascade Locks.

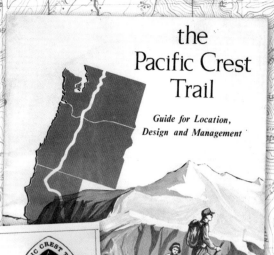

the
Pacific Crest
Trail

*Guide for Location,
Design and Management*

OF AGRICULTURE - FOREST SERVICE

18" HIGHWAY UNIFORM MARKER

9" TRAILHEAD
UNIFORM MARKER

3-1/2" TRAIL
UNIFORM MARKER

TRAIL BLAZER

Gray-white

Pacemaker Blaze

ROSE HILL 3
ROYAL GULCH 5

DIRECTION OR GUIDE SIGNING

CAIRN

NATIONAL SCENIC TRAIL SIGNING & MARKING SYSTEM

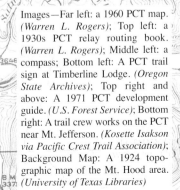

Images—Far left: a 1960 PCT map. *(Warren L. Rogers)*; Top left: a 1930s PCT relay routing book. *(Warren L. Rogers)*; Middle left: a compass; Bottom left: A PCT trail sign at Timberline Lodge. *(Oregon State Archives)*; Top right and above: A 1971 PCT development guide. *(U.S. Forest Service)*; Bottom right: A trail crew works on the PCT near Mt. Jefferson. *(Kosette Isakson via Pacific Crest Trail Association)*; Background Map: A 1924 topographic map of the Mt. Hood area. *(University of Texas Libraries)*

Tourists sit on a rock wall near Crater Lake Lodge and take in the grandeur of the brilliant blue water. Crater Lake was formed after Mt. Mazama blew its top about 7,700 years ago. *(Oregon State Archives)*

Millard Sheets painted this watercolor ski scene at Timberline Lodge for the September 1967 United Airlines calender designed to entice travel to the area. *(Friends of Timberline)*

Climbers peer into the abyss of a glacier crevass on Mt. Hood. This photo was probably taken by Ralph Gifford in the 1920s. *(Oregon State Archives)*

A man casts his fishing line into the McKenzie River just below Tamolitch Falls in 1942. *(Oregon State Archives)*

An original pen and ink drawing shows a skier on Mt. Hood. The drawing by Douglas Lynch was done circa 1937–1939 for a Timberline Lodge advertising brochure that was never published. (*Friends of Timberline*)

Barry Murray, Jr. rides the Pacific Crest Trail in 1970 along the edge of Zig Zag River Canyon while leading his pack string. Mt. Hood looms in the background. The Murray Family created indelible memories while being the first to complete the trail after its National Scenic Trail designation in 1968. Along the way, they encountered many obstacles such as disappearing trails and angry landowners. (*Barry G. Murray*)

A Mazamas climbing party ascends Mt. Hood circa 1952. *(Mazamas Library and Historical Collections Photograph, Mazamas Collection)*

A wagon train on a 1975 tour celebrating the upcoming Bicentennial of the Declaration of Independence heads along the historic Barlow Road with Mt. Hood in the background. *(Oregon State Archives)*

Kayakers paddle on Sparks Lake with the South Sister in the background. *(Oregon State Archives)*

The sun sets over the Pacific Crest Trail near McKenzie Pass east of Eugene. The trail celebrates its 50th anniversary as a national scenic trail in 2018. *(Alexander Kingsbery via Pacific Crest Trail Association)*

Bernadette Murray relaxes and bonds with her mare Chiquita during a 1970 family adventure on the Pacific Crest Trail. The pair drifted off to sleep in the bright sunshine after a long day's ride. *(Barry G. Murray)*

Bernice Murray cooks a steak, a special and rare treat, in camp near Mt. Hood on a Murray Family horse-packing adventure along the Pacific Crest Trail in 1970. *(Barry G. Murray)*

The Mahre brothers ski down Mt. Hood in 1986. Twin brothers Phil and Steve won gold and silver medals, respectively, at the 1984 Winter Olympics in Sarajevo, Yugoslavia. (*Friends of Timberline*)

Timberline LODGE

OREGON, 97028

LET'S GO

TIMBERLINE LODGE

HOWARD FISHER

Timberline Lodge, the iconic four-story resort hotel completed in 1938 on the shoulder of Mt. Hood, offers year-round recreation but is best known as a ski destination. Built by the Works Progress Administration, the structure incorporates numerous works by local artists. Top: Timberline Lodge letterhead from 1968. *(Friends of Timberline)*; Above: A 1938 *Oregon Journal* cartoon by Howard Fisher celebrates the opening of the lodge. *(Howard Fisher/Courtesy of* The Oregonian*)*; Right: A decorative woodcut by Charles Haney depicts the lodge. *(Friends of Timberline)*; Background: Timberline Lodge. *(Oregon State Archives)*

RICHARD L. KOHNSTAMM
AREA OPERATOR

ROBERT J. HOWER
MANAGER

THE BOOKS OF
TIMBERLINE

Bernadette Murray cuddles with Tagalong, her little filly horse who was born on the Pacific Crest Trail during a Murray Family horse-packing trip on the 2,650-mile long trail from Mexico to Canada in 1969 and 1970. For young Bernadette, every day with Tagalong was a new adventure. *(Barry G. Murray)*

A National Park Service Naturalist Ranger stands on the rim of the caldera at Crater Lake and speaks to a group of visitors circa 1935. The lake and Garfield Peak are in the background. *(Crater Lake National Park)*

Evening arrives at the Lava Flow Campground area of Davis Lake near the popular Cascade Lakes Highway west of La Pine. *(Oregon State Archives)*

Mountain climber Joe Leuthold, probably on Mt. Hood, is framed by rocks as he ascends circa 1950. *(Mazamas Library and Historical Collections Photograph, Al and Helen Gerding Collection.)*

Amy Nelson snowshoes through heavy snow in the Sky Lakes Wilderness Area in the Southern Oregon Cascades. *(Ian Nelson via Pacific Crest Trail Association)*

A snowboarder on Mt. Hood just above Timberline Lodge takes advantage of a sunny July day in 2014 to hit the slopes. The Palmer Snowfield draws Olympic athletes from around the country to train as well as skiers and snowboarders who attend various camps from June to September. *(Oregon State Archives)*

An original pen and ink drawing shows a ski rescue sled team on Mt. Hood. The drawing by Douglas Lynch was done circa 1937–1939 for a Timberline Lodge advertising brochure that was never published. (*Friends of Timberline*)

The first all women's Mazamas climbing party ascends Mt. Hood in 1932. (*Mazamas Library and Historical Collections Photograph, Beatrice de Lacy Collection*)

Snowmobilers take a break on a slope above Elk Lake in the Cascades west of Bend in 2016. *(Steve Mabry)*

A colorful sky lights up one of the Rosary Lakes near the Pacific Crest Trail north of Odell Lake. *(Jamie Ford via Pacific Crest Trail Association)*

End of exhibit. Learn more in an expanded Web exhibit at **bluebook.state.or.us**

Oregon State Symbols

State Flag: The front of the Oregon ceremonial flag.
Navy blue and gold are the state colors.
(Oregon State Archives)

State Flag: The reverse of the ceremonial flag. Oregon
is the only state to have different designs on two sides
of the flag.
(Oregon State Archives)

State Seal: The seal of the State of Oregon.
(Oregon State Archives)

State Animal: American Beaver *(Castor canadensis)*
(Oregon Department of Fish and Wildlife)

State Gemstone: Oregon Sunstone
(Oregon Department of Geology and Mineral Industries)

State Insect: Oregon Swallowtail *(Papilio oregonius)*
(Oregon State Capitol)

State Mushroom: Pacific Golden Chanterelle *(Cantharellus formosus)*
(Richard F. Bishop)

State Nut: Hazelnut *(Corylus avellana)*
(Oregon State Archives)

State Shell: Hairy Triton *(Fusitriton oregonesis)*
(Bill Hanshumaker, Hatfield Marine Science Center)

State Crustacean: Dungeness Crab
(Metacarcinus magister)
(Dungeness Crab Commission)

State Bird: Western Meadowlark *(Sturnella neglecta)*
(Noah Strycker)

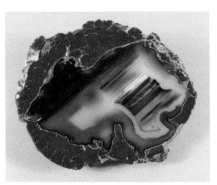

State Rock: Thunderegg (geode)
(Oregon Department of Geology and Mineral Industries)

State Fruit: Pear *(Pyrus communis)*
(Pear Bureau Northwest)

State Flower: Oregon Grape
(Mahonia Aquifolium)
(Oregon State Archives)

State Fossil: Dawn Redwood
(Metasequoia glyptostroboides)
(National Park Service, John Day Fossil Beds National Monument)

State Fish: Chinook Salmon *(Oncorhynchus tshawytscha)*
(Oregon Department of Fish and Wildlife)

State Tree: Douglas Fir *(Pseudotsuga menziesii)*
(Oregon State Archives)

The State Capitol decorated with special lighting to celebrate the 75th Anniversary of the building in 2013. *(Oregon State Archives)*

Physical Features Map

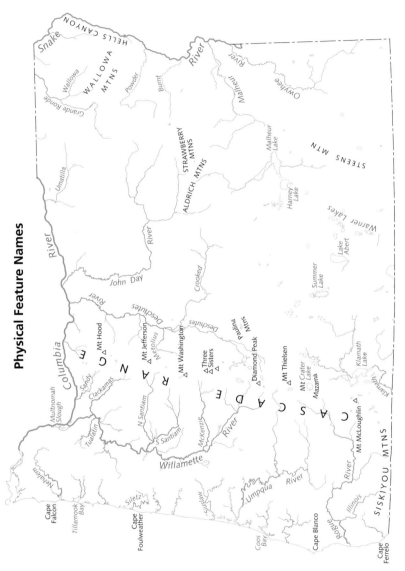

Physical Feature Names

A small sailboat sits on the shore of Waldo Lake in the Cascade Mountains.
Oregon State Archives Scenic Photograph D7K-3714

Oregon offers us a place of rich geographic diversity to establish our communities—from the Pacific Ocean beaches and Coast Range eastward to the Willamette Valley, Klamath Mountains and southwest valleys; on to the Cascade Range; then further east to the Columbia River Plateau, Blue Mountains, the southeast Basin and ranges; and on to the Snake River at our eastern border. This section identifies incorporated cities and towns, counties, regional governments and special districts.

SALEM— OREGON'S CAPITAL

Salem, with a population of 160,690, is Oregon's state capital and the third largest city. Salem is also the county seat of Marion County, but a small portion contained within its corporate limits of 44 square miles lies across the Willamette River in Polk County. Salem is situated on the 45th geographic parallel in the center of the Willamette Valley—one of the most fertile and agriculturally productive regions in the world—47 miles south of Portland and 64 miles north of Eugene.

Salem serves as the hub of both state government and the surrounding farming communities. State government is the largest employer, with approximately 17,958 state employees and offices for 69 state agencies located in Salem. Salem is also one of the largest food-processing centers in the United States.

In addition, Salem is one of Oregon's oldest cities. The tribal name for the locality was Chemeketa, said to mean "meeting or resting place." It may also have been the name of one of the bands of the Kalapuya Tribe. In 1840–1841, the Jason Lee Mission was moved from the banks of the Willamette River upstream to a site on Mill Creek. In 1842, the missionaries established the Oregon Institute. When the mission was dissolved in 1844, it was decided to lay out a townsite on the Oregon Institute lands. Either David Leslie, one of the trustees who came to Oregon from Salem, Massachusetts, or W. H. Willson, who filed plats in 1850–1851 for what is now the main part of the city, selected the name "Salem." Salem is the Anglicized form of the Hebrew word shalom, meaning peace.*

The location of the Oregon capital caused a spirited contest that lasted nearly 15 years. By a legislative act in 1851, the territorial government moved the capital to Salem from Oregon City. In 1855, it was moved to Corvallis, only to move back to Salem the same year. Destruction of the Capitol Building at Salem on December 31, 1855, was considered an incendiary part of this controversy.

The close proximity of government provides Salem citizens with a distinct opportunity to be involved in the decision-making processes of the state. The citizens of Salem also have a long history of commitment to community improvement, a committment recognized nationally through the presentation of two All-America City Awards in 1960–1961 and 1982–1983.

*Early Salem history from *Oregon Geographic Names* by Lewis A. McArthur.

State Buildings

Agriculture Building (1966)*
635 Capitol St. NE, Salem 97301

Barbara Roberts Human Services Bldg. (1992)
550 Summer St. NE, Salem 97301

Capitol Mall Parking Structure (1991)
900 Chemeketa St. NE, Salem 97301

Cecil Edwards Archives Building (1991)
800 Summer St. NE, Salem 97310

Commerce Building (1931)
158 12th St. NE, Salem 97301

Commission for the Blind (1977)
535 SE 12th Ave., Portland 97204

Employment Building (1974)
875 Union St. NE, Salem 97311

Executive Building (1979)
155 Cottage St. NE, Salem 97301

Fish and Wildlife Building (2013)
4034 Fairview Industrial Dr. SE, Salem 97302

Forestry Buildings (1938)
2600 State St., Salem 97310

General Services Building (1954)
1225 Ferry St. SE, Salem 97301

General Services Building Annex (1967)
1257 Ferry St. SE, Salem 97301

Justice Building (1930)
1162 Court St. NE, Salem 97301

Labor and Industries Building (1961)
350 Winter St. NE, Salem 97301

Liquor Control Commission Building (1955)
9201 SE McLoughlin Blvd., Milwaukie 97222

North Capitol Mall Office Building (2003)
725 Summer St. NE, Salem 97301

Public Employees' Retirement System Building (1998)
11410 SW 68th Pkwy., Tigard 97281

Public Service Building (1949)
255 Capitol St. NE, Salem 97310

Real Estate Building (1990)
1177 Center St. NE, Salem 97301

Revenue Building (1981)
955 Center St. NE, Salem 97301

State Capitol Building (1938)
900 Court St. NE, Salem 97301

State Fair Buildings, State Fairgrounds
2330 17th St. NE, Salem 97303

State Hospital Building (1883)
2600 Center St. NE, Salem 97301

State Lands Building (1990)
775 Summer St. NE, Salem 97301

State Library (1939)
250 Winter St. NE, Salem 97301

State Lottery Building (1996)
500 Airport Rd. SE, Salem 97301

State Office Building, Eugene (1961)
165 E 7th Ave., Eugene 97401

State Office Building, Pendleton (1963)
700 SE Emigrant St., Pendleton 97801

State Office Building, Portland (1992)
800 NE Oregon St., Portland 97232

State Police Salem Headquarters (2016)
3565 Trelstad Ave. SE, Salem 97317

State Printing Plant (1980)
550 Airport Rd. SE, Salem 97301

Supreme Court Building (1914)
1163 State St., Salem 97301

Transportation Building (1951)
355 Capitol St. NE, Salem 97301

Veterans' Building (1984)
700 Summer St. NE, Salem 97301

*Year is the date the building was constructed, purchased or occupied by the state.

INCORPORATED CITIES AND TOWNS

Source: Michael McCauley, Executive Director, League of Oregon Cities
Address: 1201 Court St. NE, Suite 200, Salem 97301, PO Box 928, Salem 97308
Phone: 503-588-6550
Fax: 503-399-4863
Email: loc@orcities.org
Web: www.orcities.org

There are 241 incorporated cities in Oregon. Cities are centers of population, commerce, education and services. Seventy percent of Oregonians live in cities. Nearly 70 percent of Oregon's property value is in cities. Economic activity within cities generates 83 percent of the state's income tax receipts as more than 82 percent of jobs are located in cities. There are more than 16,000 miles of city roads. Cities employ more than 3,600 police officers, comprising 60 percent of all law enforcement officers in Oregon. All of the public institutions of higher education are located in cities, as well as all but two private colleges. All but one of Oregon's 60 hospitals are located within a city. Cities form the heart of Oregon's cultural, educational, service and economic activity.

Among the services city governments typically provide are fire and police protection, streets and street maintenance, sewer and water treatment and collection systems, building permit activities, libraries, parks and recreation activities, and other numerous social services determined locally. Cities also have considerable responsibilities for land use planning within their city limits and urban growth boundaries.

City councils serve as the highest authority within city governments in deciding issues of public policy. In open public forums, city councils pass laws (ordinances), adopt resolutions and generally conduct discussions involving the governance of their communities and the welfare of their citizens.

Four forms of city government determine the administrative role of any city council. Most Oregon cities with populations over 2,500 have the council/manager or council/administrator form, in which the council hires a chief executive officer to be responsible for the daily supervision of city affairs. Portland has a commission form of government, where the elected commissioners function collectively as the city council and serve as administrators of city departments. Smaller Oregon cities typically have the mayor/council form, in which the legislative and policy-making body is a popularly-elected council.

City administrators and other city employees often participate in the policy development process but are primarily responsible for effective delivery of municipal services and programs. Under home rule, cities have latitude in managing their affairs, except where the subject matter has been preempted by state government.

Regardless of the form of government, cities find their strength in a cooperative relationship between the citizens, city officials, the private sector and other government entities. Cities recognize the positive impact of working together, both regionally and on a statewide basis, to enhance community livability.

City name origins are available from *Oregon Geographic Names* by Lewis A. McArthur.

Incorporation dates listed are based on information available.

*County seat

Adair Village
County: Benton
Address: 6030 NE Wm. R. Carr Ave., 97330
Phone: 541-745-5507
Fax: 541-230-5219
Web: www.adairvillage.org
Elevation: 330'
Incorporated: 5/25/1976
Mayor: William "Bill" Currier

Adams
County: Umatilla
Address: PO Box 20, 97810
Phone: 541-566-9380
Fax: 541-566-2077
Web: www.cityofadamsoregon.com
Elevation: 1,526'
Incorporated: 2/10/1893
Mayor: M. Dane Holmes

Adrian
County: Malheur
Address: PO Box 226, 97901
Phone: 541-372-2179
Fax: 541-372-2179
Elevation: 2,225'
Incorporated: 7/10/1972
City Council President: M. Adele Dockter

*Albany
County: Benton/Linn
Address: PO Box 490, 97321
Phone: 541-917-7500
Fax: 541-917-7511
Web: www.cityofalbany.net
Elevation: 210'
Incorporated: 10/10/1864
Mayor: Sharon Konopa

Amity
County: Yamhill
Address: PO Box 159, 109 Maddox Ave., 97101
Phone: 503-835-3711
Fax: 503-835-3780
Web: www.ci.amity.or.us
Elevation: 162'
Incorporated: 10/19/1880
Mayor: Michael Cape

Antelope
County: Wasco
Address: PO Box 105, 97001
Phone: 541-489-3201
Web: www.cityofantelope.us
Elevation: 2,654'
Incorporated: 11/12/1896
Mayor: Lacey Smith

Arlington
County: Gilliam
Address: PO Box 68, 97812
Phone: 541-454-2743
Fax: 541-454-2753
Web: http://cityofarlingtonoregon.com
Elevation: 285'
Incorporated: 11/20/1885
Mayor: Jeffery Bufton

Ashland
County: Jackson
Address: 20 E Main St., 97520
Phone: 541-488-6002
Fax: 541-488-5311
Web: www.ashland.or.us
Elevation: 1,949'
Incorporated: 10/13/1874
Mayor: John Stromberg

*Astoria
County: Clatsop
Address: 1095 Duane St., 97103
Phone: 503-325-5821
Fax: 503-325-2017
Web: www.astoria.or.us
Elevation: 23'
Incorporated: 10/20/1876
Mayor: Arline J. LaMear

Athena
County: Umatilla
Address: PO Box 686, 302 E Current St., 97813
Phone: 541-566-3862
Fax: 541-566-2781

Web: www.cityofathena.com
Elevation: 1710'
Incorporated: 2/20/1889
Mayor: John Shafer

Aumsville
County: Marion
Address: 595 Main St., 97325
Phone: 503-749-2030
Fax: 503-749-1852
Web: www.aumsville.us
Elevation: 366'
Incorporated: 8/3/1911
Mayor: Robert Baugh

Aurora
County: Marion
Address: 21420 Main St. NE, 97002
Phone: 503-678-1283, ext. 2
Fax: 503-678-2758
Web: www.ci.aurora.or.us
Elevation: 136'
Incorporated: 2/20/1893
Mayor: Bill Graupp

*Baker City
County: Baker
Address: PO Box 650, 1655 First St., 97814
Phone: 541-523-6541
Fax: 541-524-2024
Web: www.bakercity.com
Elevation: 3,451'
Incorporated: 10/13/1874
Mayor: Mike Downing

Bandon
County: Coos
Address: PO Box 67, 555 Hwy. 101, 97411
Phone: 541-347-2437
Fax: 541-347-1415
Web: www.cityofbandon.org
Elevation: 20'
Incorporated: 2/18/1891
Mayor: Mary Schamehorn

Banks
County: Washington
Address: 13680 NW Main St., 97106
Phone: 503-324-5112
Fax: 503-324-6674
Web: www.cityofbanks.org
Elevation: 250'
Incorporated: 1/16/1920
Mayor: Peter C. Edison

Barlow
County: Clackamas
Address: 106 N Main St., 97013-9191
Phone: 503-266-1330
Fax: 503-266-1330
Elevation: 103'
Incorporated: 2/13/1903
Mayor: Michael E. Lundsten

Bay City
County: Tillamook
Address: PO Box 3309, 5525 B St., 97107
Phone: 503-377-2288
Fax: 503-377-4044
Web: www.ci.bay-city.or.us
Elevation: 17'
Incorporated: 9/13/1910
Mayor: Shaena Peterson

Beaverton
County: Washington
Address: PO Box 4755, 12725 SW Millikan Way, 97005
Phone: 503-526-2222
Fax: 503-526-2479
Web: www.beavertonoregon.gov
Elevation: 189'
Incorporated: 2/10/1893
Mayor: Denny Doyle

*Bend
County: Deschutes
Address: PO Box 431, 710 NW Wall St., 97709
Phone: 541-388-5505
Fax: 541-385-6676
Web: www.bendoregon.gov
Elevation: 3,628'
Incorporated: 1/19/1905
Mayor: Casey Roats

Boardman
County: Morrow
Address: PO Box 229, 200 City Center Cir., 97818
Phone: 541-481-9252
Fax: 541-481-3244
Web: www.cityofboardman.com
Elevation: 308'
Incorporated: 5/20/1921
Mayor: Sandy Toms

Bonanza
County: Klamath
Address: PO Box 297, 97623
Phone: 541-545-6566
Fax: 541-545-1027
Email: bonanza@fireserve.net
Elevation: 4,127'
Incorporated: 2/20/1901
Mayor: Betty Tyree

Brookings
County: Curry
Address: 898 Elk Dr., 97415
Phone: 541-469-2163
Fax: 541-469-3650
Web: www.brookings.or.us
Elevation: 129'
Incorporated: 10/15/1951
Mayor: Jake Pieper

Brownsville
County: Linn
Address: PO Box 188, 255 N Main St., 97327
Phone: 541-466-5666
Fax: 541-466-5118
Web: www.ci.brownsville.or.us
Elevation: 265'
Incorporated: 10/19/1876
Mayor: Don Ware

*Burns
County: Harney
Address: 242 S Broadway Ave., 97720
Phone: 541-573-5255
Fax: 541-573-5622
Web: www.ci.burns.or.us
Elevation: 4,148'
Incorporated: 2/18/1891
Mayor: Jerry Woodfin

Butte Falls
County: Jackson
Address: PO Box 268, 431 Broad St., 97522
Phone: 541-865-3262
Fax: 541-865-3777
Email: bfcityhall@gmail.com
Elevation: 2,536'
Incorporated: 8/21/1911
Mayor: Linda Spencer

Canby
County: Clackamas
Address: PO Box 930, 222 NE 2nd Ave., 97013
Phone: 503-266-4021
Fax: 503-266-7961
Web: www.canbyoregon.gov
Elevation: 154'
Incorporated: 2/15/1893
Mayor: Brian Hodson

Cannon Beach
County: Clatsop
Address: PO Box 368, 163 E Gower St., 97110
Phone: 503-436-1581
Fax: 503-436-2050
Web: www.ci.cannon-beach.or.us
Elevation: 30'
Incorporated: 3/5/1957
Mayor: Sam Steidel

*Canyon City
County: Grant
Address: PO Box 276, 123 S Washington St., 97820
Phone: 541-575-0509
Fax: 541-575-0515
Email: tocc1862@centurylink.net
Elevation: 3,194'
Incorporated: 10/19/1864
Mayor: Steve Fischer

Canyonville
County: Douglas
Address: PO Box 765, 250 N Main, 97417
Phone: 541-839-4258
Fax: 541-839-4680
Web: www.cityofcanyonville.com
Elevation: 766'
Incorporated: 1/29/1901
Mayor: Jake Young

Carlton
County: Yamhill
Address: 191 E Main St., 97111
Phone: 503-852-7575
Fax: 503-852-7761
Web: www.ci.carlton.or.us
Elevation: 198'
Incorporated: 2/17/1899
Mayor: Kathie Oriet

Cascade Locks
County: Hood River
Address: PO Box 308, 140 SW Wa Na Pa St., 97014
Phone: 541-374-8484
Fax: 541-374-8752
Web: www.cascade-locks.or.us
Elevation: 170'
Incorporated: 6/19/1935
Mayor: Thomas Cramblett

Cave Junction
County: Josephine
Address: PO Box 1396, 222 W Lister St., 97523
Phone: 541-592-2156
Fax: 541-592-6694
Web: www.cavejunctionoregon.us
Elevation: 1,575'
Incorporated: 9/23/1946
Mayor: Daniel Dalegowski

Central Point
County: Jackson
Address: 140 S Third St., 97502
Phone: 541-664-3321
Fax: 541-664-6384
Web: www.centralpointoregon.gov
Elevation: 1,272'
Incorporated: 2/25/1889
Mayor: Henry Williams

Chiloquin
County: Klamath
Address: PO Box 196, 122 S Second Ave., 97624
Phone: 541-783-2717
Fax: 541-783-2035
Web: http://chiloquin.com
Elevation: 4,180'
Incorporated: 3/3/1926
Mayor: Mark Cobb

Clatskanie
County: Columbia
Address: PO Box 9, 75 S Nehalem St., 97016
Phone: 503-728-2622
Fax: 503-728-3297
Web: www.cityofclatskanie.com
Elevation: 45'
Incorporated: 2/18/1891
Mayor: Robert "Bob" Brajcich

Coburg
County: Lane
Address: PO Box 8316, 97408
Phone: 541-682-7850
Fax: 541-485-0655
Web: www.coburgoregon.org
Elevation: 398'
Incorporated: 2/10/1893
Mayor: Ray Smith

Columbia City
County: Columbia
Address: PO Box 189, 1840 Second St., 97018
Phone: 503-397-4010
Fax: 503-366-2870
Web: www.columbia-city.org
Elevation: 75'
Incorporated: 6/7/1926
Mayor: Cheryl Young

*Condon
County: Gilliam
Address: PO Box 445, 128 S Main St., 97823
Phone: 541-384-2711
Fax: 541-384-2700
Web: www.cityofcondon.com
Elevation: 2,831'
Incorporated: 2/10/1893
Mayor: Jim Hassing

Coos Bay
County: Coos
Address: 500 Central Ave., 97420
Phone: 541-269-1181
Fax: 541-267-5912
Web: http://coosbay.org
Elevation: 10'
Incorporated: 10/24/1874
Mayor: Joe Benetti

*Coquille
County: Coos
Address: 851 N Central Blvd., 97423
Phone: 541-396-2115
Fax: 541-396-5125
Web: www.cityofcoquille.org
Elevation: 40'
Incorporated: 2/25/1885
Mayor: Kathryn Simonetti

Cornelius
County: Washington
Address: 1355 N Barlow St., 97113
Phone: 503-357-9112
Fax: 503-357-7775
Web: www.ci.cornelius.or.us
Elevation: 179'
Incorporated: 2/10/1893
Mayor: Jeffrey C. Dalin

*Corvallis
County: Benton
Address: PO Box 1083, 97339, 501 SW Madison Ave., 97330
Phone: 541-766-6900
Fax: 541-766-6780
Web: www.corvallisoregon.gov
Elevation: 230'
Incorporated: 1/28/1857
Mayor: Biff Traber

Cottage Grove
County: Lane
Address: 400 E Main St., 97424
Phone: 541-942-5501
Fax: 541-942-1267
Web: www.cottagegrove.org
Elevation: 640'
Incorporated: 2/11/1887
Mayor: Jeff Gowing

Cove
County: Union
Address: PO Box 8, 504 Alder St., 97824
Phone: 541-568-4566
Fax: 541-568-7747
Web: http://coveoregon.org
Elevation: 2,870'
Incorporated: 3/10/1904
Mayor: Lyndon D. Rose

Creswell
County: Lane
Address: PO Box 276, 97426
Phone: 541-895-2531
Fax: 541-895-3647
Web: www.ci.creswell.or.us
Elevation: 542'
Incorporated: 7/16/1909
Mayor: David E. Stram

Culver
County: Jefferson
Address: 200 First Ave., 97734
Phone: 541-546-6494
Fax: 541-546-3624
Web: www.cityofculver.net
Elevation: 2,640'
Incorporated: 6/27/1946
Mayor: Nancy L. Diaz

*Dallas
County: Polk
Address: 187 SE Court St., 97338
Phone: 503-623-2338
Fax: 503-623-2339
Web: www.ci.dallas.or.us
Elevation: 325'
Incorporated: 2/20/1874
Mayor: Brian Dalton

Dayton
County: Yamhill
Address: PO Box 339, 416 Ferry St., 97114
Phone: 503-864-2221
Fax: 503-864-2956
Web: www.ci.dayton.or.us
Elevation: 280'
Incorporated: 10/15/1880
Mayor: Elizabeth "Beth" Wytoski

Dayville
County: Grant
Address: PO Box 321, 3 Park Ln., 97825
Phone: 541-987-2188
Fax: 541-987-2187
Email: dville@ortelco.net
Elevation: 2,369'
Incorporated: 10/25/1913
Mayor: Peter Bogardus

Depoe Bay
County: Lincoln
Address: PO Box 8, 570 SE Shell Ave., 97341
Phone: 541-765-2361
Fax: 541-765-2129
Web: www.cityofdepoebay.org
Elevation: 56'
Incorporated: 12/14/1973
Mayor: Barbra Leff

Detroit
County: Marion
Address: PO Box 589, 160 Detroit Ave., 97342
Phone: 503-854-3496
Fax: 503-854-3232
Web: http://detroitoregon.us
Elevation: 1,595'
Incorporated: 9/29/1952
Mayor: James R. Trett

Donald
County: Marion
Address: PO Box 388, 10710 Main St. NE, 97020
Phone: 503-678-5543
Fax: 503-678-2750
Web: www.donaldoregon.gov
Elevation: 198'
Incorporated: 12/6/1912
Mayor: Richard R. Olmsted

Drain
County: Douglas
Address: PO Box 158, 129 West C Ave., 97435
Phone: 541-836-2417
Fax: 541-836-7330
Web: www.cityofdrain.org
Elevation: 303'
Incorporated: 2/9/1887
Mayor: Suzanne Anderson

Dufur
County: Wasco
Address: PO Box 145, 175 NE Third St., 97021
Phone: 541-467-2349
Fax: 541-467-2353
Web: www.cityofdufur.org
Elevation: 1,345'
Incorporated: 2/10/1893
Mayor: Merle Keys

Dundee
County: Yamhill
Address: PO Box 220, 620 SW Fifth St., 97115
Phone: 503-538-3922
Fax: 503-538-1958
Web: www.dundeecity.org
Elevation: 189'
Incorporated: 2/21/1895
Mayor: David Russ

Dunes City
County: Lane
Address: PO Box 97, Westlake, 82877 Spruce St., 94793
Phone: 541-997-3338
Fax: 541-997-5751
Web: http://dunescity.com
Elevation: 39'
Incorporated: 6/13/1963
Mayor: Rebecca "Becky" Ruede

Durham
County: Washington
Address: 17160 SW Upper Boones Ferry Rd., 97224
Phone: 503-639-6851
Fax: 503-598-8595
Web: www.durham-oregon.us
Elevation: 197'
Incorporated: 7/20/1966
Mayor: Gery Schirado

Eagle Point
County: Jackson
Address: PO Box 779, 17 Buchanan Ave., 97524
Phone: 541-826-4212
Fax: 541-826-6155
Web: www.cityofeaglepoint.org
Elevation: 1,310'
Incorporated: 2/16/1911
Mayor: Robert Russell

Echo
County: Umatilla
Address: PO Box 9, 20 S Bonanza St., 97826
Phone: 541-376-8411
Fax: 541-376-8218
Web: www.echo-oregon.com
Elevation: 635'
Incorporated: 3/9/1904
Mayor: Eujeana Hampton

Elgin
County: Union
Address: PO Box 128, 180 N Eighth Ave., 97827
Phone: 541-437-2253
Fax: 541-437-0131
Web: www.cityofelginor.org
Elevation: 2,670'
Incorporated: 2/18/1891
Mayor: Allan L. Duffy

Elkton
County: Douglas
Address: PO Box 508, 366 First St., 97436
Phone: 541-584-2547
Fax: 541-584-2547
Web: www.elkton-oregon.com
Elevation: 132'
Incorporated: 11/4/1948
Mayor: Daniel Burke

*Enterprise
County: Wallowa
Address: 108 NE First St., 97828
Phone: 541-426-4196
Fax: 541-426-3395
Web: www.enterpriseoregon.org
Elevation: 3,757'
Incorporated: 2/21/1889
Mayor: Stacey Karvoski

Estacada
County: Clackamas
Address: PO Box 958, 475 SE Main St., 97023
Phone: 503-630-8270
Fax: 503-630-8280
Web: www.cityofestacada.org
Elevation: 468'
Incorporated: 1/31/1905
Mayor: Sean Drinkwine

*Eugene
County: Lane
Address: 125 E Eighth Ave., 2nd Floor, 97401
Phone: 541-682-5010
Fax: 541-682-5414
Web: www.eugene-or.gov
Elevation: 430'
Incorporated: 10/17/1862 or 10/22/1864
Mayor: Lucy Vinis

Fairview
County: Multnomah
Address: PO Box 337, 1300 NE Village St., 97024
Phone: 503-665-7929
Fax: 503-666-0888
Web: www.fairvieworegon.gov
Elevation: 114'
Incorporated: 5/11/1908
Mayor: Ted Tosterud

Falls City
County: Polk
Address: 299 Mill St., 97344
Phone: 503-787-3631
Fax: 503-787-3023
Web: www.fallscityoregon.gov
Elevation: 370'
Incorporated: 2/13/1893
Mayor: Terry Ungricht

Florence
County: Lane
Address: 250 Hwy. 101, 97439
Phone: 541-997-3437
Fax: 541-997-6814
Web: www.ci.florence.or.us
Elevation: 14'
Incorporated: 2/10/1893
Mayor: Joe Henry

Forest Grove
County: Washington
Address: PO Box 326, 1924 Council St., 97116
Phone: 503-992-3200
Fax: 503-992-3207
Web: www.forestgrove-or.gov
Elevation: 210'
Incorporated: 10/5/1872
Mayor: Peter B. Truax

*Fossil
County: Wheeler
Address: PO Box 467, 401 Main St., 97830
Phone: 541-763-2698
Fax: 541-763-2124
Web: www.cityoffossil.org
Elevation: 2,673'
Incorporated: 2/18/1891
Mayor: Carol E. MacInnes

Garibaldi
County: Tillamook
Address: PO Box 708, 107 Sixth St., 97118
Phone: 503-322-3327
Fax: 503-322-3737
Web: www.ci.garibaldi.or.us
Elevation: 22'
Incorporated: 4/8/1946
Mayor: Suzanne McCarthy

Gaston
County: Washington
Address: PO Box 129, 116 Front St., 97119
Phone: 503-985-3340
Fax: 503-985-1014
Email: gaston.city@comcast.net
Elevation: 300'
Incorporated: 12/7/1911
Mayor: Tony Hall

Gates
County: Marion
Address: 101 Sorbin Ave. W, 97346
Phone: 503-897-2669
Fax: 503-897-5046
Email: ctygtes@wbcable.net
Elevation: 945'
Incorporated: 7/7/1955
Mayor: Jerry A. Marr

Gearhart
County: Clatsop
Address: PO Box 2510, 698 Pacific Way, 97138
Phone: 503-738-5501
Fax: 503-738-9385
Web: www.ci.gearhart.or.us
Elevation: 16'
Incorporated: 1/28/1918
Mayor: Matt J. Brown

Gervais
County: Marion
Address: PO Box 329, 592 Fourth St., 97026
Phone: 503-792-4900
Fax: 503-792-3791
Web: www.gervaisoregon.org
Elevation: 184'
Incorporated: 10/29/1874
Mayor: Shanti M. Platt

Gladstone
County: Clackamas
Address: 525 Portland Ave., 97027
Phone: 503-656-5225
Fax: 503-557-2761
Web: www.ci.gladstone.or.us
Elevation: 61'
Incorporated: 1/5/1911
Mayor: Tammy Stempel

Glendale
County: Douglas
Address: PO Box 361, 124 Third St., 97442
Phone: 541-832-2106
Fax: 541-832-3221
Web: www.cityofglendaleor.com
Elevation: 1,443'
Incorporated: 2/23/1901
Mayor: Adam Jones

*Gold Beach
County: Curry
Address: 29592 Ellensburg Ave., 97444
Phone: 541-247-7029
Fax: 541-247-2212
Web: www.goldbeachoregon.gov
Elevation: 50'
Incorporated: 9/24/1945
Mayor: Karl Popoff

Gold Hill
County: Jackson
Address: PO Box 308, 420 Sixth Ave., 97525
Phone: 541-855-1525
Fax: 541-855-4501
Web: www.ci.goldhill.or.us
Elevation: 1,085'
Incorporated: 2/12/1895
Mayor: Christina Stanley

Granite
County: Grant
Address: 1378 Main St., 97877
Phone: 541-755-5100
Fax: 541-755-5100
Email: granitecity@pinetel.com
Elevation: 4,695'
Incorporated: 5/17/1900
Mayor: Ron Simonis

*Grants Pass
County: Josephine
Address: 101 NW A St., 97526
Phone: 541-450-6000
Fax: 541-479-0812
Web: www.grantspassoregon.gov
Elevation: 960'
Incorporated: 2/18/1891
Mayor: Darin Fowler

Grass Valley
County: Sherman
Address: PO Box 191, 97029
Phone: 541-333-2434
Fax: 541-333-2276
Email: cityofgv@embarqmail.com
Elevation: 2,275'
Incorporated: 10/8/1900
Mayor: Neil Pattee

Greenhorn
County: Baker
Address: 28932 S Cramer Rd., Molalla 97038
Phone: 503-310-0913
Email: hmartin@bakercounty.org
Elevation: 6,300'
Incorporated: 2/20/1903
General Manager: Baker County Commission

Gresham
County: Multnomah
Address: 1333 NW Eastman Pkwy., 97030
Phone: 503-661-3000
Fax: 503-618-3301
Web: www.greshamoregon.gov
Elevation: 301'
Incorporated: 6/3/1904
Mayor: Shane T. Bemis

Haines
County: Baker
Address: PO Box 208, 819 Front St., 97833
Phone: 541-856-3366
Fax: 541-856-3812
Web: www.cityofhainesor.org
Elevation: 3,341'
Incorporated: 3/11/1902
Mayor: Jim Brown

Halfway
County: Baker
Address: PO Box 738, 97834-0738
Phone: 541-742-4741
Fax: 541-742-4741
Email: halfwaycity@gmail.com
Elevation: 2,651'
Incorporated: 5/27/1909
Mayor: Sheila Farwell

Halsey
County: Linn
Address: PO Box 10, 100 W Halsey St., 97348
Phone: 541-369-2522
Fax: 541-369-2521
Web: www.cityofhalsey.com
Elevation: 213'
Incorporated: 10/20/1876
Mayor: Marjean Cline

Happy Valley
County: Clackamas
Address: 16000 SE Misty Dr., 97086-6299
Phone: 503-783-3800
Fax: 503-658-5174
Web: www.happyvalleyor.gov
Elevation: 377'
Incorporated: 12/4/1965
Mayor: Lori Chavez-DeRemer

Harrisburg
County: Linn
Address: PO Box 378, 120 Smith St., 97446
Phone: 541-995-6655
Fax: 541-995-9244
Web: www.ci.harrisburg.or.us
Elevation: 309'
Incorporated: 10/24/1866
Mayor: Robert "Bobby" Duncan

Helix
County: Umatilla
Address: PO Box 323, 97835
Phone: 541-457-2521
Email: cityofhelix@gmail.com
Elevation: 1,754'
Incorporated: 1/9/1903
Mayor: Jack Bascomb

*Heppner
County: Morrow
Address: PO Box 756, 111 N Main St., 97836
Phone: 541-676-9618
Fax: 541-676-9650
Web: www.cityofheppner.com
Elevation: 2,192'
Incorporated: 2/9/1887
Mayor: Cody High

Hermiston
County: Umatilla
Address: 180 NE Second St., 97838
Phone: 541-567-5521
Fax: 541-567-5530
Web: www.hermiston.or.us
Elevation: 643'
Incorporated: 7/23/1907
Mayor: David Drotzmann

*Hillsboro
County: Washington
Address: 150 E Main St., 97123
Phone: 503-681-6100
Fax: 503-681-6213
Web: http://www.hillsboro-oregon.gov
Elevation: 196'
Incorporated: 10/19/1876
Mayor: Jerry Willey

Hines
County: Harney
Address: PO Box 336, 101 E Barnes Ave., 97738
Phone: 541-573-2251
Fax: 541-573-5827
Web: www.ci.hines.or.us
Elevation: 4,155'
Incorporated: 12/13/1930
Mayor: Nikki Morgan

*Hood River
County: Hood River
Address: 211 Second St., 97031
Phone: 541-386-1488
Fax: 541-387-5289
Web: http://hood-river.or.us
Elevation: 160'
Incorporated: 2/15/1895
Mayor: Paul Blackburn

Hubbard
County: Marion
Address: PO Box 380, 3720 Second St., 97032
Phone: 503-981-9633
Fax: 503-981-8743
Web: www.cityofhubbard.org
Elevation: 181'
Incorporated: 2/18/1891
Mayor: Thia Estes

Huntington
County: Baker
Address: PO Box 369, 50 E Adams, 97907
Phone: 541-869-2202
Fax: 541-869-2550
Email: hun1891@netscape.net
Elevation: 2,110'
Incorporated: 2/18/1891
Mayor: Candy Howland

Idanha
County: Linn/Marion
Address: PO Box 430, 111 Hwy. 22 NW, 97350
Phone: 503-854-3313
Fax: 503-854-3114
Email: cityofid@bni.net
Elevation: 1,718'
Incorporated: 3/15/1950
Mayor: Jeffery Yohe

Imbler
County: Union
Address: PO Box 40, 180 Ruckman Ave., 97841
Phone: 541-534-6095
Fax: 541-534-2343
Web: www.imbleroregon.com
Elevation: 2,725'
Incorporated: 3/20/1922
Mayor: Mike McLean

Independence
County: Polk
Address: PO Box 7, 555 S Main St., 97351
Phone: 503-838-1212
Fax: 503-606-3282
Web: www.ci.independence.or.us
Elevation: 168'
Incorporated: 10/20/1874
Mayor: John McArdle

Ione
County: Morrow
Address: PO Box 361, 385 W Second St., 97843
Phone: 541-422-7414
Fax: 541-422-7179

Web: www.cityofioneoregon.com
Elevation: 1,089'
Incorporated: 7/14/1899
Mayor: Rod Taylor

Irrigon
County: Morrow
Address: PO Box 428, 500 NE Main St., 97844
Phone: 541-922-3047
Fax: 541-922-9322
Web: http://cityofirrigon.org
Elevation: 297'
Incorporated: 2/28/1957
Mayor: Sam Heath

Island City
County: Union
Address: 10605 Island Ave., 97850
Phone: 541-963-5017
Fax: 541-963-3482
Web: http://islandcityoregon.com
Elevation: 2,743'
Incorporated: 2/12/1904
Mayor: Delmer E. Hanson

Jacksonville
County: Jackson
Address: PO Box 7, 206 N Fifth St., 97530
Phone: 541-899-1231
Fax: 541-899-7882
Web: www.jacksonvilleor.us
Elevation: 1,569'
Incorporated: 10/19/1860
Mayor: Paul Becker

Jefferson
County: Marion
Address: PO Box 83, 150 N Second St., 97352
Phone: 541-327-2768
Fax: 541-327-3120
Web: http://city.jeffersonoregon.us
Elevation: 240'
Incorporated: 10/29/1870
Mayor: Cyndie Hightower

John Day
County: Grant
Address: 450 E Main St., 97845
Phone: 541-575-0028
Fax: 541-575-3668
Web: www.cityofjohnday.com
Elevation: 3,087'
Incorporated: 5/9/1900
Mayor: Ron Lundbom

Johnson City
County: Clackamas
Address: 16121 SE 81st Ave., 97267
Phone: 503-655-9710
Fax: 503-723-0317
Email: johnson.city@hotmail.com
Elevation: 114'
Incorporated: 6/23/1970
Mayor: Kay Mordock

Jordan Valley
County: Malheur
Address: PO Box 187, 306 Blackaby St., 97910
Phone: 541-586-2460
Fax: 541-586-2460
Web: www.cityofjordanvalley.com
Elevation: 4,389'
Incorporated: 3/21/1911
Mayor: Marie Kershner

Joseph
County: Wallowa
Address: PO Box 15, 201 N Main St., 97846
Phone: 541-432-3832
Fax: 541-432-3832
Web: www.josephoregon.org
Elevation: 4,200'
Incorporated: 2/9/1887
Mayor: Dennis Sands

Junction City
County: Lane
Address: PO Box 250, 680 Greenwood St., 97448
Phone: 541-998-2153
Fax: 541-998-3140
Web: www.junctioncityoregon.gov
Elevation: 325'
Incorporated: 10/29/1872
Mayor: Mark Crenshaw

Keizer
County: Marion
Address: PO Box 21000, 930 Chemawa Rd. NE, 97303
Phone: 503-390-3700
Fax: 503-393-9437
Web: www.keizer.org
Elevation: 132'
Incorporated: 11/16/1982
Mayor: Cathy Clark

King City
County: Washington
Address: 15300 SW 116th Ave., 97224-2693
Phone: 503-639-4082
Fax: 503-639-3771
Web: www.ci.king-city.or.us
Elevation: 213'
Incorporated: 7/14/1966
Mayor: Ken Gibson

*Klamath Falls
County: Klamath
Address: PO Box 237, 500 Klamath Ave., 97601
Phone: 541-883-5316
Fax: 541-883-5399
Web: https://www.klamathfalls.city
Elevation: 4,099'
Incorporated: 2/6/1893
Mayor: Carol Westfall

*La Grande
County: Union
Address: PO Box 670, 1000 Adams Ave., 97850
Phone: 541-962-1309

Fax: 541-963-3333
Web: www.cityoflagrande.org
Elevation: 2,785'
Incorporated: 12/18/1865
Mayor: Steve Clements

La Pine
County: Deschutes
Address: PO Box 2460, 16345 Sixth St., 97739
Phone: 541-536-1432
Fax: 541-536-1462
Web: www.ci.la-pine.or.us
Elevation: 4,236'
Incorporated: 12/11/2006
Mayor: Ken Mulenex

Lafayette
County: Yamhill
Address: PO Box 55, 486 Third St., 97127
Phone: 503-864-2451
Fax: 503-864-4501
Web: www.ci.lafayette.or.us
Elevation: 160'
Incorporated: 10/17/1878
Mayor: Chris Pagella

Lake Oswego
County: Clackamas
Address: PO Box 369, 380 A Ave., 97034
Phone: 503-635-0215
Fax: 503-697-6594
Web: www.ci.oswego.or.us
Elevation: 146'
Incorporated: 1/15/1910
Mayor: Kent Studebaker

Lakeside
County: Coos
Address: PO Box L, 915 North Lake Rd., 97449
Phone: 541-759-3011
Fax: 541-759-3711
Web: http://cityoflakeside.org
Elevation: 23'
Incorporated: 6/26/1974
Mayor: L. Dean Warner

*Lakeview
County: Lake
Address: 525 N First St., 97630
Phone: 541-947-2029
Fax: 541-947-2952
Web: www.lakevieworegon.org
Elevation: 4,802'
Incorporated: 2/10/1893
Mayor: Ray Turner

Lebanon
County: Linn
Address: 925 S Main St., 97355
Phone: 541-258-4900
Fax: 541-258-4950
Web: www.ci.lebanon.or.us
Elevation: 351'
Incorporated: 10/17/1878
Mayor: Paul Aziz

Lexington
County: Morrow
Address: PO Box 416, 97839
Phone: 541-989-8515
Fax: 541-989-8515
Web: www.lexingtonoregon.com
Elevation: 1,450'
Incorporated: 2/3/1903
Mayor: Arletta Arnspiger

Lincoln City
County: Lincoln
Address: PO Box 50, 801 SW Hwy. 101, 97367
Phone: 541-996-2152
Fax: 541-994-7232
Web: www.lincolncity.org
Elevation: 11'
Incorporated: 2/24/1965
Mayor: Don Williams

Lonerock
County: Gilliam
Address: Lonerock Rte., 104 SE Main St., Condon 97823
Phone: 541-384-2241
Elevation: 2,800'
Incorporated: 2/20/1901
Mayor: Paul O'Dell

Long Creek
County: Grant
Address: PO Box 489, 250 Hardisty St., 97856
Phone: 541-421-3601
Fax: 541-421-3075
Web: www.cityoflongcreek.com
Elevation: 3,754'
Incorporated: 2/18/1891
Mayor: Don Porter

Lostine
County: Wallowa
Address: PO Box 181, 97857
Phone: 541-569-2415
Fax: 541-569-5116
Elevation: 3,200'
Incorporated: 12/28/1903
Mayor: Dusty Tippet

Lowell
County: Lane
Address: PO Box 490, 107 E Third St., 97452
Phone: 541-937-2157
Fax: 541-937-2936
Web: www.ci.lowell.or.us
Elevation: 742'
Incorporated: 11/24/1954
Mayor: Don Bennett

Lyons
County: Linn
Address: 449 Fifth St., 97358
Phone: 503-859-2167
Fax: 503-859-5167
Web: www.cityoflyons.org

Elevation: 660'
Incorporated: 12/17/1958
Mayor: Troy Donohue

*Madras
County: Jefferson
Address: 125 SW E St., 97741
Phone: 541-475-2344
Fax: 541-475-7061
Web: www.ci.madras.or.us
Elevation: 2,242'
Incorporated: 3/29/1910
Mayor: Royce W. Embanks, Jr.

Malin
County: Klamath
Address: PO Box 61, 2432 Fourth St., 97632
Phone: 541-723-2021
Fax: 541-723-2011
Web: www.cityofmalin.org
Elevation: 4,062'
Incorporated: 2/22/1922
Mayor: Gary R. Zieg

Manzanita
County: Tillamook
Address: PO Box 129, 543 Laneda Ave., 97130
Phone: 503-368-5343
Fax: 503-368-4145
Web: www.ci.manzanita.or.us
Elevation: 78'
Incorporated: 4/15/1946
Mayor: Mike Scott

Maupin
County: Wasco
Address: PO Box 308, 408 Deschutes Ave., 97037
Phone: 541-395-2698
Fax: 541-395-2499
Web: www.cityofmaupin.org
Elevation: 1,047'
Incorporated: 4/17/1922
Mayor: Lynn Ewing

Maywood Park
County: Multnomah
Address: 10100 NE Prescott St., Suite 147, Portland 97220
Phone: 503-255-9805
Fax: 503-251-0366
Web: www.cityofmaywoodpark.com
Elevation: 77'
Incorporated: 10/25/1967
Mayor: Mark Hardie

*McMinnville
County: Yamhill
Address: 230 NE Second St., 97128
Phone: 503-472-4104
Fax: 503-434-7405
Web: www.mcminnvilleoregon.gov
Elevation: 157'
Incorporated: 10/20/1876
Mayor: Scott A. Hill

*Medford
County: Jackson
Address: 411 W Eighth St., Suite 310, 97501
Phone: 541-774-2000
Fax: 541-618-1700
Web: www.ci.medford.or.us
Elevation: 1,382'
Incorporated: 2/24/1885
Mayor: Gary Wheeler

Merrill
County: Klamath
Address: PO Box 487, 301 E Second St., 97633
Phone: 541-798-5808
Fax: 541-798-0145
Web: www.cityofmerrill.org
Elevation: 4,071'
Incorporated: 7/16/1908
Mayor: Timothy Saunders

Metolius
County: Jefferson
Address: 636 Jefferson Ave., 97741
Phone: 541-546-5533
Fax: 541-546-8809
Web: www.cityofmetolius.org
Elevation: 2,530'
Incorporated: 12/16/1912
Mayor: John Chavez

Mill City
County: Linn/Marion
Address: PO Box 256, 444 S First Ave., 97360
Phone: 503-897-2302
Fax: 503-897-3499
Web: www.ci.mill-city.or.us
Elevation: 862'
Incorporated: 10/15/1947
Mayor: Tim Kirsch

Millersburg
County: Linn
Address: 4222 NE Old Salem Rd., Albany 97321
Phone: 541-928-4523
Fax: 541-928-8945
Web: http://cityofmillersburg.org
Elevation: 235'
Incorporated: 11/4/1974
Mayor: Clayton Wood

Milton-Freewater
County: Umatilla
Address: PO Box 6, 722 S Main St., 97862
Phone: 541-938-5531
Fax: 541-938-8224
Web: www.mfcity.com
Elevation: 1,071'
Incorporated: 12/4/1950
Mayor: Lewis Key

Milwaukie
County: Clackamas
Address: 10722 SE Main St., 97222
Phone: 503-786-7555
Fax: 503-786-7565
Web: www.milwaukieoregon.gov
Elevation: 50'
Incorporated: 2/4/1903
Mayor: Jeremy Ferguson

Mitchell
County: Wheeler
Address: PO Box 97, 97750
Phone: 541-462-3121
Fax: 541-462-3121
Email: cityofmitchell@gmail.com
Elevation: 2,894'
Incorporated: 2/18/1891
Mayor: Vernita Jordan

Molalla
County: Clackamas
Address: PO Box 248, 117 N Molalla Ave., 97038
Phone: 503-829-6855
Fax: 503-829-3676
Web: www.cityofmolalla.com
Elevation: 375'
Incorporated: 8/23/1913
Mayor: Jimmy Thompson

Monmouth
County: Polk
Address: 151 W Main St., 97361
Phone: 503-838-0722
Fax: 503-838-0725
Web: www.ci.monmouth.or.us
Elevation: 214'
Incorporated: 10/19/1880
Mayor: Steve Milligan

Monroe
County: Benton
Address: PO Box 486, 664 Commercial St., 97456
Phone: 541-847-5175
Fax: 541-847-5177
Web: www.ci.monroe.or.us
Elevation: 298'
Incorporated: 5/16/1913
Mayor: Paul Canter

Monument
County: Grant
Address: PO Box 426, 291 Main St., 97864
Phone: 541-934-2025
Fax: 541-934-2025
Email: cityofmonument@centurytel.net
Elevation: 2,000'
Incorporated: 3/6/1905
Mayor: Sahara Derowitsch

*Moro
County: Sherman
Address: PO Box 231, 97039
Phone: 541-565-3535
Fax: 541-565-3535

Web: www.cityofmoro.net
Elevation: 1,870'
Incorporated: 2/17/1899
Mayor: Andy Anderson

Mosier
County: Wasco
Address: PO Box 456, 208 Washington St., 97040
Phone: 541-478-3505
Fax: 541-478-3810
Web: www.cityofmosier.com
Elevation: 164'
Incorporated: 10/14/1914
Mayor: Zariene Chester Burns

Mount Angel
County: Marion
Address: PO Box 960, 5 N Garfield St., 97362
Phone: 503-845-9291
Fax: 503-845-6261
Web: www.ci.mt-angel.or.us
Elevation: 168'
Incorporated: 2/10/1893
Mayor: Andrew "Andy" J. Otte

Mount Vernon
County: Grant
Address: PO Box 647, 97865
Phone: 541-932-4688
Fax: 541-932-4222
Elevation: 2,865'
Incorporated: 5/13/1949
Mayor: Kenny Delano

Myrtle Creek
County: Douglas
Address: PO Box 940, 207 NW Pleasant St., 97457
Phone: 541-863-3171
Fax: 541-863-6851
Web: www.cityofmyrtlecreek.com
Elevation: 650'
Incorporated: 2/13/1893
Mayor: Ken Brouillard

Myrtle Point
County: Coos
Address: 424 Fifth St., 97458
Phone: 541-572-2626
Fax: 541-572-3838
Web: www.ci.myrtlepoint.or.us
Elevation: 131'
Incorporated: 2/4/1887
Mayor: Barbara Carter

Nehalem
County: Tillamook
Address: PO Box 143, 35900 Eighth St., 97131
Phone: 503-368-5627
Fax: 503-368-4175
Web: www.ci.nehalem.or.us
Elevation: 11'

Incorporated: 2/2/1899
Mayor: William L. Dillard

Newberg
County: Yamhill
Address: PO Box 970, 414 E First St., 97132
Phone: 503-538-9421
Fax: 503-537-5013
Web: www.newbergoregon.gov
Elevation: 175'
Incorporated: 2/21/1889
Mayor: Bob Andrews

*Newport
County: Lincoln
Address: 169 SW Coast Hwy., 97365
Phone: 541-574-0603
Fax: 541-574-0609
Web: www.newportoregon.gov
Elevation: 134'
Incorporated: 10/23/1882
Mayor: Sandra N. Roumagoux

North Bend
County: Coos
Address: PO Box B, 835 California St., 97459
Phone: 541-756-8500
Fax: 541-756-8527
Web: http://northbendoregon.us
Elevation: 41'
Incorporated: 7/6/1903
Mayor: Rick Wetherell

North Plains
County: Washington
Address: 31360 NW Commercial St., 97133
Phone: 503-647-5555
Fax: 503-647-2031
Web: http://cityofnp.org
Elevation: 176'
Incorporated: 10/1/1963
Mayor: Teri Lenahan

North Powder
County: Union
Address: PO Box 309, 635 Third St., 97867
Phone: 541-898-2185
Fax: 541-898-2647
Email: cityofnp@eoni.com
Elevation: 3,256'
Incorporated: 7/28/1902
Mayor: Bonita E. Hebert

Nyssa
County: Malheur
Address: 301 Main St., 97913
Phone: 541-372-2264
Fax: 541-372-3737
Web: www.nyssacity.org
Elevation: 2,192'
Incorporated: 2/24/1903
Mayor: Ross Ballard

Oakland

County: Douglas
Address: 637 NE Locust St., 97462
Phone: 541-459-4531
Fax: 541-459-4472
Web: www.oaklandoregon.org
Elevation: 484'
Incorporated: 10/17/1878
Mayor: Bette Keehley

Oakridge

County: Lane
Address: PO Box 1410, 48318 E First St., 97463
Phone: 541-782-2258
Fax: 541-782-1081
Web: www.ci.oakridge.or.us
Elevation: 1,240'
Incorporated: 1/22/1934
Mayor: James B. Coey

Ontario

County: Malheur
Address: 444 SW Fourth St., 97914
Phone: 541-889-7684
Fax: 541-889-7121
Web: www.ontariooregon.org
Elevation: 2,150'
Incorporated: 9/9/1896
Mayor: Ronald Verini

*Oregon City

County: Clackamas
Address: 625 Center St., 97045
Phone: 503-657-0891
Fax: 503-657-3339
Web: www.orcity.org
Elevation: 167'
Incorporated: 12/24/1844
Mayor: Daniel Holladay

Paisley

County: Lake
Address: PO Box 100, 705 Chewaucan St., 97636
Phone: 541-943-3173
Fax: 541-943-3982
Web: www.cityofpaisley.net
Elevation: 4,369'
Incorporated: 11/18/1911
Mayor: Dale Blair

*Pendleton

County: Umatilla
Address: 500 SW Dorion Ave., 97801
Phone: 541-966-0200
Fax: 541-966-0231
Web: www.pendleton.or.us
Elevation: 1,200'
Incorporated: 10/25/1880
Mayor: John Turner

Philomath

County: Benton
Address: PO Box 400, 980 Applegate St., 97370
Phone: 541-929-6148
Fax: 541-929-3044
Web: www.ci.philomath.or.us
Elevation: 270'
Incorporated: 10/20/1882
Mayor: Rocky A. Sloan

Phoenix

County: Jackson
Address: PO Box 330, 112 W Second St., 97535
Phone: 541-535-1955
Fax: 541-535-5769
Web: www.phoenixoregon.gov
Elevation: 1,543'
Incorporated: 10/13/1910
Mayor: Chris Luz

Pilot Rock

County: Umatilla
Address: PO Box 130, 144 N Alder Pl., 97868
Phone: 541-443-2811
Fax: 541-443-2253
Web: www.cityofpilotrock.org
Elevation: 1,637'
Incorporated: 1/10/1902
Mayor: Virginia Carol Carnes

Port Orford

County: Curry
Address: PO Box 310, 555 W 20th St., 97465
Phone: 541-332-3681
Fax: 877-281-5307
Web: www.portorford.org
Elevation: 59'
Incorporated: 12/21/1911
Mayor: Tim Pogwizd

*Portland

County: Clackamas/Multnomah/Washington
Address: 1221 SW Fourth Ave., Rm. 110, 97204
Phone: 503-823-4000
Fax: 503-823-3050
Web: www.portlandoregon.gov
Elevation: 77'
Incorporated: 1/23/1851
Mayor: Ted Wheeler

Powers

County: Coos
Address: PO Box 250, 275 First St., 97466
Phone: 541-439-3331
Fax: 541-439-5555
Email: cityofpowers@msn.com
Elevation: 286'
Incorporated: 12/26/1945
Mayor: Bill Holland

Prairie City

County: Grant
Address: PO Box 370, 133 S Bridge St., 97869
Phone: 541-820-3605
Fax: 541-820-3566
Web: http://prairiecityoregon.com
Elevation: 3,548'
Incorporated: 2/19/1891
Mayor: Jim Hamsher

Prescott
County: Columbia
Address: 72742 Blakely St., Rainier 97048
Phone: 503-369-0281
Email: jl.oswald@hotmail.com
Elevation: 30'
Incorporated: 5/9/1949
Mayor: Lynette Oswald

*Prineville
County: Crook
Address: 387 NE Third St., 97754
Phone: 541-447-5627
Fax: 541-447-5628
Web: www.cityofprineville.com
Elevation: 2,868'
Incorporated: 10/23/1880
Mayor: Betty Jean Roppe

Rainier
County: Columbia
Address: PO Box 100, 106 West B St., 97048
Phone: 503-556-7301
Fax: 503-556-3200
Web: www.cityofrainier.com
Elevation: 45'
Incorporated: 11/25/1885
Mayor: Jerry Cole

Redmond
County: Deschutes
Address: 716 SW Evergreen Ave., 97756
Phone: 541-923-7710
Fax: 541-548-0706
Web: www.ci.redmond.or.us
Elevation: 3,077'
Incorporated: 7/16/1910
Mayor: George Endicott

Reedsport
County: Douglas
Address: 451 Winchester Ave., 97467
Phone: 541-271-3603
Fax: 541-271-2809
Web: www.cityofreedsport.org
Elevation: 36'
Incorporated: 8/6/1919
Mayor: Linda R. McCollum

Richland
County: Baker
Address: PO Box 266, 89 Main St., 97870
Phone: 541-893-6141
Fax: 541-893-6267
Email: richcity@eagletelephone.com
Elevation: 2,231'
Incorporated: 8/8/1902
Mayor: Dick Pedersen

Riddle
County: Douglas
Address: PO Box 143, 647 E First St., 97469
Phone: 541-874-2571
Fax: 541-874-2625
Web: www.riddleoregon.com
Elevation: 685'
Incorporated: 1/30/1893
Mayor: William "Bill" G. Duckett

Rivergrove
County: Clackamas/Washington
Address: PO Box 1104, Lake Oswego 97035
Phone: 503-639-6919
Fax: 503-624-8498
Web: www.cityofrivergrove.com
Elevation: 140'
Incorporated: 3/11/1971
Mayor: Heather Kibby

Rockaway Beach
County: Tillamook
Address: PO Box 5, 276 S Hwy. 101, 97136
Phone: 503-355-2291
Fax: 503-355-8221
Web: www.rockawaybeachor.us
Elevation: 17'
Incorporated: 7/14/1943
Mayor: Joanne Aagaard

Rogue River
County: Jackson
Address: PO Box 1137, 133 Broadway, 97537
Phone: 541-582-4401
Fax: 541-582-0937
Web: www.cityofrogueriver.org
Elevation: 1,004'
Incorporated: 10/8/1910
Mayor: Pam VanArsdale

*Roseburg
County: Douglas
Address: 900 SE Douglas Ave., 97470-3397
Phone: 541-492-6700
Web: www.cityofroseburg.org
Elevation: 475'
Incorporated: 10/26/1868
Mayor: Larry Rich

Rufus
County: Sherman
Address: PO Box 27, 304 W Second St., #100, 97050
Phone: 541-739-2321
Fax: 541-739-2460
Web: www.cityofrufus.com
Elevation: 235'
Incorporated: 11/3/1964
Mayor: Daniel L. Pehlke, Jr.

*Saint Helens
County: Columbia
Address: PO Box 278, 265 Strand St., 97051
Phone: 503-397-6272
Fax: 503-397-4016
Web: www.ci.st-helens.or.us
Elevation: 42'
Incorporated: 2/25/1889
Mayor: Rick Scholl

Saint Paul
County: Marion
Address: PO Box 7, 20239 Main St., 97137
Phone: 503-633-4971
Fax: 503-633-4972
Email: stpaulcity@stpaultel.com
Elevation: 169'
Incorporated: 2/16/1901
Mayor: Kim Wallis

*Salem
County: Marion/Polk
Address: 555 Liberty St. SE, 97301
Phone: 503-588-6255
Fax: 503-588-6354
Web: www.cityofsalem.net
Elevation: 154'
Incorporated: 1/13/1857
Mayor: Chuck Bennett

Sandy
County: Clackamas
Address: 39250 Pioneer Blvd., 97055
Phone: 503-668-5533
Fax: 503-668-8714
Web: www.ci.sandy.or.us
Elevation: 992'
Incorporated: 9/11/1911
Mayor: William "Bill" R. King

Scappoose
County: Columbia
Address: 33568 E Columbia Ave., 97056
Phone: 503-543-7146
Fax: 503-543-7182
Web: www.ci.scappoose.or.us
Elevation: 64'
Incorporated: 8/13/1921
Mayor: Scott Burge

Scio
County: Linn
Address: PO Box 37, 97374-0037
Phone: 503-394-3342
Fax: 503-394-2340
Web: http://ci.scio.or.us
Elevation: 317'
Incorporated: 10/24/1866
Mayor: Gary C. Weaver

Scotts Mills
County: Marion
Address: 265 Fourth St., PO Box 220, 97375
Phone: 503-873-5435
Fax: 503-874-4540
Web: www.scottsmills.org
Elevation: 426'
Incorporated: 8/2/1916
Mayor: Paul Brakeman

Seaside
County: Clatsop
Address: 989 Broadway, 97138
Phone: 503-738-5511
Fax: 503-738-5514
Web: www.cityofseaside.us
Elevation: 17'
Incorporated: 2/17/1899
Mayor: Don Larson

Seneca
County: Grant
Address: PO Box 208, 106 A Ave., 97873
Phone: 541-542-2161
Fax: 541-542-2161
Email: cityseneca@centurytel.net
Elevation: 4,690'
Incorporated: 8/6/1970
Mayor: Andrea Combs

Shady Cove
County: Jackson
Address: PO Box 1210, 97539
Phone: 541-878-2225
Fax: 541-878-2226
Web: www.shadycove.net
Elevation: 1,406'
Incorporated: 11/8/1972
Mayor: Tom Anderson

Shaniko
County: Wasco
Address: PO Box 17, 97057
Phone: 541-489-3447
Web: www.shanikooregon.com
Elevation: 3,344'
Incorporated: 3/13/1901
Mayor: Goldie Roberts

Sheridan
County: Yamhill
Address: 120 SW Mill St., 97378
Phone: 503-843-2347
Fax: 503-843-3661
Web: www.cityofsheridanor.com
Elevation: 189'
Incorporated: 10/25/1880
Mayor: Harry F. Cooley

Sherwood
County: Washington
Address: 22560 SW Pine St., 97140
Phone: 503-625-5522
Fax: 503-625-5524
Web: www.sherwoodoregon.gov
Elevation: 193'
Incorporated: 2/10/1893
Mayor: Krisanna Clark

Siletz
County: Lincoln
Address: PO Box 318, 215 W Buford Ave., 97380
Phone: 541-444-2521
Fax: 541-444-7371
Web: www.cityofsiletz.org
Elevation: 130'
Incorporated: 3/31/1947
Mayor: John S. Robinson

Silverton
County: Marion
Address: 306 S Water St., 97381
Phone: 503-873-5321
Fax: 503-873-3210
Web: www.silverton.or.us
Elevation: 252'
Incorporated: 2/16/1885
Mayor: Rick Lewis

Sisters
County: Deschutes
Address: PO Box 39, 520 E Cascade Ave., 97759
Phone: 541-549-6022
Fax: 541-549-0561
Web: www.ci.sisters.or.us
Elevation: 3,182'
Incorporated: 4/9/1946
Mayor: Chuck Ryan

Sodaville
County: Linn
Address: 30723 Sodaville Rd., 97355
Phone: 541-258-8882
Fax: 541-258-8882
Web: www.sodaville.org
Elevation: 492'
Incorporated: 10/25/1880
Mayor: Suzanne M. Hibbert

Spray
County: Wheeler
Address: PO Box 83, 300 Park Ave., 97874
Phone: 541-468-2069
Fax: 541-468-2044
Web: www.sprayoregon.us
Elevation: 1,801'
Incorporated: 9/18/1958
Mayor: Daniel Allen

Springfield
County: Lane
Address: 225 Fifth St., 97477
Phone: 541-726-3700
Fax: 541-726-2363
Web: www.springfield-or.gov
Elevation: 456'
Incorporated: 2/25/1885
Mayor: Christine Lundberg

Stanfield
County: Umatilla
Address: PO Box 369, 160 S Main St., 97875
Phone: 541-449-3831
Fax: 541-449-1828
Web: www.cityofstanfield.com
Elevation: 592'
Incorporated: 5/13/1910
Mayor: Thomas J. McCann

Stayton
County: Marion
Address: 362 N Third Ave., 97383
Phone: 503-769-3425
Fax: 503-769-1456
Web: www.staytonoregon.gov
Elevation: 452'
Incorporated: 2/13/1901
Mayor: Henry A. Porter

Sublimity
County: Marion
Address: PO Box 146, 245 NW Johnson St., 97385
Phone: 503-769-5475
Fax: 503-769-2206
Web: www.cityofsublimity.org
Elevation: 551'
Incorporated: 2/3/1903
Mayor: Raymond P. Heuberger

Summerville
County: Union
Address: PO Box 92, 301 Main St., 97876
Phone: 541-534-6701
Email: sheri_rogers@frontier.com
Elevation: 2,705'
Incorporated: 11/24/1885
Mayor: Sheri Rogers

Sumpter
County: Baker
Address: PO Box 68, 240 N Mill St., 97877
Phone: 541-894-2314
Fax: 541-894-2375
Email: cityofsumpter@qwestoffice.net
Elevation: 4,429'
Incorporated: 5/5/1898
Mayor: Cary Clarke

Sutherlin
County: Douglas
Address: 126 E Central Ave., 97479
Phone: 541-459-2856
Fax: 541-459-9363
Web: www.ci.sutherlin.or.us
Elevation: 516'
Incorporated: 5/4/1911
Mayor: Todd McKnight

Sweet Home
County: Linn
Address: 1140 12th Ave., 97386
Phone: 541-367-5128
Fax: 541-367-5113
Web: www.ci.sweet-home.or.us
Elevation: 537'
Incorporated: 2/10/1893
Mayor: Greg Mahler

Talent
County: Jackson
Address: PO Box 445, 110 E Main St., 97540
Phone: 541-535-1566
Fax: 541-535-7423
Web: www.cityoftalent.org
Elevation: 1,635'
Incorporated: 11/25/1910
Mayor: Darby Stricker

Tangent

County: Linn
Address: PO Box 251, 32166 Old Oak Dr., 97389
Phone: 541-928-1020
Fax: 541-928-4920
Web: www.cityoftangent.org
Elevation: 245'
Incorporated: 2/10/1893
Mayor: Loel Trulove

*The Dalles

County: Wasco
Address: 313 Court St., 97058
Phone: 541-296-5481
Fax: 541-296-6906
Web: www.ci.the-dalles.or.us
Elevation: 109'
Incorporated: 1/26/1857
Mayor: Steve Lawrence

Tigard

County: Washington
Address: 13125 SW Hall Blvd., 97223
Phone: 503-639-4171
Fax: 503-684-7297
Web: www.tigard-or.gov
Elevation: 300'
Incorporated: 10/3/1961
Mayor: John Cook

*Tillamook

County: Tillamook
Address: 210 Laurel Ave., 97141
Phone: 503-842-2472
Fax: 503-842-3445
Web: www.tillamookor.gov
Elevation: 24'
Incorporated: 2/18/1891
Mayor: Suzanne Weber

Toledo

County: Lincoln
Address: PO Box 220, 206 N Main St., 97391
Phone: 541-336-2247
Fax: 541-336-3512
Web: www.cityoftoledo.org
Elevation: 59'
Incorporated: 10/11/1893
Mayor: Billie Jo Smith

Troutdale

County: Multnomah
Address: 219 E Historic Columbia River Hwy., 97060
Phone: 503-665-5175
Fax: 503-667-6403
Web: www.troutdale.info
Elevation: 30'–200'
Incorporated: 10/3/1907
Mayor: Casey Ryan

Tualatin

County: Clackamas/Washington
Address: 18880 SW Martinazzi Ave., 97062
Phone: 503-692-2000
Fax: 503-692-5421
Web: www.tualatinoregon.gov
Elevation: 123'
Incorporated: 5/8/1913
Mayor: Lou Ogden

Turner

County: Marion
Address: PO Box 456, 5255 Chicago St., SE, 97392
Phone: 503-743-2155
Fax: 503-743-4010
Web: www.cityofturner.org
Elevation: 287'
Incorporated: 2/10/1905
Mayor: Gary Tiffin

Ukiah

County: Umatilla
Address: PO Box 265, 97880
Phone: 541-427-3900
Fax: 541-427-3902
Web: www.cityofukiahoregon.com
Elevation: 3,400'
Incorporated: 5/23/1972
Mayor: Clinton Barber

Umatilla

County: Umatilla
Address: PO Box 130, 700 Sixth St., 97882
Phone: 541-922-3226
Fax: 541-922-5758
Web: www.umatilla-city.org
Elevation: 322'
Incorporated: 10/24/1864
Mayor: David P. Trott

Union

County: Union
Address: PO Box 529, 342 S Main, 97883
Phone: 541-562-5197
Fax: 541-562-5196
Web: www.cityofunion.com
Elevation: 2,791'
Incorporated: 10/19/1878
Mayor: Leonard Flint

Unity

County: Baker
Address: 1995 Third St., Baker City 97814
Phone: 541-523-8200
Fax: 541-523-8201
Web: http://bakercounty.org
Elevation: 4,040'
Incorporated: 7/31/1972
General Manager: Mark Bennett

*Vale

County: Malheur
Address: 252 B St. W, 97918
Phone: 541-473-3133
Fax: 541-473-3895
Web: http://www.cityofvale.com

Elevation: 2,343'
Incorporated: 2/21/1889
Mayor: Mike (Mac) McLaughlin

Veneta
County: Lane
Address: PO Box 458, 88184 Eighth St., 97487
Phone: 541-935-2191
Fax: 541-935-1838
Web: www.venetaoregon.gov
Elevation: 418'
Incorporated: 5/4/1962
Mayor: Sandra H. Larson

Vernonia
County: Columbia
Address: 1001 Bridge St., 97064
Phone: 503-429-5291
Fax: 503-429-4232
Web: www.vernonia-or.gov
Elevation: 635'
Incorporated: 2/18/1891
Mayor: Mario Leonetti

Waldport
County: Lincoln
Address: PO Box 1120, 125 Alsea Hwy., 97394
Phone: 541-264-7417
Fax: 541-264-7418
Web: www.waldport.org
Elevation: 12'
Incorporated: 3/11/1911
Mayor: Susan Woodruff

Wallowa
County: Wallowa
Address: PO Box 487, 97885
Phone: 541-886-2422
Fax: 541-886-4215
Elevation: 2,950'
Incorporated: 1/18/1909
Mayor: Vikki Knifong

Warrenton
County: Clatsop
Address: PO Box 250, 225 S Main Ave., 97146
Phone: 503-861-2233
Fax: 503-861-2351
Web: www.ci.warrenton.or.us
Elevation: 8'
Incorporated: 2/11/1899
Mayor: Mark Kujala

Wasco
County: Sherman
Address: PO Box 26, 1017 Clark St., 97065
Phone: 541-442-5515
Fax: 541-442-5001
Web: www.wascooregon.com
Elevation: 1,281'
Incorporated: 4/14/1898
Mayor: Carol Mackenzie

Waterloo
County: Linn
Address: PO Box 1066, 31140 First St., Lebanon 97355
Phone: 541-451-2245
Fax: 541-451-3133
Email: cityofwaterloo@centurytel.net
Elevation: 402'
Incorporated: 2/15/1893
Mayor: Jon Arms

West Linn
County: Clackamas
Address: 22500 Salamo Rd., #100, 97068
Phone: 503-657-0331
Fax: 503-650-9041
Web: www.westlinnoregon.gov
Elevation: 642'
Incorporated: 8/15/1913
Mayor: Russell B. Axelrod

Westfir
County: Lane
Address: PO Box 296, 47441 Westoak Rd., 97492
Phone: 541-782-3983
Fax: 541-782-3983
Web: www.westfir-oregon.com
Elevation: 1,075'
Incorporated: 2/6/1979
Mayor: Matt Meske

Weston
County: Umatilla
Address: PO Box 579, 114 Main St., 97886
Phone: 541-566-3313
Fax: 541-566-2792
Web: www.cityofwestonoregon.com
Elevation: 1,796'
Incorporated: 10/19/1878
Mayor: Jennifer McClure-Spurgeon

Wheeler
County: Tillamook
Address: PO Box 177, 97147
Phone: 503-368-5767
Fax: 503-368-4273
Web: www.ci.wheeler.or.us
Elevation: 37'
Incorporated: 6/11/1913
Mayor: Stevie Stephens Burden

Willamina
County: Polk/Yamhill
Address: 411 NE C St., 97396
Phone: 503-876-2242
Fax: 503-876-1121
Web: www.willaminaoregon.gov
Elevation: 225'
Incorporated: 2/13/1903
Mayor: Ila Skyberg

Wilsonville
County: Clackamas
Address: 29799 SW Town Center Lp. E, 97070
Phone: 503-682-1011
Fax: 503-682-1015
Web: www.ci.wilsonville.or.us
Elevation: 179'
Incorporated: 2/4/1969
Mayor: Tim Knapp

Winston
County: Douglas
Address: 201 NW Douglas Blvd., 97496
Phone: 541-679-6739
Fax: 541-679-0794
Web: www.winstoncity.org
Elevation: 534'
Incorporated: 6/29/1953
Mayor: Ken Barrett

Wood Village
County: Multnomah
Address: 2055 NE 238th Dr., 97060
Phone: 503-667-6211
Fax: 503-669-8723
Web: www.ci.wood-village.or.us
Elevation: 90'–330'
Incorporated: 2/9/1951
Mayor: Timothy Clark

Woodburn
County: Marion
Address: 270 Montgomery St., 97071
Phone: 503-982-5222
Fax: 503-980-2482
Web: www.woodburn-or.gov

Elevation: 197'
Incorporated: 2/20/1889
Mayor: Kathryn Figley

Yachats
County: Lincoln
Address: PO Box 345, 441 Hwy. 101 N, #2, 97498
Phone: 541-547-3565
Fax: 541-547-3063
Web: https://yachatsoregon.org
Elevation: 45'
Incorporated: 7/18/1966
Mayor: Gerald Stanley

Yamhill
County: Yamhill
Address: PO Box 9, 205 S Maple St., 97148
Phone: 503-662-3511
Fax: 503-662-4589
Web: www.cityofyamhill.com
Elevation: 182'
Incorporated: 2/20/1891
Mayor: Paula Terp

Yoncalla
County: Douglas
Address: PO Box 508, 2640 Eagle Valley Rd., 97499
Phone: 541-849-2152
Fax: 541-849-2552
Web: www.cityofyoncalla.com
Elevation: 367'
Incorporated: 2/27/1901
Mayor: Gerald Cross

CITY POPULATIONS: 1980–2016

Source: Population Research Center, Portland State University
Phone: 503-725-3922

*Change in population between 2010 and 2016

Cities or counties that share rank numbers are tied in rank.

Rank	City	% Change*	2016	2010	2000	1990	1980
168	Adair Village	0.6	845	840	536	554	589
203	Adams	5.7	370	350	297	223	240
224	Adrian	1.7	180	177	147	131	162
11	Albany	4.7	52,540	50,158	40,852	29,540	26,511
134	Amity	0.4	1,620	1,614	1,478	1,175	1,092
237	Antelope	8.7	50	46	59	34	39
185	Arlington	3.2	605	586	524	425	521
28	Ashland	2.7	20,620	20,078	19,522	16,252	14,943
52	Astoria	3.1	9,770	9,477	9,813	10,069	9,996
152	Athena	3.9	1,170	1,126	1,221	997	965
81	Aumsville	10.6	3,965	3,584	3,003	1,650	1,432
161	Aurora	5.7	970	918	655	523	306
47	Baker City	0.6	9,890	9,828	9,860	9,140	9,471
96	Bandon	1.9	3,125	3,066	2,833	2,215	2,311
126	Banks	-0.1	1,775	1,777	1,286	563	489
231	Barlow	0.0	135	135	140	118	105
142	Bay City	3.4	1,330	1,286	1,149	1,027	986
6	Beaverton	6.2	95,385	89,803	76,129	53,307	31,962
7	Bend	9.0	83,500	76,639	52,029	20,447	17,260
86	Boardman	10.4	3,555	3,220	2,855	1,387	1,261
193	Bonanza	9.6	455	415	415	323	270
68	Brookings	3.4	6,550	6,336	5,447	4,400	3,384
132	Brownsville	1.9	1,700	1,668	1,449	1,281	1,261
100	Burns	0.9	2,830	2,806	3,064	2,913	3,579
197	Butte Falls	1.7	430	423	439	252	428
36	Canby	3.7	16,420	15,829	12,790	8,990	7,659
130	Cannon Beach	1.2	1,710	1,690	1,588	1,221	1,187
177	Canyon City	0.3	705	703	669	648	639
121	Canyonville	2.2	1,925	1,884	1,293	1,219	1,288
110	Carlton	9.1	2,190	2,007	1,514	1,289	1,302
146	Cascade Locks	9.3	1,250	1,144	1,115	930	838
120	Cave Junction	1.7	1,915	1,883	1,363	1,126	1,023
32	Central Point	2.4	17,585	17,169	12,493	7,512	6,357
174	Chiloquin	0.1	735	734	716	673	778
127	Clatskanie	0.7	1,750	1,737	1,528	1,629	1,648
158	Coburg	3.4	1,070	1,035	969	763	699
116	Columbia City	1.0	1,965	1,946	1,571	1,003	678
179	Condon	1.9	695	682	759	635	783
34	Coos Bay	4.1	16,615	15,967	15,374	15,076	14,424
84	Coquille	1.4	3,920	3,866	4,184	4,121	4,481
42	Cornelius	0.4	11,915	11,869	9,652	6,148	4,402
10	Corvallis	6.9	58,240	54,462	49,322	44,757	40,960

Rank	City	% Change*	2016	2010	2000	1990	1980
48	Cottage Grove	2.1	9,890	9,686	8,445	7,403	7,148
188	Cove	-0.4	550	552	594	507	451
75	Creswell	6.5	5,360	5,031	3,579	2,431	1,770
140	Culver	3.9	1,410	1,357	802	570	514
38	Dallas	5.2	15,345	14,583	12,459	9,422	8,530
102	Dayton	4.0	2,635	2,534	2,119	1,526	1,409
229	Dayville	0.7	150	149	138	144	199
139	Depoe Bay	3.0	1,440	1,398	1,174	870	723
219	Detroit	4.0	210	202	262	331	367
160	Donald	0.6	985	979	625	316	267
150	Drain	0.8	1,160	1,151	1,021	1,086	1,148
185	Dufur	0.2	605	604	588	527	560
94	Dundee	0.9	3,190	3,162	2,598	1,663	1,223
143	Dunes City	1.3	1,320	1,303	1,241	1,081	1,124
123	Durham	39.2	1,880	1,351	1,382	748	707
58	Eagle Point	3.5	8,765	8,469	4,797	3,008	2,764
177	Echo	0.9	705	699	650	500	624
129	Elgin	1.1	1,730	1,711	1,654	1,586	1,701
220	Elkton	5.1	205	195	147	172	155
117	Enterprise	2.3	1,985	1,940	1,895	1,905	2,003
97	Estacada	17.1	3,155	2,695	2,371	2,016	1,419
2	Eugene	6.2	165,885	156,185	137,893	112,733	105,664
55	Fairview	0.2	8,940	8,920	7,561	2,391	1,749
161	Falls City	0.3	950	947	966	818	804
59	Florence	2.5	8,680	8,466	7,263	5,171	4,411
22	Forest Grove	10.9	23,375	21,083	17,708	13,559	11,499
192	Fossil	0.4	475	473	469	399	535
172	Garibaldi	1.4	790	779	899	886	999
182	Gaston	0.5	640	637	600	563	471
191	Gates	3.0	485	471	471	499	455
138	Gearhart	1.2	1,480	1,462	995	1,027	967
103	Gervais	4.1	2,565	2,464	2,009	992	799
43	Gladstone	1.4	11,660	11,497	11,438	10,152	9,500
166	Glendale	0.1	875	874	855	707	712
107	Gold Beach	1.0	2,275	2,253	1,897	1,546	1,515
147	Gold Hill	0.0	1,220	1,220	1,073	964	904
238	Granite	5.3	40	38	24	8	17
15	Grants Pass	6.6	36,815	34,533	23,003	17,503	15,032
227	Grass Valley	0.6	165	164	171	160	164
241	Greenhorn	200.0	2	0	0	0	0
4	Gresham	2.4	108,150	105,594	90,205	68,249	33,005
201	Haines	-0.2	415	416	426	405	341
209	Halfway	0.7	290	288	337	311	380
164	Halsey	1.2	915	904	724	667	693
31	Happy Valley	34.4	18,680	13,903	4,519	1,519	1,499
85	Harrisburg	2.3	3,650	3,567	2,795	1,939	1,881
222	Helix	6.0	195	184	183	150	155
144	Heppner	0.3	1,295	1,291	1,395	1,412	1,498

Rank	City	% Change*	2016	2010	2000	1990	1980
30	Hermiston	5.9	17,730	16,745	13,154	10,047	8,408
5	Hillsboro	8.4	99,340	91,611	70,186	37,598	27,664
136	Hines	-0.2	1,560	1,563	1,623	1,452	1,632
63	Hood River	8.3	7,760	7,167	5,831	4,632	4,329
93	Hubbard	1.6	3,225	3,173	2,483	1,881	1,640
194	Huntington	1.1	445	440	515	522	539
230	Idanha	4.5	140	134	232	289	319
208	Imbler	-0.3	305	306	284	299	292
57	Independence	7.7	9,250	8,590	6,035	4,425	4,024
205	Ione	0.3	330	329	321	255	345
118	Irrigon	4.1	1,900	1,826	1,702	737	700
159	Island City	13.8	1,125	989	916	696	477
99	Jacksonville	4.8	2,920	2,785	2,235	1,896	2,030
95	Jefferson	3.1	3,195	3,098	2,487	1,805	1,702
128	John Day	-0.5	1,735	1,744	1,821	1,836	2,012
187	Johnson City	-0.2	565	566	634	586	378
225	Jordan Valley	-3.3	175	181	239	364	473
154	Joseph	1.8	1,100	1,081	1,054	1,073	999
72	Junction City	11.5	6,010	5,392	4,721	3,670	3,320
14	Keizer	2.8	37,505	36,478	32,203	21,884	--
89	King City	13.5	3,530	3,111	1,949	2,060	1,853
26	Klamath Falls	3.8	21,640	20,840	19,460	17,737	16,661
40	La Grande	0.9	13,200	13,082	12,327	11,766	11,354
133	La Pine	1.3	1,675	1,653	--	--	--
83	Lafayette	6.2	3,975	3,742	2,586	1,292	1,215
13	Lake Oswego	2.2	37,425	36,619	35,278	30,576	22,527
130	Lakeside	1.5	1,725	1,699	1,421	1,437	1,453
105	Lakeview	0.3	2,300	2,294	2,474	2,526	2,770
37	Lebanon	5.9	16,435	15,518	12,950	10,950	10,413
212	Lexington	7.1	255	238	263	286	307
60	Lincoln City	7.0	8,485	7,930	7,437	5,908	5,469
240	Lonerock	-4.8	20	21	24	11	26
222	Long Creek	-1.0	195	197	228	249	252
217	Lostine	0.9	215	213	263	231	250
156	Lowell	2.4	1,070	1,045	880	785	661
150	Lyons	0.3	1,165	1,161	1,008	938	877
70	Madras	3.8	6,275	6,046	5,078	3,443	2,235
170	Malin	1.2	815	805	640	725	539
183	Manzanita	4.5	625	598	564	513	443
198	Maupin	1.7	425	418	411	456	495
173	Maywood Park	-0.3	750	752	777	781	845
17	McMinnville	3.8	33,405	32,187	26,499	17,894	14,080
8	Medford	4.8	78,500	74,907	63,687	47,021	39,746
169	Merrill	-0.5	840	844	897	837	822
176	Metolius	4.2	740	710	729	450	451
125	Mill City	0.3	1,860	1,855	1,537	1,555	1,565
134	Millersburg	30.2	1,730	1,329	651	715	562
64	Milton-Freewater	0.3	7,070	7,050	6,470	5,533	5,086

Rank	City	% Change*	2016	2010	2000	1990	1980
27	Milwaukie	1.1	20,510	20,291	20,490	18,670	17,931
233	Mitchell	0.0	130	130	170	163	183
55	Molalla	12.0	9,085	8,108	5,647	3,651	2,992
50	Monmouth	2.2	9,745	9,534	7,741	6,288	5,594
183	Monroe	0.5	620	617	607	448	412
233	Monument	1.6	130	128	151	162	192
206	Moro	1.9	330	324	337	292	336
194	Mosier	3.9	450	433	410	244	340
90	Mount Angel	2.7	3,375	3,286	3,121	2,778	2,876
189	Mount Vernon	-0.4	525	527	595	549	569
88	Myrtle Creek	1.5	3,490	3,439	3,419	3,063	3,365
104	Myrtle Point	0.4	2,525	2,514	2,451	2,712	2,859
210	Nehalem	3.3	280	271	203	232	258
23	Newberg	6.3	23,465	22,068	18,064	13,086	10,394
46	Newport	2.0	10,190	9,989	9,532	8,437	7,519
49	North Bend	0.8	9,775	9,695	9,544	9,614	9,779
115	North Plains	3.5	2,015	1,947	1,605	997	715
194	North Powder	1.4	445	439	489	448	430
91	Nyssa	0.6	3,285	3,267	3,163	2,629	2,862
163	Oakland	1.4	940	927	954	844	886
92	Oakridge	1.6	3,255	3,205	3,172	3,063	3,680
44	Ontario	0.9	11,465	11,366	10,985	9,394	8,814
16	Oregon City	7.5	34,240	31,859	25,754	14,698	14,673
214	Paisley	0.8	245	243	247	350	343
33	Pendleton	1.6	16,880	16,612	16,354	15,142	14,521
78	Philomath	1.8	4,665	4,584	3,838	2,983	2,673
79	Phoenix	1.0	4,585	4,538	4,060	3,239	2,309
137	Pilot Rock	0.2	1,505	1,502	1,532	1,478	1,630
152	Port Orford	0.6	1,140	1,133	1,153	1,025	1,061
1	Portland	7.5	627,395	583,776	529,121	438,802	366,383
179	Powers	0.9	695	689	734	682	819
165	Prairie City	0.1	910	909	1,080	1,117	1,106
236	Prescott	0.0	55	55	72	63	73
53	Prineville	4.2	9,645	9,253	7,358	5,355	5,276
121	Rainier	0.5	1,905	1,895	1,687	1,674	1,655
18	Redmond	5.3	27,595	26,215	13,481	7,165	6,452
80	Reedsport	0.0	4,155	4,154	4,378	4,796	4,984
225	Richland	12.2	175	156	147	161	181
149	Riddle	0.0	1,185	1,185	1,014	1,143	1,265
190	Rivergrove	71.3	495	289	324	294	314
141	Rockaway Beach	1.8	1,335	1,312	1,267	970	906
108	Rogue River	3.2	2,200	2,131	1,851	1,759	1,308
25	Roseburg	7.7	22,820	21,181	20,017	17,069	16,644
210	Rufus	12.4	280	249	268	295	352
41	Saint Helens	1.8	13,120	12,883	10,019	7,535	7,064
198	Saint Paul	2.1	430	421	354	322	312
3	Salem	4.8	162,060	154,637	136,924	107,793	89,091
45	Sandy	11.3	10,655	9,570	5,385	4,152	2,905

Rank	City	% Change*	2016	2010	2000	1990	1980
66	Scappoose	2.9	6,785	6,592	4,976	3,529	3,213
167	Scio	6.2	890	838	695	623	579
204	Scotts Mills	2.2	365	357	312	283	249
67	Seaside	2.3	6,605	6,457	5,900	5,359	5,193
217	Seneca	8.0	215	199	223	191	285
98	Shady Cove	4.7	3,040	2,904	2,307	1,351	1,097
239	Shaniko	-2.8	35	36	26	26	30
71	Sheridan	-0.2	6,115	6,127	5,561	3,979	2,249
29	Sherwood	5.2	19,145	18,194	11,791	3,093	2,386
145	Siletz	1.9	1,235	1,212	1,133	992	1,001
51	Silverton	5.5	9,725	9,222	7,414	5,635	5,168
106	Sisters	17.3	2,390	2,038	959	708	696
206	Sodaville	8.8	335	308	290	192	171
228	Spray	0.0	160	160	140	149	155
9	Springfield	1.7	60,140	59,403	52,864	44,664	41,621
110	Stanfield	4.3	2,130	2,043	1,979	1,568	1,568
62	Stayton	1.3	7,745	7,644	6,816	5,011	4,396
101	Sublimity	2.8	2,755	2,681	2,148	1,491	1,077
231	Summerville	0.0	135	135	117	142	143
220	Sumpter	0.5	205	204	171	119	133
61	Sutherlin	2.8	8,025	7,810	6,669	5,020	4,560
54	Sweet Home	1.8	9,090	8,925	8,016	6,850	6,921
69	Talent	3.9	6,305	6,066	5,589	3,274	2,577
148	Tangent	3.5	1,205	1,164	933	556	478
39	The Dalles	7.4	14,625	13,620	12,156	11,021	10,820
12	Tigard	3.6	49,745	48,035	41,223	29,435	14,799
76	Tillamook	-0.3	4,920	4,935	4,352	4,001	3,991
87	Toledo	0.7	3,490	3,465	3,472	3,174	3,151
35	Troutdale	0.5	16,035	15,962	13,777	7,852	5,908
19	Tualatin	3.0	26,840	26,054	22,791	14,664	7,483
119	Turner	4.9	1,945	1,854	1,199	1,281	1,116
214	Ukiah	31.7	245	186	255	250	249
65	Umatilla	4.5	7,220	6,906	4,978	3,046	3,199
109	Union	1.4	2,150	2,121	1,926	1,847	2,062
235	Unity	5.6	75	71	131	87	115
124	Vale	0.6	1,885	1,874	1,976	1,491	1,558
77	Veneta	4.3	4,755	4,561	2,762	2,519	2,449
113	Vernonia	-4.0	2,065	2,151	2,228	1,808	1,785
112	Waldport	2.3	2,080	2,033	2,050	1,595	1,274
171	Wallowa	-0.4	805	808	869	748	847
74	Warrenton	5.5	5,265	4,989	4,096	2,681	2,493
200	Wasco	2.4	420	410	381	374	415
216	Waterloo	0.4	230	229	239	191	211
20	West Linn	2.0	25,615	25,109	22,261	16,389	11,358
212	Westfir	0.8	255	253	280	278	312
181	Weston	25.9	840	667	717	606	719
202	Wheeler	-2.2	405	414	391	335	319
114	Willamina	3.5	2,095	2,025	1,844	1,748	1,749
24	Wilsonville	21.7	23,740	19,509	13,991	7,106	2,920

Rank	City	% Change*	2016	2010	2000	1990	1980
73	Winston	0.6	5,410	5,379	4,613	3,773	3,359
82	Wood Village	1.0	3,915	3,878	2,860	2,814	2,253
21	Woodburn	3.0	24,795	24,080	20,100	13,404	11,196
175	Yachats	7.2	740	690	617	533	482
155	Yamhill	4.5	1,070	1,024	794	867	690
157	Yoncalla	1.7	1,065	1,047	1,052	919	805

COUNTY POPULATIONS: 1980–2016

Rank	County	% Change*	2016	2010	2000	1990	1980
28	Baker	2.3	16,510	16,134	16,741	15,317	16,134
11	Benton	6.7	91,320	85,579	78,153	70,811	68,211
3	Clackamas	7.7	404,980	375,992	338,391	278,850	241,911
19	Clatsop	3.2	38,225	37,039	35,630	33,301	32,489
17	Columbia	2.9	50,795	49,351	43,560	37,557	35,646
16	Coos	0.2	63,190	63,043	62,779	60,273	64,047
27	Crook	2.9	21,580	20,978	19,182	14,111	13,091
25	Curry	1.1	22,600	22,364	21,137	19,327	16,992
7	Deschutes	12.0	176,635	157,733	115,367	74,958	62,142
9	Douglas	2.5	110,395	107,667	100,399	94,649	93,748
34	Gilliam	5.8	1,980	1,871	1,915	1,717	2,057
31	Grant	-0.5	7,410	7,445	7,935	7,853	8,210
32	Harney	-1.4	7,320	7,422	7,609	7,060	8,314
24	Hood River	10.7	24,735	22,346	20,411	16,903	15,835
6	Jackson	5.2	213,675	203,206	181,269	146,389	132,456
26	Jefferson	4.9	22,790	21,720	19,009	13,676	11,599
12	Josephine	2.4	84,675	82,713	75,726	62,649	58,855
15	Klamath	1.6	67,410	66,380	63,775	57,702	59,117
30	Lake	1.5	8,015	7,895	7,422	7,186	7,532
4	Lane	4.0	365,940	351,715	322,959	282,912	275,226
18	Lincoln	3.7	47,735	46,034	44,479	38,889	35,264
8	Linn	4.8	122,315	116,672	103,069	91,227	89,495
20	Malheur	1.3	31,705	31,313	31,615	26,038	26,896
5	Marion	5.9	333,950	315,335	284,834	228,483	204,692
29	Morrow	5.1	11,745	11,173	10,995	7,625	7,519
1	Multnomah	7.5	790,670	735,334	660,486	583,887	562,647
14	Polk	5.7	79,730	75,403	62,380	49,541	45,203
35	Sherman	1.7	1,795	1,765	1,934	1,918	2,172
23	Tillamook	2.7	25,920	25,250	24,262	21,570	21,164
13	Umatilla	5.3	79,880	75,889	70,548	59,249	58,861
21	Union	3.9	26,745	25,748	24,530	23,598	23,921
33	Wallowa	1.9	7,140	7,008	7,226	6,911	7,273
22	Wasco	5.9	26,700	25,213	23,791	21,683	21,732
2	Washington	10.2	583,595	529,710	445,342	311,554	245,860
36	Wheeler	1.7	1,465	1,441	1,547	1,396	1,513
10	Yamhill	5.8	104,990	99,193	84,992	65,551	55,332
	Oregon	**6.4**	**4,076,350**	**3,831,074**	**3,421,399**	**2,842,321**	**2,633,156**

*Change in population between 2010 and 2016

COUNTY GOVERNMENT

The word "county" is from the Middle English word *conte*, meaning the office of a count. However, a county within the United States, defined by Merriam-Webster's dictionary as "the largest territorial division for local government within a state," is based on the Anglo-Saxon shire, which corresponds to the modern county. Counties were brought to the United States by the English colonists and were established in the central and western parts of the United States by the pioneers as they moved westward.

Early county governments in Oregon were very limited in the services they provided. Their primary responsibilities were forest and farm-to-market roads, law enforcement, courts, care for the needy and tax collections. In response to demands of a growing population and a more complex society, today's counties provide a wide range of important public services, including, public health, mental health, community corrections, juvenile services, criminal prosecution, hospitals, nursing homes, airports, parks, libraries, land-use planning, building regulations, refuse disposal, elections, air pollution control, veterans services, economic development, urban renewal, public housing, vector control, county fairs, museums, dog control, civil defense and senior services.

Originally, counties functioned almost exclusively as agents of the state government. Their every activity had to be either authorized or mandated by state law. However, in 1958, an amendment to the Oregon Constitution authorized counties to adopt "home rule" charters, and a 1973 state law granted all counties power to exercise broad "home rule" authority. As a result, the national Advisory Commission on Intergovernmental Relations has identified county government in Oregon as having the highest degree of local discretionary authority of any state in the nation.

Nine counties have adopted "home rule" charters, wherein voters have the power to adopt and amend their own county government organization. Lane and Washington were the first to adopt "home rule" in 1962, followed by Hood River (1964), Multnomah (1967), Benton (1972), Jackson (1978), Josephine (1980), Clatsop (1988) and Umatilla (1993).

Twenty-eight of Oregon's 36 counties, including the nine with charters, are governed by a board of commissioners comprised of three to five elected members. The remaining eight less populated counties are governed by a "county court" consisting of a county judge and two commissioners.

Baker County

County Seat: 1995 Third St., Baker City 97814
Phone: 541-523-8203 (General); 541-523-8207 (County Clerk)
Fax: 541-523-8240
Email: ccarpenter@bakercounty.org
Web: www.bakercounty.org
Established:
Sept. 22, 1862
Elev. at Baker City: 3,471'
Area: 3,089 sq. mi.
Average Temp.:
January 25.2°
July 66.6°
Assessed Value:
$1,431,477,002

Real Market Value: $2,305,372,620
(includes the value of non-taxed properties)
Annual Precipitation: 10.63"
Economy: Agriculture, forest products, manufacturing and recreation
Points of Interest: The Oregon Trail Interpretive Center and Old Oregon Trail, Sumpter Gold Dredge Park and ghost towns, Sumpter Valley Railroad, Baker City Restored Historic District (including Geiser Grand Hotel), Anthony Lakes Ski Resort and summer picnic areas, camping and hiking trails, Eagle Cap Wilderness area, Brownlee, Oxbow and Hells Canyon Reservoirs and Hells Canyon

Baker County was established from part of Wasco County and named after Colonel Edward D. Baker, a U.S. Senator from Oregon. A Union officer and close friend of President Lincoln, Colonel Baker was the only member of Congress to die in the Civil War. He was killed at Ball's Bluff, Virginia. Auburn, which no longer exists, was the first county seat. Baker City became the county seat in 1868. It was incorporated in1874, and it is the 17th oldest city in Oregon.

Before 1861, the majority of immigrants only paused in Baker County on their way west, unaware of its vast agricultural and mineral resources. Then the great gold rush began, and Baker County became one of the Northwest's largest gold producers. Farming, ranching, logging and recreation have become the chief economic bases for an area that displays spectacular scenery, including the world's deepest gorge Hells Canyon; an outstanding museum with the famous Cavin-Walfel rock collection; and numerous historic buildings with interesting architectural features.

County Officials: Commissioners—Chair William "Bill" E. Harvey 2019; Mark E. Bennett 2019, Bruce Nichols 2021, Dist. Atty. Matthew Shirtcliff 2021; Assess. Kerry Savage 2017; Clerk Cindy Carpenter 2019; Justice of the Peace Don Williams 2019; Sheriff Travis Ash 2021; Surv. Tom Hanley 2017; Treas. Alice Durflinger 2019; Co. Admin. Christena Cook; Chief Information Officer Bill Lee

Benton County

County Seat: 408 SW Monroe Ave., Corvallis 97333, 205 NW Fifth St., Corvallis 97330
Phone: 541-766-6800 (General); 541-766-6859 (Court Administrator)
Fax: 541-766-6675
Email: webmaster@co.benton.or.us
Web: www.co.benton.or.us
Established:
Dec. 23, 1847
Elev. at Corvallis:
224'
Area: 679 sq. mi.
Average Temp.:
January 39.3°
July 65.6°
Assessed Value:
$7,998,241,690
Real Market Value: $13,165,595,090
(includes the value of non-taxed properties)
Annual Precipitation: 42.71"
Economy: Agriculture, forest products, research and development, electronics and wineries
Points of Interest: Benton County Courthouse, Oregon State University Campus, Benton County Museum (Philomath), Alsea Falls, Mary's Peak, William L. Finley National Wildlife Refuge, Peavy Arboretum, McDonald Forest, Jackson-Frazier Wetland

Benton County was created from Polk County by an act of the Provisional Government of Oregon in 1847. It is one of seven counties in the United States to be named after Senator Thomas Hart Benton of Missouri, a longtime advocate of the development of the Oregon Territory. The county was created out of an area originally inhabited by the Klickitat Tribe, who rented it from the Kalapuya Tribe for use as hunting grounds. At that time, the boundaries began at the intersection of Polk County and the Willamette River, ran as far south as the California border and as far west as the Pacific Ocean. Later, portions of Benton County were taken to form Coos, Curry, Douglas, Jackson, Josephine, Lane and Lincoln Counties, leaving it in its present form with 679 square miles of land area.

Oregon State University, agriculture, and lumber and wood products manufacturing form the basis of Benton County's economy. A substantial portion of the nation's research in forestry, agriculture, engineering, education and the sciences takes place at OSU.

County Officials: Commissioners—Xanthippe "Xan" Augerot (D) 2021, Annabelle Jaramillo (D) 2021, Anne Schuster (D) 2019; Dist. Atty. John Haroldson 2021; Assess. Tami Tracy; Clerk James Morales; Sheriff Scott Jackson 2019; Surv. Joe Mardis; Tax Collector Mary Otley; Public Information Officer Lili'a Neville

Clackamas County

County Seat: County Courthouse, 2051 Kaen Rd., Oregon City 97045
Phone: 503-650-5686 (General); 503-655-8670 (Court Administrator)
Fax: 503-650-5687 (Records)
Email: sherryhal@co.clackamas.or.us
Web: www.clackamas.us
Established:
July 5, 1843
Elev. at Oregon City: 55'
Area: 1,884 sq. mi.
Average Temp.:
January 40.2°
July 68.4°
Assessed Value:
$46,405,129,768
Real Market Value: $73,944,244,111
(includes the value of non-taxed properties)
Annual Precipitation: 48.40"
Economy: Agriculture, metals manufacturing, trucking and warehousing, nursery stock, retail services, wholesale trade and construction
Points of Interest: Mount Hood and Timberline Lodge, Willamette Falls and navigation locks, McLoughlin House, Canby Ferry, Molalla Buckaroo, driving tour of Old Barlow Road, Clackamas Town Center, Museum of the Oregon Territory, North Clackamas Aquatic Park

Clackamas County was named for the resident Clackamas Tribe and was one of the four original Oregon counties created in 1843. Oregon City, the county seat, was the first incorporated city west of the Rocky Mountains, the first capital of the Oregon Territory, and the site of the first legislative session.

In 1849, when the city of San Francisco was platted, Oregon City was the site of the only federal court west of the Rockies. The plat was filed in 1850 in the first plat book of the first office of records on the West Coast and are still in Oregon City. The area's early history is featured at the Clackamas County Historical Society and Museum of the Oregon Territory.

From its 55-foot elevation at Oregon City, the county rises to 11,235 feet at the peak of Mount Hood, the only year-round ski resort in the United States and the site of the Timberline Lodge National Historical Landmark. The mountains, rivers and forests offer excellent outdoor recreation activities, from skiing and rafting to fishing and camping.

County Officials: Commissioners—Chair Jim Bernard 2021, Ken Humberston 2021, John Ludlow 2021, Paul Savas 2019, Martha Schrader 2021; Dist. Atty. John S. Foote 2021; Assess. Bob Vorman 2017; Clerk Sherry Hall 2019; Justice of the Peace Karen Brisbin 2023; Sheriff Craig Roberts 2021; Surv. Ray Griffin; Treas. Shari Anderson 2019; Co. Admin. Donald Krupp

Clatsop County

County Seat: 820 Exchange St., Suite 410, Astoria 97103
Phone: 503-325-1000 (General); 503-325-8555 (Court Administrator)
Fax: 503-325-8325
Email: clerk@co.clatsop.or.us
Web: www.co.clatsop.or.us
Established:
June 22, 1844
Elev. at Astoria:
19'
Area: 1085 sq. mi.
Average Temp.:
January 41.9°
July 60.1°
Assessed Value:
$5,875,464,334
Real Market Value: $8,351,583,284
(includes the value of non-taxed properties)
Annual Precipitation: 66.40"
Economy: Fishing, tourism and forest products
Points of Interest: Astoria Column, Port of Astoria, Flavel Mansion Museum, Lewis and Clark Expedition Salt Cairn, Fort Clatsop, Fort Stevens, Columbia River Maritime Museum

Clatsop County was created from the original Tuality District in 1844 and named for the Clatsop Tribe, one of the many Chinook tribes living in Oregon. *The Journals of Lewis and Clark* mention the tribe. Fort Clatsop, Lewis and Clark's winter headquarters in 1805 and now a national memorial near the mouth of the Columbia River, also took the tribe's name.

Astoria, Oregon's oldest city, was established as a fur trading post in 1811 and named after John Jacob Astor. The first U.S. Post Office west of the Rocky Mountains was also established in Astoria in 1847. The first county courthouse was completed in 1855. The present courthouse was erected in 1904. Records show that the summer resort of Seaside was founded by Ben Holladay, pioneer Oregon railroad builder, in the early 1870s when he constructed the Seaside House, a famous luxury hotel for which the city was finally named. The Lewis and Clark Expedition reached the Pacific Ocean at this spot.

County Officials: Commissioners—Chair Scott Lee 2019, Sarah Nebeker 2021, Kathleen Sullivan 2021, Lisa Tarabochia-Clement 2019, Lianne Thompson 2019; Dist. Atty. Joshua Marquis 2019; Assess. Suzanne Johnson; Clerk Valerie Crafard; Sheriff Thomas J. Bergin 2021; Surv. Vance Swenson; Treas. Monica Steele; County Manager Cameron Moore

Columbia County

County Seat: Courthouse, 230 Strand St., Saint Helens 97051
Phone: 503-397-3796 (General); 503-397-2327 (Court Administrator)
Fax: 503-397-7266
Email: Betty.Huser@co.columbia.or.us
Web: www.co.columbia.or.us
Established:
Jan. 16, 1854
Elev. at Saint Helens: 42'
Area: 687 sq. mi.
Average Temp.:
January 39.0°
July 68.4°
Assessed Value:
$4,911,758,978
Real Market Value: $7,376,616,652
(includes the value of non-taxed properties)
Annual Precipitation: 44.60"
Economy: Agriculture, forest products, manufacturing, surface mining and tourism
Points of Interest: Lewis and Clark Heritage Canoe Trail, Vernonia–Banks State Trail, Jewell Elk Refuge, Sauvie Island Wildlife Area, Sand Island Park, Jones Beach near Clatskanie, Prescott Beach Park, Vernonia Golf Course, Lewis and Clark Bridge at Rainier, Columbia County Fairgrounds

Chinook and Clatskanie Tribes inhabited this bountiful region centuries before Captain Robert Gray, commanding the *Columbia Rediviva,* landed on Columbia County's timbered shoreline in 1792. The Corps of Discovery expedition, led by Captain Meriwether Lewis and Lieutenant William Clark, traveled and camped along the Columbia River shore in the area later known as Columbia County in late 1805 and early 1806.

The county has 62 miles of Columbia riverfront and contains deep water ports and some of the finest industrial property in the Pacific Northwest. The Columbia River is a major route for ocean-going vessels and is a popular playground for fishing, boating, camping and windsurfing. The county has two marine parks, Sand Island and J. J. Collins Memorial Marine Park. Columbia County has a strong economic and cultural heritage centered around industries such as forest products, shipbuilding, mining and agriculture. The rural lifestyle and scenic beauty of Columbia County, coupled with its proximity to Portland, have drawn many new residents to the area.

County Officials: Commissioners—Henry Heimuller 2019, Margaret Magruder 2021, Alex Tardiff 2021; Dist. Atty. Steve Atchison 2019; Assess. Sue Martin 2019; Clerk Betty Huser 2019; Justice of the Peace Wally Thompson 2019; Sheriff Jeff Dickerson 2021; Surv. Nathan Woodward; Treas. Jennifer Cuellar-Smith 2021

Coos County

County Seat: Courthouse, 250 N Baxter, Coquille 97423
Phone: 541-396-7600 (General); 541-396-7500, ext. 4063 (Court Administrator)
Fax: 541-396-4861
Email: coosclerk@co.coos.or.us
Web: www.co.coos.or.us
Established:
Dec. 22, 1853
Elev. at Coquille:
40'
Area: 1,629 sq. mi.
Average Temp.:
January 44.2°
July 60.9°
Assessed Value:
$5,171,748,075
Real Market Value: $6,468,659,553
(includes the value of non-taxed properties)
Annual Precipitation: 56.8"
Economy: Forest products, fishing, agriculture, shipping, recreation and tourism
Points of Interest: Lumber port, myrtlewood groves, Shore Acres State Park and Botanical Gardens, beaches, Oregon Dunes National Recreation Area, museums, fishing fleets, boat basins, scenic golf courses

Coos County was created by the Territorial Legislature from parts of Umpqua and Jackson Counties in 1853 and included Curry County until 1855. The county seat was Empire City until 1896 when it was moved to Coquille. Although trappers had been in the area a quarter century earlier, the first permanent settlement in present Coos County was at Empire City, now part of Coos Bay, by members of the Coos Bay Company in 1853. The name "Coos" derives from the Coos Tribe and translates to "lake" or "place of pines."

Forest products, tourism, fishing and agriculture dominate the Coos County economy. Boating, dairy farming, myrtlewood manufacturing, shipbuilding and repair, and agriculture specialty products, including cranberries, also play an important role. The International Port of Coos Bay, considered the best natural harbor between Puget Sound and San Francisco, is the world's largest forest products shipping port.

County Officials: Commissioners—Chair Melissa Cribbins 2019, Robert "Bob" Main 2021, John Sweet 2019; Dist. Atty. Paul R. Frasier 2021; Assess. Steve Jansen 2021; Clerk Terri Turi 2019; Sheriff Craig Zanni 2019; Surv. Michael Dado 2021; Treas. Megan Simms 2021

Crook County

County Seat: Courthouse, 300 NE Third St., Room 23, Prineville 97754
Phone: 541-447-6553 (General); 541-447-6555 (Court Administrator)
Fax: 541-416-2145
Email: cheryl.seely@co.crook.or.us
Web: www.co.crook.or.us
Established:
Oct. 24, 1882
Elev. at Prineville:
2,868'
Area: 2,991 sq. mi.
Average Temp.:
January 31.8°
July 64.5°
Assessed Value:
$1,951,384,613
Real Market Value: $3,779,347,532
(includes the value of non-taxed properties)
Annual Precipitation: 10.50"
Economy: Livestock, forest products, recreation, agriculture, manufacturing and wholesale trade
Points of Interest: Pine Mills, Crooked River Canyon, Ochoco Mountains, Prineville and Ochoco Reservoirs, rockhound areas, county courthouse, Steins Pillar, Wildland Firefighters Monument, and geological formations

Crook County was formed from Wasco County in 1882 and named for Major General George Crook, U.S. Army. Geographically, the county is in the center of Oregon. It is unique in that it has only one incorporated population center, the city of Prineville founded in 1868. Prineville's colorful past was the scene of tribal raids, range wars between sheep and cattle ranchers and vigilante justice. Other communities in this sparsely settled region are Powell Butte, Post and Paulina.

Forest products, agriculture, livestock raising and recreation/tourism services constitute most of Crook County's economy. Thousands of hunters, fishers, boaters, sightseers and rockhounds are annual visitors to its streams, reservoirs and the Ochoco Mountains. Rockhounds can dig for agates, limb casts, jasper and thundereggs on more than 1,000 acres of mining claims provided by the Prineville Chamber of Commerce. Major annual events include the Prineville Rockhound Powwow, Crooked River Roundup, Crook County Fair, Old Fashioned Fourth of July Celebration, High Desert Celtic Festival and the Lord's Acre Sale.

County Officials: County Court—Judge Seth Crawford 2021, Ken Fahlgren 2021, Jerry Brummer 2021; Dist. Atty. Daina A. Vitolins 2021; Assess. Brian Huber 2019; Clerk Cheryl Seely 2019; Sheriff John Gautney 2021; Surv. Greg Kelso 2021; Treas. Kathy Gray 2021; Chief Information Officer Judge Scott Cooper

Curry County

County Seat: 94235 Moore St., Suite 212, Gold Beach 97444

Phone: 541-247-3295 (General); 541-247-4511 (Court Administrator)

Fax: 541-247-6440 (Elections Division)

Email: kolenr@co.curry.or.us

Web: www.co.curry.or.us

Established:
Dec. 18, 1855

Elev. at
Gold Beach: 60'

Area: 1,648 sq. mi.

Average Temp.:
January 45.0°
July 65.0°

Assessed Value:
$2,893,247,655

Real Market Value: $3,928,379,180
(includes the value of non-taxed properties)

Annual Precipitation: 82.67"

Economy: Forest products, agriculture, commercial and sport fishing, recreation and tourism

Points of Interest: Coastal ports, Cape Blanco Lighthouse, Cape Sebastian and Samuel H. Boardman State Parks, Rogue River Japanese Bomb Site, and Thomas Creek Bridge near Brookings – Oregon's highest bridge at 345 feet

Named after Territorial Governor George L. Curry, the county was a part of "Coose" County until it was created in 1855. Port Orford was the county seat until 1859 when it was replaced by Ellensburg (later renamed Gold Beach).

Curry County contains valuable standing timber and also offers spectacular coastal scenery, clamming and crabbing, excellent fishing (freshwater and saltwater), upriver scenic boat trips, hiking trails, and gold for the fun of panning. The Port of Brookings is considered one of the safest harbors on the coast.

Agricultural products include sheep and cattle, cranberries, blueberries, Easter lilies and horticultural nursery stock. Curry County is also a prolific producer of myrtlewood.

County Officials: Commissioners—Court Boice 2021, Sue Gold 2021, Thomas C. Huxley 2019; Dist. Atty. Everett Dial 2021; Assess. Jim Kolen 2021; Clerk Renee Kolen 2021; Sheriff John Ward 2021; Surv. Reily Smith; Treas. Debra Crumley 2021

Deschutes County

County Seat: 1300 NW Wall St., Suite 206, Bend 97701-1947

Phone: 541-388-6570 (Court Administrator)

Fax: 541-385-3202

Web: www.deschutes.org

Established:
Dec. 13, 1916

Elev. at Bend:
3,628'

Area: 3,055 sq. mi.

Average Temp.:
January 30.5°
July 65.5°

Assessed Value:
$21,975,610,092

Real Market Value: $33,133,426,787
(includes the value of non-taxed properties)

Annual Precipitation: 12"

Economy: Tourism, retail trade, forest products, recreational equipment, aviation, software and high technology

Points of Interest: Smith Rock State Park, Mount Bachelor ski area, High Desert Museum, Lava Lands, Cascade Lakes Highway, Lava River Caves State Park, Lava Cast Forests, Newberry Crater, Pilot Butte, Three Sisters Wilderness, Central Oregon Community College, Deschutes County Fairgrounds, Redmond Airport, Pine Mountain Observatory

French-Canadian fur trappers of the Hudson's Bay Company gave the name Riviere des Chutes (River of the Falls) to the Deschutes River, from which Deschutes County took its name. In 1916, Deschutes County was created from a part of Crook County.

Deschutes County, outdoor recreation capital of Oregon, with noble, snow-capped peaks dominating the skyline to the west and the wide-open high desert extending to the east, captures the awe of locals and visitors alike. Deschutes County has grown into a bustling, exciting place where progress and growth are hallmarks.

Deschutes County has experienced rapid growth largely due to its climate and year-round recreation activities. Central Oregon offers downhill and cross-country skiing, snowboarding, fishing, hunting, hiking, rockclimbing, whitewater rafting and golfing. Deschutes County is the host of diverse annual events, including the Cascade Festival of Music, the Art Hop, Cascade Children's Festival, Pole Pedal Paddle, Sisters Rodeo, Sunriver Sunfest and the Cascade Cycling Classic.

County Officials: Commissioners—Chair Tammy Baney (R) 2019, Anthony "Tony" DeBone (R) 2019, Phil Henderson (R) 2021; Dist. Atty. John Hummel 2019; Assess. Scot Langton 2019; Clerk Nancy Blankenship 2019; Sheriff L. Shane Nelson 2021; Surv. Mike Berry; Treas. Robert Wayne Lowry 2019; Justice of the Peace Charles Fadeley 2021; Co. Admin. Tom Anderson

❖❖❖

Douglas County

County Seat: Courthouse, 1036 SE Douglas Ave., Roseburg 97470
Phone: 541-440-4323 (General); 541-957-2409 (Court Administrator)
Fax: 541-440-6292
Email: HR@co.douglas.or.us
Web: www.co.douglas.or.us
Established:
  Jan. 7, 1852
Elev. at Roseburg:
  475'
Area: 5,071 sq. mi.
Average Temp.:
  January 41.2°
  July 68.4°
Assessed Value:
  $8,909,642,035
Real Market Value: $14,446,431,483
(includes the value of non-taxed properties)
Annual Precipitation: 33.35"
Economy: Forest products, mining, agriculture, fishing and recreation
Points of Interest: Winchester Bay, Salmon Harbor, Oregon Dunes National Recreation Area, North Umpqua River, Diamond Lake, historic Oakland, Wildlife Safari, Douglas County Museum, wineries

Douglas County was named for U.S. Senator Stephen A. Douglas, Abraham Lincoln's opponent in the presidential election of 1860 and an ardent congressional advocate for Oregon. Douglas County was created in 1852 from the portion of Umpqua County which lay east of the Coast Range summit. In 1862, Douglas County absorbed what remained of Umpqua County.

Douglas County extends from sea level at the Pacific Ocean to 9,182-foot Mount Thielsen in the Cascade Range. The Umpqua River marks the dividing line between northern and southern Oregon, and its entire watershed lies within the county's boundaries. The county contains nearly 2.8 million acres of commercial forest lands and the largest stand of old growth timber in the world, which still provides the region's main livelihood. Approximately 25 percent of the labor force is employed in the forest products industry. Agriculture includes field crops, orchards and livestock. Over 50 percent of the land area of the county is federal public land.
County Officials: Commissioners—Chris Boice 2019, Tim Freeman 2019, Gary Leif 2021; Dist. Atty. Richard Wesenberg 2021; Assess. Roger Hartman 2019; Clerk Patricia Hitt 2021; Justices of the Peace Candace Hissong 2019, Stephen H. Miller 2019, Carol Roberts 2019, Russell Trump 2021; Sheriff John Hanlin 2021; Surv. Kris DeGroot 2019; Treas. Dick Filley 2021

Gilliam County

County Seat: Courthouse, 221 S Oregon St., Condon 97823-0427
Phone: 541-384-2311 (General); 541-384-3303 (Court Administrator)
Fax: 541-384-2166
Email: leanne.durfey@co.gilliam.or.us
Web: www.co.gilliam.or.us
Established:
  Feb. 25, 1885
Elev. at Condon:
  2,844'
Area: 1,223 sq. mi.
Average Temp.:
  January 31.9°
  July 71.3°
Assessed Value:
  $739,396,994
Real Market Value: $1,933,989,146
(includes the value of non-taxed properties)
Annual Precipitation: 11.39"
Economy: Agriculture, recreation, environmental services and wind power generation
Points of Interest: Old Oregon Trail, Arlington Bay and Marina, Lonerock area, Condon historic district, tribal pictographs

Gilliam County was established in 1885 from a portion of Wasco County and was named after Colonel Cornelius Gilliam, a veteran of the Cayuse Indian War. The first county seat was at Alkali, now Arlington. In 1890, voters chose to move the county seat to Condon, known then as "Summit Springs." A brick courthouse was built in Condon in 1903 which was destroyed by fire in 1954. The present courthouse was built on the same site in 1955.

Gilliam County is in the heart of the Columbia Plateau wheat area. The economy is based mainly on agriculture, with an average farm size of about 4,200 acres. Wheat, barley and beef cattle are the principal crops. The largest individual employers in the county, Chemical Waste Management of the Northwest and Oregon Waste Systems, subsidiaries of Waste Management Inc., are regional waste disposal landfills.

With elevations of over 3,000 feet near Condon, in the south of the county, and 285 feet at Arlington, 38 miles north, the county offers a variety of climates. Hunting, fishing and tourism are secondary industries. Two major rivers, the John Day and Columbia, and Interstate 84 traverse the area east to west. Highway 19 connects the county's major cities north to south and serves as the gateway to the John Day Valley.
County Officials: County Court—Judge Steve Shaffer 2019, Mike Weimar (R) 2019, one position is vacant at press time; Dist. Atty. Marion Weatherford 2019; Clerk Ellen Wagenaar 2021; Justice of the Peace Cris Patnode 2019; Sheriff Gary Bettencourt 2019; Surv. Todd Catterson 2019; Treas. Nathan Hammer 2019; Assess. Chet Wilkins 2021

Grant County

County Seat: Courthouse, 201 S Humbolt St., Suite 290, Canyon City 97820
Phone: 541-575-1675 (General); 541-575-1438 (Court Administrator)
Fax: 541-575-2248
Email: percyb@grantcounty-or.gov
Web: www.gcoregonlive2.com
Established:
Oct. 14, 1864

Elev. at Canyon City: 3,194'
Area: 4,528 sq. mi.
Average Temp.:
January 30.7°
July 68.4°
Assessed Value:
$550,074,498
Real Market Value: $1,338,649,790 (includes the value of non-taxed properties)
Annual Precipitation: 14.28"
Economy: Forest products, agriculture, hunting, livestock and recreation
Points of Interest: John Day Fossil Beds National Monument, Veterans Memorial, Kam Wah Chung Museum, Joaquin Miller Cabin, Grant County Historical Museum, Sacred Totem Pole, Grant County Historical Mural, Dewitt Museum, Depot Park, Sumpter Valley Railroad, Strawberry Mountain Wilderness and North Fork John Day River Wilderness

Grant County was created in 1864 from Wasco and Umatilla Counties and was named for General Ulysses S. Grant. It shares boundaries with more counties (eight) than any other county in Oregon.

Grant County contains the headwaters of the John Day River, which has more miles of Wild and Scenic designation than any other river in the United States. More than 60 percent of the land in the county is in public ownership.

County Officials: County Court—Judge Scott Myers 2019, Boyd Britton 2019, Jim Hamsher 2021; Dist. Atty. Jim Carpenter 2019; Assess. David Thunell 2021; Clerk Brenda Percy 2019; Justice of the Peace Kathleen Stinnett 2019; Sheriff Glenn Palmer 2021; Surv. Mike Springer 2021; Treas. Julie Ellison 2021

Harney County

County Seat: Courthouse, 450 N Buena Vista Ave., Burns 97720
Phone: 541-573-6641 (General); 541-573-5207 (Court Administrator)
Fax: 541-573-8370
Email: derrin.robinson@co.harney.or.us
Web: www.co.harney.or.us
Established:
Feb. 25, 1889
Elev. at Burns:
4,118'
Area: 10,228 sq. mi.
Average Temp.:
January 27.5°
July 69.4°
Assessed Value:
$534,653,065
Real Market Value: $1,331,081,033 (includes the value of non-taxed properties)
Annual Precipitation: 10.13"
Economy: Forest products, manufacturing, livestock and agriculture
Points of Interest: Steens Mountain, Malheur National Wildlife Refuge, Alvord Desert, Alvord Hot Springs, Eastern Oregon Agricultural Research Center, "P" Ranch Round Barn, Frenchglen, Wild Horse Corrals, Delintment Lake, Yellowjacket Lake

In 1826, Peter Skene Ogden became the first white man to explore this area when he led a fur brigade for the Hudson's Bay Company. In 1889, Harney, the largest county in Oregon, was carved out of Grant County and named for Major General William S. Harney, commander of the Department of Oregon, U.S. Army, from 1858–1859. Harney was instrumental in opening areas of Eastern Oregon for settlement.

A fierce political battle, with armed night riders who spirited county records from Harney to Burns, ended with Burns as the county seat in 1890. The courthouse was constructed five years later. Burns' first newspaper was established in 1884 and its first church was established in 1887.

Harney County shares the largest ponderosa pine forest in the nation with Grant County and has more than 100,000 beef cattle on its vast ranges. Its abundance of game, campsites, excellent fishing and bird watching have stimulated fast-growing recreational activities.

County Officials: County Court—Judge Peter Runnels 2023, Mark Owens 2021; Dist. Atty. Joseph W. Lucas 2021; Assess. Ted Tiller 2019; Clerk Derrin "Dag" Robinson 2021; Justice of the Peace Donna Thomas 2019; Sheriff David Ward 2021; Surv. Kenny Delano; Treas. Ellen "Nellie" Franklin 2019

Hood River County

County Seat: 601 State St., Hood River 97031-2093

Phone: 541-386-3970 (General); 541-386-3535 (Court Administrator)

Fax: 541-387-6864

Email: brian.beebe@co.hood-river.or.us

Web: www.co.hood-river.or.us

Established:
June 23, 1908

Elev. at Hood River: 154'

Area: 533 sq. mi.

Average Temp.:
January 33.6°
July 72°

Assessed Value:
$2,347,414,882

Real Market Value: $3,814,681,047
(includes the value of non-taxed properties)

Annual Precipitation: 30.85"

Economy: Agriculture, food processing, forest products and recreation

Points of Interest: Bridge of the Gods, Cloud Cap Inn, Mount Hood Recreation Area, Mount Hood Meadows Ski Resort, Lost Lake, Panorama Point, Hood River Valley at blossom time

The first white settlers in Hood River County filed a donation land claim in 1854. The first school was built in 1863, and a road from The Dalles was completed in 1867. By 1880, there were 17 families living in the valley. Hood River County was created in 1908 from Wasco County.

Agriculture, timber, lumber and recreation are the major sources of revenue and industry. Fruit grown in the fertile valley is of such exceptional quality that the county leads the world in Anjou pear production. There are more than 14,000 acres of commercial orchards growing pears, apples, cherries and peaches. Hood River County also has two ports and two boat basins, with one serving local barge traffic, a steel boat manufacturing firm and Mid-Columbia yachting interests. Windsurfing on the Columbia River is a popular sport and attracts windsurfers from all over the world.

County Officials: Commissioners—Chair Ron Rivers 2019, Bob Benton 2019, Karen Joplin 2019, Rich McBride 2021, Les Perkins 2021; Dist. Atty. John T. Sewell 2021; Justice of the Peace John Harvey 2021; Sheriff Matt English 2021; Assess./Clerk Brian Beebe; Surv. Bradley Cross; Treas. Sandra Borowy; Co. Admin. Jeff Hecksel

Jackson County

County Seat: Courthouse, 10 S Oakdale Ave., Medford 97501

Phone: 541-774-6029 (General); 541-776-7171 (Court Administrator - Justice Bldg., 100 S Oakdale Ave., Medford 97501)

Fax: 541-774-6455

Email: walkercd@jacksoncounty.org

Web: http://jacksoncountyor.org

Established:
Jan. 12, 1852

Elev. at Medford:
1,382'

Area: 2,801 sq. mi.

Average Temp.:
January 37.6°
July 72.5°

Assessed Value:
$19,239,605,639

Real Market Value: $26,608,473,944
(includes the value of non-taxed properties)

Annual Precipitation: 19.84"

Economy: Medical, retail, tourism, agriculture, manufacturing and forest products

Points of Interest: Mount Ashland Ski Resort, Historic Jacksonville, Oregon Shakespeare Festival, Peter Britt Music Festival, Southern Oregon University, pear orchards, Howard Prairie Lake, Emigrant Lake, Hyatt Lake, Fish Lake, Rogue River, Lithia Park, Lost Creek Dam, Butte Creek Mill, Crater Lake Highway

Named for President Andrew Jackson, Jackson County was formed in 1852 from Lane County and the unorganized area south of Douglas and Umpqua Counties. It included lands which now lie in Coos, Curry, Josephine, Klamath and Lake Counties. The discovery of gold near Jacksonville in 1852 and completion of a wagon road, which joined the county with California to the south and Douglas County to the north, brought many pioneers.

County Officials: Commissioners—Chair Rick Dyer (R) 2019, Colleen Roberts (R) 2019; Bob Strosser (R) 2021; Dist. Atty. Beth Heckert 2021; Assess. David Arrasmith 2021; Clerk Chris Walker 2019; Justice of the Peace Joe Charter 2021; Sheriff Corey Falls 2019; Surv. Scott Fein 2021; Finance Director/Treas. Shannon Bell; Co. Admin. Danny Jordan

Jefferson County

County Seat: 66 SE D St., Madras 97741
Phone: 541-475-4451 (General); 541-475-3317 (Court Administrator)
Fax: 541-325-5018
Email: Kathy.Marston@co.jefferson.or.us
Web: www.co.jefferson.or.us
Established:
Dec. 12, 1914
Elev. at Madras:
2,242'
Area: 1,791 sq. mi.
Average Temp.:
January 37.4°
July 70.1°
Assessed Value:
$1,637,051,083
Real Market Value: $2,681,719,683
(includes the value of non-taxed properties)
Annual Precipitation: 10.2"
Economy: Agriculture, forest products and recreation
Points of Interest: Mount Jefferson, Warm Springs Indian Reservation, Metolius River, Black Butte, Suttle Lake, Blue Lake, Santiam Summit, Lake Billy Chinook behind Round Butte Dam, Haystack Reservoir, Priday Agate Beds

Jefferson County was established in 1914 from a portion of Crook County. It was named for Mount Jefferson on its western boundary. The county owes much of its agricultural prosperity to the railroad, which arrived in 1911, and to the development of irrigation projects in the late 1930s. The railroad, which links Madras with the Columbia River, was completed after constant feuds and battles between two lines working on opposite sides of the Deschutes River.

Vegetable, grass and flower seeds, garlic, mint and sugar beets are cultivated on some 60,000 irrigated acres. Jefferson County also has vast acreages of rangelands and a healthy industrial base related to forest products. The Warm Springs Forest Products Industry, a multi-million dollar complex owned by the Confederated Tribes of the Warm Springs Reservation—partially located in the northwestern corner of the county—is the single biggest industry. With 300 days of sunshine and a low yearly rainfall, fishing, hunting, camping, boating, water-skiing and rock hunting are popular recreations.

County Officials: Commissioners—Chair Mike Ahern 2019, Wayne Fording 2021, Mae Huston 2019; Dist. Atty. Steven Leriche 2021; Assess. Jean McCloskey 2021; Clerk Kathleen Marston 2019; Sheriff Jim Adkins 2019; Surv. Gary L. DeJarnatt 2021; Treas. Brandie McNamee 2021

Josephine County

County Seat: Courthouse, 500 NW Sixth St., Grants Pass 97526; Mailing Address: PO Box 69, Grants Pass 97526
Phone: 541-474-5243 (General); 541-476-2309 (Court Administrator)
Fax: 541-474-5246
Email: clerk@co.josephine.or.us
Web: www.co.josephine.or.us
Established:
Jan. 22, 1856
**Elev. at Grants
Pass:** 948'
Area: 1,641 sq. mi.
Average Temp.:
January 39.9°
July 71.6°
Assessed Value:
$7,203,378,002
Real Market Value: $10,341,636,145
(includes the value of non-taxed properties)
Annual Precipitation: 32.31"
Economy: Tourism, recreation, forest products, electronics and software
Points of Interest: Oregon Caves National Monument, Wolf Creek Tavern, Sunny Valley Covered Bridge and Interpretive Center, Hellgate Canyon-Rogue River, Grants Pass Historic District, Growers Market, Kalmiopsis Wilderness, Rogue Community College, Barnstormers Theater, Rogue Music Theater

Josephine County, named for Virginia "Josephine" Rollins, the first white woman to make this county her home, was established in 1856 out of the western portion of Jackson County. The county seat was originally located in Sailor Diggings (later, Waldo), but in July of 1857 was relocated to Kerbyville, situated on the main route between the port of Crescent City, California and the gold fields.

The discovery of rich placers at Sailor Diggings in 1852 and the resulting gold rush brought the first settlers to this region. Several U.S. Army forts were maintained in the county and many engagements during the Rogue River Indian War (1855–1858) took place within its boundaries. In 1886, the county seat was finally relocated to Grants Pass, a new town on the railroad that was completed through Oregon that same year. Grants Pass is now the departure point for most Rogue River scenic waterway guided fishing and boat trips. The Illinois River, one of the Rogue's tributaries, has also been designated a scenic waterway.

County Officials: Commissioners—Dan DeYoung 2021, Simon Hare 2019 Lily Morgan 2021; Dist. Atty. Ryan A. Mulkins 2021; Assess. Connie Roach 2021; Clerk Trisha Myers 2021; Sheriff Dave R. Daniel 2019; Surv. Peter D. Allen 2021; Treas. Eve Arce 2021

Klamath County

County Seat: 305 Main St., Klamath Falls 97601-6391

Phone: 541-883-5134 (General); 541-883-5503 (Court Administrator)

Fax: 541-885-6757

Email: lsmith@co.klamath.or.us

Web: www.klamathcounty.org

Established:
Oct. 17, 1882

Elev. at Klamath Falls: 4,105'

Area: 6,135 sq. mi.

Average Temp.:
January 29.8°
July 68.0°

Assessed Value:
$5,070,507,145

Real Market Value: $7,196,478,061 (includes the value of non-taxed properties)

Annual Precipitation: 14.31"

Economy: Forest products, agriculture, geothermal energy, tourism and recreation

Points of Interest: Crater Lake National Park, Collier Memorial State Park and Logging Museum, Klamath Lake (largest lake in Oregon), seven National Wildlife Refuges, Oregon Institute of Technology (OIT), Klamath County Museum, Favell Museum of Western Art, Ross Ragland Performing Arts Theatre

The Klamath or "Clamitte" Tribe, for which Klamath County was named, has had a presence for 10,000 years. White settlement began in 1846 along the Applegate Immigrant Trail, which precipitated clashes between the two cultures and led to the Modoc Indian War of 1872. The Oregon Legislature created Klamath County by dividing Lake County in 1882. Linkville was named county seat and its name was changed to Klamath Falls in 1893.

Klamath County's present-day position as a great lumber, agriculture and distribution center was assured in the early 1900s with the coming of the railroad and the start of one of the most successful of all federal reclamation projects—the Klamath Project, which drained much of the 128 square mile Lower Klamath Lake to provide 188,000 acres of irrigable land.

Natural geothermal hot wells provide heat for many homes, businesses and the OIT campus. The full potential of this energy resource continues to be studied. Klamath County is recognized for its scenic beauty, outdoor recreation, abundant waterfowl and diverse landscape.

County Officials: Commissioners—Donnie Boyd 2021, Derrick DeGroot 2021, Kelley Minty Morris 2019; Dist. Atty. Rob Patridge 2019; Assess. Leonard Hill 2021; Clerk Linda Smith 2019; Justice of the Peace Karen Oakes 2023; Sheriff Chris Kaber 2021; Surv. Michael Markus 2021; Treas. Jason Link 2021

Lake County

County Seat: Courthouse, 513 Center St., Lakeview 97630

Phone: 541-947-6006 (General); 541-947-6051 (Court Administrator)

Fax: 541-947-6015

Email: sgeaney@co.lake.or.us

Web: www.lakecountyor.org

Established:
October 24, 1874

Elev. at Lakeview: 4,800'

Area: 8,359 sq. mi.

Average Temp.:
January 28.4°
July 67.0°

Assessed Value:
$990,014,492

Real Market Value: $3,113,612,384 (includes the value of non-taxed properties)

Annual Precipitation: 15.80"

Economy: Livestock, forest products, agriculture and recreation

Points of Interest: Hart Mountain Antelope Refuge, Fort Rock and Fort Rock Homestead Village Museum, Abert Lake and Rim, Goose Lake, Hunter's Hot Springs, Old Perpetual Geyser, Schminck Memorial Museum and Lake County Museum, Lake County Round-Up Museum, Warner Canyon Ski Area, Gearhart Wilderness, Lost Forest, Crack-in-the-Ground, Sheldon National Wildlife Refuge, Summer Lake Hot Springs, Hole-in-the-Ground, sunstones (Oregon's state gemstone) near Plush, Warner Wetlands, Summer Lake Wildlife Area

Lake County was created from Jackson and Wasco Counties by the 1874 Legislature. It then included the present Klamath County and all of the present Lake County except Warner Valley. In 1882, Klamath was removed and in 1885, the Warner area from Grant County was added.

Linkville, now Klamath Falls, was the first county seat. M. Bullard gave 20 acres as the Lakeview townsite. In the 1875 election, the county seat was moved to Lakeview. The Hart Mountain Antelope Refuge is a 270,000 acre wildlife haven for antelope, mule deer, bighorn sheep and upland birds. A number of migratory waterfowl flyways converge on Goose Lake, south of Lakeview, the Warner Wetlands near Plush and the Summer Lake Wildlife area. Lakeview has been deemed the hang gliding capital of the West.

County Officials: Commissioners—Chair Bradley Winters 2021, Ken Kestner 2019, Dan Shoun 2019; Dist. Atty. Sharon Forster 2021; Assess. Dave Knowles 2021; Clerk Stacie Geaney 2021; Sheriff Michael Taylor 2019; Surv. Darryl Anderson 2019; Treas. Ann Crumrine 2021

Lane County

County Seat: Courthouse, 125 E Eighth Ave., Eugene 97401
Phone: 541-682-4203 (General); 541-682-4166 (Court Administrator)
Fax: 541-682-4616
Web: www.lanecounty.org
Established:
Jan. 28, 1851
Elev. at Eugene:
422'
Area: 4,620 sq. mi.
Average Temp.:
January 40°
July 70°
Assessed Value:
$31,441,712,573
Real Market Value: $52,783,387,805
(includes the value of non-taxed properties)
Annual Precipitation: 46"
Economy: Agriculture, higher education, high technology, forest products, recreation, recreational vehicle manufacturing and tourism
Points of Interest: Twenty historic covered bridges, Bohemia Mines, coastal sand dunes, Darlingtonia Botanical Wayside, Fern Ridge Reservoir, Heceta Head Lighthouse, Hendricks Park Rhododendron Garden, hot springs, Hult Center for the Performing Arts, Lane Community College, Lane ESD Planetarium, Martin Rapids whitewater, McKenzie Pass, Mt. Pisgah Arboretum, Old Town Florence, Pac-12 sports events, Proxy Falls, Sea Lion Caves, University of Oregon, vineyards and wineries, Waldo Lake, Carl G. Washburne State Park tide pools, Willamette Pass ski area

Lane County was named for General Joseph Lane, a rugged frontier hero who was Oregon's first territorial governor. Pioneers traveling the Oregon Trail in the late 1840s came to Lane County mainly to farm. The county's first district court met under a large oak tree until a clerk's office could be built in 1852. A few years later, the first courthouse opened in what is now downtown Eugene. With the building of the railroads, the market for timber opened in the 1880s. Today, wood products are still an important part of the economy in addition to high-technology manufacturing and tourism. Lane County government operates under a home rule charter approved by voters in 1962.

Although 90 percent of Lane County is forest land, Eugene and Springfield comprise the second largest urban area in Oregon.

County Officials: Commissioners—Jay Bozievich 2019, Pat Farr 2021, Sid Leiken 2019, Peter Sorenson 2021, Faye Stewart 2019; Dist. Atty. Patricia Perlow 2021; Assess. Mike Cowles 2019; Clerk Cheryl Betschart; Justice of the Peace Rick Brissenden 2021; Sheriff Byron Trapp 2021; Surv. Jay Blomme; Co. Admin. Steve Mokrohisky

Lincoln County

County Seat: Courthouse, 225 W Olive St., Newport 97365
Phone: 541-265-6611 (General); 541-265-4236 (Court Administrator)
Fax: 541-265-4176
Email: webmaster@co.lincoln.or.us
Web: www.co.lincoln.or.us
Established:
Feb. 20, 1893
Elev. at Newport:
134'
Area: 992 sq. mi.
Average Temp.:
January 44.4°
July 57.6°
Assessed Value:
$7,320,749,420
Real Market Value: $9,944,047,930
(includes the value of non-taxed properties)
Annual Precipitation: 71.93"
Economy: Tourism, government, services and retail, forest products and fishing
Points of Interest: Agate Beach, Alsea Bay Interpretive Center, Beverly Beach State Park, Boiler Bay, Cape Perpetua Visitors' Center, Cascade Head, Connie Hansen Garden Conservancy, Devils Lake, Lincoln County Historical Museum, Newport Performing and Visual Arts Centers, OSU Hatfield Marine Science Center and Interpretive Center, Oregon Coast Aquarium, Otter Crest Viewpoint, Seal Rock Park, South Beach State Park, Yaquina Arts Center, Yaquina Bay State Park and Lighthouse, Yaquina Head Outstanding Natural Area

With miles of beach and coastline, Lincoln County is one of the most popular visitor destinations on the Oregon Coast. Named for President Abraham Lincoln, Lincoln County was created by the Oregon Legislature in 1893. Lincoln County has a very temperate climate and a short, but productive, growing season.

Depoe Bay is known as "the whale watching capital of the world." Lincoln City offers more than 2,000 hotel, motel and bed and breakfast rooms and resorts, as well as the Siletz Tribe's Chinook Winds Casino. Newport, known as Oregon's oceanography research center, features numerous interpretive centers and the Oregon Coast Aquarium, along with a large fishing fleet and working bay front. Siletz is the home of the Administration Center and reservation of the Confederated Tribes of Siletz Indians of Oregon. Toledo is known as Lincoln County's industrial center. Waldport features the Alsea Bay Interpretive Center. Yachats is known as the "Gem of the Oregon Coast."

County Officials: Commissioners—Chair Terry N. Thompson (D) 2019, Bill Hall (D) 2021, Doug Hunt (D) 2019; Dist. Atty. Michelle Branam 2019; Assess. Joe Davidson 2021; Clerk Dana Jenkins 2019; Sheriff Curtis Landers 2021; Surv. John Waffenschmidt; Treas. Linda Pilson 2021

Linn County

County Seat: Courthouse, 300 SW Fourth Ave., Albany 97321
Phone: 541-967-3825 (General); 541-967-3802 (Court Administrator)
Fax: 541-926-8226
Email: sdruckenmiller@co.linn.or.us
Web: www.co.linn.or.us
Established:
 Dec. 28, 1847
Elev. at Albany:
 210'
Area: 2,297 sq. mi.
Average Temp.:
 January 39.0°
 July 65.6°
Assessed Value:
 $9,390,023,954
Real Market Value: $13,241,005,083
(includes the value of non-taxed properties)
Annual Precipitation: 42.55"
Economy: Agriculture, forest products, rare metals, manufacturing and recreation
Points of Interest: Willamette and Santiam Rivers; Foster, Green Peter and Detroit Reservoirs; Cascade Range mountains with Mount Jefferson, Hoodoo Ski Bowl and the Pacific Crest Trail; covered bridges; Fair and Expo Center; Brownsville Museum and Albany historic districts

Linn County was created in 1847 and named for U.S. Senator Lewis F. Linn of Missouri, who was the author of the Donation Land Act which provided free land to settlers in the West. Linn County is in the center of the Willamette Valley, with the Willamette River as its western boundary and the crest of the Cascades as its eastern boundary. The climate and soil conditions provide one of Oregon's most diversified agriculture areas, allowing a wide variety of specialty crops and leading the nation in the production of common and perennial ryegrass. Linn County is also home to major producers of processed food, manufactured homes and motor homes, as well as the traditional logging and wood products industries.

Recreational opportunities are extensive and include hiking, climbing and skiing; picnicking and camping in county and state parks; boating, water skiing and fishing on lakes and rivers; petrified wood and agate beds; covered bridges and historic districts and events.

County Officials: Commissioners—John K. Lindsey (R) 2019, Roger Nyquist (R) 2021, William Tucker (R) 2021; Dist. Atty. Douglas Marteeny 2021; Assess. Dave Swartzlender 2021; Clerk Steven Druckenmiller 2019; Justice of the Peace Jad Lemhouse 2021; Sheriff Bruce Riley 2019; Surv. Charles Gibbs 2021; Treas. Michelle Hawkins 2021; Co. Admin. Ralph Wyatt

Malheur County

County Seat: 251 B St. W, Vale 97918
Phone: 541-473-5183 (General); 541-473-5171 (Court Administrator)
Fax: 541-473-5523
Email: ddelong@malheurco.org
Web: www.malheurco.org
Established:
 Feb. 17, 1887
Elev. at Vale:
 2,243'
Area: 9,926 sq. mi.
Average Temp.:
 January 28.7°
 July 75.6°
Assessed Value:
 $1,974,258,249
Real Market Value: $3,309,903,160
(includes the value of non-taxed properties)
Annual Precipitation: 9.64"
Economy: Agriculture, livestock, food processing and recreation
Points of Interest: Oregon Trail, Keeney Pass, Owyhee Lake, Succor Creek State Park, Leslie Gulch Canyon, Jordan Craters, grave of trapper John Baptiste Charbonneau, Nyssa Agricultural Museum, Vale Oregon Trail Murals, Jordan Valley Basque Pelota Court, the Four Rivers Cultural Center

Malheur County was created in 1887 from Baker County. Malheur County derives its name from the "Riviere au Malheur" or "Unfortunate River" (later changed to "Malheur River"), named by French trappers whose property and furs were stolen from their river encampment.

Malheur County is a place filled with fascinating history, diverse landscape and friendly people. The landscape is enchanting and provides for a wide variety of excellent recreation such as hunting, fishing, hiking, rock climbing, rock hounding, boating and water skiing. The county is 94 percent rangeland. Basques, primarily shepherds, settled in Jordan Valley in the 1890s. Irrigated fields in the county's northeast corner, known as Western Treasure Valley, are the center of intensive and diversified farming.

County Officials: County Court—Judge Dan Joyce (R) 2023, Donald Hodge (R) 2019, Lawrence "Larry" P. Wilson (R) 2021; Dist. Atty. David M. Goldthorpe 2021; Assess. Dave Ingram 2021; Clerk Deborah DeLong 2019; Justice of the Peace Margaret "Margie" Mahony 2019; Sheriff Brian E. Wolfe 2021; Surv. Tom Edwards; Treas. Jennifer Forsyth 2019; Co. Admin. and Chief Information Officer Lorinda DuBois

Marion County

County Seat: 100 High St. NE, Salem 97301
Phone: 503-588-5225 (General); 503-588-5105 (Court Administrator)
Fax: 503-373-4408
Email: clerksoffice@co.marion.or.us
Web: www.co.marion.or.us
Established:
July 5, 1843
Elev. at Salem:
154'
Area: 1,194 sq. mi.
Average Temp.:
January 39.3°
July 66.3°
Assessed Value:
$23,371,520,094
Real Market Value: $39,002,299,869
(includes the value of non-taxed properties)
Annual Precipitation: 40.35"
Economy: Government, agriculture, food processing, forest products, manufacturing, education and tourism
Points of Interest: State Capitol, Champoeg State Park, Silver Falls State Park, The Oregon Garden, Wheatland Ferry, Buena Vista Ferry, Detroit Dam and Santiam River, Breitenbush Hot Springs, Mount Angel Abbey, food processing plants, Willamette University, Chemeketa Community College, Willamette Heritage Center and Mission Mill Museum Village, Bush House, Deepwood House and the Gilbert House Children's Museum

Marion County, then called Champooick, was created by the Provisional Government in 1843, 16 years before Oregon gained statehood. In 1849, the name was changed to Marion in honor of General Francis Marion.

The county, located in the heart of the Willamette Valley, has the Willamette River as its western boundary and the Cascade Range on the east. Salem, the county seat, is one of the valley's oldest cities. Among its public buildings are the Marion County Courthouse, State Capitol, Capitol Mall buildings and Salem Civic Center. The county was presided over by the Marion County Court until January 1, 1963, when the court was abolished and replaced by a Board of Commissioners.

County Officials: Commissioners—Chair Sam Brentano 2021, Janet Carlson 2019, Kevin Cameron 2019; Dist. Atty. Walter Beglau 2019; Assess. Tom Rohlfing 2021; Clerk Bill Burgess 2021; Justice of the Peace Janice D. Zyryanoff 2019; Sheriff Jason Myers 2019; Surv. Mark Riggins; Treas. Laurie Steele 2019; Co. Admin. John Lattimer

Morrow County

County Seat: Courthouse, 100 S Court St., Heppner 97836; PO Box 788, Heppner 97836
Phone: 541-676-5604 (General); 541-676-5264 (Court Administrator)
Fax: 541-676-9876
Email: bchilders@co.morrow.or.us
Web: http://morrowcountyoregon.com
Established:
Feb. 16, 1885
Elev. at Heppner:
1,955'
Area: 2,049 sq. mi.
Average Temp.:
January 33.1°
July 69.0°
Assessed Value:
$2,261,682,093
Real Market Value: $4,078,799,116
(includes the value of non-taxed properties)
Annual Precipitation: 12.5"
Economy: Agriculture, food processing, dairies, utilities, forest products, livestock and recreation
Points of Interest: Columbia River, coal-fired generating plant, Blue Mountains, Umatilla National Forest, Oregon Trail, Blue Mountain Scenic Byway, Morrow County Museum, Port of Morrow and the Lewis and Clark Route

Morrow County, created from Umatilla County in 1885, is located east of the Cascades in north-central Oregon. It was named for J. L. Morrow, an early resident. Morrow County contains more than one million acres of gently rolling plains and broad plateaus. This rich agricultural land can be roughly divided into three occupational zones—increasing amounts of irrigation farming in the north, vast fields of wheat yielding to cattle ranches in the center, and timber products in the south. With the advent of center pivot irrigation technology, Morrow County became one of Oregon's fastest growing areas in terms of population, personal income, and agricultural and industrial development. The Port of Morrow, second largest in the state in terms of tonnage, serves as a gateway to the Pacific Northwest and Pacific Rim markets.

County Officials: Commissioners—Jim Doherty 2021, Melissa J. Lindsay 2023, Don Russell 2019; Dist. Atty. Justin Nelson 2019; Assess. Mike Gorman 2019; Clerk Bobbi Childers 2021; Justice of the Peace Annetta Spicer 2021; Sheriff Kenneth Matlack 2021; Surv. Stephen Haddock 2021; Treas. Gayle Gutierrez 2021

Multnomah County

County Seat: 501 SE Hawthorne Blvd., Portland 97214

Phone: 503-823-4000 (General); 503-988-3957 (Court Administrator)

Web: http://web.multco.us

Established:
Dec. 22, 1854

Elev. at Portland:
77'

Area: 465 sq. mi.

Average Temp.:
January 38.9°
July 67.7°

Assessed Value:
$75,599,622,697

Real Market Value: $169,161,437,156 (includes the value of non-taxed properties)

Annual Precipitation: 37.39"

Economy: Manufacturing, transportation, whole-sale and retail trade, and tourism

Points of Interest: Oregon History Center, Oregon Museum of Science and Industry, Oregon Zoo, Portland Art Museum, Washington Park, International Rose Test Gardens, Japanese Gardens, Columbia River Gorge, Multnomah Falls, Blue Lake Park, Oxbow Park, Pittock Mansion, Port of Portland, Memorial Coliseum and Rose Quarter, Oregon Convention Center, Moda Center Arena, Vista House

Lewis and Clark made note of "Multnomah," the tribal village on Sauvie Island, in 1805 and applied that name to all tribal people of the area. The name is derived from "nematlnomaq," probably meaning "downriver." Multnomah County was created from parts of Washington and Clackamas Counties by the Territorial Legislature in 1854, five years before Oregon became a state, because citizens found it inconvenient to travel to Hillsboro to conduct county business.

The county is both the smallest in size and largest in population in Oregon. Over 50 percent of its people live in Portland, a busy metropolis dominated by rivers and greenery. The remaining area includes picturesque rural land, from pastoral farms on Sauvie Island to the rugged Columbia River Gorge and the western slopes of Mount Hood.

County Officials: Commissioners—Chair Deborah Kafoury 2018, Sharon Meieran 2020, Loretta Smith 2018, Lori Stegmann 2020, Jessica Vega Pederson 2020; Dist. Atty. Rod Underhill 2021; Sheriff Mike Reese 2018; Auditor Steve March 2018; Assess. Michael Vaughn; Recorder Ron Weldon; Surv. James Clayton; Chief Finance Officer Mark Campbell; Chief Information Officer Sherry Swackhamer; Attorney Jenny Madkour; Engineer Ian Cannon

Polk County

County Seat: Courthouse, 850 Main St., Dallas 97338

Phone: 503-623-8173 (General); 503-623-3154 (Court Administrator)

Fax: 503-623-0896

Email: unger.valerie@co.polk.or.us

Web: www.co.polk.or.us

Established:
Dec. 22, 1845

Elev. at Dallas: 325'

Area: 745 sq. mi.

Average Temp.:
January 39.1°
July 65.6°

Assessed Value:
$5,621,923,862

Real Market Value: $8,121,188,858 (includes the value of non-taxed properties)

Annual Precipitation: 51.66"

Economy: Agriculture, forest products, manufacturing, electronics and education

Points of Interest: Western Oregon University, covered bridges, historic courthouse, Brunk House, Baskett Slough Wildlife Refuge, mountain scenery, wineries, National Historic Trail, Confederated Tribes of Grand Ronde Headquarters and Spirit Mountain Casino

Polk County was created from the original Yamhill district in 1845 by the Provisional Legislature. It was named for then President James Knox Polk. The first county seat was at Cynthia Ann. City officials later changed its name to Dallas, after Vice-President George M. Dallas, and moved the community about a mile to improve its water supply.

The first courthouse was at Cynthia Ann. A second courthouse burned in 1898 and was replaced with the present building built with sandstone quarried three miles west of Dallas. A three-story office annex was completed in 1966. Polk County Human Services was consolidated in the newly acquired Academy Building in 1989.

Traveling back roads in Polk County will reveal many attractions, from covered bridges and pleasant parks to vineyards, wineries, and bed and breakfast lodgings spotting the surrounding hills. Many roads meander through beautiful fertile valleys from the Willamette River to the timbered foothills of the Coast Range. Polk County was the primary destination of early wagon trains which took the southern route to Oregon. Cities located in Polk County include Dallas, Independence, Monmouth, Falls City and portions of Salem and Willamina.

County Officials: Commissioners—Chair Craig Pope 2019, Mike Ainsworth 2019, Jennifer Wheeler 2021; Dist. Atty. Aaron Felton 2021; Assess. Douglas P. Schmidt 2021; Clerk Valerie Unger 2021; Sheriff Mark A. Garton 2021; Surv. Eric Berry; Treas. Linda Fox 2021; Co. Admin. Greg P. Hansen

Sherman County

County Seat: Courthouse, 500 Court St., Moro 97039
Phone: 541-565-3606 (Clerk); 541-565-3650 (Court Clerk)
Fax: 541-565-3771
Email:countyclerk@shermancounty.net
Web: www.co.sherman.or.us
Established:
    Feb. 25, 1889
Elev. at Moro:
    1,807'
Area: 831 sq. mi.
Average Temp.:
    January 30.7°
    July 67.9°
Assessed Value:
    $428,564,210
Real Market Value: $1,602,917,944
(includes the value of non-taxed properties)
Annual Precipitation: 9.15"
Economy: Tourism, wind energy, wheat, barley and cattle
Points of Interest: Historic county courthouse, Sherman County Museum, Gordon Ridge, John Day Dam, Sherar's Grade, Deschutes State Park, LePage Park, Giles French Park, Sherman County Fairgrounds and Recreational Vehicle Park

Sherman County, created in 1889 from the northeast corner of Wasco County, was named for General William Tecumseh Sherman. It was separated from Wasco County as much for its unique geological setting as for the settlers' desire to have their own political process. The rolling hills are bordered by the deep canyons of the John Day River to the east, the Columbia River to the north, and the Deschutes River and Buck Hollow to the west and south.

The county was settled in the 1870s by stockmen. By 1881, the homesteaders arrived, permanently changing the area by plowing and fencing the land. Since then, the county has been a wheat-growing area with miles of waving grain on rolling hills of wind-blown glacial silt. The total absence of timber in the county exemplifies the true meaning of the "wide open spaces of the West." Its pastoral landscape has spectacular views of canyons and rivers with mountains silhouetted in the distance. Recreation abounds on the rivers, from the famous and scenic fly-fishing and whitewater rafting stream of the Deschutes to water-skiing, wind-surfing, boating, fishing and rafting on the John Day and Columbia Rivers. Sherman County is one of Oregon's leaders in soil and water conservation.
County Officials: County Court—Judge Gary Thompson 2019, Joe Dabulskis (R) 2021, Tom McCoy (R) 2019; Dist. Atty. Wade McLeod 2019; Assess. Ross Turney 2019; Clerk Jenine McDermid 2021; Treas. Marnene Benson-Wood 2019; Justice of the Peace Ron McDermid 2021; Sheriff Brad Lohrey 2021; Surv. Daryl Ingebo

Tillamook County

County Seat: Courthouse, 201 Laurel Ave., Tillamook 97141
Phone: 503-842-2034 (General); 503-842-2596, ext. 124 (Court Administrator)
Fax: 503-842-2721
Email: toneil@co.tillamook.or.us
Web: www.co.tillamook.or.us
Established:
    Dec. 15, 1853
Elev. at Tillamook:
    22'
Area: 1,125 sq. mi.
Average Temp.:
    January 42.2°
    July 58.2°
Assessed Value:
    $4,643,768,539
Real Market Value: $6,008,465,936
(includes the value of non-taxed properties)
Annual Precipitation: 90.90"
Economy: Agriculture, forest products, fishing and recreation
Points of Interest: Neah-Kah-Nie Mountain; Tillamook, Nehalem, Netarts and Nestucca Bays; Oswald West State Park, Nehalem Bay State Park, Bob Straub State Park, Cape Lookout State Park; Pioneer Museum, Blue Heron Cheese Factory, Tillamook Cheese Factory, Naval Air Station Museum, Haystack Rock at Cape Kiwanda, Whalen Island State Park

Tillamook County was formed in 1853 from Yamhill and Clatsop Counties. The name Tillamook comes from the Tillamook (or Killamook) Tribe.

Dairy farms dominate the county's fertile valley. It is the home of the world famous Tillamook Cheese Factory. The reforested 355,000-acre "Tillamook Burn" area continues to mature. Commercial thinning will become increasingly evident. With 75 miles of scenic coastline, four bays and nine rivers, Tillamook County offers the finest deep-sea and stream fishing, charter and dory boats, clamming, crabbing, beachcombing and hiking. Its forests also furnish excellent hunting.
County Officials: Commissioners—Chair Tim Josi 2019, Bill Baertlein 2021, David Yamamoto 2021; Dist. Atty. William Porter 2019; Assess. Denise Vandecoevering 2021; Clerk Tassi O'Neil 2021; Justice of the Peace Joel Stevens 2021; Sheriff Andy Long 2021; Surv. Michael Rice; Treas. Debbie Clark 2021

Umatilla County

County Seat: Courthouse, 216 SE Fourth St., Pendleton 97801

Phone: 541-276-7111 (General); 541-278-0341, Pendleton, 541-667-3020, Hermiston (Court Administrators)

Email: adminservices@umatillacounty.net

Web: www.co.umatilla.or.us

Established:
  Sept. 27, 1862

Elev. at Pendleton:
  1,069'

Area: 3,231 sq. mi.

Average Temp.:
  January 31.9°
  July 73.6°

Assessed Value:
  $5,398,880,336

Real Market Value: $8,313,097,425
(includes the value of non-taxed properties)

Annual Precipitation: 12.97"

Economy: Agriculture, food processing, forest products, tourism, manufacturing, recreation, aggregate production and wind power generation

Points of Interest: Pendleton Round-Up, Pendleton Woolen Mills, Old Town Pendleton, County Historical Society, Pendleton Underground, McNary Dam and Recreation Area, Echo Museum and Historic Area, Hat Rock, Battle Mountain and Emigrant Springs State Parks, Weston Historic District, Frazier Farmstead Museum in Milton-Freewater, North Fork Umatilla Wilderness Area, Tollgate-Spout Springs Recreation Area, Courthouse Clock Tower, Stateline Wind Project, Confederated Tribes of the Umatilla Indian Reservation's Wildhorse Casino and Tamastslikt Cultural Center

Umatilla County traces its creation in 1862 to the regional gold rushes, which spawned the riverport of Umatilla City and brought stockraisers to the lush grasslands.

Although Lewis and Clark and the Oregon Trail pioneers passed through Umatilla County, it did not bloom until the arrival of the railroad in 1881 and the development of dryland wheat farming.

Water in the form of irrigation has been key to economic diversification and growth, most recently in the Hermiston area, where the desert now yields lush watermelons and other products. Tourism is also increasingly important to Umatilla County where "Let-er-Buck" is heard by Pendleton Round-Up crowds.

County Officials: Commissioners—Chair Bill Elfering 2021, Larry Givens 2019, George Murdock 2019; Dist. Atty. Daniel R. Primus 2021; Sheriff Terry Rowan 2021; Assess. Paul Chalmers; Rec. Mgr. Steve Churchill; Surv. David Krumbein; Financial Mgr. Robert Pahl; Admin. Serv. Dir. Dan Lonai

Union County

County Seat: Union County Commissioners, 1106 K Ave., La Grande 97850

Phone: 541-963-1001 (General); 541-962-9500, ext. 232 (Court Administrator)

Fax: 541-963-1079

Email: rchurch@union-county.org

Web: http://union-county.org

Established:
  Oct. 14, 1864

Elev. at La Grande:
  2,788'

Area: 2,038 sq. mi.

Average Temp.:
  January 30.9°
  July 70.4°

Assessed Value:
  $1,859,413,405

Real Market Value: $2,937,637,140
(includes the value of non-taxed properties)

Annual Precipitation: 18.79"

Economy: Agriculture, forest products, education and government

Points of Interest: Meacham and Tollgate winter sports areas, Grande Ronde Valley, Eastern Oregon University (La Grande)

Union County was created in 1864 and named for the town of Union, which had been established two years before and named by its founders for patriotic reasons during the Civil War. The county comprised a part of the northern portion of Baker County. In 1899, Union County gave up its eastern portion to Wallowa County.

The Grande Ronde Valley in Union County is nearly table flat and is covered with the rich silt of an old lake bed. Highly diversified, with a 160-day growing season and an annual rainfall of 20 inches, the valley boasts of never having had a general crop failure. The county's 1,092 farms average 473 acres a unit.

Union County's front door opens to the rugged Wallowa Mountains. Its back door faces the Blue Mountains, which attract hikers, skiers and hunters.

County Officials: Commissioners—Chair Steve McClure 2019, Donna Beverage 2021, Jack Howard 2019, ; Dist. Atty. Kelsie McDaniel 2019; Assess. Cody Vavra 2021; Clerk Robin Church 2021; Sheriff Boyd Rasmussen 2021; Surv. Rick Robinson 2021; Treas. Donna Marshall 2021; Co. Admin. and Chief Info. Officer Shelley Burgess

Wallowa County

County Seat: Courthouse, 101 S River St., Enterprise 97828
Phone: 541-426-4543 ext. 15 (General); 541-426-4991 (Court Administrator)
Fax: 541-426-0582
Email: wcclerk@co.wallowa.or.us
Web: www.co.wallowa.or.us
Established:
Feb. 11, 1887
Elev. at Enterprise:
3,757'
Area: 3,153 sq. mi.
Average Temp.:
January 24.2°
July 63.0°
Assessed Value: $748,518,338
Real Market Value: $1,802,556,330
(includes the value of non-taxed properties)
Annual Precipitation: 13.08"
Economy: Agriculture, art, livestock, forest products and recreation
Points of Interest: Wallowa Lake; art galleries; Mount Howard gondola; Eagle Cap Wilderness; Hells Canyon National Recreation Area; Minam, Wallowa and Grande Ronde Rivers

This rather isolated area was claimed by the Chief Joseph band of the Nez Perce as its hunting and fishing grounds. The Nez Perce used the word "wallowa" to designate a tripod of poles used to support fish nets. In 1871, the first white settlers came to Wallowa County crossing the mountains in search of livestock feed in the Wallowa Valley. The area had been part of Union County since 1864, but it was carved from that county in 1887 by a legislative act.

Wallowa County is a land of rugged mountains, gentle valleys and deep canyons. Peaks in the Wallowa Mountains soar to almost 10,000 feet in elevation and the Snake River drops over 8,500 feet in elevation over its length. Hells Canyon, carved by the Snake, is the nation's deepest gorge averaging 5,500 feet from rim to river.

The scenery in the county is spectacular and serves as a magnet for tourists. Unrivaled opportunities for outdoor recreation create the county's reputation as a visitors' paradise. Permanent residents enjoy the same recreation opportunities, adding to a high quality of life supported by traditional farm and forest industries, as well as art and tourism.

County Officials: Commissioners—Chair Susan Roberts 2021, Paul Castilleja 2019, Todd Nash 2021; Dist. Atty. Mona K. Williams 2019; Assess. Randy Wortman 2021; Clerk Sandy Lathrop 2019; Sheriff Steve Rogers 2021; Treas. Shonelle Dutcher-Pryse 2021; Surv. Richard Shaver

Wasco County

County Seat: Courthouse, 511 Washington St., The Dalles 97058
Phone: 541-506-2500 (General); 541-506-2700 (Court Administrator)
Fax: 541-506-2531
Email: countyclerk@co.wasco.or.us
Web: www.co.wasco.or.us
Established:
Jan. 11, 1854
Elev. at The Dalles:
98'
Area: 2,396 sq. mi.
Average Temp.:
January 33.4°
July 73.1°
Assessed Value:
$2,211,557,753
Real Market Value: $4,230,566,627
(includes the value of non-taxed properties)
Annual Precipitation: 14.9"
Economy: Agriculture, forest products, manufacturing, electric power, aluminum and transportation
Points of Interest: Columbia and Deschutes Rivers, Fort Dalles Museum, Pulpit Rock, The Dalles Dam, Celilo Converter Station, Confederated Tribes of the Warm Springs Reservation and Kah-Nee-Ta Resort, Mount Hood, Sorosis Park, original Wasco County Courthouse, St. Peter's Landmark and the Columbia River Gorge Discovery Center

When the Territorial Legislature created Wasco County in 1854 from parts of Clackamas, Lane, Linn and Marion Counties, it embraced all of Oregon east of the Cascade Range, most of Idaho and parts of Montana and Wyoming. It was named for the Wasco, or Wascopam, Tribe.

Wasco's county seat is The Dalles. Now the trading hub of north-central Oregon, The Dalles gained earlier fame as the town at the end of the Oregon Trail. Thousands of years before that, humans scratched pictographs on rocks overlooking the Columbia River in this area. Later, tribes gathered for generations near Celilo Falls to trade and fish. The county's tribal heritage continues in evidence today. Kah-Nee-Ta, a popular Oregon resort, is located on the Confederated Tribes of the Warm Springs Reservation in southern Wasco County.

County Officials: Commissioners—Scott Hege 2021, Steve Kramer 2021, Rod Runyon, 2019; Dist. Atty. Eric J. Nisley 2021; Assess. Jill Filla Amery 2021; Clerk Lisa Gambee 2021; Sheriff Lane Magill 2021; Surv. Dan Boldt; Treas. Elijah Preston 2021

Washington County

County Seat: 155 N First Ave., Suite 300, Hillsboro 97124
Phone: 503-846-8611 (General); 503-846-8888 (Court Administrator)
Fax: 503-846-4545
Email: elections@co.washington.or.us
Web: www.co.washington.or.us
Established:
   July 5, 1843
Elev. at Hillsboro:
   196'
Area: 727 sq. mi.
Average Temp.:
   January 39.9°
   July 66.6°
Assessed Value:
   $59,446,698,455
Real Market Value: $108,038,519,766 (includes the value of non-taxed properties)
Annual Precipitation: 37.71"
Economy: Agriculture, horticulture, forest products, food processing, high tech, sports equipment and apparel
Points of Interest: Tualatin Valley orchards and vineyards, Pacific University, Wilson River and Sunset Highways, Hagg Lake, Old Scotch Church

The original four counties created by the Provisional Government of Oregon were Twality, Clackamas, Yamhill and Champoick. Twality was changed to Washington in honor of President George Washington by the Territorial Legislature on September 3, 1849. The actual organization of Washington County government followed several years later.

Now one of the state's fastest developing areas, the fertile Tualatin Valley was once filled with beaver and was a favorite hunting ground for Hudson's Bay Company trappers. The first white settlers arrived around 1840, lured by rich soil. Despite its rapid urbanization, the valley still contains prime agricultural land. Many small towns rich in history dot the area. Pacific University, founded as Tualatin Academy in 1849, is one of the oldest colleges in the West. Washington County operates under a home rule charter approved by voters in 1962. The Northwest's largest enclosed shopping center, Washington Square, is located south of Beaverton.

County Officials: Commissioners—Chair Andy Duyck 2019, Greg Malinowski 2019, Roy Rogers 2021, Dick Schouten 2021, Bob Terry 2019; Dist. Atty. Robert Hermann 2019; Justice of the Peace Dan Cross 2023; Sheriff Pat Garrett 2021; Auditor John Hutzler 2019; Assess./Clerk Richard Hobernicht; Surv. James Elam; Co. Admin. Robert Davis; Chief Info. Officer Phillip Bransford

Wheeler County

County Seat: Courthouse, 701 Adams St., Fossil 97830
Phone: 541-763-2400 (General); 541-763-2541 (Court Administrator)
Fax: 541-763-2026
Email: bsitton@co.wheeler.or.us
Web: www.wheelercountyoregon.com
Established:
   Feb. 17, 1899
Elev. at Fossil:
   2,654'
Area: 1,715 sq. mi.
Average Temp.:
   January 35°
   July 66°
Assessed Value:
   $132,050,568
Real Market Value: $636,195,413 (includes the value of non-taxed properties)
Annual Precipitation: 14.66"
Economy: Livestock and tourism
Points of Interest: Painted Hills, John Day Fossil Beds, John Day River

Wheeler County was formed by the Oregon Legislature in 1899 from parts of Grant, Gilliam and Crook Counties and was named for Henry H. Wheeler, who operated the first mail stage line from The Dalles to Canyon City. The new county consisted of 1,656 square miles with an estimated 46 townships, a population of 1,600 and taxable property worth one million dollars.

Wheeler County is as rugged and uneven as any Oregon county, with the terrain varying widely from sagebrush, juniper and rim rock to stands of pine and fir. Portions of two national forests lie within its boundaries with forest lands covering nearly one-third of the county. The area is probably best known as one of the most outstanding depositories of prehistoric fossils on the North American continent.

County Officials: County Court—Judge Lynn Morley 2023; Rob Ordway 2021, Debra Starkey 2019, ; Dist. Atty. Gretchen Ladd 2021; Assess. Donald R. Cossitt 2019; Clerk Alicia Hankins 2021; Justice of the Peace Robin Ordway 2021; Sheriff Chris Humphreys 2021; Surv. Jason Hatfield 2021; Treas. Sandra K. Speer 2019

Yamhill County

County Seat: Courthouse, 535 NE Fifth St., McMinnville 97128
Phone: 503-434-7501 (General); 503-434-7530 (Court Administrator)
Fax: 503-434-7553
Email: clerk@co.yamhill.or.us
Web: www.co.yamhill.or.us
Established:
July 5, 1843
Elev. at
McMinnville:
157'
Area: 718 sq. mi.
Average Temp.:
January 39.0°
July 65.0°
Assessed Value: $8,299,206,770
Real Market Value: $13,292,164,397
(includes the value of non-taxed properties)
Annual Precipitation: 43.6"
Economy: Agriculture, wine production, steel manufacturing, forest products, dental instruments and aircraft servicing
Points of Interest: Linfield College, George Fox University, Herbert Hoover House, Yamhill County Historical Museum, Wheatland Ferry, Captain Michael Smith Evergreen Aviation and Space Museum, Rogers Landing

Created in 1843, Yamhill County was one of Oregon's original four districts. Its current boundaries were established in 1860. The county was named after the Yamhelas, members of the Kalapuya Tribe, who lived along the Yamhill River in the western Willamette Valley.

Agriculture is still the county's primary industry. Nursery and greenhouse crops; fruits, nuts, berries, hay, silage, field and grass seeds are major agricultural products. Yamhill County ranks sixth among the counties in annual market value of its agricultural production. Yamhill County is also the heart of Oregon's wine industry. Thirty-six wineries represent the largest concentration of wineries in any county and produce the greatest number of award-winning wines in the state. A third of the county is covered with commercial timber. The mainstay of the western valley area is logging and timber products. Nonseasonal industries include a steel rolling mill, electronic and dental equipment manufacturing and a newsprint mill.

County Officials: Commissioners—Stan Primozich 2019, Rick Olson 2021, Mary Starrett 2019; Dist. Atty. Bradley Berry 2021; Assess. Derrick Wharff 2021; Clerk Brian Van Bergen 2021; Sheriff Tim Svenson 2019; Treas. Michael Green 2021; Acting Surveyor Bill Gille

REGIONAL GOVERNMENTS

Formed in 1984 under ORS Chapter 190, the Oregon Regional Councils Association (ORCA) promotes cooperation between levels of government.

The multi-jurisdictional councils are voluntary associations cooperating on issues and problems which cross city, county and, in some cases, state boundaries. The association provides a forum for exchanging and discussing common issues.

Central Oregon Intergovernmental Council

Contact: Andrew Spreadborough, Executive Director
Address: 334 NE Hawthorne Ave., Bend 97701
Phone: 541-548-8163
Fax: 541-923-3416
Web: https://coic2.org

Lane Council of Governments

Contact: Brenda Wilson, Executive Director
Address: 859 Willamette St., Suite 500, Eugene 97401
Phone: 541-682-4283
Fax: 541-682-4099
Web: www.lcog.org

Mid-Columbia Council of Governments

Contact: Bob Francis, Executive Director
Address: 1113 Kelly Ave., The Dalles 97058
Phone: 541-298-4101
Fax: 541-298-2084
Web: http://mccog.com

Mid-Willamette Valley Council of Governments

Contact: Nancy Boyer, Executive Director
Address: 100 High St. SE, Suite 200, Salem 97301
Phone: 503-588-6177
Web: www.mwvcog.org:8080/2

Northwest Senior and Disability Services

Contact: Melinda Compton, Executive Director (Program);
Rodney Schroeder, Executive Director (Operations)
Address: 3410 Cherry Ave. NE, Salem 97303
Phone: 503-304-3400; Toll-free: 1-800-469-8772
Fax: 503-304-3434
Web: www.nwsds.org

Oregon Cascades West Council of Governments

Contact: Fred Abousleman, Executive Director
Address: 1400 Queen Ave. SE, Suite 205A, Albany 97322
Phone: 541-967-8720

Fax: 541-967-6123
Web: www.ocwcog.org

Rogue Valley Council of Governments

Contact: Michael Cavallaro, Executive Director
Address: 155 N First St., PO Box 3275, Central Point 97502
Phone: 541-664-6674
Fax: 541-664-7927
Web: www.rvcog.org

METRO

Contact: Tom Hughes, Council President
Address: Metro Regional Center, 600 NE Grand Ave., Portland 97232-2736
Phone: 503-797-1700
Fax: 503-797-1799
Web: www.oregonmetro.gov

Councilors: President Tom Hughes 2018, District 1: Shirley Craddick 2018, District 2: Carlotta Collette 2018, District 3: Craig Dirksen 2020, District 4: Kathryn Harrington 2018, District 5: Sam Chase 2020, District 6: Bob Stacey 2020, Auditor: Brian Evans 2018

The council president and auditor are elected regionally. The remaining six councilors are elected by district. All serve four-year terms. The auditor reviews Metro's operations.

Metro is a regional government responsible for managing issues that cross city and county lines and serving more than 1.5 million residents in the 25 cities and three counties in the Portland area. Metro's core responsibilities include management of the region's garbage, compost and recycling system; support of the economy through management of the Oregon Convention Center and Expo Center; maintaining what makes this place great and preserving farm and forestland through regional planning and management of the region's urban growth boundary; preservation of our environment through management of more than 18,000 acres of parks and natural areas; and management of some of the state's top entertainment venues, including the Oregon Zoo and Portland'5 Centers for the Arts.

Every day, Metro's 765 full-time equivalent employees work to make sure the Portland region maintains its quality of life through supporting livable communities, waste reduction, environmental restoration and economic opportunity. An elected seven-member council oversees Metro, and its day-to-day affairs are managed by a chief operating officer, who is appointed by the council.

The Portland region has been coming together to manage regional planning since the 1940s. In 1957, representatives from Clackamas, Multnomah and Washington Counties formed a Metropolitan Planning Commission to handle some research related to long-range planning. The Metropolitan

Service District was formed in 1970, and voters gave it expanded powers in 1979.

In 1990, voters in the Portland region granted Metro home rule power. The current Metro charter, enacting the seven-member council and appointed chief operating officer, was approved in 2002.

PORT DISTRICTS OF OREGON

Port of Alsea, Established 1910
Address: 365-A Port St., PO Box 1060, Waldport 97394
Phone: 541-563-3872
Web: www.portofalsea.com
Commissioners: Chair Rob Bishop, Chuck Pavlik, Lou Piette, Jan Power, Joe Rohleder; Port Mgr. Roxie Cuellar. Meets third Tuesday of the month.

Port of Arlington, Established 1933
Address: 100 Island Pkwy., PO Box 279, Arlington 97812
Phone: 541-454-2868
Web: www.PortofArlington.com
Commissioners: President Ron Wilson; Aaron Fitzsimmons, Kevin Hunking, Dewey Kennedy, Scott Nation; Port Mgr. Peter Mitchell. Meets Second Tuesday of the month.

Port of Astoria, Established 1914
Address: 10 Pier One Bldg., Suite 308, Astoria 97103
Phone: 503-741-3300
Fax: 503-741-3345
Web: www.portofastoria.com
Commissioners: President Robert Mushen, James Campbell, Stephen Fulton, Bill Hunsinger, John P. Raichl; Exec. Dir. Jim Knight. Meets third Tuesday of the month.

Port of Bandon, Established 1913
Address: 390 First St. SW, PO Box 206, Bandon 97411
Phone: 541-347-3206
Fax: 541-347-4645
Web: www.portofbandon.com
Commissioners: President Reg Pullen, Wayne Butler, Rick Goche, Donny Goddard, Kelly Nelson Miles; Port Mgr. Gina Dearth; Harbor Master Bob Shammot. Meets fourth Thursday of the month at 5:00 p.m.

Port of Brookings Harbor, Established 1956
Address: 16340 Lower Harbor Rd., Suite. 103, PO Box 848, Brookings 97415
Phone: 541-469-2218
Fax: 541-469-0672
Web: www.portofbrookingsharbor.com

Commissioners: Roy Davis, Sue Gold, Roger Thompson, Tim Patterson, Sharon Hartung; Port Mgr. Gary Dehlinger. Meets third Tuesday of the month.

Port of Cascade Locks, Estab. 1937

Address: 427 Portage Rd., PO Box 307, Cascade Locks 97014
Phone: 541-374-8619
Fax: 541-374-8428
Web: www.portofcascadelocks.org
Commissioners: President Jess Groves, Joeinne Caldwell, Brad Lorang, John Stipan, **VACANT**; Port Mgr. Paul Koch. Meets first and third Thursdays of the month.

International Port of Coos Bay, Established 1909

Address: 125 Central Ave., Suite. 300, PO Box 1215, Coos Bay 97420
Phone: 541-267-7678
Fax: 541-269-1475
Web: http://portofcoosbay.com
Commissioners: President David Kronsteiner, Eric Farm, Robert Garcia, Brianna Hanson, James Martin; CEO David Koch. Meets third Monday of the month.

Port of Garibaldi, Established 1910

Address: 402 S Seventh St., PO Box 10, Garibaldi 97118
Phone: 503-322-3292
Fax: 503-322-0029
Web: www.portofgaribaldi.org
Commissioners: President Valerie Folkema, Kelly Barnett, Robert Browning, Paul Daniels, John Luquette; Port Mgr. Michael Saindon. Meets second Wednesday of the month.

Port of Gold Beach, Established 1955

Address: 29891 Harbor Way, PO Box 1126, Gold Beach 97444
Phone: 541-247-6269
Fax: 541-247-6268
Web: www.portofgoldbeach.com
Commissioners: President Milt Walker, William Fowler, Mark Lottis, Bill McNair, Charles Riddle; Port Mgr. James Clemens. Meets third Thursday of the month.

Port of Hood River, Established 1933

Address: 1000 E Port Marina Dr., Hood River 97031
Phone: 541-386-1645
Fax: 541-386-1395
Web: www.portofhoodriver.com
Commissioners: President Jon Davies, Fred Duckwall, Richard McBride, Brian Shortt, Hoby Streich; Exec. Dir. Michael McElwee. Meets first and third Tuesdays of the month at 5:00 p.m.

Port of Morrow, Established 1958

Address: 2 Marine Dr., PO Box 200, Boardman 97818
Phone: 541-481-7678
Fax: 541-481-2679
Web: www.portofmorrow.com
Commissioners: President Joe Taylor, Jerry Healy, Larry Lindsay, Marv Padberg, Rick Stokoe; Gen. Mgr. Gary Neal. Meets second Wednesday of the month.

Port of Nehalem, Established 1909

Address: 36060 6th St., PO Box 476, Nehalem 97131-0476
Phone: 503-368-7212
Fax: 503-368-7234
Web: portofnehalem.org
Commissioners: President Lindy Scovell, Rick R. Dart, Terry Fullan, Steve Huber, Loren Remy; Adm. Sec. Karrie Purdom. Meets fourth Wednesday of the month; third Wednesday in November and December.

Port of Newport, Established 1910

Address: 600 SE Bay Blvd., Newport 97365
Phone: 541-265-7758
Fax: 541-265-4235
Web: www.portofnewport.com
Commissioners: Steve Beck, Ken Brown, Walter Chuck, Stewart Lamerdin, Patricia Patrick-Joling; Gen. Mgr. Kevin Greenwood. Meets fourth Tuesday of the month.

Port of Port Orford, Established 1919

Address: 300 Dock Rd., PO Box 490, Port Orford 97465
Phone: 541-332-7121
Web: www.portofportorford.com
Commissioners: President Brett Webb, Gary Anderson, David Bassett, Tom Calvanese, Sam Scaffo; Port Mgr. Steve Courtier. Meets third Tuesday of the month.

International Port of Portland, Established 1891

Address: 7200 NE Airport Wy., Portland 97208; PO Box 3529, Portland 97218
Phone: 503-415-6000; 1-800-547-8411
Web: www2.portofportland.com
Commissioners: President Jim Carter, Michael Alexander, Tom Chamberlain, Alice Cuprill-Comas, Robert L. Levy, Pat McDonald, Linda Pearce, Tom Tsuruta, Gary Young; Exec. Dir. Bill Wyatt. Meets second Wednesday of the month.

Port of Saint Helens, Established 1941

Address: 100 E St., PO Box 190, Columbia City 97018
Phone: 503-397-2888
Fax: 503-397-6924

Web: www.portsh.org

Commissioners: President Mike Avent, Larry Ericksen, Chris Iverson, Paulette Lichatowich, Terry Luttrell; Exec. Dir. Patrick Trapp. Meets second Wednesday of the month.

Port of Siuslaw, Established 1909

Address: 100 Harbor St., PO Box 1220, Florence 97439
Phone: 541-997-3426
Fax: 541-997-9407
Web: http://portofsiuslaw.com

Commissioners: President Ron Caputo, Mike Buckwald, Terry Duman, David Huntington, Nancy Rickard; Port Mgr. Steven Leskin. Meets third Wednesday of the month.

Port of The Dalles, Established 1933

Address: 3636 Klindt Dr., The Dalles 97058
Phone: 541-298-4148
Fax: 541-298-2136
Web: http://portofthedalles.com

Commissioners: President Greg Weast, Staci Coburn, Mike Courtney, David Griffith, Kristi Timmons; Exec. Dir. Andrea Klaas. Meets second Wednesday of the month.

Port of Tillamook Bay, Estab. 1953

Address: 4000 Blimp Blvd., Suite 100, Tillamook 97141
Phone: 503-842-2413
Fax: 503-842-3680
Web: www.potb.org

Commissioners: President Jim Young, Carolyn Decker, Jack Mulder, Bob Olsen, Gerald Opdahl; General Mgr. Michele Bradley. Meets the first Tuesday after the 15th of each month.

Port of Toledo, Established 1910

Address: 496 NE Hwy. 20, Unit #1, PO Box 428 Toledo 97391-9720
Phone: 541-336-5207
Fax: 541-336-5160
Web: http://portoftoledo.org

Commissioners: President Michael Kriz, Chuck Gerttula, Rick Graff, Gregg Harrison, Penny Ryerson; Port Mgr. Bud Shoemake. Meets third Tuesday of the month.

Port of Umatilla, Established 1940

Address: 500 Willamette Ave., PO Box 879, Umatilla 97882
Phone: 541-922-3224
Fax: 541-922-5609
Email: kimpuzey@uci.net

Commissioners: President Kurt Bendixsen, Jerry Baker, Jerry Imsland, Jerry Simpson, John Turner; Gen. Mgr. Kim Puzey. Meets Tuesday after first Wednesday of the month.

Port of Umpqua, Established 1913

Address: 1877 Winchester Ave., PO Box 388, Reedsport 97467
Phone: 541-271-2232
Fax: 541-271-2747
Web: www.portofumpqua.net

Commissioners: President Steve Reese, Leon Bridge, Carey Jones, Barry Nelson, Keith Tymchuk; Port Mgr. Charmaine Vitek. Meets third Wednesday of the month.

SPECIAL SERVICE DISTRICTS

Contact: Frank Stratton, Executive Director
Address: Special Districts Association of Oregon, PO Box 12613, Salem 97309-0613
Phone: 503-371-8667; Toll-free: 1-800-285-5461
Fax: 503-371-4781
Web: www.sdao.com

ORS 198.010 and 198.335 authorize 28 types of districts: water control, irrigation, ports, regional air quality control authorities, fire, hospital, mass transit, sanitary districts and authorities, people's utility, domestic water supply districts and authorities, cemetery, park and recreation, metropolitan service, special road, road assessment, highway lighting, health, vector control, water improvement, weather modification, geothermal heating, transportation, county service, chemical control, weed control, emergency communications, diking, and soil and water conservation districts.

Special Districts are financed through property taxes, fees for services, or a combination thereof. Most special districts are directed by a governing body elected by the voters.

Formed in 1979, the Special Districts Association of Oregon (SDAO) provides support services to member districts throughout the state in the areas of research and technical assistance, legislative representation, training programs, insurance services, information and reference materials, financing services, and employee benefits programs.

TRANSIT DISTRICTS

Basin Transit Service Transportation District

Contact: Ernest Palmer, General Manager
Address: 1130 Adams St., Klamath Falls 97601
Phone: 541-883-2877
Fax: 541-884-6287
Web: www.basintransit.com

Grant County Transportation District

Contact: Shelley Bezona, Chair
Address: 229 NE Dayton St., John Day 97845
Phone: 541-575-2370

Fax: 541-575-2162
Web: www.grantcountypeoplemover.com

Hood River County Transportation District

Contact: Deanna Bisbee and Ron Nails, Co-Executive Directors
Address: 224 Wasco Loop, PO Box 1147, Hood River 97031
Phone: 541-386-4202
Fax: 541-386-1228
Web: http://community.gorge.net/hrctd/

Lane Transit District

Contact: Aurora Jackson, General Manager
Address: PO Box 7070, Springfield 97475
Phone: 541-687-5555
Fax: 541-682-6111
Web: www.ltd.org/

Lincoln County Transit

Contact: Cynda Bruce, General Manager
Address: 410 NE Harney St., Newport 97365
Phone: 541-265-4900
Fax: 541-574-1296
Web: www.co.lincoln.or.us/transit

Rogue Valley Transportation District

Contact: Julie A. Brown, General Manager
Address: 3200 Crater Lake Ave., Medford 97504
Phone: 541-779-5821
Fax: 541-773-2877
Web: www.rvtd.org/

Salem-Keizer Transit District

Contact: Allan Pollock, General Manager
Address: 555 Court St. NE, Suite 5230, Salem 97301

Phone: 503-588-2424
Fax: 503-566-3933
Web: www.cherriots.org/

South Clackamas Transportation District

Contact: Shirley Lyons, Manager
Address: PO Box 517, Molalla 97038
Phone: 503-632-7000
Fax: 503-632-5214
Web: http://www.sctd.org

Sunset Empire Transportation District

Contact: Jeff Hazen, Executive Director
Address: 900 Marine Dr., Astoria 97103
Phone: 503-861-7433
Fax: 503-325-1606
Web: www.ridethebus.org/

Tillamook County Transportation District

Contact: Doug Pilant, General Manager
Address: 3600 Third St., Suite A, Tillamook 97141
Phone: 503-815-8283
Fax: 503-815-8005
Web: www.tillamookbus.com

Tri-County Metropolitan Transportation District of Oregon (TriMet)

Contact: Neil McFarlane, General Manager
Address: 1800 SW 1st Ave. Suite. 300, Portland 97201
Phone: 503-962-7505
Fax: 503-962-6451
Web: http://trimet.org/

ELEMENTARY SCHOOL STUDENT ESSAY

Apple Gate Lake

Cora Snoke, Essay Contest Runner-up
Sara Major's Fourth/Fifth Grade Class
Rush Community School, Jacksonville

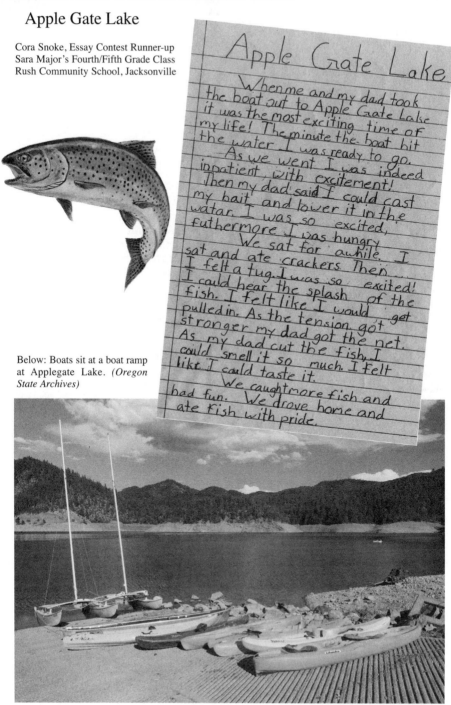

Apple Gate Lake

When me and my dad took the boat out to Apple Gate Lake it was the most exciting time of my life! The minute the boat hit the water I was ready to go.

As we went I was indeed inpatient with excitement! Then my dad said I could cast my bait and lower it in the watar. I was so excited, futhermore I was hungry.

We sat for awhile. I sat and ate crackers. Then I felt a tug. I was so excited! I could hear the splash of the fish. I felt like I would get pulled in. As the tension got stronger my dad got the net. As my dad cut the fish, I could smell it so much. I felt like I could taste it.

We caught more fish and had fun. We drove home and ate fish with pride.

Below: Boats sit at a boat ramp at Applegate Lake. *(Oregon State Archives)*

A man standing in a boat hands fish to a woman on the shore of Diamond Lake with
Mount Thielsen in the background, east of Roseburg in 1937.
Oregon State Archives OHD Photograph

The "Oregon System"—procedures for initiative, referendum and
recall—gained Oregon national recognition for the degree of citizen
involvement in the processes of self-government. Most recently,
vote-by-mail and the Oregon Motor Voter processes have drawn
national attention to Oregon. This detailed history of elections in
Oregon illustrates the tangible results of participation in our
government.

Voting and Voter Registration

Source: Office of the Secretary of State, Elections Division

Address: 255 Capitol St. NE, Suite 501, Salem 97310

Phone: 503-986-1518

Web: http://sos.oregon.gov/voting-elections/Pages/default.aspx

Elections in Oregon

All regular elections in Oregon are held on one of four days each year, except in cases of emergency. The election days are:

- the second Tuesday in March,
- the third Tuesday in May,
- the third Tuesday in September, and
- the first Tuesday after the first Monday in November.

Elections are conducted by mail. Voters who are registered as of the 21st day before an election are mailed a ballot to vote and return by election day.

The use of vote-by-mail was first approved on a limited basis by the Legislature in 1981 and was made a permanent feature of some elections in 1987. In 1998, Oregon voters amended state law to require that the primary and general elections in May and November of even-numbered years also be conducted through vote-by-mail. Beginning in 2000, primary and general elections have been conducted by mail. In 2007, the Legislature provided that all elections will be conducted by mail.

At the primary election, voters who are registered in the major political parties, currently the Democratic, Republican and Independent parties, nominate candidates to run in the general election. All voters may vote on nonpartisan contests, such as judicial elections, which are also held at the primary election. Most statewide ballot measures are on the general election ballot.

Registering to Vote

Oregon's new voter registration law, Oregon Motor Voter, took effect on January 1, 2016, making Oregon the first state in the nation to implement automatic voter registration. The program, which modernizes voter registration in Oregon and provides a secure, simple and convenient way for more Oregonians to become registered voters, was created by House Bill 2177, passed by the 2015 Legislature and signed into law by Governor Kate Brown.

With Oregon Motor Voter, automatic voter registration is available if you are eligible to register to vote* and you apply for your original, renewal or replacement driver's license, permit or identification card at a Driver and Motor Vehicle Division office (DMV).

Once you engage the Oregon Motor Voter process by visiting the DMV, you will receive a card and a prepaid postage return envelope from the Elections Division. With this card, you have three options:

1. **Do nothing.** You will be registered to vote as a nonaffiliated voter (not a member of a political party).

2. **Choose a political party by returning the card.** Joining a political party will allow you to vote in its primary elections.

3. **Use the card to opt out** and decline to register to vote.

Once registered, you will automatically receive a ballot and instructions in the mail about two weeks before an election. When you vote, your ballot is secret and your choices cannot be matched up with your name.

Registration by mail was authorized by the 1975 Legislature and can also be used to register to vote in Oregon. Forms are located in most banks and public buildings, in every county elections office and in many state agencies.

Forms also can be obtained from the Office of the Secretary of State, Elections Division, 255 Capitol St. NE, Suite 501, Salem 97310.

Date of Election	Deadline to Register**
March 14, 2017	February 21, 2017
May 16, 2017	April 25, 2017
September 19, 2017	August 29, 2017
November 7, 2017	October 17, 2017

Oregon residents who are not U.S. citizens by the deadline to register to vote, but who will be citizens by election day, should contact their county elections office for information about how to register to vote.

Persons who become residents of Oregon after the deadline to register for a U.S. presidential election may be eligible to vote for U.S. president and vice president. Contact your county elections office for more information.

---

*To register to vote, a person must be a resident of Oregon and be able to answer "yes" to the following questions on the voter registration card:

- "Are you a citizen of the United States of America?" and
- "Are you at least 17 years of age?"

**A voter registration card received in an elections office after the deadline date meets the registration deadline if it has a timely, valid postmark.

Important! Persons registered to vote in other states may not transfer their voter registration to Oregon. To register to vote in Oregon, a person must go through the Oregon Motor Voter process or complete either an Oregon voter registration card or a Federal Post Card Application, which is available in most states.

How to Maintain a Current Voter Registration

Registered voters must notify their county elections office in writing if:

- their residence or mailing address changes,
- their name changes, or
- they wish to change political party affiliation.

A voter may notify county elections officials of changes to the above by sending a new voter registration card to the appropriate county.

A voter may update voter registration information as late as election day and vote in that election.

If a voter has moved from one county in Oregon to another, the voter should fill out a voter registration card and send it to the new county elections office. If the voter registration card is sent after the 21st day before an election, the voter should call the county elections official to find out how to receive a ballot for that election.

Voting Absentee

Absentee ballots are mailed to military and other out-of-state voters in advance of the regular mailing of ballots. Voters should contact their local elections office to obtain an absentee ballot.

Voters' Pamphlets

For each primary and general election and for most special elections, the Elections Division produces and distributes to every household, one or more pamphlets containing information about candidates and measures that will appear on the ballot at the election. Many county elections offices also produce pamphlets that contain information about local candidates and measures.

2018 FILING DEADLINES

- The candidate filing period for the May 15, 2018, primary election begins on September 7, 2017, and ends on March 6, 2018. The deadline for filing *Voters' Pamphlet* material with the Elections Division is no sooner than January 15, 2018, and no later than March 8, 2018.
- The candidate filing period for the November 6, 2018, general election begins on May 30, 2018, and ends on August 28, 2018. The deadline for filing *Voters' Pamphlet* material with the Elections Division is not sooner than July 9, 2018, and no later than August 28, 2018.

RECENT ELECTION HISTORY

2016 Primary Election

Election Date: May 17, 2016
Source: Abstracts of Votes, available from the Office of the Secretary of State, Elections Division, 255 Capitol St. NE, Suite 501, Salem 97310

Web: http://sos.oregon.gov/voting-elections/Pages/default.aspx

Key: *Nominated; **Elected; WI = Write In

United States President

Democrat	Total
Clinton, Hillary	269,846
Sanders, Bernie*	360,829
Miscellaneous	10,920
Independent	
Trump, Donald J. (WI)*	8,795
Miscellaneous	15,017
Republican	
Cruz, Ted	65,513
Kasich, John R.	62,248
Trump, Donald J.*	252,748
Miscellaneous	13,411

United States Senator

Democrat	Total
Stine, Kevin H.	78,287
Weaver, Paul B.	20,346
Wyden, Ron*	501,903
Miscellaneous	2,740
Independent	
Reynolds, Steven C.*	10,497
Sandnes, Marvin	4,733
Miscellaneous	10,496
Republican	
Callahan, Mark*	123,473
Carpenter, Sam	104,494
Laschober, Dan	34,157
Stewart, Faye	57,399
Miscellaneous	3,357

United States Representative

1st Congressional District

Democrat	Total
Bonamici, Suzanne*	99,153
Woodley, Shabba	10,961
Miscellaneous	375
Independent	
Bonamici, Suzanne (WI)*	855
Miscellaneous	613
Republican	
Burgess, Jonathan E.	9,127
Heinrich, Brian J.*	19,290
Morgan, Delinda	10,640
Miscellaneous	768

2nd Congressional District

Democrat	Total
Crary, James (Jim)*	53,484
Miscellaneous	1,295
Independent	
Walden, Greg (WI)*	1,725
Miscellaneous	1,090

Republican

Romero, Jr., Paul J.	21,099
Walden, Greg*	85,039
Miscellaneous	238

3rd Congressional District

Democrat	Total
Blumenauer, Earl*	144,706
Miscellaneous	2,511
Independent	
Walker, David W.*	2,529
Miscellaneous	856
Republican	
Walker, David W. (WI)*	217
Miscellaneous	2,160

4th Congressional District

Democrat	Total
DeFazio, Peter A.*	113,816
McKinney, Joseph	9,894
Miscellaneous	601
Independent	
DeFazio, Peter A. (WI)*	1,223
Miscellaneous	1,654
Republican	
Perkins, Jo Rae	26,375
Robinson, Art*	55,557
Miscellaneous	620

5th Congressional District

Democrat	Total
McTeague, Dave	28,184
Schrader, Kurt*	72,643
Miscellaneous	549
Independent	
Schrader, Kurt (WI)*	792
Miscellaneous	1,601
Republican	
Allan, Seth	10,799
Rainey, Earl D.	3,783
West, Ben	14,696
Willis, Colm*	40,568
Miscellaneous	665

Governor

Democrat	Total
Bell, Julian	49,313
Brown, Kate*	494,890
Chance, Chet	5,636
Forsythe, Kevin M.	10,147
Johnson, Steve	13,363
Stauffer, Dave	16,108
Miscellaneous	6,595
Independent	
Barney, Patrick	6,840
Thomason, Cliff*	9,806
Miscellaneous	11,460
Republican	
Alley, Allen	103,388
Cuff, Bruce	41,598
Forthan, Bob	4,290
Niemeyer, Bob	35,669

Pierce, Bud*	171,158
Miscellaneous	3,020

Secretary of State

Democrat	Total
Avakian, Brad*	204,135
Devlin, Richard	137,612
Hoyle, Val	178,829
Miscellaneous	4,462
Independent	
Wells, Paul Damian*	17,124
Miscellaneous	9,245
Republican	
Leiken, Sid	74,237
Richardson, Dennis*	269,790
Miscellaneous	2,086

State Treasurer

Democrat	Total
Read, Tobias*	405,364
Miscellaneous	7,058
Independent	
Telfer, Chris*	20,517
Miscellaneous	5,100
Republican	
Gudman, Jeff*	254,216
Miscellaneous	3,802

Attorney General

Democrat	Total
Rosenblum, Ellen*	425,670
Miscellaneous	4,973
Independent	
Rosenblum, Ellen (WI)*	4,629
Miscellaneous	3,820
Republican	
Crowe, Daniel Zene*	227,985
Miscellaneous	3,138

Judge of the Supreme Court

Nonpartisan	Total

Position 4

Kistler, Revas**	645,539
Miscellaneous	8,781

Position 5

Landau, Jack L.**	644,620
Miscellaneous	7,817

Judge of the Court of Appeals

Nonpartisan	Total

Position 2

Duncan, Rebecca**	645,237
Miscellaneous	7,368

Position 3

Ortega, Darleen**	657,261
Miscellaneous	7,375

Position 7

Flynn, Meagan A.**	653,981
Miscellaneous	6,842

Judge of the Circuit Court
Nonpartisan

	Total

1st District—Position 4

Crain, Patricia**	30,484
Orr, David J.	22,378
Miscellaneous	138

2nd District—Position 5

Rooke-Ley. Ilisa H. R.**	64,690
Miscellaneous	675

2nd District—Position 6

Merten, Maurice K.**	64,490
Miscellaneous	695

2nd District—Position 9

Chanti, Suzanne B.**	64,482
Miscellaneous	642

2nd District—Position 11

Holland, Lauren S.**	64,467
Miscellaneous	703

3rd District—Position 4

Burton, Claudia M.**	46,256
Miscellaneous	516

3rd District—Position 6

James, Mary M.**	46,164
Miscellaneous	493

3rd District—Position 9

Broyles, Audrey J.**	46,517
Miscellaneous	461

3rd District—Position 13

Hart, Tom**	46,594
Miscellaneous	452

4th District—Position 9

Rees, David F.**	122,281
Miscellaneous	1,969

4th District—Position 15

James, Bronson D.**	123,408
Miscellaneous	1,895

4th District—Position 17

Skye, Kelly**	122,566
Miscellaneous	1,855

4th District—Position 20

Bloch, Eric J.**	121,805
Miscellaneous	1,911

4th District—Position 22

Lopez, Angel**	125,646
Miscellaneous	1,775

4th District—Position 25

Dailey, Kathleen M.**	122,947
Miscellaneous	1,831

4th District—Position 26

Immergut, Karin J.**	122,704
Miscellaneous	1,911

5th District—Position 2

Miller, Eve L.**	62,308
Miscellaneous	888

5th District—Position 4

Van Dyk, Douglas V.**	62,002
Miscellaneous	890

5th District—Position 5

Weber, Katherine E.**	62,051
Miscellaneous	820

5th District—Position 7

Herndon, Robert D.**	62,594
Miscellaneous	865

5th District—Position 10

Rastetter, Thomas J.**	61,875
Miscellaneous	831

6th District—Position 2

Ballard, John L.	4,756
Lieuallen, Jon S.**	9,750
Miscellaneous	27

6th District—Position 3

Hill, Daniel J.	11,459
Miscellaneous	84

7th District—Position 2

Stauffer, Janet L.**	10,188
Miscellaneous	119

7th District—Position 4

Wolf, John A.**	9,799
Miscellaneous	93

11th District—Position 4

Adler, A. Michael**	29,646
Miscellaneous	209

11th District—Position 6

Ashby, Wells B.**	30,219
Miscellaneous	199

12th District—Position 2

Campbell, Monte S.**	14,250
Miscellaneous	113

13th District—Position 2

Osborne, Roxanne B.**	14,269
Miscellaneous	190

13th District—Position 3

Adkisson, Marci W.**	13,948
Miscellaneous	170

Elections and Records

13th District—Position 4

Wogan, Cameron F.**	13,552
Miscellaneous	174

13th District—Position 5

Bunch, Dan**	13,600
Miscellaneous	121

14th District—Position 3

Newman, Michael**	16,334
Miscellaneous	270

14th District—Position 4

Baker, Lindi L.**	17,040
Miscellaneous	252

15th District—Position 1

Stone, Martin**	18,512
Miscellaneous	151

15th District—Position 2

Barron, Richard L.**	18,673
Miscellaneous	184

15th District—Position 4

Hughes, Ryan P.	8,217
Inokuchi, Rick	2,419
Jacquot, Megan L.**	10,984
Miscellaneous	61

16th District—Position 2

Marshall, William**	18,327
Miscellaneous	213

16th District—Position 3

Griffin, Anthony F.	4,096
Hoddle, Steve	3,785
Johnson, Kathleen*	7,198
Lee, Charles	4,180
McKinney, Dan G.*	5,823
Miscellaneous	66

16th District—Position 4

Burge, Frances E.**	18,550
Miscellaneous	185

18th District—Position 2

Goldthorpe, David M.	2,970
McIntosh, Dawn M.**	5,146
Woltjer, Ronald D.	2,106
Miscellaneous	27

20th District—Position 1

Marble, Tim	35,166
Sims, Ted**	62,286
Miscellaneous	514

20th District—Position 4

Butterfield, Eric**	79,388
Miscellaneous	950

20th District—Position 10

Upton, Suzanne**	81,836
Miscellaneous	967

21st District—Position 3

Connell, David B.**	17,222
Miscellaneous	174

23rd District—Position 1

Bispham, Carol R.**	18,063
Miscellaneous	337

23rd District—Position 5

McHill, Tom**	17,739
Miscellaneous	249

25th District—Position 1

Collins, John L.**	18,292
Miscellaneous	160

25th District—Position 3

Easterday, Cynthia**	17,526
Miscellaneous	164

27th District—Position 1

Hill, Jonathan R.**	4,901
Miscellaneous	64

2016 General Election

Election Date: November 8, 2016

Source: *Abstracts of Votes,* available from the Office of the Secretary of State, Elections Division, 255 Capitol St. NE, Suite 501, Salem 97310

Web: http://sos.oregon.gov/voting-elections/Pages/default.aspx

Key: *Elected; WI = Write In
C = Constitution Party
D = Democratic Party
I = Independent Party
L = Libertarian Party
NA = Nonaffiliated
PG = Pacific Green Party
P = Progressive Party
R = Republican Party
WF = Working Families Party

United States President

	Total
Clinton, Hillary—D*	1,002,106
Johnson, Gary—L	94,231
Stein, Jill—PG	50,002
Trump, Donald J.—R	782,403
Miscellaneous	72,594

United States Senator

	Total
Callahan, Mark—R	651,106
Lewallen, Shanti S.—WF	61,915
Lindsay, Jim—L	23,941
Navickas, Eric—PG	48,823
Reynolds, Steven C.—I	59,516
Wyden, Ron—D*	1,105,119
Miscellaneous	2,058

United States Representative

1st Congressional District

	Total
Bonamici, Suzanne—D*	225,391
Heinrich, Brian J.—R	139,756
Sheahan, Kyle—L	12,257
Miscellaneous	691

2nd Congressional District

	Total
Crary, James (Jim)—D	106,640
Walden, Greg—R*	272,952
Miscellaneous	1,147

3rd Congressional District

	Total
Blumenauer, Earl—D*	274,687
Delk, David—P	27,978
Walker, David W.—I	78,154
Miscellaneous	1,536

4th Congressional District

	Total
Beilstein, Mike—PG	12,194
DeFazio, Peter A.—D*	220,628
Guthrie, Gil—L	6,527
Robinson, Art—R	157,743
Miscellaneous	476

5th Congressional District

	Total
Sandnes, Marvin—PG	12,542
Schrader, Kurt—D*	199,505
Willis, Colm—R	160,443
Miscellaneous	618

Governor

	Total
Auer, Aaron Donald—C	19,400
Brown, Kate—D*	985,027
Foster, James—L	45,191
Pierce, Bud—R	845,609
Thomason, Cliff—I	47,481
Miscellaneous	3,338

Secretary of State

	Total
Avakian, Brad—D	814,089
Durbin, Sharon L.—L	46,975
Marsh, Michael—C	15,269
Richardson, Dennis—R*	892,669
Wells, Paul Damian—I	64,956
Zundel, Alan—PG	47,576
Miscellaneous	2,646

State Treasurer

	Total
Gudman, Jeff—R	766,680
Henry, Chris—P	90,507
Read, Tobias—D*	808,998
Telfer, Chris—I	173,878
Miscellaneous	2,624

Attorney General

	Total
Crowe, Daniel Zene—R	766,753
Hedbor, Lars D. H.—L	58,609
Rosenblum, Ellen—D*	1,011,761
Miscellaneous	3,507

Judge of the Supreme Court
Nonpartisan

	Total

Position 6

	Total
Nakamoto, Lynn R.*	1,140,090
Miscellaneous	25,033

Judge of the Court of Appeals
Nonpartisan

	Total

Position 5

	Total
Shorr, Scott*	1,113,271
Miscellaneous	21,131

Position 8

DeHoog, Roger J.*	1,083,621
Miscellaneous	20,663

Judge of the Circuit Court
Nonpartisan

	Total

2nd District—Position 13

McIntyre, Karrie*	94,957
Miscellaneous	1,654

3rd District—Position 1

Bennett, Channing*	79,492
Miscellaneous	1,376

3rd District—Position 7

Armstrong, Sean E.*	78,956
Miscellaneous	1,380

4th District—Position 6

Bottomly, Leslie G.*	209,675
Miscellaneous	4,143

4th District—Position 24

Dahlin, Eric L.*	205,548
Miscellaneous	4,011

4th District—Position 35

Henry, Patrick W.*	202,173
Miscellaneous	4,026

9th District—Position 1

Carlson, David R.	3,590
Landis, Erin K.*	5,464
Miscellaneous	22

11th District—Position 3

Flint, Bethany P.*	54,703
Miscellaneous	747

13th District—Position 1

Janney, Andrea M.*	17,769
Miscellaneous	316

16th District—Position 3		20th District—Position 14	
Johnson, Kathleen*	21,579	Pagán, Ramón*	150,498
McKinney, Dan G.	19,094	Miscellaneous	2,988
Miscellaneous	174		

Voter Participation 1986–2016
*Presidential election year

Primary Election

Year	Registered Voters	Voted	Percent
1986	1,458,300	693,821	47.6
1988*	1,366,294	753,112	55.1
1990	1,437,462	660,990	46.0
1992*	1,543,353	758,459	49.1
1994	1,730,562	661,717	38.2
1996*	1,851,499	698,990	37.8
1998	1,906,677	665,340	34.9
2000*	1,808,080	927,351	51.3
2002	1,839,072	858,524	46.6
2004*	1,862,919	864,833	46.4
2006	1,965,939	758,393	38.6
2008*	2,008,957	1,170,526	58.3
2010	2,033,951	846,515	41.6
2012*	2,021,263	787,847	38.9
2014	2,113,430	758,604	35.9
2016*	2,281,555	1,231,843	54.0

General Election

Year	Registered Voters	Voted	Percent
1986	1,502,244	1,088,140	72.4
1988*	1,528,478	1,235,199	80.8
1990	1,476,500	1,133,125	76.7
1992*	1,775,416	1,498,959	84.4
1994	1,832,774	1,254,265	68.4
1996*	1,962,155	1,399,180	71.3
1998	1,965,981	1,160,400	59.0
2000*	1,954,006	1,559,215	79.8
2002	1,872,615	1,293,756	69.1
2004*	2,141,243	1,851,593	86.5
2006	1,976,669	1,399,650	70.8
2008*	2,153,914	1,845,251	85.7
2010	2,068,798	1,487,210	71.9
2012*	2,199,360	1,820,507	82.8
2014	2,174,763	1,541,782	70.9
2016*	2,561,657	2,056,310	80.3

Voter Registration by County—November 8, 2016

County	Democrat	Republican	Independent	*Nonaffiliated	**Other	Total
Baker	2,157	5,417	574	2,835	182	11,165
Benton	26,452	14,211	2,505	13,945	1,248	58,361
Clackamas	97,563	83,253	12,371	69,438	6,141	268,766
Clatsop	9,504	6,671	1,149	6,995	627	24,946
Columbia	12,271	9,820	1,547	9,740	866	34,244
Coos	12,687	13,412	2,026	11,187	1,014	40,326
Crook	3,320	6,698	900	4,007	299	15,224
Curry	4,445	5,776	995	4,324	325	15,865
Deschutes	38,928	41,291	7,652	31,663	2,682	122,216
Douglas	17,847	29,171	3,659	19,078	1,710	71,465
Gilliam	315	572	53	301	34	1,275

County	Democrat	Republican	Independent	*Nonaffiliated	**Other	Total
Grant	1,048	2,566	285	1,186	53	5,138
Harney	944	2,466	199	1,098	61	4,768
Hood River	5,766	3,138	635	3,758	257	13,554
Jackson	45,837	48,297	7,774	37,660	3,338	142,906
Jefferson	3,270	4,581	716	3,704	337	12,608
Josephine	15,272	23,121	3,371	16,828	1,812	60,404
Klamath	8,475	17,600	2,138	10,857	732	39,802
Lake	813	2,508	223	1,136	66	4,746
Lane	104,554	60,836	10,977	59,882	6,375	242,624
Lincoln	12,586	7,857	1,724	9,325	613	32,105
Linn	21,738	27,366	3,986	21,538	1,653	76,281
Malheur	2,620	6,154	466	4,725	200	14,165
Marion	59,477	58,682	8,171	51,782	3,979	182,091
Morrow	1,264	2,070	258	1,833	115	5,540
Multnomah	276,137	65,773	18,344	127,255	17,470	504,979
Polk	16,816	18,024	2,624	13,554	846	51,864
Sherman	288	601	45	281	26	1,241
Tillamook	6,181	5,327	800	4,747	367	17,422
Umatilla	8,897	14,036	1,792	13,192	956	38,873
Union	3,890	7,466	825	4,091	378	16,650
Wallowa	1,241	2,575	215	1,113	67	5,211
Wasco	5,193	4,635	714	4,662	399	15,603
Washington	134,023	88,231	14,546	97,051	6,794	340,645
Wheeler	243	458	53	217	85	986
Yamhill	19,091	26,837	3,077	17,087	1,506	67,598
Totals	**981,153**	**717,497**	**117,389**	**682,075**	**63,543**	**2,561,657**

*A "nonaffiliated" voter is one who has chosen not to be a member of any political party and has indicated this on his or her voter registration card.

**"Other" includes all voters registered with minor political parties.

OREGON ELECTION HISTORY

Voter Registration for General Elections 1950–2016

Year	Democrat	Republican	Other	Total
1950	378,357	361,158	11,755	751,270
1952	416,589	421,681	13,246	851,516
1954	402,283	404,694	12,562	819,539
1956	451,179	413,659	13,114	877,952
1958	447,198	395,089	12,759	855,046
1960	480,588	405,195	14,833	900,616
1962	473,561	395,351	14,778	883,690
1964	511,973	402,336	18,152	932,461
1966	518,228	412,586	19,011	949,825
1968	530,074	420,943	20,834	971,851
1970	521,662	410,693	23,104	955,459
1972	673,710	473,907	50,059	1,197,676
1974	652,414	439,667	50,992	1,143,073
1976	794,218	497,297	128,631	1,420,146
1978	808,182	511,621	163,536	1,482,339
1980	784,129	564,771	220,322	1,569,222
1982	751,100	551,718	213,771	1,516,589
1984	792,208	594,387	222,098	1,608,693
1986	728,177	587,154	186,913	1,502,244
1988	737,489	590,648	200,341	1,528,478
1990	692,100	570,933	213,467	1,476,500
1992	792,551	642,206	340,659	1,775,416
1994	786,990	665,956	379,828	1,832,774
1996	805,286	714,548	442,321	1,962,155
1998	791,970	704,593	469,418	1,965,981

Year	Democrat	Republican	Other	Total
2000	769,195	699,179	485,632	1,954,006
2002	729,460	680,444	462,711	1,872,615
2004	829,193	761,715	550,335	2,141,243
2006	767,562	706,365	502,742	1,976,669
2008	929,741	695,677	528,496	2,153,914
2010	863,322	664,123	541,353	2,068,798
2012	872,361	684,858	642,141	2,199,360
2014	825,701	653,048	696,014	2,174,763

Year	Democrat	Republican	Independent	Other	Total
2016	981,153	717,497	117,389	745,618	2,561,657

Votes Cast in Oregon for United States President 1860–2016

Key: *Elected; **Received highest vote in Oregon but lost election nationwide

Year	Candidate	Party	Votes
1860	John Bell	Constitutional Union	212
	John C. Breckenridge	Democrat	5,074
	Stephen Douglas	Douglas Democrat	4,131
	Abraham Lincoln*	Republican	5,344
1864	Abraham Lincoln*	Republican	9,888
	George McClellan	Democrat	8,457
1868	U.S. Grant*	Republican	10,961
	Horatio Seymour**	Democrat	11,125
1872	U.S. Grant*	Republican	11,818
	Horace Greeley	Democrat-Liberal Republicans	7,742
	Charles O'Connor	National Labor Reformers	587
1876	Peter Cooper	Greenback	510
	Rutherford B. Hayes*	Republican	15,214
	Samuel Tilden	Democrat	14,157
1880	James A. Garfield*	Republican	20,619
	Winfield Hancock	Democrat	19,955
	James B. Weaver	Greenback Labor	249
1884	James G. Blaine**	Republican	26,860
	General B.F. Butler	Greenback Labor (Workingman)	726
	Grover Cleveland*	Democrat	24,604
	John P. St. John	Prohibition	492
1888	Grover Cleveland	Democrat	26,522
	Robert H. Cowdrey	United Labor	363
	Clinton B. Fisk	Prohibition	1,677
	Benjamin Harrison*	Republican	33,291
1892	John Bidwell	Prohibition	2,281
	Grover Cleveland*	Democrat	14,243
	Benjamin Harrison**	Republican	35,002
	James B. Weaver[1]	Populist	26,965
1896	William J. Bryan	Democrat, People's Party and Silver Republican	46,739
	Joshua Levering	Prohibition	919
	William McKinley*	Republican	48,779
	John M. Palmer	National (Gold) Democrat	977
1900	Wharton Barker	Regular People's	275
	William J. Bryan	Democrat People's	33,385
	Eugene V. Debs	Social-Democrats	1,494
	William McKinley*	Republican	46,526
	John G. Woolley	Prohibition	2,536
1904	Eugene V. Debs	Socialist	7,619
	Alton Parker	Democrat	17,327
	Theodore Roosevelt*	Republican	60,455
	Silas C. Swallow	Prohibition	3,806
	Thomas E. Watson	People's	753

Year	Candidate	Party	Votes
1908	William J. Bryan	Democrat	38,049
	Eugene W. Chafin	Prohibition	2,682
	Eugene V. Debs	Socialist	7,339
	Thomas L. Hisgen	Independence	289
	William H. Taft*	Republican	62,530
1912	Eugene W. Chafin	Prohibition	4,360
	Eugene V. Debs	Socialist	13,343
	Theodore Roosevelt	Progressive	37,600
	William H. Taft	Republican	34,673
	Woodrow Wilson*	Democrat	47,064
1916	Allan L. Benson	Socialist	9,711
	J. Frank Hanley	Prohibition	4,729
	Charles Evans Hughes**	Republican	126,813
	John M. Parker[2]	Progressive	310
	Woodrow Wilson*	Democrat	120,087
1920	James M. Cox	Democrat	80,019
	William W. Cox	Industrial Labor	1,515
	Eugene V. Debs	Socialist	9,801
	Warren G. Harding*	Republican	143,592
	Aaron S. Watkins	Prohibition	3,595
1924	Calvin Coolidge*	Republican	142,579
	John W. Davis	Democrat	67,589
	Frank T. Johns	Socialist Labor	917
	Robert M. LaFollette	Independent	68,403
1928	William Z. Foster	Independent	1,094
	Herbert Hoover*	Republican	205,341
	Verne L. Reynolds	Socialist Labor	1,564
	Alfred E. Smith	Democrat	109,223
	Norman Thomas	Socialist Principles-Independent	2,720
1932	William Z. Foster	Communist	1,681
	Herbert Hoover	Republican	136,019
	Verne L. Reynolds	Socialist Labor	1,730
	Franklin D. Roosevelt*	Democrat	213,871
	Norman Thomas	Socialist	15,450
1936	John W. Aiken	Socialist Labor	500
	Alfred M. Landon	Republican	122,706
	William Lemke	Independent	21,831
	Franklin D. Roosevelt*	Democrat	266,733
	Norman Thomas	Independent	2,143
1940	John W. Aiken	Socialist Labor	2,487
	Franklin D. Roosevelt*	Democrat	258,415
	Wendell L. Willkie	Republican	219,555
1944	Thomas E. Dewey	Republican	225,365
	Franklin D. Roosevelt*	Democrat	248,635
	Norman Thomas	Independent	3,785
	Claude A. Watson	Independent	2,362
1948	Thomas E. Dewey**	Republican	260,904
	Norman Thomas	Independent	5,051
	Harry S. Truman*	Democrat	243,147
	Henry A. Wallace	Progressive	14,978
1952	Dwight D. Eisenhower*	Republican	420,815
	Vincent Hallinan	Independent	3,665
	Adlai Stevenson	Democrat	270,579
1956	Dwight D. Eisenhower*	Republican	406,393
	Adlai Stevenson	Democrat	329,204
1960	John F. Kennedy*	Democrat	367,402
	Richard M. Nixon**	Republican	408,060
1964	Barry M. Goldwater	Republican	282,779
	Lyndon B. Johnson*	Democrat	501,017
1968	Hubert H. Humphrey	Democrat	358,866
	Richard M. Nixon*	Republican	408,433
	George C. Wallace	Independent	49,683

Year	Candidate	Party	Votes
1972	George S. McGovern	Democrat	392,760
	Richard M. Nixon*	Republican	486,686
	John G. Schmitz	Independent	46,211
1976	Jimmy Carter*	Democrat	490,407
	Gerald Ford**	Republican	492,120
	Eugene J. McCarthy	Independent	40,207
1980	John Anderson	Independent	112,389
	Jimmy Carter	Democrat	456,890
	Ed Clark	Libertarian	25,838
	Barry Commoner	Independent	13,642
	Ronald Reagan*	Republican	571,044
1984	Walter F. Mondale	Democrat	536,479
	Ronald Reagan*	Republican	685,700
1988	George Bush*	Republican	560,126
	Michael S. Dukakis**	Democrat	616,206
	Lenora B. Fulani	Independent	6,487
	Ron Paul	Libertarian	14,811
1992	George Bush	Republican	475,757
	Bill Clinton*	Democrat	621,314
	Lenora Fulani	New Alliance Party	3,030
	Andre Marrou	Libertarian	4,277
	Ross Perot	Independent Initiative Party of Oregon	354,091
1996	Harry Browne	Libertarian	8,903
	Bill Clinton*	Democrat	649,641
	Bob Dole	Republican	538,152
	John Hagelin	Natural Law	2,798
	Mary Cal Hollis	Socialist	1,922
	Ralph Nader	Pacific	49,415
	Ross Perot	Reform	121,221
	Howard Phillips	U.S. Taxpayers	3,379
2000	Harry Browne	Libertarian	7,447
	Patrick J. Buchanan	Independent	7,063
	George W. Bush*	Republican	713,577
	Al Gore**	Democrat	720,342
	John Hagelin	Reform	2,574
	Ralph Nader	Pacific Green	77,357
	Howard Phillips	Constitution	2,189
2004	Michael Badnarik	Libertarian	7,260
	George W. Bush*	Republican	866,831
	David Cobb	Pacific Green	5,315
	John F. Kerry**	Democrat	943,163
	Michael Anthony Peroutka	Constitution	5,257
2008	Baldwin, Chuck	Constitution	7,693
	Barr, Bob	Libertarian	7,635
	McCain, John	Republican	738,475
	McKinney, Cynthia	Pacific Green	4,543
	Nader, Ralph	Peace	18,614
	Obama, Barack*	Democrat	1,037,291
2012	Anderson, Ross C. (Rocky)	Progressive	3,384
	Christensen, Will	Constitution	4,432
	Johnson, Gary	Libertarian	24,089
	Obama, Barack*	Democrat	970,488
	Romney, Mitt	Republican	754,175
	Stein, Jill	Pacific Green	19,427
2016	Clinton, Hillary**	Democrat	1,002,106
	Johnson, Gary	Libertarian	94,231
	Stein, Jill	Pacific Green	50,002
	Trump, Donald J.*	Republican	782,403

[1]One Weaver elector was endorsed by the Democrats and elected as a Fusionist, receiving 35,811 votes.
[2]Vice-presidential candidate

Initiative, Referendum and Recall

In 1902, Oregon voters overwhelmingly approved a legislatively referred ballot measure that created Oregon's initiative and referendum process. In 1904, voters enacted the direct primary and, in 1908, Oregon's Constitution was amended to allow for recall of public officials. These were the culmination of efforts by the Direct Legislation League, a group of political activists that progressive leader William S. U'Ren founded in 1898.

This system of empowering the people to propose new laws or change the Constitution of Oregon through a general election ballot measure became nationally known as "the Oregon System."

Initiative: Registered voters may place on the ballot any issue that amends the Oregon Constitution or changes the Oregon Revised Statutes (ORS).

Referendum: Registered voters may attempt to reject any bill passed by the Legislature by placing a referendum on the ballot.

Referral: The Legislature may refer any bill it passes to voters for approval. It must do so for any amendment to the Oregon Constitution.

Since 1902, the people have passed 127 of the 367 initiative measures placed on the ballot and 23 of the 65 referenda on the ballot. During the same period, the Legislature has referred 434 measures to the people, of which 257 have passed.

Both houses of the Legislature must vote to refer a statute or constitutional amendment for popular vote. Such referrals cannot be vetoed by the governor.

To place an initiative or referendum on the ballot, supporters must obtain a specified number of signatures from registered voters. The number required is determined by a fixed percentage of the votes cast for all candidates for governor at the general election preceding the filing of the petition. In the 2016 General Election, 1,946,046 votes were cast for governor. Therefore:

- Referendum petitions require four percent, or 77,842 signatures.
- Initiative petitions for statutory enactments require six percent, or 116,763 signatures.
- Initiative petitions for constitutional amendments require eight percent, or 155,684 signatures.

The original constitutional amendment, passed in 1902, provided that a fixed percentage of the votes cast for justice of the Supreme Court would determine the number of signatures required to place an initiative or referendum on the ballot. Both a statutory enactment and a constitutional amendment required eight percent of the votes cast, while a referendum required five percent of the votes cast. In 1954, the people amended the Oregon Constitution to increase the required number of signatures to 10 percent for a constitutional amendment. In 1968, a vote of the people established the current requirements.

Prior to 1954, measures on the ballot were not numbered. They are listed below in order of appearance on the ballot. The 2001 Legislature amended state law to require that ballot measure numbers not repeat in any subsequent election. Numbers assigned for each election begin with the next number after the last number assigned in the previous election.

Key: *Adopted; L = Referred by the Legislature; I = Submitted by initiative petition; R = Referendum by petition; (Also, see footnotes on pp. 312, 313.)

Election Date/Measure Number/Ballot Title	Yes	No
June 2, 1902		
1. Limits Uses Initiative and Referendum—L[1]	*62,024	5,668
June 6, 1904		
1. Office of State Printer—L[1]	*45,334	14,031
2. Direct Primary Nominating Convention Law—I[2]	*56,205	16,354
3. Local Option Liquor Law—I[2]	*43,316	40,198
June 4, 1906		
1. Shall act appropriating money maintaining Insane Asylum, Penitentiary, Deaf-Mute, Blind School, University, Agricultural College, and Normal Schools be approved—R	*43,918	26,758
2. Equal Suffrage Constitutional Amendment—I[1]	36,902	47,075
3. Amendment to local option law giving anti-prohibitionists and prohibitionists equal privileges—I[2]	35,297	45,144
4. Law to abolish tolls on the Mount Hood and Barlow Road and providing for its ownership by the State—I[2]	31,525	44,527
5. Constitutional amendment providing method of amending constitution and applying the referendum to all laws affecting constitutional conventions and amendments—I[1]	*47,661	18,751
6. Constitutional amendment giving cities and towns exclusive power to enact and amend their charters—I[1]	*52,567	19,852
7. Constitutional amendment to allow the state printing, binding, and Printers' compensation to be regulated by law at any time—I[1]	*63,749	9,571

Election Date/Measure Number/Ballot Title	Yes	No
8. Constitutional amendment for the initiative and referendum on local, special and municipal laws and parts of laws—I[1]	*47,678	16,735
9. Bill for a law prohibiting free passes and discrimination by railroad companies and other public service corporations—I[2]	*57,281	16,779
10. An act requiring sleeping car companies, refrigerator car companies and oil companies to pay an annual license upon gross earnings—I[2]	*69,635	6,441
11. An act requiring express companies, telegraph companies and telephone companies to pay an annual license upon gross earnings—I[2]	*70,872	6,360
June 1, 1908		
1. To Increase Compensation of Legislators from $120 to $400 Per Session—L[1]	19,691	68,892
2. Permitting Location of State Institutions at Places Other than the State Capitol—L[1]	*41,975	40,868
3. Reorganization System of Courts and Increasing the Number of Supreme Judges from Three to Five—L[1]	30,243	50,591
4. Changing Date of General Elections from June to November—L[1]	*65,728	18,590
5. Giving Sheriffs Control of County Prisoners—R	*60,443	30,033
6. Requiring Railroads to Give Public Officials Free Passes—R	28,856	59,406
7. Appropriating $100,000 for Building Armories—R	33,507	54,848
8. Increasing Annual Appropriation for University of Oregon from $47,500 to $125,000—R	*44,115	40,535
9. Equal Suffrage—I[1]	36,858	58,670
10. Fishery Law Proposed by Fishwheel Operators—I[2]	*46,582	40,720
11. Giving Cities Control of Liquor Selling, Poolrooms, Theaters, etc., subject to local option law—I[1]	39,442	52,346
12. Modified Form of Single Tax Amendment—I[1]	32,066	60,871
13. Recall Power on Public Officials—I[1]	*58,381	31,002
14. Instructing Legislature to Vote for People's Choice for United States Senator—I[2]	*69,668	21,162
15. Authorizing Proportional Representation Law—I[1]	*48,868	34,128
16. Corrupt Practices Act Governing Elections—I[2]	*54,042	31,301
17. Fishery Law Proposed by Gillnet Operators—I[2]	*56,130	30,280
18. Requiring Indictment To Be By Grand Jury—I[1]	*52,214	28,487
19. Creating Hood River County—I[2]	*43,948	26,778
November 8, 1910		
1. Permitting Female Taxpayers to Vote—I[1]	35,270	59,065
2. Establishing Branch Insane Asylum in Eastern Oregon—L[2]	*50,134	41,504
3. Calling Convention to Revise State Constitution—L[2]	23,143	59,974
4. Providing Separate Districts for Election of Each State Senator and Representative—L[1]	24,000	54,252
5. Repealing Requirements That All Taxes Shall Be Equal and Uniform—L[1]	37,619	40,172
6. Permitting Organized Districts to Vote Bonds for Construction of Railroads by Such Districts—L[1]	32,884	46,070
7. Authorizing Collection of State and County Taxes on Separate Classes of Property—L[1]	31,629	41,692
8. Requiring Baker County to Pay $1,000 a Year to Circuit Judge in Addition to His State Salary—R	13,161	71,503
9. Creating Nesmith County From Parts of Lane and Douglas—I[2]	22,866	60,951
10. To Establish a State Normal School at Monmouth—I[2]	*50,191	40,044
11. Creating Otis County From Parts of Harney, Malheur and Grant—I[2]	17,426	62,016
12. Annexing Part of Clackamas County to Multnomah—I[2]	16,250	69,002
13. Creating Williams County From Parts of Lane and Douglas—I[2]	14,508	64,090
14. Permitting People of Each County to Regulate Taxation for County Purposes and Abolishing Poll Taxes—I[1]	*44,171	42,127
15. Giving Cities and Towns Exclusive Power to Regulate Liquor Traffic Within Their Limits—I[1]	*53,321	50,779
16. For Protection of Laborers in Hazardous Employment, Fixing Employers' Liability, etc.—I[2]	*56,258	33,943

Election Date/Measure Number/Ballot Title	Yes	No
17. Creating Orchard County From Part of Umatilla—I^2	15,664	62,712
18. Creating Clark County From Part of Grant—I^2	15,613	61,704
19. To Establish State Normal School at Weston—I^2	40,898	46,201
20. To Annex Part of Washington County to Multnomah—I^2	14,047	68,221
21. To Establish State Normal School at Ashland—I^2	38,473	48,655
22. Prohibiting Liquor Traffic—I^1	43,540	61,221
23. Prohibiting the Sale of Liquors and Regulating Shipments of Same, and Providing for Search for Liquor—I^2	42,651	63,564
24. Creating Board to Draft Employers' Liability Law for Submission to Legislature—I^2	32,224	51,719
25. Prohibiting Taking of Fish in Rogue River Except With Hook and Line—I^2	*49,712	33,397
26. Creating Deschutes County Out of Part of Crook—I^2	17,592	60,486
27. Bill for General Law Under Which New Counties May Be Created or Boundaries Changed—I^2	37,129	42,327
28. Permitting Counties to Vote Bonds for Permanent Road Improvement—I^1	*51,275	32,906
29. Permitting Voters in Direct Primaries to Express Choice for President and Vice President, to Select Delegates to National Convention and Nominate Candidates for Presidential Electors—I^2	*43,353	41,624
30. Creating Board of People's Inspectors of Government, Providing for Reports of Board in Official State Gazette to be Mailed to All Registered Voters Bi-monthly—I^2	29,955	52,538
31. Extending Initiative and Referendum, Making Term of Members of Legislature Six Years, Increasing Salaries, Requiring Proportional Representation in Legislature, Election of President of Senate and Speaker of House Outside of Members, etc.—I^1	37,031	44,366
32. Permitting Three-Fourths Verdict in Civil Cases—I^1	*44,538	39,399
November 5, 1912		
1. Equal Suffrage Amendment—I^1	*61,265	57,104
2. Creating Office of Lieutenant Governor—L^1	50,562	61,644
3. Divorce of Local and State Taxation—L^1	51,582	56,671
4. Permitting Different Tax Rates on Classes of Property—L^1	52,045	54,483
5. Repeal of County Tax Option—L^1	*63,881	47,150
6. Majority Rule on Constitutional Amendments—L^1	32,934	70,325
7. Double Liability on Bank Stockholders—L^1	*82,981	21,738
8. Statewide Public Utilities Regulation—R	*65,985	40,956
9. Creating Cascade County—I^2	26,463	71,239
10. Millage Tax for University and Agricultural College—I^2	48,701	57,279
11. Majority Rule on Initiated Laws—I^1	35,721	68,861
12. County Bond and Road Construction Act—Grange Bill—I^2	49,699	56,713
13. Creating State Highway Department—Grange Bill—I^2	23,872	83,846
14. Changing Date State Printer Bill Becomes Effective—I^2	34,793	69,542
15. Creating Office of Hotel Inspector—I^2	16,910	91,995
16. Eight-hour Day on Public Works—I^2	*64,508	48,078
17. Blue Sky Law—I^2	48,765	57,293
18. Relating to Employment of State Prisoners—I^2	*73,800	37,492
19. Relating to Employment of County and City Prisoners—I^2	*71,367	37,731
20. State Road Bonding Act—I^2	30,897	75,590
21. Limiting State Road Indebtedness—I^1	*59,452	43,447
22. County Bonding Act—I^2	43,611	60,210
23. Limiting County Road Indebtedness—I^1	*57,258	43,858
24. Providing Method for Consolidating Cities and Creating New Counties—I^2	40,199	56,992
25. Income Tax Amendment—I^1	52,702	52,948
26. Tax Exemption on Household Effects—I^2	*60,357	51,826
27. Tax Exemption on Moneys and Credits—I^2	42,491	66,540
28. Revising Inheritance Tax Laws—I^2	38,609	63,839
29. Freight Rates Act—I^2	*58,306	45,534
30. County Road Bonding Act—I^1	38,568	63,481
31. Abolishing Senate; Proxy Voting; U'Ren Constitution—I^1	31,020	71,183

Election Date/Measure Number/Ballot Title	Yes	No
32. Statewide Single Tax with Graduated Tax Provision—I[1]	31,534	82,015
33. Abolishing Capital Punishment—I[2]	41,951	64,578
34. Prohibits Boycotts and Pickets—I[2]	49,826	60,560
35. Prohibits Use of Public Streets, Parks and Grounds in Cities over 5,000 Without Permit—I[2]	48,987	62,532
36. Appropriation for University of Oregon—R	29,437	78,985
37. Appropriation for University of Oregon—R	27,310	79,376
November 4, 1913 (Special Referendum Election)		
1. State University Building Repair Fund—R	*56,659	40,600
2. University of Oregon New Building Appropriation—R	*53,569	43,014
3. Sterilization Act—R	41,767	53,319
4. County Attorney Act—R	*54,179	38,159
5. Workmen's Compensation Act—R	*67,814	28,608
November 3, 1914		
1. Requiring Voters to be Citizens of the United States—L[1]	*164,879	39,847
2. Creating Office of Lieutenant Governor—L[1]	52,040	143,804
3. Permitting Certain City and County Boundaries to be Made Identical, and Governments Consolidated—L[1]	77,392	103,194
4. Permitting State to Create an Indebtedness Not to Exceed Two Percent of Assessed Valuation for Irrigation and Power Projects and Development of Untilled Lands—L[1]	49,759	135,550
5. Omitting Requirement that "All Taxation Shall Be Equal And Uniform"—L[1]	59,206	116,490
6. Changing Existing Rule of Uniformity and Equality of Taxation—Authorizing Classification of Property for Taxation Purposes—L[1]	52,362	122,704
7. To Establish State Normal School at Ashland—L[2]	84,041	109,643
8. Enabling Incorporated Municipalities to Surrender Charters and To Be Merged in Adjoining City or Town—L[1]	*96,116	77,671
9. To Establish State Normal School at Weston—L[2]	87,450	105,345
10. Providing Compensation for Members of Legislature at Five Dollars Per Day—L[1]	41,087	146,278
11. Universal Constitutional Eight Hour Day Amendment—I[1]	49,360	167,888
12. Eight-hour Day and Room-Ventilation Law for Female Workers—I[2]	88,480	120,296
13. Nonpartisan Judiciary Bill Prohibiting Party Nominations for Judicial Officers—I[2]	74,323	107,263
14. $1,500 Tax Exemption Amendment—I[1]	65,495	136,193
15. Public Docks and Water Frontage Amendment—I[1]	67,128	114,564
16. Municipal Wharves and Docks Bill—I[2]	67,110	111,113
17. Prohibition Constitutional Amendment—I[1]	*136,842	100,362
18. Abolishing Death Penalty—I[1]	*100,552	100,395
19. Specific Personal Graduated Extra-tax Amendment of Article IX, Oregon Constitution—I[1]	59,186	124,943
20. Consolidating Corporation and Insurance Departments—I[2]	55,469	120,154
21. Dentistry Bill—I[2]	92,722	110,404
22. County Officers Term Amendment—I[1]	82,841	107,039
23. A Tax Code Commission Bill—I[2]	34,436	143,468
24. Abolishing Desert Land Board and Reorganizing Certain State Offices—I[2]	32,701	143,366
25. Proportional Representation Amendment to Oregon Constitution—I[1]	39,740	137,116
26. State Senate Constitutional Amendment—I[1]	62,376	123,429
27. Department of Industry and Public Works Amendment—I[1]	57,859	126,201
28. Primary Delegate Election Bill—I[2]	25,058	153,638
29. Equal Assessment and Taxation and $300 Exemption Amendment—I[1]	43,280	140,507
November 7, 1916		
1. Single Item Veto Amendment—L[1]	*141,773	53,207
2. Ship Tax Exemption Amendment—L[1]	*119,652	65,410
3. Negro and Mulatto Suffrage Amendment—L[1]	100,027	100,701
4. Full Rental Value Land Tax and Homemakers' Loan Fund Amendment—I[1]	43,390	154,980

Election Date/Measure Number/Ballot Title	Yes	No
5. For Pendleton Normal School and Ratifying Location Certain State Institutions—I[1]	96,829	109,523
6. Anti-compulsory Vaccination Bill—I[2]	99,745	100,119
7. Bill Repealing and Abolishing the Sunday Closing Law—I[2]	*125,836	93,076
8. Permitting Manufacture and Regulating Sale 4 Percent Malt Liquors—I[1]	85,973	140,599
9. Prohibition Amendment Forbidding Importation of Intoxicating Liquors for Beverage Purposes—I[1]	*114,932	109,671
10. Rural Credits Amendment—I[1]	*107,488	83,887
11. State-wide Tax and Indebtedness Limitation Amendment—I[1]	*99,536	84,031

June 4, 1917 (Special Election)

1. Authorizing Ports to Create Limited Indebtedness to Encourage Water Transportation—L[1]	*67,445	54,864
2. Limiting Number of Bills Introduced and Increasing Pay of Legislators—L[1]	22,276	103,238
3. Declaration Against Implied Repeal of Constitutional Provisions by Amendments Thereto—L[1]	37,187	72,445
4. Uniform Tax Classification Amendment—L[1]	*62,118	53,245
5. Requiring Election City, Town and State Officers at Same Time—L[1]	*83,630	42,296
6. Four Hundred Thousand Dollar Tax Levy for a New Penitentiary—L[2]	46,666	86,165
7. Six Million Dollar State Road Bond Issue and Highway Bill—L[2]	*77,316	63,803

November 5, 1918

1. Establishing and Maintaining Southern and Eastern Oregon Normal Schools—L[1]	49,935	66,070
2. Establishing Dependent, Delinquent and Defective Children's Home, Appropriating Money Therefor—L[2]	43,441	65,299
3. Prohibiting Seine and Setnet Fishing in Rogue River and Tributaries—R	45,511	50,227
4. Closing the Willamette River to Commercial Fishing South of Oswego—R	*55,555	40,908
5. Delinquent Tax Notice Bill—I[2]	*66,652	41,594
6. Fixing Compensation for Publication of Legal Notice—I[2]	*50,073	41,816
7. Authorizing Increase in Amount of Levy of State Taxes for Year 1919 (submitted by state tax commission under chapter 150, Laws 1917)	41,364	56,974

June 3, 1919 (Special Election)

1. Six Percent County Indebtedness for Permanent Roads Amendment—L[1]	*49,728	33,561
2. Industrial and Reconstruction Hospital Amendment—L[1]	38,204	40,707
3. State Bond Payment of Irrigation and Drainage District Bond Interest—L[1]	*43,010	35,948
4. Five Million Dollar Reconstruction Bonding Amendment—L[1]	39,130	40,580
5. Lieutenant Governor Constitutional Amendment—L[1]	32,653	46,861
6. The Roosevelt Coast Military Highway Bill—L[2]	*56,966	29,159
7. Reconstruction Bonding Bill—L[2]	37,294	42,792
8. Soldiers', Sailors' and Marines' Educational Financial Aid Bill—L[2]	*49,158	33,513
9. Market Roads Tax Bill—L[2]	*53,191	28,039

May 21, 1920 (Special Election)

1. Extending Eminent Domain Over Roads and Ways—L[1]	*100,256	35,655
2. Limitation of 4 Percent State Indebtedness for Permanent Roads—L[1]	*93,392	46,084
3. Restoring Capital Punishment—L[1]	*81,756	64,589
4. Crook and Curry Counties Bonding Amendment—L[1]	*72,378	36,699
5. Successor to Governor—L[1]	*78,241	56,946
6. Higher Educational Tax Act—L[2]	*102,722	46,577
7. Soldiers', Sailors' and Marines' Educational Aid Revenue Bill—L[2]	*91,294	50,482
8. State Elementary School Fund Tax—L[2]	*110,263	39,593
9. Blind School Tax Measure—L[2]	*115,337	30,739

November 2, 1920

1. Compulsory Voting and Registration Amendment—L[1]	61,258	131,603
2. Constitutional Amendment Regulating Legislative Sessions and the Payment of Legislators—L[1]	80,342	85,524
3. Oleomargarine Bills—R	67,101	119,126
4. Single Tax Constitutional Amendment—I[1]	37,283	147,426
5. Fixing Term of Certain County Officers—I[1]	*97,854	80,983

Election Date/Measure Number/Ballot Title	Yes	No
6. Port of Portland Dock Commission Consolidation—I[2]	80,493	84,830
7. Anti-compulsory Vaccination Amendment—I[1]	63,018	127,570
8. Constitutional Amendment Fixing Legal Rate of Interest in Oregon—I[1]	28,976	158,673
9. Roosevelt Bird Refuge—I[2]	78,961	107,383
10. Divided Legislative Session Constitutional Amendment—I[1]	57,791	101,179
11. State Market Commission Act—I[2]	51,605	119,464
June 7, 1921 (Special Election)		
1. Legislative Regulation and Compensation Amendment—L[1]	42,924	72,596
2. World War Veterans' State Aid Fund, Constitutional Amendment—L[1]	*88,219	37,866
3. Emergency Clause Veto Constitutional Amendment—L[1]	*62,621	45,537
4. Hygiene Marriage Examination and License Bill—L[2]	56,858	65,793
5. Women Jurors and Revised Jury Law—L[2]	*59,882	59,265
November 7, 1922		
1. Amendment Permitting Linn County Tax Levy to Pay Outstanding Warrants—L	*89,177	57,049
2. Amendment Permitting Linn and Benton Counties to Pay Outstanding Warrants—L[1]	*86,547	53,844
3. Single Tax Amendment—I[1]	39,231	132,021
4. 1925 Exposition Tax Amendment—I[2]	82,837	95,587
5. Income Tax Amendment—I[2]	54,803	112,197
6. Compulsory Education Bill—I[2]	*115,506	103,685
November 6, 1923 (Special Election)		
1. Income Tax Act—L[2]	*58,647	58,131
November 4, 1924		
1. Voters' Literacy Amendment—L[1]	*184,031	48,645
2. Public Use and Welfare Amendment—L[1]	*134,071	65,133
3. Bonus Amendment—L[1]	*131,199	92,446
4. Oleomargarine Condensed Milk Bill—R	91,597	157,324
5. Naturopath Bill—I[2]	75,159	122,839
6. Workmen's Compulsory Compensation Law for Hazardous Occupations—I[1]	73,270	151,862
7. Income Tax Repeal—I[2]	*123,799	111,055
November 2, 1926		
1. Klamath County Bonding Amendment—L[1]	*81,954	68,128
2. Six Percent Limitation Amendment—L[1]	54,624	99,125
3. Repeal of Free Negro and Mulatto Section of the Constitution—L[1]	*108,332	64,954
4. Amendment Prohibiting Inheritance and Income Taxes—L[1]	59,442	121,973
5. The Seaside Normal School Act—L[2]	47,878	124,811
6. The Eastern Oregon State Normal School Act—L[2]	*101,327	80,084
7. The Recall Amendment—L[1]	*100,324	61,307
8 Curry County Bonding or Tax Levy Amendment—L[1]	*78,823	61,472
9. Amendment Relating to Elections to Fill Vacancies in Public Offices—L[1]	*100,397	54,474
10. Klamath and Clackamas County Bonding Amendment—L[1]	*75,229	61,718
11. The Eastern Oregon Tuberculosis Hospital Act—L[2]	*131,296	48,490
12. Cigarette and Tobacco Tax Bill—R	62,254	123,208
13. Motor Bus and Truck Bill—R	*99,746	78,685
14. Act Appropriating Ten Percent of Self-sustaining Boards' Receipts—R	46,389	97,460
15. Income Tax Bill With Property Tax Offset—I[2]	50,199	122,512
16. Bus and Truck Operating License Bill—I[2]	76,164	94,533
17. Fish Wheel, Trap, Seine and Gillnet Bill—I[2]	*102,119	73,086
18. Income Tax Bill—I[2]	83,991	93,997
19. Oregon Water and Power Board Development Measure—I[1]	35,313	147,092
20. Amendment Fixing Salaries of County Officers of Umatilla County—L[2]	1,988	2,646
21. To Provide Salaries for Certain Officials of Clackamas County—L[2]	2,826	6,199
June 28, 1927 (Special Election)		
1. Repeal of Negro, Chinaman and Mulatto Suffrage Section of Constitution—L[1]	*69,373	41,887
2. Portland School District Tax Levy Amendment—L[1]	46,784	55,817
3. Criminal Information Amendment—L[1]	*64,956	38,774

Election Date/Measure Number/Ballot Title	Yes	No
4. Legislators' Pay Amendment—L[1]	28,380	81,215
5. Voters' Registration Amendment—L[1]	*55,802	49,682
6. State and County Officers, Salary Amendment—L[1]	46,999	61,838
7. City and County Consolidation Amendment—L[1]	41,309	57,613
8. Veterans' Memorial and Armory Amendment—L[1]	25,180	80,476
9. State Tax Limitation Amendment—L[1]	19,393	84,697
10. Income Tax Bill—L[2]	48,745	67,039
11. Property Assessment and Taxation Enforcement Bill—L[2]	31,957	70,871
12. Nestucca Bay Fish Closing Bill—R	*53,684	47,552
November 6, 1928		
1. Five Cent Gasoline Tax Bill—I[1]	71,824	198,798
2. Bill for Reduction of Motor Vehicle License Fees—I[1]	98,248	174,219
3. Income Tax Bill—I[2]	118,696	132,961
4. Limiting Power of Legislature Over Laws Approved by the People—I[1]	108,230	124,200
5. Deschutes River Water and Fish Bill—I[2]	78,317	157,398
6. Rogue River Water and Fish Bill—I[2]	79,028	156,009
7. Umpqua River Water and Fish Bill—I[2]	76,108	154,345
8. McKenzie River Water and Fish Bill—I[2]	77,974	153,418
November 4, 1930		
1. Repeal of State Payment of Irrigation and Drainage District Interest—L[1]	*96,061	74,892
2. State Cabinet Form of Government Constitutional Amendment—L[1]	51,248	135,412
3. Bonus Loan Constitutional Amendment—L[1]	92,602	101,785
4. Motor Vehicle License Tax Constitutional Amendment—L[1]	71,557	115,480
5. Motor Vehicle License Tax Constitutional Amendment—L[1]	63,683	111,441
6. Constitutional Amendment for Filling Vacancies in the Legislature—L[1]	*85,836	76,455
7. Legislators' Compensation Constitutional Amendment—L[1]	70,937	108,070
8. Two Additional Circuit Judges Bill—R	39,770	137,549
9. Income Tax Bill—R	*105,189	95,207
10. Anti-cigarette Constitutional Amendment—I[1]	54,231	156,265
11. Rogue River Fishing Constitutional Amendment—I[1]	96,596	99,490
12. Lieutenant Governor Constitutional Amendment—I[1]	92,707	95,277
13. People's Water and Power Utility Districts Constitutional Amendment—I[1]	*117,776	84,778
November 8, 1932		
1. Taxpayer Voting Qualification Amendment—L[1]	*189,321	124,160
2. Amendment Authorizing Criminal Trials Without Juries by Consent of Accused—L[1]	*191,042	111,872
3. Six Percent Tax Limitation Amendment—L[1]	*149,833	121,852
4. Oleomargarine Tax Bill—R	131,273	200,496
5. Bill Prohibiting Commercial Fishing on the Rogue River—R	127,445	180,527
6. Higher Education Appropriation Bill—R	58,076	237,218
7. Bill to Repeal State Prohibition Law of Oregon—I[2]	*206,619	138,775
8. The Freight Truck and Bus Bill—I[2]	151,790	180,609
9. Bill Moving University, Normal and Law Schools, Establishing Junior Colleges—I[2]	47,275	292,486
10. Tax and Debt Control Constitutional Amendment—I[1]	99,171	162,552
11. Tax Supervising and Conservation Bill—I[2]	117,940	154,206
12. Personal Income Tax Law Amendment—I[2]	144,502	162,468
13. State Water Power and Hydroelectric Constitutional Amendment—I[1]	*168,937	130,494
July 21, 1933 (Special Election)		
1. An Amendment to the Constitution of the United States of America—L[0]	*136,713	72,854
2. Soldiers and Sailors Bonus Limitation Amendment—L[1]	*113,267	75,476
3. County Manager Form of Government Constitutional Amendment—L[1]	66,425	117,148
4. Prosecution by Information and Grand Jury Modification Amendment—L[1]	67,192	110,755
5. Debt and Taxation Limitations for Municipal Corporations Constitutional Amendment—L[1]	82,996	91,671
6. State Power Fund Bonds—L[2]	73,756	106,153
7. Sales Tax Bill—L[2]	45,603	167,512
8. Repeal of Oregon Prohibition Constitutional Amendment—L[1]	*143,044	72,745

Election Date/Measure Number/Ballot Title	Yes	No
9. Oleomargarine Tax Bill—R	66,880	144,542
May 18, 1934 (Special Election)		
1. County Indebtedness and Funding Bond Constitutional Amendment—L[1]	83,424	96,629
2. Criminal Trial Without Jury and Non-unanimous Verdict Constitutional Amendment—L[1]	*117,446	83,430
3. Bill Authorizing a State Tuberculosis Hospital in Multnomah County—L[2]	*104,459	98,815
4. Bill Authorizing a State Insane Hospital in Multnomah County—L[2]	92,575	108,816
5. School Relief Sales Tax Bill—R	64,677	156,182
November 6, 1934		
1. Grange Power Bill—R	124,518	139,283
2. Limitations of Taxes on Taxable Property Constitutional Amendment—I[1]	100,565	161,644
3. Healing Arts Constitutional Amendment—I[1]	70,626	191,836
January 31, 1936 (Special Election)		
1. Bill Changing Primary Elections to September With Other Resulting Changes—L[2]	61,270	155,922
2. Compensation of Members of the Legislature Constitutional Amendment—L[1]	28,661	184,332
3. Sales Tax Bill—L[2]	32,106	187,319
4. Bill Authorizing Student Activity Fees in State Higher Educational Institutions—R	50,971	163,191
November 3, 1936		
1. Bill Amending Old Age Assistance Act of 1935—R	174,293	179,236
2. Amendment Forbidding Prevention or Regulation of Certain Advertising If Truthful—I[1]	100,141	222,897
3. Tax Limitation Constitutional Amendment for School Districts Having 100,000 Population—I[1]	112,546	203,693
4. Noncompulsory Military Training Bill—I[2]	131,917	214,246
5. Amendment Limiting and Reducing Permissible Taxes on Tangible Property—I[1]	79,604	241,042
6. State Power Bill—I[2]	131,489	208,179
7. State Hydroelectric Temporary Administrative Board Constitutional Amendment—I[1]	100,356	208,741
8. State Bank Bill—I[2]	82,869	250,777
November 8, 1938		
1. Governor's 20-day Bill Consideration Amendment—L[1]	*233,384	93,752
2. Amendment Repealing the Double Liability of Stockholders in Banking Corporations—L[1]	133,525	165,797
3. Legislators Compensation Constitutional Amendments—L[1]	149,356	169,131
4. Bill Requiring Marriage License Applicants Medically Examined; Physically and Mentally—L[2]	*277,099	66,484
5. Slot Machines Seizure by Sheriffs and Destruction on Court Order—R	*204,561	126,580
6. Prohibiting Slot Machines, Pin-ball, Dart and Other Similar Games—R	*197,912	129,043
7. Townsend Plan Bill—I[3]	*183,781	149,711
8. Citizens' Retirement Annuity Bill; Levying Transactions Tax to Provide Fund—I[2]	112,172	219,557
9. Bill Regulating Picketing and Boycotting by Labor Groups and Organizations—I[2]	*197,771	148,460
10. Water Purification and Prevention of Pollution Bill—I[2]	*247,685	75,295
11. Bill Regulating Sale of Alcoholic Liquor for Beverage Purposes—I[2]	118,282	222,221
12. Constitutional Amendment Legalizing Certain Lotteries and Other Forms of Gambling—I[1]	141,792	180,329
November 5, 1940		
1. Amendment Removing Office Time Limit of State Secretary and Treasurer—L[1]	163,942	213,797
2. Amendment Making Three Years' Average People's Voted Levies, Tax Base—L[1]	129,699	183,488

Election Date/Measure Number/Ballot Title	Yes	No
3. Amendment Repealing the Double Liability of Stockholders of State Banks—L[1]	157,891	191,290
4. Legislators' Compensation Constitutional Amendment—L[1]	186,830	188,031
5. Bill Changing the Primary Nominating Elections from May to September—R	156,421	221,203
6. Bill to Further Regulate Sale and Use of Alcoholic Liquor—R	158,004	235,128
7. Bill Repealing Present Liquor Law; Authorizing Private Sale, Licensed, Taxed—I[2]	90,681	309,183
8. Amendment Legalizing Certain Gambling and Gaming Devices and Certain Lotteries—I[1]	150,157	258,010
9. Bill to Repeal the Oregon Milk Control Law—I[2]	201,983	213,838
November 3, 1942		
1. Legislators' Compensation Constitutional Amendment—L[1]	*129,318	109,898
2. Rural Credits Loan Fund Repeal Amendment—L[1]	*101,425	88,857
3. Amendment Specifying Exclusive Uses of Gasoline and Motor Vehicle Taxes—L[1]	*125,990	86,332
4. Amendment Authorizing Regulation by Law of Voting Privilege Forfeiture—L[1]	101,508	103,404
5. Cigarette Tax Bill—R	110,643	127,366
6. Bill Restricting and Prohibiting Net Fishing Coastal Streams and Bays—R	97,212	137,177
7. Bill Distributing Surplus Funds to School Districts, Reducing Taxes Therein—I[2]	*136,321	92,623
November 7, 1944		
1. Amendment To Provide Alternative Means for Securing Bank Deposits—L[1]	*228,744	115,745
2. Amendment Authorizing Change to Managerial Form of County Government—L[1]	*175,716	154,504
3. Amendment Authorizing "Oregon War Veterans' Fund," Providing Tax Therefor—L[1]	*190,520	178,581
4. Amendment to Authorize Legislative Regulation of Voting Privilege Forfeiture—L[1]	*183,855	156,219
5. Bill Providing Educational Aid to Certain Veterans World War II—L[2]	*238,350	135,317
6. Bill Imposing Tax on Retail Sales of Tangible Personal Property—L[2]	96,697	269,276
7. Burke Bill; Only State Selling Liquor over 14 Hundredths Alcohol—R	*228,853	180,158
8. Constitutional Amendment Increasing State Tax Fund for Public School Support—I[1]	177,153	186,976
9. Constitutional Amendment Providing Monthly Annuities From a Gross Income Tax—I[1]	180,691	219,981
June 22, 1945 (Special Election)		
1. Bill Authorizing Tax Levy for State Building Fund—L[2]	*78,269	49,565
2. Bill Authorizing Cigarette Tax to Support Public Schools—L[2]	60,321	67,542
November 5, 1946		
1. Constitutional Amendment Providing for Succession to Office of Governor—L[1]	*221,547	70,322
2. Bill Authorizing Tax for Construction and Equipment of State Armories—L[2]	75,693	219,006
3. Bill Establishing Rural School Districts and School Boards—L[2]	*155,733	134,673
4. Bill Authorizing Chinamen to Hold Real Estate and Mining Claims—L[1]	*161,865	133,111
5. Amendment Permitting Legislative Bills to be Read by Title Only—L[1]	*145,248	113,279
6. Constitutional Amendment Increasing Number of Senators to Thirty-one—L[1]	88,717	185,247
7. Bill Regulating Fishing in Coastal Streams and Inland Waters—R	*196,195	101,398
8. To Create State Old-age and Disability Pension Fund—I[2]	86,374	244,960
9. To Create Basic School Support Fund by Annual Tax Levy—I[2]	*157,904	151,765
October 7, 1947 (Special Election)		
1. Bill Taxing Retail Sales for School, Welfare and Governmental Purposes—L[2]	67,514	180,333
2. Cigarette Tax Bill—R	103,794	140,876

Election Date/Measure Number/Ballot Title	Yes	No
November 2, 1948		
1. Constitutional Six Percent Tax Limitation Amendment—L^1	150,032	268,155
2. Constitutional Amendment Authorizing Indebtedness for State Forestation—L^1	*211,912	209,317
3. Bill Authorizing State Boys' Camp Near Timber, Oregon—L^2	*227,638	219,196
4. Bill Amending Licensing and Acquisition Provisions for Hydroelectric Commission Act—R	173,004	242,100
5. Constitutional Amendment Fixing Qualifications of Voters in School Elections—I^1	*284,776	164,025
6. Oregon Old Age Pension Act—I^2	*313,212	172,531
7. Bill Increasing Personal Income Tax Exemptions—I^2	*405,842	63,373
8. Oregon Liquor Dispensing Licensing Act—I^2	210,108	273,621
9. World War II Veterans' Bonus Amendment—I^1	198,283	265,805
10. Prohibiting Salmon Fishing in Columbia River With Fixed Appliances—I^2	*273,140	184,834
11. Question of Authorizing Additional State Tax, to be Offset by Income Tax Funds—R	143,856	256,167
November 7, 1950		
1. Constitutional Amendment Fixing Legislators' Annual Compensation—L^1	*243,518	205,361
2. Constitutional Amendment Lending State Tax Credit for Higher Education Buildings—L^1	*256,895	192,573
3. Constitutional Amendment Augmenting "Oregon War Veterans' Fund"—L^1	*268,171	183,724
4. Increasing Basic School Support Fund by Annual Tax Levy—L^2	*234,394	231,856
5. Needy Aged Persons Public Assistance Act—R	*310,143	158,939
6. Providing Uniform Standard Time in Oregon—R	*277,633	195,319
7. World War II Veterans' Compensation Fund—I^1	*239,553	216,958
8. Constitutional Amendment for Legislative Representation Reapportionment—I^1	190,992	215,302
9. Making Sale of Promotively Advertised Alcoholic Beverage Unlawful—I^2	113,524	378,732
November 4, 1952		
1. Amendment Making Superintendent of Public Instruction Appointive—L^1	282,882	326,199
2. World War Veterans' State Aid Sinking Fund Repeal—L^1	*454,898	147,128
3. Act Authorizing Domiciliary State Hospital for Aged Mentally Ill—L^2	*480,479	153,402
4. Amendment Legal Voters of Taxing Unit Establish Tax Base—L^1	*355,136	210,373
5. Amendment to Augment Oregon War Veterans' Fund—L^1	*465,605	132,363
6. Amendment Creating Legislative Assembly Emergency Committee—L^1	*364,539	194,492
7. Amendment Fixing Elective Terms of State Senators and Representatives—L^1	*483,356	103,357
8. Amendatory Act Title Subject Amendment—L^1	*315,071	191,087
9. Act Limiting State Property Tax—L^2	*318,948	272,145
10. Motor Carrier Highway Transportation Tax Act—R	*409,588	230,241
11. School District Reorganization Act—R	295,700	301,974
12. Cigarette Stamp Tax Revenue Act—R	233,226	413,137
13. Establishing United States Standard Time in Oregon—I^2	*399,981	256,981
14. Constitutional Amendment Prohibiting Lotteries, Bookmaking, Pari-mutuel Betting on Animal Racing—I^1	230,097	411,884
15. Constitutional Amendment Authorizing Alcoholic Liquor Sale by Individual Glass—I^1	*369,127	285,446
16. Constitutional Amendment Providing Equitable Taxing Method for Use of Highways—I^1	135,468	484,730
17. Milk Production and Marketing Act Bill—I^2	313,629	337,750
18. Constitutional Legislative Senator and Representative Apportionment Enforcement Amendment—I^1	*357,550	194,292
November 2, 1954		
1. Salaries of State Legislators—L^1	216,545	296,008
2. Subdividing Counties for Electing State Legislators—L^1	*268,337	208,077

Election Date/Measure Number/Ballot Title	Yes	No
3. Mental Hospital In or Near Portland—L²	*397,625	128,685
4. Constitutional Amendments—How Proposed by People—L¹	*251,078	230,770
5. State Property Tax—L¹	208,419	264,569
6. Establishing Daylight Saving Time—I²	252,305	300,007
7. Prohibiting Certain Fishing in Coastal Streams—I²	232,775	278,805
8. Repealing Milk Control Law—I²	*293,745	247,591
November 6, 1956		
1. State Tax Laws—Immediate Effect Authorized—L¹	175,932	487,550
2. Authorizing State Acceptance of Certain Gifts—L¹	*498,633	153,033
3. Salaries of Certain State Officers—L¹	*390,338	263,155
4. Qualifications for County Coroner and Surveyor—L¹	*455,485	182,550
5. Salaries of State Legislators—L¹	320,741	338,365
6. Cigarette Tax—R	280,055	414,613
7. Prohibiting Certain Fishing in Coastal Streams—I²	*401,882	259,309
November 4, 1958		
1. Fixing State Boundaries—L¹	*399,396	114,318
2. Increasing Funds for War Veterans' Loans—L¹	232,246	318,685
3. Salaries of State Legislators—L¹	236,000	316,437
4. Capital Punishment Bill—L¹	264,434	276,487
5. Financing Urban Redevelopment Projects—L¹	221,330	268,716
6. Modifying County Debt Limitation—L¹	*252,347	224,426
7. Special Grand Jury Bill—L¹	*357,792	136,745
8. Authorizes Different Use of State Institution—L¹	*303,282	193,177
9. Temporary Appointment and Assignment of Judges—L¹	*373,466	125,898
10. State Power Development—L¹	218,662	291,210
11. County Home Rule Amendment—L¹	*311,516	157,023
12. Authorizing Discontinuing Certain State Tuberculosis Hospitals—L¹	*319,790	195,945
13. Persons Eligible to Serve in Legislature—I¹	*320,751	201,700
May 20, 1960		
1. Salaries of State Legislators—L¹	250,456	281,542
November 8, 1960		
1. Fixing Commencement of Legislators' Term—L¹	*579,022	92,187
2. Daylight Saving Time—L²	357,499	393,652
3. Financing Urban Redevelopment Projects—L¹	*335,792	312,187
4. Permitting Prosecution by Information or Indictment—L¹	306,190	340,197
5. Authorizing Legislature to Propose Revised Constitution—L¹	*358,367	289,895
6. State Bonds for Higher Education Facilities—L¹	*467,557	233,759
7. Voter Qualification Amendment—L¹	*508,108	183,977
8. Authorizing Bonds for State Building Program—L¹	232,250	433,515
9. Compulsory Retirement for Judges—L¹	*578,471	123,283
10. Elective Offices: When to Become Vacant—L¹	*486,019	169,865
11. Financing Improvements in Home Rule Counties—L¹	*399,210	222,736
12. Continuity of Government in Enemy Attack—L¹	*578,266	88,995
13. War Veterans' Bonding and Loan Amendment—L¹	*415,931	266,630
14. Personal Income Tax Bill—R	115,610	570,025
15. Billboard Control Measure—I²	261,735	475,290
May 18, 1962		
1. Six Percent Limitation Amendment—L¹	141,728	262,140
2. Salaries of State Legislators—L¹	*241,171	178,749
November 6, 1962		
1. Reorganize State Militia—L¹	*312,680	234,440
2. Forest Rehabilitation Debt Limit Amendment—L¹	*323,799	199,174
3. Permanent Road Debt Limit Amendment—L¹	*319,956	200,236
4. Power Development Debt Limit Amendment—L¹	*298,255	208,755
5. State Courts Creation and Jurisdiction—L¹	*307,855	193,487
6. Daylight Saving Time—L²	*388,154	229,661
7. Constitutional Six Percent Limitation Amendment—L¹	*270,637	219,509
8. Legislative Apportionment Constitutional Amendment—I¹	197,322	325,182
9. Repeals School District Reorganization Law—I²	206,540	320,917

Election Date/Measure Number/Ballot Title	Yes	No
October 15, 1963 (Special Election)		
1. Personal and Corporation Income Tax Bill—R	103,737	362,845
May 15, 1964		
1. Authorizing Bonds for Education Building Program—L[1]	*327,220	252,372
November 3, 1964		
1. Capital Punishment Bill—L[1]	*455,654	302,105
2. Leasing Property for State Use—L[1]	*477,031	238,241
3. Amending State Workmen's Compensation Law—I[2]	205,182	549,414
4. Prohibiting Commercial Fishing for Salmon, Steelhead—I[2]	221,797	534,731
May 24, 1966		
1. Cigarette Tax Bill—L[2]	*310,743	181,957
2. Superintendent of Public Instruction Constitutional Amendment—L[1]	197,096	267,319
November 8, 1966		
1. Public Transportation System Employes Constitutional Amendment—L[1]	*468,103	123,964
2. State Bonds for Educational Facilities—L[1]	237,282	332,983
May 28, 1968		
1. Common School Fund Constitutional Amendment—L[1]	*372,915	226,191
2. Constitutional Amendment Changing Initiative — Referendum Requirements—L[1]	*321,731	244,750
3. Higher Education and Community College Bonds—L[1]	*353,383	261,014
November 5, 1968		
1. Constitutional Amendment Broadening Veterans Loan Eligibility—L[1]	*651,250	96,065
2. Constitutional Amendment for Removal of Judges—L[1]	*690,989	56,973
3. Empowering Legislature to Extend Ocean Boundaries—L[1]	*588,166	143,768
4. Constitutional Amendment Broadening County Debt Limitation—L[1]	331,617	348,866
5. Government Consolidation City-County Over 300,000—L[1]	*393,789	278,483
6. Bond Issue to Acquire Ocean Beaches—I[1]	315,175	464,140
7. Constitutional Amendment Changing Property Tax Limitation—I[1]	276,451	503,443
June 3, 1969 (Special Election)		
1. Property Tax Relief and Sales Tax—L[1]	65,077	504,274
May 26, 1970		
1. Capital Construction Bonds for State Government—L[1]	190,257	300,126
2. Repeals "White Foreigner" Section of Constitution—L[1]	*326,374	168,464
3. Revised Constitution for Oregon—L[1]	182,074	322,682
4. Pollution Control Bonds—L[1]	*292,234	213,835
5. Lowers Oregon Voting Age to 19—L[1]	202,018	336,527
6. Local School Property Tax Equalization Measure—L[1]	180,602	323,189
November 3, 1970		
1. Constitutional Amendment Concerning Convening of Legislature—L[1]	261,428	340,104
2. Automatic Adoption, Federal Income Tax Amendments—L[1]	*342,138	269,467
3. Constitutional Amendment Concerning County Debt Limitation—L[1]	283,629	294,186
4. Investing Funds Donated to Higher Education—L[1]	*332,188	268,588
5. Veterans' Loan Amendment—L[1]	*481,031	133,564
6. Limits Term of Defeated Incumbents—L[1]	*436,897	158,409
7. Constitutional Amendment Authorizing Education Bonds—L[1]	269,372	318,651
8. Allows Penal Institutions Anywhere in Oregon—L[1]	*352,771	260,100
9. Scenic Waterways Bill—I[2]	*406,315	214,243
10. New Property Tax Bases for Schools—I[1]	223,735	405,437
11. Restricts Governmental Powers Over Rural Property—I[1]	272,765	342,503
January 18, 1972 (Special Election)		
1. Increases Cigarette Tax—R	*245,717	236,937
May 23, 1972		
1. Eliminates Literacy Requirement; Lowers Voting Age—L[1]	327,231	349,746
2. Repeals Requirement for Decennial State Census—L[1]	*420,568	206,436
3. Allows Legislators to Call Special Sessions—L[1]	241,371	391,698
4. Capital Construction Bonds for State Government—L[1]	232,391	364,323
5. Irrigation and Water Development Bonds—L[1]	233,175	374,295
6. Enabling County-City Vehicle Registration Tax—R	120,027	491,551

Election Date/Measure Number/Ballot Title	Yes	No
November 7, 1972		
1. Eliminates Location Requirements for State Institutions—L[1]	*594,080	232,948
2. Qualifications for Sheriff Set By Legislature—L[1]	*572,619	281,720
3. Amends County Purchase and Lease Limitations—L[1]	329,669	462,932
4. Changes State Constitution Provision Regarding Religion—L[1]	336,382	519,196
5. Minimum Jury Size of Six Members—L[1]	*591,191	265,636
6. Broadens Eligibility for Veterans' Loans—L[1]	*736,802	133,139
7. Repeals Governor's Retirement Act—I[2]	*571,959	292,561
8. Changes Succession to Office of Governor—I[1]	*697,297	151,174
9. Prohibits Property Tax for School Operations—I[1]	342,885	558,136
May 1, 1973 (Special Election)		
1. Property Tax Limitation; School Tax Revision—L[2]	253,682	358,219
May 28, 1974		
1. Income, Corporate Tax, School Support Increase—L[2]	136,851	410,733
2. Highway Fund Use for Mass Transit—L[1]	190,899	369,038
3. New School District Tax Base Limitation—L[1]	166,363	371,897
4. Authorizes Bonds for Water Development Fund—L[1]	198,563	328,221
5. Increases Veterans' Loan Bonding Authority—L[1]	*381,559	164,953
6. Permits Legislature to Call Special Session—L[1]	246,525	298,373
November 5, 1974		
1. Liquor Licenses for Public Passenger Carriers—L[1]	353,357	384,521
2. Opens All Legislative Deliberations to Public—L[1]	*546,255	165,778
3. Revises Constitutional Requirements for Grand Juries—L[1]	*437,557	246,902
4. Governor Vacancy Successor Age Requirement Eliminated—L[1]	*381,593	331,756
5. The measure designated as Number 5 by the 1973 Legislature was moved to the May 28, 1974 primary election by the 1974 special session. On the advice of the Attorney General, this measure number was left blank.		
6. Permits Establishing Qualifications for County Assessors—L[1]	*552,737	146,364
7. Tax Base Includes Revenue Sharing Money—L[1]	322,023	329,858
8. Revises School District Election Voting Requirements—L[1]	337,565	378,071
9. Permits State Employes to be Legislators—L[1]	218,846	476,547
10. Revises Oregon Voter Qualification Requirements—L[1]	*362,731	355,506
11. Right to Jury in Civil Cases—L[1]	*480,631	216,853
12. Community Development Fund Bonds—L[1]	277,723	376,747
13. Obscenity and Sexual Conduct Bill—R	*393,743	352,958
14. Public Officials' Financial Ethics and Reporting. This measure was also referred to all 36 counties, with 30 voting yes and 6 voting no; and all cities with governing bodies, with 153 voting yes and 90 voting no.—L[2]	*498,002	177,946
15. Prohibits Purchase or Sale of Steelhead—I[2]	*458,417	274,182
May 25, 1976		
1. Expands Veterans' Home-Farm Loan Eligibility—L[1]	*549,553	158,997
2. Discipline of Judges—L[1]	*639,977	59,774
3. Housing Bonds—L[1]	*315,588	362,414
4. Authorizes Vehicle Tax Mass Transit Use—L[1]	170,331	531,219
November 2, 1976		
1. Validates Inadvertently Superseded Statutory Amendments—L[1]	*607,325	247,843
2. Allows Changing City, County Election Days—L[1]	376,489	536,967
3. Lowers Minimum Age for Legislative Service—L[1]	285,777	679,517
4. Repeals Emergency Succession Provision—L[1]	*507,308	368,646
5. Permits Legislature to Call Special Session—L[1]	*549,126	377,354
6. Allows Charitable, Fraternal, Religious Organizations Bingo—L[1]	*682,252	281,696
7. Partial Public Funding of Election Campaigns—L[2]	263,738	659,327
8. Increases Motor Fuel, Ton-Mile Taxes—R	465,143	505,124
9. Regulates Nuclear Power Plant Construction Approval—I[2]	423,008	584,845
10. Repeals Land Use Planning Coordination Statutes—I[2]	402,608	536,502
11. Prohibits Adding Fluorides to Water Systems—I[2]	419,567	555,981
12. Repeals Intergovernmental Cooperation, Planning District Statutes—I[2]	333,933	525,868

Election Date/Measure Number/Ballot Title	Yes	No
May 17, 1977 (Special Election)		
1. School Operating Levy Measure—L[1]	112,570	252,061
2. Authorizes Additional Veterans' Fund Uses—L[1]	*200,270	158,436
3. Increases Veterans' Loan Bonding Authority—L[1]	*250,783	106,953
November 8, 1977 (Special Election)		
1. Water Development Loan Fund Created—L[1]	*124,484	118,953
2. Development of Nonnuclear Energy Resources—L[1]	105,219	137,693
May 23, 1978		
1. Home Rule County Initiative-Referendum Requirements—L[1]	*306,506	156,623
2. Open Meetings Rules for Legislature—L[1]	*435,338	80,176
3. Housing for Low Income Elderly—L[1]	*291,778	250,810
4. Domestic Water Fund Created—L[1]	148,822	351,843
5. Highway Repair Priority, Gas Tax Increase—L[2]	190,301	365,170
6. Reorganizes Metropolitan Service District, Abolishes CRAG—L[2,4]	*110,600	91,090
November 7, 1978		
1. Appellate Judge Selection, Running on Record—L[1]	358,504	449,132
2. Authorizes Senate Confirmation of Governor's Appointments—L[1]	*468,458	349,604
3. Vehicle and Fee Increase Referendum—R	208,722	673,802
4. Shortens Formation Procedures for People's Utility Districts—I[2]	375,587	471,027
5. Authorizes, Regulates Practice of Denture Technology—I[2]	*704,480	201,463
6. Limitations on Ad Valorem Property Taxes—I[1]	424,029	453,741
7. Prohibits State Expenditures, Programs or Services for Abortion—I[1]	431,577	461,542
8. Requires Death Penalty for Murder under Specified Conditions—I[2]	*573,707	318,610
9. Limitations on Public Utility Rate Base—I[2]	*589,361	267,132
10. Land Use Planning, Zoning Constitutional Amendment—I[1]	334,523	515,138
11. Reduces Property Tax Payable by Homeowner and Renter—L[1]	383,532	467,765
12. Support of Constitutional Amendment (Federal) Requires Balance Budget—L[5]	*641,862	134,758
May 20, 1980		
1. Constitutional Amendment Limits Uses of Gasoline and Highway User Taxes—L[1]	*451,695	257,230
2. Amends Liquor by the Drink Constitutional Provision—L[1]	325,030	384,346
3. State Bonds for Small Scale Local Energy Project Loan Fund—L[1]	*394,466	278,125
4. Veterans' Home and Farm Loan Eligibility Changes—L[1]	*574,148	130,452
5. Continues Tax Reduction Program—L[2]	*636,565	64,979
6. Definition of Multifamily Low Income Elderly Housing—L[1]	*536,002	138,675
November 4, 1980		
1. Repeal of Constitutional Provision Requiring Elected Superintendent of Public Instruction—L[1]	291,142	820,892
2. Guarantees Mentally Handicapped Voting Rights, Unless Adjudged Incompetent to Vote—L[1]	*678,573	455,020
3. Dedicates Oil, Natural Gas Taxes to Common School Fund—L[1]	*594,520	500,586
4. Increases Gas Tax from Seven to Nine Cents per Gallon—L[2]	298,421	849,745
5. Forbids Use, Sale of Snare, Leghold Traps for Most Purposes—I[2]	425,890	728,173
6. Constitutional Real Property Tax Limit Preserving 85% Districts' 1977 Revenue—I[1]	416,029	711,617
7. Nuclear Plant Licensing Requires Voter Approval, Waste Disposal Facility Existence—I[2]	*608,412	535,049
8. State Bonds for Fund to Finance Correctional Facilities—L[1]	523,955	551,383
May 18, 1982		
1. Use of State Bond Proceeds to Finance Municipal Water Projects—L[1]	*333,656	267,137
2. Multifamily Housing for Elderly and Disabled Persons—L[1]	*389,820	229,049
3. State Bonds for Fund to Finance Corrections Facilities—L[1]	281,548	333,476
4. Raises Taxes on Commercial Vehicles, Motor Vehicles Fuels for Roads—L[2]	308,574	323,268
5. Governor to Appoint Chief Justice of Oregon Supreme Court—L[2]	159,811	453,415
November 2, 1982		
1. Increases Tax Base When New Property Construction Increases District's Value—L[1]	219,034	768,150

Election Date/Measure Number/Ballot Title	Yes	No
2. Lengthens Governor's Time for Postsession Veto or Approval of Bills—L[1]	385,672	604,864
3. Constitutional Real Property Tax Limit Preserving 85% Districts' 1979 Revenue—I[1]	504,836	515,626
4. Permits Self-Service Dispensing of Motor Vehicle Fuel at Retail—I[2]	440,824	597,970
5. People of Oregon Urge Mutual Freeze on Nuclear Weapons Development—I[3]	*623,089	387,907
6. Ends State's Land Use Planning Powers, Retains Local Planning—I[2]	461,271	565,056
May 15, 1984		
1. State May Borrow and Lend Money for Public Works Projects—L[1]	332,175	365,571
2. Increases Fees for Licensing and Registration of Motor Vehicles—L[2]	234,060	487,457
November 6, 1984		
1. Changes Minimum Requirements for Recall of Public Officers—L[1]	*664,464	470,139
2. Constitutional Real Property Tax Limit—I[1]	599,424	616,252
3. Creates Citizens' Utility Board to Represent Interests of Utility Consumers—I[2]	*637,968	556,826
4. Constitutional Amendment Establishes State Lottery, Commission; Profits for Economic Development—I[1]	*794,441	412,341
5. Statutory Provisions for State Operated Lottery if Constitutionally Authorized—I[2]	*786,933	399,231
6. Exempts Death Sentences from Constitutional Guarantees Against Cruel, Vindictive Punishments—I[1]	*653,009	521,687
7. Requires by Statute Death or Mandatory Imprisonment for Aggravated Murder—I[2]	*893,818	295,988
8. Revises Numerous Criminal Laws Concerning Police Powers, Trials, Evidence, Sentencing—I[2]	552,410	597,964
9. Adds Requirements for Disposing Wastes Containing Naturally Occurring Radioactive Isotopes—I[2]	*655,973	524,214
September 17, 1985 (Special Election)		
1. Amends Constitution. Approves Limited 5% Sales Tax for Local Education—L[1]	189,733	664,365
May 20, 1986		
1. Constitutional Amendment: Bans Income Tax on Social Security Benefits—L[1]	*534,476	118,766
2. Constitutional Amendment: Effect on Merger of Taxing Units on Tax Base—L[1]	*333,277	230,886
3. Constitutional Amendment: Verification of Signatures on Initiative and Referendum Petitions—L[1]	*460,148	132,101
4. Requires Special Election for U.S. Senator Vacancy, Removes Constitutional Provision—L[1]	*343,005	269,305
5. Constitutional Amendment: $96 Million Bonds for State-County Prison Buildings—L[1]	300,674	330,429
November 4, 1986		
1. Deletes Constitutional Requirement that Secretary of State Live in Salem—L[1]	*771,959	265,999
2. Constitutional Amendment Revising Legislative District Reapportionment Procedures After Federal Census—L[1]	*637,410	291,355
3. Constitutional Amendment Allows Charitable, Fraternal, Religious Organizations to Conduct Raffles—L[1]	*736,739	302,957
4. Replaces Public Utility Commissioner with Three Member Public Utility Commission—L[2]	*724,577	297,973
5. Legalizes Private Possession and Growing of Marijuana for Personal Use—I[2]	279,479	781,922
6. Constitutional Amendment Prohibits State Funding Abortions. Exception: Prevent Mother's Death—I[1]	477,920	580,163
7. Constitutional 5% Sales Tax, Funds Schools, Reduces Property Tax—I[1]	234,804	816,369
8. Prohibits Mandatory Local Measured Telephone Service Except Mobile Phone Service—I[2]	*802,099	201,918

Election Date/Measure Number/Ballot Title	Yes	No
9. Amends Constitution. Limits Property Tax Rates and Assessed Value Increases—I[1]	449,548	584,396
10. Revises Many Criminal Laws Concerning Victims' Rights, Evidence, Sentencing, Parole—I[2]	*774,766	251,509
11. Homeowner's, Renter's Property Tax Relief Program; Sales Tax Limitation Measure—I[1]	381,727	639,034
12. State Income Tax Changes, Increased Revenue to Property Tax Relief—I[2]	299,551	720,034
13. Constitutional Amendment: Twenty Day Pre-election Voter Registration Cutoff—I[1]	*693,460	343,450
14. Prohibits Nuclear Power Plant Operation Until Permanent Waste Site Licensed—I[2]	375,241	674,641
15. Supersedes "Radioactive Waste" Definition; Changes Energy Facility Payment Procedure—I[2]	424,099	558,741
16. Phases Out Nuclear Weapons Manufactured With Tax Credits, Civil Penalty—I[2]	400,119	590,971

May 19, 1987 (Special Election)

	Yes	No
1. State Role In Selection of High-Level Nuclear Waste Repository Site—L[2]	*299,581	100,854
2. Continues Existing Levies To Prevent School Closures: Tax Base Elections—L[1]	*223,417	178,839

May 17, 1988

	Yes	No
1. Authorizes Water Development Fund Loans for Fish Protection, Watershed Restoration—L[1]	*485,629	191,008
2. Protective Headgear for Motorcycle Operators and Passengers and Moped Riders—L[2]	*486,401	224,655

November 8, 1988

	Yes	No
1. Extends Governor's Veto Deadline After Legislature Adjourns; Requires Prior Announcement—L[1]	*615,012	520,939
2. Common School Fund Investments; Using Income for State Lands Management—L[1]	*621,894	510,694
3. Requires the Use of Safety Belts—L[2]	528,324	684,747
4. Requires Full Sentences Without Parole, Probation for Certain Repeat Felonies—I[2]	*947,805	252,985
5. Finances Intercollegiate Athletic Fund by Increasing Malt Beverage, Cigarette Taxes—I[2]	449,797	759,360
6. Indoor Clean Air Law Revisions Banning Public Smoking—I[2]	430,147	737,779
7. Oregon Scenic Waterway System—I[2]	*663,604	516,998
8. Revokes Ban on Sexual Orientation Discrimination in State Executive Branch—I[2]	*626,751	561,355

May 16, 1989 (Special Election)

	Yes	No
1. Establishes New Tax Base Limits on Schools—L[1]	183,818	263,283

June 27, 1989 (Special Election)

	Yes	No
1. Removes Constitutional Limitation on Use of Property Forfeited To State—L[1]	*340,506	141,649
2. Prohibits Selling/Exporting Timber from State Lands Unless Oregon Processed—L[1]	*446,151	48,558

May 15, 1990

	Yes	No
1. Permits Using Local Vehicle Taxes for Transit if Voters Approve—L[1]	294,099	324,458
2. Amends Constitution; Allows Pollution Control Bond Use for Related Activities—L[1]	*352,922	248,123
3. Amends State Constitution; Requires Annual Legislative Sessions of Limited Duration—L[1]	294,664	299,831
4. Amends Laws on Organization of International Port of Coos Bay—L[2]	4,234	4,745
5A. Advisory Vote: Changing the School Finance System—L[5]	*462,090	140,747
5B. Advisory Vote: Income Tax Increase Reducing Homeowner School Property Taxes—L[5]	177,964	408,842
5C. Advisory Vote: Income Tax Increase Eliminating Homeowner School Property Taxes—L[5]	128,642	449,725

Election Date/Measure Number/Ballot Title	Yes	No
5D. Advisory Vote: Sales Tax Reducing School Property Taxes—L[5]	202,367	385,820
5E. Advisory Vote: Sales Tax Eliminating School Property Taxes—L[5]	222,611	374,466
November 6, 1990		
1. Grants Metropolitan Service District Electors Right to Home Rule—L[1]	*510,947	491,170
2. Constitutional Amendment Allows Merged School Districts to Combine Tax Bases—L[1]	*680,463	354,288
3. Repeals Tax Exemption, Grants Additional Benefit Payments for PERS Retirees—R	406,372	617,586
4. Prohibits Trojan Operation Until Nuclear Waste, Cost, Earthquake Standards Met—I[2]	446,795	660,992
5. State Constitutional Limit on Property Taxes for Schools, Government Operations—I[1]	*574,833	522,022
6. Product Packaging Must Meet Recycling Standards or Receive Hardship Waiver—I[2]	467,418	636,804
7. Six-County Work in Lieu of Welfare Benefits Pilot Program—I[2]	*624,744	452,853
8. Amends Oregon Constitution to Prohibit Abortion With Three Exceptions—I[1]	355,963	747,599
9. Requires the Use of Safety Belts—I[2]	*598,460	512,872
10. Doctor Must Give Parent Notice Before Minor's Abortion—I[2]	530,851	577,806
11. School Choice System, Tax Credit for Education Outside Public Schools—I[1]	351,977	741,863
May 19, 1992		
1. Amends Constitution: Future Fuel Taxes May Go to Police—L[1]	244,173	451,715
November 3, 1992		
1. Bonds May be Issued for State Parks—L[1]	653,062	786,017
2. Future Fuel Taxes May Go to Parks—L[1]	399,259	1,039,322
3. Limits Terms for Legislature, Statewide Offices, Congressional Offices—I[1]	*1,003,706	439,694
4. Bans Operation of Triple Truck-Trailer Combinations on Oregon Highways—I[2]	567,467	896,778
5. Closes Trojan Until Nuclear Waste, Cost, Earthquake, Health Conditions Met—I[2]	585,051	874,636
6. Bans Trojan Power Operation Unless Earthquake, Waste Storage Conditions Met—I[2]	619,329	830,850
7. Raises Tax Limit on Certain Property; Residential Renters' Tax Relief—I[1]	362,621	1,077,206
8. Restricts Lower Columbia Fish Harvests to Most Selective Means Available—I[2]	576,633	828,096
9. Government Cannot Facilitate, Must Discourage Homosexuality, Other "Behaviors"—I[1]	638,527	828,290
June 29, 1993 (Special Election)		
1. Allows Voter Approval of Urban Renewal Bond Repayment Outside Limit—L[1]	180,070	482,714
November 9, 1993 (Special Election)		
1. Should We Pass A 5% Sales Tax for Public Schools with these Restrictions?—L[1]	240,991	721,930
May 17, 1994		
2. Allows New Motor Vehicle Fuel Revenues for Dedicated Purposes—L[1]	158,028	446,665
November 8, 1994		
3. Amends Constitution: Changes Deadline for Filling Vacancies at General Election—L[1]	*776,197	382,126
4. Amends Constitution: Creates Vacancy if State Legislator Convicted of Felony—L[1]	*1,055,111	145,499
5. Amends Constitution: Bars New or Increased Taxes without Voter Approval—I[1]	543,302	671,025
6. Amends Constitution: Candidates May Use Only Contributions from District Residents—I[1]	*628,180	555,019
7. Amends Constitution: Guarantees Equal Protection: Lists Prohibited Grounds of Discrimination—I[1]	512,980	671,021

Election Date/Measure Number/Ballot Title	Yes	No
8. Amends Constitution: Public Employees Pay Part of Salary for Pension—I[1]	*611,760	610,776
9. Adopts Contribution and Spending Limits, Other Campaign Finance Law Changes—I[2]	*851,014	324,224
10. Amends Constitution: Legislature Cannot Reduce Voter-Approved Sentence Without 2/3 Vote—I[1]	*763,507	415,678
11. Mandatory Sentences for Listed Felonies; Covers Persons 15 and Up—I[2]	*788,695	412,816
12. Repeals Prevailing Rate Wage Requirement for Workers on Public Works—I[2]	450,553	731,146
13. Amends Constitution: Governments Cannot Approve, Create Classifications Based on, Homosexuality—I[1]	592,746	630,628
14. Amends Chemical Process Mining Laws: Adds Requirements, Prohibitions, Standards, Fees—I[1]	500,005	679,936
15. Amends Constitution: State Must Maintain Funding for Schools, Community Colleges—I[1]	438,018	760,853
16. Allows Terminally Ill Adults to Obtain Prescription for Lethal Drugs—I[2]	*627,980	596,018
17. Amends Constitution: Requires State Prison Inmates to Work Full Time—I[1]	*859,896	350,541
18. Bans Hunting Bears with Bait, Hunting Bears, Cougars with Dogs—I[2]	*629,527	586,026
19. Amends Constitution: No Free Speech Protection for Obscenity, Child Pornography—I[1]	549,754	652,139
20. Amends Constitution: "Equal Tax" on Trade Replaces Current Taxes—I[1]	284,195	898,416

May 16, 1995 (Special Election)

21. Dedication of Lottery Funds to Education—L[1]	*671,027	99,728
22. Inhabitancy in State Legislative Districts—L[1]	*709,931	45,311

May 21, 1996

23. Amends Constitution: Increases Minimum Value in Controversy Required to Obtain Jury Trial—L[1]	*466,580	177,218
24. Amends Constitution: Initiative Petition Signatures Must Be Collected From Each Congressional District—L[1]	279,399	360,592
25. Amends Constitution: Requires 3/5 Majority in Legislature to Pass Revenue-Raising Bills—L[1]	*349,918	289,930

November 5, 1996

26. Amends Constitution: Changes the Principles that Govern Laws for Punishment of Crime—L[1]	*878,677	440,283
27. Amends Constitution: Grants Legislature New Power Over Both New, Existing Administrative Rules—L[1]	349,050	938,819
28. Amends Constitution: Repeals Certain Residency Requirements for State Veterans' Loans—L[1]	*708,341	593,136
29. Amends Constitution: Governor's Appointees Must Vacate Office If Successor Not Timely Confirmed—L[1]	335,057	958,947
30. Amends Constitution: State Must Pay Local Governments Costs of State-Mandated Programs—L[1]	*731,127	566,168
31. Amends Constitution: Obscenity May Receive No Greater Protection Than Under Federal Constitution—L[1]	630,980	706,974
32. Authorizes Bonds for Portland Region Light Rail, Transportation Projects Elsewhere—R[2]	622,764	704,970
33. Amends Constitution: Limits Legislative Change to Statutes Passed by Voters—I[1]	638,824	652,811
34. Wildlife Management Exclusive to Commission; Repeals 1994 Bear/Cougar Initiative—I[2]	570,803	762,979
35. Restricts Bases for Providers to Receive Pay for Health Care—I[2]	441,108	807,987
36. Increases Minimum Hourly Wage to $6.50 Over Three Years—I[2]	*769,725	584,303
37. Broadens Types of Beverage Containers Requiring Deposit and Refund Value—I[2]	540,645	818,336
38. Prohibits Livestock in Certain Polluted Waters or on Adjacent Lands—I[2]	479,921	852,661
39. Amends Constitution: Government, Private Entities Cannot Discriminate Among Health Care Provider Categories—I[1]	569,037	726,824

Election Date/Measure Number/Ballot Title	Yes	No
40. Amends Constitution: Gives Crime Victims Rights, Expands Admissible Evidence, Limits Pretrial Release—I[1]	*778,574	544,301
41. Amends Constitution: States How Public Employee Earnings Must Be Expressed—I[1]	446,115	838,088
42. Amends Constitution: Requires Testing of Public School Students; Public Report—I[1]	460,553	857,878
43. Amends Collective Bargaining Law for Public Safety Employees—I[2]	547,131	707,586
44. Increases, Adds Cigarette and Tobacco Taxes; Changes Tax Revenue Distribution—I[2]	*759,048	598,543
45. Amends Constitution: Raises Public Employees' Normal Retirement Age; Reduces Benefits—I[1]	458,238	866,461
46. Amends Constitution: Counts Non-Voters As "No" Votes on Tax Measures—I[1]	158,555	1,180,148
47. Amends Constitution: Reduces and Limits Property Taxes; Limits Local Revenues, Replacement Fees—I[1]	*704,554	642,613
48. Amends Constitution: Instructs State, Federal Legislators to Vote for Congressional Term Limits—I[1,3]	624,771	671,095
May 20, 1997 (Special Election)		
49. Amends Constitution: Restricts Inmate Lawsuits; Allows Interstate Shipment of Prison Made Products—L[1]	*699,813	70,940
50. Amends Constitution: Limits Assessed Value of Property for Tax Purposes; Limits Property Tax Rates—L[1]	*429,943	341,781
November 4, 1997 (Special Election)		
51. Repeals Law Allowing Terminally Ill Adults To Obtain Lethal Prescription—L[2]	445,830	666,275
52. Authorizes State Lottery Bond Program To Finance Public School Projects—L[2]	*805,742	293,425
May 19, 1998		
53. Amends Constitution: Eliminates Voter Turnout Requirement For Passing Certain Property Tax Measures—L[1]	303,539	319,871
November 3, 1998		
54. Amends Constitution: Authorizes State To Guarantee Bonded Indebtedness Of Certain Education Districts—L[1]	*569,982	474,727
55. Amends Constitution: Permits State To Guarantee Earnings On Prepaid Tuition Trust Fund—L[1]	456,464	579,251
56. Expands Notice To Landowners Regarding Changes To Land Use Laws—L[2]	*874,547	212,737
57. Makes Possession Of Limited Amount Of Marijuana Class C Misdemeanor—R[2]	371,967	736,968
58. Requires Issuing Copy Of Original Oregon Birth Certificate to Adoptees—I[2]	*621,832	462,084
59. Amends Constitution: Prohibits Using Public Resources To Collect Money For Political Purposes—I[1]	539,757	561,952
60. Requires Vote By Mail In Biennial Primary, General Elections—I[2]	*757,204	334,021
61. Vote Not Tallied By Court Order		
62. Amends Constitution: Requires Campaign Finance Disclosures; Regulates Signature Gathering; Guarantees Contribution Methods—I[1]	*721,448	347,112
63. Amends Constitution: Measures Proposing Supermajority Voting Requirements Require Same Supermajority For Passage—I[1]	*566,064	457,762
64. Prohibits Many Present Timber Harvest Practices, Imposes More Restrictive Regulations—I[2]	215,491	897,535
65. Amends Constitution: Creates Process For Requiring Legislature To Review Administrative Rules—I[1]	483,811	533,948
66. Amends Constitution: Dedicates Some Lottery Funding To Parks, Beaches; Habitat, Watershed Protection—I[1]	*742,038	362,247
67. Allows Medical Use Of Marijuana Within Limits; Establishes Permit System—I[2]	*611,190	508,263
November 2, 1999 (Special Election)		
68. Amends Constitution: Allows Protecting Business, Certain Government Programs From Prison Work Programs—L[1]	*406,526	289,407

Elections and Records

Election Date/Measure Number/Ballot Title	Yes	No
69. Amends Constitution: Grants Victims Constitutional Rights In Criminal Prosecutions, Juvenile Court Delinquency Proceedings—L[1]	*406,393	292,419
70. Amends Constitution: Gives Public, Through Prosecutor, Right To Demand Jury Trial In Criminal Cases—L[1]	289,783	407,429
71. Amends Constitution: Limits Pretrial Release Of Accused Person To Protect Victims, Public—L[1]	*404,404	292,696
72. Amends Constitution: Allows Murder Conviction By 11 To 1 Jury Verdict—L[1]	316,351	382,685
73. Amends Constitution: Limits Immunity From Criminal Prosecution Of Person Ordered To Testify About His Or Her Conduct—L[1]	320,160	369,843
74. Amends Constitution: Requires Terms Of Imprisonment Announced In Court Be Fully Served, With Exceptions—L[1]	*368,899	325,078
75. Amends Constitution: Persons Convicted Of Certain Crimes Cannot Serve On Grand Juries, Criminal Trial Juries—L[1]	*399,671	292,445
76. Amends Constitution: Requires Light, Heavy Motor Vehicle Classes Proportionately Share Highway Costs—L[1]	*372,613	314,351
May 16, 2000		
77. Amends Constitution: Makes Certain Local Taxing Districts' Temporary Property Tax Authority Permanent—L[1]	336,253	432,541
78. Amends Constitution: Lengthens Period For Verifying Signatures On Initiative And Referendum Petitions—L[1]	*528,129	327,440
79. Amends Constitution: Increases Signatures Required To Place Initiative Amending Constitution On Ballot—L[1]	356,912	505,081
80. Amends Constitution: Authorizes Using Fuel Tax, Vehicle Fees For Increasing Highway Policing—L[1]	310,640	559,941
81. Amends Constitution: Allows Legislature To Limit Recovery Of Damages In Civil Actions—L[1]	219,009	650,348
82. Repeals Truck Weight-Mile Tax; Establishes And Increases Fuel Taxes—R[2]	109,741	767,329
November 7, 2000		
83. Amends Constitution: Authorizes New Standards, Priorities For Veterans' Loans; Expands Qualified Recipients—L[1]	*1,084,870	365,203
84. Amends Constitution: State Must Continue Paying Local Governments For State-Mandated Programs—L[1]	*1,211,384	222,723
85. Amends Constitution: Modifies Population, Minimum Area Requirements For Formation Of New Counties—L[1]	634,307	767,366
86. Amends Constitution: Requires Refunding General Fund Revenues Exceeding State Estimates To Taxpayers—L[1]	*898,793	550,304
87. Amends Constitution: Allows Regulation Of Location Of Sexually Oriented Businesses Through Zoning—L[1]	694,410	771,901
88. Increases Maximum Deductible In Oregon For Federal Income Taxes Paid—L[2]	*739,270	724,097
89. Dedicates Tobacco Settlement Proceeds To Specified Health, Housing, Transportation Programs—L[2]	622,814	828,117
90. Authorizes Rates Giving Utilities Return On Investments In Retired Property—R[2]	158,810	1,208,545
91. Amends Constitution: Makes Federal Income Taxes Fully Deductible On Oregon Tax Returns—I[1]	661,342	814,885
92. Amends Constitution: Prohibits Payroll Deductions For Political Purposes Without Specific Written Authorization—I[1]	656,250	815,338
93. Amends Constitution: Voters Must Approve Most Taxes, Fees; Requires Certain Approval Percentage—I[1]	581,186	865,091
94. Repeals Mandatory Minimum Sentences For Certain Felonies, Requires Resentencing—I[2]	387,068	1,073,275
95. Amends Constitution: Student Learning Determines Teacher Pay; Qualifications, Not Seniority, Determine Retention—I[1]	514,926	962,250
96. Amends Constitution: Prohibits Making Initiative Process Harder, Except Through Initiative; Applies Retroactively—I[1]	527,613	866,588
97. Bans Body-Gripping Animal Traps, Some Poisons; Restricts Fur Commerce—I[2]	606,939	867,219

Election Date/Measure Number/Ballot Title	Yes	No
98. Amends Constitution: Prohibits Using Public Resources For Political Purposes; Limits Payroll Deductions—I[1]	678,024	776,489
99. Amends Constitution: Creates Commission Ensuring Quality Home Care Services For Elderly, Disabled—I[1]	*911,217	539,414
1. Amends Constitution: Legislature Must Fund School Quality Goals Adequately; Report; Establish Grants—I[1]	*940,223	477,461
2. Amends Constitution: Creates Process For Requiring Legislature To Review Administrative Rules—I[1]	605,575	779,190
3. Amends Constitution: Requires Conviction Before Forfeiture; Restricts Proceeds Usage; Requires Reporting, Penalty—I[1]	*952,792	465,081
4. Dedicates Tobacco-Settlement Proceeds; Earnings Fund Low-Income Health Care—I[2]	650,850	789,543
5. Expands Circumstances Requiring Background Checks Before Transfer Of Firearm—I[2]	*921,926	569,996
6. Provides Public Funding To Candidates Who Limit Spending, Private Contributions—I[2]	586,910	838,011
7. The Secretary of State has been enjoined from canvassing the votes for this measure—I[1]		
8. Amends Constitution: Limits State Appropriations To Percentage Of State's Prior Personal Income—I[1]	608,090	789,699
9. Prohibits Public School Instruction Encouraging, Promoting, Sanctioning Homosexual, Bisexual Behaviors—I[2]	702,572	788,691
May 21, 2002		
10. Amends Constitution: Allows Public Universities to Receive Equity in Private Companies as Compensation for Publicly Created Technology—L[1]	*608,640	177,004
11. Amends Constitution: Authorizes Less Expensive General Obligation Bond financing for OHSU Medical Research and other Capital Costs—L[1]	*589,869	190,226
12. Removed from Ballot		
13. Amends Constitution: Authorizes Using Education Fund Principal in Specified Circumstances; Transfers $220 Million to School Fund—L[1]	376,605	411,923
September 17, 2002 (Special Election, see Note below)		
19. Amends Constitution: Authorizes Using Education Stability Fund Principal in Specified Circumstances; Transfers $150 Million to State School Fund; Creates School Capital Matching Subaccount in Stability Fund—L[1]	*496,815	306,440
20. Increases Cigarette Tax; Uses Revenue for Health Plan, Other Programs—L[2]	*522,613	289,119
November 5, 2002		
14. Amends Constitution: Removes Historical Racial References in Obsolete Sections of Constitution—L[1]	*867,901	352,027
15. Amends Constitution: Authorizes State to Issue General Obligation Bonds for Seismic Rehabilitation of Public Education Buildings—L[1]	*671,640	535,638
16. Amends Constitution: Authorizes State to Issue General Obligation Bonds for Seismic Rehabilitation of Emergency Services Buildings—L[1]	*669,451	530,587
17. Amends Constitution: Reduces Minimum Age Requirement to Serve as State Legislator from 21 Years to 18 Years—L[1]	341,717	910,331
18. Allows Certain Tax Districts to Establish Permanent Property Tax Rates and Divide into Tax Zones—L[1]	450,444	704,116
Note: An early Special Election was held for Measures 19 and 20 (see above)		
21. Amends Constitution: Revises Procedure for Filling Judicial Vacancies, Electing Judges; Allows Vote for "None of the Above"—I[1]	526,450	668,256
22. Amends Constitution: Requires Supreme Court Judges and Court of Appeals Judges to be Elected by District—I[1]	595,936	610,063
23. Creates Health Care Finance Plan for Medically Necessary Services; Creates Additional Income, Payroll Taxes—I[2]	265,310	969,537
24. Allows Licensed Denturists to Install Partial Dentures; Authorizes Cooperative Dentist-Denturist Business Ventures—I[2]	*907,979	286,492
25. Increases Minimum Wage to $6.90 in 2003; Increases for Inflation in Future Years—I[2]	*645,016	611,658
26. Amends Constitution: Prohibits Payment, Receipt of Payment Based on the Number of Initiative, Referendum Petition Signatures Obtained—I[1]	*921,606	301,415

Elections and Records

Election Date/Measure Number/Ballot Title	Yes	No
27. Requires Labeling of Genetically-Engineered Foods Sold or Distributed in or from Oregon—I[2]	371,851	886,806
January 28, 2003 (Special Election)		
28. Temporarily Increases Income Tax Rates—L[2]	575,846	676,312
September 16, 2003 (Special Election)		
29. Amends Constitution: Authorizes State of Oregon to Incur General Obligation Debt for Savings on Pension Liabilities—L[1]	*360,209	291,778
February 3, 2004 (Special Election)		
30. Enacts Temporary Personal Income Tax Surcharge; Increases, Changes Corporate, Other Taxes; Avoids Specific Budget Cuts—R[2]	481,315	691,462
November 2, 2004		
31. Amends Constitution: Authorizes Law Permitting Postponement of Election for Particular Public Office When Nominee for Office Dies—L[1]	*1,122,852	588,502
32. Amends Constitution: Deletes Reference to Mobile Homes from Provision Dealing with Taxes and Fees on Motor Vehicles—L[1]	*1,048,090	661,576
33. Amends Medical Marijuana Act: Requires Marijuana Dispensaries for Supplying Patients/Caregivers; Raises Patients' Possession Limit—I[2]	764,015	1,021,814
34. Requires Balancing Timber Production, Resource Conservation/Preservation in Managing State Forests; Specifically Addresses Two Forests—I[2]	659,467	1,060,496
35. Amends Constitution: Limits Noneconomic Damages (Defined) Recoverable for Patient Injuries Caused by Healthcare Provider's Negligence or Recklessness—I[1]	869,054	896,857
36. Amends Constitution: Only Marriage Between One Man and One Woman Is Valid or Legally Recognized as Marriage—I[1]	*1,028,546	787,556
37. Governments Must Pay Owners, or Forgo Enforcement, when Certain Land Use Restrictions Reduce Property Value—I[2]	*1,054,589	685,079
38. Abolishes SAIF; State Must Reinsure, Satisfy SAIF's Obligations; Dedicates Proceeds, Potential Surplus to Public Purposes—I[2]	670,935	1,037,722
November 7, 2006		
39. Prohibits Public Body from Condemning Private Real Property If Intends to Convey to Private Party—I[2]	*881,820	431,844
40. Amends Constitution: Requires Oregon Supreme Court Judges and Court of Appeals Judges To Be Elected by District—I[1]	576,153	749,404
41. Allows Income Tax Deduction Equal to Federal Exemptions Deduction to Substitute for State Exemption Credit—I[2]	483,443	818,452
42. Prohibits Insurance Companies from Using Credit Score or "Credit Worthiness" in Calculating Rates or Premiums—I[2]	479,935	876,075
43. Requires 48-Hour Notice to Unemancipated Minor's Parent Before Providing Abortion; Authorizes Lawsuits, Physician Discipline—I[2]	616,876	746,606
44. Allows Any Oregon Resident Without Prescription Drug Coverage to Participate in Oregon Prescription Drug Program—I[2]	*1,049,594	296,649
45. Amends Constitution: Limits State Legislators: Six Years as Representative, Eight Years as Senator, Fourteen Years in Legislature—I[1]	555,016	788,895
46. Amends Constitution: Allows Laws Regulating Election Contributions, Expenditures Adopted by Initiative or 3/4 of Both Legislative Houses—I[1]	520,342	770,251
47. Revises Campaign Finance Laws: Limits or Prohibits Contributions and Expenditures; Adds Disclosure, New Reporting Requirements—I[2]	*694,918	615,256
48. Amends Constitution: Limits Biennial Percentage Increase in State Spending to Percentage Increase in State Population, Plus Inflation—I[1]	379,971	923,629
November 6, 2007 (Special Election)		
49. Modifies Measure 37: Clarifies Right to Build Homes; Limits Large Developments; Protects Farms, Forests, Groundwater—L[2]	*718,023	437,351
50. Amends Constitution: Dedicates Funds to Provide Health Care for Children, Fund Tobacco Prevention, Through Increased Tobacco Tax—L[1]	472,063	686,470
May 20, 2008		
51. Amends Constitution: Enables Crime Victims to Enforce Existing Constitutional Rights in Prosecutions, Delinquency Proceedings; Authorizes Implementing Legislation—L[1]	*744,195	249,143

Election Date/Measure Number/Ballot Title	Yes	No
52. Amends Constitution: Enables Crime Victims to Enforce Existing Constitutional Rights in Prosecutions, Delinquency Proceedings; Authorizes Implementing Legislation—L[1]	*738,092	247,738
53. Amends Constitution: Modifies Provisions Governing Civil Forfeitures Related to Crimes; Permits Use of Proceeds by Law Enforcement—L[1]	*490,158	489,477
November 4, 2008		
54. Amends Constitution: Standardizes Voting Eligibility for School Board Elections with Other State and Local Elections—L[1]	*1,194,173	450,979
55. Amends Constitution: Changes Operative Date of Redistricting Plans; Allows Affected Legislators to Finish Term in Original District—L[1]	*1,251,478	364,993
56. Amends Constitution: Provides that May and November Property Tax Elections are Decided by Majority of Voters Voting—L[1]	*959,118	735,500
57. Increases Sentences for Drug Trafficking, Theft Against Elderly and Specified Repeat Property and Identity Theft Crimes; Requires Addiction Treatment for Certain Offenders—L[2]	*1,058,955	665,942
58. Prohibits Teaching Public School Student in Language Other Than English for More Than Two Years—I[2]	756,903	977,696
59. Creates an Unlimited Deduction for Federal Income Taxes on Individual Taxpayers' Oregon Income-Tax Returns—I[2]	615,894	1,084,422
60. Teacher "Classroom Performance," Not Seniority, Determines Pay Raises; "Most Qualified" Teachers Retained, Regardless of Seniority—I[2]	673,296	1,070,682
61. Creates Mandatory Minimum Prison Sentences for Certain Theft, Identity Theft, Forgery, Drug, and Burglary Crimes—I[2]	848,901	887,165
62. Amends Constitution: Allocates 15% of Lottery Proceeds to Public Safety Fund for Crime Prevention, Investigation, Prosecution—I[2]	674,428	1,035,756
63. Exempts Specified Property Owners From Building Permit Requirements for Improvements Valued At/Under 35,000 Dollars—I[2]	784,376	928,721
64. Penalizes Person, Entity for Using Funds Collected with "Public Resource" (Defined) for "Political Purpose"—I[2]	835,563	854,327
65. Changes General Election Nomination Processes for Major/Minor Party, Independent Candidates for Most Partisan Offices—I[2]	553,640	1,070,580
January 26, 2010 (Special Election)		
66. Raises tax on household income at and above $250,000 (and $125,000 for individual filers). Reduces income taxes on unemployment benefits in 2009. Provides funds currently budgeted for education, health care, public safety, other services—R[2]	*692,687	583,707
67. Raises $10 corporate minimum tax, business minimum tax, corporate profits tax. Provides funds currently budgeted for education, health care, public safety, other services—R[2]	*682,720	591,188
May 18, 2010		
68. Revises Constitution: Allows State To Issue Bonds To Match Voter Approved School District Bonds For School Capital Costs—L[1]	*498,073	267,052
69. Amends Constitution: Continues And Modernizes Authority For Lowest Cost Borrowing For Community Colleges And Public Universities—L[1]	*546,649	216,157
November 2, 2010		
70. Amends Constitution: Expands availability of home ownership loans for Oregon veterans through Oregon War Veterans' Fund—L[1]	*1,180,933	217,679
71. Amends Constitution: Requires legislature to meet annually; limits length of legislative sessions; provides exceptions—L[1]	*919,040	435,776
72. Amends Constitution: Authorizes exception to $50,000 state borrowing limit for state's real and personal property projects—L[1]	*774,582	536,204
73. Requires increased minimum sentences for certain repeated sex crimes, incarceration for repeated driving under influence—I[2]	*802,388	608,317
74. Establishes medical marijuana supply system and assistance and research programs; allows limited selling of marijuana—I[2]	627,016	791,186
75. Authorizes Multnomah County casino; casino to contribute monthly revenue percentage to state for specified purposes—I[2]	448,162	959,342
76. Amends Constitution: Continues lottery funding for parks, beaches, wildlife habitat, watershed protection beyond 2014; modifies funding process—I[1]	*972,825	432,552

Election Date/Measure Number/Ballot Title	Yes	No
November 6, 2012		
77. Amends Constitution: Governor may declare "catastrophic disaster" (defined); requires legislative session; authorizes suspending specified constitutional spending restrictions—L[1]	*957,646	673,468
78. Amends Constitution: Changes constitutional language describing governmental system of separation of powers; makes grammatical and spelling changes—L[1]	*1,165,963	458,509
79. Amends Constitution: Prohibits real estate transfer taxes, fees, other assessments, except those operative on December 31, 2009—I[1]	*976,587	679,710
80. Allows personal marijuana, hemp cultivation/use without license; commission to regulate commercial marijuana cultivation/sale—I[2]	810,538	923,071
81. Prohibits commercial non-tribal fishing with gillnets in Oregon "inland waters," allows use of seine nets—I[2]	567,996	1,072,614
82. Amends Constitution: Authorizes establishment of privately-owned casinos; mandates percentage of revenues payable to dedicated state fund—I[1]	485,240	1,226,331
83. Authorizes privately-owned Wood Village casino; mandates percentage of revenues payable to dedicated state fund—I[2]	500,123	1,207,508
84. Phases out existing inheritance taxes on large estates, and all taxes on intra-family property transfers—I[2]	776,143	912,541
85. Amends Constitution: Allocates corporate income/excise tax "kicker" refund to additionally fund K through 12 public education—I[1]	*1,007,122	672,586
November 4, 2014		
86. Amends Constitution: Requires creation of fund for Oregonians pursuing post-secondary education, authorizes state indebtedness to finance fund—L[1]	614,439	821,596
87. Amends Constitution: Permits employment of state judges by National Guard (military service) and state public universities (teaching)—L[1]	*817,709	600,015
88. Provides Oregon resident "driver card" without requiring proof of legal presence in the United States—R[2]	506,751	983,576
89. Amends Constitution: State/political subdivision shall not deny or abridge equality of rights on account of sex—I[1]	*925,892	514,907
90. Changes general election nomination processes: provides for single primary ballot listing candidates; top two advance—I[2]	459,629	987,050
91. Allows possession, manufacture, sale of marijuana by/to adults, subject to state licensing, regulation, taxation—I[2]	*847,865	663,346
92. Requires food manufacturers, retailers to label "genetically engineered" foods as such; state, citizens may enforce—I[2]	752,737	753,574
May 17, 2016		
93. Majority yes vote disincorporates City of Damascus; property to Clackamas County, net assets to taxpayers—I[6]	*2,834	1,400
November 8, 2016		
94. Amends Constitution: Eliminates mandatory retirement age for state judges—L[1]	699,689	1,194,167
95. Amends Constitution: Allows investments in equities by public universities to reduce financial risk and increase investments to benefit students—L[1]	*1,301,183	546,919
96. Amends Constitution: Dedicates 1.5% of state lottery net proceeds to funding support services for Oregon veterans—L[1]	*1,611,367	312,526
97. Increases corporate minimum tax when sales exceed $25 million; funds education, healthcare, senior services—I[2]	808,310	1,164,658
98. Requires state funding for dropout-prevention, career and college readiness programs in Oregon high schools—I[2]	*1,260,163	650,347
99. Creates "Outdoor School Education Fund," continuously funded through Lottery, to provide outdoor school programs statewide—I[2]	*1,287,095	630,735
100. Prohibits purchase or sale of parts or products from certain wildlife species; exceptions; civil penalties—I[2]	*1,306,213	574,631

[0]Repeal of federal prohibition amendment
[1]Constitutional amendment
[2]Statutory enactment
[3]Required communication to federal officials on behalf of people of Oregon

[4]Tri-county measure voted on in Clackamas, Multnomah and Washington Counties
[5]Advisory vote for legislators' information
[6]Voted on in Clackamas County

Earliest Authorities in Oregon

Pacific Fur Company*
Fort Astoria

Name	Term of Service	By What Authority/Remarks
McDougall, Duncan	Mar. 22, 1811–Feb. 15, 1812 Aug. 4, 1812–Aug. 20, 1813 Aug. 26, 1813–Oct. 16, 1813	Acting agent and partner; served in absence of Wilson Price Hunt by agreement with partners
Hunt, Wilson Price	Feb. 15, 1812–Aug. 4, 1812 Aug. 20, 1813–Aug. 26, 1813	Agent and partner by Articles of Agreement, June 23, 1810, Article 21

*Sold to John George McTavish and John Stuart, partners of the North West Company, Oct. 16, 1813; sale confirmed by Wilson Price Hunt, agent, March 10, 1814

North West Company
Headquarters, Columbia District, Fort George (Astoria)

McTavish, John George	Oct. 16, 1813–Dec. 1, 1813	Acting governor and partner
McDonald, John (of Garth)	Dec. 1, 1813–Apr. 4, 1814	Governor and partner, Alexander Henry, trader
McTavish, Donald	Apr. 23, 1814–May 22, 1814	Governor and partner; with Alexander Henry, drowned in the Columbia River
Keith, James	May 22, 1814–June 7, 1816	Acting governor and partner

Chief of the Coast	Term of Service	Chief of the Interior
Keith, James	June 7, 1816–Mar. 21, 1821	McKenzie, Donald

Hudson's Bay Company*
Headquarters, Columbia District, Fort George (Astoria) 1821–1825; Fort Vancouver, 1825–1846

Chief Factor	Term of Service	Junior Chief Factor
McMillan, James	Spring, 1821–Fall, 1821	Cameron, John Dougald
Cameron, John Dougald	Fall, 1821–Spring, 1824	Kennedy, Alexander
Kennedy, Alexander	Spring, 1824–Mar. 18, 1825	McLoughlin, John
McLoughlin, John	Mar. 18, 1825–May 31, 1845	None appointed

*Appointments in 1821 by agreement with North West Company; and 1822–1825 by council of Northern Department, Sir George Simpson, Governor

Oregon (Walamet) Mission of the Methodist Episcopal Church
Mission Bottom 1834–1841; Chemeketa (Salem) 1841–1847

Name	Term of Service	Position
Lee, Jason	Oct. 6, 1834–Mar. 26, 1838	Appointed superintendent upon recommendation of the Board of Managers of the Missionary Society
Leslie, David	Mar. 26, 1838–May 27, 1840	Acting superintendent in absence of Lee
Lee, Jason	May 27, 1840–Dec. 25, 1843	Superintendent
Leslie, David	Dec. 25, 1843–June 1, 1844	Acting superintendent in absence of Lee
Gary, George	June 1, 1844–July 18, 1847	Appointed superintendent; instructed to dissolve the mission properties

Provisional Government Executive Committee

Name	Term of Service	By What Authority/Remarks
Hill, David; Beers, Alanson; Gale, Joseph	July 5, 1843–May 25, 1844	Elected by meeting of inhabitants of the Oregon Territory

Name/Political Party	Term of Service	By What Authority/Remarks
Stewart, P.G.; Russell Osborn; Bailey, W.J.	May 25, 1844–July 14, 1845	By vote of the people

Governors of Oregon

Under Provisional Government

Abernethy, George	July 14, 1845–Mar. 3, 1849	By people at 1845 general election; reelected 1848

Under Territorial Government

Name/Political Party[1]	Term of Service	By What Authority/Remarks
Lane, Joseph—D	Mar. 3, 1849–June 18, 1850	Appointed by President Polk; resigned
Prichette, Kintzing—D	June 18, 1850–Aug. 18, 1850	Acting governor, was secretary
Gaines, John P.—W	Aug. 18, 1850–May 16, 1853	Appointed by President Taylor
Lane, Joseph—D	May 16, 1853–May 19, 1853	Appointed by President Pierce; resigned
Curry, George L.—D	May 19, 1853–Dec. 2, 1853	Acting governor, was secretary
Davis, John W.—D	Dec. 2, 1853–Aug. 1, 1854	Appointed by President Pierce; resigned
Curry, George L.—D	Aug. 1, 1854–Mar. 3, 1859	Acting governor, was secretary; appointed by President Pierce, Nov. 1, 1854

Under State Government

Whiteaker, John—D	Mar. 3, 1859–Sept. 10, 1862	Elected 1858
Gibbs, A.C.—R	Sept. 10, 1862–Sept. 12, 1866	Elected 1862
Woods, George L.—R	Sept. 12, 1866–Sept. 14, 1870	Elected 1866
Grover, LaFayette—D	Sept. 14, 1870–Feb. 1, 1877	Elected 1870; reelected 1874; resigned
Chadwick, Stephen F.—D	Feb. 1, 1877–Sept. 11, 1878	Was secretary of state
Thayer, W.W.—D	Sept. 11, 1878–Sept. 13, 1882	Elected 1878
Moody, Z.F.—R	Sept. 13, 1882–Jan. 12, 1887	Elected 1882
Pennoyer, Sylvester—DP	Jan. 12, 1887–Jan. 14, 1895	Elected 1886; reelected 1890
Lord, William Paine—R	Jan. 14, 1895–Jan. 9, 1899	Elected 1894
Geer, T.T.—R	Jan. 9, 1899–Jan. 14, 1903	Elected 1898
Chamberlain, George E.—D	Jan. 15, 1903–Feb. 28, 1909	Elected 1902; reelected 1906; resigned
Benson, Frank W.—R	Mar. 1, 1909–June 17, 1910	Was secretary of state; resigned
Bowerman, Jay[2]—R	June 17, 1910–Jan. 8, 1911	Was president of Senate
West, Oswald—D	Jan. 11, 1911–Jan. 12, 1915	Elected 1910
Withycombe, James—R	Jan. 12, 1915–Mar. 3, 1919	Elected 1914; reelected 1918; died in office
Olcott, Ben W.—R	Mar. 3, 1919–Jan. 8, 1923	Was secretary of state
Pierce, Walter M.—D	Jan. 8, 1923–Jan. 10, 1927	Elected 1922
Patterson, I.L.—R	Jan. 10, 1927–Dec. 21, 1929	Elected 1926; died in office
Norblad, A.W.[3]—R	Dec. 22, 1929–Jan. 12, 1931	Was president of Senate
Meier, Julius L.—I	Jan. 12, 1931–Jan. 14, 1935	Elected 1930
Martin, Charles H.—D	Jan. 14, 1935–Jan. 9, 1939	Elected 1934
Sprague, Charles A.—R	Jan. 9, 1939–Jan. 11, 1943	Elected 1938
Snell, Earl—R	Jan. 11, 1943–Oct. 28, 1947	Elected 1942; reelected 1946; died in office
Hall, John H.[4]—R	Oct. 30, 1947–Jan. 10, 1949	Was speaker of House
McKay, Douglas—R	Jan. 10, 1949–Dec. 27, 1952	Elected 1948; reelected 1950; resigned
Patterson, Paul L.—R	Dec. 27, 1952–Jan. 31, 1956	Was president of Senate; elected 1954; died in office
Smith, Elmo—R	Feb. 1, 1956–Jan. 14, 1957	Was president of Senate
Holmes, Robert D.—D	Jan. 14, 1957–Jan. 12, 1959	Elected 1956
Hatfield, Mark O.—R	Jan. 12, 1959–Jan. 9, 1967	Elected 1958; reelected 1962
McCall, Tom—R	Jan. 9, 1967–Jan 13, 1975	Elected 1966; reelected 1970
Straub, Robert W.—D	Jan. 13, 1975–Jan. 8, 1979	Elected 1974

Name/Political Party[1]	Term of Service	By What Authority/Remarks
Atiyeh, Victor G.—R	Jan. 8, 1979–Jan. 12, 1987	Elected 1978; reelected 1982
Goldschmidt, Neil—D	Jan. 12, 1987–Jan. 14, 1991	Elected 1986
Roberts, Barbara—D	Jan. 14, 1991–Jan. 9, 1995	Elected 1990
Kitzhaber, John—D	Jan. 9, 1995–Jan. 13, 2003	Elected 1994; reelected 1998
Kulongoski, Theodore R.—D	Jan. 13, 2003–Jan. 10, 2011	Elected 2002; reelected 2006
Kitzhaber, John—D	Jan. 10, 2011–Feb. 18, 2015	Elected 2010; reelected 2014; resigned
Brown, Kate[5]—D	Feb. 18, 2015–	Succeeded Kitzhaber; elected 2016

[1]D = Democrat; R = Republican; DP = Democrat People's; I = Independent; W = Whig

[2]Jay Bowerman became governor when Frank Benson, who was serving as both governor and secretary of state, became incapacitated. Benson resigned as governor but continued as secretary of state until his death.

[3]In 1920, the Constitution was changed to allow the president of the Senate to succeed as governor.

[4]A plane crash on October 28, 1947, killed Governor Earl Snell, Secretary of State Robert S. Farrell, Jr., President of the Senate Marshall E. Cornett and the pilot, Cliff Hogue. John H. Hall, Speaker of the House and next in line of succession, automatically became governor. Earl Newbry was appointed by John H. Hall to the position of secretary of state.

[5]Kate Brown was serving as secretary of state when John Kitzhaber vacated the office of governor. The Oregon Constitution requires that the secretary of state is next in line to fill the vacancy. In 2016, Brown was elected to serve the remaining two years of Kitzhaber's term.

Secretaries of State of Oregon

Under Provisional Government

Name/Political Party	Term of Service	By What Authority/Remarks
LeBreton, George W.	Feb. 18, 1841–Mar. 4, 1844	Elected by meeting of inhabitants of the Willamette Valley to office of clerk of courts and public recorder, thus served as first secretary; reelected 1843; died in office
Johnson, Overton	Mar. 4, 1844–May 25, 1844	Appointed clerk and recorder
Long, Dr. John E.	May 25, 1844–June 21, 1846	Elected clerk and recorder by people at first 1844 general election; reelected 1845 general election; reelected 1845 by Legislature; drowned
Prigg, Frederick	June 26, 1846–Sept. 16, 1848	Appointed secretary to succeed Long; elected 1846 by Legislature; resigned
Holderness, Samuel M.	Sept. 19, 1848–Mar. 10, 1849	Appointed to succeed Prigg; elected 1848 by Legislature

Under Territorial Government

Magruder, Theophilus	Mar. 10, 1849–Apr. 9, 1849	Elected by Legislature
Prichette, Kintzing—D	Apr. 9, 1849–Sept. 18, 1850	Appointed by President Polk
Hamilton, Gen. E.D.—W	Sept. 18, 1850–May 14, 1853	Appointed by President Taylor
Curry, George L.—D	May 14, 1853–Jan. 27, 1855	Appointed by President Pierce
Harding, Benjamin—D	Jan. 27, 1855–Mar. 3, 1859	Appointed by President Pierce

Under State Government

Heath, Lucien—D	Mar. 3, 1859–Sept. 8, 1862	Elected 1858
May, Samuel E.—R	Sept. 8, 1862–Sept. 10, 1870	Elected 1862; reelected 1866
Chadwick, Stephen F.[1]—D	Sept. 10, 1870–Sept. 2, 1878	Elected 1870; reelected 1874
Earhart, R.P.—R	Sept. 2, 1878–Jan. 10, 1887	Elected 1878; reelected 1882
McBride, George W.—R	Jan. 10, 1887–Jan. 14, 1895	Elected 1886; reelected 1890
Kincaid, Harrison R.—R	Jan. 14, 1895–Jan. 9, 1899	Elected 1894
Dunbar, Frank I.—R	Jan. 9, 1899–Jan. 14, 1907	Elected 1898; reelected 1902

Name/Political Party	Term of Service	By What Authority/Remarks
Benson, Frank W.[2]—R	Jan. 15, 1907–Apr. 14, 1911	Elected 1906; reelected 1910; died in office
Olcott, Ben W.[3]—R	Apr. 17, 1911–May 28, 1920	Appointed by Governor West; elected 1912; reelected 1916; resigned
Kozer, Sam A.—R	May 28, 1920–Sept. 24, 1928	Appointed by Governor Olcott; elected 1920; reelected 1924; resigned
Hoss, Hal E.—R	Sept. 24, 1928–Feb. 6, 1934	Appointed by Governor Patterson; elected 1928; reelected 1932; died in office
Stadelman, P.J.—R	Feb. 9, 1934–Jan. 7, 1935	Appointed by Governor Meier
Snell, Earl—R	Jan. 7, 1935–Jan. 4, 1943	Elected 1934; reelected 1938
Farrell, Robert S., Jr.—R	Jan. 4, 1943–Oct. 28, 1947	Elected 1942; reelected 1946; died in office
Newbry, Earl T.—R	Nov. 3, 1947–Jan. 7, 1957	Appointed by Governor Hall; elected 1948; reelected 1952
Hatfield, Mark O.—R	Jan. 7, 1957–Jan. 12, 1959	Elected 1956; resigned
Appling, Howell, Jr.—R	Jan. 12, 1959–Jan. 4, 1965	Appointed by Governor Hatfield; elected 1960
McCall, Tom—R	Jan. 4, 1965–Jan. 9, 1967	Elected 1964; resigned
Myers, Clay—R	Jan. 9, 1967–Jan. 3, 1977	Appointed by Governor McCall; elected 1968; reelected 1972
Paulus, Norma—R	Jan. 3, 1977–Jan. 7, 1985	Elected 1976; reelected 1980
Roberts, Barbara—D	Jan. 7, 1985–Jan. 14, 1991	Elected 1984; reelected 1988; resigned
Keisling, Phil—D	Jan. 14, 1991–Nov. 8, 1999	Appointed by Governor Roberts; elected 1992; reelected 1996; resigned
Bradbury, Bill—D	Nov. 8, 1999–Jan. 5, 2009	Appointed by Governor Kitzhaber; elected 2000; reelected 2004
Brown, Kate[4]—D	Jan. 5, 2009–Feb. 17, 2015	Elected 2008; reelected 2012; succeeded Governor Kitzhaber
Atkins, Jeanne P.—D	Mar. 11, 2015–Jan. 2, 2017	Appointed by Governor Brown
Richardson, Dennis—R	Jan. 2, 2017–	Elected 2016

[1]When Stephen Chadwick succeeded L. F. Grover as governor in 1877, he did not resign as secretary of state. He signed documents and proclamations twice—as governor and as secretary of state—until September 1878.

[2]Frank Benson served as both secretary of state and governor. See Footnote 2 under Governors of Oregon.

[3]When James Withycombe died in office on March 3, 1919, Ben W. Olcott succeeded him as governor. However, Governor Olcott did not resign or appoint a new secretary of state until May 28, 1920.

[4]When Governor John Kitzhaber resigned during office, Secretary of State Kate Brown became governor according to the order of succession required by the Oregon Constitution.

Treasurers of Oregon

Under Provisional Government

Name/Political Party	Term of Service	By What Authority/Remarks
Gray, W.H.	Mar. 1, 1843–July 5, 1843	Elected by meeting of citizens of the Willamette Valley
Willson, W.H.	July 5, 1843–May 14, 1844	Elected by meeting of the inhabitants of the Willamette settlements
Foster, Phillip	July 2, 1844–July 7, 1845	Elected by people at first 1844 general election

Name/Political Party	Term of Service	By What Authority/Remarks
Ermatinger, Francis	July 7, 1845–Mar. 3, 1846	Elected by people at 1845 general election; reelected 1845 by Legislature; resigned
Couch, John H.	Mar. 4, 1846–Sept. 27, 1847	Appointed to succeed Ermatinger; elected by Legislature 1846; resigned
Kilbourn, William K.	Oct. 11, 1847–Sept. 28, 1849	Appointed to succeed Couch; elected by Legislature 1849

Under Territorial Government

Taylor, James	Sept. 28, 1849–Feb. 8, 1851	Elected by Legislature
Rice, L.A.	Feb. 8, 1851–Sept. 22, 1851	Elected by Legislature; resigned
Buck, William W.	Sept. 27, 1851–Dec. 16, 1851	Appointed to succeed Rice
Boon, John D.—D	Dec. 16, 1851–Mar. 1, 1855	Elected by Legislature
Lane, Nat H.—D	Mar. 1, 1855–Jan. 10, 1856	Elected by Legislature
Boon, John D.—D	Jan. 10, 1856–Mar. 3, 1859	Elected by Legislature

Under State Government

Boon, John D.—D	Mar. 3, 1859–Sept. 8, 1862	Elected 1858
Cooke, E.N.—R	Sept. 8, 1862–Sept. 12, 1870	Elected 1862; reelected 1866
Fleischner, L.—D	Sept. 12, 1870–Sept. 14, 1874	Elected 1870
Brown, A.H.—D	Sept. 14, 1874–Sept. 9, 1878	Elected 1874
Hirsch, E.—R	Sept. 9, 1878–Jan. 10, 1887	Elected 1878; reelected 1882
Webb, G.W.—D	Jan. 10, 1887–Jan. 12, 1891	Elected 1886
Metschan, Phil—R	Jan. 12, 1891–Jan. 9, 1899	Elected 1890; reelected 1894
Moore, Charles S.—R	Jan. 9, 1899–Jan. 14, 1907	Elected 1898; reelected 1902
Steel, George A.—R	Jan. 15, 1907–Jan. 3, 1911	Elected 1906
Kay, Thomas B.—R	Jan. 4, 1911–Jan. 6, 1919	Elected 1910; reelected 1914
Hoff, O.P.—R	Jan. 6, 1919–Mar. 18, 1924	Elected 1918; reelected 1922; died in office
Myers, Jefferson—D	Mar. 18, 1924–Jan. 4, 1925	Appointed by Governor Pierce
Kay, Thomas B.—R	Jan. 4, 1925–April 29, 1931	Elected 1924; reelected 1928; died in office
Holman, Rufus C.—R	May 1, 1931–Dec. 27, 1938	Appointed by Governor Meier; elected 1932; reelected 1936; resigned
Pearson, Walter E.—D	Dec. 27, 1938–Jan. 6, 1941	Appointed by Governor Martin
Scott, Leslie M.—R	Jan. 6, 1941–Jan. 3, 1949	Elected 1940; reelected 1944
Pearson, Walter J.—D	Jan. 3, 1949–Jan. 5, 1953	Elected 1948
Unander, Sig—R	Jan. 5, 1953–Dec. 31, 1959	Elected 1952; reelected 1956; resigned
Belton, Howard C.—R	Jan. 4, 1960–Jan. 4, 1965	Appointed by Governor Hatfield; elected 1960
Straub, Robert—D	Jan. 4, 1965–Jan. 1, 1973	Elected 1964; reelected 1968
Redden, James A.—D	Jan. 1, 1973–Jan. 3, 1977	Elected 1972
Myers, Clay—R	Jan. 3, 1977–Apr. 1, 1984	Elected 1976; reelected 1980; resigned
Rutherford, Bill—R	Apr. 1, 1984–July 9, 1987	Appointed by Governor Atiyeh; elected 1984; resigned
Meeker, Tony—R	July 9, 1987–Jan. 4, 1993	Appointed by Governor Goldschmidt; elected 1988
Hill, Jim—D	Jan. 4, 1993–Jan. 1, 2001	Elected 1992; reelected 1996
Edwards, Randall—D	Jan. 1, 2001–Jan. 5, 2009	Elected 2000; reelected 2004
Westlund, Ben—D	Jan. 5, 2009–Mar. 7, 2010	Elected 2008; died in office
Ted Wheeler—D	Mar. 11, 2010–Jan. 2, 2017	Appointed by Governor Kulongoski; elected 2010; reelected 2012
Read, Tobias—D	Jan. 2, 2017–	Elected 2016

Oregon Supreme Court Justices[1]

Under Provisional Government

Name	Term of Service	By What Authority/Remarks
Babcock, Dr. Ira L.	Feb. 18, 1841–May 1, 1843	Supreme judge with probate powers elected at meeting of inhabitants of the Willamette Valley
Wilson, W.E.	No record of service	Supreme judge with probate powers; elected at meeting of inhabitants of the Willamette Settlements, May 2, 1843
Russell, Osborn	Oct. 2, 1843–May 14, 1844	Supreme judge and probate judge; appointed by the Executive Committee
Babcock, Dr. Ira L.	June 27, 1844–Nov. 11, 1844	Presiding judge, Circuit Court; elected at first general election May 1844; resigned
Nesmith, James W.	Dec. 25, 1844–Aug. 9, 1845	Presiding judge, Circuit Court; appointed by Executive Committee; elected by people 1845
Ford, Nathaniel	Declined service	Supreme judge; elected by Legislature Aug. 9, 1845; declined to serve
Burnett, Peter H.	Sept. 6, 1845–Dec. 29, 1846	Supreme judge; elected by Legislature; declined appointment to Supreme Court 1848
Thornton, J. Quinn	Feb. 20, 1847–Nov. 9, 1847	Supreme judge; appointed by Governor Abernethy; resigned
Lancaster, Columbia	Nov. 30, 1847–Apr. 9, 1849	Supreme judge; appointed by Governor Abernethy
Lovejoy, A.L.	No record of service	Supreme judge; elected by Legislature Feb. 16, 1849

Under Territorial[2] and State Government[3]

Name	Term of Service	By What Authority/Remarks
Bryant, William P.	1848–1850	Appointed 1848; resigned 1850; chief justice 1848–1850
Pratt, Orville C.	1848–1852	Appointed 1848; term ended 1852
Nelson, Thomas	1850–1853	Appointed 1850 to succeed Bryant; term ended 1853; chief justice 1850–1853
Strong, William	1850–1853	Appointed 1850 to succeed Burnett; term ended 1853
Williams, George H.	1853–1858	Appointed 1853, 1857; resigned 1858; chief justice 1853–1858
Olney, Cyrus	1853–1858	Appointed 1853, 1857; resigned 1858
Deady, Matthew P.	1853–1859	Appointed 1853, 1857; elected 1858; resigned 1859
McFadden, Obadiah B.	1853–1854	Appointed 1853; term ended 1854
Boise, Reuben P.	1858–1870, 1876–1880	Appointed 1858 to succeed Olney; elected 1859; reelected 1864; term ended 1870; elected 1876; term ended 1878; appointed 1878; term ended 1880; chief justice 1862–1864, 1867–1870
Wait, Aaron E.	1859–1862	Elected 1858; resigned May 1, 1862; chief justice 1859–1862
Stratton, Riley E.	1859–1866	Elected 1858, 1864; died Dec. 26, 1866
Prim, Paine Page	1859–1880	Appointed 1859 to succeed Deady; elected 1860; reelected 1866, 1872; term ended 1878; appointed 1878; term ended 1880; chief justice 1864–1866, 1870–1872, 1876–1878
Page, William W.	1862	Appointed May 1862 to succeed Wait; term ended Sept. 1862
Shattuck, Erasmus D.	1862–1867, 1874–1878	Elected 1862; resigned Dec. 1867; elected 1874; term ended 1878; chief justice 1866–1867

Name	Term of Service	By What Authority/Remarks
Wilson, Joseph G.	1862–1870	New appointment Oct. 17, 1862; elected 1864; resigned May 1870
Skinner, Alonzo A.	1866–1867	Appointed 1866 to succeed Stratton; term ended 1867
Upton, William W.	1867–1874	Appointed Dec. 1867 to succeed Shattuck; elected 1868; term ended 1874; chief justice 1872–1874
Kelsay, John	1868–1870	Elected 1868 to succeed Stratton; term ended 1870
Whitten, Benoni	1870	Appointed May 1870 to succeed Wilson; term ended Sept. 1870
McArthur, Lewis L.	1870–1878	Elected 1870; reelected 1876; term ended 1878
Thayer, Andrew J.	1870–1873	Elected 1870; died Apr. 26, 1873
Bonham, Benjamin F.	1870–1876	Elected 1870; term ended 1876; chief justice 1874–1876
Moser, Lafayette F.	1873–1874	Appointed May 1873 to succeed A.J. Thayer; term ended 1874
Burnett, John	1874–1876	Elected 1874; term ended 1876
Watson, James F.	1876–1878	Elected 1876; term ended 1878
Kelly, James K.	1878–1880	Appointed 1878; term ended 1880; chief justice 1878–1880
Lord, William P.	1880–1894	Elected 1880; reelected 1882, 1888; term ended 1894; chief justice 1880–1882, 1886–1888, 1892–1894
Watson, Edward B.	1880–1884	Elected 1880; term ended 1884; chief justice 1882–1884
Waldo, John B.	1880–1886	Elected 1880; term ended 1886; chief justice 1884–1886
Thayer, William W.	1884–1890	Elected 1884; term ended 1890; chief justice 1888–1890
Strahan, Reuben S.	1886–1892	Elected 1886; term ended 1892; chief justice 1890–1892
Bean, Robert S.	1890–1909	Elected 1890; reelected 1896, 1902, 1908; resigned May 1, 1909; chief justice 1894–1896, 1900–1902, 1905–1909
Moore, Frank A.	1892–1918	Elected 1892; reelected 1898, 1904, 1910, 1916; died Sept. 25, 1918; chief justice 1896–1898, 1902–1905, 1909–1911, 1915–1917
Wolverton, Charles E.	1894–1905	Elected 1894, 1900; resigned Dec. 4, 1905; chief justice 1898–1900, 1905
Hailey, Thomas G.	1905–1907	Appointed Dec. 5, 1905 to succeed Wolverton; term ended Jan. 15, 1907
Eakin, Robert	1907–1917	Elected 1906, 1912; resigned Jan. 8, 1917; chief justice 1911–1913
King, William R.	1909–1911	Appointed Feb. 12, 1909; term ended Jan. 1, 1911
Slater, Woodson T.	1909–1911	Appointed Feb. 12, 1909; term ended Jan. 1, 1911
McBride, Thomas A.	1909–1930	Appointed May 1, 1909 to succeed Robert S. Bean; elected 1914; reelected 1920, 1926; died Sept. 9, 1930; chief justice 1913–1915, 1917–1921, 1923–1927
Bean, Henry J.	1911–1941	Elected 1910; reelected 1914, 1920, 1926, 1932, 1938; died May 8, 1941; chief justice 1931–1933, 1937–1939
Burnett, George H.	1911–1927	Elected 1910; reelected 1916, 1922; died Sept. 10, 1927; chief justice 1921–1923, 1927
McNary, Charles L.	1913–1915	Appointed June 3, 1913; term ended Jan. 4, 1915
Ramsey, William M.	1913–1915	Appointed June 3, 1913; term ended Jan. 4, 1915
Benson, Henry L.	1915–1921	Elected 1914; reelected 1920; died Oct. 16, 1921
Harris, Lawrence T.	1915–1924	Elected 1914; reelected 1920; resigned Jan. 15, 1924

Name	Term of Service	By What Authority/Remarks
McCamant, Wallace	1917–1918	Appointed Jan. 8, 1917 to succeed Eakin; resigned June 4, 1918
Johns, Charles A.	1918–1921	Appointed June 4, 1918 to succeed McCamant; elected 1918; resigned Oct. 7, 1921
Olson, Conrad P.	1918–1919	Appointed Sept. 27, 1918 to succeed Moore; term ended Jan. 7, 1919
Bennett, Alfred S.	1919–1920	Elected 1918; resigned Oct. 5, 1920
Brown, George M.	1920–1933	Appointed Oct. 14, 1920 to succeed Bennett; elected 1920; reelected 1926; term ended 1933
McCourt, John	1921–1924	Appointed Oct. 8, 1921 to succeed Johns; elected 1922; died Sept. 12, 1924
Rand, John L.	1921–1942	Appointed Oct. 18, 1921 to succeed Benson; elected 1922; reelected 1928, 1934, 1940; died Nov. 19, 1942; chief justice 1927–1929, 1933–1935, 1939–1941
Coshow, Oliver P.	1924–1931	Appointed Jan. 15, 1924 to succeed Harris; elected 1924; term ended 1931; chief justice 1929–1931
Pipes, Martin L.	1924	Appointed Sept. 1924 to succeed McCourt; term ended Dec. 31, 1924
Belt, Harry H.	1925–1950	Elected 1924; reelected 1930, 1936, 1942, 1948; died Aug. 6, 1950; chief justice 1945–1947
Rossman, George	1927–1965	Appointed Sept. 13, 1927 to succeed George H. Burnett; elected 1928; reelected 1934, 1940, 1946, 1952, 1958; term ended 1965; chief justice 1947–1949
Kelly, Percy R.	1930–1949	Appointed Sept. 24, 1930 to succeed McBride; elected 1930; reelected 1936, 1942, 1948; died June 14, 1949; chief justice 1941–1943
Campbell, James U.	1931–1937	Elected 1930; reelected 1936; died July 16, 1937; chief justice 1935–1937
Bailey, John O.	1933–1950	Elected 1932; reelected 1938, 1944; resigned Nov. 15, 1950; chief justice 1943–1945
Lusk, Hall S.	1937–1960	Appointed July 22, 1937 to succeed Campbell; elected 1938; reelected 1944, 1950, 1956; resigned Mar. 15, 1960; 1961–1968 recalled to temporary active service 1961 through 1968; chief justice 1949–1951
Brand, James T.	1941–1958	Appointed May 14, 1941 to succeed Henry J. Bean; elected 1942; reelected 1948, 1954; resigned June 30, 1958; chief justice 1951–1953
Hay, Arthur D.	1942–1952	Appointed Nov. 28, 1942 to succeed Rand; elected 1944; reelected 1950; died Dec. 19, 1952
Page, E.M.	1949–1950	Appointed July 8, 1949 to succeed Percy R. Kelly; resigned Jan. 18, 1950
Latourette, Earl C.	1950–1956	Appointed Jan. 19, 1950 to succeed E.M. Page; elected 1950; died Aug. 18, 1956; chief justice 1953–1955
Warner, Harold J.	1950–1963	Appointed Sept. 5, 1950 to succeed Belt; elected 1950; reelected 1956; term ended 1963; chief justice 1955–1957
Tooze, Walter L.	1950–1956	Appointed Nov. 16, 1950 to succeed Bailey; elected 1950; reelected 1956; died Dec. 21, 1956
Perry, William C.	1952–1970	Appointed Dec. 26, 1952 to succeed Hay; elected 1954; reelected 1960, 1966; resigned June 1, 1970; chief justice 1957–1959, 1967–1970
McAllister, William M.	1956–1976	Appointed Aug. 24, 1956 to succeed Latourette; elected 1956; reelected 1962, 1968, 1974; resigned Dec. 31, 1976; chief justice 1959–1967

Name	Term of Service	By What Authority/Remarks
Kester, Randall B.	1957–1958	Appointed Jan. 3, 1957 to succeed Tooze; resigned Mar. 1, 1958
Sloan, Gordon	1958–1970	Appointed Mar. 1, 1958 to succeed Kester; elected 1958; reelected 1964; resigned Oct. 1, 1970
O'Connell, Kenneth J.	1958–1977	Appointed July 1, 1958 to succeed Brand; elected 1958; reelected 1964, 1970; term ended 1977; chief justice 1970–1976
Goodwin, Alfred T.	1960–1969	Appointed Mar. 18, 1960 to succeed Lusk; elected 1960; reelected 1966; resigned Dec. 19, 1969
Denecke, Arno H.	1963–1982	Elected 1962; reelected 1968, 1974, 1980; resigned June 30, 1982; chief justice 1976–1982
Holman, Ralph M.	1965–1980	Elected 1964; reelected 1970, 1976; resigned Jan. 20, 1980
Tongue, Thomas H.	1969–1982	Appointed Dec. 29, 1969 to succeed Goodwin; elected 1970; reelected 1976; resigned Feb. 7, 1982
Howell, Edward H.	1970–1980	Appointed June 1, 1970 to succeed Perry; elected 1970; reelected 1976; resigned Nov. 30, 1980
Bryson, Dean F.	1970–1979	Elected 1970; appointed Oct. 23, 1970 (before elective term began) to succeed Sloan; reelected 1976; resigned April 1, 1979
Lent, Berkeley	1977–1988	Elected 1976; reelected 1982; resigned Sept. 30, 1988; chief justice 1982–1983
Linde, Hans	1977–1990	Appointed Jan. 3, 1977 to succeed McAllister; elected 1978; reelected 1984; resigned Jan. 31, 1990
Peterson, Edwin J.	1979 –1993	Appointed May 15, 1979 to succeed Bryson; elected 1980; reelected 1986, 1992; resigned Dec. 31, 1993; chief justice 1983–1991
Tanzer, Jacob	1980–1982	Appointed Jan. 21, 1980 to succeed Holman; elected 1980; resigned Dec. 31, 1982
Campbell, J.R.	1980–1988	Appointed Dec. 1, 1980 to succeed Howell; elected 1982; resigned Dec. 31, 1988
Roberts, Betty	1982–1986	Appointed Feb. 8, 1982 to succeed Tongue; elected 1982; resigned Feb. 7, 1986
Carson, Wallace P., Jr.	1982–2006	Appointed July 14, 1982 to succeed Denecke; elected 1982; reelected 1988, 1994, 2000; chief justice 1991–2005; resigned Dec. 31, 2006
Jones, Robert E.	1983–1990	Appointed Dec. 16, 1982 to succeed Tanzer; elected 1984; resigned April 30, 1990
Gillette, W. Michael	1986–2011	Appointed Feb. 10, 1986 to succeed Roberts; elected 1986; reelected 1992, 1998, 2004
Van Hoomissen, George	1988–2001	Elected May 17, 1988 to succeed Lent; reelected 1994; resigned Dec. 31, 2000
Fadeley, Edward N.	1988–1998	Elected Nov. 8, 1988 to succeed Campbell; reelected 1994; resigned Jan. 31, 1998
Unis, Richard	1990–1996	Appointed Feb. 1, 1990 to succeed Linde; elected 1990; resigned June 30, 1996
Graber, Susan P.[4]	1990–1998	Appointed May 2, 1990 and Jan. 7, 1991 to succeed Jones; elected 1992; resigned April 1, 1998
Durham, Robert D.	1994–2013	Appointed Jan. 4, 1994 to succeed Peterson; elected 1994; reelected 2000, 2006
Kulongoski, Ted	1997–2001	Elected May, 1996; resigned June 14, 2001
Leeson, Susan M.	1998–2003	Appointed Feb. 26, 1998 to succeed Fadeley; elected 1998; resigned Jan. 31, 2003
Riggs, R. William	1998–2006	Appointed Sept. 8, 1998 to succeed Graber; elected 1998; reelected 2004, resigned Sept. 30, 2006
De Muniz, Paul J.	2001–2013	Elected Nov. 7, 2000 to succeed Van Hoomissen; reelected 2006; chief justice 2006–2012

Name	Term of Service	By What Authority/Remarks
Balmer, Thomas A.	2001–	Appointed Sept. 20, 2001 to succeed Kulongoski; elected 2002; reelected 2008, 2014; chief justice 2012 to date
Kistler, Rives	2003–	Appointed Aug. 15, 2003 to succeed Leeson; elected 2004; reelected 2010, 2016
Walters, Martha Lee	2006–	Appointed Oct. 1, 2006 to succeed Riggs; elected 2008; reelected 2014
Linder, Virginia L.	2007–2015	Elected Nov. 7, 2006 to succeed Carson; reelected 2012; retired Dec. 31, 2015
Landau, Jack L.	2011–	Elected 2010 to succeed Gillette; reelected 2016
Brewer, Dave	2013–	Elected 2012 to succeed De Muniz
Baldwin, Richard C.	2013–	Elected 2012 to succeed Durham
Nakamoto, Lynn	2016–	Appointed Dec. 7, 2015 to succeed Linder; elected 2016

[1]Unless otherwise noted, justices took office in the year in which elected until 1905. Since then, terms have started on the first Monday in January and continued until the first Monday six years hence or until a successor has been sworn in, if later.

[2]Appointments under territorial government were made by the president of the United States.

[3]From 1859 to 1862, there were four Supreme Court justices. In 1862, a fifth justice was added. The justices at that time also rode circuit. In 1878, the Supreme Court and Circuit Court were separated; the Supreme Court then had three justices. In 1910, the number increased to five. The final increase to the present seven occurred in 1913.

[4]When Justice Jones resigned, he had already filed to run for another term and his name appeared on the ballot at the 1990 primary election. Because he was elected for another term, which began January 7, 1991, he had to resign from his new term, and Justice Graber was appointed again at that time.

Judges of the Oregon Court of Appeals

The Oregon Court of Appeals was established July 1, 1969 with five members, expanded to six members October 5, 1973 and to ten members September 1, 1977.

Name	Term of Service	By What Authority/Remarks
Langtry, Virgil	1969–1976	Appointed July 1, 1969; elected 1970; resigned Sept. 15, 1976
Foley, Robert H.	1969–1976	Appointed July 1, 1969; elected 1970; resigned Aug. 16, 1976
Schwab, Herbert M.	1969–1980	Appointed July 1, 1969; elected 1970; reelected 1976; resigned Dec. 31, 1980; chief judge 1969–1980
Fort, William S.	1969–1977	Appointed July 1, 1969; elected 1970; term ended 1977
Branchfield, Edward	1969–1971	Appointed July 1, 1969; term ended 1971
Thornton, Robert Y.	1971–1983	Elected 1970; reelected 1976; term ended 1983
Tanzer, Jacob	1973–1975, 1976–1980	Appointed to new seat Oct. 5, 1973; term ended Jan. 6, 1975; elected 1976; appointed Aug. 16, 1976 (before elective term began) to succeed Foley; resigned Jan. 21, 1980
Lee, Jason	1975–1980	Elected 1974; died Feb. 19, 1980
Johnson, Lee	1977–1978	Elected 1976; resigned Dec. 18, 1978
Richardson, William L.	1976–1997	Elected 1976; appointed Oct. 15, 1976 (before elective term began) to succeed Langtry; reelected 1982, 1988, 1994; chief judge 1993–1997; resigned June 30, 1997
Buttler, John H.	1977–1992	Appointed to new seat Sept. 1, 1977; elected 1978; reelected 1984, 1990; resigned Dec. 31, 1992
Joseph, George M.	1977–1992	Appointed to new seat Sept. 1, 1977; elected 1978; reelected 1984, 1990; resigned Dec. 31, 1992; chief judge 1981–1992
Gillette, W. Michael	1977–1986	Appointed to new seat Sept. 1, 1977; elected 1978; reelected 1984; resigned Feb. 10, 1986
Roberts, Betty	1977–1982	Appointed to new seat Sept. 1, 1977; elected 1978; resigned Feb. 8, 1982

Name	Term of Service	By What Authority/Remarks
Campbell, J.R.	1979–1980	Appointed Mar. 19, 1979 to succeed Johnson; elected 1980; resigned Nov. 30, 1980
Warden, John C.	1980–1988	Appointed Feb. 19, 1980 to succeed Tanzer; term ended Jan. 5, 1981; appointed Jan. 6, 1981 to succeed Schwab; elected 1982; resigned Dec. 30, 1988
Warren, Edward H.	1980–1999	Appointed Mar. 10, 1980 to succeed Lee; elected 1980; reelected 1986, 1992, 1998; resigned 1999
Van Hoomissen, George A.	1981–1988	Elected 1980; reelected 1986; resigned Sept. 30, 1988
Young, Thomas F.	1981–1988	Appointed Jan. 5, 1981 to succeed Campbell; elected 1982; died Jan. 3, 1988
Rossman, Kurt C.	1982–1994	Appointed Mar. 2, 1982 to succeed Roberts; elected 1982; reelected 1988; resigned Dec. 31, 1994
Newman, Jonathan	1983–1991	Elected 1982; reelected 1988; resigned Aug. 31, 1991
Deits, Mary J.	1986–2004	Appointed Feb. 28, 1986 to succeed Gillette; elected 1986; reelected 1992, 1998; chief judge 1997–2004; resigned Oct. 31, 2004
Riggs, R. William	1988–1998	Appointed Oct. 24, 1988 to fill Van Hoomissen position; elected 1988 to succeed Warden; reelected 1994; resigned Sept. 8, 1998
Graber, Susan P.	1988–1990	Appointed Feb. 11, 1988 to succeed Young; elected 1988; resigned May 2, 1990
Edmonds, Walter I., Jr.	1989–2009	Appointed Jan. 1, 1989 to succeed Van Hoomissen; elected 1990; reelected 1996, 2002, 2008; retired Dec. 31, 2009
De Muniz, Paul J.	1990–2000	Appointed May 11, 1990 to succeed Graber; elected 1990; reelected 1996; resigned Dec. 29, 2000
Durham, Robert D.	1991–1994	Appointed Nov. 14, 1991 to succeed Newman; elected 1992; resigned Jan. 4, 1994
Landau, Jack L.	1993–2011	Appointed Dec. 15, 1992 to succeed Joseph; elected 1994; reelected 2000, 2006; resigned Jan. 3, 2011
Leeson, Susan M.	1993–1998	Appointed Dec. 15, 1992 to succeed Buttler; elected 1994; resigned Feb. 26, 1998
Haselton, Rick T.	1994–2015	Appointed Mar. 4, 1994 to succeed Durham; elected 1994; reelected 2000, 2006, 2012; retired Dec. 31, 2015
Armstrong, Rex	1995–	Elected 1994; reelected 2000, 2006, 2012
Linder, Virginia L.	1997–2007	Appointed Sept. 24, 1997 to succeed Richardson; elected 1998; reelected 2004; resigned Jan. 2, 2007
Wollheim, Robert D.	1998–2014	Appointed Feb. 27, 1998 to succeed Leeson; elected 1998; reelected 2004, 2010; retired Oct. 31, 2014
Brewer, Dave	1999–2012	Appointed Jan. 14, 1999 to succeed Warren; elected 2000; reelected 2006; chief judge 2004–2012
Kistler, Rives	1999–2003	Appointed Jan. 14, 1999 to succeed Riggs; elected 2000; resigned Aug. 14, 2003
Schuman, David	2001–2014	Appointed March 19, 2001 to succeed De Muniz; elected 2002; reelected 2008; retired Jan. 31, 2014
Ortega, Darleen	2003–	Appointed Oct. 13, 2003 to succeed Kistler; elected 2004; reelected 2010, 2016
Rosenblum, Ellen F.	2007–2011	Elected 2006; retired May 1, 2011
Sercombe, Timothy	2007–	Appointed March 26, 2007 to succeed Linder; elected 2008; reelected 2014
Duncan, Rebecca	2010–	Appointed Jan. 7, 2010 to succeed Edmonds; elected 2010; reelected 2016
Nakamoto, Lynn	2011–2015	Appointed Dec. 7, 2010 to succeed Landau; elected 2012; resigned Dec. 31, 2015

Elections and Records

Name	Term of Service	By What Authority/Remarks
Hadlock, Erika	2011–	Appointed July 7, 2011 to succeed Rosenblum; elected 2012
Egan, James C.	2013–	Elected 2012
DeVore, Joel	2013–	Appointed Oct. 17, 2013; elected 2014
Lagesen, Erin C.	2013–	Appointed Oct. 17, 2013; elected 2014
Tookey, Douglas L.	2013–	Appointed Oct. 17, 2013; elected 2014
Garrett, Chris	2014–	Appointed Dec. 24, 2013 to succeed Schuman; elected 2014
Flynn, Meagan A.	2014–	Appointed Sept. 25, 2014 to succeed Wollheim; elected 2016
DeHoog, Roger J.	2016–	Appointed Dec. 7, 2015 to succeed Nakamoto; elected 2016
Shorr, Scott A.	2016–	Appointed Dec. 7, 2015 to succeed Haselton; elected 2016

Judges of the Oregon Tax Court

The Oregon Tax Court was established January 1, 1962.

Name	Term of Service	By What Authority/Remarks
Gunnar, Peter M.	1962–1965	Appointed by Governor Hatfield Jan. 1, 1962; elected 1962; resigned Feb. 18, 1965
Howell, Edward H.	1965–1970	Appointed by Governor Hatfield Feb. 19, 1965; elected 1966; resigned May 31, 1970
Roberts, Carlisle B.	1970–1983	Appointed by Governor McCall June 1, 1970; elected 1970; reelected 1976; term ended 1983
Stewart, Samuel B.	1983–1985	Elected 1982; died Feb. 25, 1985
Byers, Carl N.	1985–2001	Appointed by Governor Atiyeh Mar. 6, 1985; elected 1986; reelected 1992, 1998; retired 2001
Breithaupt, Henry C.	2001–	Appointed by Governor Kitzhaber June 29, 2001 to succeed Byers; elected 2002; reelected 2008, 2014

Attorneys General of Oregon

Name/Political Party	Term of Service	By What Authority/Remarks
Chamberlain, George E.—D	May 20, 1891–Jan. 14, 1895	Appointed by Governor Pennoyer; elected June 1892
Idleman, Cicero M.—R	Jan. 14, 1895–Jan. 9, 1899	Elected 1894
Blackburn, D.R.N.—R	Jan. 9, 1899–Jan. 12, 1903	Elected 1898
Crawford, Andrew M.—R	Jan. 13, 1903–Jan. 3, 1915	Elected 1902; reelected 1906, 1910
Brown, George M.—R	Jan. 4, 1915–Oct. 14, 1920	Elected 1914; reelected 1918; resigned
Van Winkle, Isaac H.—R	Oct. 14, 1920–Dec. 14, 1943	Appointed by Governor Olcott; elected 1920; reelected 1924, 1928, 1932, 1936, 1940; died in office
Neuner, George—R	Dec. 21, 1943–Jan. 5, 1953	Appointed by Governor Snell; elected 1944; reelected 1948
Thornton, Robert Y.—D	Jan. 5, 1953–May 20, 1969	Elected 1952; reelected 1956, 1960, 1964
Johnson, Lee—R	May 20, 1969–Jan. 3, 1977	Elected 1968; reelected 1972
Redden, James—D	Jan. 3, 1977–Mar. 24, 1980	Elected 1976
Brown, James M.—D	Mar. 24, 1980–Jan. 4, 1981	Appointed by Governor Atiyeh
Frohnmayer, David B.—R	Jan. 5, 1981–Dec. 31, 1991	Elected 1980; reelected 1984, 1988; resigned 1991
Crookham, Charles S.—R	Jan. 2, 1992–Jan. 3, 1993	Appointed by Governor Roberts
Kulongoski, Ted—D	Jan. 4, 1993–Jan. 4, 1997	Elected 1992
Myers, Hardy—D	Jan. 6, 1997–Jan. 5, 2009	Elected 1996; reelected 2000, 2004
Kroger, John R.—D	Jan. 5, 2009–June 29, 2012	Elected 2008; resigned 2012
Rosenblum, Ellen—D	June 29, 2012–	Appointed by Governor Kitzaber; elected 2012; reelected 2016

Commissioners of the Bureau of Labor and Industries[1]

Name/Political Party	Term of Service	By What Authority/Remarks
Hoff, O.P.—R	June 2, 1903–Jan. 6, 1919	Appointed by Governor Chamberlain; elected 1906; reelected 1910, 1914
Gram, C.H.—R	Jan. 6, 1919–Jan. 4, 1943	Elected 1918; reelected 1922, 1926, 1930, 1934, 1938
Kimsey, W.E.—R	Jan. 4, 1943–Jan. 3, 1955	Elected 1942; reelected 1946, 1950
Nilsen, Norman O.—D	Jan. 3, 1955–Jan. 6, 1975	Elected 1954; reelected 1958, 1962, 1966, 1970
Stevenson, Bill—D	Jan. 6, 1975–Jan. 1, 1979	Elected 1974
Roberts, Mary Wendy—D.	Jan. 1, 1979–Jan 2, 1995	Elected 1978; reelected 1982, 1986, 1990
Roberts, Jack—R	Jan. 2, 1995–Jan. 6, 2003	Elected 1994; reelected 1998
Gardner, Dan[2]	Jan. 6, 2003–April 7, 2008	Elected 2002; reelected 2006; resigned 2008
Avakian, Brad[3]	Apr. 8, 2008–	Appointed by Governor Kulongoski; elected 2008; reelected 2012, 2014

[1]This position, originally called Labor Commissioner, was changed to Commissioner of the Bureau of Labor Statistics and Inspector of Factories and Workshops in 1918. In 1930, the name changed to Commissioner of the Bureau of Labor. The 1979 Legislature changed the name to Commissioner of the Bureau of Labor and Industries.

[2]The 1995 Legislature made this position nonpartisan, and the 1998 election was the first for this position after the change.

[3]Due to the appointment and election of Brad Avakian in 2008, the 2009 Legislature's House Bill 2095 provided that the Commissioner of the Bureau of Labor and Industries position be placed on the 2012 ballot for a two-year term. This restored the position to its regular election schedule in 2014.

Presidents of the Senate

Session	Name/Political Party	City	County
1860	Elkins, Luther—D		Linn
1862	Bowlby, Wilson—R		Washington
1864	Mitchell, J.H.—R	Portland	Multnomah
1865[1]	Mitchell, J.H.—R	Portland	Multnomah
1866	Cornelius, T.R.—R		Washington
1868	Burch, B.F.—D		Polk
1870	Fay, James D.—D		Jackson
1872	Fay, James D.—D		Jackson
1874	Cochran, R.B.—D		Lane
1876	Whiteaker, John—D		Lane
1878	Whiteaker, John—D		Lane
1880	Hirsch, Sol—R	Portland	Multnomah
1882	McConnell, W.J.—R		Yamhill
1885[2]	Waldo, William—R	Salem	Marion
1887	Carson, John C.—R	Portland	Multnomah
1889	Simon, Joseph—R	Portland	Multnomah
1891	Simon, Joseph—R	Portland	Multnomah
1893	Fulton, C.W.—R	Astoria	Clatsop
1895	Simon, Joseph—R	Portland	Multnomah
1897	Simon, Joseph—R	Portland	Multnomah
1898[1]	Simon, Joseph—R	Portland	Multnomah
1899	Taylor, T.C.—R	Pendleton	Umatilla
1901	Fulton, C.W.—R	Astoria	Clatsop
1903[2]	Brownell, George C.—R	Oregon City	Clackamas
1905	Kuykendall, W.—R	Eugene	Lane
1907	Haines, E.W.—R	Forest Grove	Washington
1909[2]	Bowerman, Jay—R	Condon	Gilliam
1911	Selling, Ben—R	Portland	Multnomah
1913	Malarkey, Dan J.—R	Portland	Multnomah
1915	Thompson, W. Lair—R	Lakeview	Lake

Session	Name/Political Party	City	County
1917	Moser, Gus C.—R	Portland	Multnomah
1919	Vinton, W.T.—R	McMinnville	Yamhill
1920[1]	Vinton, W.T.—R	McMinnville	Yamhill
1921[2]	Ritner, Roy W.—R	Pendleton	Umatilla
1923	Upton, Jay—R	Prineville	Crook
1925	Moser, Gus C.—R	Portland	Multnomah
1927	Corbett, Henry L.—R	Portland	Multnomah
1929	Norblad, A.W.—R	Astoria	Clatsop
1931	Marks, Willard L.—R	Albany	Linn
1933[3]	Kiddle, Fred E.—R	Island City	Union
1935[2]	Corbett, Henry L.—R	Portland	Multnomah
1937	Franciscovich, F.M.—R	Astoria	Clatsop
1939	Duncan, Robert M.—R	Burns	Harney
1941	Walker, Dean H.—R	Independence	Polk
1943	Steiwer, W.H.—R	Fossil	Wheeler
1945	Belton, Howard C.—R	Canby	Clackamas
1947	Cornett, Marshall E.—R	Klamath Falls	Klamath
1949	Walsh, William E.—R	Coos Bay	Coos
1951	Patterson, Paul L.—R	Hillsboro	Washington
1953	Marsh, Eugene E.—R	McMinnville	Yamhill
1955	Smith, Elmo—R	John Day	Grant
1957[2]	Overhulse, Boyd R.—D	Madras	Jefferson
1959	Pearson, Walter J.—D	Portland	Multnomah
1961	Boivin, Harry D.—D	Klamath Falls	Klamath
1963[2]	Musa, Ben—D	The Dalles	Wasco
1965[2]	Boivin, Harry D.—D	Klamath Falls	Klamath
1967[2]	Potts, E.D.—D	Grants Pass	Josephine
1969	Potts, E.D.—D	Grants Pass	Josephine
1971[2]	Burns, John D.—D	Portland	Multnomah
1973	Boe, Jason—D	Reedsport	Douglas
1974[1]	Boe, Jason—D	Reedsport	Douglas
1975	Boe, Jason—D	Reedsport	Douglas
1977	Boe, Jason—D	Reedsport	Douglas
1978[1]	Boe, Jason—D	Reedsport	Douglas
1979	Boe, Jason—D	Reedsport	Douglas
1980[1]	Boe, Jason—D	Reedsport	Douglas
1981[4]	Heard, Fred W.—D	Klamath Falls	Klamath
1983[3]	Fadeley, Edward N.—D	Eugene	Lane
1985	Kitzhaber, M.D., John A.—D	Roseburg	Douglas
1987	Kitzhaber, M.D., John A.—D	Roseburg	Douglas
1989[2]	Kitzhaber, M.D., John A.—D	Roseburg	Douglas
1991	Kitzhaber, M.D., John A.—D	Roseburg	Douglas
1993	Bradbury, Bill—D	Bandon	Coos
1995[2]	Smith, Gordon H.—R	Pendleton	Umatilla
1997	Adams, Brady—R	Grants Pass	Josephine
1999	Adams, Brady—R	Grants Pass	Josephine
2001[5]	Derfler, Gene—R	Salem	Marion
2003	Courtney, Peter—D	Salem	Marion
2005	Courtney, Peter—D	Salem	Marion
2007	Courtney, Peter—D	Salem	Marion
2009	Courtney, Peter—D	Salem	Marion
2011	Courtney, Peter—D	Salem	Marion
2013	Courtney, Peter—D	Salem	Marion
2015	Courtney, Peter—D	Salem	Marion
2017	Courtney, Peter—D	Salem	Marion

[1]Special session
[2]Regular and special session
[3]Regular and two special sessions
[4]Regular and four special sessions
[5]Regular and five special sessions

Speakers of the House of Representatives

Session	Name/Political Party	City	County
1860	Harding, B.F.—D		Marion
1862	Palmer, Joel—R		Yamhill
1864	Moores, I.R.—R		Marion
1865[1]	Moores, I.R.—R		Marion
1866	Chenoweth, F.A.—R		Benton
1868	Whiteaker, John J.—D		Lane
1870	Hayden, Benjamin—D		Polk
1872	Mallory, Rufus—R		Marion
1874	Drain, J.C.—D		Douglas
1876	Weatherford, J.K.—D	Albany	Linn
1878	Thompson, J.M.—D		Lane
1880	Moody, Z.F.—R	The Dalles	Wasco
1882	McBride, George W.—R		Columbia
1885[2]	Keady, W.P.—R	Corvallis	Benton
1887	Gregg, J.T.—R	Salem	Marion
1889	Smith, E.L.—R	Hood River	Hood River
1891	Geer, T.T.—R	Macleay	Marion
1893	Keady, W.P.—R	Portland	Multnomah
1895	Moores, C.B.—R	Salem	Marion
1897[4]	House failed to organize		
1898[1]	Carter, E.V.—R	Ashland	Jackson
1899	Carter, E.V.—R	Ashland	Jackson
1901	Reeder, L.B.—R	Pendleton	Umatilla
1903[2]	Harris, L.T.—R	Eugene	Lane
1905	Mills, A.L.—R	Portland	Multnomah
1907	Davey, Frank—R	Salem	Marion
1909[2]	McArthur, C.N.—R	Portland	Multnomah
1911	Rusk, John P.—R	Joseph	Wallowa
1913	McArthur, C.N.—R	Portland	Multnomah
1915	Selling, Ben—R	Portland	Multnomah
1917	Stanfield, R.N.—R	Stanfield	Umatilla
1919	Jones, Seymour—R	Salem	Marion
1920[1]	Jones, Seymour—R	Salem	Marion
1921[2]	Bean, Louis E.—R	Eugene	Lane
1923	Kubli, K.K.—R	Portland	Multnomah
1925	Burdick, Denton G.—R	Redmond	Deschutes
1927	Carkin, John H.—R	Medford	Jackson
1929	Hamilton, R.S.—R	Bend	Deschutes
1931	Lonergan, Frank J.—R	Portland	Multnomah
1933[3]	Snell, Earl W.—R	Arlington	Gilliam
1935	Cooter, John E.—D	Toledo	Lincoln
1935[1]	Latourette, Howard—D	Portland	Multnomah
1937	Boivin, Harry D.—D	Klamath Falls	Klamath
1939	Fatland, Ernest R.—R	Condon	Gilliam
1941	Farrell, Robert S., Jr.—R	Portland	Multnomah
1943	McAllister, William M.—R	Medford	Jackson
1945	Marsh, Eugene E.—R	McMinnville	Yamhill
1947	Hall, John H.—R	Portland	Multnomah
1949	Van Dyke, Frank J.—R	Medford	Jackson
1951	Steelhammer, John F.—R	Salem	Marion
1953	Wilhelm, Rudie, Jr.—R	Portland	Multnomah
1955	Geary, Edward A.—R	Klamath Falls	Klamath
1957[2]	Dooley, Pat—D	Portland	Multnomah
1959	Duncan, Robert B.—D	Medford	Jackson
1961	Duncan, Robert B.—D	Medford	Jackson
1963[2]	Barton, Clarence—D	Coquille	Coos
1965[2]	Montgomery, F.F.—R	Eugene	Lane
1967[2]	Montgomery, F.F.—R	Eugene	Lane

Session	Name/Political Party	City	County
1969	Smith, Robert F.—R	Burns	Harney
1971[2]	Smith, Robert F.—R	Burns	Harney
1973	Eymann, Richard O.—D	Springfield	Lane
1974[1]	Eymann, Richard O.—D	Springfield	Lane
1975	Lang, Philip D.—D	Portland	Multnomah
1977	Lang, Philip D.—D	Portland	Multnomah
1978[1]	Lang, Philip D.—D	Portland	Multnomah
1979	Myers, Hardy—D	Portland	Multnomah
1980[1]	Myers, Hardy—D	Portland	Multnomah
1981[5]	Myers, Hardy—D	Portland	Multnomah
1983[3]	Kerans, Grattan—D	Eugene	Lane
1985	Katz, Vera—D	Portland	Multnomah
1987	Katz, Vera—D	Portland	Multnomah
1989[2]	Katz, Vera—D	Portland	Multnomah
1991	Campbell, Larry—R	Eugene	Lane
1993	Campbell, Larry—R	Eugene	Lane
1995[2]	Clarno, Bev—R	Bend	Deschutes
1997	Lundquist, Lynn—R	Powell Butte	Deschutes
1999	Snodgrass, Lynn—R	Boring	Clackamas
2001[6]	Simmons, Mark—R	Elgin	Union
2003	Minnis, Karen—R	Wood Village	Multnomah
2005	Minnis, Karen—R	Wood Village	Multnomah
2007	Merkley, Jeff—D	Portland	Multnomah
2009	Hunt, Dave—D	Gladstone	Clackamas
2011	Hanna, Bruce (co-speaker)—R	Roseburg	Douglas, Lane
2011	Roblan, Arnie (co-speaker)—D	Coos Bay	Coos, Douglas, Lane
2013	Kotek, Tina—D	Portland	Multnomah
2015	Kotek, Tina—D	Portland	Multnomah
2017	Kotek, Tina—D	Portland	Multnomah

[1]Special session
[2]Regular and special session
[3]Regular and two special sessions
[4]E.J. Davis was elected speaker by less than a quorum. Subsequently, Henry L. Benson was elected speaker by less than a quorum. The Supreme Court revised an 1871 decision and ordered the secretary of state to audit claims and draw warrants for all claims which the Legislature, through its enactments, permitted and directed, either expressly or by implication.
[5]Regular and four special sessions
[6]Regular and five special sessions

U.S. Senators from Oregon

First Position[2]

Name/Political Party	Term of Service[1]	By What Authority/Remarks
Smith, Delazon[3]—D	Feb. 14–Mar. 3, 1859	Elected by Legislature 1858
Baker, Edward[4]—R	Dec. 5, 1860–Oct. 21, 1861	Elected by Legislature 1860; died in office
Stark, Benjamin—D	Oct. 29, 1861–Sept. 11, 1862	Appointed by Governor Whiteaker to succeed Baker
Harding, Benjamin F.—D	Sept. 11, 1862–1865	Elected by Legislature to succeed Baker
Williams, George H.—R	1865–1871	Elected by Legislature 1864
Kelly, James K.—D	1871–1877	Elected by Legislature 1870
Grover, LaFayette—D	1877–1883	Elected by Legislature 1876
Dolph, Joseph N.—R	1883–1895	Elected by Legislature 1882; reelected 1889
McBride, George W.—R	1895–1901	Elected by Legislature 1895
Mitchell, John H.—R	1901–1905	Elected by Legislature 1901; died in office Dec. 8, 1905

Name/Political Party	Term of Service[1]	By What Authority/Remarks
Gearin, John M.—D	Dec. 12, 1905–Jan. 23, 1907	Appointed by Governor Chamberlain to succeed Mitchell
Mulkey, Fred W.—R	Jan. 23–Mar. 2, 1907	Selected by general election 1906 for short term; elected by Legislature to serve remaining term of Mitchell and Gearin
Bourne, Jonathan, Jr.—R	1907–1913	Selected by general election 1906; elected by Legislature 1907
Lane, Harry—D	1913–May 23, 1917	Selected by general election 1912; elected by Legislature 1913; died in office
McNary, Charles L.—R	May 29, 1917–Nov. 5, 1918	Appointed by Governor Withycombe to succeed Lane
Mulkey, Fred W.—R	Nov. 5–Dec. 17, 1918	Elected 1918 for short term; resigned to permit reappointment of McNary
McNary, Charles L.—R	Dec. 17, 1918–Feb. 24, 1944	Appointed 1918 for unexpired short term; elected 1918; reelected 1924, 1930, 1936, 1942; died in office
Cordon, Guy—R	Mar. 4, 1944–1955	Appointed by Governor Snell to succeed McNary; elected 1944; reelected 1948
Neuberger, Richard L.—D	1955–Mar. 9, 1960	Elected 1954; died in office
Lusk, Hall S.—D	Mar. 16, 1960–Nov. 8, 1960	Appointed by Governor Hatfield to succeed Neuberger
Neuberger, Maurine—D	Nov. 8, 1960–1967	Elected 1960 for short and full terms
Hatfield, Mark O.—R	1967–1997	Elected 1966; reelected 1972, 1978, 1984, 1990
Smith, Gordon H.—R	1997–2009	Elected 1996; reelected 2002
Merkley, Jeff—D	2009–	Elected 2008; reelected 2014

Second Position[2]

Lane, Joseph—D	Feb. 14, 1859–1861	Elected by Legislature 1858
Nesmith, James W.—D	1861–1867	Elected by Legislature 1860
Corbett, Henry W.—R	1867–1873	Elected by Legislature 1866
Mitchell, John H.—R	1873–1879	Elected by Legislature 1872
Slater, James H.—D	1879–1885	Elected by Legislature 1878
Mitchell, John H.—R	1885–1897	Elected by Legislature 1885; reelected 1891
Corbett, Henry W.—R[5]	March, 1897	Appointed by Governor Lord, not seated
Simon, Joseph—R	Oct. 6, 1898–1903	Elected by Legislature to fill vacancy
Fulton, Charles W.—R	1903–1909	Elected by Legislature 1903
Chamberlain, George E.—D[6]	1909–1921	Selected by general election 1908; elected by Legislature; reelected by people 1914
Stanfield, Robert N.—R	1921–1927	Elected 1920
Steiwer, Frederick—R	1927–Feb. 1, 1938	Elected 1926; reelected 1932; resigned
Reames, Alfred Evan—D	Feb. 1–Nov. 9, 1938	Appointed by Governor Martin to succeed Steiwer
Barry, Alex G.—R	Nov. 9, 1938–1939	Elected 1938 for short term
Holman, Rufus C.—R	1939–1945	Elected 1938
Morse, Wayne[7]—D	1945–1969	Elected 1944; reelected 1950, 1956, 1962
Packwood, Robert—R	1969–1995	Elected 1968; reelected 1974, 1980, 1986, 1992; resigned 1995
Wyden, Ron[8]—D	1996–	Elected 1996; reelected 1998, 2004, 2010, 2016

[1]Unless otherwise noted, normal terms of office began on the fourth day of March and ended on the third day of March until 1933 when terms were changed to begin and end on the third day of January, unless a different date was set by Congress.

[2]Delazon Smith and Joseph Lane drew lots in 1859 for the short and long term senate seats. Smith won the short term of only 17 days expiring March 3, 1859 (designated first position). Lane won the long term expiring March 3, 1861 (designated second position).

[3]When the Legislature first met after statehood in May 1859, Smith was defeated for reelection, and no successor was named. Consequently, Oregon had only one U.S. senator from March 3, 1859 until Baker was elected October 1, 1860.

[4]Senator Edward Baker was killed in the Battle of Balls Bluff, Virginia while serving as a colonel in the Civil War, the only U.S. senator to serve in military action while a senator. His statue, cast of horatio stone and marble, stands 6 ft. 5 in. tall in the Capitol rotunda in Washington, D.C.

[5]When the Legislature failed to elect a successor to Mitchell, Governor Lord appointed Henry Corbett. After conflict, however, the U.S. Senate decided the governor did not have this authority and refused to seat Corbett. Therefore, Oregon was represented by only one U.S. senator from March 4, 1897 to October 6, 1898.

[6]Direct election of U.S. senators resulted from Oregon's ratification of Article XVII of the U.S. Constitution on January 23, 1913 (effective May 31, 1913). Oregon initiated a direct primary for selecting candidates in 1904.

[7]Wayne Morse was elected as a Republican in 1944 and reelected as a Republican in 1950. He changed to Independent in 1952, and to Democrat in 1955. He was reelected as a Democrat in 1956 and 1962.

[8]Elected to fill the unexpired term of Robert Packwood due to Senator Packwood's resignation. The elections, both primary and general, to fill Senator Packwood's seat were conducted by mail. The special primary and general elections were the first statewide vote-by-mail elections to fill a federal office in United States history.

U.S. Representatives from Oregon

Name/Political Party	Term of Service[1]	By What Authority/Remarks
Thurston, Samuel R.—D	June 6, 1849–Apr. 9, 1851	Territorial Delegate elected 1849; died at sea returning home from first session
Lane, Joseph—D	June 2, 1851–Feb. 14, 1859	Territorial Delegate elected 1851; reelected 1853, 1855, 1857
Grover, LaFayette—D	Feb. 15–Mar. 3, 1859	First Representative at large, elected 1858 for short term
Stout, Lansing—D	1859–1861	Elected 1858
Shiel, George K.—D	1861–1863	Elected 1860
McBride, John R.—R	1863–1865	Elected 1862
Henderson, J.H.D.—R	1865–1867	Elected 1864
Mallory, Rufus—R	1867–1869	Elected 1866
Smith, Joseph S.—D	1869–1871	Elected 1868
Slater, James H.—D	1871–1873	Elected 1870
Wilson, Joseph G.—R	1873	Elected 1872; died in July, 1873 before qualifying
Nesmith, James W.—D	1873–1875	Elected 1873
La Dow, George A.—D	1875	Elected 1874; died Mar. 4, 1875 before qualifying
Lane, Lafayette—D	Oct. 25, 1875–1877	Elected 1875
Williams, Richard—R	1877–1879	Elected 1876
Whiteaker, John—D	1879–1881	Elected 1878
George, Melvin C.—R	1881–1885	Elected 1880; reelected 1882
Hermann, Binger—R	1885–1893	Elected 1884; reelected 1886, 1888, 1890

1st District

Hermann, Binger—R	1893–1897	Elected 1892; reelected 1894
Tongue, Thomas H.—R	1897–Jan. 11, 1903	Elected 1896; reelected 1898, 1900, 1902; died in office
Hermann, Binger—R	June 1, 1903–1907	Elected 1903 to succeed Tongue; reelected 1904

Name/Political Party	Term of Service[1]	By What Authority/Remarks
Hawley, Willis C.—R	1907–1933	Elected 1906; reelected 1908, 1910, 1912, 1914, 1916, 1918, 1920, 1922, 1924, 1926, 1928, 1930
Mott, James W.—R	1933–Nov. 12, 1945	Elected 1932; reelected 1934, 1936, 1938, 1940, 1942, 1944; died in office
Norblad, A. Walter, Jr.—R	Jan. 11, 1946–Sept. 20, 1964	Elected 1945 to succeed Mott; reelected 1946, 1948, 1950, 1952, 1954, 1956, 1958, 1960, 1962; died in office
Wyatt, Wendell—R	Nov. 3, 1964–1975	Elected 1964 to succeed Norblad; reelected 1966, 1968, 1970, 1972
AuCoin, Les—D	1975–1993	Elected 1974; reelected 1976, 1978, 1980, 1982, 1984, 1986, 1988, 1990
Furse, Elizabeth—D	1993–1999	Elected 1992; reelected 1994, 1996
Wu, David—D	1999–2011	Elected 1998; reelected 2000, 2002, 2004, 2006, 2008, 2010; resigned 2011
Bonamici, Suzanne—D[2]	2012–	Elected 2012; reelected 2012, 2014, 2016

2nd District

Ellis, William R.—R	1893–1899	Elected 1892; reelected 1894, 1896
Moody, Malcolm A.—R	1899–1903	Elected 1898; reelected 1900
Williamson, John N.—R	1903–1907	Elected 1902; reelected 1904
Ellis, William R.—R	1907–1911	Elected 1906; reelected 1908
Lafferty, Abraham W.—R.	1911–1913	Elected 1910
Sinnott, N.J.—R	1913–May 31, 1928	Elected 1912; reelected 1914, 1916, 1918, 1920, 1922, 1924, 1926; resigned
Butler, Robert R.—R	Nov. 6, 1928–Jan. 7, 1933	Elected 1928 to succeed Sinnott; reelected 1930; died in office
Pierce, Walter M.—D	1933–1943	Elected 1932; reelected 1934, 1936, 1938, 1940
Stockman, Lowell—R	1943–1953	Elected 1942; reelected 1944, 1946, 1948, 1950
Coon, Samuel H.—R	1953–1957	Elected 1952; reelected 1954
Ullman, Albert C.—D	1957–1981	Elected 1956; reelected 1958, 1960, 1962, 1964, 1966, 1968, 1970, 1972, 1974, 1976,1978
Smith, Denny—R	1981–1983	Elected 1980
Smith, Robert F.—R	1983–1995	Elected 1982; reelected 1984, 1986, 1988, 1990, 1992
Cooley, Wes—R	1995–1997	Elected 1994
Smith, Robert F.—R	1997–1999	Elected 1996
Walden, Greg—R	1999–	Elected 1998; reelected 2000, 2002, 2004, 2006, 2008, 2010, 2012, 2014, 2016

3rd District

Lafferty, Abraham W.—R	1913–1915	Elected 1912
McArthur, Clifton N.—R	1915–1923	Elected 1914; reelected 1916, 1918, 1920
Watkins, Elton—D	1923–1925	Elected 1922
Crumpacker, Maurice E.—R	1925–July 25, 1927	Elected 1924; reelected 1926; died in office
Korell, Franklin F.—R	Oct. 18, 1927–1931	Elected 1927; reelected 1928
Martin, Charles H.—D	1931–1935	Elected 1930; reelected 1932
Ekwall, William A.—R	1935–1937	Elected 1934

Name/Political Party	Term of Service[1]	By What Authority/Remarks
Honeyman, Nan Wood—D	1937–1939	Elected 1936
Angell, Homer D.—R	1939–1955	Elected 1938; reelected 1940, 1942, 1944, 1946, 1948, 1950, 1952
Green, Edith S.—D	1955–1975	Elected 1954; reelected 1956, 1958, 1960, 1962, 1964, 1966, 1968, 1970, 1972
Duncan, Robert B.—D	1975–1981	Elected 1974; reelected 1976, 1978
Wyden, Ron—D	1981–1996	Elected 1980; reelected 1982, 1984, 1986, 1988, 1990, 1992, 1994
Blumenauer, Earl—D[3]	1996–	Elected 1996; reelected 1998, 2000, 2002, 2004, 2006, 2008, 2010, 2012, 2014, 2016

4th District

Ellsworth, Harris—R	1943–1957	Elected 1942; reelected 1944, 1946, 1948, 1950, 1952, 1954
Porter, Charles O.—D	1957–1961	Elected 1956; reelected 1958
Durno, Edwin R.—R	1961–1963	Elected 1960
Duncan, Robert B.—D	1963–1967	Elected 1962; reelected 1964
Dellenback, John—R	1967–1975	Elected 1966; reelected 1968, 1970, 1972
Weaver, James—D	1975–1987	Elected 1974; reelected 1976, 1978, 1980, 1982, 1984
DeFazio, Peter A.—D	1987–	Elected 1986; reelected 1988, 1990, 1992, 1994, 1996, 1998, 2000, 2002, 2004, 2006, 2008, 2010, 2012, 2014, 2016

5th District

Smith, Denny—R	1983–1991	Elected 1982; reelected 1984, 1986, 1988
Kopetski, Mike	1991–1995	Elected 1990; reelected 1992
Bunn, Jim—R	1995–1997	Elected 1994
Hooley, Darlene—D	1997–2009	Elected 1996; reelected 1998, 2000, 2002, 2004, 2006
Schrader, Kurt—D	2009–	Elected 2008, reelected 2010, 2012, 2014, 2016

[1]Unless otherwise noted, normal terms of office began on the fourth day of March and ended on the third day of March until 1933 when terms were changed to begin and end on the third day of January, unless a different date was set by Congress.

[2]Elected in the January 31, 2012, Special Election to finish the unexpired term of Representative David Wu.

[3]Elected in 1996 to finish the unexpired term of Representative Ron Wyden. Reelected to a full term at the November 5, 1996, General Election.

Backcountry skier Jeff Lokting descends near the 10,000-foot level of Mount Hood in 1985.
Photo courtesy Mt. Hood Museum

The splendor of Oregon began well before it became a territory or a state. Historian Stephen Dow Beckham's finely executed history introduces the reader to the physical and geological changes that created the land we know as Oregon. He escorts us through the times when the Northwest was occupied by the first tribal people and the events that have occurred since Lewis and Clark spread word of the Columbia River and the Pacific Northwest to the rest of the nation.

OREGON HISTORY

Written by Stephen Dow Beckham
Pamplin Professor of History
Lewis & Clark College

An Inhabited Land

Nature marked time. Spring followed winter, passed into summer, merged into fall and, inevitably, gave birth to another winter. The progression was endless and predictable. Water was a consistent ingredient. The steady rain and mist fed the coast and western valleys, nourishing lush forests and grasslands. Salmon surged up the streams, filling the water from bank to bank in a cycle of birth and dying. The fish, exhausted after their journey and spawning, were dragged back downstream by the current. Bears and eagles watched and feasted, while the smolts stirred from the gravel to slip unnoticed down the rivers to the sea and renew the endless process.

Beyond the Cascade Mountains in the vast, arid stretches of central and eastern Oregon, the rainfall was less but life was nevertheless abundant. Aromatic sagebrush, hardy juniper, the sunny faces of balsam root, and tufts of lomatium gave form and color to the landscape. In the fall, countless birds passed across the sky winging their way southward on their annual migration. Geese, ducks, pelicans, and sandhill cranes settled down to search for seeds, feed on brine shrimp in the alkaline lakes, or gain energy for their push to their winter rookeries. Nature constructed elaborate stage sets in the mountains, as tamarack, vine maple, big-leaf maple and alder shed their chlorophyll and transformed from green to red, gold and brown. The turning of the leaves, like the migration of birds and of salmon, steelhead, sturgeon and smelt, marked the change of seasons. Winter brought quiet. Life slowed and snow blanketed part of the land. Living things battened down and endured. Then, as always in nature, the process started over again.

The inevitable exceptions to these predictable events were dramatic and often inexplicable. From time to time, the Cascade peaks shuddered and erupted with uncommon fury, releasing ash flows, watery floods of muddy debris, plumes of smoke, and slowly oozing lava. Occasionally, a rupture appeared in the earth and, as in ancient times when the great basalt flows spread like taffy, layer upon layer, to form the Columbia Plateau, lavas poured out on the surface. They diverted rivers and formed a jumbled landscape, almost fortified in appearance, before ceasing their advance and cooling. Sometimes the earth simply shook and, with great drama, rose or fell. These massive quakes plunged forests surrounding wetlands into estuaries or the sea; they unleashed landslides that sometimes dammed rivers. The earthquakes, driven by the thrust of the Pacific Plate under the continent, changed the face of the land.

Humans witnessed these things.

For at least 10,000 years, and perhaps for another 5,000 to 10,000 years before that, they were in Oregon. Their names for themselves, their languages and their lifeways are unknown, but they were here. Evidence of their presence is subtle but certain. In central and eastern Oregon, where discovery of prehistory is easier because the vegetation is sparse and artifacts are more likely to be preserved in dry rock shelters, archaeologists have found numerous traces. The record, while incomplete, is compelling.

Humans hunted the megafauna of the Late Pleistocene. Massive creatures, far larger than any alive today, lived during the Wisconsin Ice Age, which began to end about 15,000 years ago. Mammoths, mastodons, horses and camels lived contemporaneously with Oregon's first human inhabitants. Scattered in the sands of the High Desert are a mix of camel bones and pieces of fluted projectile points. Big-game hunters using the atlatl—a spear-throwing device that gave them greater leverage and improved both distance and velocity—killed the big-game animals that were yet in the land. Whether hunting hastened the animals' passing or whether environmental conditions drove them to extinction is not clear, but the animals and humans were neighbors in Oregon ten or more millennia ago.

Archaeological work in a cave near Fort Rock revealed that humans had lived in the area for more than 10,000 years. (Oregon State Archives scenic photo)

The story of prehistory in Oregon has unfolded steadily since the advent of archaeological investigations mounted in the 1870s by Paul Schumacher and A.W. Chase along the coast. While the early researchers were primarily relic collectors, Dr. Luther S. Cressman of the University of Oregon helped in the 1930s to develop the discipline of systematic scientific research verifying the deep time frame of people's presence in Oregon. Cressman's primary contributions unfolded at Fort Rock Cave, a deep rock shelter that, 10,000 years ago, was home to people living on an island in a vast inland lake in south-central Oregon. Cressman and his students investigated several sites, testing and excavating, but leaving portions of each location. How fortunate was that discipline, for following World War II and the development of radiocarbon dating, Cressman returned to Fort Rock to open new units of the site and established that, more than 10,000 years ago the region had been occupied by humans.

Oregon's archaeological record grows fuller each year. It documents more than ten millennia of human habitation and successive adaptations to changing environmental conditions. At the end of the 18th century, Oregon possessed several distinctive lifeways. These, for the convenience of description, have been described in geographical terms as Coast, Plateau and Great Basin. While this lumping violates some of the integrity of distinctive cultural practices, it helps clarify the complex human adaptations to distinctive biotic regions of the state.

Northwest Coast

The people of the shoreline and western Oregon valleys, in general, shared lifeways common with native people residing along the North Pacific from Cape Mendocino to southeast Alaska. From the Clatsop at the mouth of the Columbia to the Chetco at the California border and from the Clackamas near the falls of the Willamette to the Takelma and Shasta of the Rogue River Valley—these people shared a common setting: a wet, temperate region, heavily forested, connected by rivers running into the sea. Their environment provided the essentials of life: cedar to frame and cover their houses, materials for clothing and dugout canoes, salmon and other fish as primary subsistence, and a bounty of game, roots and berries to supplement their diet.

For these people life was predictable and generally easy. They had to work hard to secure and maintain supplies of firewood, repair their fishing traps, weirs, and nets, and engage in extensive gathering activities, but for them, nature was generous. Shoreline residents harvested vast quantities of mollusks and crustaceans from the intertidal zones. Valley natives dug camas and wapato, gathered and processed acorns, hunted deer and elk and worked a bit harder to survive. Annually, they set fire to the meadows, opening and shaping the landscapes of the Willamette, Umpqua, and Rogue River valleys. Burning stimulated nutritious browse for deer, assisted women in the harvest of tarweed seeds, stimulated the regeneration of berries and maintained an open understory, which undoubtedly enhanced the security of settlements.

Oregon natives of the western part of the state possessed sufficient time and wealth to develop special arts. The Chinookans of the Columbia River carved handsome, high-prowed canoes with animal effigies on their bows and erected remarkable wooden spirit figures at vigil and grave sites. The Tututni and Chetco of the south coast bartered for raw materials and made massive obsidian wealth-display

blades; wove intricately decorated basketry with geometric designs of beargrass, maidenhair fern, and wild hazel bark; and sent their young people off on spirit quests to sacred sites atop mountain peaks or promontories overlooking the sea. The Coquille, Coos, Lower Umpqua, Siuslaw, Alsea, and Tillamook occupied estuaries that carry their names. A dozen bands from the Tualatin to the Santiam and Yoncalla lived in the Willamette Valley and northern Umpqua Valley. South of them resided the Upper Umpqua, Cow Creek, Shasta Costa, Takelma, and Shasta. Western Oregon people had connections of trade and commerce reaching into northern California and to coastal Washington and British Columbia. They were involved in the flow of dentalium shells, elk hide armor, slaves, and surplus foods. Their lifeways echoed the strong traditions of art, ceremony, social class distinction and emphasis on wealth that ran for hundreds of miles along the North Pacific Coast.

Columbia Plateau

Living east of the Cascades, the people of Oregon's interior nevertheless had access to unparalleled riverine resources. The Columbia and its tributaries—Deschutes, John Day, Umatilla, Snake, Grande Ronde, and Owyhee—were filled with fish. For at least 10,000 years, Celilo Falls, the place where the Columbia dropped over a series of basalt ledges and surged almost on its side through Five Mile Rapids, was their major fishery. So vast were the harvests of fish, the tribes that gathered at Celilo controlled one of the greatest, longest-operating trade centers in the American West. The commerce of Celilo was varied. Arriving from the coast were sleek dugout canoes, paddles, cattail matting, prized shells, and special foodstuffs such as smelt. From the south came war captives to be bartered into slavery, obsidian from more than twenty quarry sites destined for the hands of craftsmen in Washington and British Columbia (where none of this vital projectile material existed naturally), and, just prior to Euro-American contact, herds of horses. From the east came carefully preserved beargrass for basketry, buffalo hides and saddles and, again, just before the arrival of American explorers, remarkable trade goods—glass beads, weapons, metal-tipped tools, and cotton and woolen cloth and clothing.

The Plateau people occupied a challenging environment. Summers were hot and windy; winters were cold and windy. The lodges to shelter human activities thus varied from pole-frame, mat-covered summer encampments to semisubterranean pit houses, framed with a cone of rafters covered with brush and earth to provide a refuge from the icy cold, snow, and darkness of winter. In spite of its harshness, the region abounded in life. Following annual ceremonies, the women harvested the roots of wild celeries, balsams, and lomatiums. They picked huckleberries in the nearby mountains and gathered nutritious moss. The men ran down deer in the snow to secure not only meat but hides to tan for clothing and moccasins. They dipped, clubbed, netted, and speared salmon and wind-dried them in curing sheds along the river.

Oregon's Plateau tribes included the Wasco, Wishram, Warm Springs (or Tenino), John Day, Cayuse, Umatilla, and Nez Perce. They lived from the Cascade Mountains to the Wallowas, from the margins of the rivers to summer camps at high elevations. Their seasonal round responded to the rhythms of nature and took them from fishing camps to berry-picking sites and hunting camps high in the mountains. With the onset of winter, they returned to lower elevations and their permanent villages along the margins of the principal streams.

Great Basin

The high desert region is majestic and harsh. It is an unforgiving landscape where, at times, life is a scramble. For the Northern Paiute, Western Shoshoni, Bannock, Klamath and Modoc, survival demanded unremitting labor and almost constant movement. While the Klamath and Modoc possessed staple foods such as suckers, trout, wocus (water lily seed) and huckleberries, the tribes to the east had a more marginal existence. Their resilience in coping with high elevation, extreme temperatures, arid conditions and isolation spoke to their time-tested survival skills in a challenging environment. The Klamath Basin peoples actually lived at a point of transition between Plateau, Basin, Coast and California lifeways, whereas the Northern Paiute, who held vast stretches of central and southeastern Oregon, were more closely tied to the basin environment.

The harsh environment of the Great Basin challenged the survival skills of the native inhabitants. (Oregon State Archives scenic photo)

Oregon's Great Basin peoples engaged in a seasonal round that often required 200 or more miles of travel per year. In winter, they resided on the margins of lakes and rivers, seeking the lowest elevation and most moderate temperatures in harsh conditions. Their homes included rock shelters as well as lodges covered with brush and tule mats. In winters, confinement and the months of the long moons

encouraged storytelling and necessitated tapping the food resources carefully stored in the previous seasons. When spring became summer, these people were on the move. They hunted waterfowl, antelope, and deer; gathered roots, berries, seeds and nuts; fished; and traveled. They moved to higher and higher elevations following food sources, until the aspen leaves turned to bright gold, telling them it was time to leave the high country and return to the winter encampments.

The peoples of the Great Basin traveled in extended family groups but sometimes gathered as bands for communal hunts. Women and children fanned out through the countryside and, moving slowly toward a ravine and making great noise, drove all creatures before them. Far down the trace, etched eons ago by erosion through basalt, the men stretched fiber nets. Here they clubbed frightened rabbits or, when lucky, killed deer and antelope with bow and arrow. Paddling carefully in the predawn cold onto the waters of the lakes in the middle of the High Desert, the men silently stretched nets between poles and, with a great noise, spooked the unsuspecting water birds. The birds rose to flee in the mist, only to become entangled in the mesh of netting, which the men then collapsed into the water, harvesting a bountiful supply of food for their families.

Great Basin residents practiced a mixed economy. They hunted, fished, trapped, dug, and picked food resources. They moved with the seasons in an almost continuous quest for subsistence. They covered a vast, open country, leaving their petroglyphs at sacred sites, caching foods, camping in rock shelters used by the ancient inhabitants of the region. Their finely developed survival skills enabled them to endure and prosper in a land that held them, at times, at the edge of existence.

The first inhabitants occupied three distinct biotic provinces or geographical areas. Their adaptation and mastery of the environment reached from the margins of the fog-shrouded and wet Pacific shoreline to the arid reaches of sagebrush and bunchgrass of the interior. Their subsistence activities took them from sea level to tree line in the Wallowas and on Steens Mountain. They were at home in the desert and in the grasslands of the Columbia Plateau. In the fall, they set fire to the meadows to keep open the western Oregon valleys as well as to maintain the bald headlands along the Oregon coast. At the south-facing bases of the headlands, they often erected their plank houses facing into the sun. They plied the rivers with dugout canoes; they hunted for ducks and geese on the lakes with balsa rafts made of dried tules.

The first inhabitants knew this land. They gave it names. They explained its features in their oral histories, through experienced storytellers reciting the stories. They told of the myth age when only animals and no humans were in the land. They recounted tales of transition, when animals and humans interacted on a personal basis, a time when humans were not quite fully formed. They told of the historic past, of things remembered and partly remembered. They did this with gesture, eye contact, voice modulation, and sometimes by musical interlude wherein they or someone in the crowd sang a song relevant to the story. Their techniques varied. The Tillamook, for example, repeated stories line-by-line as they listened to the teller, thereby memorizing over a period of years the stories and history of their tribe. The challenge to the storyteller was thus to deliver with talent and stay true to the story elements, yet build the drama and unleash creativity.

The first inhabitants held a rich land. Its resources far exceeded their needs and their wants. They lived fully. While there is some evidence of migration and population dynamics, those tales of prehistory are lost in the mists of time. What is known is that Oregon was fully occupied by the 18th century. people of more than 30 different languages lived throughout the state. They knew and loved the land. It was their home.

Some Came By Sea

The first moment of contact was not recorded. Possibly, it occurred when a Manila Galleon made a landfall somewhere along the Oregon Coast. How the viewers must have wondered when, looking out to sea, they saw a great ship, propelled by billowing sails, not paddles, scudding to the wind and laboring through the waves. The prospect for such an encounter unfolded in 1565 when the Spanish, after several years of probing for a route, finally found a means to catch the great Japanese Current for a sweeping circular transit of the North Pacific. While normally the galleons—one per year for 250 years—did not make a landfall until south of Cape Mendocino in northern California, some did go farther north.

The *San Francisco Xavier,* one of 30 vessels that failed to arrive in Acapulco or any of the other destination ports along the west coast of New Spain (Mexico), likely wrecked in 1707 on the Nehalem sand spit near the base of Neahkahnie Mountain. Tillamook tribal tales of strangers in their midst, discoveries of large chunks of beeswax and a lidded silver vase, and legends of buried treasure hint that a wayward galleon may have crashed into the shore. A thousand-ton vessel, it was probably laden with silk, porcelain, altar pieces reworked in Asia from gold and silver shipped from Central America, pepper, cloves, and other luxury items—each stored in cargo space allotted to the merchants who controlled the monopoly of the galleon trade.

Spanish voyages in the North Pacific were part of the nation's efforts to seek colonies, mission fields, and wealth. As early as 1543, Bartolome Ferrelo, a surviving captain of the ill-fated expedition under Juan Cabrillo, may have sailed as far north as the Oregon-California border. He and his shipmates sought the fabled Straits of Anian—a passage through the continent. Cape Ferrelo on the south coast bears his name. Some also believe that

Francis Drake sojourned on the *Golden Hind* in 1579 in coastal Oregon. Having raided Spanish ports and stolen immense wealth in his voyage northward from Cape Horn, Drake was hiding out before crossing the Pacific and rounding the world to return to England. Although his anchorage is claimed at sites in California, heralded in a marker at Cape Arago, and said to have been at Whale Cove, no one has produced conclusive evidence of his visit to Oregon. Sebastian Vizcaino, sailing for Spain in 1603, possibly sighted and named Cape Sebastian north of the California border. The promontory marked his northernmost exploration along the Pacific shoreline.

Tillamook tribal tales tell of a Spanish ship wrecked on the Nehalem sand spit in 1707. (Oregon State Archives scenic photo)

Then came silence. As had been the case for thousands of years, Oregon was wholly an indigenous people's land. The mid-1700s, however, unleashed forces that would forever change native dominion in the American West. The forces were in part intellectual. Europe had engaged in a Renaissance, a rekindling of energies and rediscovery of classical learning. Emerging nation-states took pride in commerce, art, and education. The turning point, however, was the Enlightenment. By the early 18th century, several nations had philosophical societies whose members hungered for knowledge and who sought natural laws or evidence for what governed the universe. They became eager students of the world. Carl Linne, a Swede, developed systems to classify all living things as plants or animals, seeking to order the descriptions and terminologies. Luke Howard, an Englishman, developed a nomenclature for clouds. Isaac Newton provided mathematical evidence on the working of gravity and descriptions of optics. The quest for knowledge, developing collections of "curiosities," and, in time, exploring unknown lands took on national significance.

The reaching out of Russians to the Aleutians and into Alaska between 1728 and 1769 shocked the Spanish. Following the discoveries of Vitus Bering, Russian fur seekers swept into the region, destroying Aleut villages, enslaving the natives, and securing riches by shipping furs to the Asian and European markets. A cardinal principle of Spain, exercised since the 1520s, was to create protective borderlands to insulate her wealthiest colonies from foreign predators. By the 1760s, officials in New Spain were gravely worried that the Russians, somewhere to the north, might fall upon their outlying colonies in Baja California, Pimeria Alta (Arizona), or New Mexico. Viceroy Antonio de Bucareli in 1769 thus dispatched Gaspar de Portola by sea and Juan Batista de Anza by land with priests, soldiers, and families of workers to establish a new borderland—Alta California. Within two decades, these Spanish colonists had a chain of missions, presidios, and pueblos extending from San Diego to San Francisco Bay.

When the Russians did not appear, the Spanish reached out again. In 1775, the viceroy ordered the first of a series of maritime expeditions to explore the coastline northward. The voyages of Juan Perez, Bruno Hezeta, and Bodega y Quadra gave more form to the European understanding of the coast. Working under wretched conditions, sailing against the current and suffering from ill health and spoiled water, the mariners nevertheless began an important era in exploration.

The British came next. In 1778, Captain James Cook, aboard H.M.S. Resolution, made a landfall on the central Oregon coast. He commemorated the day by naming the headland Cape Foulweather. A famed mariner who had twice before explored the Pacific, Cook was sent to find the Northwest Passage, a mythical sea route through the continent. He could not find what did not exist, but Cook sailed north to the Arctic Ocean and charted much of the outer coast. The Spanish responded immediately and dispatched Ignacio de Arteaga and Bodega y Quadra in 1779 to explore parts of coastal Alaska. In the 1780s, the French expedition under Comte de Laperouse and the Spanish expedition under Alessandro Malaspina sailed the shore to chart, collect specimens of natural history and native culture, and assess the prospects of new colonies.

Significant in discerning the features of coastal Oregon were the labors of independent mariners, dispatched not by their governments but by investors who sought wealth through the fur trade. Cook's men discovered when they reached China in 1779 that a sea otter pelt purchased for a broken file or a few brass buttons brought a thousand-fold return when bartered to the merchants of the Pearl River delta. Captain John Meares of England and Captain Robert Gray of Boston both sailed the coast of Oregon in 1788–89 and traded with natives who paddled out to sea in their canoes or who, in Gray's trade at Tillamook Bay, dared to barter with the foreigners who sailed across the bar and dropped anchor near their villages.

On a second voyage to the coast in 1792, Gray decided to risk a perilous crossing, the unknown bar of the Columbia River. Although the river had been discerned by Hezeta and tentatively designated Rio San Roque, no mariner had entered it. Gray did. He and his men sailed through the breakers and over the shoals, passing the base of Cape Disappointment, named in frustration by Meares on a previous voyage, and dropped anchor in the broad estuary of the great river. Gray named it Columbia in honor of his ship, the Columbia Rediviva. A few weeks later, Gray encountered the exploring party headed by Captain George Vancouver, another British expedition in search of the Northwest Passage. Gray told Vancouver of his "discovery" of the Columbia, a watershed known and occupied by thousands of people for at least 10,000 years. Vancouver could not resist. He dispatched Lieutenant William Broughton aboard the Chatham into the Columbia to chart its course. Broughton and his crew used two whaleboats to conduct reconnaissance as far east as the entrance to the Columbia Gorge, noting depths of the channel and tribal villages along the shore, persuaded, at last, that the river did not pass through the continent.

By the end of the 18th century, an estimated 300 vessels from a dozen different countries had sailed to the Northwest Coast. Some of these had passed along the shores of Oregon. The logs of James Cook, John Meares, Robert Gray, John Boit and Robert Haswell, as well as eight diaries of George Vancouver's shipmates recorded first impressions of the land and its people. "They were of a middling size with mild pleasing features & nowise sullen or distrustful in their behaviour," wrote Dr. Archibald Menzies in 1792 when describing the Quah-to-mah Tribe near Cape Blanco.

The mariners named headlands, charted offshore rocks, explored some of the estuaries, notably the Columbia and Puget Sound, and obtained useful knowledge. The narratives of Cook and Vancouver were published shortly after their journeys. They whetted the appetite of others who wanted to know more about these lands. The collections of bows, arrows, baskets and plants secured by Vancouver's expedition went into the holdings of the British Museum. What had been unknown was now better understood. The currents of the Enlightenment had swept halfway round the world and touched the Oregon Country.

Land-based Fur Trade and Exploration

The mariners who sailed the coast or ran their vessels tentatively into the estuaries and harbors of Oregon initiated inexorable forces of change. They introduced trade goods that swept in swift current through the traditional cultures of the native peoples, altering forever their clothing, technology, and means of subsistence. They introduced diseases such as smallpox, measles, and fevers; in time these pathogens decimated the Indian population. However, an event that would have even greater consequence was the November, 1805, arrival at the mouth of the Columbia River of a weary, but eager, exploring party under the command of Meriwether Lewis and William Clark.

Dispatched in 1804 by President Thomas Jefferson, this military expedition, financed at public expense and underwritten in part by the American Philosophical Society, was the American nation's belated commitment to the Enlightenment. Ostensibly, the party was to explore the newly acquired Louisiana Territory. Jefferson, however, wanted to find a water route, so far as practical, for the transit of commerce across North America. An avid student of nature and civilization, he laid out detailed instructions for the explorers to observe the flora, fauna, geology, climate and tribal culture. They were to map the land, take temperatures of hot springs, note locations of major geographical features, record tribal vocabularies and open diplomatic relations between the tribes and the United States.

The scripting of the expedition could not have been more perfect. The cast of characters included two stalwart leaders, young Army recruits, French-Canadian hunters, a Shoshoni woman—Sacagawea—and her infant son—Baptiste Charbonneau—York, an African-American slave of William Clark's, and a shaggy Newfoundland dog. The success of the Corps of Discovery in carrying out its multiple missions gave it luster while heightening interest in western lands and in government-financed exploration.

Explorers Lewis and Clark view the Columbia River from Rock Fort in this mural in The Dalles by Robert Thomas. (Oregon State Archives scenic photo)

Lewis and Clark accomplished their mission with verve. They crossed the Rockies, entered the Bitterroot Valley of Montana, followed the Nez Perce Trail west of Lolo Pass and, then, embarked by dugouts to descend the Clearwater, Snake and Columbia Rivers. They camped on the north and south banks of the Columbia, portaged at Celilo Falls, passed through the Gorge and established their winter quarters at Fort Clatsop on the Oregon shore near the river's mouth. During the rain-soaked winter of 1805–06, they wrote their journals, boiled salt from seawater on the nearby beach of the Pacific, recorded cultural information from the Clatsop and Chinook people, drew numerous maps, and hoped a trading vessel might carry some of their treasured notes safely to the president. None appeared. The following spring, the party departed for home, paddling against the swift current until it reached the mouth of the Umatilla River. Having bartered for horses

sufficient to carry the party and its supplies, the men set out overland to retrace their steps across the mountains and plains.

News of the Lewis and Clark Expedition enlivened interest in distant frontiers. Already, fur seekers were pushing up the Missouri, Arkansas and Red Rivers. The descriptions of swift streams and ponds filled with beaver, mink, otter and marten in the mountains persuaded several investors to send men with traps and trade goods to exploit those resources. John Colter, a member of the Corps of Discovery, turned around before reaching St. Louis and signed on with a fur trapping party headed for the Yellowstone country. The rush for furs had taken on a new life. This time Americans were major players.

Jefferson turned over the journals of the leaders to Nicholas Biddle, who edited them in an abridged two-volume edition, *The Journals of Lewis & Clark* (1814). So popular were their accounts of adventure that an eager public literally read the books to pieces.

Lewis and Clark had created a remarkable legacy. They had dramatically enhanced the geographical understanding of a far-flung part of North America. They collected 178 plant specimens—140 in the Oregon Country. They made notes upon or brought home specimens of 122 species and subspecies of animals—65 west of the Continental Divide. They expanded a nation's horizon and understanding in noteworthy ways.

The stirrings of change picked up momentum in 1808 when Simon Fraser and other employees of the North West Company, a fur-trading enterprise based in Montreal, crossed the Rockies and descended a mighty stream—the Fraser—to the Pacific Ocean. David Thompson, a skilled cartographer also in the employ of the North West Company, came next. He and his party crossed the Rockies and descended the Columbia. When he reached the ocean in 1811, he found an American fur trade post on the south shore. The Pacific Fur Company had already established a toehold, the first permanent Euro-American settlement in the region, at Astoria.

The new post on the lower Columbia River fulfilled the speculative dream of John Jacob Astor. An emigrant from Germany who prospered as a middleman in the fur trade and investor in New York real estate, Astor had listened keenly to reports of the Lewis and Clark Expedition. One of America's first millionaires, Astor thought big. His vision was to establish a post near the ocean shore in the Pacific Northwest. Land-based trappers and traders would secure furs for his rich trade in Canton. His warehouses on the lower Pearl River would exchange otter pelts for silks and porcelains for the American market. His sailing vessels would supply both his Columbia River post and the Russian American Company in Alaska. These ambitions led Astor to found the American Fur Company for the Rocky Mountain region in 1808, the Pacific Fur Company for the Columbia watershed in 1810, and the South West Company in 1811.

To attain his goals in Oregon, Astor planned a two-pronged approach. He outfitted the *Tonquin,* a ship under Captain Jonathan Thorn, with trade goods, tools and everything needed to sustain his new fort on the Columbia. Sailing in September, 1810, the *Tonquin* arrived in March, 1811, at the Columbia River. Astor also ordered Wilson Price Hunt to lead an overland party, which departed from St. Louis in September, 1810, for an arduous and nearly fatal winter crossing of the continent. Ultimately, in spite of drownings at the mouth of the Columbia and terrible privations for the overland party, the Astorians began clearing the dense spruce forest to erect their fort. "The buildings consisted of apartments for the proprietors and clerks, with a capacious dining-hall for both, extensive warehouses for the trading goods and furs, a provision store, a trading shop, smith's forge, carpenter's workshop," noted Ross Cox. All was enclosed by a log stockade with two bastions in which the Astorians mounted six-pound cannon.

Although the Pacific Fur Company's outpost appeared substantial when David Thompson arrived at its doorstep in 1812, its tenure proved fragile. The *Tonquin* was blown up and sank on a trading voyage north along the coast. Supplies were infrequent. The men at Astoria were driven by starvation to establish Willamette Post in the lower Willamette Valley to relieve some of the pressure on stores at the river's mouth. The connections with China were infrequent. When the partners-in-the-field at Astoria learned of the outbreak of the War of 1812, they rightly feared a British naval vessel might enter the river and seize their post. Thus, in 1813, they sold out to the North West Company. The sale ended Astor's dreams for the Pacific Fur Company. His investment, however, proved highly consequential for the United States.

The Treaty of Ghent (1814) provided in the peace terms ending the war with Great Britain that all conditions would revert to "status ante bellum." The Americans subsequently interpreted this clause to mean that the American claim to the Oregon Country—enhanced by the construction of the fort at Astoria—remained unextinguished. To buttress this prospect, the U.S. Navy dispatched Captain James Biddle on the U.S.S. *Ontario* to the Columbia River. In 1818, Biddle declared American possession of both shores of the estuary. John B. Prevost, an American special agent, arrived later that year and symbolically reasserted his nation's interest by raising The Stars and Stripes on the flagpole at Fort George, the post purchased and named by the North West Company for King George III of England.

During the 1810s, the competition between the North West Company and the Hudson's Bay Company, the older, larger rival for control of the fur trade, erupted into bloodshed in the Red River Valley in Canada. Determined to end the conflict and to bring stability to the frontier, the British parliament, in 1821, forcibly merged the companies. One firm survived—the Hudson's Bay Company, founded in 1670. This British corporation took over the inter-

ests of the North West Company in the Oregon Country. For the next 25 years, the Hudson's Bay Company helped shape the destiny of the region.

The Hudson's Bay Company had a single concern: profit. To satisfy investors interested in return on their money, the directors in London named George Simpson to superintend the field operations. Simpson, in turn, named Dr. John McLoughlin, a former North West Company employee, to serve as Chief Factor in the watershed of the Columbia River. The directions of Simpson and steady hand of McLoughlin proved highly significant in the history of Oregon. Collectively, they agreed on a simple, effective set of policies: peace with the tribes, fair prices for furs secured through trade and self-sufficiency for the posts in the region.

The Oregon Country was so distant that the company workers in the region had to provide for their own subsistence. Vessels could bring in tools and trade goods, but they could not provide food to sustain the nearly 600 men working for the company and their families. Simpson and McLoughlin thus developed the post system. Fort Vancouver, founded in 1822 near the confluence of the Willamette and Columbia rivers, was the hub. The spokes of connection reached to Fort George at the mouth of the Columbia, Fort Umpqua in southwestern Oregon, Fort Boise on the western Snake Plain in Idaho, and to Fort Nisqually, Fort Okanogan, and Fort Walla Walla in Washington. A series of more distant forts in British Columbia and southeast Alaska completed the system. Post traders were encouraged to plant vegetables, lay out orchards and raise livestock. These stations tested the region's agricultural potentials. They found considerable promise in their ventures.

Hudson's Bay Company Chief Factor Dr. John McLoughlin was a powerful force in the Oregon Country. (Oregon State Archives scenic photo)

Simpson and McLoughlin also instituted the brigade system. In addition to the posts where nearby tribes bartered furs for trade goods, the company outfitted brigades of 20 to 50 or more employees who, with their Indian wives and children, went into the field to trap and trade for months. Brigade leaders in Oregon included John Work, Michel LaFramboise, Alexander Roderick McLeod, and Peter Skene Ogden. The brigades penetrated the far reaches of the state. McLeod, for example, explored the Oregon coast south to the Rogue River in the 1820s. Work led brigades back and forth via the Willamette, Umpqua and Rogue Valleys to the Sacramento Valley of California. Ogden mounted five brigades to the upper Snake River. His mission, defined by Simpson, was to eradicate the fur-bearing animals of the region. The plan of ecological disruption mounted by the company was to create an area so devoid of furs that Americans crossing the Rockies would become discouraged and turn back. The Hudson's Bay Company largely succeeded in all these objectives.

Simpson and McLoughlin also launched other initiatives. They established a coastal maritime trade. The *Beaver,* a steam-powered sidewheeler, brought manufactured items to native villages along the shore north to Alaska. They opened retail stores in San Francisco and Honolulu and offered lumber cut at the company mill on the north bank of the Columbia as well as salted salmon from Pillar Rock and Cascades fisheries on the river. They established the Puget Sound Agricultural Company with farms at Nisqually and Cowlitz Landings.

The legacies of the Hudson's Bay Company were many. Its employees fished for salmon, felled the towering firs, manufactured lumber, grew bountiful gardens, raised cereal crops, tended horses on the plateau and cows on the meadows west of the Cascades, and trapped and traded for furs. The brigade leaders mapped much of the land; their diaries, closely held by the company, contained valuable geographical information. The company had great impact on the tribes. It spread manufactured goods, hastened cultural change and introduced new diseases. Most of the firm's employees—including natives from Hawaii and Polynesia—married native women creating a mixed-blood population. Their children had connections with both local and foreign worlds and often grew up bilingual. The company spread the Chinook Jargon far and wide. This trade vocabulary of nearly 1,000 words was founded on the Chinookan language of the Columbia River. It became the primary means of communication across tribal lines and with Euro-Americans throughout the region.

The success of the Hudson's Bay Company in the Pacific Northwest did not pass unnoticed. In the 1820s, Hall Jackson Kelley, an ardent, visionary schoolteacher in Massachusetts, began promoting American colonization of the region. Kelley printed circulars and pamphlets that raved about the region's potentials. He talked about the "spontaneous growth of the soil" and the "fruits of laborious industry," which would make Americans rich if they would settle in Oregon. Nathaniel Jarvis Wyeth, a wealthy Boston ice merchant, responded and, when Kelley's colony failed to develop, he formed the Pacific Trading Company, a joint-stock venture, to develop Oregon.

Wyeth's plans echoed those of John Jacob Astor. In 1832, he set out with uniformed associates to cross the continent and locate forts in the Oregon Country. His plan was to supply his land-based traders from western stations and ship furs and salmon to Asia. Desertions reduced his party to 11. John McLoughlin played the good host and extended the hospitality of Fort Vancouver to the American but did little to encourage his enterprise. In 1834, Wyeth returned to Oregon. He traveled with companions overland, driving wagons across the Great Plains and to South Pass, the subsequent route of the Oregon Trail. His party built Fort Hall on the upper Snake and erected Fort William on Sauvie Island at the mouth of the Willamette. Wyeth then set out to trap for furs in the Deschutes watershed. His diary documented his lonely, fruitless efforts to wrest a fortune from the fur-bearing animals of central Oregon. Wyeth's competitors were too powerful. The American Fur Company commanded the trade in the Rockies; the Hudson's Bay Company had a firm grip on the Pacific Northwest. Wyeth's supply ship arrived late and carried out a cargo of poorly preserved salmon. In 1836, he gave up. His business, which showed so much promise, had foundered on the realities of competition and demanding conditions in Oregon.

A fascinating legacy from the fur trade era was how its operators played host to wandering naturalists. David Douglas was singular among these. A Scotsman in the employ of the Royal Horticultural Society of London, Douglas came to Oregon in 1825–27 and 1830–32 to collect plants of potential uses in European landscapes as well as to obtain herbarium specimens to enlarge the understanding of botany. Douglas was ardent in his assignment. In 1826, he traveled alone into the South Umpqua watershed of southwestern Oregon in a quest for the sugar pine trees that produced the handsome seeds he had viewed at Fort Vancouver. His diaries documented his explorations; his name became popularly attached to *Pseudotsuga menziesii,* the famed Douglas Fir. In 1834, Thomas Nuttall, of Harvard University's Arnold Arboretum, and naturalist John Kirk Townsend accompanied Wyeth on his second overland journey. Townsend's *Narrative of Travels Beyond the Rocky Mountains* (1839) gave a positive account of the American West. The duplicates of his bird and mammal skins he sold to John James Audubon. These specimens added to scientific understanding and were rendered into lifelike images by the famed painter in his books on North American birds and the quadrupeds.

By the early 1840s, the fur trade was in decline. Changes in fashion had significantly reduced the interest in men's top hats made of hair stripped from beaver pelts. Extermination of fur-bearing animals in vast parts of the American West was another factor. Furs were neither abundant nor cheap. The days of the fur trade were ending, but the legacy of the enterprise was large. The fur trade had opened primary routes of travel, altered tribal lifeways, filled in geographical information and produced an important literature about Oregon. The Astorians—Ross Cox, Alexander Ross, Gabriel Franchere, Robert Stuart and Peter Corney—all produced books in the 19th century describing Oregon. More significant, however, were the companion volumes penned by Washington Irving. His works, *Astoria or Anecdotes of an Enterprise Beyond the Rocky Mountains* (1836) and *Adventures of Captain Bonneville* (1837), were read by an eager public. Irving described the temperate climate and abundant resources of Oregon, portraying the land as a place of adventure and possible prosperity.

Federal Interests

The government of the United States maintained special interests in Oregon. It founded its claims on the "doctrine of the right of discovery." Although Robert Gray was a mariner for a private fur-trading company, he sailed under a sea letter issued by President George Washington. His crossing of the bar of the Columbia initiated the U.S. claim to having "discovered" Oregon. The Lewis and Clark Expedition was a military expedition financed and directed by the government. Fort Clatsop, though occupied less than five months in 1805–1806, was deemed an American outpost. So, too, the Pacific Fur Company's Fort Astoria was an American venture, and the United States through the actions of Captain Biddle and John Prevost asserted national interests in 1818, pursuant to the terms of the Treaty of Ghent.

In 1818, the United States and Great Britain met in diplomatic conference to try to resolve their interests in the Oregon Country. The negotiators, at loggerheads over the extension of the 49th parallel to the Pacific, reached a compromise. In the Convention of 1818, they agreed to shared spheres of interest in the Columbia watershed, deferring the question of sovereignty for the time being.

The Americans were not idle. In the 1819 Adams-Onis Treaty, whereby Spain ceded Florida to the United States, American negotiators secured all of the Spanish "discovery rights" north of the 42nd parallel—the northern boundary of California. In 1824, the United States negotiated an agreement permitting trade for ten years in Alaska and fixing Russia's southern boundary at 50° 40'. Slowly, steadily, the United States had narrowed the field among the nations vying for control of the Oregon Country. Great Britain, the United States and the indigenous people remained as competitors. In 1827, the two countries agreed to extend indefinitely their earlier agreement that each had a sphere of interest in the region. The new condition added to the convention was that either nation might give notice and demand a resolution of the issue within one year.

American "discovery rights" gained Supreme Court sanction when, in 1823, Chief Justice John Marshall ruled in a matter involving former tribal lands. Marshall opined in *Johnson v. McIntosh* that because natives were wanderers over the face of the earth, their rights were impaired and subordinate to the "discovery rights" of Europeans. While tribes retained an occupancy right, title was not vested in

them. The Marshall ruling became a convenient justification to dispossess hundreds of tribes of their homelands.

President Andrew Jackson, an expansionist with interests in the West, attempted in 1835 to purchase the harbor of San Francisco for $500,000 from Mexico. The following year he dispatched the brig *Loriot* to the West Coast. Lieutenant William A. Slacum carried a presidential commission to examine Puget Sound, the Columbia estuary, and San Francisco Bay, assess those anchorages for strategic value, and examine the frontier economy of the region. Slacum's report, printed in the *United States Congressional Serial Set,* made a strong case for American acquisition of all three harbors.

Jackson next endorsed, and Congress funded, the multifaceted U.S. Exploring Expedition. Under the command of Lieutenant Charles Wilkes, this Navy party included five vessels, more than 300 seamen, and a corps of talented scientists, artists and officers. After exploring the coasts of South America, Australia and Hawaii, the expedition, in 1841, sailed to Puget Sound and the Columbia River. Overland parties traveled south via the Cowlitz to Fort Vancouver, east through the Gorge to Fort Walla Walla, and south through the Willamette Valley to Sutter's Fort on the Sacramento River. James Dwight Dana collected fossils at Saddle Mountain at the mouth of the Columbia; Titian Ramsay Peale sketched the Umpqua Mountains; Horatio Hale compiled tribal vocabularies; and Charles Wilkes penned a fact-filled description of western Oregon.

In 1845, the narrative and scientific reports of the Wilkes Expedition, as it was popularly called, began to appear. Volumes four and five contained candid information about Oregon. Wilkes described the Willamette Valley and its "advantages for raising crops, pasturage of stock, and the facilities of settlers becoming rich." He wrote: "The salmon-fishery may be classed as one of the great sources of wealth, for it affords a large amount of food at a very low price, and of the very best quality. . . ." The sixth volume of reports, an atlas, included numerous charts of Puget Sound and the Columbia River useful for mariners. Over the next dozen years, specialists wrote scientific assessments of the flora and fauna collected by the expedition and published 14 oversized folios of hand-colored illustrations of the specimens. The knowledge about Oregon had increased dramatically and was based on sound authority.

While the Wilkes party was on the high seas headed to the Pacific Northwest, Robert Greenhow, librarian to the Department of State, compiled his *Memoir, Historical and Political, on the Northwest Coast of North America* (1840). Senator Lewis Linn of Missouri had the report printed for the Select Committee on Oregon Territory and requested the immediate publication of an additional 2,500 copies for the Senate to distribute. Greenhow presented a history of exploration, covered the diplomacy of sovereignty issues, discussed the fur trade and argued that Oregon was a region "lying entirely within the undisputed limits of the Republic." Therein he revealed his agenda. Greenhow's memoir was a brief to make the case for American sovereignty over the Pacific Northwest.

Explorer John C. Fremont gathered invaluable information that attracted travelers to Oregon. (Courtesy Wikimedia)

Thomas Hart Benton, senator from Missouri and, for more than 20 years, a champion of American expansion, in 1842, secured congressional funding for his son-in-law, John Charles Fremont, to explore west to South Pass. The following year, Fremont, a member of the U.S. Topographical Engineers, set out again, guided by Kit Carson, to follow overland emigrants across the Oregon Trail. Fremont kept a diary and collected minerals, plants and zoological specimens. Charles Preuss, his cartographer, prepared eight detailed strip maps showing the route of the trail to Fort Walla Walla. In the map margins were notations on fords, grazing sites, camping locations, and the availability of firewood. Fremont's wife, Jessie, turned her husband's diaries into flowing prose. Published by the Government Printing Office in large numbers, the Fremont narratives and Preuss maps became a major publicity piece for Oregon and a virtual travelers' guide to the trail.

In early 1846, Lieutenant Neil M. Howison sailed to Oregon on the *Shark* to carry out another reconnaissance. Delayed by the wreck of the ship on the Columbia bar, Howison sojourned for five months and examined the land, interviewed residents, visited tribal villages and reflected on what he saw. He noted that the influence of Dr. John McLoughlin had "done more than any other man toward the rapid development of the resources of the country." Howison described wolves, grizzly bears, elk and the thriving condition of cattle and sheep. "I can think of nothing vegetable in nature," he commented, "that Oregon will not produce." His report was ultimately issued in the *United States Congressional Serial Set* in 1848. It was another candid assessment of Oregon by an objective observer.

During the period 1792 to 1846, the U.S. government thus aided and abetted American interest in Oregon. The nation's leaders, both public and private, took actions to help buttress claims to Oregon through discovery, diplomacy, exercise of will, and the persuasive historical research of Robert Greenhow. The explorations of Lewis and Clark, Slacum, the Wilkes expedition, John Fremont and Neil M. Howison generated maps, reports and collections of specimens. These were analyzed and published. The evidence was growing about the prospects of the Pacific Northwest and Oregon, in particular.

Souls to Save

The first three decades of the 19th century were a time of intense religious fervor in America. The Second Great Awakening, kindled by the exhortations of Rev. Timothy Dwight, swept across the land. Camp meetings, revivals, sectarian controversies, the founding of home and foreign mission societies, building of seminaries to educate the ministry, and publication of books, tracts, hymns, and translations of the scriptures into native languages were all part of the religious commitment. Shakers gathered in celibate communities. Mormon converts followed the teachings of Joseph Smith, Jr. Revivals sweeping over the country produced conversions and, in some, anticipation of the return of Christ to Earth.

In 1832, the *Christian Advocate and Journal* carried a feature story about four Indians from the interior of the Pacific Northwest who had arrived in St. Louis. Although they may have come to confer with William Clark, the explorer and then superintendent of tribal affairs in the Louisiana Territory, the press interpreted their visit as a cry from heathens seeking the white man's book of God. This news proved electrifying to a population eager to promote evangelical Christianity. With the alleged request from the "savages of Oregon" for the word of God, mission societies were ready to send workers to the field to reap souls.

Rev. Jason Lee was first to respond. In 1833, the Methodist Episcopal Church authorized Lee, his nephew, Daniel Lee, and three lay assistants to go to Oregon. With mission board underwriting and a determination to preach to the tribes people, this party embraced its calling and joined Nathaniel Wyeth in 1834 on his second overland trek to the Columbia estuary. Thus Nuttall and Townsend, with interests in natural history; Wyeth, who hoped to compete with the Hudson's Bay Company; and a cadre of missionaries joined forces to traverse the continent.

Although the initial request for missionaries had presumably come from the Nez Perces or Flatheads in the interior, Lee conferred with McLoughlin on a likely location for a mission west of the Cascades. He selected Mission Bottom on the southwest side of French Prairie in the northern Willamette Valley. Proximity to Fort Vancouver, the proven agricultural potential of the area, the nearby population of retired fur trappers, and the isolation of any site east of the mountains weighed heavily in Lee's decision.

History

The Methodists tried hard. They built a station, fenced and tilled fields, opened a school, and ministered to the Kalapuyans, whose villages had been ravaged by a horrendous fever starting in 1829. By the mid-1830s, as many as 70 percent had perished. Lee and his associates thus coped with orphans, solitary survivors of families or entire villages and the aged. To cope with the challenges, Lee ambitiously planned to increase his crew of workers. He sent back positive reports, and in 1838, returned to the East to seek money and recruits. He raised an estimated $100,000 and brought 32 adults and 18 of their children to Oregon in 1839. The expanded staff opened a mission on the Clatsop Plains, another among the Clackamas people at Oregon City, a third at The Dalles, and yet another at the southern end of Puget Sound. In spite of their efforts, the Methodist laborers were not good linguists nor effective missionaries. The converts were few. Dr. Elijah White, a recruit, fired off criticisms to the mission board, which suspended Lee and closed the operations in 1843.

The Methodists, though converting few Indians, had tested the potentials of Oregon and succeeded in raising cereal crops, vegetables and livestock. Their families prospered. They staked out land claims, including one which encroached on Dr. McLoughlin's milling site at Willamette Falls. Writing home about what they found, they gave good reports of Oregon. These Americans helped set the stage for overland emigration.

In the 1820s, the American Board of Commissioners for Foreign Missions (ABCFM) had sent workers among the Cherokee, Creek, Choctaw and other tribes. An ecumenical project drawing on the resources of the Congregational, Presbyterian, and Dutch Reformed denominations, the ABCFM also responded to the alleged request of Oregon Indians for missionaries. In 1835, Rev. Samuel Parker and Rev. Marcus Whitman traveled west to survey prospects. Although Whitman turned back at Green River in the Rocky Mountains, Parker continued to Oregon, explored widely and, after returning home by sea via Hawaii, published *Journal of an Exploring Tour Beyond the Rocky Mountains* (1838). Whitman had seen enough to persuade him to devote his energies to the natives of the Pacific Northwest.

In 1836, Whitman, his new wife Narcissa, Rev. Henry H. Spalding and his wife Eliza, set out for Oregon. Both women kept diaries, leaving a fascinating chronicle of the journey of the first white women across the continent. Jane Barnes, a barmaid from Portsmouth, England, had lived for a few months at Astoria during the tenure of the North West Company, but she had traveled by sea. The transit of two missionary women overland was duly noted by residents of the American frontier interested in lands in Oregon.

After visiting Fort Vancouver and obtaining supplies from the Hudson's Bay Company, the Whitmans settled at Waiilatpu, "the place of the rye grass," on the margins of the Walla Walla River near the base of the Blue Mountains. Their mission was to the Cayuse, Umatilla, and Nez Perce people. The Spaldings selected a site at Lapwai, Idaho on the lower Clearwater River in Nez Perce country. For the next 11 years these missionaries and their associates who founded other stations on the Columbia Plateau wrestled with survival, mastering native languages and trying to convert the tribal people. An issue facing all was whether or not it was essential to transform Indians into sedentary farmers dressed like white people as a precondition to conversion to Christianity. The Indians found little attraction in the hard labor of farming, were reluctant to give up their traditional fisheries and hunting, and seemed generally disinterested in the whites' teachings. When Whitman whipped them for disobedience, he fell in their esteem. Conversions were few; troubles accumulated.

In 1838, Fathers Francois N. Blanchet and Modest Demers set out with a Hudson's Bay Company brigade from Red River. They crossed overland through Canada and descended the Columbia to found Catholic missions in the region. The Anglican ministry of Rev. Herbert Beaver at Fort Vancouver in 1836–38 was short-lived and controversial. The fur trappers, many of them nominally Catholic or possessing Catholic ancestors, were receptive to Blanchet and Demers, who moved swiftly, marrying couples, baptizing Indian wives and children, and recording an impressive tally in their sacramental ledgers. They established missions at Fort Vancouver, Cowlitz Prairie, and French Prairie.

Where the protestants had only marginal success in gaining converts, the Catholics prospered. There were several reasons. They did not insist on a change in lifeways as a condition for baptism. They wore vestments, burned incense, rang handbells, recited a ritualistic mass and generated a sense of mystery and interest in their services. They were single men governed by vows of chastity and steadfast purpose of ministry to their flock. They were bound by a commitment to poverty and not engaged in staking land claims or contesting McLoughlin for a mill site. They had a distant but consistent base of support through the Catholic Church. They had already established connections to the native peoples because women from almost every tribe or band in the Pacific Northwest had married Catholic men. They were skilled linguists and were willing to undergo years of patient work to master the native languages.

In 1834 and 1835, a group of retired fur trappers, most of them French-Canadians living on French Prairie, had petitioned the Bishop of Red River in Canada for a priest. In 1836, they had built a log chapel. Blanchet and Demers thus found a receptive audience when they established the St. Paul Mission in October, 1839. The parishioners erected a meeting hall and lodgings for the priests in 1841. The grandly named St. Joseph's College, a school funded in part by a bequest from a French philanthropist, opened in 1843 with 30 boys and three instructors. Nuns arrived in 1844 to establish Saint Marie de Willamette, a girls' school. Parishioners between 1844 and 1846 kilned bricks and erected the St. Paul Church.

Missions further accelerated changes in the lives of Oregon tribes. Many tribes, particularly in western Oregon, were imprinted by the itinerant priests and carried for generations a commitment to Catholicism. This was especially the case among the Kalapuyans and Upper Chinookans. Adrian Croquet, a Belgian priest, ministered to them on the Grand Ronde Reservation from 1860 to 1898. Catholic Oblate missions of St. Ann, St. Rose of the Cayouse, Walla Walla, St. Anthony, and Frenchtown likewise led to conversions among the Confederated Tribes of the Umatilla.

The protestants largely failed in their missionary efforts but left an impact in other ways. They proved that Euro-American families could thrive in the Oregon Country. They grew vegetables and fruit and raised livestock. They wrote reports and lectured in the East about the prospects of the region. They spoke of its mild climate, fertile soil, towering forests, abundant fish and wild game. They helped set the stage for the opening of the Oregon Trail.

Overland to Oregon

Some said there was a contagion in the land and called it the "Oregon Fever." It caused dreams, persuaded men and women to give up all that was familiar, risk their lives and fortunes, and set out for the far shores of the Pacific. The overland emigrations of the mid-nineteenth century were one of the epochal events of human history. Seldom had so many people traveled so far by land to seek a new beginning.

The motives for moving to Oregon were clear. Tens of thousands of Americans residing along the frontier from Minnesota to Texas were land speculators. Many had moved before, to buy a new farm, erect a home and barn, clear and fence fields and sell their "improvements." They were poised to do so again, particularly when senators Lewis Linn and Thomas Hart Benton of Missouri repeatedly introduced bills in Congress calling for grants of up to 1,000 free acres for those who would settle in Oregon. Land speculation ran in their veins. Even when the bills did not pass, thousands were ready to take the risk and hope, in time, Congress would reward their labors.

Oregon had a good press founded on careful observations and scientific authority. The reports of Lewis and Clark, the Astorians, the narratives of John B. Wyeth (1833), Samuel Parker (1838), William Slacum (1838), John Kirk Townsend (1839), Lieutenant John C. Fremont (1845), Lieutenant Charles Wilkes (1846), and Lieutenant Neil Howison (1848) described a rich land with attractive potentials. Letters from missionaries to newspapers and magazines, sermons and lectures delivered during fund-raising in the East, summary reports such as that by Robert Greenhow (1840)—

all laid before the public the region's prospects. The pull factors attracting emigration to Oregon were land, timber, salmon, a climate favorable for agriculture, sites for water power and a peaceful environment. Relations with natives had remained positive and stable throughout the fur-trade era.

On the other end, several push factors motivated frontier residents to consider relocating. The late 1830s and early 1840s were a period of calamitous flooding along the Missouri, Mississippi, and Ohio Rivers. Many who had foolishly built on the floodplains watched their cabins, barns, and split-rail fences wash away in freshets and waited anxiously for weeks as floodwaters drowned their fields and ruined their crops. The Panic of 1837 plunged the country toward depression. Bank failures, currency problems, poor credit, and the inability to pay off loans beset millions. Many hungered for a chance to walk away from their losses and heartaches for a new beginning. Recurrent fevers, particularly malaria, beset many who lived on the frontier. Oregon had a good reputation for health; though thousands of indigenous people perished in the 1830s, most Euro-Americans remained well.

Travel on the Oregon Trail accelerated in the 1840s. Shown above is a covered wagon at Flagstaff Hill. (Oregon State Archives scenic photo)

So the stage was set: Oregon's allure was strong, and the pressure to move out pushed many. A small emigration of about 100 people in 1842 followed Dr. Elijah White westward. The following spring, nearly a thousand emigrants gathered along the Missouri frontier to wait until the prairies were dry enough to permit travel. They had loaded their wagons with dried fruit and vegetables, flour, bran, cornmeal, beans, bacon, ham and kegs of vinegar. They brought weapons, clothing, tools, blankets and quilts and a few treasured possessions. Most carried light tinware for eating, a reflector oven for baking biscuits, a spider for holding the coffee pot and a frying pan. Musicians put in a violin, accordion or Jew's harp. All else they sold or gave away to family and friends. Those who brought too much were compelled to abandon their possessions along the trail.

No one had ever seen anything like it before. The waves of emigrants grew. More than 3,000 traveled overland to Oregon in 1845; by 1850, an estimated 9,000 had crossed the trail to the Pacific Northwest. They knew their journey was a rite of passage. For the first time in their lives, and for many the only time, they penned daily entries in diaries. Their trip was epochal. They were part of history and wanted to record their participation in it.

The overland journey exacted many tolls. For some it was death on the trail. In many respects, the Oregon Trail became one continuous, linear cemetery. Along its course lay the remains of men, women, and children who died of cholera, measles, dysentery, drownings and accidents. Guns misfired; wagons overturned; cattle bolted; clothing caught on fire—the calamities that befell those on a four- to six-month camping trip were many. In spite of the hardships of 1,950 miles of trail between St. Joseph, Missouri, and Oregon City, Oregon, the trip was a great adventure. Vast herds of buffalo, visits by tribal people wanting to trade, the distant Wind River Mountains, basalt flows and canyons along the Snake, and the succession of sunrises and sunsets were all part of the experience. Boys found swimming holes. Women and girls did their best to create a semblance of home by cooking creatively and maintaining norms of domesticity. The men went hunting and fishing, bartered with one another for horses and gear, and carved or marked their names in axle grease on prominent rocks near the trail.

The overland journey was often the migration of an extended family. Parents, children, and grandparents made up the parties. Sometimes several brothers, their families, their sisters and their families, and young hired hands from the neighborhood constituted the group. If one family migrated in 1846, three related families might migrate in 1847 to join them in Oregon. The Applegate family, immigrants of 1843 to Polk County and settlers by 1848 of the Umpqua Valley, were illustrative. Three brothers, their wives, and 39 children constituted this clan. The families took adjoining land claims near Yoncalla. The connections of kinship and friendship were part of the social fabric that knit frontier Oregon in the mid-nineteenth century.

The primary Oregon Trail ran from Fort Hall to Fort Boise in Idaho, then via Burnt River to the Grande Ronde Valley. It crossed the Blue Mountains and the Columbia Plateau, running up to 20 miles south of the river almost to The Dalles. Travelers then made a perilous trip by canoe, bateau, or log raft through the Columbia Gorge to western Oregon. By 1846, they had another option, transit of the Barlow Road, a rugged, rock-filled trace through the forests across the Cascade Mountains to Oregon City.

In 1845, Stephen H. L. Meek led nearly a thousand emigrants with their 200 wagons and livestock east from the Snake River onto Oregon's high desert. The shortcut he proposed over the Cascades proved a terrible trail. Eventually, the wagon train had to work its way through the Deschutes River watershed to regain the old trail at The Dalles. That same year Samuel Barlow, Joel Palmer, William Rector and

others blazed a trace around the southern slopes of Mount Hood. They were compelled to abandon their wagons in the mountains, but the following year workmen opened the Barlow Road, a final overland segment of the Oregon Trail. Thousands traveled its course and paid the toll until 1919, when it passed to the State of Oregon. In 1846, explorers from the Willamette Valley opened the Applegate Trail. This route cut southwest from Fort Hall, crossed the deserts of northern Nevada, passed through the Klamath Basin and Rogue River Valley, and then entered the Willamette Valley from the south. Many who settled in southwestern Oregon in the 1850s and 1860s were emigrants on the Applegate Trail.

The Oregon Trail pioneers were creatures of habit. They carried their attitudes, prejudices and ideas as part of their baggage. They were imitators rather than innovators. They attempted, as best they could remember, to recreate the governmental and social institutions they had left behind. They founded schools and academies and erected Federal, Greek Revival and Gothic Revival buildings to house them—just like at home. Although they saw themselves as stalwart, brave and independent, they were actually a highly dependent people, demanding righteously that the federal government give them land, survey their claims, guard them from Indians, erect lighthouses, establish postal routes and construct wagon roads. They saw themselves as makers of history but seldom perceived they were locked into the historical fabric of which they were merely threads.

The "Oregon Question" and Provisional Government

Oregon was a prize lusted for by two partisans. In 1845, President James K. Polk informed Great Britain he wanted resolution of the issue of sovereignty in the Pacific Northwest. In the agreement reached in 1828, the nations had one year in which to resolve the long-simmering "Oregon Question." Polk was an avowed expansionist. A Democrat, he sought the presidency in 1844 on a simple platform: the annexation of Texas and the occupation of Oregon. The Tyler administration took care of acquiring Texas before Polk was sworn into office, but he persisted in an aggressive agenda of American expansion. Polk campaigned under the popular slogan "54 40 or fight," a contention that the southern boundary of Russian America was the northern boundary of Oregon. He pressed through diplomatic channels and used his inaugural address to assert American rights to all of Oregon. His ambitions far exceeded the area of American activity.

Resolution came on June 15, 1846, in the Oregon Treaty. Polk was already in pursuit of a greater prize—California—and had helped engineer a declaration of war against Mexico by massing troops along the Texas border until they were attacked by Mexican soldiers. Oregon became a sidebar in the unfolding story of the Mexican War. While Congress was willing to plunge the country into a war against its neighbor to the south, it was opposed to entering a conflict with Great Britain. That nation, beset with internal disputes over Corn Law reform, was likewise eager to reach a settlement. Thus, in 1846, the two countries agreed to extend the boundary on the 49th parallel westward from the crest of the Rockies to the primary channel between Vancouver Island and the continent. British citizens and the Hudson's Bay Company retained trading and navigational rights in the Columbia River, though the United States subsequently terminated those privileges in 1859.

By 1846, the arguments of the United States to claim the Oregon Country were founded on more than "discovery rights." Several thousand Americans had settled in the region. Every year, the arrival of new emigrants tipped the scale against the Hudson's Bay Company. The Americans had also established a Provisional Government. Its genesis came with the death in 1841 of Ewing Young. A former mountain man who had built up cattle herds in the Chehalem Valley and owned more than $3,000 in promissory notes from his neighbors, Young died without heirs. Residents gathered after his funeral to discuss what to do with his property. They agreed to name a committee to draft a civil code. Father Blanchet served as chair. When they assembled four months later, Blanchet reported his committee had not met. Disagreements between French-Canadians and Americans about the form of self-government and its powers had created an impasse.

The creation of the Provisional Government helped tip the balance in the dispute between the United States and Great Britain. (Oregon State Archives scenic photo)

The arrival of overland emigrants in 1842, and the increase of retired fur trappers who settled in the Willamette Valley with their mixed-blood families complicated matters. Old settlers and new arrivals worried about their land claims. They wondered what might happen if Congress passed Linn's bills granting lands to Americans who settled in Oregon. Wild animals brought to a head the decisions for a government. Grizzlies, black bears, cougars, and wolves ranged freely in the Willamette Valley. Their destruction of livestock gave cause in the spring of 1843 for a "Wolf Meeting." A second Wolf Meeting led to the decision to create a system of government. On May 2, 1843, at Champoeg, Joseph Meek posed the critical question: "Who's for a divide? All for the report of the committee and organization follow me," he shouted. By a close vote, perhaps 52 to 50, those wanting the government prevailed.

What was the significance of the Provisional Government? In spite of claims that the vote in the spring of 1843 on French Prairie sealed the fate of American sovereignty to the Oregon Country, there is no evidence that the Polk administration weighed the action. What was important and known to the decision-makers across the continent was that an American colony had developed on the shores of the far Pacific Ocean. The Provisional Government informed the Polk administration of its existence. It passed memorials in 1843 and 1845 seeking congressional attention to the needs of Americans in Oregon. The memorial of June 28, 1845, petitioned for naval yards, mail service, land grants, military protection and territorial status. On December 8, 1845, Thomas Hart Benton presented the document to the Senate. These endorsements and his election were all the expansionist President Polk needed in an era when many felt it was America's manifest destiny to spread from sea to sea. Whitman's ride across the continent in 1838 and the events at Champoeg—the lore of Oregon history—did not tip the scales. The United States had embarked on a grand scheme of territorial growth. Oregon was only part of the plan.

The Oregon Provisional Government played an important role in creating order on a frontier. For more than two decades, the Hudson's Bay Company held and exercised civil authority and control of the fur trade, while maintaining peace in dealing with tribes. Its power did not extend to American settlers and ended in 1846 with the Oregon Treaty. The Provisional Government filled the void. It provided for laws governing land claims, instituted taxation, formed counties, created the offices of governor and legislators, and set up a court system. Popularly elected representatives hammered out these decisions between 1843 and 1845. The proposals were often revised, for newly arrived emigrants increased the electorate and brought their experience and men with political ambitions. The Provisional Government was in constant flux, but George Abernethy, a former lay worker for the Methodist Mission, continued as governor.

J. Henry Brown collected the correspondence and decisions made in Oregon City and published them as *Brown's Political History of Oregon* (1892). He dedicated his documentary volume to the "intrepid men and women" who helped lay the foundation of the Pacific states and "builded better than they knew." The legislature patterned many of its laws on those of the Iowa Territory, including weights and measures, criminal codes, and vagrancy. In 1843, the legislature put bounties on wolves, panthers, bears, and lynxes. Cash payments for the skin of the head with ears of these animals soon decimated their population and led to the extinction of several species in Oregon. The Law of Land Claims permitted individuals to file on as much as a square mile, but only one claim at a time, and restricted filings on key town sites or waterpower locations.

The Provisional Legislature banned permanent residency of free African-Americans and mulattoes. Any reaching age 18 had two years to leave the Oregon Country, as did anyone held in slavery. The initial penalty for failure to leave was not less than 20 nor more than 39 lashes. In 1844, the legislature amended the law to put violators out to low bid for public labor and removal. The law, though never enforced, confirmed the racial prejudice of the frontier generation moving into the Willamette Valley.

Cayuse Indian War

Cold winds swept across the Columbia Plateau. In November, 1847, they heralded the onset of the winter of discontent. Too long had the Cayuse tribe suffered from new diseases and the failed ministrations of Dr. Marcus Whitman. In their culture, a shaman or curer who failed was subject to death. This doctor, a strapping, determined white man had come into their lands uninvited. The mission he and his wife established worked like a magnet to draw emigrants. Each year, the wagon trains descended the Blue Mountains and, like the grasshoppers that swept across the countryside, they heralded discomforting changes. Smallpox, measles, fevers, death and mourning came in their wake.

On November 29, 1847, a band of Cayuse men, fed by fear and resentment, fell upon the missionary station. In a matter of hours, they murdered Marcus and Narcissa Whitman and a dozen others. Two more died subsequently of exposure and 47, many orphaned children of emigrants, were taken captive. The Spaldings fled Lapwai and skirted the Cayuse homeland in their dash to safety. Panic swept through the Willamette settlements. Initially, the settlers thought the tribes of the Columbia Plateau might drive through the Gorge and attempt to murder them, too.

The Provisional Legislature faced its greatest test. While Peter Skene Ogden of the Hudson's Bay Company was rushing east with 16 men to try to ransom the hostages, Governor Abernethy called for "immediate and prompt action." The legislature authorized raising companies of volunteers to go to war against the Cayuse Tribe. It entrusted command to Colonel Cornelius Gilliam and named a committee to negotiate with the Hudson's Bay Company for loans of arms, ammunition, and supplies to mount the campaign. The government wrestled with two approaches: one, to send peace commissioners to try to persuade the Cayuse to turn over the perpetrators; or, two, to wage a war of retribution. In short order, it did both. Governor Abernethy appointed a peace commission—Joel Palmer, Henry A. G. Lee, and Robert Newell. Gilliam, who did not approve of the commission, set out in January, 1848 with more than 500 volunteers.

The Cayuse War became, at times, a war of nerves. The peace commissioners tried to end hostilities and get the Cayuse to turn over the killers

of those at the Whitman station. Gilliam and his forces, eager for action, provoked conflicts with both friendly and hostile Cayuse. In March, having persuaded the Cayuse to surrender five men, the military brought them to Oregon City. They were charged, tried, and hanged in 1850. The guilt of the five men and the jurisdiction of the court were not fully established. Controversy swirled for decades after this trial—the first culminating in capital punishment following legal proceedings in the Oregon Territory.

Territorial Government

The Oregon Country lay in limbo following the 1846 treaty with Great Britain. Congress had not acted and was diverted by both the Mexican War and the slavery question. The tragedy at the Whitman Mission demanded action. In December, 1847, the Provisional Legislature drafted another memorial to lay again before Congress its "situation and wants." The petition discussed the deaths at Waiilatpu, lack of revenue laws and uneasiness about land claims. Should Congress act, the memorial pointed out that "the present citizens of this country have strong claims upon the patronage of the General Government" for any appointments. Joseph Meek with nine compatriots carried the petition east in early spring of 1848.

Much was at stake. If Congress created the Oregon Territory, the region would fall under the mantle of federal authority and funding. The residents of the region might expect, at last, action on the free land proposals and a host of benefits from the creation of a vital infrastructure to enhance security, improve commerce, and ease communication problems. On August 14, 1848, President Polk signed the Organic Act creating the Oregon Territory. Uncle Sam could now begin his labors in the Pacific Northwest in earnest.

Joseph Lane, a Mexican War hero and resident of Indiana, was appointed governor. He set out overland for Oregon City, where he was inaugurated on March 3, 1849, proclaiming the sprawling region under the administration of the United States. The event was of singular consequence. Territorial status brought not only a governor but also three judges, an attorney, and a marshal—all federal appointees. Oregonians who were male, 21 years or older, and citizens of the United States had the franchise and could elect a territorial legislature. Its laws, however, were subject to veto by Congress, and the legislature had limited power to incur debt. The residents could elect a delegate to speak for their interests before Congress. Samuel R. Thurston, the first named, lacked the power to vote, but he could advocate territorial interests.

The Organic Act extended the Northwest Ordinance of 1787 to the region. This legislation of the Continental Congress articulated the philosophy for development of new territories in the Ohio and upper Mississippi Valleys. It prohibited slavery, provided land grants for support of public schools, and affirmed "utmost good faith" in dealing with tribes. The ordinance and its inclusion in the Organic Act thus recognized aboriginal land title throughout the region. It voided the land laws of the Provisional Government, except for the claims to 640 acres of the various missions to the tribes. Oregon's act granted two square miles of land per township to fund schools.

Land remained foremost in the minds of the Oregonians. Thurston knew the anxiety and jockeying for claims. Thousands had risked their lives and futures on the prospect of getting free farms in Oregon. On September 29, 1850, Congress passed what became known as the Oregon Donation Land Act, establishing the system of land survey prior to deeding properties. By 1851, John P. Preston, surveyor-general, and his crews had established the Willamette Meridian running north and south between Canada and California and begun survey of the east and west Baseline. The coordinates met at Willamette Stone Park in the west hills above Portland. The system left an indelible imprint. From the beginning of time, nature, had etched the land in gentle contours. Henceforth straight lines, section corners and a massive grid system—followed by roads, timber harvests and fields—imprinted the landscape. The beauty of the system was that it was regular. It gave every parcel of land a unique address based on its distance from the primary coordinates.

Congress also established the General Land Office, the first of which opened in Oregon City and was followed, in time, by branches in The Dalles, La Grande, and Roseburg. Seekers of Donation Lands—ultimately 7,437 successful claimants in Oregon—could register their claims and await the surveys of the townships and their particular claims. Once the surveys were completed, they could obtain title, subdivide and sell. Speculation was built into the fabric of the act, particularly because it permitted both men and women to acquire up to 320 acres—a square mile for married couples. This was far more land than any farmer might till or manage.

Territorial status brought highly significant investments in Oregon. The U.S. Coast Survey dispatched William Pope McArthur and the vessel *Ewing* to begin charting the coastline. Over the next several years, the Coast Survey examined the shoreline and the estuaries. It produced charts with depth readings, noted dangerous rocks, and gave form to the shore. Its reports included handsome engravings of coastal headlands as mariners saw them from sea.

Dr. Elijah White had served since 1843 as Indian agent in Oregon. His appointment was strange in that he worked on federal salary when American sovereignty was not established. In 1849, Joseph Lane began duties both as governor and ex-officio superintendent of Indian affairs. He was succeeded by Anson Dart of Wisconsin and next by Joel Palmer, negotiator of several of the region's ratified treaties. The superintendents named Indian agents to serve at The Dalles, Clatsop Plains, Willamette Valley,

Umpqua Valley, Rogue River Valley and Port Orford.

Important federal services that came with territorial status included opening of postal routes and offices, federal courts and customs houses. John Shively, an 1843 emigrant, was appointed as Oregon's first postmaster in 1847 in Astoria. Postal routes created vital communication links along a frontier. Congress established customs districts with agents at Port Orford, Umpqua River and Astoria. In later years, it opened offices for the Yaquina District and Portland. Federal officials were charged with collecting duties and recording statistical information on the ebb and flow of commerce. Their reports showed the rise of agriculture and industry, particularly the impact of the markets produced by the California Gold Rush for Oregon crops and lumber. Court officials had charge of dispute resolution. With three districts, they had a wide geographical reach and traveled a circuit to adjudicate complaints.

Using executive authority, U.S. presidents in the 1850s began withdrawing land from public entry to set aside sites for federal projects, including reservations for lighthouses, forts, and tribes. Several instances of the withdrawals proved unwise. In the case of lighthouses, some sites were too high above the sea or too remote from supplies to permit economical construction of stations. Most forts, though constructed, were of limited utility and were soon abandoned. The Coast (or Siletz) Reservation and the Grand Ronde Reservation, however, were two instances where presidential withdrawals helped shape both indigenous history and settlement patterns. The large Siletz Reservation was dismembered in 1865 and 1875 and again after 1892. The tribal tenure, though diminishing, slowed pioneer settlement along much of the central coast.

Fort Yamhill, now in Dayton, is one of many forts built in Oregon during the 1850s by the U.S. Army. (Oregon State Archives scenic photo)

Territorial status meant the arrival of the U.S. Army. Congress appropriated $76,500 in 1846 to establish garrisons along the Oregon Trail, but the project was diverted by the Mexican War. In 1849, the Mounted Riflemen finally headed west under the command of Major Osborne Cross. Their assignment was to build and staff forts to preclude further difficulties with the tribes. When the Riflemen's heavy wagons bogged down on the southern slopes of Mount Hood, the soldiers dug pits and cached many of their supplies at a place later known as Government Camp. They then pushed on to occupy temporary quarters at Oregon City and Astoria. During the 1850s, the U.S. Army established Fort Orford (1851), Fort Dalles (1852), Fort Lane (1853), Fort Cascades (1855) on the north bank of the Columbia in the Gorge, Fort Umpqua, Fort Yamhill and Fort Hoskins (all 1856). Construction created jobs for carpenters, brick masons and laundresses. Soldiers brought payrolls flowing into the local economy as well as a sense of security from the tribes.

The Army provided another important service. Its engineers were authorized by Congress to survey and construct the Scottsburg-Myrtle Creek and Myrtle Creek-Camp Stuart military wagon roads. These routes connected in 1853–55 to carry freight and travelers from the head of tidewater on the Umpqua River to the mining districts in the Rogue River Valley and northern California. The Army also dispatched Lieutenant George Derby to survey a road over the Coast Range between Astoria and Salem. Although opened by axemen, the route drew only limited use. Derby, in 1855, surveyed and supervised construction of the Fort Vancouver-Fort Cascades Military Portage Road into the Columbia Gorge. Uncle Sam's engineers, soldiers and laborers helped create primary travel corridors to remote parts of the territory. As college graduates, the military officers also recorded weather data, collected fossils, pickled zoological specimens, wrote down tribal word lists and sent interesting materials and communications to the Smithsonian Institution. These labors contributed to further understanding about the region.

While the federal government annually considered projects in the Oregon Territory, the legislature wrestled with local issues. These included frustration with the repeated appointment of nonresidents of the region to key positions; political fighting among Whigs, Democrats and Know-Nothings; and the outbreak of warfare with the tribes. Residents of Puget Sound and the Walla Walla district were especially restive with a government located in Oregon City or, after 1851, in Salem. Congress addressed this matter and on March 2, 1853, President Millard Fillmore signed legislation creating the Washington Territory. This action gave final definition to Oregon's geography.

Another important consequence of territorial status was the extension of the Pacific Railroad Surveys into Oregon in 1855–56. Funded by Congress and staffed by the Topographical Engineers, this project sought five alternative routes across the continent to connect the Mississippi Valley with the Pacific Ocean. Additionally, the surveyors examined possibilities for north-south connections between the rail lines. Lieutenants Robert Stockton Williamson and Henry L. Abbot directed the surveys through the Willamette and Rogue River Valleys and along the eastern flank of the Cascade Mountains. Their handsome reports, accompanied by geological observations by Dr. John Strong Newberry, included hand-colored plates showing the countryside, botanical, zoological, and paleontological collections, and profiles of possible grades for railroad routes.

Territorial government catapulted the residents of Oregon into the nexus of federal authority. Although cheerfully independent, Oregonians embraced territorial status with expectation. They had frustration about political cronies named to top government posts, but they gained important services and facilities funded at national expense.

Spread of Settlement

Euro-American settlement in Oregon spread rapidly. Retired mountain men settled in French Prairie, Tualatin Plains and the Chehalem Valley. By 1843, overland emigrants had crossed to the west bank of the Willamette to stake claims along Rickreall and Salt Creeks. By 1845, they were at the lower reaches of the Santiam and Mary's Rivers. Settlers reached the southern end of the Willamette Valley in 1848, and, within a year, were pouring over the hills into the Umpqua Valley. Parties coming by sea settled in 1851 at the mouth of the Umpqua River and at Port Orford on the south coast. Others, restless with their sandy claims on the Clatsop Plains, braved the Indian trail across Neahkahnie Mountain to establish a colony on Tillamook Bay.

The field notes of the land surveyors and their township maps of the 1850s work like a time machine to reveal settlement patterns. Sometimes they noted tribal villages, often located at the confluences of stream courses or at the base of south-facing slopes to catch the rays of sunlight. They charted a network of trails transforming into wagon roads with ferries at river crossings. They showed house locations confirming that many settlers, savvy about flooding in mid-America, built their claim cabins far back from the riverbanks and often positioned them facing fields, the back door to the forest and its generous supplies of firewood. They documented the prairie condition of the western Oregon valleys, the consequence of tribal fire ecology.

The Bureau of the Census in 1850 recorded 11,873 Oregonians: 4,671 females and 7,202 males—a gender disparity of 40 to 60 percent. In towns, nearly 70 percent of the residents were men. "At Astoria, Milton City, and Portland," wrote demographer William Bowen, "they outnumbered women more than three to one." Bowen also found the imprint of kinship as an integrating force in frontier Oregon. "The neighborhood was one of the most basic associations of rural frontier life," he said, "a union of persons with similar backgrounds in small, fairly homogeneous communities, each slightly different from the rest." This meant that closely knit neighborhoods were quick to meet individual needs, prone to exclude outsiders (especially minorities, foreigners and single men), but open to individuals who married into families and thereby joined the community. Bowen thus concluded that Oregon had two societies in the 1850s: a rural frontier dominated by extended families or clans and an urban frontier "drawing its members disproportionately from the ranks of unmarried men from the Northeast or abroad."

Urban development and farm improvements were driven by the California Gold Rush. A number of Oregonians headed south for the diggings in 1848 and many more did so in 1849. The men plowed and planted crops, departed for the mines, and left the women and children to weed, combat birds and varmints, water the vegetables and mind the claim. Hundreds returned in the fall for harvest, their saddlebags heavy with leather pouches of gold dust and nuggets. Most discovered that the boom in California created a lucrative market for wheat, apples, vegetables, oysters, shingles, piling and lumber. The influx of 100,000 new residents and statehood for California in 1850 became an important stimulus and force of stability in the Oregon economy.

Opportunities beckoned. Captain Asa Mead Simpson of Brunswick, Maine, grasped some. Six months in the Sierras convinced him in 1849 that there were better ways to find fortune in the West. He opened lumberyards in Stockton, Sacramento and San Francisco. In the early 1850s, he laid the foundations of a commercial empire stretching from Monterey Bay to Puget Sound. He shipped steam engines and saws for mills at Port Orford, Coos Bay, Umpqua River, Astoria and Gray's Harbor in the Washington Territory. With his partner, Captain George Flavel, he constructed and operated steam tugs to provide bar pilot service for his vessels and those of others. Simpson ran his enterprises for 64 years. His crews built more than 50 ships at his yards on the southern Oregon coast at North Bend.

Aaron Meier, a Jewish emigrant from Germany, worked his way north in the mid-1850s from the Sierra gold fields to new mines in the Rogue River Valley. He carried needles, thread, buttons and bolts of cloth in his traveling dry goods business. He worked hard, saved, and, in 1857, opened a small retail store in Portland, then a town of 1,300 residents. The city's boom during the 1860s with opening of new mining fields in the interior and the flow of capital through the emerging city gave him the chance to expand his business. In time, Sigmund Frank, his son-in-law, joined him. Meier & Frank Department Store was on its way to becoming one of the nation's largest retail outlets.

In 1852, Abigail Scott Duniway arrived in Oregon after her mother and a brother died during the overland crossing. Abigail married young and with her husband, Ben Duniway, selected a donation claim near Lafayette in Yamhill County. Then misfortune struck. Ben signed a note, using the farm as collateral. They lost the farm and Ben, injured in a farming accident, was an invalid for the rest of his life. Having a young family and no options, Abigail assumed full responsibilities. She taught school, made hats, ran a boarding house and aspired to be somebody. By 1859, she had started to define her future. She wrote *Captain Gray's Company,* a novel based on her Oregon Trail diary. Having found her voice, in later years she became a nationally known suffrage advocate and for 16 years was editor and publisher of *The New Northwest,* a weekly newspaper.

Joel Palmer visited Oregon in 1845 and helped open the Barlow Road. He was much impressed with what he saw and described it in *Journal of Travels Over the Rocky Mountains* (1847). He emigrated with his family from Indiana in 1847, and platted Dayton on his farm at the falls of the Yamhill River. Palmer's opportunities came in public service. He served as commissary-general and a peace commissioner in the Cayuse War and, in 1853, was appointed superintendent of Indian affairs. Over the next 24 months, he negotiated ten treaties, eight of which were ratified. A humane man, he nevertheless implemented a program of dramatic reduction of tribal domain but tried to provide reservations close to aboriginal areas and sought to preserve peace.

Matthew Paul Deady, a lawyer from Ohio, began teaching school in 1849 in Yamhill County. He soon returned to the practice of law, was elected to the Territorial Legislature, and, in 1853, was named judge of the territorial supreme court. Deady served in the constitutional convention, as federal district judge, drafter of civil and criminal codes, compiler of Oregon laws, and a founder of the University of Oregon. His diary, published long after his death as *Pharisee Among Philistines* (1975), confirmed his biting intellect and close observations of society.

As the Willamette Valley became more developed in the 1860s, many settlers moved east of the Cascades to the Klamath Basin. (Oregon State Archives scenic photo)

Simpson, Meier, Duniway, Palmer and Deady were representative of the newcomers. Thousands aspired to make something of themselves. Oregon was a great platform for dreaming dreams and improving one's lot. A number rose to the surface early, finding their callings in business, public service, literature and social reform. Thousands of others engaged in hard work, some laboring in quiet desperation and others for a modest improvement in condition.

By the early 1860s, settlement moved in new directions. Some overland emigrants had stopped at The Dalles. The community emerged by 1850 as a primary outfitting point on the western Columbia Plateau and grew steadily. By 1862, settlers were claiming lands in the Grande Ronde and Powder River Valleys, along the John Day, in the Crooked River and Ochoco region of central Oregon, and in the Klamath Basin. The children of Oregon Trail pioneers were engaged in eastward migration. Precluded by high land prices or multiple heirs in large families from owning farms in western Oregon, they took surplus livestock and headed over the Cascades to the lush meadows along the margins of the region's streams and lakes. Members of the Riddle family, who settled in 1851 in the South Umpqua Valley, were pioneer settlers in the Harney Basin. James and Elizabeth Foster in 1872 moved their large family to Summer Lake. Foster's parents had emigrated through central Oregon in 1845 in the party led by Stephen H. L. Meek. Thousands of others followed this pattern.

Oregon remained a rural, small-town region in the 19th century. The Donation Land Act, by allowing claims from 160 to 320 acres per person, effectively dispersed the population. A number of townsites became ghost towns. Randolph, Waldo, Dardanelles, Elizabethtown and Sailor's Diggings in the mines of southern Oregon vanished when the gold was gone. Cincinnati, Champoeg, Multnomah City, Peoria and Lancaster were once thriving communities along the Willamette. Auburn, Greenhorn, Granite and Bourne for a time served the mining populations of northeastern Oregon. Floods, fires, playing out of mineral deposits and changing travel patterns pushed them into oblivion.

Baker City grew rich from mining, timber and railroads in the late 1800s. Shown above is the ornate Geiser Grand Hotel. (Oregon State Archives scenic photo)

Some communities naturally attracted growth. Ashland at the base of the Siskiyous in the Bear Creek Valley, Roseburg in the Umpqua Valley,

Marshfield on upper Coos Bay, Prineville on the Crooked River, Pendleton at the base of the Blue Mountains and Baker City near the mines in the Blue Mountains became crossroads communities. For many towns, the key to success was to capture county government. Promoters vied for such locations, for they guaranteed a flow of people recording deeds, appearing in court, securing contracts or coping with society's needs. County government was as important as a good mill site, coal mine, or wagon road crossing in helping to anchor a community.

Indian Wars

Camas lilies bloomed in such profusion that meadows looked like lakes amid the forests. The tarweed seeds ripened and the women set the fires. Armed with beaters and funnel-shaped baskets, they began the annual cycle of gathering. Acorns ripened, matured, and fell from the oaks. Their flour, when leached of tannic acid, provided a nutritious gruel or bread when baked on flat stones near the fires. Salmon surged up the rivers. Eels clung to the rocks as they ascended the rapids. Deer and elk browsed on the nutritious plants in the foothills. Flecks of gold glistened in the crystal-clear water of the streambeds.

This was the setting when, during the winter of 1851–52, packers on the trail to California discovered the placer mines of southwestern Oregon. Within weeks, a reckless population, most of them hardened miners from California, surged over the Siskiyous or stepped off the gangplanks of ships putting in at Crescent City, Port Orford, Umpqua City or Scottsburg. The rush was on. It meant quick riches for those who found the right pothole in bedrock filled with nuggets or the fortunate miners whose riffle boxes captured the fine particles of gold that glistened in the black sand. For the tribes of the Rogue River country, it meant that all they had known and their very lives were at stake.

The causes of conflict erupted everywhere. The Donation Land Act became law in 1850. Years passed before treaties, negotiated in 1853 and 1854, were ratified. Some, such as those of Anson Dart or the Willamette Valley Treaty Commission of 1851, never gained Senate approval. In spite of the promises of superintendents of Indian Affairs, Dart and Palmer, the white people poured in. Dispossession ruled. The miners drove the Takelma, Shasta, Chetco, Shasta Costa, Mikonotunne, Tututni, Galice Creeks and Cow Creeks from their villages. Located on old stream terraces, these villages were prime locations for placer deposits.

The hungry newcomers hunted the game, decimating the deer and elk populations. The Territorial Legislature in 1854 prohibited sale of ammunition or guns to Indians, deepening their disadvantage. The miners and residents of Jacksonville, Canyonville, Kerbyville and Gold Beach liked bacon and ham. They let hogs run wild, catching them in baited traps. The hogs ate the acorns, a primary subsistence food for the tribes.

Mining debris poured down the Illinois, Rogue, South Coquille and South Umpqua Rivers. The salmon runs diminished; the eels died. Crayfish, fresh water mussels and trout choked on the flood of mud. Starvation threatened. The claimants of Donation Lands fenced their fields with split-rail fences and built log cabins. They worked with a will to stop tribal field burning. The tribal women found it impossible to harvest tarweed seeds and the blackberries that formerly regenerated with the annual fires did not grow back. The settlers turned under the fields of camas lilies, and their cattle and horses grazed off the blue-flowering plants.

The mining districts—whether in the Rogue River country or the Blue Mountains of northeastern Oregon—caused major ecological disruption. The rush for quick wealth through mineral exploitation unraveled nature's ways and long-established human subsistence activities. Then came the "exterminators"—unprincipled men who believed that "the only good Indian was a dead Indian." They formed volunteer companies and perpetrated massacres against the Chetco tribe in 1853, the Lower Coquille Tribe in 1854, and in wanton aggression against Takelma people camped near the Table Rock Reservation in 1855.

Frederick M. Smith, sub-Indian agent at Port Orford, in 1854 addressed the attacks on the tribes in his district. They were ravaged by hunger, dispossession of their villages, onset of new and fatal diseases, and overt murders. Reporting the massacre of the Lower Coquille Tribe, he wrote: *"Bold, brave, courageous men! to attack a friendly and defenceless tribe; to burn, roast, and shoot sixteen of their number, and all on suspicion that they were about to rise and drive from their country three hundred white men!"* Smith's lament, the mourning cries of the Indian women, the death rituals of rubbing the hair with pitch and the inexorable course of hunger, attack and death precipitated the conflicts known as the Rogue River Wars. The troubles seethed between 1852 and 1856. Finally, the U.S. Army had sufficient forces to mount a campaign in 1855–56 to destroy the tribes' ability to resist.

Vanquished by the combined operations of the Oregon Volunteers and Army regulars, the tribes of the Rogue and Umpqua Valleys and the southwestern Oregon coast were then removed to the Siletz and Grand Ronde reservations. Forced marches through winter snows or over the rocky headlands and through the sand dunes of coastal Oregon became trails of tears for hundreds driven to the distant reservations. Other survivors were herded aboard the *Columbia,* a sidewheel steamer, which removed them from Port Orford to the Columbia and lower Willamette River area. Then, they had to walk the muddy trail to the reservations.

The myth of independence was shattered by the actions of Oregon's frontier residents. For their "services rendered" in the conflicts of 1853, the volunteers billed the federal government for $107,287, and they were the primary cause of the hostilities. When the conflicts ended in 1856, they worked for years to gain settlement. Finally, in 1890, Congress passed the Oregon Indian Depredation Claims Act. Aged pioneers filed affidavits to claim reimbursement for lost pillows, ricks of hay, rail fences and beans and bacon during the conflicts of the 1850s. A dependent generation's elders once again tapped the federal treasury for support.

Troubles with the tribes erupted anew in the 1850s on the Columbia Plateau. In 1855, Superintendent Joel Palmer and Governor Isaac I. Stevens of Washington Territory summoned the tribes of the eastern plateau to the Walla Walla Treaty Council. In a matter of days, they hammered out agreements, ceding lands but reserving others with the Nez Perce, Cayuse, Umatilla, and Yakima. Subsequently, Palmer met the Wasco, Wishram and Warm Springs (or Tenino) at The Dalles and entered into a treaty with them. All of these agreements were noteworthy for enumerating rights. The tribes, who had engaged in traditional subsistence activities from time immemorial, reserved rights to fish "at usual and accustomed grounds and stations," to erect fish-processing sheds for drying their catch, and to hunt, gather and graze livestock on unenclosed lands.

While Congress was considering the treaties, the Bureau of Indian Affairs began urging the tribes to remove to their new reservations and take up an agrarian lifestyle. Few wanted to engage in such backbreaking labor or give up fishing, hunting and gathering. The pressure was on. Immigrants arrived every fall and settlement spread east from The Dalles. Pioneer cabins lined the shores of the Gorge, threatening to disrupt the tribal fisheries. Then came gold discoveries on the Fraser and Thompson Rivers in British Columbia and in the Colville district on the north-central plateau. The influx of miners led to an eruption of troubles and, in time, to the Yakima Indian War of 1855–58. The forces of the U.S. Army, supplemented by companies of Oregon Volunteers, defeated the hostile bands.

The 1850s were a wrenching time of transition. Steadily, tribal numbers diminished, their food sources destroyed and their lands appropriated. These were terrible times for the region's native people.

Statehood

Issues far from Oregon shaped affairs along the Pacific Coast in the 1850s. Sectional tensions heightened during the bumbling presidencies of Millard Fillmore, Franklin Pierce and James Buchanan. The Compromise of 1850 gained a little time, but its concessions satisfied neither pro-slavery extremists in the South nor abolitionists in the North. The nation was on its course to the Civil War. Harriet Beecher Stowe's novel, *Uncle Tom's Cabin,* enraged slaveowners as it swept across the country in a powerful indictment of the "peculiar institution." Formation of the Republican Party in 1854, troubles in "Bleeding Kansas" in 1856, the Dred Scott decision in 1857, and John Brown's raid on the federal arsenal at Harper's Ferry in 1859 confirmed the divisions and tensions. The Republicans had drawn the line—no further expansion of slavery. They nominated John C. Fremont, a popular western explorer, for the presidency. Although Fremont lost, within four years their candidate, Abraham Lincoln, was headed to Washington, D.C., as the 16th president. Passions were high. Then came secession and war.

Three parties vied for political control in Oregon. The Democrats were an odd lot, including northerners opposed to slavery and southern diehards who supported an institution barred by the Organic Act of 1848. The Whigs held political patronage in the early 1850s but watched their party disintegrate nationally. The Know-Nothings were opposed to the political clique that had managed territorial government in Salem. These divisions confirmed the heavy hold of old persuasions and attitudes—the intellectual baggage carried by the immigrants.

Without enabling legislation from Congress, Oregonians voted in June 1857 to hold a constitutional convention. The delegates assembled in Salem during the summer and drafted a governing document. It was modeled on those of Iowa, Indiana, and Michigan. The constitution limited public debt and placed tight controls on banks and corporations. An agricultural people, the convention delegates argued, had little use for frivolous expenditures or unnecessary institutions. In the fall voters faced three questions. Did they approve the constitution? They voted yes. Did they want slavery? They voted 7,727 no and 2,645 yes. Did they want freed African-Americans to live in Oregon? They voted eight to one against permitting their residency.

The actions in 1857 were predictable. Oregonians hungered for control of their own government and an end to the patronage appointments produced by shifting administrations in Washington, D.C. They also affirmed they did not want slavery in Oregon. The question of driving free African-Americans from the new state revealed resoundingly racist attitudes. They did not see freed slaves, Indians or women standing equally before the law. In this Oregonians differed little from Thomas Jefferson. Architect of the Declaration of Independence and its gracefully worded affirmations of natural rights, Jefferson was a slave-owner all his adult life. He could not rise to the noble philosophy of personal freedom he articulated in the 1770s. Oregonians in 1857 appeared to have drunk from the same well.

In June, 1858, residents of the territory elected officials as defined by their new constitution. For months the fate of Oregon statehood floated on shifting political coalitions distrustful of changing the fragile balance of power in Congress. It was known Oregon would be a free state, yet its newly elected senators—Joseph Lane and Delazon Smith—were proslavery Democrats. Finally Congress acted and on February 14, 1859, President Buchanan signed the bill. Oregon joined the federal union.

Civil War in Oregon

The plunge to Civil War exploded on April 12, 1861, in the bombardment of Fort Sumter in Charleston Harbor. When it became apparent the conflict would not be short, the Army began removing regular soldiers from the District of Oregon. Because of the responsibility to guard the reservations and maintain a military presence, especially in central and eastern Oregon where gold discoveries generated a rapid influx of miners and settlers, federal and state officials scrambled to find replacement troops. The Department of the Pacific raised recruits and dispatched companies of California Volunteers to Fort Yamhill, Fort Hoskins and Siletz Blockhouse. The Army abandoned Fort Umpqua in 1862. The First Oregon Volunteer Cavalry and the First Washington Territory Infantry went to central Oregon. During the Civil War, Oregon raised six companies of cavalry. Known officially as the First Oregon Cavalry, they served until June, 1865.

Secessionist sympathizers surfaced in Oregon. The Knights of the Golden Circle, an anti-Union group, reportedly plotted the seizure of Fort Vancouver, military headquarters on the Columbia River. They did not act. When pro-Confederate partisans raised their flag in Jacksonville, they faced opposition and backed down. The Long Tom Rebellion was perhaps the most noteworthy outbreak of secessionist feeling. Emboldened by the assassination of President Lincoln, Philip Henry Mulkey walked the streets of Eugene on May 6, 1865, shouting: "Hurrah for Jeff Davis, and damn the man that won't!" The First Oregon Volunteer Infantry arrested Mulkey, who promptly grabbed a glass of water and toasted Jeff Davis, the Confederate president. A pro-Union mob, wanting to lynch Mulkey, broke down the jail door. Mulkey slashed one of the men with a hidden knife. Mulkey's supporters from the Long Tom district were ready to fight, but the infantry slipped Mulkey out of town under an armed guard, loaded him on a steamboat, and sent him off to three months in jail at Fort Vancouver. Mulkey sued for $10,000 for false arrest. After 14 court appearances over a two-year period, he settled for $200.

For many of the soldiers, the Civil War in Oregon was a monotonous, numbing assignment. In their monthly post returns, officers recorded desertions, suicides and bouts in the brig because of drunkenness and misbehavior. The tribes were quiet on the Siletz and Grand Ronde Reservations. The rain was predictable and depressing. "Nothing transpired of importance," recorded Royal A. Bensell, a soldier at Fort Yamhill. Too many days brought that refrain in his Civil War diary.

East of the Cascades, the troops had active engagement. Gold discoveries at Canyon City and other diggings on the headwaters of the John Day River and in the Powder River country on the eastern slopes of the Blue Mountains had drawn thousands of miners. The Northern Paiute, disrupted in their seasonal round and tempted by the easy pickings of clothing, food, and horses, embarked on raids and conflicts that demanded military intervention. The Oregon Volunteer Infantry and Cavalry established Camp Watson (1864) after placing troops at temporary stations: Dahlgren, Currey, Gibbs, Henderson and Maury. The forces engaged in lengthy and often fruitless explorations searching for the elusive Indians.

Gold strikes near the headwaters of the John Day River led to disputes with Native Americans. (Oregon State Archives scenic photo)

Realizing that the problems east of the Cascades were of long duration, the U.S. Army established Fort Klamath (1863), Camp Warner (1866), and Fort Harney (1867). During the summer of 1864, Captains John M. Drake, George B. Curry and Lieutenant-Colonel Charles Drew led troops on sweeps through southeastern Oregon, northern Nevada and southwestern Idaho. They had little success in finding the "enemy." "These tribes can be gathered upon a reservation, controlled, subsisted for a short time, and afterwards be made to subsist themselves," commented the superintendent of Indian affairs, "for one-tenth the cost of supporting military forces in pursuit of them." In time, that happened. The Klamath Reservation and the short-lived Malheur Reservation included various bands of Northern Paiute. The Civil War in Oregon mostly involved guarding reservations or pursuing native people who were masters of escape in their own homelands.

Uncle Sam's Handiwork

Statehood meant that Oregonians had two senators and a representative to make their case in Congress. The congressional delegation delivered. Some argued it was critical to open communications across the new state. The Republican Party was not of a mind to continue projects wholly in the control and labor of federal employees. Its philosophy was to throw as much action as possible into the private sector. Thus, between 1865 and 1869 Congress liberally awarded land grants to the State of Oregon to pass on to companies constructing "military wagon roads." Theoretically, the routes were to link strategic locations suitable for use by troops during emergencies.

The new roads were the Oregon Central, Corvallis-Yaquina Bay, Willamette Valley and Cascade Mountain, The Dalles-Boise and the Coos Bay. Two provided routes from Willamette Valley points in Albany and Springfield eastward to Boise. A third connected The Dalles via the John Day watershed to Boise. Two ran toward the coast: one from Albany to Yaquina City and another from Roseburg to Coos Bay. Under the terms of the grants, as soon as a company had completed a stretch of road, it could apply to the governor for certification of its success. The governor or his designated official would visit the route. If the road was deemed suitable for wagon use, the company then received three square miles of land for every mile of road. The tally for the five roads ran into millions of acres.

Land-grant wagon roads were founded on speculation and fraud. None of the companies had the experience, capital or leadership to build satisfactory routes through such challenging terrain. They cleared and carved out traces, leaving many streams unbridged and routes subject to slides and frequent closures. The Oregon Central Military Wagon Road Company was unblushing in its scam. When its surveyors reached the Cascade summit, rather than heading east toward Boise, they swept south through the upper Deschutes and into the Klamath Reservation, cutting a swath of checkerboard lands out of the lush meadows along the Williamson and Sprague Rivers. They moved on toward Goose Lake into Guano Valley, then over the southern slopes of Steens Mountain into the Pueblo Valley before turning northeasterly toward Boise. Their meandering route captured tens of thousands of acres of prime grazing land, dismembered the Klamath Reservation and ensured a much larger grant than if they had surveyed a route directly toward Idaho.

Wagon road companies locked up land for years. The General Land Office held hundreds of thousands of acres of unclaimed grants. As long as the company or its successor purchasers did not take title, they did not have to pay taxes. The longer they waited, the greater the appreciation of value in timber, minerals or grazing. By avoiding paying taxes and letting land values increase, the companies—or those who bought them to speculate in the grants—calculated a better return. Further, the companies did not maintain the roads yet dared to demand tolls from travelers. Lamentations of local residents who lived in the alternate sections along the routes finally compelled Congress to investigate and the courts to take back the remaining portions of the grants.

Among the loudest critics of the wagon road companies were land seekers. In the Homestead Act (1862), Congress gave the land-hungry an unparalleled opportunity. For a modest filing fee, five years of residency and claim improvements, homesteaders could receive as much as 160 acres of the public domain for free. Congress became increasingly generous in giving away federal lands. It passed bounty land acts for veterans of wars, the Desert Land Act (1877), Enlarged Homestead Act (1909), and Stock

Raising Homestead Act (1916). Shrewd speculators might accumulate hundreds of acres by working the system. Between 1850 and 1940, millions of acres in Oregon passed from public to private ownership through the land distribution acts promoted by developers of the American West.

Congressional action shaped Oregon in other areas. The coast was a dangerous place where strong winds buffeted the shore. Narrow channels led over fluctuating bars into the estuaries. The headlands were remote, hulking forms on the eastern landscape. Mariners desperately needed services. The bar of the Columbia gained a reputation as the "graveyard of the Pacific." Boats foundered, grounded and smashed on rocky headlands, taking hundreds of lives. The U.S. Coast Survey continued to chart the estuaries and compile information in the *Coast Pilot,* an annual publication with data on landmarks, rocks, buoys and anchorages. The U.S. Light-House Board was called upon to provide more assistance.

On a case-by-case basis, Congress appropriated funds for design and construction of important facilities. These included lighthouses: Cape Arago (1866), Cape Blanco (1870), Yaquina Bay (1872), Cape Foulweather (1873), Point Adams (1875), Tillamook Rock (1881), Warrior Rock (1888) at the mouth of the Willamette River, Cape Meares (1890), Umpqua River, Heceta Head, Coquille River (all 1894), and Desdemona Sands (1905). The goal was to create a system of stations with interlocking lights. On a clear night at sea, a mariner might expect to sight at any point a distinctive beacon on shore to pinpoint the location. Fog signals powered by steam engines blasted warnings from a number of the stations to tell captains to drop anchor or beat a retreat until the mists cleared.

In 1892, an appropriation of $60,000 funded construction of *Columbia River Lightship No. 50.* Anchored off the treacherous bar of the Columbia, the lightship had a lonely crew of eight who, for decades, kept watch, maintained kerosene lights, and fed coal into boilers to power a massive fog signal. Their wave-tossed perch with booming horn drew hardy men who, like those at remote lighthouses, endured modest pay and isolation.

Congress also funded construction of stations and staffing for the U.S. Life-Saving Service. The first station opened in 1878 at the Cape Arago Lighthouse near the entrance to Coos Bay. Numerous shipwrecks and loss of life associated with the export of coal and lumber from the harbor brought federal action. The small building had a surfboat and one oarsman. Launching the craft and rowing to a vessel in distress depended upon volunteers. By the end of the 19th century, the U.S. Life-Saving Service had stations at Warrenton, Tillamook Bay, Yaquina Bay, Coos Bay and the Umpqua and Coquille Rivers. Each had crew quarters, a boat house and a practice mast for breeches-buoy drill. In the early 20th century, the USLSS erected stations at Port Orford and Siuslaw River.

In the 1870s, the U.S. Geological Survey (USGS) began work in Oregon. John Evans, U.S. Geologist for the Oregon Territory, had mounted initial surveys of mining areas in 1855–56. In the final three decades of the 19th century, the agency inaugurated studies of mining districts to assess coal and gold deposits. Its skilled cartographers also commenced topographic mapping in conjunction with the National Geodetic Survey. These maps, revised at 20-to-30 year intervals in the 20th century, gave form to the land. They provided vital information on roads, settlements, and terrain. In the 1890s, the USGS performed a remarkable service. Its employees mounted the first comprehensive assessment of forests in the state. They estimated standing volumes of hardwoods and softwoods, mapped areas ravaged by forest fires, photographed the terrain and published technical reports on forest conditions and grazing impacts.

By 1856, the Bureau of Indian Affairs had embarked on its mission to attempt to transform tribes into the mainstream culture in one generation. It founded its work upon an agrarian economy regardless of the terrain, elevation or traditional subsistence patterns of the tribes. Oregon's reservations were Siletz, Grand Ronde, Warm Springs, Umatilla, Klamath and Malheur. The tribes retained but a fraction of their aboriginal lands. The Nez Perce, whose 1855 treaty reserved their tribal lands in northeastern Oregon, were beset by trespassers who, in 1877, provoked the Nez Perce War and the exodus of Chief Joseph's band. This band orchestrated a brilliant retreat through the Pacific Northwest, for months eluding the U.S. Army. When they finally surrendered, the government confined them first in Oklahoma and, after 1885, on the Colville Reservation in Washington.

Indian agents, subagents, farmers, teachers, and doctors—all in the employ of the federal government—mounted the programs. They created farms and insisted, in spite of the weather, that tribes raise wheat in the boggy soil along the Oregon coast. Hundreds died in this ill-fated experiment. They also attempted to compel the Klamath and Warm Springs tribes to become farmers. The setting for their farms was amenable to gathering root crops or berries, but not to cereal or vegetable crop production. Terrible hardship ensued.

In 1879, Lt. Melville C. Wilkinson of the U.S. Army opened the Indian Training School in Forest Grove, on four acres of land rented from Pacific University. $5,000 was provided to start the school. Wilkinson, with the help of eight Puyallup Indian boys began construction on the buildings in 1880. The initial class of students consisted of fourteen boys and four girls. All the students came from the State of Washington, seventeen of them from the Puyallup Reservation on the Puget Sound and one boy from the Nisqually Reservation. These students were taught blacksmithing, shoemaking, carpentering, wagon making, girl's industries and advancement in studies. The local community did not support expansion of the campus. So Henry J. Minthorn, the second superintendent of the school, considered three sites for a new school. Newberg offered 100 acres of heavily timbered land, Forest Grove offered 23 acres with a pasture parcel of 75 acres approximately four miles away from the main site, and Salem offered 171 partially cleared, sparsely timbered land north of town. He chose the Salem site since it was close to the state capital and had the most acreage and, in 1885, he moved the school, changing its name to Chemawa Indian School.

In 1887, the General Allotment Act launched a major assault on tribalism. The law, extended over the next few years to Oregon reservations, provided for dividing up the tribal estate into individual allotments of 80 to 160 acres. The plan was for each Indian to receive a tract, farm it, transform in lifeways, master English and, after the passage of 25 years, gain certification as "competent." He then became a citizen of the United States, received title to the allotment, and could pay taxes on the land! The program fostered a dramatic loss in tribal lands and created a nightmare of checkerboard ownerships within reservations.

Jetties, such as this one at the mouth of the Columbia River, were part of a growing federal investment in Oregon. (Oregon State Archives scenic photo)

The Army Corps of Engineers was also on duty in 19th century Oregon. Its employees mounted river navigability studies on the Columbia, Umpqua and Willamette, and planned dredging and jetty projects at several estuaries. These men charted the rivers, designed improvements and, with federal appropriations, oversaw blasting of rocks and reefs. Between 1878 and 1896, the Corps of Engineers supervised the region's most expensive "pork barrel" project—construction of the massive bypass canal and locks at the Cascades of the Columbia. The Corps also constructed the Yamhill River Locks (1900) and, starting in 1888, initiated jetty projects at Coquille River, Coos Bay, Siuslaw River, Yaquina Bay and Columbia River. By 1920, the Corps of Engineers had spent $4.7 million on river and harbor projects; local contributions added nearly a fifth more when required by legislation. The flow of federal dollars was an immense benefit to Oregonians, for the state did not have the resources to fund such large-scale projects.

Uncle Sam delivered. Federal projects included land grants for wagon roads, homesteads, and war veterans. Congress paid for soldiers to fight Indians, personnel to manage reservations, funds to build and staff lighthouses and lifesaving stations, operation of postal routes, post offices, the federal court system, customs houses, the General Land Office, mapping and mineral assessments by the U.S. Geological Survey, and updating of navigational information by the U.S. Coast Survey. Uncle Sam was a key player in a state populated by farmers, stockraisers, fishers, miners, loggers, sawmill workers and small-town business people.

Minorities

The welcome mat was not out. Oregon's early generations defined opportunity narrowly. The land and resources were the domain of men and women of Caucasian background; others need not apply. Even when the Donation Land Act provided that women qualified for claims, brothers and brothers-in-law tried to wrest claims away from widows. Entreaties of women for fairer treatment finally led to passage of the Married Women's Property Act in 1866, the right to vote in school elections in 1878, and admission to the bar in 1886. Women were a minority in Oregon. The frontier demography, especially in mining districts and rural areas, remained predominantly male for decades. Women's efforts to gain the general franchise were repeatedly rebuffed and not realized until the 20th century.

African-Americans were unequivocally not wanted. Some, nevertheless, persisted quietly and settled in the state. The Census of 1850 reported either 54 or 56 African-Americans in the entire Pacific Northwest. The Census of 1860 identified 124 blacks and mulattoes, a tiny fraction of the more than 52,000 residents enumerated. Those who settled in Oregon took risks, but they had known prejudice and discrimination far worse in other parts of the country. Sometimes, however, racial episodes erupted. These occurred sporadically in several parts of the state over a period of 70 years. By 1890, for example, the African-American population of Coos County was 36. Most worked for the local railroad or at the Beaver Hill and Libby coal mines. Recruited in West Virginia, they had migrated across the country and walked through the Coast Range from Roseburg to the lower Coquille River, only to find that they and their families were expected to live in leaking boxcars. The men had to work in the deep shafts reaching below sea level for 90 cents per day. When they complained, they were accused of fomenting labor strife and compelled to leave.

Alonzo Tucker was an African-American who worked as a bootblack and operator of a gym in Marshfield. In 1902, dubious charges of rape were leveled against him by a white woman. When a mob of 200 armed men marched on the jail, the marshal lost control of Tucker, who hid beneath a dock. He was twice shot the next morning and then hanged from the Fourth Street Bridge by a mob that had grown to more than 300. The coroner's inquest found no fault; the victim, the report said, had died of loss of blood from a gunshot wound. No indictments were brought. The local newspaper observed that the lynch mob was "quiet and orderly" and that the vigilante proceeding was no "unnecessary disturbance of the peace." In 1907, the Marshfield School Board instituted segregated education, alleging that the four African-American students "will materially retard the progress of the five hundred white children."

Not all African-Americans faced treatments like those in turn-of-the-century Coos County. Some found steady employment with the railroads, both on construction crews and on Pullman cars. Others opened restaurants, barber shops, beauty shops, and saloons. In 1903, McCants Stewart passed the Oregon bar exam and began legal practice. Dr. J. A. Merriam entered medical practice in Portland in that decade. A number entered the ministry and labored at the pulpit, in choirs and in social halls to influence the spirituality of their families, friends, and neighbors. Outreach came in many forms. The Colored Benevolent Association of Portland, founded in 1867, fraternal lodges, baseball teams and women's clubs were other means for African-Americans to help their communities.

Chinese-Americans

Poverty, warfare, overpopulation and ambition racked the peoples of the Pearl River Delta in the mid-19th century. Foreigners carved out enclaves in Macao, Hong Kong and Canton, bribed their way into the Chinese economy by importing opium and siphoned off a rich trade in luxury items. Many Chinese aspired to a better life and Gum San—Gold Mountain—beckoned. Tales of gold discoveries along the Pacific Coast proved irresistible. Thousands of men responded. Their plan was simple—go to Gum San, work hard every day, store up gold and return to purchase land and hold position in Chinese society.

As the gold rush drifted northward into Oregon, the Chinese followed the discoveries. They were relegated to the worked-over placers, barred from some districts altogether, and compelled to pay a head tax because of race. They worked, paid and endured. By the 1870s, for example, Chinese males constituted nearly half the population of Grant County. They lived frugally and labored hard. They moved tons of rock to get to pay dirt in crevices and potholes in the upper John Day diggings. They ran restaurants, laundries, herbal pharmacies and gambling dens.

Because of their distinctive dress, language, religion and difference from the surrounding culture, the Chinese were treated brutally. The editor of the *Grant County News* on October 15, 1885, observed: "To every one it is apparent that the Chinese are a curse and a blight to this county, not only financially, but socially and morally. . . . What the Chinaman wears, he brings from China, and what he eats (except rats and lizards), he brings across the ocean, and thus American trade or production reaps no benefit from

his presence." The presence of tongs—kinship and social organizations—and Chinese determination to carry wealth home fostered intense discrimination. Murders, assaults, segregation, intimidation, special taxation and opposition confronted the Chinese at every turn.

What did they do? They persevered and many achieved their goals. They found employment in railroad construction. Chinese laborers provided much of the backbreaking toil to make the cuts for the Oregon & California Railroad as it inched southward through the Umpqua Mountains to the Rogue River Valley or on the line of the Oregon Railway & Navigation Company as it stretched eastward in 1880–82 through the Columbia Gorge. Willing to endure cannery work, Chinese men by the 1870s had acquired a near monopoly of work in canneries from Astoria to The Dalles. They gutted the fish, operated the steam pressure cookers, fastened the labels, and prepared tons of cases for shipment to a world market. They labored at nearly 40 canneries lining the shores of the Columbia for low wages and compulsory residency in company dormitories.

The Chinese congregated in Chinatown in Portland or, when their seasonal work diminished, traveled to communities in San Francisco, Seattle, or Vancouver, British Columbia. Anti-Chinese bigotry grew in the 1880s. Chinese were driven out of several communities—Oregon City, Albina and Mount Tabor. In 1887, vigilantes murdered ten or twelve Chinese miners in Hells Canyon on the Oregon-Idaho border. The Chinese Exclusion Act then cut off immigration, leaving nearly 9,000 Chinese men in Oregon with little prospect of bringing a bride from home or paying for passage of family members. The downward spiral began. Each year, Oregon had fewer residents of Chinese ancestry. Those who had resources returned home. Others, like Doc Hay and Lung On, remained, running an herbal drug store and car dealership in John Day. Bert Why operated a grocery store in North Bend. Most of the men who stayed remained single and lived lonely lives in Gum San.

Japanese-Americans

Jobs and land lured Japanese immigrants by the last decade of the 19th century. Overpopulation and limited opportunity at home, the favorable publicity of labor recruiters and adventure drew Japanese to Oregon. They found places to work and live. Many men hired on as laborers to build railroads. Tadashichi Tanaka, Shinzaburo Ban and Shintaro Takaki were all involved in 1891 in recruiting rail workers. The men helped build the Union Pacific, Southern Pacific, feeder lines and logging railroads.

Japanese immigrant families settled in the Treasure Valley near Ontario, Hood River Valley, and at Gresham. The prospect of gaining a few acres, planting a garden, setting out an orchard, and producing high-quality vegetables and fruits drew husbands, wives, and children to work together to establish a substantial hold in a new land. Others settled on Second, Third and Fourth streets in

Northwest Portland, where they became shopkeepers. Some men worked in sawmills, but at risk. In 1925, for example, a woman in Toledo on Yaquina Bay sparked a nasty attack on Japanese families. Threats of violence and bricks thrown through windows drove 25 Japanese men, women and children from the town, and earned Rosemary Shenk a court appearance.

Other Newcomers

Oregon, by the end of the 19th century, in spite of exclusionist attitudes and wars fought against Indians by the pioneer generation, had a changing complexion. Jewish merchants operated mercantile stores, enriched cultural life through their love of music and literature and founded synagogues. Japanese and Chinese workers took some of the worst but necessary jobs. They helped build the state's vital transportation links. They canned fish, raised fruit and ran small businesses. African-Americans dominated the Pullman services, mined coal and grew steadily in numbers. Oregon was not a comfortable place for minorities, but negative treatment was also dished out to "dumb Swedes," "beer-drinking Germans" and Irish and Italian Catholics. Many Oregonians wore their fears of those who were different on their shirtsleeves.

Emerging Economies

Natural resources drove economic development. A popular song said: "There'll be apples on each branch in Oregon; there'll be valleys filled with golden grain. There'll be cattle on each ranch in Oregon; and there'll be plenty of sun and rain." Farming, stockraising, mining, fishing and logging became mainstays. Land became the target. The trick was to find, coax, extricate and harvest everything useful the state had to offer, provided it was possible to get it to market.

Stockraising, for both beef and milk products, saw rapid growth in the late 1800s. (Oregon State Archives scenic photo)

Farmers took their oxen with plows and harrows into the prairies of the Rogue, Umpqua and Willamette valleys to turn the sod and sow crops. They raised wheat, oats, barley, corn and potatoes.

Swampy lands at Cipole, Gaston and Lake Labish produced fabulous onions. In time, experimentation led to specialty crops: hops for making malt in the brewing business, flax for linen manufacturing, hemp for paper and rope, and grapes for wine. Oregon farmers, by the 1880s, went wild for prunes. Thousands of acres of hillside lands were opened and groomed as orchards. Investors erected prune dryers and flooded the world market with more prunes than could be consumed. Some directed their energies next into filberts, walnuts, turkey raising and hog production. The agricultural potentials of western Oregon were varied.

Stockraising attracted a number of investors. Dairy farmers began their workday before sunrise and were still milking cows after sunset. Their cows grazed on the meadows surrounding Tillamook Bay, Nestucca, Salmon River, Coos Bay, Coquille River and in the Willamette Valley. The sprawling hinterlands of Oregon—two-thirds of the state laying beyond the Cascades—became cattle, sheep and horse country in the 19th century. The dramatic rise of livestock production occurred between 1862 and 1882. It responded to the presence of hungry men in the mines of the Blue Mountains, transcontinental railroad connections in Nevada with boxcars and refrigerator cars to haul meat to major cities, woolen mills demanding material for their spindles, and land amenable to pastoral labors. Pete French, Ben Snipes, David Shirk, John S. Devine, W. B. Todhunter, Dr. Bernard Daly, and others became barons of the ranges. By strategically gaining control of springs, streambanks, and lake margins, they were able to run their vast herds on the public domain without competition. David Shirk's herds ranged up and down Guano Valley. Devine and Todhunter ran the Whitehorse Ranch in the Pueblo Valley. Pete French, whose kingdom lay at the base of Steens Mountain, was gunned down by an angry homesteader in 1897. The jury trying the alleged murderer ruled that French had died of "natural causes"—a bullet in the head. There was no conviction.

Smaller producers also came into Trans-Cascadia. Some tended herds of sheep—as many as 5,000 in a flock—in lonely labor. The work entailed months driving the sheep to summer range at high elevation, backbreaking days of shearing and wrestling wool bales onto wagons, and marking and doctoring the critters. Sheep and cattle raisers did not mix. Angry words sometimes led to gunshots that felled livestock and nearly plunged Central Oregon partisans into a cycle of sheep and cattle wars. Basque and Mexican shepherds brought their skills to Jordan Valley, Catlow Valley and Treasure Valley. Some filed on homesteads. Donato Uvernaga and Simon Acordagoitia, Basques who settled on the Owyhee, hand-dug canals and built a hulking waterwheel. The steady current lifted metal buckets of life-giving water from the river to nourish the fields these immigrants cleared of sagebrush deep in the canyons below the Mahogany Mountains.

Mining shifted rapidly from placer deposits to lode claims. In that transition, the mining moved from an individual to a corporate enterprise, for shared capital and risk were usually necessary to open adits, erect a shaft house, install a stamp mill or flotation table and hire the crews necessary to operate a mine. Cooks and flunkies produced the grub served in the mess hall. Miners rode the ore buckets or climbed rickety ladders into the mine. The company engineer or mine manager directed the flow of ore through the processing plants. Oregon's 19th century ventures included gold mines in the Bohemia District of the Western Cascades, Siskiyous and Blue Mountains. Much of the gold and silver produced in Oregon and farther east in Idaho flowed through Portland, stimulating the development of the state's largest city. Between 1864 and 1870, for example, $29.8 million in mineral wealth passed through Portland. Between 1852 and 1964, Oregon produced an estimated $136 million in gold and silver. Approximately 73 percent came from the mines of Baker and Grant Counties.

Quicksilver mines tapped deposits in Lane and Douglas Counties. Brave miners engaged in the risky business of smelting the ores to fill flasks of mercury at London, Nonpareil, Milltown Hill and other small communities that grew up at the mine portals. In the 1880s, Will Q. Brown opened nickel deposits at Riddle in the South Umpqua Valley. Over the next 90 years, this mine produced more than $1 billion in nickel, generating an important payroll for Douglas County.

The Mary D. Hume, *shown here wrecked in Gold Beach, is one of many vessels that carried salmon to markets. (Oregon State Archives scenic photo)*

The need for fuel for steam engines drove Oregon's coal mining industry. Steam schooners, locomotives, donkey engines and mill equipment depended on cheap, plentiful coal. The mines at Coos Bay opened in 1853, and, for nearly a century, the coal fields of the lower Coquille River and Coos Bay fired Oregon industry and helped heat San Francisco. The Beaver Hill Mine, one of the largest on the coast, had shafts reaching nearly 1,100 feet below sea level. The Coos Bay, Roseburg & Eastern Railroad moved coal from the mines to the bunkers

at Coos Bay where it was loaded on steamers that would take it to distant markets.

Salmon annually filled the rivers. Some say the runs were so thick that it was possible to walk dryshod across the streams! Robert Deniston Hume grasped the potential. His brothers were pioneer cannery operators on the Sacramento and, starting in 1867, on the Columbia River. In 1876, Hume settled at the mouth of the Rogue River. By bravado and cunning, he carved out such an empire that, in time, he was referred to as a "pygmy monopolist." Hume gained ownership of both banks of the river from the Pacific upstream to the head of tidewater. This holding made it impossible for any competitor to land a boat or draw nets filled with fish without trespassing on his land. In time, Hume constructed a company town—Wedderburn—where he ran a cannery, store, race track and cold storage plant. His vessels, the *Alexander Duncan, Berwick,* and *Mary D. Hume,* transported his catch to markets. Hume became a pioneer in the hatchery business when, in 1877, he began experimenting with raising fish on Indian Creek, near the mouth of the Rogue River.

Canneries at Coos Bay, Umpqua River, Kernville and the Nestucca River processed the runs on the coastal streams. Canneries lined the banks of the Columbia between The Dalles and the sea. Samuel Elmore, Ben Young, Frank Warren and Frank Seufert were major players in the salmon canning business. The trick was to move quickly when new technology gave advantage. Laborers caught the fish in traps, seine nets, set nets and at fishwheels whose paddles scooping with the current, pulled salmon, sturgeon, eels and steelhead from the river and dumped them into fish boxes headed for a cannery.

Transportation systems were central to the future of most investments and profits in Oregon enterprise. Packet service and schooners carried passengers and freight along the coast. Sternwheelers picked up and delivered milk on the estuaries and carried commerce and passengers on most of the larger streams. Steamboats plied the Willamette, transforming landings into sites for warehouses, grist mills and small towns. Steamboats traversed Upper Klamath Lake and Goose Lake, taking children to school and tourists or shoppers to specific destinations. Investors constructed steamboats above the Cascades for water travel on the Columbia east to The Dalles and also on the upper river above Celilo Falls with connections to the mouth of the Snake and on to Lewiston, Idaho.

Packing companies and teamsters responded to the needs of mining communities and residents of distant communities. Outfitted with mules and horses, they carried the food, clothing and tools demanded by the miners in Canyon City, Auburn and Baker City or the farmers along Crooked River and Ochoco Creek. Teamsters like Henry H. Wheeler braved blizzards in winter and scorching heat in summer to carry mail, passengers and freight across the Columbia Plateau and into the mountains of eastern Oregon.

Railroads heralded the most significant advances in transportation. Between 1855 and 1862, Joseph Ruckel and Harrison Olmstead laid the foundation. They hired men, secured a right-of-way, and constructed roadbed and trestles for a horse-drawn cart to travel their "railway" along the Oregon shore at the Cascade Rapids of the Columbia. They were locked in bitter competition with Bradford & Company, competitors on the north bank. Pressing against both firms was the Oregon Steam Navigation Company which had developed in the 1850s a significant hold on steamboat service on the lower Willamette and Columbia Rivers. In 1860, Jacob Kamm, John C. Ainsworth and other investors in the OSN Company incorporated and, in rapid steps, bought out the Bradfords, Ruckel, and Olmstead. Holding the critical sea-level portages through the Columbia Gorge, they were ready to craft a major transportation system. Within months, they accomplished their goal.

Salmon canneries, with their colorful labels, lined the banks of the lower Columbia River in the late 1800s. (Oregon State Archives image)

The OSN Company, one of the state's first large corporations, developed an intricate system of steamboats, portage railroads and freight lines that gave it a hold on much of the commerce of the Pacific Northwest. It also built Oregon's first railroad. In 1862, as word of rich mines in the interior hit the front pages of newspapers, Ainsworth was in San Francisco purchasing rails and a small locomotive, the Oregon Pony, for shipment to the Gorge. Within a few months, workers transformed the old cart-rail system of Ruckel and Olmstead into Oregon's first railroad line—a five-mile route from Tanner Creek to the head of the Cascades. Other crews had taken on the bigger task of building a railroad for 14 miles from The Dalles to Celilo. Although its investors sold a major interest to the Northern Pacific in 1872, they bought back the shares following the Panic of 1873. They finally sold out in 1880. Those who held stock in the OSN Company were worth millions. Their daring and commitment had played a major role in helping anchor Portland as a hub of commerce and trade in the Pacific Northwest.

Railroads provided critical links to Oregon towns. In many instances they created towns. In 1880, Henry Villard headed a group of investors who bought out the OSN Company. Their firm, the

Oregon Railway & Navigation Company, built a railroad along the south bank of the Columbia east to the Umatilla River. In 1883, having gained control of the Northern Pacific, Villard created Oregon's first transcontinental link with the OR&N. His Oregon Short Line Railroad ran southeast over the Blue Mountains to Huntington and, in 1884, joined a connection into Idaho to the Union Pacific. This provided a second transcontinental connection for the state.

Construction of the Oregon & California Railroad, a north-south line to run from Portland to the Sacramento Valley, was a long-desired goal, but its completion proved frustrating. Driven by a fabulous land grant of nearly five million acres from Congress, rival companies vied for the right to construct the route. Ben Holladay, operator of the Overland Mail and the Pacific Mail Steamship Company, ultimately prevailed. He formed the Oregon & California Railroad Company, sold bonds and began building. The line reached Roseburg in 1872, and then stopped. Bad times in national finances were part of the problem. Poor potentials for returns on exceedingly expensive construction into the Rogue River Valley and over the Siskiyou Mountains were another. Construction resumed in 1882, and ultimately linked the line into the Southern Pacific system in California.

The primary lines of the OR&N to the interior and the O&C through the western Oregon valleys encouraged logging, lumber manufacturing, export of wool and livestock, and sale of fruit, cereal crops, and other agricultural commodities to a vastly expanded market. The primary lines also encouraged two generations of smaller operators such as T. Egenton Hogg to dream of connecting units or even of new transcontinental linkages. Hogg managed in the 1880s to build a line from salt water at Yaquina City over the Coast Range and east via the Santiam as far as Detroit. The route of his Oregon Pacific Railroad appeared on maps in the 1890s, but it never reached the Deschutes or the Harney Basin, where speculators laid out towns in anticipation of its arrival.

The pieces were mostly in place by the latter 19th century for the state to sustain steady growth. Oregon had a resource-dependent economy driven by exploitation of fish, timber, minerals and agricultural lands. The state had steamboats, stage lines, pack teams, and railroads to serve residents of small towns as well as emerging cities. Oregon's population grew steadily. At statehood in 1859, Oregon had 52,465 residents. The figure more than tripled to 174,768 in 1880, and reached 413,536 in 1900.

Troubled Times

Discontents stirred in the hearts and minds of Oregonians in the last three decades of the 19th century. Life left some feeling cheated. Hard work did not bring sufficient wages or sale of farm commodities to secure a decent living. Many jobs took place in the midst of danger in poorly lighted sawmills, dust-filled coal mines, slippery canneries,or woolen mills with whirling spindles. Loggers confronted falling trees, flying cables, surging freshets and wretched living conditions in the camps where they lived. Clerks were underpaid and labored six days a week in monotonous jobs where they had neither health nor retirement plans and little prospect for advancement. Women attended academies, public schools, normal schools, colleges and universities, but male Oregonians refused to grant them the right to vote. Too many, it seemed, coped with alcoholic husbands who plundered the egg and butter money for a few more coins to spend on "demon liquor."

The disenchanted found inspiration for reconstructing their world. Ideologies beckoned alluringly and became part of an interesting mix of forces that set the stage for significant changes in Oregon. They ranged from arguments for women's suffrage to the pleas of the Christian Women's Temperance Union to control, if not suspend, the manufacture and sale of alcoholic beverages. The ideologies ran from economic and social theories to racist and bigoted attacks on minorities and immigrants. Many suggested political action might solve a state's or a nation's problems in a time of increasing industrialization.

California journalist Henry George promoted a simple solution to destitution. He argued in *Progress and Poverty* (1879) that the United States could eradicate poverty by implementing a tax of 100 percent on the "unearned increment," the inflationary value of real estate. The redistribution of the "single tax," he said, could meet need and solve societal problems. Tens of thousands read his book and became "single taxers."

Edward Bellamy's *Looking Backward* (1887) intrigued others. Bellamy used a shallow plot line about a man who fell into a mesmeric trance in 1887 — a time of labor strife, urban pollution, slums and poverty — and who awakened in 2000. He found a reconstructed American society and economy with abundant prosperity and peace. All had changed through the miracle of "nationalism." In Bellamy's world, the solution was government ownership of all means of production, transportation, housing and basic utilities.

Hard rock miners listened to the speakers from the Knights of Labor and the Western Federation of Miners. Many were not happy with their lot. Coal miners on Oregon's southwest coast endured low wages, explosions, and horrendous working conditions. Men extracting quicksilver in Douglas County slowly poisoned themselves tending the furnaces to produce flasks of mercury. Gold miners labored hundreds of feet below ground in the quartz deposits of the Bohemia Mining District in the Western Cascades and in mine shafts in the Blue and Wallowa Mountains of eastern Oregon. They were inspired by the prospect of forming unions and joining with fellow miners to wrest better pay and safer working conditions from the companies for which they labored.

Grange halls served as local social centers throughout rural Oregon. Their members advocated for agrarian issues. (Oregon State Archives scenic photo)

Thousands of farmers turned first to the Patrons of Husbandry, joining Granges, engaging in the rituals of the organization, and pressing the legislature to meet the needs of agrarians. Others joined the Northwestern Alliance, a nonpartisan organization of farmers who hoped for reform. Alliance members and Grangers lobbied for collection and publication of agricultural statistics, strengthening of education at Oregon Agricultural College in Corvallis, development of experimental farms to test crops, breeds of livestock, and the impact of fertilizer and chemical sprays. And not a few heard about Mary Elizabeth Lease of Kansas, who told farmers in America's heartland that they should "raise less corn and more hell!"

Many agrarians embraced the People's Party. In 1892, its platform attempted to create an agenda to meet their needs. The populists endorsed limits on immigration, government ownership of railroads, telegraph and telephone, free coinage of silver to stimulate western mining, secret ballot, direct election of senators, and the subtreasury system whereby the government would buy unsold farm commodities, hold them, and then unload the products on the world market. Farmers would receive subtreasury notes — backed by the government — when they deposited potatoes, wheat, barley or apples at the federal warehouse — and could pay off their loans. William Hope Harvey's *Coin's Financial School* (1892) made the case for expanding the amount of money in circulation. Professor Coin argued that if the federal government would purchase and coin all available silver, the nation's economy could be corrected, farmers could pay off the mortgages for steam tractors and combines, and prosperity would return.

As these ideas swept through the newspapers, out of the mouths of speakers, and through books, they found believers. In 1890, Oregon had 2,555 men employed in logging and log transportation, 1,962 working in sawmills, 2,756 engaged in fishing or the oyster harvest, 2,308 mining, and 17,316 working as agricultural laborers. Tens of thousands more Oregonians lived on family farms. Men rode the range to tend cattle, sheep and horses, while women preserved food and cooked huge meals at roundup and shearing times. The farm population—owners and hired laborers—endured continuous work, dark nights, isolation, taxes on their lands, and uncertainty.

In 1889, many of the discontented met in Salem to form the Union Party. The meeting drew Prohibition advocates, members of the Knights of Labor, and the interest of Democrat Sylvester Pennoyer, seeking another term as governor. This was the atmosphere of social and political discontent that brought Oregonians to the People's Party. Hundreds turned out for rallies to meet General James B. Weaver, populist candidate for president. Abigail Scott Duniway, continuing her unrelenting campaign for women's suffrage, in 1892 introduced Mary Elizabeth Lease, the "Kansas Pythoness" and populist stump speaker, to an eager audience in Portland. Duniway's 1894 speech to an estimated 2,800 strikers inspired some to call her the "Patrick Henry of the Northwest" and led her brother, editor of *The Oregonian,* to refuse to print the text of her address.

While the Republicans and Democrats continued their hold on the majority of state offices, they found populists among their ranks in the Legislature. Oregon Democrats got the reform message in the 1890s. Historian Dorothy O. Johansen quoted the saying "Scratch a Western Democrat and you find a Populist," an apt assessment of the Democrats' embrace of free silver, banking reform, income tax, and reform in government.

Oregon government needed change. Oregon Senator John Hipple Mitchell, a slippery man when it came to wives and influence peddling, reportedly said: "Ben Holladay's politics are my politics and what Ben Holladay wants I want." Holladay's hold on regional transportation systems and Mitchell's retainer as legal counsel for both the Oregon & California Railroad and the Northern Pacific left little doubt about the senator's loyalties. He may have been elected by the Legislature, but he appeared to be in the pocket of special interests.

Frustrated Oregonians also turned to the pathetic performance of the builders of the state's military wagon roads. The grants locked up hundreds of thousands of acres in checkerboard sections on both margins of the traces and, by the 1890s, many of the holdings had passed to out-of-state owners. The grant for the Coos Bay Wagon Road—105,120 acres—passed quickly into the hands of speculators little interested in the road or its operation. For a time, Californians Leland Stanford, Mark Hopkins, Charles Crocker and Collis P. Huntington owned much of the grant. Other portions went to the Southern Oregon Improvement Company, a pool of investors in Boston and New Bedford, Massachusetts. Edward Martin of San Francisco formed the Eastern Oregon Land Company when he secured 450,000 acres of the land grant for The Dalles-Boise Military Wagon Road.

By not taking title to the grants, the owners avoided taxation, yet no settler could homestead or purchase the land from the General Land Office. A few Oregonians perpetrated unblushing frauds in the scramble for properties under the Swamp Lands Act. Ostensibly the law encouraged reclamation and irrigation. It created, however, a situation where unscrupulous public officials conspired with speculators to gain ownership of tidelands, lush lake margins and even dry ground. Plunderers also took advantage of the 1887 decision of the Legislature to sell school lands, sections 16 and 36, in each township. Had the lands or revenues gone into a school fund, the endowment could have financed public education in Oregon in perpetuity.

In the 1890s, neither the ideologues nor the political activists carried the day. Society, business and political affairs continued much as usual. The times of discontent, however, set the stage for change. Ideas circulated that posed the prospect for deep-seated reform. All that was needed was some principled leadership, public indignation with the corruption, and the will to try something new.

The Oregon System

William U'Ren was a quiet, contemplative man. Little in his countenance or demeanor betrayed the inner fire that drove his determination to change public participation in Oregon government. A single-tax advocate, U'Ren moved on to embrace the ideas of James W. Sullivan, author of *Direct Legislation by the Citizenship Through the Initiative and Referendum* (1892). If U'Ren could empower common citizens, he could wage war on vested interests, corruption, and the tensions that set classes against each other. U'Ren jettisoned the single tax, embraced Sullivan's philosophy, converted to populism and, in 1897, gained a seat in the Legislature as a candidate of the People's Party. U'Ren was in a position to cut a deal because populists held 13 critical votes to swing power in the legislature.

William U'Ren.
(Courtesy Wikimedia)

The time for dealing was at hand. Senator John H. Mitchell, despised by many, came out firmly for the Republican platform and the gold standard. Jonathan Bourne, Jr., a Republican and silver mine owner, saw a chance to dump Mitchell, provided he could win populist votes. U'Ren set the price: initiative, referendum, voter registration, and an elections procedure law. Bourne bought the package but had to play a cat-and-mouse game in what was known as the "Holdup of '97." Bourne, U'Ren, and others forged a coalition and blocked the House from organizing. The Committee on Credentials declined to report, the anti-Mitchell representatives refused to take their oaths of office, and the Mitchell forces could not elect him, lacking a quorum in the House. U'Ren and Bourne pushed through each of the promised measures. By a cumbersome process, the legislature twice approved a constitutional amendment and, after ratification by a resounding public vote in 1902, Oregonians instituted the initiative and referendum, having amended the state constitution for the first time since 1859.

The combination of voter commitment to enact long-needed laws and the ability to do so with the initiative helped propel Oregon to national attention as a state leading in progressivism. The largely non-partisan Oregon System, as it was heralded, addressed the accumulated social evils that had grown in numbers and complexity. The means were at hand to make government more efficient, honest, and responsive to human need.

Oregonians tallied important enactments: Direct Primary Law (1904), extension of initiative and referendum to local laws, city home rule, indictment by grand jury, taxes on telephone, telegraph, and railroad companies (all 1906), a recall amendment to the State Constitution, the Corrupt Practices Act (both 1908), three-fourths verdict in civil cases, and employers' liability act (both 1910), women's suffrage, prohibition on private employment of convict labor, eight-hour day on public works (all 1912), presidential preference primary (1913), Prohibition, and an eight-hour day and room ventilation for women workers (both 1914). Other laws abolished capital punishment, the infamous Oregon Boot, a heavy manacle attached to legs of prisoners, and required publication of the *Oregon Blue Book*.

The Oregon Land Fraud trials captured local and national interest. Francis Heney, special federal prosecutor, brought to justice 33 who had pillaged federal lands, state school lands and the timbered resources of the Siletz Indian Reservation. The kingpin of the Oregon Land Fraud Ring, Stephen A. D. Puter, penned in his prison cell *Looters of the Public Domain* (1908), a tell-all book with portraits of his co-conspirators and copies of documents confirming their criminal acts. Heney's prosecutions cleaned out many of the personnel of the General Land Office; twice indicted, but failed to convict, Binger Hermann, an Oregonian and former commissioner of the General Land Office in Washington, D.C.; and obtained prison sentences for Senator John H. Mitchell and Congressman John N. Williamson.

Oregon governors George E. Chamberlain, who served from 1903 to 1909, and Oswald West, who served from 1911 to 1915, were in office during the era of progressivism and each, in a nonpartisan manner, helped facilitate the Oregon System. To persuade the legislature that he intended for progressive reform to prevail, in 1911, West vetoed 63 bills. When good legislation failed, he saw that it surfaced as initiative measures. As a consequence, Oregonians

gained a workers' compensation act, banking laws, and a Public Utility Commission. By executive order in 1913, West declared that Oregon beaches were public highways and set the precedent for the much-litigated but protected right of public access to the entire state shoreline. He gave full authority to his secretary, Fern Hobbs, and sent her with members of the National Guard to Copperfield, a notorious boom town on the railroad in Baker County. With a declaration of martial law on January 1, 1914, she closed all saloons and houses of prostitution. She left the guardsmen to monitor the situation. West never minced words. In his reminiscences he wrote about Oregon's land fraud ring: "These looters of the public domain—working with crooked federal and state officials—through rascality and fraud, gained title to thousands of acres of valuable, publicly-owned timber lands, and at minimum prices." West pounded them, even when penning his recollections in 1950.

Progressivism touched Oregon in another way. In 1907, Congress considered a crucial agricultural appropriations bill. Powerful lobbyists for timber companies persuaded Senator Charles Fulton from Astoria to attach to it an amendment rescinding presidential authority to create any more forest reserves in the Pacific Northwest under the Forest Reserve Act of 1891. In less than ten days, Gifford Pinchot, new head of the U.S. Forest Service, and President Theodore Roosevelt poured over maps and identified millions of acres of critical forests. Roosevelt exercised the last hours of his executive authority and created the "Midnight Reserves." Oregon's national forests multiplied severalfold by the stroke of a pen and the willpower of two conservationists.

The Oregon System was the creative response to a mix of ideologies and discontents. It broke the power of many special interests and old political coalitions. It became a model for the rest of the country and was emulated in dozens of states and cities drawing inspiration from the power of a determined citizenry.

Mixed Blessings

Progressivism waned with World War I. Oregonians and other Americans began to tire of crusades. The entry into the Great War tested the resolution to continue problem-solving. Peace and commitment to its maintenance were casualties of both the war and the postwar world.

Industrial strife mounted when worker expectations remained unrealized as prosperity increased after 1900. Alienated, fearful and distrustful of the establishment, some workers gravitated toward the Socialist Party and militant labor unions. The West Coast Shingle Weaver's Union as chartered by the American Federation of Labor and the International Union of Shingle Weavers, Sawmill Workers and Woodsmen sought recruits. The Industrial Workers of the World grew by the thousands when disgruntled loggers and mill workers enlisted in its ranks. Known to most by its initials, IWW, the union was perceived by management as the "I Won't Work" contingent. Free speech fights, confrontations, strikes, and demands for better working conditions and higher wages became the tense legacy of workers and management on the eve of World War I.

Illustrative of the tensions were the vigilante actions of the businessmen of Bandon. In 1913, enraged by the publication of *Social Justice*, they seized its editor and publisher. Dr. Bailey K. Leach had used his newspaper to denounce vigilantism, the Boy Scouts of America as a paramilitary organization, and perceived thought control in the public library, which refused to accession Socialist literature. A mob grabbed Dr. Leach, placed a noose around his neck and "deported" him from Bandon. Beaten and left barefoot on the North Spit at Coos Bay, having been compelled to kneel and kiss the American flag, he walked through the sand dunes and up the Umpqua River to the office of Governor Oswald West to complain of his treatment. An investigation mounted by the State Supreme Court led to the disbarment of an attorney in Marshfield. Leach was lucky. When IWW organizer Wesley Everest was deported in similar fashion from Coos Bay, he went to Centralia, Washington, to promote the union. In 1919, he was seized by a mob, castrated, and hanged from a railroad bridge. No one was charged with Everest's murder. To many, the rousing hymn of the IWW, "Hallelujah, I'm a Bum," justified violations of civil liberties and the law.

To counter the growth of labor unions and the Socialist Party, the federal government took control of spruce production in Western Oregon and Washington. Deemed an essential material for airplane manufacturing, spruce became the assignment of the U.S. Army's Spruce Production Division. It assumed responsibilities for logging, lumbering, and filling orders. In 1917, General Brice P. Disque took command of troops who erected mills at Coquille and Toledo, Oregon and Vancouver and Port Gamble, Washington. The Spruce Division produced 54 million board feet of airplane wing beams in Oregon and left a modern electrical sawmill and extensive railroad network in Lincoln County, which, in time, passed into private ownership.

The federal government also created the Loyal Legion of Loggers and Lumbermen. Ostensibly an employer-employee union, the 4-Ls recruited thousands of workers who pledged not to strike and to help the nation in its production of war materials. The Emergency Fleet Corporation, a federal agency, contracted with yards to turn out vessels for the war effort. Shipbuilders in Portland, Astoria, Tillamook and Marshfield produced steel and wooden-hull vessels for the EFC. Fort Stevens at Warrenton took on new life since its primary construction during the Civil War and Spanish-American War. Troops drilled and trained on its parade grounds; some departed with other Oregonians for service on the battlefields of Europe.

World War I was a mixed blessing for Oregon. Initially, it stimulated the economy with the production of war materials, foodstuffs, and ships, but it set the stage for the collapse of shipbuilding and the falloff of lumber production in the 1920s. Everywhere were signs of trouble: few housing starts, instability in banking, speculation in the stock market and migration. More than 50,000 people left Oregon following World War I. Opportunities beckoned elsewhere.

In a sense, Oregon made their transit possible. Between 1911 and 1922, state, county, and local funds helped build the Columbia River Highway. The Columbia Gorge section, designed by Samuel Lancaster, an engineer brought in from Tennessee, ran eastward with gentle grades and sensitive integration with the environment to open access to scenic waterfalls, hiking trails, and spectacular vistas between Portland and

A World War I pilot from Oregon. (Oregon State Archives photo)

The Dalles. Modern construction techniques, including steel-reinforced poured-concrete bridges, created the region's first paved highway. In 1913, Oregon created the State Highway Commission. Four years later, it expanded its membership and the legislature began steady appropriations to "Get Oregon Out of the Mud." The "good roads" campaign took on real life in 1919 when Oregon enacted a gasoline tax. The first state in the country to pay for roads through a gas tax, Oregon embraced the automobile age and began construction of the Pacific Highway. From its crossing at the Interstate Bridge across the Willamette, the route ran south via the Willamette, Umpqua, and Rogue Valleys to California. Paved in concrete, its gentle course ran through productive farmlands, crossed rivers on major bridges, wended its way up the slopes of the Siskiyous and confirmed Oregon's commitment to good roads.

Road construction led to legislation in 1921, promoted by Governor Ben Olcott, to authorize the State Highway Commission to acquire rights-of-way for scenic conservation and roadside forest preserves. In 1922, the state accepted the gift of Sarah Helmick State Park in Polk County. These actions received legislative direction in 1925 with authorization to acquire lands for park purposes for waysides and natural areas. Governor I. L. Patterson, in 1929, named the first State Park Commission, which worked closely with Samuel H. Boardman, the state parks engineer, for building a land base of state-owned park properties.

Although highway construction helped one sector of the economy, the advent of automobile traffic sounded the death knell for steamboats on the rivers and, in time, Oregon's electrical railroad system. The Oregon Electric Railway operated daily trains over 122 miles of track by 1912 between Portland and

Eugene. A "No Soot-No Cinders" route, the commuter line also ran west to Forest Grove. The Southern Pacific's Red Electric began connections in 1914. It ran from Portland to Corvallis via Lake Oswego and Newberg. A branch line swung west to Hillsboro, Forest Grove and McMinnville. For a time, travelers had the choice of ten departures from Portland and at least two from McMinnville. The efficiency of the electrics and the interurban lines was eclipsed by cars and buses. The 1920s were a time of transition. Smells of draft animals and the clacking sound of horseshoes mixed with the swift movement of electrical railroads and gasoline-driven cars and trucks. In time, the familiar "Galloping Goose," the solitary passenger-mail car that ran on many of Oregon's short lines, disappeared. Residents of Friend, Shaniko, Prairie City, Cherry Grove, Bull Run, and other small towns would have to travel by road, not rail.

Wartime stress, emphasis on patriotism, distrust of German-Americans, eugenics campaigns championed by Dr. Bethenia Owens-Adair, and anti-Catholic bigotry created fertile ground in Oregon for the rise of the American Protective Association, Federation of Patriotic Societies, and the Ku Klux Klan. With a combined membership estimated at more than 64,000 Oregonians, these organizations fed on the fear and distrust of residents in a period of social flux and uncertainty. Although minorities were few in number, racism and bigotry were imported ideas. They came with newcomers from other parts of the country and grew in soil that already nurtured suspicion and tendencies to vigilante action. Chapters of the Ku Klux Klan formed in Tillamook, Medford, Eugene and Portland, as well as many other towns. Robed Klansmen paraded in the streets, ignited crosses on hillsides, nailed American flags to the doors of Catholic schools, and intimidated African-Americans.

The Klan, FOPS, and Scottish Rite Masons sponsored a bill, passed in 1922 in the general election, to compel all children to attend public schools. The overtly anti-Catholic measure threatened to close all parochial schools and military academies. The state Supreme Court ruled the law unconstitutional in 1924, and the U.S. Supreme Court concurred in 1925. The Ku Klux Klan found a strange champion in the Oregon legislature. Kaspar K. Kubli, speaker of the House of Representatives, happened to possess winning initials and became a rallying point for efforts to drive through the Alien Property Act of 1923. The law prohibited Japanese from purchasing or leasing land in Oregon. The legislature also passed a law forbidding wearing of sectarian clothing, namely priestly vestments or nuns' habits, in classrooms.

A number of historians have written about the flaws of the 1920s and the nation's serious engagement with public-sanctioned bigotry. While some of the laws were overt, many more went on quietly but consistently. Oregon's indigenous people, who became citizens of the United States in 1924, were forbidden to purchase alcohol, though some applied for a special card that certified their entitlement to drink. Oregon realtors declined to sell homes in certain areas to minorities. Oregon developers wrote into deeds restrictive covenants that prohibited holding ducks and geese and sale of the house and land to anyone of Chinese or Japanese ancestry. Large neighborhoods of Portland—Garthwick, Dunthorpe, Eastmoreland, Westmoreland—and Lake Oswego were kept "white" for decades by subtle but effective discrimination.

One of the hard-fought agendas of the 1920s was the encouragement of public power. In 1930, Oregonians approved the creation of public utility districts. The action shook some of the well-established utility companies, for they now faced the prospect that if their rates and actions were out of line with public interest, voters could set up their own company, and vie for hydropower rights on a stream or build a sawdust-fired electrical plant and offer service to consumers.

The 1920s were a period of rapid adjustment from wartime preparedness and boom to an uneven and deteriorating economy. Oregon moved from progressivism to the rise of selfish interests and secret societies that threatened liberties and promoted bigotry. Yet, in spite of following strange paths, the state laid the foundation of a fine highway system, state parks, and competitive rates for electrical power.

The Great Depression

On October 29, 1929, a calamity rocked the United States. Within hours the stock market, buoyed by speculation and unreasonable expectations, plunged into the abyss of "Black Tuesday." The onset of the Great Depression meant little to tens of thousands of Oregonians. They were already living in depressed circumstances, trying to make a go of arid homesteads, stump farms, or underpaid jobs in sawmills. Those who had savings, however, felt the debacle acutely. Banks went bankrupt. In spite of handsome buildings and facades of stability, white marble counters, brass grills at the teller cages, and hulking vaults, their resources were vulnerable and they fell by the droves, wiping out the accumulated resources of depositors. Bank failures led to foreclosures on homes, farms, and businesses and contributed to the general malaise that had seized the country.

In spite of his reputation as a humanitarian, President Herbert Hoover, a sometime Oregonian who had grown up in Newberg, wrestled unsuccessfully with checking the economic free-fall. Hoover was trapped both by his political philosophy

Herbert Hoover grew up in Newberg. (Courtesy Wikimedia)

and by problems so complex that no one really had a viable solution for them.

So, in 1933, the nation turned to a pragmatist—Franklin Delano Roosevelt—who also did not have solutions but who had promised to try to remedy the Great Depression through bold actions. Roosevelt began deliberately in March. He declared a national "bank holiday," closing all financial institutions across the country so that federal inspectors could examine their books. If a bank reopened, it would do so because the government found it sound. It could be trusted. If a bank's affairs were beyond redemption, it remained closed. Roosevelt also spoke to all Americans—including hundreds of thousands of Oregonians who, since 1921, had purchased radios. In a series of "fireside chats" broadcast from the White House, he waged a campaign to build confidence. He promoted the reform, relief, and recovery agendas of the New Deal.

While few believe the Democrat programs of the 1930s effectively turned around the Great Depression, they were of immense consequence to Oregon. Through deficit spending and passing on payment obligations to succeeding generations, Congress authorized programs that helped change the face of Oregon. The Beer Act of March, 1933 set the stage for repeal of Prohibition and permitted hop-raisers and brewers like Blitz-Weinhard to resume production. Far more significant, however, was the creation that same month of the Civilian Conservation Corps. Intended to provide unemployment relief for several million young Americans, the CCC developed projects in public land states like Oregon. The CCC established base camps and spike camps in most of the national forests and began a remarkable program of construction. The workers cut trails; built roads; constructed bridges; built campgrounds with handsome log facilities for cooking, eating, and public meetings; laid telephone wires; constructed drift fences to manage cattle; built log corrals; enclosed springs; dammed creeks to create small reservoirs; constructed guard stations and ranger stations; and carried the materials board-by-board to lofty peaks for fire lookouts. From Hells Canyon to the Chetco River and from the Oriana Corral on the Fremont National Forest to the campground at Eagle Creek in the Columbia Gorge, the CCC made enduring, handsome improvements on federal lands.

Similarly, the Works Projects Administration drew unemployed architects, stone masons, painters, weavers, metal workers, plumbers, and artisans into special Oregon projects. The WPA built Timberline Lodge, a dramatic recreation hotel, on the southern slopes of Mount Hood. WPA artisans created towering murals, iron gates, and furniture for the new library on the campus of the University of Oregon. WPA laborers erected post offices, customs buildings, and federal buildings from Burns to Tillamook. Not since Andrew Carnegie's matching-funds projects for public libraries in the 1910s had Oregon seen such a profusion of public structures.

The Public Works Administration and the Public Buildings Administration worked with the WPA in other ways to transform Oregon. Projects included a city hall in Canby, a dramatic capitol and state library in Salem, an armory in Klamath Falls, a high school in Corvallis, a dormitory at the State School for the Blind, a sewage disposal plant in Medford, and five stunning bridges spanning major estuaries on the Oregon coast. The bridges, completed in 1936, cost $5.4 million. In the midst of the Great Depression, Oregon embarked on grading and paving Highway 101 to forge another important transportation link.

The WPA also employed teachers, lawyers, and architects. It mounted the Oregon Folklore Project, the Oregon Writers' Program and the Inventory of the County Archives of Oregon. These workers published *Oregon: End of the Trail* (1940), *Mount Hood: A Guide* (1940), the annual *Oregon Almanac: A Handbook of Fact and Fancy, Oregon Oddities*—a magazine used in public schools—and 14 of a projected 35 descriptive guides to records in county courthouses. Each of the guides included an overview of county history based upon a review of the archives. In many instances, these were the first historical assessments of Oregon counties. Working almost in tandem with the WPA were drafters, historians and photographers engaged in the Historic American Buildings Survey. They compiled information, including measured drawings, on nearly a hundred significant structures in Oregon.

The New Deal had a grassroots impact in Oregon. This was most dramatically confirmed when, in 1935, Congress funded construction of a project that Roosevelt had promised during his 1932 campaign swing through the state. Bonneville Dam, one of the great engineering marvels of the early 20th century, was to span the Columbia River at the western end of the Gorge. Its massive reservoir would back up waters to The Dalles. Its locks would lift ships and barges for easy transit to the grain elevators on the western plateau. Its turbines would generate massive amounts of electricity to power industry and diversify the region's economy. Above all, construction of the dam would provide employment for 4,000 laborers and the multiplier effect would generate thousands more jobs to feed, house and provide services to these workers and their families. Because navigation was a critical element with the building of the locks, the Army Corps of Engineers secured project supervision. Initial estimates for the dam, lock, powerhouse and federal townsites for management personnel ran to $81 million.

As the dam neared completion, the Bonneville Power Administration in 1937 took over responsibility for construction of transmission lines and marketing of power to utility companies, public utility districts, and industrial users such as aluminum plants in Troutdale and The Dalles. In 1941, the BPA hired Woody Guthrie to compose and sing songs celebrating power development on the Columbia River. Guthrie's 17 songs included the popular "Roll

On, Columbia." Its lyrics touted the New Deal achievements:

"At Bonneville now there are ships in the locks,
The waters have risen and cleared all the rocks,
Shiploads of plenty will steam past the docks,
So roll on, Columbia, roll on."

The New Deal touched the lives of Oregonians in other ways. The Taylor Grazing Act in 1934 changed the free-for-all of livestock using the public domain. Henry Gerber and local ranchers in the Langell Valley of Klamath County were acutely aware of the need to allocate grazing rights. The Bonanza Grazing Unit, headed by Gerber, was the first organized in the United States under the Taylor Act. In time, the law brought 152 million acres under the U.S. Grazing Service and called for local boards of landowners to allocate the animal units per month allowed in national forests or on lands administered by the General Land Office. In 1946, Congress merged the land office and the grazing service to create the Bureau of Land Management.

The Soil Conservation Service, created in 1936, provided counsel and assistance to farmers faced with erosion by wind and water on the Columbia Plateau. The Production Credit Association worked with farmers to scale down mortgage payments by extending the length of their loans. The Federal Housing Administration, set up in 1934, provided low-interest loans to try to encourage home construction. The Bankhead-Jones Act of 1937 provided federal dollars to buy out impoverished homesteaders and transform the lands into federal holdings. The National Grasslands between Madras and Prineville was a product of the Bankhead-Jones Act. The Rural Electrification Administration worked with private utilities and public utility districts to extend lines to remote areas. By the late 1930s, thousands of rural Oregonians for the first time had electrical service and would be able to use a radio, refrigerator, vacuum cleaner, electric stove, washing machine and lights.

The Great Depression took a toll on Oregon but created a setting for massive improvement of infrastructure. Roads, bridges, buildings, dams, locks, powerhouses, electrical transmission lines, recreation facilities and range management were an impressive tally of accomplishments. While many Oregonians were driven into a subsistence lifestyle of "making do" with homemade clothing, a garden and austerity, the federal projects had infused confidence, generated payrolls, and laid the foundations for new industries and much wider use of public lands in the state.

World War II

The attack on Pearl Harbor on December 7, 1941, pulled the United States out of neutrality and plunged the nation again into world war. Because Oregon lay along the nation's Pacific Coast, it was considered in the war zone. The consequences were almost immediate. To create a wartime mentality as well as to prepare against attack, residents of coastal communities faced nightly blackouts. Block wardens monitored compliance. Shades and blankets covered windows and many painted over the upper half of their car headlamps. Volunteers joined the Ground Observer Corps to log the make and identity of airplanes. Soldiers maintained coastal patrols, supplementing Coast Guard personnel in their watch of the sea. Jeeps ran along the beaches to isolated dugouts where foot patrols with dogs stood duty.

War preparedness had begun in the late 1930s with scrap drives. Schoolchildren competed to see who could tally the heaviest pile of metal. The occasional school that located an old logging railroad locomotive surged to top honors. With the declaration of war, Oregonians confronted rationing of tires, gasoline, meat, sugar, and clothing. For those who lived far from town, rationing necessitated careful trip planning.

Executive Order 9066 of February 19, 1942, fell heavily on the Japanese-American population of Oregon. Although most were American citizens and many had sons, brothers, and fathers who had enlisted or were drafted into military service, the families of Japanese background living west of the Cascades in Oregon were placed under curfew and ordered to report to evacuation centers, preliminaries to removal to distant relocation camps. Over 120,000 Japanese-Americans from Oregon, Washington, and California endured relocation. Japanese-Americans in Hawaii—more fully in the war zone—were exempted from relocation. Those who were removed, lost homes, crops, farm animals, property, bank accounts and personal possessions.

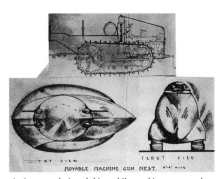

An inventor designed this mobile machine gun nest during World War II. Oregonians pulled together on the home front. (Oregon State Archives photo)

The war gripped the United States and Oregonians. Dozens of towns erected permanent billboards that carried the names of citizens killed in defense of their country. Oregon had 2,826 wartime deaths and over 5,000 wounded. Tensions rose when a Japanese submarine surfaced off the mouth of the Columbia River and on June 21, 1942, fired 17 shells at Fort Stevens. Concern rose again on September 9 of the same year, when a small airplane, launched by a catapult from the deck of a Japanese submarine off Brookings, carried Nubuo Fujita and Shoji Okuda over the Siskiyou National Forest to drop incendiary bombs on Mount Emily. Oregon suffered civilian casualties on May 5, 1945, when participants in a church picnic near Bly poked an incendiary balloon that had floated across the Pacific. The device, intended to set forest fires, exploded and killed the minister's wife and five children.

A wartime economy helped pull Oregon out of the Great Depression. Federal expenditures mounted dramatically. The investment included facilities, construction salaries, and assembling of large numbers of personnel who needed housing, food, clothing and other services. The U.S. Army built Camp Adair north of Corvallis and Camp Abbott on the upper Deschutes River south of Bend. These troop-training facilities served thousands of recruits. Camp Adair even included a fake Japanese village where soldiers practiced assaults should they reach the main islands of Japan. The Umatilla Army Depot near Hermiston became a sprawling repository for munitions in hundreds of semisubterranean silos. The Army also constructed hangars and airfields at Portland, Astoria, Newport, North Bend and Floras Lake. The U.S. Navy built the Tongue Point Naval Station at Astoria, and at the Tillamook Naval Air Station, erected two of the largest wood-frame buildings in the world. Blimps, stationed at Blimperon 33, moved out of these massive hangars and glided up and down the coast to patrol for enemy ships and submarines.

The electricity from Bonneville, dubbed by some in 1939 as the "dam of doubt," moved through the BPA grid to aluminum plants from Longview to Spokane. Inexpensive electricity heated the smelters to process bauxite into rolls of aluminum, which moved by rail to the Boeing manufacturing plants on Puget Sound. There was no doubt about the dramatic rise of employment where nearly 50,000 workers by 1944 were able to produce 16 airplanes every 24 hours. In Portland and nearby Vancouver, Henry J. Kaiser's shipyards employed an estimated 100,000 workers. Men and women worked side by side to build "Baby Flattops" and "Liberty Ships." By 1945, some 150,000 workers were engaged in 85 shipyards in Oregon and Washington.

Jobs in aluminum plants, shipyards, military bases, and lumber production for the war effort created a surge of migration. During World War II, an estimated 194,000 people moved into the state. For the first time, Oregon's African-American population grew substantially—in Portland increasing from 2,565 in 1940 to 25,000 in 1944. Drawn by jobs, steady salaries, and the area's reputation as a decent place to live, newcomers coped with inflated rents, shantytowns, camps, and trailer parks. In 1942, Edgar Kaiser met some of the housing problem by building Vanport on the south bank of the Columbia. With 35,000 residents, the community became Oregon's second largest town until destroyed in May 1948 by breaking levees during a major flood. Public housing projects, dubbed "cardboard palaces" by some, met short-term needs and, in some instances, were used for years or were transformed into student housing on college campuses.

The GI Bill helped veterans return to civilian life with home loans and educational funding. (Oregon State Archives photo)

When World War II ended, Oregon was a different place. The economy was good, even when labor disputes erupted with the West Coast Longshoremen's Union. The federal projects of the 1930s created an extensive infrastructure for the use and enjoyment of national forests and the public domain. Many Oregonians had disposable income and savings. The future beckoned far more brightly than during the drab years of the Great Depression or the uncertainties of World War II.

Rapid Developments

Postwar Oregon prospered. Although housing was short, residents made do. The GI Bill provided funding for a generation eager for higher education but blocked from the opportunity because of the Great Depression and World War II. College enrollments swelled as returning veterans and recent high school graduates settled down to earn degrees and pursue civilian careers. The state's college campuses grew in response to the increasing numbers of students. The legislature appropriated funds for new facilities at La Grande, Monmouth, Eugene, Klamath Falls and Corvallis. From its beginnings at Vanport College, Portland State University emerged as a new urban campus in the state's largest city. In addition, the state's private colleges and universities likewise grew in enrollments and transformed from their sectarian origins to independent liberal arts institutions.

Savings that had accumulated during the war, low-interest FHA loans, and dramatic population growth in California fueled a booming logging and lumbering economy. Between 1945 and 1990, the state became a national leader in manufacture of forest products. For decades, Coos Bay held the title as the world's largest lumber shipping port. Oregon sawmills' wigwam burners belching smoke and sawdust cinders and heavily laden log trucks were icons for a thriving industry.

The infrastructure of roads, guard stations and ranger stations—a legacy of labors by the CCC—improved forest access. The shift from custodial care of the national forests to full-scale harvest of timber was the most dramatic factor in the growth of logging and lumber manufacturing. Court rulings to take back the O&C Railroad grant in 1915 brought 2.3 million acres and an estimated 50 billion board feet of timber to federal control. In 1919, recapture of the Coos Bay Wagon Road grant brought back another 96,000 acres of virgin forest and 2.5 billion board feet of timber. The Stanfield Act of 1926 set a formula for the revenues, later revised in 1937 and 1953 by Congress. The final distribution called for 50 percent of the timber receipts from O&C and Coos Bay Wagon Road lands to go to western Oregon counties, 25 percent to the federal treasury, and 25 percent to the U.S. Forest Service or the BLM for reforestation. The demand for lumber and the vested interest of Oregon counties in securing income from the sale of trees from federally managed forests helped drive the boom in this segment of Oregon's economy.

Logging and lumbering enterprises were highly competitive. Small operators, known as gyppos, struggled to hold together their businesses while they moved from contract to contract, cutting logs, running small mills, and seizing a share of the market. Some, like Kenneth Ford of Roseburg Lumber Company, persevered and became major figures in the industry. Many more ran small operations, employed several dozen workers, and, when fortunes changed, closed out their operations. Outside capital flowed into Oregon after 1945. Weyerhaeuser Corporation, Menasha Corporation, Evans Products, and Georgia-Pacific were among several firms with national connections that turned to old timber holdings or purchased unlogged forests from Oregon companies. These larger firms embraced new technologies and products, developing plywood and particleboard in addition to dimensional lumber. They created cost savings through greater efficiencies and research and development.

While some enterprises were thriving, others struggled. The salmon catch and pack in Oregon canneries peaked in the 1890s and headed steadily downward. Efforts to check the trend, especially in the Columbia River, led to construction of the state's Central Hatchery in 1909 at Bonneville and in 1926 to abolition of fishwheels. The hulking fishwheels, turned by the river's current, had scooped up tons of fish. While horse-drawn seine nets and mesh fishtraps at the river's mouth may have taken a greater toll on the salmon, the fishwheels were a visible symbol of overharvest. After 1950, Oregon's fish canneries steadily diminished; the last closed in 1979. The great silvery horde of fish no longer filled the streams. Conservation of remaining stocks dictated sharp restrictions on commercial and sport fishing.

Dam construction, an enduring commitment of federal investment in Oregon, moved steadily forward. It took a tremendous toll on anadromous fish, but so did logging, urbanization, and agricultural activities. During the 1950s and 1960s, the Army Corps of Engineers had oversight of massive new projects—The Dalles, John Day and McNary Dams on the main stem of the Columbia, several more dams upstream, and Oxbow and Brownlee Dams on the Snake River along Oregon's eastern border. Federal projects also checked the Willamette. Pre-1940 Corps projects had included Fern Ridge, Cottage Grove, and Dorena Reservoirs. Postwar construction, financed by multimillion-dollar congressional appropriations, built Detroit, Big Cliff, Green Peter, and Foster Dams on the Santiam forks; Lookout Point, Dexter, and Hills Creek Dams on the Middle Fork of the Willamette; Cougar and Blue River Dams in the McKenzie watershed; and Fall Creek Dam near Eugene. By 1960, these facilities had largely tamed the Willamette River, checking floodwaters and generating electricity.

Federal improvements touched Oregon in other significant ways. Beginning in the 1870s, renewing in the 1890s, and proceeding regularly through the 20th century, Congress made appropriations in the 1899 Rivers and Harbors Act for major construction in Oregon. Projects included jetties at the mouths of the Columbia, Yaquina, Coquille, and Coos Bay. Congress also funded the Celilo Canal and Locks, (1906–16), a complicated transportation system blasted through basalt to provide ship passage around Five Mile Rapids and Celilo Falls into the upper Columbia River. Congress regularly renewed or funded start-up projects that dredged channels, removed rocks, and led to construction of new jetties on most of Oregon's coastal estuaries. Singularly significant in the postwar era was the Interstate Highway Act of 1956. Billions of federal dollars began flowing back to the states, allowing construction in Oregon of nonstop freeways—I-5 running north and south through western Oregon valleys between Washington and California and I-84 running east and west from Portland to Boise, Idaho. These projects created not only payrolls but significant contributions to the state's economy through efficient shipment of commodities.

Postwar changes swept through Oregon agriculture. While cattle-raising and wheat production remained mainstays in eastern Oregon, specialized crops of alfalfa, sugar beets, and potatoes drew a number of farmers to focus their energies on lands watered by turn-of-the-century reclamation projects. Farmers in the Treasure Valley near Ontario, the upper Deschutes watershed, and the Klamath Basin tapped irrigation water to embark on these ventures. On Oregon's southwestern coast, cranberry production, founded in 1887, became important as Ocean Spray diversified its product line to include ruby-red juice fortified by Oregon cranberries. Walnuts, filberts and turkeys created income for farmers in Yamhill and Washington Counties. Pear, peach, apple, and cherry production prospered in the Hood River and Rogue River Valleys. Slowly, but steadily, grass seed and nursery products grew in acreage in the Willamette Valley. Rose bushes, irises, grafted fruit trees, and ornamental shrubs grew in the valley's fertile soils. Workers dug, baled, and shipped these specialty products to national markets. Venturesome investors cleared old prune orchards and forested hillsides, planted vineyards, and constructed wineries. A new industry found a good market for Oregon wines.

Tourists flocked to the Tillamook Cheese Factory and other popular destinations, adding to the state's prosperity. (Oregon State Archives scenic photo)

Tourism emerged as a major industry. Oregon's scenic beauty of mountains, forests, deserts and Pacific shoreline proved an irresistible attraction. Good roads, one of the largest state park systems in the country, restaurants, and hotels and motels facilitated the annual surge of visitors. Millions traveled Highway 101, exploring the cheese factory at Tillamook, gift shops in Lincoln City, and the Sea Lion Caves. They toured sawmills at North Bend, rode a mail boat on the Rogue River, or purchased salt water taffy, carved myrtlewood, seashells, and cranberry candy. Others flocked to the Shakespearean plays in Ashland, marveled at Crater Lake, went bow-and-arrow hunting for deer at Hart Mountain, skied at Mount Bachelor, stayed overnight at Timberline Lodge, took a jetboat into Hells Canyon, or visited the John Day Fossil Beds National Monument. Those who came to visit bought meals, lodging and keepsakes. They added to the state's prosperity.

Postwar Oregon was a troubled time for the state's Native Americans. Douglas O. McKay, former governor, had been appointed as Secretary of the Interior in the Eisenhower Cabinet. Believing strongly in economy in government and seeing the Bureau of Indian Affairs as an anachronism of inefficiency, McKay joined others in pressing to sever ties with tribes. House Concurrent Resolution 108 in 1952 stated that it was the sense of Congress that the federal government should set indigenous people

free. Between 1954 and 1960, Congress terminated all government-to-government relationships with the Klamath and every tribe and band west of the Cascades in Oregon. The program required sale of reservation lands, issuance of deeds for individual trust lands, and curtailment of all BIA and Indian Health Service benefits. Then the momentum waned. Thousands of Oregon's native peoples had fallen into limbo as "terminated Indians." Finally, in 1977, Senator Mark O. Hatfield introduced legislation to amend the situation for the Confederated Tribes of the Siletz. On a case-by-case basis, the terminated tribes sought and won, by 1989, the restoration of their federal relations. The road back was, for some, a frustrating journey of years of waiting, petitioning, and documenting their ongoing tribal life.

Elements of boom and bust coursed through Oregon in the years between 1945 and 1990. Booming conditions drove new construction and business prosperity in many small towns. Tens of thousands of new residents moved into the state. Yet, not all was well in Oregon. The measures were visible: diminishing runs of fish, a vast checkerboard of clearcuts on the sides of mountains, a Willamette River so fetid that only the foolhardy dared to swim in it, spread of cheat grass and Russian olive, and other invading species like shad, bass, and squawfish. It was time to consider the consequences of rapid development.

Taking Stock

In 1962, Thomas Lawson McCall, a journalist, caught the state's attention with a television documentary, *"Pollution in Paradise."* In his clipped, forceful narration and with compelling photography, McCall showed what had happened to the Willamette River. Sewage, industrial wastes, garbage, abandoned docks and warehouses, tires, and hulks of automobiles befouled a once pristine, fish-filled stream. Between 1850 and 1920, the Willamette had served as western Oregon's artery of commerce and transportation. Use had bred abuse and, almost without seeing it, Oregonians had transformed the stream into an open sewer.

Tom McCall was elected governor in 1966. Stressing an eleventh commandment, "Thou shalt not pollute," McCall, a Republican, forged a broad-based coalition to address the consequences of rapid development, growing population, and ecological changes in the state. McCall's ideas were not always popular and his commentary sometimes appeared quirky. His approach, however, was earnest and, for a majority, compelling. During his eight years in office, he and like-minded leaders—Stafford Hansell, a hogfarmer from Boardman, L. B. Day, a labor leader from Salem, and others—began a process of moving Oregonians from outright "ownership" of land to "stewardship."

The tally of accomplishments during the McCall years included creation of the Department of Environmental Quality (1969), extensive research and solution to Willamette Valley fieldburning, blocking of shipment of additional tons of nerve gas to the Umatilla Army Depot, creation of the Willamette Greenway—a 170-mile-long corridor of easements and park properties, the Bottle Bill (1971) requiring deposits on returnable beverage containers, and Senate Bill 100. This much-debated bill created the Land Conservation and Development Commission (1973). The LCDC moved every county and incorporated town into a system of statewide land-use planning. Hearings on draft goals and guidelines drew thousands of participants to meetings. Volunteers and staff hammered out a system for evaluating, in light of the statewide guidelines, comprehensive land-use plans required of all government entities. Repeatedly, critics tried to overturn the LCDC. Each time, a majority of voters sustained the system. Oregonians had started to come to terms with the realities of growth and the responsibilities inherent in sustaining livability.

The 1990s were a sobering decade for dozens of small towns and for the thousands involved in logging and lumbering. The boom ended in the forest products industry. Shrill voices decried the Endangered Species Act of 1973 and charged that spotted owls and marbled murrelets were not worth jobs and payrolls. The reality was that Oregon had not attained sustained yield in management of forests and that overharvest, similar to overfishing, forced adjustment. Sawmills closed. Towns like Powers, West Fir, Oakridge, Swiss Home, Hines, Valsetz and Vernonia were shaken by the closures and departure of residents. Most communities adjusted. Some Oregonians, however, wrestled with difficulty when they discovered that the national forests and lands administered by the Bureau of Land Management— acreage on the other side of their fence—belonged to all the people of the United States, not the locals, and that interest groups thousands of miles away had a valid voice in crafting land policy and use of public resources.

Bill Bowerman cofounded Nike with Phil Knight. (Courtesy Wikimedia)

The 1990s was also a decade of diversification in Oregon's economy. High-tech industries came of age. From modest beginnings in a garage in 1948, Howard Vollum and Jack Murdock built Tektronix, an electronics company, into one of the nation's largest companies by the mid-1980s. Oregon's reputation as a decent place to live with willing workers encouraged several corporations—among them Hewlett-Packard, Intel and Wacker Siltronics—to construct fabrication plants and manufacture computer components. These billion-dollar facilities contributed to a thriving urban Oregon economy. While many rural Oregonians

struggled with survival, many urban Oregonians found good jobs in new industries. Phil Knight and Bill Bowerman, longtime track coach at the University of Oregon, transformed the tennis shoe into a styled, engineered icon of the "fitness generation." Their Nike Corporation grew by the 1990s into a major manufacturer and retailer of sports and casual clothing. Its distinctive "swoosh" logo appeared on the outfits of professional athletes, amateurs, and even great-grandmothers who found ease and comfort wearing nonlacing tennis shoes or fleece jogging outfits.

In 1984, residents of the state approved a lottery. It grew rapidly in popularity as new games and promotions increased player options. Gambling profits proved irresistible to legislators who appropriated them to meet costs of basic social services and education. In 1992, the Cow Creek Band of the Umpqua Tribe negotiated the first gaming compact with the governor under the Indian Gaming Regulatory Act. Within five years, the tribe was the second largest employer in Douglas County, operating a casino, restaurants, hotel, truck stop and other businesses at Canyonville. Other tribes followed. In 1998, Spirit Mountain Casino, owned by the Confederated Tribes of the Grand Ronde community, surpassed Multnomah Falls as the most visited traveler destination in Oregon.

Oregon had not solved all its problems. Adequate financing for education at all levels eluded legislators, governors, teachers' unions and students. Salmon recovery plans, at times, seemed more abundant than fish. Tribes, federal and state agencies, sport and commercial fishing organizations, and fish biologists all wrestled with finding ways to save remaining runs and rebuilding those that teetered on the edge of extinction. Poverty continued to grip Oregonians. Thousands of new residents—many of them Hispanics who had found hard jobs and tough living conditions in following the harvests and working in the state's nursery business—tried to make do.

A willingness to embrace new ventures has persisted in Oregon. In 1990, Measure 5 placed severe limitations on property taxes to support schools and government. In 1993, Oregonians were first in the nation to hold a vote-by-mail election. The following year they approved a Death With Dignity Act, permitting doctor-assisted suicide. In 1998, Oregon raised the minimum wage to the highest in the nation, easing for the hourly worker some of the struggle for existence but threatening enterprises operating on a shoestring. Oregonians refused to approve a sales tax, but continued to pay high property taxes and income taxes.

Such is the course of Oregon history. A majestic territory of immense potentials drew newcomers in the 1840s. In less than a decade, they wrested control from the tribes, changed the face of the land with surveys and property ownership, and engaged in ambitious exploitation of the state's resources. When it finally became evident that nature's plenty could not continue to yield in profusion, Oregonians embraced new models for doing things.

The state's history has stories of triumph and tragedy, hope and perseverance, and taking risks. The Oregon System became a national model for improving government in the 20th century. Oregon has served as a great testing ground for federal projects which have provided a medley of benefits—electricity, navigation, irrigation, timber harvests, tourist facilities, and jobs. Oregon has led the nation in environmental legislation and commitment to working for quality of life for all of its citizens. For generations, Oregonians have celebrated the special words in their state song: "Hail to thee, Land of Promise, My Oregon." Oregon's promise is strong and therein lies the state's future.

ACT OF CONGRESS ADMITTING OREGON INTO THE UNION

Preamble
Whereas the people of Oregon have framed, ratified and adopted a constitution of state government which is republican in form, and in conformity with the Constitution of the United States and have applied for admission into the Union on an equal footing with the other states; therefore —

1. Admission of State—Boundaries
That Oregon be, and she is hereby, received into the Union on an equal footing with the other states in all respects whatever, with the following boundaries: In order that the boundaries of the state may be known and established, it is hereby ordained and declared that the State of Oregon shall be bounded as follows, to wit: Beginning one marine league at sea, due west from the point where the forty-second parallel of north latitude intersects the same, thence northerly, at the same distance from the line of the coast lying west and opposite the state, including all islands within the jurisdiction of the United States, to a point due west and opposite the middle of the north ship channel of the Columbia River; thence easterly, to and up the middle channel of said river, and, where it is divided by islands, up the middle and widest channel thereof, to a point near Fort Walla Walla, where the forty-sixth parallel of north latitude crosses said river, thence east, on said parallel, to the middle of the main channel of the Shoshone or Snake River; thence up the middle of the main channel of said river, to the mouth of the Owyhee River; thence due south, to the parallel of latitude forty-two degrees north; thence west, along said parallel, to the place of beginning, including jurisdiction in civil and criminal cases upon the Columbia River and Snake River, concurrently with states and territories of which those rivers form a boundary in common with this state.

2. Concurrent Jurisdiction on Columbia & Other Rivers—Navigable Waters to be Common Highways
The said State of Oregon shall have concurrent jurisdiction on the Columbia and all other rivers and waters bordering on the said State of Oregon, so far as the same shall form a common boundary to said state, and any other state or states now or hereafter to be formed or bounded by the same; and said rivers and waters, and all the navigable waters of said state, shall be common highways and forever free, as well as to the inhabitants of said state as to all other citizens of the United States, without any tax, duty & impost, or toll thereof.

3. Representation in Congress
Until the next census and apportionment of representatives, the State of Oregon shall be entitled to one representative in the Congress of the United States.

4. Propositions Submitted to People of State
The following propositions be and the same are hereby offered to the said people of Oregon for their free acceptance or rejection, which, if accepted, shall be obligatory on the United States and upon the said State of Oregon, to wit:

School Lands
First, that sections numbered sixteen and thirty-six in every township of public lands in said state, and where either of said sections, or any part thereof, has been sold or otherwise disposed of, other lands equivalent thereto, and as contiguous as may be, shall be granted to said state for the use of schools.

University Lands
Second, the seventy-two sections of land shall be set apart and reserved for the use and support of a state university, to be selected by the Governor of said state, subject to the approval of the Commissioner of the General Land Office, and to be appropriated and applied in such manner as the legislature of said state may prescribe for the purpose aforesaid, but for no other purpose.

Lands For Public Buildings
Third, that ten entire sections of land, to be selected by the Governor of said state, in legal subdivisions, shall be granted to said state for the purpose of completing the public buildings, or for the erection of others at the seat of government, under the direction of the legislature thereof.

Salt Springs & Contiguous Lands
Fourth, that all salt springs within said state, not exceeding twelve in number, with six sections of land adjoining, or as contiguous as may be to each, shall be granted to said state for its use, the same to be selected by the Governor thereof within one year

after the admission of said state, and when so selected, to be used or disposed of on such terms, conditions and regulations as the legislature shall direct; provided, that no salt spring or land, the right whereof is now vested in any individual or individuals, or which may be hereafter confirmed or adjudged to any individual or individuals, shall by this article be granted to said state.

Percentage on Land Sales

Fifth, that 5 per centum of the net proceeds of sales of all public lands lying within said state which shall be sold by Congress after the admission of said state into the Union, after deducting all the expenses incident to the same, shall be paid to said state, for the purpose of making public roads and internal improvements, as the legislature shall direct; provided, that the foregoing propositions, hereinbefore offered, are on the condition that the people of Oregon shall provide by an ordinance, irrevocable without the consent of the United States, that said state shall never interfere with the primary disposal of the soil within the same by the United States, or with any regulations Congress may find necessary for securing the title in said soil to bona fide purchasers thereof; and that in no case shall nonresident proprietors be taxed higher than residents.

Conditions on Which Propositions Are Offered

Sixth, and that the state shall never tax the lands or the property of the United States in said state; provided, however, that in case any of the lands herein granted to the State of Oregon have heretofore been confirmed to the Territory of Oregon for the purposes specified in this act, the amount so confirmed shall be deducted from the quantity specified in this act.

5. Residue of Territory

Until Congress shall otherwise direct, the residue of the Territory of Oregon shall be and is hereby incorporated into and made a part of the Territory of Washington.

Approved February 14, 1859.

Proposition of Congress accepted by the Legislative Assembly of the State of Oregon on June 3, 1859.

HISTORY OF RECREATION IN OREGON

Written by Katherine E. Hill

Oregon is blessed with some of the most striking natural wonders in the nation. The state's stunning coastline, Cascade Mountain Range and abundant rivers form a unique geography that has captivated Oregonians for generations. Very few aspects of Oregon's past express this enduring relationship quite so well as the state's history of outdoor recreation. Popular pastimes such as gathering plants,

hunting, fishing and animal husbandry arose out of the traditions of the state's earliest inhabitants and remain important symbols of Oregon's rich, natural heritage. As Oregon has grown, its outdoor culture has grown alongside it, and activities like biking, running and winter sports have made the state a mecca for outdoor recreation. Meanwhile, conservation efforts like the development of the state parks system, have ensured the preservation of the state's natural resources. Over time, Oregon's history of outdoor recreation has given it a distinct identity, rooted in a deep appreciation for the state's natural beauty and an active commitment to its preservation.

Some of Oregon's most popular recreation activities such as hunting and fishing, have been crucial to life in Oregon for centuries. Native tribes of the Pacific Northwest have long placed economic and cultural importance on fishing. For centuries before the arrival of Europeans in Oregon, fishing sites such as Celilo Falls supported enormous intertribal trading centers which attracted as many as 5,000 people.[1] Although the construction of The Dalles Dam in 1957 submerged this area,[2] these early fishing traditions established fishing as a key element of Oregon's cultural identity. As the region developed, the commercial importance of fishing continued to grow as evidenced by the production of 450,000 cases of canned salmon in 1878[3] — only 11 years after the opening of the state's first cannery.[4]

Oregon's population eventually placed undue pressure on fishing and game stocks and, in response, Oregonians looked to balance commercial and recreational demands on natural resources. Oregon founded its first fishing commission in 1878 to address this issue and protect the state's marine habitats.

Later, in 1893, this commission was expanded to create a combined fish and game commission. Under director Hollister McGuire, the commission limited the game bird season for the first time and began marking salmon in order to monitor the population and make recommendations to the Legislature. Oregon created its first official Game Board in 1899 and further restricted hunting and fishing in the state by instituting a closed season on beaver hunting and requiring fishing licenses for the first time in the state's history.

The next few decades saw more significant milestones in wildlife management. In 1911, the state established 1.5 million acres of wildlife refuges, and, in 1938, Oregon State University graduated its first class of fish and wildlife students. By 1975, the newly formed Department of Fish and Wildlife managed 766,000 anglers and 390,000 hunters who spent $190,000,000 each year,[5] and according to the most recent economic survey in 2008, Oregonians and visitors spent $2.5 billion annually on fish and wildlife recreational activities.[6] Oregon's Department of Fish and Wildlife uses these funds to regulate outdoor recreation in Oregon and assist with long-term conservation strategies. Most of the state's wildlife use now comes from sport fishing. Through outdoor recreation, salmon and steelhead still play an important role in Oregon's outdoor culture. The Deschutes, Rogue and McKenzie Rivers are internationally known as blue ribbon fly-fishing destinations.

The boating that takes place on these rivers also has deep roots in Oregon's history. In the 1890s when much of the state was still remote wilderness, the Rogue River was used to deliver mail to surrounding communities.[7] Navigation of the Rogue and McKenzie Rivers also inspired the development of the drift boat and river dory. These new designs were created to help river guides maneuver river rapids as recreational boating became more popular at the turn of the century.[8] Since 1958, Oregon's Marine Board has kept the state's waterways safe and clean by overseeing boater registration, safety education and law enforcement.[9] Today, Oregon's contributions to river travel and efforts to protect its natural areas have made it a popular area for boating and rafting.

A cowboy rides a bucking bronco during the 1956 Pendleton Round-Up. (Oregon State Archives photo)

Rodeo is also a sport whose history is intimately linked with Oregon's heritage. This highly competitive sport combines a variety of events such as barrel racing, bull riding and calf roping designed to demonstrate each participant's horsemanship skills. Several Oregon rodeo competitions have become well known in the rodeo community over the course of their long history. The first Pendleton show in 1910 was intended to be an exhibition of frontier life. That year, it attracted a crowd of 7,000 and has exploded in popularity over the years. High community involvement and enthusiasm made the four-day show a success. Today, over 60,000 attendees descend annually on Pendleton for the rodeo.[10, 11]

Many other rodeos in Oregon have become part of Oregon's storied history of outdoor recreation. Just three years after the founding of the Pendleton Round-up, the Molalla Buckeroo was established, making it only the third organized rodeo in the state's history. Originally planned to celebrate the town's

first railroad in 1913, the rodeo as we know it today soon became an annual tradition.[12] For decades now, the Molalla Buckeroo has been held each year during the week of July 4th and incorporates a large community parade in addition to the rodeo. The Saint Paul Rodeo in Marion County is also a long-running fourth of July tradition. Since 1935, the rodeo in Saint Paul has been a community cornerstone and is considered one of the best rodeo exhibitions in the nation. It also incorporates the entire community through parades and cook-offs.[13] Rodeos like these aim to foster a stronger sense of community and keep Oregon's rich frontier traditions alive. Oregon's many rodeos serve as a testament to its agricultural heritage and multifaceted culture.

Although traditions like fishing, boating and rodeo have contributed to Oregon's unique identity, perhaps the oldest and most iconic symbol of recreation in Oregon is the beauty of the land itself. Over time, Oregon has become well known for its devotion to protect and share this land with the public through the parks system. The seeds of the public parks system originated with efforts towards highway beautification around the turn of the century. With the development of the automobile, tourism within the state grew, as did public demand for scenic preservation. In his Biennial Report in 1919–1920, State Highway Attorney J. M. Devers wrote that state highways might be improved if the State Highway Commission had some mechanism to acquire nearby land for public use.[14]

The following year, Governor Ben Olcott addressed the Oregon State Legislature on the importance of conserving scenic beauty in Oregon and noted the urgent demands for conservation that recreational tourism had placed on the state. He remarked, "All of the things we have been striving for, the development of tourist travel; the urge to make and keep our state the most livable in the Union; the desire to keep our children in God's own environment, surrounded by the beauties to which they are the true heirs, all of these will be surrendered and lost unless we act and act promptly."[15]

Subsequent action by the Legislature made it possible for the State Highway Commission to acquire wayside land for beautification, and, as tourism increased, more communities requested public lands for recreation. This arrangement was especially influenced by the nature of the early Model T automobile that most families used for camping outings. Because these vehicles traveled only 30 miles an hour, families had to be highly strategic about the distance of their trips, and many families simply stopped along the highway where water was accessible.[16]

The growing need for overnight accommodations prompted the State Highway Commission to take further measures to acquire lands outside the highway right of way. Revisions to the 1921 Highway law widened the scope of the law and allowed the State Highway Commission to develop additional land. Expansion of the State Highway Commission's land management program created the foundation for the state parks system and gifts of land soon followed. By 1929, the area managed by the commission was large enough that a State Parks Commission was founded to oversee further management of these areas. Railroad engineer and homesteader Samuel H. Boardman managed the newly formed State Parks Commission. During his tenure from 1929 to 1950, Boardman proved to be skilled at persuading local donors to support the parks effort, and, under his direction, park acreage grew from 4,000 to 66,000.

Beginning in 1933, these efforts were aided by members of the Civilian Conservation Corps. Oregon was a major site for CCC projects during the Great Depression, and the group employed thousands of young people across the state. CCC projects focused mainly on forestry, fire protection, flood control and other land management tasks. Groups constructed trails and campgrounds still used today. Silver Creek Falls camp just east of Salem and Multnomah's Eagle Creek campground are results of CCC efforts.

Oregon is home to four national parks: Crater Lake, John Day Fossil Beds, Nez Perce National Historic Park and the Lewis & Clark National Historic Trail. These parks provide habitats for 11 endangered species while drawing over $81 million in tourism revenue. Oregon's robust state parks system includes 193 parks covering 86,000 acres of land. Oregon's Department of Parks and Recreation oversees state park lands and protects these "outstanding natural, scenic, cultural, historic and recreational sites for the enjoyment and education of present and future generations."[17] This includes not only managing state parks but also providing conservation grants and organizing historic preservation efforts.

Cyclists, such as these in front of Portland's City Bicycle Hospital in 1910, were part of a bicycling craze in the early 1900s. (Oregon State Archives photo)

Two-wheeled transportation has also had a significant effect on outdoor recreation since long before the development of the automobile. As early as the 1880s, Salem and Portland residents can be seen riding "penny-farthing bicycles" in archival photos. With the transition from these large front-wheeled "penny-farthing" bicycles to modern designs, the bicycling craze exploded in popularity, and advertisements for bicycles ran in the Salem Daily Capital Journal and other Oregon newspapers. The trend even inspired early "celebrity athlete" endorsements for various products as cycling grew from a novelty into a more common form of transportation and recreation. [18]

However, with the advent of auto transportation, cycling mostly fell out of favor until late in the 20th Century. It was around this time that Oregon was heavily involved with reigniting interest in cycling. Portland unveiled a Bicycle Master Plan in 1973, which improved riding and parking accommodations for bikes and organized promotional programs. Further improvements put additional biking infrastructure in place and integrated bike use with public transport systems. Today, Oregon's largest city is consistently ranked as one of the bike-friendliest cities in the country, with 7.2 percent of commuters travelling by bike compared to 0.5 percent nationwide.[19]

Rural Oregon also provides ample opportunity for recreational cycling in the form of scenic bikeways throughout the state. Oregon's 15 state designated scenic bikeways showcase the best road biking routes in the state with options available for riders of all skill levels. Trails range from the casual 17-mile Covered Bridges Scenic Bikeway along the Row River Trail to the rugged 108-mile Blue Mountain Scenic Bikeway in Heppner. Every September, Heppner's Blue Mountain Bikeway hosts a challenging ride which leads riders through the Umatilla National Forest to Highway 395 up a nearly 4,000-foot climb.[20] Other popular rides, such as Cycle Oregon, attract cyclists from around the world. Ashland innkeeper Jim Beaver originally proposed the ride in 1987, as a coastal ride between sister cities Astoria and Ashland. With support from the Oregon Department of Transportation and the local Chamber of Commerce, the inaugural Cycle Oregon ride took place in September 1988. In this 320-mile ride, 1,006 riders from 20 states traveled from Salem to Brookings, generating $360,000 for local communities along the way. Cycle Oregon is still going strong with over 2,000 participants each year.[21]

Though automobiles and bikes have played a large role in outdoor recreation history, some of Oregon's rich scenery is best experienced on foot. With countless trails through both cities and scenic natural areas, Oregon's outdoors is loved by hikers and runners alike. Events like Oregon's popular Hood to Coast Relay race allow long-distance runners to experience Oregon's natural areas while enjoying a difficult and unique run. Each August, Hood to Coast attracts thousands of runners for the 198-mile run from the base of Mount Hood to Seaside. Experienced marathoner Bob Foote organized the first race in 1982 with eight teams of 10 members each. Since then, the relay has expanded considerably and filled its team limit on Opening Day for the past 18 years. Race organizers have also added a Portland to Coast

Walk event and High School Challenge.[22] The popularity of running in the state has even lead to considerable athletic success. Dubbed "Tracktown, USA," Eugene is the only site to host three consecutive Olympic track and field trials, which has happened there twice, first in 1972, 1976 and 1980, and again in 2008, 2012 and 2016.

For the more hiking inclined, Oregon's state parks offer hundreds of hiking opportunities from day trips conveniently located near city centers to backpacking adventures in more remote regions. The state's incredible wealth of trails includes pristine coastal areas, old growth forests, high desert expanses and world-class mountain views.

Oregon's Cascade Range is one of the state's most dominant geographical features, and many consider it the backbone of local outdoor recreation. Organized hiking and climbing groups have a long history in Oregon beginning with the founding of the Mazama Club in 1894. For over a century, outdoor groups like the Mazama Club have explored Oregon's natural resources and created international impact in backpacking and mountaineering. The earliest origins of the well-known Pacific Crest Trail can be traced back to a conversation between outdoors woman and educator Catherine Montgomery and a member of the Seattle offshoot of the Mazama Club, the Mountaineers. At the close of their 1926 meeting, Montgomery wondered aloud, "Why do not you Mountaineers do something big for Western America. . . . A high winding trail down the heights of our western mountains with mile markers and shelter huts – like these pictures I'll show you of the 'Long Trail of the Appalachians' — from the Canadian Border to the Mexican Boundary Line!"[23] Two years later, this idea was presented at a meeting of the Seattle-based Mountaineers Club attended by Clinton C. Clarke, another hiker who would eventually become famous for his efforts to promote the trail. The project was later completed with the help of a diverse group of local organizations, including the Sierra Club, YMCA, Boy Scouts and Civilian Conservation Corps.[24] Today, the Pacific Crest Trail is one of the most famous and enduring icons of outdoor recreation on the West Coast and stretches 2,659 miles from the Mexican border just south of Campo, California, to the Canadian border at Manning Park, British Columbia. The Oregon leg of the trail carries thousands of visitors each year over the Cascade Range from Southern Oregon's Siskiyou Mountains summit to the Washington state border at the Bridge of the Gods. The trail features spectacular views of Crater Lake and the entire Cascade Range, including Mount McLoughlin, Diamond Peak, the Three Sisters, Mount Washington, Three Fingered Jack, Mount Jefferson and Mount Hood.[25]

It's not only hikers that enjoy Oregon's Cascade Range. In winter, Oregon is a mountaineer's paradise and an international skiing and snowboarding destination. During the 1920s, Scandinavian immigrants brought skiing and ski jumping experience to the region and founded ski clubs like the Bend Skyliners and the Cascade Ski Club. These clubs laid the foundation for the establishment of ski areas in Oregon.[26] After lumber workers founded the Bend Skyliners Mountaineering club in 1928 and created a ski jump 11 miles west of Bend, winter sports began growing in the state. In 1958, Bill Healy, a U.S. Army 10th Mountain Division veteran opened Mount Bachelor—Oregon's largest ski area. The mountaineering expertise Healy gained during his service in this elite group of ski-troopers inspired him to create a ski resort at Bachelor Butte. Mount Bachelor now caters to nearly 500,000 visitors each year.[27]

About the same time, Loop Road was completed around the base of Mount Hood allowing more recreational access. A year later, the area was designated a public recreation area by the federal government. In 1928, Cascade Ski Club was founded and a ski jumping tournament was started at Multipor in January 1929. The group expanded in the following years and competed with local groups at Mount Hood and even had some competitors from as far off as Seattle and Vancouver, B.C.[28]

A skier gets airborne on Mt. Hood in 1937. Ski resorts grew rapidly in Oregon in the mid 1900s. (Oregon State Archives photo)

Soon, Mount Hood's popularity created a demand for overnight facilities, and plans were created for a lodge at the site. With the nation in the grip of the Great Depression, Timberline Lodge was seen as an ideal project for the Works Progress Administration (WPA), and, after three proposals, the project was scheduled for completion in 1938. In September 1937, President Franklin Roosevelt dedicated the site and remarked that "thousands and thousands of visitors in the coming years" would be impressed with Oregon's ranching, farming and forestry as "important elements of northwestern prosperity." He also spoke of the recreational value of the region. In a speech at the historic hotel, he remarked that "those who follow us to Timberline Lodge on their holidays and vacations will represent the enjoyment of new opportunities for play in every season of the year. . . . I look forward to the day when many, many people from this region of the Nation are going to come here for skiing and tobogganing and various other forms of winter sports." Today, the lodge has fulfilled Roosevelt's vision. With two million visitors annually, Timberline Lodge is a testament to the popularity of winter sports in the state and the recreation value of the Cascade Range as a whole.[29]

Of course, no discussion of outdoor recreation in Oregon is complete without mentioning its scenic coastline. Oregon's beaches were declared a public highway by Governor Oswald West in 1913 in order to protect the beaches from private encroachment. Later, the passage of the Beach Bill in 1967 solidified public claims to Oregon's beaches and ensured access for growing numbers of beachgoers. Oregon's 363 miles of coastline are used today for swimming, horse-riding, windsurfing and more.

Outdoor sports like windsurfing benefit from natural resources in other locations as well. The state's famous Columbia River Gorge acts as a funnel for wind and offers an ideal environment for water sports. Small towns like Hood River have become popular spots for windsurfers of every skill level to enjoy the sport. During the summer, the Gorge hosts both serious athletic competitions like the Gorge Cup and friendly celebrations like the annual King of the Hook.[30] Windsurfing in the state is widely known as a fun and colorful spectator sport showcasing Oregon's natural treasures.

Oregon's rich natural beauty has also created a home for many nationally renowned golf courses. Since 1904, the Oregon Golf Association has assisted with tournaments and promoted golf in the state through its network of 45,000 members.[31] Fortunately, the state has no shortage of quality courses for Oregon's golfers. Some of the sport's most well-known architects such as Bob Cupp, Arnold Palmer and David McLay Kidd have been drawn to Oregon's natural beauty. Public courses in Central Oregon like the Pronghorn Club, Crosswater at Sunriver, and Tetherow are all nationally ranked.[32] The southern Oregon coast's Bandon Dunes resort also offers world-class golf. The course regularly stages major national tournaments and has been ranked the best public golf course in America after Pebble Beach.[33]

Outdoor activities like these have become beloved traditions for many Oregonians and a source of state pride. In 1941, Oregon's first state parks superintendent Samuel Boardman wrote in a letter to Newton Drury, National Park Service Director, that he felt Oregon's citizens had been given a "recreational kingdom" at their disposal. Indeed, Oregon's vast and varied geography has provided opportunities for outdoor recreation of every kind throughout the years. From fishing to skiing and countless other pursuits, Oregon remains a remarkable outdoor paradise and "recreational kingdom," just as it was nearly a century ago.

For Further Information:

Columbia River Gorge Commission
Department of Environmental Quality
Department of Fish and Wildlife

Department of State Lands
Oregon Forest Resources Institute
Forestry Department
Land Conservation and Development Department
Land Use Board of Appeals
Landscape Architect Board
Landscape Contractors Board
Oregon Department of Transportation
Oregon Parks and Recreation Department
State Fair and Exposition Center
Travel Oregon
Travel Information Council
Water Resources Department
Watershed Enhancement

Endnotes:

[1] "Celilo Falls." Columbia River Inter-Tribal Fish Commission. 2016 http://www.critfc.org/salmon-culture/tribal-salmon-culture/celilo-falls

[2] "Historic Columbia River Highway: One Hundred Years of The Poem in Stone-Before the Highway" Oregon Secretary of State. http://sos.oregon.gov/archives/exhibits/columbia-river-highway/Pages/history-before.aspx

[3] "Fishing Timeline" The Oregon Story http://www.opb.org/programs/oregonstory/fishing/timeline.html

[4] "ODFW History" ODFW History June 23, 2015 http://www.dfw.state.or.us/agency/history.asp

[5] Ibid.

[6] "Economic Impact" Oregon Department of Fish and Wildlife http://www.dfw.state.or.us/agency/economic_impact.asp

[7] "Mail Boat History" Jerry's Rogue Jets http://www.roguejets.com/about/mail-boat-history

[8] "The Oregon Drift Boat" 1859: Oregon's Magazine https://www.1859oregonmagazine.com/outdoors/the-oregon-drift-boat

[9] "About Us" Oregon State Marine Board http://www.oregon.gov/OSMB/info/Pages/AboutUs.aspx

[10] "Round-Up History" Round-Up History http://www.pendletonroundup.com/p/about/147

[11] "2010 Pendleton Round up attendance highest on recent record" KVEW-TV http://www.kvewtv.com/article/2010/sep/20/2010-pendleton-round-attendance-highest-recent-rec

[12] "The Molalla Buckeroo Story" Molalla Buckeroo, http://molallabuckeroo.com/story.html

[13] "History." St. Paul Rodeo http://www.stpaulrodeo.com/p/about/147

[14] "History of the Oregon State Parks — 1917-1963 (Section 1: Formation of a Park System)" National Parks Service History E-Library, http://npshistory.com/publications/oregon/history/sec1.htm

[15] "Governor Ben W. Olcott's Administration." Oregon State Archives http://arcweb.sos.state.or.us/pages/records/governors/guides/state/olcott/scenic1921.html

[16] National Parks Service History E-Library

[17] "Oregon Parks and Recreation Department About Us" Oregon Parks and Recreation Department About Us

http://www.oregon.gov/oprd/Pages/about_us.aspx

[18] "Oregon On Two Wheels: The History of Cycling in Our Historic Newspapers" Oregon Digital Newspaper Program

http://odnp.uoregon.edu/2011/07/25/oregon-on-two-wheels-the-history-of-cycling-in-our-historic-newspapers

[19] Ibid.

[20] "State of Oregon: Oregon Parks and Recreation Department: Scenic Bikeways" State of Oregon: Oregon Parks and Recreation Department: Scenic Bikeways

https://www.oregon.gov/oprd/BIKE/Pages/index.aspx

[21] "History of Cycle Oregon" Cycle Oregon RSS http://cycleoregon.com/aboutus/history

[22] "Race History | Hood to Coast" Hood to Coast http://www.hoodtocoastrelay.com/race-history

[23] Mann, Barney "Scout" "Where the Pacific Crest Trail Begins: Is It Campo? Manning Park, No, It's Montgomery" PCT Communicator, March 2011

[24] "Pacific Crest Trail History | Pacific Crest Trail Association" Pacific Crest Trail Association. http://www.pcta.org/about-us/history

[25] "Oregon - Pacific Crest Trail Association" Pacific Crest Trail Association Accessed August 07, 2016. http://www.pcta.org/discover-the-trail/geography/oregon

[26] "History" — Cascade Ski Club & Lodge http://www.cascadeskiclub.com/content/history.aspx

[27] "History" Mt. Bachelor, http://www.mtbachelor.com/info/history

[28] Cascade Ski Club

[29] "Explore the Lodge" Timberline http://www.timberlinelodge.com/plan-your-visit/explore-the-lodge

[30] Duffy, Lizzy. "Windsurfers Flock to Columbia Gorge to Ride Waves Air" http://www.opb.org/news/series/greetings-northwest/windsurfers-hood-river-columbia-river-gorge

[31] "History of the OGA" Oregon Golf Association. http://oga.org/about/history-oga

[32] "Golf Courses in Central Oregon Ranked Among Golf Digest's Top 100" Visit Central Oregon http://visitcentraloregon.com/central-oregon-stories/eat-drink-stories/golf-courses-central-oregon-ranked-among-golf-digests-top-100

[33] Whitten, Ron. "America's Greatest Public Courses" Golf Digest http://www.golfdigest.com/gallery/americas-100-greatest-public-courses-ranking

Katie Hill was born and raised in Salem, Oregon. She graduated from South Salem High School in 2015 and is entering her second year as an undergraduate at the University of Chicago. While at home, she enjoys cycling, swimming, and spending New Year's with family on the Oregon Coast.

CHRONOLOGICAL HISTORY OF OREGON

Oregon's history contains many more significant dates than space will permit, but this list may prove helpful to those embarking on a study of the state.

Oregon Country 1543–1847

1543—Bartolome Ferrelo possibly reaches southwest coast

1565—Manila Galleon trade route opens across North Pacific

1579—Sir Francis Drake allegedly visits Oregon

1603—Sebastian Vizcaino possibly sights Cape Sebastian

1707—*San Francisco Xavier* probably wrecks at Nehalem

1738—Pierre Gaultier de la Verendrye leads first expedition into Oregon

1765—First use of word "Ouragon" in Maj. Robert Rogers' petition to explore American West

1774—Capt. Juan Perez sails to Northwest Coast for Spain

1775—Capt. Bruno Hezeta sees mouth of Columbia River and names it Rio San Roque

1775–1780—First smallpox outbreak among Oregon's indigenous people

1778—Capt. James Cook makes landfall at Cape Foulweather and discovers fur wealth of Northwest Coast

1788—Capt. Robert Gray trades with tribes in Tillamook Bay

Markus Lopius, Black African traveling with Gray, probably killed at Tillamook

1792—Capt. Robert Gray enters and names the Columbia River

Capt. George Vancouver expedition charts Columbia estuary

Lt. William E. Broughton names Mount Hood after British naval officer Alexander Arthur Hood

1801–1802—Second smallpox outbreak among Oregon's Tribes

1803—Louisiana Purchase extends United States to Rocky Mountains

1804—President Thomas Jefferson dispatches Lewis and Clark Expedition

1805—Lewis and Clark Expedition explores lower Snake and Columbia Rivers and establishes Fort Clatsop

1806—Lewis and Clark Expedition returns to the United States

1811—John Jacob Astor's Pacific Fur Company establishes Fort Astoria

1812—Overland Astorians discover South Pass in Wyoming, later route of Oregon Trail

1813 — North West Company purchases Fort Astoria and names it Fort George

1814 — First English woman, Jane Barnes, visits Fort George

First domestic livestock imported by sea from California

1817 — William Cullen Bryant refers to "Oregon" in poem *Thanatopsis*

1818 — North West Company establishes Fort Nez Perce

James Biddle and John Prevost assert United States interests in Oregon

United States and Great Britain agree to "joint occupancy" of Oregon

1819 — Adams-Onis Treaty cedes Spain's discovery rights north of 42 degrees to the U.S.

1821 — Hudson's Bay Company subsumes North West Company

1824 — U.S. and Russia agree to 50 degrees latitude as southern boundary of Russian interests

Dr. John McLoughlin begins long tenure as Chief Factor for Hudson's Bay Company

1825 — Workmen build Fort Vancouver on Columbia River

1827 — U.S. and Great Britain agree to indefinite "joint occupancy"

First sawmill begins cutting lumber near Fort Vancouver

1828 — Jedediah Smith's party travels overland from California but Indians kill 15 men on the Umpqua River

First grist mill starts making flour at Fort Vancouver

1829 — Dr. John McLoughlin establishes claim at Willamette Falls, later Oregon City

1830 — Fever pandemic begins calamitous death toll of tribes

1832 — Newspapers report four Indians from Pacific Northwest in St. Louis seeking missionaries

Nathaniel Wyeth enters Oregon fur trade

Capt. B. L. E. Bonneville arrives overland to trap and trade for furs on Columbia Plateau

Hudson's Bay Company establishes Fort Umpqua at Elkton

1833 — First school opens at Fort Vancouver

First lumber exports by Hudson's Bay Company to China

1834 — Jason Lee's party establishes Methodist Mission near Wheatland

1836 — First steamship *Beaver* begins service for Hudson's Bay Company on the Columbia River

Lt. William Slacum mounts reconnaissance of western Oregon

Whitman-Spalding mission party, including Narcissa Whitman and Eliza Spalding, arrives overland via Oregon Trail

Washington Irving publishes *Astoria*

1838 — Willamette Cattle Company drives livestock overland from California

Priests Blanchet and Demers arrive overland from Canada

1839 — Catholics establish mission at St. Paul

1841 — Lt. Charles Wilkes mounts reconnaissance with U.S. Exploring Expedition

Ewing Young's death leads to public meetings

First Catholic boys' school founded at Saint Paul

First ship, *Star of Oregon*, built by settlers

1842 — Methodist missionaries found the Oregon Institute in Salem, an antecedent to Willamette University

First brick building, a house, erected by George Gay in Polk County

1843 — First large migration of over 900 immigrants arrives via Oregon Trail

Lt. John C. Fremont mounts reconnaissance of Oregon Trail

"Wolf Meetings" lead to Provisional Government

Oregonians submit petition to Senate seeking U.S. jurisdiction

1844 — First town plat surveyed at Oregon City

First Catholic girls' school founded at Saint Paul

Acts to prohibit slavery and exclude blacks and mulattoes from Oregon Territory were passed and the "Lash Law" enacted requiring Blacks – "be they free or slave – be whipped twice a year until he or she shall quit the territory"

1845 — Meek Cut off opens as alleged short cut to Oregon Trail

Estimated 3,000 overland immigrants arrive

Oregonians petition Congress for federal services

First Provisional governor, George Abernethy, elected

Francis Pettygrove and A. L. Lovejoy name Portland and commence plat of city

1846 — Lt. Neil Howison mounts reconnaissance of western Oregon

Barlow Road opens as toll route

Applegate Trail, alternative to Oregon Trail, opens

Oregon Treaty affirms U.S. sovereignty to Pacific Northwest

First newspaper on the west coast, *Oregon Spectator*, founded in Oregon City

1847 — Cayuse Tribe attacks Whitman Mission

Oregon Volunteers engage in Cayuse Indian War

First postmaster, John Shively, named at Astoria

First English book, a *Blue Back Speller*, printed in Oregon City

Oregon Territory 1848–1858

1848—Joseph Meek carries petition east seeking federal "patronage"

Organic Act creates Oregon Territory

James Marshall discovers gold in California

First U.S. Customs Service office opens in Astoria

1849—First territorial governor, Joseph Lane, assumes duties

First Mounted Riflemen of U.S. Army arrive overland

First "Beaver" gold coins minted in Oregon City

1850—Congress passes Oregon Donation Land Act

First capital punishment—five Cayuse are hanged in Oregon City

Investors start printing *The Oregonian* in Portland

U.S. Census enumerates 11,873 Oregonians

1851—First General Land Office opens in Oregon City

Willamette Valley Treaty Commission negotiates treaties

Teamsters discover gold in Rogue River Valley

Anson Dart convenes Tansy Point Treaty Council at mouth of Columbia River

First U.S. Army post, Fort Orford, built at Port Orford

U.S. Coast Survey begins charting shoreline

1852—U.S. Army establishes Fort Dalles on Oregon Trail

Congress names Salem capital of Oregon Territory

1853—Territorial legislature adopts Oregon law code

U.S. Army establishes Fort Lane in Rogue River Valley

Territorial legislature publishes *Oregon Archives*

Congress funds Scottsburg-Myrtle Creek Wagon Road

Cow Creek and Rogue River Tribes negotiate treaties with U.S.

Oregon Institute becomes Willamette University

Congress carves Washington Territory out of Oregon Territory

First coal exports begin on southwest Oregon coast

1854—Volunteers massacre Coquille Indians

Legislature prohibits sale of ardent spirits, arms and ammunition to tribes

Legislature bars testimony of "Negroes, mulattoes, and Indians, or persons one half or more of Indian blood" in proceedings involving a white person

1855—Pacific Railroad Surveys examine potential routes

Umatilla and Nez Perce tribes sign treaties at Walla Walla Treaty Council, reserving land and rights to food resources

Warm Springs tribes sign treaty reserving land and rights to food resources

Rogue River Indian War and Yakima Indian War commence

President James Buchanan creates Siletz Reservation

Territorial capitol burns in Salem

1856—U.S. Army establishes Forts Umpqua, Hoskins, and Yamhill

President James Buchanan creates Grand Ronde Reservation

U.S. Army orders closure of settlement east of Cascades because of warfare with tribes

1857—Constitutional Convention meets in Salem

Draft constitution bans slavery and bars African-Americans from residency

Aaron Meier and Emil Frank found Meier & Frank Department Store

1858—First election selects state officials

State of Oregon 1859–Present

1859—Congress grants Oregon statehood on February 14, becoming only state admitted to Union with exclusion laws in their constitution

First bank established by Ladd & Tilton in Portland

First elected governor of state John Whiteaker inaugurated

1860—U.S. Census enumerates 52,465 residents

Oregon Steam Navigation Company commences service

First daily stage operates between Portland and Sacramento

1861—First Oregon State Fair held at Oregon City

1862—Congress passes Homestead Act

First Oregon Cavalry raises six companies

Gold rush commences to Blue Mountains

First portage railroad completed at Cascades

Laws passed banning interracial marriages; requiring Blacks, Chinese, Hawaiians (Kanakas) and Mulattos to pay annual $5 tax, those not able to pay required to perform road maintenance

1863—U.S. Army establishes Fort Klamath

1864—Telegraph line connects Portland-Sacramento

U.S. Army establishes Camp Watson

Treaty creates Klamath Reservation

Popular vote approves Salem as state capital

1865—Long Tom Rebellion confirms pro-southern sympathies

Congress authorizes Oregon Central Military Wagon Road

History

1866 — First lighthouse, Cape Arago, illuminates light signal

U.S. Army establishes Camp Warner

Married Women's Property Act protects women's rights

Congress authorizes Corvallis-Yaquina Bay Military Wagon Road and Willamette Valley-Cascade Mountain Military Wagon Road

1867 — U.S. Army establishes Fort Harney

Congress authorizes The Dalles-Boise Military Wagon Road

1868 — Oregon State Agricultural College opens (later becomes Oregon State University)

1869 — Direct export of wheat to Europe begins

Congress authorizes Coos Bay Military Wagon Road

1870 — U.S. Census enumerates 90,923 residents

Abigail Scott Duniway launches suffrage campaign

Despite failing in Oregon election, U.S. Constitution adds 15th Amendment granting African-American men the right to vote

1872 — Oregon & California Railroad completes line to Roseburg

Modoc Indian War commences

1873 — Oregon Patrons of Husbandry (Grange) forms chapters

Modoc tribesmen face trial and execution at Fort Klamath

Oregon Pioneer Association forms

Great fire destroys much of downtown Portland

1875 — First U.S. Life-Saving Service station opens near Coos Bay

1876 — University of Oregon opens

Robert D. Hume builds salmon cannery on Rogue River

1877 — Nez Perce Indian War involves Chief Joseph's band

Congress passes Desert Land Act

1878 — High schools authorized for districts with 1,000 students

Bannock-Paiute Indian War sweeps into southeastern Oregon

Women gain right to vote in school elections

1879 — BIA Indian Training School opens in Forest Grove, third boarding school of its type, designed to assimilate tribal children into white culture, teach vocational skills

1880 — Great Gale snow and wind storm devastates parts of Oregon and Washington

U.S. Census enumerates 174,768 residents

O. R. & N. Company begins railroad through Gorge

1882 — Normal schools open in Monmouth, Ashland and Drain to train teachers

1883 — O. R. & N. Company railroad reaches Umatilla providing transcontinental links

1884 — Oregon Short Line railroad extends to Huntington

1885 — BIA Indian Training School opens near Salem, is renamed Chemawa Indian School

1886 — Oregon Supreme Court admits Oregon's first female lawyer Mary Gysin Leonard to the state bar

Chief Joseph's Nez Perce band locates on Colville Reservation

1887 — Locals rob and massacre 34 Chinese gold miners at Deep Creek in Hells Canyon

General Allotment Act assaults tribal lands on reservations

Cranberry harvests commence

First in U.S. to make Labor Day a holiday

1888 — First Agricultural Experiment Station opens at Corvallis

1890 — Congress passes Oregon Indian Depredation Claims Act

U.S. Census enumerates 313,767 residents

Chinese Consolidated Benevolent Association founded

1891 — Congress passes Forest Reserve Act

1892 — Congress authorizes Columbia River Lightship No. 50

1894 — Mazama Club forms to promote outdoor adventure

1896 — Workmen complete Cascade Locks

1897 — Holdup of '97 blocks state legislature

1898 — Oregon Historical Society receives charter

1900 — Workmen complete Yamhill River Locks

U.S. Census enumerates 413,536 residents

1902 — Crater Lake National Park opens

Congress passes Federal Reclamation Act

Voters amend Constitution for Initiative and Referendum, allowing citizens to propose new laws and constitutional amendments

1903 — Heppner Flood kills 225 people

First *Voters' Pamphlet* published

1904 — Direct primary law passes

First African-American George Hardin named officer in Portland Police Bureau

1905 — Lewis and Clark Centennial Exposition commemorates the 100th anniversary of the Lewis and Clark Expedition

Klamath Irrigation Project commences

Oregon land fraud trials pursue wrongdoers

1906 — City home rule law approved allowing extensive city lawmaking authority

Indictment by grand jury law approved

Taxes begin on telephone, telegraph and railroads

First meeting of Association of Oregon Counties

1907 — President Theodore Roosevelt creates "Midnight Reserves" setting aside millions of acres of national forests

1908—Constitution amended for Recall provision
First woman Lola Baldwin named head of Women's Division, Portland Police

1909—State's Central Fish Hatchery opens at Bonneville
Oregon Caves National Monument created
Pendleton Round-Up begins
Congress passes Enlarged Homestead Act

1910—U.S. Census enumerates 672,765 residents
Three-fourths verdict in civil cases approved
Employers' Liability Act approved

1911—Columbia River Gorge Highway construction begins
First U.S. primary elections held in Oregon
Oregon Trunk Railroad completes line to Bend

1912—Women's suffrage approved
Prohibition of private convict labor approved
Eight-hour day on public works approved
First U.S. minimum wage law approved

1913—Presidential preference primary law approved
Governor Oswald West declares beaches open to public

1914—Death penalty abolished
Prohibition approved
Eight-hour day approved for women
Congress revests O & C Railroad land grant
Legislature requires publication of *Oregon Blue Book*

1916—Workmen complete Celilo Locks and Canal
Congress passes Stock-Raising Homestead Act

1917—U.S. Army Spruce Production Division begins logging

1918—Influenza pandemic kills hundreds
Emergency Fleet Corporation contracts for ships
Oregonians enlist to serve in World War I

1919—First gasoline tax in U.S. authorized to fund highways
Congress revests Coos Bay Wagon Road land grant

1920—Death penalty reinstated
Oregon League of Women Voters founded
U.S. Census enumerates 783,389 residents

1921—Ku Klux Klan organizes chapters
Hurricane hits Oregon and Washington

1922—First state park opened by Oregon Highway Commission south of Monmouth, named for Sarah Helmick
Compulsory School Act approved outlawing private and parochial schools and requiring children aged 8 to 18 to attend public school
First African-American woman Beatrice Cannady graduates from Lewis & Clark Law School
Japanese American Citizens' League founded

1923—Alien Land Law approved preventing first generation Japanese Americans from owning or leasing land
Alien Business Restriction Law approved denying business licenses to first generation Japanese Americans
Prohibition of sectarian garb in schools approved

1924—Compulsory School Act held unconstitutional
Congress extends citizenship to Native Americans
Clarke-McNary Act aids federal-state forest fire protection

1925—State parks and waysides authorized
League of Oregon Cities founded

1926—Fishwheels abolished
Astor Column completed
Exclusion of African-Americans clause removed from Constitution

1927—State Constitution amended to remove voting restrictions against African and Chinese Americans

1929—State Park Commission created

1930—Vale Irrigation Project begins water delivery
U.S. Census enumerates 953,786 residents
First Oregon woman judge Mary Jane Spurlin appointed to Multnomah County District Court

1933—Tillamook Burn destroys 240,000 forest acres
Civilian Conservation Corps and Works Projects Administration start projects

1934—First grazing district under Taylor Grazing Act forms at Bonanza

1935—Congress authorizes Bonneville Dam
Fire destroys State Capitol

1936—Bandon Fire destroys town, 11 residents die
Work completed on five major bridges on Highway 101
First Oregon woman Nan Wood Honeyman elected to U.S. House of Representatives

1937—President Franklin D. Roosevelt dedicates Timberline Lodge and Bonneville Dam
Gas chamber built for capital punishments
Oregon Shakespeare Festival forms in Ashland
Congress creates Bonneville Power Administration
Bankhead-Jones Act authorizes buyout of homesteaders

1938—544 Report approved for Willamette River flood control
Bonneville Dam completed

1939—Tillamook Burn destroys 190,000 forest acres
State capitol completed in Salem

1940—U.S. Census enumerates 1,089,684 residents

1941—Oregonians enlist to serve in World War II

1942—Executive Order 9066 authorizes removal of Japanese-Americans to internment camps

Japanese submarine shells Fort Stevens

Siskiyou National Forest firebombed by Japanese

U.S. Army builds Camp Adair and Camp Abbot

U.S. Navy builds Tillamook and Tongue Point Naval Air Stations

Vanport founded to house wartime workers

1945—Six Oregonians die in explosion of Japanese incendiary balloon

Tillamook Burn destroys 180,000 forest acres

Supplement to 1923 Alien Land Law passes

1946—Portland State University (PSU) founded

Rural School Law encourages consolidation of districts

1947—Plane crash kills Governor Snell, Secretary of State Farrell, and others

1948—Columbia River Flood destroys Vanport

Vollum and Murdock found Tektronix

1949—State Department of Forestry begins replanting Tillamook Burn

Fair Labor Practices Commission established

State Supreme Court invalidates 1923 and 1945 Alien Land acts

First woman Dorothy McCullough Lee elected Portland mayor

1950—U.S. Census enumerates 1,521,341 residents

1951—Law prohibiting interracial marriages repealed

1952—Constitution amended to provide for equal representation in state legislature

1953—Public Accommodations Law prohibits racial discrimination by businesses

1954—Congress terminates Western Oregon tribes

Supreme Court upholds *Brown v. Board of Education of Topeka*, abolishing segregated schools

1956—Congress authorizes Interstate freeway system

Congress terminates Klamath Tribe

1957—Oregon Fair Housing Act passes

1959—Oregon ratifies 15th Amendment to the U.S. Constitution, granting African American men the right to vote, 89 years after its adoption

1960—Census enumerates 1,768,687 residents

Congress passes Multiple Use-Sustained Yield Act for management of national forests

First female U.S. Senator from Oregon Maurine Neuberger elected

1962—Columbus Day Storm causes major damage in Western Oregon

Oregon State University football player Terry Baker (QB) becomes state's first Heisman Trophy winner

1964—Death penalty abolished

National Civil Rights Act outlaws unequal voter registation requirements; racial segregation in schools, workplace, public places

1965—Congress passes Voting Rights Act prohibiting qualifications or prerequisites to voting

1966—Workmen complete Astoria-Megler Bridge spanning Columbia River estuary

I-5 affords non-stop driving through Oregon

1967—Beach Bill approved, ensuring public access to all of Oregon's coastal beaches

Racial tensions escalate into riots in Portland

1969—Federal District Court in *Sohappy v. Smith* affirms tribal treaty fishing rights in Columbia River

1970—U.S. Census enumerates 2,091,000 resident

1971—Bottle Bill approved

Congress confirms Burns Paiute Reservation

1973—Land Conservation and Development Commission created

Public Meetings Law approved

Public Records Law approved

Tillamook State Forest created

Congress approves Endangered Species Act

Oregon ratifies U.S. Equal Rights Amendment

1974—Congress creates John Day Fossil Beds National Monument

Oregon Health Sciences University forms out of mergers

Governor Tom McCall sets odd/even gasoline refueling days

1975—Congress creates Hells Canyon National Recreation Area

1976—First woman Norma Paulus elected secretary of state

First Oregon nuclear power plant Trojan built north of Saint Helens

1977—Aerosol sprays banned by law

Congress restores Confederated Tribes of Siletz

First woman Betty Roberts appointed to Oregon Court of Appeals

1978—Death penalty reinstated

1979—Federal District Court in *Kimball v. Callahan* affirms Klamath tribal hunting and fishing rights within former reservation

1980—U.S. Census enumerates 2,633,000 residents

Congress creates new Siletz Reservation

Mount Saint Helens eruption disrupts ship traffic on Columbia River

1981—Bhagwan Shree Rajneesh establishes Rajneeshpuram near Antelope

1982—Congress restores Cow Creek Band of Umpqua Tribe

First woman Betty Roberts appointed justice of Oregon Supreme Court

1983—Congress restores Confederated Tribes of Grand Ronde

1984—Congress restores Confederated Tribes of Coos, Lower Umpqua and Siuslaw

First Oregon lottery ratified by voters

First African-American woman Margaret Carter elected to state legislature

1985—Bhagwan Shree Rajneesh deported and fined $400,000

First woman Vera Katz selected speaker of Oregon House

1986—Congress restores Klamath Tribe

Metropolitan Area Express (MAX) begins light-rail service in Portland

1988—Congress creates Grand Ronde Reservation

Congress approves Civil Liberties Act paying $20,000 to each surviving interned Japanese-American

Ballot Measure 8 bans discrimination based on sexual orientation

1989—Congress restores Coquille Tribe

African exchange student Mulugeta Seraw killed by racist skinheads in Portland

1990—U.S. Census enumerates 2,842,000 residents

Ballot Measure 5 limits property taxes to support schools and government

U.S. Department of Fish and Wildlife lists Northern Spotted Owl as endangered

1991—First woman Barbara Roberts elected governor

1992—First African-American James A. Hill, Jr. elected to statewide office as state treasurer

First gaming compact for casinos signed with Cow Creek and Umpqua Tribes

1993—First statewide vote-by-mail election held in U.S.

1994—First Death With Dignity Act approved permitting doctor-assisted suicide

1996—First vote-by-mail election for federal office held

1998—Metropolitan Area Express (MAX) extends light-rail service 18 miles west from Portland

1999—*New Carissa,* freighter runs aground near Coos Bay

U.S. Department of Fish and Wildlife lists several salmon species from Columbia and Willamette Rivers as endangered

2000—U.S. Census enumerates 3,421,399 residents

Measure requiring removal of racist language from state Constitution passes

2001—Metropolitan Area Express (MAX) extends light-rail service to Portland Airport

2002—Susan Castillo first Hispanic woman elected to statewide office as school superintendent

Near record forest fire season leaves 1,000,000 acres burned

2003—Oregon begins 10-year plan to fix deteriorating bridges

2004—Trojan, Oregon's only nuclear power plant, decommissioned

L. L. Stub Stewart State Park opens, Oregon's first new state park campground in more than 30 years

2005—Oregon State Quarter released with design featuring Crater Lake

2006—Trojan, Oregon's decommissioned nuclear power plant, imploded

2007—Oregon's constitution 150 years old

Sandy River's Marmot Dam, built in 1912, removed

Oregon Equality Act passes

2008—*New Carissa,* freighter that ran aground on Coos Bay beach in 1999, dismantled and removed

2009—Oregon celebrates its sesquicentennial on February 14, 2009

Oregon unemployment rate tops 12% amid recession

2010—Governor's panel predicts 10 years of state budget deficits

2012—Oregon legislature begins annual sessions, with the even-numbered years having a month-long session in February

2013—Klamath Tribes' senior water rights in Upper Klamath Basin reaffirmed by courts

Drought and lightning produced most expensive wildfire season on record

Josephine County's last sawmill closes for lack of logs

2014—U.S. District court strikes down same-sex marriage ban; Voters approve recreational marijuana use; Equal Rights for Women in Oregon Constitution

University of Oregon football player Marcus Mariota (QB) wins the Heisman Trophy

2015—Governor John Kitzhaber resigned Feb. 18, 2015, Secretary of State Kate Brown became governor according to the order of succession required by the Oregon Constitution

Minoru Yasui, Hood River Attorney, was posthumously awarded the Presidential Medal of Freedom in recognition of his challenge of a military curfew placed on Japanese Americans during World War II and for his lifetime of civil rights work.

2016—Armed militants seized and occupied the headquarters of Harney County's Malheur National Wildlife Refuge for 41 days.

ELEMENTARY SCHOOL STUDENT ESSAY

The Sandy Hill

Quinton Smith, Essay Contest Runner-up
Mrs. Wright's Third Grade Class
Island City Elementary, Island City

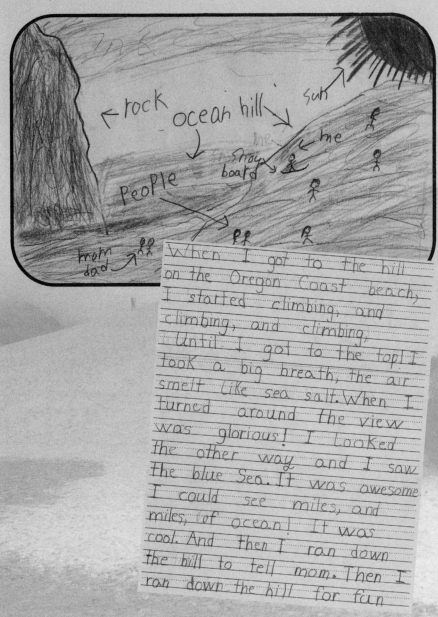

When I got to the hill on the Oregon Coast beach, I started climbing, and climbing, and climbing, Until I got to the top! I took a big breath, the air smelt like sea salt. When I turned around the view was glorious! I looked the other way and I saw the blue Sea. It was awesome. I could see miles, and miles, of ocean! It was cool. And then I ran down the hill to tell mom. Then I ran down the hill for fun

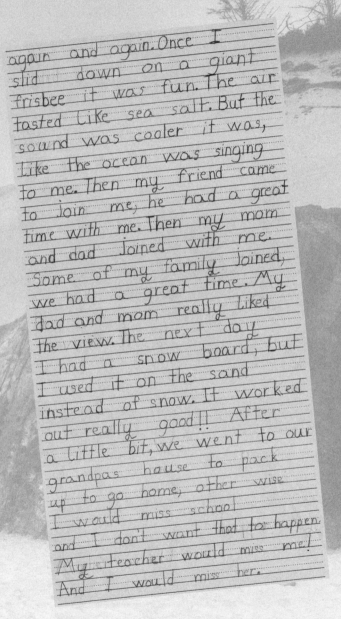

again and again. Once I slid down on a giant frisbee it was fun. The air tasted like sea salt. But the sound was cooler it was, like the ocean was singing to me. Then my friend came to join me, he had a great time with me. Then my mom and dad joined with me. Some of my family joined, we had a great time. My dad and mom really liked the view. The next day I had a snow board, but I used it on the sand instead of snow. It worked out really good!! After a little bit, we went to our grandpas house to pack up to go home, other wise I would miss school and I don't want that to happen. My teacher would miss me! And I would miss her.

Background image: A sandy hill at Cape Kiwanda in Pacific City.
(Oregon State Archives)

A car pulls a camping trailer east along U.S. Highway 20 west of Sisters in 1964.
Oregon State Archives Photograph OHD7318

The Oregon Constitution has been the foundation of government in Oregon since 1859. Oregonians have amended it repeatedly, and, since 1902, citizens have been able to place amendments on the statewide ballot by means of the initiative process. This section contains the full text of the Oregon Constitution.

CONSTITUTION OF OREGON
2015 EDITION

The Constitution of Oregon was framed by a convention of 60 delegates chosen by the people. The convention met on August 17, 1857, the third Monday in August, and adjourned on September 18 of the same year. On November 9, 1857, the Constitution was approved by vote of the people of the Oregon Territory. The Act of Congress admitting Oregon into the Union was approved February 14, 1859, and on that date the Constitution went into effect.

The Constitution is here published as it is in effect following the approval of amendments and revisions on November 4, 2014. The text of the original signed copy of the Constitution filed in the Office of the Secretary of State is retained unless it has been repealed or superseded by amendment or revision. Where the original text has been amended or revised or where a new provision has been added to the original Constitution, the source of the amendment, revision or addition is indicated in the source note immediately following the text of the amended, revised or new section. Notations also have been made setting out the history of repealed sections.

Unless otherwise specifically noted, the leadlines for the sections have been supplied by the Office of the Legislative Counsel.

PREAMBLE

We the people of the State of Oregon to the end that Justice be established, order maintained, and liberty perpetuated, do ordain this Constitution. —

ARTICLE I
BILL OF RIGHTS

Section 1. Natural rights inherent in people. We declare that all men, when they form a social compact are equal in right: that all power is inherent in the people, and all free governments are founded on their authority, and instituted for their peace, safety, and happiness; and they have at all times a right to alter, reform, or abolish the government in such manner as they may think proper.—

Section 2. Freedom of worship. All men shall be secure in the Natural right, to worship Almighty God according to the dictates of their own consciences.—

Section 3. Freedom of religious opinion. No law shall in any case whatever control the free exercise, and enjoyment of religeous [sic] opinions, or interfere with the rights of conscience.—

Section 4. No religious qualification for office. No religious test shall be required as a qualification for any office of trust or profit.—

Section 5. No money to be appropriated for religion. No money shall be drawn from the Treasury for the benefit of any religeous [sic], or theological institution, nor shall any money be appropriated for the payment of any religeous [sic] services in either house of the Legislative Assembly.—

Section 6. No religious test for witnesses or jurors. No person shall be rendered incompetent as a witness, or juror in consequence of his opinions on matters of religeon [sic]; nor be questioned in any Court of Justice touching his religeous [sic] belief to affect the weight of his testimony.—

Section 7. Manner of administering oath or affirmation. The mode of administering an oath, or affirmation shall be such as may be most consistent with, and binding upon the conscience of the person to whom such oath or affirmation may be administered.—

Section 8. Freedom of speech and press. No law shall be passed restraining the free expression of opinion, or restricting the right to speak, write, or print freely on any subject whatever; but every person shall be responsible for the abuse of this right.—

Section 9. Unreasonable searches or seizures. No law shall violate the right of the people to be secure in their persons, houses, papers, and effects, against unreasonable search, or seizure; and no warrant shall issue but upon probable cause, supported by oath, or affirmation, and particularly describing the place to be searched, and the person or thing to be seized.—

Section 10. Administration of justice. No court shall be secret, but justice shall be administered, openly and without purchase, completely and without delay, and every man shall have remedy by due course of law for injury done him in his person, property, or reputation.—

Section 11. Rights of Accused in Criminal Prosecution. In all criminal prosecutions, the accused shall have the right to public trial by an impartial jury in the county in which the offense shall have been committed; to be heard by himself and counsel; to demand the nature and cause of the accusation against him, and to have a copy thereof; to meet the witnesses face to face, and to have compulsory process for obtaining witnesses in his favor; provided, however, that any accused person, in other than capital cases, and with the consent of the trial judge, may elect to waive trial by jury and consent to be tried by the judge of the court alone, such election to be in writing; provided, however, that in the circuit court ten members of the jury may render a verdict of guilty or not guilty, save and except a verdict of guilty of first degree murder, which shall be found only by a unanimous verdict, and not otherwise; provided further, that the existing laws and constitutional provisions relative to criminal prosecutions shall be continued and remain in effect as to all prosecutions for crimes committed before the taking effect of this amendment. [Constitution of 1859; Amendment proposed by S.J.R. 4, 1931, and adopted by the people Nov. 8, 1932; Amendment proposed by S.J.R. 4, 1931 (2d s.s.), and adopted by the people May 18, 1934]

Note: The leadline to section 11 was a part of the measure submitted to the people by S.J.R. 4, 1931.

Section 12. Double jeopardy; compulsory self-incrimination. No person shall be put in jeopardy twice for the same offence [sic], nor be compelled in any criminal prosecution to testify against himself.—

Section 13. Treatment of arrested or confined persons. No person arrested, or confined in jail, shall be treated with unnecessary rigor.—

Section 14. Bailable offenses. Offences [sic], except murder, and treason, shall be bailable by sufficient sureties. Murder or treason, shall not be bailable, when the proof is evident, or the presumption strong.—

Section 15. Foundation principles of criminal law. Laws for the punishment of crime shall be founded on these principles: protection of society, personal responsibility, accountability for one's actions and reformation. [Constitution of 1859; Amendment proposed by S.J.R. 32, 1995, and adopted by the people Nov. 5, 1996]

Section 16. Excessive bail and fines; cruel and unusual punishments; power of jury in criminal case. Excessive bail shall not be required, nor excessive fines imposed. Cruel and unusual punishments shall not be inflicted, but all penalties shall be proportioned to the offense.— In all criminal cases whatever, the jury shall have the right to determine the law, and the facts under the direction of the Court as to the law, and the right of new trial, as in civil cases.

Section 17. Jury trial in civil cases. In all civil cases the right of Trial by Jury shall remain inviolate.—

Section 18. Private property or services taken for public use. Private property shall not be taken for public use, nor the particular services of any man be demanded, without just compensation; nor except in the case of the state, without such compensation first assessed and tendered; provided, that the use of all roads, ways and waterways necessary to promote the transportation of the raw products of mine or farm or forest or water for beneficial use or drainage is necessary to the development and welfare of the state and is declared a public use. [Constitution of 1859; Amendment proposed by S.J.R. 17, 1919, and adopted by the people May 21, 1920; Amendment proposed by S.J.R. 8, 1923, and adopted by the people Nov. 4, 1924]

Section 19. Imprisonment for debt. There shall be no imprisonment for debt, except in case of fraud or absconding debtors.—

Section 20. Equality of privileges and immunities of citizens. No law shall be passed granting to any citizen or class of citizens privileges, or immunities, which, upon the same terms, shall not equally belong to all citizens.—

Section 21. Ex-post facto laws; laws impairing contracts; laws depending on authorization in order to take effect; laws submitted to electors. No ex-post facto law, or law impairing the obligation of contracts shall ever be passed, nor shall any law be passed, the taking effect of which shall be made to depend upon any authority, except as provided in this Constitution; provided, that laws locating the Capitol of the State, locating County Seats, and submitting town, and corporate acts, and other local, and Special laws may take effect, or not, upon a vote of the electors interested.—

Section 22. Suspension of operation of laws. The operation of the laws shall never be suspended, except by the Authority of the Legislative Assembly.

Section 23. Habeas corpus. The privilege of the writ of habeas corpus shall not be suspended unless in case of rebellion, or invasion the public safety require it.—

Section 24. Treason. Treason against the State shall consist only in levying war against it, or adhering to its enemies, giving them aid or comfort.— No person shall be convicted of treason unless on the testimony of two witnesses to the same overt act, or confession in open Court.—

Section 25. Corruption of blood or forfeiture of estate. No conviction shall work corruption of blood, or forfeiture of estate.—

Section 26. Assemblages of people; instruction of representatives; application to legislature. No law shall be passed restraining any of the inhabitants of the State from assembling together in a peaceable manner to consult for their common good; nor from instructing their Representatives; nor from applying to the Legislature for redress of greviances [sic].—

Section 27. Right to bear arms; military subordinate to civil power. The people shall have the right to bear arms for the defence [sic] of themselves, and the State, but the Military shall be kept in strict subordination to the civil power[.]

Section 28. Quartering soldiers. No soldier shall, in time of peace, be quartered in any house, without the consent of the owner, nor in time of war, except in the manner prescribed by law.

Section 29. Titles of nobility; hereditary distinctions. No law shall be passed granting any title of Nobility, or conferring hereditary distinctions.—

Section 30. Emigration. No law shall be passed prohibiting emigration from the State.—

Section 31. Rights of aliens; immigration to state. [Constitution of 1859; repeal proposed by H.J.R. 16, 1969, and adopted by the people May 26, 1970]

Section 32. Taxes and duties; uniformity of taxation. No tax or duty shall be imposed without the consent of the people or their representatives in the Legislative Assembly; and all taxation shall be uniform on the same class of subjects within the territorial limits of the authority levying the tax. [Constitution of 1859; Amendment proposed by H.J.R. 16, 1917, and adopted by the people June 4, 1917]

Section 33. Enumeration of rights not exclusive. This enumeration of rights, and privileges shall not be construed to impair or deny others retained by the people.—

Section 34. Slavery or involuntary servitude. There shall be neither slavery, nor involuntary servitude in the State, otherwise than as a punishment for crime, whereof the party shall have been duly convicted.— [Added to Bill of Rights as unnumbered section by vote of the people at time of adoption of the Oregon Constitution in accordance with section 4 of Article XVIII thereof]

Section 35. Restrictions on rights of certain persons. [Added to Bill of Rights as unnumbered section by vote of the people at time of adoption of the Oregon Constitution in accordance with Section 4 of Article XVIII thereof; Repeal proposed by H.J.R. 8, 1925, and adopted by the people Nov. 2, 1926]

Section 36. Liquor prohibition. [Created through initiative petition filed July 1, 1914, and adopted by the people Nov. 3, 1914; Repeal proposed by initiative petition filed March 20, 1933, and adopted by the people July 21, 1933]

Section 36. Capital punishment abolished. [Created through initiative petition filed July 2, 1914, and adopted by the people Nov. 3, 1914; Repeal proposed by S.J.R. 8, 1920 (s.s.), and adopted by the people May 21, 1920, as Const. Art. I, §38]

Note: At the general election in 1914 two sections, each designated as section 36, were created and added to the Constitution by separate initiative petitions. One of these sections was the prohibition section and the other abolished capital punishment.

Section 36a. Prohibition of importation of liquors. [Created through initiative petition filed July 6, 1916, and adopted by the people Nov. 7, 1916; Repeal proposed by initiative petition filed March 20, 1933, and adopted by the people July 21, 1933]

Section 37. Penalty for murder in first degree. [Created through S.J.R. 8, 1920, and adopted by the people May 21, 1920; Repeal proposed by S.J.R. 3, 1963, and adopted by the people Nov. 3, 1964]

Section 38. Laws abrogated by amendment abolishing death penalty revived. [Created through S.J.R. 8, 1920, and adopted by the people May 21, 1920; Repeal proposed by S.J.R. 3, 1963, and adopted by the people Nov. 3, 1964]

Section 39. Sale of liquor by individual glass. The State shall have power to license private clubs, fraternal organizations, veterans' organizations, railroad corporations operating interstate trains and commercial establishments where food is cooked and served, for the purpose of selling alcoholic liquor by the individual glass at retail, for consumption on the premises, including mixed drinks and cocktails, compounded or mixed on the premises only. The Legislative Assembly shall provide in such detail as it shall deem advisable for carrying out and administering the provisions of this amendment and shall provide adequate safeguards to carry out the original intent and purpose of the Oregon Liquor Control Act, including the promotion of temperance in the use and consumption of alcoholic beverages, encourage the use and consumption of lighter beverages and aid in the establishment of Oregon industry. This power is subject to the following:

(1) The provisions of this amendment shall take effect and be in operation sixty (60) days after the approval and adoption by the people of Oregon; provided, however, the right of a local option election exists in the counties and in any incorporated city or town containing a population of at least five hundred (500). The Legislative Assembly shall prescribe a means and a procedure by which the voters of any county or incorporated city or town as limited above in any county, may through a local option election determine whether to prohibit or permit such power, and such procedure shall specifically include that whenever fifteen per cent (15%) of the registered voters of any county in the state or of any incorporated city or town as limited above, in any county in the state, shall file a petition requesting an election in this matter, the question shall be voted upon at the next regular November biennial election, provided said petition is filed not less than sixty (60) days before the day of election.

(2) Legislation relating to this matter shall operate uniformly throughout the state and all individuals shall be treated equally; and all provisions shall be liberally construed for the accomplishment of these purposes. [Created through initiative petition filed July 2, 1952, and adopted by the people Nov. 4, 1952]

Section 40. Penalty for aggravated murder. Notwithstanding sections 15 and 16 of this Article, the penalty for aggravated murder as defined by law shall be death upon unanimous affirmative jury findings as provided by law and otherwise shall be life imprisonment with minimum sentence as provided by law. [Created through initiative petition filed July 6, 1983, and adopted by the people Nov. 6, 1984]

Section 41. Work and training for corrections institution inmates; work programs; limitations; duties of corrections director. (1) Whereas the people of the state of Oregon find and declare that inmates who are confined in corrections institutions should work as hard as the taxpayers who provide for their upkeep; and whereas the people also find and declare that inmates confined within corrections institutions must be fully engaged in productive activity if they are to successfully re-enter society with practical skills and a viable work ethic; now, therefore, the people declare:

(2) All inmates of state corrections institutions shall be actively engaged full-time in work or on-the-job training. The work or on-the-job training programs shall be established and overseen by the corrections director, who shall ensure that such programs are cost-effective and are designed to develop inmate motivation, work capabilities and cooperation. Such programs may include boot camp prison programs. Education may be provided to inmates as part of work or on-the-job training so long as each inmate is engaged at least half-time in hands-on training or work activity.

(3) Each inmate shall begin full-time work or on-the-job training immediately upon admission to a corrections institution, allowing for a short time for administrative intake and processing. The specific quantity of hours per day to be spent in work or on-the-job training shall be determined by the corrections director, but the overall time spent in work or training shall be full-time. However, no inmate has a legally enforceable right to a job or to otherwise participate in work, on-the-job training or educational programs or to compensation for work or labor performed while an inmate of any state, county or city corrections facility or institution. The corrections director may reduce or exempt participation in work or training programs by those inmates deemed by corrections officials as physically or mentally disabled, or as too dangerous to society to engage in such programs.

(4) There shall be sufficient work and training programs to ensure that every eligible inmate is productively involved in one or more programs. Where an inmate is drug and alcohol addicted so as to prevent the inmate from effectively participating in work or training programs, corrections officials shall provide appropriate drug or alcohol treatment.

(5) The intent of the people is that taxpayer-supported institutions and programs shall be free to benefit from inmate work. Prison work programs shall be designed and carried out so as to achieve savings in government operations, so as to achieve a net profit in private sector activities or so as to benefit the community.

(6) The provisions of this section are mandatory for all state corrections institutions. The provisions of this section are permissive for county or city corrections facilities. No law, ordinance or charter shall prevent or restrict a county or city governing body from implementing all or part of the provisions of this section. Compensation, if any, shall be determined and established by the governing body of the county or city which chooses to engage in prison work programs, and the governing body may choose to adopt any power or exemption allowed in this section.

(7) The corrections director shall contact public and private enterprises in this state and seek proposals to use inmate work. The corrections director may: (a) install and equip plants in any state corrections institution, or any other location, for the employment or training of any of the inmates therein; or (b) purchase, acquire, install, maintain and operate materials, machinery and appliances necessary to the conduct and operation of such plants. The corrections director shall use every effort to enter into contracts or agreements with private business concerns or government agencies to accomplish the production or marketing of products or services produced or performed by inmates. The corrections director may carry out the director's powers and duties under this section by delegation to others.

(8) Compensation, if any, for inmates who engage in prison work programs shall be determined and established by the corrections director. Such compensation shall not be subject to existing public or private sector minimum or prevailing wage laws, except where required to comply with federal law. Inmate compensation from enterprises entering into agreements with the state shall be exempt from unemployment compensation taxes to the extent allowed under federal law. Inmate injury or disease attributable to any inmate work shall be covered by a corrections system inmate injury fund rather than the workers compensation law. Except as otherwise required by federal law to permit transportation in interstate commerce of goods, wares or merchandise manufactured, produced or mined, wholly or in part by inmates or except as otherwise required by state law, any compensation earned through prison work programs shall only be used for the following purposes: (a) reimbursement for all or a portion of the costs of the inmate's rehabilitation, housing, health care, and living costs; (b) restitution or compensation to the victims of the particular inmate's crime; (c) restitution or compensation to the victims of crime generally through a fund designed for that purpose; (d) financial support for immediate family of the inmate outside the corrections institu-

Constitution

tion; and (e) payment of fines, court costs, and applicable taxes.

(9) All income generated from prison work programs shall be kept separate from general fund accounts and shall only be used for implementing, maintaining and developing prison work programs. Prison industry work programs shall be exempt from statutory competitive bid and purchase requirements. Expenditures for prison work programs shall be exempt from the legislative appropriations process to the extent the programs rely on income sources other than state taxes and fees. Where state taxes or fees are the source of capital or operating expenditures, the appropriations shall be made by the legislative assembly. The state programs shall be run in a businesslike fashion and shall be subject to regulation by the corrections director. Expenditures from income generated by state prison work programs must be approved by the corrections director. Agreements with private enterprise as to state prison work programs must be approved by the corrections director. The corrections director shall make all state records available for public scrutiny and the records shall be subject to audit by the Secretary of State.

(10) Prison work products or services shall be available to any public agency and to any private enterprise of any state, any nation or any American Indian or Alaskan Native tribe without restriction imposed by any state or local law, ordinance or regulation as to competition with other public or private sector enterprises. The products and services of corrections work programs shall be provided on such terms as are set by the corrections director. To the extent determined possible by the corrections director, the corrections director shall avoid establishing or expanding for-profit prison work programs that produce goods or services offered for sale in the private sector if the establishment or expansion would displace or significantly reduce preexisting private enterprise. To the extent determined possible by the corrections director, the corrections director shall avoid establishing or expanding prison work programs if the establishment or expansion would displace or significantly reduce government or nonprofit programs that employ persons with developmental disabilities. However, the decision to establish, maintain, expand, reduce or terminate any prison work program remains in the sole discretion of the corrections director.

(11) Inmate work shall be used as much as possible to help operate the corrections institutions themselves, to support other government operations and to support community charitable organizations. This work includes, but is not limited to, institutional food production; maintenance and repair of buildings, grounds, and equipment; office support services, including printing; prison clothing production and maintenance; prison medical services; training other inmates; agricultural and forestry work, especially in parks and public forest lands; and environmental clean-up projects. Every state agency shall cooperate with the corrections director in establishing inmate work programs.

(12) As used throughout this section, unless the context requires otherwise: "full-time" means the equivalent of at least forty hours per seven day week, specifically including time spent by inmates as required by the Department of Corrections, while the inmate is participating in work or on-the-job training, to provide for the safety and security of the public, correctional staff and inmates; "corrections director" means the person in charge of the state corrections system.

(13) This section is self-implementing and supersedes all existing inconsistent statutes. This section shall become effective April 1, 1995. If any part of this section or its application to any person or circumstance is held to be invalid for any reason, then the remaining parts or applications to any persons or circumstances shall not be affected

but shall remain in full force and effect. [Created through initiative petition filed Jan. 12, 1994, and adopted by the people Nov. 8, 1994; Amendment proposed by H.J.R. 2, 1997, and adopted by the people May 20, 1997; Amendment proposed by H.J.R. 82, 1999, and adopted by the people Nov. 2, 1999]

Note: Added to Article I as unnumbered section by initiative petition (Measure No. 17, 1994) adopted by the people Nov. 8, 1994.

Note: An initiative petition (Measure No. 40, 1996) proposed adding a new section relating to crime victims' rights to the Oregon Constitution. That section, appearing as section 42 of Article I in previous editions of this Constitution, was declared void for not being enacted in compliance with section 1, Article XVII of this Constitution. See Armatta v. Kitzhaber, 327 Or. 250, 959 P.2d 49 (1998).

Section 42. Rights of victim in criminal prosecutions and juvenile court delinquency proceedings. (1) To preserve and protect the right of crime victims to justice, to ensure crime victims a meaningful role in the criminal and juvenile justice systems, to accord crime victims due dignity and respect and to ensure that criminal and juvenile court delinquency proceedings are conducted to seek the truth as to the defendant's innocence or guilt, and also to ensure that a fair balance is struck between the rights of crime victims and the rights of criminal defendants in the course and conduct of criminal and juvenile court delinquency proceedings, the following rights are hereby granted to victims in all prosecutions for crimes and in juvenile court delinquency proceedings:

(a) The right to be present at and, upon specific request, to be informed in advance of any critical stage of the proceedings held in open court when the defendant will be present, and to be heard at the pretrial release hearing and the sentencing or juvenile court delinquency disposition;

(b) The right, upon request, to obtain information about the conviction, sentence, imprisonment, criminal history and future release from physical custody of the criminal defendant or convicted criminal and equivalent information regarding the alleged youth offender or youth offender;

(c) The right to refuse an interview, deposition or other discovery request by the criminal defendant or other person acting on behalf of the criminal defendant provided, however, that nothing in this paragraph shall restrict any other constitutional right of the defendant to discovery against the state;

(d) The right to receive prompt restitution from the convicted criminal who caused the victim's loss or injury;

(e) The right to have a copy of a transcript of any court proceeding in open court, if one is otherwise prepared;

(f) The right to be consulted, upon request, regarding plea negotiations involving any violent felony; and

(g) The right to be informed of these rights as soon as practicable.

(2) This section applies to all criminal and juvenile court delinquency proceedings pending or commenced on or after the effective date of this section. Nothing in this section reduces a criminal defendant's rights under the Constitution of the United States. Except as otherwise specifically provided, this section supersedes any conflicting section of this Constitution. Nothing in this section is intended to create any cause of action for compensation or damages nor may this section be used to invalidate an accusatory instrument, conviction or adjudication or otherwise terminate any criminal or juvenile delinquency proceedings at any point after the case is commenced or on appeal. Except as otherwise provided in subsections (3) and (4) of this section, nothing in this section may be used to invalidate a ruling of a court or to suspend any criminal or juvenile delinquency proceedings at any point after the case is commenced.

(3)(a) Every victim described in paragraph (c) of subsection (6) of this section shall have remedy by due course of law for violation of a right established in this section.

(b) A victim may assert a claim for a right established in this section in a pending case, by a mandamus proceeding if no case is pending or as otherwise provided by law.

(c) The Legislative Assembly may provide by law for further effectuation of the provisions of this subsection, including authorization for expedited and interlocutory consideration of claims for relief and the establishment of reasonable limitations on the time allowed for bringing such claims.

(d) No claim for a right established in this section shall suspend a criminal or juvenile delinquency proceeding if such a suspension would violate a right of a criminal defendant guaranteed by this Constitution or the Constitution of the United States.

(4) Upon the victim's request, the prosecuting attorney, in the attorney's discretion, may assert and enforce a right established in this section.

(5) Upon the filing by the prosecuting attorney of an affidavit setting forth cause, a court shall suspend the rights established in this section in any case involving organized crime or victims who are minors.

(6) As used in this section:

(a) "Convicted criminal" includes a youth offender in juvenile court delinquency proceedings.

(b) "Criminal defendant" includes an alleged youth offender in juvenile court delinquency proceedings.

(c) "Victim" means any person determined by the prosecuting attorney or the court to have suffered direct financial, psychological or physical harm as a result of a crime and, in the case of a victim who is a minor, the legal guardian of the minor.

(d) "Violent felony" means a felony in which there was actual or threatened serious physical injury to a victim or a felony sexual offense.

(7) In the event that no person has been determined to be a victim of the crime, the people of Oregon, represented by the prosecuting attorney, are considered to be the victims. In no event is it intended that the criminal defendant be considered the victim. [Created through H.J.R. 87, 1999, and adopted by the people Nov. 2, 1999; Amendment proposed by H.J.R. 49, 2007, and adopted by the people May 20, 2008]

Note: The effective date of House Joint Resolutions 87, 89, 90 and 94, compiled as sections 42, 43, 44 and 45, Article I, is Dec. 2, 1999.

Note: Sections 42, 43, 44 and 45, were added to Article I as unnumbered sections by the amendments proposed by House Joint Resolutions 87, 89, 90 and 94, 1999, and adopted by the people Nov. 2, 1999.

Section 43. Rights of victim and public to protection from accused person during criminal proceedings; denial of pretrial release. (1) To ensure that a fair balance is struck between the rights of crime victims and the rights of criminal defendants in the course and conduct of criminal proceedings, the following rights are hereby granted to victims in all prosecutions for crimes:

(a) The right to be reasonably protected from the criminal defendant or the convicted criminal throughout the criminal justice process and from the alleged youth offender or youth offender throughout the juvenile delinquency proceedings.

(b) The right to have decisions by the court regarding the pretrial release of a criminal defendant based upon the principle of reasonable protection of the victim and the public, as well as the likelihood that the criminal defendant will appear for trial. Murder, aggravated murder and treason shall not be bailable when the proof is evident or the presumption strong that the person is guilty. Other violent felonies shall not be bailable when a court has determined there is probable cause to believe the criminal defendant committed the crime, and the court finds, by clear and convincing evidence, that there is danger of physical injury or sexual victimization to the victim or members of the public by the criminal defendant while on release.

(2) This section applies to proceedings pending or commenced on or after the effective date of this section. Nothing in this section abridges any right of the criminal defendant guaranteed by the Constitution of the United States, including the rights to be represented by counsel, have counsel appointed if indigent, testify, present witnesses, cross-examine witnesses or present information at the release hearing. Nothing in this section creates any cause of action for compensation or damages nor may this section be used to invalidate an accusatory instrument, conviction or adjudication or otherwise terminate any criminal or juvenile delinquency proceeding at any point after the case is commenced or on appeal. Except as otherwise provided in paragraph (b) of subsection (4) of this section and in subsection (5) of this section, nothing in this section may be used to invalidate a ruling of a court or to suspend any criminal or juvenile delinquency proceedings at any point after the case is commenced. Except as otherwise specifically provided, this section supersedes any conflicting section of this Constitution.

(3) As used in this section:

(a) "Victim" means any person determined by the prosecuting attorney or the court to have suffered direct financial, psychological or physical harm as a result of a crime and, in the case of a victim who is a minor, the legal guardian of the minor.

(b) "Violent felony" means a felony in which there was actual or threatened serious physical injury to a victim or a felony sexual offense.

(4)(a) The prosecuting attorney is the party authorized to assert the rights of the public established by this section.

(b) Upon the victim's request, the prosecuting attorney, in the attorney's discretion, may assert and enforce a right established in this section.

(5)(a) Every victim described in paragraph (a) of subsection (3) of this section shall have remedy by due course of law for violation of a right established in this section.

(b) A victim may assert a claim for a right established in this section in a pending case, by a mandamus proceeding if no case is pending or as otherwise provided by law.

(c) The Legislative Assembly may provide by law for further effectuation of the provisions of this subsection, including authorization for expedited and interlocutory consideration of claims for relief and the establishment of reasonable limitations on the time allowed for bringing such claims.

(d) No claim for a right established in this section shall suspend a criminal or juvenile delinquency proceeding if such a suspension would violate a right of a criminal defendant or alleged youth offender guaranteed by this Constitution or the Constitution of the United States.

(6) In the event that no person has been determined to be a victim of the crime, the people of Oregon, represented by the prosecuting attorney, are considered to be the victims. In no event is it intended that the criminal defendant be considered the victim. [Created through H.J.R. 90, 1999, and adopted by the people Nov. 2, 1999; Amendment proposed by H.J.R. 50, 2007, and adopted by the people May 20, 2008]

Note: See notes under section 42 of this Article.

Section 44. Term of imprisonment imposed by court to be fully served; exceptions. (1)(a) A term of imprisonment imposed by a judge in open court may not be set aside or otherwise not carried out, except as authorized by the sentencing court or through the subsequent exercise of:

(A) The power of the Governor to grant reprieves, commutations and pardons; or

(B) Judicial authority to grant appellate or post-conviction relief.

(b) No law shall limit a court's authority to sentence a criminal defendant consecutively for crimes against different victims.

(2) This section applies to all offenses committed on or after the effective date of this section. Nothing in this section reduces a criminal defendant's rights under the Constitution of the United States. Except as otherwise specifically provided, this section supersedes any conflicting section of this Constitution. Nothing in this section creates any cause of action for compensation or damages nor may this section be used to invalidate an accusatory instrument, ruling of a court, conviction or adjudication or otherwise suspend or terminate any criminal or juvenile delinquency proceedings at any point after the case is commenced or on appeal.

(3) As used in this section, "victim" means any person determined by the prosecuting attorney to have suffered direct financial, psychological or physical harm as a result of a crime and, in the case of a victim who is a minor, the legal guardian of the minor. In the event no person has been determined to be a victim of the crime, the people of Oregon, represented by the prosecuting attorney, are considered to be the victims. In no event is it intended that the criminal defendant be considered the victim. [Created through H.J.R. 94, 1999, and adopted by the people Nov. 2, 1999]

Note: See notes under section 42 of this Article.

Section 45. Person convicted of certain crimes not eligible to serve as juror on grand jury or trial jury in criminal case. (1) In all grand juries and in all prosecutions for crimes tried to a jury, the jury shall be composed of persons who have not been convicted:

(a) Of a felony or served a felony sentence within the 15 years immediately preceding the date the persons are required to report for jury duty; or

(b) Of a misdemeanor involving violence or dishonesty or served a sentence for a misdemeanor involving violence or dishonesty within the five years immediately preceding the date the persons are required to report for jury duty.

(2) This section applies to all criminal proceedings pending or commenced on or after the effective date of this section, except a criminal proceeding in which a jury has been impaneled and sworn on the effective date of this section. Nothing in this section reduces a criminal defendant's rights under the Constitution of the United States. Except as otherwise specifically provided, this section supersedes any conflicting section of this Constitution. Nothing in this section is intended to create any cause of action for compensation or damages nor may this section be used to disqualify a jury, invalidate an accusatory instrument, ruling of a court, conviction or adjudication or otherwise suspend or terminate any criminal proceeding at any point after a jury is impaneled and sworn or on appeal. [Created through H.J.R. 89, 1999, and adopted by the people Nov. 2, 1999]

Note: See notes under section 42 of this Article.

Section 46. Prohibition on denial or abridgment of rights on account of sex. (1) Equality of rights under the law shall not be denied or abridged by the State of Oregon or by any political subdivision in this state on account of sex.

(2) The Legislative Assembly shall have the power to enforce, by appropriate legislation, the provisions of this section.

(3) Nothing in this section shall diminish a right otherwise available to persons under section 20 of this Article or

any other provision of this Constitution. [Created through initiative petition filed Oct. 24, 2013, and adopted by the people Nov. 4, 2014]

ARTICLE II
SUFFRAGE AND ELECTIONS

Sec. 1. Elections free
  2. Qualifications of electors
  3. Rights of certain electors
  4. Residence
  5. Soldiers, seamen and marines; residence; right to vote
  7. Bribery at elections
  8. Regulation of elections
  9. Penalty for dueling
  10. Lucrative offices; holding other offices forbidden
  11. When collector or holder of public moneys ineligible to office
  12. Temporary appointments to office
  13. Privileges of electors
  14. Time of holding elections and assuming duties of office
  14a. Time of holding elections in incorporated cities and towns
  15. Method of voting in legislature
  16. Election by plurality; proportional representation
  17. Place of voting
  18. Recall; meaning of words "the legislative assembly shall provide"
  22. Political campaign contribution limitations
  23. Approval by more than majority required for certain measures submitted to people
  24. Death of candidate prior to election

Section 1. Elections free. All elections shall be free and equal.—

Section 2. Qualifications of electors. (1) Every citizen of the United States is entitled to vote in all elections not otherwise provided for by this Constitution if such citizen:

(a) Is 18 years of age or older;

(b) Has resided in this state during the six months immediately preceding the election, except that provision may be made by law to permit a person who has resided in this state less than 30 days immediately preceding the election, but who is otherwise qualified under this subsection, to vote in the election for candidates for nomination or election for President or Vice President of the United States or elector of President and Vice President of the United States; and

(c) Is registered not less than 20 calendar days immediately preceding any election in the manner provided by law.

(2) Provision may be made by law to require that persons who vote upon questions of levying special taxes or issuing public bonds shall be taxpayers. [Constitution of 1859; Amendment proposed by initiative petition filed Dec. 20, 1910, and adopted by the people Nov. 5, 1912; Amendment proposed by S.J.R. 6, 1913, and adopted by the people Nov. 3, 1914; Amendment proposed by S.J.R. 6, 1923, and adopted by the people Nov. 4, 1924; Amendment proposed by H.J.R. 7, 1927, and adopted by the people June 28, 1927; Amendment proposed by H.J.R. 5, 1931, and adopted by the people Nov. 8, 1932; Amendment proposed by H.J.R. 26, 1959, and adopted by the people Nov. 8, 1960; Amendment proposed by H.J.R. 41, 1973, and adopted by the people Nov. 5, 1974; Amendment proposed by initiative petition filed July 20, 1986, and adopted by the people Nov. 4, 1986; Amendment proposed by H.J.R. 4, 2007, and adopted by the people Nov. 4, 2008]

Note: The leadline to section 2 was a part of the measure submitted to the people by initiative petition (Measure No. 13, 1986) and adopted by the people Nov. 4, 1986.

Section 3. Rights of certain electors. A person suffering from a mental handicap is entitled to the full rights of an elector, if otherwise qualified, unless the person has been adjudicated incompetent to vote as provided by law. The privilege of an elector, upon conviction of any crime which is punishable by imprisonment in the penitentiary, shall be forfeited, unless otherwise provided by law. [Constitution of 1859; Amendment proposed by S.J.R. 9, 1943, and adopted by the people Nov. 7, 1944; Amendment proposed by S.J.R. 26, 1979, and adopted by the people Nov. 4, 1980]

Section 4. Residence. For the purpose of voting, no person shall be deemed to have gained, or lost a residence, by reason of his presence, or absence while employed in the service of the United States, or of this State; nor while engaged in the navigation of the waters of this State, or of the United States, or of the high seas; nor while a student of any Seminary of Learning; nor while kept at any alms house, or other assylum [sic], at public expence [sic]; nor while confined in any public prison.—

Section 5. Soldiers, seamen and marines; residence; right to vote. No soldier, seaman, or marine in the Army, or Navy of the United States, or of their allies, shall be deemed to have acquired a residence in the state, in consequence of having been stationed within the same; nor shall any such soldier, seaman, or marine have the right to vote.—

Section 6. Right of suffrage for certain persons. [Constitution of 1859; Repeal proposed by H.J.R. 4, 1927, and adopted by the people June 28, 1927]

Section 7. Bribery at elections. Every person shall be disqualified from holding office, during the term for which he may have been elected, who shall have given, or offered a bribe, threat, or reward to procure his election.—

Section 8. Regulation of elections. The Legislative Assembly shall enact laws to support the privilege of free suffrage, prescribing the manner of regulating, and conducting elections, and prohibiting under adequate penalties, all undue influence therein, from power, bribery, tumult, and other improper conduct.—

Section 9. Penalty for dueling. Every person who shall give, or accept a challenge to fight a duel, or who shall knowingly carry to another person such challenge, or who shall agree to go out of the State to fight a duel, shall be ineligible to any office of trust, or profit.—

Section 10. Lucrative offices; holding other offices forbidden. No person holding a lucrative office, or appointment under the United States, or under this State, shall be eligible to a seat in the Legislative Assembly; nor shall any person hold more than one lucrative office at the same time, except as in this Constitution [sic] expressly permitted; Provided, that Officers in the Militia, to which there is attached no annual salary, and the Office of Post Master, where the compensation does not exceed One Hundred Dollars per annum, shall not be deemed lucrative.—

Section 11. When collector or holder of public moneys ineligible to office. No person who may hereafter be a collector, or holder of public moneys, shall be eligible to any office of trust or profit, until he shall have accounted for, and paid over according to law, all sums for which he may be liable.—

Section 12. Temporary appointments to office. In all cases, in which it is provided that an office shall not be filled by the same person, more than a certain number of years continuously, an appointment pro tempore shall not be reckoned a part of that term.—

Section 13. Privileges of electors. In all cases, except treason, felony, and breach of the peace, electors shall be free from arrest in going to elections, during their attendance there, and in returning from the same; and no elector shall be obliged to do duty in the Militia on any day of election, except in time of war, or public danger.—

Section 14. Time of holding elections and assuming duties of office. The regular general biennial election in Oregon for the year A. D. 1910 and thereafter shall be held on the first Tuesday after the first Monday in November. All officers except the Governor, elected for a six year term in 1904 or for a four year term in 1906 or for a two year term in 1908 shall continue to hold their respective offices until the first Monday in January, 1911; and all officers, except the Governor elected at any regular general biennial election after the adoption of this amendment shall assume the duties of their respective offices on the first Monday in January following such election. All laws pertaining to the nomination of candidates, registration of voters and all other things incident to the holding of the regular biennial election shall be enforced and be effected the same number of days before the first Tuesday after the first Monday in November that they have heretofore been before the first Monday in June biennially, except as may hereafter be provided by law. [Constitution of 1859; Amendment proposed by H.J.R. 7, 1907, and adopted by the people June 1, 1908]

Section 14a. Time of holding elections in incorporated cities and towns. Incorporated cities and towns shall hold their nominating and regular elections for their several elective officers at the same time that the primary and general biennial elections for State and county officers are held, and the election precincts and officers shall be the same for all elections held at the same time. All provisions of the charters and ordinances of incorporated cities and towns pertaining to the holding of elections shall continue in full force and effect except so far as they relate to the time of holding such elections. Every officer who, at the time of the adoption of this amendment, is the duly qualified incumbent of an elective office of an incorporated city or town shall hold his office for the term for which he was elected and until his successor is elected and qualified. The Legislature, and cities and towns, shall enact such supplementary legislation as may be necessary to carry the provisions of this amendment into effect. [Created through H.J.R. 22, 1917, and adopted by the people June 4, 1917]

Section 15. Method of voting in legislature. In all elections by the Legislative Assembly, or by either branch thereof, votes shall be given openly or viva voce, and not by ballot, forever; and in all elections by the people, votes shall be given openly, or viva voce, until the Legislative Assembly shall otherwise direct.—

Section 16. Election by plurality; proportional representation. In all elections authorized by this constitution until otherwise provided by law, the person or persons receiving the highest number of votes shall be declared elected, but provision may be made by law for elections by equal proportional representation of all the voters for every office which is filled by the election of two or more persons whose official duties, rights and powers are equal and concurrent. Every qualified elector resident in his precinct and registered as may be required by law, may vote for one person under the title for each office. Provision may be made by law for the voter's direct or indirect expression of his first, second or additional choices among the candidates for any office. For an office which is filled by the election of one person it may be required by law that the person elected shall be the final choice of a majority of the electors voting for candidates for that office. These principles may be applied by law to nominations by political parties and organizations. [Constitution of 1859; Amendment proposed by initiative petition filed Jan. 29, 1908, and adopted by the people June 1, 1908]

Section 17. Place of voting. All qualified electors shall vote in the election precinct in the County where they may reside, for County Officers, and in any County in the State for State Officers, or in any County of a Congressional

District in which such electors may reside, for Members of Congress.—

Section 18. Recall; meaning of words "the legislative assembly shall provide." (1) Every public officer in Oregon is subject, as herein provided, to recall by the electors of the state or of the electoral district from which the public officer is elected.

(2) Fifteen per cent, but not more, of the number of electors who voted for Governor in the officer's electoral district at the most recent election at which a candidate for Governor was elected to a full term, may be required to file their petition demanding the officer's recall by the people.

(3) They shall set forth in the petition the reasons for the demand.

(4) If the public officer offers to resign, the resignation shall be accepted and take effect on the day it is offered, and the vacancy shall be filled as may be provided by law. If the public officer does not resign within five days after the petition is filed, a special election shall be ordered to be held within 35 days in the electoral district to determine whether the people will recall the officer.

(5) On the ballot at the election shall be printed in not more than 200 words the reasons for demanding the recall of the officer as set forth in the recall petition, and, in not more than 200 words, the officer's justification of the officer's course in office. The officer shall continue to perform the duties of office until the result of the special election is officially declared. If an officer is recalled from any public office the vacancy shall be filled immediately in the manner provided by law for filling a vacancy in that office arising from any other cause.

(6) The recall petition shall be filed with the officer with whom a petition for nomination to such office should be filed, and the same officer shall order the special election when it is required. No such petition shall be circulated against any officer until the officer has actually held the office six months, save and except that it may be filed against a senator or representative in the legislative assembly at any time after five days from the beginning of the first session after the election of the senator or representative.

(7) After one such petition and special election, no further recall petition shall be filed against the same officer during the term for which the officer was elected unless such further petitioners first pay into the public treasury which has paid such special election expenses, the whole amount of its expenses for the preceding special election.

(8) Such additional legislation as may aid the operation of this section shall be provided by the legislative assembly, including provision for payment by the public treasury of the reasonable special election campaign expenses of such officer. But the words, "the legislative assembly shall provide," or any similar or equivalent words in this constitution or any amendment thereto, shall not be construed to grant to the legislative assembly any exclusive power of lawmaking nor in any way to limit the initiative and referendum powers reserved by the people. [Created through initiative petition filed Jan. 29, 1908, and adopted by the people June 1, 1908; Amendment proposed by S.J.R. 16, 1925, and adopted by the people Nov. 2, 1926; Amendment proposed by H.J.R. 1, 1983, and adopted by the people Nov. 6, 1984]

Note: "Recall." constituted the leadline to section 18 and was a part of the measure submitted to the people by S.J.R. 16, 1925.

Note: An initiative petition (Measure No. 3, 1992) proposed adding new sections relating to term limits to the Oregon Constitution. Those sections, appearing as sections 19, 20 and 21 of Article II in previous editions of this Constitution, were declared void for not being enacted in compliance with section 1, Article XVII of this Constitution. See Lehman v. Bradbury, 333 Or. 231, 37 P.3d 989 (2002).

Section 22. Political campaign contribution limitations. Section (1) For purposes of campaigning for an elected public office, a candidate may use or direct only contributions which originate from individuals who at the time of their donation were residents of the electoral district of the public office sought by the candidate, unless the contribution consists of volunteer time, information provided to the candidate, or funding provided by federal, state, or local government for purposes of campaigning for an elected public office.

Section (2) Where more than ten percent (10%) of a candidate's total campaign funding is in violation of Section (1), and the candidate is subsequently elected, the elected official shall forfeit the office and shall not hold a subsequent elected public office for a period equal to twice the tenure of the office sought. Where more than ten percent (10%) of a candidate's total campaign funding is in violation of Section (1) and the candidate is not elected, the unelected candidate shall not hold a subsequent elected public office for a period equal to twice the tenure of the office sought.

Section (3) A qualified donor (an individual who is a resident within the electoral district of the office sought by the candidate) shall not contribute to a candidate's campaign any restricted contributions of Section (1) received from an unqualified donor for the purpose of contributing to a candidate's campaign for elected public office. An unqualified donor (an entity which is not an individual and who is not a resident of the electoral district of the office sought by the candidate) shall not give any restricted contributions of Section (1) to a qualified donor for the purpose of contributing to a candidate's campaign for elected public office.

Section (4) A violation of Section (3) shall be an unclassified felony. [Created through initiative petition filed Jan. 25, 1993, and adopted by the people Nov. 8, 1994]

Note: An initiative petition (Measure No. 6, 1994) adopted by the people Nov. 8, 1994, proposed a constitutional amendment as an unnumbered section. Section 22 sections (1), (2), (3) and (4) were designated in the proposed amendment as "SECTION 1.," "SECTION 2.," "SECTION 3." and "SECTION 4.," respectively.

Section 23. Approval by more than majority required for certain measures submitted to people. (1) Any measure that includes any proposed requirement for more than a majority of votes cast by the electorate to approve any change in law or government action shall become effective only if approved by at least the same percentage of voters specified in the proposed voting requirement.

(2) For the purposes of this section, "measure" includes all initiatives and all measures referred to the voters by the Legislative Assembly.

(3) The requirements of this section apply to all measures presented to the voters at the November 3, 1998 election and thereafter.

(4) The purpose of this section is to prevent greater-than-majority voting requirements from being imposed by only a majority of the voters. [Created through initiative petition filed Jan. 15, 1998, and adopted by the people Nov. 3, 1998]

Note: Added as unnumbered section to the Constitution but not to any Article therein by initiative petition (Measure No. 63, 1998) adopted by the people Nov. 3, 1998.

Note: An initiative petition (Measure No. 62, 1998) proposed adding new sections and a subsection relating to political campaigns to the Oregon Constitution. Those sections, appearing as sections 24 to 32 of Article II and sections 1 (6), 1b and 1c of Article IV in previous editions of this Constitution, were declared void for not being enacted in compliance with section 1, Article XVII of this Constitution. See Swett v. Bradbury, 333 Or. 597, 43 P.3d 1094 (2002).

Section 24. Death of candidate prior to election. When any vacancy occurs in the nomination of a candidate for elective public office in this state, and the vacancy is due to the death of the candidate, the Legislative Assembly may provide by law that:

(1) The regularly scheduled election for that public office may be postponed;

(2) The public office may be filled at a subsequent election; and

(3) Votes cast for candidates for the public office at the regularly scheduled election may not be considered. [Created through S.J.R. 19, 2003, and adopted by the people Nov. 2, 2004]

ARTICLE III
DISTRIBUTION OF POWERS

Sec. 1. Separation of powers
 2. Budgetary control over executive and administrative officers and agencies
 3. Joint legislative committee to allocate emergency fund appropriations and to authorize expenditures beyond budgetary limits
 4. Senate, confirmation of executive appointments

Section 1. Separation of powers. The powers of the Government shall be divided into three separate branches, the Legislative, the Executive, including the administrative, and the Judicial; and no person charged with official duties under one of these branches, shall exercise any of the functions of another, except as in this Constitution expressly provided. [Constitution of 1859; Amendment proposed by H.J.R. 44, 2011, and adopted by the people Nov. 6, 2012]

Section 2. Budgetary control over executive and administrative officers and agencies. The Legislative Assembly shall have power to establish an agency to exercise budgetary control over all executive and administrative state officers, departments, boards, commissions and agencies of the State Government. [Created through S.J.R. 24, 1951, and adopted by the people Nov. 4, 1952]

Note: Section 2 was designated as "Sec. 1" by S.J.R. 24, 1951, and adopted by the people Nov. 4, 1952.

Section 3. Joint legislative committee to allocate emergency fund appropriations and to authorize expenditures beyond budgetary limits. (1) The Legislative Assembly is authorized to establish by law a joint committee composed of members of both houses of the Legislative Assembly, the membership to be as fixed by law, which committee may exercise, during the interim between sessions of the Legislative Assembly, such of the following powers as may be conferred upon it by law:

(a) Where an emergency exists, to allocate to any state agency, out of any emergency fund that may be appropriated to the committee for that purpose, additional funds beyond the amount appropriated to the agency by the Legislative Assembly, or funds to carry on an activity required by law for which an appropriation was not made.

(b) Where an emergency exists, to authorize any state agency to expend, from funds dedicated or continuously appropriated for the uses and purposes of the agency, sums in excess of the amount of the budget of the agency as approved in accordance with law.

(c) In the case of a new activity coming into existence at such a time as to preclude the possibility of submitting a budget to the Legislative Assembly for approval, to approve, or revise and approve, a budget of the money appropriated for such new activity.

(d) Where an emergency exists, to revise or amend the budgets of state agencies to the extent of authorizing transfers between expenditure classifications within the budget of an agency.

(2) The Legislative Assembly shall prescribe by law what shall constitute an emergency for the purposes of this section.

(3) As used in this section, "state agency" means any elected or appointed officer, board, commission, department, institution, branch or other agency of the state government.

(4) The term of members of the joint committee established pursuant to this section shall run from the adjournment of one odd-numbered year regular session to the organization of the next odd-numbered year regular session. No member of a committee shall cease to be such member solely by reason of the expiration of his term of office as a member of the Legislative Assembly. [Created through S.J.R. 24, 1951, and adopted by the people Nov. 4, 1952; Amendment proposed by S.J.R. 41, 2010, and adopted by the people Nov. 2, 2010]

Note: Section 3 was designated as "Sec. 2" by S.J.R. 24, 1951, and adopted by the people Nov. 4, 1952.

Section 4. Senate confirmation of executive appointments. (1) The Legislative Assembly in the manner provided by law may require that all appointments and reappointments to state public office made by the Governor shall be subject to confirmation by the Senate.

(2) The appointee shall not be eligible to serve until confirmed in the manner required by law and if not confirmed in that manner, shall not be eligible to serve in the public office.

(3) In addition to appointive offices, the provisions of this section shall apply to any state elective office when the Governor is authorized by law or this Constitution to fill any vacancy therein, except the office of judge of any court, United States Senator or Representative and a district, county or precinct office. [Created through S.J.R. 20, 1977, and adopted by the people Nov. 7, 1978]

ARTICLE IV
LEGISLATIVE BRANCH

Sec. 1. Legislative power; initiative and referendum
 1b. Payment for signatures
 2. Number of Senators and Representatives
 3. How Senators and Representatives chosen; filling vacancies; qualifications
 4. Term of office of legislators; classification of Senators
 6. Apportionment of Senators and Representatives; operative date
 7. Senatorial districts; senatorial and representative subdistricts
 8. Qualification of Senators and Representatives; effect of felony conviction
 9. Legislators free from arrest and not subject to civil process in certain cases; words uttered in debate
 10. Annual regular sessions of the Legislative Assembly; organizational session; extensions of regular sessions
 10a. Emergency sessions of the Legislative Assembly
 11. Legislative officers; rules of proceedings; adjournments
 12. Quorum; failure to effect organization
 13. Journal; when yeas and nays to be entered
 14. Deliberations to be open; rules to implement requirement
 15. Punishment and expulsion of members
 16. Punishment of nonmembers
 17. General powers of Legislative Assembly
 18. Where bills to originate
 19. Reading of bills; vote on final passage
 20. Subject and title of Act
 21. Acts to be plainly worded
 22. Mode of revision and amendment
 23. Certain local and special laws prohibited
 24. Suit against state

Constitution

25. Majority necessary to pass bills and resolutions; special requirements for bills raising revenue; signatures of presiding officers required
26. Protest by member
27. All statutes public laws; exceptions
28. When Act takes effect
29. Compensation of members
30. Members not eligible to other offices
31. Oath of members
32. Income tax defined by federal law; review of tax laws required
33. Reduction of criminal sentences approved by initiative or referendum process

Section 1. Legislative power; initiative and referendum. (1) The legislative power of the state, except for the initiative and referendum powers reserved to the people, is vested in a Legislative Assembly, consisting of a Senate and a House of Representatives.

(2)(a) The people reserve to themselves the initiative power, which is to propose laws and amendments to the Constitution and enact or reject them at an election independently of the Legislative Assembly.

(b) An initiative law may be proposed only by a petition signed by a number of qualified voters equal to six percent of the total number of votes cast for all candidates for Governor at the election at which a Governor was elected for a term of four years next preceding the filing of the petition.

(c) An initiative amendment to the Constitution may be proposed only by a petition signed by a number of qualified voters equal to eight percent of the total number of votes cast for all candidates for Governor at the election at which a Governor was elected for a term of four years next preceding the filing of the petition.

(d) An initiative petition shall include the full text of the proposed law or amendment to the Constitution. A proposed law or amendment to the Constitution shall embrace one subject only and matters properly connected therewith.

(e) An initiative petition shall be filed not less than four months before the election at which the proposed law or amendment to the Constitution is to be voted upon.

(3)(a) The people reserve to themselves the referendum power, which is to approve or reject at an election any Act, or part thereof, of the Legislative Assembly that does not become effective earlier than 90 days after the end of the session at which the Act is passed.

(b) A referendum on an Act or part thereof may be ordered by a petition signed by a number of qualified voters equal to four percent of the total number of votes cast for all candidates for Governor at the election at which a Governor was elected for a term of four years preceding the filing of the petition. A referendum petition shall be filed not more than 90 days after the end of the session at which the Act is passed.

(c) A referendum on an Act may be ordered by the Legislative Assembly by law. Notwithstanding section 15b, Article V of this Constitution, bills ordering a referendum and bills on which a referendum is ordered are not subject to veto by the Governor.

(4)(a) Petitions or orders for the initiative or referendum shall be filed with the Secretary of State. The Legislative Assembly shall provide by law for the manner in which the Secretary of State shall determine whether a petition contains the required number of signatures of qualified voters. The Secretary of State shall complete the verification process within the 30-day period after the last day on which the petition may be filed as provided in paragraph (e) of subsection (2) or paragraph (b) of subsection (3) of this section.

(b) Initiative and referendum measures shall be submitted to the people as provided in this section and by law not inconsistent therewith.

(c) All elections on initiative and referendum measures shall be held at the regular general elections, unless otherwise ordered by the Legislative Assembly.

(d) Notwithstanding section 1, Article XVII of this Constitution, an initiative or referendum measure becomes effective 30 days after the day on which it is enacted and approved by a majority of the votes cast thereon. A referendum ordered by petition on a part of an Act does not delay the remainder of the Act from becoming effective.

(5) The initiative and referendum powers reserved to the people by subsections (2) and (3) of this section are further reserved to the qualified voters of each municipality and district as to all local, special and municipal legislation of every character in or for their municipality or district. The manner of exercising those powers shall be provided by general laws, but cities may provide the manner of exercising those powers as to their municipal legislation. In a city, not more than 15 percent of the qualified voters may be required to propose legislation by the initiative, and not more than 10 percent of the qualified voters may be required to order a referendum on legislation. [Created through H.J.R. 16, 1967, and adopted by the people May 28, 1968 (this section adopted in lieu of former sections 1 and 1a of this Article); Amendment proposed by S.J.R. 27, 1985, and adopted by the people May 20, 1986; Amendment proposed by S.J.R. 3, 1999, and adopted by the people May 16, 2000]

Note: An initiative petition (Measure No. 62, 1998) proposed adding new sections and a subsection relating to political campaigns to the Oregon Constitution. Those sections, appearing as sections 24 to 32 of Article II and sections 1 (6), 1b and 1c of Article IV in previous editions of this Constitution, were declared void for not being enacted in compliance with section 1, Article XVII of this Constitution. See Swett v. Bradbury, 333 Or. 597, 43 P.3d 1094 (2002).

Section 1. Legislative authority vested in assembly; initiative and referendum; style of bills. [Constitution of 1859; Amendment proposed by H.J.R. 1, 1901, and adopted by the people June 2, 1902; Amendment proposed by S.J.R. 6, 1953, and adopted by the people Nov. 2, 1954; Repeal proposed by H.J.R. 16, 1967, and adopted by the people May 28, 1968 (present section 1 of this Article adopted in lieu of this section)]

Section 1a. Initiative and referendum on parts of laws and on local, special and municipal laws. [Created through initiative petition filed Feb. 3, 1906, and adopted by the people June 4, 1906; Repeal proposed by H.J.R. 16, 1967, and adopted by the people May 28, 1968 (present section 1 of this Article adopted in lieu of this section)]

Note: Section 1b as submitted to the people was preceded by the following: To protect the integrity of initiative and referendum petitions, the People of Oregon add the following provisions to the Constitution of the State of Oregon:

Section 1b. Payment for signatures. It shall be unlawful to pay or receive money or other thing of value based on the number of signatures obtained on an initiative or referendum petition. Nothing herein prohibits payment for signature gathering which is not based, either directly or indirectly, on the number of signatures obtained. [Created through initiative petition filed Nov. 7, 2001, and adopted by the people Nov. 5, 2002]

Note: Added as unnumbered section to the Constitution but not to any Article therein by initiative petition (Measure No. 26, 2002) adopted by the people Nov. 5, 2002.

Section 1d. Effective date of amendment to section 1, Article IV, by S.J.R. 3, 1999. [Created through S.J.R. 3, 1999, and adopted by the people May 16, 2000; Repealed Dec. 31, 2002, as specified in text of section adopted by the people May 16, 2000]

Section 2. Number of Senators and Representatives. The Senate shall consist of sixteen, and the House of

Representatives of thirty four members, which number shall not be increased until the year Eighteen Hundred and Sixty, after which time the Legislative Assembly may increase the number of Senators and Representatives, always keeping as near as may be the same ratio as to the number of Senators, and Representatives: Provided that the Senate shall never exceed thirty and the House of Representatives sixty members.—

Section 3. How Senators and Representatives chosen; filling vacancies; qualifications. (1) The senators and representatives shall be chosen by the electors of the respective counties or districts or subdistricts within a county or district into which the state may from time to time be divided by law.

(2)(a) If a vacancy occurs in the office of senator or representative from any county or district or subdistrict, the vacancy shall be filled as may be provided by law.

(b) Except as provided in paragraph (c) of this subsection, a person who is appointed to fill a vacancy in the office of senator or representative must be an inhabitant of the district the person is appointed to represent for at least one year next preceding the date of the appointment.

(c) For purposes of an appointment occurring during the period beginning on January 1 of the year a reapportionment becomes operative under section 6 of this Article, the person must have been an inhabitant of the district for one year next preceding the date of the appointment or from January 1 of the year the reapportionment becomes operative to the date of the appointment, whichever is less. [Constitution of 1859; Amendment proposed by S.J.R. 20, 1929, and adopted by the people Nov. 4, 1930; Amendment proposed by H.J.R. 20, 1953, and adopted by the people Nov. 2, 1954; Amendment proposed by S.J.R. 14, 1995, and adopted by the people May 16, 1995; Amendment proposed by H.J.R. 31, 2007, and adopted by the people Nov. 4, 2008]

Section 3a. Applicability of qualifications for appointment to legislative vacancy. [Section 3a was designated section 1b, which was created by S.J.R. 14, 1995, and adopted by the people May 16, 1995; Repealed Dec. 31, 1999, as specified in text of section adopted by the people May 16, 1995]

Section 4. Term of office of legislators; classification of Senators. (1) The Senators shall be elected for the term of four years, and Representatives for the term of two years. The term of each Senator and Representative shall commence on the second Monday in January following his election, and shall continue for the full period of four years or two years, as the case may be, unless a different commencing day for such terms shall have been appointed by law.

(2) The Senators shall continue to be divided into two classes, in accordance with the division by lot provided for under the former provisions of this Constitution, so that one-half, as nearly as possible, of the number of Senators shall be elected biennially.

(3) Any Senator or Representative whose term, under the former provisions of this section, would have expired on the first Monday in January 1961, shall continue in office until the second Monday in January 1961. [Constitution of 1859; Amendment proposed by S.J.R. 23, 1951, and adopted by the people Nov. 4, 1952; Amendment proposed by S.J.R. 28, 1959, and adopted by the people Nov. 8, 1960]

Section 5. Census. [Constitution of 1859; Repeal proposed by H.J.R. 16, 1971, and adopted by the people May 23, 1972]

Section 6. Apportionment of Senators and Representatives. [Constitution of 1859; Amendment proposed by initiative petition filed July 3, 1952, and adopted by the people Nov. 4, 1952; Repeal proposed by H.J.R. 6, 1985, and adopted by the people Nov. 4, 1986 (present section 6 of this Article adopted in lieu of this section)]

Section 6. Apportionment of Senators and Representatives; operative date. (1) At the odd-numbered year regular session of the Legislative Assembly next following an enumeration of the inhabitants by the United States Government, the number of Senators and Representatives shall be fixed by law and apportioned among legislative districts according to population. A senatorial district shall consist of two representative districts. Any Senator whose term continues through the next odd-numbered year regular legislative session after the operative date of the reapportionment shall be specifically assigned to a senatorial district. The ratio of Senators and Representatives, respectively, to population shall be determined by dividing the total population of the state by the number of Senators and by the number of Representatives. A reapportionment by the Legislative Assembly becomes operative as described in subsection (6) of this section.

(2) This subsection governs judicial review and correction of a reapportionment enacted by the Legislative Assembly.

(a) Original jurisdiction is vested in the Supreme Court, upon the petition of any elector of the state filed with the Supreme Court on or before August 1 of the year in which the Legislative Assembly enacts a reapportionment, to review any reapportionment so enacted.

(b) If the Supreme Court determines that the reapportionment thus reviewed complies with subsection (1) of this section and all law applicable thereto, it shall dismiss the petition by written opinion on or before September 1 of the same year and the reapportionment becomes operative as described in subsection (6) of this section.

(c) If the Supreme Court determines that the reapportionment does not comply with subsection (1) of this section and all law applicable thereto, the reapportionment shall be void. In its written opinion, the Supreme Court shall specify with particularity wherein the reapportionment fails to comply. The opinion shall further direct the Secretary of State to draft a reapportionment of the Senators and Representatives in accordance with the provisions of subsection (1) of this section and all law applicable thereto. The Supreme Court shall file its order with the Secretary of State on or before September 15. The Secretary of State shall conduct a hearing on the reapportionment at which the public may submit evidence, views and argument. The Secretary of State shall cause a transcription of the hearing to be prepared which, with the evidence, shall become part of the record. The Secretary of State shall file the corrected reapportionment with the Supreme Court on or before November 1 of the same year.

(d) On or before November 15, the Supreme Court shall review the corrected reapportionment to assure its compliance with subsection (1) of this section and all law applicable thereto and may further correct the reapportionment if the court considers correction to be necessary.

(e) The corrected reapportionment becomes operative as described in subsection (6) of this section.

(3) This subsection governs enactment, judicial review and correction of a reapportionment if the Legislative Assembly fails to enact any reapportionment by July 1 of the year of the odd-numbered year regular session of the Legislative Assembly next following an enumeration of the inhabitants by the United States Government.

(a) The Secretary of State shall make a reapportionment of the Senators and Representatives in accordance with the provisions of subsection (1) of this section and all law applicable thereto. The Secretary of State shall conduct a hearing on the reapportionment at which the public may submit evidence, views and argument. The Secretary of State shall cause a transcription of the hearing to be prepared which, with the evidence, shall become part of the record. The reapportionment so made shall be filed with the Supreme Court by August 15 of the same year. The reapportionment becomes operative as described in subsection (6) of this section.

(b) Original jurisdiction is vested in the Supreme Court upon the petition of any elector of the state filed with the Supreme Court on or before September 15 of the same year to review any reapportionment and the record made by the Secretary of State.

(c) If the Supreme Court determines that the reapportionment thus reviewed complies with subsection (1) of this section and all law applicable thereto, it shall dismiss the petition by written opinion on or before October 15 of the same year and the reapportionment becomes operative as described in subsection (6) of this section.

(d) If the Supreme Court determines that the reapportionment does not comply with subsection (1) of this section and all law applicable thereto, the reapportionment shall be void. The Supreme Court shall return the reapportionment by November 1 to the Secretary of State accompanied by a written opinion specifying with particularity wherein the reapportionment fails to comply. The opinion shall further direct the Secretary of State to correct the reapportionment in those particulars, and in no others, and file the corrected reapportionment with the Supreme Court on or before December 1 of the same year.

(e) On or before December 15, the Supreme Court shall review the corrected reapportionment to assure its compliance with subsection (1) of this section and all law applicable thereto and may further correct the reapportionment if the court considers correction to be necessary.

(f) The reapportionment becomes operative as described in subsection (6) of this section.

(4) Any reapportionment that becomes operative as provided in this section is a law of the state except for purposes of initiative and referendum.

(5) Notwithstanding section 18, Article II of this Constitution, after the convening of the next odd-numbered year regular legislative session following the reapportionment, a Senator whose term continues through that legislative session is subject to recall by the electors of the district to which the Senator is assigned and not by the electors of the district existing before the latest reapportionment. The number of signatures required on the recall petition is 15 percent of the total votes cast for all candidates for Governor at the most recent election at which a candidate for Governor was elected to a full term in the two representative districts comprising the senatorial district to which the Senator was assigned.

(6)(a) Except as provided in paragraph (b) of this subsection, a reapportionment made under this section becomes operative on the second Monday in January of the next odd-numbered year after the applicable deadline for making a final reapportionment under this section.

(b) For purposes of electing Senators and Representatives to the next term of office that commences after the applicable deadline for making a final reapportionment under this section, a reapportionment made under this section becomes operative on January 1 of the calendar year next following the applicable deadline for making a final reapportionment under this section. [Created through H.J.R. 6, 1985, and adopted by the people Nov. 4, 1986 (this section adopted in lieu of former section 6 of this Article); Amendment proposed by H.J.R. 31, 2007, and adopted by the people Nov. 4, 2008; Amendment proposed by S.J.R. 41, 2010, and adopted by the people Nov. 2, 2010]

Section 7. Senatorial districts; senatorial and representative subdistricts. A senatorial district, when more than one county shall constitute the same, shall be composed of contiguous counties, and no county shall be divided in creating such senatorial districts. Senatorial or representative districts comprising not more than one county may be divided into subdistricts from time to time by law. Subdistricts shall be composed of contiguous territory within the district; and the ratios to population of senators or representatives, as the case may be, elected from the subdistricts, shall be substantially equal within the district. [Constitution of 1859; Amendment proposed by H.J.R. 20, 1953, and adopted by the people Nov. 2, 1954]

Section 8. Qualification of Senators and Representatives; effect of felony conviction. (1)(a) Except as provided in paragraph (b) of this subsection, a person may not be a Senator or Representative if the person at the time of election:

(A) Is not a citizen of the United States; and

(B) Has not been for one year next preceding the election an inhabitant of the district from which the Senator or Representative may be chosen.

(b) For purposes of the general election next following the applicable deadline for making a final apportionment under section 6 of this Article, the person must have been an inhabitant of the district from January 1 of the year following the applicable deadline for making the final reapportionment to the date of the election.

(2) Senators and Representatives shall be at least twenty one years of age.

(3) A person may not be a Senator or Representative if the person has been convicted of a felony during:

(a) The term of office of the person as a Senator or Representative; or

(b) The period beginning on the date of the election at which the person was elected to the office of Senator or Representative and ending on the first day of the term of office to which the person was elected.

(4) A person is not eligible to be elected as a Senator or Representative if that person has been convicted of a felony and has not completed the sentence received for the conviction prior to the date that person would take office if elected. As used in this subsection, "sentence received for the conviction" includes a term of imprisonment, any period of probation or post-prison supervision and payment of a monetary obligation imposed as all or part of a sentence.

(5) Notwithstanding sections 11 and 15, Article IV of this Constitution:

(a) The office of a Senator or Representative convicted of a felony during the term to which the Senator or Representative was elected or appointed shall become vacant on the date the Senator or Representative is convicted.

(b) A person elected to the office of Senator or Representative and convicted of a felony during the period beginning on the date of the election and ending on the first day of the term of office to which the person was elected shall be ineligible to take office and the office shall become vacant on the first day of the next term of office.

(6) Subject to subsection (4) of this section, a person who is ineligible to be a Senator or Representative under subsection (3) of this section may:

(a) Be a Senator or Representative after the expiration of the term of office during which the person is ineligible; and

(b) Be a candidate for the office of Senator or Representative prior to the expiration of the term of office during which the person is ineligible.

(7)(a) Except as provided in paragraph (b) of this subsection, a person may not be a Senator or Representative if the person at all times during the term of office of the person as a Senator or Representative is not an inhabitant of the district from which the Senator or Representative may be chosen or which the Senator or Representative has been appointed to represent. A person does not lose status as an inhabitant of a district if the person is absent from the district for purposes of business of the Legislative Assembly.

(b) Following the applicable deadline for making a final apportionment under section 6 of this Article, until the expiration of the term of office of the person, a person may be an inhabitant of any district. [Constitution of 1859; Amendment proposed by H.J.R. 6, 1985, and adopted by the people Nov. 4, 1986; Amendment proposed by S.J.R. 33, 1993, and adopted by the people Nov. 8, 1994; Amendment proposed by S.J.R. 14, 1995, and adopted by the people May 16, 1995; Amendment proposed by H.J.R. 31, 2007, and adopted by the people Nov. 4, 2008]

Section 8a. Applicability of qualification for legislative office. [Created by S.J.R. 14, 1995, and adopted by the people May 16, 1995; Repealed Dec. 31, 1999, as specified in text of section adopted by the people May 16, 1995]

Section 9. Legislators free from arrest and not subject to civil process in certain cases; words uttered in debate. Senators and Representatives in all cases, except for treason, felony, or breaches of the peace, shall be privileged from arrest during the session of the Legislative Assembly, and in going to and returning from the same; and shall not be subject to any civil process during the session of the Legislative Assembly, nor during the fifteen days next before the commencement thereof: Nor shall a member for words uttered in debate in either house, be questioned in any other place.—

Section 10. Annual regular sessions of the Legislative Assembly; organizational session; extension of regular sessions. (1) The Legislative Assembly shall hold annual sessions at the Capitol of the State. Each session must begin on the day designated by law as the first day of the session. Except as provided in subsection (3) of this section:

(a) A session beginning in an odd-numbered year may not exceed 160 calendar days in duration; and

(b) A session beginning in an even-numbered year may not exceed 35 calendar days in duration.

(2) The Legislative Assembly may hold an organizational session that is not subject to the limits of subsection (1) of this section for the purposes of introducing measures and performing the duties and effecting the organization described in sections 11 and 12 of this Article. The Legislative Assembly may not undertake final consideration of a measure or reconsideration of a measure following a gubernatorial veto when convened in an organizational session.

(3) A regular session, as described in subsection (1) of this section, may be extended for a period of five calendar days by the affirmative vote of two-thirds of the members of each house. A session may be extended more than once. An extension must begin on the first calendar day after the end of the immediately preceding session or extension except that if the first calendar day is a Sunday, the extension may begin on the next Monday. [Constitution of 1859; Amendment proposed by S.J.R. 41, 2010, and adopted by the people Nov. 2, 2010]

Section 10a. Emergency sessions of the Legislative Assembly. In the event of an emergency the Legislative Assembly shall be convened by the presiding officers of both Houses at the Capitol of the State at times other than required by section 10 of this Article upon the written request of the majority of the members of each House to commence within five days after receipt of the minimum requisite number of requests. [Created through H.J.R. 28, 1975, and adopted by the people Nov. 2, 1976]

Section 11. Legislative officers; rules of proceedings; adjournments. Each house when assembled, shall choose its own officers, judge of the election, qualifications, and returns of its own members; determine its own rules of proceeding, and sit upon its own adjournments; but neither house shall without the concurrence of the other, adjourn for more than three days, nor to any other place than that in which it may be sitting.—

Section 12. Quorum; failure to effect organization. Two thirds of each house shall constitute a quorum to do business, but a smaller number may meet; adjourn from day to day, and compel the attendance of absent members. A quorum being in attendance, if either house fail to effect an organization within the first five days thereafter, the members of the house so failing shall be entitled to no compensation from the end of the said five days until an organization shall have been effected.—

Section 13. Journal; when yeas and nays to be entered. Each house shall keep a journal of its proceedings.—The yeas and nays on any question, shall at the request of any two members, be entered, together with the names of the members demanding the same, on the journal; provided that on a motion to adjourn it shall require one tenth of the members present to order the yeas and nays.

Section 14. Deliberations to be open; rules to implement requirement. The deliberations of each house, of committees of each house or joint committees and of committees of the whole, shall be open. Each house shall adopt rules to implement the requirement of this section and the houses jointly shall adopt rules to implement the requirements of this section in any joint activity that the two houses may undertake. [Constitution of 1859; Amendment proposed by S.J.R. 36, 1973, and adopted by the people Nov. 5, 1974; Amendment proposed by H.J.R. 29, 1977, and adopted by the people May 23, 1978]

Section 15. Punishment and expulsion of members. Either house may punish its members for disorderly behavior, and may with the concurrence of two thirds, expel a member; but not a second time for the same cause.—

Section 16. Punishment of nonmembers. Either house, during its session, may punish by imprisonment, any person, not a member, who shall have been guilty of disrespect to the house by disorderly or contemptious [sic] behavior in its presence, but such imprisonment shall not at any time, exceed twenty [sic] twenty four hours.—

Section 17. General powers of Legislative Assembly. Each house shall have all powers necessary for a chamber of the Legislative Branch, of a free, and independent State. [Constitution of 1859; Amendment proposed by H.J.R. 44, 2011, and adopted by the people Nov. 6, 2012]

Section 18. Where bills to originate. Bills may originate in either house, but may be amended, or rejected in the other; except that bills for raising revenue shall originate in the House of Representatives.—

Section 19. Reading of bills; vote on final passage. Every bill shall be read by title only on three several days, in each house, unless in case of emergency two-thirds of the house where such bill may be pending shall, by a vote of yeas and nays, deem it expedient to dispense with this rule; provided, however, on its final passage such bill shall be read section by section unless such requirement be suspended by a vote of two-thirds of the house where such bill may be pending, and the vote on the final passage of every bill or joint resolution shall be taken by yeas and nays. [Constitution of 1859; Amendment proposed by S.J.R. 15, 1945, and adopted by the people Nov. 5, 1946]

Section 20. Subject and title of Act. Every Act shall embrace but one subject, and matters properly connected therewith, which subject shall be expressed in the title. But if any subject shall be embraced in an Act which shall not be expressed in the title, such Act shall be void only as to so much thereof as shall not be expressed in the title. This section shall not be construed to prevent the inclusion in an amendatory Act, under a proper title, of matters otherwise germane to the same general subject, although the title or titles of the original Act or Acts may not have been sufficiently broad to have permitted such matter to have been so included in such original Act or Acts, or any of them. [Constitution of 1859; Amendment proposed by S.J.R. 41, 1951, and adopted by the people Nov. 4, 1952]

Section 21. Acts to be plainly worded. Every act, and joint resolution shall be plainly worded, avoiding as far as practicable the use of technical terms.—

Section 22. Mode of revision and amendment. No act shall ever be revised, or amended by mere reference to its title, but the act revised, or section amended shall be set forth, and published at full length. However, if, at any session of the Legislative Assembly, there are enacted two or more acts amending the same section, each of the acts shall be given effect to the extent that the amendments do not conflict in purpose. If the amendments conflict in purpose, the act last signed by the Governor shall control. [Constitution of 1859; Amendment proposed by S.J.R. 28, 1975, and adopted by the people Nov. 2, 1976]

Section 23. Certain local and special laws prohibited. The Legislative Assembly, shall not pass special or local laws, in any of the following enumerated cases, that is to say:—

Regulating the jurisdiction, and duties of justices of the peace, and of constables;

For the punishment of Crimes, and Misdemeanors;

Regulating the practice in Courts of Justice;

Providing for changing the venue in civil, and Criminal cases;

Granting divorces;

Changing the names of persons;

For laying, opening, and working on highways, and for the election, or appointment of supervisors;

Vacating roads, Town plats, Streets, Alleys, and Public squares;

Summoning and empanneling [sic] grand, and petit jurors;

For the assessment and collection of Taxes, for State, County, Township, or road purposes;

Providing for supporting Common schools, and for the preservation of school funds;

In relation to interest on money;

Providing for opening, and conducting the elections of State, County, and Township officers, and designating the places of voting;

Providing for the sale of real estate, belonging to minors, or other persons laboring under legal disabilities, by executors, administrators, guardians, or trustees.—

Section 24. Suit against state. Provision may be made by general law, for bringing suit against the State, as to all liabilities originating after, or existing at the time of the adoption of this Constitution; but no special act authorizeing [sic] such suit to be brought, or making compensation to any person claiming damages against the State, shall ever be passed.—

Section 25. Majority necessary to pass bills and resolutions; special requirements for bills raising revenue; signatures of presiding officers required. (1) Except as otherwise provided in subsection (2) of this section, a majority of all the members elected to each House shall be necessary to pass every bill or Joint resolution.

(2) Three-fifths of all members elected to each House shall be necessary to pass bills for raising revenue.

(3) All bills, and Joint resolutions passed, shall be signed by the presiding officers of the respective houses.

[Constitution of 1859; Amendment proposed by H.J.R. 14, 1995, and adopted by the people May 21, 1996]

Section 26. Protest by member. Any member of either house, shall have the right to protest, and have his protest, with his reasons for dissent, entered on the journal.—

Section 27. All statutes public laws; exceptions. Every Statute shall be a public law, unless otherwise declared in the Statute itself.—

Section 28. When Act takes effect. No act shall take effect, until ninety days from the end of the session at which the same shall have been passed, except in case of emergency; which emergency shall be declared in the preamble, or in the body of the law.

Section 29. Compensation of members. The members of the Legislative Assembly shall receive for their services a salary to be established and paid in the same manner as the salaries of other elected state officers and employes. [Constitution of 1859; Amendment proposed by S.J.R. 3, 1941, and adopted by the people Nov. 3, 1942; Amendment proposed by H.J.R. 5, 1949, and adopted by the people Nov. 7, 1950; Amendment proposed by H.J.R. 8, 1961, and adopted by the people May 18, 1962]

Section 30. Members not eligible to other offices. No Senator or Representative shall, during the time for which he may have been elected, be eligible to any office the election to which is vested in the Legislative Assembly; nor shall be appointed to any civil office of profit which shall have been created, or the emoluments of which shall have been increased during such term; but this latter provision shall not be construed to apply to any officer elective by the people.—

Section 31. Oath of members. The members of the Legislative Assembly shall before they enter on the duties of their respective offices, take and subscribe the following oath or affirmation;—I do solemnly swear (or affirm as the case may be) that I will support the Constitution of the United States, and the Constitution of the State of Oregon, and that I will faithfully discharge the duties of Senator (or Representative as the case may be) according to the best of my Ability, And such oath may be administered by the Govenor [sic], Secretary of State, or a judge of the Supreme Court.—

Section 32. Income tax defined by federal law; review of tax laws required. Notwithstanding any other provision of this Constitution, the Legislative Assembly, in any law imposing a tax or taxes on, in respect to or measured by income, may define the income on, in respect to or by which such tax or taxes are imposed or measured, by reference to any provision of the laws of the United States as the same may be or become effective at any time or from time to time, and may prescribe exceptions or modifications to any such provisions. At each regular session the Legislative Assembly shall, and at any special session may, provide for a review of the Oregon laws imposing a tax upon or measured by income, but no such laws shall be amended or repealed except by a legislative Act. [Created through H.J.R. 3, 1969, and adopted by the people Nov. 3, 1970]

Section 33. Reduction of criminal sentences approved by initiative or referendum process. Notwithstanding the provisions of section 25 of this Article, a two-thirds vote of all the members elected to each house shall be necessary to pass a bill that reduces a criminal sentence approved by the people under section 1 of this Article. [Created through initiative petition filed Nov. 16, 1993, and adopted by the people Nov. 8, 1994]

ARTICLE V
EXECUTIVE BRANCH

Section 1. Governor as chief executive; term of office; period of eligibility. The cheif [sic] executive power of the State, shall be vested in a Governor, who shall hold his office for the term of four years; and no person shall be eligible to such office more than Eight, in any period of twelve years.—

Section 2. Qualifications of Governor. No person except a citizen of the United States, shall be eligible to the Office of Governor, nor shall any person be eligible to that office who shall not have attained the age of thirty years, and who shall not have been three years next preceding his election, a resident within this State. The minimum age requirement of this section does not apply to a person who succeeds to the office of Governor under section 8a of this Article. [Constitution of 1859; Amendment proposed by H.J.R. 52, 1973, and adopted by the people Nov. 5, 1974]

Section 3. Who not eligible. No member of Congress, or person holding any office under the United States, or under this State, or under any other power, shall fill the Office of Governor, except as may be otherwise provided in this Constitution.—

Section 4. Election of Governor. The Governor shall be elected by the qualified Electors of the State at the times, and places of choosing members of the Legislative Assembly; and the returns of every Election for Governor, shall be sealed up, and transmitted to the Secretary of State; directed to the Speaker of the House of Representatives, who shall open, and publish them in the presence of both houses of the Legislative Assembly.—

Section 5. Greatest number of votes decisive; election by legislature in case of tie. The person having the highest number of votes for Governor, shall be elected; but in case two or more persons shall have an equal and the highest number of votes for Governor, the two houses of the Legislative Assembly at the next regular session thereof, shall forthwith by joint vote, proceed to elect one of the said persons Governor.—

Section 6. Contested elections. Contested Elections for Governor shall be determined by the Legislative Assembly in such manner as may be prescribed by law.—

Section 7. Term of office. The official term of the Governor shall be four years; and shall commence at such times as may be prescribed by this constitution, or prescribed by law.—

Section 8. Vacancy in office of Governor. [Constitution of 1859; Amendment proposed by S.J.R. 10, 1920 (s.s.), and adopted by the people May 21, 1920; Amendment proposed by S.J.R. 8, 1945, and adopted by the people Nov. 5, 1946; Repeal proposed by initiative petition filed July 7, 1972, and adopted by the people Nov. 7, 1972 (present section 8a of this Article adopted in lieu of this section)]

Section 8a. Vacancy in office of Governor. In case of the removal from office of the Governor, or of his death, resignation, or disability to discharge the duties of his office as prescribed by law, the Secretary of State; or if there be none, or in case of his removal from office, death, resignation, or disability to discharge the duties of his office as prescribed by law, then the State Treasurer; or if there be none, or in case of his removal from office, death, resignation, or disability to discharge the duties of his office as prescribed by law, then the President of the Senate; or if there be none, or in case of his removal from office, death, resignation, or disability to discharge the duties of his office as prescribed by law, then the Speaker of the House of Representatives, shall become Governor until the disability be removed, or a Governor be elected at the next general biennial election. The Governor elected to fill the vacancy shall hold office for the unexpired term of the outgoing Governor. The Secretary of State or the State Treasurer shall appoint a person to fill his office until the election of a Governor, at which time the office so filled by appointment shall be filled by election; or, in the event of a disability of the Governor, to be Acting Secretary of State or Acting State Treasurer until the disability be removed. The person so appointed shall not be eligible to succeed to the office of Governor by automatic succession under this section during the term of his appointment. [Created through initiative petition filed July 7, 1972, and adopted by the people Nov. 7, 1972 (this section adopted in lieu of former section 8 of this Article)]

Section 9. Governor as commander in chief of state military forces. The Governor shall be commander in cheif [sic] of the military, and naval forces of this State, and may call out such forces to execute the laws, to suppress insurection [sic], or to repel invasion.

Section 10. Governor to see laws executed. He shall take care that the Laws be faithfully executed.—

Section 11. Recommendations to legislature. He shall from time to time give to the Legislative Assembly information touching the condition of the State, and reccomend [sic] such measures as he shall judge to be expedient[.]

Section 12. Governor may convene legislature. He may on extraordinary occasions convene the Legislative Assembly by proclamation, and shall state to both houses when assembled, the purpose for which they shall have been convened.—

Section 13. Transaction of governmental business. He shall transact all necessary business with the officers of government, and may require information in writing from the offices of the Administrative, and Military Departments upon any subject relating to the duties of their respective offices.—

Section 14. Reprieves, commutations and pardons; remission of fines and forfeitures. He shall have power to grant reprieves, commutations, and pardons, after conviction, for all offences [sic] except treason, subject to such regulations as may be provided by law. Upon conviction for treason he shall have power to suspend the execution of the sentence until the case shall be reported to the Legislative Assembly, at its next meeting, when the Legislative Assembly shall either grant a pardon, commute the sentence, direct the execution of the sentence, or grant a farther [sic] reprieve.—

He shall have power to remit fines, and forfeitures, under such regulations as may be prescribed by law; and shall report to the Legislative Assembly at its next meeting each case of reprieve, commutation, or pardon granted, and the reasons for granting the same; and also the names of all persons in whose favor remission of fines, and forfeitures shall have been made, and the several amounts remitted[.]

Section 15. [This section of the Constitution of 1859 redesignated as section 15b by the amendment proposed by S.J.R. 12, 1915, and adopted by the people Nov. 7, 1916]

Section 15a. Single item and emergency clause veto. The Governor shall have power to veto single items in appropriation bills, and any provision in new bills declaring an emergency, without thereby affecting any other provision of such bill. [Created through S.J.R. 12, 1915, and adopted by the people Nov. 7, 1916; Amendment proposed by S.J.R. 13, 1921, and adopted by the people June 7, 1921]

Section 15b. Legislative enactments; approval by Governor; notice of intention to disapprove; disapproval and reconsideration by legislature; failure of Governor to return bill. (1) Every bill which shall have passed the Legislative Assembly shall, before it becomes a law, be presented to the Governor; if the Governor approve, the Governor shall sign it; but if not, the Governor shall return it with written objections to that house in which it shall have originated, which house shall enter the objections at large upon the journal and proceed to reconsider it.

(2) If, after such reconsideration, two-thirds of the members present shall agree to pass the bill, it shall be sent, together with the objections, to the other house, by which it shall likewise be reconsidered, and, if approved by two-thirds of the members present, it shall become a law. But in all such cases, the votes of both houses shall be determined by yeas and nays, and the names of the members voting for or against the bill shall be entered on the journal of each house respectively.

(3) If any bill shall not be returned by the Governor within five days (Saturdays and Sundays excepted) after it shall have been presented to the Governor, it shall be a law without signature, unless the general adjournment shall prevent its return, in which case it shall be a law, unless the Governor within thirty days next after the adjournment (Saturdays and Sundays excepted) shall file such bill, with written objections thereto, in the office of the Secretary of State, who shall lay the same before the Legislative Assembly at its next session in like manner as if it had been returned by the Governor.

(4) Before filing a bill after adjournment with written objections, the Governor must announce publicly the possible intention to do so at least five days before filing the bill with written objections. However, nothing in this subsection requires the Governor to file any bill with objections because of the announcement. [Created through S.J.R. 12, 1915, and adopted by the people Nov. 7, 1916; Amendment proposed by H.J.R. 9, 1937, and adopted by the people Nov. 8, 1938; Amendment proposed by S.J.R. 4, 1987, and adopted by the people Nov. 8, 1988]

Note: See note at section 15, Article V.

Section 16. Governor to Fill Vacancies by Appointment. When during a recess of the legislative assembly a vacancy occurs in any office, the appointment to which is vested in the legislative assembly, or when at any time a vacancy occurs in any other state office, or in the office of judge of any court, the governor shall fill such vacancy by appointment, which shall expire when a successor has been elected and qualified. When any vacancy occurs in any elective office of the state or of any district

or county thereof, the vacancy shall be filled at the next general election, provided such vacancy occurs more than sixty-one (61) days prior to such general election. [Constitution of 1859; Amendment proposed by H.J.R. 5, 1925, and adopted by the people Nov. 2, 1926; Amendment proposed by H.J.R. 30, 1985, and adopted by the people May 20, 1986; Amendment proposed by S.J.R. 4, 1993, and adopted by the people Nov. 8, 1994]

Note: The leadline to section 16 was a part of the measure submitted to the people by H.J.R. 5, 1925.

Section 17. Governor to issue writs of election to fill vacancies in legislature. He shall issue writs of Election to fill such vacancies as may have occured [sic] in the Legislative Assembly.

Section 18. Commissions. All commissions shall issue in the name of the State; shall be signed by the Govenor [sic], sealed with the seal of the State, and attested by the Secretary of State.—

ARTICLE VI
ADMINISTRATIVE DEPARTMENT

Section 1. Election of Secretary and Treasurer of state; terms of office; period of eligibility. There shall be elected by the qualified electors of the State, at the times and places of choosing Members of the Legislative Assembly, a Secretary, and Treasurer of State, who shall severally hold their offices for the term of four years; but no person shall be eligible to either of said offices more than Eight in any period of Twelve years.—

Section 2. Duties of Secretary of State. The Secretary of State shall keep a fair record of the official acts of the Legislative Assembly, and Executive Branch; and shall when required lay the same, and all matters relative thereto before either chamber of the Legislative Assembly. The Secretary of State shall be by virtue of holding the office, Auditor of Public Accounts, and shall perform such other duties as shall be assigned to the Secretary of State by law. [Constitution of 1859; Amendment proposed by H.J.R. 44, 2011, and adopted by the people Nov. 6, 2012]

Section 3. Seal of state. There shall be a seal of State, kept by the Secretary of State for official purposes, which shall be called "The seal of the State of Oregon".—

Section 4. Powers and duties of Treasurer. The powers, and duties of the Treasurer of State shall be such as may be prescribed by law.—

Section 5. Offices and records of executive officers. The Governor, Secretary of State, and Treasurer of State shall severally keep the public records, books and papers at the seat of government in any manner relating to their respective offices. [Constitution of 1859; Amendment proposed by S.J.R. 13, 1985, and adopted by the people Nov. 4, 1986]

Section 6. County Officers: There shall be elected in each county by the qualified electors thereof at the time of holding general elections, a county clerk, treasurer and sheriff who shall severally hold their offices for the term of four years. [Constitution of 1859; Amendment proposed by initiative petition filed June 9, 1920, and adopted by the people Nov. 2, 1920; Amendment proposed by H.J.R. 7, 1955, and adopted by the people Nov. 6, 1956]

Note: The leadline to section 6 was a part of the measure proposed by initiative petition filed June 9, 1920, and adopted by the people Nov. 2, 1920.

Section 7. Other officers. Such other county, township, precinct, and City officers as may be necessary, shall be elected, or appointed in such manner as may be prescribed by law.—

Section 8. County officers' qualifications; location of offices of county and city officers; duties of such officers. Every county officer shall be an elector of the county, and the county assessor, county sheriff, county coroner and county surveyor shall possess such other qualifications as may be prescribed by law. All county and city officers shall keep their respective offices at such places therein, and perform such duties, as may be prescribed by law. [Constitution of 1859; Amendment proposed by H.J.R. 7, 1955, and adopted by the people Nov. 6, 1956; Amendment proposed by H.J.R. 42, 1971, and adopted by the people Nov. 7, 1972; Amendment proposed by H.J.R. 22, 1973, and adopted by the people Nov. 5, 1974]

Section 9. Vacancies in county, township, precinct and city offices. Vacancies in County, Township, precinct and City offices shall be filled in such manner as may be prescribed by law.—

Section 9a. County manager form of government. [Created through H.J.R. 3, 1943, and adopted by the people Nov. 7, 1944; Repeal proposed by H.J.R. 22, 1957, and adopted by the people Nov. 4, 1958]

Section 10. County home rule under county charter. The Legislative Assembly shall provide by law a method whereby the legal voters of any county, by majority vote of such voters voting thereon at any legally called election, may adopt, amend, revise or repeal a county charter. A county charter may provide for the exercise by the county of authority over matters of county concern. Local improvements shall be financed only by taxes, assessments or charges imposed on benefited property, unless otherwise provided by law or charter. A county charter shall prescribe the organization of the county government and shall provide directly, or by its authority, for the number, election or appointment, qualifications, tenure, compensation, powers and duties of such officers as the county deems necessary. Such officers shall among them exercise all the powers and perform all the duties, as distributed by the county charter or by its authority, now or hereafter, by the Constitution or laws of this state, granted to or imposed upon any county officer. Except as expressly provided by general law, a county charter shall not affect the selection, tenure, compensation, powers or duties prescribed by law for judges in their judicial capacity, or for justices of the peace or for district attorneys. The initiative and referendum powers reserved to the people by this Constitution hereby are further reserved to the legal voters of every county relative to the adoption, amendment, revision or repeal of a county charter and to legislation passed by counties which have adopted such a charter; and no county shall require that referendum petitions be filed less than 90 days after the provisions of the charter or the legislation proposed for referral is adopted by the county governing body. To be circulated, referendum or initiative petitions shall set forth in full the charter or legislative provisions proposed for adoption or referral. Referendum petitions shall not be required to include a ballot title to be circulated. In a county a number of signatures of qualified voters equal to but not greater than four percent of the total number of all votes cast in the county for all candidates for Governor at the election at which a Governor was elected for a term of four years next preceding the filing of the petition shall be required for a petition to order a referendum on county legislation or a part thereof. A number of signatures equal to but not greater than six percent of the total number of votes cast in the county for all candidates for Governor at the election at which a Governor was elected for a term of four years next preceding the filing of the petition shall be required for a petition to propose an initiative ordinance. A number of signatures equal to but not greater than eight percent of the total number of votes cast in the county for all candidates for Governor at the election at which a Governor was elected for a term of four years next preceding the filing of the petition shall be required for a petition to propose a charter amendment. [Created through H.J.R. 22, 1957, and adopted by the people Nov. 4, 1958; Amendment proposed by S.J.R. 48, 1959, and adopted by the people Nov. 8, 1960; Amendment proposed by H.J.R. 21, 1977, and adopted by the people May 23, 1978]

ARTICLE VII (Amended)
THE JUDICIAL BRANCH

Section 1. Courts; election of judges; term of office; compensation. The judicial power of the state shall be vested in one supreme court and in such other courts as may from time to time be created by law. The judges of the supreme and other courts shall be elected by the legal voters of the state or of their respective districts for a term of six years, and shall receive such compensation as may be provided by law, which compensation shall not be diminished during the term for which they are elected. [Created through initiative petition filed July 7, 1910, and adopted by the people Nov. 8, 1910]

Section 1a. Retirement of judges; recall to temporary active service. Notwithstanding the provisions of section 1, Article VII (Amended) of this Constitution, a judge of any court shall retire from judicial office at the end of the calendar year in which he attains the age of 75 years. The Legislative Assembly or the people may by law:

(1) Fix a lesser age for mandatory retirement not earlier than the end of the calendar year in which the judge attains the age of 70 years;

(2) Provide for recalling retired judges to temporary active service on the court from which they are retired; and

(3) Authorize or require the retirement of judges for physical or mental disability or any other cause rendering judges incapable of performing their judicial duties. This section shall not affect the term to which any judge shall have been elected or appointed prior to or at the time of approval and ratification of this section. [Created through S.J.R. 3, 1959, and adopted by the people Nov. 8, 1960]

Section 2. Amendment's effect on courts, jurisdiction and judicial system; Supreme Court's original jurisdiction. The courts, jurisdiction, and judicial system of Oregon, except so far as expressly changed by this amendment, shall remain as at present constituted until otherwise provided by law. But the supreme court may, in its own discretion, take original jurisdiction in mandamus, quo warranto and habeas corpus proceedings. [Created through initiative petition filed July 7, 1910, and adopted by the people Nov. 8, 1910]

Section 2a. Temporary appointment and assignment of judges. The Legislative Assembly or the people may by law empower the Supreme Court to:

(1) Appoint retired judges of the Supreme Court or judges of courts inferior to the Supreme Court as temporary members of the Supreme Court.

(2) Appoint members of the bar as judges pro tempore of courts inferior to the Supreme Court.

(3) Assign judges of courts inferior to the Supreme Court to serve temporarily outside the district for which they were elected.A judge or member of the bar so appointed or assigned shall while serving have all the judicial powers and duties of a regularly elected judge of the court to which he is assigned or appointed. [Created through S.J.R. 30, 1957, and adopted by the people Nov. 4, 1958]

Section 2b. Inferior courts may be affected in certain respects by special or local laws. Notwithstanding the provisions of section 23, Article IV of this Constitution, laws creating courts inferior to the Supreme Court or prescribing and defining the jurisdiction of such courts or the manner in which such jurisdiction may be exercised, may be made applicable:

(1) To all judicial districts or other subdivisions of this state; or

(2) To designated classes of judicial districts or other subdivisions; or

(3) To particular judicial districts or other subdivisions. [Created through S.J.R. 34, 1961, and adopted by the people Nov. 6, 1962]

Section 3. Jury trial; re-examination of issues by appellate court; record on appeal to Supreme Court; affirmance notwithstanding error; determination of case by Supreme Court. In actions at law, where the value in controversy shall exceed $750, the right of trial by jury shall be preserved, and no fact tried by a jury shall be otherwise re-examined in any court of this state, unless the court can affirmatively say there is no evidence to support the verdict. Until otherwise provided by law, upon appeal of any case to the supreme court, either party may have attached to the bill of exceptions the whole testimony, the instructions of the court to the jury, and any other matter material to the decision of the appeal. If the supreme court shall be of opinion, after consideration of all the matters thus submitted, that the judgment of the court appealed from was such as should have been rendered in the case, such judgment shall be affirmed, notwithstanding any error committed during the trial; or if, in any respect, the judgment appealed from should be changed, and the supreme court shall be of opinion that it can determine what judgment should have been entered in the court below, it shall direct such judgment to be entered in the same manner and with like effect as decrees are now entered in equity cases on appeal to the supreme court. Provided, that nothing in this section shall be construed to authorize the supreme court to find the defendant in a criminal case guilty of an offense for which a greater penalty is provided than that of which the accused was convicted in the lower court. [Created through initiative petition filed July 7, 1910, and adopted by the people Nov. 8, 1910; Amendment proposed by H.J.R. 71, 1973, and adopted by the people Nov. 5, 1974; Amendment proposed by H.J.R. 47, 1995, and adopted by the people May 21, 1996]

Section 4. Supreme Court; terms; statements of decisions of court. The terms of the supreme court shall be appointed by law; but there shall be one term at the seat of government annually. At the close of each term the judges shall file with the secretary of state concise written statements of the decisions made at that term. [Created through initiative petition filed July 7, 1910, and adopted by the people Nov. 8, 1910]

Section 5. Juries; indictment; information. [Created through initiative petition filed July 7, 1910, and adopted by the people Nov. 8, 1910; Amendment proposed by S.J.R. 23, 1957, and adopted by the people Nov. 4, 1958; Repeal proposed by S.J.R. 1, 1973, and adopted by the people Nov. 5, 1974 (present section 5 of this Article adopted in lieu of this section)]

Section 5. Juries; indictment; information; verdict in civil cases. (1) The Legislative Assembly shall provide by law for:

(a) Selecting juries and qualifications of jurors;

(b) Drawing and summoning grand jurors from the regular jury list at any time, separate from the panel of petit jurors;

(c) Empaneling more than one grand jury in a county; and

(d) The sitting of a grand jury during vacation as well as session of the court.

(2) A grand jury shall consist of seven jurors chosen by lot from the whole number of jurors in attendance at the court, five of whom must concur to find an indictment.

(3) Except as provided in subsections (4) and (5) of this section, a person shall be charged in a circuit court with the commission of any crime punishable as a felony only on indictment by a grand jury.

(4) The district attorney may charge a person on an information filed in circuit court of a crime punishable as a felony if the person appears before the judge of the circuit court and knowingly waives indictment.

(5) The district attorney may charge a person on an information filed in circuit court if, after a preliminary hearing before a magistrate, the person has been held to answer upon a showing of probable cause that a crime punishable as a felony has been committed and that the person has committed it, or if the person knowingly waives preliminary hearing.

(6) An information shall be substantially in the form provided by law for an indictment. The district attorney may file an amended indictment or information whenever, by ruling of the court, an indictment or information is held to be defective in form.

(7) In civil cases three-fourths of the jury may render a verdict. [Created through S.J.R. 1, 1973, and adopted by the people Nov. 5, 1974 (this section adopted in lieu of former section 5 of this Article)]

Section 6. Incompetency or malfeasance of public officer. Public officers shall not be impeached; but incompetency, corruption, malfeasance or delinquency in office may be tried in the same manner as criminal offenses, and judgment may be given of dismissal from office, and such further punishment as may have been prescribed by law. [Created through initiative petition filed July 7, 1910, and adopted by the people Nov. 8, 1910]

Section 7. Oath of office of Judges of Supreme Court. Every judge of the supreme court, before entering upon the duties of his office, shall take and subscribe, and transmit to the secretary of state, the following oath:

"I, _____, do solemnly swear (or affirm) that I will support the constitution of the United States, and the constitution of the State of Oregon, and that I will faithfully and impartially discharge the duties of a judge of the supreme court of this state, according to the best of my ability, and that I will not accept any other office, except judicial offices, during the term for which I have been elected." [Created through initiative petition filed July 7, 1910, and adopted by the people Nov. 8, 1910]

Section 8. Removal, suspension or censure of judges. (1) In the manner provided by law, and notwithstanding section 1 of this Article, a judge of any court may be removed or suspended from his judicial office by the Supreme Court, or censured by the Supreme Court, for:

(a) Conviction in a court of this or any other state, or of the United States, of a crime punishable as a felony or a crime involving moral turpitude; or

(b) Wilful misconduct in a judicial office where such misconduct bears a demonstrable relationship to the effective performance of judicial duties; or

(c) Wilful or persistent failure to perform judicial duties; or

(d) Generally incompetent performance of judicial duties; or

(e) Wilful violation of any rule of judicial conduct as shall be established by the Supreme Court; or

(f) Habitual drunkenness or illegal use of narcotic or dangerous drugs.

(2) Notwithstanding section 6 of this Article, the methods provided in this section, section 1a of this Article and in section 18, Article II of this Constitution, are the exclusive methods of the removal, suspension, or censure of a judge. [Created from S.J.R. 9, 1967, and adopted by the people Nov. 5, 1968; Amendment proposed by S.J.R. 48, 1975, and adopted by the people May 25, 1976]

Section 9. Juries of less than 12 jurors. Provision may be made by law for juries consisting of less than 12 but not less than six jurors. [Created through S.J.R. 17, 1971, and adopted by the people Nov. 7, 1972]

ARTICLE VII (Original)
THE JUDICIAL BRANCH

Note: Original Article VII, compiled below, has been supplanted in part by amended Article VII and in part by statutes enacted by the Legislative Assembly. The provisions of original Article VII relating to courts, jurisdiction and the judicial system, by the terms of section 2 of amended Article VII, are given the status of a statute and are subject to change by statutes enacted by the Legislative Assembly, except so far as changed by amended Article VII.

Section 1. Courts in which judicial power vested. The Judicial power of the State shall be vested in a Suprume [sic] Court, Circuits [sic] Courts, and County Courts, which shall be Courts of Record having general jurisdiction, to be defined, limited, and regulated by law in accordance with this Constitution.— Justices of the Peace may also be invested with limited Judicial powers, and Municipal Courts may be created to administer the regulations of incorporated towns, and cities. —

Section 2. Supreme Court. The Supreme Court shall consist of Four Justices to be chosen in districts by the electors thereof, who shall be citizens of the United States, and who shall have resided in the State at least three years next preceding their election, and after their election to reside in their respective districts: The number of Justices, the Districts may be increased, but shall never exceed seven; and the boundaries of districts may be changed, but no Change of Districts, shall have the effect to remove a Judge from office, or require him to change his residence without his consent. [Constitution of 1859; Amendment proposed by S.J.R. 7, 2001, and adopted by the people Nov. 5, 2002]

Section 3. Terms of office of Judges. The Judges first chosen under this Constitution shall allot among themselves, their terms of office, so that the term of one of them shall expire in Two years, one in Four years, and Two in Six years, and thereafter, one or more shall be chosen every Two years to serve for the term of Six years. —

Section 4. Vacancy. Every vacancy in the office of Judge of the Supreme Court shall be filled by election for the remainder of the vacant term, unless it would expire at the next election, and until so filled, or when it would so expire, the Governor shall fill the vacancy by appointment. —

Section 5. Chief Justice. The Judge who has the shortest term to serve, or the oldest of several having such shortest term, and not holding by appointment shall be the Chief [sic] Justice. —

Section 6. Jurisdiction. The Supreme Court shall have jurisdiction only to revise the final decisions of the Circuit Courts, and every cause shall be tried, and every decision shall be made by those Judges only, or a majority of them, who did not try the cause, or make the decision in the Circuit Court. —

Section 7. Term of Supreme Court; statements of decisions of court. The terms of the Supreme Court shall be appointed by Law; but there shall be one term at the seat of Government annually: —

And at the close of each term the Judges shall file with the Secretary of State, Concise written Statements of the decisions made at that term. —

Note: Section 7 is in substance the same as section 4 of amended Article VII.

Section 8. Circuit court. The Circuits [sic] Courts shall be held twice at least in each year in each County organized for judicial purposes, by one of the Justices of the Supreme Court at times to be appointed by law; and at such other times as may be appointed by the Judges severally in pursuance of law. —

Section 9. Jurisdiction of circuit courts. All judicial power, authority, and jurisdiction not vested by this Constitution, or by laws consistent therewith, exclusively in some other Court shall belong to the Circuit Courts, and they shall have appellate jurisdiction, and supervisory control over the County Courts, and all other inferior Courts, Officers, and tribunals. —

Section 10. Supreme and circuit judges; election in classes. The Legislative Assembly, may provide for the election of Supreme, and Circuit Judges, in distinct classes, one of which classes shall consist of three Justices of the Supreme Court, who shall not perform Circuit duty, and the other class shall consist of the necessary number of Circuit Judges, who shall hold full terms without allotment, and who shall take the same oath as the Supreme Judges. [Constitution of 1859; Amendment proposed by S.J.R. 7, 2001, and adopted by the people Nov. 5, 2002]

Constitution

Section 11. County judges and terms of county courts. There shall be elected in each County for the term of Four years a County Judge, who shall hold the County Court at times to be regulated by law. —

Section 12. Jurisdiction of county courts; county commissioners. The County Court shall have the jurisdiction pertaining to Probate Courts, and boards of County Commissioners, and such other powers, and duties, and such civil Jurisdiction, not exceeding the amount or value of five hundred dollars, and such criminal jurisdiction not extending to death or imprisonment in the penitentiary, as may be prescribed by law. — But the Legislative Assembly may provide for the election of Two Commissioners to sit with the County Judge whilst transacting County business, in any, or all of the Counties, or may provide a seperate [sic] board for transacting such business. —

Section 13. Writs granted by county judge; habeas corpus proceedings. The County Judge may grant preliminary injuctions [sic], and such other writs as the Legislative Assembly may authorize him to grant, returnable to the Circuit Court, or otherwise as may be provided by law; and may hear, and decide questions arising upon habeas corpus; provided such decision be not against the authority, or proceedings of a Court, or Judge of equal, or higher jurisdiction. —

Section 14. Expenses of court in certain counties. The Counties having less than ten thousand inhabitants, shall be reimbursed wholly or in part for the salary, and expenses of the County Court by fees, percentage, & other equitable taxation, of the business done in said Court & in the office of the County Clerk. [Constitution of 1859; Amendment proposed by S.J.R. 7, 2001, and adopted by the people Nov. 5, 2002]

Section 15. County clerk; recorder. A County Clerk shall be elected in each County for the term of Two years, who shall keep all the public records, books, and papers of the County; record conveyances, and perform the duties of Clerk of the Circuit, and County Courts, and such other duties as may be prescribed by law: — But whenever the number of voters in any County shall exceed Twelve Hundred, the Legislative Assembly may authorize the election of one person as Clerk of the Circuit Court, one person as Clerk of the County Court, and one person Recorder of conveyances. —

Section 16. Sheriff. A sheriff shall be elected in each County for the term of Two years, who shall be the ministerial officer of the Circuit, and County Courts, and shall perform such other duties as may be prescribed by law.—

Section 17. Prosecuting attorneys. There shall be elected by districts comprised of one, or more counties, a sufficient number of prosecuting Attorneys, who shall be the law officers of the State, and of the counties within their respective districts, and shall perform such duties pertaining to the administration of Law, and general police as the Legislative Assembly may direct. —

Section 18. Verdict by Three-fourths Jury in Civil Cases; Jurors; Grand Jurors; Indictment May Be Amended, When. [Constitution of 1859; Amendment proposed by initiative petition filed Jan. 30, 1908, and adopted by the people June 1, 1908; Amendment proposed by H.J.R. 14, 1927, and adopted by the people June 28, 1927; Repeal proposed by S.J.R. 23, 1957, and adopted by the people Nov. 4, 1958]

Section 19. Official delinquencies. Public Officers shall not be impeached, but incompetency, corruption, malfeasance, or delinquency in office may be tried in the same manner as criminal offences [sic], and judgment may be given of dismissal from Office, and such further punishment as may have been prescribed by law. —

Note: Section 19 is the same as section 6 of amended Article VII.

Section 20. Removal of Judges of Supreme Court and prosecuting attorneys from office. The Govenor [sic] may remove from Office a Judge of the Supreme Court, or Prosecuting Attorney upon the Joint resolution of the Legislative Assembly, in which Two Thirds of the members elected to each house shall concur, for incompetency, Corruption, malfeasance, or delinquency in office, or other sufficient cause stated in such resolution. —

Section 21. Oath of office of Supreme Court Judges. Every judge of the Supreme Court before entering upon the duties of his office shall take, subscribe, and transmit to the Secretary of State the following oath. — I _____ do solemnly swear (or affirm) that I will support the Constitution of the United States, and the constitution of the State of Oregon, and that I will faithfully, and impartially discharge the duties of a Judge of the Supreme, and Circuits [sic] Courts of said State according to the best of my ability, and that I will not accept any other office, except Judicial offices during the term for which I have been elected. —

ARTICLE VIII
EDUCATION AND SCHOOL LANDS

Sec. 1. Superintendent of Public Instruction
    2. Common School Fund
    3. System of common schools
    4. Distribution of school fund income
    5. State Land Board; land management
    7. Prohibition of sale of state timber unless timber processed in Oregon
    8. Adequate and Equitable Funding

Section 1. Superintendent of Public Instruction. The Governor shall be superintendent of public instruction, and his powers, and duties in that capacity shall be such as may be prescribed by law; but after the term of five years from the adoption of this Constitution, it shall be competent for the Legislative Assembly to provide by law for the election of a superintendent, to provide for his compensation, and prescribe his powers and duties.—

Section 2. Common School Fund. (1) The sources of the Common School Fund are:

(a) The proceeds of all lands granted to this state for educational purposes, except the lands granted to aid in the establishment of institutions of higher education under the Acts of February 14, 1859 (11 Stat. 383) and July 2, 1862 (12 Stat. 503).

(b) All the moneys and clear proceeds of all property which may accrue to the state by escheat.

(c) The proceeds of all gifts, devises and bequests, made by any person to the state for common school purposes.

(d) The proceeds of all property granted to the state, when the purposes of such grant shall not be stated.

(e) The proceeds of the five hundred thousand acres of land to which this state is entitled under the Act of September 4, 1841 (5 Stat. 455).

(f) The five percent of the net proceeds of the sales of public lands to which this state became entitled on her admission into the union.

(g) After providing for the cost of administration and any refunds or credits authorized by law, the proceeds from any tax or excise levied on, with respect to or measured by the extraction, production, storage, use, sale, distribution or receipt of oil or natural gas and the proceeds from any tax or excise levied on the ownership of oil or natural gas. However, the rate of such taxes shall not be greater than six percent of the market value of all oil and natural gas produced or salvaged from the earth or waters of this state as and when owned or produced. This paragraph does not include proceeds from any tax or excise as described in section 3, Article IX of this Constitution.

(2) All revenues derived from the sources mentioned in subsection (1) of this section shall become a part of the Common School Fund. The State Land Board may expend moneys in the Common School Fund to carry out its powers and duties under subsection (2) of section 5 of this Article. Unexpended moneys in the Common School Fund shall be invested as the Legislative Assembly shall provide by law and shall not be subject to the limitations of section 6, Article XI of this Constitution. The State Land Board may apply, as it considers appropriate, income derived from the investment of the Common School Fund to the operating expenses of the State Land Board in exercising its powers and duties under subsection (2) of section 5 of this Article. The remainder of the income derived from the investment of the Common School Fund shall be applied to the support of primary and secondary education as prescribed by law. [Constitution of 1859; Amendment proposed by H.J.R. 7, 1967, and adopted by the people May 28, 1968; Amendment proposed by H.J.R. 6, 1979, and adopted by the people Nov. 4, 1980; Amendment to subsection (2) proposed by S.J.R. 1, 1987, and adopted by the people Nov. 8, 1988; Amendment to paragraph (b) of subsection (1) proposed by H.J.R. 3, 1989, and adopted by the people June 27, 1989]

Section 3. System of common schools. The Legislative Assembly shall provide by law for the establishment of a uniform, and general system of Common schools.

Section 4. Distribution of school fund income. Provision shall be made by law for the distribution of the income of the common school fund among the several Counties of this state in proportion to the number of children resident therein between the ages, four and twenty years.—

Section 5. State Land Board; land management. (1) The Governor, Secretary of State and State Treasurer shall constitute a State Land Board for the disposition and management of lands described in section 2 of this Article, and other lands owned by this state that are placed under their jurisdiction by law. Their powers and duties shall be prescribed by law.

(2) The board shall manage lands under its jurisdiction with the object of obtaining the greatest benefit for the people of this state, consistent with the conservation of this resource under sound techniques of land management. [Constitution of 1859; Amendment proposed by H.J.R. 7, 1967, and adopted by the people May 28, 1968]

Section 6. Qualifications of electors at school elections. [Created through initiative petition filed June 25, 1948, and adopted by the people Nov. 2, 1948; Repeal proposed by H.J.R. 4, 2007, and adopted by the people Nov. 4, 2008]

Note: The leadline to section 6 was a part of the measure proposed by initiative petition filed June 25, 1948, and adopted by the people Nov. 2, 1948.

Section 7. Prohibition of sale of state timber unless timber processed in Oregon. (1) Notwithstanding subsection (2) of section 5 of this Article or any other provision of this Constitution, the State Land Board shall not authorize the sale or export of timber from lands described in section 2 of this Article unless such timber will be processed in Oregon. The limitation on sale or export in this subsection shall not apply to species, grades or quantities of timber which may be found by the State Land Board to be surplus to domestic needs.

(2) Notwithstanding any prior agreements or other provisions of law or this Constitution, the Legislative Assembly shall not authorize the sale or export of timber from state lands other than those described in section 2 of this Article unless such timber will be processed in Oregon. The limitation on sale or export in this subsection shall not apply to species, grades or quantities of timber which may be found by the State Forester to be surplus to domestic needs.

(3) This section first becomes operative when federal law is enacted allowing this state to exercise such authority or when a court or the Attorney General of this state determines that such authority lawfully may be exercised. [Created through S.J.R. 8, 1989, and adopted by the people June 27, 1989]

Section 8. Adequate and Equitable Funding. (1) The Legislative Assembly shall appropriate in each biennium a sum of money sufficient to ensure that the state's system of public education meets quality goals established by law, and publish a report that either demonstrates the appropriation is sufficient, or identifies the reasons for the insufficiency, its extent, and its impact on the ability of the state's system of public education to meet those goals.

(2) Consistent with such legal obligation as it may have to maintain substantial equity in state funding, the Legislative Assembly shall establish a system of Equalization Grants to eligible districts for each year in which the voters of such districts approve local option taxes as described in Article XI, section 11 (4)(a)(B) of this Constitution. The amount of such Grants and eligibility criteria shall be determined by the Legislative Assembly. [Created through initiative petition filed Oct. 22, 1999, and adopted by the people Nov. 7, 2000]

Note: Added to Article VIII as unnumbered section by initiative petition (Measure No. 1, 2000) adopted by the people Nov. 7, 2000.

Note: The leadline to section 8 was a part of the measure submitted to the people by Measure No. 1, 2000.

ARTICLE IX
FINANCE

Section 1. Assessment and taxation; uniform rules; uniformity of operation of laws. The Legislative Assembly shall, and the people through the initiative may, provide by law uniform rules of assessment and taxation. All taxes shall be levied and collected under general laws operating uniformly throughout the State. [Constitution of 1859; Amendment proposed by H.J.R. 16, 1917, and adopted by the people June 4, 1917]

Constitution

411

Section 1a. Poll or head tax; declaration of emergency in tax laws. No poll or head tax shall be levied or collected in Oregon. The Legislative Assembly shall not declare an emergency in any act regulating taxation or exemption. [Created through initiative petition filed June 23, 1910, and adopted by the people Nov. 8, 1910; Amendment proposed by S.J.R. 10, 1911, and adopted by the people Nov. 5, 1912]

Section 1b. Ships exempt from taxation until 1935. All ships and vessels of fifty tons or more capacity engaged in either passenger or freight coasting or foreign trade, whose home ports of registration are in the State of Oregon, shall be and are hereby exempted from all taxes of every kind whatsoever, excepting taxes for State purposes, until the first day of January, 1935. [Created through S.J.R. 18, 1915, and adopted by the people Nov. 7, 1916]

Section 1c. Financing redevelopment and urban renewal projects. The Legislative Assembly may provide that the ad valorem taxes levied by any taxing unit, in which is located all or part of an area included in a redevelopment or urban renewal project, may be divided so that the taxes levied against any increase in the assessed value, as defined by law, of property in such area obtaining after the effective date of the ordinance or resolution approving the redevelopment or urban renewal plan for such area, shall be used to pay any indebtedness incurred for the redevelopment or urban renewal project. The legislature may enact such laws as may be necessary to carry out the purposes of this section. [Created through S.J.R. 32, 1959, and adopted by the people Nov. 8, 1960; Amendment proposed by H.J.R. 85, 1997, and adopted by the people May 20, 1997]

Section 2. Legislature to provide revenue to pay current state expenses and interest. The Legislative Assembly shall provide for raising revenue sufficiently to defray the expenses of the State for each fiscal year, and also a sufficient sum to pay the interest on the State debt, if there be any.—

Section 3. Laws imposing taxes; gasoline and motor vehicle taxes. [Constitution of 1859; Amendment proposed by S.J.R. 11, 1941, and adopted by the people Nov. 3, 1942; Repeal proposed by S.J.R. 7, 1979, and adopted by the people May 20, 1980]

Section 3. Tax imposed only by law; statement of purpose. No tax shall be levied except in accordance with law. Every law imposing a tax shall state distinctly the purpose to which the revenue shall be applied. [Created through S.J.R. 7, 1979, and adopted by the people May 20, 1980 (this section and section 3a adopted in lieu of former section 3 of this Article)]

Section 3a. Use of revenue from taxes on motor vehicle use and fuel; legislative review of allocation of taxes between vehicle classes. (1) Except as provided in subsection (2) of this section, revenue from the following shall be used exclusively for the construction, reconstruction, improvement, repair, maintenance, operation and use of public highways, roads, streets and roadside rest areas in this state:

(a) Any tax levied on, with respect to, or measured by the storage, withdrawal, use, sale, distribution, importation or receipt of motor vehicle fuel or any other product used for the propulsion of motor vehicles; and

(b) Any tax or excise levied on the ownership, operation or use of motor vehicles.

(2) Revenues described in subsection (1) of this section:

(a) May also be used for the cost of administration and any refunds or credits authorized by law.

(b) May also be used for the retirement of bonds for which such revenues have been pledged.

(c) If from levies under paragraph (b) of subsection (1) of this section on campers, motor homes, travel trailers, snowmobiles, or like vehicles, may also be used for the acquisition, development, maintenance or care of parks or recreation areas.

(d) If from levies under paragraph (b) of subsection (1) of this section on vehicles used or held out for use for commercial purposes, may also be used for enforcement of commercial vehicle weight, size, load, conformation and equipment regulation.

(3) Revenues described in subsection (1) of this section that are generated by taxes or excises imposed by the state shall be generated in a manner that ensures that the share of revenues paid for the use of light vehicles, including cars, and the share of revenues paid for the use of heavy vehicles, including trucks, is fair and proportionate to the costs incurred for the highway system because of each class of vehicle. The Legislative Assembly shall provide for a biennial review and, if necessary, adjustment, of revenue sources to ensure fairness and proportionality. [Created through S.J.R. 7, 1979, and adopted by the people May 20, 1980 (this section and section 3 adopted in lieu of former section 3 of this Article); Amendment proposed by S.J.R. 44, 1999, and adopted by the people Nov. 2, 1999; Amendment proposed by S.J.R. 14, 2003, and adopted by the people Nov. 2, 2004]

Section 3b. Rate of levy on oil or natural gas; exception. Any tax or excise levied on, with respect to or measured by the extraction, production, storage, use, sale, distribution or receipt of oil or natural gas, or the ownership thereof, shall not be levied at a rate that is greater than six percent of the market value of all oil and natural gas produced or salvaged from the earth or waters of this state as and when owned or produced. This section does not apply to any tax or excise the proceeds of which are dedicated as described in sections 3 and 3a of this Article. [Created through H.J.R. 6, 1979, and adopted by the people Nov. 4, 1980]

Note: Section 3b was designated as "Section 3a" by H.J.R. 6, 1979, and adopted by the people Nov. 4, 1980.

Section 4. Appropriation necessary for withdrawal from treasury. No money shall be drawn from the treasury, but in pursuance of appropriations made by law.—

Section 5. Publication of accounts. An accurate statement of the receipts, and expenditures of the public money shall be published with the laws of each odd-numbered year regular session of the Legislative Assembly. [Constitution of 1859; Amendment proposed by S.J.R. 41, 2010, and adopted by the people Nov. 2, 2010]

Section 6. Deficiency of funds; tax levy to pay. Whenever the expenses, of any fiscal year, shall exceed the income, the Legislative Assembly shall provide for levying a tax, for the ensuing fiscal year, sufficient, with other sources of income, to pay the deficiency, as well as the estimated expense of the ensuing fiscal year.—

Section 7. Appropriation laws not to contain provisions on other subjects. Laws making appropriations, for the salaries of public officers, and other current expenses of the State, shall contain provisions upon no other subject.—

Section 8. Stationery for use of state. All stationary [sic] required for the use of the State shall be furnished by the lowest responsible bidder, under such regulations as may be prescribed by law. But no State Officer, or member of the Legislative Assembly shall be interested in any bid, or contract for furnishing such stationery.—

Section 9. Taxation of certain benefits prohibited. Benefits payable under the federal old age and survivors insurance program or benefits under section 3(a), 4(a) or 4(f) of the federal Railroad Retirement Act of 1974, as amended, or their successors, shall not be considered income for the purposes of any tax levied by the state or by a local government in this state. Such benefits shall not be used in computing the tax liability of any person under any such tax. Nothing in this section is intended to affect any benefits to which the beneficiary would otherwise be entitled. This section applies to tax periods beginning on or after January 1, 1986. [Created through H.J.R. 26, 1985, and adopted by the people May 20, 1986]

Section 10. Retirement plan contributions by governmental employees. (1) Notwithstanding any existing State or Federal laws, an employee of the State of Oregon or any political subdivision of the state who is a member of a retirement system or plan established by law, charter or ordinance, or who will receive a retirement benefit from a system or plan offered by the state or a political subdivision of the state, must contribute to the system or plan an amount equal to six percent of their salary or gross wage.

(2) On and after January 1, 1995, the state and political subdivisions of the state shall not thereafter contract or otherwise agree to make any payment or contribution to a retirement system or plan that would have the effect of relieving an employee, regardless of when that employee was employed, of the obligation imposed by subsection (1) of this section.

(3) On and after January 1, 1995, the state and political subdivisions of the state shall not thereafter contract or otherwise agree to increase any salary, benefit or other compensation payable to an employee for the purpose of offsetting or compensating an employee for the obligation imposed by subsection (1) of this section. [Created through initiative petition filed May 10, 1993, and adopted by the people Nov. 8, 1994]

Section 11. Retirement plan rate of return contract guarantee prohibited. (1) Neither the state nor any political subdivision of the state shall contract to guarantee any rate of interest or return on the funds in a retirement system or plan established by law, charter or ordinance for the benefit of an employee of the state or a political subdivision of the state. [Created through initiative petition filed May 10, 1993, and adopted by the people Nov. 8, 1994]

Section 12. Retirement not to be increased by unused sick leave. (1) Notwithstanding any existing Federal or State law, the retirement benefits of an employee of the state or any political subdivision of the state retiring on or after January 1, 1995, shall not in any way be increased as a result of or due to unused sick leave. [Created through initiative petition filed May 10, 1993, and adopted by the people Nov. 8, 1994]

Section 13. Retirement plan restriction severability. If any part of Sections 10, 11 or 12 of this Article is held to be unconstitutional under the Federal or State Constitution, the remaining parts shall not be affected and shall remain in full force and effect.[Created through initiative petition filed May 10, 1993, and adopted by the people Nov. 8, 1994]

Section 14. Revenue estimate; retention of excess corporate tax revenue in General Fund for public education funding; return of other excess revenue to taxpayers; legislative increase in estimate. (1) As soon as is practicable after adjournment sine die of an odd-numbered year regular session of the Legislative Assembly, the Governor shall cause an estimate to be prepared of revenues that will be received by the General Fund for the biennium beginning July 1. The estimated revenues from corporate income and excise taxes shall be separately stated from the estimated revenues from other General Fund sources.

(2) As soon as is practicable after the end of the biennium, the Governor shall cause actual collections of revenues received by the General Fund for that biennium to be determined. The revenues received from corporate income and excise taxes shall be determined separately from the revenues received from other General Fund sources.

(3) If the revenues received by the General Fund from corporate income and excise taxes during the biennium exceed the amount estimated to be received from corporate income and excise taxes for the biennium, by two percent or more, the total amount of the excess shall be retained in the General Fund and used to provide additional funding for public education, kindergarten through twelfth grade.

(4) If the revenues received from General Fund revenue sources, exclusive of those described in subsection (3) of this section, during the biennium exceed the amount estimated to be received from such sources for the biennium, by two percent or more, the total amount of the excess shall be returned to personal income taxpayers.

(5) The Legislative Assembly may enact laws:

(a) Establishing a tax credit, refund payment or other mechanism by which the excess revenues are returned to taxpayers, and establishing administrative procedures connected therewith.

(b) Allowing the excess revenues to be reduced by administrative costs associated with returning the excess revenues.

(c) Permitting a taxpayer's share of the excess revenues not to be returned to the taxpayer if the taxpayer's share is less than a de minimis amount identified by the Legislative Assembly.

(d) Permitting a taxpayer's share of excess revenues to be offset by any liability of the taxpayer for which the state is authorized to undertake collection efforts.

(6)(a) Prior to the close of a biennium for which an estimate described in subsection (1) of this section has been made, the Legislative Assembly, by a two-thirds majority vote of all members elected to each House, may enact legislation declaring an emergency and increasing the amount of the estimate prepared pursuant to subsection (1) of this section.

(b) The prohibition against declaring an emergency in an act regulating taxation or exemption in section 1a, Article IX of this Constitution, does not apply to legislation enacted pursuant to this subsection.

(7) This section does not apply:

(a) If, for a biennium or any portion of a biennium, a state tax is not imposed on or measured by the income of individuals.

(b) To revenues derived from any minimum tax imposed on corporations for the privilege of carrying on or doing business in this state that is imposed as a fixed amount and that is nonapportioned (except for changes of accounting periods).

(c) To biennia beginning before July 1, 2001. [Created through H.J.R. 17, 1999, and adopted by the people Nov. 7, 2000; Amendment proposed by S.J.R. 41, 2010, and adopted by the people Nov. 2, 2010; Amendment proposed by initiative petition filed Dec. 7, 2011, and adopted by the people Nov. 6, 2012]

Section 15. Prohibition on tax, fee or other assessment upon transfer of interest in real property; exception. The state, a city, county, district or other political subdivision or municipal corporation of this state shall not impose, by ordinance or other law, a tax, fee or other assessment upon the transfer of any interest in real property, or measured by the consideration paid or received upon the transfer of any interest in real property. This section does not apply to any tax, fee or other assessment in effect and operative on December 31, 2009. [Created through initiative petition filed March 4, 2010, and adopted by the people Nov. 6, 2012]

Note: Added to Article IX as unnumbered section by initiative petition (Measure No. 79, 2012) adopted by the people Nov. 6, 2012.

ARTICLE X
THE MILITIA

Sec. 1. State militia
  2. Persons exempt
  3. Officers

Section 1. State militia. The Legislative Assembly shall provide by law for the organization, maintenance and discipline of a state militia for the defense and protection of the State. [Constitution of 1859; Amendment proposed by H.J.R. 5, 1961, and adopted by the people Nov. 6, 1962]

Section 2. Persons exempt. Persons whose religious tenets, or conscientious scruples forbid them to bear arms shall not be compelled to do so. [Constitution of 1859; Amendment proposed by H.J.R. 5, 1961, and adopted by the people Nov. 6, 1962]

Section 3. Officers. The Governor, in his capacity as Commander-in-Chief of the military forces of the State, shall appoint and commission an Adjutant General. All other officers of the militia of the State shall be appointed and commissioned by the Governor upon the recommendation of the Adjutant General. [Constitution of 1859; Amendment proposed by H.J.R. 5, 1961, and adopted by the people Nov. 6, 1962]

Section 4. Staff officers; commissions. [Constitution of 1859; Repeal proposed by H.J.R. 5, 1961, and adopted by the people Nov. 6, 1962]

Section 5. Legislature to make regulations for militia. [Constitution of 1859; Repeal proposed by H.J.R. 5, 1961, and adopted by the people Nov. 6, 1962]

Section 6. Continuity of government in event of enemy attack. [Created through H.J.R. 9, 1959, and adopted by the people Nov. 8, 1960; Repeal proposed by H.J.R. 24, 1975, and adopted by the people Nov. 2, 1976]

ARTICLE X-A
CATASTROPHIC DISASTERS

Sec. 1. Definitions; declaration of catastrophic disaster; convening of Legislative Assembly
  2. Additional powers of Governor; use of General Fund moneys and lottery funds
  3. Procedural requirements for Legislative Assembly
  4. Additional powers of Legislative Assembly
  5. Participation in session of Legislative Assembly by electronic or other means
  6. Termination of operation of this Article; extension by Legislative Assembly; transition provisions; limitation on power of Governor to invoke this Article

Section 1. Definitions; declaration of catastrophic disaster; convening of Legislative Assembly. (1) As used in this Article, "catastrophic disaster" means a natural or human-caused event that:

(a) Results in extraordinary levels of death, injury, property damage or disruption of daily life in this state; and

(b) Severely affects the population, infrastructure, environment, economy or government functioning of this state.

(2) As used in this Article, "catastrophic disaster" includes, but is not limited to, any of the following events if the event meets the criteria listed in subsection (1) of this section:

(a) Act of terrorism.

(b) Earthquake.

(c) Flood.

(d) Public health emergency.

(e) Tsunami.

(f) Volcanic eruption.

(g) War.

(3) The Governor may invoke the provisions of this Article if the Governor finds and declares that a cata-

strophic disaster has occurred. A finding required by this subsection shall specify the nature of the catastrophic disaster.

(4) At the time the Governor invokes the provisions of this Article under subsection (3) of this section, the Governor shall issue a proclamation convening the Legislative Assembly under section 12, Article V of this Constitution, unless:

(a) The Legislative Assembly is in session at the time the catastrophic disaster is declared; or

(b) The Legislative Assembly is scheduled to convene in regular session within 30 days after the date the catastrophic disaster is declared.

(5) If the Governor declares that a catastrophic disaster has occurred, the Governor shall manage the immediate response to the disaster. The actions of the Legislative Assembly under sections 3 and 4 of this Article are limited to actions necessary to implement the Governor's immediate response to the disaster and to actions necessary to aid recovery from the disaster. [Created through H.J.R. 7, 2011, and adopted by the people Nov. 6, 2012]

Section 2. Additional powers of Governor; use of General Fund moneys and lottery funds. (1) If the Governor declares that a catastrophic disaster has occurred, the Governor may:

(a) Use moneys appropriated from the General Fund to executive agencies for the current biennium to respond to the catastrophic disaster, regardless of the legislatively expressed purpose of the appropriation at the time the appropriation was made.

(b) Use lottery funds allocated to executive agencies for the current biennium to respond to the catastrophic disaster, regardless of the legislatively expressed purpose of the allocation at the time the allocation was made. The Governor may not reallocate lottery funds under this paragraph for purposes not authorized by section 4, Article XV of this Constitution.

(2) The authority granted to the Governor by this section terminates upon the taking effect of a law enacted after the declaration of a catastrophic disaster that specifies purposes for which appropriated General Fund moneys or allocated lottery funds may be used, or upon the date on which the provisions of sections 1 to 5 of this Article cease to be operative as provided in section 6 of this Article, whichever is sooner. [Created through H.J.R. 7, 2011, and adopted by the people Nov. 6, 2012]

Section 3. Procedural requirements for Legislative Assembly. If the Governor declares that a catastrophic disaster has occurred:

(1) Notwithstanding sections 10 and 10a, Article IV of this Constitution, the Legislative Assembly may convene in a place other than the Capitol of the State if the Governor or the Legislative Assembly determines that the Capitol is inaccessible.

(2) Notwithstanding section 12, Article IV of this Constitution, during any period of time when members of the Legislative Assembly are unable to compel the attendance of two-thirds of the members of each house because the catastrophic disaster has made it impossible to locate members or impossible for them to attend, two-thirds of the members of each house who are able to attend shall constitute a quorum to do business.

(3) In a session of the Legislative Assembly that is called because of the catastrophic disaster or that was imminent or ongoing at the time the catastrophic disaster was declared, the number of members of each house that constitutes a quorum under subsection (2) of this section may suspend the rule regarding reading of bills under the same circumstances and in the same manner that two-

thirds of the members may suspend the rule under section 19, Article IV of this Constitution.

(4) Notwithstanding section 25, Article IV of this Constitution, during any period of time when members of the Legislative Assembly are unable to compel the attendance of two-thirds of the members of each house because the catastrophic disaster has made it impossible to locate members or impossible for them to attend, three-fifths of the members of each house who are able to attend a session described in subsection (3) of this section shall be necessary to pass every bill or joint resolution.

(5) Notwithstanding section 1a, Article IX of this Constitution, the Legislative Assembly may declare an emergency in any bill regulating taxation or exemption, including but not limited to any bill that decreases or suspends taxes or postpones the due date of taxes, if the Legislative Assembly determines that the enactment of the bill is necessary to provide an adequate response to the catastrophic disaster. [Created through H.J.R. 7, 2011, and adopted by the people Nov. 6, 2012]

Section 4. Additional powers of Legislative Assembly. (1) If the Governor declares that a catastrophic disaster has occurred:

(a) The Legislative Assembly may enact laws authorizing the use of revenue described in section 3a, Article IX of this Constitution, for purposes other than those described in that section.

(b) The Legislative Assembly may, by a vote of the number of members of each house that constitutes a quorum under subsection (2) of section 3 of this Article, appropriate moneys that would otherwise be returned to taxpayers under section 14, Article IX of this Constitution, to state agencies for the purpose of responding to the catastrophic disaster.

(c) Notwithstanding section 7, Article XI of this Constitution, the Legislative Assembly may lend the credit of the state or create debts or liabilities in an amount the Legislative Assembly considers necessary to provide an adequate response to the catastrophic disaster.

(d) The provisions of section 15, Article XI of this Constitution, do not apply to any law that is approved by three-fifths of the members of each house who are able to attend a session described in subsection (3) of section 3 of this Article.

(e) The Legislative Assembly may take action described in subsection (6) of section 15, Article XI of this Constitution, upon approval by three-fifths of the members of each house who are able to attend a session described in subsection (3) of section 3 of this Article.

(f) Notwithstanding section 4, Article XV of this Constitution, the Legislative Assembly may allocate proceeds from the State Lottery for any purpose and in any ratio the Legislative Assembly determines necessary to provide an adequate response to the catastrophic disaster.

(2) Nothing in this section overrides or otherwise affects the provisions of section 15b, Article V of this Constitution. [Created through H.J.R. 7, 2011, and adopted by the people Nov. 6, 2012]

Section 5. Participation in session of Legislative Assembly by electronic or other means. For purposes of sections 3 and 4 of this Article, a member of the Legislative Assembly who cannot be physically present at a session convened under section 1 of this Article shall be considered in attendance if the member is able to participate in the session through electronic or other means that enable the member to hear or read the proceedings as the proceedings are occurring and enable others to hear or read the member's votes or other contributions as the votes or other contributions are occurring. [Created through H.J.R. 7, 2011, and adopted by the people Nov. 6, 2012]

Section 6. Termination of operation of this Article; extension by Legislative Assembly; transition provisions; limitation on power of Governor to invoke this Article. (1) Except as provided in subsection (2) of this section, the provisions of sections 1 to 5 of this Article, once invoked, shall cease to be operative not later than 30 days following the date the Governor invoked the provisions of sections 1 to 5 of this Article, or on an earlier date recommended by the Governor and determined by the Legislative Assembly. The Governor may not recommend a date under this subsection unless the Governor finds and declares that the immediate response to the catastrophic disaster has ended.

(2) Prior to expiration of the 30-day limit established in subsection (1) of this section, the Legislative Assembly may extend the operation of sections 1 to 5 of this Article beyond the 30-day limit upon the approval of three-fifths of the members of each house who are able to attend a session described in subsection (3) of section 3 of this Article.

(3) The determination by the Legislative Assembly required by subsection (1) of this section or an extension described in subsection (2) of this section shall take the form of a bill. A bill that extends the operation of sections 1 to 5 of this Article shall establish a date upon which the provisions of sections 1 to 5 of this Article shall cease to be operative. A bill described in this subsection shall be presented to the Governor for action in accordance with section 15b, Article V of this Constitution.

(4) A bill described in subsection (3) of this section may include any provisions the Legislative Assembly considers necessary to provide an orderly transition to compliance with the requirements of this Constitution that have been overridden under this Article because of the Governor's declaration of a catastrophic disaster.

(5) The Governor may not invoke the provisions of sections 1 to 5 of this Article more than one time with respect to the same catastrophic disaster. A determination under subsection (1) of this section or an extension described in subsection (2) of this section that establishes a date upon which the provisions of sections 1 to 5 of this Article shall cease to be operative does not prevent invoking the provisions of sections 1 to 5 of this Article in response to a new declaration by the Governor that a different catastrophic disaster has occurred. [Created through H.J.R. 7, 2011, and adopted by the people Nov. 6, 2012]

ARTICLE XI
CORPORATIONS AND INTERNAL IMPROVEMENTS

11d. Effect of section 11b on exemptions and assessments
11e. Severability of sections 11b, 11c and 11d
11k. Limitation on applicability of section 11(8) voting requirements to elections on measures held in May or November of any year
11L. Limitation on applicability of sections 11 and 11b on bonded indebtedness to finance capital costs
12. People's utility districts
13. Interests of employes when operation of transportation system assumed by public body
14. Metropolitan service district charter
15. Funding of programs imposed upon local governments; exceptions

Section 1. Prohibition of state banks. The Legislative Assembly shall not have the power to establish, or incorporate any bank or banking company, or monied [sic] institution whatever; nor shall any bank company, or instition [sic] exist in the State, with the privilege of making, issuing, or putting in circulation, any bill, check, certificate, prommisory [sic] note, or other paper, or the paper of any bank company, or person, to circulate as money. —

Note: The semicolon appearing in the signed Constitution after the word "whatever" in section 1 was not in the original draft reported to and adopted by the convention and is not part of the Constitution. State v. H.S. & L.A., 8 Or. 396, 401 (1880).

Section 2. Formation of corporations; municipal charters; intoxicating liquor regulation. Corporations may be formed under general laws, but shall not be created by the Legislative Assembly by special laws. The Legislative Assembly shall not enact, amend or repeal any charter or act of incorporation for any municipality, city or town. The legal voters of every city and town are hereby granted power to enact and amend their municipal charter, subject to the Constitution and criminal laws of the State of Oregon, and the exclusive power to license, regulate, control, or to suppress or prohibit, the sale of intoxicating liquors therein is vested in such municipality; but such municipality shall within its limits be subject to the provisions of the local option law of the State of Oregon. [Constitution of 1859; Amendment proposed by initiative petition filed Dec.13, 1905, and adopted by the people June 4, 1906; Amendment proposed by initiative petition filed June 23, 1910, and adopted by the people Nov. 8, 1910]

Section 2a. Merger of adjoining municipalities; county-city consolidation. (1) The Legislative Assembly, or the people by the Initiative, may enact a general law providing a method whereby an incorporated city or town or municipal corporation may surrender its charter and be merged into an adjoining city or town, provided a majority of the electors of each of the incorporated cities or towns or municipal corporations affected authorize the surrender or merger, as the case may be.

(2) In all counties having a city therein containing over 300,000 inhabitants, the county and city government thereof may be consolidated in such manner as may be provided by law with one set of officers. The consolidated county and city may be incorporated under general laws providing for incorporation for municipal purposes. The provisions of this Constitution applicable to cities, and also those applicable to counties, so far as not inconsistent or prohibited to cities, shall be applicable to such consolidated government. [Created through H.J.R. 10, 1913, and adopted by the people Nov. 3, 1914; Amendment proposed by S.J.R. 29, 1967, and adopted by the people Nov. 5, 1968]

Section 3. Liability of stockholders. The stockholders of all corporations and joint stock companies shall be liable for the indebtedness of said corporation to the amount of their stock subscribed and unpaid and no more, excepting that the stockholders of corporations or joint stock companies conducting the business of banking shall be individually liable equally and ratably and not one for another, for the benefit of the depositors of said bank, to the amount of their stock, at the par value thereof, in addition to the par value of such shares, unless such banking corporation shall have provided security through membership in the federal deposit insurance corporation or other instrumentality of the United States or otherwise for the benefit of the depositors of said bank equivalent in amount to such double liability of said stockholders. [Constitution of 1859; Amendment proposed by S.J.R. 13, 1911, and adopted by the people Nov. 5, 1912; Amendment proposed by H.J.R. 2, 1943, and adopted by the people Nov. 7, 1944]

Section 4. Compensation for property taken by corporation. No person's property shall be taken by any corporation under authority of law, without compensation being first made, or secured in such manner as may be prescribed by law. —

Section 5. Restriction of municipal powers in Acts of incorporation. Acts of the Legislative Assembly, incorporating towns, and cities, shall restrict their powers of taxation, borrowing money, contracting debts, and loaning their credit. —

Section 6. State not to be stockholder in company; exceptions. (1) The state shall not subscribe to, or be interested in the stock of any company, association or corporation. However, as provided by law the state may hold and dispose of stock, including stock already received, that is donated or bequeathed; and may invest, in the stock of any company, association or corporation, any funds or moneys that:

(a) Are donated or bequeathed for higher education purposes;

(b) Are the proceeds from the disposition of stock that is donated or bequeathed for higher education purposes, including stock already received; or

(c) Are dividends paid with respect to stock that is donated or bequeathed for higher education purposes, including stock already received.

(2) Notwithstanding the limits contained in subsection (1) of this section, the state may hold and dispose of stock:

(a) Received in exchange for technology created in whole or in part by a public institution of post-secondary education; or

(b) Received prior to December 5, 2002, as a state asset invested in the creation or development of technology or resources within Oregon. [Constitution of 1859; Amendment proposed by H.J.R. 11, 1955, and adopted by the people Nov. 6, 1956; Amendment proposed by H.J.R. 27, 1969, and adopted by the people Nov. 3, 1970; Amendment proposed by S.J.R. 17, 2001, and adopted by the people May 21, 2002]

Section 7. Credit of State Not to Be Loaned; Limitation Upon Power of Contracting Debts. The Legislative Assembly shall not lend the credit of the state nor in any manner create any debt or liabilities which shall singly or in the aggregate with previous debts or liabilities exceed the sum of fifty thousand dollars, except in case of war or to repel invasion or suppress insurrection or to build and maintain permanent roads; and the Legislative Assembly shall not lend the credit of the state nor in any manner create any debts or liabilities to build and maintain permanent roads which shall singly or in the aggregate with previous debts or liabilities incurred for that purpose exceed one percent of the true cash value of all the property of the state taxed on an ad valorem basis; and every contract of indebtedness entered into or assumed by or on behalf of the state in violation of the provisions of this section shall be void and of no effect. This section does not apply to any agreement entered into pursuant to law by the state or any agency thereof for the lease of real property to the state or agency for any period not exceeding 20 years and for a public purpose. [Constitution of 1859; Amendment proposed by initiative petition filed July 2, 1912, and adopted by the people Nov. 5, 1912; Amendment proposed by H.J.R. 11, 1920 (s.s.), and adopted by the people May 21, 1920; Amendment proposed by S.J.R. 4, 1961, and adopted by the people Nov. 6, 1962; Amendment proposed by S.J.R. 19, 1963, and adopted by the people Nov. 3, 1964]

Note: The leadline to section 7 was a part of the measure submitted to the people by H.J.R. 11, 1920 (s.s.).

Section 8. State not to assume debts of counties, towns or other corporations. The State shall never assume the debts of any county, town, or other corporation whatever, unless such debts, shall have been created to repel invasion, suppress insurrection, or defend the State in war. —

Section 9. Limitations on powers of county or city to assist corporations. No county, city, town or other municipal corporation, by vote of its citizens, or otherwise, shall become a stockholder in any joint company, corporation or association, whatever, or raise money for, or loan its credit to, or in aid of, any such company, corporation or association. Provided, that any municipal corporation designated as a port under any general or special law of the state of Oregon, may be empowered by statute to raise money and expend the same in the form of a bonus to aid in establishing water transportation lines between such port and any other domestic or foreign port or ports, and to aid in establishing water transportation lines on the interior rivers of this state, or on the rivers between Washington and Oregon, or on the rivers of Washington and Idaho reached by navigation from Oregon's rivers; any debts of a municipality to raise money created for the aforesaid purpose shall be incurred only on approval of a majority of those voting on the question, and shall not, either singly or in the aggregate, with previous debts and liabilities incurred for that purpose, exceed one per cent of the assessed valuation of all property in the municipality. [Constitution of 1859; Amendment proposed by S.J.R. 13, 1917, and adopted by the people June 4, 1917]

Section 10. County debt limitation. No county shall create any debt or liabilities which shall singly or in the aggregate, with previous debts or liabilities, exceed the sum of $5,000; provided, however, counties may incur bonded indebtedness in excess of such $5,000 limitation to carry out purposes authorized by statute, such bonded indebtedness not to exceed limits fixed by statute. [Constitution of 1859; Amendment proposed by initiative petition filed July 7, 1910, and adopted by the people Nov. 8, 1910; Amendment proposed by initiative petition filed July 2, 1912, and adopted by the people Nov. 5, 1912; Amendment proposed by S.J.R. 11, 1919, and adopted by the people June 3, 1919; Amendment proposed by H.J.R. 7, 1920 (s.s.), and adopted by the people May 21, 1920; Amendment proposed by S.J.R. 1, 1921 (s.s.), and adopted by the people Nov. 7, 1922; Amendment proposed by S.J.R. 5, 1921 (s.s.), and adopted by the people Nov. 7, 1922; Amendment proposed by H.J.R. 3, 1925, and adopted by the people Nov. 2, 1926; Amendment proposed by S.J.R. 18, 1925, and adopted by the people Nov. 2, 1926; Amendment proposed by H.J.R. 19, 1925, and adopted by the people Nov. 2, 1926; Amendment proposed by H.J.R. 21, 1957, and adopted by the people Nov. 4, 1958]

Section 11. Tax and indebtedness limitation. [Created through initiative petition filed July 6, 1916, and adopted by the people Nov. 7, 1916; Amendment proposed by H.J.R. 9, 1931, and adopted by the people Nov. 8, 1932; Amendment proposed by H.J.R. 9, 1951, and adopted by the people Nov. 4, 1952; Repeal proposed by S.J.R. 33, 1961, and adopted by the people Nov. 6, 1962 (second section 11 of this Article adopted in lieu of this section)]

Section 11. Tax base limitation. [Created through S.J.R. 33, 1961, and adopted by the people Nov. 6, 1962 (this section adopted in lieu of first section 11 of this Article); Amendment proposed by H.J.R. 28, 1985, and adopted by the people May 20,

1986; Repeal proposed by H.J.R. 85, 1997, and adopted by the people May 20, 1997 (present section 11 of this Article adopted in lieu of this section and sections 11a, 11f, 11g, 11h, 11i and 11j of this Article)]

Section 11. Property tax limitations on assessed value and rate of tax; exceptions. (1)(a) For the tax year beginning July 1, 1997, each unit of property in this state shall have a maximum assessed value for ad valorem property tax purposes that does not exceed the property's real market value for the tax year beginning July 1, 1995, reduced by 10 percent.

(b) For tax years beginning after July 1, 1997, the property's maximum assessed value shall not increase by more than three percent from the previous tax year.

(c) Notwithstanding paragraph (a) or (b) of this subsection, property shall be valued at the ratio of average maximum assessed value to average real market value of property located in the area in which the property is located that is within the same property class, if on or after July 1, 1995:

(A) The property is new property or new improvements to property;

(B) The property is partitioned or subdivided;

(C) The property is rezoned and used consistently with the rezoning;

(D) The property is first taken into account as omitted property;

(E) The property becomes disqualified from exemption, partial exemption or special assessment; or

(F) A lot line adjustment is made with respect to the property, except that the total assessed value of all property affected by a lot line adjustment shall not exceed the total maximum assessed value of the affected property under paragraph (a) or (b) of this subsection.

(d) Property shall be valued under paragraph (c) of this subsection only for the first tax year in which the changes described in paragraph (c) of this subsection are taken into account following the effective date of this section. For each tax year thereafter, the limits described in paragraph (b) of this subsection apply.

(e) The Legislative Assembly shall enact laws that establish property classes and areas sufficient to make a determination under paragraph (c) of this subsection.

(f) Each property's assessed value shall not exceed the property's real market value.

(g) There shall not be a reappraisal of the real market value used in the tax year beginning July 1, 1995, for purposes of determining the property's maximum assessed value under paragraph (a) of this subsection.

(2) The maximum assessed value of property that is assessed under a partial exemption or special assessment law shall be determined by applying the percentage reduction of paragraph (a) and the limit of paragraph (b) of subsection (1) of this section, or if newly eligible for partial exemption or special assessment, using a ratio developed in a manner consistent with paragraph (c) of subsection (1) of this section to the property's partially exempt or specially assessed value in the manner provided by law. After disqualification from partial exemption or special assessment, any additional taxes authorized by law may be imposed, but in the aggregate may not exceed the amount that would have been imposed under this section had the property not been partially exempt or specially assessed for the years for which the additional taxes are being collected.

(3)(a)(A) The Legislative Assembly shall enact laws to reduce the amount of ad valorem property taxes imposed by local taxing districts in this state so that the total of all ad valorem property taxes imposed in this state for the tax year beginning July 1, 1997, is reduced by 17 percent from the total of all ad valorem property taxes that would have been imposed under repealed sections 11 and 11a of this Article (1995 Edition) and section 11b of this Article but not taking into account Ballot Measure 47 (1996), for the tax year beginning July 1, 1997.

(B) The ad valorem property taxes to be reduced under subparagraph (A) of this paragraph are those taxes that would have been imposed under repealed sections 11 or 11a of this Article (1995 Edition) or section 11b of this Article, as modified by subsection (11) of this section, other than taxes described in subsection (4), (5), (6) or (7) of this section, taxes imposed to pay bonded indebtedness described in section 11b of this Article, as modified by paragraph (d) of subsection (11) of this section, or taxes described in section 1c, Article IX of this Constitution.

(C) It shall be the policy of this state to distribute the reductions caused by this paragraph so as to reflect:

(i) The lesser of ad valorem property taxes imposed for the tax year beginning July 1, 1995, reduced by 10 percent, or ad valorem property taxes imposed for the tax year beginning July 1, 1994;

(ii) Growth in new value under subparagraph (A), (B), (C), (D) or (E) of paragraph (c) of subsection (1) of this section, as added to the assessment and tax rolls for the tax year beginning July 1, 1996, or July 1, 1997 (or, if applicable, for the tax year beginning July 1, 1995); and

(iii) Ad valorem property taxes authorized by voters to be imposed in tax years beginning on or after July 1, 1996, and imposed according to that authority for the tax year beginning July 1, 1997.

(D) It shall be the policy of this state and the local taxing districts of this state to prioritize public safety and public education in responding to the reductions caused by this paragraph while minimizing the loss of decision-making control of local taxing districts.

(E) If the total value for the tax year beginning July 1, 1997, of additions of value described in subparagraph (A), (B), (C), (D) or (E) of paragraph (c) of subsection (1) of this section that are added to the assessment and tax rolls for the tax year beginning July 1, 1996, or July 1, 1997, exceeds four percent of the total assessed value of property statewide for the tax year beginning July 1, 1997 (before taking into account the additions of value described in subparagraph (A), (B), (C), (D) or (E) of paragraph (c) of subsection (1) of this section), then any ad valorem property taxes attributable to the excess above four percent shall reduce the dollar amount of the reduction described in subparagraph (A) of this paragraph.

(b) For the tax year beginning July 1, 1997, the ad valorem property taxes that were reduced under paragraph (a) of this subsection shall be imposed on the assessed value of property in a local taxing district as provided by law, and the rate of the ad valorem property taxes imposed under this paragraph shall be the local taxing district's permanent limit on the rate of ad valorem property taxes imposed by the district for tax years beginning after July 1, 1997, except as provided in subsection (5) of this section.

(c)(A) A local taxing district that has not previously imposed ad valorem property taxes and that seeks to impose ad valorem property taxes shall establish a limit on the rate of ad valorem property tax to be imposed by the district. The rate limit established under this subparagraph shall be approved by a majority of voters voting on the question. The rate limit approved under this subparagraph shall serve as the district's permanent rate limit under paragraph (b) of this subsection.

(B) The voter participation requirements described in subsection (8) of this section apply to an election under this paragraph.

(d) If two or more local taxing districts seek to consolidate or merge, the limit on the rate of ad valorem property tax to be imposed by the consolidated or merged district shall be the rate that would produce the same tax revenue as the local taxing districts would have cumulatively produced in the year of consolidation or merger, if the consolidation or merger had not occurred.

(e)(A) If a local taxing district divides, the limit on the rate of ad valorem property tax to be imposed by each local taxing district after division shall be the same as the local taxing district's rate limit under paragraph (b) of this subsection prior to division.

(B) Notwithstanding subparagraph (A) of this paragraph, the limit determined under this paragraph shall not be greater than the rate that would have produced the same amount of ad valorem property tax revenue in the year of division, had the division not occurred.

(f) Rates of ad valorem property tax established under this subsection may be carried to a number of decimal places provided by law and rounded as provided by law.

(g) Urban renewal levies described in this subsection shall be imposed as provided in subsections (15) and (16) of this section and may not be imposed under this subsection.

(h) Ad valorem property taxes described in this subsection shall be subject to the limitations described in section 11b of this Article, as modified by subsection (11) of this section.

(4)(a)(A) A local taxing district other than a school district may impose a local option ad valorem property tax that exceeds the limitations imposed under this section by submitting the question of the levy to voters in the local taxing district and obtaining the approval of a majority of the voters voting on the question.

(B) The Legislative Assembly may enact laws permitting a school district to impose a local option ad valorem property tax as otherwise provided under this subsection.

(b) A levy imposed pursuant to legislation enacted under this subsection may be imposed for no more than five years, except that a levy for a capital project may be imposed for no more than the lesser of the expected useful life of the capital project or 10 years.

(c) The voter participation requirements described in subsection (8) of this section apply to an election held under this subsection.

(5)(a) Any portion of a local taxing district levy shall not be subject to reduction and limitation under paragraphs (a) and (b) of subsection (3) of this section if that portion of the levy is used to repay:

(A) Principal and interest for any bond issued before December 5, 1996, and secured by a pledge or explicit commitment of ad valorem property taxes or a covenant to levy or collect ad valorem property taxes;

(B) Principal and interest for any other formal, written borrowing of moneys executed before December 5, 1996, for which ad valorem property tax revenues have been pledged or explicitly committed, or that are secured by a covenant to levy or collect ad valorem property taxes;

(C) Principal and interest for any bond issued to refund an obligation described in subparagraph (A) or (B) of this paragraph; or

(D) Local government pension and disability plan obligations that commit ad valorem property taxes and to ad valorem property taxes imposed to fulfill those obligations.

(b)(A) A levy described in this subsection shall be imposed on assessed value as otherwise provided by law in an amount sufficient to repay the debt described in this subsection. Ad valorem property taxes may not be imposed under this subsection that repay the debt at an earlier date

418

or on a different schedule than established in the agreement creating the debt.

(B) A levy described in this subsection shall be subject to the limitations imposed under section 11b of this Article, as modified by subsection (11) of this section.

(c)(A) As used in this subsection, "local government pension and disability plan obligations that commit ad valorem property taxes" is limited to contractual obligations for which the levy of ad valorem property taxes has been committed by a local government charter provision that was in effect on December 5, 1996, and, if in effect on December 5, 1996, as amended thereafter.

(B) The rates of ad valorem property taxes described in this paragraph may be adjusted so that the maximum allowable rate is capable of raising the revenue that the levy would have been authorized to raise if applied to property valued at real market value.

(C) Notwithstanding subparagraph (B) of this paragraph, ad valorem property taxes described in this paragraph shall be taken into account for purposes of the limitations in section 11b of this Article, as modified by subsection (11) of this section.

(D) If any proposed amendment to a charter described in subparagraph (A) of this paragraph permits the ad valorem property tax levy for local government pension and disability plan obligations to be increased, the amendment must be approved by voters in an election. The voter participation requirements described in subsection (8) of this section apply to an election under this subparagraph. No amendment to any charter described in this paragraph may cause ad valorem property taxes to exceed the limitations of section 11b of this Article, as amended by subsection (11) of this section.

(d) If the levy described in this subsection was a tax base or other permanent continuing levy, other than a levy imposed for the purpose described in subparagraph (D) of paragraph (a) of this subsection, prior to the effective date of this section, for the tax year following the repayment of debt described in this subsection the local taxing district's rate of ad valorem property tax established under paragraph (b) of subsection (3) of this section shall be increased to the rate that would have been in effect had the levy not been excepted from the reduction described in subsection (3) of this section. No adjustment shall be made to the rate of ad valorem property tax of local taxing districts other than the district imposing a levy under this subsection.

(e) If this subsection would apply to a levy described in paragraph (d) of this subsection, the local taxing district imposing the levy may elect out of the provisions of this subsection. The levy of a local taxing district making the election shall be included in the reduction and ad valorem property tax rate determination described in subsection (3) of this section.

(6)(a) The ad valorem property tax of a local taxing district, other than a city, county or school district, that is used to support a hospital facility shall not be subject to the reduction described in paragraph (a) of subsection (3) of this section. The entire ad valorem property tax imposed under this subsection for the tax year beginning July 1, 1997, shall be the local taxing district's permanent limit on the rate of ad valorem property taxes imposed by the district under paragraph (b) of subsection (3) of this section.

(b) Ad valorem property taxes described in this subsection shall be subject to the limitations imposed under section 11b of this Article, as modified by subsection (11) of this section.

(7) Notwithstanding any other existing or former provision of this Constitution, the following are validated, ratified, approved and confirmed:

(a) Any levy of ad valorem property taxes approved by a majority of voters voting on the question in an election held before December 5, 1996, if the election met the voter participation requirements described in subsection (8) of this section and the ad valorem property taxes were first imposed for the tax year beginning July 1, 1996, or July 1, 1997. A levy described in this paragraph shall not be subject to reduction under paragraph (a) of subsection (3) of this section but shall be taken into account in determining the local taxing district's permanent rate of ad valorem property tax under paragraph (b) of subsection (3) this section. This paragraph does not apply to levies described in subsection (5) of this section or to levies to pay bonded indebtedness described in section 11b of this Article, as modified by subsection (11) of this section.

(b) Any serial or one-year levy to replace an existing serial or one-year levy approved by a majority of the voters voting on the question at an election held after December 4, 1996, and to be first imposed for the tax year beginning July 1, 1997, if the rate or the amount of the levy approved is not greater than the rate or the amount of the levy replaced.

(c) Any levy of ad valorem property taxes approved by a majority of voters voting on the question in an election held on or after December 5, 1996, and before the effective date of this section if the election met the voter participation requirements described in subsection (8) of this section and the ad valorem property taxes were first imposed for the tax year beginning July 1, 1997. A levy described in this paragraph shall be treated as a local option ad valorem property tax under subsection (4) of this section. This paragraph does not apply to levies described in subsection (5) of this section or to levies to pay bonded indebtedness described in section 11b of this Article, as modified by subsection (11) of this section.

(8) An election described in subsection (3), (4), (5)(c)(D), (7)(a) or (c) or (11) of this section shall authorize the matter upon which the election is being held only if:

(a) At least 50 percent of registered voters eligible to vote in the election cast a ballot; or

(b) The election is a general election in an even-numbered year.

(9) The Legislative Assembly shall replace, from the state's General Fund, revenue lost by the public school system because of the limitations of this section. The amount of the replacement revenue shall not be less than the total replaced in fiscal year 1997-1998.

(10)(a) As used in this section:

(A) "Improvements" includes new construction, reconstruction, major additions, remodeling, renovation and rehabilitation, including installation, but does not include minor construction or ongoing maintenance and repair.

(B) "Ad valorem property tax" does not include taxes imposed to pay principal and interest on bonded indebtedness described in paragraph (d) of subsection (11) of this section.

(b) In calculating the addition to value for new property and improvements, the amount added shall be net of the value of retired property.

(11) For purposes of this section and for purposes of implementing the limits in section 11b of this Article in tax years beginning on or after July 1, 1997:

(a)(A) The real market value of property shall be the amount in cash that could reasonably be expected to be paid by an informed buyer to an informed seller, each acting without compulsion in an arm's length transaction occurring as of the assessment date for the tax year, as established by law.

(B) The Legislative Assembly shall enact laws to adjust the real market value of property to reflect a substantial casualty loss of value after the assessment date.

(b) The $5 (public school system) and $10 (other government) limits on property taxes per $1,000 of real market value described in subsection (1) of section 11b of this Article shall be determined on the basis of property taxes imposed in each geographic area taxed by the same local taxing districts.

(c)(A) All property taxes described in this section are subject to the limits described in paragraph (b) of this subsection, except for taxes described in paragraph (d) of this subsection.

(B) If property taxes exceed the limitations imposed under either category of local taxing district under paragraph (b) of this subsection:

(i) Any local option ad valorem property taxes imposed under this subsection shall be proportionally reduced by those local taxing districts within the category that is imposing local option ad valorem property taxes; and

(ii) After local option ad valorem property taxes have been eliminated, all other ad valorem property taxes shall be proportionally reduced by those taxing districts within the category, until the limits are no longer exceeded.

(C) The percentages used to make the proportional reductions under subparagraph (B) of this paragraph shall be calculated separately for each category.

(d) Bonded indebtedness, the taxes of which are not subject to limitation under this section or section 11b of this Article, consists of:

(A) Bonded indebtedness authorized by a provision of this Constitution;

(B) Bonded indebtedness issued on or before November 6, 1990; or

(C) Bonded indebtedness:

(i) Incurred for capital construction or capital improvements; and

(ii)(I) If issued after November 6, 1990, and approved prior to December 5, 1996, the issuance of which has been approved by a majority of voters voting on the question; or

(II) If approved by voters after December 5, 1996, the issuance of which has been approved by a majority of voters voting on the question in an election that is in compliance with the voter participation requirements in subsection (8) of this section.

(12) Bonded indebtedness described in subsection (11) of this section includes bonded indebtedness issued to refund bonded indebtedness described in subsection (11) of this section.

(13) As used in subsection (11) of this section, with respect to bonded indebtedness issued on or after December 5, 1996, "capital construction" and "capital improvements":

(a) Include public safety and law enforcement vehicles with a projected useful life of five years or more; and

(b) Do not include:

(A) Maintenance and repairs, the need for which could reasonably be anticipated.

(B) Supplies and equipment that are not intrinsic to the structure.

(14) Ad valorem property taxes imposed to pay principal and interest on bonded indebtedness described in section 11b of this Article, as modified by subsection (11) of this section, shall be imposed on the assessed value of the property determined under this section or, in the case of specially assessed property, as otherwise provided by law or as limited by this section, whichever is applicable.

(15) If ad valorem property taxes are divided as provided in section 1c, Article IX of this Constitution, in order to fund a redevelopment or urban renewal project, then notwithstanding subsection (1) of this section, the ad valorem property taxes levied against the increase shall be used exclusively to pay any indebtedness incurred for the redevelopment or urban renewal project.

(16) The Legislative Assembly shall enact laws that allow collection of ad valorem property taxes sufficient to pay, when due, indebtedness incurred to carry out urban renewal plans existing on December 5, 1996. These collections shall cease when the indebtedness is paid. Unless excepted from limitation under section 11b of this Article, as modified by subsection (11) of this section, nothing in this subsection shall be construed to remove ad valorem property taxes levied against the increase from the dollar limits in paragraph (b) of subsection (11) of this section.

(17)(a) If, in an election on November 5, 1996, voters approved a new tax base for a local taxing district under repealed section 11 of this Article (1995 Edition) that was not to go into effect until the tax year beginning July 1, 1998, the local taxing district's permanent rate limit under subsection (3) of this section shall be recalculated for the tax year beginning on July 1, 1998, to reflect:

(A) Ad valorem property taxes that would have been imposed had repealed section 11 of this Article (1995 Edition) remained in effect; and

(B) Any other permanent continuing levies that would have been imposed under repealed section 11 of this Article (1995 Edition), as reduced by subsection (3) of this section.

(b) The rate limit determined under this subsection shall be the local taxing district's permanent rate limit for tax years beginning on or after July 1, 1999.

(18) Section 32, Article I, and section 1, Article IX of this Constitution, shall not apply to this section.

(19)(a) The Legislative Assembly shall by statute limit the ability of local taxing districts to impose new or additional fees, taxes, assessments or other charges for the purpose of using the proceeds as alternative sources of funding to make up for ad valorem property tax revenue reductions caused by the initial implementation of this section, unless the new or additional fee, tax, assessment or other charge is approved by voters.

(b) This subsection shall not apply to new or additional fees, taxes, assessments or other charges for a government product or service that a person:

(A) May legally obtain from a source other than government; and

(B) Is reasonably able to obtain from a source other than government.

(c) As used in this subsection, "new or additional fees, taxes, assessments or other charges" does not include moneys received by a local taxing district as:

(A) Rent or lease payments;

(B) Interest, dividends, royalties or other investment earnings;

(C) Fines, penalties and unitary assessments;

(D) Amounts charged to and paid by another unit of government for products, services or property; or

(E) Payments derived from a contract entered into by the local taxing district as a proprietary function of the local taxing district.

(d) This subsection does not apply to a local taxing district that derived less than 10 percent of the local taxing district's operating revenues from ad valorem property taxes, other than ad valorem property taxes imposed to pay bonded indebtedness, during the fiscal year ending June 30, 1996.

(e) An election under this subsection need not comply with the voter participation requirements described in subsection (8) of this section.

(20) If any provision of this section is determined to be unconstitutional or otherwise invalid, the remaining provisions shall continue in full force and effect. [Created through H.J.R. 85, 1997, and adopted by the people May 20, 1997 (this section adopted in lieu of former sections 11, 11a, 11f, 11g, 11h, 11i and 11j of this Article)]

Note: The effective date of House Joint Resolution 85, 1997, is June 19, 1997.

Section 11a. School district tax levy. [Created through S.J.R. 3, 1987, and adopted by the people May 19, 1987; Repeal proposed by H.J.R. 85, 1997, and adopted by the people May 20, 1997 (present section 11 adopted in lieu of this section and sections 11, 11f, 11g, 11h, 11i and 11j of this Article)]

Section 11b. Property tax categories; limitation on categories; exceptions. (1) During and after the fiscal year 1991-92, taxes imposed upon any property shall be separated into two categories: One which dedicates revenues raised specifically to fund the public school system and one which dedicates revenues raised to fund government operations other than the public school system. The taxes in each category shall be limited as set forth in the table which follows and these limits shall apply whether the taxes imposed on property are calculated on the basis of the value of that property or on some other basis:

MAXIMUM ALLOWABLE TAXES

For Each $1000.00 of Property's Real Market Value

Fiscal Year	School System	Other than Schools
1991-1992	$15.00	$10.00
1992-1993	$12.50	$10.00
1993-1994	$10.00	$10.00
1994-1995	$ 7.50	$10.00
1995-1996	$ 5.00	$10.00 and thereafter

Property tax revenues are deemed to be dedicated to funding the public school system if the revenues are to be used exclusively for educational services, including support services, provided by some unit of government, at any level from pre-kindergarten through post-graduate training.

(2) The following definitions shall apply to this section:

(a) "Real market value" is the minimum amount in cash which could reasonably be expected by an informed seller acting without compulsion, from an informed buyer acting without compulsion, in an "arms-length" transaction during the period for which the property is taxed.

(b) A "tax" is any charge imposed by a governmental unit upon property or upon a property owner as a direct consequence of ownership of that property except incurred charges and assessments for local improvements.

(c) "Incurred charges" include and are specifically limited to those charges by government which can be controlled or avoided by the property owner.

(i) because the charges are based on the quantity of the goods or services used and the owner has direct control over the quantity; or

(ii) because the goods or services are provided only on the specific request of the property owner; or

(iii) because the goods or services are provided by the governmental unit only after the individual property owner has failed to meet routine obligations of ownership and such action is deemed necessary to enforce regulations pertaining to health or safety. Incurred charges shall not exceed the actual costs of providing the goods or services.

(d) A "local improvement" is a capital construction project undertaken by a governmental unit

(i) which provides a special benefit only to specific properties or rectifies a problem caused by specific properties, and

(ii) the costs of which are assessed against those properties in a single assessment upon the completion of the project, and

(iii) for which the payment of the assessment plus appropriate interest may be spread over a period of at least ten years. The total of all assessments for a local improvement shall not exceed the actual costs incurred by the governmental unit in designing, constructing and financing the project.

(3) The limitations of subsection (1) of this section apply to all taxes imposed on property or property ownership except

(a) Taxes imposed to pay the principal and interest on bonded indebtedness authorized by a specific provision of this Constitution.

(b) Taxes imposed to pay the principal and interest on bonded indebtedness incurred or to be incurred for capital construction or improvements, provided the bonds are offered as general obligations of the issuing governmental unit and provided further that either the bonds were issued not later than November 6, 1990, or the question of the issuance of the specific bonds has been approved by the electors of the issuing governmental unit.

(4) In the event that taxes authorized by any provision of this Constitution to be imposed upon any property should exceed the limitation imposed on either category of taxing units defined in subsection (1) of this section, then, notwithstanding any other provision of this Constitution, the taxes imposed upon such property by the taxing units in that category shall be reduced evenly by the percentage necessary to meet the limitation for that category. The percentages used to reduce the taxes imposed shall be calculated separately for each category and may vary from property to property within the same taxing unit. The limitation imposed by this section shall not affect the tax base of a taxing unit.

(5) The Legislative Assembly shall replace from the State's general fund any revenue lost by the public school system because of the limitations of this section. The Legislative Assembly is authorized, however, to adopt laws which would limit the total of such replacement revenue plus the taxes imposed within the limitations of this section in any year to the corresponding total for the previous year plus 6 percent. This subsection applies only during fiscal years 1991-92 through 1995-96, inclusive. [Created through initiative petition filed May 8, 1990, and adopted by the people Nov. 6, 1990]

Section 11c. Limits in addition to other tax limits. The limits in section 11b of this Article are in addition to any limits imposed on individual taxing units by this Constitution. [Created through initiative petition filed May 8, 1990, and adopted by the people Nov. 6, 1990]

Section 11d. Effect of section 11b on exemptions and assessments. Nothing in sections 11b to 11e of this Article is intended to require or to prohibit the amendment of any current statute which partially or totally exempts certain classes of property or which prescribes special rules for assessing certain classes of property, unless such amendment is required or prohibited by the implementation of the limitations imposed by section 11b of this Article. [Created through initiative petition filed May 8, 1990, and adopted by the people Nov. 6, 1990]

Section 11e. Severability of sections 11b, 11c and 11d. If any portion, clause or phrase of sections 11b to 11e of this Article is for any reason held to be invalid or unconstitutional by a court of competent jurisdiction, the remaining portions, clauses and phrases shall not be affected but

Constitution

shall remain in full force and effect. [Created through initiative petition filed May 8, 1990, and adopted by the people Nov. 6, 1990]

Section 11f. School district tax levy following merger. [Created through H.J.R. 14, 1989, and adopted by the people Nov. 6, 1990; Repeal proposed by H.J.R. 85, 1997, and adopted by the people May 20, 1997 (present section 11 adopted in lieu of this section and sections 11, 11a, 11g, 11h, 11i and 11j of this Article)]

Note: Section 11f was designated as "Section 11b" by H.J.R. 14, 1989, and adopted by the people Nov. 6, 1990.

Section 11g. Tax increase limitation; exceptions. [Created through initiative petition filed Dec. 8, 1995, and adopted by the people Nov. 5, 1996; Repeal proposed by H.J.R. 85, 1997, and adopted by the people May 20, 1997 (present section 11 adopted in lieu of this section and sections 11, 11a, 11f, 11h, 11i and 11j of this Article)]

Section 11h. Voluntary contributions for support of schools or other public entities. [Created through initiative petition filed Dec. 8, 1995, and adopted by the people Nov. 5, 1996; Repeal proposed by H.J.R. 85, 1997, and adopted by the people May 20, 1997 (present section 11 adopted in lieu of this section and sections 11, 11a, 11f, 11g, 11i and 11j of this Article)]

Section 11i. Legislation to implement limitation and contribution provisions. [Created through initiative petition filed Dec. 8, 1995, and adopted by the people Nov. 5, 1996; Repeal proposed by H.J.R. 85, 1997, and adopted by the people May 20, 1997 (present section 11 adopted in lieu of this section and sections 11, 11a, 11f, 11g, 11h and 11j of this Article)]

Section 11j. Severability of sections 11g, 11h and 11i. [Created through initiative petition filed Dec. 8, 1995, and adopted by the people Nov. 5, 1996; Repeal proposed by H.J.R. 85, 1997, and adopted by the people May 20, 1997 (present section 11 adopted in lieu of this section and sections 11, 11a, 11f, 11g, 11h and 11i of this Article)]

Section 11k. Limitation on applicability of section 11 (8) voting requirements to elections on measures held in May or November of any year. Notwithstanding subsection (8) of section 11 of this Article, subsection (8) of section 11 of this Article does not apply to any measure voted on in an election held in May or November of any year. [Created through H.J.R. 15, 2007, and adopted by the people Nov. 4, 2008]

Section 11L. Limitation on applicability of sections 11 and 11b on bonded indebtedness to finance capital costs. (1) The limitations of sections 11 and 11b of this Article do not apply to bonded indebtedness incurred by local taxing districts if the bonded indebtedness was incurred on or after January 1, 2011, to finance capital costs as defined in subsection (5) of this section.

(2) Bonded indebtedness described in subsection (1) of this section includes bonded indebtedness issued to refund bonded indebtedness described in subsection (1) of this section.

(3) Notwithstanding subsection (1) of this section, subsection (8) of section 11 of this Article, as limited by section 11k of this Article, applies to measures that authorize bonded indebtedness described in subsection (1) of this section.

(4) The weighted average life of bonded indebtedness incurred on or after January 1, 2011, to finance capital costs may not exceed the weighted average life of the capital costs that are financed with that indebtedness.

(5)(a) As used in this section, "capital costs" means costs of land and of other assets having a useful life of more than one year, including costs associated with acquisition, construction, improvement, remodeling, furnishing, equipping, maintenance or repair.

(b) "Capital costs" does not include costs of routine maintenance or supplies. [Created through H.J.R. 13, 2009, and adopted by the people May 18, 2010]

Section 12. People's utility districts. Peoples' [sic] Utility Districts may be created of territory, contiguous or otherwise, within one or more counties, and may consist of an incorporated municipality, or municipalities, with or without unincorporated territory, for the purpose of supplying water for domestic and municipal purposes; for the development of water power and/or electric energy; and for the distribution, disposal and sale of water, water power and electric energy. Such districts shall be managed by boards of directors, consisting of five members, who shall be residents of such districts. Such districts shall have power:

(a) To call and hold elections within their respective districts.

(b) To levy taxes upon the taxable property of such districts.

(c) To issue, sell and assume evidences of indebtedness.

(d) To enter into contracts.

(e) To exercise the power of eminent domain.

(f) To acquire and hold real and other property necessary or incident to the business of such districts.

(g) To acquire, develop, and/or otherwise provide for a supply of water, water power and electric energy.

Such districts may sell, distribute and/or otherwise dispose of water, water power and electric energy within or without the territory of such districts. The legislative assembly shall and the people may provide any legislation, that may be necessary, in addition to existing laws, to carry out the provisions of this section. [Created through initiative petition filed July 3, 1930, and adopted by the people Nov. 4, 1930]

Section 13. Interests of employes when operation of transportation system assumed by public body. Notwithstanding the provisions of section 20, Article I, section 10, Article VI, and sections 2 and 9, Article XI, of this Constitution, when any city, county, political subdivision, public agency or municipal corporation assumes responsibility for the operation of a public transportation system, the city, county, political subdivision, public agency or municipal corporation shall make fair and equitable arrangements to protect the interests of employes and retired employes affected. Such protective arrangements may include, without being limited to, such provisions as may be necessary for the preservation of rights, privileges and benefits (including continuation of pension rights and payment of benefits) under existing collective bargaining agreements, or otherwise. [Created through H.J.R. 13, 1965, and adopted by the people Nov. 8, 1966]

Section 14. Metropolitan service district charter. (1) The Legislative Assembly shall provide by law a method whereby the legal electors of any metropolitan service district organized under the laws of this state, by majority vote of such electors voting thereon at any legally called election, may adopt, amend, revise or repeal a district charter.

(2) A district charter shall prescribe the organization of the district government and shall provide directly, or by its authority, for the number, election or appointment, qualifications, tenure, compensation, powers and duties of such officers as the district considers necessary. Such officers shall among them exercise all the powers and perform all the duties, as granted to, imposed upon or distributed among district officers by the Constitution or laws of this state, by the district charter or by its authority.

(3) A district charter may provide for the exercise by ordinance of powers granted to the district by the Constitution or laws of this state.

(4) A metropolitan service district shall have jurisdiction over matters of metropolitan concern as set forth in the charter of the district.

(5) The initiative and referendum powers reserved to the people by this Constitution hereby are further reserved to the legal electors of a metropolitan service district relative to the adoption, amendment, revision or repeal of a district charter and district legislation enacted thereunder. Such powers shall be exercised in the manner provided for county measures under section 10, Article VI of this Constitution. [Created by S.J.R. 2, 1989, and adopted by the people Nov. 6, 1990]

Section 15. Funding of programs imposed upon local governments; exceptions. (1) Except as provided in subsection (7) of this section, when the Legislative Assembly or any state agency requires any local government to establish a new program or provide an increased level of service for an existing program, the State of Oregon shall appropriate and allocate to the local government moneys sufficient to pay the ongoing, usual and reasonable costs of performing the mandated service or activity.

(2) As used in this section:

(a) "Enterprise activity" means a program under which a local government sells products or services in competition with a nongovernment entity.

(b) "Local government" means a city, county, municipal corporation or municipal utility operated by a board or commission.

(c) "Program" means a program or project imposed by enactment of the Legislative Assembly or by rule or order of a state agency under which a local government must provide administrative, financial, social, health or other specified services to persons, government agencies or to the public generally.

(d) "Usual and reasonable costs" means those costs incurred by the affected local governments for a specific program using generally accepted methods of service delivery and administrative practice.

(3) A local government is not required to comply with any state law or administrative rule or order enacted or adopted after January 1, 1997, that requires the expenditure of money by the local government for a new program or increased level of service for an existing program until the state appropriates and allocates to the local government reimbursement for any costs incurred to carry out the law, rule or order and unless the Legislative Assembly provides, by appropriation, reimbursement in each succeeding year for such costs. However, a local government may refuse to comply with a state law or administrative rule or order under this subsection only if the amount appropriated and allocated to the local government by the Legislative Assembly for a program in a fiscal year:

(a) Is less than 95 percent of the usual and reasonable costs incurred by the local government in conducting the program at the same level of service in the preceding fiscal year; or

(b) Requires the local government to spend for the program, in addition to the amount appropriated and allocated by the Legislative Assembly, an amount that exceeds one-hundredth of one percent of the annual budget adopted by the governing body of the local government for that fiscal year.

(4) When a local government determines that a program is a program for which moneys are required to be appropriated and allocated under subsection (1) of this section, if the local government expended moneys to conduct the program and was not reimbursed under this section for the usual and reasonable costs of the program, the local government may submit the issue of reimbursement to non-binding arbitration by a panel of three arbitrators. The panel shall consist of one representative from the Oregon Department of Administrative Services, the League of Oregon Cities and the Association of Oregon Counties.

The panel shall determine whether the costs incurred by the local government are required to be reimbursed under this section and the amount of reimbursement. The decision of the arbitration panel is not binding upon the parties and may not be enforced by any court in this state.

(5) In any legal proceeding or arbitration proceeding under this section, the local government shall bear the burden of proving by a preponderance of the evidence that moneys appropriated by the Legislative Assembly are not sufficient to reimburse the local government for the usual and reasonable costs of a program.

(6) Except upon approval by three-fifths of the membership of each house of the Legislative Assembly, the Legislative Assembly shall not enact, amend or repeal any law if the anticipated effect of the action is to reduce the amount of state revenues derived from a specific state tax and distributed to local governments as an aggregate during the distribution period for such revenues immediately preceding January 1, 1997.

(7) This section shall not apply to:

(a) Any law that is approved by three-fifths of the membership of each house of the Legislative Assembly.

(b) Any costs resulting from a law creating or changing the definition of a crime or a law establishing sentences for conviction of a crime.

(c) An existing program as enacted by legislation prior to January 1, 1997, except for legislation withdrawing state funds for programs required prior to January 1, 1997, unless the program is made optional.

(d) A new program or an increased level of program services established pursuant to action of the Federal Government so long as the program or increased level of program services imposes costs on local governments that are no greater than the usual and reasonable costs to local governments resulting from compliance with the minimum program standards required under federal law or regulations.

(e) Any requirement imposed by the judicial branch of government.

(f) Legislation enacted or approved by electors in this state under the initiative and referendum powers reserved to the people under section 1, Article IV of this Constitution.

(g) Programs that are intended to inform citizens about the activities of local governments.

(8) When a local government is not required under subsection (3) of this section to comply with a state law or administrative rule or order relating to an enterprise activity, if a nongovernment entity competes with the local government by selling products or services that are similar to the products and services sold under the enterprise activity, the nongovernment entity is not required to comply with the state law or administrative rule or order relating to that enterprise activity.

(9) Nothing in this section shall give rise to a claim by a private person against the State of Oregon based on the establishment of a new program or an increased level of service for an existing program without sufficient appropriation and allocation of funds to pay the ongoing, usual and reasonable costs of performing the mandated service or activity.

(10) Subsection (4) of this section does not apply to a local government when the local government is voluntarily providing a program four years after the effective date of the enactment, rule or order that imposed the program.

(11) In lieu of appropriating and allocating funds under this section, the Legislative Assembly may identify and direct the imposition of a fee or charge to be used by a local government to recover the actual cost of the program.

[Created through H.J.R. 2, 1995, and adopted by the people Nov. 5, 1996]

Section 15a. Subsequent vote for reaffirmation of section 15. [Created through H.J.R. 2, 1995, and adopted by the people Nov. 5, 1996; Repeal proposed by S.J.R. 39, 1999, and adopted by the people Nov. 7, 2000]

ARTICLE XI-A
RURAL CREDITS

[Created through initiative petition filed July 6, 1916, and adopted by the people Nov. 7, 1916; Repeal proposed by S.J.R. 1, 1941, and adopted by the people Nov. 3, 1942]

ARTICLE XI-A
FARM AND HOME LOANS TO VETERANS

Sec. 1. State empowered to make farm and home loans to veterans; standards and priorities for loans
2. Bonds
3. Eligibility to receive loans
4. Tax levy
5. Repeal of conflicting constitutional provisions
6. Refunding bonds

Section 1. State empowered to make farm and home loans to veterans; standards and priorities for loans. (1) Notwithstanding the limits contained in section 7, Article XI of this Constitution, the credit of the State of Oregon may be loaned and indebtedness incurred in an amount not to exceed eight percent of the true cash value of all the property in the state, for the purpose of creating a fund, to be known as the "Oregon War Veterans' Fund," to be advanced for the acquisition of farms and homes for the benefit of male and female residents of the State of Oregon who served in the Armed Forces of the United States. Secured repayment thereof shall be and is a prerequisite to the advancement of money from such fund, except that moneys in the Oregon War Veterans' Fund may also be appropriated to the Director of Veterans' Affairs to be expended, without security, for the following purposes:

(a) Aiding veterans' organizations in connection with their programs of service to veterans;

(b) Training service officers appointed by the counties to give aid as provided by law to veterans and their dependents;

(c) Aiding the counties in connection with programs of service to veterans;

(d) The duties of the Director of Veterans' Affairs as conservator of the estates of beneficiaries of the United States Veterans' Administration; and

(e) The duties of the Director of Veterans' Affairs in providing services to veterans, their dependents and survivors.

(2) The Director of Veterans' Affairs may establish standards and priorities with respect to the granting of loans from the Oregon War Veterans' Fund that, as determined by the director, best accomplish the purposes and promote the financial sustainability of the Oregon War Veterans' Fund, including, but not limited to, standards and priorities necessary to maintain the tax-exempt status of earnings from bonds issued under authority of this section and section 2 of this Article. [Created through H.J.R. 7, 1943, and adopted by the people Nov. 7, 1944; Amendment proposed by H.J.R. 1, 1949, and adopted by the people Nov. 7, 1950; Amendment proposed by H.J.R. 14, 1951, and adopted by the people Nov. 4, 1952; Amendment proposed by S.J.R. 14, 1959, and adopted by the people Nov. 8, 1960; Amendment proposed by H.J.R. 9, 1967, and adopted by the people Nov. 5, 1968; Amendment proposed by H.J.R. 33, 1969, and adopted by the people Nov. 3, 1970; Amendment proposed by H.J.R. 12, 1973, and adopted by the people May 28, 1974; Amendment proposed by H.J.R. 10, 1977, and adopted by the people May 17, 1977;

Amendment proposed by S.J.R. 53, 1977, and adopted by the people May 17, 1977; Amendment proposed by S.J.R. 2, 1999, and adopted by the people Nov. 7, 2000; Amendment proposed by H.J.R. 7, 2009, and adopted by the people Nov. 2, 2010]

Section 2. Bonds. Bonds of the state of Oregon containing a direct promise on behalf of the state to pay the face value thereof, with the interest therein provided for, may be issued to an amount authorized by section 1 hereof for the purpose of creating said "Oregon War Veterans' Fund." Said bonds shall be a direct obligation of the state and shall be in such form and shall run for such periods of time and bear such rates of interest as provided by statute. [Created through H.J.R. 7, 1943, and adopted by the people Nov. 7, 1944; Amendment proposed by H.J.R. 1, 1949, and adopted by the people Nov. 7, 1950]

Section 3. Eligibility to receive loans. No person shall receive money from the Oregon War Veterans' Fund except the following:

(1) A person who:

(a) Resides in the State of Oregon at the time of applying for a loan from the fund;

(b) Is a veteran, as that term is defined by Oregon law;

(c) Served under honorable conditions on active duty in the Armed Forces of the United States; and

(d) Satisfies the requirements applicable to the funding source for the loan from the Oregon War Veterans' Fund.

(2)(a) The spouse of a person who is qualified to receive a loan under subsection (1) of this section but who has either been missing in action or a prisoner of war while on active duty in the Armed Forces of the United States even though the status of missing or being a prisoner occurred prior to completion of a minimum length of service or the person never resided in this state, provided the spouse resides in this state at the time of application for the loan.

(b) The surviving spouse of a person who was qualified to receive a loan under subsection (1) of this section but who died while on active duty in the Armed Forces of the United States even though the death occurred prior to completion of a minimum length of service or the person never resided in this state, provided the surviving spouse resides in this state at the time of application for the loan.

(c) The eligibility of a surviving spouse under this subsection shall terminate on the spouse's remarriage.

(3) As used in this section, "active duty" does not include attendance at a school under military orders, except schooling incident to an active enlistment or a regular tour of duty, or normal military training as a reserve officer or member of an organized reserve or National Guard unit. [Created through H.J.R. 7, 1943, and adopted by the people Nov. 7, 1944; Amendment proposed by H.J.R. 1, 1949, and adopted by the people Nov. 7, 1950; Amendment proposed by H.J.R. 14, 1951, and adopted by the people Nov. 4, 1952; Amendment proposed by S.J.R. 14, 1959, and adopted by the people Nov. 8, 1960; Amendment proposed by H.J.R. 9, 1967, and adopted by the people Nov. 5, 1968; Amendment proposed by S.J.R. 23, 1971, and adopted by the people Nov. 7, 1972; Amendment proposed by H.J.R. 23, 1975, and adopted by the people May 25, 1976; Amendment proposed by H.J.R. 23, 1979, and adopted by the people May 20, 1980; Amendment proposed by S.J.R. 3, 1995, and adopted by the people Nov. 5, 1996; Amendment proposed by S.J.R. 2, 1999, and adopted by the people Nov. 7, 2000; Amendment proposed by H.J.R. 7, 2009, and adopted by the people Nov. 2, 2010]

Section 4. Tax levy. There shall be levied each year, at the same time and in the same manner that other taxes are levied, a tax upon all property in the state of Oregon not exempt from taxation, not to exceed two (2) mills on each dollar valuation, to provide for the payment of principal and interest of the bonds authorized to be issued by this article. The two (2) mills additional tax herein provided for hereby is specifically authorized and said tax levy hereby authorized shall be in addition to all other taxes which may be levied according to law. [Created through H.J.R. 7, 1943, and adopted by the people Nov. 7, 1944; Amendment proposed by H.J.R. 85, 1997, and adopted by the people May 20, 1997]

Section 5. Repeal of conflicting constitutional provisions. The provisions of the constitution in conflict with this amendment hereby are repealed so far as they conflict herewith. [Created through H.J.R. 7, 1943, and adopted by the people Nov. 7, 1944]

Section 6. Refunding bonds. Refunding bonds may be issued and sold to refund any bonds issued under authority of sections 1 and 2 of this article. There may be issued and outstanding at any one time bonds aggregating the amount authorized by section 1 hereof, but at no time shall the total of all bonds outstanding, including refunding bonds, exceed the amount so authorized. [Created through H.J.R. 7, 1943, and adopted by the people Nov. 7, 1944]

ARTICLE XI-B
STATE PAYMENT OF IRRIGATION AND DRAINAGE DISTRICT INTEREST

[Created through H.J.R. 32, 1919, and adopted by the people June 3, 1919; Repeal proposed by H.J.R. 1, 1929, and adopted by the people Nov. 4, 1930]

ARTICLE XI-C
WORLD WAR VETERANS' STATE AID SINKING FUND

[Created through H.J.R. 12, 1921, and adopted by the people June 7, 1921; Amendment proposed by H.J.R. 7, 1923, and adopted by the people Nov. 4, 1924; Repeal proposed by S.J.R. 12, 1951, and adopted by the people Nov. 4, 1952]

ARTICLE XI-D
STATE POWER DEVELOPMENT

Sec. 1. State's rights, title and interest to water and water-power sites to be held in perpetuity
   2. State's powers enumerated
   3. Legislation to effectuate article
   4. Construction of article

Section 1. State's rights, title and interest to water and water-power sites to be held in perpetuity. The rights, title and interest in and to all water for the development of water power and to water power sites, which the state of Oregon now owns or may hereafter acquire, shall be held by it in perpetuity. [Created through initiative petition filed July 7, 1932, and adopted by the people Nov. 8, 1932]

Section 2. State's powers enumerated. The state of Oregon is authorized and empowered:

(1) To control and/or develop the water power within the state;

(2) To lease water and water power sites for the development of water power;

(3) To control, use, transmit, distribute, sell and/or dispose of electric energy;

(4) To develop, separately or in conjunction with the United States, or in conjunction with the political subdivisions of this state, any water power within the state, and to acquire, construct, maintain and/or operate hydroelectric power plants, transmission and distribution lines;(

(5) To develop, separately or in conjunction with the United States, with any state or states, or political subdivisions thereof, or with any political subdivision of this state, any water power in any interstate stream and to acquire, construct, maintain and/or operate hydroelectric power plants, transmission and distribution lines;

(6) To contract with the United States, with any state or states, or political subdivisions thereof, or with any political subdivision of this state, for the purchase or acquisition of water, water power and/or electric energy for use, transmission, distribution, sale and/or disposal thereof;

(7) To fix rates and charges for the use of water in the development of water power and for the sale and/or disposal of water power and/or electric energy;

(8) To loan the credit of the state, and to incur indebtedness to an amount not exceeding one and one-half percent of the true cash value of all the property in the state taxed on an ad valorem basis, for the purpose of providing funds with which to carry out the provisions of this article, notwithstanding any limitations elsewhere contained in this constitution;

(9) To do any and all things necessary or convenient to carry out the provisions of this article. [Created through initiative petition filed July 7, 1932, and adopted by the people Nov. 8, 1932; Amendment proposed by S.J.R. 6, 1961, and adopted by the people Nov. 6, 1962]

Section 3. Legislation to effectuate article. The legislative assembly shall, and the people may, provide any legislation that may be necessary in addition to existing laws, to carry out the provisions of this article; Provided, that any board or commission created, or empowered to administer the laws enacted to carry out the purposes of this article shall consist of three members and be elected without party affiliation or designation. [Created through initiative petition filed July 7, 1932, and adopted by the people Nov. 8, 1932]

Section 4. Construction of article. Nothing in this article shall be construed to affect in any way the laws, and the administration thereof, now existing or hereafter enacted, relating to the appropriation and use of water for beneficial purposes, other than for the development of water power. [Created through initiative petition filed July 7, 1932, and adopted by the people Nov. 8, 1932]

ARTICLE XI-E
STATE REFORESTATION

Section 1. State empowered to lend credit for forest rehabilitation and reforestation; bonds; taxation. The credit of the state may be loaned and indebtedness incurred in an amount which shall not exceed at any one time 3/16 of 1 percent of the true cash value of all the property in the state taxed on an ad valorem basis, to provide funds for forest rehabilitation and reforestation and for the acquisition, management, and development of lands for such purposes. So long as any such indebtedness shall remain outstanding, the funds derived from the sale, exchange, or use of said lands, and from the disposal of products therefrom, shall be applied only in the liquidation of such indebtedness. Bonds or other obligations issued pursuant hereto may be renewed or refunded. An ad valorem tax shall be levied annually upon all the property in the state of Oregon taxed on an ad valorem basis, in sufficient amount to provide for the payment of such indebtedness and the interest thereon. The legislative assembly may provide other revenues to supplement or replace the said tax levies. The legislature shall enact legislation to carry out the provisions hereof. This amendment shall supersede all constitutional provisions in conflict herewith. [Created through H.J.R. 24, 1947, and adopted by the people Nov. 2, 1948; Amendment proposed by S.J.R. 7, 1961, and adopted by the people Nov. 6, 1962; Amendment proposed by H.J.R. 85, 1997, and adopted by the people May 20, 1997]

ARTICLE XI-F(1)
HIGHER EDUCATION BUILDING PROJECTS

Sec. 1. State empowered to lend credit for higher education building projects
2. Limitation on authorization to incur indebtedness
3. Sources of revenue
4. Bonds
5. Legislation to effectuate Article

Section 1. State empowered to lend credit for higher education building projects. The credit of the state may be loaned and indebtedness incurred in an amount which shall not exceed at any one time three-fourths of one percent of the true cash value of all the taxable property in the state, as determined by law to provide funds with which to acquire, construct, improve, repair, equip and furnish buildings, structures, land and other projects, or parts thereof, that the legislative assembly determines will benefit higher education institutions or activities. [Created through H.J.R. 26, 1949, and adopted by the people Nov. 7, 1950; Amendment proposed by H.J.R. 12, 1959, and adopted by the people Nov. 8, 1960; Amendment proposed by H.J.R. 101, 2010, and adopted by the people May 18, 2010]

Section 2. Limitation on authorization to incur indebtedness. Indebtedness shall not be incurred to finance projects described in section 1 of this Article unless the constructing authority conservatively estimates that the constructing authority will have sufficient revenues to pay the indebtedness and operate the projects financed with the proceeds of the indebtedness. For purposes of this section, "revenues" includes all funds available to the constructing authority except amounts appropriated by the legislative assembly from the General Fund. [Created through H.J.R. 26, 1949, and adopted by the people Nov. 7, 1950; Amendment proposed by H.J.R. 101, 2010, and adopted by the people May 18, 2010]

Section 3. Sources of revenue. Ad valorem taxes shall be levied annually upon all the taxable property in the state of Oregon in sufficient amount, with the aforesaid revenues, to provide for the payment of such indebtedness and the interest thereon. The legislative assembly may provide other revenues to supplement or replace such tax levies. [Created through H.J.R. 26, 1949, and adopted by the people Nov. 7, 1950; Amendment proposed by H.J.R. 101, 2010, and adopted by the people May 18, 2010]

Section 4. Bonds. Bonds issued pursuant to this article shall be the direct general obligations of the state, and be in such form, run for such periods of time, and bear such rates of interest, as shall be provided by statute. Such bonds may be refunded with bonds of like obligation. Unless provided by statute, no bonds shall be issued pursuant to this article for the construction of buildings or other structures for higher education until after all of the aforesaid outstanding revenue bonds shall have been redeemed or refunded. [Created through H.J.R. 26, 1949, and adopted by the people Nov. 7, 1950]

Section 5. Legislation to effectuate Article. The legislative assembly shall enact legislation to carry out the provisions hereof. This article shall supersede all conflicting constitutional provisions. [Created through H.J.R. 26, 1949, and adopted by the people Nov. 7, 1950]

ARTICLE XI-F(2)
VETERANS' BONUS

Sec. 1. State empowered to lend credit to pay veterans' bonus; issuance of bonds
2. Definitions
3. Amount of bonus
4. Survivors of certain deceased veterans entitled to maximum amount

5. Certain persons not eligible
6. Order of distribution among survivors
7. Bonus not saleable or assignable; bonus free from creditors' claims and state taxes
8. Administration of Article; rules and regulations
9. Applications
10. Furnishing forms; printing, office supplies and equipment; employes; payment of expenses

Section 1. State empowered to lend credit to pay veterans' bonus; issuance of bonds. Notwithstanding the limitations contained in Section 7 of Article XI of the constitution, the credit of the State of Oregon may be loaned and indebtedness incurred to an amount not exceeding 5 percent of the assessed valuation of all the property in the state, for the purpose of creating a fund to be paid to residents of the State of Oregon who served in the armed forces of the United States between September 16, 1940, and June 30, 1946, and were honorably discharged from such service, which fund shall be known as the "World War II Veterans' Compensation Fund."

Bonds of the State of Oregon, containing a direct promise on behalf of the state to pay the face value thereof with the interest thereon provided for may be issued to an amount authorized in Section 1 hereof for the purpose of creating said World War II Veterans' Compensation Fund. Refunding bonds may be issued and sold to refund any bonds issued under authority of Section 1 hereof. There may be issued and outstanding at any one time bonds aggregating the amount authorized by Section 1, but at no time shall the total of all bonds outstanding, including refunding bonds, exceed the amount so authorized. Said bonds shall be a direct obligation of the State and shall be in such form and shall run for such periods of time and bear such rates of interest as shall be provided by statute. No person shall be eligible to receive money from said fund except the veterans as defined in Section 3 of this act [sic]. The legislature shall and the people may provide any additional legislation that may be necessary, in addition to existing laws, to carry out the provisions of this section. [Created through initiative petition filed June 30, 1950, and adopted by the people Nov. 7, 1950]

Section 2. Definitions. The following words, terms, and phrases, as used in this act [sic] shall have the following meaning unless the text otherwise requires:

(1) "Domestic service" means service within the continental limits of the United States, excluding Alaska, Hawaii, Canal Zone and Puerto Rico.

(2) "Foreign Service" means service in all other places, including sea duty.

(3) "Husband" means the unremarried husband, and "wife" means the unremarried wife.

(4) "Child or Children" means child or children of issue, child or children by adoption or child or children to whom the deceased person has stood in loco parentis for one year or more immediately preceding his death.

(5) "Parent or Parents" means natural parent or parents; parent or parents by adoption; or, person or persons, including stepparent or stepparents, who have stood in loco parentis to the deceased person for a period of one year or more immediately prior to entrance into the armed service of the United States.

(6) "Veterans" means any person who shall have served in active duty in the armed forces of the United States at any time between September 16, 1940, and June 30, 1946, both dates inclusive, and who, at the time of commencing such service, was and had been a bona fide resident of the State of Oregon for at least one year immediately preceding the commencement of such service, and who shall have been separated from such service under honorable conditions, or who is still in such service, or who has been retired. [Created through initiative petition filed June 30, 1950, and adopted by the people Nov. 7, 1950]

Section 3. Amount of bonus. Every veteran who was in such service for a period of at least 90 days shall be entitled to receive compensation at the rate of Ten Dollars ($10.00) for each full month during which such veteran was in active domestic service and Fifteen Dollars ($15.00) for each full month during which such veteran was in active foreign service within said period of time. Any veteran who was serving on active duty in the armed forces between September 16, 1940, and June 30, 1946, whose services were terminated by reason of service-connected disabilities, and who, upon filing a claim for disabilities with the United States Veterans' Administration within three months after separation from the armed service, was rated not less than 50% disabled as a result of such claim, shall be deemed to have served sufficient time to entitle him or her to the maximum payment under this act [sic] and shall be so entitled. The maximum amount of compensation payable under this act [sic] shall be six hundred dollars ($600.00) and no such compensation shall be paid to any veteran who shall have received from another state a bonus or compensation because of such military service. [Created through initiative petition filed June 30, 1950, and adopted by the people Nov. 7, 1950]

Section 4. Survivors of certain deceased veterans entitled to maximum amount. The survivor or survivors, of the deceased veteran whose death was caused or contributed to by a service-connected disease or disability incurred in service under conditions other than dishonorable, shall be entitled, in the order of survivorship provided in this act [sic], to receive the maximum amount of said compensation irrespective of the amount such deceased would have been entitled to receive if living. [Created through initiative petition filed June 30, 1950, and adopted by the people Nov. 7, 1950]

Section 5. Certain persons not eligible. No compensation shall be paid under this act [sic] to any veteran who, during the period of service refused on conscientious, political or other grounds to subject himself to full military discipline and unqualified service, or to any veteran for any periods of time spent under penal confinement during the period of active duty, or for service in the merchant marine: Provided, however, that for the purposes of this act [sic], active service in the chaplain corps, or medical corps shall be deemed unqualified service under full military discipline. [Created through initiative petition filed June 30, 1950, and adopted by the people Nov. 7, 1950]

Section 6. Order of distribution among survivors. The survivor or survivors of any deceased veteran who would have been entitled to compensation under this act [sic], other than those mentioned in Section 4 of this act [sic], shall be entitled to receive the same amount of compensation as said deceased veteran would have received, if living, which shall be distributed as follows:

(1) To the husband or wife, as the case may be, the whole amount.

(2) If there be no husband or wife, to the child or children, equally; and

(3) If there be no husband or wife or child or children, to the parent or parents, equally. [Created through initiative petition filed June 30, 1950, and adopted by the people Nov. 7, 1950]

Section 7. Bonus not saleable or assignable; bonus free from creditors' claims and state taxes. No sale or assignment of any right or claim to compensation under this act [sic] shall be valid, no claims of creditors shall be enforcible against rights or claims to or payments of such compensation, and such compensation shall be exempt from all taxes imposed by the laws of this state. [Created through initiative petition filed June 30, 1950, and adopted by the people Nov. 7, 1950]

Section 8. Administration of article; rules and regulations. The director of Veterans' Affairs, State of Oregon, referred to herein as the "director" hereby is authorized and empowered, and it shall be his duty, to administer the provisions of this act [sic], and with the approval of the veterans advisory committee may make such rules and regulations as are deemed necessary to accomplish the purpose hereof. [Created through initiative petition filed June 30, 1950, and adopted by the people Nov. 7, 1950]

Section 9. Applications. All applications for certificates under this act [sic] shall be made within two years from the effective date hereof and upon forms to be supplied by the director. Said applications shall be duly verified by the claimant before a notary public or other person authorized to take acknowledgments, and shall set forth applicant's name, residence at the time of entry into the service, date and place of enlistment, induction or entry upon active federal service, beginning and ending dates of foreign service, date of discharge, retirement or release from active federal service, statement of time lost by reason of penal confinement during the period of active duty; together with the applicant's original discharge, or certificate in lieu of lost discharge, or certificate of service, or if the applicant has not been released at the time of application, a statement by competent military authority that the applicant during the period for which compensation is claimed did not refuse to subject himself to full military discipline and unqualified service, and that the applicant has not been separated from service under circumstances other than honorable. The director may require such further information to be included in such application as deemed necessary to enable him to determine the eligibility of the applicant. Such applications, together with satisfactory evidence of honorable service, shall be filed with the director. The director shall make such reasonable requirements for applicants as may be necessary to prevent fraud or the payment of compensation to persons not entitled thereto. [Created through initiative petition filed June 30, 1950, and adopted by the people Nov. 7, 1950]

Section 10. Furnishing forms; printing, office supplies and equipment; employes; payment of expenses. The director shall furnish free of charge, upon request, the necessary forms upon which applications may be made and may authorize the county clerks, Veterans organizations and other organizations, and notaries public willing to assist veterans without charge, to act for him in receiving application under this act [sic], and shall furnish such clerks, organizations and notaries public, with the proper forms for such purpose. The director hereby is authorized and directed with the approval of the veterans' advisory committee, to procure such printing, office supplies and equipment and to employ such persons as may be necessary in order to properly carry out the provisions of this act [sic], and all expense incurred by him in the administration thereof shall be paid out of the World War II Veterans' Compensation Fund, in the manner provided by law for payment of claims from other state funds. [Created through initiative petition filed June 30, 1950, and adopted by the people Nov. 7, 1950]

ARTICLE XI-G
HIGHER EDUCATION INSTITUTIONS AND ACTIVITIES; COMMUNITY COLLEGES

Section 1. State empowered to lend credit for financing higher education institutions and activities, and community colleges. (1) Notwithstanding the limitations contained in section 7, Article XI of this Constitution, and in addition to other exceptions from the limitations of such section, the credit of the state may be loaned and indebtedness incurred in an amount not to exceed at any time three-fourths of one percent of the true cash value of all taxable property in the state, as determined by law.

(2) Proceeds from any loan authorized or indebtedness incurred under this section shall be used to provide funds with which to acquire, construct, improve, repair, equip and furnish buildings, structures, land and other projects, or parts thereof, that the Legislative Assembly determines will benefit higher education institutions or activities or community colleges authorized by law to receive state aid.

(3) The amount of any indebtedness incurred under this section in any biennium shall be matched by an amount that is at least equal to the amount of the indebtedness. The matching amount must be used for the same or similar purposes as the proceeds of the indebtedness and may consist of moneys appropriated from the General Fund or any other moneys available to the constructing authority for such purposes. However, the matching amount may not consist of proceeds of indebtedness incurred by the state under any other Article of this Constitution. Any matching amount appropriated from the General Fund to meet the requirements of this subsection must be specifically designated therefor by the Legislative Assembly.

(4) Nothing in this section prevents the financing of projects, or parts thereof, by a combination of the moneys available under this section, under Article XI-F(1) of this Constitution, and from other lawful sources. [Created through H.J.R. 8, 1963 (s.s.), and adopted by the people May 15, 1964; Amendment proposed by H.J.R. 2, 1967 (s.s.), and adopted by the people May 28, 1968; Amendment proposed by H.J.R. 101, 2010, and adopted by the people May 18, 2010]

Section 2. Bonds. Bonds issued pursuant to this Article shall be the direct general obligations of the state and shall be in such form, run for such periods of time, and bear such rates of interest as the Legislative Assembly provides. Such bonds may be refunded with bonds of like obligation. [Created through H.J.R. 8, 1963 (s.s.), and adopted by the people May 15, 1964]

Section 3. Sources of revenue. Ad valorem taxes shall be levied annually upon the taxable property within the State of Oregon in sufficient amount to provide for the prompt payment of bonds issued pursuant to this Article and the interest thereon. The Legislative Assembly may provide other revenues to supplement or replace, in whole or in part, such tax levies. [Created through H.J.R. 8, 1963 (s.s.), and adopted by the people May 15, 1964]

ARTICLE XI-H
POLLUTION CONTROL

Sec. 1. State empowered to lend credit for financing pollution control facilities or related activities
2. Only facilities 70 percent self-supporting and self-liquidating authorized; exceptions
3. Authority of public bodies to receive funds
4. Sources of revenue
5. Bonds
6. Legislation to effectuate Article

Section 1. State empowered to lend credit for financing pollution control facilities or related activities. In the manner provided by law and notwithstanding the limitations contained in sections 7 and 8, Article XI, of this Constitution, the credit of the State of Oregon may be loaned and indebtedness incurred in an amount not to

exceed, at any one time, one percent of the true cash value of all taxable property in the state:

(1) To provide funds to be advanced, by contract, grant, loan or otherwise, to any municipal corporation, city, county or agency of the State of Oregon, or combinations thereof, for the purpose of planning, acquisition, construction, alteration or improvement of facilities for or activities related to, the collection, treatment, dilution and disposal of all forms of waste in or upon the air, water and lands of this state; and

(2) To provide funds for the acquisition, by purchase, loan or otherwise, of bonds, notes or other obligations of any municipal corporation, city, county or agency of the State of Oregon, or combinations thereof, issued or made for the purposes of subsection (1) of this section. [Created through H.J.R. 14, 1969, and adopted by the people May 26, 1970; Amendment proposed by S.J.R. 41, 1989, and adopted by the people May 22, 1990]

Section 2. Only facilities 70 percent self-supporting and self-liquidating authorized; exceptions. The facilities for which funds are advanced and for which bonds, notes or other obligations are issued or made and acquired pursuant to this Article shall be only such facilities as conservatively appear to the agency designated by law to make the determination to be not less than 70 percent self-supporting and self-liquidating from revenues, gifts, grants from the Federal Government, user charges, assessments and other fees. This section shall not apply to any activities for which funds are advanced and shall not apply to facilities for the collection, treatment, dilution, removal and disposal of hazardous substances. [Created through H.J.R. 14, 1969, and adopted by the people May 26, 1970; Amendment proposed by S.J.R. 41, 1989, and adopted by the people May 22, 1990]

Section 3. Authority of public bodies to receive funds. Notwithstanding the limitations contained in section 10, Article XI of this Constitution, municipal corporations, cities, counties, and agencies of the State of Oregon, or combinations thereof, may receive funds referred to in section 1 of this Article, by contract, grant, loan or otherwise and may also receive such funds through disposition to the state, by sale, loan or otherwise, of bonds, notes or other obligations issued or made for the purposes set forth in section 1 of this Article. [Created through H.J.R. 14, 1969, and adopted by the people May 26, 1970]

Section 4. Sources of revenue. Ad valorem taxes shall be levied annually upon all taxable property within the State of Oregon in sufficient amount to provide, together with the revenues, gifts, grants from the Federal Government, user charges, assessments and other fees referred to in section 2 of this Article for the payment of indebtedness incurred by the state and the interest thereon. The Legislative Assembly may provide other revenues to supplement or replace such tax levies. [Created through H.J.R. 14, 1969, and adopted by the people May 26, 1970]

Section 5. Bonds. Bonds issued pursuant to section 1 of this Article shall be the direct obligations of the state and shall be in such form, run for such periods of time, and bear such rates of interest, as shall be provided by law. Such bonds may be refunded with bonds of like obligation. [Created through H.J.R. 14, 1969, and adopted by the people May 26, 1970]

Section 6. Legislation to effectuate Article. The Legislative Assembly shall enact legislation to carry out the provisions of this Article. This Article shall supersede all conflicting constitutional provisions and shall supersede any conflicting provision of a county or city charter or act of incorporation. [Created through H.J.R. 14, 1969, and adopted by the people May 26, 1970]

ARTICLE XI-I(1)
WATER DEVELOPMENT PROJECTS

Sec. 1. State empowered to lend credit to establish Water Development Fund; eligibility; use
2. Bonds
3. Refunding bonds
4. Sources of revenue
5. Legislation to effectuate Article

Section 1. State empowered to lend credit to establish Water Development Fund; eligibility; use. Notwithstanding the limits contained in sections 7 and 8, Article XI of this Constitution, the credit of the State of Oregon may be loaned and indebtedness incurred in an amount not to exceed one and one-half percent of the true cash value of all the property in the state for the purpose of creating a fund to be known as the Water Development Fund. The fund shall be used to provide financing for loans for residents of this state for construction of water development projects for irrigation, drainage, fish protection, watershed restoration and municipal uses and for the acquisition of easements and rights of way for water development projects authorized by law. Secured repayment thereof shall be and is a prerequisite to the advancement of money from such fund. As used in this section, "resident" includes both natural persons and any corporation or cooperative, either for profit or nonprofit, whose principal income is from farming in Oregon or municipal or quasi-municipal or other body subject to the laws of the State of Oregon. Not less than 50 percent of the potential amount available from the fund will be reserved for irrigation and drainage projects. For municipal use, only municipalities and communities with populations less than 30,000 are eligible for loans from the fund. [Created through S.J.R. 1, 1977, and adopted by the people Nov. 8, 1977; Amendment proposed by S.J.R. 6, 1981, and adopted by the people May 18, 1982; Amendment proposed by H.J.R. 45, 1987, and adopted by the people May 17, 1988]

Section 2. Bonds. Bonds of the State of Oregon containing a direct promise on behalf of the state to pay the face value thereof, with the interest therein provided for, may be issued to an amount authorized by section 1 of this Article for the purpose of creating such fund. The bonds shall be a direct obligation of the state and shall be in such form and shall run for such periods of time and bear such rates of interest as provided by statute. [Created through S.J.R. 1, 1977, and adopted by the people Nov. 8, 1977]

Section 3. Refunding bonds. Refunding bonds may be issued and sold to refund any bonds issued under authority of sections 1 and 2 of this Article. There may be issued and outstanding at any time bonds aggregating the amount authorized by section 1 of this Article but at no time shall the total of all bonds outstanding, including refunding bonds, exceed the amount so authorized. [Created through S.J.R. 1, 1977, and adopted by the people Nov. 8, 1977]

Section 4. Sources of revenue. Ad valorem taxes shall be levied annually upon all the taxable property in the State of Oregon in sufficient amount to provide for the payment of principal and interest of the bonds issued pursuant to this Article. The Legislative Assembly may provide other revenues to supplement or replace, in whole or in part, such tax levies. [Created through S.J.R. 1, 1977, and adopted by the people Nov. 8, 1977]

Section 5. Legislation to effectuate Article. The Legislative Assembly shall enact legislation to carry out the provisions of this Article. This Article supersedes any conflicting provision of a county or city charter or act of incorporation. [Created through S.J.R. 1, 1977, and adopted by the people Nov. 8, 1977]

ARTICLE XI-I(2)
MULTIFAMILY HOUSING FOR ELDERLY AND DISABLED

Sec. 1. State empowered to lend credit for multifamily housing for elderly and disabled persons
2. Sources of revenue
3. Bonds
4. Legislation to effectuate Article

Section 1. State empowered to lend credit for multifamily housing for elderly and disabled persons. In the manner provided by law and notwithstanding the limitations contained in section 7, Article XI of this Constitution, the credit of the State of Oregon may be loaned and indebtedness incurred in an amount not to exceed, at any one time, one-half of one percent of the true cash value of all taxable property in the state to provide funds to be advanced, by contract, grant, loan or otherwise, for the purpose of providing additional financing for multifamily housing for the elderly and for disabled persons. Multifamily housing means a structure or facility designed to contain more than one living unit. Additional financing may be provided to the elderly to purchase ownership interest in the structure or facility. [Created through H.J.R. 61, 1977, and adopted by the people May 23, 1978; Amendment proposed by S.J.R. 34, 1979, and adopted by the people May 20, 1980; Amendment proposed by H.J.R. 1, 1981, and adopted by the people May 18, 1982]

Section 2. Sources of revenue. The bonds shall be payable from contract or loan proceeds; bond reserves; other funds available for these purposes; and, if necessary, state ad valorem taxes. [Created through H.J.R. 61, 1977, and adopted by the people May 23, 1978]

Section 3. Bonds. Bonds issued pursuant to section 1 of this Article shall be the direct obligations of the state and shall be in such form, run for such periods of time and bear such rates of interest as shall be provided by law. The bonds may be refunded with bonds of like obligation. [Created through H.J.R. 61, 1977, and adopted by the people May 23, 1978]

Section 4. Legislation to effectuate Article. The Legislative Assembly shall enact legislation to carry out the provisions of this Article. This Article shall supersede all conflicting constitutional provisions. [Created through H.J.R. 61, 1977, and adopted by the people May 23, 1978]

ARTICLE XI-J
SMALL SCALE LOCAL ENERGY LOANS

Sec. 1. State empowered to loan credit for small scale local energy loans; eligibility; use
2. Bonds
3. Refunding bonds
4. Sources of revenue
5. Legislation to effectuate Article

Section 1. State empowered to loan credit for small scale local energy loans; eligibility; use. Notwithstanding the limits contained in sections 7 and 8, Article XI of this Constitution, the credit of the State of Oregon may be loaned and indebtedness incurred in an amount not to exceed one-half of one percent of the true cash value of all the property in the state for the purpose of creating a fund to be known as the Small Scale Local Energy Project Loan Fund. The fund shall be used to provide financing for the development of small scale local energy projects. Secured repayment thereof shall be and is a prerequisite to the advancement of money from such fund. [Created through S.J.R. 24, 1979, and adopted by the people May 20, 1980]

Section 2. Bonds. Bonds of the State of Oregon containing a direct promise on behalf of the state to pay the face value thereof, with the interest therein provided for,

Constitution

may be issued to an amount authorized by section 1 of this Article for the purpose of creating such fund. The bonds shall be a direct obligation of the state and shall be in such form and shall run for such periods of time and bear such rates of interest as provided by statute. [Created through S.J.R. 24, 1979, and adopted by the people May 20, 1980]

Section 3. Refunding bonds. Refunding bonds may be issued and sold to refund any bonds issued under authority of sections 1 and 2 of this Article. There may be issued and outstanding at any time bonds aggregating the amount authorized by section 1 of this Article but at no time shall the total of all bonds outstanding including refunding bonds, exceed the amount so authorized. [Created through S.J.R. 24, 1979, and adopted by the people May 20, 1980]

Section 4. Sources of revenue. Ad valorem taxes shall be levied annually upon all the taxable property in the State of Oregon in sufficient amount to provide for the payment of principal and interest of the bonds issued pursuant to this Article. The Legislative Assembly may provide other revenues to supplement or replace, in whole or in part, such tax levies. [Created through S.J.R. 24, 1979, and adopted by the people May 20, 1980]

Section 5. Legislation to effectuate Article. The Legislative Assembly shall enact legislation to carry out the provisions of this Article. This Article supersedes any conflicting provision of a county or city charter or act of incorporation. [Created through S.J.R. 24, 1979, and adopted by the people May 20, 1980]

ARTICLE XI-K
GUARANTEE OF BONDED INDEBTEDNESS OF EDUCATION DISTRICTS

Section 1. State empowered to guarantee bonded indebtedness of education districts. To secure lower interest costs on the general obligation bonds of school districts, education service districts and community college districts, the State of Oregon may guarantee the general obligation bonded indebtedness of those districts as provided in sections 2 to 6 of this Article and laws enacted pursuant to this Article. [Created through H.J.R. 71, 1997, adopted by the people Nov. 3, 1998]

Section 2. State empowered to lend credit for state guarantee of bonded indebtedness of education districts. In the manner provided by law and notwithstanding the limitations contained in sections 7 and 8, Article XI of this Constitution, the credit of the State of Oregon may be loaned and indebtedness incurred, in an amount not to exceed, at any one time, one-half of one percent of the true cash value of all taxable property in the state, to provide funds as necessary to satisfy the state guaranty of the bonded general obligation indebtedness of school districts, education service districts and community college districts that qualify, under procedures that shall be established by law, to issue general obligation bonds that are guaranteed by the full faith and credit of this state. The state may guarantee the general obligation debt of qualified school districts, education service districts and community college districts and may guarantee general obligation bonded indebtedness incurred to refund the school district, education service district or community college district general obligation bonded indebtedness. [Created through H.J.R. 71, 1997, and adopted by the people Nov. 3, 1998]

Section 3. Repayment by education districts. The Legislative Assembly may provide that reimbursement to the state shall be obtained from, but shall not be limited to, moneys that otherwise would be used for the support of the educational programs of the school district, the education service district or the community college district that incurred the bonded indebtedness with respect to which any payment under the state's guaranty is made. [Created through H.J.R. 71, 1997, and adopted by the people Nov. 3, 1998]

Section 4. Sources of revenue. The State of Oregon may issue bonds if and as necessary to provide funding to satisfy the state's guaranty obligations undertaken pursuant to this Article. In addition, notwithstanding anything to the contrary in Article VIII of this Constitution, the state may borrow available moneys from the Common School Fund if such borrowing is reasonably necessary to satisfy the state's guaranty obligations undertaken pursuant to this Article. The State of Oregon also may issue bonds if and as necessary to provide funding to repay the borrowed moneys, and any interest thereon, to the Common School Fund. The bonds shall be payable from any moneys reimbursed to the state under section 3 of this Article, from any moneys recoverable from the school district, the education service district or the community college district that incurred the bonded indebtedness with respect to which any payment under the state's guaranty is made, any other funds available for these purposes and, if necessary, from state ad valorem taxes. [Created through H.J.R. 71, 1997, and adopted by the people Nov. 3, 1998]

Section 5. Bonds. Bonds of the state issued pursuant to this Article shall be the direct obligations of the state and shall be in such form, run for such periods of time and bear such rates of interest as shall be provided by law. The bonds may be refunded with bonds of like obligation. [Created through H.J.R. 71, 1997, and adopted by the people Nov. 3, 1998]

Section 6. Legislation to effectuate Article. The Legislative Assembly shall enact legislation to carry out the provisions of this Article, including provisions that authorize the state's recovery, from any school district, education service district or community college district that incurred the bonded indebtedness with respect to which any payment under the state's guaranty is made, any amounts necessary to make the state whole. This Article shall supersede all conflicting constitutional provisions and shall supersede any conflicting provision of any law, ordinance or charter pertaining to any school district, education service district or community college district. [Created through H.J.R. 71, 1997, and adopted by the people Nov. 3, 1998]

ARTICLE XI-L
OREGON HEALTH AND SCIENCE UNIVERSITY

Section 1. State empowered to lend credit for financing capital costs of Oregon Health and Science University; bonds. (1) In the manner provided by law and notwithstanding the limitations contained in section 7, Article XI of this Constitution, the credit of the State of Oregon may be loaned and indebtedness incurred, in an aggregate outstanding principal amount not to exceed, at any one time, one-half of one percent of the real market value of all property in the state, to provide funds to finance capital costs of Oregon Health and Science

University. Bonds issued under this section may not be paid from ad valorem property taxes.

(2) Any indebtedness incurred under this section shall be in the form of general obligation bonds of the State of Oregon containing a direct promise on behalf of the State of Oregon to pay the principal, premium, if any, and interest on such bonds, in an aggregate outstanding principal amount not to exceed the amount authorized in subsection (1) of this section. The bonds shall be the direct obligation of the State of Oregon and shall be in such form, run for such period of time, have such terms and bear such rates of interest as may be provided by statute. The full faith and credit and taxing power of the State of Oregon shall be pledged to the payment of the principal, premium, if any, and interest on such bonds provided, however, that the ad valorem taxing power of the State of Oregon may not be pledged to the payment of such bonds.

(3) The proceeds from bonds issued under this section shall be used to finance capital costs of Oregon Health and Science University and costs of issuing bonds pursuant to this Article. Bonds issued under this section to finance capital costs of Oregon Health and Science University shall be issued in an aggregate principal amount that produces net proceeds for the university in an amount that does not exceed $200 million.

(4) The proceeds from bonds issued under this section may not be used to finance operating costs of Oregon Health and Science University.

(5) As used in this Article, "bonds" means bonds, notes or other financial obligations of the State of Oregon issued under this section. [Created through H.J.R. 19, 2001, and adopted by the people May 21, 2002]

Section 2. Sources of repayment. The principal, premium, if any, interest and any other amounts payable with respect to bonds issued under section 1 of this Article shall be repaid as determined by the Legislative Assembly from the following sources:

(1) Amounts appropriated for such purpose by the Legislative Assembly from the General Fund, including any taxes levied to pay the bonds other than ad valorem property taxes;

(2) Amounts allocated for such purpose by the Legislative Assembly from the proceeds of the State Lottery or from the Master Settlement Agreement entered into on November 23, 1998, by the State of Oregon and leading United States tobacco product manufacturers; and

(3) Amounts appropriated or allocated for such purpose by the Legislative Assembly from other sources of revenue. [Created through H.J.R. 19, 2001, and adopted by the people May 21, 2002]

Section 3. Refunding bonds. Bonds issued under section 1 of this Article may be refunded with bonds of like obligation. [Created through H.J.R. 19, 2001, and adopted by the people May 21, 2002]

Section 4. Legislation to effectuate Article. The Legislative Assembly may enact legislation to carry out the provisions of this Article. [Created through H.J.R. 19, 2001, and adopted by the people May 21, 2002]

Section 5. Relationship to conflicting provisions of Constitution. This Article shall supersede all conflicting provisions of this constitution. [Created through H.J.R. 19, 2001, and adopted by the people May 21, 2002]

ARTICLE XI-M
SEISMIC REHABILITATION OF PUBLIC EDUCATION BUILDINGS

Sec. 1. State empowered to lend credit for seismic rehabilitation of public education buildings; bonds
2. Sources of repayment

3. Refunding bonds
4. Legislation to effectuate Article
5. Relationship to conflicting provisions of Constitution
Note: Article XI-M was designated as "Article XI-L" by S.J.R. 21, 2001, and adopted by the people Nov. 5, 2002.

Section 1. State empowered to lend credit for seismic rehabilitation of public education buildings; bonds. (1) In the manner provided by law and notwithstanding the limitations contained in section 7, Article XI of this Constitution, the credit of the State of Oregon may be loaned and indebtedness incurred, in an aggregate outstanding principal amount not to exceed, at any one time, one-fifth of one percent of the real market value of all property in the state, to provide funds for the planning and implementation of seismic rehabilitation of public education buildings, including surveying and conducting engineering evaluations of the need for seismic rehabilitation.

(2) Any indebtedness incurred under this section must be in the form of general obligation bonds of the State of Oregon containing a direct promise on behalf of the State of Oregon to pay the principal, premium, if any, interest and other amounts payable with respect to the bonds, in an aggregate outstanding principal amount not to exceed the amount authorized in subsection (1) of this section. The bonds are the direct obligation of the State of Oregon and must be in a form, run for a period of time, have terms and bear rates of interest as may be provided by statute. The full faith and credit and taxing power of the State of Oregon must be pledged to the payment of the principal, premium, if any, and interest on the general obligation bonds; however, the ad valorem taxing power of the State of Oregon may not be pledged to the payment of the bonds issued under this section.

(3) As used in this section, "public education building" means a building owned by the State Board of Higher Education, a school district, an education service district, a community college district or a community college service district. [Created through S.J.R. 21, 2001, and adopted by the people Nov. 5, 2002]

Section 2. Sources of repayment. The principal, premium, if any, interest and other amounts payable with respect to the general obligation bonds issued under section 1 of this Article must be repaid as determined by the Legislative Assembly from the following sources:

(1) Amounts appropriated for the purpose by the Legislative Assembly from the General Fund, including taxes, other than ad valorem property taxes, levied to pay the bonds;

(2) Amounts allocated for the purpose by the Legislative Assembly from the proceeds of the State Lottery or from the Master Settlement Agreement entered into on November 23, 1998, by the State of Oregon and leading United States tobacco product manufacturers; and

(3) Amounts appropriated or allocated for the purpose by the Legislative Assembly from other sources of revenue. [Created through S.J.R. 21, 2001, and adopted by the people Nov. 5, 2002]

Section 3. Refunding bonds. General obligation bonds issued under section 1 of this Article may be refunded with bonds of like obligation. [Created through S.J.R. 21, 2001, and adopted by the people Nov. 5, 2002]

Section 4. Legislation to effectuate Article. The Legislative Assembly may enact legislation to carry out the provisions of this Article. [Created through S.J.R. 21, 2001, and adopted by the people Nov. 5, 2002]

Section 5. Relationship to conflicting provisions of Constitution. This Article supersedes conflicting provisions of this Constitution. [Created through S.J.R. 21, 2001, and adopted by the people Nov. 5, 2002]

Constitution

431

ARTICLE XI-N
SEISMIC REHABILITATION OF EMERGENCY SERVICES BUILDINGS

Sec. 1. State empowered to lend credit for seismic rehabilitation of emergency services buildings; bonds
2. Sources of repayment
3. Refunding bonds
4. Legislation to effectuate Article
5. Relationship to conflicting provisions of Constitution

Note: Article XI-N was designated as "Article XI-L" by S.J.R. 22, 2001, and adopted by the people Nov. 5, 2002.

Section 1. State empowered to lend credit for seismic rehabilitation of emergency services buildings; bonds. (1) In the manner provided by law and notwithstanding the limitations contained in section 7, Article XI of this Constitution, the credit of the State of Oregon may be loaned and indebtedness incurred, in an aggregate outstanding principal amount not to exceed, at any one time, one-fifth of one percent of the real market value of all property in the state, to provide funds for the planning and implementation of seismic rehabilitation of emergency services buildings, including surveying and conducting engineering evaluations of the need for seismic rehabilitation.

(2) Any indebtedness incurred under this section must be in the form of general obligation bonds of the State of Oregon containing a direct promise on behalf of the State of Oregon to pay the principal, premium, if any, interest and other amounts payable with respect to the bonds, in an aggregate outstanding principal amount not to exceed the amount authorized in subsection (1) of this section. The bonds are the direct obligation of the State of Oregon and must be in a form, run for a period of time, have terms and bear rates of interest as may be provided by statute. The full faith and credit and taxing power of the State of Oregon must be pledged to the payment of the principal, premium, if any, and interest on the general obligation bonds; however, the ad valorem taxing power of the State of Oregon may not be pledged to the payment of the bonds issued under this section.

(3) As used in this section:

(a) "Acute inpatient care facility" means a licensed hospital with an organized medical staff, with permanent facilities that include inpatient beds, and with comprehensive medical services, including physician services and continuous nursing services under the supervision of registered nurses, to provide diagnosis and medical or surgical treatment primarily for but not limited to acutely ill patients and accident victims. "Acute inpatient care facility" includes the Oregon Health and Science University.

(b) "Emergency services building" means a public building used for fire protection services, a hospital building that contains an acute inpatient care facility, a police station, a sheriff's office or a similar facility used by a state, county, district or municipal law enforcement agency. [Created through S.J.R. 22, 2001, and adopted by the people Nov. 5, 2002]

Section 2. Sources of repayment. The principal, premium, if any, interest and other amounts payable with respect to the general obligation bonds issued under section 1 of this Article must be repaid as determined by the Legislative Assembly from the following sources:

(1) Amounts appropriated for the purpose by the Legislative Assembly from the General Fund, including taxes, other than ad valorem property taxes, levied to pay the bonds;

(2) Amounts allocated for the purpose by the Legislative Assembly from the proceeds of the State Lottery or from the Master Settlement Agreement entered into on November 23, 1998, by the State of Oregon and leading United States tobacco product manufacturers; and

(3) Amounts appropriated or allocated for the purpose by the Legislative Assembly from other sources of revenue. [Created through S.J.R. 22, 2001, and adopted by the people Nov. 5, 2002]

Section 3. Refunding bonds. General obligation bonds issued under section 1 of this Article may be refunded with bonds of like obligation. [Created through S.J.R. 22, 2001, and adopted by the people Nov. 5, 2002]

Section 4. Legislation to effectuate Article. The Legislative Assembly may enact legislation to carry out the provisions of this Article. [Created through S.J.R. 22, 2001, and adopted by the people Nov. 5, 2002]

Section 5. Relationship to conflicting provisions of Constitution. This Article supersedes conflicting provisions of this Constitution. [Created through S.J.R. 22, 2001, and adopted by the people Nov. 5, 2002]

ARTICLE XI-O
PENSION LIABILITIES

Sec. 1. State empowered to lend credit for pension liabilities
2. Refunding obligations
3. Legislation to effectuate Article
4. Relationship to conflicting provisions of Constitution

Section 1. State empowered to lend credit for pension liabilities. (1) In the manner provided by law and notwithstanding the limitations contained in section 7, Article XI of this Constitution, the credit of the State of Oregon may be loaned and indebtedness incurred to finance the State of Oregon's pension liabilities. Indebtedness authorized by this section also may be used to pay costs of issuing or incurring indebtedness under this section.

(2) Indebtedness incurred under this section is a general obligation of the State of Oregon and must contain a direct promise on behalf of the State of Oregon to pay the principal, premium, if any, and interest on that indebtedness. The State of Oregon shall pledge its full faith and credit and taxing power to pay that indebtedness; however, the ad valorem taxing power of the State of Oregon may not be pledged to pay that indebtedness. The amount of indebtedness authorized by this section and outstanding at any time may not exceed one percent of the real market value of all property in the state. [Created through H.J.R. 18, 2003, and adopted by the people Sept. 16, 2003]

Section 2. Refunding obligations. Indebtedness incurred under section 1 of this Article may be refunded with like obligations. [Created through H.J.R. 18, 2003, and adopted by the people Sept. 16, 2003]

Section 3. Legislation to effectuate Article. The Legislative Assembly may enact legislation to carry out the provisions of this Article. [Created through H.J.R. 18, 2003, and adopted by the people Sept. 16, 2003]

Section 4. Relationship to conflicting provisions of Constitution. This Article supersedes all conflicting provisions of this Constitution. [Created through H.J.R. 18, 2003, and adopted by the people Sept. 16, 2003]

ARTICLE XI-P
SCHOOL DISTRICT CAPITAL COSTS

Sec. 1. State empowered to lend credit for grants or loans to school districts to finance capital costs; general obligation bond proceeds as matching funds
2. Sources of repayment
3. Refunding bonds
4. School capital matching fund
5. "Capital costs" defined
6. Legislation to effectuate Article

7. Relationship to conflicting provision of Constitution

Section 1. State empowered to lend credit for grants or loans to school districts to finance capital costs; general obligation bond proceeds as matching funds. (1) In the manner provided by law and notwithstanding the limitations contained in section 7, Article XI of this Constitution, the State of Oregon may loan its credit and incur indebtedness, in an aggregate outstanding principal amount not to exceed, at any one time, one-half of one percent of the real market value of the real property in this state, to provide funds to be advanced by grant or loan to school districts to finance the capital costs of the school districts. Bonds issued under this section may not be paid from ad valorem property taxes.

(2) Indebtedness incurred under this section must be in the form of general obligation bonds of the State of Oregon containing a direct promise to pay the principal, interest and premium, if any, of the bonds in an aggregate outstanding principal amount not to exceed the amount authorized in subsection (1) of this section. The bonds are the direct obligation of the State of Oregon and must be in such form, run for such periods of time, have such terms and bear such rates of interest as may be provided by statute. The State of Oregon shall pledge its full faith and credit and taxing power to the payment of the principal, interest and premium, if any, of the bonds. However, the State of Oregon may not pledge its ad valorem taxing power to the payment of the bonds.

(3) The proceeds from bonds issued under this section may be used only to provide matching funds to finance the capital costs of school districts that have received voter approval for local general obligation bonds and to provide for the costs of issuing bonds and the payment of debt service.

(4) The proceeds from bonds issued under this section may not be used to finance the operating costs of school districts. [Created through H.J.R. 13, 2009, and adopted by the people May 18, 2010]

Section 2. Sources of repayment. The principal, interest and premium, if any, of the bonds issued under section 1 of this Article must be repaid as determined by the Legislative Assembly from the following sources:

(1) Amounts appropriated for repayment by the Legislative Assembly from the General Fund, including taxes levied to pay the bonds except ad valorem property taxes;

(2) Amounts appropriated or allocated for repayment by the Legislative Assembly from other sources of revenue; or

(3) Any other available moneys. [Created through H.J.R. 13, 2009, and adopted by the people May 18, 2010]

Section 3. Refunding bonds. Bonds issued under section 1 of this Article may be refunded with bonds of like obligation. [Created through H.J.R. 13, 2009, and adopted by the people May 18, 2010]

Section 4. School capital matching fund. (1) There is created a school capital matching fund. Moneys in the fund may be invested and the earnings shall be retained in the fund or expended as provided by the Legislative Assembly.

(2) The Legislative Assembly may by law appropriate, allocate or transfer moneys or revenue to the school capital matching fund.

(3) The Legislative Assembly may appropriate, allocate or transfer moneys in the school capital matching fund and earnings on moneys in the fund for the purposes of providing:

(a) State matching funds to school districts to finance capital costs; and

(b) Payment of debt service for general obligation bonds issued pursuant to this Article. [Created through H.J.R. 13, 2009, and adopted by the people May 18, 2010]

Section 5. "Capital costs" defined. As used in this Article, "capital costs" means costs of land and of other assets having a useful life of more than one year, including costs associated with acquisition, construction, improvement, remodeling, furnishing, equipping, maintenance or repair. [Created through H.J.R. 13, 2009, and adopted by the people May 18, 2010]

Section 6. Legislation to effectuate Article. The Legislative Assembly may enact legislation to carry out the provisions of this Article. [Created through H.J.R. 13, 2009, and adopted by the people May 18, 2010]

Section 7. Relationship to conflicting provision of Constitution. This Article supersedes any conflicting provision of this Constitution. [Created through H.J.R. 13, 2009, and adopted by the people May 18, 2010]

ARTICLE XI-Q
REAL OR PERSONAL PROPERTY OWNED OR OPERATED BY STATE

Sec. 1. State empowered to lend credit for real or personal property to be owned or operated by state; refinancing authority

2. Limit on indebtedness; general obligation of state

3. Legislation to effectuate Article

4. Relationship to conflicting provisions of Constitution

Note: Article XI-Q was designated as "Article XI-P" by S.J.R. 48, 2010, and adopted by the people Nov. 2, 2010.

Section 1. State empowered to lend credit for real or personal property to be owned or operated by state; refinancing authority. (1) In the manner provided by law and notwithstanding the limitations contained in section 7, Article XI of this Constitution, the credit of the State of Oregon may be loaned and indebtedness incurred to finance the costs of:

(a) Acquiring, constructing, remodeling, repairing, equipping or furnishing real or personal property that is or will be owned or operated by the State of Oregon, including, without limitation, facilities and systems;

(b) Infrastructure related to the real or personal property; or

(c) Indebtedness incurred under this subsection.

(2) In the manner provided by law and notwithstanding the limitations contained in section 7, Article XI of this Constitution, the credit of the State of Oregon may be loaned and indebtedness incurred to refinance:

(a) Indebtedness incurred under subsection (1) of this section.

(b) Borrowings issued before the effective date of this Article to finance or refinance costs described in subsection (1) of this section. [Created through S.J.R. 48, 2010, and adopted by the people Nov. 2, 2010]

Note: The effective date of Senate Joint Resolution 48, 2010, is Dec. 2, 2010.

Section 2. Limit on indebtedness; general obligation of state. (1) Indebtedness may not be incurred under section 1 of this Article if the indebtedness would cause the total principal amount of indebtedness incurred under section 1 of this Article and outstanding to exceed one percent of the real market value of the property in this state.

(2) Indebtedness incurred under section 1 of this Article is a general obligation of the State of Oregon and must contain a direct promise on behalf of the State of Oregon to pay the principal, premium, if any, and interest on the obligation. The full faith and credit and taxing power of the State of Oregon must be pledged to payment of the indebtedness. However, the State of Oregon may not pledge or levy an ad valorem tax to pay the indebtedness. [Created through S.J.R. 48, 2010, and adopted by the people Nov. 2, 2010]

Section 3. Legislation to effectuate Article. The Legislative Assembly may enact legislation to carry out the provisions of this Article. [Created through S.J.R. 48, 2010, and adopted by the people Nov. 2, 2010]

Section 4. Relationship to conflicting provisions of Constitution. This Article supersedes conflicting provisions of this Constitution. [Created through S.J.R. 48, 2010, and adopted by the people Nov. 2, 2010]

ARTICLE XII
STATE PRINTING

Section 1. State printing; State Printer. Laws may be enacted providing for the state printing and binding, and for the election or appointment of a state printer, who shall have had not less than ten years' experience in the art of printing. The state printer shall receive such compensation as may from time to time be provided by law. Until such laws shall be enacted the state printer shall be elected, and the printing done as heretofore provided by this constitution and the general laws. [Constitution of 1859; Amendment proposed by S.J.R. 1, 1901, and adopted by the people June 6, 1904; Amendment proposed by initiative petition filed Feb. 3, 1906, and adopted by the people June 4, 1906]

ARTICLE XIII
SALARIES

Section 1. Salaries or other compensation of state officers. [Constitution of 1859; Repeal proposed by S.J.R. 12, 1955, and adopted by the people Nov. 6, 1956]

ARTICLE XIV
SEAT OF GOVERNMENT

Sec. 1. Seat of government
 2. Erection of state house prior to 1865

Section 1. Seat of government. [Constitution of 1859; Repeal proposed by S.J.R. 41, 1957, and adopted by the people Nov. 4, 1958 (present section 1 and former 1958 section 3 of this Article adopted in lieu of this section and former original section 3 of this Article)]

Section 1. Seat of government. The permanent seat of government for the state shall be Marion County. [Created through S.J.R. 41, 1957, and adopted by the people Nov. 4, 1958 (this section and former 1958 section 3 of this Article adopted in lieu of former original sections 1 and 3 of this Article)]

Section 2. Erection of state house prior to 1865. No tax shall be levied, or money of the State expended, or debt contracted for the erection of a State House prior to the year eighteen hundred and sixty five. —

Section 3. Limitation on removal of seat of government; location of state institutions. [Constitution of 1859; Amendment proposed by S.J.R. 1, 1907, and adopted by the people June 1, 1908; Repeal proposed by S.J.R. 41, 1957, and adopted by the people Nov. 4, 1958 (present section 1 and former 1958 section 3 of this Article adopted in lieu of this section and former section 1 of this Article)]

Section 3. Location and use of state institutions. [Created through S.J.R. 41, 1957, and adopted by the people Nov. 4, 1958 (this section, designated as "Section 2" by S.J.R. 41, 1957, and present section 1 of this Article adopted in lieu of former original sections 1 and 3 of this Article; Repeal proposed by S.J.R. 9, 1971, and adopted by the people Nov. 7, 1972]

ARTICLE XV
MISCELLANEOUS

Sec. 1. Officers to hold office until successors elected; exceptions; effect on defeated incumbent
 2. Tenure of office; how fixed; maximum tenure

 3. Oaths of office
 4. Regulation of lotteries; state lottery; use of net proceeds from state lottery
 4a. Use of net proceeds from state lottery for parks and recreation areas
 4b. Use of net proceeds from state lottery for fish and wildlife, watershed and habitat protection
 4c. Audit of agency receiving certain net proceeds from state lottery
 5. Property of married women not subject to debts of husband; registration of separate property
 5a. Policy regarding marriage
 6. Minimum area and population of counties
 7. Officers not to receive fees from or represent claimants against state
 8. Persons eligible to serve in legislature
 9. When elective office becomes vacant
 10. The Oregon Property Protection Act of 2000
 11. Home Care Commission

Section 1. Officers to hold office until successors elected; exceptions; effect on defeated incumbent. (1) All officers, except members of the Legislative Assembly and incumbents who seek reelection and are defeated, shall hold their offices until their successors are elected, and qualified.

(2) If an incumbent seeks reelection and is defeated, he shall hold office only until the end of his term; and if an election contest is pending in the courts regarding that office when the term of such an incumbent ends and a successor to the office has not been elected or if elected, has not qualified because of such election contest, the person appointed to fill the vacancy thus created shall serve only until the contest and any appeal is finally determined notwithstanding any other provision of this constitution. [Constitution of 1859; Amendment proposed by H.J.R. 51, 1969, and adopted by the people Nov. 3, 1970]

Section 2. Tenure of office; how fixed; maximum tenure. When the duration of any office is not provided for by this Constitution, it may be declared by law; and if not so declared, such office shall be held during the pleasure of the authority making the appointment. But the Legislative Assembly shall not create any office, the tenure of which shall be longer than four years.

Section 3. Oaths of office. Every person elected or appointed to any office under this Constitution, shall, before entering on the duties thereof, take an oath or affirmation to support the Constitution of the United States, and of this State, and also an oath of office.—

Note: The amendments to sections 4, 4a, 4b and 4c and the repeal of section 4d by Measure No. 76, 2010, as submitted to the people was preceded by a preamble that reads as follows:

PREAMBLE: The people of the State of Oregon find that renewing the current dedication in the Oregon Constitution of fifteen percent of lottery revenues to parks, water quality and fish and wildlife habitats will provide lasting social, economic, environmental and public health benefits. The people of the State of Oregon also find that renewal of the Parks and Natural Resources Fund will support voluntary efforts to:

(1) Protect and restore water quality, watersheds and habitats for native fish and wildlife that provide a healthy environment for current and future generations of Oregonians;

(2) Maintain and expand public parks, natural areas and recreation areas to meet the diverse needs of a growing population and to provide opportunities for [sic] to experience nature and enjoy outdoor recreation activities close to home and in the many special places throughout Oregon;

(3) Provide jobs and economic opportunities improving the health of our forests, prairies, lakes, streams, wetlands, rivers, and parks, including efforts to halt the spread of invasive species;

(4) Strengthen the audit and reporting requirements, identify desired outcomes and specify allowable uses of the fund in order to provide more strategic, accountable and efficient uses of the Parks and Natural Resources Fund; and

(5) Enhance the ability of public land managers, private organizations, individuals and businesses to work together in local, regional and statewide partnerships to expand recreation opportunities, improve water quality and conserve fish and wildlife habitat.

Section 4. Regulation of lotteries; state lottery; use of net proceeds from state lottery. (1) Except as provided in subsections (2), (3), (4), (8) and (9) of this section, lotteries and the sale of lottery tickets, for any purpose whatever, are prohibited, and the Legislative Assembly shall prevent the same by penal laws.

(2) The Legislative Assembly may provide for the establishment, operation, and regulation of raffles and the lottery commonly known as bingo or lotto by charitable, fraternal, or religious organizations. As used in this section, charitable, fraternal or religious organization means such organizations or foundations as defined by law because of their charitable, fraternal, or religious purposes. The regulations shall define eligible organizations or foundations, and may prescribe the frequency of raffles, bingo or lotto, set a maximum monetary limit for prizes and require a statement of the odds on winning a prize. The Legislative Assembly shall vest the regulatory authority in any appropriate state agency.

(3) There is hereby created the State Lottery Commission which shall establish and operate a State Lottery. All proceeds from the State Lottery, including interest, but excluding costs of administration and payment of prizes, shall be used for any of the following purposes: creating jobs, furthering economic development, financing public education in Oregon or restoring and protecting Oregon's parks, beaches, watersheds and native fish and wildlife.

(4)(a) The State Lottery Commission shall be comprised of five members appointed by the Governor and confirmed by the Senate who shall serve at the pleasure of the Governor. At least one of the Commissioners shall have a minimum of five years experience in law enforcement and at least one of the Commissioners shall be a certified public accountant. The Commission is empowered to promulgate rules related to the procedures of the Commission and the operation of the State Lottery. Such rules and any statutes enacted to further implement this article shall insure the integrity, security, honesty, and fairness of the Lottery. The Commission shall have such additional powers and duties as may be provided by law.

(b) The Governor shall appoint a Director subject to confirmation by the Senate who shall serve at the pleasure of the Governor. The Director shall be qualified by training and experience to direct the operations of a state-operated lottery. The Director shall be responsible for managing the affairs of the Commission. The Director may appoint and prescribe the duties of no more than four Assistant Directors as the Director deems necessary. One of the Assistant Directors shall be responsible for a security division to assure security, integrity, honesty, and fairness in the operations and administration of the State Lottery. To fulfill these responsibilities, the Assistant Director for security shall be qualified by training and experience, including at least five years of law enforcement experience, and knowledge and experience in computer security.

(c) The Director shall implement and operate a State Lottery pursuant to the rules, and under the guidance, of the Commission. The State Lottery may operate any game procedure authorized by the commission, except parimutuel racing, social games, and the games commonly known in Oregon as bingo or lotto, whereby prizes are distributed using any existing or future methods among adult persons who have paid for tickets or shares in that game; provided that, in lottery games utilizing computer terminals or other devices, no coins or currency shall ever be dispensed directly to players from such computer terminals or devices.

(d) There is hereby created within the General Fund the Oregon State Lottery Fund which is continuously appropriated for the purpose of administering and operating the Commission and the State Lottery. The State Lottery shall operate as a self-supporting revenue-raising agency of state government and no appropriations, loans, or other transfers of state funds shall be made to it. The State Lottery shall pay all prizes and all of its expenses out of the revenues it receives from the sale of tickets or shares to the public and turnover the net proceeds therefrom to a fund to be established by the Legislative Assembly from which the Legislative Assembly shall make appropriations for the benefit of any of the following public purposes: creating jobs, furthering economic development, financing public education in Oregon or restoring and protecting Oregon's parks, beaches, watersheds and native fish and wildlife. Effective July 1, 1997, 15% of the net proceeds from the State Lottery shall be deposited, from the fund created by the Legislative Assembly under this paragraph, in an education stability fund. Effective July 1, 2003, 18% of the net proceeds from the State Lottery shall be deposited, from the fund created by the Legislative Assembly under this paragraph, in an education stability fund. Earnings on moneys in the education stability fund shall be retained in the fund or expended for the public purpose of financing public education in Oregon as provided by law. Except as provided in subsection (6) of this section, moneys in the education stability fund shall be invested as provided by law and shall not be subject to the limitations of section 6, Article XI of this Constitution. The Legislative Assembly may appropriate other moneys or revenue to the education stability fund. The Legislative Assembly shall appropriate amounts sufficient to pay lottery bonds before appropriating the net proceeds from the State Lottery for any other purpose. At least 84% of the total annual revenues from the sale of all lottery tickets or shares shall be returned to the public in the form of prizes and net revenues benefiting the public purpose.

(5) Notwithstanding paragraph (d) of subsection (4) of this section, the amount in the education stability fund created under paragraph (d) of subsection (4) of this section may not exceed an amount that is equal to five percent of the amount that was accrued as revenues in the state's General Fund during the prior biennium. If the amount in the education stability fund exceeds five percent of the amount that was accrued as revenues in the state's General Fund during the prior biennium:

(a) Additional net proceeds from the State Lottery may not be deposited in the education stability fund until the amount in the education stability fund is reduced to less than five percent of the amount that was accrued as revenues in the state's General Fund during the prior biennium; and

(b) Fifteen percent of the net proceeds from the State Lottery shall be deposited into the school capital matching fund created under section 4, Article XI-P of this Constitution.

(6) The Legislative Assembly may by law appropriate, allocate or transfer any portion of the principal of the education stability fund created under paragraph (d) of subsection (4) of this section for expenditure on public education if:

(a) The proposed appropriation, allocation or transfer is approved by three-fifths of the members serving in each house of the Legislative Assembly and the Legislative Assembly finds one of the following:

(A) That the last quarterly economic and revenue forecast for a biennium indicates that moneys available to the state's General Fund for the next biennium will be at least three percent less than appropriations from the state's General Fund for the current biennium;

(B) That there has been a decline for two or more consecutive quarters in the last 12 months in seasonally adjusted nonfarm payroll employment; or

(C) That a quarterly economic and revenue forecast projects that revenues in the state's General Fund in the current biennium will be at least two percent below what the revenues were projected to be in the revenue forecast on which the legislatively adopted budget for the current biennium was based; or

(b) The proposed appropriation, allocation or transfer is approved by three-fifths of the members serving in each house of the Legislative Assembly and the Governor declares an emergency.

(7) The Legislative Assembly may by law prescribe the procedures to be used and identify the persons required to make the forecasts described in subsection (6) of this section.

(8) Effective July 1, 1999, 15% of the net proceeds from the State Lottery shall be deposited in a parks and natural resources fund created by the Legislative Assembly. Of the moneys in the parks and natural resources fund, 50% shall be deposited in a parks subaccount and distributed for the public purposes of financing the protection, repair, operation, and creation of state, regional and local public parks, ocean shore and public beach access areas, historic sites and recreation areas, and 50% shall be deposited in a natural resources subaccount and distributed for the public purposes of financing the restoration and protection of native fish and wildlife, watersheds and water quality in Oregon. The Legislative Assembly shall not limit expenditures from the parks and natural resources fund, or from the parks or natural resources subaccounts. The Legislative Assembly may appropriate other moneys or revenue to the parks and natural resources fund.

(9) Only one State Lottery operation shall be permitted in the State.

(10) The Legislative Assembly has no power to authorize, and shall prohibit, casinos from operation in the State of Oregon. [Constitution of 1859; Amendment proposed by H.J.R. 14, 1975, and adopted by the people Nov. 2, 1976; Amendment proposed by initiative petition filed April 3, 1984, and adopted by the people Nov. 6, 1984 (paragraph designations in subsection (4) were not included in the petition); Amendment proposed by H.J.R. 20, 1985, and adopted by the people Nov. 4, 1986; Amendment proposed by H.J.R. 15, 1995, and adopted by the people May 16, 1995; Amendment proposed by initiative petition filed March 11, 1998, and adopted by the people Nov. 3, 1998; Amendment proposed by H.J.R. 80, 2002 (3rd s.s.), and adopted by the people Sept. 17, 2002; Revision proposed by H.J.R. 13, 2009, and adopted by the people May 18, 2010; Amendment proposed by initiative petition filed Dec. 22, 2009, and adopted by the people Nov. 2, 2010]

Note: The amendments to section 4, as adopted by the people in Measure No. 66, 1998, incorrectly set forth the text of section 4 as it existed at the time the measure was submitted to the people. The text of the measure, as approved by the voters, was printed here.

Note: The amendments to section 4, as adopted by the people in Measure No. 76, 2010, at the Nov. 2010 general election did not set forth the text of section 4 as it was revised by the people in Measure No. 68, 2010 (H.J.R. 13, 2009), at the May 2010 primary election. The text of section 4, as revised by Measure No. 68, 2010, and amended by Measure No. 76, 2010, is printed here.

Section 4a. Use of net proceeds from state lottery for parks and recreation areas. (1) In each biennium the Legislative Assembly shall appropriate all of the moneys in the parks subaccount of the parks and natural resources fund established under section 4 of this Article for the uses allowed in subsection (2) of this section, and to achieve all of the following:

(a) Provide additional public parks, natural areas or outdoor recreational areas to meet the needs of current and future residents of the State of Oregon;

(b) Protect natural, cultural, historic and outdoor recreational resources of state or regional significance;

(c) Manage public parks, natural areas and outdoor recreation areas to ensure their long-term ecological health and provide for the enjoyment of current and future residents of the State of Oregon; and

(d) Provide diverse and equitable opportunities for residents of the State of Oregon to experience nature and participate in outdoor recreational activities in state, regional, local or neighborhood public parks and recreation areas.

(2) The moneys in the parks subaccount shall be used only to:

(a) Maintain, construct, improve, develop, manage and operate state parks, ocean shores, public beach access areas, historic sites, natural areas and outdoor and recreation areas;

(b) Acquire real property, or interests therein, that has significant natural, scenic, cultural, historic or recreational values, for the creation or operation of state parks, ocean shores, public beach access areas, outdoor recreation areas and historic sites; and

(c) Provide grants to regional or local government entities to acquire property for public parks, natural areas or outdoor recreation areas, or to develop or improve public parks, natural areas or outdoor recreation areas.

(3) In each biennium the Legislative Assembly shall appropriate no less than twelve percent of the moneys in the parks subaccount for local and regional grants as authorized under paragraph (c) of subsection (2) of this section. However, if in any biennium the amount of net proceeds deposited in the parks and natural resources fund created under section 4 of this Article increases by more than fifty percent above the amount deposited in the 2009-2011 biennium, the Legislative Assembly shall appropriate no less than twenty-five percent of the moneys in the parks subaccount for local and regional grants as authorized under paragraph (c) of subsection (2) of this section. The grants shall be administered by a single state agency. The costs of the state agency in administering the grants shall not be paid out of the portion of the moneys in the parks subaccount appropriated for local and regional grants. [Created through initiative petition filed March 11, 1998, and adopted by the people Nov. 3, 1998; Amendment proposed by initiative petition filed Dec. 22, 2009, and adopted by the people Nov. 2, 2010]

Section 4b. Use of net proceeds from state lottery for fish and wildlife, watershed and habitat protection. (1) In each biennium the Legislative Assembly shall appropriate all of the moneys in the natural resources subaccount of the parks and natural resources fund established under section 4 of this Article for the uses allowed in subsections (2) and (3) of this section, and to accomplish all of the following:

(a) Protect and improve water quality in Oregon's rivers, lakes, and streams by restoring natural watershed functions or stream flows;

(b) Secure long-term protection for lands and waters that provide significant habitats for native fish and wildlife;

(c) Restore and maintain habitats needed to sustain healthy and resilient populations of native fish and wildlife;

(d) Maintain the diversity of Oregon's plants, animals and ecosystems;

(e) Involve people in voluntary actions to protect, restore and maintain the ecological health of Oregon's lands and waters; and

(f) Remedy the conditions that limit the health of fish and wildlife, habitats and watershed functions in greatest need of conservation.

(2) In each biennium the Legislative Assembly shall appropriate no less than sixty-five percent of the moneys in the natural resources subaccount to one state agency, and that agency shall distribute those moneys as grants to entities other than state or federal agencies for projects that achieve the outcomes specified in subsection (1) of this section. However, if in any biennium the amount of net proceeds deposited in the parks and natural resources fund created under section 4 of this Article increases by more than fifty percent above the amount deposited in the 2009-2011 biennium, the Legislative Assembly shall appropriate no less than seventy percent of the moneys in the natural resources subaccount to one state agency, and that agency shall distribute those moneys as grants to entities other than state or federal agencies for projects that achieve the outcomes specified in subsection (1) of this section. In addition, these moneys shall be used only to:

(a) Acquire from willing owners interests in land or water that will protect or restore native fish or wildlife habitats, which interests may include but are not limited to fee interests, conservation easements or leases;

(b) Carry out projects to protect or restore native fish or wildlife habitats;

(c) Carry out projects to protect or restore natural watershed functions to improve water quality or stream flows; and

(d) Carry out resource assessment, planning, design and engineering, technical assistance, monitoring and outreach activities necessary for projects funded under paragraphs (a) through (c) of this subsection.

(3) In each biennium the Legislative Assembly shall appropriate that portion of the natural resources subaccount not appropriated under subsection (2) of this section to support all of the following activities:

(a) Develop, implement or update state conservation strategies or plans to protect or restore native fish or wildlife habitats or to protect or restore natural watershed functions to improve water quality or stream flows;

(b) Develop, implement or update regional or local strategies or plans that are consistent with the state strategies or plans described in paragraph (a) of this subsection;

(c) Develop, implement or update state strategies or plans to prevent, detect, control or eradicate invasive species that threaten native fish or wildlife habitats or that impair water quality;

(d) Support local delivery of programs or projects, including watershed education activities, that protect or restore native fish or wildlife habitats or watersheds;

(e) Pay the state agency costs of administering subsection (2) of this section, which costs shall not be paid out of the moneys available for grants under subsection (2) of this section; and

(f) Enforce fish and wildlife and habitat protection laws and regulations. [Created through initiative petition filed March 11, 1998, and adopted by the people Nov. 3, 1998; Amendment

proposed by initiative petition filed Dec. 22, 2009, and adopted by the people Nov. 2, 2010]

Section 4c. Audit of agency receiving certain net proceeds from state lottery. The Secretary of State shall regularly audit any state agency that receives moneys from the parks and natural resources fund established under section 4 of this Article to address the financial integrity, compliance with applicable laws, efficiency and effectiveness of the use of the moneys. The costs of the audit shall be paid from the parks and natural resources fund. However, such costs may not be paid from the portions of such fund, or the subaccounts of the fund, that are dedicated to grants. The audit shall be submitted to the Legislative Assembly as part of a biennial report to the Legislative Assembly. In addition, each agency that receives moneys from the parks and natural resources fund shall submit a biennial performance report [sic] the Legislature [sic] Assembly that describes the measurable biennial and cumulative results of activities and programs financed by the fund. [Created through initiative petition filed March 11, 1998, and adopted by the people Nov. 3, 1998; Amendment proposed by initiative petition filed Dec. 22, 2009, and adopted by the people Nov. 2, 2010]

Note: Added as section 4c to the Constitution but not to any Article therein by initiative petition (Measure No. 66, 1998) adopted by the people Nov. 3, 1998.

Section 4d. Subsequent vote for reaffirmation of sections 4a, 4b and 4c and amendment to section 4. [Created through initiative petition filed March 11, 1998, and adopted by the people Nov. 3, 1998; Repeal proposed by initiative petition filed Dec. 22, 2009, and adopted by the people Nov. 2, 2010]

Section 4e. Transfer of moneys in school capital matching subaccount to school capital matching fund created under section 4, Article XI-P. [Created through H.J.R. 13, 2009, and adopted by the people May 18, 2010; Repealed Jan. 2, 2011, as specified in text of section adopted by the people May 18, 2010]

Section 5. Property of married women not subject to debts of husband; registration of separate property. The property and pecuniary rights of every married woman, at the time of marriage or afterwards, acquired by gift, devise, or inheritance shall not be subject to the debts, or contracts of the husband; and laws shall be passed providing for the registration of the wife's seperate [sic] property.

Section 5a. Policy regarding marriage. It is the policy of Oregon, and its political subdivisions, that only a marriage between one man and one woman shall be valid or legally recognized as a marriage. [Created through initiative petition filed March 2, 2004, and adopted by the people Nov. 2, 2004]

Note: Added as unnumbered section to the Constitution but not to any Article therein by initiative petition (Measure No. 36, 2004) adopted by the people Nov. 2, 2004.

Section 6. Minimum area and population of counties. No county shall be reduced to an area of less than four hundred square miles; nor shall any new county be established in this State containing a less area, nor unless such new county shall contain a population of at least twelve hundred inhabitants.

Section 7. Officers not to receive fees from or represent claimants against state. No State officers, or members of the Legislative Assembly, shall directly or indirectly receive a fee, or be engaged as counsel, agent, or Attorney in the prosecution of any claim against this State.—

Section 8. Certain persons not to hold real estate or mining claims; working mining claims. [Constitution of 1859; Repeal proposed by S.J.R. 14, 1945, and adopted by the people Nov. 5, 1946]

Section 8. Persons eligible to serve in legislature; employment of judges by Oregon National Guard or public university. Notwithstanding the provisions of section 1, Article III and section 10, Article II of this Constitution:

(1) A person employed by any board or commission established by law to supervise and coordinate the activities of Oregon's institutions of post-secondary education, a person employed by a public university as defined by law or a member or employee of any school board is eligible to serve as a member of the Legislative Assembly, and membership in the Legislative Assembly does not prevent the person from being employed by any board or commission established by law to supervise and coordinate the activities of Oregon's post-secondary institutions of education or by a public university as defined by law, or from being a member or employee of a school board.

(2) A person serving as a judge of any court of this state may be employed by the Oregon National Guard for the purpose of performing military service or may be employed by any public university as defined by law for the purpose of teaching, and the employment does not prevent the person from serving as a judge. [Created through initiative petition filed June 13, 1958, and adopted by the people Nov. 4, 1958; Amendment proposed by S.J.R. 203, 2014, and adopted by the people Nov. 4, 2014]

Section 8a. [Created through S.J.R. 203, 2014, and adopted by the people Nov. 4, 2014; Section not compiled because of its temporary nature]

Section 9. When elective office becomes vacant. The Legislative Assembly may provide that any elective public office becomes vacant, under such conditions or circumstances as the Legislative Assembly may specify, whenever a person holding the office is elected to another public office more than 90 days prior to the expiration of the term of the office he is holding. For the purposes of this section, a person elected is considered to be elected as of the date the election is held. [Created through S.J.R. 41, 1959, and adopted by the people Nov. 8, 1960]

Section 10. The Oregon Property Protection Act of 2000. (1) This section may be known and shall be cited as the "Oregon Property Protection Act of 2000."

(2) Statement of principles. The People, in the exercise of the power reserved to them under the Constitution of the State of Oregon, declare that:

(a) A basic tenet of a democratic society is that a person is presumed innocent and should not be punished until proven guilty;

(b) The property of a person generally should not be forfeited in a forfeiture proceeding by government unless and until that person is convicted of a crime involving the property;

(c) The value of property forfeited should be proportional to the specific conduct for which the owner of the property has been convicted; and

(d) Proceeds from forfeited property should be used for treatment of drug abuse unless otherwise specified by law for another purpose.

(3) Forfeitures prohibited without conviction. Except as provided in this section, a judgment of forfeiture of property in a civil forfeiture proceeding by the State or any of its political subdivisions may not be entered until and unless the person claiming the property is convicted of a crime in Oregon or another jurisdiction and the property:

(a) Constitutes proceeds of the crime for which the claimant has been convicted;

(b) Was instrumental in committing or facilitating the crime for which the claimant has been convicted;

(c) Constitutes proceeds of one or more other crimes similar to the crime for which the claimant was convicted; or

(d) Was instrumental in committing or facilitating one or more other crimes similar to the crime for which the claimant was convicted.

(4) Forfeiture based on similar crimes. Property may be forfeited under paragraph (c) or (d) of subsection (3) of this section only if the claimant is notified in writing of the other crime or crimes claimed to be similar to the crime for which the claimant was convicted. The notice must be given at the time the claimant is given notice of the seizure of the property for forfeiture, and the claimant must have an opportunity to challenge the seizure and forfeiture of the property.

(5) Forfeiture without conviction of claimant. The property of a claimant who has not been convicted of a crime may be forfeited in a civil forfeiture proceeding only if the claimant consents to the forfeiture of the property or the forfeiting agency proves the property constitutes proceeds or an instrumentality of crime committed by another person as described in subsection (3) of this section and:

(a) The claimant took the property with the intent to defeat forfeiture of the property;

(b) The claimant knew or should have known that the property constituted proceeds or an instrumentality of criminal conduct; or

(c) The claimant acquiesced in the criminal conduct. A person shall be considered to have acquiesced in criminal conduct if the person knew of the criminal conduct and failed to take reasonable action under the circumstances to terminate the criminal conduct or prevent use of the property to commit or facilitate the criminal conduct.

(6) Standard of proof. (a) Except as provided in paragraph (b) of this subsection, if the property to be forfeited in a civil forfeiture action is personal property, the forfeiting agency must prove the elements specified in subsection (3) or (5) of this section by a preponderance of the evidence. If the property to be forfeited in a civil forfeiture action is real property, the forfeiting agency must prove the elements specified in subsection (3) or (5) of this section by clear and convincing evidence.

(b) If a forfeiting agency establishes in a forfeiture proceeding that cash, weapons or negotiable instruments were found in close proximity to controlled substances or to instrumentalities of criminal conduct, the burden is on any person claiming the cash, weapons or negotiable instruments to prove by a preponderance of the evidence that the cash, weapons or negotiable instruments are not proceeds of criminal conduct or an instrumentality of criminal conduct.

(7) Value of property forfeited. The value of the property forfeited under the provisions of this section may not be excessive and shall be substantially proportional to the specific conduct for which the owner of the property has been convicted. For purposes of this section, "property" means any interest in anything of value, including the whole of any lot or tract of land and tangible and intangible personal property, including currency, instruments or securities or any other kind of privilege, interest, claim or right whether due or to become due. Nothing in this section shall prohibit a person from voluntarily giving a judgment of forfeiture.

(8) Financial institutions. In a civil forfeiture proceeding, if a financial institution claiming an interest in the property demonstrates that it holds an interest, the financial institution's interest is not subject to forfeiture.

(9) Exception for unclaimed property and contraband. Notwithstanding the provisions of subsection (3) of this section, if, following notice to all persons known to have

an interest or who may have an interest, no person claims an interest in the seized property or if the property is contraband, a judgment of forfeiture may be allowed and entered without a criminal conviction. For purposes of this subsection, "contraband" means personal property, articles or things, including but not limited to controlled substances or drug paraphernalia, that a person is prohibited by Oregon statute or local ordinance from producing, obtaining or possessing.

(10) Exception for forfeiture of animals. This section does not apply to the forfeiture of animals that have been abused, neglected or abandoned.

(11) Law enforcement seizures unaffected. Nothing in this section shall be construed to affect the temporary seizure of property for evidentiary, forfeiture, or protective purposes, or to alter the power of the Governor to remit fines or forfeitures under Article V, Section 14, of this Constitution.

(12) Disposition of property to drug treatment. Any sale of forfeited property shall be conducted in a commercially reasonable manner. Property forfeited in a civil forfeiture proceeding shall be distributed or applied in the following order:

(a) To the satisfaction of any foreclosed liens, security interests and contracts in the order of their priority;

(b) To the State or any of its political subdivisions for actual and reasonable expenses related to the costs of the forfeiture proceeding, including attorney fees, storage, maintenance, management, and disposition of the property incurred in connection with the sale of any forfeited property; and

(c) To the State or any of its political subdivisions to be used exclusively for drug treatment, unless another disposition is specially provided by law.

(13) Restrictions on State transfers. Neither the State of Oregon, its political subdivisions, nor any forfeiting agency shall transfer forfeiture proceedings to the federal government unless a state court has affirmatively found that:

(a) The activity giving rise to the forfeiture is interstate in nature and sufficiently complex to justify the transfer;

(b) The seized property may only be forfeited under federal law; or

(c) Pursuing forfeiture under state law would unduly burden the state forfeiting agencies.

(14) Penalty for violations. Any person acting under color of law, official title or position who takes any action intending to conceal, transfer, withhold, retain, divert or otherwise prevent any moneys, conveyances, real property, or any things of value forfeited under the law of this State or the United States from being applied, deposited or used in accordance with the requirements of this section shall be subject to a civil penalty in an amount treble the value of the forfeited property concealed, transferred, withheld, retained or diverted. Nothing in this subsection shall be construed to impair judicial immunity if otherwise applicable.

(15) Reporting requirement. All forfeiting agencies shall report the nature and disposition of all property seized for forfeiture or forfeited to a State asset forfeiture oversight committee that is independent of any forfeiting agency. The asset forfeiture oversight committee shall generate and make available to the public an annual report of the information collected. The asset forfeiture oversight committee shall also make recommendations to ensure that asset forfeiture proceedings are handled in a manner that is fair to innocent property owners and interest holders.

(16) Severability. If any part of this section or its application to any person or circumstance is held to be invalid for any reason, then the remaining parts or applications to any persons or circumstances shall not be affected but shall remain in full force and effect. [Created through initiative petition filed Jan. 5, 2000, and adopted by the people Nov. 7, 2000; Amendment proposed by S.J.R. 18, 2007, and adopted by the people May 20, 2008]

Note: The leadlines to section 10 and subsections (2), (3), (9) and (11) to (16) of section 10 were a part of the measure submitted by initiative petition (Measure No. 3, 2000) adopted by the people Nov. 7, 2000. The leadlines to subsections (4) to (8) and (10) of section 10 were a part of S.J.R. 18, 2007, which was adopted by the people May 20, 2008.

Note: The text of section 11 (sections 1 to 3, Measure No. 99, 2000) as submitted to the people was preceded by a preamble that reads as follows:

WHEREAS, thousands of Oregon seniors and persons with disabilities live independently in their own homes, which they prefer and is less costly than institutional care (i.e. nursing homes), because over 10,000 home care workers, (also known as client employed providers), paid by the State of Oregon provide in-home support services;

WHEREAS, home care workers provide services that range from housekeeping, shopping, meal preparation, money management and personal care to medical care and treatment, but receive little, if any, training in those areas resulting in a detrimental impact on quality of care;

WHEREAS, the quality of care provided to seniors and people with disabilities is diminished when there is a lack of stability in the workforce which is the result of home care workers receiving low wages, minimal training and benefits;

WHEREAS, both home care workers and clients receiving home care services would benefit from creating an entity which has the authority to provide, and is held accountable for the quality of services provided in Oregon's in-home system of long-term care.

Section 11. Home Care Commission. (1) Ensuring High Quality Home Care Services: Creation and Duties of the Quality Home Care Commission. (a) The Home Care Commission is created as an independent public commission consisting of nine members appointed by the Governor.

(b) The duties and functions of the Home Care Commission include, but are not limited to:

(A) Ensuring that high quality, comprehensive home care services are provided to the elderly and people with disabilities who receive personal care services in their homes by home care workers hired directly by the client and financed by payments from the State or by payments from a county or other public agency which receives money for that purpose from the State;

(B) Providing routine, emergency and respite referrals of qualified home care providers to the elderly and people with disabilities who receive personal care services by home care workers hired directly by the client and financed in whole or in part by the State, or by payment from a county or other public agency which receives money for that purpose from the State;

(C) Provide training opportunities for home care workers, seniors and people with disabilities as consumers of personal care services;

(D) Establish qualifications for home care workers;

(E) Establish and maintain a registry of qualified home care workers;

(F) Cooperate with area agencies on aging and disability services and other local agencies to provide the services described and set forth in this section.

(2) Home Care Commission Operation/Selection. (a) The Home Care Commission shall be comprised of nine members. Five members of the Commission shall be current or former consumers of home care services for the eld-

erly or people with disabilities. One member shall be a representative of the Oregon Disabilities Commission, (or a successor entity, for as long as a comparable entity exists). One member shall be a representative of the Governor's Commission on Senior Services, (or a successor entity, for as long as a comparable entity exists). One member shall be a representative of the Oregon Association of Area Agencies on Aging and Disabilities, (or a successor entity, for as long as a comparable entity exists). One member shall be a representative of the Senior and Disabled Services Division, (or a successor entity, for as long as a comparable entity exists).

(b) The term of office of each member is three years, subject to confirmation by the Senate. If there is a vacancy for any cause, the Governor shall make an appointment to become immediately effective for the unexpired term. A member is eligible for reappointment and may serve no more than three consecutive terms. In making appointments to the Commission, the Governor may take into consideration any nominations or recommendations made by the representative groups or agencies.

(3) Other Provisions — Legal Duties and Responsibilities of the Commission. (a) The Home Care Commission shall, in its own name, for the purpose of carrying into effect and promoting its functions, have authority to contract, lease, acquire, hold, own, encumber, insure, sell, replace, deal in and with and dispose of real and personal property.

(b) When conducting any activities in this Section or in subsection (1) of this section, and in making decisions relating to those activities, the Home Care Commission shall first consider the effect of its activities and its decisions on improving the quality of service delivery and ensuring adequate hours of service are provided to clients who are served by home care workers.

(c) Clients of home care services retain their right to select the providers of their choice, including family members.

(d) Employees of the Commission are not employees of the State of Oregon for any purpose.

(e) Notwithstanding the provisions in paragraph (d) of this subsection, the State of Oregon shall be held responsible for unemployment insurance payments for home care workers.

(f) For purposes of collective bargaining, the Commission shall be the employer of record of home care workers hired directly by the client and paid by the State, or by a county or other public agency which receives money for that purpose from the State. Home care workers have the right to form, join and participate in the activities of labor organizations of their own choosing for the purpose of representation and collective bargaining with the Commission on matters concerning employment relations. These rights shall be exercised in accordance with the rights granted to public employees with mediation and interest arbitration as the method of concluding the collective bargaining process. Home care workers shall not have the right to strike.

(g) The Commission may adopt rules to carry out its functions. [Created through initiative petition filed Nov. 10, 1999, and adopted by the people Nov. 7, 2000]

Note: The leadlines to subsections (1), (2) and (3) of section 11, except the periods in subsections (2) and (3), were a part of the measure submitted to the people by initiative petition (Measure No. 99, 2000) and adopted by the people Nov. 7, 2000.

Note: Section 11 was submitted to the voters as sections 1, 2 and 3 and added to the Constitution but not to any Article therein by Measure No. 99, 2000.

Note: In Measure No. 99, 2000, subsection (1)(a) and (b)(A) to (F) were designated as section 1 (A) and (B)(1) to (6); subsection (2)(a) and (b) as section 2 (A) and (B); and subsection (3)(a) to (g)

as section 3 (A) to (G). The reference to subsection (1) of this section was a reference to Section 1 above, and the reference to paragraph (d) of this subsection was a reference to subsection (D) of this section.

Note: In Measure No. 99, 2000, the period in subsection (1)(b)(F) appeared as a semicolon, and there was no period in subsection (3)(e).

ARTICLE XVI
BOUNDARIES

Section 1. State boundaries. The State of Oregon shall be bounded as provided by section 1 of the Act of Congress of February 1859, admitting the State of Oregon into the Union of the United States, until:

(1) Such boundaries are modified by appropriate interstate compact or compacts heretofore or hereafter approved by the Congress of the United States; or

(2) The Legislative Assembly by law extends the boundaries or jurisdiction of this state an additional distance seaward under authority of a law heretofore or hereafter enacted by the Congress of the United States. [Constitution of 1859; Amendment proposed by S.J.R. 4, 1957, and adopted by the people Nov. 4, 1958; Amendment proposed by H.J.R. 24, 1967, and adopted by the people Nov. 5, 1968]

ARTICLE XVII
AMENDMENTS AND REVISIONS

Sec. 1.   Method of amending Constitution
      2.   Method of revising Constitution

Section 1. Method of amending Constitution. Any amendment or amendments to this Constitution may be proposed in either branch of the legislative assembly, and if the same shall be agreed to by a majority of all the members elected to each of the two houses, such proposed amendment or amendments shall, with the yeas and nays thereon, be entered in their journals and referred by the secretary of state to the people for their approval or rejection, at the next regular general election, except when the legislative assembly shall order a special election for that purpose. If a majority of the electors voting on any such amendment shall vote in favor thereof, it shall thereby become a part of this Constitution. The votes for and against such amendment, or amendments, severally, whether proposed by the legislative assembly or by initiative petition, shall be canvassed by the secretary of state in the presence of the governor, and if it shall appear to the governor that the majority of the votes cast at said election on said amendment, or amendments, severally, are cast in favor thereof, it shall be his duty forthwith after such canvass, by his proclamation, to declare the said amendment, or amendments, severally, having received said majority of votes to have been adopted by the people of Oregon as part of the Constitution thereof, and the same shall be in effect as a part of the Constitution from the date of such proclamation. When two or more amendments shall be submitted in the manner aforesaid to the voters of this state at the same election, they shall be so submitted that each amendment shall be voted on separately. No convention shall be called to amend or propose amendments to this Constitution, or to propose a new Constitution, unless the law providing for such convention shall first be approved by the people on a referendum vote at a regular general election. This article shall not be construed to impair the right of the people to amend this Constitution by vote upon an initiative petition therefor. [Created through initiative petition filed Feb. 3, 1906, and adopted by the people June 4, 1906]

Note: The above section replaces sections 1 and 2 of Article XVII of the original Constitution.

Section 2. Method of revising Constitution. (1) In addition to the power to amend this Constitution granted by section 1, Article IV, and section 1 of this Article, a revision of all or part of this Constitution may be proposed in either house of the Legislative Assembly and, if the proposed revision is agreed to by at least two-thirds of all the members of each house, the proposed revision shall, with the yeas and nays thereon, be entered in their journals and referred by the Secretary of State to the people for their approval or rejection, notwithstanding section 1, Article IV of this Constitution, at the next regular state-wide primary election, except when the Legislative Assembly orders a special election for that purpose. A proposed revision may deal with more than one subject and shall be voted upon as one question. The votes for and against the proposed revision shall be canvassed by the Secretary of State in the presence of the Governor and, if it appears to the Governor that the majority of the votes cast in the election on the proposed revision are in favor of the proposed revision, he shall, promptly following the canvass, declare, by his proclamation, that the proposed revision has received a majority of votes and has been adopted by the people as the Constitution of the State of Oregon or as a part of the Constitution of the State of Oregon, as the case may be. The revision shall be in effect as the Constitution or as a part of this Constitution from the date of such proclamation.

(2) Subject to subsection (3) of this section, an amendment proposed to the Constitution under section 1, Article IV, or under section 1 of this Article may be submitted to the people in the form of alternative provisions so that one provision will become a part of the Constitution if a proposed revision is adopted by the people and the other provision will become a part of the Constitution if a proposed revision is rejected by the people. A proposed amendment submitted in the form of alternative provisions as authorized by this subsection shall be voted upon as one question.

(3) Subsection (2) of this section applies only when:

(a) The Legislative Assembly proposes and refers to the people a revision under subsection (1) of this section; and

(b) An amendment is proposed under section 1, Article IV, or under section 1 of this Article; and

(c) The proposed amendment will be submitted to the people at an election held during the period between the adjournment of the legislative session at which the proposed revision is referred to the people and the next regular legislative session. [Created through H.J.R. 5, 1959, and adopted by the people Nov. 8, 1960]

ARTICLE XVIII
SCHEDULE

Section 1. Election to accept or reject Constitution. For the purpose of taking the vote of the electors of the State, for the acceptance or rejection of this Constitution, an election shall be held on the second Monday of November, in the year 1857, to be conducted according to existing laws regulating the election of Delegates in Congress, so far as applicable, except as herein otherwise provided.

Section 2. Questions submitted to voters. Each elector who offers to vote upon this Constitution, shall be asked by the judges of election this question:

Do you vote for the Constitution? Yes, or No.

And also this question:

Do you vote for Slavery in Oregon? Yes, or No.

And in the poll books shall be columns headed respectively.

"Constitution, Yes."   "Constitution, No"

"Slavery, Yes."   "Slavery, No".

And the names of the electors shall be entered in the poll books, together with their answers to the said questions, under their appropriate heads. The abstracts of the votes transmitted to the Secretary of the Territory, shall be publicly opened, and canvassed by the Governor and Secretary, or by either of them in the absence of the other; and the Governor, or in his absence the Secretary, shall forthwith issue his proclamation, and publish the same in the several newspapers printed in this State, declaring the result of the said election upon each of said questions. [Constitution of 1859; Amendment proposed by S.J.R. 7, 2001, and adopted by the people Nov. 5, 2002]

Section 3. Majority of votes required to accept or reject Constitution. If a majority of all the votes given for, and against the Constitution, shall be given for the Constitution, then this Constitution shall be deemed to be approved, and accepted by the electors of the State, and shall take effect accordingly; and if a majority of such votes shall be given against the Constitution, then this Constitution shall be deemed to be rejected by the electors of the State, and shall be void.—

Section 4. Vote on certain sections of Constitution. If this Constitution shall be accepted by the electors, and a majority of all the votes given for, and against slavery, shall be given for slavery, then the following section shall be added to the Bill of Rights, and shall be part of this Constitution:

"Sec. ___ "Persons lawfully held as slaves in any State, Territory, or District of the United States, under the laws thereof, may be brought into this State, and such Slaves, and their descendants may be held as slaves within this State, and shall not be emancipated without the consent of their owners."

And if a majority of such votes shall be given against slavery, then the foregoing section shall not, but the following sections shall be added to the Bill of Rights, and shall be a part of this Constitution.

"Sec. ___ There shall be neither slavery, nor involuntary servitude in the State, otherwise than as a punishment for crime, whereof the party shall have been duly convicted." [Constitution of 1859; Amendment proposed by S.J.R. 7, 2001, and adopted by the people Nov. 5, 2002]

Note: See sections 34 and 35 of Article I, Oregon Constitution.

Section 5. Apportionment of Senators and Representatives. Until an enumeration of the inhabitants of the State shall be made, and the senators and representatives apportioned as directed in the Constitution, the County of Marion shall have two senators, and four representatives.

Linn two senators, and four representatives.

Lane two senators, and three representatives.

Clackamas and Wasco, one senator jointly, and Clackamas three representatives, and Wasco one representative.

Yamhill one senator, and two representatives.

Polk one senator, and two representatives.

Benton one senator, and two representatives.

Multnomah, one senator, and two representatives.

Washington, Columbia, Clatsop, and Tillamook one senator jointly, and Washington one representative, and Washington and Columbia one representative jointly, and Clatsop and Tillamook one representative jointly.

Douglas, one senator, and two representatives.

Jackson one senator, and three representatives.

Josephine one senator, and one representative.

Umpqua, Coos and Curry, one senator jointly, and Umpqua one representative, and Coos and Curry one representative jointly. [Constitution of 1859; Amendment proposed by S.J.R. 7, 2001, and adopted by the people Nov. 5, 2002]

Section 6. Election under Constitution; organization of state. If this Constitution shall be ratified, an election shall be held on the first Monday of June 1858, for the election of members of the Legislative Assembly, a Representative in Congress, and State and County officers, and the Legislative Assembly shall convene at the Capital on the first Monday of July 1858, and proceed to elect two senators in Congress, and make such further provision as may be necessary to the complete organization of a State government.—

Section 7. Former laws continued in force. All laws in force in the Territory of Oregon when this Constitution takes effect, and consistent therewith, shall continue in force until altered, or repealed.—

Section 8. Officers to continue in office. All officers of the Territory of Oregon, or under its laws, when this Constitution takes effect, shall continue in office, until superseded by the State authorities.—

Section 9. Crimes against territory. Crimes and misdemeanors committed against the Territory of Oregon shall be punished by the State, as they might have been punished by the Territory, if the change of government had not been made.—

Section 10. Saving existing rights and liabilities. All property and rights of the Territory, and of the several counties, subdivisions, and political bodies corporate, of, or in the Territory, including fines, penalties, forfeitures, debts and claims, of whatsoever nature, and recognizances, obligations, and undertakings to, or for the use of the Territory, or any county, political corporation, office, or otherwise, to or for the public, shall inure to the State, or remain to the county, local division, corporation, officer, or public, as if the change of government had not been made. And private rights shall not be affected by such change.—

Section 11. Judicial districts. Until otherwise provided by law, the judicial districts of the State, shall be constituted as follows: The counties of Jackson, Josephine, and Douglas, shall constitute the first district. The counties of Umpqua, Coos, Curry, Lane, and Benton, shall constitute the second district.—The counties of Linn, Marion, Polk, Yamhill and Washington, shall constitute the third district.—The counties of Clackamas, Multnomah, Wasco, Columbia, Clatsop, and Tillamook, shall constitute the fourth district—and the County of Tillamook shall be attached to the county of Clatsop for judicial purposes.—

A cross section of a log advertises a free naturalist-guided drive for tourists at Crater Lake in 1933.
Photo courtesy Crater Lake National Park

Index

Alphabetization is word-by-word (e.g., "Labor unions" precedes "Laboratories").

Note: Names that begin with Oregon and that are not listed under O are located in the index under the next word in the name.

A

Abbreviation, postal, 2

Absentee voting, 279

Abuse

    child. *See* Child abuse

    Temporary Assistance for Domestic Violence Survivors, 66

Access and Habitat Board (Department of Fish and Wildlife), 53

Accidents, workplace, 40–41

Accounting and auditing

    Accountancy Board, 29–30

    Audit Committee, Joint Legislative, 134

    Auditor of public accounts, 15, 21

    Auditors (Accountancy Board), 29–30

    Audits Division (Secretary of State), 22

    Enterprise Goods and Services (Department of Administrative Services), 31

    Tax Practitioners, Board of, 85

ACLB (Appraiser Certification and Licensure Board), 36

Acupuncturists (Medical Board), 71

Adams-Onis Treaty (1819), 342

Addictions and Mental Health Division (Health Authority), 57

Administrative Hearings Office (Employment Department), 49

Administrative law judges, 49

Administrative rules, 22

    Office of Legislative Counsel's review, 133

Administrative Services, Department of (DAS), 30–32

Administrative Services Division (Department of Corrections), 42

Adult Education and Literacy programs (Office of Community Colleges and Workforce Development), 60

Advanced Estheticians, Board of Certified, 57

Advisory Councils and Committees

    Bicycle and Pedestrian Advisory Committee (Department of Transportation), 88

    Child Welfare Advisory Committee (Department of Human Services), 64

    Citizen Involvement Advisory Committee (Department of Land Conservation and Development), 68

    Driving under the Influence of Intoxicants (DUII), Governor's Advisory Committee on, 88

    Employment Department, 49

    Forest Trust Land Advisory Committee (State Forestry Department), 54

    Freight Advisory Committee (Department of Transportation), 88

    Grants Advisory Committee (Department of Land Conservation and Development), 67

    Groundwater Advisory Committee (Water Resources Department), 91

    Hearing Aids (Health Licensing Office), 58

    Historic Trails (State Parks and Recreation Department), 76, 181

    Local Officials Advisory Committee (Department of Land Conservation and Development), 68

    Medicaid Advisory Committee (Health Authority), 59

    Medicaid Long-Term Care Quality and Reimbursement (Department of Human Services), 64

    Prevailing Wage Advisory Committee, Wage and Hour Division (Bureau of Labor and Industries), 29

    Public Lands Advisory Committee (Department of Administrative Services), 32

    Savings Growth Plan Advisory Committee (Public Employees Retirement System), 80

    Smoke Management Advisory Committee (State Forestry Department), 55

    State Advisory Committee on Historic Preservation (State Parks and Recreation Department), 75

    State Forests Advisory Committee, 55

    Tualatin Arts Advisory Committee, 179

    Veterans' Affairs, Advisory Committee to the Director of, 89

    Workers' Compensation Management-Labor Advisory Committee, 41

Advocacy

    Advocacy Commissions Office, 32–33

    Child Advocacy Services (Justice Department), 26

    Governor's Advocacy Office (Department of Human Services), 63

Aeronautics. *See* Airplanes and airports

Affirmative action, 19

Affordable housing, 61, 62

African Americans. *See also* Minorities

    Commission on Black Affairs, 33

    history of, in Oregon, 357–358

Index

Arts Council of Lake Oswego, 178
Arts in Education of the Gorge, 178
Asian and Pacific Islander Affairs, Commission on, 32–33
Asians. *See* Minorities
Assembly, right of (Oregon Bill of Rights), 392
Asset management (Department of Administrative Services), 30–32
Assisted living facilities (Office of the Long-Term Care Ombudsman), 70
Assisted suicide, 372
Astor, John Jacob, 339–340
Astor Street Opry Company, 177
Athletic Trainers, Board of (Health Licensing Office), 57–58
Attorney General, 17, 25
list of, by date, 324
Attorneys
admission to practice, 94, 123
Board of Bar Examiners, 123
discipline of, 94
Oregon State Bar, 124
Audiology, State Board of Examiners for Speech-Language Pathology and, 83
Auditing. *See* Accounting and auditing
Aurora Colony Historical Society, 182
Autism, 58
Auto registration, 86
Autopsies (Medical Examiner Division), 79
Avakian, Brad (Commissioner of Bureau of Labor and Industries), 18, 27
Aviation Department, 37

B

Background checks (Department of State Police), 77
Bail (Oregon Bill of Rights), 391
Baker Heritage Museum, 182
Ballot initiatives. *See* Initiative, referendum and recall
Ballot Measures. *See* headings starting with "Measure"
Bankhead-Jones Act of 1937, 368
Banks and banking
Constitution of Oregon, 416
Financial Regulation Division (Department of Consumer and Business Services), 40
Bar Examiners, Board of, 123
Barbers, 58
Beaches. *See* Coastline
Beauticians, 58
"Beaver State," 2
Beaverton Arts Commission, 177
Beef Council (Department of Agriculture), 35
Beer
Liquor Control Commission, 69

Oregon Hop Commission (Department of Agriculture), 35
Behavior Analysis Regulatory Board (Health Licensing Office), 58
Benefits counseling (Department of Veterans' Affairs), 89
Benton, Thomas Hart, 343
Benton County Historical Society, 182
Beverage, state (milk), 2
Bicycle and Pedestrian Advisory Committee (Department of Transportation), 88
Bicycle Master Plan (Portland), 376
Bill of Rights (Constitution of Oregon), 391–396
Bingo, 26
Birds. *See also* headings starting with "Wildlife"
hunting regulation, 51–53
state bird, 2
Birth
Board of Direct Entry Midwifery (Health Licensing Office), 58
statistics, 2
Black Affairs, Commission on, 33
Blackberry Commission, Oregon Raspberry and (Department of Agriculture), 36
Blind persons
Commission for the Blind, 37
Talking Book and Braille Services, 69
Blue Mountain Community College, 169
Blue Mountain Scenic Bikeway, 376
Blue Mountains, 6
Blueberry Commission (Department of Agriculture), 35
Blumenauer, Earl (U.S. Representative), 214
Board of Accountancy, 29–30
Board of Advanced Estheticians, 57
Board of Agriculture, 34, 35
Board of Architect Examiners, 37
Board of Bar Examiners, 123
Board of Boiler Rules, 39
Board of Chiropractic Examiners, 38
Board of Cosmetology (Health Licensing Office), 58
Board of Dentistry, 46
Board of Denture Technology (Health Licensing Office), 58
Board of Direct Entry Midwifery (Health Licensing Office), 58
Board of Education, 46–47, 167
Board of Electrologists and Body Art Practitioners (Health Licensing Office), 58
Board of Examiners for Engineering and Land Surveying, 50
Board of Examiners for Speech-Language Pathology and Audiology, 83
Board of Forestry, 54
Board of Geologist Examiners, 55

Casinos
    Indian tribes, 218, 372
    prohibition on, 436
Catastrophic disasters (Constitution of Oregon), 414–415
Cattle. *See* Livestock
Cayuse Indian War, 348
Cemeteries
    national, 6
    Oregon Commission on Historic Cemeteries, 75–76, 180
    State Mortuary and Cemetery Board, 73
Censure of judges, 409
Central Oregon Community College, 169
Central Oregon Intergovernmental Council, 271
Charitable Activities Section (Justice Department), 26
Check-cashing businesses, Financial Regulation Division (Department of Consumer and Business Services), 40
Chemeketa Community College, 170
Chief Clerk of the House of Representatives, 128
Chief Education Office, 19–20, 164
Chief Financial Officer
    Department of Administrative Services, 30
    Department of Corrections, 42–43
    Housing and Community Services Department, 62
Chief Human Resources Office (Department of Administrative Services), 30–31
Chief Operating Officer, Office of (Department of Administrative Services), 30
Child abuse
    Child Welfare Programs (Department of Human Services), 64
    Civil Enforcement Division (Justice Department), 26
Child Advocacy Services (Justice Department), 26
Child care (Department of Human Services), 65–66
Child labor regulation, 29
Child Support Division (Justice Department), 26
Child support enforcement, 26
Childbirth
    Board of Direct Entry Midwifery, 58
    statistics, 2
Children
    Child Welfare Advisory Committee (Department of Human Services), 64
    Child Welfare Programs (Department of Human Services), 64–65
    Early Learning Division (ELD), 47, 165, 167
    education. *See* Education; Schools
    Family Services Review Commission (Department of Human Services), 64
    Internet crimes against, 27
    juvenile corrections. *See* Juvenile delinquency and corrections
    labor regulation, 29
    National Guard Youth Challenge Program, 72–73
    Refugee Child Welfare Advisory (Department of Human Services), 64–65
    with special needs, 59
    support enforcement, 26
    Youth Authority, 92
    Youth Challenge Program (Oregon Military Department), 72–73
    Youth Development Division (Department of Education), 47–48
Children's Wraparound Program, 59
Chinese Americans, 358, 366
Chinook salmon (state fish), 3. *See also* Salmon
Chiropractic Examiners, State Board of, 38
Christmas trees (Department of Agriculture), 35
Chronological history by year, 379–385
Circuit Courts, 95–98, 100–123, 408
    photographs of judges, 100–119
Circuit Judges Association, 123
Cities, 227–252. *See also headings starting with "Municipal"*
    Constitution of Oregon, 415–424
    finance, 159–160. *See also* Taxation
    largest, 3
    map, 12
    merger of, 416
    Municipal Courts, 125
    population (1980–2016), 247–252
    total number of, 3
    types of government, 227
Citizen Involvement Advisory Committee (Department of Land Conservation and Development), 68
Civil commitment (Psychiatric Security Review Board), 79
Civil Enforcement Division (Justice Department), 26
Civil Litigation Section, Trial Division (Justice Department), 27
Civil Recovery Section (Justice Department), 26
Civil Rights Division (Bureau of Labor and Industries), 29
Civil War, 353–354
Civilian Conservation Corps (CCC), 367, 376, 377
Clackamas Community College, 170
Clackamas County
    Arts Alliance, 179
    Historical Society and Museum of the Oregon Territory, 183
Class-action lawsuits, 27
Clatsop Community College, 170

Congress, U.S.
  Governor's Washington, D.C., Office as
    liaison with, 21
  Representatives, U.S., 2, 213–215,
    330–332, 441–442
  Senators, U.S., 328–330
Conservation. *See* Environment; Natural
  resources; Wildlife
Constituent Services Office (Governor's
  Office), 19
Constitution of Oregon, 389–442
  Bill of Rights, 391–396
  election to accept or reject, 441
Construction Contractors Board, 38
Construction industry, 190. *See also* Building
  regulation
Construction Industry Energy Board
  (Department of Consumer and Business
  Services), 39
Consular Corps, 223–224
Consumer and Business Services, Department of
  (DCBS), 38–42
Consumer protection, 26
  agricultural products, 34
  Department of Consumer and Business
    Services, 38–42
  Weights and Measures Program, 34
Contractors. *See specific type*
Cook, James (Captain), 338
Coos, Lower Umpqua and Siuslaw, Confederated
  Tribes of, 219
Coos Art Museum, 178
Coos History Museum and Maritime Collection,
  183
Coquille Indian Tribe, 9, 220
Coquille Valley Art Association, 178
Corban University, 173
Cornucopia Arts Council and Pine Fest, 178
Coroners (Constitution of Oregon), 407
Corporate excise tax, 160, 192, 413
Corporate income tax, 160, 192
Corporation Division (Secretary of State), 22
Correctional institutions, 5, 43–45. *See also*
  Prisons and prisoners
  juveniles. *See* Juvenile delinquency and cor-
    rections
Corrections, Department of, 42–45
Corrections Enterprises, Oregon (Department of
  Corrections), 43–44
Cosmetology, Board of, 58
Council on Court Procedures, 124
Council on Developmental Disabilities
  (Department of Human Services), 66–67
Counselors and Therapists, Oregon Board of
  Licensed Professional, 45
Counties, 253–271. *See also* Local government;
  specific counties

circuit courts. *See* Circuit Courts
city-county consolidation, 416
Constitution of Oregon, 406–407
corrections activities, 42
district attorneys, 27
finance, 159–160. *See also* Taxation
government, 406–407
home rule, 407
largest, 3
map, 12
minimum area and population, 437
number of, 3
population (1980–2016), 252
smallest, 3
County Courts, 125
Court of Appeals, Oregon, 94–95, 322–324
  photographs of judges, 97–98
Court Procedures, Council on, 124
Courtney, Peter (President of State
  Senate), 128, 138
Courts, 93–126. *See also* Judges
  cases filed in Oregon courts
    (2010–2015), 99
  Circuit Courts, 95–98, 100–123, 408
  Circuit Courts, photographs of judges,
    100–119
  Constitution of Oregon, 407–409
  Council on Court Procedures, 124
  County Courts, 125
  Court of Appeals, 94–95, 97–98, 322–324
  District Courts, U.S., 217
  judges by district, 119–123
  Justice Courts, 125
  Municipal Courts, 125
  State Court Administrator, 99
  Supreme Court, 94, 96, 318–322
  Tax Court, 95, 98, 324
Covered Bridges Scenic Bikeway, 376
Cow Creek Band of Umpqua Tribe of
  Indians, 9, 220
CPAs (Accountancy Board), 29–30
Crabs, Dungeness, 3
  Commission, 35
Crafts. *See* Arts
Credit unions, Financial Regulation Division
  (Department of Consumer and Business
  Services), 40
Crimes, victims of
  Crime Victims' Services Division (Justice
    Department), 26
  rights of (Oregon Bill of Rights), 394–395
Criminal and Collateral Remedies Litigation
  Section, Trial Division (Justice
  Department), 27
Criminal Investigations Division (Department of
  State Police), 78

Index

Dietitians, Board of Licensed (Health Licensing Office), 58
Director's Office
  Department of Transportation, 86
  Water Resources Department, 90
Disabilities Commission, Oregon, 65
Disabled persons. *See also* Developmental disabilities
  Aging and People with Disabilities Programs (Department of Human Services), 63–64
  Council on Developmental Disabilities (Department of Human Services), 66–67
  Deaf and Hard of Hearing Services Program, 64
  Disabilities Commission, Oregon, 65
  Home Care Commission, 439–440
  housing for, 429
  Northwest Senior and Disability Services, 271
  Oregon ABLE (Achieving a Better Life Experience) Savings Plan, 25
  Residential Service Protection Fund (Public Utility Commission), 81
  Vocational Rehabilitation Services, Office of (Department of Human Services), 66
Disasters
  Constitution of Oregon, 414–415
  Department of Geology and Mineral Industries, 56
  earthquakes, 431–432
  forest fires, 54
Discrimination. *See also* Minorities
  Bill of Rights, Oregon, 391
  Civil Rights Division (Bureau of Labor and Industries), 29
  Diversity, Equity and Inclusion Office, 19
  equal employment opportunity, 29
  history of, 357–359, 366
  housing discrimination, 29
  sex discrimination prohibited (Bill of Rights, Oregon), 396
Diseases, animal, 34
Diseases, occupational, 40
Diseases, plant, 35
District Attorneys (Justice Department), 27
District Courts. *See* Circuit Courts
Diversity, Equity and Inclusion Office (Governor's Office), 19
Divorce statistics, 3
DLCD (Department of Land Conservation and Development), 67–68
DMV (Driver and Motor Vehicle Division), 86–87
DNA identification (Department of State Police), 77
Doctor-assisted suicide, 372

Domestic Violence Survivors, Temporary Assistance for, 66
Dotterer, Dave (Interim Deputy Secretary of State), 21
Double jeopardy (Oregon Bill of Rights), 391
Double majority vote to increase property tax rate, 159
Douglas, David, 341
Douglas County Museum and Umpqua River Lighthouse Museum, 183
Douglas Fir (state tree), 9, 341
Downhill skiing, 8
DPSST (Department of Public Safety Standards and Training), 80–81
Driver and Motor Vehicle Division (DMV; Department of Transportation), 86–87
Driver licenses, 86
Driving under the Influence of Intoxicants, Governor's Advisory Committee on, 88
Drug use and abuse
  Addictions and Mental Health Division (Health Authority), 57
  High Intensity Drug Trafficking Area Investigation Service Center, 27
  legal use of recreational marijuana, 69, 385
Drunk driving, Governor's Advisory Committee on DUII, 88
Dueling penalty, 397
DUII, Governor's Advisory Committee on, 88
Dungeness crabs, 3
  Commission (Department of Agriculture), 35
Duniway, Abigail Scott, 351, 363

E

Ear piercing, 58
Early Head Start, 167
Early Learning Council (ELC), 167
Early Learning Division (Department of Education), 47, 165, 167
Earthquakes
  Department of Geology and Mineral Industries, 56
  seismic rehabilitation of emergency services and public education buildings, 431–432
Eastern Oregon Correctional Institution, 44
Eastern Oregon University (EOU), 172
Economic Analysis Office (Department of Administrative Services), 31–32
Economy, 189–192. *See also specific industries and sectors (e.g., Agriculture)*
  employment. *See* Employment and labor
  forecasting, economic, 32
  high tech sector. *See* High-tech industries
  historic development, 359–361
  impact of growth, 190

Emergencies. *See also* Disasters
Emergency Management Office (Military Department), 72
National Guard, 72
seismic rehabilitation of emergency services and public education buildings, 431–432
Emergency Board (Legislative Assembly), 134
Emergency Fire Cost Committee (State Forestry Department), 54
Emergency Management Office (Military Department), 72
Emergency preparedness (Department of Corrections), 43
Emigration rights (Oregon Bill of Rights), 392
Eminent domain
Bill of Rights of Oregon, 392
Constitution of Oregon, 416
Employment and labor
Bureau of Labor and Industries, 27–29
Economic Analysis Office (Department of Administrative Services), 31–32
equal employment opportunity, 29
Jobs and Economy Policy Advisor, 20
Labor and Workforce Policy Advisor, 20
Occupational Safety and Health Division (Department of Consumer and Business Services), 40
statistics, 190–191
Technical Assistance for Employers Program, 29
workers' compensation. See headings starting with "Workers' Compensation"
Workforce Operations Division (Employment Department), 48–49
Employment Appeals Board, 49
Employment Department, 48–49
Employment Department Advisory Council, 49
Employment Relations Board, 49
Endangered plants, 35
Endangered Species Act of 1973, 372
Energy
alternative energy projects, 2
Constitution of Oregon, 425
Construction Industry Energy Board (Department of Consumer and Business Services), 39
Department of Energy, 50
geothermal projects, 2
history of, 366, 369, 370
local energy loans, 429–430
Pacific Northwest Electric Power and Conservation Planning Council, 74
policy advisor, 20
Public Utility Commission, 81
Energy Department, 50
Energy Facility Siting Council, 50
Energy policy advisor (Governor's Office), 20

Engineering and Land Surveying, State Board of Examiners for, 50
Enterprise Asset Management (Department of Administrative Services), 31
Enterprise Goods and Services (Department of Administrative Services), 31
Enterprise Information Resource Management Strategy, 31
Entrepreneurship, 22
Environment. *See also* Natural resources
Constitution of Oregon, 428
Department of Energy, 50
Department of Environmental Quality, 50–51
Department of Geology and Mineral Industries, 55–56
emphasis on, 371–372
health issues. See headings starting with "Health"
Malheur Field Station, 185
pesticides, 34–35
water. See Water
woodlands. See Forests
Environmental Health Registration Board (Health Licensing Office), 58
Environmental Quality Commission, 51
Environmental Quality Department (DEQ), 50–51
Environmental Solutions Division (Department of Environmental Quality), 51
EOU (Eastern Oregon University), 172
Equity and Inclusion Office, 57
Escrow agents (Real Estate Agency), 82
ESD (Environmental Solutions Division), 51
Estuarine reserves and sanctuaries (South Slough National Estuarine Research Reserve), 84–85
Ethics in government. *See also* Conflict of interest
Government Ethics Commission, 56
Eugene as "Tracktown, USA," 377
European explorers, 337–338
Evergreen Aviation & Space Museum, 185
Ex post facto laws (Oregon Bill of Rights), 392
Examiners for professional licensing. *See* specific profession
Executive branch of government, 13–92. *See also* Governor
Constitution of Oregon, 405–406
Executive Division (State Treasury), 23
Exports. *See* International trade
Exposition Center and State Fair, 83
Extradition, 19

F

Facilities Authority, Oregon (State Treasury), 24
Fair, State, 3, 83–84

Forfeiture of property and Oregon Property Protection Act of 2000, 438–439
Fort McDermitt Paiute-Shoshone Tribe, 9
Fossil, state, 4
Foster care, 64
Four Rivers Cultural Center, 179, 183
Fraud
    Financial Fraud/Consumer Protection Section (Justice Department), 26
    Land Fraud trials, 364
    Medicaid Fraud Unit (Justice Department), 26
Freedom of assembly (Oregon Bill of Rights), 392
Freedom of speech (Oregon Bill of Rights), 391
Freight Advisory Committee (Department of Transportation), 88
Fremont, John Charles, 343
Fruit
    Blueberry Commission (Department of Agriculture), 35
    Raspberry and Blackberry Commission (Department of Agriculture), 36
    state, 4
    Strawberry Commission (Department of Agriculture), 36
    Sweet Cherry Commission (Department of Agriculture), 36
Fuel. *See also* Energy; *specific type (e.g., Oil)*
    Department of Energy, 50
    gasoline tax, 412
Funeral homes (State Mortuary and Cemetery Board), 73
Fur trade, 338–341

G

Gambling. *See also* Casinos; Lottery, Oregon State
    Gaming Division (Department of State Police), 78–79
    Racing Commission, Oregon, 82
Game hunting regulation, Department of Fish and Wildlife, 51–53
Gaming Division (Department of State Police), 78–79
Gasoline. *See* Fuel
Gasoline tax, 412
Gemstone, state, 4
Gender. *See* Women
Genealogical Forum of Oregon, 183
General Counsel Division (Justice Department), 27
General Fund, 156, 158–159, 165, 166, 192
    Rainy Day Fund to cover decline in, 158
Geographic center of state, 4
Geographic Names Board, 180

Geologist Examiners, State Board of, 55
Geology. *See also* Minerals
    formation of Oregon, 334
Geology and Mineral Industries, State Department of, 55–56
Geology and Mineral Industries Governing Board, 56
George Fox University, 174
Geothermal projects, 2
Gilliam County Historical Society, 183
Gold strikes, 353–355
Golden Chanterelle (state mushroom), 6
Golf courses, 378
Gorge, deepest, 4
Government Ethics Commission, Oregon, 56
Government finance, 155–161
    budget. *See* Budget, state
    Common School Fund, 84, 410–411
    Constitution of Oregon, 411–413
    Enterprise Goods and Services (Department of Administrative Services), 31
    federal funds, 157
    local governments, 159–160
    pension liabilities, state empowered to borrow to fund, 432
    Rainy Day Fund and Education Stability Fund, 158–159
    revenue. *See* Taxation
    state spending limit, 159
Government jobs, 191
Governor, 14, 19–21
    additional powers, 414
    Constitution of Oregon, 405–406
    list of governors by date, 314–315
    Senate confirmation of appointments by, 129, 399
    vacancy in office of, 405
    veto of legislation, 19, 129, 406
Governor's Advocacy Office (Department of Human Services), 63
Governor's Commission on Senior Services (Department of Human Services), 64
Governor's Council of Economic Advisors (Department of Administrative Services), 32
Governor's Natural Resource Office, 20–21
Governor's Office of Labor and Workforce Policy, 20
Grand jury, 408
    disqualification from service (Oregon Bill of Rights), 396
Grande Ronde Community, Confederated Tribes of, 221, 266, 372
Granges, 362
Grant County Historical Museum, 183
Grants. *See also* Educational assistance

Patrol Services Division (Department of State Police), 79
Hiking, 377
Hill, Katherine E., 374, 379
Hillsboro Arts & Culture Council, 178
Hispanic Affairs, Commission on, 33
Hispanics, 372. *See also* Minorities
Historic Cemeteries, Commission on, 75–76, 180
Historic markers (Travel Information Council), 88
Historic preservation (State Parks and Recreation Department)
    Historic Trails Advisory Council, 76, 181
    Oregon Heritage Commission, 75, 181
    State Advisory Committee on Historic Preservation, 75
    State Historic Preservation Office, 75, 181–182
Historic sites, national, 6
Historic Trails Advisory Council (State Parks and Recreation Department), 181
Historical Records Advisory Board, Archives Division (Secretary of State), 22
Historical Society, 181
History, 333–385
    agriculture, 359, 370–371
    automobiles, effect of, 365
    British settlement, 338
    cattle and sheep business, 359
    chronological history by year, 379–385
    Civil War, 353–354
    Depression era, 366–368
    discovery of Columbia River, 338
    discrimination, 357–359, 366
    earliest authorities governing state, 313–314
    economy, 369–371
    environmental concerns, 371–372
    European explorers, 337–338
    evangelical movement and missionaries, 343–345
    federal action in 1800s, 355–357
    federal action post-World War II, 369–371
    first natives, 334–336
    fur trade, 338–341
    geologic formation of Oregon, 334
    gold strikes in Oregon, 353–355
    Indian wars, 348, 352–353
    lumber industry, 370, 372
    minorities, 357–359, 366, 368
    Oregon System, 363–364, 373
    organizations, 182–184
    political parties, 361–363
    post-WWII development, 369–371
    progressivism, 363–364
    Provisional Government, 347–348
    railroads, 361

salmon fishing, 360, 370
settlement of state, 342–343
settlements, spread of, 348–350
statehood, 355, 361, 373–374
territorial status, 348–350
tourism, 371
transportation systems, 360–361
World Wars, effect of, 365–366, 368–369
History Museum of Hood River County, 183
HMSC (Hatfield Marine Science Center), 186–187
Holidays, legal, 5
Home Care Commission, 439–440
Home Loan Program for veterans, 89
Home rule
    Charter (Metro), 272
    Constitution of Oregon, 407
Homeland security coordination (Department of State Police), 78
Homicide, aggravated murder penalty (Oregon Bill of Rights), 392
Hood River County History Museum, 183
Hood to Coast Relay race, 376–377
Hop Commission (Department of Agriculture), 35
Horse racing (Oregon Racing Commission), 82
Hospital, State (Health Authority), 59
Hospitals and seismic rehabilitation, 432
Hot springs, 4
Hours of work (Wage and Hour Division), 29
House of Representatives, State. *See* Legislative Assembly
House of Representatives, U.S. *See* Congress, U.S.
Housing
    disabled and elderly, 429
    equal opportunity in, 29
    Housing and Community Services Department (OHCSD), 61–63
    Residential and Manufactured Structures Board (Department of Consumer and Business Services), 40
    veterans. *See* Veterans
Housing and Community Services Department (OHCSD), 61–63
Housing Finance Division (Housing and Community Services Department), 62
Housing Stability Council (Housing and Community Services Department), 61–62
Hudson's Bay Company, 313, 340, 344, 347
Human Resources Division (Secretary of State), 23
Human Services, Department of (DHS), 63–67
Human trafficking, 27
Hunting regulation, Department of Fish and Wildlife, 51–53

senior judges, 95–98
Supreme Court Justices, 94, 96
temporary assignment of, 408
term of office, 407
Judicial branch of government, 93–126. *See also*
Courts; Judges
Constitution of Oregon, 407–409
districts, 5, 95
Judicial Conference, 98–99
Judicial Fitness and Disability, Commission
on, 124
Jurisdiction of courts. *See specific court*
Jury trials (Constitution of Oregon)
civil cases, 408
disqualification from jury service, 396
number of jurors, 409
Oregon Bill of Rights, 391, 392
selection of jurors, 408
Justice Courts, 125
Justice Department, 25–27
Justice of the peace, 125
Justices. *See* Supreme Court, Oregon
Juvenile delinquency and corrections
correctional facilities, 92
victim's rights in court proceedings,
394–395
Youth Authority, 92

K

Keizer Art Association, 178
Kicker provision, income tax refunds, 158
Klamath Art Association, 178
Klamath Arts Council, 178
Klamath Community College, 170
Klamath Mountains, 6
Klamath River Basin Compact, 91
Klamath Tribes, 9, 221
Kotek, Tina (Speaker of the House), 128, 143
Ku Klux Klan, 366

L

Labeling
agricultural commodity commissions,
35–36
Animal Health Program (Department of
Agriculture), 34
Food Safety Program (Department of
Agriculture), 34
Labor. *See* Employment and labor
Labor and Industries Bureau, 27–29
Labor and Industries Commissioner, 18, 27
list of, by date, 325
Labor and Workforce policy advisor (Governor's
Office), 20
Labor unions, 49, 364–365

Laboratories
agricultural laboratory services, 34
Forensic Services Division (Department of
State Police), 78
Laboratory and Environmental Assessment
Office (Department of Environmental
Quality), 51
State Public Health Laboratory (Health
Authority), 59
Laboratory and Environmental Assessment
Office (Department of Environmental
Quality), 51
Lake County Museum, 183
Lake Oswego, Arts Council of, 178
Lakes
statistics on, 5
Lakewood Center for the Arts, 179
Land Board. *See* State Land Board
Land Conservation and Development,
Department of (DLCD), 67–68
Land Conservation and Development
Commission (LCDC), 372
Land Fraud trials, 364
Land Surveying, State Board of Examiners for
Engineering and, 50
Land use. *See also* Eminent domain
Metro planning, 272
Land Use Board of Appeals (LUBA), 68
Lands, state. *See* State buildings and lands
Landscape Architect Board, State, 68
Landscape Contractors Board, State, 69
Landslides (Department of Geology and Mineral
Industries), 56
Lane Arts Council, 177
Lane Community College, 170
Lane Council of Governments, 271
Lane County Historical Society and
Museum, 183
Law Commission, 133–134
Law Enforcement Data System, 78
Law enforcement officers. *See* Police
Law Library, State of Oregon, 99, 123
Laws. *See also* Legislative Assembly
effective date, 129
ex post facto laws (Oregon Bill of
Rights), 392
Office of Legislative Counsel's role, 133
Oregon Law Commission's role, 133
process of passing laws, 129, 403–404
publication of, 133
veto of legislation, 19, 129, 406
Lawsuits against state
Constitution of Oregon, 404
liability limitations under Oregon Tort
Claims Act, 99
state officers not to represent plaintiffs
in, 437

history of cattle and sheep
business, 359, 368
Livestock Identification Program
(Department of Agriculture), 34
Sheep Commission (Department of
Agriculture), 36
Loans
Housing and Community Services
Department, 61–63
local energy loans, 429–430
veterans, farm and home loans to, 89,
424–425
Lobbyists (Government Ethics Commission), 56
Local and regional arts agencies, 177–180
Local government, 225–275. *See also* Cities;
Counties
budget, 159–160
Constitution of Oregon, 406–407
employees. *See* Local government
employees
finance, 159–160. *See also* Taxation
Investment Pool, 24
Local government employees
Employment Relations Board, 49
Public Employees Retirement System
(PERS), 80
retirement benefits and plans, tax status,
413
Local Officials Advisory Committee
(Department of Land Conservation and
Development), 68
Logging industry. *See* Lumber industry
Long-term care
Long-Term Care Ombudsman Office, 70
Medicaid Long-Term Care Quality and
Reimbursement Advisory Council
(Department of Human Services), 64
Lottery, Oregon State, 70, 372
Constitution of Oregon, 414–415, 435–437
education support from, 156, 157, 166
Gaming Division (Department of State
Police), 78–79
Lottery Fund, 156–157, 165, 166
state parks support from, 75, 436
watershed support from, 91
Low-income households
energy bill assistance (Housing and
Community Services Department), 62
housing (Housing and Community Services
Department), 61
LUBA (Land Use Board of Appeals), 68
Lumber industry, 370, 372, 411. *See also* Forests

M

Magazines, 200–201
Magistrate Division, Oregon Tax Court, 95

Malheur Country Historical Society, 184
Malheur Field Station, 185
Mandamus, 408
Manley Art Center, 178
Manufacturing, 191. *See also* Economy
Maps
Congressional Districts for U.S. House of
Representatives, 215
Oregon, cities and counties, 12
State Representative Districts, 136–137
State Senate Districts, 135, 137
Marijuana, recreational use, 69, 385
Marine Board, State, 70–71
Maritime Pilots, Oregon Board of, 81–82
Markers, historic (Travel Information
Council), 88
Market Access and Certification Programs
(Department of Agriculture), 34
Marriage
divorce statistics, 3
between man and woman, 437
same-sex, 385
separate property of husband and
spouse, 437
statistics, 5
Marylhurst University, 174
Mass transit, 274–275
Rail and Public Transit Division
(Department of Transportation), 87
Massage Therapists, Board of, 71
Mazama Club, 377
McCall, Thomas Lawson, 371
McLoughlin, Dr. John, 3, 340–341
Measure 5 (1990), 156, 160–161, 192, 372
Measure 50 (1997), 160–161, 192
Measure 66 (2010), 160
Measure 85 (2012), 158
Measurement standards, Weights and Measures
Program (Department of Agriculture), 34
Mechanical Board (Department of Consumer and
Business Services), 39
Media
directories, 193–210
freedom of press (Oregon Bill of Rights),
391
Mediation
in appeals, 94
in workers' compensation, 42
Medicaid. *See* Oregon Health Plan
Medicaid Advisory Committee (Health
Authority), 59
Medicaid Fraud Unit (Justice Department), 26
Medicaid Long-Term Care Quality and
Reimbursement Advisory Council
(Department of Human Services), 64
Medical assistance. *See also* Oregon Health Plan
Medicaid Advisory Committee, 59

Heritage Station Museum, 184
High Desert Museum, 185
Hood River County History Museum, 183
Jewish Museum and Center for Holocaust
 Education, 184
Lake County Museum, 183
Lane County Historical Society and
 Museum, 183
Linn County Historical Museum, 184
Museum at Warm Springs, 184
Museum of the Oregon Territory, 183
Natural and Cultural History, University of
 Oregon Museum of, 187–188
North Lincoln County Historical
 Museum, 184
Old Aurora Colony Museum, 182
Oregon Historical Society Museum, 181
Oregon Museum of Science and Industry
 (OMSI), 186
Portland Art Museum, 176–177
Tillamook County Pioneer Museum, 184
University of Oregon Museum of Natural
 and Cultural History, 187–188
Wasco County Museum, 183
Washington County Museum, 184
Yamhill County Historical Society and
 Museum, 184
Mushroom, state, 6

N

Nail technology regulation, Board of
 Cosmetology, 58
Name of Oregon, 6
National cemeteries, 6
National fish hatcheries, 6
National forests. *See* Forests
National Governors Association, 21
National grassland, 6
National Guard, 72, 438
National Guard Youth Challenge Program, 72–73
National Historic Oregon Trail Interpretive
 Center, 180
National historic sites, 6
National Indian Gaming Regulatory Act
 (NIGRA), 218
National memorials and monuments, 6–7
National parks, 7, 376
National recreation areas, 7
National scenic areas, 7
 Columbia River Gorge Commission, 38
National trails, historic, 7
National University of Natural Medicine, 174
National wildlife refuges, 7
Native Americans. *See* Indian tribes
Natural and Cultural History, University of
 Oregon Museum of, 187–188

Natural disasters. *See* Disasters
Natural gas taxation, 412
Natural resources. *See also* Environment
 conservation of, 375
 Department of Fish and Wildlife, 51–53
 fish. *See* Fish and fishing; *headings starting
  with "Fish and Wildlife"*
 forests. *See* Forests
 Governor's Natural Resource Office, 20–21
 history of economic development, 359–361
 Land Conservation and Development,
  Department of, 67–68
 museums, aquariums, etc., 184–188
 Natural Resources Office, 21–22
 Natural Resources Programs (Department of
  Agriculture), 34–35
 Plant Protection and Conservation Programs
  (Department of Agriculture), 35
 scenic areas. *See* National scenic areas
 wildlife. *See* Wildlife
Naturopathic Medicine, Board of, 73
New Deal, 367–368
Newspapers, 194–199
 freedom of press (Oregon Bill of
  Rights), 391
Nez Perce. *See* Indian tribes
Nike Corporation, 372
Nikkei Legacy Center and Endowment,
 Oregon, 184
Nobel prize winners from Oregon, 2
North Clackamas Arts Guild, 179
North Lincoln County Historical Museum, 184
North West Company, 313, 340
Northwest Christian University, 174
Northwest Ordinance of 1787, 348
Northwest Power and Conservation Council, 73
Northwest Senior and Disability Services, 271
Nuclear energy/waste
 Department of Energy, 50
 Hanford Cleanup Board (Department of
  Energy), 50
Nuclear medicine (Board of Medical
 Imaging), 71
Nurseries, plant. *See* Plants
Nursing, Oregon State Board of, 74
Nursing homes
 Medicaid Long-Term Care Quality and
  Reimbursement Advisory Council
  (Department of Human Services), 64
 Nursing Home Administrators Board
  (Health Licensing Office), 58
 Office of the Long-Term Care
  Ombudsman, 70
Nuts
 Hazelnut Commission (Department of
  Agriculture), 35
 state nut, 7

O

Index

removal from office for incompetency or malfeasance, 408

term of office, 434

vacancies in elected offices, 398, 399, 401, 405, 407, 438

Public records

Archives Division's duties and responsibilities, 22, 180

Constitution of Oregon requirements, 406–407

Secretary of State's duties and responsibilities, 22

Public Safety and Oregon Military Department policy advisor, 21

Public Safety Memorial Fund, 80

Public Safety Standards and Training, Board on, 81

Public Safety Standards and Training, Department of (DPSST), 80–81

Public transit. *See* Mass transit

Public Utility Commission (PUC), 81–82

Public works projects

employment of workers, 29

prevailing wage rate, 29

Pulitzer prize winners from Oregon, 2

Q

Quality Education Commission, 47

Quo warranto, 408

R

Racing Commission, Oregon, 82

Racketeering, 26, 27

Radio stations, 201–206

public educational radio, 207–210

Rail and Public Transit Division (Department of Transportation), 87

Railroads

history of, 361

Oregon & California Railroad lands, 361

Rail and Public Transit Division (Department of Transportation), 87

Rainfall, 7

Rainy Day Fund, 158–159

Ranches. *See* Agriculture

Raspberry and Blackberry Commission (Department of Agriculture), 36

Read, Tobias (State Treasurer), 16, 23

Real Estate Agency, 82

Real estate appraisers (Appraiser Certification and Licensure Board), 36

Real Estate Board, 82

Reclamation (Mineral Land Regulation and Reclamation program), 56

Records, public. *See* Public records

Records Center, State (Secretary of State), 22

Recreation. *See also* Parks; Tourism

history of, 374–379

national recreation areas, 7

Recreational marijuana industry, 69, 385

Reed College, 174

Reforestation, 425

Refugees

Refugee Child Welfare Advisory (Department of Human Services), 64–65

Refugee Program (Self-Sufficiency Programs), 65

Regional Arts and Culture Council, 177

Regional Forest Practice Committees (State Forestry Department), 55

Regional governments, 271–272

Regional Solutions Centers, 21

Registration of business entities and secured transactions, 22

Registration of corporate names, 22

Regular Division, Oregon Tax Court, 95

Rehabilitation

Offender Management and Rehabilitation Division (Department of Corrections), 43

Rehabilitation Council (Department of Human Services), 65

Vocational Rehabilitation Services Office (Department of Human Services), 66

Religion not to be supported by public funds (Oregon Bill of Rights), 391

Religious freedom (Oregon Bill of Rights), 391

Religious services (Department of Corrections), 43

Representatives, State. *See* Legislative Assembly

Representatives, U.S., 2, 213–215, 330–332

Republican Party, 217

Reservoirs, 7

Residential and Manufactured Structures Board (Department of Consumer and Business Services), 40

Residential Service Protection Fund (Public Utility Commission), 81

Respiratory Therapist and Polysomnographic Technologist Licensing Board (Health Licensing Office), 58

Restoration and Enhancement Board (Department of Fish and Wildlife), 52

Retirement Savings Board, Oregon, 25

Retirement Savings Plan, Oregon, 25

Revenue, Department of, 82–83

Revenue, state and local governments. *See* Taxation

Richardson, Dennis (Secretary of State), 15, 21

Right to bear arms (Oregon Bill of Rights), 392

Right to die legislation, 372

Rivers, 7

Army Corps of Engineers' projects, 357

Columbia River, discovery of, 338

Index

State employees
    Chief Human Resources Office
        (Department of Administrative Services),
        30–31
    Employment Relations Board, 49
    pension liabilities, state empowered to bor-
        row to fund, 432
    Public Employees' Benefit Board (Health
        Authority), 59
    Public Employees Retirement System
        (PERS), 80
    Public Officials Compensation Commission
        (Department of Administrative Services), 32
    retirement plan contributions, 413
State Fair Council, 83–84
State Fire Marshal (Department of State
    Police), 79
State Fish and Wildlife Commission (Department
    of Fish and Wildlife), 52
State Forestry Department, 53–55
State Forests Advisory Committee, 55
State General Fund, 156, 165, 166, 192
State Highway Commission, 375
State Historic Preservation Office (State Parks
    and Recreation Department), 75
State Land Board, 23, 411
State lands. See State buildings and lands
State Lands, Department of, 84
State Landscape Architect Board, 68
State Landscape Contractors Board, 69
State Law Library, 99, 123
State Library, 69
State Lottery. See Lottery, Oregon State
State Marine Board, 70–71
State Mortuary and Cemetery Board, 73
State parks. See Parks
State Parks and Recreation Department, 74–76
State Parks Commission, 376
State Penitentiary, 44
State Police Department, 77–79
State printer (Constitution of Oregon), 434
State prisons, 43–45. See also Prisons and
    prisoners
State Rehabilitation Council (Department of
    Human Services), 65
State stationary, 412
Statehood, 355, 373–374, 440
Statewide Transportation Improvement
    Program, 88
Stationary, state, 412
Steens Mountain, 6
Strawberry Commission (Department of
    Agriculture), 36
Streams. See Rivers
Student Access and Completion Office (Higher
    Education Coordinating Commission), 61,
    168–169

Student aid. See Educational assistance
Student essays
    "Apple Gate Lake" by Cora Snoke
        (elementary school runner-up), 276
    "Frog Lake" by Colton Anderson
        (elementary school runner-up), 188
    "Mending Lila" by Jada Jones
        (elementary school winner), 162
    "Oregon Adventure!" by Jake Hale (middle
        school runner-up), 154
    "Oregon Surf" by Hayes Blackman (middle
        school runner-up), 126
    "The Sandy Hill" by Quinton Smith
        (elementary school runner-up), 386–387
    "Wahclella Falls" by Soren Nilsen-Goodin
        (middle school winner), viii
Students. See Colleges and universities;
    Education; Schools
Substance abuse. See Alcoholic beverages and
    alcohol abuse; Drug use and abuse
Suicide, doctor-assisted, 372
Sunstone (state gemstone), 4
Superintendent of Public Instruction, 410
Supplemental Nutritional Assistance Program, 66
Supreme Court, Oregon, 94
    Constitution of Oregon, 407–408
    judicial discipline, enforcement of, 409
    list of justices, by date, 318–322
    oath of office of justices, 408–409
    original jurisdiction, 408
    photographs of justices, 96
    terms of office, 408
Suspension of operation of laws (Oregon Bill of
    Rights), 392
Swallowtail Butterfly (state insect), 4
Sweet Cherry Commission (Department of
    Agriculture), 36

T

Tall Fescue Commission (Department of
    Agriculture), 36
Tamástslikt Cultural Institute, 182
Tattoo artists, 58
Tax Court, Oregon, 95, 98, 324
Tax preparers
    Accountancy Board, 29–30
    Tax Practitioners, Board of, 85
Taxation. See also specific type of tax (e.g.,
    income, property, sales)
    Bill of Rights of Oregon, 392
    business taxes, 160, 192
    Constitution of Oregon, 411–413
    Department of Revenue, 82–83
    excess revenues, return of, 413
    kicker, income tax refunds, 158
    Legislative Revenue Office's role, 134

Wasco County Museum, 183
Washington, D.C., Office (Governor's Office), 21
Washington County Museum, 184
Water. *See also* Lakes; Rivers; *following headings starting with "Water"*
  Constitution of Oregon, 429
  Department of Environmental Quality (DEQ), 50
  Groundwater Advisory Committee (Water Resources Department), 91
  Natural Resources Programs (Department of Agriculture), 34
  rainfall, 7
  Western States Water Council, 91
Water power. *See* Electricity
Water quality program (Department of Environmental Quality), 50
Water Resources Commission, 90
Water Resources Department, 90–91
Water resources development
  Constitution of Oregon, 429
  Western States Water Council, 91
Water Right Services Division (Water Resources Department), 91
Waterfalls, 9–10
  Wahclella Falls by Soren Nilsen-Goodin (middle school essay winner), viii
Watershed management. *See also* Natural resources
  Constitution of Oregon, 429
  Watershed Enhancement Board, Oregon (OWEB), 91
Waterways. *See also* Rivers
  Constitution of Oregon, 429
  Department of State Lands, 84
Ways and Means, Joint Committee on (Legislative Assembly), 134
Web sites
  URLs are given as part of addresses for state departments, agencies, officers, etc., in Executive and Legislative sections.
Weeds (Department of Agriculture), 35
Weights and Measures Program, 34
Welfare. *See also* Medical assistance
  Child Welfare Advisory Committee (Department of Human Services), 64
  Child Welfare Programs (Department of Human Services), 64–65
  Supplemental Nutritional Assistance Program, 66
  Temporary Assistance for Needy Families (TANF), 66
Wells (Groundwater Advisory Committee), 91
Western Governors' Association, 21
Western Interstate Commission for Higher Education, 173

Western Meadowlark (state bird), 2
Western Oregon University (WOU), 172
Western Seminary, 174
Western States Water Council, 91
Western University of Health Sciences, 174
Wetlands (Department of State Lands), 84
Wheat Commission (Department of Agriculture), 36
Wildlife. *See also* Natural resources
  Access and Habitat Program (Department of Fish and Wildlife), 53
  Conservation Program, 53
  Department of Fish and Wildlife, 51–53
  Fish and Wildlife Division (Department of State Police), 77
  The High Desert Museum, 185
  hunting regulation, 51–53
  lottery proceeds for restoration and protection, 436–437
  Malheur Field Station, 185
Wildlife Division (Department of Fish and Wildlife), 52
Wildlife refuges, national, 6
Wilkes Expedition, 343
Willamette Heritage Center, 182
Willamette University, 174
Wilsonville Arts and Cultural Council, 179
Wind energy, 2
Windsurfing, 378
Wine
  Liquor Control Commission, 69
  Wine Board, 91–92
  wineries, 371
Witnesses in criminal trials (Oregon Bill of Rights), 391
Women
  Commission for Women, 33
  Diversity, Equity and Inclusion Office, 19
  equal rights, 385, 396
  property rights of, 437
Wood. *See* Lumber industry
Woodburn Art Center, 180
Woodlands. *See* Forests
Woody, Elizabeth (poet laureate), 7
Workers' Compensation Board, 42
Workers' Compensation Division (Department of Consumer and Business Services), 41
Workers' Compensation Management-Labor Advisory Committee, 41
Workers' Compensation Ombudsman (Department of Consumer and Business Services), 41
Workforce and Economic Research Division (Employment Department), 48
Workforce Operations Division (Employment Department), 48–49

Working conditions, regulation
Bureau of Labor and Industries, 29
Occupational Safety and Health Division
(Department of Consumer and Business
Services), 40
Works Projects Administration (WPA), 367
World Forestry Center, 188
World War I, 365
World War II, 368–369
WOU (Western Oregon University), 172
WPA (Works Projects Administration), 367
Wyden, Ron (U.S. Senator), 212
Wy'East Artisans Guild, 179
Wyeth, Nathaniel Jarvis, 341, 343

X

X-ray technicians (Board of Medical
Imaging), 71

Y

Yakima Indian War, 353
Yamhill County Historical Society and
Museum, 184
Yamhill Valley Heritage Center, 184
Yaquina Art Association and Gallery, 179
YDD (Youth Development Division),
47–48, 165
Youth. *See* Children; Juvenile delinquency and
corrections
Youth Authority, Oregon, 92
Youth Challenge Program (Oregon Military
Department), 72–73
Youth Conservation Corps, 169
Youth Development Division (Education
Department), 47–48, 165

Z

Zoo, Oregon, 187

Index